ELLIOTT AND QUINN'S ENGLISH LEGAL SYSTEM

ELLIOTT AND QUINN'S ENGLISH LEGAL SYSTEM

Emily Allbon and Sanmeet Kaur Dua

Twentieth Edition

Pearson

Harlow, England • London • New York • Boston • San Francisco • Toronto • Sydney • Dubai • Singapore • Hong Kong
Tokyo • Seoul • Taipei • New Delhi • Cape Town • São Paulo • Mexico City • Madrid • Amsterdam • Munich • Paris • Milan

PEARSON EDUCATION LIMITED
KAO Two, KAO Park
Harlow CM17 9SR
United Kingdom
Tel: +44 (0)1279 623623
Web: www.pearson.com/uk

Previously published 1996, 1998, 2000, 2002, 2004, 2005, 2006, 2007, 2008, 2009, 2010, 2010 (print); 2012, 2013, 2014, 2015, 2016, 2017, 2018 (print and electronic).
Twentieth edition published 2019 (print and electronic)

ISBN: 978-1-292-25105-9 (print)
          978-1-292-25107-3 (PDF)
          978-1-292-25108-0 (ePub)

British Library Cataloguing-in-Publication Data
A catalogue record for the print edition is available from the British Library

Library of Congress Cataloging-in-Publication Data
A catalog record for the print edition is available from the Library of Congress

10 9 8 7 6 5 4 3 2 1
23 22 21 20 19

Cover image: AlonzoDesign/DigitalVision Vectors/Getty Images

Print edition typeset in 9.5/12pt ITC Galliard Pro by Pearson CSC.
Printed in Slovakia by Neografia

NOTE THAT ANY PAGE CROSS REFERENCES REFER TO THE PRINT EDITION

In loving memory of Catherine Elliott, creator and author of numerous best-selling law titles, whose writing has inspired generations of law students across the world.

Brief contents

Preface   xviii
Publisher's acknowledgements   xx
Table of cases   xxix
Table of statutes   xxxvi
Table of statutory materials   xli
Cases, law reports and case references: a guide   xliii

Introduction   2

Part 1 Sources of law   10

1   Case law   12
2   Statute law   46
3   Statutory interpretation   60
4   Delegated legislation   86
5   European law   100
6   Custom   128
7   Equity   134
8   Treaties   142
9   Law reform   146

Part 2 People working in the legal system   176

10   The judges   178
11   The legal professions   214
12   The jury   264
13   Magistrates   304
14   Administration of justice   326
15   Paying for legal services   334

Part 3 Human rights   372

   16   Introduction to human rights   374
   17   Remedies for infringement of human rights   404

Part 4 Criminal justice system   418

   18   The police   420
   19   The criminal trial process   474
   20   Sentencing   524
   21   Young offenders   570
   22   Criminal appeals   596

Part 5 Civil justice system   622

   23   The civil trial process   624
   24   Tribunals   672
   25   Alternative methods of dispute resolution   688
   26   Civil appeals and judicial review   710

Part 6 Concepts of law   726

   27   Law and rules   728
   28   Law and morals   740
   29   Law and justice   756

       Glossary   766
       Select bibliography   768
       Index   784

Companion website

To access additional resources to support your study, including multiple choice questions and answers to the end of chapter questions and web updates, please visit **www.pearsoned.co.uk/elliottquinn**

Contents

Preface   xviii

Publisher's acknowledgements   xx

Table of cases   xxix

Table of statutes   xxxvi

Table of statutory materials   xli

Cases, law reports and case references: a guide   xliii

Introduction   2

The legal system in context   4

The unwritten constitution   4

A written constitution?   8

Reading list   8

On the internet   9

Part 1 Sources of law   10

1   Case law   12

Historical background   14

Judicial precedent   18

The hierarchy of the courts   19

How do judges really decide cases?   28

Do judges make law?   31

When should judges make law?   34

Advantages of case law   37

Disadvantages of case law   38

Answering questions   41

Summary of Chapter 1: Case law   41

Reading list   43

On the internet   43

2   Statute law   46

Introduction   48

House of Commons   48

House of Lords   48

Making an Act of Parliament   49

Reforms to legislative procedures   56

Answering questions   57

Summary of Chapter 2: Statute law   57

Reading list 58
On the internet 58

3 Statutory interpretation 60

Introduction 62
How are statutes interpreted? 63
Rules of interpretation 63
Interpreting European legislation 72
Aids to interpretation 72
How do judges really interpret statutes? 80
Reform of statutory interpretation 82
Answering questions 83
Summary of Chapter 3: Statutory interpretation 84
Reading list 85
On the internet 85

4 Delegated legislation 86

Introduction 88
The power to make delegated legislation 88
Why is delegated legislation necessary? 90
Control of delegated legislation 90
Criticism of delegated legislation 95
Answering questions 96
Summary of Chapter 4: Delegated legislation 98
Reading list 99
On the internet 99

5 European law 100

Introduction 102
The aims of the European Union 105
Modernising the European Union 107
The institutions of the European Union 107
Making European legislation 114
Types of European legislation 115
How does EU law affect the UK? 121
Answering questions 125
Summary of Chapter 5: European law 126
Reading list 127
On the internet 127

6 Custom 128

Introduction 130
When can custom be a source of law? 130
Answering questions 132
Summary of Chapter 6: Custom 132
Reading list 133

7   Equity   134

Introduction   136
How equity began   136
Common law and equity   137
The Judicature Acts   137
Equity today   138
Answering questions   140
Summary of Chapter 7: Equity   140
Reading list   141

8   Treaties   142

Introduction   144
Implementation of treaties   144
Answering questions   144
On the internet   145

9   Law reform   146

Introduction   148
Judicial change   148
Reform by Parliament   149
Pressures for reform   151
Agencies of law reform   164
Royal Commissions   165
Performance of the law reform bodies   168
Problems with law reform agencies   172
Answering questions   173
Summary of Chapter 9: Law reform   174
Reading list   174
On the internet   175

Part 2 People working in the legal system   176

10   The judges   178

The role of the judges   180
Judicial hierarchy   180
Appointments to the judiciary   182
Wigs and gowns   188
Training   188
Pay   189
Promotion   190
Termination of appointment   190
Independence of the judiciary   193
Criticisms of the judiciary   195
Answering questions   209
Summary of Chapter 10: The judges   209

	Reading list	211
	On the internet	212
11	**The legal professions**	**214**
	Introduction	216
	Solicitors	216
	Barristers	224
	Complaints	230
	Background of barristers and solicitors	232
	Performance of the legal professions	239
	The future of the professions	241
	Fusion of the professions	250
	Other legal personnel	255
	Do we need legal professionals?	257
	Answering questions	259
	Summary of Chapter 11: The legal professions	259
	Reading list	261
	On the internet	262
12	**The jury**	**264**
	History	266
	The function of the jury	267
	When are juries used?	269
	Qualifications for jury service	273
	Summoning the jury	276
	Jury vetting	277
	Challenges	278
	Discharging the jury	279
	The secrecy of the jury	280
	The verdict	282
	Strengths of the jury system	283
	Criticisms of the jury system	285
	Reform of the jury	294
	Answering questions	299
	Summary of Chapter 12: The jury	299
	Reading list	300
	On the internet	302
13	**Magistrates**	**304**
	The magistrates' courts	306
	Magistrates	307
	Suggested reforms	320
	Answering questions	322
	Summary of Chapter 13: Magistrates	323
	Reading list	324
	On the internet	324

14   **Administration of justice**   326

The Ministry of Justice and the Home Office   328
The Lord Chancellor   329
The Law Officers' Department   331
Answering questions   333
Summary of Chapter 14: Administration of justice   333
Reading list   333
On the internet   333

15   **Paying for legal services**   334

Introduction   336
Unmet need for legal services   336
The historical development of legal aid   339
Legal aid today   340
Problems with the legal aid system   345
Not-for-profit agencies   353
Conditional fee agreements   355
Contingency fees   358
Third party funding   360
Reform   361
Answering questions   367
Summary of Chapter 15: Paying for legal services   367
Reading list   368
On the internet   369

Part 3 Human rights   372

16   **Introduction to human rights**   374

Introduction   376
The European Convention on Human Rights   377
The scope of the Convention   377
The administration   378
The Human Rights Act 1998   380
Advantages of the Human Rights Act 1998   385
Disadvantages of the Human Rights Act 1998   387
A Bill of Rights for the UK?   389
The European Court of Human Rights and the CJEU   393
The European Charter of Fundamental Rights   394
Today's debates   395
Answering questions   400
Summary of Chapter 16: Introduction to human rights   401
Reading list   402
On the internet   402

17   Remedies for infringement of human rights   404

Introduction   406
Judicial review   406
Habeas corpus   406
Civil action for negligence   406
Compensation   410
Criminal proceedings   411
Criminal Injuries Compensation Scheme   411
The Independent Office for Police Conduct   412
The admissibility of evidence   413
The right to exercise self-defence   413
Parliamentary controls   414
The Ombudsman   414
Answering questions   414
Summary of Chapter 17: Remedies for infringement of human rights   415
Reading list   416
On the internet   416

Part 4   Criminal justice system   418

18   The police   420

Introduction   422
Miscarriages of justice   422
The response to the miscarriages of justice   425
Human Rights Act 1998   426
The organisation of the police   426
Police powers   429
Criticism and reform   460
Answering questions   467
Summary of Chapter 18: The police   468
Reading list   469
On the internet   472

19   The criminal trial process   474

The adversarial process   476
Criminal Procedure Rules   477
The Crown Prosecution Service   478
Appearance in court   486
Classification of offences   487
Allocation procedure   489
Sending for trial   490
Plea and trial preparation hearing   490
Disclosure   491
Plea bargaining   494

The trial 495
Models of criminal justice systems 501
Criticism and reform 502
Answering questions 517
Summary of Chapter 19: The criminal trial process 518
Reading list 520
On the internet 521

20 Sentencing 524

Purposes of sentencing 526
Sentencing practice 529
Guidance for the court when sentencing 530
Types of sentence 533
Reform 560
Answering questions 561
Summary of Chapter 20: Sentencing 561
Reading list 564
On the internet 566

21 Young offenders 570

Introduction 572
Criminal liability 573
Young people and the police 573
Remand and bail 574
Youth cautions 574
Trial 575
Sentencing 576
Key reports 588
Answering questions 590
Summary of Chapter 21: Young offenders 591
Reading list 593
On the internet 593

22 Criminal appeals 596

Appeals 598
The power of the prosecution to appeal 606
The Supreme Court 608
Privy Council 609
Criticism and reform of the appeal system 609
Answering questions 618
Summary of Chapter 22: Criminal appeals 619
Reading list 620
On the internet 621

Part 5 Civil justice system

Part 5 Civil justice system   622

23   The civil trial process   624

Introduction   626
History   626
The civil courts   627
The civil justice system before April 1999   628
The civil justice system after April 1999   631
Interim assessment of LASPO   649
Criticism of the civil justice system   650
Reform   662
Answering questions   666
Summary of Chapter 23: The civil trial process   666
Reading list   668
On the internet   670

24   Tribunals   672

Introduction   674
History   674
Reforming the tribunals   675
Tribunals today   677
Advantages of tribunals   682
Disadvantages of tribunals   683
Answering questions   683
Summary of Chapter 24: Tribunals   684
Reading list   686
On the internet   686

25   Alternative methods of dispute resolution   688

Introduction   690
Problems with court hearings   691
Alternative dispute resolution mechanisms   692
Examples of ADR   694
Advantages of ADR   701
Problems with ADR   702
The future for ADR   703
Answering questions   705
Summary of Chapter 25: Alternative methods of dispute resolution   705
Reading list   707
On the internet   708

26   Civil appeals and judicial review   710

Appeals in civil law cases   712
Judicial review   714
Answering questions   723
Summary of Chapter 26: Civil appeals and judicial review   724
Reading list   724
On the internet   725

Part 6 Concepts of law   726

27 Law and rules   728

Introduction   730
Austin: the command theory   730
Hart: primary and secondary rules   730
Dworkin: legal principles   732
The natural law theory   732
The function of law   732
Why are laws obeyed?   736
Answering questions   737
Summary of Chapter 27: Law and rules   737
Reading list   739

28 Law and morals   740

Introduction   742
Law and morality   743
Changes in law and morality   744
Differences between law and morality   744
Should law and morality be separate?   745
Answering questions   753
Summary of Chapter 28: Law and morals   753
Reading list   755
On the internet   755

29 Law and justice   756

Introduction   758
Aristotle   758
Natural law theories   758
Utilitarianism   758
The economic analysis of law   759
Rawls: *A Theory of Justice*   759
Nozick and the minimal state   760
Karl Marx   761
Kelsen and positivism   761
Justice in practice   761
Answering questions   762
Summary of Chapter 29: Law and justice   762
Reading list   764

Glossary   766
Select bibliography   768
Index   784

Preface

As with the previous edition, we hope that this edition does justice to the work done by both Catherine and Francis over many years. We have continued to employ our signature style of writing by engaging students via topical and current examples in order to help them understand how the law, processes and procedures that are discussed in this book relate to their everyday lives.

The key updates to this edition can be found in Parts 1, 2 and 4, although other necessary updates appear throughout. Some updates were more challenging than others. For example, with Brexit on the horizon and negotiations ongoing, the updates only reflect the state of affairs up to the point of writing. Anything could happen on this front by the time of publication! Some significant updates have been made to Chapter 9 on law reform. In particular, there is discussion of the Upskirting Bill and how that was brought about through a Private Members' Bill and the #MeToo movement. This movement has courted much publicity in recent times but actually the action does not require there to be reform of the law but rather reliance on existing law to deal with such issues. A further important update to Chapter 9 relates to the series of cases that have been heard on the so called 'gig' economy involving the likes of Uber and Deliveroo and the status of those who work for them. Are they employees or workers with better rights than are afforded to those who are self-employed? Chapter 10 has seen some interesting updates around the changing judicial role; in particular the increased incidences of judges speaking out on legal issues, and adapting their judgments to ensure they are understood. There have been updates across various chapters in relation to access to justice and the role technology is to play moving forward. This edition includes updates on the reforms brought in to improve the situation concerning young offenders, as well as the proposals for those in the slightly older age bracket (18–25). Diversity remains a strong thread throughout the book and there have been updates to a number of chapters in relation to this. Finally, we have been thrilled to have our academic colleague (and criminal law practitioner) Ffyon Reilly involved in this edition, and her thorough reworking of chapters 19, 20 and 22 has been invaluable.

The ethos of the book remains the same in that this text is designed to provide a clear explanation of the English legal system and how it works in practice today. As ever, the legal system and its operation are currently the subject of heated public debate, and we hope that the material here will allow you to enter into some of that debate and develop your own views as to how the system should develop.

One of our priorities in writing this text has been to explain the material clearly, so that it is easy to understand, without lowering the quality of the content. Too often, law is avoided as a difficult subject, when the real difficulty is the vocabulary and style of legal textbooks. For that reason, we have aimed to use 'plain English' as far as possible and explain the more complex legal terminology where it arises. There is also a glossary of difficult words at the back of the text. In addition, chapters are structured so that material is in a systematic order for the purposes of both learning and revision, and clear subheadings make specific points easy to locate.

Although we hope that many readers will use this text to satisfy a general interest in law and the legal system, we recognise that the majority will be those who have to sit an examination on the subject. Therefore, each chapter features typical examination questions (with detailed guidance on answering them, using the material in the text, available on the companion website at **www.pearsoned.co.uk/elliottquinn**). This is obviously useful at revision time, but we recommend that when first reading the text, you take the opportunity offered by the question sections to think through the material that you have just read and look at it from different angles. This will help you both to understand and to remember it. You will also find a section at the end of the text which gives useful general advice on answering examination questions on the English legal system.

We would like to thank our families for their encouragement, support and, most of all, patience when writing this edition.

We have endeavoured to state the law as at 31 October 2018.

Emily Allbon and Sanmeet Kaur Dua
City, University of London
October 2018

Publisher's acknowledgements

Text Credits:
15 Crown Copyright: Constitutional reform: A Supreme Court for the United Kingdom **20 BBC:** Lord Neuberger **21 Parliamentary Copyright:** *R v Reid* (1992) **22 Crown Copyright:** Supreme Court **23 Crown Copyright:** James and Karimi, The Court of Appeal **23 Crown Copyright:** Attorney General for *Jersey v Holley* (2005) **23 Crown Copyright:** Court of Appeal, Lord Woolf, *R v Simpson* (2003) **24 Crown Copyright:** *R v Simpson* (Ian McDonald) (2003) (Post Judgment Discussion) **26 Crown Copyright:** *Manchester City Council v Pinnock* (No. 2) (2011) **26 Parliamentary Copyright:** *Regina v Boyd* (2002) **27 Crown Copyright:** *AlKhawaja and Tahery v UK* (2009) **28 Oxford University Press:** William Blackstone, *Commentaries on the Laws of England* Vol 1, (Oxford: Clarendon Press, 1765, facsimile version Legal Classics Library, 1983) **30 Hachette Book Group:** In Kairys, D. (1998). *The Politics of law: A Progressive Critique.* **30 HarperCollins:** Griffith, J. A. G. (1997) *The Politics of the Judiciary*, London: Fontana. **31 Taylor & Francis:** Waldron, J. (2002). *The Law.* **31 Parliamentary Copyright:** *Arthur J.S. Hall & Co v Simons* (2000) **32 Parliamentary Copyright:** *Airedale NHS Trust v Bland* (1993) **33 Parliamentary Copyright:** *C (A Minor) v DPP* (1995) **33 Parliamentary Copyright:** *Violence: Reforming the Offences Against the Person Act 1861* (1998) **33 Francis Bennion:** New Law Journal in 1999, Francis Bennion, a former parliamentary counsel **33 Parliamentary Copyright:** *Kleinwort Benson Ltd v Lincoln City Council* (1998) **34 Crown Copyright:** *Simmons v Castle* [2012] EWCA Civ **36 Parliamentary Copyright:** *President of India v La Pintada Compañia Navigación SA* (1984) **37 Crown Copyright:** *R (on the application of Nicklinson) v Ministry of Justice* (2014) **38 Taylor & Francis:** The Spirit of the Common Law (1963) © Transaction Publishers, 1963 **40 Crown Copyright:** *R v Bentley* (1953) **41 Mr Justice Peak:** Mr Justice Peak, 1833 **48 Lloyd George:** The former Prime Minister, Lloyd George **56 Parliamentary Copyright:** The House of Lords Constitutional Committee Report, Preparing Legislation for Parliament (2017) **50 Crown Copyright:** The Stationery Office © Crown Copyright 2001 **62 Butterworths Publishers:** Bennion, F.A.R. (2005) *Statutory Interpretation.* London: Butterworths. **63 Crown Copyright:** *R v City of London Court Judge* (1892) **64 Crown Copyright:** *Whiteley v Chappell* (1868) **64 Cambridge University Press:** Zander, M. (2004). *The Law Making Process.* Cambridge: Cambridge University Press. **65 Crown Copyright:** The Serious Organised Crime and Police Act 2005 **65 Presscom:** Haw's demonstration **65 Parliamentary Copyright:** *Grey v Pearson* (1857) **66 Crown Copyright:** *R v Allen* (1872) LR 1 CCR 367 **66 Crown Copyright:** *Maddox v Storer*: QBD 1962 **66 Crown Copyright:** *Adler v George* [1964] 2 QB 7 **68 Parliamentary Copyright:** *Magor and St Mellons Rural District Council v Newport Corporation*: HL 1951 **68 Parliamentary Copyright:** *Pepper v Hart* (1993) **69 Parliamentary Copyright:** *R (on the application of Quintavalle) v Secretary of State for Health* (2003) **70 Crown Copyright:** Section 3 of the Human Rights Act 1998 **70 Parliamentary Copyright:** *R v A* (2001) **71 Crown Copyright:** Youth Justice and Criminal Evidence Act 1999 **71 Parliamentary Copyright:** *Ghaidan v Godin Mendoza* (2004) **76 Parliamentary Copyright:** Bill of Rights 1689 **77, 78 Parliamentary Copyright:** *Davis v Johnson* [1978] 2 WLR 553 **78 Oxford University Press:** Pepper

(Inspector of Taxes) Respondent and Hart Appellant 78 **Parliamentary Copyright:** *Wilson v Secretary of State for Trade and Industry* (2003) 79 **Crown Copyright:** Highways Act 1835 79 **Parliamentary Copyright:** *Turkington* v *Times Newspapers* (2000) 80 **Parliamentary Copyright:** *R* v *Ireland and Burstow* (1997) 81 **Crown Copyright:** Transport (London) Act 1969 82 **Parliamentary Copyright:** *Bromley London Borough Council* v *Greater London Council* (1982) 82 **HarperCollins:** Griffith, J. A. G. (1997) The Politics of the Judiciary, London: Fontana. 90 **Crown Copyright:** Legislative and Regulatory Reform Act 2006 90 **Crown Copyright:** *R* v *Brent London Borough Council*, ex parte Gunning (1985) 93 **Crown Copyright:** *Customs and Excise Commissioners* v *Cure & Deeley Ltd* (1962) 97 **Crown Copyright:** The Police and Criminal Evidence Act 1984 (Tape recording of Interviews) (No. 1) Order 1991 103, 105 **Crown Copyright:** European Union (Withdrawal) Act 2018 111 **European Union:** Article 267 of the treaty on the functioning of the European Union 111 **European Union:** *Cilfit* v *Ministry of Health* (1983) 115 **European Union:** Three systems of voting in the Council European legislation 116 **European Union:** Article 288 of the Treaty on the Functioning of the European Union 116 **European Union:** Article 157 of the Treaty on the Functioning of the European Union 119 **European Union:** *Foster* v *British Gas plc* (1990) 122 **Crown Copyright:** 2(4) of the European Communities Act 122 **Crown Copyright:** European Communities Act 1972 123 **Parliamentary Copyright:** Article 9 of the Bill of Rights 123 **Parliamentary Copyright:** *Pepper (Inspector of Taxes)* v *Hart* 124 **Crown Copyright:** *Bulmer* v *Bollinger* 125 **The Independent:** *The Independent*, 16 July 1996 125 **New Law Journal:** Burns, S. (2008) An incoming tide. *New Law Journal*, 158: 44. 125 **Crown Copyright:** Status of EU law dependent on continuing statutory basis 104 **Crown Copyright:** The Stationery Office. ©Crown Copyright 2017 130 **Court of Munster:** Tanistry Case (1608) 148 **Parliamentary Copyright:** *R* v *R* (1991) 150 **Crown Copyright:** Sexual Offences (Scotland) Act 2009 151 **Crown Copyright:** Sexual Offences Act 2003 155 **Crown Copyright:** Equality Act 2010 159 **Crown Copyright:** Employment Tribunal's judgment 160 **Crown Copyright:** The Supreme Court Practice direction 3 168, 169 **Oxford University Press:** Zander, M. (1988) *A Matter of Justice.* Oxford: Oxford University Press. 172 **Elseiver:** Zander, M. (2004) *The Law Making Process.* London: Butterworths. 183 **Helena Kennedy:** Helena Kennedy QC (1992) 183 **The Bar Council:** Holland, L. and Spencer, L. (1992) *Without Prejudice? Sex Equality at the Bar and in the Judiciary.* London: Bar Council. 183 **Oxford University Press:** Devlin, P. (1979). *The Judge.* Oxford: Oxford University Press. 184 **Crown Copyright:** *Constitutional Reform: a new way of appointing judges* (2003) 187 **Crown Copyright:** The Governance of Britain: Judicial Appointments (2007) 189 **Crown copyright:** The Strategy of the Judicial College 2018–2020 189 **Crown Copyright:** Ministry of Justice Judicial salaries from 1 April 2017 191 **Crown copyright:** The Constitutional Reform Act 2005 193 **Crown copyright:** Constitutional Reform Act 2005 194 **Crown copyright:** *R (Miller and Dos Santos)* v *Secretary of State for Exiting the European Union* (2017) 194 **Guy Mansfield QC:** A letter from 17 QCs at One Crown Office Row had further reproof for Truss's 'inadequate defence': 194 **Crown copyright:** Crown copyright 195 **Oxford University Press:** Pannick, D. (1988). *Judges.* Oxford: Oxford University Press. 196 **Crown copyright:** The attractiveness of senior judicial appointment to highly qualified practitioners (2008) 196 **Edward Sparrow:** Chairman of the City of London Law Society, Edward Sparrow, has spoken about cherry picking and fast tracking senior City solicitors to the High Court bench 196 **Crown copyright:** Constitutional Reform Act 2005 197 **Crown copyright:** Minister for Constitutional Affairs Government to Attract More Women, Ethnics & Disabled Judges 198 **Lady Hale:** Lady Hale, speech in 2015 at Birmingham University 199 **Sir Geoffrey Vos:** Sir Geoffrey Vos, head of the High Court's Chancery Division **199 Lord Burnett:** Lord Chief Justice, Lord Burnett **201 Lord Woolf:** Lord Woolf, wrote a memo to the House of Commons Public Administration Select Committee expressing concern that Lord Hutton had been used as a political tool by the Government **201 Emma Dent Coad:** MP Emma Dent Coad **201 David Lammy:** David Lammy, Labour MP for Tottenham **201 Parliamentary Copyright:** *Liversidge* v *Anderson* (1942) **202 TREE & Trees Centre:** *McIlkenny* v *Chief Constable of the West Midlands* (1980) **202 Crown copyright:** Attorney General to the Court of Appeal. In response, a spokesperson from the Judicial Communications Office stated: **203 Crown copyright:** Iain Duncan Smith, MP for Chingford and Woodford Green and former Leader of the Conservative Party (2001–03) alarmingly had this to say in January 2017 **203, 204 Kirsty Brimelow QC:** Kirsty Brimelow QC **205 LexisNexis:** Judicial criticism raises hackles 14 November 2008 **205 The Judicial Communications Office:** The Judicial Communications Office **205 The Independent:** J.K. Rowling responds perfectly to Mail Online headline referencing judges's sexuality after Brexit High Court ruling **205 LexisNexis:** Jon Robins, 'Too little, too late', *New Law Journal* 10 November 2016 https://www.newlawjournal.co.uk/content/too-little-too-late-1 **206 HarperCollins:** Griffith, J. A. G. (1997) *The Politics of the Judiciary*, London: Fontana. **208 Lord McKay:** Lord McKay **210 Crown copyright:** Section 3 of the Constitutional Reform Act 2005 **181 Crown copyright:** Ministry of Justice, Civil Justice Statistics (quarterly) January–March 2018. Graph created from data contained in the Court Statistics, Table 5.2 'Royal Courts of Justice tables' (https://www.gov.uk/government/statistics/civil-justice-statistics-quarterly-january-to-march-2018) **223 Crown copyright:** Common Sense, Common Safety (2010) **225 Crown copyright:** *Fawaz Al Attiya* v *Hamad Bin Jassim Bin Jabber Al Thani* (2016) **228 The Law Society:** Commenting on the new appointment procedures, the Law Society president **228 Thomson Reuters:** Blackwell, M. (2012) Old boys' networks, family connections and the English legal profession. *Public Law*, 3: 426. **233 The Law Society:** Insight Oxford Ltd's 2010 report Obstacles and Barriers to the career development of woman solicitors **234 International In-House Counsel Journal Ltd.:** Cruickshank, E. (2007) Sisters in the law, *Solicitors Journal*, 1510. **238 Legal Education and Training Review:** Legal education and training **240 Infobase Publishing:** Bloom, H. (1987). *Charles Dickens's Bleak House*. New York: Chelsea House Publishers. **241 Legal Ombudsman:** Costs and customer service in a changing legal services market Legal Ombudsman **242 International In-House Counsel Journal Ltd.:** Zander, M. (2001b) A question of trust. *Solicitors Journal*, 1100 **242 Sir David Clementi:** Report of the Review of the Regulatory Framework for Legal Services in England and Wales. **242 Sir David Clementi:** Sir David Clementi **245 The Law Society:** Chief executive of the Law Society **249 Crown copyright:** The Future of Legal Services: Putting the Consumer First (2005) **217 The Law Society:** Available from Chart 1 from Trends in the solicitors' profession, Annual Statistics Report 2016 June 2017 **232 Legal Ombudsman:** Graph created from data held in the table labelled 'What the complaints were about' which is hosted on the following page: http://www.legalombudsman.org.uk/raising-standards/data-and-decisions/\#complaints-data. **235 The Law Society:** Page 9 of the law society report 'Diversity Profile of the Profession 2014, A Short Synopsis' published in June 2015. The report can be accessed at: http://www.lawsociety.org.uk/support-services/research-trends/diversity-in-the-profession/ **266, 267 Parliamentary Copyright:** *R* v *Wang* (2005) **267 HarperCollins:** de Tocqueville, A. (2000) *Democracy in America* (Lawrence, G. (trans.); Mayer, J.P. (ed.)). New York: Perennial Classics (first published 1835). **267 Stevens, Shanks & Sons Ltd.:** Devlin, P. (1956) *Trial by Jury*. London: Stevens. **267 Criminal Law Review:** Darbyshire, P. (1991) The lamp that shows that freedom lives – is it worth the candle? *Criminal Law Review*, 740. **270 Thomas of Cwmgiedd:** Lord Thomas of Cwmgiedd in September 2017 **271 Crown copyright:** Criminal Justice Act 2003 **271 Crown copyright:** *R* v *JSM* (2010) **271 Crown copyright:** *R* v *Twomey* 2009 **272 Crown copyright:** Senior Courts Act 1981 **273 Crown copyright:** Criminal Justice Act 2003 **274, 275 Parliamentary Copyright:** *R* v *Abdroikof* (2007) **279 European Court of Human Rights:** *Sander* v *United Kingdom* (2001) **282 US Supreme Court:** *Peña Rodriguez* v *Colorado* (2017) **282 US Supreme Court:** *Peña Rodriguez* v *Colorado* (2017) **285 Central Criminal Court:** *R* v *Ponting* (1985) **285 Oxford University Press:** Denning, A. (2004). *What Next in the Law*. London: Butterworth. **286 Parliamentary Copyright:** *R* v *Rayment and others* (2005) **287 Crown copyright:** Wooler, S. (2006) *Review of the Investigation and Criminal Proceedings Relating to the Jubilee Line Cases*. London: HM CPS Inspectorate. **287 Criminal Law Review:** Lloyd Bostock, S. (2007) The Jubilee Line jurors: does their experience strengthen the argument for judge only trial in long and complex fraud cases? *Criminal Law Review*, 255. **292 Crown copyright:** *R* v *Hussain and Others* **295 Douglas Mill:** former chief executive of the Law Society in Scotland, Douglas Mill, told the BBC **296 Crown copyright:** Review of Efficiency in Criminal Proceedings (2015) **297 International InHouse Counsel Journal Ltd.:** Zander, M. (2001b) A question of trust. *Solicitors Journal*, 1100. **299 University of London:** University of London, International Programmes LLB **299 Crown copyright:** Lord Justice Auld (2001) Review of the Criminal Courts of England and Wales, chapter 5, para. 1 **299 Crown copyright:** *Lord Denning MR in R* v *Sheffield Crown Court*, ex parte Brownlow (1980)) **290 Crown copyright:** The Lammy Review: An independent review into the treatment of, and outcomes for, Black, Asian and Minority Ethnic individuals in the Criminal Justice System (8 September 2017) https://www.gov.uk/government/publications/lammy-review-final-report **306 LexisNexis:** Zander, M. (2004) *The Law Making Process*. London: Butterworths. **307 Shailesh Vara:** Justice Minister Shailesh Vara **309 Steve Molyneux:** Tweet by Steve Molyneux **309 Roger Warrington JP:** Roger Warrington JP **311 Times Newspapers Limited:** Crisis of plummeting magistrate numbers, *The Times*, July 12 2018 **310, 311 Crown copyright:** Judicial Diversity Statistics 2017 **313 Parliamentary Copyright:** https://publications.parliament.uk/pa/bills/cbill/2014-2015/0004/en/15004en.htm **314 Crown copyright:** Criminal Justice Statistics Quarterly **315, 316 Crown copyright:** Morgan and Russell (2000) The Judiciary in the Magistrates' Courts, Home Office RDS Occasional Paper No. 66 **318 Crown copyright:** The Strengths and Skills of the Judiciary in the Magistrates' Courts (2011) **318 Crown copyright:** *R* v *Bingham Justices*, ex parte Jowitt (1974) **319 Cambridge University Press:** Jackson, R.M. (1989) *The Machinery of Justice in England*. Cambridge: Cambridge University Press. **322 The Howard League:** Frances Crook, chief executive of the Howard League **331 Crown copyright:** Constitutional Reform Act 2005 **336 Amnesty International:** Amnesty International, Cuts that hurt: The impact of legal aid cuts in England on access to justice (2016) can be downloaded at: https://www.amnesty.org/en/documents/eur45/4936/2016/en/ **337, 338 Crown copyright:** Pereira, I., Perry C., Greevy, H. and Shrimpton, H. (2015), The varying paths to justice. Mapping problem resolution routes for users and nonusers of the civil, administrative and family justice systems. London: Ministry of Justice Analytical Series. **341 The Law Society:** Richard Miller, head of legal aid at the Law Society **345 Times Newspapers Limited:** Sir Andrew McFarlane, President of the Family Division of the High Court **346 Mr Justice Bodey:** Mr Justice Bodey **346 Crown copyright:** *Re D* (a child) 2014 **347 Citizens Advice Bureau:** Citizens Advice Bureau (2004a) *Geography of Advice*. London: Citizens Advice Bureau. **347 Parliamentary Copyright:** Enforcing Human Rights 2018 **347 Crown copyright:** *R (on* *the application of Unison)* v *Lord Chancellor* (2017) **349 Lord Carlile:** Lord Carlile **349 Desmond Hudson:** Desmond Hudson **349 Crown copyright:** Access to Justice Act 1999: Breaking the Code: The Impact of Legal Aid Reforms on General Civil Litigation (Goriely and Gysta, 2001) **351 Parliamentary Copyright:** Criminal legal aid: reforms risk undermining rule of law **361 The Royal Courts of Justice:** *Excalibur Ventures* v *Psari Holdings* (2016) **361 The Law Society:** Melanie Newman, 'Strength in numbers' *New Law Journal* (23 July 2018) **362 Lord Carter's Review of Legal Aid Procurement:** Legal Aid: A Market Based Approach to Reform (2006) **345 Crown copyright:** Ministry of Justice, *Family Court Statistics Quarterly,* England and Wales, April to June 2017 (published 28 June 2018) **383 Crown copyright:** The Lord Chancellor **383 Elseiver:** Raine, J. and Walker, C. (2002) *The Impact on the Courts and the Administration of Justice of the Human Rights Act 1998.* London: Lord Chancellor's Department, Research Secretariat. **384 Lord Bingham:** Lord Bingham **384 Crown copyright:** *Secretary of State for Social Security* v *Tunnicliffe* (1991) **392 Lord Lester:** Lord Lester **393 Lord Chancellor, Kenneth Clarke:** Lord Chancellor, Kenneth Clarke **394 European Union Agency for Fundamental Right:** EU Charter of Fundamental Rights Article 52 Scope and interpretation **395 European Union:** *McB* v *E* (2011) **397 Crown copyright:** *Secretary of State for the Home Department* v *MB* (2007) **397 Lord Carlile:** Lord Carlile **408 European Court of Human Rights:** *Osman* v *UK* **409 Crown copyright:** *Lee* v *Ashers* Baking Company Ltd & Ors [2018] UKSC 49 **410 Crown copyright:** Criminal Justice Act 1988 **411 Crown copyright:** Health and Safety at Work etc. Act 1974 **447 Crown copyright:** Police and Criminal Evidence Act 1984, Section 78 **425 Lord Lane:** Lord Lane **426 John Wiley & Sons, Inc.:** Steven Greer 'Miscarriages of Criminal Justice Reconsidered' 1994 John Wiley & Sons, Inc. **426 Crown copyright:** Police and Magistrates' Courts Act 1994 **427 Police Federation:** The Police Federation of England **428 Parliamentary Copyright:** The Home Affairs Committee (2002) **430 Crown copyright:** Police and Criminal Evidence Act 1984 (PACE) – Code A **430 Crown copyright:** *Rice* v *Connolly* (1966) **432 Crown copyright:** Police and Criminal Evidence Act 1984 (PACE) – Code A **433 Ipsos MORI:** Ipsos MORI Report for Her Majesty's Inspectorate of Constabulary and Fire & Rescue Services, Public Perceptions of Policing in England and Wales 2017 Page 18. **438 Parliamentary Copyright:** *Christie* v *Leachinsky* (1947) **438 Crown copyright:** Criminal Justice Act 1988 **442 Crown copyright:** PACE Code of Practice C **445 Crown copyright:** Baldwin, J. (1992a) The Role of Legal Representatives at the Police Station. Royal Commission on Criminal Justice Research Study No. 2. London: HMSO. **455 Crown copyright:** *Thomas* v *Sawkins* (1935) **455 Crown copyright:** *McLeod* v *UK* (1998) **460 POLICE NOW:** Mission statement of POLICE NOW **461 Crown copyright:** The Stephen Lawrence Independent Review **461 Parliamentary Copyright:** Memorandum submitted by Ionann Management Consultants Limited **433 Crown copyright:** Ipsos MORI Report for Her Majesty's Inspectorate of Constabulary and Fire & Rescue Services, Public Perceptions of Policing in England and Wales 2017 Page 16. **464 Crown copyright:** Police Integrity: Securing and Maintaining Public Confidence (1999) **465 John Fitzpatrick:** John Fitzpatrick, Legal Action, May 1994 **466 Crown copyright:** The Report of the Independent Review of Deaths and Serious Incidents in Police Custody **453 Crown copyright:** Graph created from the gov.uk National DNA Database Statistics site, made available by clicking on National DNA Database Statistics, Q2, 2018-2019 **458 Crown copyright:** Graph created from Table Q2.2 'Offenders cautioned, by offence group, 12 months ending March 2008 to 12 months ending March 2018' which is available by clicking on 'Overview tables' on the following Ministry of Justice website: https://www.gov.uk/government/statistics/criminal-justice-system-statistics-quarterly-march-2018 **467**

INQUEST: From Inquest, statistics and monitoring, at: https://www.inquest.org.uk/ deaths-in-police-custody **477 Crown copyright:** Criminal Procedure Rules: Rule 1 2005 **477 Crown copyright:** Criminal Procedure Rules: Rule 3 **478 Parliamentary Copyright:** *R* v *Clarke and McDaid* (2008) **480 Williams Lea Tag:** Glidewell, Sir I. (1998) Review of the Crown Prosecution Service. Cm 3960. London: Stationery Office. **480 Karl Turner:** Attorney General Karl Turner **480 Michael Zander:** Professor Michael Zander writing in a letter to The Times (29 December 1998) **482 Crown Copyright:** *R (on the application of Corner House Research and others)* v *Director of the Serious Fraud Office* (2008) EWHC 714 **483 Crown Copyright:** The President of the Queen's Bench Division, Sir Brian Leveson **487 Crown Copyright:** Criminal Practice Direction 14E.2 **491 Crown copyright:** Act 1996 (the CPIA) and the CPIA Code of Practice. **493 Guardian News and Media Limited:** Minister Nick Hurd **493 Parliamentary Copyright:** Angela Rafferty QC **493 Crown Copyright:** Sir Brian Leveson (currently the President of the Queen's Bench Division and Head of Criminal Justice) speech at UCL in April 2018 **493 Ian Dennis:** Professor Ian Dennis **493 The Bar Council:** chairperson of the Bar Council, Andrew Walker QC **497 Crown copyright:** *R* v *Hanson* (2005) **498 Crown copyright:** *R* v *Clark* (2003)). **499 Crown copyright:** the Deputy Chief Justice, Lord Justice Judge, *R* v *Cannings* [2004] EWCA **501 Crown copyright:** James Sturman QC in Dallagher case **501 LexisNexis:** Enright, S. (1993) 'Cost effective criminal justice', 143 *New Law Journal* 1023. **502 Houghton Mifflin Harcourt Learning Technology:** Mansfield, M. (1993) *Presumed Guilty: The British Legal System Exposed*, London: Heinemann. **502 Sylvia Denman:** A report prepared by the Crown Prosecution Inspectorate in 2003 **503 Crown copyright:** David Lammy, in his 2017 The Lammy Review **507 William Clegg:** Jury in Michael Stone's trial **508 Crown copyright:** Audit Commission (2003) *Victims and Witnesses*, London: Audit Commission. **509 Lexis Nexis:** Zander, M. (2007d) Change of PACE. *New Law Journal*, 157: 504. **512 Crown copyright:** Department for Constitutional Affairs (2004) Broadcasting Courts, CP 28/04, London: DCA. **513 Falconer:** The Lord Chancellor Falconer **515 Andrew Walker:** Andrew Walker QC Chair of the Bar, on the 24th November 2018 **516 Julia Macur:** Lady Justice Macur **516 Crown copyright:** The Lord Chief Justice in his 2017 annual report **517 Andrew Walker:** Speech to Annual Bar and Young Bar Conference, 24 November 2018, Andrew Walker QC, Chair of the Bar **488 Crown copyright:** Page 7, *Criminal Court Statistics Quarterly*, England and Wales, October to December 2014, published by Ministry of Justice on 26 March 2015 **506 Crown copyright:** Graph created from data in Table C2 'Effectiveness of Crown Court trials' in 'Criminal Court Statistics: April to June 2018. **512 Crown copyright:** Page 3, Ministry of Justice, Analytical Summary 2015. **526 Crown copyright:** Section 142 of the Criminal Justice Act 2003 **527 Crown copyright:** Home Office (1990) Crime, Justice and Protecting the Public, Cm 965, London: HMSO. **528 Crown copyright:** Council Guideline on the Imposition of Community Order **528 Crown copyright:** Criminal Justice Act 2003 **529 Parliamentary Copyright:** Ministry of Justice **529 The Pennsylvania State University:** John Braithwaite's 'the good society' **529 Taylor & Francis:** Restorative justice for victims: inherent limits?, Gerry Johnstone, 2017 **530 Centre for Crime and Justice Studies:** 'Gun Crime' A Review Of Evidence And Policy (2008), **532 Crown copyright:** Criminal Justice Act 2003 **533 Crown copyright:** Section 143 of Criminal Justice Act 2003 **535 Crown copyright:** The Parole Board **536 Crown copyright:** David Gauke **545 Crown copyright:** Criminal Justice Act 2003 **537 Crown copyright:** *R* v *Blackshaw* (2011) EWCA **538 Kenneth Donald John Macdonald:** Kenneth Donald John Macdonald **539 Penguin random house:** Vivien Stern, *Bricks of Shame: Britain's Prisons*, Penguin, 1987 **542 Crown copyright:** Graph based on data contained in

Table Q5.2 Criminal Justice System statistics quarterly: March 2017, Ministry of Justice. **543 Lord Carter:** Lord Carter (2007) **543 Crown copyright:** Page 6, Criminal Justice Statistics Quarterly Update to March 2017, published 17 August 2017. **544 Parliamentary Copyright:** Joint Committee on the draft Voting Eligibility (Prisoners) Bill **545 Crown copyright:** Criminal Justice Act 2003 **546 Crown copyright:** Sentencing Council Guidelines **556 Taylor & Francis:** Carlen, P. (1983) *Women's Imprisonment: A Study in Social Control*, London: Routledge. **557 Hamida Ali:** Hamida Ali, Croydon council's cabinet **557 David Ramsbotham:** A former HM Chief Inspector of Prisons, Sir David Ramsbotham, Report on Holloway Prison (unpublished, 1997) **558 Francis Crook:** Francis Crook Chief executive of the Howard League **559 Parliamentary Copyright:** Transforming Rehabilitation, 2017–2018 **559 Parliamentary Copyright:** Transforming Rehabilitation, 2017–2018 **560 Crown copyright:** The Law Commission **560 Crown copyright:** The Rt Hon the Lord Thomas of Cwmgiedd, Lord Chief Justice of England and Wales **561, 562 Crown copyright:** Criminal Justice Act 2003 **575 European Court of Human Rights:** European Convention on Human Rights **577 Crown copyright:** Criminal Justice and Immigration Act 2008 **578 British Medical Association:** Our joint position statement on the medical role in solitary confinement **581 Crown copyright:** Justice Minister outlines vision for Secure Schools **581 Parliamentary Copyright:** The Secretary of State for the Home Department (Mr. Jack Straw) 8 Jul 1999: Column 1224 **588 Crown copyright:** Review of the Youth Justice System in England and Wales By Charlie Taylor **589 Parliamentary Copyright:** Page 10, The treatment of young adults in the criminal justice system, House of Commons Justice Committee **588 Parliamentary Copyright:** The treatment of young adults in the criminal justice system, House of Commons Justice Committee **572 Crown copyright:** Page 6 of Youth Justice Statistics 2016/17 **578 Crown copyright:** Ministry of Justice Youth Custody report: August 2017 **580 Crown copyright:** Page 76, of the Youth Justice Statistics 2015/16 available online at: https://www.gov.uk/government/uploads/system/uploads/attachment_data/file/585897/youth-justice-statistics-2015-2016.pdf **586 Crown copyright:** Page 5, Under 18 secure population by ethnicity 2005/05–2017/ **598 Crown copyright:** SCA 1981, s 48 **599 Crown copyright:** *R* v *Mildenhall Magistrates' Court*, ex parte Forest Heath DC (1997) **601 Crown copyright:** Page 36 of Court Statistics Quarterly January to March 2014, Ministry of Justice Statistics bulletin, published 19 June 2014, **602 Crown copyright:** Section 2(1) of the Criminal Appeal Act 1968 **603 Crown copyright:** *R* v *Williams* [2001] EWCA Crim 932, Dyson LJ (at [28]) **603 Crown copyright:** *R* v *Boal* [1992] QB 591 **604 Crown copyright:** Criminal Appeal Act 1968, Court of Appeal **603 Crown copyright:** Ekaireb [2015] EWCA Crim 1936 **605 Crown copyright:** *R* v *Pendleton* (2001) **606 Crown copyright:** Lady Justice Hale, President of the Supreme Court states this about Court of Appeal judges **607 Crown copyright:** Davis L.J. **608 Council of Europe/European Court of Human Rights:** Art. 4(2) of Protocol 7 of the European Convention **610 Crown copyright:** Judicial Statistics Annual Report 2004, p. 3 **611 Stevens and Sons:** Williams, G. (1983) *Textbook of Criminal Law*, London: Stevens and Sons. **612 Crown copyright:** Review of the Criminal Courts (2001), Sir Robin Auld **613 Crown copyright:** Criminal Appeal Act 1995 **614 Crown copyright:** s. 17 appeal from the Birmingham Six **616 Crown copyright:** Birmingham Six in 1991, Court of Appeal **618 Crown copyright:** *McIlkenny* v *Chief Constable of the West Midlands* (1980) **618 Parliamentary Copyright:** 1707 Act of Union **617 Crown copyright:** Lord Atkin,1933 **629, 631 Crown copyright:** Woolf, Lord Justice H. (1996) Access to Justice. London: Lord Chancellor's Department. **632 Lord Justice Sedley:** *Ablett* v *Devon County Council* (2000), Lord Justice Sedley **634 Crown copyright:** Claim form, https://hmctsformfinder.justice.gov.uk/HMCTS/GetForm.

do?court_forms_id=338 **635 Crown copyright:** *Broadhurst* v *Tan* (2016) **639 Crown copyright:** Woolf, Lord Justice H. (1996) Access to Justice. London: Lord Chancellor's Department. **639 Crown copyright:** Page 7 of Civil Justice Statistics Quarterly July to September 2018, Ministry of Justice Statistics bulletin, published 6 December 2018 **640 Crown copyright:** Graph created from data contained in file 'csv_timeliness_national_final.csv', which can be found by clicking on 'Civil' at the following link: https://www.gov.uk/government/statistics/court-statistics-quarterly-january-to-march-2014 **642 Crown copyright:** Civil Justice Council **646 Crown copyright:** Civil Courts Structure Review: Final Report (2016) **650 Crown copyright:** Post implementation review of part 2 of legal aid sentencing and punishment of offenders (LASPO) act 2012: Initial assessment by MOJ **651 Crown copyright:** Page 10, of the Civil Justice Statistics Quarterly, England and Wales, April to June 2016 published 1 September 2016 and available online at: https://www.gov.uk/government/statistics/civil-justice-statistics-quarterly-april-to-june-2016 **654 Crown copyright:** Queen's Speech 2017: what it means for you **657 Crown copyright:** *Bannister* v *SGB plc* (1997) **659 Crown copyright:** *Feltham* v *Commissioners for HM Revenue and Customs* (2011) **661 Parliamentary Copyright:** *Attorney General* v *Leveller Magazine* (1979) **661 Crown copyright:** PART 39 – Miscellaneous Provisions Relating to Hearings **662, 663 Crown copyright:** Civil Courts Structure Review: Final Report (2016). **664 The Bar Council:** Reforming Civil Litigation (2013) **680 Crown copyright:** Tribunals and Gender Recognition Statistics Quarterly, April to June 2018 (Provisional) **678 Crown copyright:** https://www.judiciary.gov.uk/wp-content/uploads/2010/02/tribunals-chart-171005.pdf **690 Crown copyright:** Civil Procedure Rule **690 Crown copyright:** *Halsey* v *Milton Keynes General NHS Trust* (2004) **691 Crown copyright:** *Kupeli* v *Sirketi* (2016) **693 Crown copyright:** Civil Procedure Rule 1.4 **694 Crown copyright:** *Rolf* v *De Guerin* (2011) **696 Crown copyright:** Pereira, I., Perry C., Greevy, H. and Shrimpton, H. (2015), The Varying Paths to Justice Mapping problem resolution routes for users and nonusers of the civil, administrative and family justice systems. Ministry of Justice Analytical Series. **697 Crown copyright:** Lord Chancellor's Department (2002) *Further Findings: A Continuing Evaluation of the Civil Justice Reforms.* London: Lord Chancellor's Department. **700 Crown copyright:** *R* v *Local Commissioner for Administration for the North and East Area of England, ex parte Bradford City Council* (1979) **700 Crown copyright:** *AI* v *MT* (2013) **701 Crown copyright:** *Thakkar* v *Patel* (2017) **702 Hazel Genn:** Hazel Genn (2009) **703 Hazel Genn:** Hazel Genn's research (2002) **716 Parliamentary Copyright:** Council of Civil Service Unions v Minister for the Civil Service (1984) **736 Pearson Education:** Aristotle, & Grant, A. (1885). *The Ethics.* London: Longmans, Green. **742 Cardiff University:** Warnock, M. (1986) *Morality and the Law.* Cardiff: University College Cardiff. **743 Crown copyright:** *Re A* (Children) (Conjoined Twins: Surgical Separation) (2000) **746 Yale University:** Fuller, L. (1969) *The Morality of Law.* London: Yale UP. **747 Crown copyright:** Wolfenden, J. (1957) Report of the Committee on Homosexual Offences and Prostitution. Cm 2471. London: HMSO. **748 Parliamentary Copyright:** *Shaw* v *Director of Public Prosecutions* (1961) **749 Lord Reid:** Lord Reid **749 Viscount Simonds:** Viscount Simonds **749 Parliamentary Copyright:** *Knuller Ltd* v *Director of Public Prosecutions* (1972) **750 Crown copyright:** Report of the Committee of Inquiry into Human Fertilisation and Embryology, London Her Majesty's Stationery Office, Reprinted 1988 **761 Karl Marx:** Karl Marx

Photo Credits:
15 Alamy: Justin Kase z10z/Alamy Stock Photo **54 Shutterstock:** Maksym Gorpenyuk/Shutterstock **107 Pearson Education:** Jules Selmes/Pearson Education Ltd **108 Getty**

Images: Luke1138/iStock/Getty Images **152 Shutterstock:** Sundry Photography/ Shutterstock **156 123RF:** daisydaisy/123RF **166 Alamy:** Trinity Mirror/Mirrorpix/Alamy Stock Photo **170 Getty Images:** Handout/Getty Images **207 Alamy:** Alex Segre/Alamy Stock Photo **188 Crown Copyright:** www.judiciary.gov.uk **197 Getty Images:** Dan Kitwood/ Getty Images **217 Shutterstock:** Spiroview Inc/Shutterstock **270 Shutterstock:** BasPhoto/Shutterstock **379 123RF:** Arseniy Chervonenkis/123RF **396 Alamy:** DBURKE/ Alamy Stock Photo **399 Shutterstock:** Blend Images/Shutterstock **399 Shutterstock:** Duplass/Shutterstock **399 Pearson Education:** Sophie Bluy/Pearson Education Ltd **409 Shutterstock:** Ivonne Wierink/Shutterstock **424 Getty Images:** David Cannon Collection/Getty Images **429 Shutterstock:** pcruciatti/shutterstock **429 Shutterstock:** miamia/ Shutterstock **439 Shutterstock:** Kbiros/Shutterstock **453 Shutterstock:** PeJo/Shutterstock **628 Alamy:** Alex Segre/Alamy Stock Photo **645 Getty Images:** Scott Barbour/Getty Images **693 ABTA:** ABTA – The Travel Association

Table of cases

A (Children) (Conjoined Twins: Surgical Separation), Re [2001] Fam 147, [2000] All ER 961 **743**

A (Letter to a Young Person) (Rev 1), Re [2017] EWFC 48 (26 July 2017) **204**

A and M *v* Royal Mail Group [2015] EW Misc B24 (CC) **357**

A and X and others *v* Secretary of State for the Home Department [2004] UKHL 56, [2005] 2 AC 68 **180, 396**

A *v* Hoare [2008] UKHL 6, [2008] 1 AC 844 **632**

A *v* Secretary of State for the Home Department (No. 2) [2005] UKHL 71, [2006] 2 AC 221 **447**

Abdulaziz *v* United Kingdom (No 4) [1985] 7 EHRR 471 **386**

Ablett (William) *v* Devon County Council [2000] All ER Official Transcript 4 December, CA Civil Division **632**

A Council *v* Jack's Mother, Jack's Dad and Jack (2018) **204**

Adler *v* George [1964] 2 QB 7 **66**

Agricultural, Horticultural and Forestry Industry Training Board *v* Aylesbury Mushrooms [1972] 1 WLR 190, [1972] 1 All ER 280 **93**

AI *v* MT (Alternative dispute resolution) [2013] EWHC 100 (Fam), [2013] Fam Law 373 **700**

Airedale NHS Trust *v* Bland [1993] AC 789 **32, 149**

Al Rawi *v* Security Service [2010] EWCA Civ 482 **661**

Ali *v* Head Teacher and Governors of Lord Grey School [2006] UKHL 14, [2006] 2 AC 363 **400**

Al Attiya, Fawaz *v* Hamad Bin Jassim Bin Jabber Al Thani (2016) [2016] EWHC 212 (QB) **225**

Al-Khawaja and Tahery *v* United Kingdom [2009] ECHR 110 **26, 27**

Appleton and Gallagher *v* News Group Newspapers [2015] EWHC 2689 **644**

Arkin *v* Borchard Lines [2005] EWCA Civ 655, [2005] 3 All ER 613 **360**

Armstrong *v* UK [2014] ECHR 1368 **275**

Arthur JS Hall & Co *v* Simons [2000] 3 WLR 543 **20, 31, 231, 232**

Aslam *v* Uber BV [2016] EW Misc B68 (ET) (28 October 2016); [2018] EWCA Civ 2748 **159, 175**

Assange *v* Swedish Prosecution Authority [2012] UKSC 22, [2012] 2 WLR 1275 **21**

Associated Provincial Picture Houses Ltd *v* Wednesbury Corp [1948] 1 KB 223 **599, 715, 721, 767**

Attorney General for Jersey *v* Holley [2005] UKPC 23, [2005] 2 AC 580 **22–24**

Attorney General *v* Dallas [2012] EWHC 156 **268**

Attorney General *v* Fraill and Sewart. See R *v* Fraill and Sewart

Attorney General *v* Guardian Newspapers Ltd (No. 1) [1987] 1 WLR 1248 **206**

Attorney General *v* Leveller Magazine [1979] AC 440 **661**

Attorney General *v* Scotcher [2005] UKHL 36, [2005] 1 WLR 1867 **281**

Attorney General *v* Seckerson and Times Newspapers Ltd [2009] EWHC 1023 (Admin), [2009] EMLR 371 **281**

Austin *v* Metropolitan Police Commissioner [2009] UKHL 5, [2009] 3 All ER 455 **464**

Bannister *v* SGB plc [1997] 4 All ER 129, [1998] 1 WLR 1123 **657**

BBC and Others, Re (2016) **268**

Bhamjee *v* Forsdick (No. 2) [2003] EWCA Civ 1113, [2004] 1 WLR 88 **660**

Black Clawson International Ltd *v* Papierwerke Waldhof-Aschaffenburg AG [1975] AC 591 **75**

Bowers *v* Hardwick, 478 US 186, US Ct [1986] **390**

Brasserie du PêcheurSA *v* Germany (C-46/93); R *v* Secretary of State for Transport, ex p Factortame Ltd (No. 4) (Case C-48/93) [1996] QB 404 **116**

Briggs *v* First Choice Holidays & Flights Limited (2017) QBD (Singh J) 08/02/2017 (unreported) **691, 696**

British Oxygen Co Ltd *v* Minister of Technology [1971] AC 610 **717**

Broadhurst *v* Tan [2016] EWCA Civ 94 **635, 649**

Brogan *v* United Kingdom (Application Nos 11209/84, 11234/84, 11266/84 and 11386/85) [1989] 11 EHRR 117, [1988] The Times, 30 November **386**

Bromley LBC *v* Greater London Council [1982] 1 All ER 153 **81, 84, 206**

Brooks *v* Metropolitan Police Commissioner [2005] UKHL 24, [2005] 2 All ER 489 **407**

Brown (Margaret) *v* Stott [2001] 2 WLR 817, 2000 JC **383**

Bulmer *v* Bollinger (No. 2) [1974] Ch 401 **112, 124**

Bushell's Case [1670] 124 ER 1006 **266**

C (A Minor) *v* DPP [1996] AC 1, [1995] 2 All ER 43 **32**

Caballero *v* United Kingdom [2000] 30 EHRR 643 **426**

Chappell *v* Times Newspapers Ltd [1975] 1 WLR 482 **138**

Christie *v* Leachinsky [1947] AC 573 **438**

CIA Security International SA *v* Signalson (Case C-194/94) [1996] ECR I-2201 **119**

Cilfit *v* Ministry of Health [1983] 1 CMLR 472 **111**

Cochrane v HM Advocate [2010] HCJAC 117 **530**

Commissioner of Police of the Metropolis v Caldwell [1982] AC 341, [1981] 1 All ER 961 **20, 21**

Commissioner of Police of the Metropolis v DSD and another [2018] UKSC 11 **536**

Condron v United Kingdom (35718/97) (No. 2) [2001] 31 EHRR 1, [2000] Crim LR 679 **449, 604, 606**

Conway v Rimmer [1968] AC 910, [1968] 1 All ER 874 **662**

Council of Civil Service Unions v Minister for the Civil Service [1985] AC 374, [1984] 1 WLR 1174 **206, 330, 390, 716, 721, 722**

Coventry v Lawrence (No. 2) [2014] UKSC 46, [2015] AC 106, [2014] 4 All ER 517 **357**

CTB v News Group Newspapers Ltd [2011] EWHC 1232 (QB), [2011] All ER (D) 142 (May) **399**

Cusack v London Borough of Harrow [2013] UKSC 40, [2013] 1 WLR 2022 **63**

Customs and Excise Commissioners v APS Samex [1983] 1 All ER 1042 **112**

Customs and Excise Commissioners v Cure & Deeley Ltd [1962] 1 QB 340 **93**

D (A Child), Re (2014) [2014] EWCA Civ 315 **346**

D (A Child), Re (2017) [2017] EWCA Civ 1695 **203**

D v East Berkshire Community NHS Trust [2003] EWCA Civ 1151, [2004] QB 558 **28**

D&C Builders Ltd v Rees [1966] 2 QB 617 **138**

Davis v Johnson [1979] AC 264, [1978] 2 WLR 553 **75, 77**

de Lasala v de Lasala [1980] AC 546 **22**

Denton v T H White Ltd [2014] EWCA Civ 906, [2015] 1 All ER 880, [2014] 1 WLR 3926 **648**

Dimes v Grand Junction Canal Proprietors [1852] 3 HL Cas 759 **714**

Director General of Fair Trading v Proprietary Association of Great Britain [2001] 1 WLR 700 **715**

Director of Public Prosecutions v Jones (Margaret) [1998] QB 563; reversing [1999] 2 AC 240 **33, 34**

Donnelly v Jackman [1970] 1 WLR 562 **431**

Donoghue v Stevenson [1932] AC 562 **743**

Douglas v Hello! Ltd [2001] 2 WLR 992 **380**

DSD v Commissioner of Police of the Metropolis (2014) [2014] EWCA 436 **535**

Dunnett v Railtrack plc [2002] EWCA Civ 303, [2002] 2 All ER 850 **694**

Earl of Oxford's Case [1615] 1 Ch Rep 1 **137, 141**

Elliott v Grey [1960] 1 QB 367 **67**

Elvanite Full Circle Ltd v AMEC Earth and Environmental (UK) Ltd [2013] EWHC 1643 (TCC), [2013] 4 All ER 765 **648**

Evans v Amicus Healthcare Ltd [2004] EWCA Civ 727, [2005] Fam 1 **751**

Evans v United Kingdom [2007] 1 FLR 1990, [2007] 2 FCR5 671 **751**

Eweida v United Kingdom [2013] ECHR 48420/10, [2013] IRLR 231 **400**

Excalibur Ventures v Psari Holdings [2016] EWCA Civ 1144 **361**

Feltham v Commissioners of HM Revenue and Customs [2011] UKFTT 612 (TC) **658**

Fisher v Bell [1961] 1 QB 394 **64**

Fitzpatrick v Sterling Housing Association Ltd [2001] 1 AC 27, [2000] 1 FLR 271 **35**

Fleet Street Casuals Case. See R v Inland Revenue Commissioners, ex p National Federation of Self Employed and Small Businesses

Foster v British Gas plc (Case C-188/89) [1991] 1 QB 405, [1990] 3 All ER 897 **119**

Francovich v Italy (Case C-6/90) [1991] ECR I-5357, [1992] IRLR 84 **116**

G v Director of Public Prosecutions [1989] Crim LR 150 **436**

GCHQ Case. See Council of Civil Service Unions v Minister for the Civil Service

Ghaidan v Godin-Mendoza [2004] UKHL 30, [2004] 2 AC 557, [2004] 3 All ER 411 **71**

Gillick v West Norfolk and Wisbech Area Health Authority [1986] AC 112, [1985] 3 All ER 402 **36, 612, 744**

Goswell v Commissioner of Metropolitan Police , Lawtel 7/4/98 **408**

Greens and MT v United Kingdom [2010] 53 EHRR 710, [2010] ECHR 60041/08 **387, 544**

Gregory v United Kingdom [1998] 25 EHRR 577, [1997] The Times, 27 February **279, 280**

Grey v Pearson [1857] 6 HL Cas 61 **65**

Grobbelaar v News Group Newspapers Ltd [2001] EWCA Civ 33, [2001] 2 All ER 437 **289**

Hall v Simons. See Arthur JS Hall & Co v Simons

Halsey v Milton Keynes General NHS Trust [2004] EWCA Civ 576, [2004] 4 All ER 920 **690, 691**

Hanif and Khan v United Kingdom (Application Nos 52999/08 and 61779/08) [2012] Crim LR 295, [2011] Times, 27 December **275**

Hanningfield (Lord) v Chief Constable of Essex Police [2013] EWHC 243 (QB), [2013] 1 WLR 3632 **437**

Heydon's Case [1584] 3 Co Rep 7a **66, 67**

Hill v Chief Constable of West Yorkshire [1989] AC 53 **406, 407**

Hirst v United Kingdom (No. 2) [2005] 42 EHRR 849, [2005] ECHR 74025/01 **544**

HM Advocate v Cadder [2010] UKSC 43, [2010] 1 WLR 2601 **2010**

HMA v Edwin McLaren and Lorraine McLaren (2017) **294**

Hunter v Chief Constable of the West Midlands [1982] AC 529, affirming [1980] QB **202, 618**

Hurst v Leeming [2002] EWHC 2401 (Ch) **694**

Hutchinson v United Kingdom (Application No. 57592/08) [2015] 61 EHRR 393, [2015] 38 BHRC 67 **541**

Hyam v DPP [1975] AC 55

Inco Europe Ltd *v* First Choice Distribution [2000] 1 WLR 586 **69, 70**

Independent Workers' Union of Great Britain (IWGB) *v* RooFoods Limited T/A Deliveroo (2016) TUR1/985(2016) **162, 175**

JJ (Control Orders), Re. See Secretary of State for the Home Department *v* JJ

Kate Wilson *v* (1) Commissioner Of Police of the Metropolis and (2) Association of Chief Police Officers **153**

Kay *v* Lambeth London Borough Council [2006] EWCA Civ 926, [2005] QB 352 **27**

Kenlin *v* Gardiner [1967] 2 QB 510 **431**

Kennedy *v* Charity Commission [2014] UKSC 20 **718**

Kent *v* Commissioner of Police of the Metropolis [1981] The Times 15 May **390**

Kinsley *v* Commissioner of Police of the Metropolis [2010] EWCA Civ 953, [2010] 25 LS Gaz R 17 **659**

Kleinwort Benson Ltd *v* Lincoln City Council [1999] 2 AC 349, [1998] 3 WLR 1095 **33**

Knuller (Publishing, Printing and Promotions) Ltd *v* DPP [1973] AC 435, [1972] 3 WLR 143 **749**

Kucukdeveci *v* Swedex GmbH & Co KG (Case C-555/07) [2010] ECR I-365, [2010] All ER (EC) 867 **120**

Kupeli *v* Sirketi [2016] EWHC 1478 **691**

L'Office Cherifien des Phosphates Unitramp SA *v* Yamashita-Shinnihon Steamship Co Ltd (The Boucraa) [1994] 1 AC 486 **73**

Laporte *v* Commissioner of Police of the Metropolis [2015] EWHC 371 **690**

Leaf *v* International Galleries [1950] 2 KB 86 **138**

Lee *v* Ashers Baking Company (2018) [2018 UKSC 49 **409**

Leonesio *v* Italian Ministry for Agriculture and Forestry (Case 93/71) [1972] ECR 287, [1973] CMLR 343 **117**

Liversidge *v* Anderson [1942] AC 206 **201**

London and North Eastern Railway Co *v* Berriman [1946] AC 278 **64**

Macarthys Ltd *v* Smith [1979] 1 WLR 1189 **116**

Maddox *v* Storer [1963] 1 QB 451 **66**

Magor and St Mellons Rural DC *v* Newport Corporation [1952] AC 189 **68**

Malone *v* Commissioner of Police of the Metropolis [1980] QB 49, [1979] 2 WLR 700 **376**

Manchester City Council *v* Pinnock (No. 2) [2011] UKSC 6, [2011] 2 All ER 586 **26**

Mangold *v* Helm [2006] All ER (EC) 383 **120**

Marleasing SA *v* La Comercial Internacional de Alimentacion SA (Case C-106/89) [1990] ECR 1–4135 **119, 124**

Marshall *v* Southampton and South West Hampshire AHA (No.1) (Case C-152/84) [1986] QB 401 **113, 119**

McB *v* E (Case C-400/10 PPU) [2011] Fam 364, [2011] 3 WLR 699 **395**

McKenzie *v* McKenzie [1970] 3 All ER 1034, [1970] 3 WLR 472 **257**

McLeod *v* United Kingdom [1999] 27 EHRR 493, [1998] 2 FLR 1048 **455**

McIlkenny *v* Chief Constable of the West Midlands. See Hunter *v* Chief Constable of the West Midlands

McLoughlin *v* O'Brian [1983] 1 AC 410, [1982] 2 WLR 982 **35**

MGN Ltd *v* United Kingdom [2011] 53 EHRR 195, [2011] ECHR 39401/04 **356**

Mills *v* Colchester Corporation [1867] LR 2 CP 476 **131**

Mitchell *v* News Group Newspapers [2013] EWCA Civ 1537, [2014] 2 All ER 430, [2014] 1 WLR 795 **648**

Morris *v* United Kingdom [2002] 34 EHRR 1253 **26**

Motto *v* Trafigura [2011] EWCA Civ 1150, [2012] 2 All ER 181 **357**

Murray *v* United Kingdom (Right to Silence) [1996] 22 EHRR 29 **448**

O'Hara *v* Chief Constable of the Royal Ulster Constabulary [1997] AC 286, [1996] 146 NW Rep 1852

O'Hara *v* United Kingdom [2002] 34 EHRR 32

OB *v* Director of the Serious Fraud Office [2012] EWCA Crim 901, [2012] 3 All ER 1017 **70**

Osman *v* United Kingdom [1999] 1 FLR 193, [2000] 29 EHRR 245 **407, 408**

Othman (Abu Qatada) *v* United Kingdom [2012] ECHR 8139/09 **392**

P *v* S and Cornwall CC (Case C-13/94) [1996] All ER (EC) 397 **394**

Peña-Rodriguez *v* Colorado 580 U. S. ____ (2017) **282**

Pepper (Inspector of Taxes) *v* Hart [1993] AC 593, [1993] 1 All ER 42 **68, 75, 76, 78, 84, 123**

Perotti *v* Collyer-Bristow [2004] EWCA Civ 1019, [2004] All ER (D) 463 (Jul) **660**

PGF II SA *v* OMFS Co 1 Ltd [2013] EWCA Civ 1288, [2014] 1 All ER 970 **690**

Pham *v* Secretary of State of the Home Department [2015] UKSC 19. On appeal from: [2013] EWCA Civ 616 **718**

Pickstone *v* Freemans plc [1989] AC 66, [1988] 2 All ER 803, [1988] 3 WLR 265 **68**

Pimlico Plumber Ltd *v* Smith (2018) [2018 UKSC 29 **160, 161, 175**

Pinochet Ugarte, Re. See R *v* Bow Street Metropolitan Stipendiary Magistrate, ex p Pinochet Ugarte (No. 2)

Practice Direction (Alert to jury) **281**

Practice Direction (CPD III Custody and bail 14E Trials in absence) [2015] EWCA Crim 1567 **487**

Practice Direction (Judicial Precedent) [1966] 1 WLR 1234 **20, 32, 33, 42, 159, 175**

Practice Direction (Justices: Clerk to Court) [2000] 1 WLR 1886 **315**

Practice Direction (Reliable scientific basis for evidence to be admitted) [2014] EWCA Crim 1569 **501**

Practice Direction (Solicitors: Rights of Audience Supreme Court) (1985) **252**

Practice Direction (Solicitors: Rights of Audience) [1972] 1 All ER 608, [1972] 1 WLR 307 **252**

Practice Direction (Special measures: young defendants) **576, 575, 591**

Practice Direction (Third tier courts over-rule their own decisions) (1966) **611**

President of India *v* La Pintada Campañia Navigación SA (The La Pintada) (No. 1) [1985] AC 104, [1984] 2 All ER 773 **36, 172**

Procurator Fiscal *v* Brown. See Brown (Margaret) *v* Stott

Pubblico Ministero *v* Ratti (Case 148/78) [1979] ECR 1629, [1980] 1 CMLR 96 **118**

R (on the application of Al Skeini) *v* Secretary of State for Defence [2007] UKHL 26, [2008] 1 AC 153 **381**

R (on the application of Anderson) *v* Secretary of State for the Home Department [2002] UKHL 46, [2003] 1 AC 837 **540**

R (on the application of B) *v* secretary of state for Justice (2017) **578**

R (on the application of Cart) *v* Upper Tribunal [2011] UKSC 28, [2012] 1 AC 663 **681**

R (on the application of Chester) *v* Secretary of State for Justice; McGeoch *v* The Lord President of the Council [2013] UKSC 63, [2014] AC 271, [2014] 1 All ER 683 **387**

R (on the application of Corner House Research and others) (DAE Systems pic, interested party) *v* Director of the Serious Fraud Office [2008] UKHL 60, [2008] 4 All ER 927 **482**

R (on the application of Crawford) *v* University of Newcastle Upon Tyne [2014] EWHC 1197 (Admin), [2014] All ER (D) 07 (May) **690**

R (on the application of DSD and NBV & Ors) *v* Parole Board of England and Wales & Ors and John Radford [2018] EWHC 694 (Admin) **154**

R (on the application of Gentle) *v* Prime Minister [2008] UKHL 20; affirming [2006] EWCA Civ 1689, [2007] 2 WLR 195 **171**

R (on the application of Gillan) *v* Metropolitan Police Commissioner [2006] UKHL 12, [2006] 2 WLR 537 **435**

R (on the application of Gujra) *v* Crown Prosecution Service [2012] UKSC 52, [2013] 1 AC 484 **484**

R (on the application of Haw) *v* Secretary of State for the Home Department [2006] EWCA Civ 532, [2006] QB 780 **65**

R (on the application of HC) *v* Secretary of State for the Home Department [2013] EWHC 982 (Admin), [2014] 1 WLR 1234 **574**

R (on the application of HS2 Action Alliance Ltd) *v* Secretary of State for Transport [2015] EWCA Civ 203, [2015] All ER (D) 132 (Mar) **123, 124**

R (on the application of Jackson and others) *v* Attorney General [2005] UKHL 56, [2005] 3 WLR 733 **52**

R (on the application of Kadhim) *v* Brent London Borough Housing Benefit Review Board [2001] QB 955, [2001] 2 WLR 1674 **24**

R (on the application of LG) *v* Independent Appeal Panel for Tom Hood School [2010] EWCA Civ 142, [2010] All ER (D) 292 (Feb) **400**

R (on the application of Miller and Dos Santos *v* Secretary of State for Exiting the European Union [2017] UKSC 5 **6, 17–19, 103, 125, 194, 203, 205, 225**

R (on the application of Mohamed) *v* Secretary of State for Foreign and Commonwealth Affairs [2008] EWHC 2048 (Admin), [2009] 1 WLR 2579 **661**

R (on the application of Morrison) *v* Independent Police Complaints Commission [2009] EWHC 2589 (Admin), [2009] All ER (D) 257 (Oct) **438**

R (on the application of Moseley) *v* London Borough of Haringey [2014] UKSC 56, [2015] 1 All ER 495, [2014] 1 WLR 3947 **91**

R (on the application of Mousa) *v* Secretary of State for Defence [2011] EWCA Civ 1334, [2011] 47 LS Gaz R 19 **171**

R (on the application of Mullen) *v* Secretary of State for the Home Department [2004] UKHL 18, [2005] 1 AC 1 **612**

R (on the application of Nicklinson) *v* Ministry of Justice [2014] UKSC 38, [2014] 3 WLR 200 **36**

R (Nunn) *v* Chief Constable of Suffolk Constabulary [2014] UKSC 37 **604**

R (on the application of O'Brien) *v* Independent Assessor [2007] UKHL 10, [2007] 2 AC 312 **410**

R (on the application of Purdy) *v* DPP [2009] UKHL 45, [2010] 1 AC 345, [2009] 4 All ER 1147 **148, 485**

R (on the application of Quintavalle) *v* Human Fertilisation and Embryology Authority [2005] UKHL 28; [2005] 2 AC 561 **752**

R (on the application of Quintavalle) *v* Secretary of State for Health [2003] UKHL 13, [2003] 2 AC 687, [2003] 2 All ER 113 **69**

R (on the application of Roberts) *v* Commissioner of Police of the Metropolis [2015] UKSC 79 **434**

R (on the application of Saunders) *v* Independent Police Complaints Commission [2008] EWHC 2372 (Admin), [2009] 1 All ER 379 **465**

R (on the application of Shabina Begum) *v* Headteacher and Governors of Denbigh School [2006] UKHL 15, [2007] 1 AC 100 **400**

R (Unison) *v* Lord Chancellor (2017) [2017] UKSC 51 **204, 347, 680**

R (on the application of Virgin Media Ltd) *v* Zinga [2014] EWCA Crim 52, [2014] 3 All ER 90, [2014] 1 WLR 2228 **485**

R (on the application of W) *v* Metropolitan Police Commissioner [2006] EWCA Civ 458; reversing [2005] EWHC 1586 (Admin), [2005] 3 All ER 749 **583**

R (on the application of Wells) *v* Secretary of State for Transport, Local Government and the Regions (Case C-201/02) [2005] All ER (EC) 323, [2004] ECR 1-723 **120**

R (on the application of Westminster City Council) *v* Mayor of London [2002] EWHC 2440 (Admin), [2003] LGR 611, [2002] All ER (D) 494 (Jul) **118**

R R *v* Emmens. See R *v* Hollington

R *v* A [2001] UKHL 25, [2001] 3 All ER 1 **70**

R *v* Abdroikof [2007] UKHL 37, [2008] 1 All ER 315 **274–276**

R *v* Alladice (Colin Carlton) [1988] 87 Cr App R 380 **444**

R *v* Allen [1872] LR 1 CCR 367 **66**

R *v* Andrews (Tracey) [1999] Crim LR 156, [1998] 95 (43) LSG **279**

R *v* Aubrey, Berry and Campbell [1978] (unreported) **277**

R *v* Bansal, Bir, Mahio and Singh [1985] Crim LR 151 **290**

R *v* Bentley [1953] The Times 14 January, CA **40**

R *v* Bingham Justices, ex p Jowitt [1974] The Times, 3 July, DC **318**

R *v* Blackshaw [2011] EWCA Crim 2312, [2012] 1 WLR 1126 **531, 537**

R. *v* Boal (Francis) [1992] 2 WLR 890 **603**

R *v* Boundary Commission for England, ex p Foot [1983] 1 All ER 1099 **719, 722**

R *v* Bow County Court, ex p Pelling (No. 1) [1999] 4 All ER 751, [1999] 1 WLR 1807 **257**

R *v* Bow Street Metropolitan Stipendiary Magistrate, ex p Pinochet Ugarte (No. 2) [2000] 1 AC 119, [1999] 1 All ER 577 **21, 80, 715**

R *v* Boyd [2002] UKHL 31, [2002] 3 All ER 1074 **26**

R *v* Brent London Borough Council, ex p Gunning [1985] 84 LGR 168 **90**

R *v* Bristol [2007] EWCA Crim 3214, [2007] All ER (D) 47 (Dec) **432**

R *v* Brown [1994] 1 AC 212, HL, affirming [1992] QB 491, [1992] 2 WLR 441 **749**

R *v* C [2004] EWCA Crim 292, [2004] 1 WLR 2098 **40**

R *v* Caldwell. See Commissioner of Police of the Metropolis *v* Caldwell

R *v* Canale [1990] 2 All ER 187 **447**

R *v* Chief Constable of Sussex, ex p International Trader's Ferry Ltd [1999] 2 AC 418, [1998] 3 WLR 1260, affirming [1997] 2 All ER 65 **716, 721**

R *v* Chief Constable of the Royal Ulster Constabulary, ex p Begley [1997] 1 WLR 1475 **443**

R *v* City of London Court Judge [1892] 1 QB 273 **63**

R *v* Clarence [1888] 22 QBD 23 **33**

R *v* Clark [2003] EWCA Crim 1020, [2003] 2 FCR 447 **498**

R *v* Clarke (2006) **603**

R *v* Clarke [2009] EWCA Crim 1074, [2009] 4 All ER 298 **25**

R *v* Clarke and McDaid [2008] UKHL 8, [2008] 1 WLR 338 **478**

R *v* Condron [1997] 1 WLR 287, [1997] 1 Cr App R 185 **449**

R *v* Cooper [2011] EWCA Crim 1872, [2012] 1 Cr App Rep (S) 529 **24**

R *v* Dallagher [2002] EWCA Crim 1903 **501**

R *v* Davis [2008] EWCA Crim 1735, [2008] All ER (D) 78 (Sep) **510**

R *v* Deacon and Others, AG's Reference Nos 4, 5, 6, 7 and 8 of 2014 [2014] EWCA Crim 651 **607**

R *v* Derbyshire CC, ex p Times Supplements [1991] 3 Admin LR 241, [1990] The Times, 19 July **717**

R *v* Dica [2004] EWCA Crim 1103, [2004] QB 1257 **33**

R *v* Ekaireb [2015] EWCA Crim 1936 **603**

R *v* Ellis (Alexander Tyrone) [2013] EWCA Crim 213 **538**

R *v* Erskine [2009] EWCA Crim 1425, [2010] 1 All ER 1196, [2010] 1 WLR 183 **19**

R *v* F [2009] EWCA Crim 2377, [2010] 1 All ER 1084, [2010] 1 WLR 2511 **267**

R *v* F and D (2016) **268**

R *v* Ford (Royston) [1989] QB 868 **290, 298**

R *v* Fraill and Sewart, sub nom Attorney General *v* Fraill and Sewart, R *v* Knox [2011] EWHC 1629 (Admin) 228 **268**

R *v* Fulling [1987] QB 426; [1987] 2 WLR 923 **413**

R *v* G and another [2003] UKHL 50, [2003] 4 All ER 765 **20**

R *v* Gibson [1990] 2 QB 619 **749**

R *v* Goodyear [2005] EWCA Crim 888, [2005] 3 All ER 117 **494**

R *v* Hanratty [2002] EWCA Crim 1141, [2002] 3 All ER 534 **605**

R *v* Hanson [2005] EWCA Crim 824, [2005] 1 WLR 3169 **497**

R *v* Hollington (David John); R *v* Emmens (George Michael) [1986] Cr App R 281 **291**

R *v* Horncastle [2009] UKSC 14, [2010] 2 All ER 352 **26**

R *v* Human Fertilisation and Embryology Authority, ex p Blood [1997] 2 WLR 807 **750**

R *v* Hussain and Others [2010] EWCA Crim 1327 **292**

R *v* Inland Revenue Commissioners, ex p National Federation of Self-Employed and Small Businesses Ltd [1982] AC 617 **720**

R *v* Innospec Ltd [2010] Crim LR 665 **483, 494**

R *v* International Stock Exchange of the United Kingdom and the Republic of Ireland, ex p Else [1982] Ltd [1993] QB 534 **113**

R *v* Ireland; R *v* Burstowe [1998] AC 147, [1997] 4 All ER 225 **80**

R *v* James and Karimi [2006] EWCA Crim 14, [2006] 1 All ER 759 **23, 24**

R *v* Jogee and Ruddock [2016] UKSC 8; [2016] UKPC 7; On appeal from [2013] EWCA Crim 1433 and JCPC 0020 of 2015 **21, 22**

R *v* Jones [2002] EWCA Crim 2167, [2002] All ER (D) 189 (Sept) **495**

R *v* Jones (Steven Martin) [1997] 1 Cr App R 86, [1996] The Times, 23 July **604**

R v JSM [2010] EWCA Crim 1755, [2011] 1 Cr App Rep 42 **271**

R v Kansal (No. 2) [2001] UKHL 62, [2002] 2 AC 69 **20**

R v Kronlid [1996] The Times, 31 July **284, 285**

R v KS [2009] EWCA Crim 2377, [2010] 1 All ER 1084, [2010] 1 WLR 2511 **271**

R v Lambert (2006) **603**

R v Lambert (Steven) [2001] UKHL 37, [2002] 2 AC 545 **20, 384**

R v Latif (Khalid); R v Shahzad (Mohammed Khalid) [1996] 1 WLR 104 **447**

R v Local Commissioner for Administration for the North and East Area of England, ex p Bradford City Council [1979] 2 All ER 881 **700**

R v Lord Saville of Newdigate, ex p B (No. 2) [2000] 1 WLR 1855, [1999] 4 All ER 860 **716**

R v Magro [2010] EWCA Crim 1575, [2011] QB 398 **25**

R v Marshall and Crump [2007] EWCA Crim 35, [2007] All ER (D) 76 (Jan) **268**

R v Mason [1981] QB 881, [1980] 3 WLR 617 **277**

R v McGarry [1998] 3 All ER 805, [1999] 1 WLR 1500 **448**

R v McLoughlin; R v Newell [2014] EWCA Crim 188, [2014] 3 All ER 73, [2014] 1 WLR 3964 **541**

R v Mildenhall Magistrates' Court, ex p Forest Heath DC [1997] 161 JP 401 **599**

R v Ministry of Defence ex p Smith [1995] 4 All ER 427 **721**

R v Mirza [2004] UKHL 2, [2004] 1 AC 118 **281**

R v Momodou and Limani [2005] EWCA Crim 177, [2005] 2 All ER 571 **464**

R v Morrissey (Ian Patrick); R v Staines (Lorelie Marion) [1997] 2 Cr App R 426 **386**

R v N (Right to Silence) [1998] The Times, 13 February **449**

R v National Lottery Commission, ex p Camelot Group plc [2000] The Times, 12 October **715**

R v Obellim [1997] 1 Cr App R 355, [1996] Crim LR 601 **277**

R v Owen [1991] The Times, 12 December **285**

R v Parliamentary Commissioner for Standards, ex p Al Fayed [1998] 1 WLR 669 **714**

R v Pendleton [2001] UKHL 66, [2002] 1 All ER 524 **605**

R v Ponting [1985] Crim LR 318 **202, 284**

R v Powell and English [1999]1 AC 1, [1997] 4 All ER 545 **21, 40**

R v R (Rape: Marital Exemption) [1992] 1 AC 599, [1991] 4 All ER 481 **40, 148, 612**

R v Rayment and others (23 March 2005, unreported) **286, 294**

R v Reid [1992] 3 All ER 673 **21**

R v Rochford [2010] EWCA Crim 1928, [2011] 1 Cr App R 11, [2011] 1 WLR 534 **491**

R v Samuel (Cornelius Joseph) [1988] QB 615 **444**

R v Saunders [1996] 1Cr App Rep 463 **386**

R v Seaton [2010] EWCA Crim 1980, [2011] 1 All ER 932 **449**

R v Secretary of State for Employment, ex p Equal Opportunities Commission [1995] 1 AC 1, [1994] 1 All ER 910 **122**

R v Secretary of State for Foreign and Commonwealth Affairs, ex p Lord Rees-Mogg [1994] QB 552 **125**

R v Secretary of State for Social Security, ex p Joint Council for the Welfare of Immigrants [1997] 1 WLR 275, [1996] 4 All ER 385 **93**

R v Secretary of State for the Environment, ex p Norwich City Council [1982] QB 808 **721**

R v Secretary of State for the Environment, Transport and the Regions, ex p Spath Holme Ltd [2001] 2 AC 349, [2001] 1 All ER 195 **76**

R v Secretary of State for the Home Department, ex p Brind [1991] 1 AC 696 HL, affirming [1990] 2 Env 787 CA (Civ Div); affirming [1989] Admin LR 169 **390, 721**

R v Secretary of State for the Home Department, ex p Hosenball [1977] 1 WLR 766 **722**

R v Secretary of State for the Home Department, ex p Venables; R v Secretary of State for the Home Department, ex p Thompson [1998] AC 407, [1997] 3 WLR 23 **579**

R v Secretary of State for Transport, ex p Factortame (No. 1) [1990] 2 AC 85 **72, 116, 122, 123, 125**

R v Sheffield Crown Court, ex p Brownlow [1980] QB 530 **277, 299**

R v Simpson [2003] EWCA Crim 1499, [2003] 3 All ER 531 **24, 25**

R v Smith (1999) **603**

R v Smith (Morgan James) [2000] 4 All ER 289 **22–24**

R v Somerset CC, ex p Fewings [1995] 1 WLR 1037 **717**

R v Southwark LBC, ex p Udu [1996] 8 Admin LR 25, [1995] Times, 30 October **718**

R v Staines. See R v Morrissey

R v Suleimanov (Ucha) (2013) [2013] EWCA Crim 32 **538**

R v Thompson [2010] EWCA Crim 2955, [2011] 2 Cr App Rep (S) 131 **297**

R v Tisdall [1984] 6 Cr App R (S) 155 **285**

R v Turner (Frank Richard) (No. 1) [1970] 2 QB 321 **494**

R v Twomey [2009] EWCA Crim 1035, [2009] 3 All ER 1002 **271**

R v Wang [2005] UKHL 9, [2005] 1 WLR 661 **266**

R v Williams (2001) **602**

R v Young [1995] QB 324 **286**

Rees, Re [1986] AC 937 **394**

Rice v Connolly [1966] 2 QB 414 **430**

Richardson (Mark) v Chief Constable of West Midlands Police [2011] EWHC 773 (QB), [2011] 2 Cr App Rep 1 **436**

Ricketts v Cox [1982] 74 Cr App R 298 **430**

Rolf v De Guerin [2011] EWCA Civ 78, [2011] NLJR 290, [2011] All ER (D) 169 (Feb) **694**

Rondel v Worsley [1969] 1 AC 191 **20, 231**

Royal College of Nursing of the United Kingdom *v* Department of Health and Social Security [1981] AC 800 **67**

S (A Minor), Re [2002] All ER (D) 14 (Dec) **71**

S and Michael Marper *v* United Kingdom (Application Nos 30562/04 and 30566/04) [2008] ECHR 178 **451**

Sander *v* United Kingdom [2001] 31 EHRR 44 **279, 280**

Saunders *v* United Kingdom [1997] 23 EHRR 313 **384, 386**

Scandinavian Trading Tanker Co AB *v* Flota Petrolera Ecuatoriana (The Scaptrade) [1983] 2 AC 694, [1983] 2 All ER 763 **140**

Secretary of State for Social Security *v* Tunnicliffe [1991] 2 All ER 712 **384**

Secretary of State for the Home Department *v* JJ [2007] UKHL 45, [2008] 1 AC 385; affirming [2006] EWCA Civ 1141, [2007] QB 446 **397**

Secretary of State for the Home Department *v* MB [2007] UKHL 46, [2008] 1 AC 440 **397**

SG *v* St Gregory's Catholic Science College [2011] EWHC 1452 (Admin), [2011] NLJR 884 **399**

Shaw *v* DPP [1962] AC 220, [1961] 2 All ER 446 **748, 749**

Simmons *v* Castle [2012] EWCA Civ 1288, [2013] 1 All ER 334, [2013] 1 WLR 1239 **34, 649**

Simpson *v* Wells (1871–72) LR 7 QB 2 **130**

Singh *v* London Underground Ltd [1990] The Independent, 25 April, [1990] The Times, 25 April **272**

Smith and Grady *v* United Kingdom [1999] 29 EHRR 493, [1999] ECHR 33985/96 **721**

Smith *v* Hughes [1960] 1 WLR 830 **67**

Smith *v* Ministry of Defence [2013] UKSC 41, [2014] AC 52, [2013] 4 All ER 794 **381**

Sport International Bussum BV *v* Inter-Footwear Ltd [1984] 1 WLR 776 **140**

Stafford *v* DPP [1973] 3 All ER 762 **604, 605**

Steel *v* United Kingdom [1999] 28 EHRR 603, [1998] Crim LR 893 **551**

Steel *v* United Kingdom (The McLibel Two) [2005] 41 EHRR 22 **353, 370**

Stock *v* Frank Jones (Tipton) Ltd [1978] 1 All ER 948, [1978] 1 WLR 231 **41**

Sutcliffe *v* Pressdram Ltd [1991] 1 QB 153, [1990] 1 All ER 269 **289**

SW *v* United Kingdom (Application Nos 20166/92, 20190/92) [1995] 21 EHRR 363, [1996] 1 FLR 434 **40**

T *v* United Kingdom; *v* United Kingdom [2000] 2 All ER 1024, [2000] 30 EHRR 121 **575, 579**

Tachographs, Re (Case 128/78); sub nom Commission of the European Communities *v* United Kingdom (Case 128/78) [1979] ECR 419 **111**

Tanistry Case [1608] Dav Ir 28 **130, 766**

Taxquet *v* Belgium [2009] (unreported) (Application no. 926/05), January 13, 2009, ECHR **293**

Taylor *v* Goodwin [1879] 4 QBD 228, 43 JP 653 **79**

Taylor *v* Lawrence [2002] EWCA Civ 90, [2003] QB 528 **602, 713**

Thakkar *v* Patel [2017] EWCA Civ 117 **701**

Thoburn *v* Sunderland City Council [2002] EWHC 195 (Admin), [2003] QB 151 **123, 376**

Thomas *v* National Union of Mineworkers (South Wales Area) [1986] Ch 20, [1985] 2 WLR 1081 **206**

Thomas *v* Sawkins [1935] 2 KB 249 **455**

Three Rivers DC *v* Bank of England (No. 2) [1996] 2 All ER 363 **75**

Turkington *v* Times Newspapers [2000] 4 All ER 913, [2000] 3 WLR 1670 **79**

Twomey *v* United Kingdom (Application Nos 67318/09 and 22226/12) [2013] ECHR 578 **271**

Uber London Limited *v* Transport for London [2018] EWCA Civ 1213 **158, 175**

United Kingdom *v* Council of the European Union (Case C-84/94) [1996] All ER (EC) 877, [1996] ECR 1-5755 **111**

United States *v* Windsor, 133 S. Ct. 2675 [2013] **390**

Van Duyn *v* Home Office [1974] 1 WLR 1107 **118**

Van Gend en Loos *v* Nederlandse Tariefcommissie (Case 26/62) [1963] ECR 3 **115, 117**

Veluppillai *v* Veluppillai [2015] EWHC 3095 **659**

Vinter *v* United Kingdom [2013] ECHR 66069/09, [2013] All ER (D) 158 (Jul) **541**

Volker und Markus Schecke *v* Land Hessen [2012] All ER (EC) 127 **395**

Von Colson *v* Land Nordrhein-Westfalen (Case C-14/83) [1984] ECR 1891 **119**

Waddington *v* Miah (Otherwise Ullah) [1974] 1 WLR 683 **377**

Walters *v* WH Smith & Son Ltd [1914] 1 KB 595 **437**

Ward *v* James (No. 2) [1966] 1QB 273 **272**

Whitely *v* Chapell [1868] LR 4 QB 147 **64**

Willers *v* Joyce [2016] UKSC 43 & 44 **22, 24**

Willis *v* MRJ Rundell & Associates Ltd [2013] EWHC 2923 (TCC), [2013] 3 EGLR 13, [2013] All ER (D) 36 (Oct) **647**

Wilson *v* First County Trust Ltd [2003] UKHL 40, [2004] 1 AC 816 **383**

Wilson *v* Secretary of State for Trade and Industry [2003] UKHL 40, [2004] 1 AC 816 **76–78, 384, 401**

Wilson *v* Willes [1806] 7 East 121 **131**

Wolstanton Ltd *v* Newcastle-under-Lyme Corp [1940] AC 860, [1940] 3 All ER 101 **130**

Wyld *v* Silver [1963] 1 QB 169 **131**

X (A Child), Re [2017] EWHC 158 **203**

X *v* Mid-Sussex Citizens Advice Bureau [2012] UKSC 59, [2013] 1 All ER 1038 **113**

YL *v* Birmingham City Council [2007] UKHL 27, [2008] 1 AC 95; [2007] 3 All ER 957 **382**

Young *v* Bristol Aeroplane Co Ltd [1944] KB 718; affirmed [1946] AC 163, [1946] 1 All ER 98 **24**

Z *v* United Kingdom (Case 29392/95) [2001] 2 FLR 612, [2002] 34 EHRR 3 **407**

Table of statutes

Abortion Act 1967 51, 67, 150, 163
Access to Justice Act 1999 218, 250, 251, 253, 307,
    308, 312, 335, 339, 343, 349, 356, 364, 367,
    480, 486, 712, 724
    s. 37 480
Act of Settlement 1700 28, 190
Act of Union 1707 618
Administration of Justice Act 1960 70
Administration of Justice Act 1969 713, 767
Anti-Social Behaviour Act 2003 583
Anti-Social Behaviour, Crime and Policing Act 2014
    553, 585
    s. 1 585
    s. 22 585
Anti-Terrorism, Crime and Security Act 2001 180,
    388, 396
Arbitration Act 1996 697, 698
Armed Forces Act 2006 70
Asylum and Immigration Appeals Act 1993 93, 94
Bail Act 1976 459, 574
Bill of Rights 1689 76, 123
    Art. 9 76, 123
Bribery Act 2010 483
Children Act 1989 71, 189
Children Act 2004 432
    s. 11 432
Children and Young Persons Act 1969 576, 577
Civil Partnership Act 2004 361
Civil Procedure Act 1997 631, 641
Companies Act 1980 149
Compensation Act 2006 223, 655
    Pt. 2 223
Computer Misuse Act 1990 169
Constitutional Reform Act 2005 8, 14, 180, 182, 184,
    191, 193, 198, 200, 205, 209, 210, 307–309,
    330, 608, 609, 619
    s. 2 331
    s. 2(2) 331
    s. 3 193, 210
    s. 7 180
    s. 64 196
    s. 65 194
    s. 108(1) 191
    s. 108(3) 191

Constitutional Reform and Governance Act 2010 144
Consumer Credit Act 1974 383
Consumer Rights Act 2015 365
Contempt of Court Act 1981 281, 288, 511
    s. 8 281
Coroners and Justice Act 2009 510, 512, 531
Corporate Manslaughter and Corporate Homicide Act
    2007 466
Counter-Terrorism Act 2008 440
    s. 22 440
Courts Act 1971 190
Courts Act 2003 306, 308, 309, 314, 315, 328, 478,
    506, 512
    s. 29 315
Courts and Legal Services Act 1990 182, 195, 196,
    218, 222, 224, 251, 253, 254, 256, 289, 355,
    367, 626, 629
Crime (Sentences) Act 1997 541
    s. 30 541
Crime and Courts Act 2013 185, 194, 198, 306, 482,
    495, 513, 545, 627, 644, 723
    Pt2, Sch. 13 185
Crime and Disorder Act 1998 313, 459, 486, 538,
    572–575, 584–586
    s. 8 585
    ss. 11–13 584
    s. 37 572
    s. 39 573
    s. 40 573
    s. 41 572
    s. 44 586
    s. 49 313
    s. 49(2) 315
    s. 57 486
    s. 65 574
    s. 66ZA 575
Crime and Security Act 2010 433
    s. 1 433
Criminal Appeal Act 1968 202, 423, 602, 605, 606,
    613, 614, 616
    s. 2 606, 616
    s. 2(1) 602
    s. 17 202, 423, 613, 614
    s. 23 605

Criminal Appeal Act 1995 **170, 600, 613, 617**

Criminal Attempts Act 1981 **149**

Criminal Defence Service (Advice and Assistance) Act
    2001 **50**

Criminal Defence Service Act 2006 **343**

Criminal Evidence (Witness Anonymity) Act 2008 **510**

Criminal Justice Act 1967 **535**

Criminal Justice Act 1972 **608**

Criminal Justice Act 1988 **410, 415, 606**

    s. 133 **410**

    s. 134 **438**

Criminal Justice Act 2003 **270, 271, 273, 292, 299,**
    322, 432, 438, 440, 457, 460, 481, 491, 497,
    525, 526, 528, 531–533, 538, 541, 545, 561,
    562, 607, 608, 619

    Pt. 10 (ss. 75–97) **619**

    s. 43 **271**

    s. 44 **271**

    s. 46 **292**

    s. 75 **607**

    ss. 101–103 **497**

    s. 142 **526, 561**

    s. 143 **533**

    s. 144 **532**

    s. 148 **545**

    s. 153 **533**

    s. 154 **270, 322**

    ss. 189–194 **538**

    s. 321 **273**

    Sch. 21 **541**

    Sch. 33 **273**

    Sch. ? **608**

Criminal Justice and Court Services Act 2000 **451**

Criminal Justice and Courts Act 2015 **269, 280, 313,**
    457, 579, 641, 714, 723

Criminal Justice and Immigration Act 2008 **41, 410,**
    460, 480, 487, 538, 575, 577, 581, 582, 592,
    601, 612

    s. 55 **480**

    s. 76 **438**

Criminal Justice and Police Act 2001 **554**

    s. 2 **554**

Criminal Justice and Public Order Act 1994 **8, 170,**
    181, 292, 314, 389, 430, 440, 448–451, 459,
    535, 766

    s. 34 **440, 448–450**

    s. 34(2A) **448**

    s. 35 **448**

    s. 36 **440, 448**

    s. 37 **440, 448**

    s. 48 **292**

    s. 51 **292**

    s. 60 **434**

    s. 65 **434**

    s. 71 **434**

Criminal Law Act 1967 **148, 149, 284, 438**

    s. 3 **284, 438**

Criminal Law Act 1977 **169, 270, 313**

Criminal Procedure and Investigations Act 1996 **292,**
    491, 504, 505, 608

    s. 3(1) **491**

    s. 6 **505**

    s. 54 **292**

    Code of Practice **491**

Crown Proceedings Act 1947 **406**

Data Retention and Investigatory Powers Act 2014 **456**

Defamation Act 2013 **272, 273**

Domestic Violence and Matrimonial Proceedings Act
    1976 **75**

Employment Protection (Consolidation) Act 1978 **122**

Employment Rights Act 1996 **159, 160, 310**

    s. 12(3)(a) **160**

    s. 50(1) **310**

    s. 230 **159**

Enterprise and Regulatory Reform Act 2013 **679**

Equality Act 2006 **385, 399**

Equality Act 2010 **155, 432, 461, 579**

    s. 26 **155**

    s. 149 **432**

European (Notification of Withdrawal) Act 2017 **6, 103,**
    104

European Communities Act 1972 **62, 72, 73, 88, 103,**
    115, 121–125

    s. 2 **88**

    s. 2(1) **115, 125**

    s. 2(4) **72, 84, 121, 122**

    s. 3(1) **19**

European Parliamentary Elections Act 1999 **52**

European Union Act 2011 **117, 125**

    s. 18 **125**

European Union (Withdrawal) Act 2018 **103, 105**

    s. 2 **103**

    s. 3 **103**

    s. 9 **105**

Fair Trading Act 1973 **696, 706**

Family Law Act 1996 **695, 706**

Finance (No. 2) Act 1940 **93**

Finance Act 1976 **75**

Financial Services Act 1986 **386**

    s. 177 **386**

Firearms Act **530**

Government of Wales Act 1998 **7**

Government of Wales Act 2006 **55**

    Sch. 7 **55**

Health and Safety at Work Act 1974 **411**
Highways Act 1835 **79**
Homicide Act 1957 **23**
  s. 3 **22**
House of Lords Act 1999 **49, 57**
Housing Act 1980 **721**
Human Fertilisation and Embryology Act 1990 **69, 750, 752, 755**
  s. 1 **69**
Human Fertilisation and Embryology Act 2008 **752, 753, 755**
Human Reproductive Cloning Act 2001 **751**
Human Rights Act 1998 **5, 8, 15, 20, 28, 61, 70–72, 76, 79, 84, 123, 155, 180, 184, 189, 200, 202, 315, 375–377, 380–393, 397, 400–402, 407, 408, 415, 422, 426, 675, 712**
  s. 2 **26, 70, 380, 386, 387, 400, 401**
  s. 2(1)(a) **26**
  s. 3 **70, 71, 380, 386, 390, 401**
  s. 3(1) **70, 84**
  s. 4 **70, 71, 382, 401**
  s. 6 **380, 382, 401**
  s. 6(3)(b) **380, 382**
  s. 7 **380, 401**
  s. 10 **6, 70, 382, 383**
  s. 19 **6, 382, 389**
Hunting Act 2004 **52**
Identity Cards Act 2006 **398**
Identity Documents Act 2010 **398**
Immigration Act 1971 **377**
  s. 34 **377**
Inquiries Act 2005 **167, 171, 172**
Interpretation Act 1978 **63**
Judicature Act 1873 **135, 137, 138, 141, 609**
Judicature Act 1875 **135, 137, 138, 141**
Judicial Committee Act 1833 **22**
Juries Act 1974 **267, 273, 277, 282**
Justice and Security Act 2013 **661**
Justices of the Peace Act 1361 **306, 551**
Landlord and Tenant Act 1985 **76**
  s. 31 **76**
Law Commission Act 2009 **169**
Law Commissions Act 1965 **164**
Law of Libel Amendment Act 1888 **79**
Law Officers Act 1997 **332**
Legal Aid, Sentencing and Punishment of Offenders Act 2012 **34, 244, 259, 340–343, 350, 351, 354, 357, 358, 363, 365, 367, 371, 427, 515, 574, 575, 645, 649, 654, 658, 679, 696**
  Pt. 2 **645, 649, 650, 654**
  s. 55 **649**
  Sch. 1 **340**

Legal Aid, Sentencing and Rehabilitation of Offenders Act 2013 **644**
Legal Services Act 2007 **216, 230, 242–244, 246, 247, 250, 253, 255, 260, 660**
  s. 30 **244**
Legislative and Regulatory Reform Act 2006 **89, 90**
Limitation Act 1980 **632**
Local Government Act 1972 **89, 94, 717**
  s. 120(1)(b) **717**
  s. 235 **89**
  s. 235(2) **94**
Local Government and Public Involvement in Health Act 2007 **89, 94**
Localism Act 2011 **92, 94**
Magistrates' Courts (Procedure) Act 1998 **486**
Magistrates' Courts Act 1980 **313, 435, 486, 487, 551**
  s. 1 **435, 486**
  s. 11 **487**
  s. 12 **486**
  s. 16A **313**
Magna Carta 1215 **123, 266**
Marriage (Same Sex Couples) Act 2013 **742**
Matrimonial Homes Act 1967 **140**
Mental Health Act 1983 **548**
Merchant Shipping Act 1988 **122**
Misuse of Drugs Act 1971 **434**
  s. 23 **434**
National Assistance Act 1948 **90, 382**
National Health Service Redress Act 2006 **665**
Northern Ireland Act 1998 **6**
Offences Against the Person Act 1861 **65, 163**
  s. 57 **65**
  s. 58 **163**
  s. 59 **163**
Official Secrets Act 1911 **202, 277, 284, 389**
Official Secrets Act 1920 **66**
Parliament Act 1911 **49, 52, 53, 57, 92**
Parliament Act 1949 **49, 52, 53, 57, 92**
Parliamentary Commissioner Act 1967 **700**
Police Act 1997 **456**
Police and Criminal Evidence Act 1984 **63, 97, 149, 169, 172, 344, 413, 429–445, 447, 448, 450, 451, 454–456, 468, 472, 481, 507, 573, 593**
  Codes of Practice **430, 446, 447, 449, 450, 472, 593**
  Code A **430, 432, 434**
  Code B **455**
  Code C **442, 444, 445, 573, 574**
  Code E **442**
  Code G **435**
  Code G, para. 2.9 **436**

Code H **440**
s. 1 **434, 468**
s. 1(3) **431**
s. 1(6) **431, 433**
s. 2 **432**
s. 2(3) **432**
s. 2(9) **433**
ss. 8-18 **454**
s. 8 **454**
s. 17 **455**
s. 17(6) **455**
s. 18 **455**
s. 19 **456**
s. 24 **436**
s. 24A **437, 468**
s. 25 **431**
s. 28 **438**
s. 30 **439**
ss. 30A–30D **439**
s. 32 **450, 455**
s. 37 **439, 481**
s. 38(1) **439**
s. 40 **440**
s. 41 **440**
s. 46 **439**
s. 54 **450**
s. 55 **451**
s. 56 **443**
s. 58 **344, 443**
s. 60 **97, 442**
s. 60(1)(b) **97**
s. 60(11) **434**
ss. 61–64 **451**
s. 65 **451**
s. 66 **430**
s. 76 **447**
s. 76(1) **413**
s. 76(2) **413, 447**
s. 76(4) **413**
s. 76(8) **413, 447**
s. 78 **413, 447**
s. 117 **433, 436, 438, 454**
Pt. II (ss. 8-18) **454**
Police and Justice Act 2006 **427, 428, 459**
Police and Magistrates' Courts Act 1994 **426**
Police Reform Act 2002 **412, 426, 428, 431, 468**
s. 50 **431**
Police Reform and Social Responsibility Act 2011 **65, 413, 427, 436**
s. 1(2) **427**
Policing and Crime Act 2009 **552**
Policing and Crime Act 2017 **428**

Powers of Criminal Courts (Sentencing) Act 2000 **537, 552, 572, 579–582, 584, 592**
s. 1 **552**
s. 16 **581**
s. 73 **582**
s. 74 **582**
s. 90 **579**
s. 91 **579, 581, 592**
s. 96 **537**
s. 100 **580**
ss. 146–147 **552**
s. 150 **584**
Prevention of Terrorism (Temporary Provisions) Act 1984 **386**
s. 14(1)(a) **97, 98**
Prevention of Terrorism Act 2005 **396, 397**
Proceeds of Crime Act 2002 **550**
s. 6 **550**
s. 38 **550**
Prosecution of Offences Act 1985 **479, 481, 484**
s. 10 **481**
s. 23(3) **484**
Protection of Children Act 1978 **151**
Protection of Freedoms Act 2012 **271, 435, 451**
Public Bodies Act 2011 **92, 95, 329**
Public Order Act 1986 **65, 150, 169, 314, 389**
Race Relations Act 1976 **461**
Regulation of Investigatory Powers Act 2000 **456, 457**
Rent Act 1977 **35**
Restriction of Offensive Weapons Act 1959 **64**
Road Traffic Act 1930 **67**
Road Traffic Act 1960 **66**
Scotland Act 1998 **6, 55, 618**
Senior Courts Act 1981 **272, 598**
s. 48 **598**
Serious Crime Act 2007 **21, 550**
Pt. 1 **550**
s. 5 **550**
Serious Organised Crime and Police Act 2005 **65, 427, 430, 433, 436, 454, 468, 497**
ss. 71–75 **497**
s. 117 **433**
s. 132(1) **65**
s. 133(1) **65**
Sex Disqualification (Removal) Act 1919 **233**
Sexual Offences (Amendment) Act 2000 **52**
Sexual Offences Act 1967 **148, 749**
Sexual Offences Act 2003 **150, 151**
s. 67 **150, 151**
Sexual Offences (Scotland) Act 2009 **150**
s. 9(4) **150**
Sporting Events (Control of Alcohol etc.) Act 1985 **434**

State Immunity Act 1978 80
Statutes of Labourers (14C) 130
Statutory Instruments Act 1946 88
Street Offences Act 1959 67
Suicide Act 1961 485
Taking of Hostages Act 1982 144
Terrorism Act 2000 434, 440
   s. 44 434, 435
   s. 47A 435
Terrorism Prevention and Investigation Measures Act
   2011 398
Transport (London) Act 1969 81, 82
   s. 1 81, 82
   s. 1(1) 82
Tribunals and Inquiries Act 1992 681

Tribunals, Courts and Enforcement Act 2007 184, 185,
   673, 675, 677, 681–685
   Pt. 1 677, 685
   Pt. 2 198
   s. 64 185
   Sch. 6 677
Unfair Contract Terms Act 1977 169
Vaccine Damage Payments Act 1971 681
Violent Crime Reduction Act 2006 451
War Crimes Act 1991 52
Weights and Measures Act 1985 123
Youth Justice and Criminal Evidence Act 1999 71, 496,
   510, 581
   s. 41 71

Table of statutory materials

Statutory Instruments

Civil Procedure Rules 1998 (SI 1998/3132) **625, 631, 632, 635, 637, 641, 648, 649, 659–661, 666, 679, 690, 693, 703, 713, 719**
- Pt 1 **631, 640**
- r. 1.1(2) **631**
- r. 1.4 **637, 690, 693**
- r. 1.4(2)(e) **636**
- r. 3.4 **641**
- r. 3.9 **641**
- Pt 7 **633**
- r. 24.6(1) **637**
- r. 26.4 **637, 690**
- r. 26.6 **637**
- r. 28.14 **635**
- Pt 36 **635, 649**
- r. 39.2 **661**
- r. 44.5 **690**
- r. 52 **713**
- r. 52.17 **602, 713**
- Pt 54 **719**

Civil Service (Amendment) Order in Council 1997 **99**

County Court Rules 1981 (SI 1981/1687) **628, 632, 657, 666**
- Ord. 17 **657**

Criminal Procedure Rules 2005 (SI 2005/384) **477, 478, 491, 494, 501, 504, 505, 518**
- r. 1 **477**
- r. 3 **477**

Equality Act (Sexual orientation) Regulations (Northern Ireland) 2006 (SI 2006/439) **410**

Police and Criminal Evidence Act 1984 (Taperecording of Interviews) (No. 1) Order 1991 (SI 1991/2687) **97**

Rent Acts (Maximum Fair Rent) Order 1999 (SI 1999/6) **76**

Rules of the Supreme Court 2009 (SI 2009/1603) **160, 628, 632, 666**

Practice Direction 1 **160**
- Para. 1.2.17 **160**

Practice Direction 3 (Applications for Permission to Appeal) **160**
- Para 3.6.1 **160**
- Para 3.6.12 **160**

European legislation

Directives

Directive 76/207/EEC (Equal Treatment Directive) **394**

Directive 85/337/EEC (Environmental Impact Assessment Directive) **120**

Directive 98/34/EC (Notification Directive) **119**

Directive 2008/52/EC (Mediation Directive) **705**

Directive 2013/11/EU (Alternative dispute resolution for consumer disputes) **704**

Treaties

European Atomic Energy Community Treaty 1951 (Euratom) 94 **102, 105**

European Charter of Fundamental Rights **341, 393–395**
- Art. 47 **341**
- Art. 51 **395**
- Art. 53(2) **394**

European Coal and Steel Community Treaty 1951 (ECSC) **102**

European Community Treaty See Treaty of Rome

European Treaty See Treaty of Rome

Maastricht Treaty See Treaty on the European Union

Single European Act 1986 **102, 105, 115**

Treaty of Amsterdam 1997 **106, 115**

Treaty of Lisbon 2009 **102, 107–110, 114, 115**
- Art. 6 **394**
- Art. 49 **102**
- Art. 50 **6, 17, 102, 103, 194**

Treaty of Paris 1951 **105**

Treaty of Rome 1957 (EEC Treaty now renamed as the EC Treaty) **102, 116, 118, 124, 394**
- Art. 164 **394**

Treaty on the European Union 1992 (Maastricht Treaty) **102, 106, 111, 115, 116, 125**

Treaty on the Functioning of the European Union 2009 (TFEU) **102, 111–116**
- Art. 157 **116**
- Art. 218(3) **102**
- Art. 238(3)(b) **102**
- Art. 267 **111–114, 126**
- Art. 288 **116**

International legislation and conventions

Bill of Rights (USA) 187, 390, 746
Civil Justice Reform Act 1990 (USA) 657
Constitution (USA)
European Convention for the Protection of Human
    Rights and Fundamental Freedoms 1950 5, 6, 8,
    26, 28, 70, 71, 76, 110, 144, 145, 163, 171,
    279, 293, 315, 330, 344, 346, 352, 353, 356,
    357, 361, 375–390, 392–394, 396–398, 400,
    401, 407, 410, 415, 422, 426, 434, 435, 447,
    448, 451, 455, 456, 458, 459, 464, 477, 487,
    517, 540, 541, 544, 551, 552, 574, 575, 579,
    591, 606, 608, 612, 618, 660, 676, 690, 691,
    714, 718, 751
  Art. 2 171, 377, 381, 401, 408
  Art. 3 377, 381, 401, 426, 438, 541
  Art. 4 377, 381, 401
  Art. 5 377, 381, 386, 388, 396, 397, 401, 426,
    459, 464, 551, 552
  Art. 6 16, 26, 71, 271, 275, 276, 293, 346, 352,
    353, 357, 377, 381, 384, 392, 397, 400, 401,
    407, 408, 415, 422, 426, 575, 591, 606, 660,
    676, 690, 714
  Art. 6(1) 280

Art. 7 40, 377, 381, 401, 477, 487, 517
Art. 8 346, 361, 377, 381, 401, 408, 426, 435,
    447, 455, 456, 574, 751
Art. 8(2) 447
Art. 9 377, 381, 399, 401, 410
Art. 10 281, 353, 356, 377, 378, 381, 401, 408,
    410, 551, 552, 691
Art. 11 162, 377, 381, 401, 691
Art. 12 377, 381, 401
Art. 14 361, 377, 381, 396
Art. 15 378, 386, 396
Art. 26 378
Art. 27 378
Art. 50 6, 15, 379
Preamble
Protocol 1 378, 381
Protocol 1, Art. 1 378, 381
Protocol 1, Art. 2 378, 381, 399
Protocol 1, Art. 3 378, 381
Protocol 4 378
Protocol 7, Art. 4(2) 608
Geneva Conventions 132
Harrison Act 1914 (US) 744
Vienna Convention 21

Cases, law reports and case references: a guide

In order to understand the table of cases and the reference to cases in this text generally, you need to know about the naming of cases, law reports and case references.

Case names

Each legal case that is taken to court is given a name. The name of the case is usually based on the family name of the parties involved. Where there are more than two parties on each side, the case name tends to be shortened to just include one name for each side. In essays, the name of the case should normally be put into italics or underlined, though in this text we have chosen to put them in bold italics. The exact case names in civil law and criminal law are slightly different so we will consider each in turn.

Criminal law case names

If Ms Smith steals Mr Brown's car, then a criminal action is likely to be brought by the state against her. The written name of the case would then be ***R* v *Smith***. The letter 'R' stands for the Latin *Rex* (King) or *Regina* (Queen) depending on whether there was a king or queen on the throne at the time of the decision. Sometimes the full Latin terms are used rather than the simple abbreviation R, so that the case ***R* v *Smith*** if brought in 2004 while Queen Elizabeth is on the throne could also be called ***Regina* v *Smith***. The idea is that the action is ultimately being brought by the state against Ms Smith.

The 'v' separating the two parties' names is short for 'versus', in the same way as one might write ***Nottingham Forest Football Club* v *Arsenal Football Club*** when the two teams are going to play a match against each other. When speaking, instead of saying 'R versus Smith' one should really say 'The Crown against Smith'.

If Ms Smith is only 13, and therefore still a minor, the courts cannot reveal the identity of the child to the public and therefore the case will be referred to by her initial rather than her full name: ***R* v *S***.

Occasionally, criminal prosecutions are brought by the Government's law officers. If an action was brought by the Attorney General against Ms Smith it would be called ***AG* v *Smith***. If it was brought by the Director of Public Prosecutions it would be called ***DPP* v *Smith***. Should the state fail to bring an action at all, Mr Brown might choose to bring a private prosecution himself and the case would then be called ***Brown* v *Smith***.

Civil law case names

In civil law, if Mr Brown is in a neighbour dispute with Ms Smith and decides to bring an action against Ms Smith, the name of the case will be ***Brown* v *Smith***. This is orally expressed as 'Brown and Smith', rather than 'Brown versus Smith'. At the original trial, the first name used is the name of the person bringing the action (the claimant) and the second name used is that of the defendant. If there is an appeal against the original decision, then the first name will usually be the name of the appellant and the second name that of the respondent, though there are some exceptions to this.

In civil law, the state can have an interest in what are described as judicial review cases. For example, Mr Brown may be unhappy with his local council, Hardfordshire City Council, for failing to take action against his neighbour. He may bring an action against the council and the action would be called *R v Hardfordshire City Council, ex parte Brown*.

In certain family and property actions, a slightly different format may be used. For example, if Ms Smith's child, James Smith, is out of control and needs to be taken into care, a resulting legal action might be called *Re Smith* or *In re Smith*. '*Re*' is Latin and simply means 'in the matter of' or 'concerning'. So the name *Re Smith* really means 'in the matter of James Smith'.

As with civil cases, there is sometimes a need to prevent the public from knowing the name of the parties, particularly where children are involved. The initials of the child are then used rather than his or her full name. So the above case might be called *Re S* rather than *Re Smith* to protect James.

The Law Reports

Because some cases lay down important legal principles, over 2,000 each year are published in law reports. Some of these law reports date back over 700 years. Perhaps the most respected series of law reports are those called *The Law Reports*, because before publication the report of each case included in them is checked for accuracy by the judge who tried it. It is this series that should be cited before a court in preference to any other. The series is divided into several sub-series depending on the court which heard the case, as follows:

Appeal Cases (containing decisions of the Court of Appeal, the former House of Lords, the Supreme Court and the Privy Council).

Chancery Division (decisions of the Chancery Division of the High Court and their appeals to the Court of Appeal).

Family Division (decisions of the Family Division of the High Court and their appeals to the Court of Appeal).

Queen's Bench (decisions of the Queen's Bench Division of the High Court and their appeals to the Court of Appeal).

Neutral citation

Following the Practice Direction (Judgments: Form and Citation), a system of neutral citation was introduced in 2001 in the Court of Appeal and the High Court. This form of citation was introduced to facilitate reference to cases reported on the internet and on electronic databases. Unlike reports in books, these reports do not have fixed page numbers and volumes. A unique number is now given to each approved judgment and the paragraphs in each judgment are numbered. The system of neutral citation is as follows:

Civil Division of the Court of Appeal:	[2018] EWCA Civ 1, 2, 3, etc.
Criminal Division of the Court of Appeal:	[2018] EWCA Crim 1, 2, 3, etc.
Administrative Court:	[2018] EWHC Admin 1, 2, 3, etc.

The letters 'EW' stand for England and Wales. For example, if *Brown* v *Smith* is the fifth numbered judgment of 2018 in the Civil Division of the Court of Appeal, it would be cited: *Brown* v *Smith* [2018] EWCA Civ 5. If you wished to refer to the fourth paragraph of the judgment, the correct citation is [2018] EWCA Civ 5 at [4]. The neutral citation must always be used on at least one occasion when the judgment is cited before a court.

Case reference

Each case is given a reference(s) to explain exactly where it can be found in a law report(s). This reference consists of a series of letters and numbers that follow the case name. The pattern of this reference varies depending on the law report being referred to. The usual format is to follow the name of the case by:

A year Where the date reference tells you the year in which the case was decided, the date is normally enclosed in round brackets (often where the reference includes a volume number). If the date is the year in which the case is reported, it is given in square brackets. The most common law reports tend to use square brackets.

A volume number Not all law reports have a volume number; sometimes they simply identify their volumes by year.

The law report abbreviation Each series of law reports has an abbreviation for its title so that the whole name does not need to be written out in full. The main law reports and their abbreviations are as follows:

All England Law Reports	(All ER)
Appeal Cases	(AC)
Chancery Division	(Ch D)
Criminal Appeal Reports	(Cr App R)
Family Division	(Fam)
King's Bench Division	(KB)
Queen's Bench Division	(QB)
Weekly Law Reports	(WLR)

A page number This is the page at which the report of the case commences. For example, *Cozens* v *Brutus* [1973] AC 854 means that the case was reported in the Appeal Cases law report in 1973 at page 854; *DPP* v *Hawkins* [1988] 1 WLR 1166 means that the case was reported in the first volume of the Weekly Law Reports of 1988 at page 1166; and *R* v *Angel* (1968) 52 Cr App R 280 means that the case was reported in the 52nd volume of the Criminal Appeal Reports at page 280.

These references can be used to go to find and read the case in a law library which stocks the relevant law reports. This is important as a textbook can only provide a summary of the case and has no legal status in itself – it is the actual case which contains the law.

Where a case has been decided after the Practice Direction of 2001 introducing neutral citations for the Court of Appeal and Administrative Court, the neutral citation will appear in front of the law report citation. For example: *Brown* v *Smith* [2004] EWCA Civ 5, [2004] QB 432, [2004] 3 All ER 21.

ELLIOTT AND QUINN'S
ENGLISH LEGAL SYSTEM

Introduction

This introduction discusses:

- the principle that too much power should not be invested in the hands of a single person or body (known as the separation of powers);

- the supremacy of Parliament; and

- the rule of law, which means that the state should govern according to agreed rules.

The legal system in context

This book examines the legal system of England and Wales, looking at how our law is made and applied. To understand the legal system, however, you first need to know something about the context in which this legal system is operating: the constitution. A constitution is a set of rules which details a country's system of government; in most cases it will be a written document, but in some countries, including Britain, the constitution cannot be found written down in one document, and is known as an unwritten constitution.

Constitutions essentially set out broad principles concerning who makes law and how, and allocate power between the main institutions of the state – Government, Parliament and the judiciary. They may also indicate the basic values on which the country should expect to be governed, such as the idea that citizens should not be punished unless they have broken the law, or that certain rights and freedoms should be guaranteed, and the state prevented from overriding them.

The unwritten constitution

Britain is very unusual in not having a written constitution – every other Western democracy has one. In many cases, the document was written after a major political change, such as a revolution or securing independence from a colonial power. The fact that the British constitution is not to be found in a specific document does not mean that we do not have a constitution: if a country has rules about who holds the power to govern, what they can and cannot do with that power, and how that power is to be passed on or transferred, it has a constitution, even though there is no single constitutional document. In our constitution, for example, it is established that the Government is formed by the political party which wins a general election, and that power is transferred from that party when they lose an election.

Having said that, the exact details of some areas of our constitution are subject to debate. This is because its sources include not only Acts of Parliament and judicial decisions, which are of course written down (although not together in one document), but also what are known as conventions. Conventions are not law, but are long-established traditions which tend to be followed, not because there would be any legal sanction if they were not, but because they have simply become the right way to behave. In this respect they are a bit like the kind of social rules that most people follow – for example, it is not against the law to pick your nose in public, but doing so usually invites social disapproval, so we generally avoid it. In the same way, failing to observe a constitutional convention is not against the law, but provokes so much political disapproval that conventions generally are followed, and most people concerned would see them as binding. Some well-established examples of conventions are that the Queen does not refuse to give her consent to Acts of Parliament; judges do not undertake activities associated with a political party; and the Speaker of the House of Commons does his or her job impartially, despite being a member of one of the parties represented in the House.

Because conventions are not law, they are not enforced by the courts; but someone who has broken a convention may end up being forced to resign as a result of the disapproval it causes.

Three basic principles underlying the British constitution are the separation of powers, the supremacy of Parliament and the rule of law.

The separation of powers

One of the fundamental principles underlying our constitution is that of the separation of powers. According to this principle, developed by the eighteenth-century French philosopher, Montesquieu (see Cohler *et al.*, 1989), all state power can be divided into three types: executive, legislative and judicial. The executive represents what we would call the Government and its servants, such as the police and civil servants; the legislative power is Parliament; and judicial authority is exercised by the judges.

The basis of Montesquieu's theory was that these three types of power should not be concentrated in the hands of one person or group, since this would give them absolute control, with no one to check that the power was exercised for the good of the country. Instead, Montesquieu argued, each type of power should be exercised by a different body, so that they can each keep an eye on the activities of the other and make sure that they do not behave unacceptably.

Montesquieu believed that England, at the time when he was writing, was an excellent example of this principle being applied in practice. Whether that was true even then is debatable, and there are certainly areas of weakness now, as we shall see in later chapters.

The supremacy of Parliament

A second fundamental principle of our constitution has traditionally been the supremacy of Parliament (also called parliamentary sovereignty). This means that Parliament is the highest source of English law; so as long as a law has been passed according to the rules of parliamentary procedure, it must be applied by the courts. The legal philosopher, Dicey (1982), famously explained that according to the principle of parliamentary sovereignty Parliament has 'under the English Constitution, the right to make or unmake any law whatever; and, further, that no person or body is recognised by the law of England as having a right to override or set aside the legislation of Parliament'. So if, for example, Parliament had passed a law stating that all newborn boys had to be killed, or that all dog owners had to keep a cat as well, there might well be an enormous public outcry, but the laws would still be valid and the courts would, in theory at least, be obliged to uphold them. The reasoning behind this approach is that Parliament, unlike the judiciary, is democratically elected, and therefore ought to have the upper hand when making the laws that every citizen has to live by.

This approach is unusual in democratic countries. Most comparable nations have what is known as a Bill of Rights. This is a statement of the basic rights which citizens can expect to have protected from state interference; it may form part of a written constitution, or be a separate document. In many countries, the job of a Bill of Rights is done by incorporating into national law the European Convention on Human Rights, an international Treaty which was agreed after the Second World War, and seeks to protect basic human rights such as freedom of expression, of religion and of movement. A Bill of Rights takes pre-cedence over other laws and the courts are able to refuse to apply legislation which infringes any of the rights protected by it.

Although Britain is one of the original signatories of the European Convention on Human Rights, for many years it was not incorporated into English law. Parliament has now passed the Human Rights Act 1998, which came into force in October 2000. This Act at last incorporates the Convention into domestic law, but it does not give the Convention superiority over English law. It requires that, wherever possible, legislation should be interpreted in line with the principles of the Convention, but it does not allow the courts to override statutes that are incompatible with it, nor does it prevent Parliament from making laws that are in conflict with it.

Section 19 of the Act requires that when new legislation is made, a Government Minister must make a statement before the second reading of the Bill in Parliament, saying either that in their view the provisions of the Bill are compatible with the Convention or that, even if they are not, the Government wishes to proceed with the Bill anyway. Although the implication is obviously that, in most cases, Ministers will be able to say that a Bill conforms with the Convention, the Act's provision for the alternative state-ment confirms that parliamentary supremacy is not intended to be overridden. The Act does make one impact on parliamentary supremacy, though a small one: s. 10 allows a Minister of the Crown to amend by order any Act which has been found by the courts to be incompatible with the Convention, whereas normally an Act of Parliament could only be changed by another Act. However, there is no obligation to do this and a piece of legislation which has been found to be incompatible with the Convention would remain valid if the Government chose not to amend it.

Membership of the European Union left the fundamental principle of parliamentary sovereignty intact. This was the conclusion of the Supreme Court in *R (on the application of Miller and Dos Santos* v *Secretary of State for Exiting the European Union* (2017). The Supreme Court ruled that Government Ministers could only withdraw the United Kingdom from the European Union after Parliament had passed an Act of Parliament giving the Ministers the authority to do so. In March 2017, the European (Notification of Withdrawal) Act 2017 was passed allowing the UK to formally trigger the withdrawal process through Article 50.

An interesting and unusual view of the present constitutional position has been put forward by John Laws (1998), writing in the academic journal *Public Law*. He suggests that, even without a Bill of Rights, it can be argued that Parliament is not quite so all-powerful as traditional constitutional doctrine would suggest. His point is that Parliament draws its power from the fact that it is democratically elected: we accept its authority to make law because we all have a say in who makes up Parliament. Therefore, says Laws J, it must follow that Parliament's power is restricted to making laws which are consistent with democracy, and with the idea that if we are all entitled to a vote, we must also be entitled to a certain minimum level of treatment. That would mean that our example of a law that all newborn boys had to be killed, which would clearly conflict with this entitlement, might actually be beyond Parliament's law-making powers and, according to Laws J, the courts, therefore, would be constitutionally entitled to refuse to uphold it. This view has not been tested by the courts, but it certainly provides an interesting contribution to the debate.

In 1998, some important constitutional changes were made which passed some of the powers of the Westminster Parliament to new bodies in Scotland and Northern Ireland. The new Scottish Parliament, created by the Scotland Act 1998, can make laws affecting Scotland only, on many important areas, including health, education, local government, criminal justice, food standards and agriculture, though legislation on foreign affairs, defence, national security, trade and industry and a number of other areas will still be made for the whole of the UK by the Westminster Parliament. In September 2014 a referendum was held in Scotland, asking its populace whether they would want to remain part of the UK or declare independence. Following a vote to remain part of the UK, further powers were promised to the Scottish Parliament, including full control over taxation. The Northern Ireland Act 1998 similarly gives the Northern Ireland Assembly power to make legislation for Northern

Ireland in some areas, though again, foreign policy, defence and certain other areas are still to be covered by Westminster.

In the same year, the Government of Wales Act established a new body for Wales, the Welsh Assembly but, unlike the other two bodies, the Welsh Assembly has only limited powers to make primary legislation; legislation made in Westminster will continue to cover Wales. However, the Welsh Assembly is able to make what is called delegated legislation (discussed in Chapter 4).

The rule of law

The third basic principle of our constitution is known as the rule of law. It is developed from the writings of the nineteenth-century writer Dicey. According to Dicey, the rule of law had three elements. First, that there should be no sanction without breach, meaning that nobody should be punished by the state unless they had broken a law. Secondly, that one law should govern everyone, including both ordinary citizens and state officials. Thirdly, that the rights of the individual were not secured by a written constitution, but by the decisions of judges in ordinary law.

The real importance of the rule of law today lies in the basic idea underlying all three of Dicey's points (but especially the first) that the state should use its power according to agreed rules, and not arbitrarily. The issue has arisen frequently in the context of the state's response to terrorism. For example, opposition to an alleged shoot to kill policy by the armed forces in Northern Ireland against suspected terrorists was based on the principle that suspected criminals should be fairly tried, according to the law, and punished only if convicted.

The pressure group JUSTICE issued a manifesto for the rule of law in 2007. This suggests that the rule of law can be broken down into a set of values that governments should accept as matters of constitutional principle which should not be breached. Thus JUSTICE suggests that under the rule of law, governments should:

- adhere to international standards of human rights;
- uphold the independence of judges and the legal profession;
- protect the right to a fair trial and due process;
- champion equality before the law;
- ensure access to justice;
- accept rigorous powers of scrutiny by the legislature; and
- ensure that greater cooperation between governments within Europe is matched by increased rights for citizens.

A practice that has recently come to light which appears to breach the rule of law is that of 'extraordinary rendition'. This describes the kidnapping of people by state representatives and their subsequent detention, without recourse to established legal procedures (such as a formal request for the extradition of a suspect). The US intelligence service has kidnapped a large number of foreign nationals suspected of involvement with the terrorist organisation, Al Qaeda, from around the world and removed them to secret locations without following any established legal procedures. It has been alleged that the UK has provided the US with some assistance in this practice through, in particular, the provision of information about suspects and the use of UK airports.

The Constitutional Reform Act 2005 introduced some major reforms to the British constitution. This Act expressly states in its first section that it 'does not adversely affect . . . the existing constitutional principle of the rule of law'.

A written constitution?

There has been much debate in recent years about whether the UK should have a written constitution. The main reasons put forward in favour of this are that it would clear up some of the grey areas concerning conventions, make the constitution accessible to citizens, and, some argue, provide greater protection of basic rights and liberties, such as freedom of speech.

Written constitutions can be changed, but usually only by means of a special procedure, more difficult than that for changing ordinary law. Thus, it might be necessary to hold a referendum on the proposed change, or gain a larger than usual majority in Parliament, or both. This contrasts with our unwritten constitution, which can be altered by an ordinary piece of legislation. So, some people have argued that the right of people suspected of committing a crime to remain silent when questioned, without this being taken as evidence of guilt, was part of our constitution; nevertheless, that right was essentially abolished by the Criminal Justice and Public Order Act 1994. If the UK had had a written constitution, then this right would probably have been contained in it and a special procedure would have had to be followed to amend the constitution to remove that right. The integration of the European Convention on Human Rights into domestic law may prove to be the first step towards a fully-fledged written constitution. However, the Conservative Government is considering repealing the Human Rights Act 1998, which incorporated the European Convention on Human Rights into domestic law, and replacing it with a British Bill of Rights. The proposals are short on detail, and it is unclear what difference this would make if it occurred. This possibility underscores the ability of successive governments to change the unwritten constitution as they see fit.

Those in favour of our unwritten constitution argue that it is the product of centuries of gradual development, forming part of our cultural heritage which it would be wrong to destroy. They also point out that the lack of any special procedural requirements for changing it allows flexibility, so that the constitution develops along with the changing needs of society.

Reading list

Cohler, A.M., Miller, B.C. and Stone, H.S. (eds) (1989) *Montesquieu: The Spirit of the Laws*. Cambridge: Cambridge University Press.

Dicey, A. (1982) *Introduction to the Study of the Law of the Constitution*. Indianapolis: Liberty Classics.

Horowitz, M.J. (1977) The rule of law: an unqualified good? *Yale Law Journal*, 86: 561.

Laws, J. (1998) The limitations of human rights. *Public Law*, 254.

Raz, J. (1972) The rule of law and its virtue. *Law Quarterly Review*, 93: 195.

On the internet

The manifesto for the rule of law prepared by JUSTICE is available on its website:
http://www.justice.org.uk

Part 1
Sources of law

The word 'source' can mean several different things with regard to law, but for our purposes it primarily describes the means by which the law comes into existence. English law stems from eight main sources, though these vary a great deal in importance:

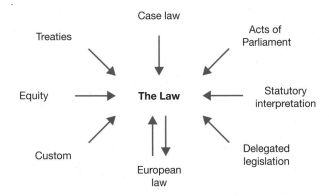

The basis of our law today is case law, a mass of judge-made decisions which lay down rules to be followed in future court cases. For many centuries case law was the main form of law and it is still very important today. However, Acts of Parliament (also known as statutes) are the most important source of law, in the sense that they prevail over most of the other sources. As well as being a source of law in their own right, Acts of Parliament contribute to case law, since the courts occasionally have to interpret the Acts, and such decisions lay down new precedents. Delegated legislation is made by the administration rather than the legislature, and lays down detailed rules to implement the broader provisions of Acts of Parliament. Custom, equity and international treaties are minor sources of law.

Over the years an important source of law has been the legislation of the European Union, which is the only type of law that can take precedence over Acts of Parliament in the UK. Following on from our decision to Brexit, there will be considerable unravelling of our laws in order to separate UK law from European law. It appears that the UK will absorb into its laws many EU laws that currently permeate throughout UK law as it will be difficult to undo so many years of integration of our laws. This is further discussed in Chapter 5.

Part 1 concludes with a discussion of the process of law reform, whereby these sources of law can be changed to reflect the changes taking place in society.

Chapter 1
Case law

This chapter contains:

- an introduction to judicial precedent;

- a description of the hierarchy of the courts and judicial precedent;

- an analysis of how judicial precedent works in practice;

- a discussion of whether judges actually make the law, rather than simply declaring the law;

- consideration of whether judges should be allowed to make law; and

- an overview of the advantages and disadvantages of binding precedent.

1.1 Historical background

Before the Norman Conquest, different areas of England were governed by different systems of law, often adapted from those of the various invaders who had settled there; roughly speaking, Dane law applied in the north, Mercian law around the midlands and Wessex law in the south and west. Each was based largely on local custom and, even within the larger areas, these customs, and hence the law, varied from place to place. The king had little control over the country as a whole, and there was no effective central government.

When William the Conqueror gained the English throne in 1066, he established a strong central government and began, among other things, to standardise the law. Representatives of the king were sent out to the countryside to check local administration, and were given the job of adjudicating in local disputes, according to local law.

When these 'itinerant justices' returned to Westminster, they were able to discuss the various customs of different parts of the country and, by a process of sifting, reject unreasonable ones and accept those that seemed rational, to form a consistent body of rules. During this process – which went on for around two centuries – the principle of *stare decisis* ('let the decision stand') grew up. Whenever a new problem of law came to be decided, the decision formed a rule to be followed in all similar cases, making the law more predictable.

The result of all this was that by about 1250, a 'common law' had been produced, that ruled the whole country, would be applied consistently and could be used to predict what the courts might decide in a particular case. It contained many of what are now basic points of English law – the fact that murder is a crime, for example.

The principles behind this 'common law' are still used today in creating case law (which is in fact often known as common law). From the basic idea of *stare decisis,* a hierarchy of precedent grew up, in line with the hierarchy of the modern court system, so that, in general, a judge must follow decisions made in courts which are higher up the hierarchy than his or her own (the detailed rules on precedent are discussed later in this section). This process was made easier by the establishment of a regular system of publication of reports of cases in the higher courts. The body of decisions made by the higher courts, which the lower ones must respect, is known as case law.

The English common law system was exported around the world wherever British influence dominated during the colonial period. These countries, including the US and many Commonwealth countries, are described as having common law systems. They are often contrasted with civil law systems, which can be found in Continental Europe and countries over which European countries have had influence. The best-known civil law system is the French legal system, whose civil code has been highly influential.

1.1.1 The Supreme Court

Rather unexpectedly, the Labour Government announced in June 2003 that it was going to abolish the House of Lords (which had existed since 1876) and replace it with a Supreme Court. It subsequently issued a consultation paper, *Constitutional Reform: A Supreme Court for the United Kingdom,* which considered the shape that this reform should take. The Constitutional Reform Act 2005 was passed, which contained provisions for the creation of the new court. The Supreme Court (Photo 1.1) was established in 2009 and replaced the House of Lords. The term 'House of Lords' is slightly confusing because this name was used to describe both the highest court, which sat in the Palace of Westminster, and the upper

Photo 1.1 The Supreme Court in Parliament Square

Source: © Justin Kase Zelevenez/Alamy

chamber of Parliament. The upper chamber still remains; it is the Committee of the House of Lords sitting as a court that has been abolished. The last case to be heard by the House of Lords was the high-profile case of Debbie Purdy, who suffered from multiple sclerosis and who was seeking clarification on the criminalisation of individuals who assist the terminally ill to commit suicide.

The Labour Government was anxious to point out that the reform did not imply any dissatisfaction with the performance of the House of Lords as the country's highest court of law:

> On the contrary its judges have conducted themselves with the utmost integrity and independence. They are widely and rightly admired, nationally and internationally. The Government believes, however, that the time has come to establish a new court regulated by statute as a body separate from Parliament.

Six of the Law Lords opposed the reform, considering the change to be unnecessary and harmful.

1.1.2 Separation from Parliament

The consultation paper stated that this reform was necessary to enhance the independence of the judiciary from both the legislature and the executive. It pointed to the growth of judicial review cases and the passing of the Human Rights Act 1998 as two key reasons why this reform was becoming urgent. Article 6 of the European Convention on Human Rights requires not only that the judges should be independent but also that they should be seen to be independent. The fact that the Law Lords sat as a Committee of the House of Lords in Parliament raised issues about whether it appeared to be dependent on the legislature rather than independent.

The new Supreme Court is completely separate from Parliament. Its judges have no rights to sit and vote in the upper chamber. Only the Law Lords who sat in the House of Lords before it was abolished have the right to sit and vote in the House of Lords in its legislative capacity after their retirement from the judiciary.

One advantage of this change is that the court no longer sits in the Palace of Westminster, where there is a shortage of space. The Supreme Court is based in a refurbished Neo-Gothic building opposite Parliament in Parliament Square. A disadvantage is proving to be the financial arrangements for the court. In the past, the House of Lords' running expenses fell within Parliament's budget and did not attract much attention. Now its budget falls within the accounts of the Ministry of Justice and is exposed to the general cuts being made by politicians to reduce the nation's debt.

1.1.3 Jurisdiction

The Supreme Court can hear appeals from the whole of the United Kingdom. It can hear both civil and criminal appeals from England and Wales and Northern Ireland, and civil appeals from Scotland. It is the ultimate arbiter on questions of domestic law. Cases from the Supreme Court raising human rights issues can be heard by the European Court of Human Rights, and cases raising European law issues can be heard by the Court of Justice of the European Union. A case can only be heard by the Supreme Court if the lower court or, more normally, the Supreme Court itself, gives permission to appeal. In 2018, 28 per cent of applications for permission to appeal were successful. This is in line with the trend in previous years. Quite often a lot of publicity surrounds cases which are not in relation to a judgment on appeal but rather in relation to the decision whether permission to appeal should be granted. For example in 2017, the unfortunate case of terminally ill Charlie Gard that courted much public interest, in fact so much so, that supporters of Charlie and his parents became known as 'Charlie's Army'. The case also attracted comment from Donald Trump and the Pope. This was a case in relation to an application for permission to appeal, not in relation to the decision itself. Charlie's parents mounted an appeal against Great Ormond Street Hospital's ('GOSH') decision to withdraw Charlie's life support machine. Charlie's parents did not want GOSH to continue treatment but rather just to continue to keep Charlie alive through artificial ventilation until they could take him to the US for treatment, for which they had raised funds. GOSH denied this as it had determined that such an endeavour would be futile. The Supreme Court agreed with GOSH and with the utmost sympathy, denied permission to appeal this decision.

The Supreme Court does not have the power to overturn legislation, a power enjoyed by the Supreme Court in America. It is not a purely constitutional court (like the *Conseil constitutionnel* in France), partly because we do not have a written constitution so it would be difficult to determine the jurisdiction of a constitutional court for the United Kingdom. The new court does not have the power to give preliminary rulings on difficult points of law because English courts do not traditionally consider issues in the abstract, so giving such a power to the Supreme Court would sit uneasily with our judicial traditions.

1.1.4 Membership

The full-time Law Lords from the former House of Lords are the first judges of the Supreme Court. It has a maximum of 12 full-time judges, but can call on the help of other judges on a part-time basis. Members of the Supreme Court are called 'Justices of the Supreme Court'. The Lord Chancellor was a member of the Appellate Committee of the House of Lords, but does not have a right to sit in the Supreme Court. The judges no longer automatically become Lords, instead the new male appointments take the title of 'Sir' and the female appointments 'Dame'. Quite a remarkable and long-awaited moment in legal history was marked in October 2018 when a majority of female justices sat in the Supreme Court (see Chapter 10).

Qualifications for membership have remained the same as for the House of Lords. The Government rejected the idea that changes should be made to make it easier for distinguished academics to be appointed in order to enhance the diversity of the court. This is disappointing, as the Government itself acknowledges that the current pool of candidates for the court is very narrow, and the Government's statistics show that the current senior judiciary are not representative of society. Candidates are not subjected to confirmation hearings before Parliament as these would risk politicising the appointment process (discussed in Chapter 10).

In the Supreme Court five judges normally hear each case but in important cases seven or nine judges sit together. The rules for permission to appeal have remained largely unchanged, so the range and number of cases heard is just slightly higher than those of the House of Lords – about 90 cases each year.

1.1.5 The Supreme Court at work

In the past, the public was confused as to the identity of the House of Lords and its relationship with Parliament. Increasingly the public understands the role of the Supreme Court. It is open to the public and it is physically easier to visit than the old House of Lords which was hidden inside the long corridors of the Palace of Westminster.

Having moved into separate buildings from Parliament, the Supreme Court has tried to be more open, accessible and media friendly. All of its hearings are open to the public. The judge giving the lead, majority verdict will give a short oral explanation of the judgment in the morning it is released. This is televised and is occasionally shown on a news programme. There is more media interest in its work, particularly with its growing case load involving human rights law. It is gradually getting a higher profile and moving into the role of a constitutional court.

In 2018 the Supreme Court heard 85 cases and just under half of these appeals were successful. It is arguable that this high success rate suggests more cases should be given permission to appeal.

The physical layout of the Supreme Court building provides more opportunity for the judges to chat with each other informally when they are preparing their judgments than the offices on the long corridor in the House of Lords (Paterson (2013)). Through this process of discussion they can iron out some of their differences, so there are fewer divergent views being expressed in the individual judgments, reducing uncertainty. In 2014, only one-fifth of cases included a dissenting judgment. There is still a role for a minority dissenting judgment as this can help shape the law where the court later decides it got the law wrong.

As mentioned earlier, the Supreme Court sits in panels containing an odd number of judges, normally five, but sometimes they sit in panels of seven or even nine. It is worthy of particular note that in the Article 50 case of *R (on the application of Miller and Dos*

Santos) v *The Secretary of State for Exiting the European Union* (2017), 11 judges sat to hear the case. On one occasion in 2017, nine judges sat to hear a case and on nine other occasions seven judges decided the case.

Hearings in the Supreme Court are relatively short, lasting an average of two days. In 2016, the longest hearing was with regard to the aforementioned *Miller* case, which lasted four days. From the trial hearing, the Supreme Court takes on average three and a half months to give its decision. Its judgments are on average 30 pages long. In over half of the cases heard by the Supreme Court, one of the parties is a public authority (such as the HM Revenue & Customs, the Crown Prosecution Service and local authorities).

1.2 Judicial precedent

Case law comes from the decisions made by judges in the cases before them (the decisions of juries do not make case law). In deciding a case, there are two basic tasks: first, establishing what the facts are, meaning what actually happened; and, secondly, how the law applies to those facts. It is the second task that can make case law, and the idea is that once a decision has been made on how the law applies to a particular set of facts, similar facts in later cases should be treated in the same way, following the principle of *stare decisis* described earlier. This is obviously fairer than allowing each judge to interpret the law differently, and also provides predictability, which makes it easier for people to live within the law.

The judges listen to the evidence and the legal argument and then prepare a written decision as to which party wins, based on what they believe the facts were, and how the law applies to them. This decision is known as the judgment, and is usually long, containing quite a lot of comment which is not strictly relevant to the case, as well as an explanation of the legal principles on which the judge has made a decision. The explanation of the legal principles on which the decision is made is called the *ratio decidendi* – Latin for the 'reason for deciding'. It is this part of the judgment, known as binding precedent, which forms case law.

All the parts of the judgment which do not form part of the *ratio decidendi* of the case are called *obiter dicta* – which is Latin for 'things said by the way'. These are often discussions of hypothetical situations: for example, the judge might say 'Jones did this, but if she had done that, my decision would have been . . . '. None of the *obiter dicta* forms part of the case law, though judges in later cases may be influenced by it, and it is said to be a persuasive precedent.

In deciding a case, a judge must follow any decision that has been made by a higher court in a case with similar facts. The rules concerning which courts are bound by which are known as the rules of judicial precedent, or *stare decisis*. As well as being bound by the decisions of courts above them, some courts must also follow their own previous decisions; they are said to be bound by themselves.

When faced with a case on which there appears to be a relevant earlier decision, the judges can do any of the following.

Follow If the facts are sufficiently similar, the precedent set by the earlier case is followed, and the law applied in the same way to produce a decision.

Distinguish Where the facts of the case before the judge are significantly different from those of the earlier one, then the judge distinguishes the two cases and need not follow the earlier one.

Figure 1.1 How judicial precedent works

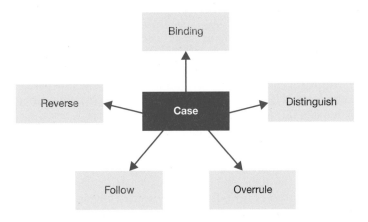

Overrule Where the earlier decision was made in a lower court, the judges can overrule that earlier decision if they disagree with the lower court's statement of the law. The outcome of the earlier decision remains the same, but will not be followed. The power to overrule cases is only used sparingly because it weakens the authority and respect of the lower courts.

Reverse If the decision of a lower court is appealed to a higher one, the higher court may change it if they feel the lower court has wrongly interpreted the law. Clearly when a decision is reversed, the higher court is usually also overruling the lower court's statement of the law.

In practice, the process is rather more complicated than this, since decisions are not always made on the basis of only one previous case; there are usually several different cases offered in support of each side's view of the question.

Numerous cases are published in law reports, legal databases and online. In *R v Erskine* (2009) the Court of Appeal said lawyers needed to select carefully the cases they referred to in court or the justice system would be 'suffocated'. Only cases which established the principle of law under consideration should be cited. Authorities that merely illustrated the principle, or restated it, should not be cited. The court was thereby seeking to ensure that the doctrine of precedent is not overwhelmed by the sheer number of published judgments.

1.3 The hierarchy of the courts

1.3.1 Court of Justice of the European Union

At present, decisions of the Court of Justice of the European Union (CJEU) on European law are binding on all English courts (European Communities Act 1972, s. 3(1)). Although the European Court tends to follow its own previous decisions, it is not bound to do so, but we need to know what the position will be post-Brexit. Indeed, Lord Neuberger, prior to stepping down as the President of the Supreme Court having presided over the *Miller* judgment, impressed upon the Government to clarify the position. He is mindful of the separation of powers and has maintained that 'If [the Government] doesn't express clearly what the judges should do about decisions of the European Court of Justice after Brexit, or indeed any other topic after Brexit, then the judges will simply have to do their best.' This would mean that the judges need to be guided by statute otherwise they will be left with little guidance from the Government. A year later, things are unfortunately not that much clearer although some guidance can be garnered from the Government's White Paper entitled 'Legislating for the Withdrawal Agreement between the United Kingdom and the European Union'. This White Paper states that the proposed EU (Withdrawal Agreement) Bill will legislate for the time-limited implementation period. This effectively suggests that following 29 March 2019, which is when the UK will officially leave the EU, there will be a time-limited implementation period which will last until 31 December 2020. In other words, EU law will remain in place to ensure some certainty for businesses although it will be under the umbrella of the Withdrawal Agreement. Perhaps with some cynicism, one might say that this 'transitional period' is another way of buying more time for the inevitable. The paper also explains that the direct jurisdiction of the CJEU in the UK will come to an end over the period of eight years in relation to the rights of EU citizens who continue to live in the UK following Brexit; the UK will continue to seek guidance from the CJEU through the usual referral procedure. The UK courts will continue to deliver the final judgment in all decisions, not the CJEU.

1.3.2 Supreme Court

Apart from cases concerning European law, the Supreme Court is the highest appeal court on civil and criminal matters, and all other English courts are bound by it. The Supreme Court replaced the long-established House of Lords in 2009 and the rules of precedent are exactly the same for the Supreme Court as they were for the House of Lords before it. The House of Lords was traditionally bound by its own decisions, but in 1966 the Lord Chancellor issued a Practice Statement saying that the House of Lords was no longer bound by its previous decisions. In practice, the House of Lords only rarely overruled one of its earlier decisions, and this reluctance is illustrated by the case of *R v Kansal (No. 2)* (2001). In that case the House of Lords held that it had probably got the law wrong in its earlier decision of *R v Lambert* (2001). The latter case had ruled that the Human Rights Act 1998 would not have retrospective effect in relation to appeals heard by the House of Lords after the Act came into force, but which had been decided by the lower courts before the Act came into force. Despite the fact that the majority thought the earlier judgment of *Lambert* was wrong, the House decided in *Kansal* to follow it. This was because *Lambert* was a recent decision, it represented a possible interpretation of the statute that was not unworkable and it only concerned a temporary transitional period.

There is, however, a range of cases where the House of Lords had been prepared to apply the **1966 Practice Direction**. In *Hall v Simons* (2000), the House of Lords refused to follow the earlier case of *Rondel v Worsley* (1969), which had given barristers immunity against claims for negligence in their presentation of cases.

In *R v G and another* (2003), the House of Lords overruled an established criminal case of *R v Caldwell* (1981). Under *R v Caldwell*, the House had been prepared to convict people for criminal offences where the prosecution had not proved that the defendant personally had intended, or seen the risk of causing, the relevant harm, but had simply shown that a reasonable person would have had this state of mind on the facts. This was particularly harsh where the actual defendant was incapable of seeing the risk of harm, because, for example, they were very young or of low intelligence. ***Caldwell*** had been heavily criticised by academics over the years, but when the House of Lords originally reconsidered the matter, in ***R v Reid*** (1992), it confirmed its original decision. However, when the matter again came to the House of Lords in 2003, the House dramatically admitted that it had got the law wrong. It stated:

> The surest test of a new legal rule is not whether it satisfies a team of logicians but how it performs in the real world. With the benefit of hindsight the verdict must be that the rule laid down by the majority in **Caldwell** failed this test. It was severely criticised by academic lawyers of distinction. It did not command respect among practitioners and judges. Jurors found it difficult to understand; it also sometimes offended their sense of justice. Experience suggests that in **Caldwell** the law took a wrong turn.

In ***R v Jogee*** (2016), the Supreme Court was looking at the law on accomplice liability. The law on this subject had been developed by the House of Lords in ***R v Powell and English*** (1999). The Supreme Court decided that the House of Lords had got the law wrong on this area and that it was appropriate to change back the law to how it had been before ***Powell and English***. It was justified in making this change because when the House of Lords had decided ***Powell and English*** not all relevant authorities were considered; the law laid down in ***Powell and English*** was not satisfactory and caused problems leading to a large number of appeals; and it was wrong for accomplice liability to be imposed when the accomplice had less culpability than the murderer. A change in the law did not need to be left to Parliament because accomplice liability is governed by the common law and should be corrected by the courts. This change in the law would also bring the common law into line with legislation made by Parliament (the Serious Crime Act 2007) in an overlapping area of criminal liability. The law was therefore changed even though the Supreme Court was mindful of the fact that this change was likely to lead to a number of appeals by people who had been convicted as accomplices in earlier cases under ***Powell and English***.

In ***Re Pinochet Ugarte*** (1999), the House of Lords stated that it had the power to reopen an appeal where, through no fault of his or her own, one of the parties has been subjected to an unfair procedure. The case was part of the litigation concerning General Augusto Pinochet, the former Chilean head of state. The Lords reopened the appeal because one of the Law Lords who heard the original appeal, Lord Hoffmann, was connected with the human rights organisation Amnesty International, which had been a party to the appeal. This meant that there was a possibility of bias and so the proceedings could be viewed as unfair. The Lords stressed, however, that there was no question of them being able to reopen an appeal because the decision made originally was thought to be wrong; the Pinochet appeal was reopened because it could be said that there had not been a fair hearing, and not because the decision reached was wrong (although at the second hearing of the appeal, the Lords did in fact come to a slightly different decision).

Assange* v *Swedish Prosecution Authority (2012) concerned an application by the Swedish authorities for Julian Assange (involved in the Wikileaks scandal) to be extradited to Sweden to face charges concerning accusations of sexual assault. The Supreme Court allowed this application but Assange's lawyer argued that the case should be reopened because the Supreme Court had decided the case on the basis of the Vienna Convention, which had not been discussed during the hearing. This argument to reopen the case was subsequently rejected.

1.3.3 Privy Council

The Privy Council was established by the Judicial Committee Act 1833. It is the final appeal court for outlying British or formerly British territories, such as Jamaica, Gibraltar and the Isle of Man. The judges of the Supreme Court sit in the Privy Council. It is based in the buildings of the Supreme Court but remains a separate entity. In 2018, it heard 43 appeals.

Under the traditional rules of precedent, the decisions of the Privy Council do not bind English courts, but have strong persuasive authority because of the seniority of the judges who sit in the Privy Council (*de Lasala* v *de Lasala* (1980)). A national court will therefore usually follow a Privy Council decision (unless there is a decision of a superior court to the contrary), but it is not bound by precedent to do so. A judge of the Courts of England and Wales should not follow a decision of the Privy Council if it is inconsistent with the decision of a court by which the judge is otherwise bound, because the Privy Council is not part of the hierarchy of the national court structure.

Some recent cases, particularly in the context of criminal law, had thrown doubt on this limited role of the Privy Council in developing judicial precedent in England, but the traditional approach has been confirmed by the Supreme Court in *Willers* v *Joyce* (2016). The Supreme Court stated that a first instance judge or the Court of Appeal cannot decide to ignore this rule of precedent simply because they consider it a 'foregone conclusion' that the Privy Council view will be accepted by the Supreme Court in the future. Judges should never follow a decision of the Privy Council, if it is inconsistent with the decision of a court which is binding on them.

However, in *Willers* v *Joyce* the Supreme Court did state that, while a first instance judge or Court of Appeal judge cannot themselves ignore the traditional rules of precedent, the Privy Council itself can state its decision should be followed by the lower domestic courts. In an appeal to the Privy Council involving an issue of English law on which a previous decision of the House of Lords, Supreme Court or Court of Appeal is challenged, the Privy Council can expressly direct that the previous decision was wrong and that domestic courts should treat the Privy Council's decision as representing English law. The Supreme Court remarked that such an approach 'is plainly sensible in practice and justified by experience'. It takes advantage of the fact that the Privy Council judges normally consist of Justices of the Supreme Court.

In 2016 the Supreme Court and the Privy Council sat together for the first time. In *R* v *Jogee and Ruddock* (2016) the two courts heard two appeals jointly so that a united approach was taken to the legal issues that arose in the cases. *R* v *Jogee* was a domestic appeal to the Supreme Court and *R* v *Ruddock* was a Jamaican case on appeal to the Privy Council. The same panel of judges gave a joint judgment in the cases.

Willers v *Joyce* lays down as a matter of principle what effectively happened in practice in *Jersey* v *Holley* (2005). That case concerned the old defence of provocation in criminal law which if successful reduced a defendant's liability from murder to manslaughter.

The defence was laid down in s. 3 of the Homicide Act 1957. This section was interpreted as laying down a two-part test. The first part of the test required the defendant to have suffered from a sudden and temporary loss of self-control when he or she killed the victim. The second part of the test provided that the defence would only be available if a reasonable person would have reacted as the defendant did. This was described as an objective test, because it was judging the defendant's conduct according to objective standards, rather than their own standards. However, in practice, reasonable people almost never kill, so if this second requirement was interpreted strictly, the defence would rarely have succeeded. As a result, in *R* v *Smith (Morgan James)* (2000) the House of Lords held that, in determining whether a reasonable person would have reacted in this way, a court could take into account the actual characteristics of the defendant. So if the defendant had been depressed and was of low intelligence, then the test would become whether a reasonable person suffering from depression and of low intelligence would have reacted by killing the victim.

In an appeal from Jersey on the defence of provocation, *Attorney General for Jersey* v *Holley* (2005), the Privy Council refused to follow the case of *Smith (Morgan James)*, stating the case misinterpreted Parliament's intention when it passed the Homicide Act 1957. It considered the only characteristics that should be taken into account when considering whether the defendant had reacted reasonably were characteristics that were directly relevant to the provocation itself, but not general characteristics which simply affected a person's ability to control him- or herself.

The Court of Appeal in *James and Karimi* (2006) decided to apply the Privy Council's judgment in *Holley* rather than the House of Lords' judgment in *Smith (Morgan James)*. The Court of Appeal acknowledged this went against the established rules of judicial precedent. It gave various justifications for treating this as an exceptional case in which those established rules should not apply. It pointed out that the Privy Council had realised the importance of its judgment and had chosen to have an enlarged sitting of nine judges, all drawn from the House of Lords:

> The procedure adopted and the comments of members of the Board in **Holley** suggest that a decision must have been taken by those responsible for the constitution of the Board in **Holley** . . . to use the appeal as a vehicle for reconsidering the decision of the House of Lords in **Morgan Smith**, not just as representing the law of Jersey but as representing the law of England. A decision was taken that the Board hearing the appeal to the Privy Council should consist of nine of the twelve Lords of Appeal in Ordinary.

The judges in *Holley* were divided in their verdict six to three. The start of the first judgment of the majority stated:

> This appeal, being heard by an enlarged board of nine members, is concerned to resolve this conflict [between the House of Lords and the Privy Council] and clarify definitively the present state of English law, and hence Jersey law, on this important subject.

The dissenting judges stated:

> We must however accept that the effect of the majority decision is as stated in paragraph 1 of the majority judgment.

Thus, even the dissenting judges appear to accept that the majority decision laid down the law in England. The Court of Appeal also considered that if an appeal was taken to the House of Lords, the outcome was 'a foregone conclusion' and the House would take the same approach as *Holley*:

> Half of the Law Lords were party to the majority decision in **Holley**. Three more in that case accepted that the majority decision represented a definitive statement of English law on the issue in question. The choice of those to sit on the appeal might raise some nice questions, but we cannot conceive that, whatever the precise composition of the Committee, it would do other than rule that the majority decision in **Holley** represented the law of England. In effect, in the long term at least, **Holley** has overruled **Morgan Smith**.

This argument would be more convincing if the *Holley* case had been decided by a unanimous verdict. In fact, there were still potentially six House of Lords judges who preferred the

Smith (Morgan James) approach: the three dissenting judges and the three House of Lords judges who did not hear the *Holley* case. The 'foregone conclusion' test has been rejected by the Supreme Court in *Willers* v *Joyce*. What matters is whether the Privy Council has expressly stated that it is laying down the law for England and Wales.

Lord Woolf recognised in *R* v *Simpson* (2003) that the rules of judicial precedent must provide certainty but at the same time they themselves must be able to evolve in order to do justice:

> The rules as to precedent reflect the practice of the courts and have to be applied bearing in mind that their objective is to assist in the administration of justice. They are of considerable importance because of their role in achieving the appropriate degree of certainty as to the law. This is an important requirement of any system of justice. The principles should not, however, be regarded as so rigid that they cannot develop in order to meet contemporary needs.

The Court of Appeal presumably concluded in *James and Karimi* that this was a situation where justice could only be achieved by shifting the established rules of judicial precedent. The actual outcome of the case made it more difficult for a partial defence to murder, reducing liability to manslaughter, to succeed. This may be considered to achieve justice for victims' families, but it may be an injustice to the mentally ill defendant.

1.3.4 Court of Appeal

This is split into Civil and Criminal Divisions; they do not bind each other. Both are bound by decisions of the old House of Lords, and the new Supreme Court.

Key case

In *Young* v *Bristol Aeroplane Co Ltd* (1946) the Court of Appeal stated that the Civil Division is usually bound by its own previous decisions. There are four exceptions to this general rule.

1   The previous decision was made in ignorance of a relevant law (it is said to have been made *per incuriam*). This *per incuriam* rule was interpreted in *R* v *Cooper* (2011) as extending beyond decisions made in ignorance of legal authorities, to include decisions made in ignorance of relevant 'material and argument'. On the facts of that case, the material and arguments concerned the history of legislation banning sex offenders from working with children. Without this information the Court of Appeal had misinterpreted the legislation in an earlier case and this interpretation was corrected in the present case.

2   There are two previous conflicting decisions.

3   There is a House of Lords (or Supreme Court) decision which conflicts with the earlier Court of Appeal decision.

4   A proposition of law was assumed to exist by an earlier court and was not subject to argument or consideration by that court.

The last of these exceptions was added by *R (on the application of Kadhim)* v *Brent London Borough Housing Benefit Review Board* (2001).

Legal principle
The Civil Division of the Court of Appeal is usually bound by its own previous decisions.

In the Criminal Division, the results of cases heard may decide whether or not an individual goes to prison, so the Criminal Division takes a more flexible approach to its previous decisions and does not follow them where doing so could cause injustice. In *R v Simpson* (2003) the Court of Appeal stated that it had a degree of discretion to decide whether one of its earlier decisions should be treated as binding on itself when there were grounds for saying the earlier decision was wrong. This *dicta* was narrowly interpreted in *R v Magro* (2010), where the Court of Appeal held that its earlier decision in *R v Clarke* (2009) was wrong, but it was still not able to overrule it because the earlier decision had benefited from full argument of the relevant legislation and case law and the judges closely analysed the point. Thus *R v Simpson* was interpreted as simply referring to the *per incuriam* rule that an earlier case would not be binding if it was made in ignorance of a relevant law (at least when the earlier case benefits the defendant).

1.3.5 High Court

This court is divided between the Divisional Courts and the ordinary High Court. All are bound by the Court of Appeal, the old House of Lords and the new Supreme Court.

The Divisional Courts are the Queen's Bench Division, which deals with criminal appeals and judicial review, the Chancery Division and the Family Division, which both deal with civil appeals. The two civil Divisional Courts are bound by their previous decisions, but the Divisional Court of the Queen's Bench is more flexible about this, for the same reason as the Criminal Division of the Court of Appeal. The Divisional Courts bind the ordinary High Court.

The ordinary High Court is not bound by its own previous decisions. It can produce precedents for courts below it, but these are of a lower status than those produced by the Court of Appeal, the old House of Lords or the new Supreme Court.

1.3.6 Crown Court

The Crown Court is bound by all the courts above it. Its decisions do not form binding precedents, though when High Court judges sit in the Crown Court, their judgments form persuasive precedents, which must be given serious consideration in successive cases, though it is not obligatory to follow them. When a circuit or district judge is sitting, no precedents are formed. Since the Crown Court cannot form binding precedents, it is obviously not bound by its own decisions.

1.3.7 Magistrates' courts

The magistrates' courts hear mainly summary criminal cases. They are bound by the High Court, the Court of Appeal and the Supreme Court. Their own decisions are not reported, and cannot produce binding precedents, or even persuasive ones. Like the Crown Court, they are therefore not bound by their own decisions.

1.3.8 County Court

The County Court hears low-value civil cases. It is a court of record so it can set precedents for itself, but not for higher courts. It is bound by the High Court, the Court of Appeal and the Supreme Court.

1.3.9 European Court of Human Rights

The European Court of Human Rights (ECtHR) is an international court based in Strasbourg. It hears cases alleging that there has been a breach of the European Convention on Human Rights. This court does not fit neatly within the hierarchy of the courts. Under s. 2 of the Human Rights Act 1998, an English court 'must take account of' the cases decided by the ECtHR. This would suggest that the decisions of the ECtHR are not completely binding on UK courts. Usually the jurisprudence of the ECtHR, having been taken into account, would be followed, but the domestic courts are not bound to do so. There is considerable debate about how s. 2 should be interpreted which is linked to a broader debate about how much influence the ECtHR should have in the United Kingdom. Under what has become known as the 'mirror principle', it has been suggested that the domestic courts should seek to mirror the interpretation of Convention rights to the interpretation given by the ECtHR. In *Manchester City Council* v *Pinnock (No. 2)* (2011) the Supreme Court stated:

> Where . . . there is a clear and constant line of decisions whose effect is not inconsistent with some fundamental substantive or procedural aspect of our law, and whose reasoning does not appear to overlook or misunderstand some argument or point of principle, we consider that it would be wrong for this court not to follow that line.

Despite this, the Supreme Court (and the House of Lords before it) has, on occasion, refused to follow an earlier decision of the ECtHR on the basis that the ECtHR has not fully understood the UK common law on this subject. In *Morris* v *UK* (2002), the ECtHR ruled that the courts martial system (which is the courts system used by the army) breached the European Convention on Human Rights as it did not guarantee a fair trial within the meaning of Art. 6 of the Convention. Subsequently, in *R* v *Boyd* (2002), three soldiers who had been convicted of assault by a court martial argued before the House of Lords that the court martial had violated their right to a fair trial under the Convention. This argument was rejected and the House of Lords refused to follow the earlier decision of the ECtHR. It stated:

> While the decision in **Morris** is not binding on the House, it is of course a matter which the House must take into account [s. 2(1)(a) of the Human Rights Act 1998] and which demands careful attention, not least because it is a recent expression of the European Court's view on these matters.

The House considered that the European Court was given 'rather less information than the House' about the courts martial system, and in the light of this additional information it concluded that there had been no violation of the Convention.

In *R* v *Horncastle* (2009), two appeals were heard together by the Supreme Court where defendants had been convicted using witness statements and the witness was not available to be cross-examined. In one case, the defendant was on trial for causing grievous bodily harm and the victim was a key witness but had died of natural causes before the trial. In the other case, the trial was for kidnapping and the victim had run away the day before the trial because she was too frightened to give evidence. The defendants appealed against their convictions, arguing that they had not received a fair trial in breach of Art. 6 of the European Convention. They referred, in particular, to the case of *Al-Khawaja and Tahery* v *UK* (2009) where the ECtHR had stated that convictions could not be based 'solely or to a decisive extent' on the evidence of a witness who could not be cross-examined (known as hearsay evidence). The defendants' appeals were rejected by the Supreme Court, which refused to follow the *Al-Khawaja* case. It commented that the ECtHR had developed its case law without giving full consideration to the safeguards against an unfair trial that existed under the common law. The Supreme Court stated:

> The requirement to 'take into account' the Strasbourg jurisprudence will normally result in this court applying principles that are clearly established by the Strasbourg Court. There will, however, be rare occasions where this court has concerns as to whether a decision of the Strasbourg Court sufficiently appreciates or accommodates particular aspects of our domestic process. In such circumstances it is open to this court to decline to follow the Strasbourg decision, giving reasons for adopting this course. This is likely to give the Strasbourg Court the opportunity to reconsider the particular aspect of the decision that is in issue, so that there takes place what may prove to be a valuable dialogue between this court and the Strasbourg court.

The original *Al-Khawaja and Tahery* v *UK* decision was given in Chamber and the UK Government requested that the case be reheard by the Grand Chamber (see pp. 378–9). The Grand Chamber accepted in 2001 that hearsay evidence could be admissible provided there were sufficient counterbalancing safeguards. Thus, a healthy dialogue between the ECtHR and the national court resulted in modification of the European Court's position.

Where there is a conflict between a decision of the ECtHR and a national court which binds a lower court, the lower court should usually follow the decision of the binding higher national court, but give permission to appeal. Thus, in *Kay* v *Lambeth London Borough Council* (2006) the Court of Appeal had been faced with a binding precedent of the House of Lords which conflicted with a decision of the ECtHR. The Court of Appeal had applied the House of Lords' decision but gave permission to appeal. In the subsequent appeal the

Figure 1.2 The routes for civil and criminal cases

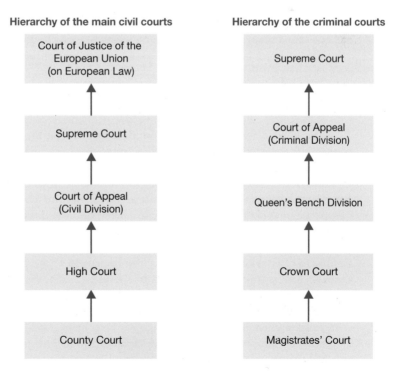

House had agreed that this was the appropriate course of action. We can expect to see similar tensions in the relationship between the Supreme Court and the ECtHR.

There is one exception where the usual English rules of precedent will not apply and the decision of the ECtHR will be followed rather than the decision of the House of Lords. This exception was identified in the case of *D* v *East Berkshire Community NHS Trust* (2003). In that case the Court of Appeal did not follow a decision of the House of Lords which was incompatible with the Convention because:

- the Strasbourg court had disagreed with the earlier House of Lords decision in an application made in the same case;
- the House of Lords' decision had been given before the Human Rights Act 1998;
- there had been no reference in the House of Lords' decision to the Convention;
- the policy considerations underlying the earlier House of Lords decision had been largely eroded.

1.4 How do judges really decide cases?

The independence of the judiciary was ensured by the Act of Settlement 1700, which transferred the power to sack judges from the Crown to Parliament. Consequently, judges should theoretically make their decisions based purely on the logical deductions of precedent, uninfluenced by political or career considerations.

The eighteenth-century legal commentator, William Blackstone, introduced the declaratory theory of law, stating that judges do not make law, but merely, by the rules of precedent, discover and declare the law that has always been: '[the judge] being sworn to determine, not according to his private sentiments . . . not according to his own private judgment, but according to the known laws and customs of the land: not delegated to pronounce a new law, but to maintain and expound the old one'. Blackstone does not accept that precedent ever offers a choice between two or more interpretations of the law: where a bad decision is made, he states, the new one that reverses or overrules it is not a new law, nor a statement that the old decision was bad law, but a declaration that the previous decision was 'not law', in other words that it was the wrong answer. His view presupposes that there is always one right answer, to be deduced from an objective study of precedent.

Today, however, this position is considered somewhat unrealistic. If the operation of precedent is the precise science Blackstone suggests, a large majority of cases in the higher courts would never come to court at all. The lawyers concerned could simply look up the relevant case law and predict what the decision would be, then advise whichever of the clients would be bound to lose not to bother bringing or fighting the case. In a civil case, or any appeal case, no good lawyer would advise a client to bring or defend a case that they had no chance of winning. Therefore, where such a case is contested, it can be assumed that, unless one of the lawyers has made a mistake, it could go either way, and still be in accordance with the law. Further evidence of this is provided by the fact that one can read a judgment of the Court of Appeal, argued as though it were the only possible decision in the light of the cases that had gone before, and then discover that this apparently inevitable decision has promptly been reversed by the House of Lords.

In practice, then, judges' decisions may not be as neutral as Blackstone's declaratory theory suggests: they have to make choices which are by no means spelled out by precedents. Yet, rather than openly stating that they are choosing between two or more equally relevant precedents, the courts find ways to avoid awkward ones, which give the impression that the precedents they do choose to follow are the only ones that could possibly apply. In theory, only the Supreme Court, which can overrule its own decisions as well as those of other courts, can depart from precedent: all the other courts must follow the precedent that applies in a particular case, however much they dislike it. In fact, there are a number of ways in which judges may avoid awkward precedents that at first sight might appear binding:

- By distinguishing the awkward precedent on its facts – arguing that the facts of the case under consideration are different in some important way from those of the previous case, and therefore the rule laid down does not apply to them. Since the facts are unlikely to be identical, this is the simplest way to avoid an awkward precedent, and the courts have made some extremely narrow distinctions in this way.

- By distinguishing the point of law – arguing that the legal question answered by the precedent is not the same as that asked in the present case.

- By stating that the precedent has been superseded by more recent decisions, and is therefore outdated.

- By giving the precedent a very narrow *ratio decidendi*. The only part of a decision that forms binding precedent is the *ratio*, the legal principle on which the decision is based. Since judges never state 'this is the *ratio decidendi*', it is possible to argue at some length about which bits of the judgment actually form the *ratio* and therefore bind courts in later cases. Judges wishing to avoid an awkward precedent may reason that those parts of the judgment which seem to apply to their case are not part of the *ratio*, and are only *obiter dicta*, which they are not obliged to follow.

- By arguing that the precedent has no clear *ratio decidendi*. There are usually three judges sitting in Court of Appeal cases, and five in the Supreme Court. Where each judge in the former case has given a different reason for coming to the same decision, or where, for example, two judges of the Supreme Court take one view, two more another, and the fifth agrees with none of them, it can be argued that there is no one clear *ratio decidendi* for the decision.

- By claiming that the precedent is inconsistent with a later decision of a higher court, and has been overruled by implication.

- By stating that the previous decision was made *per incuriam*, meaning that the court failed to consider some relevant statute or precedent. This method is used only rarely, since it clearly undermines the status of the court below.

- By arguing that the precedent is outdated, and no longer in step with modern thinking.

We can see that there is considerable room for manoeuvre within the doctrine of precedent, so what factors guide judicial decisions, and to what extent? The following are some of the answers that have been suggested.

1.4.1 Dworkin: a seamless web of principles

Ronald Dworkin argues that judges have no real discretion in making case law. He sees law as a seamless web of principles, which supply a right answer – and only one – to every possible problem. Dworkin reasons that although stated legal rules may 'run out' (in the sense of not being directly applicable to a new case) legal principles never do, and therefore judges never need to use their own discretion.

In his book *Law's Empire* (1986), Professor Dworkin claims that judges first look at previous cases, and from those deduce which principles could be said to apply to the case before them. Then they consult their own sense of justice as to which apply, and also consider what the community's view of justice dictates. Where the judge's view and that of the community coincide, there is no problem, but if they conflict, the judges then ask themselves whether or not it would be fair to impose their own sense of justice over that of the community. Dworkin calls this the interpretive approach and, although it may appear to involve a series of choices, he considers that the legal principles underlying the decisions mean that in the end only one result could possibly surface from any one case.

Dworkin's approach has been heavily criticised as being unrealistic: opponents believe that judges do not consider principles of justice but take a much more pragmatic approach, looking at the facts of the case, not the principles.

1.4.2 Critical theorists: precedent as legitimation

Critical legal theorists, such as David Kairys (1998), take a quite different view. They argue that judges have considerable freedom within the doctrine of precedent. Kairys suggests that there is no such thing as legal reasoning, in the sense of a logical, neutral method of determining rules and results from what has gone before. He states that judicial decisions are actually based on 'a complex mixture of social, political, institutional, experiential and personal factors', and are simply legitimated, or justified, by reference to previous cases. The law provides 'a wide and conflicting variety' of such justifications 'from which courts pick and choose'.

The process is not necessarily as cynical as it sounds. Kairys points out that he is not saying that judges actually make the decision and then consider which precedents they can pick to justify it; rather their own beliefs and prejudices naturally lead them to give more weight to precedents which support those views. Nevertheless, for critical legal theorists, all such decisions can be seen as reflecting social and political judgments, rather than objective, purely logical deductions.

Critical theory argues that the neutral appearance of so-called 'legal reasoning' disguises the true nature of legal decisions which, by the choices made, uphold existing power relations within society, tending to favour, for example, employers over employees, property owners over those without, men over women, and rich developed countries over poor undeveloped ones.

1.4.3 Griffith: political choices

In similar vein, Griffith (1997) argues in his book *The Politics of the Judiciary* that judges make their decisions based on what they see as the public interest, but that their view of this interest is coloured by their background and their position in society. He suggests that the narrow social background – usually public school and Oxbridge – of the highest judges (see p. 195), combined with their position as part of established authority, leads them to believe that it is in the public interest that the established order should be maintained: in other words, that those who are in charge – whether of the country or, for example, in the workplace – should stay in charge, and that traditional values should be maintained. This leads them to 'a tenderness for private property and dislike of trade unions, strong adherence to the maintenance of order, distaste for minority opinions, demonstrations and protests, the avoidance of conflict with Government policy even where it is manifestly oppressive of the most vulnerable, support of governmental secrecy, concern for the preservation of the moral and social behaviour [to which they are] accustomed'.

As Griffith points out, the judges' view of public interest assumes that the interests of all the members of society are roughly the same, ignoring the fact that within society, different groups – employers and employees, men and women, rich and poor – may have interests which are diametrically opposed. What appears to be acting in the public interest will usually mean in the interest of one group over another, and therefore cannot be seen as neutral.

1.4.4 Waldron: political choices, but why not?

In his book, *The Law* (1989), Waldron agrees that judges do exercise discretion, and that they are influenced in those choices by political and ideological considerations, but argues that this is not necessarily a bad thing. He contends that while it would be wrong for judges to be biased towards one side in a case, or to make decisions based on political factors in the hope of promotion, it is unrealistic to expect a judge to be 'a political neuter – emasculated of all values and principled commitments'.

Waldron points out that to be a judge at all means a commitment to the values surrounding the legal system: recognition of Parliament as supreme, the importance of precedent, fairness, certainty, the public interest. He argues that this itself is a political choice, and further choices are made when judges have to balance these values against one another where they conflict. The responsible thing to do, according to Waldron, is to think through such conflicts in advance, and to decide which might generally be expected to give way to which. These will inevitably be political and ideological decisions. Waldron argues that since such decisions have to be made 'the thing to do is not to try to hide them, but to be as explicit as possible'. Rather than hiding such judgments behind 'smokescreens of legal mystery . . . if judges have developed particular theories of morals, politics and society, they should say so up front, and incorporate them explicitly into their decision-making'.

Waldron suggests that where judges feel uncomfortable about doing this, it may be a useful indication that they should re-examine their bias, and see whether it is an appropriate consideration by which they are to be influenced. In addition, if the public know the reasoning behind judicial decisions 'we can evaluate them and see whether we want to rely on reasons like that for the future'.

Some support for Waldron's analysis can be found in Lord Hoffmann's judgment in ***Arthur J.S. Hall & Co v Simons*** (2000). In that case the House of Lords dramatically removed the established immunity of barristers from liability in negligence for court work. Lord Hoffmann stated:

> I hope that I will not be thought ungrateful if I do not encumber this speech with citations. The question of what the public interest now requires depends upon the strength of the arguments rather than the weight of authority.

1.5 Do judges make law?

Although judges have traditionally seen themselves as declaring or finding rather than creating law, and frequently state that making law is the prerogative of Parliament, there are several areas in which they clearly do make law.

In the first place, historically, a great deal of our law is and always has been case law, made by judicial decisions. Contract and tort law are still largely judge-made, and many of the most important developments – for example, the development of negligence as a tort – have had profound effects. Even though statutes have later been passed on these subjects, and occasionally Parliament has attempted to embody whole areas of common law in statutory form, these still embody the original principles created by the judges.

Secondly, the application of law, whether case law or statute, to a particular case is not usually an automatic matter. Terminology may be vague or ambiguous, new developments in social life have to be accommodated, and the procedure requires interpretation as well as application. As we have suggested, judicial precedent does not always make a particular decision obvious and obligatory – there may be conflicting precedents, their implications may be unclear, and there are ways of getting round a precedent that would otherwise produce an undesirable decision. If it is accepted that Blackstone's declaratory theory does not apply in practice, then clearly the judges do make law, rather than explaining the law that is already there. The theories advanced by Kairys, Griffith and Waldron all accept that judges do have discretion, and therefore they do to some extent make law.

Where precedents do not spell out what should be done in a case before them, judges nevertheless have to make a decision. They cannot simply say that the law is not clear and refer it back to Parliament, even though in some cases they point out that the decision before them would be more appropriately decided by those who have been elected to make decisions on changes in the law. This was the case in *Airedale NHS Trust* v *Bland* (1993), where the House of Lords considered the fate of Tony Bland, the football supporter left in a coma after the Hillsborough stadium disaster. The court had to decide whether it was lawful to stop supplying the drugs and artificial feeding that were keeping Mr Bland alive, even though it was known that doing so would mean his death soon afterwards. Several Law Lords made it plain that they felt that cases raising 'wholly new moral and social issues' should be decided by Parliament, the judges' role being to 'apply the principles which society, through the democratic process, adopts, not to impose their standards on society'. Nevertheless, the court had no option but to make a decision one way or the other, and the judges decided the action was lawful in the circumstances, because it was in the patient's best interests.

Thirdly, our judges have been left to define their own role, and the role of the courts generally in the political system, more or less as they please. They have, for example, given themselves the power to review decisions of any public body, even when Parliament has said those decisions are not to be reviewed. And despite their frequent pronouncements that it is not for them to interfere in Parliament's law-making role, the judges have made it plain that they will not, unless forced by very explicit wording, interpret statutes as encroaching on common law rights or judge-made law (see p. 65). They also control the operation of case law without reference to Parliament: an obvious example is that the 1966 Practice Direction announcing that the House of Lords would no longer be bound by its own decisions, which made case law more flexible and thereby gave the judges more power, was made on the court's own authority, without needing permission from Parliament.

The House of Lords has explained its approach to judicial law-making (which is the same for the Supreme Court) in the case of *C (A Minor)* v *DPP* (1995) which raised the issue of children's liability for crime. The common law defence of *doli incapax* provided that a defendant aged between 10 and 14 could be liable for a crime only if the prosecution could prove that the child knew that what he or she did was seriously wrong. On appeal from the magistrates' court, the Divisional Court held that the defence was outdated and should no longer exist in law. An appeal was brought before the House of Lords, arguing that the

Divisional Court was bound by precedent and not able to change the law in this way. The House of Lords agreed, and went on to consider whether it should change the law itself (as the 1966 Practice Direction clearly allowed it to do), but decided that this was not an appropriate case for judicial law-making. Explaining this decision, Lord Lowry suggested five factors were important:

- Where the solution to a dilemma was doubtful, judges should be wary of imposing their own answer.

- Judges should be cautious about addressing areas where Parliament had rejected opportunities of clearing up a known difficulty, or had passed legislation without doing so.

- Areas of social policy over which there was dispute were least likely to be suitable for judicial law-making.

- Fundamental legal doctrines should not be lightly set aside.

- Judges should not change the law unless they can be sure that doing so is likely to achieve finality and certainty on the issue.

This guidance suggests that the judges should take quite a cautious approach to changing the law. In practice, however, the judges do not always seem to be following these guidelines. For example, in an important criminal case of *R v Dica* (2004) the Court of Appeal overruled an earlier case of *R v Clarence* (1888) and held that criminal liability could be imposed on a defendant for recklessly infecting another person with HIV. This change in the law was made despite the fact that the Home Office had earlier decided that legislation should not be introduced which would have imposed liability in this situation (*Violence: Reforming the Offences Against the Person Act 1861* (1998)). The Home Office had observed that 'this issue had ramifications going beyond the criminal law into wider considerations of social and public health policy'.

Some commentators feel that the judiciary's current approach is tending to go too far, and straying outside its constitutional place. Writing in the *New Law Journal* in 1999, Francis Bennion, a former parliamentary counsel, criticised what he called the 'growing appetite of some judges for changing the law themselves, rather than waiting for Parliament to do it'. Bennion cites two cases as examples of this. The first, *Kleinwort Benson Ltd v Lincoln City Council* (1998), concerns contract law, and in particular, a long-standing rule, originating from case law, that where someone made a payment as a result of a mistake about the law, they did not have the right to get the money back. The rule had existed for nearly two centuries, and been much criticised in recent years – so much so that a previous Lord Chancellor had asked the Law Commission to consider whether it should be amended by legislation, and they had concluded that it should. This would normally be taken by the courts as a signal that they should leave the issue alone and wait for Parliament to act, but in this case the Lords decided to change the rule. In doing so, Lord Keith expressed the view that 'a robust view of judicial development of the law' was desirable. Bennion argues that, in making this decision, the Lords were usurping the authority which constitutionally belongs to Parliament. He also points out that judicial, rather than parliamentary, change of the law in this kind of area causes practical difficulties, because it has retrospective effect; a large number of transactions which were thought to be settled under the previous rule can now be reopened. This would not usually be the case if Parliament changed the law.

The second case Bennion criticises is *DPP v Jones* (1999), which concerned a demonstration on the road near Stonehenge. In that case the Lords looked at another long-held rule, that the public have a right to use the highway for 'passing and repassing' (in other words, walking along the road), and for uses which are related to that, but that there is no right to use the highway in other ways, such as demonstrating or picketing. In *Jones*, the House of Lords stated that this rule placed unrealistic and unwarranted restrictions on everyday activities, and that the highway is a public place that the public has a right to enjoy for any reasonable purpose. This decision clearly has major implications for the powers of the police to break up demonstrations and pickets.

Bennion argues that, in making decisions like these, the judiciary are taking powers to which they are not constitutionally entitled, and that they should not extend their law-making role into such controversial areas.

Key case

An interesting recent example of judicial law-making is the Court of Appeal decision of ***Simmons v Castle*** (2012). The background to the case was that Lord Jackson (a senior judge) had produced a report recommending certain reforms should be made to the civil justice system to try to reduce the cost of litigation (see p. 645). Some of the key recommendations of this report were included by the Government in the Legal Aid, Sentencing and Punishment of Offenders Act 2012. But the legislation did not include a proposed reform to increase the award of damages by 10 per cent. The Government stated that calculation of damages was governed by the common law and it would be left to the courts to make this change. The Court of Appeal subsequently announced, in ***Simmons v Castle*** (2012), that this increase would take effect from 1 April 2013 at the same time as the 2012 Act would come into force. The Court of Appeal stated that when the 2012 Act was passed there was a 'clear understanding that the judges would implement the ten per cent increase', and that it would be 'little short of a breach of faith' if the judges failed to do so. The problem with the courts changing the law in this way is that it throws into doubt how independent they are from the politicians. Also, the judges do not have the benefit of the tight parliamentary scrutiny. After the case was decided, the Association of British Insurers applied for the Court of Appeal to reopen its decision because it was unhappy that the decision would apply retrospectively to cases that had commenced before the April deadline and thereby increase the cost of these cases for the insurance companies.

Legal principle
Judges should change the law if Parliament intended them to do so and a failure to do so would be a breach of faith.

1.6 When should judges make law?

Again, this is a subject about which there are different views, not least among the judiciary, and the following are some of the approaches which have been suggested.

1.6.1 Adapting to social change

In 1952, Lord Denning gave a lecture called 'The Need for a New Equity', arguing that judges had become too timid about adapting the law to the changing conditions of society. They were, he felt, leaving this role too much to Parliament, which was too slow and cumbersome to do the job well (by 1984, he felt that judges had taken up the task again).

Lord Scarman, in *McLoughlin* v *O'Brian* (1982), stated that the courts' function is to adjudicate according to principle, and if the results are socially unacceptable Parliament can legislate to overrule them. He felt that the risk was not that case law might develop too far, but that it stood still and did not therefore adapt to the changing needs of society.

Paterson's (1982) survey of 19 Law Lords active between 1967 and 1973 found that at least 12 thought that the Law Lords had a duty to develop the common law in response to changing social conditions. A case where the judges did eventually show themselves willing to change the law in the light of social change is *Fitzpatrick* v *Sterling Housing Association Ltd* (2000). The case concerned a homosexual man, Mr Fitzpatrick, who had lived with his partner, Mr Thompson, for 18 years, nursing and caring for him after Mr Thompson suffered an accident which caused irreversible brain damage and severe paralysis. Mr Thompson was the tenant of the flat in which they lived and, when he died in 1994, Mr Fitzpatrick applied to take over the tenancy, which gave the tenant certain protections under the Rent Acts. The landlords refused. The Rent Act 1977 states that when a statutory tenant dies, the tenancy can be taken over by a spouse, a person living with the ex-tenant as wife or husband, or a member of the family who was living with the tenant. Mr Fitzpatrick's case sought to establish that he was a member of Mr Thompson's family, by virtue of their close and loving relationship.

The Court of Appeal agreed that 'if endurance, stability, interdependence and devotion were the sole hallmarks of family membership', there could be no doubt that the couple were a family. They also pointed out that discriminating against stable same-sex relationships was out of step with the values of modern society. However, they recognised that the law on succession to statutory tenancies was firmly rooted in the idea that families were based on marriage or kinship, and this had only ever been relaxed in terms of heterosexual couples living together, who were treated as if married. As a result, the court concluded that it would be wrong to change the law by interpreting the word family to include same-sex couples; all three judges agreed that such a change should be made, in order to reflect modern values, but it should be made by Parliament. The House of Lords, however, overturned the Court of Appeal's decision. It ruled that the appellant could not be treated as the spouse of the deceased tenant, but as a matter of law a same-sex partner could establish the necessary familial link for the purposes of the legislation.

1.6.2 Types of law

Lord Reid has suggested that the basic areas of common law are appropriate for judge-made law, but that the judges should respect the need for certainty in property and contract law, and that criminal law, except for the issue of *mens rea*, was best left to Parliament.

1.6.3 Consensus law-making

Lord Devlin (1979) has distinguished between activist law-making and dynamic law-making. He saw new ideas within society as going through a long process of acceptance. At first society will be divided about them, and there will be controversy, but eventually such ideas may come to be accepted by most members of society, or most members will at least become prepared to put up with them. At this second stage we can say there is a consensus. We can see this process in the way that views have changed over recent decades on subjects such as homosexuality and sex before marriage.

Law-making which takes one side or another while an issue is still controversial is what Devlin called dynamic law-making, and he believed judges should not take part in it because it endangered their reputation for independence and impartiality. Their role is in activist law-making, concerning areas where there is a consensus. The problem with Devlin's view is that in practice the judges sometimes have no choice but to embark on dynamic law-making. In *Gillick* v *West Norfolk and Wisbech Area Health Authority* (1985), the House of Lords was asked to consider whether a girl under the age of 16 needed her parents' consent before she could be given contraceptive services. It was an issue on which there was by no means a consensus, with one side claiming that teenage pregnancies would increase if the courts ruled that parental consent was necessary, and the other claiming that the judges would be encouraging under-age sex if they did not. The House of Lords held, by a majority of three to two, that a girl under 16 did not have to have parental consent if she was mature enough to make up her own mind. But the decision did not end the controversy, and it was widely suggested that the judges were not the right people to make the choice. However, since Parliament had given no lead, they had no option but to make a decision one way or the other, and were therefore forced to indulge in what Devlin would call dynamic law-making.

1.6.4 Respecting parliamentary opinion

It is often stated that judges should not make law where there is reason to believe Parliament does not support such changes. In *President of India* v *La Pintada Compañia Navigación SA* (1984), the House of Lords felt that there was a strong case for overruling a nineteenth-century decision that a party could receive no interest on a contract debt, but they noted that the Law Commission had recommended that this rule should be abolished and the legislators specifically decided not to do so. Lord Brandon said that to make new law in these circumstances would be an 'unjustifiable usurpation of the function which properly belongs to Parliament'.

Similarly, it is sometimes argued that judges should avoid making law in areas of public interest which Parliament is considering at the time. Lord Radcliffe suggested that, in such areas, judges should be cautious 'not because the principles adopted by Parliament are more satisfactory or more enlightened, but because it is unacceptable constitutionally that there should be two independent sources of law-making at work at the same time'.

The Bigger Picture: Assisted voluntary euthanasia

There is an ongoing debate about whether someone should be able to lawfully assist another person to die. Under the current law such assistance could amount to murder. Campaigners in favour of voluntary euthanasia argue that the law should be changed either by Parliament or by the courts. In *R (on the application of Nicklinson)* v *Ministry of Justice* (2014) the applicant, Tony Nicklinson, had led an active life until, at the age of 51, he suffered a catastrophic stroke. This left him paralysed below the neck, unable to speak and only able to move his head and eyes. His condition is sometimes described as 'locked-in syndrome', because his active mind is locked into a virtually useless body. Tony summed up his life as 'dull, miserable, demeaning, undignified and intolerable'. He decided that he wanted to die but due to his disabilities he was not able to commit suicide without assistance unless he starved himself, which is a slow and very uncomfortable death. He sought a declaration from the courts that any doctors who assisted him in dying (known as assisted voluntary euthanasia (AVE)), would not be committing the offence of murder because they would have a defence of necessity. This declaration was refused. The court ruled that the defence of necessity was not available on these facts. To allow the defence of necessity would amount to a major change in the common law. This change could not be made by the courts, because any such change raised controversial social policy issues: parliamentary legislation would instead be required. The High Court noted that 'the subject is profoundly difficult and complex, raising a myriad of moral, medical and practical considerations'. As a result, a court hearing an individual case, concentrating on the dire circumstances of the claimant, is not in a position to decide such broader questions, but its decision would create a precedent which would affect many other cases. The High Court commented:

> . . . it is one thing for the courts to adopt and develop the principles of the common law incrementally in order to keep up with the requirements of justice in a changing society, but major changes involving matters of controversial social policy are for Parliament.

The High Court's decision has been confirmed by the Court of Appeal, and the Supreme Court. Parliament, unlike the courts, can control the consequences of such a move. If assisted voluntary euthanasia were legalised in this way, then the legislation would be able to put into place a surrounding framework regarding end-of-life care and procedural safeguards. The case, in effect, confirms the supremacy of Parliament. The judges did not want to be seen to be taking over the role of Parliament in making laws. The court followed the traditional role of judges as declarers of law, rather than makers of law. While the judiciary will not make law in this area, with every high-profile case the pressure for Parliament to review this area of law increases.

1.6.5 Protecting individual rights

In a 1992 lecture, the human rights lawyer, Anthony Lester QC, argued that while judges must have regard to precedent, they could still use their discretion within the system of precedent more effectively. He argued that, in the past, judges have abdicated responsibility for law-making by surrounding themselves with self-made rules (such as the pre-1966 rule that the House of Lords was bound by its own decisions). Since the 1960s, however, he feels that this tendency has gradually been reduced, with judges taking on more responsibility for developing the common law in accordance with contemporary values, and being more willing to arbitrate fairly between the citizen and the state. Lester praises this development, arguing that the judges can establish protection for the individual against misuse of power, where Parliament refuses to do so.

1.7 Advantages of case law

1.7.1 Certainty

Judicial precedent means litigants can assume that like cases will be treated alike, rather than judges making their own random decisions, which nobody could predict. This helps people to plan their affairs.

1.7.2 Detailed practical rules

Case law is a response to real situations, as opposed to statutes, which may be more heavily based on theory and logic. Case law shows the detailed application of the law to various circumstances, and thus gives more information than statute. The academic Roscoe Pound (1963) has written on the doctrine of precedent:

> Growth is ensured in that the limits of the principle are not fixed authoritatively once and for all but are discovered gradually by a process of inclusion and exclusion as cases arise which bring out its practical workings and prove how far it may be made to do justice in its actual operation.

1.7.3 Free market in legal ideas

The right-wing philosopher Hayek (1982) has argued that there should be as little legislation as possible, with case law becoming the main source of law. He sees case law as developing in line with market forces: if the *ratio* of a case is seen not to work, it will be abandoned; if it works, it will be followed. In this way the law can develop in response to demand. Hayek sees statute law as imposed by social planners, forcing their views on society whether the majority of people like it or not, and threatening the liberty of the individual.

1.7.4 Flexibility

Law needs to be flexible to meet the needs of a changing society, and case law can make changes far more quickly than Parliament. The most obvious signs of this are the radical changes the House of Lords made in the field of criminal law, following announcing in 1966 that its judges would no longer be bound by their own decisions.

1.8 Disadvantages of case law

1.8.1 Complexity and volume

There are hundreds of thousands of decided cases, comprising several thousand volumes of law reports, and more are added all the time. With the development of the internet, almost every decided case is available online or in legal databases. Judgments themselves are long, with many judges making no attempt at readability, and the *ratio decidendi* of a case may be buried in a sea of irrelevant material. This can make it very difficult to pinpoint appropriate principles.

A possible solution to these difficulties would be to follow the example of some European systems, where courts hand down a single concise judgment with no dissenting judgments. However, some of these decisions can become so concise that lawyers are required to do considerable research around the specific words used to discover the legal impact of the case, because no detailed explanation is provided by the judges.

1.8.2 Rigid

The rules of judicial precedent mean that judges should follow a binding precedent even where they think it is bad law, or inappropriate. This can mean that bad judicial decisions are perpetuated for a long time before they come before a court high enough to have the power to overrule them.

1.8.3 Illogical distinctions

The fact that binding precedents must be followed unless the facts of the case are significantly different can lead to judges making minute distinctions between the facts of a previous case and the case before them, so that they can distinguish a precedent which they consider inappropriate. This in turn leads to a mass of cases all establishing different precedents in very similar circumstances, and further complicates the law.

1.8.4 Unpredictable

The advantages of certainty can be lost if too many of the kind of illogical distinctions referred to above are made, and it may be impossible to work out which precedents will be applied to a new case.

1.8.5 Dependence on chance

Case law changes only in response to those cases brought before it, so important changes may not be made unless someone has the money and determination to push a case far enough through the appeal system to allow a new precedent to be created.

1.8.6 Unsystematic progression

Case law develops according to the facts of each case and so does not provide a comprehensive code. A whole series of rules can be built on one case, and if this is overruled the whole structure can collapse.

1.8.7 Lack of research

When making case law the judges are only presented with the facts of the case and the legal arguments, and their task is to decide on the outcome of that particular dispute. Technically, they are not concerned with the social and economic implications of their decisions, and so they cannot commission research or consult experts as to these implications, as Parliament can when changing the law. Increasingly, the senior courts have been willing to allow interveners to make representations in the public interest during court proceedings. Such an intervener might be, for example, a charitable body, such as Liberty or JUSTICE, and it will present to the court arguments about the broader impact of the case on society, provide comparisons with practice abroad and refer to socioeconomic research in the field. In the House of Lords' last year of operation, it allowed third-party interveners to make representations in almost a third of its cases.

1.8.8 Retrospective effect

Changes made by case law apply to events which happened before the case came to court, unlike legislation, which usually only applies to events after it comes into force. This may be considered unfair, since if a case changes the law, the parties concerned in that case could not have known what the law was before they acted. US courts sometimes get around the problems by deciding the case before them according to the old law, while declaring that in future the new law will prevail: or they may determine with what degree of retroactivity a new rule is to be enforced.

The same issue came before the courts again in **R v C** (2004). In that case the defendant was convicted in 2002 of raping his wife in 1970. On appeal, he argued that this conviction breached Art. 7 of the European Convention and tried to distinguish the earlier case of **SW v United Kingdom** (1995). He said that while in **SW v United Kingdom** the defendant could have foreseen in 1989 when he committed the offence that his conduct would be regarded as criminal, this was not the case in 1970. This argument was rejected by the Court of Appeal. It claimed, rather unconvincingly, that a husband in 1970 could have anticipated this development in the law. In fact, the leading textbooks at the time clearly stated that husbands were not liable for raping their wives.

Key case

In **SW v United Kingdom** (1995), two men, who had been convicted of the rape and attempted rape of their wives, brought a case before the European Court of Human Rights, alleging that their convictions violated Art. 7 of the European Convention on Human Rights, which provides that criminal laws should not have retrospective effect. The men argued that when the incidents which gave rise to their convictions happened, it was not a crime for a man to force his wife to have sex; it only became a crime after the decision in **R v R** (1991). The court dismissed the men's argument: Art. 7 did not prevent the courts from clarifying the principles of criminal liability, providing the developments could be clearly foreseen. In this case, there had been mounting criticism of the previous law, and a series of cases which had chipped away at the marital rape exemption, before the **R v R** decision.

Legal principle

There is no breach of the European Convention when courts clarify the law, provided legal developments can be foreseen.

Recent criminal cases have shown that the retrospective effect of case law can also work to the benefit of the defendant. In **R v Powell and English** (1999) the House of Lords clarified the law that should determine the criminal liability of accomplices. An earlier controversial case that had involved the criminal liability of an accomplice was that of **R v Bentley** (1953), whose story was made into the 1992 film *Let Him Have It*. Bentley was caught and arrested after being chased across rooftops by police. Craig had a gun and Bentley is alleged to have said to Craig, 'Let him have it'. Craig then shot and killed a policeman. Craig was charged with murdering a police officer (at that time a hanging offence) and Bentley was charged as his accomplice. In court Bentley argued that when he shouted, 'Let him have it', he was telling Craig to hand over his gun rather than, as the prosecution claimed, encouraging him to shoot the police officer. Nevertheless both were convicted. Craig was under the minimum age for the death sentence, and was given life imprisonment. Bentley, who was older, was hanged. The conviction was subsequently overturned by the Court of Appeal in July 1998, following a long campaign by his family. In considering the trial judge's summing up to the jury, the Court of Appeal said that criminal liability 'must be determined according to the common law as now understood'. The common law that applied in 1998 to accomplice liability was more favourable than the common law that applied in 1952. The danger in practice is that every time the common law shifts to be more favourable to defendants, the floodgates are potentially opened for defendants to appeal against their earlier convictions.

To try to avoid this problem, the Criminal Justice and Immigration Act 2008 provides that the Court of Appeal can reject as out of time references made to it by the Criminal Cases Review Commission which are based purely on a change in the common law. The court is likely to do this where a rejection of the appeal will not cause substantial injustice.

1.8.9 Undemocratic

Lord Scarman pointed out in **Stock** v **Jones** (1978) that the judge cannot match the experience and vision of the legislator; and that unlike the legislator the judge is not answerable to the people. Theories, like Griffith's, which suggest that precedent can actually give judges a good deal of discretion, and allow them to decide cases on grounds of political and social policy, raise the question of whether judges, who are unelected, should have such freedom.

Answering questions

1 What do we mean when we say that the English Legal System is a common law system? *University of London, International Programmes LLB*

2 Judicial reasoning in case law 'consists in the applying to new combinations of circumstances those rules of law which we derive from legal principles and judicial precedents . . . and we are not at liberty to reject them, and to abandon all analogy to them'. (Mr Justice Peak, 1833)

   Does this statement reflect the operation of precedent today? *University of London, International Programmes LLB*

3 Precedent must, on the one hand, provide certainty, but on the other hand, it must be flexible in adapting to social change. In view of the so-called binding nature of precedent, how are judges able to reconcile these seemingly contradictory characteristics in their use of precedent?

4 Critically evaluate the extent to which the doctrine of binding precedent inhibits judicial creativity.

5 Evaluate the advantages of abolishing the doctrine of binding judicial precedent.

For answers to these questions, visit the companion website at www.pearsoned.co.uk/ elliottquinn

SUMMARY OF CHAPTER 1: CASE LAW

Judicial precedent

In deciding a case, a judge must follow any decision that has been made by a higher court in a case with similar facts. Judges are bound only by the part of the judgment that forms the legal principle that was the basis of the earlier decision, known as the *ratio decidendi*. The rest of the judgment is known as *obiter dicta* and is not binding.

The hierarchy of the courts

The Court of Justice of the European Union is the highest authority on European law; in other matters the Supreme Court is the highest court in the UK. Under the 1966 Practice Direction, the Supreme Court is not bound by its previous decisions.

How do judges really decide cases?

According to the traditional declaratory theory laid down by William Blackstone, judges do not make law but merely discover and declare the law that has always been. Ronald Dworkin also accepts that the judges have no real discretion in making case law, but he bases this view on his concept that law is a seamless web of principles.

Very different views have been put forward by other academics. Critical theorists argue that judicial decisions are actually influenced by social, political and personal factors and that the doctrine of judicial precedent is merely used to legitimate the judges' decisions. Griffith also thinks that judges are influenced by their personal background. Waldron accepts that judges make political choices but sees no fundamental problem with this.

When should judges make law?

There is no doubt that on occasion judges make law. There is some debate as to when judges ought to make law. When judges make law they can adapt it to social change, but Francis Bennion has highlighted the danger that if the courts are too willing to make law, they undermine the position of Parliament.

Advantages of binding precedent

The doctrine of judicial precedent provides:

- certainty;
- detailed practical rules;
- a free market in legal ideas; and
- flexibility.

Disadvantages of binding precedent

Case law has been criticised because of its:

- complexity and volume;
- rigidity;
- illogical distinctions;
- unpredictability;
- dependence on chance;
- retrospective effect; and
- undemocratic character.

Reading list

Bennion, F.A.R. (1999) A naked usurpation. *New Law Journal*, 149: 421.

Devlin, P. (1979) *The Judge*. Oxford: Oxford University Press.

Dworkin, R. (1986) *Law's Empire*. London: Fontana.

Griffith, J.A.G. (1997) *The Politics of the Judiciary*. London: Fontana.

Hale, Sir M. (1979) *The History of the Common Law of England*. Chicago: University of Chicago Press.

Hayek, F. (1982) *Law, Legislation and Liberty: A New Statement of the Liberal Principles of Justice and Political Economy*. London: Routledge.

Hohfeld, W.N. and Cook, W.W. (1919) *Fundamental Legal Concepts as Applied in Judicial Reasoning*. London: Greenwood Press.

Kairys, D. (1998) *The Politics of Law: A Progressive Critique*. New York: Basic Books.

Lawson, C.M. (1982) The family affinities of common law and civil law legal systems. *Hastings International Comparative Law Review*, 6: 85.

Lennan, J. (2010) A Supreme Court for the United Kingdom: a note on early days. *Civil Justice Quarterly*, 29(2): 139.

MacCormick, N. (1978) *Legal Rules and Legal Reasoning*. Oxford: Clarendon.

Paterson, A. (1982) *The Law Lords*. London: Macmillan.

———— (2013) *Final Judgment: The Last Law Lords and the Supreme Court*. Oxford: Hart Publishing.

Pound, R. (1963) *The Spirit of the Common Law*. Boston: Beacon Press.

Prime, T. and Scanlan, G. (2004) *Stare decisis* and the Court of Appeal: judicial confusion and judicial reform. *Civil Justice Quarterly*, 23: 212.

Summers, R. (1992) *Essays on the Nature of Law and Legal Reasoning*. Berlin: Duncker & Humblot.

Waldron, J. (1989) *The Law*. London: Routledge.

Weinreb, L. (2004) *Legal Reason: The Use of Analogy in Legal Argument*. Cambridge: Cambridge University Press.

1

CASE LAW

On the internet

Government White Paper, Legislating for the Withdrawal Agreement between the United Kingdom and the European Union:

https://assets.publishing.service.gov.uk/government/uploads/system/uploads/attachment_data/file/728757/6.4737_Cm9674_Legislating_for_the_withdrawl_agreement_FINAL_230718_v3a_WEB_PM.pdf

European (Withdrawal) Act 2018:

http://www.legislation.gov.uk/ukpga/2018/16/enacted

Draft withdrawal agreement March 2018:

https://ec.europa.eu/commission/sites/beta-political/files/draft_agreement_coloured.pdf

Decisions of the Supreme Court can be found on the website of the Supreme Court at:
https://www.supremecourt.uk/decided-cases/

The Supreme Court YouTube channel provides video-clips of the Justices of the Supreme Court handing down summaries of their judgments:
http://www.youtube.com/user/UKSupremeCourt

You can watch live broadcasts of the Supreme Court at work on the Sky News website at:
http://news.sky.com/supreme-court-live

The Supreme Court Annual Report and Accounts 2017–2018 can be found at:
https://www.supremecourt.uk/docs/annual-report-2017-18.pdf

The former House of Lords judgments are available on the House of Lords' judicial business website at:
http://www.publications.parliament.uk/pa/ld/ldjudgmt.htm

Some important judgments are published on the Court Service website at:
http://www.justice.gov.uk/about/hmcts/

You can watch an introductory film about the Supreme Court on the Supreme Court website at:
https://www.supremecourt.uk/about/introductory-film.html

Chapter 2
Statute law

This chapter discusses:

- the House of Commons;
- the House of Lords;
- how an Act of Parliament is made; and
- post-legislative scrutiny.

2.1 Introduction

Statutes are made by Parliament, which consists of the House of Commons, the House of Lords and the Monarch. Another term for a statute is an Act of Parliament. In Britain, Parliament is sovereign, which has traditionally meant that the law it makes takes precedence over law originating from any other source though, as we shall see, membership of the European Union (EU) has compromised this principle. EU law aside, Parliament can make or cancel any law it chooses, and the courts must enforce it. In other countries, such as the United States of America, the courts can declare such legislation unconstitutional, but our courts are not allowed to do that.

2.2 House of Commons

The House of Commons is the democratically elected chamber of Parliament. Every four to five years Members of Parliament (MPs) are elected in a general election. There are 650 MPs who discuss the big political issues of the day and proposals for new laws.

2.3 House of Lords

The House of Lords acts as a revising chamber for legislation and its work complements the business of the Commons. Members of the House of Lords are not elected by the general public, instead the majority are appointed by the Queen on the recommendation of the House of Lords Appointments Commission. The House of Lords currently has close to 800 members, divided into four different types:

- Life peers
- Retired judges of the former House of Lords' judicial committee
- Bishops
- Elected hereditary peers.

Life peers are appointed for their lifetime only, so the right to sit in the House of Lords is not passed on to their children.

The Bigger Picture: Modernising the House of Lords

The former Prime Minister, Lloyd George, described the House of Lords as 'a body of five hundred men chosen at random from amongst the unemployed'. Today's desire for reform might partly reflect public discontent at the 'cash for honours' controversy, when there were suggestions that individuals had been made Lords in return for donations to political parties. Such a reform could also provide a response to the recent scandal that some members of the Lords appear to have arranged for legislation to be amended in return for receiving large sums of money from private companies. At the moment the House of Lords is a chamber which legislates on behalf of the people but is not held to account by the people.

Traditionally, hereditary peers have sat in the House of Lords and this right was passed down from father to son. Membership of the House is currently undergoing a major reform to remove the role of the hereditary peers. Their right to sit and vote in the House of Lords was ended in 1999 by the House of Lords Act, but 92 members were elected internally to remain until the next stage of the Lords reform process.

The Royal Commission for the Reform of the House of Lords, chaired by Lord Wakeham, published its report in January 2000. It recommended that there should be a chamber of about 550 members. Only a minority would be elected, to represent the regions; the remainder would be appointed by an independent Appointments Commission. It would be responsible for selecting members who were broadly representative of British society. Approximately 20 per cent of the House of Lords' members would be politically independent and the others would reflect the political balance as expressed by the last general election. The Appointments Commission would be under a statutory duty to ensure that at least 30 per cent of new members were women and that minorities were represented in numbers at least proportionate to their representation in the total population. The powers of the new chamber would be broadly comparable with the present House of Lords.

In 2011, the coalition Government announced its proposals for House of Lords reform, with the publication of a White Paper and a House of Lords Reform Draft Bill. The key proposals were that there should be a smaller chamber of 300 members with 80 per cent elected and 20 per cent appointed. Elected members would be elected for a 15-year term on a staged basis – one third every five years. The appointed members would be chosen by an Appointments Commission, with 20 members being appointed at the same time as the elected members. The appointed members would be expected to make a 'non-party political' contribution to the work of the chamber. All members would be allowed to serve only one 15-year term.

The representatives of the Church of England would be retained but reduced in number from 26 to 12. The Prime Minister would also be able to make an unspecified number of Ministerial appointments to the House in addition to the 300 elected and appointed members. Anyone appointed in this way would only be a member of the House whilst he or she retained Ministerial office.

The existing life and hereditary peers have been removed from office. The primacy of the House of Commons over the House of Lords has been retained, as have the Parliament Acts of 1911 and 1949 (discussed on p. 52). These key recommendations, with a few minor amendments, were included in a House of Lords Bill which was presented to Parliament in 2012. However, following opposition by Conservative MPs, the Bill was abandoned after its Second Reading in the House of Commons.

2.4 Making an Act of Parliament

2.4.1 Policy development

Before the parliamentary legislative process begins, usually a policy objective will have been identified by the Government of the day. This policy objective may have been set out in an election manifesto or included in an official consultation document, known as a Green Paper. The latter document puts forward tentative proposals, which interested parties may consider and give their views on. The Green Paper will be followed by a White Paper, which contains the specific reform plans. The Government's legislative plans for a parliamentary session are outlined in the Queen's Speech in May.

Figure 2.1 An example of a statute: Criminal Defence (Advice and Assistance) Act 2001

ELIZABETH II   c. 4

Criminal Defence Service (Advice and Assistance) Act 2001

2001 CHAPTER 4

An Act to clarify the extent of the duty of the Legal Services Commission under section 13(1) of the Access to Justice Act 1999.   [10th April 2001]

B E IT ENACTED by the Queen's most Excellent Majesty, by and with the advice and consent of the Lords Spiritual and Temporal, and Commons, in this present Parliament assembled, and by the authority of the same, as follows: —

1   Extent of duty to fund advice and assistance

(1)   Subsection (1) of section 13 of the Access to Justice Act 1999 (c. 22) (duty of Legal Services Commission to fund advice and assistance as part of Criminal Defence Service) shall be treated as having been enacted with the substitution of the following for paragraph (b) and the words after it—

"(b)   in prescribed circumstances, for individuals who—

(i)   are not within paragraph (a) but are involved in investigations which may lead to criminal proceedings,

(ii)   are before a court or other body in such proceedings, or

(iii)   have been the subject of such proceedings;

and the assistance which the Commission may consider appropriate includes assistance in the form of advocacy."

(2)   Regulations under subsection (1) of section 13 (as amended above) may include provision treating them as having come into force at the same time as that subsection.

2   Short title

This Act may be cited as the Criminal Defence Service (Advice and Assistance) Act 2001.

Figure 2.2 Parliamentary Bills

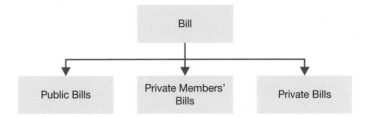

2.4.2 Bills

All statutes begin as a Bill, which is a proposal for a piece of legislation. There are three types of Bill:

Public Bills These are written by parliamentary counsel who specialise in drafting legislation. They are presented to Parliament by Government ministers and change the general law of the whole country.

Private Members' Bills These are prepared by an individual backbench MP (someone who is not a member of the Cabinet). MPs wanting to put forward a Bill have to enter a ballot to win the right to do so, and then persuade the Government to allow enough parliamentary time for the Bill to go through. Consequently very few such Bills become Acts, and they tend to function more as a way of drawing attention to particular issues. Some, however, have made important contributions to legislation, an example being the Abortion Act 1967 which stemmed from a Private Members' Bill put forward by David Steel.

Private Bills These are usually proposed by a local authority, public corporation or large public company, and usually only affect that sponsor. An example might be a local authority seeking the right to build a bridge or road.

The actual preparation of Bills is done by expert draftsmen known as parliamentary counsel.

2.4.3 First reading

The title of the prepared Bill is read to the House of Commons. This is called the first reading, and acts as a notification of the proposed measure.

2.4.4 Second reading

At the second reading, the proposals are debated fully, and may be amended, and members vote on whether the legislation should proceed. In practice, the whip system (party officials whose job is to make sure MPs vote with their party) means that a Government with a reasonable majority can almost always get its legislation through at this and subsequent stages.

2.4.5 Committee stage

The Bill is then referred to a committee of the House of Commons for detailed examination, bearing in mind the points made during the debate. At this point further amendments to the Bill may be made.

2.4.6 Report stage

The committee then reports back to the House, and any proposed amendments are debated and voted upon.

2.4.7 Third reading

The Bill is re-presented to the House. There may be a short debate, and a vote on whether to accept or reject the legislation as it stands.

2.4.8 House of Lords

The Bill then goes to the House of Lords, where it goes through a similar process of three readings. If the House of Lords alters anything, the Bill returns to the Commons for further consideration. The Commons then responds with agreement, reasons for disagreement, or proposals for alternative changes.

At one time legislation could not be passed without the agreement of both Houses, which meant that the unelected House of Lords could block legislation put forward by the elected House of Commons. The Parliament Acts of 1911 and 1949 lay down special procedures by which proposed legislation can go for Royal Assent without the approval of the House of Lords after specified periods of time. These procedures are only rarely used, because the House of Lords usually drops objections that are resisted by the Commons, though their use has increased in recent years. Four Acts of Parliament have been passed to date relying on the Parliament Act 1949:

- War Crimes Act 1991
- European Parliamentary Elections Act 1999
- Sexual Offences (Amendment) Act 2000
- Hunting Act 2004.

Key case

It is of particular note that the procedures were used to pass the controversial Hunting Act 2004. This Act bans hunting wild animals with dogs and a form of hunting known as hare coursing. It was passed despite the House of Lords' opposition, by using the Parliament Act 1949. Members of the pressure group the Countryside Alliance brought a legal challenge to the Act in *R (on the application of Jackson and others)* v *Attorney General* (2005). They argued that the Parliament Act 1949 was itself unlawful and that therefore the Hunting Act, which was passed relying on the procedures it laid down, was also unlawful. The initial Act of 1911 had required a two-year delay between the first vote in the House of Commons and reliance on the special procedures in the Act. The 1949 Act reduced this delay to one year and was itself passed using the special procedures in the 1911 Act. The Countryside Alliance claimed that the 1949 Act was unlawful because it had been passed relying on the procedures laid down in the 1911 Act, when the 1911 Act was not drafted to allow its procedures to be used to amend itself. This argument was rejected by the courts. The Law Lords stated that the 1911 and 1949 Acts could not be used to enact major constitutional reforms, such as the abolition of the House of Lords. Since the 1949 Act was simply reducing the House of Lords' delaying power from two years to one, this did not amount to a major constitutional reform and so the 1949 Act was lawful and so also, therefore, was the Hunting Act.

Legal principle

The Parliament Acts of 1911 and 1949 cannot be used to enact major constitutional reforms.

2.4.9 Royal Assent

In the vast majority of cases, agreement between the Lords and Commons is reached, and the Bill is then presented for Royal Assent. Technically, the Queen must give her consent to all legislation before it can become law, but in practice that consent is never refused.

The Bill is then an Act of Parliament, and becomes law, though most do not take effect from the moment the Queen gives her consent, but on a specified date in the near future or when a commencement order has been issued by a Government Minister.

Figure 2.3 Making an Act of Parliament

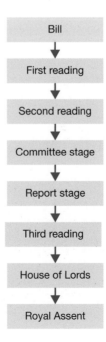

2.4.10 Accelerated procedures

In the case of legislation about which there is no controversy, the procedure may be simplified, with the first three readings in the Lords, then three in the Commons, with the Bill passing back to the Lords only if there is disagreement. Private Bills technically go through the above procedure, and are examined to make sure that adequate warning has been given to anyone affected by the provisions, but there is little debate on them. Consolidating Acts, which simply bring together all the existing law on one topic, also go through an accelerated procedure, with no debate, because they do not change the law; codification Bills, on the other hand, go through the normal process (see p. 149).

2.4.11 Post-legislative scrutiny

The Law Commission (a body responsible for looking at how the law needs to be reformed) has considered whether a formal procedure should be introduced to scrutinise legislation after it has been passed. Following a consultation process the Commission issued a report on the subject entitled *Post-Legislative Scrutiny* (2006). This report strongly supported the creation

Photo 2.1 The Houses of Parliament

Source: © Maksym Gorpenyuk/Shutterstock.com

of a joint parliamentary committee on post-legislative scrutiny which would routinely check whether new legislation – both Acts of Parliament and delegated legislation (discussed in Chapter 4) – is working effectively. These recommendations were accepted by the Labour Government in its report *Post-legislative scrutiny – The Government's approach* (2008). As a result, three to five years after an Act has been passed, the relevant Government department has to produce a memorandum summarising the impact of the Act, which is given to the relevant department committee in Parliament to consider.

2.4.12 Devolution

Devolution is a process of decentralisation, and puts power closer to the citizen so that local factors are better recognised in decision-making. Following referendums in 1997 and 1998, a Scottish Parliament, a Welsh Assembly and a Northern Irish Assembly have been established with legislative powers. These three legislative bodies have been given some power that was previously held by the Westminster Parliament. The Westminster Parliament remains sovereign: it can change the Acts of Parliament that established these devolved legislative bodies and can legislate on anything that has been devolved. However, the Government has made it clear it will not normally do so without the consent of the devolved legislatures.

Under the Government of Wales Act 2006, the Welsh Assembly can legislate on 20 subjects listed in Schedule 7 to that Act dealing with the delivery of local services, including education, agriculture, housing and transport. This type of legislation is known as Assembly Acts. The Scotland Act 1998 specifies those matters that are reserved to the Westminster Parliament (such as defence and foreign policy) and anything else falls within the remit of the Scottish Parliament. After the Scottish Independence Referendum of September 2014, which resulted in a vote for Scotland to remain part of the UK, further powers were promised to be devolved to the Scottish Parliament, including full control over taxation. The Scottish Parliament has full legislative powers over devolved matters. Its laws are known as Acts of the Scottish Parliament. All of these devolved bodies have the power to pass primary legislation (with the authority of law in its own right) rather than just secondary legislation (discussed in Chapter 4). So Acts of these devolved bodies do not need the approval of the UK Government to take effect.

The Bigger Picture: English votes for English laws

Devolution of legislative powers to Scotland, Wales and Northern Ireland raised questions about who should vote for legislation which had an impact only on England. In simple terms, why should Scottish MPs vote on legislation that only affected education in England, when English MPs no longer had the right to vote on legislation on education in Scotland? In 2015 Parliament's Standing Orders were changed to give 'English votes for English laws'. The new Standing Orders mean that prior to the second reading the Speaker can certify a Bill, or provisions within a Bill, as 'relating exclusively to England or to England and Wales'. English-only Bills are then considered by a Committee made up of only English MPs. After the report stage, English MPs sit in a Legislative Grand Committee and are asked to consent to the Bill through a Legislative Consent Motion. Thus English MPs have effectively a veto on English Bills. Once the Legislative Consent Motion has been passed, then the Bill can proceed to its third reading. So, apart from these Committee stages, all MPs vote as normal on the Bill.

> The Housing and Planning Bill was the first Bill to be certified under the new Standing Orders and, in 2016, was the first in respect of which the new Legislative Grand Committee processes operated. The Housing Bill included an extension of the right-to-buy for housing association tenants in England and was approved by all MPs at the third reading stage.
> The new rules have been criticised as unduly complicated, and for creating two tiers of MPs: English MPs who can always vote, and other MPs who can sometimes vote. An alternative would be to have a separate English Parliament.

2.5 Reforms to legislative procedures

An experiment was carried out in 2012 looking at whether there would be benefits in introducing a new 'public reading stage' for Bills to give the public an opportunity to comment on proposed legislation online, and a dedicated 'public reading day' within a Bill's committee stage where those comments would be debated by the committee scrutinising the Bill. This procedure was piloted on three Bills, but its use has not been extended further.

More recently, in September 2016, the House of Lords Constitutional Committee launched an inquiry into the legislative process. This was in part a follow up on its previous work carried out in 2004 on the passage of legislation through Parliament. The purpose of this inquiry was to consider how outside organisations and the public are involved in the legislative process and indeed how their role could be developed. Of course Brexit was also firmly on the agenda as well. The four central questions on which evidence was sought were related to the arrangements for delivering clear draft legislation; the improvements that can be made to deliver clearer laws; the impact of Brexit; and how technology can be used to enhance the process of developing legislation.

The inquiry closed in September 2017. The final report that was published (*Preparing Legislation for Parliament* (2017)) made the following recommendations.

- That legislation should be made more accessible and easier to understand, for practitioners and the public.

- That consolidation is urgently needed in several areas of the law (for example immigration law and sentencing law).

- That the Government should routinely publish the evidence base for proposals and that, if a robust evidence base is not available, the Government should explain why it is nevertheless appropriate to proceed.

- That piloting the application of policy is an important way of developing effective policies over time, and that the Government should develop guidance for departments, setting out when piloting is appropriate or desirable.

- That the Government should publish draft Bills for pre-legislative scrutiny more frequently and that it should become a regular feature of the legislative process.

The broad needs that this inquiry appears to have identified are the need for better scrutiny, a tidying up of related areas of law and ensuring that legislation is comprehensible, which in turn must contribute to facilitating access to justice.

Answering questions

1   There has been some disagreement as to the way in which the House of Lords should be reformed. What are the various options, and how do these differ from its present composition?

2   Describe the stages of the law-making process in Parliament: to what extent is approval of the House of Lords always required?

For answers to these questions, visit the companion website at www.pearsoned.co.uk/ elliottquinn

SUMMARY OF CHAPTER 2: STATUTE LAW

Introduction

Statutes are made by Parliament, which consists of the House of Commons, the House of Lords and the Monarch.

House of Commons

The House of Commons is the democratically elected chamber of Parliament.

House of Lords

Following the House of Lords Act 1999, membership of the House of Lords is currently undergoing a major reform to remove the role of the hereditary peers. The Government is considering removing the remaining 92 hereditary peers. An independent Appointments Commission selects some non-party members for the upper House and vets party appointments.

Making an Act of Parliament

All statutes begin as a Bill. There are three types of Bill:

- Public Bills
- Private Members' Bills
- Private Bills.

The legislative process usually starts in the House of Commons and proceeds as follows.

- First reading
- Second reading
- Committee stage
- Report stage
- Third reading
- House of Lords
- Royal Assent.

Role of the House of Lords

The Parliament Acts of 1911 and 1949 lay down special procedures by which proposed legislation can go for Royal Assent without the approval of the House of Lords after specified periods of time. These procedures are only rarely used, because the House of Lords usually drops objections that are resisted by the Commons, though their use has increased in recent years.

Reading list

Law Commission (2006) *Post-Legislative Scrutiny*. Cm 6945. London: HMSO.

Renton, D. (1975) *The Preparation of Legislation*. London: HMSO.

Royal Commission for the Reform of the House of Lords (2000) *A House for the Future*. Cm 4534. London: HMSO.

On the internet

Copies of Public Bills currently being considered by Parliament can be found at:
http://www.parliament.uk/business/bills-and-legislation/

Copies of recent legislation can be found at:
http://www.legislation.gov.uk/ukpga

Useful explanatory notes prepared by the Government to explain the implications of recent legislation can be found at:
http://www.legislation.gov.uk/browse

The House of Lords Constitutional Committee Report, *The Legislative Process: Preparing Legislation for Parliament* (2017), is available at:
https://www.parliament.uk/business/committees/committees-a-z/lords-select/ constitution-committee/news-parliament-2017/legislative-process-part-one-report/

Chapter 3
Statutory interpretation

This chapter discusses:

- the meaning of parliamentary intention;

- the rules of statutory interpretation;

- internal aids to statutory interpretation;

- external aids to statutory interpretation, including the Human Rights Act 1998 and the official record of what was said in Parliament (known as *Hansard*); and

- theories about how judges interpret statutes in practice.

3.1 Introduction

Although Parliament makes legislation, it is left to the courts to apply it. The general public imagines that this is simply a case of looking up the relevant law and ruling accordingly, but the reality is not so simple. Despite the fact that Acts of Parliament are carefully written by expert draftsmen, there are many occasions in which the courts find that the implications of a statute for the case before them are not at all clear.

Bennion (2005) has identified a number of factors that may cause this uncertainty:

- A word is left out because the draftsman thought it was automatically implied. For example, a draftsman writing a statute banning men with facial hair from parks might write that 'men with beards or moustaches are prohibited from parks'. Does this mean that a man who has a beard **and** a moustache would be allowed in? If the words 'and/or' were used it would be clear, but the draftsman may have thought this was automatically implied.

- A broad term was used, leaving it to the user to decide what it includes. Where a statute bans vehicles from the park, this obviously includes cars and lorries, but the courts would have to decide whether it also prohibited skateboards, bikes or roller skates, for example.

- An ambiguous word or phrase was used on purpose, perhaps because the provision is politically contentious. The European Communities Act 1972 was ambiguous about the position of UK legislation.

- The wording is inadequate because of a printing, drafting or other error.

- The events of the case before the court were not foreseen when the legislation was produced. In the example given above regarding vehicles, skateboards might not have been invented when the statute was drafted, so it would be impossible for Parliament to say whether they should be included in the term 'vehicles'.

In any of these cases, the job of the courts – in theory at least – is to discover how Parliament intended the law to apply and put that into practice. This is because, as you know, in our constitution, Parliament is the supreme source of law (excluding EU law, which will be discussed later), and therefore the judiciary's constitutional role is to put into practice what they think Parliament actually intended when it made a particular law, rather than simply what the judges themselves might think is the best interpretation in the case before them. However, as we shall see, the practice is not always as straightforward as the constitutional theory suggests.

3.1.1 What is parliamentary intention?

The idea of parliamentary intention is a very slippery concept in practice. The last example above is one illustration of this: how could Parliament have had any intention at all of how skateboards should be treated under the legislation, if skateboards were not invented when the legislation was passed?

More problems are revealed if we try to pin down precisely what parliamentary intention means. Is it the intention of every individual Member of Parliament at the time the law was passed? Obviously not, since not every member will have voted for the legislation or even necessarily been present when it was passed. The intention of all those who did support a particular piece of legislation is no easier to define either, since some of those are likely to be acting from loyalty to their party, and will not necessarily have detailed knowledge of the provisions, much less have thought hard about how they might apply in as yet unseen circumstances. Even among those MPs who have considered the detailed provisions, there may be many different opinions as to how they should apply in different situations. And even if one of these groups was taken to represent true parliamentary intention, how are their views to be assessed? It is hardly feasible to conduct a poll every time a legislative provision is found to be unclear.

In fact, the people who will have paid most attention to the wording of a statute are the Ministers who seek to get them through Parliament, the civil servants who advise the Ministers and the draftsmen who draw up the legislation. None of these can really be said to amount to Parliament.

3.1.2 Statutory interpretation and case law

Once the courts have interpreted a statute, or a section of one, that interpretation becomes part of case law in just the same way as any other judicial decision, and subject to the same rules of precedent. A higher court may decide that the interpretation is wrong, and reverse the decision if it is appealed, or overrule it in a later case but, unless and until this happens, lower courts must interpret the statute in the same way.

3.2 How are statutes interpreted?

Parliament has given the courts some sources of guidance on statutory interpretation. The Interpretation Act 1978 provides certain standard definitions of common provisions, such as the rule that the singular includes the plural and 'he' includes 'she', while interpretation sections at the end of most modern Acts define some of the words used within them – the Police and Criminal Evidence Act 1984 contains such a section. A further source of help has been provided since the beginning of 1999: all Bills passed since that date are the subject of special explanatory notes, which are made public. These detail the background to the legislation and explain the effects particular provisions are intended to have.

Apart from this assistance, it has been left to the courts to decide what method to use to interpret statutes, and four basic approaches have developed, in conjunction with certain aids to interpretation. These approaches should not be considered as rules to be followed. The Supreme Court made clear in *Cusack* v *London Borough of Harrow* (2013) that while these approaches have a valuable part to play in interpreting statutes, they should be treated as 'guidelines rather than railway lines'.

3.3 Rules of interpretation

3.3.1 The literal rule

This rule gives all the words in a statute their ordinary and natural meaning, on the principle that the best way to interpret the will of Parliament is to follow the literal meaning of the words they have used. Under this rule, the literal meaning must be followed, even if the result is silly; for example, Lord Esher stated, in *R* v *City of London Court Judge* (1892): 'If the words of an Act are clear, you must follow them, even though they lead to a manifest absurdity. The court has nothing to do with the question of whether the legislature has committed an absurdity.'

Examples of the literal rule in use are:

Whiteley v *Chappell* **(1868)** A statute aimed at preventing electoral malpractice made it an offence to impersonate 'any person entitled to vote' at an election. The accused was acquitted because he impersonated a dead person and a dead person was clearly not entitled to vote!

London and North Eastern Railway Co v *Berriman* **(1946)** A railway worker was knocked down and killed by a train, and his widow attempted to claim damages. The relevant statute provided that this was available to employees killed while engaging in 'relaying or repairing' tracks; the dead man had been doing routine maintenance and oiling, which the court held did not come within the meaning of 'relaying and repairing'.

Fisher v *Bell* **(1961)** After several violent incidents in which the weapon used was a flick-knife, Parliament decided that these knives should be banned. The Restriction of Offensive Weapons Act 1959 consequently made it an offence to 'sell or offer for sale' any flick-knife. The defendant had flick-knives in his shop window and was charged with offering these for sale. The courts held that the term 'offers for sale' must be given its ordinary meaning in law, and that in contract law this was not an offer for sale but only an invitation to people to make an offer to buy. The defendant was therefore not guilty of a crime under the Act, despite the fact that this was obviously just the sort of behaviour that Act was set up to prevent.

Advantages of the literal rule

It respects parliamentary sovereignty, giving the courts a restricted role and leaving law-making to those elected for the job.

Disadvantages of the literal rule

Where use of the literal rule does lead to an absurd or obviously unjust conclusion, it can hardly be said to be enacting the will of Parliament, since Parliament is unlikely to have intended absurdity and injustice. The case of *London and North Eastern Railway Co* v *Berriman* (above) is an example of literal interpretation creating injustice where Parliament probably never intended any – the difference in the type of work being done does not change the degree of danger to which the workers were exposed.

In addition, the literal rule is useless where the answer to a problem simply cannot be found in the words of the statute. As Hart (1994) has pointed out, some terms have a core of very clear meaning, but it may still be unclear how far that word stretches: the example above of an imaginary law banning 'vehicles' from the park clearly illustrates this. Where such a broad term is used, the answer is simply not there in the words of the statute, and the courts have to use some other method.

The Law Commission in 1969 pointed out that interpretation based only on literal meanings 'assumes unattainable perfection in draftsmanship'; even the most talented and experienced draftsmen cannot predict every situation to which legislation may have to be applied. One should not expect too much of words, which are always an imperfect means of communication. The same word may mean different things to different people, and words also shift their meanings over time.

Zander, in his book *The Law-Making Process* (2004), describes the literal approach as 'mechanical, divorced both from the realities of the use of language and from the expectations and aspirations of the human beings concerned . . . in that sense it is irresponsible'.

In *R (on the application of Haw)* v *Secretary of State for the Home Department* (2006), the Court of Appeal refused to apply a literal interpretation to a new piece of legislation, as it considered that this would not reflect the intention of Parliament. The case concerned Brian Haw, who had been holding a protest in Parliament Square, opposite Parliament, against the war in Iraq since June 2001. He lived on the pavement and displayed a large number of placards protesting about Government policy in Iraq. The demonstration had earlier been held to be lawful, since it neither caused an obstruction nor gave rise to any fear that a breach of the peace might arise. The Serious Organised Crime and Police Act 2005, s. 133(1) was subsequently passed, which required any person who intended to organise a demonstration in the vicinity of Parliament to apply to the police for authorisation to do so. Section 132(1) provided that a person who carried on a demonstration in the designated area was guilty of an offence if, when the demonstration started, appropriate authorisation had not been given:

(1) Any person who –

    (a) organises a demonstration in a public place in the designated area, or

    (b) takes part in a demonstration in a public place in the designated area, or

    (c) carries on a demonstration by himself in a public place in the designated area, is guilty of an offence if, when the demonstration **starts**, authorisation for the demonstration has not been given under section 134(2).

Haw argued that the Act did not apply to his demonstration because it had started before the Act came into force. The Court of Appeal held that the Act did in fact apply to Haw's demonstration: 'Any other conclusion would be wholly irrational and could fairly be described as manifestly absurd.' Construing the statutory language in context, Parliament's intention was clearly to regulate all demonstrations in the designated area, whenever they began. Thus, rather than following a literal interpretation of the legislation, the court looked at its context to determine the intention of Parliament. The court gave particular weight to the fact that the 2005 Act repealed a provision in the Public Order Act 1986. That provision had provided for controls to be placed on public demonstrations and would have applied to demonstrations which had been started since 1986. The Court of Appeal thought it was inconceivable that Parliament would have intended to repeal that power to control demonstrations started before 2005 and replace it with legislation which could only control demonstrations started after 2005, as this would leave a significant gap in the power of the state to control demonstrations.

Conditions were subsequently imposed on Haw's demonstration in accordance with the provisions of the 2005 Act, aimed primarily at restricting the size of the demonstration. It was accepted that Haw's demonstration in itself did not pose a security risk, but if a large number of people joined his demonstration this could be an opportunity for terrorists to join in and conceal an explosive device. A new framework for regulating protests around Parliament Square is contained in the Police Reform and Social Responsibility Act 2011, replacing the relevant provisions in the 2005 Act.

3.3.2 The golden rule

This provides that if the literal rule gives an absurd result, which Parliament could not have intended, then (and only then) the judge can substitute a reasonable meaning in the light of the statute as a whole. It was defined by Lord Wensleydale in *Grey* v *Pearson* (1857): 'The grammatical and ordinary sense of the words is to be adhered to, unless that would lead to some absurdity, or some repugnance or inconsistency with the rest of the instrument, in which case the grammatical and ordinary sense of the words may be modified so as to avoid that absurdity and inconsistency, but no further.'

Examples of the golden rule in use are:

R v *Allen* (1872) Section 57 of the Offences Against the Person Act 1861 stated that 'Whosoever being married shall marry any other person during the life of the former husband or wife . . . shall be guilty of bigamy.' It was pointed out that it was impossible for a person already married to 'marry' someone else – they might go through a marriage ceremony, but would not actually be married; using the literal rule would make the statute useless. The courts therefore held that 'shall marry' should be interpreted to mean 'shall go through a marriage ceremony'.

Maddox v *Storer* (1963) Under the Road Traffic Act 1960, it was an offence to drive at more than 30 mph in a vehicle 'adapted to carry more than seven passengers'. The vehicle in the case was a minibus made to carry 11 passengers, rather than altered to do so, and the court held that 'adapted to' could be taken to mean 'suitable for'.

Adler v *George* (1964) The defendant was charged under s. 3 of the Official Secrets Act 1920, with obstructing a member of the armed forces 'in the vicinity of any prohibited place'. He argued that the natural meaning of 'in the vicinity of' meant near to, whereas the obstruction had actually occurred in the prohibited place itself, an air force station. The court held that while in many circumstances 'in the vicinity' could indeed only be interpreted as meaning near to, in this context it was reasonable to construe it as including being within the prohibited place.

Advantages of the golden rule

The golden rule can prevent the absurdity and injustice caused by the literal rule, and help the courts put into practice what Parliament really means.

Disadvantages of the golden rule

The Law Commission noted in 1969 that the 'rule' provided no clear meaning of an 'absurd result'. As in practice that was judged by reference to whether a particular interpretation was irreconcilable with the general policy of the legislature, the golden rule turns out to be a less explicit form of the mischief rule (discussed next).

3.3.3 The mischief rule

Key case

The mischief rule was laid down in **Heydon's Case** in the sixteenth century, and provides that judges should consider three factors:

- what the law was before the statute was passed;
- what problem, or 'mischief', the statute was trying to remedy;
- what remedy Parliament was trying to provide.

The judge should then interpret the statute in such a way as to put a stop to the problem that Parliament was addressing.

Legal principle

Judges can interpret a statute so that it effectively tackles the problem that Parliament wanted to deal with: the mischief rule.

Examples of the mischief rule in use are:

Smith v *Hughes* **(1960)** The Street Offences Act 1959 made it a criminal offence for a prostitute to solicit potential customers in a street or public place. In this case, the prostitute was not actually in the street, but was sitting in a house, on the first floor, and tapping on the window to attract the attention of the men walking by. The judge decided that the aim of the Act was to enable people to walk along the street without being solicited, and since the soliciting in question was aimed at people in the street, even though the prostitute was not in the street herself, the Act should be interpreted to include this activity.

Elliott v *Grey* **(1960)** The Road Traffic Act 1930 provided that it was an offence for an uninsured car to be 'used on the road'. The car in this case was on the road, but jacked up, with its battery removed, but the court held that, as it was nevertheless a hazard of the type which the statute was designed to prevent, it was covered by the phrase 'used on the road'.

Royal College of Nursing v *DHSS* **(1981)** The Abortion Act 1967 stated that terminations of pregnancy were legal only if performed by a 'registered medical practitioner'. By 1972, surgical abortions were largely being replaced by drug-induced ones, in which the second stage of the process (attaching the patient to a drip), was carried out by nurses, under the instructions of a doctor. The House of Lords ruled that the mischief which the Act sought to remedy was the uncertain state of the previous law, which drove many women to dangerous back-street abortionists. It sought to do this by widening the grounds on which abortions could be obtained, and ensuring that they were carried out with proper skill in hygienic conditions, and the procedure in question promoted this aim, and was not unlawful. It was a controversial decision, with Lords Wilberforce and Edmund Davies claiming that the House was not interpreting legislation but rewriting it.

Advantages of the mischief rule

The mischief rule helps avoid absurdity and injustice, and promotes flexibility. It was described by the Law Commission in 1969 as a 'rather more satisfactory approach' than the two other established rules.

Disadvantages of the mischief rule

Heydon's Case was the product of a time when statutes were a minor source of law, compared to the common law. Drafting was by no means as exact a process as it is today, and the supremacy of Parliament was not really established. At that time too, what statutes there were tended to include a lengthy preamble, which more or less spelt out the 'mischief' with which the Act was intended to deal. Judges of the time were very well qualified to decide what the previous law was and what problems a statute was intended to remedy, since they had usually drafted statutes on behalf of the king, and Parliament only rubber-stamped them. Such a rule may be less appropriate now that the legislative situation is so different.

3.3.4 The purposive approach

Historically, the preferred approach to statutory interpretation was to look for the statute's literal meaning. However, over the last three decades, the courts have accepted that the literal approach can be unsatisfactory. Instead, the judges have been increasingly influenced by the European approach to statutory interpretation which focuses on giving effect to the purpose of the legislation. During his judicial career, Lord Denning was at the forefront of moves to establish a more purposive approach, aiming to produce decisions that put into practice the spirit of the law, even if that meant paying less than usual regard to the letter of the law – the actual words of the statute. He felt that the mischief rule could be interpreted broadly, so that it would not just allow the courts to look at the history of the case, but it would also allow them to carry out the intention of Parliament, however imperfectly this might have been expressed in the words used. In reality, the purposive approach that has developed takes a more liberal approach to statutory interpretation than is traditionally associated with the mischief rule. Denning stated his views in *Magor and St Mellons Rural District Council* v *Newport Corporation* (1952):

> We do not sit here to pull the language of Parliament to pieces and make nonsense of it . . . we sit here to find out the intention of Parliament and carry it out, and we do this better by filling in the gaps and making sense of the enactment than by opening it up to destructive analysis.

On appeal, the House of Lords described this approach as 'a naked usurpation of the judicial function, under the guise of interpretation . . . If a gap is disclosed, the remedy lies in an amending Act.'

In fact, over time, the House of Lords has come to accept that a purposive approach to statutory interpretation can, in certain cases, be appropriate. The move towards a purposive approach has been particularly marked in relation to the interpretation of European legislation and national legislation that is designed to implement European legislation, as the Court of Justice of the European Union (like most civil law countries) tends itself to adopt a purposive approach to statutory interpretation. Thus, in *Pickstone* v *Freemans* (1988) the House of Lords held that it had to read words into inadequate domestic legislation in order to give effect to European legislation which was intended to tackle the problem of women being paid less than men for the same work.

But the purposive approach has not been restricted to the context of European law, and has been applied to pure domestic legislation. In *Pepper* v *Hart* (1993) the House of Lords stated:

> The days have long passed when the court adopted a strict constructionist view of interpretation which required them to adopt the literal meaning of the language. The courts now adopt a purposive approach which seeks to give effect to the true purpose of legislation and are prepared to look at much extraneous material that bears on the background against which the legislation was enacted.

Key case

In *R (on the application of Quintavalle)* v *Secretary of State for Health* (2003) the House of Lords was required to interpret the Human Fertilisation and Embryology Act 1990. Section 1 of this Act defines an embryo as 'a live human embryo where fertilisation is complete' and their use was regulated by the Human Fertilisation and Embryology Authority (HFEA). After the Act had been passed, scientists developed a cloning technique whereby embryos were not created by fertilising an egg, but by replacing the nucleus of an egg with a cell from another person. The Labour Government had issued a statement saying that medical research involving cloned embryos did fall within the Act and could be regulated by HFEA. The pressure group, Pro-Life Alliance, was opposed to such research and sought a declaration of the courts that HFEA was acting outside its statutory powers. The House of Lords gave the Act a purposive interpretation to give effect to the intention of Parliament. It observed that under the influence of European legal culture 'the pendulum has swung towards purposive methods of construction':

> The basic task of the court is to ascertain and give effect to the true meaning of what Parliament has said in the enactment to be construed. But that is not to say that attention should be confined and a literal interpretation given to the particular provisions which give rise to difficulty . . . The court's task, within the permissible bounds of interpretation, is to give effect to Parliament's purpose. So the controversial provisions should be read in the context of the statute as a whole, and the statute as a whole should be read in the historical context of the situation which led to its enactment.

It concluded that Parliament could not have intended to exclude cloned embryos from being regulated by HFEA.

Legal principle
Legislation can be interpreted using a purposive approach.

3

STATUTORY INTERPRETATION

3.3.5 Rectification

Words can be added to a statute by a judge to give effect to Parliament's intention where an obvious error has been made in drafting a statute. This was the conclusion of the House of Lords in *Inco Europe Ltd* v *First Choice Distribution* (2000) and this process of correcting mistakes is known as rectification. To be able to read words into a statute, the court must be in no doubt about what provision needs to be added. The power of rectification is restricted to plain cases of drafting mistakes. The court must not do anything that might look like judicial legislation; its role is purely interpretative. Since a statute is expressed in language that is approved and enacted by the legislature, the courts must exercise considerable caution before adding, omitting or substituting words. Therefore, before interpreting a statute in this way, the court must be sure:

- of the intended purpose of the statute;
- that the draftsman and Parliament have, by accident, failed to give effect to that purpose;
- how Parliament would have written the provision if the error had been spotted, though not necessarily the precise words Parliament would have used, had the error in the Bill been noticed.

Even where these conditions are satisfied, a court may be unable to imply a change of wording in the Act if the change in language is considered too far-reaching.

The case of ***Inco Europe Ltd*** was considered in ***OB v Director of the Serious Fraud Office*** (2012). The defendant had been sent to prison for contempt of court and sought to appeal against this decision from the Criminal Division of the Court of Appeal to the Supreme Court. The old Administration of Justice Act 1960 contained a right to appeal in such cases, but this right was not mentioned when the legislation was amended by the Armed Forces Act 2006. The defendant argued that this omission was simply a legislative error and he should still have a right of appeal. The Court of Appeal accepted that the case satisfied the requirements laid down in ***Inco Europe Ltd***. In particular, when enacting the 2006 Act, Parliament had no intention of removing the right of appeal in contempt cases. In summary, the courts will correct an error in legislative drafting where common sense requires it.

The Bigger Picture: The Human Rights Act 1998

The Human Rights Act 1998 incorporates into UK law the European Convention on Human Rights, which is an international treaty signed by most democratic countries, and designed to protect basic human rights. In much of Europe, the Convention has been incorporated into national law as a Bill of Rights, which means that the courts can overrule domestic legislation which is in conflict with it. This is not the case in the UK. Instead, s. 3(1) of the Human Rights Act requires that:

> So far as it is possible to do so, primary legislation and subordinate legislation must be read and given effect in a way which is compatible with the Convention rights.

Section 2 further requires that, in deciding any question which arises in connection with a right protected by the Convention, the courts 'must take into account' any relevant judgments made by the European Court of Human Rights (see p. 26). If it is impossible to find an interpretation which is compatible with the Convention, the court concerned can make a declaration of incompatibility under s. 4 of the Act. This does not affect the validity of the statute in question, but it is designed to draw attention to the conflict so that the Government can change the law to bring it in line with the Convention (although the Act does not oblige the Government to do this). Under s. 10 there is a special 'fast track' procedure by which a Minister can make the necessary changes.

When new legislation is being made, the relevant Bill must carry a statement from the relevant Minister, saying either that its provisions are compatible with the Convention, or that, even if they are not, the Government wishes to go ahead with the legislation anyway. In the latter case, the Government would be specifically saying that the legislation must override Convention rights if there is a clash, but clearly any Government intent on passing such legislation would be likely to face considerable opposition and so would have to have a very good reason, in the eyes of the public, for doing so.

If the courts consider that a literal interpretation of an Act would render the legislation in breach of the European Convention, under s. 3 the precise wording of the Act may in certain circumstances be ignored and the Act given an interpretation which conforms with the Convention. In ***R v A*** (2001) the House of Lords noted that:

> Under ordinary methods of interpretation a court may depart from the language of the statute to avoid absurd consequences: section 3 goes much further . . . In accordance with the will of Parliament as reflected in section 3 it will sometimes be necessary to adopt an interpretation which linguistically may appear strained.

This case was concerned with the prosecution of rape. Evidence of a complainant's past sexual experience is sometimes admissible as evidence in court in rape trials. Such evidence has in the past been used to give the jury a bad impression of the victim and make it appear that she was not a credible witness – the insinuation being that a woman who has had an active sex life with men other than a husband is immoral and cannot be trusted generally. The Labour Government was concerned that rape victims were not being adequately protected in court proceedings and legislation was passed on the matter. The Youth Justice and Criminal Evidence Act 1999, s. 41 provided that evidence of the complainant's past sexual behaviour could only be given if 'a refusal of leave might have the result of rendering unsafe a conclusion of the jury or . . . the court on any relevant issue in the case'. The clear intention of Parliament was to significantly restrict the use of past sexual history evidence in rape trials. Unfortunately, in the first case to reach the House of Lords concerning this section, the House relied on the Human Rights Act 1998 in order to ignore the clear intention of Parliament. It ruled that a defendant had to be given the opportunity to adduce evidence as to the complainant's past sexual behaviour with the defendant which had taken place over a week before the purported rape. It considered that otherwise this section would be in breach of Art. 6 of the European Convention on Human Rights guaranteeing a fair trial. The interpretation of the legislation ran contrary to Parliament's intention when it passed that Act, though it is arguable that Parliament's ultimate intention was being respected as provided for in the Human Rights Act 1998.

In *Ghaidan v Godin-Mendoza* (2004) the House of Lords encouraged the courts to use s. 3 to interpret statutes in accordance with the European Convention. Lord Steyne noted that, at the time of the judgment, ten declarations of incompatibility had been made under s. 4, of which five had been overturned on appeal, and s. 3 had only been relied on 10 times. He concluded from these statistics that s. 4 was being relied on too often, when it should only be used as a last resort, and that instead the courts should make greater use of s. 3 to interpret legislation in accordance with the Convention.

The House felt that, in the context of s. 3, the courts should be prepared to move away from the 'semantic lottery' of the words used by the draftsman and interpret the statute in the light of Convention rights:

> [O]nce it is accepted that section 3 may require legislation to bear a meaning which departs from the unambiguous meaning the legislation would otherwise bear, it becomes impossible to suppose Parliament intended that the operation of section 3 should depend critically upon the particular form of words adopted by the parliamentary draftsman in the statutory provision under consideration.

The House simply requires the courts to make sure that the meaning given to the legislation is consistent with the 'fundamental features' of the statute and the judges must avoid deciding issues calling for legislative deliberation. This potentially gives the courts considerable flexibility when relying on s. 3 to interpret a statute which risks breaching the European Convention.

The Court of Appeal went too far in *Re S (A Minor)* (2002). It attempted to interpret the Children Act 1989 by adding a new procedure requiring the local authority to contact the guardian of a child subjected to a care order in particular circumstances. The House of Lords allowed an appeal as it considered that the Court of Appeal had crossed the boundary between interpretation and amendment. The new procedure created by the Court of Appeal conflicted with a fundamental feature of the 1989 Act that judicial supervision of care orders was very restricted.

Thus, there are certain limits on the courts' powers of interpretation when applying s. 3 of the Human Rights Act 1998, but they still appear to have greater powers of interpretation in this context than when they are exercising their ordinary powers of statutory interpretation.

3

STATUTORY INTERPRETATION

3.4 Interpreting European legislation

Section 2(4) of the European Communities Act 1972 provides that all parliamentary legislation (whether passed before or after the European Communities Act) must be construed and applied in accordance with European law. The case of *R v Secretary of State for Transport, ex parte Factortame* (1990) makes it clear that the English courts must apply European law which is directly effective even if it conflicts with English law, including statute law (these issues are discussed more fully in Chapter 5: European law).

3.5 Aids to interpretation

Whichever approach the judges take to statutory interpretation, they have at their disposal a range of material to help. Some of these aids may be found within the piece of legislation itself, or in certain rules of language commonly applied in statutory texts – these are called internal aids. Others, outside the piece of legislation, are called external aids. Since 1995, a very important new external aid has been added in the form of the Human Rights Act 1998.

3.5.1 Internal aids

The literal rule and the golden rule both direct the judge to internal aids, though they are taken into account whatever the approach.

The statute itself

To decide what a provision of the Act means the judge may draw a comparison with provisions elsewhere in the statute. Clues may also be provided by the long title of the Act or the subheadings within it.

Explanatory notes

Acts passed since the beginning of 1999 are provided with explanatory notes, published at the same time as the Act.

Rules of language

Developed by lawyers over time, these rules are really little more than common sense, despite their intimidating names. As with the rules of interpretation, they are not always precisely applied. Examples include:

Ejusdem generis General words which follow specific ones are taken to include only things of the same kind. For example, if an Act used the phrase 'dogs, cats and other animals' the phrase 'and other animals' would probably include other domestic animals, but not wild ones.

Expressio unius est exclusio alterius Express mention of one thing implies the exclusion of another. If an Act specifically mentioned 'Persian cats', the term would not include other breeds of cat.

Noscitur a sociis A word draws meaning from the other words around it. If a statute mentioned 'cat baskets, toy mice and food', it would be reasonable to assume that 'food' meant cat food, and dog food was not covered by the relevant provision.

Presumptions

The courts assume that certain points are implied in all legislation. These presumptions include the following.

- Statutes do not change the common law.
- The legislature does not intend to remove any matters from the jurisdiction of the courts.
- Existing rights are not to be interfered with.
- Laws which create crimes should be interpreted in favour of the citizen where there is ambiguity.
- Legislation does not operate retrospectively: its provisions operate from the day it comes into force, and are not backdated.
- Statutes do not affect the Monarch.
- Statutes are 'always speaking' (see p. 79).

It is always open to Parliament to go against these presumptions if it sees fit – for example, the European Communities Act 1972 makes it clear that some of its provisions are to be applied retrospectively. But, unless the wording of a statute makes it absolutely clear that Parliament has chosen to go against one or more of the presumptions, the courts can assume that the presumptions apply.

Some indication of the weight which judges feel should be attached to presumptions can be seen in the case of ***L'Office Cherifien des Phosphates Unitramp SA* v *Yamashita-Shinnihon Steamship Co Ltd (The Boucraa)*** (1994), which concerned the presumption against retrospective effect. The House of Lords stated that the important issue was 'simple fairness': if they read the relevant statute as imposing the suggested degree of retrospective effect, would the result be so unfair that Parliament could not have intended it, even though their words might suggest retrospective effect? This could be judged by balancing a number of factors, including the nature of the rights affected, the clarity of the words used and the background to the legislation.

What remains unclear is how judges decide between different presumptions if they conflict, and why certain values are selected for protection by presumptions, and not others. For example, the presumption that existing rights are not to be interfered with serves to protect

Figure 3.1 Approaches to statutory interpretation

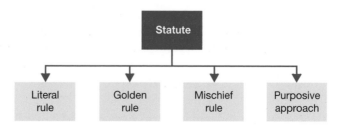

Figure 3.2 Internal aids to interpretation

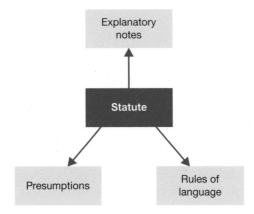

the existing property or money of individuals, but there is no presumption in favour of people claiming state benefits.

3.5.2 External aids

The mischief rule directs the judge to external aids, including the following:

Historical setting

A judge may consider the historical setting of the provision that is being interpreted, as well as other statutes dealing with the same subjects.

Dictionaries and textbooks

These may be consulted to find the meaning of a word, or to gather information about the views of legal academics on a point of law.

Reports

Legislation may be preceded by a report of a Royal Commission, the Law Commission or some other official advisory committee (see pp. 164–5). The House of Lords stated in ***Black Clawson International Ltd*** v ***Papierwerke Waldhof-Aschaffenburg AG*** (1975) that official reports may be considered as evidence of the pre-existing state of the law and the mischief that the legislation was intended to deal with.

Treaties

Treaties and international conventions can be considered when following the presumption that Parliament does not legislate in such a way that the UK would be in breach of its international obligations.

Previous practice

General practice and commercial usage in the field covered by the legislation may shed light on the meaning of a statutory term.

Hansard

This is the official daily report of parliamentary debates, and therefore a record of what was said during the introduction of legislation. For over 100 years, the judiciary held that such documents could not be consulted for the purpose of statutory interpretation. During his career, Lord Denning made strenuous efforts to do away with this rule and, in ***Davis* v *Johnson*** (1978), justified his interpretation of the Domestic Violence and Matrimonial Proceedings Act 1976 by reference to the parliamentary debates during its introduction. The House of Lords, however, rebuked him for doing so, and maintained that the rule should stand.

Key case

In 1993, the case of **Pepper v Hart** overturned the rule against consulting *Hansard*, and such consultation is clearly now allowed. The case was between teachers at a fee-paying school (Malvern College) and the Inland Revenue, and concerned the tax which employees should have to pay on perks (benefits related to their job). Malvern College allowed its teachers to send their sons there for one-fifth of the usual fee, if places were available. Tax law requires employees to pay tax on perks, and the amount of tax is based on the cost to the employer of providing the benefit, which is usually taken to mean any extra cost that the employer would not otherwise incur. The amount paid by Malvern teachers for their sons' places covered the extra cost to the school of having the child there (in books, food and so on), but did not cover the school's fixed costs, for paying teachers, maintaining buildings and so on, which would have been the same whether the teachers' children were there or not. Therefore the perk cost the school little or nothing, and so the teachers maintained that they should not have to pay tax on it. The Inland Revenue disagreed, arguing that the perk should be taxed on the basis of the amount it saved the teachers on the real cost of sending their children to the school.

The reason why the issue of consulting parliamentary debates arose was that, during the passing of the Finance Act 1976 which laid down the tax rules in question, the then Secretary to the Treasury, Robert Sheldon, had specifically mentioned the kind of situation that arose in **Pepper v Hart**. He had stated that where the cost to an employer of a perk was minimal, employees should not have to pay tax on the full cost of it. The question was, could the judges take into account what the Minister had said? The House of Lords convened a special court of seven judges, which decided that they could look at *Hansard* to see what the Minister had said, and that his remarks could be used to decide what Parliament had intended.

Legal principle

When interpreting a statute the courts can consult *Hansard* to see what a Minister had said about a piece of legislation in order to decide what Parliament had intended.

The decision in ***Pepper* v *Hart*** was confirmed in ***Three Rivers District Council* v *Bank of England (No. 2)*** (1996), which concerned the correct interpretation of legislation passed in order to fulfil obligations arising from an EC directive. Although the legislation was not itself ambiguous, the claimants claimed that, if interpreted in the light of the information contained in *Hansard*, the legislation imposed certain duties on the defendants, which were not obvious from the legislation itself. The defendants argued that *Hansard* could only be consulted where legislation contained ambiguity, but the court disagreed, stating that where legislation was passed in order to give effect to international obligations, it was important to make sure that it did so, and consulting legislative materials was one way of helping to ensure this. The result would appear to be that *Hansard* can be consulted not just to explain ambiguous phrases, but to throw light on the general purpose of legislation.

In ***R*** v ***Secretary of State for the Environment, Transport and the Regions, ex parte Spath Holme Ltd*** (2001), the House of Lords gave a restrictive interpretation of the application of ***Pepper*** v ***Hart***. The applicant was a company that was the landlord of certain properties. It sought judicial review of the Rent Acts (Maximum Fair Rent) Order 1999, made by the Secretary of State under s. 31 of the Landlord and Tenant Act 1985. The applicant company contended that the 1999 Order was unlawful as the Secretary of State had made it to alleviate the impact of rent increases on certain categories of tenants, when a reading of *Hansard* showed that Parliament's intention was that such orders would only be made to reduce the impact of inflation. On the use of *Hansard* to interpret the intention of Parliament, the House of Lords pointed out that the case of ***Pepper*** v ***Hart*** was concerned with the meaning of an expression used in a statute ('the cost of a benefit'). The Minister had given a statement on the meaning of that expression. By contrast, the present case was concerned with a matter of policy, and in particular the meaning of a statutory power rather than a statutory expression. Only if a Minister were, improbably, to give a categorical assurance to Parliament that a power would not be used in a given situation would a parliamentary statement on the scope of a power be admissible.

Key case

In **Wilson** v **Secretary of State for Trade and Industry** (2003) the House of Lords again gave a restrictive interpretation to **Pepper** v **Hart**. It held that only statements in *Hansard* made by a Minister or other promoter of legislation could be looked at by the court; other statements recorded in *Hansard* had to be ignored.

Under the British constitution, Parliament and the courts have separate roles. Parliament enacts legislation, the courts interpret and apply it. Due to the principle of the separation of powers (see p. 5), neither institution should stray into the other's domain. Thus, Art. 9 of the Bill of Rights 1689 provides that 'the freedom of speech and debates or proceedings in Parliament ought not to be impeached or questioned in any court or place out of Parliament'. In **Wilson**, the House of Lords emphasised the importance of the courts not straying into Parliament's constitutional role. It concluded from this that *Hansard* could only be used to interpret the meaning of words in legislation; it could not be used to discover the reasons for the legislation. The Court of Appeal in **Wilson** had used *Hansard* to look at the parliamentary debates concerning a particular Act. It was not trying to discover the meaning of words, as their meaning was not in doubt, but to discover the reason which led Parliament to think that it was necessary to pass the Act. The House of Lords held that the Court of Appeal had been wrong to do this. Referring to *Hansard* simply to check the meaning of enacted words supported the principle of parliamentary sovereignty (see p. 5). Referring to *Hansard* to discover the reasoning of Parliament, where there was no ambiguity as to the meaning of the words, would go against the sovereignty of Parliament.

The Human Rights Act 1998 requires the courts to exercise a new role in respect of Acts of Parliament. This new role is fundamentally different from interpreting and applying legislation. The courts are now required to determine whether the legislation violates a right laid down in the European Convention on Human Rights. If the Act does violate the Convention, the courts have to issue a declaration of incompatibility. In order to determine this question, the House of Lords stated in **Wilson** that the courts can only refer to *Hansard* for background information, such as the social policy aim of the Act. Poor reasoning in the course of parliamentary debate was not a matter which could count against the legislation when determining the question of compatibility.

Legal principle

When interpreting a statute, only statements in *Hansard* made by a Minister or other promoter of legislation can be looked at by the court.

Although it is now clear that *Hansard* can be referred to in order to find evidence of parliamentary intention, there is still much debate as to how useful it is, and whether it can provide good evidence of what Parliament intended.

Below are three key arguments in favour of using *Hansard* to assist statutory interpretation.

Usefulness

Lord Denning's argument, advanced in **Davis v Johnson**, was that to ignore it would be to 'grope in the dark for the meaning of an Act without switching on the light'. When such an obvious source of enlightenment was available, it was ridiculous to ignore it – in fact Lord Denning said after the case that he intended to continue to consult *Hansard*, but simply not say he was doing so.

Other jurisdictions

Legislative materials are used in many foreign jurisdictions, including many other European countries and the US. In such countries, these materials tend to be more accessible and concise than *Hansard* – it is difficult to judge whether they are consulted because of this quality, or whether the fact that they are consulted has encouraged those who produce them to make them more readable. It is argued that the latter might be a useful side-effect of allowing the judges to consult parliamentary materials.

Media reports

Parliamentary proceedings are reported in newspapers and on radio and television. Since judges are as exposed to these as anyone else, it seems ridiculous to blinker themselves in court, or to pretend that they are blinkered.

Below are four key arguments against the use of *Hansard*.

Lack of clarity

The House of Lords, admonishing Lord Denning for his behaviour in **Davis v Johnson**, and directing that parliamentary debates were not to be consulted, stated that the evidence provided by the parliamentary debates might not be reliable; what was said in the cut and thrust of public debate was not 'conducive to a clear and unbiased explanation of the meaning of statutory language'.

Time and expense

Their Lordships also suggested that, if debates were to be used, there was a danger that the lawyers arguing a case would devote too much time and attention to ministerial statements and so on, at the expense of considering the language used in the Act itself.

> It would add greatly to the time and expense involved in preparing cases involving the construction of a statute if counsel were expected to read all the debates in *Hansard,* and it would often be impracticable for counsel to get access to at least the older reports of debates in select committees in the House of Commons; moreover, in a very large proportion of cases such a search, even if practicable, would throw no light on the question before the court . . .

This criticism of the use of *Hansard* was highlighted by Lord Steyn, a judge in the House of Lords, in his article '*Pepper* v *Hart*: a re-examination' (2001). He suggests that much of the work of the appellate courts is now concerned with the interpretation of documents, such as statutes, rather than the examination of precedents.

Parliamentary intention

The nature of parliamentary intention is difficult, if not impossible, to pin down. Parliamentary debates usually reveal the views of only a few members and, even then, those words may need interpretation too.

Lord Steyn (2001) criticised the way the use of *Hansard* in **Pepper v Hart** gives pre-eminence to the Government Minister's interpretation of the statute and ignores any dissenting voices by opposition MPs. The Minister only spoke in the House of Commons and the detail of what he said was unlikely to have been known by the House of Lords. Lord Steyn therefore queries how the Minister's statement can be said to reflect the intention of Parliament, which is made up of both Houses. He points to the nature of the parliamentary process:

> The relevant exchanges sometimes take place late at night in nearly empty chambers. Sometimes it is a party political debate with whips on. The questions are often difficult but political warfare sometimes leaves little time for reflection. These are not ideal conditions for the making of authoritative statements about the meaning of a clause in a Bill. In truth a Minister speaks for the Government and not for Parliament. The statements of a Minister are no more than indications of what the Government would like the law to be. In any event, it is not discoverable from the printed record whether individual members of the legislature, let alone a plurality in each chamber, understood and accepted a ministerial explanation of the suggested meaning of the words.

This criticism has been partly tackled by the House of Lords in **Wilson v Secretary of State for Trade and Industry** (2003). The House stated that the courts must be careful not to treat the ministerial statement as indicative of the intention of Parliament:

> Nor should the courts give a ministerial statement, whether made inside or outside Parliament, determinative weight. It should not be supposed that members necessarily agreed with the Minister's reasoning or his conclusions.

The House emphasised that the will of Parliament is expressed in the language used in its enactments.

Statutes are always speaking

The courts have developed a presumption that 'statutes are always speaking', which means they have to be interpreted in the modern-day legal context, rather than being fixed with the same meaning they had when they were originally passed. For example, s. 72 of the Highways Act 1835 provides a person is committing an offence if they:

> . . . wilfully ride upon any footpath or causeway by the side of any road made or set apart for the use or accommodation of foot passengers; or shall wilfully lead or drive any horse, ass, sheep, mule, swine, or cattle or carriage of any description, or any truck or sledge, upon any such footpath or causeway; or shall tether any horse, ass, mule, swine, or cattle, on any highway, so as to suffer or permit the tethered animal to be thereon.

This piece of legislation was passed before bicycles had been invented, but in ***Taylor* v *Goodwin*** (1879) the High Court held that the statute should be interpreted as applying to bicycles because they could come within the concept of a 'carriage' and the defendant was liable for the 'furious driving of a bicycle' on a pavement.

In ***Turkington* v *Times Newspapers*** (2000), *The Times* had published an article which reported a press conference in which a law firm had been criticised. *The Times* argued that they had a defence under the Law of Libel Amendment Act 1888, which applied when newspapers published accounts of certain public meetings. The claimant argued that the defence could not apply because when the statute had been passed there was no such thing as a 'press conference'. The House of Lords held:

> There is a clear answer to this appeal to Victorian history. Unless they reveal a contrary intention all statutes are to be interpreted as 'always speaking statutes'.

There are two aspects of the 'always speaking' principle. The first is that courts must interpret and apply a statute to the world as it exists today. The second is that the statute must be interpreted in the light of the legal system as it exists today: a statutory provision has to be considered as a norm of the current legal system, rather than just as a product of a historically defined parliamentary assembly. The House of Lords concluded:

> . . . on ordinary principles of construction the question before the House must be considered in the light of the law of freedom of expression as it exists today. The appeal to the original meaning of the words of the statute must be rejected.

Figure 3.3 External aids to interpretation

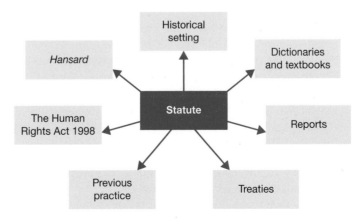

In **R v *Ireland and Burstow*** (1997) the House of Lords stated:

> Statutes dealing with a particular grievance or problem may sometimes require to be historically interpreted. But . . . statutes will generally be found to be of the 'always speaking' variety.

As a result, any reference to *Hansard* that determines the meaning of words at the time an Act was passed will not be conclusive about how the words will be interpreted today.

3.6 How do judges really interpret statutes?

This question has much in common with the discussion of case law and the operation of precedent (p. 18); in both cases, discussion of rules conceals a certain amount of flexibility. The so-called 'rules of interpretation' are not rules at all, but different approaches. Judges do not methodically apply these rules to every case and, in any case, the fact that they can conflict with each other and produce different results necessarily implies some choice as to which is used. There is choice too in the relative weight given to internal and external aids, and rules of language, and approaches have varied over the years.

Just as with judicial precedent, the idea that statutory interpretation is an almost scientific process that can be used to produce a single right answer is simply nonsense. There is frequently room for more than one interpretation (otherwise the question would never reach the courts) and judges must choose between them. For clear evidence of this, there is no better example than the litigation concerning Augusto Pinochet, the former head of state of Chile. He had long been accused of crimes against humanity, including torture and murder and conspiracy to torture and to murder. When he made a visit to the UK, the Spanish Government requested that he should be extradited to Spain so that they could put him on trial. This led to protracted litigation concerning whether it was legal for Britain to extradite him to Spain, and eventually the question came before the House of Lords. Pinochet's defence argued on the basis of the State Immunity Act 1978, which gives other states immunity from prosecution in English courts; the Act provides that 'states' includes heads of state. The Lords were therefore asked to decide whether this immunity extended to Pinochet's involvement in the acts he was accused of and, by a majority of three to two, they decided that it did not. Yet when the appeal was reopened (because one of the judges, Lord Hoffmann, was found to have links with Amnesty International, which was a party to the case), this time with seven Law Lords sitting, a different decision was reached. Although the Lords still stated that the General did not have complete immunity, by a majority of six to one, they restricted his liability to those acts which were committed after 1978, when torture committed outside the UK became a crime in the UK. This gave General Pinochet immunity for the vast majority of the torture allegations, and complete immunity for the allegations of murder and conspiracy to murder.

The reasoning behind both the decisions is complex and does not really need to concern us here; the important point to note is that in both hearings the Lords were interpreting the same statutory provisions, yet they came up with significantly different verdicts. Because of the way it was reopened, the case gives us a rare insight into just how imprecise and unpredictable statutory interpretation can be, and it is hard to resist the implication that if you put any other case involving statutory interpretation before two separate panels of judges, they might well come up with different judgments too.

Given then that judges do have some freedom over questions of statutory interpretation, what influences the decisions they make? As with case law, there are a number of theories.

3.6.1 Dworkin: fitting in with principles

Dworkin (1986) claims that, in approaching a case, the job of judges is to develop a theory about how the particular measure they are dealing with fits with the rest of the law as a whole. If there are two possible interpretations of a word or phrase, the judge should favour the one that allows the provision to sit most comfortably with the purpose of the rest of the law and with the principles and ideals of law and legality in general. This should be done, not for any mechanical reason, but because a body of law which is coherent and unified is, just for that reason, a body of law more entitled to the respect and allegiance of its citizens.

3.6.2 Cross: a contextual approach

Sir Rupert Cross (Bell and Engle, 1995) suggests that the courts take a 'contextual' approach in which, rather than choosing between different rules, they conduct a progressive analysis, considering first the ordinary meaning of the words in the context of the statute (taking a broad view of context), and then moving on to consider other possibilities if this provides an absurd result. Cross suggests that the courts can read in words that are necessarily implied, and have a limited power to add to, alter or ignore words that would otherwise make a provision unintelligible, absurd, totally unreasonable, unworkable or completely inconsistent with the rest of the Act.

3.6.3 Willis: the just result

John Willis's influential article 'Statute interpretation in a nutshell' (1938) was cynical about the use of the three 'rules'. He points out that a statute is often capable of several different interpretations, each in line with one of the rules. Despite the emphasis placed on literal interpretation, Willis suggests that the courts view all three rules as equally valid. He claims they use whichever rule will produce the result that they themselves believe to be just.

3.6.4 Griffith: political choices

As with case law (see p. 30), Griffith (1997) claims that, where there is ambiguity, the judiciary choose the interpretation that best suits their view of policy. An example of this was the 'Fares Fair' case, *Bromley London Borough Council* v *Greater London Council* (1982). The Labour-controlled GLC had enacted a policy – which was part of their election manifesto – to lower the cost of public transport in London, by subsidising it from the money paid in rates (what we now call Council Tax). This meant higher rates. Conservative-controlled Bromley Council challenged the GLC's right to do this.

The powers of local authorities (which then included the GLC) are defined entirely by statute, and there is an assumption that if a power has not been granted to a local authority by Parliament, then it is not a power the authority is entitled to exercise. The judges' job then was to discover what powers Parliament had granted the GLC, and to determine whether their action on fares and rates was within those powers.

Section 1 of the Transport (London) Act 1969 stated: 'It shall be the general duty of the Greater London Council to develop policies, and to encourage, organise and where appropriate, carry out measures which will promote the provision of integrated, efficient and economic transport facilities and services in Greater London.' The key word here was 'economic', with each side taking a different view of its meaning.

The GLC said 'economic' meant 'cost-effective', in other words, giving good value for money. They stated that good value covered any of the policy goals that transport services could promote: efficient movement of passengers, reduction of pollution and congestion, possibly even social redistribution. Bromley Council, on the other hand, said that 'economic' meant 'breaking even': covering the expenses of its operation out of the fares charged to the passengers and not requiring a subsidy.

It is not difficult to see that both sides had a point – the word 'economic' could cover either meaning, making the literal rule more or less useless. Because of this, Lord Scarman refused to consult a dictionary, stating that: 'The dictionary may tell us the several meanings the word can have but the word will always take its specific meaning (or meanings) from its surroundings.' Lord Scarman stressed that those surroundings meant not just the statute as a whole, but also the general duties of the GLC to ratepayers; that duty must coexist with the duty to the users of public transport.

Lord Scarman concluded:

'Economic' in s. 1 must, therefore, be construed widely enough to embrace both duties. Accordingly, I conclude that in s. 1(1) of the Act 'economic' covers not only the requirement that transport services be cost-effective but also the requirement that they be provided so as to avoid or diminish the burden on the ratepayers so far as it is practicable to do so.

Griffith has argued that the idea of a 'duty' to ratepayers as explained in the case is entirely judge-made, and that the Law Lords' ruling that the interests of transport users had been preferred over those of ratepayers is interfering with the role of elected authorities. He suggests that 'public expenditure can always be criticised on the ground that it is excessive or wrongly directed', but that it is the role of elected bodies to make such decisions, and if the public does not like them 'the remedy lies in their hands at the next election'.

It is certainly odd that when the judges make so much play of the fact that Parliament should legislate because it is elected and accountable, they do not consider themselves bound to respect decisions made in fulfilment of an elected body's manifesto. What the Lords were doing, argues Griffith, was making a choice between two interpretations, based not on any real sense of what Parliament intended, but 'primarily [on] the Law Lords' strong preference for the principles of the market economy with a dislike of heavy subsidisation for social purposes' – in other words a political choice.

The judiciary would argue against this proposition, but it is certainly difficult to see where any of the 'rules of interpretation' fitted into this case: none of the rules of interpretation or the aids to interpretation forced the judges to favour Bromley Council's interpretation of the law over that of the GLC. They could have chosen either interpretation and still been within the law, so that choice must have been based on something other than the law.

3.7 Reform of statutory interpretation

The problems with statutory interpretation have been recognised for decades but, despite several important reports, little has changed. The Law Commission examined the interpretation of statutes in 1967 and had 'little hesitation in suggesting that this is a field not suitable for codification'. Instead, it proposed certain improvements within the present system:

- More liberal use should be made of internal and external aids.
- In the event of ambiguity, the construction which best promoted the 'general legislative purpose' should be adopted. This could be seen as supporting Denning's approach.

The Renton Committee on the Preparation of Legislation produced its report in 1975, making many proposals for improving the procedure for making and drafting statutes, including the following.

- Acts could begin with a statement of purpose in the same way that older statutes used to have preambles.
- There should be a move towards including less detail in the legislation, introducing the simpler style used in countries such as France.
- More use could be made in statutes of examples showing the courts how an Act was intended to work in particular situations.
- Long, un-paragraphed sentences should be avoided.
- Statutes should be arranged to suit the convenience of the ultimate users.
- There should be more consolidation of legislation.

In 1978, Sir David Renton, in a speech entitled 'Failure to implement the Renton Report', noted that there had been a small increase in the number of draftsmen and increased momentum in the consolidation process, but that Parliament had continued to pass a huge amount of legislation, with no reduction in the amount of detail and scarcely any use of statements of purpose. Fifteen years later, in 1992, a Commission appointed by the *Hansard* Society for Parliamentary Government reported that little had changed. Having consulted widely, it concluded that there was widespread dissatisfaction with the situation, and suggested that the drafting style adopted should be appropriate for the main end users of legislation, with the emphasis on clarity, simplicity and certainty. There should be some means of informing citizens, lawyers and the courts about the general purpose behind a particular piece of legislation, and unnecessary detail should be avoided. The Commission suggested that an increase in the number of draftsmen might be necessary to achieve these aims; since its report, four more draftsmen have been recruited, but otherwise there was no immediate response to the proposals. The Labour Government, however, placed a high priority on making the workings of law and government accessible to ordinary people, and the introduction of explanatory notes to Bills passed from 1999 is an important step forward.

Answering questions

1 Using appropriate examples, explain three judicial rules of statutory interpretation.
2 The four approaches to statutory interpretation are so inconsistent with each other that a different result could be reached in the same case if the judges simply followed a different approach. Discuss.
3 Why do judges sometimes refer to *Hansard*?

For answers to these questions, visit the companion website at www.pearsoned.co.uk/ elliottquinn

3

STATUTORY INTERPRETATION

SUMMARY OF CHAPTER 3: STATUTORY INTERPRETATION

Parliamentary intention

In interpreting statutes the courts are looking for the intention of Parliament, but this intention is frequently difficult to find.

Rules of statutory interpretation

There are four approaches to statutory interpretation:

- the literal rule;
- the golden rule;
- the mischief rule; and
- the purposive approach.

Human Rights Act 1998

Under s. 3 of the 1998 Act the courts are required to read legislation in a way that is compatible with Convention rights.

Interpreting European legislation

Under s. 2(4) of the European Communities Act 1972, all parliamentary legislation must be construed in accordance with European law.

Internal aids to statutory interpretation

Internal aids consist of the statute itself, explanatory notes (post-1999) and rules of language.

External aids to statutory interpretation

These include:

- dictionaries and textbooks;
- reports that preceded the legislation;
- treaties;
- the Human Rights Act 1998; and
- *Hansard*, following the decision of **Pepper v Hart**.

How do judges really interpret statutes?

Different academics have put forward arguments as to how judges really interpret statutes. John Willis argues that the courts use whichever rule will produce the result that they themselves believe to be just. Griffith thinks that judges interpret statutes in a way that coincides with their political preferences, referring to the case of **Bromley London Borough Council v Greater London Council** to support his arguments.

Reform of statutory interpretation

The Renton Committee on the Preparation of Legislation in 1975 recommended reforms of the procedure for making and drafting statutes, but little has changed.

Reading list

Bell, J. and Engle, G. (eds) (1995) *Cross: Statutory Interpretation* (3rd edn). London: LexisNexis/ Butterworths.

Bennion, F.A.R. (2005) *Statutory Interpretation*. London: Butterworths.

(2007) Executive estoppel: *Pepper* v *Hart* revisited. *Public Law*, Spring 1.

Dworkin, R. (1986) *Law's Empire*. London: Fontana.

Griffith, J.A.G. (1997) *The Politics of the Judiciary*. London: Fontana.

Hart, H.L.A. (1994) *The Concept of Law*. Oxford: Clarendon.

Manchester, C., Salter, D. and Moodie, P. (2000) *Exploring the Law: The Dynamics of Precedent and Statutory Interpretation* (2nd edn). London: Sweet & Maxwell.

Renton, D. (1975) *The Preparation of Legislation*. London: HMSO.

Steyn, J. (2001) *Pepper* v *Hart*: a re-examination. *Oxford Journal of Legal Studies,* 59.

Willis, J. (1938) Statute interpretation in a nutshell. *Canadian Bar Review,* 16: 13.

Zander, M. (2004) *The Law-Making Process*. London: Butterworths.

On the internet

Hansard is available at:
https://www.hansard.parliament.uk

Chapter 4
Delegated legislation

This chapter discusses:

- the three forms of delegated legislation;
- why delegated legislation is necessary;
- how delegated legislation is controlled; and
- criticism made of delegated legislation.

4.1 Introduction

In many cases the statutes passed by Parliament lay down a basic framework of the law, with creation of the detailed rules delegated to others. There are three main forms of delegated legislation: statutory instruments, bye-laws and Orders in Council.

4.1.1 Statutory instruments

Statutory instruments were created by the Statutory Instruments Act 1946. There are four forms of statutory instrument (Pywell, 2013):

- **Regulations.** These are used to make substantive law.
- **Orders in Council.** These are made by the Privy Council and usually involve rubber-stamping the detailed rules regulating the professions.
- **Orders.** These are usually made by Government Ministers and serve a narrow purpose, such as commencement orders (stating when a statutory provision will come into force) and legislative reform orders (discussed below).
- **Rules.** These are procedural rules which lay down how things should be done, rather than what should be done, such as the Civil Procedure Rules (discussed in Chapter 23).

4.1.2 Bye-laws

Bye-laws are made by local authorities, public and nationalised bodies and deal with matters within their limited jurisdiction. Bye-laws have to be approved by central Government.

4.1.3 Orders in Council

Orders in Council are approved by the Privy Council and signed by the Queen. They are used when an ordinary statutory instrument made by a Minister would be inappropriate, such as in times of emergency or where the order involves the transfer of ministerial power. For example, under the Civil Service (Amendment) Order in Council 1997, Tony Blair gave himself the power to appoint up to three people to the Prime Minister's Office outside the normal Civil Service recruitment procedure. He used this power to appoint his two most trusted political advisers: Alastair Campbell and Jonathan Powell. The involvement of the monarch is necessary because of the potentially far-reaching consequences of Orders in Council.

4.2 The power to make delegated legislation

Ordinary members of the public cannot decide on a whim to make delegated legislation. Instead, usually an Act of Parliament is required, known as an enabling Act, which gives this power to a branch of the state. The Act can be quite specific, giving a limited power to make legislation on a very narrow issue, or it can be quite general and allow for a wide range of delegated legislation to be made. An example of such a general provision is the European Communities Act 1972, s. 2, which allows the executive to make delegated legislation to bring into force in the UK relevant European legislation. Local authorities have been given a general power to make bye-laws under s. 235 of the Local Government Act 1972. Recent years have seen a move towards centralised government and therefore a reduced role for bye-laws. The Labour Government, however, favoured the use of local bye-laws to strengthen community involvement in regulating behaviour in their local areas. To facilitate the use of bye-laws the Local Government and Public Involvement in Health Act 2007 was passed containing provisions for a faster legislative process for some bye-laws.

The Bigger Picture: Legislative reform orders

The **Legislative and Regulatory Reform Act 2006** gives the executive very wide powers to make delegated legislation. This Act was introduced following a report of the Better Regulation Task Force, *Regulation – Less is More* (2005). The official aim of the Act is to make it simpler and faster to amend existing legislation. It allows Ministers to issue statutory instruments to amend legislation to reduce a burden (such as unnecessary cost or administrative inconvenience) caused by legislation in order to promote better regulation. European Union obligations can also be implemented using this Act. Orders made under this Act are known as legislative reform orders. The first draft of the Bill was severely criticised by a panel of MPs for giving excessive powers to make delegated legislation which were disproportionate to the Bill's stated aims. In the light of this criticism some amendments were made. Thus, the effect of the order must be proportionate, it must strike a fair balance between the different interests involved and it must not be of constitutional significance. Sometimes a super-affirmative procedure (see p. 92) will have to be followed to pass a legislative reform order. Concerns remain that this is an unnecessary shift of power from a democratically elected Parliament, to the executive.

4

DELEGATED LEGISLATION

Figure 4.1 Sources of delegated legislation

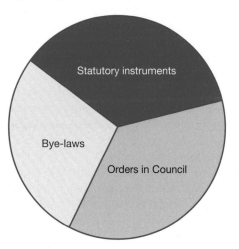

4.3 Why is delegated legislation necessary?

Delegated legislation is necessary for a number of reasons:

Insufficient parliamentary time Parliament does not have the time to debate every detailed rule necessary for efficient government.

Speed It allows rules to be made more quickly than they could by Parliament. Parliament does not sit all the time, and its procedure is slow and cumbersome; delegated legislation often has to be made in response to emergencies and urgent problems.

Technicality of the subject matter Modern legislation often needs to include detailed, technical provisions – those in building regulations or safety at work rules, for example. MPs do not usually have the technical knowledge required, whereas delegated legislation can use experts who are familiar with the relevant areas.

Need for local knowledge Local bye-laws in particular can only be made effectively with awareness of the locality. Recognition of the importance of local knowledge can be found with the devolved assemblies for Scotland, Wales and Northern Ireland. These democratic bodies have important powers to make delegated legislation.

Flexibility Statutes require cumbersome procedures for enactment, and can only be revoked or amended by another statute. Delegated legislation, however, can be put into action quickly, and easily revoked if it proves problematic.

Future needs Parliament cannot hope to foresee every problem that might arise as a result of a statute, especially concerning areas such as health provision or welfare benefits. Delegated legislation can be put in place as and when such problems arise.

4.4 Control of delegated legislation

Because it is not directly made by elected representatives, delegated legislation is subject to the following range of controls, designed to ensure that the power delegated is not abused.

4.4.1 Consultation

Those who make delegated legislation often consult experts within the relevant field, and those bodies which are likely to be affected by it. In the case of road traffic regulations, for example, Ministers are likely to seek the advice of police, motoring organisations, vehicle manufacturers and local authorities before making the rules. Often the relevant statute makes such consultation obligatory and names the bodies which should be consulted. Under the National Insurance Act 1946, for example, draft regulations must be submitted to the National Insurance Advisory Committee. In other cases there may be a general statutory requirement for 'such consultation as the minister thinks appropriate with such organisations as appear to him to represent the interest concerned'. Statutory instruments made under the Legislative and Regulatory Reform Act 2006 (see p. 89) can only be made after interested parties have been consulted.

In *R* v *Brent London Borough Council, ex parte Gunning* (1985) it was stated that consultations had to be fair and to be fair they must:

- take place at a formative stage;
- give adequate reasons for the proposals to allow for intelligent consideration and response;

- allow adequate time for consideration and response; and
- ensure that the product of the consultation is conscientiously taken into account in finalising the proposals.

In *R (on the application of Moseley)* v *London Borough of Haringey* (2014) the Supreme Court stated that the consultation documentation needed to refer to alternative legislative options that had been rejected by the public body so that the people consulted were aware of these.

4.4.2 Publication

All delegated legislation is published, and therefore available for public scrutiny. Alongside the statutory instrument, the Government now publishes an explanatory memorandum detailing the statutory instrument's policy objective and legislative context. The importance of publishing legislation was emphasised in a European case in 2009. A man had been prevented from getting on a plane with a tennis racket as hand luggage. The airline had pointed to some European regulations that prohibited certain articles from being taken on board the plane for security reasons. The relevant items were listed in an appendix which had been published but when the appendix was amended the amended version was not published. The passenger claimed that the amended regulations could not be enforced against him because they had never been published. This argument was accepted by the court because governments should not be allowed to pass secret legislation; the public should be able to ascertain the scope of their rights and obligations under the law.

4.4.3 Supervision by Parliament

There are a number of ways in which Parliament can oversee delegated legislation.

Revocation

Parliamentary sovereignty means that Parliament can at any time revoke a piece of delegated legislation itself, or pass legislation on the same subject as the delegated legislation.

The negative resolution procedure

Much delegated legislation is put before Parliament for MPs under the negative resolution procedure. Within a specified time (usually 40 days), any member may put down a motion to annul it. An annulment motion put down by a backbencher is not guaranteed to be dealt with, but one put down by the Official Opposition (the party with the second largest number of MPs) usually will be. If, after debate, either House passes an annulment motion, the delegated legislation is cancelled.

The affirmative resolution procedure

Enabling Acts dealing with subjects of special, often constitutional, importance may require Parliament to vote its approval of the delegated legislation. This is called the affirmative resolution procedure, whereby delegated legislation is laid before one or both Houses (sometimes in draft), and becomes law only if a motion approving it is passed within a specified time (usually 28 or 40 days). Since a vote has to be taken, the procedure means that the Government must

4

DELEGATED LEGISLATION

find parliamentary time for debate, and opposition parties have an opportunity to raise any objections. In practice, though, it is very rare for the Government not to achieve a majority when such votes are taken and the process amounts to little more than a rubber-stamping exercise. An instrument has not been struck down under this procedure since 1969.

The super-affirmative procedure

The super-affirmative procedure is sometimes required to check legislative reform orders (see p. 89) and is required for some orders made under the Public Bodies Act 2011 and the Localism Act 2011. Under this procedure Parliament has more power to scrutinise the proposed delegated legislation than under the ordinary affirmative resolution procedure. First, the Minister must lay before Parliament for 60 days a draft of the proposed legislative reform order. During this period two parliamentary committees will automatically review the order and produce a report. The Minister then takes into account these reports and any other representations and decides whether to proceed with the legislation and whether to make any amendments to it. If he or she decides to proceed, the draft order, with any amendments, is formally made available in each House (described as 'being laid before Parliament'). This ability to make changes to the draft order is a key feature of the procedure, which is not available to statutory instruments made under the ordinary negative or affirmative resolution procedures. The two committees then produce a report, normally within 15 days. Each House considers the relevant committee report on the draft order. An order dealt with under this procedure must be expressly approved by both Houses of Parliament before it can be made.

Committee supervision

Several parliamentary committees monitor new delegated legislation. The Joint Committee on Statutory Instruments watches over the making of delegated legislation and reports to each House on any delegated legislation which requires special consideration, including any regulations made under an Act that prohibit challenge by the courts, or which seem to make unusual or unexpected use of the powers granted by the enabling Act. However, the Committee may not consider the merits of any piece of delegated legislation. This is the responsibility of the House of Lords' Merits of Statutory Instruments Committee. In addition, the House of Lords' Select Committee on Delegated Powers and Regulatory Reform looks at the extent of legislative powers proposed to be delegated by Parliament to Government Ministers. It is required to report on whether the provision of any Bill inappropriately delegates legislative power, or subjects the exercise of legislative power to an inappropriate level of parliamentary scrutiny.

Questions from MPs

MPs can ask Ministers questions about delegated legislation at a ministerial question time, or raise them in debates.

The House of Lords

Although the House of Lords cannot veto proposed Acts following the Parliament Acts 1911 and 1949 (see p. 52), the same does not apply to delegated legislation. Instead there is a Convention that dates back to 1968 that the House of Lords should only exceptionally reject a statutory instrument. This has only happened five times since 1968. Most recently, in 2015

the House of Lords rejected the draft Tax Credits (Income Thresholds and Determination of Rates) (Amendment) Regulations 2015. As a result of this defeat, the Government commissioned the former leader of the House of Lords, Lord Strathclyde, to carry out a review looking at the relationship between the two Houses of Parliament in the context of delegated legislation, and to ensure that the elected chamber plays the decisive role in the passage of such legislation. The Strathclyde Review was published in December 2015. It outlined three options for change:

- no power of scrutiny by the House of Lords;
- the passing of a resolution by the House of Lords establishing a convention that the Lords' ability to reject secondary legislation would be left unused; or
- new legislation removing the Lords' powers to reject secondary legislation, but allowing them to ask the Commons to 'think again'.

The House of Lords has rejected all three of these recommendations and the Government has not yet acted upon them.

4.4.4 Control by the courts: judicial review

While the validity of a statute can never be challenged by the courts because of parliamentary sovereignty, delegated legislation can. It may be challenged on any of the following grounds under the procedure for judicial review.

Procedural *ultra vires*

Here the complainant claims that the procedures laid down in the enabling Act for producing delegated legislation have not been followed. In *Agricultural, Horticultural and Forestry Industry Training Board* v *Aylesbury Mushrooms Ltd* (1972), an order was declared invalid because the requirement to consult with interested parties before making it had not been properly complied with.

Substantive *ultra vires*

This is usually based on a claim that the measure under review goes beyond the powers Parliament granted under the enabling Act. In *Customs and Excise Commissioners* v *Cure & Deeley Ltd* (1962), the powers of the Commissioners to make delegated legislation under the Finance (No. 2) Act 1940 were challenged. The Act empowered them to produce regulations 'for any matter for which provision appears to them necessary for the purpose of giving effect to the Act'. The Commissioners held that this included allowing them to make a regulation giving them the power to determine the amount of tax due where a tax return was submitted late. The High Court invalidated the regulation on the ground that the Commissioners had given themselves powers far beyond what Parliament had intended; they were empowered only to collect such tax as was due by law, not to decide what amount they thought fit.

   R v *Secretary of State for Social Security, ex parte Joint Council for the Welfare of Immigrants* (1996) concerned the Asylum and Immigration Appeals Act 1993 which provided a framework for determining applications for asylum, and for appeals after unsuccessful applications. It allowed asylum seekers to apply for social security benefits while they were waiting for their applications or appeals to be decided, at a cost of over £200 million per year

4

DELEGATED LEGISLATION

to British taxpayers. This led to concern from some quarters that the provisions might attract those who were simply seeking a better lifestyle than that available in their own countries (often called economic migrants), as opposed to those fleeing persecution, whom the provisions were actually designed to help.

In order to discourage economic migrants, the then Secretary of State for Social Security exercised his powers to make delegated legislation under the Social Security (Contributions and Benefits) Act 1992, and produced regulations which stated that social security benefits would no longer be available to those who sought asylum after they had entered the UK, rather than immediately on entry, or those who had been refused leave to stay here and were awaiting the outcome of appeals against the decision.

The Joint Council for the Welfare of Immigrants challenged the regulations, claiming that they fell outside the powers granted by the 1992 Act. The Court of Appeal upheld their claim, stating that the 1993 Act was clearly intended to give asylum seekers rights which they did not have previously. The effect of the regulations was effectively to take those rights away again since, without access to social security benefits, most asylum seekers would either have to return to the countries from which they had fled, or live on nothing while their claims were processed. The court ruled that Parliament could not have intended to give the Secretary of State powers to take away the rights it had given in the 1993 Act: this could only be done by a new statute, and therefore the regulations were *ultra vires.*

The decision was a controversial one, because the regulations had themselves been approved by Parliament, and overturning them could be seen as a challenge to the power of the legislature, despite the decision being explained by the court as upholding that power.

Unreasonableness

If rules are manifestly unjust, have been made in bad faith (for example, by someone with a financial interest in their operation) or are otherwise so perverse that no reasonable official could have made them, the courts can declare them invalid.

4.4.5 Confirmation by Government Minister

Under s. 235(2) of the Local Government Act 1972, bye-laws passed by local authorities often need to be confirmed by the relevant Government Minister. This confirmation process checks that:

- the local authority had the power to make the legislation;
- the consultation process was undertaken;
- there is no duplication or conflict with existing legislation;
- the bye-law deals with a genuine and specific local problem (rather than a national issue); and
- there is no conflict with Government policy.

Following the passing of the Local Government and Public Involvement in Health Act 2007, regulations can be passed allowing bye-laws dealing with specified issues to be made under an accelerated procedure which does not require confirmation by a Government Minister. This power has been extended to where councils want to repeal outdated bye-laws under the Localism Act 2011.

Figure 4.2 Control of delegated legislation

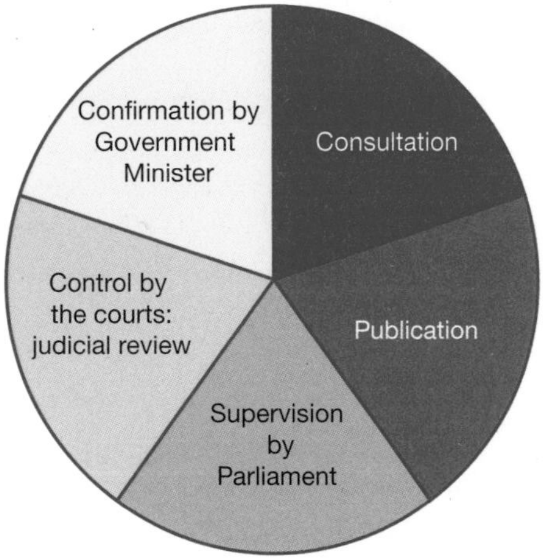

4.6 Criticism of delegated legislation

4.6.1 Lack of democratic involvement

This argument is put forward because delegated legislation is usually made by civil servants, rather than elected politicians. This is not seen as a particular problem where the delegated legislation takes the form of detailed administrative rules, since these would clearly take up impossible amounts of parliamentary time otherwise. However, in the latter years of the John Major-led Conservative Government (1990–97) there was increasing concern that delegated legislation was being used to implement important policies.

The power to overturn an Act of Parliament by ministerial order is known as a Henry VIII power because Henry VIII legislated to give his declarations the same legal status as Acts of Parliament. Henry VIII clauses in legislation amount to an attack on parliamentary supremacy. While ordinary delegated powers create a mechanism for the executive to supplement parliamentary statutes, Henry VIII clauses allow the executive to amend or repeal such statutes. The executive should not be able to overrule primary legislation because this undermines Parliament's power. The Public Bodies Act 2011 contains a list of public bodies (called quangos) which the Government is entitled to abolish by delegated legislation – the media has called this the 'bonfire of the quangos'. This power amounts to a Henry VIII power because it allows Ministers by order to amend or abolish bodies that were established by primary legislation.

The role of the Privy Council in passing delegated legislation is particularly sensitive because it is not a democratic body. The civil rights group, JUSTICE, published a report in 2009 pointing out that Orders in Council made by the Privy Council had been used to abolish the right of trade union membership for some civil servants and to force residents of the Chagos Islands to leave their homes and prevent them from returning.

4

DELEGATED LEGISLATION

4.6.2 Overuse

Critics argue that there is too much delegated legislation; this is linked to the point above, as there would be little problem with increasing amounts of delegated legislation if its purpose was merely to flesh out technical detail.

4.6.3 Sub-delegation

Delegated legislation is sometimes made by people other than those who were given the original power to do so.

4.6.4 Lack of control

Despite the above list of controls over delegated legislation, the reality is that effective super-vision is difficult. First, publication has only limited benefits, given that the general public are frequently unaware of the existence of delegated legislation, let alone on what grounds it can be challenged and how to go about doing so. This in turn has an effect on the ability of the courts to control delegated legislation, since judicial review relies on individual challenges being brought before the courts. This may not happen until years after a provision is enacted, when it finally affects someone who is prepared and able to challenge it. The obvious result is that legislation which largely affects a class of individuals who are not given to questioning official rules, are unaware of their rights, or who lack the financial resources to go to court, will rarely be challenged.

A further problem is that some enabling Acts confer extremely wide discretionary powers on Ministers; a phrase such as 'the Minister may make such regulations as he sees fit for the purpose of bringing the Act into operation' would not be unusual. This means that there is very little room for anything to be considered *ultra vires*, so judicial review is effectively frustrated.

The main method of control over delegated legislation is therefore parliamentary, but this too has its drawbacks. Although the affirmative resolution procedure usually ensures that parliamentary attention is drawn to important delegated legislation, it is rarely possible to prevent such legislation being passed. The Select Committee on the Scrutiny of Delegated Powers makes an important contribution, and has been able to secure changes to a number of important pieces of legislation. However, it too lacks real power, as it is unable to consider the merits of delegated legislation (as opposed to whether the delegated powers have been correctly used) and its reports have no binding effect.

Answering questions

1   To what extent is there any parliamentary or judicial control over delegated legislation?

2   The effect that delegated legislation has on daily life is significantly greater than that of primary legislation (Acts of Parliament). What are the benefits of delegated legislation? In your view, do its benefits outweigh its weaknesses?

3   Read the source material below and answer parts (a), (b) and (c) which follow.

Exercise on Delegated Legislation

Source A

Police and Criminal Evidence Act 1984

(1984 c.60)
Section 60

Tape-recording of Interviews

(1) It shall be the duty of the Secretary of State –

  . . .

(b) to make an order requiring the tape-recording of interviews of persons suspected of the commission of criminal offences, or of such descriptions of criminal offences as may be specified in the order . . .

(2) An order under subsection (1) above shall be made by statutory instrument and shall be subject to annulment in pursuance of a resolution of either House of Parliament.

Source B

Statutory Instrument
1991 No. 2687
The Police and Criminal Evidence Act 1984

(Tape-recording of Interviews) (No. 1) Order 1991

Made	29th November 1991
Laid before Parliament	6th December 1991
Coming into force	1st January 1992

Now, therefore, in pursuance of the said section 60(1)(b), the Secretary of State hereby orders as follows:
  . . .

2. This Order shall apply to interviews of persons suspected of the commission of indictable offences which are held by police officers at police stations in the police areas specified in the schedule to this Order and which commence after midnight on 31st December 1991.

3. (1) Subject to paragraph (2) below, interviews to which this Order applies shall be tape-recorded in accordance with the requirements of the code of practice on tape-recording which came into operation on 29th July 1988 . . .

  (2) The duty to tape-record interviews under paragraph (1) above shall not apply to interviews –

  (a) where the offence of which a person is suspected is one in respect of which he has been arrested or detained under section 14(1)(a) of the Prevention of Terrorism (Temporary Provisions) Act 1989; . . .

(a) Using Sources A and B to illustrate your answer, compare the legislative process in relation to an Act of Parliament on the one hand and delegated legislation on the other.

(b) What are the advantages and disadvantages of delegated legislation?

(c) Each of the following interviews was conducted by police officers and took place at a police station covered by SI 1991/2687, but none of the interviews was tape-recorded.

(i) On 30th November 1991 Alice was charged with an indictable offence and interviewed;

(ii) Bertie, who was suspected of an indictable offence, was interviewed on 1st April 1998;

(iii) Cedric, detained under s. 14(1)(a) of the Prevention of Terrorism (Temporary Provisions) Act 1989 was interviewed in April 1998.

Discuss interviews (i), (ii) and (iii) with reference to Source B.

For answers to these questions, visit the companion website at www.pearsoned.co.uk/elliottquinn

SUMMARY OF CHAPTER 4: DELEGATED LEGISLATION

There are three main forms of delegated legislation:

- Statutory instruments
- Bye-laws
- Orders in Council.

The power to make delegated legislation

Usually an Act of Parliament is required giving the power to make delegated legislation to a branch of the state.

Why is delegated legislation necessary?

Delegated legislation is necessary because it saves parliamentary time, constitutes a quick form of legislation, and is suited to technical subject areas or where local knowledge is needed.

Control of delegated legislation

Delegated legislation is controlled through:

- the consultation of experts;
- publication of the legislation;
- supervision by Parliament;
- the courts with the judicial review procedure; and
- confirmation by a Government Minister.

Criticism of delegated legislation

Delegated legislation has been criticised due to:

- lack of democratic involvement;
- overuse;
- sub-delegation; and
- lack of controls.

Reading list

Better Regulation Task Force (2005) *Regulation – Less is More: Reducing Burdens, Improving Outcomes*. London: Cabinet Office.

Burns, S. (2006) Tipping the balance. *New Law Journal*, 156: 787.

McHarg, A. (2006) What is delegated legislation? *Public Law*, Autumn: 539.

Pywell, S. (2013) Untangling the law. *New Law Journal*, 163: 321.

On the internet

Statutory instruments are published on the legislation.gov.uk website at:
www.legislation.gov.uk/uksi

Chapter 5
European law

This chapter discusses:

- the six key institutions of the European Union: the Council of Ministers, the European Council, the Commission, the European Parliament, the Court of Justice of the European Union and the European Central Bank;

- how European law is made;

- the four main sources of European law: treaties, regulations, directives and decisions; and

- the impact of European Union law on the UK.

5.1 Introduction

The European Union (EU) currently comprises 28 European countries. The original members – France, West Germany, Belgium, Luxembourg, Italy and the Netherlands – laid the foundations in 1951, when they created the European Coal and Steel Community (ECSC). Six years later, they signed the Treaty of Rome, creating the European Economic Community (EEC) and the European Atomic Energy Community (Euratom). The original six were joined by the UK, Ireland and Denmark in 1973, Greece in 1981 and Spain and Portugal in 1986 and, in the same year, the member countries signed the Single European Act, which developed free movement of goods and people within the Community (the single market), and greater political unity. Finland, Austria and Sweden joined in 1995. Following the Nice summit in 2004, the EU increased its membership from 15 to 27, with most of the new members coming from eastern Europe. The last country to join was Croatia in 2013. Five countries are currently in formal negotiations to join the EU: Iceland, Macedonia, Montenegro, Serbia and Turkey. Due to its financial difficulties there is a possibility that Greece may leave the EU.

In 1993 the Maastricht Treaty renamed the European Economic Community the European Community and also created the European Union (EU). Following the Lisbon Treaty in 2009 the European Community has now been totally replaced by the European Union.

The Bigger Picture: BREXIT

In June 2016 a referendum was held to decide whether the United Kingdom should remain a member of the European Union or withdraw. The citizens of the United Kingdom voted by a small majority in favour of leaving the European Union (sometimes described in the media as Brexit). The political and legal implications of this withdrawal are very significant, though the precise impact of this planned withdrawal is still unclear. A formal procedure has to be followed under Article 50 of the Treaty on European Union before the withdrawal takes effect. The terms of Article 50 are as follows:

1 Any Member State may decide to withdraw from the Union in accordance with its own constitutional requirements.

2 A Member State which decides to withdraw shall notify the European Council of its intention. In the light of the guidelines provided by the European Council, the Union shall negotiate and conclude an agreement with that State, setting out the arrangements for its withdrawal, taking account of the framework for its future relationship with the Union. That agreement shall be negotiated in accordance with Article 218(3) of the Treaty on the Functioning of the European Union. It shall be concluded on behalf of the Union by the Council, acting by a qualified majority, after obtaining the consent of the European Parliament.

3 The Treaties shall cease to apply to the State in question from the date of entry into force of the withdrawal agreement or, failing that, two years after the notification referred to in paragraph 2, unless the European Council, in agreement with the Member State concerned, unanimously decides to extend this period.

4 For the purposes of paragraphs 2 and 3, the member of the European Council or of the Council representing the withdrawing Member State shall not participate in the discussions of the European Council or Council or in decisions concerning it. A qualified majority shall be defined in accordance with Article 238(3)(b) of the Treaty on the Functioning of the European Union.

5 If a State which has withdrawn from the Union asks to rejoin, its request shall be subject to the procedure referred to in Article 49.

The Article 50 procedure commences with the UK contacting the European Council by letter informing them of their intention to withdraw. Following the decision of the Supreme Court in *R (on the application of Miller and Dos Santos)* v *The Secretary of State for Exiting the European Union* (2017) Parliament has to pass an Act of Parliament to authorise Government Ministers to initiate the withdrawal process. Once the withdrawal process has begun by this notification, two years are allowed to complete the withdrawal process. In March 2017 the European Union (Notification of Withdrawal) Act 2017 was passed with two seemingly simple lines.

The Prime Minister wrote to the President of the European Council, Donald Tusk on 29 March 2017 to begin the process of withdrawal under Article 50. The withdrawal process is scheduled to be completed by 29 March 2019. The terms of the withdrawal have to be negotiated and agreed with the Council acting by qualified majority vote with the consent of the European Parliament. If the two-year period ends without agreement, the withdrawing country is no longer a member. Article 50 does not provide for a cancellation of the notification. Following the March 2017 notification, negotiations of the withdrawal have taken place through monthly meetings each extending over four days. The fifth round of negotiations in October 2018 closed with progress being cited as being made on the rights of British citizens residing in the EU and vice versa once withdrawal takes place. However, it was also widely reported that negotiations thus far remained deadlocked on the vital issue of the financial settlement which needs to be reached for withdrawal to take place. This has been a thorny issue and the cause of much political and financial uncertainty. Essentially it has been debated and some might say disputed, what level of financial contribution the UK is expected to make after leaving the EU. The debates about financial contributions have been so fragile that the Government has remarked several times during the process that 'no deal is better than a bad deal'.

At a national level, the UK Parliament will repeal the European Communities Act 1972 (discussed on p. 121), removing the automatic incorporation of European law into UK law. The European Parliament and European Court of Justice will stop having any direct power over the courts and Parliament in the United Kingdom. In terms of what will become of current EU legislation, the UK has introduced the European Union (Withdrawal) Act 2018 which will repeal and replace existing law within the UK that gives effect to EU law but it appears that relevant EU law will indeed be absorbed into domestic law. For instance, sections 2 and 3 convert all delegated and direct EU legislation into domestic law.

Section 2 of the European Union (Withdrawal) Act 2018 states: '(1) EU-derived domestic legislation, as it has effect in domestic law immediately before exit day, continues to have effect in domestic law on and after exit day'. Section 3 states: 'Direct EU legislation, so far as operative immediately before exit day, forms part of domestic law on and after exit day.' The drive to provide certainty and continuity to what is one of the biggest changes to our legal system is of paramount importance. However, there is concern that law created for and to apply within a supranational legal order will struggle within a national legal order such as that of the UK. This may place a lot of pressure on the UK's judiciary to interpret such laws in a way that gives them purpose but in such a tense political climate this may prove to be very controversial.

It is anticipated and one is hopeful, that an agreement between the EU and the UK will be reached. Should that happen, the EU and the UK will enter into a withdrawal agreement which will set out the basis of the UK's withdrawal and how the EU Treaties are to be disapplied. The EU published in March 2018, a draft Withdrawal Agreement which gives an indication of some but certainly not all of the matters on which agreement has started to progress. For instance, there is some agreement on citizen's rights after Brexit, the financial settlement and a transition period during which Treaties are disapplied.

Figure 5.1 European Union (Notification of Withdrawal) Act 2017

ELIZABETH II   c. **9**

European Union (Notification of Withdrawal) Act 2017

2017 CHAPTER 9

An Act to confer power on the Prime Minister to notify, under Article 50(2) of the Treaty on European Union, the United Kingdom's intention to withdraw from the EU.   [16th March 2017]

B E IT ENACTED by the Queen's most Excellent Majesty, by and with the advice and consent of the Lords Spiritual and Temporal, and Commons, in this present Parliament assembled, and by the authority of the same, as follows:—

1   Power to notify withdrawal from the EU

(1)   The Prime Minister may notify, under Article 50(2) of the Treaty on European Union, the United Kingdom's intention to withdraw from the EU.

(2)   This section has effect despite any provision made by or under the European Communities Act 1972 or any other enactment.

2   Short title

This Act may be cited as the European Union (Notification of Withdrawal) Act 2017.

However, the European Union (Withdrawal) Act ties the hands of the UK Government by affording Parliament a greater role in the process of the UK exiting the EU. This is summed up by s. 9 of the European Union (Withdrawal) Act: 'A Minister of the Crown may by regulations make such provision as the Minister considers appropriate for the purposes of implementing the withdrawal agreement if the Minister considers that such provision should be in force on or before exit day, *subject to the prior enactment of a statute by Parliament approving* the final terms of withdrawal of the United Kingdom from the EU.' (own emphasis). To this end the UK's Department for Exiting the European Union issued a White Paper entitled 'Legislating for the Withdrawal Agreement between the United Kingdom and the European Union' in July 2018 which sets out proposals for a European Union (Withdrawal Agreement) Bill 2018. It is now this Bill and its contents within, that is telling of how Brexit will play out in the UK. In particular, the Bill sets out details for a transition period until December 2020 which is designed to promote greater certainty for UK businesses. Effectively, this will buy us more time. Of course, negotiations between the UK and the EU are currently under way but with every tentative step forward, and the corresponding scrutiny that ensues this renders progress almost at a standstill. Proposed plans are heavily scrutinised and shrouded with high levels of scepticism. If no deal is reached, then the EU Treaties will automatically cease to apply on exit day without any further arrangements.

5.2 The aims of the European Union

The original aim of the first treaty signed, the Treaty of Paris (1951), was to create political unity within Europe and prevent another world war. The ECSC placed the production of steel and coal in all the member states under the authority of a single community organisation, with the object of indirectly controlling the manufacture of arms and therefore helping to prevent war between member states. The ECSC ceased to exist in 2002. Euratom was designed to produce cooperative nuclear research, and the EEC to improve Europe's economic strength.

It is the EEC (now known as the EU) that has had the most significance, particularly for law. Its object now is to weld Europe into a single prosperous area by abolishing all restrictions affecting the movement of people, goods and money between member states, producing a single market of over 500 million people, available to all producers in the member states. This, it is hoped, will help Europe to compete economically with countries such as the US, Japan, China and India, the member states being stronger as a block than they could possibly be alone. The Single European Act 1986 was a major step towards this goal, setting a target of 1992 for the abolition of trade barriers between member states. The practical effect is that, for example, a company manufacturing rivets in Leeds, with an order from a company in Barcelona, can send the rivets all the way there by lorry without the driver having to fill in customs forms as he or she crosses every border. The rivets will be made to a common EU standard, so the Spanish firm will know exactly what they are going to receive, while any trademarks or other rights over the design of the rivets will be protected throughout the member states. Just as goods can now move freely throughout the EU, so can workers: for example, a designer from Paris can go and work in London, or Milan, or Dublin, with no need for a work permit and no problem with immigration controls.

Table 5.1 Membership of the European Union

Year	Country
1951	Belgium France Italy Luxembourg Netherlands West Germany
1973	Denmark Ireland United Kingdom
1981	Greece
1986	Portugal Spain
1995	Austria Finland Sweden
2004	Cyprus Czech Republic Estonia Hungary Latvia Lithuania Malta Poland Slovakia Slovenia
2007	Bulgaria Romania
2013	Croatia

Along with these closer economic ties, it is intended that there should be increasing political unity, though there is some disagreement – particularly, though not exclusively, in Britain – as to how far this should go. Nevertheless, progress is being made: the Treaty on European Union (TEU, also known as the Maastricht Treaty), signed in 1992, was the first major move in this direction, establishing the aims of a single currency (the euro), joint defence and foreign policies, and inter-governmental cooperation on justice and home affairs. The introduction of the euro began in 1999 (though not in the UK, which had negotiated the right to opt out of the programme), and the Amsterdam Treaty, signed in 1997, gave more precise definition to the common foreign and security policy and cooperation in justice and home affairs. These matters now fall within the scope of the EU.

Photo 5.1 The European flag

Source: © Jules Selmes/Pearson Education Ltd. 2008

5.3 Modernising the European Union

The European institutions and decision-making structures were originally designed 50 years ago for a small community of six countries. These structures became out of date and inadequate to cope with the expanded membership of Europe. A new European Constitution was drawn up with a view to modernising the European institutions, making them more democratic and efficient. However, referendums in the Netherlands and France rejected this Constitution. After a two-year period of reflection, the Lisbon Treaty was agreed in 2007 adopting the most important of the planned reforms of the failed Constitution in a pragmatic and minimalist format, rather than the more grandiose presentation of the Constitution (which would have got rid of all the previous EU treaties and replaced them with a single Constitution). The Lisbon Treaty leaves all the existing European treaties in place and simply makes key amendments. It was ratified by all the member states and came into force in December 2009.

5.4 The institutions of the European Union

There are six key European institutions: the Commission, the Council of Ministers, the European Council, the European Parliament of the European Union, the Court of Justice of the European Union and the European Central Bank. Each of these institutions will be considered in turn.

5.4.1 The Commission

The Commission is composed of 28 members, called Commissioners, who are each appointed by the member states, subject to approval by the European Parliament, for five years. During the preparation of the Lisbon Treaty, efforts were made to include provisions to reduce the number of Commissioners to make the organisation more streamlined and potentially more efficient, but these efforts proved unsuccessful. They must be nationals of a member state, and in practice there tend to be two each from the largest states – France, Germany, Italy, Spain and the UK – and one each from the rest. However, the Commissioners do not represent their own countries: they are independent, and their role is to represent the interests of the EU overall. The idea is that the Commission's commitment to furthering EU interests balances the role of the European Council, whose members represent national interests.

In addition to its part in making EU legislation (see p. 114), the Commission is responsible for ensuring that member states uphold EU law, and has powers to investigate breaches by member states and, where necessary, bring them before the Court of Justice. It also plays an important role in the relationship of the EU with the rest of the world, negotiating trade agreements and the accession of new members, and draws up the annual draft budget for the EU. It is assisted in all these functions by an administrative staff, which has a similar role to that of the civil service in the UK.

The reputation of the Commission was seriously damaged in 1999 when an independent report found evidence of fraud, mismanagement and nepotism, forcing all the Commissioners to resign.

Photo 5.2 The European Commission

Source: © Luke1138/iStock/Getty Images

5.4.2 European Council

The members of the European Council are the president of the European Commission and the 28 heads of state of the member countries (for example, the Prime Minister of the United Kingdom, the President of France and the Chancellor of Germany). The European Council meets twice a year and has the same powers as the Council of Ministers, though the two are technically separate institutions. Many of the key decisions affecting the future direction of Europe are taken at these meetings. The Presidency of the Council is held by each member state, in rotation, for a period of six months.

Following the Lisbon Treaty, the President of the European Council will be elected by a qualified majority for a term of two-and-a-half years (renewable once), replacing the six-monthly rotating presidency. The newly defined role of the President includes ensuring the 'external representation of the Union on issues concerning its common foreign and security policy', which has led those opposed to a stronger Europe to be concerned that the President could effectively become a head of state for Europe – a move towards a president of the United States of Europe. In fact, the office enjoys only limited powers which cannot be compared with the extensive executive powers of an American president. The former British Prime Minister, Tony Blair, was considered for this position, but was found to be too controversial a figure due to his involvement in instigating the Iraq War. Instead, a former Prime Minister of Belgium was selected to be the first person to hold this prestigious position.

5.4.3 The Council of Ministers

The Council of Ministers represents the interests of individual member states. It is a very powerful body in Europe and plays an important role in the passing of legislation. It does not have a permanent membership – in each meeting the members, one from each country, are national government ministers chosen according to the subject under discussion (so, for example, a discussion of matters relating to farming would usually be attended by the Ministers for Agriculture of each country). The Council meets most weeks to agree legislation and policy.

The Council may be questioned by the European Parliament, but the chief control is exercised by the national governments controlling their ministers who attend the Council.

5.4.4 The European Parliament

The Parliament is composed of 751 members (MEPs), including one President, who are directly elected in their own countries. In Britain they are elected to represent a geographical area which is much larger than for MPs, since there are only 73 MEPs for the whole country. Elections are held every five years.

The individual member countries are each allocated a number of seats, roughly according to population, although on this basis the smaller countries are over-represented. Members sit in political groupings rather than with others from their own country.

The Treaty of Lisbon has increased the powers of the European Parliament, to try and strengthen the democratic process within Europe. As well as taking part in the legislative process (discussed below), the Parliament has a variety of roles to play in connection with the other institutions. Over the Commission, it exercises a supervisory power. It has a right of veto over the appointment of the Commission as a whole, and can also sack the whole Commission by a vote of censure. In 1999, the entire Commission resigned during a crisis over fraud and mismanagement within the Commission, to avoid a vote of censure. The Commission must make an annual report to Parliament, and Parliament can also require Commissioners to answer written or oral questions. The Commission has to submit each proposed budget of the European Union to the European Parliament for its approval.

The Council is not accountable to Parliament in the same way, but the Parliament reports on it three times a year, and the President of the Council is obliged to address the Parliament once a year, followed by a debate. The Parliament can also bring actions against other EU institutions for failure to implement EU law.

The Parliament appoints an Ombudsman, who investigates complaints of maladministration by EU institutions from individuals and MEPs. It can also be petitioned by any natural or legal person living or having an office within a member state, on any issue within the EU field which affects that person directly.

5.4.5 Court of Justice of the European Union

The whole court system of the European Union is known as the Court of Justice of the European Union. This, in fact, consists of three courts: the main Court of Justice of the European Union, the General Court, and the Civil Service Tribunal.

Following the Lisbon Treaty of 2009, the official court name is the 'Court of Justice of the European Union (CJEU)' but it is still often referred to as the 'European Court of Justice' (ECJ). The CJEU has the task of supervising the uniform application of EU law throughout the member states, and in so doing it can create case law. It is important not to confuse it with the European Court of Human Rights, which deals with alleged breaches of human rights by countries that are signatories to the European Convention on Human Rights. That court is completely separate, and not an institution of the EU.

The CJEU, which sits in Luxembourg, has 28 judges, appointed for a period of six years (which may be renewed). The judges are assisted by nine Advocates General, who produce opinions on the cases assigned to them, indicating the issues raised and suggesting conclusions. These are not binding, but are nevertheless usually followed by the court. Both judges and Advocates General are chosen from those who are eligible for the highest judicial posts in their own countries.

Most cases are heard in plenary session, that is, with all the judges sitting together. Only one judgment will be delivered, giving no indication of the extent of agreement between the judges, and these often consist of fairly brief propositions, from which it can be difficult to discern any *ratio decidendi*. Consequently, lawyers seeking precedents often turn to the opinions written by the Advocates General. Since September 1989 the full CJEU has been assisted by a new Court of First Instance (now known as the General Court) to deal with specialist economic law cases. Parties in such cases may appeal to the full CJEU on a point of law.

The majority of cases heard by the CJEU are brought by member states and institutions of the Community, or are referred to it by national courts. It has only limited power to deal with cases brought by individual citizens, and such cases are rarely heard.

The CJEU has two separate functions: a judicial role, deciding cases of dispute; and a supervisory role.

The judicial role of the CJEU

The CJEU hears cases of dispute between parties, which fall into two categories: proceedings against member states, and proceedings against European institutions.

Proceedings against member states may be brought by the Commission, or by other member states, and involve alleged breaches of European law by the country in question. For example, in ***Re Tachographs: EC Commission* v *UK*** (1979), the CJEU upheld a complaint against the UK for failing to implement a European regulation making it compulsory for lorries used to carry dangerous goods to be fitted with tachographs (devices used to record the speed and distance travelled, with the aim of preventing lorry drivers from speeding, or from driving for longer than the permitted number of hours). The Commission usually gives the member state the opportunity to put things right before bringing the case to the CJEU.

Proceedings against EU institutions may be brought by member states, other EU institutions and, in limited circumstances, by individual citizens or organisations. The procedure can be used to review the legality of EU regulations, directives or decisions, on the grounds that proper procedures have not been followed, the provisions infringe a European Treaty or any rule relating to its application, or powers have been misused. In ***United Kingdom* v *Council of the European Union*** (1996) the UK sought to have the Directive on the 48-hour working week annulled on the basis that it had been unlawfully adopted by the Council. The application was unsuccessful.

In the past, there was no machinery for enforcing judgments against states. Following the Maastricht Treaty, there is now provision for member states to be fined.

Decisions made in these kinds of cases cannot be questioned in UK courts.

The supervisory role of the CJEU

Article 267 of the Treaty on the Functioning of the European Union provides that any court or tribunal in a member state may refer a question on EU law to the CJEU if it considers that 'a decision on that question is necessary to enable it to give judgment'. The object of this referral system is to make sure that the law is interpreted in the same way throughout Europe.

Article 267 states that a reference must be made if the national court is one from which there is no further appeal – so in Britain, the Supreme Court must refer such questions, while the lower courts usually have some discretion about whether or not to do so. The European Court has clarified in ***Cilfit* v *Ministry of Health*** (1983) when a court is required to refer a point of law for its consideration. It stated that a reference should be made by the final appellate court where a question of European law is raised unless:

1   The question raised is irrelevant.
2   The provision of European law has already been interpreted by the European Court.
3   The correct application of European law is so obvious as to leave no scope for any reasonable doubt (known as *acte claire*). This must be assessed in the light of the specific characteristics of European law, the particular difficulties to which its interpretation gives rise and the risk of divergence in judicial decisions between European member states.

About 20 references a year are made from UK courts. The Article 267 procedure is expensive and time-consuming, often delaying a decision on the case for a long time (about nine months), and so lower courts have been discouraged from using it. Consequently, attempts have been made to set down guidelines by which a lower court could determine when a referral to the CJEU would or would not be necessary.

5

EUROPEAN LAW

Figure 5.2 Institutions of the European Union

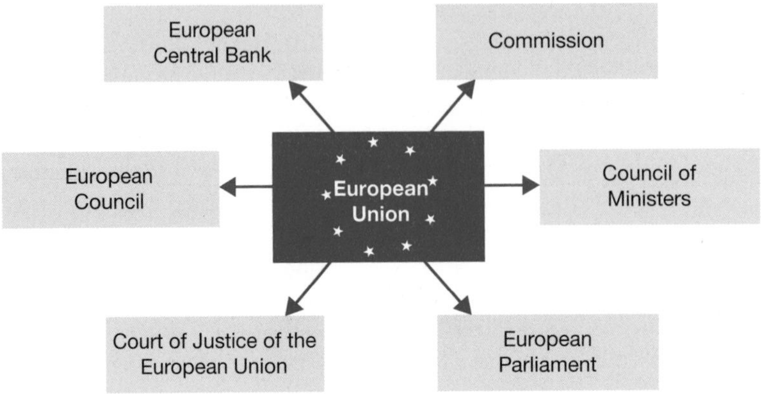

Key case

In **Bulmer v Bollinger** (1974), the Court of Appeal was asked to review a judge's exercise of discretion to refer a question under what is now Art. 267. They pointed out that the European Court could not interfere with the exercise of a judge's discretion to refer, and Lord Denning set down guidelines on the points which should be taken into account in considering whether a reference was necessary. He emphasised the cost and delay that a reference could cause, and stated that no reference should be made:

● where it would not be conclusive of the case, and other matters would remain to be decided;

● where there had been a previous ruling on the same point;

● where the court considers that point to be reasonably clear and free from doubt; and

● where the facts of the case had not yet been decided.

Unless the point to be decided could be considered 'really difficult and important', said Lord Denning, the court should save the expense and delay of a reference and decide the issue itself.

Denning's view has since been criticised by academics, who point out that it can be cheaper and quicker to refer a point at an early stage, than to drag the case up through the English courts first. In addition, the clear and consistent interpretation of EU law can come to depend on whether individual litigants have the resources to take their cases all the way up to the Supreme Court. Critics also note that the apparent importance of the case should not be decisive, as many important decisions of the CJEU have arisen from cases where the parties actually had little at stake.

Legal principle

Lord Denning laid down guidance on when courts should make references to the Court of Justice of the European Union under Art. 267.

Although the judiciary still use Denning's **Bulmer** guidelines, in the 1980s and 1990s there appeared to be a greater willingness to refer cases under the Art. 267 procedure. In **Customs and Excise Commissioners v APS Samex** (1983), Bingham J pointed out that, in interpreting European law, the Court of Justice has certain advantages over national courts: it can take a panoramic view of the whole of European law, compare the legislation as it is written in different member states' languages, and it is experienced in the purposive approach to interpretation for which European legislation was designed. In addition, it has the facility to allow member states to make their views on an issue known. As a result, it is better placed than a national court to decide issues of interpretation. In *R v International Stock Exchange, ex parte Else* (1993), the same judge (by then Master of the Rolls), said that if, once the facts have been found, it is clear that an issue of European law is vital to a court's final decision, that court should normally make an Art. 267 referral: English courts should only decide such issues without referral if they have real confidence that they can do so correctly, without the help of the CJEU.

More recently, as euro-scepticism has increased, the Supreme Court has again become reluctant to refer cases to the CJEU, relying on the fact that the interpretation of the EU legislation is obvious: an *acte claire*. For example, in *X v Mid-Sussex Citizens Advice Bureau* (2012), the Supreme Court stated that the word 'occupation' in a European Directive obviously did not extend to volunteers.

Where a case is submitted, proceedings will be suspended in the national court until the CJEU has given its verdict. This verdict does not tell the national court how to decide the case, but simply explains what EU law on the matter is. The national court then has the duty of making its decision in the light of this.

Regardless of which national court submitted the point for consideration, a ruling from the CJEU should be followed by all other courts in the EU – so, theoretically, a point raised by a County Court in England may result in a ruling that the highest courts in all the member states have to follow. Where a ruling reveals that national legislation conflicts with EU law, the national Government usually enacts new legislation to put the matter right.

The court's decisions can be changed only by its own subsequent decision or by an amendment of the Treaty, which would require the unanimous approval of member states through their own Parliaments. Decisions of the European Court cannot be questioned in English courts. This principle has limited the jurisdiction of the Supreme Court as a final appellate court.

An illustration of the use of Art. 267 is the case of *Marshall v Southampton and South West Hampshire Area Health Authority* (1986). Miss Marshall, a dietician, was compulsorily retired by the Authority from her job when she was 62, although she wished to continue to 65. It was the Authority's policy that the normal retiring age for its employees was the age at which state retirement pensions became payable: for women this was 60, though the

5

EUROPEAN LAW

Table 5.2 Membership of the European institutions

Commission	28 Commissioners
European Council	The president of the European Commission and 28 heads of state
Council of Ministers	It does not have a permanent membership. For each meeting one minister is chosen from each country according to the subject of the meeting
European Parliament	A maximum of 751 Members of the European Parliament (MEPs)
Court of Justice of the European Union	28 judges
European Central Bank	It manages the Euro and EU economic and monetary policy

Authority had waived the rule for two years in Miss Marshall's case. She claimed that the Authority was discriminating against women by adopting a policy that employees should retire at state pension age, hence requiring women to retire before men. This policy appeared to be legal under the relevant English legislation but was argued to be contrary to a Council directive providing for equal treatment of men and women. The national court made a reference to the CJEU asking for directions on the meaning of the directive. The CJEU found that there was a conflict with UK law, and the UK later changed its legislation to conform.

It is important to note that the CJEU is not an appeal court from decisions made in the member states. It does not substitute its own decisions for those of a lower court (except those of its own Court of First Instance, discussed below). It will assist a national court at any level in reaching a decision, but the actual decision remains the responsibility of the national court. When parties in an English case talk of taking the case to Europe, the only way they can do this is to get an English court to make a referral for an Art. 267 ruling, and they may have to take their case all the way to the Supreme Court to ensure this.

General Court

This court was originally known as the European Court of First Instance and was established in 1988 to reduce the workload of the then European Court of Justice. It was renamed by the Lisbon Treaty in 2009, becoming the General Court. It primarily hears direct actions against EU institutions. Appeals on points of law are heard by the Court of Justice of the European Union.

Civil Service Tribunal

The Civil Service Tribunal hears disputes between the European Union and its civil servants.

5.4.6 European Central Bank

The European Central Bank (ECB) gained the official status of being an institution of the European Union under the Lisbon Treaty in 2009. The ECB was established in 1998 and has its headquarters in Frankfurt in Germany. It is responsible for the economic and monetary policy of the 18 member states that have adopted the euro as their national currency, known together as the eurozone. The primary objective of the ECB is to maintain price stability within the eurozone, in other words to keep inflation below 2 per cent. It has responsibility for fixing the interest rate within the eurozone. It takes its decisions independently of governments and the other European institutions.

5.5 Making European legislation

The Council of Ministers (often called simply 'the Council'), the Commission and the European Parliament all play a role in making EU legislation. A complicated range of different procedures has been developed to make these laws. All legislation starts with a proposal from the Commission, and the Council enjoys the most power in the legislative process.

Parliament's legislative role was historically purely advisory, with the Commission and the Council having a much more powerful role in the legislative process. This led to concern over the lack of democracy within Europe, for while Parliament is directly elected by the citizens of Europe, the Commission and Council members are not. The role of the European Parliament in the passing of European legislation has gradually been increased by the Single European Act, the Maastricht Treaty, the Amsterdam Treaty and the Lisbon Treaty. Increasingly, the passing of EU legislation requires the approval of the European Parliament as well as the Council, through the co-decision process.

The Council continues to play an important role in the passing of European legislation. There are three systems of voting in the Council:

- **unanimity,** where proposals are only passed if all members vote for them;
- **simple majority,** where proposals only require more votes for than against; and
- **qualified majority,** which allows each state a specified number of votes (the larger the state, the more votes it has), and provides that a proposal can only be agreed if there are a specified number of votes in its favour.

These voting procedures have been controversial, because where unanimity is not required a member state can be forced to abide by legislation for which it has not voted, and which it believes is against its interests. This is seen as compromising national sovereignty. However, requiring unanimity makes it difficult to get things done quickly (or sometimes at all) and, as a result, initial progress towards the single market was very slow. The need to speed up progress led to both the Single European Act and the Maastricht Treaty requiring only qualified majority voting more often. The Amsterdam Treaty and the Lisbon Treaty extended its use a little more, and it is now the norm for many areas.

5.6 Types of European legislation

There is a range of different forms of European legislation: treaties, regulations, directives and decisions. In considering the impact of this legislation on UK law a distinction has to be drawn between direct applicability and direct effect. Direct applicability refers to the fact that treaty articles, regulations and some decisions immediately become part of the law of each member state. Directives are not directly applicable.

Where European legislation has direct effect, it creates individual rights which national courts must protect without any need for implementing legislation in that member state. In the UK the national courts were given this power under s. 2(1) of the European Communities Act 1972.

There are two types of direct effect: vertical direct effect gives individuals rights against Governments; and horizontal direct effect gives rights against other people and organisations.

Provisions of treaties, regulations and directives only have direct effect if they are clear, unconditional and their implementation requires no further legislation in member states. These conditions were first laid down in the context of treaties in ***Van Gend en Loos*** v ***Nederlandse Tariefcommissie*** (1963).

The ability of individuals to rely on European law before their national courts greatly enhances its effectiveness. National courts can quickly apply directly effective legislation and can draw on a wide range of remedies. Where legislation does not have direct effect, the only method of enforcement available in the past was an action brought by the Commission or a member state against a member state before the CJEU. This process can be slow and provides no direct remedy for the individual.

However, in the 1990s the European Court recognised the right of individuals to be awarded damages by their national courts for breach of European legislation by a member state, even where the legislation did not have direct effect. Originally, in *Francovich* v *Italy* (1991), this right was applied where directives had not been implemented but it has been developed to extend to any violation of European law. In *Francovich*, an Italian company went into liquidation, leaving its employees, including Francovich, unpaid arrears of salary. Italy had not set up a compensation scheme for employees in such circumstances as was required by a European directive. Francovich sued in the Italian courts. The court held that although the directive was not sufficiently precise to have direct effect it gave a right to damages.

Liability will be imposed on a member state if:

- the legislation was intended to confer rights on individuals;
- the content of those rights is clear from the provisions of the legislation; and
- there is a direct causal link between the breach of the member state's obligation and the damage sustained by the individual.

In addition, a fourth condition was added by *Brasserie du Pêcheur SA* v *Germany* (1996) and *R* v *Secretary of State for Transport, ex parte Factortame* (1990):

- there was a serious breach of European law.

Article 288 of the Treaty on the Functioning of the European Union states:

> To exercise the Union's competences, the institutions shall adopt regulations, directives, decisions, recommendations and opinions.
>
> A regulation shall have general application. It shall be binding in its entirety and directly applicable in all Member States.
>
> A directive shall be binding, as to the result to be achieved, upon each Member State to which it is addressed, but shall leave to the national authorities the choice of form and methods.
>
> A decision shall be binding in its entirety. A decision which specifies those to whom it is addressed shall be binding only on them.
>
> Recommendations and opinions shall have no binding force.

The four different types of European law will now be examined in turn.

5.6.1 Treaties

The Treaties of the European Union are international treaties agreed between all the member states. They effectively constitute the European Constitution, establishing the six key European institutions and the aims of the European Union. There are now two main treaties of equal importance: the Treaty on European Union (also known as the Maastricht Treaty) and the Treaty on the Functioning of the European Union (historically known as the Rome Treaty). These treaties have been amended over the years and their article numbers changed as the European Union has evolved. Treaty provisions can create rights and obligations.

An example of a directly effective treaty provision is Art. 157 of the Treaty on the Functioning of the European Union. This provides 'equal pay for male and female workers for equal work of equal value'. In *Macarthys Ltd* v *Smith* (1979), Art. 157 was held to give a woman in the UK the right to claim the same wages as were paid to the male predecessor in her job, even though she had no such right under the UK equal pay legislation passed in 1970, before the UK joined the EEC.

Treaty provisions which are merely statements of intent or policy, rather than establishing clear rights or duties, require detailed legislation to be made before they can be enforced in the member states.

Parliament has passed the European Union Act 2011 which requires a national referendum before the EU treaties can be amended or a new treaty signed involving a transfer of power or competence from the UK to the EU.

5.6.2 Regulations

A regulation is the nearest European law comes to an English Act of Parliament. Regulations apply throughout the EU, usually to people in general, and they become part of the law of each member nation as soon as they come into force, without the need for each country to make its own legislation.

> ### Key case
>
> The case of *Van Gend en Loos* (1963) decided that a treaty provision has direct effect if it is unconditional, clear and precise as to the rights or obligations it creates, and leaves member states no discretion on implementing it. Treaty provisions which are unconditional, clear and precise, and allow no discretion on implementation, have both horizontal and vertical direct effect.
>
> #### Legal principle
> Treaty provisions have direct effect if they are unconditional, clear and precise and impose an obligation on member states to implement them.

Regulations must be applied even if the member state has already passed legislation which conflicts with them. In *Leonesio* v *Italian Ministry for Agriculture and Forestry* (1972), a regulation to encourage reduced dairy production stated that a cash premium should be payable to farmers who slaughtered cows and agreed not to produce milk for five years. Leonesio had fulfilled this requirement, but was refused payment because the Italian constitution required legislation to authorise government expenditure. The CJEU said that once Leonesio had satisfied the conditions, he was entitled to the payment; the Italian Government could not use its own laws to block that right.

5.6.3 Directives

Directives are less precisely worded than regulations, because they aim to set out broad policy objectives, leaving the member states to create their own detailed legislation in order to put those objectives into practice (within specified time limits). As a result, it was originally assumed by most member states that directives could not have direct effect, and would not create individual rights until they had been translated into domestic legislation. However, the CJEU has consistently refused to accept this view, arguing that direct effect is an essential weapon if the EU is to ensure that member states implement directives.

Key case

The case which initially established direct effect for directives was ***Van Duyn* v *Home Office*** (1974). The Home Office had refused Van Duyn permission to enter the UK because she was a member of a religious group, the Scientologists, which the Government wanted to exclude from the country at the time. Van Duyn argued that her exclusion was contrary to provisions in the Treaty of Rome on freedom of movement. The Government responded by pointing out that the Treaty allowed exceptions on public policy grounds, but Van Duyn then relied on a later directive which said that public policy could only be invoked on the basis of personal conduct, and Van Duyn herself had done nothing to justify exclusion. The case was referred to the CJEU, which found that the obligation conferred on the Government was clear and unconditional, and so created enforceable rights.

Legal principle

Directives have direct effect where they impose clear and unconditional obligations on a government.

The reasoning behind the approach taken in ***Van Duyn*** was explained in ***Pubblico Ministero* v *Ratti*** (1979), where the European Court pointed out that member states could not be allowed to rely on their own wrongful failure to implement directives as a means of denying individual rights.

Directives have vertical direct effect but not horizontal direct effect. This means that they impose obligations on the state and not individuals. Thus, they have direct effect in proceedings against a member state (vertical) but not in proceedings between individuals (horizontal). A directive with direct effect can be utilised by an individual against the state when the state has failed to implement the directive properly or on time.

The issue of direct effect was important in the high-profile case of ***R (on the application of Westminster City Council)* v *Mayor of London*** (2002). Westminster Council had applied for judicial review of the decision to introduce a congestion charge to enter central London. The decision had been taken by the Mayor of London, Ken Livingstone. The High Court rejected the application. Westminster Council had sought to rely on a provision of a directive. The High Court stated that the Council could not do this, as when directives had direct effect they only gave rights to individuals and not to Government institutions.

Table 5.3 Impact of European legislation

Impact	Meaning of term
Direct applicability	Legislative provisions immediately become part of the law of each member state.
Direct effect	Legislation creates individual rights which national courts must protect without any need for implementing legislation in the member state.
Horizontal direct effect	Legislation gives rights against governments, individuals and private organisations.
Vertical direct effect	Legislation gives rights against governments.
Indirect effect	National courts should interpret national law in accordance with relevant European legislation.

The CJEU has found a number of ways to widen access where the principle of vertical direct effect applies. First, it has defined 'the state' very broadly to include all public bodies and 'emanations of the state', including local authorities and nationalised industries. In *Foster v British Gas plc* (1990) the CJEU stated that:

> [A] body, whatever its legal form, which has been made responsible, pursuant to a measure adopted by the State, for providing a public service under the control of the State and has for that purpose special powers beyond those which result from the normal rules applicable in relations between individuals, is included in any event among the bodies against which the provisions of a directive capable of having direct effect may be relied upon. (para 20)

This meant, for example, that in *Marshall v Southampton and South West Hampshire Area Health Authority* (discussed at p. 113), Miss Marshall was able to take advantage of the relevant directive even though she was not suing the Government itself, because her employer was a health authority and therefore considered to be a public body.

Secondly, in *Von Colson v Land Nordrhein-Westfalen* (1984), the court introduced the principle of indirect effect, stating that national courts should interpret national law in accordance with relevant directives, whether the national law was designed to implement a directive or not. The principle was confirmed in *Marleasing SA v La Comercial Internacional de Alimentación SA* (1990). Here, Marleasing alleged that La Comercial, a Spanish company, had been formed with the express purpose of defrauding creditors (of which they were one) and sought to have its articles of association (the document under which a company is formed) declared void. Spanish contract law allowed this, but the EU had passed a directive which did not. Which should the member state court follow? The European Court held that where a provision of domestic law was 'to any extent open to interpretation', national courts had to interpret that law 'as far as possible' in line with the wording and purpose of any relevant directive. This would apply whether the domestic law was passed before or after the directive, except that domestic law passed before a directive would only be affected once the time limit for implementation of the directive had expired.

Marleasing has been much discussed by academics, but it is still unclear quite how far national courts are expected to go in implementing directives having indirect effect. EU law experts Craig and de Búrca (2007) suggest, however, that the principle of indirect effect probably only applies where national law is sufficiently ambiguous to allow it to be interpreted in line with directives; where there is a conflict, but the national law is clear, member state courts are unlikely to be required to override that law.

Thirdly, some recent cases have allowed an unimplemented directive to act as a shield, though not as a sword, to the benefit of private individuals. In other words, the directive could be relied upon to provide a defence but not to provide a right of action. For example, *CIA Security International SA v Signalson* (1996) concerned the failure by the Belgian Government to notify the Commission of its law on security systems in accordance with a European directive on the subject (Notification Directive 98/34). Litigation arose between two private companies, CIA Security and Signalson. Signalson tried to prevent CIA from marketing an alarm system which had not been approved under Belgian law. CIA successfully argued that the Belgian law did not apply because the Commission had not been notified about it in accordance with the European directive. Thus, CIA was able to rely on the directive to provide a defence in the litigation between two private individuals. On the surface it looked as if the directive was being given horizontal direct effect in breach of established principles of European law, but in fact the case has been interpreted as merely allowing a directive to give private individuals a defence. Another interpretation of the case was that

5

EUROPEAN LAW

Figure 5.3 European legislation

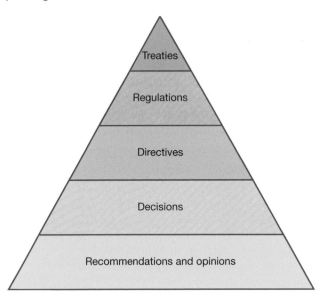

Signalson was effectively acting as an agent of the state, bringing proceedings for the withdrawal of a product which potentially did not conform with Belgian law.

In *R (on the application of Wells)* v *Secretary of State for Transport, Local Government and the Regions* (2005), there was a plan by a private company to reopen a quarry in an environmentally sensitive area. No environmental impact assessment had been carried out by the state in accordance with the Environmental Impact Assessment Directive (Directive 85/337). A local resident asked the Secretary of State to remove or modify the planning permission pending the carrying out of the assessment, but he refused. In the subsequent litigation, the court had to consider whether the local resident could rely on the directive. The court acknowledged that a directive cannot be used as a sword to impose obligations on a private individual. But a directive could be used as a shield, even if in doing so there would be a negative impact on a private individual: in this case the quarry owners would have to stop work on the quarry until the completion of the environmental impact assessment. As the quarry owners were not required to carry out an obligation, this did not amount to the imposition of direct horizontal effect.

Finally, the European Court has suggested in *Kucukdeveci* v *Swedex GmbH* (2009) that where a general principle of European law is being applied by a directive, the provisions of the directive can be applied by a private individual against another private individual. Thus, the national court can refuse to apply a national law in breach of a directive in litigation between private parties. On the facts of the case, the general principle identified was the principle of equal treatment and the directive was concerned with age discrimination. German national legislation would have allowed a person to be discriminated against on the basis of his or her age, and the European Court said the national court would be entitled not to apply the national law. It is understandable that the European Court wanted to give the employee a remedy, but the private employer had acted in accordance with clear provisions of German employment law, and found themselves penalised for the German Government's mistake. This is a new development in European law, but its impact remains uncertain, as it is difficult to predict what will be treated as a general principle of European law. In *Mangold* v *Helm* (2006),

Figure 5.4 Impact of European legislation

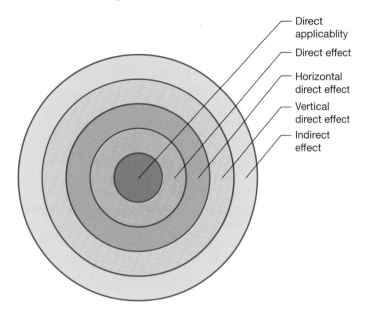

Direct applicablity

Direct effect

Horizontal direct effect

Vertical direct effect

Indirect effect

which also involved age discrimination, the European Court stated that the general principle of equality was found 'in various international instruments and in the constitutional traditions common in the member states'.

5.6.4 Decisions

A decision may be addressed to a state, a person or a company and is binding only on the recipient. Examples include granting, or refusing, export licences to companies from outside the EU.

5.6.5 Recommendations and opinions

The Council and the Commission may issue recommendations and opinions which, although not to be disregarded, are not binding law.

5.7 How does EU law affect the UK?

Membership of the EU has had a number of effects on UK law and our legal system.

5.7.1 New sources of law

Joining the original EEC created new and very important sources of law for the UK. Section 2(4) of the European Communities Act 1972 provides that English law should be interpreted and have effect subject to the principle that European law is supreme; this means that

European law now takes precedence over all domestic sources of law. As a result, it has had a profound effect on the rights of citizens in this country and, in particular, on the rights of employees, especially female workers. For example, in **R v Secretary of State for Employment, ex parte Equal Opportunities Commission** (1994), the House of Lords found that parts of the Employment Protection (Consolidation) Act 1978 were incompatible with European law on equal treatment for male and female employees, because the Act gave part-time workers fewer rights than full-timers. Since most part-time workers were women, this was held to discriminate on the basis of sex, and the UK Government was forced to change the law, and greatly improve the rights of part-time workers.

5.7.2 The role of the courts

Because EU law takes precedence over domestic legislation, the role of the courts has changed as a result of membership. Before the UK joined the EEC, statutes were the highest form of law, and judges had no power to refuse to apply them. Now, however, they can – in fact they should – refuse to apply statutes which are in conflict with directly effective EU law.

Key case

The leading case in this area is **R v Secretary of State for Transport, ex parte Factortame** (1990). It arose from the fishing policy decided by member states in 1983, which allowed member states to limit fishing within 12 miles of their own shores to boats from their own country, and left the remainder of the seas around the European Community open to fishing boats from any member state. In addition, to preserve stocks of fish, each state was allocated a quota of fish, and required not to exceed it. Soon after the new rules were in place, the UK Government became concerned that Spanish fishing boats were registering as British vessels, so that their catches counted against the British quota rather than the Spanish, and genuine British fishermen were as a result getting a smaller share. The Government therefore passed the Merchant Shipping Act 1988, which contained provisions to prevent the Spanish trawlers taking advantage of the British quota.

Spanish boat owners challenged the Act, claiming it was in conflict with EU law on the freedom to set up business anywhere in Europe, and the House of Lords agreed. They stated that s. 2(4) of the European Communities Act 'has precisely the same effect as if a section were incorporated in . . . [the 1988 Act, saying] that the provisions with respect to registration of British fishing vessels were to be without prejudice to the directly enforceable Community rights of nationals of any member state . . . '

The decision was criticised as compromising the rights of the UK Parliament to make law for this country, as the House of Lords rendered effectively unenforceable the Merchant Shipping Act. But the House of Lords was firm in dismissing such complaints, pointing out that it was very clear before the UK joined the EEC that doing so would mean giving up some degree of sovereignty over domestic law, and that this was accepted voluntarily when the UK joined the Community. 'Under . . . the Act of 1972, it has always been clear that it was the duty of a United Kingdom court, when delivering final judgment, to override any rule of national law found to be in conflict with any directly enforceable rule of Community law . . . '

Legal principle
Judges should refuse to apply statutes which are in conflict with directly effective EU law.

Lord Justice Laws stated in ***Thoburn* v *Sunderland City Council*** (2002) that the European Communities Act 1972 was a constitutional Act which could only be repealed by express provisions of an Act of Parliament (and not by implication). The case concerned a group of market stallholders who became known in the tabloid press as the 'metric martyrs'. They had refused to sell their fruits and vegetables in kilos and grammes, preferring to stick to the old weighing system of pounds and ounces. They argued they had not breached the law because part of the 1972 Act had been impliedly repealed by a later Act of Parliament: the Weights and Measures Act 1985, which allowed for the use of the old imperial measures. In essence, they were arguing that it was not a criminal offence to sell a pound of bananas.

In his judgment, Lord Justice Laws stated that Acts of Parliament should be divided between 'ordinary' statutes and 'constitutional' statutes. The European Communities Act was a constitutional Act and could only be repealed if Parliament used express words to show its intention to do so.

In ***R (on the application of HS2 Action Alliance Ltd)* v *Secretary of State for Transport*** (2014), the Supreme Court considered that Art. 9 of the Bill of Rights of 1689 was unquestionably part of whatever constitution the UK has. Article 9 prevents courts from considering proceedings in Parliament, and the Supreme Court would take a lot of persuasion that EU legislation could change that position. The case was concerned with the development of a high-speed rail link between London and Birmingham known as HS2. EU directives laid down procedures that had to be followed before giving permission for this type of project, to ensure the environmental impact of the project would be carefully considered. The government proposed agreeing to the construction of the HS2 using an Act of Parliament. The claimants argued that the parliamentary procedures followed to pass the Act of Parliament approving the HS2 project would not satisfy these EU directives, partly because they would not allow effective public participation in the consultation process. The appeal was rejected by the Supreme Court, as the Court was not prepared to question the parliamentary procedures involved in passing an Act of Parliament because Art. 9 of the Bill of Rights 1689 bans it from doing so in order to respect Parliamentary sovereignty in a democratic system.

The Supreme Court noted that if there is a conflict between a constitutional principle, such as that embodied in Art. 9 of the Bill of Rights 1689, and EU law, that conflict has to be resolved by our courts as an issue arising under the constitutional law of the United Kingdom. The impact of ***Factortame*** and the principle of the Supremacy of Europe was restricted by pointing out that ***Factortame*** was not concerned with a principle of constitutional law. While ***Thoburn* v *Sunderland City Council*** drew a simple binary distinction between constitutional and ordinary legislation, the Supreme Court in the HS2 case seems to suggest a distinction should also be drawn between fundamental constitutional principles in legislation and common law and less important constitutional principles. The United Kingdom does not have a written constitution, but it has a number of constitutional instruments, such as the Magna Carta, the Bill of Rights, the European Communities Act 1972 and the Human Rights Act 1998. The Supreme Court observed: 'Article 9 of the Bill of Rights, one of the pillars of the constitutional settlement which established the rule of law in England in the seventeenth century, precludes the impeaching or questioning in any court of debates or proceedings in Parliament.' Article 9 was described by Lord Browne-Wilkinson in the House of Lords in ***Pepper* v *Hart*** as 'a provision of the highest constitutional importance' which 'should not be narrowly construed'.

An EU directive could not succeed in setting aside such a fundamental constitutional principle. The interpretation in ***Factortame*** of the European Communities Act 1972 does not require national courts to accord primacy to EU law over *all* domestic law. ***Thoburn*** treats

5

EUROPEAN LAW

the European Communities Act as a constitutional statute which was therefore immune from implied repeal, so later legislation that was inconsistent (but not *explicitly* inconsistent) with EU law would cede priority to the 1972 Act and hence to the EU law to which that Act gives effect. But the ***HS2*** case goes further by introducing the notion that not all constitutional measures are equal; some constitutional measures are more fundamental than others. Parliament in a given constitutional measure, such as the 1972 Act, may not have intended the repeal of a more fundamental, but conflicting, constitutional measure. Whilst ordinary legislation will always (unless explicitly inconsistent) yield in the face of conflicting European law, a fundamental constitutional measure will not.

So there are two fundamental limitations on the principle of the Supremacy of European Union law:

1 Parliament cannot bind itself so it can expressly repeal the European Communities Act 1972.

2 Parliament can impliedly repeal European Community law which conflicts with a fundamental constitutional principle in the UK constitution.

The role of the courts is also affected by the principle stated in ***Marleasing*** (see p. 119), which effectively means that the courts now have a new external aid to consider when interpreting statutes, and should take notice of it wherever they can do so without straining the words of the statute.

The UK courts are subjected to the supervisory jurisdiction of the CJEU (as explained on p. 110), and this gives a further source of law, since the courts of all member states are bound by CJEU decisions on the interpretation and application of EU law.

5.7.3 The future

One view of the influence of UK membership of Europe on our national law was given by Lord Denning, in poetic mood, in ***Bulmer v Bollinger***: 'The Treaty is like an incoming tide. It flows into the estuaries and up the rivers. It cannot be held back.' Lord Scarman, obviously in an equally lyrical frame of mind, commented:

> For the moment, to adopt Lord Denning's imagery, the incoming tide has not yet mingled with the home waters of the common law: but it is inconceivable that, like the Rhone and the Arve where those two streams meet at Geneva, they should move on, side by side, one grey with the melted snows and ice of the distant mountains of our legal history, the other clear blue and clean, reflecting modern opinion. If we stay in the Common Market, I would expect to see its principles of legislation and statutory interpretation, and its conception of an activist court whose role is to strengthen and fulfil the purpose of statute law, replace the traditional attitudes of English judges and lawyers to statute law and the current complex style of statutory drafting.

What Lord Scarman was referring to was the difference in approach between the English legal system and those in mainland Europe. When drafting statutes, for example, English law has tended towards tightly written, very precise rules, whereas the continental style is looser, setting out broad principles to be followed. As a result, the continental style of statutory interpretation takes a very purposive approach, paying most attention to putting into practice the spirit of the legislation, and filling in any gaps in the wording if necessary, as opposed to the more literal style traditionally associated with English judges. The CJEU tends to take the continental approach, and it has been suggested that, as time goes on, this will influence our own judges more and more, leading to more creative judicial decision-making, with corresponding changes in the drafting of statutes.

Following the *Factortame* litigation there was concern that Europe was threatening the sovereignty of the UK Parliament, as the European Court ruling had caused an Act of Parliament to be set aside. Lord Denning revised his description of European law as like an 'incoming tide' and stated:

> No longer is European law an incoming tide flowing up the estuaries of England. It is now like a tidal wave bringing down our sea walls and flowing inland over our fields and houses – to the dismay of all. (*The Independent,* 16 July 1996)

The academic Seamus Burns (2008) has suggested that, in the light of subsequent legal developments, Lord Denning 'might have to revise his image of EU law being like an incoming tide permeating our existing legal order, and more realistically compare it to a tsunami, enveloping everything in its path with irresistible force'.

In *R v Secretary of State for Foreign and Commonwealth Affairs, ex parte Lord Rees-Mogg* (1994) an unsuccessful attempt was made to demonstrate that the UK could not legally ratify the Maastricht Treaty. In rejecting this claim, the court pointed out that the Treaty did not involve the abandoning or transferring of powers, so that a Government could choose later to denounce the Treaty, or fail to honour its obligations under it.

Parliament has passed the European Union Act 2011 which includes a provision to protect the sovereignty of Parliament. Section 18 of the Act states that the status of EU law is dependent on the continuing statutory authority of the European Communities Act 1972. So if this statute is repealed by Parliament then EU law would cease to have effect in the United Kingdom. Section 18 states:

Section 18. Status of EU law dependent on continuing statutory basis

> Directly applicable or directly effective EU law (that is, the rights, powers, liabilities, obligations, restrictions, remedies and procedures referred to in section 2(1) of the European Communities Act 1972) falls to be recognised and available in law in the United Kingdom only by virtue of that Act or where it is required to be recognised and available in law by virtue of any other Act.

In 2016, the UK voted in a referendum to leave the EU. Brexit will constitute a major change in the UK's relationship with the EU. The extent of this change will depend on the exit negotiations. In *R (Miller and Dos Santos) v Secretary of State for Exiting the European Union* the Supreme Court confirmed the fundamental principle of the Supremacy of Parliament and that the United Kingdom could only withdraw from the European Union if Parliament had voted an Act authorising it to do so which it now has (see p. 105).

Answering questions

1   What have been the major consequences of the United Kingdom's membership of the European Union for the character of the English legal system? *University of London, International Programmes LLB*

2   European law provisions have had a profound impact on UK law. In particular, explain how it has affected the use of precedent by judges in UK courts.

3   To what extent has the English legal system irrevocably accommodated European Union law?

4   Explain the role of the Court of Justice of the European Union.

For answers to these questions, visit the companion website at www.pearsoned.co.uk/ elliottquinn

SUMMARY OF CHAPTER 5: EUROPEAN LAW

Introction

The European Union currently has 28 members. It was established to create political unity within Europe and to prevent another world war. In 2016 the UK voted in a referendum to leave the EU, and the withdrawal process is scheduled to be completed by 29 March 2019.

The institutions of the European Union

There are six key institutions of the European Union: the Commission, the Council of Ministers, the European Council, the European Parliament, Court of Justice of the European Union and the European Central Bank. The Court of Justice of the European Union has two separate functions: a judicial role where it decides cases of dispute and a supervisory role under Art. 267 of the Treaty on the Functioning of the European Union.

Making European legislation

The Council of Ministers, the Commission and the European Parliament all play a role in making European legislation. All legislation starts with a proposal from the Commission, though the Council enjoys the most power in the legislative process. Increasingly, the qualified majority system of voting is being used by the Council in agreeing new legislation.

Types of European legislation

The different forms of European legislation are:

- treaties;
- regulations;
- directives; and
- decisions.

How does EU law affect the UK?

Membership of the EU has had a number of effects on UK law and on our legal system. Joining the original EEC created new and very important sources of law for the UK. Because EU law takes precedence over domestic legislation, the role of the courts has changed as a result of membership of the Union. Now judges should refuse to apply statutes which are in conflict with directly effective European law. Post Brexit, however, the judiciary needs guidance from the Government on how to manage the juxtaposition of English law and EU law.

Reading list

Booth, A. (2002) Direct effect. *Solicitors Journal*, 924.

Burns, S. (2008) An incoming tide. *New Law Journal*, 158: 44.

Craig, P. and de Búrca, G. (2007) *EU Law: Text, Cases and Materials*. Oxford: Oxford University Press.

Levitsky, J. (1994) The Europeanization of the British legal style. *American Journal of Comparative Law*, 42: 347.

On the internet

Access to the homepages of the European institutions can be obtained from the following website:
http://europa.eu/about-eu/institutions-bodies/index_en.htm

European legislation is available at:
http://eur-lex.europa.eu/en/index.htm

A European Commission Fact Sheet on Brexit is at:
http://europa.eu/rapid/press-release_MEMO-17-648_en.htm

Parliament's perspective on how Brexit will work in the UK is at:
http://www.parliament.uk/business/publications/research/eu-referendum/how-will-brexit-work/

5

EUROPEAN LAW

Chapter 6
Custom

This chapter discusses:

- the history of custom as a source of law; and
- when custom can be a source of law today.

6.1 Introduction

As we have seen, the basis of the common law was custom. The itinerant justices sent out by William the Conqueror (see p. 14) examined the different local practices of dealing with disputes and crime, filtered out the less practical and reasonable ones, and ended up with a set of laws that were to be applied uniformly throughout the country. As Sir Henry Maine, a nineteenth-century scholar who studied the evolution of legal systems, has pointed out, this did not mean that custom itself was ever law – the law was created by the decisions of judges in recognising some customs and not others.

Custom still plays a part in modern law, but a very small one. Its main use is in cases where a traditional local practice – such as fishermen being allowed to dry their nets on a particular piece of land, or villagers holding a fair in a certain place – is being challenged. Custom was defined in the *Tanistry Case* (1608) as 'such usage as has obtained the force of law' and, in these cases, those whose practices are being challenged assert that the custom has existed for so long that it should be given the force of law, even though it may conflict with the general common law.

6.2 When can custom be a source of law?

To be regarded as conferring legally enforceable rights, a custom must fulfil several criteria.

6.2.1 'Time immemorial'

It must have existed since 'Time immemorial'. This was fixed by a statute in 1275 as meaning 'since at least 1189'. In practice today claimants usually seek to prove the custom has existed as far back as living memory can go, often by calling the oldest local inhabitant as a witness. However, this may not always be sufficient. In a dispute over a right to use local land in some way, for example, if the other side could prove that the land in question was under water until the seventeenth or eighteenth century, the right could therefore not have existed since 1189. In *Simpson* v *Wells* (1872), a charge of obstructing the public footway by setting up a refreshment stall was challenged by a claim that there was a customary right to do so derived from 'statute sessions', ancient fairs held for the purpose of hiring servants. It was then proved that statute sessions were first authorised by the Statute of Labourers in the fourteenth century, so the right could not have existed since 1189.

6.2.2 Reasonableness

A legally enforceable custom cannot conflict with fundamental principles of right and wrong, so a customary right to commit a crime, for example, could never be accepted. In *Wolstanton Ltd* v *Newcastle-under-Lyme Corporation* (1940) the lord of a manor claimed a customary right to take minerals from under a tenant's land, without paying compensation for any damage caused to buildings on the land. It was held that this was unreasonable.

6.2.3 Certainty and clarity

It must be certain and clear. The locality in which the custom operates must be defined, along with the people to whom rights are granted (local fishermen, for example, or tenants of a particular estate) and the extent of those rights. In *Wilson* v *Willes* (1806) the tenants of a manor claimed the customary right to take as much turf as they needed for their lawns from the manorial commons. This was held to be too vague, since there appeared to be no limit to the amount of turf which could be taken.

6.2.4 Locality

It must be specific to a particular geographic area. Where a custom is recognised as granting a right, it grants that right only to those specified – a custom giving fishermen in Lowestoft the right to dry their nets on someone else's land would not give the same right to fishermen in Grimsby. Custom is only ever a source of local law.

6.2.5 Continuity

It must have existed continuously. The rights granted by custom do not have to have been exercised continuously since 1189, but it must have been possible to exercise them at all times since then. In *Wyld* v *Silver* (1963), a landowner, wishing to build on land where the local inhabitants claimed a customary right to hold an annual fair, argued that the right had not been exercised within living memory. The court nevertheless granted an injunction preventing the building.

6.2.6 Exercised as of right

It must have been exercised peaceably, openly and as of right. Customs cannot create legal rights if they are exercised only by permission of someone else. In *Mills* v *Colchester Corporation* (1867) it was held that a customary right to fish had no legal force where the right had always depended on the granting of a licence, even though such licences had traditionally been granted to local people on request.

6.2.7 Consistency

It must be consistent with other local customs. For example, if a custom is alleged to give the inhabitants of one farm the right to fish in a lake, it cannot also give the inhabitants of another the right to drain the lake. The usual course where a conflict arises is to deny that the opposing custom has any force, though this is not possible if it has already been recognised by a court.

6.2.8 Obligatory

Where a custom imposes a specific duty, that duty must be obligatory – a custom cannot provide that the lord of a manor grants villagers a right of way over his land only if he likes them, or happens not to mind people on his land that day.

6

CUSTOM

> **The Bigger Picture:** Custom in international law
>
> Custom is particularly important in the context of international law where fixed legal rules (for example in treaties and the Geneva Conventions) are less developed. In 2005, the International Committee of the Red Cross published a study aimed at promoting customary international humanitarian law. It identified 161 rules of customary international humanitarian law, which provide legal protection for people affected by armed conflict. These customs derive from the practice of states as expressed, for example, in military manuals, national legislation and diplomatic statements. They are considered to be binding custom in international law if they reflect the widespread, representative and uniform practice of states and are accepted as law.
>
> These customs are particularly important during civil wars as treaty law is primarily concerned with international conflicts. The study showed that customary international humanitarian law applicable in non-international armed conflict goes beyond the rules of treaty law. While treaty law covering internal armed conflict does not expressly prohibit attacks on civilians, international customs do. Customs are particularly important in this context because, while only states are bound by international treaties, all those involved in internal fighting, including rebel groups, are bound by international customs.

6.2.9 Conformity with statute

A custom which is in conflict with a statute will not be held to give rise to law.

Answering questions

1   Custom is one of the sources of UK law. In reality, how useful is it as such a source?

For the answer to this question, visit the companion website at www.pearsoned.co.uk/ elliottquinn

SUMMARY OF CHAPTER 6: CUSTOM

Introduction

The basis of the common law was custom. Custom still plays a part in modern law, but a very small one. Its main use is in cases where a traditional local practice is being challenged.

When can custom be a source of law?

To be regarded as conferring legally enforceable rights, a custom must fulfil several criteria:

'Time immemorial'

It must have existed since 'Time immemorial'. This was fixed by a statute in 1275 as meaning 'since at least 1189'.

Reasonableness

A legally enforceable custom cannot conflict with fundamental principles of right and wrong.

Certainty and clarity

It must be certain and clear.

Locality

It must be specific to a particular geographic area.

Continuity

It must have existed continuously.

Exercised as of right

It must have been exercised peaceably, openly and as of right.

Consistency

It must be consistent with other local customs.

Obligatory

Where a custom imposes a specific duty, that duty must be obligatory.

Conformity with statute

A custom which is in conflict with a statute will not be held to give rise to law.

Reading list

Maine, Sir H. (2001) *Ancient Law*. London: Dent.

Chapter 7
Equity

This chapter looks at:

- how equity became a source of law;

- the difference between common law and equity;

- reforms introduced by the Judicature Acts 1873–75;

- equity today; and

- the future of equity as a source of law.

7.1 Introduction

In ordinary language, equity simply means fairness, but in law it applies to a specific set of legal principles, which add to those provided in the common law. It was originally inspired by ideas of fairness and natural justice, but is now no more than a particular branch of English law. Lawyers often contrast 'law' and equity, but it is important to know that when they do this they are using 'law' to mean common law. Equity and common law may be different, but both are laws. Equity is an area of law which can only be understood in the light of its historical development.

7.2 How equity began

As we have seen, the common law was developed after the Norman Conquest through the 'itinerant justices' travelling around the country and sorting out disputes. By about the twelfth century, common law courts had developed which applied this common law. Civil actions in these courts had to be started by a writ, which set out the cause of the action or the grounds for the claim made, and there grew up different types of writ. Early on, new writs were created to suit new circumstances, but in the thirteenth century this was stopped. Litigants had to fit their circumstances to one of the available types of writ: if the case did not fall within one of those types, there was no way of bringing the case to the common law court. At the same time, the common law was itself becoming increasingly rigid, and offered only one remedy, damages, which was not always an adequate solution to every problem – if a litigant had been promised the chance to buy a particular piece of land, for example, and the seller then went back on the agreement, damages might not be an adequate remedy since the buyer really wanted the land, and may have made arrangements on the basis that it would be acquired.

Consequently, many people were unable to seek redress for wrongs through the common law courts. Many of these dissatisfied parties petitioned the king, who was thought of as the 'fountain of justice'. These petitions were commonly passed to the Chancellor, the king's chief minister, as the king did not want to spend time considering them. The Chancellor was usually a member of the clergy, and was thought of as 'keeper of the king's conscience'. Soon litigants began to petition the Chancellor himself and, by 1474, the Chancellor had begun to make decisions on the cases on his own authority, rather than as a substitute for the king. This was the beginning of the Court of Chancery.

Litigants appeared before the Chancellor, who would question them, and then deliver a verdict based on his own moral view of the question. The court could insist that relevant documents be disclosed, as well as questioning the parties in person, unlike the common law courts which did not admit oral evidence until the sixteenth century, and had no way of extracting the truth from litigants. Because the court followed no binding rules, relying entirely on the Chancellor's view of right and wrong, it could enforce rights not recognised by the common law, which, restricted by precedent, was failing to adapt to new circumstances. The Court of Chancery could provide whatever remedy best suited the case – the decree of specific performance, for example, would have meant that the seller of land referred to above could be forced to honour the promise. This type of justice came to be known as equity.

7.3 Common law and equity

Not surprisingly, the Court of Chancery became popular, and caused some resentment among common lawyers, who argued that the quality of decisions varied with the length of the Chancellor's foot – in other words, that it depended on the qualities of the individual Chancellor. Because precedents were not followed and each case was considered purely on its merits, justice could appear arbitrary, and nobody could predict what a decision might be.

On the other hand, this very flexibility was seen as the great advantage of equity – where any rules are laid down, there will always be situations in which those rules produce injustice. The more general the rule, the more likely this is, yet it is impossible to foresee and lay down all the specific exceptions in which it should not apply. Equity dealt with these situations by applying notions of good sense and fairness, but in doing so laid itself open to the charge that fairness is a subjective quality.

The common lawyers particularly resented the way in which equity could be used to restrict their own jurisdiction. Where the common law gave a litigant a right which, in the circumstances, it would be unjust to exercise, the Court of Chancery could issue a common injunction, preventing the exercise of the common law right. An example might be where a litigant had made a mistake in drawing up a document. Under common law the other party could enforce the document anyway, even if they were aware of the mistake but failed to draw attention to it. This was considered inequitable, and a common injunction would prevent the document being enforced.

Nevertheless, the rivalry continued for some time, but gradually abated as equity too began to be ruled by precedent and standard principles, a development related to the fact that it was becoming established practice to appoint lawyers rather than clergy to the office of Lord Chancellor. By the nineteenth century, equity had a developed case law and recognisable principles, and was no less rigid than the common law.

Key case

Tensions between equity and the common law came to a head in 1615 in **The Earl of Oxford's Case**, where conflicting judgments of the common law courts and the Court of Chancery were referred to the king for a decision; he advised that where there was conflict, equity should prevail. Had this decision not been made, equity would have been worthless – it could not fulfil its role of filling in the gaps of the common law unless it was dominant.

Legal principle
Where there is a conflict between equity and the common law, then equity should prevail.

7.4 The Judicature Acts

Once equity became a body of law, rather than an arbitrary exercise of conscience, there was no reason why it needed its own courts. Consequently, the Judicature Acts of 1873–75, which established the basis of the court structure we have today, provided that equity and common law could both be administered by all courts, and that there would no longer be

7

EQUITY

different procedures for seeking equitable and common law remedies. Although the Court of Chancery remained as a division of the High Court, like all other courts it can now apply both common law and equity.

7.5 Equity today

It is important to note that the Judicature Acts did not fuse common law and equity, only their administration. There is still a body of rules of equity which is distinct from common law rules, and acts as an addition to it. Although they are implemented by the same courts, the two branches of the law are separate. Where there is conflict, equity still prevails.

7.5.1 Equitable maxims

Although both the common law and equity lay down rules developed from precedents, equity also created maxims which had to be satisfied before equitable rules could be applied. These maxims were designed to ensure that decisions were morally fair. The following are some of them.

'He who comes to equity must come with clean hands'

This means that claimants who have themselves been in the wrong in some way will not be granted an equitable remedy. In *D&C Builders* v *Rees* (1966) a small building firm did some work on the house of a couple named Rees. The bill came to £732, of which the Reeses had already paid £250. When the builders asked for the balance of £482, the Reeses announced that the work was defective, and they were only prepared to pay £300. As the builders were in serious financial difficulties (as the Reeses knew), they reluctantly accepted the £300 'in completion of the account'. The decision to accept the money would not normally be binding in contract law, and afterwards the builders sued the Reeses for the outstanding amount. The Reeses claimed that the court should apply the doctrine of equitable estoppel, which can make promises binding when they would normally not be. However, Lord Denning refused to apply the doctrine, on the grounds that the Reeses had taken unfair advantage of the builders' financial difficulties, and therefore had not come 'with clean hands'.

'He who seeks equity must do equity'

Anyone who seeks equitable relief must be prepared to act fairly towards their opponent. In *Chappell* v *Times Newspapers Ltd* (1975), newspaper employees who had been threatened that they would be sacked unless they stopped their strike action applied for an injunction to prevent their employers from carrying out the threat. The court held that, in order to be awarded the remedy, the strikers should undertake that they would withdraw their strike action if the injunction was granted. Since they refused to do this, the injunction was refused.

'Delay defeats equity'

Where a claimant takes an unreasonably long time to bring an action, equitable remedies will not be available. The unreasonableness of any delay will be a matter of fact to be assessed in view of the circumstances in each case. In *Leaf* v *International Galleries* (1950) the claimant bought a painting of Salisbury Cathedral described (innocently) by the seller as a genuine Constable. Five years later, the buyer discovered that it was nothing of the sort, and claimed the equitable remedy of rescission, but the court held that the delay had been too long.

These maxims (there are several others) mean that where a claimant's case relies on a rule of equity, rather than a rule of common law, that rule can only be applied if the maxims are satisfied – unlike common law rules which have no such limitations.

7.5.2 Equitable remedies

Equity substantially increased the number of remedies available to a wronged party. The following are the most important:

Injunction This orders the defendants to do or not to do something.

Specific performance This compels a party to fulfil a previous agreement.

Rectification This order alters the words of a document which does not express the true intentions of the parties to it.

Rescission This restores parties to a contract to the position they were in before the contract was signed.

Equitable remedies are discretionary. A claimant who wins the case is awarded the common law remedy of damages as of right, but the courts may choose whether or not to award equitable remedies. They are very much an addition to common law remedies, and usually only available if common law remedies are plainly inadequate.

Equitable principles have had their greatest impact in the development of the law of property and contract, and remain important in these areas today. The two best-known contributions come from property law, and are the developments of the law of trusts, and the basis of the rules which today govern mortgages. The creation of alternative remedies has also been extremely important.

Figure 7.1 Equitable remedies

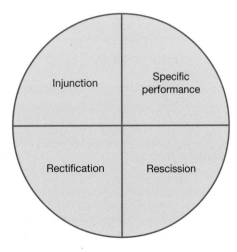

The Bigger Picture: Equity's future?

Equity has shown itself capable of adapting and expanding to meet new needs, and so creating law reform. During the 1950s and 1960s, it responded to increasing marital breakdown by stating that a deserted wife could acquire an equitable interest in the family home, providing an interim solution to a growing problem until legislation could be passed in the form of the Matrimonial Homes Act 1967. And in the 1970s, two important new remedies were created by extending the scope of injunctions: the Anton Piller order, by which the court can order defendants to allow their premises to be searched and relevant documents to be removed, and the Mareva injunction, a court order to a third party, such as a bank, to freeze the assets of a party to a dispute where there is a danger that they may be removed from the court's jurisdiction (by being taken out of the country, for example, and therefore made unavailable if damages were ordered by the court).

However, further attempts to extend equitable jurisdiction, notably in *Scandinavian Trading Tanker Co AB* v *Flota Petrolera Ecuatoriana* (1983) and *Sport International Bussum BV* v *Inter-Footwear Ltd* (1984), have been firmly resisted by the House of Lords.

The availability of discretionary remedies means that equity still fulfils the traditional function of supplementing the common law, providing just and practical remedies where the common law alone is not enough, but restricting itself to cases where those remedies are felt to be genuinely and justly deserved.

Answering questions

1   Critically analyse the role of equity – both historical and modern – in the English and Welsh legal system today.

2   To what extent does equity remain a separate source of law?

For answers to these questions, visit the companion website at www.pearsoned.co.uk/ elliottquinn

SUMMARY OF CHAPTER 7: EQUITY

Introduction

In law the term 'equity' refers to a specific set of legal principles, which add to those provided in the common law.

How equity began

By the thirteenth century the common law had become inflexible and, in order to obtain justice in specific cases, individuals petitioned the king who passed the cases to the Lord Chancellor to consider. By 1474, the Chancellor had begun to make decisions on the cases on his own authority, rather than as a substitute for the king. This was the beginning of the Court of Chancery.

Common law and equity

Tensions developed between the common law and the Court of Chancery. Matters came to a head in 1615 in **The Earl of Oxford's Case**, where conflicting judgments of the common law courts and the Court of Chancery were referred to the king for a decision; he advised that where there was conflict, equity should prevail. By the nineteenth century, equity had a developed case law and recognisable principles, and was no less rigid than the common law.

The Judicature Acts

The Judicature Acts of 1873–75 provided that there would no longer be separate courts administering equity and common law.

Equity today

Although equity and the common law are implemented by the same courts, the two branches of the law are separate. Where there is conflict, equity still prevails.

Equitable maxims

Equity developed maxims to ensure that decisions are morally fair. The following are some of them.

- 'He who comes to equity must come with clean hands.'
- 'He who seeks equity must do equity.'
- 'Delay defeats equity.'

Equitable remedies

The following are the most important equitable remedies, all of which are available at the discretion of the court.

- injunction;
- specific performance;
- rectification;
- rescission.

Reading list

Burrows, A. (2002) We do this at common law but that in equity. *Oxford Journal of Legal Studies*, 22: 1.

Millett, L. (2000) Modern equity: a means of escape. *Judicial Studies Board Journal*, 21.

Salter, M. and Doupe, M. (2006) Concealing the past? Questioning textbook interpretations of the history of equity and trusts. *Liverpool Law Review*, 22: 253.

Chapter 8
Treaties

This chapter discusses:

- treaties as an important source of international and national law; and

- the implementation of treaties.

8.1 Introduction

When the UK enters into treaties with other countries, it undertakes to implement domestic laws that are in accordance with the provisions of those treaties. For the purposes of the legal system, probably the most important treaties signed by the UK Government are those setting up and developing the European Union, and the European Convention on Human Rights (discussed on p. 377).

8.2 Implementation of treaties

In many countries, treaties automatically become part of domestic law when the country signs them. However, in the UK, the position is that signing treaties usually does not instantly make them law, so citizens cannot rely on them in proceedings brought in UK courts. Only when Parliament produces legislation to enact its treaty commitments do those commitments become law – the Taking of Hostages Act 1982 is an example of legislation incorporating the provisions of international treaties. Until such legislation is produced, individuals cannot usually take advantage of the protections envisaged by treaties.

However, there are some treaties which do not precisely follow this rule. Parts of the treaties setting up the European Communities are directly applicable in British courts, and can be relied on to create rights and duties just like an English statute (this subject is discussed in Chapter 5: European law).

The Bigger Picture: Treaties under a modern constitution

In 2008, the Minister of Justice published a White Paper looking at ways to improve the current constitution: *The Governance of Britain: Constitutional Renewal* (2008). The Constitutional Reform and Governance Act 2010 puts on a statutory footing the procedures followed for the ratification of a treaty. In essence, it provides for treaties to be ratified by following a negative resolution procedure (see p. 91). The relevant Government Minister has to lay a copy of the treaty before Parliament and 21 days have to pass without either of the parliamentary Houses resolving that the treaty should not be ratified. If either House resolves that the treaty should not be ratified, a further condition is triggered requiring the Secretary of State to lay a statement before Parliament explaining why he or she is of the opinion that the treaty should nevertheless be ratified. Should it be the House of Commons that has resolved that the treaty should not be ratified, the Minister has to wait a further 21 days after the above statement has been laid, and the treaty cannot be ratified if the Commons again resolves to oppose it within that period. In exceptional circumstances, these procedures do not have to be followed.

Answering questions

1   In what way can treaties be said to be a source of law?

For the answer to this question, visit the companion website at www.pearsoned.co.uk/ elliottquinn

On the internet

The European Convention on Human Rights is available on the website of the European Court of Human Rights at:

http://www.echr.coe.int/Documents/Convention_ENG.pdf

8

TREATIES

Chapter 9
Law reform

This chapter discusses:

- judicial and parliamentary law reform in practice;

- the impetus for law reform from pressure groups, political parties, the civil service, treaty obligations, public opinion and media pressure;

- the different agencies that have been set up to consider the need for reform in areas referred to them by the Government, including the Law Commission, Royal Commissions and public inquiries; and

- the success of these agencies of law reform.

9.1 Introduction

An effective legal system cannot stand still. Both legal procedures and the law itself must adapt to social change if they are to retain the respect of at least most of society, without which they cannot survive. Many laws which were made even as short a time ago as the nineteenth century simply do not fit the way we see society today – until the early part of the twentieth century, for example, married women were legally considered the property of their husbands, while, not much earlier, employees could be imprisoned for breaking their employment contracts.

Most legislation in this country stands until it is repealed – the fact that it may be completely out of date does not mean it technically ceases to apply. The offences of challenging to fight, eavesdropping and being a common scold for example, which long ago dropped out of use, nevertheless remained on the statute book until they were abolished by the Criminal Law Act 1967. In practice, of course, many such provisions simply cease to be used, but where it becomes clear that the law may be out of step with social conditions, or simply ineffective, change can be brought about in a range of ways.

9.2 Judicial change

Case law can bring about some reform – a notable example was the decision in **R v R** (1991), in which the House of Lords declared that a husband who has sexual intercourse with his wife without her consent may be guilty of rape. Before this decision, the law on rape within marriage was based on an assertion by the eighteenth-century jurist Sir Matthew Hale, that 'by marrying a man, a woman consents to sexual intercourse with him, and may not retract that consent'. This position had been found offensive for many years before **R v R**. In 1976, Parliament considered it during a debate on the Sexual Offences Act, but decided not to make changes at that time, and it was not until 1991 that the Court of Appeal and then the House of Lords held that rape within marriage should be considered an offence.

Lord Keith stated that Hale's assertion reflected the status of women within marriage in his time, but since then both the status of women and the marriage relationship had completely changed. The modern view of husband and wife as equal partners meant that a wife could no longer be considered to have given irrevocable consent to sex with her husband; the common law was capable of evolving to reflect such changes in society, and it was the duty of the court to help it do so.

Sometimes individuals try to force a change in the law by bringing a case to court. Debbie Purdy suffered from multiple sclerosis. When her condition deteriorated, she wanted her husband to be able to assist her to commit suicide without facing the risk of prosecution for the offence of assisting suicide. She successfully brought legal proceedings to force the Director of Public Prosecutions to publish guidelines on when he would prosecute for this offence – **R (on the application of Purdy) v Director of Public Prosecutions** (2009).

In practice, however, major reforms like this are rarely produced by the courts, and would not be adequate as the sole agency of reform. Norman Marsh's article 'Law reform in the United Kingdom' (1971) puts forward a number of reasons for this.

1   First, as we saw in the chapter on case law, there is no systematic, state-funded process for bringing points of law in need of reform to the higher courts. The courts can only deal with such points as they arise in the cases before them, and this depends on the

parties involved having sufficient finance, determination and interest to take their case up through the courts. Consequently, judge-made reform proceeds not on the basis of which areas of law need changes most, but on a haphazard presentation of cases.

2   Secondly, judges have to decide cases on the basis of the way the issues are presented to them by the parties concerned. They cannot commission research, or consult with interested bodies to find out the possible effects of a decision on individuals and organisations other than those in the case before them – yet their decision will apply to future cases.

3   Thirdly, judges have to recognise the doctrine of precedent, and for much of the time this prohibits any really radical reforms.

4   Marsh's fourth point is that reforming decisions by judges have the potential to be unjust to the losing party. Law reforms made by Parliament are prospective – they come into force on a specified date, and we are not usually expected to abide by them until after that date. Judicial decisions, on the other hand, are retrospective, affecting something that happened before the judges decided what the law was. The more reformatory such a decision is, the less the likelihood that the losing party could have abided by the law, even if they wanted to.

5   Finally, Marsh argues, judges are not elected, and therefore feel they should not make decisions which change the law in areas of great social or moral controversy. They themselves impose limits on their ability to make major changes and will often point out to Parliament the need for it to make reforms, as happened in the ***Bland*** case concerning the Hillsborough stadium disaster victim (see p. 32).

9.3 Reform by Parliament

The majority of law reform is therefore carried out by Parliament. It is done in four ways:

- **Repeal** of old and/or obsolete laws.

- **Creation** of completely new law, or adaptation of existing provisions, to meet new needs. The creation of the offence of insider dealing (where company officials make money by using information gained by virtue of a privileged position) in the Companies Act 1980 was a response to public concern about 'sharp practice' in the City.

- **Consolidation.** When a new statute is created, problems with it may become apparent over time, in which case further legislation may be enacted to amend it. Consolidation brings together successive statutes on a particular subject and puts them into one statute. For example, the legislation in relation to companies was consolidated in 1985.

- **Codification.** Where a particular area of the law has developed over time to produce a large body of both case law and statute, a new statute may be created to bring together all the rules on that subject (case law and statute) in one place. That statute then becomes the starting point for cases concerning that area of the law, and case law, in time, builds up around it. The Criminal Attempts Act 1981 and the Police and Criminal Evidence Act 1984 are examples of codifying statutes. Codification is thought to be most suitable for areas of law where the principles are well worked out; areas that are still developing, such as tort, are less suitable for codifying.

Figure 9.1 Reforming legislation

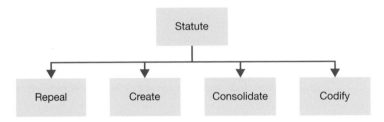

These types of reform often happen together – the Public Order Act 1986, for example, created new public order offences designed to deal with specific problems of the time, such as football hooliganism and, at the same time, repealed out-of-date public order offences.

Some significant law reforms have come about as a result of Private Members' Bills (see p. 51) – an example is the Abortion Act 1967 which resulted from a Private Members' Bill put forward by David Steel. A well-publicised Private Members' Bill came in 2018 which was introduced by Gina Martin in relation to upskirting. Upskirting refers to the instance where a person takes a picture up someone's skirt without their consent. There is a big market for such pictures on certain websites. Gina was attending a music festival in Hyde Park when she observed two men who were standing close to her and looking at a picture on a phone. She became quickly aware that they were looking at a picture of a girl's crotch and she realised that they had managed to take a picture up her skirt in between her legs. She then managed to take the phone from the men and ran to show security. When the police arrived, Gina says that the police asked the man whose phone it was to delete it, which he did. No criminal charges were brought against the man who had taken this photo.

Gina felt completely unsupported and turned to social media, posting a status update on Facebook and Twitter with a picture of the men who had taken the upskirt picture in the background. Gina wanted to expose these men and establish their identities through the help of social media. The posts went viral and sparked considerable public debate, with a number of other women sharing similar experiences with Gina. It was then that Gina felt that this was a bigger issue that needed more attention and identified law that requires reform. To start with, Gina set up the campaign #StopSkirtingTheIssue.

Presently we have section 67 on voyeurism in the Sexual Offences Act 2003, which does not consider upskirting a sexual offence. The trouble with s. 67 is that the offence covered by it turns on whether the alleged offender has without consent witnessed a person doing a private act for sexual gratification. Upskirting is also usually an incident that takes place in a public as opposed to a private place. Gina was not engaged in a private act and it is not clear whether the photo was taken for the purposes of sexual gratification and so charges could not be brought under this section. By contrast, Scotland has already amended its Sexual Offences Act to include the offence of upskirting, and section 9(4) of the Scottish Act states that:

9 Voyeurism

1   A person ("A") commits an offence, to be known as the offence of voyeurism, if A does any of the things mentioned in subsections (2) to (5) . . .

4   The third thing is that A—

(a) without another person ("B") consenting, and

(b) without any reasonable belief that B consents,

records B doing a private act with the intention that A or another person ("C"), for a purpose mentioned in subsection (7), will look at an image of B doing the act.

By contrast s. 67 of the Sexual Offences Act 2003 for England and Wales states:

67 Voyeurism

1   A person commits an offence if—

   (a) for the purpose of obtaining sexual gratification, he observes another person doing a private act, and

   (b) he knows that the other person does not consent to being observed for his sexual gratification.

2   A person commits an offence if—

   (a) he operates equipment with the intention of enabling another person to observe, for the purpose of obtaining sexual gratification, a third person (B) doing a private act, and

   (b) he knows that B does not consent to his operating equipment with that intention.

A frustrated Gina Martin then initiated a Private Members' Bill which garnered much publicity but upon its second reading it was blocked by one MP, Sir Christopher Chope. He objected to the Bill on principle because it was not debated. The Government of the day has since shown considerable support for making upskirting an offence and the Private Members' Bill has now been superseded by the Government's Voyeurism (Offences) (No.2) Bill which at the time of writing is scheduled for its second reading. This latest Bill will see upskirting become a criminal offence by looking to capture instances where the purpose of an act is to obtain sexual gratification or cause humiliation, distress or alarm. The offence will carry with it up to two years' imprisonment. (See p. 51 for the process of creating a Bill.)

What we can see from this incident is the speed at which reform can take place, the power of social media, the impact of a Private Members' Bill and the need for the law to be responsive to modern day problems.

9.4 Pressures for reform

The inspiration for reform may come from a variety of sources, alone or in combination. As well as encouraging Parliament to consider particular issues in the first place, they may have an influence during the consultation stage of legislation.

9.4.1 Pressure groups

Groups concerned with particular subjects may press for law reform in those areas – examples include charities such as Shelter, Age UK and the Child Poverty Action Group; professional organisations such as the Law Society and the British Medical Association; and business representatives such as the Confederation of British Industry. JUSTICE is a pressure group specifically concerned with promoting law reform in general.

Pressure groups use a variety of tactics, including lobbying MPs, gaining as much publicity as possible for their cause, organising petitions, and encouraging people to write to their own MP and/or relevant Ministers. Some groups are more effective than others: size obviously helps, but sheer persistence and a knack for grabbing headlines can be just as productive – the anti-porn campaigner Mary Whitehouse almost single-handedly pressurised the Government to create the Protection of Children Act 1978, which sought to prevent child pornography. The amount of power wielded by the members of a pressure group is

9

LAW REFORM

also extremely important – organisations involved with big business tend to be particularly effective in influencing legislation, and there is a growing industry set up purely to help them lobby effectively, for a price. On the other hand, pressure groups made up of ordinary individuals can be very successful, particularly if the issue on which they are campaigning is one which stirs up strong emotion in the general public. An example was the Snowdrop Petition, organised after the shooting of 16 young children and their teacher in Dunblane, Scotland. Despite enormous opposition from shooting clubs, it managed to persuade the then Government to ban most types of handguns.

Quite apart from the established pressure groups a new wave of pressure has found its form through social media and the use of hashtags in particular. A prominent global and infamous example is the #MeToo movement. It is incredible how social media has proven its prowess on a global stage, producing a phenomenal domino effect in helping females who have been subject to sexual assault and/or harassment come forward and discuss their experience. The movement is based on a desire to find a public presence for females opening up about their experiences and having them acknowledged. The point about this movement is not that such victims have not had a voice to talk about this but rather that they have not had the listeners who would believe them about their experiences. This in turn meant that there had been no accountability for their unfortunate experiences. They have decided to use their voice in a different way, namely through social media to unveil the magnitude of the problem. Facebook, Twitter and Instagram have been inundated with #MeToo at a pace that has astounded some but not others who have felt that finally such behaviour is being uncovered and social media has allowed them to display the true scale of the problem. The hashtag has, to use a modern phrase, gone viral.

Photo 9.1 #MeToo protest

Source: © Sundry Photography/Shutterstock

The phrase 'Me Too' was first put forward by Tarana Burke who founded an activist group and this phrase was then converted into a hashtag by American actress Alyssa Milano in the wake of allegations against the Hollywood film producer Harvey Weinstein that he had sexually assaulted, abused, harassed and/or raped dozens of women over nearly 30 years. Some have claimed that when they spoke up they were given a financial settlement in return for their silence. Others have said that their complaints were not taken seriously whilst others were not able to talk about their experiences at that time. It is claimed that Harvey Weinstein's 'casting couch' practices would require young actresses who were auditioning to engage in sexual acts on the promise that they would effectively get ahead in the industry and have a career boost. The claims against Weinstein appear to be the tip of an iceberg. Through the use of #MeToo on social media, the movement has given women across the world the confidence to speak out about their experience of sexual harassment and/or misconduct in their place of work, whether they are prominent in their industry or not. Law firms are not immune either. Bill Voge, the global chairman of Latham & Watkin stepped down after admitting that he made inappropriate sexual communications. It was reported that the communications were made with someone outside of the firm. It would appear that women are starting to lose the apprehension surrounding their experience and gaining solidarity in looking for justice and accountability for what they have had to endure.

It would seem that #MeToo has effectively reached a critical mass as a movement. Famous women finding the courage to discuss their experiences are giving confidence to other women to talk about their experience, creating a domino effect which is impacting on the public's understanding of such experiences. This confidence has spread into other areas such as the victims of the UK police spying scandal in which it is alleged that undercover police officers deceived, abused and manipulated their position of trust. One such recent claim in relation to this scandal was brought by Kate Wilson against a police officer Mark Kennedy whom was undercover unbeknown to Kate and engaged in a sexual relationship with her to the knowledge of his line manager (***Kate Wilson* v *(1) Commissioner Of Police of the Metropolis and (2) Association of Chief Police Officers*** (2016)). At the time of writing, this claim is being investigated by the Investigatory Powers Tribunal (IPT). Thus far, papers seen by the inquiry admit that it was known by Kennedy's managers that he was engaged in a relationship with Wilson whilst being undercover. Kennedy all the while, was married with children in his 'real' life. This case is pending before the IPT. Other similar claims have been made which the police have attempted to settle out of court. Settling out of court in this way minimises what information the police have to disclose compared with if these cases went to trial and were contested. Wilson however, according to media reports, is determined to unearth just how far this level of deceit goes in the policing institution and appears determined to demonstrate that there was complicity and widespread condonation of such behaviour. Unfortunately, this type of claim is not an isolated event. In fact, in 2015 a public inquiry called the Undercover Policing Inquiry was created and is currently headed up by Sir John Mitting for the purposes of investigating and reporting on the actions and behaviour of undercover police officers (see Chapter 18). It was in part spurred by the shocking revelation that a police spy had infiltrated the family of Stephen Lawrence. Whilst it should not be forgotten that there is a huge value to undercover policing in the prevention and detection of crime, there is however by its very nature a risk of an abuse of a position of trust and it is these occurrences that seem to attract more publicity rather than the prevention and detection of crime that undercover policing achieves. The review is set to be completed by December 2023 whereupon the final report will be delivered to the Home Secretary. There is large-scale criticism of the review in the media as it was due to complete in 2018 but the timescale has been pushed back to 2023.

The concerns about such a delay centre around the time that this will afford the police to 'cover up' such abuses of power and trust. Furthermore, there is a concern about whether Mitting is right for the job. He is white, male, from an upper/middle-class background and elderly (see Chapter 10). Questions are therefore raised as to whether he can empathise and relate sufficiently to the experiences of the victims that have suffered.

With all of the campaigns within this movement, whether it be #MeToo or Time's Up, the investigations have an immense and important social worth in bringing those responsible to account but how can the law help such women? Or indeed, is such social awakening enough without using the tools of the law? A critical feature of this movement has been that a large proportion of the claims that are levied relate to an event that took place many years ago. This of course does not make it any less deserving of attention but it creates layers of difficulty and expense. It is immensely expensive to finance legal actions of this nature. New mechanisms for financing legal actions like these have emerged such as CrowdJustice and The Justice and Equality Fund, which is a UK-wide fund set up in the wake of the #MeToo and Time's Up movement to offer a network of advice and support to those who have suffered sexual harassment at work. This is backed by many celebrities, with Emma Watson (who played Hermione in the Harry Potter films) donating £1 million, and support from many others such as Kiera Knightly (who played Elizabeth Swann in *Pirates of the Caribbean*). CrowdJustice operates in the same way as one would ask for sponsorship online but instead you are asking for pledges of money to fund your legal action. This opens up access to justice in a novel way (see Chapter 15). One of the first examples of CrowdJustice funding an action relates to the much publicised decision of the Parole Board of England and Wales to recommend that John Worboys be released for parole, in *The Queen on the application of DSD and NBV & Ors v The Parole Board of England and Wales & Ors and John Radford* (2018). Worboys, was convicted of 19 serious sexual offences which took place between 2006 and 2009 and was sentenced to an indeterminate sentence with a minimum term of eight years' imprisonment. It is thought that he sexually assaulted women since 2003, but victims have unsuccessfully brought claims against him. At any rate, after this period, Worboys was eligible to be considered for release. The Parole Board did indeed consider Worboys for release and satisfied itself that it was no longer necessary for Worboys to be held in prison. This decision was met with some upset and three sets of judicial review proceedings were instituted. One of the proceedings was bought by two of the victims of Worboys claiming that the Parole Board had acted *ultra vires* especially because it had not undertaken sufficient inquiry into his offending and the limited way in which Worboys described this in his parole hearing; namely, that he only admitted to offending for a period of around three years when he had in fact offended for a much longer period. The High Court quashed the decision of the Parole Board. This decision is important for two reasons. First, never previously had a judicial review been sought over such a decision other than by the parties to whom it relates, that is, Worboys or the Secretary of State. This action was brought by two of the victims after learning about Worboys' potential release in the media. Second, action for judicial review by the two victims was funded by CrowdJustice who helped finance the action and indeed protect the victims financially as they would have been eligible to pay costs if they lost in this action. In January 2018, this action had raised £66,278 from pledges by 2,549 people. It is remarkable that such publicity and support from the public has led to such a decision. The impact of social media on the law and the momentum of this social awakening cannot be underestimated.

As for the law, this movement is based on existing law around fundamental human rights which are enshrined in the Human Rights Act 1998, particularly on rights protected under s. 26 of the Equality Act 2010 which defines sexual harassment as:

Harassment

1   A person (A) harasses another (B) if—

   (a) A engages in unwanted conduct related to a relevant protected characteristic, and

   (b) the conduct has the purpose or effect of—

      (i)   violating B's dignity, or

      (ii) creating an intimidating, hostile, degrading, humiliating or offensive environment for B.

2   A also harasses B if—

   (a) A engages in unwanted conduct of a sexual nature, and

   (b) the conduct has the purpose or effect referred to in subsection (1)(b).

3   A also harasses B if—

   (a) A or another person engages in unwanted conduct of a sexual nature or that is related to gender reassignment or sex,

   (b) the conduct has the purpose or effect referred to in subsection (1)(b), and

   (c) because of B's rejection of or submission to the conduct, A treats B less favourably than A would treat B if B had not rejected or submitted to the conduct.

4   In deciding whether conduct has the effect referred to in subsection (1)(b), each of the following must be taken into account—

   (a) the perception of B;

   (b) the other circumstances of the case;

   (c) whether it is reasonable for the conduct to have that effect.

5   The relevant protected characteristics are—

   - age;
   - disability;
   - gender reassignment;
   - race;
   - religion or belief;
   - sex;
   - sexual orientation.

This is important as it covers a wide remit of conduct such as but not limited to, sexual comments, jokes, comments about someone's appearance, sexual advances, wolf whistles and groping. The key as with most of the law on harassment and bullying is the effect this has on the victim and that it is unwanted.

Then there is of course the possibility and risk, with the recent momentum and publicity of these campaigns, that innocent men might suffer – so caution must be heeded in the midst of such a big movement.

9

LAW REFORM

Whilst we may think that we have come far in relation to achieving equality, and in many respects we have, it is clear that we still have a long way to go especially in some of the more subtle forms of discriminatory behaviour that is condoned within the culture of many types of industry. A lot of the perpetrators, whether they are the employers or individuals, unfairly use non-disclosure agreements (also commonly known as NDAs), to pay off the alleged victims of sexual harassment so that they will not bring a claim and therefore not attract publicity of the nature that we are now seeing in the media. The trouble with these is that they are attractive to the victims in the sense that funding a claim is a costly business as has already been mentioned but on the other hand, we do not see the full application and therefore force of the law in these areas. There is nothing illegal about the use of such agreements but it does feel immoral and unethical on a number of levels. These agreements stifle the development of the law in these areas all too often. This is why the new mechanisms of funding legals actions, such as CrowdJustice and the Justice and Equality Fund, are so instrumental in the development and reform not necessarily of the law itself but rather the power and ability to use the existing law.

9.4.2 Clarity in the gig economy

A further pressure for development is sparked by our demands for the so-called 'gig-economy'. The gig economy has rapidly gained popularity but has the law been able to keep up with all the ramifications of this?

The gig economy can be described as a flexible pattern of work based around a worker's availability, dependent on technology, most notably an app, used to supplement an income where the worker can set their hours and days of work.

Photo 9.2 Food delivery courier working in the 'gig economy'

Source: © daisydaisy/123RF

The trouble with this type of work is the employment status of such workers. Whether they are an employee or whether they are self-employed has significant implications for their rights. Recognising the problems that this throws up, the Government commissioned an independent review of the gig economy which was conducted by Matthew Taylor, chief executive of the Royal Society of the Arts and called: *Good Work, The Taylor Review of Modern Working Practices*, published in July 2017. The work of the review was based on a single overriding ambition: all work in the UK economy should be fair and decent with realistic scope for development and fulfilment. In relation to the gig economy, the review states: 'Technology has facilitated new business models based around matching sellers and buyers of goods and services. This means that people can make money from assets that they own or their ability to do a certain type of work. The gig economy tends to refer to people using apps to sell their labour. Two of most well-known examples are Uber and Deliveroo . . . '

The review details that the Chartered Institute of Personnel and Development (CIPD) estimate there are approximately 1.3 million people (4 per cent of all in employment) working in the gig economy in the UK and that at least half are using it to top-up income from their regular employment. The research also suggests that the gig economy will continue to grow. This means that workers are potentially more vulnerable and could be taken advantage of when engaging in this sort of work, especially if there is uncertainty over their employment status.

The Government has since issued its response to the Taylor Review in early 2018, proclaiming that the UK will become one of the first countries to address the challenges of the changing world of work in the modern economy by giving millions of flexible workers new rights under major Government reforms. It is necessary for the UK to pay attention to this area to future-proof the economy and to protect businesses and workers whilst doing so. The problems presented by this flexible method of working can be seen from the series of cases that appear in Table 9.1 on the following pages, together with relevant commentary from the Taylor Review and the Government's response.

So, as the case list in relation to the gig economy grows, what does this mean for the law and how it should reform? A lot of this work is perceived as something one would do when they need to pick up extra work, work that is attractive as it is of low skill and perhaps work someone only does for a limited period. This type of work is very useful and fulfils an important economic and social function; many years ago this type of work could be found in the retail sector. There is a level of mutuality in these arrangements but there is then the danger of those undertaking the work being exploited. This is why it is so important for these workers to be classified as workers rather than independent contractors. The possibilities to reform this area of law could be: (a) do nothing; (b) do something for this particular sector, that is, the gig economy way of working flexibly; or (c) have a complete overhaul of our employment law. The Taylor Review cautiously recommends something close to option (b). In relation to digital platform sectors, that is, the gig economy sector, it recommends an intermediate category covering casual, independent relationships, with a more limited set of key employment rights applying. It states that greater clarity is needed on how to distinguish between employees and workers and therefore the category of workers should be replaced with 'dependent contractors'. It goes on to state: 'The status of "dependent contractor" should have a clearer definition which better reflects the reality of modern working arrangements, properly capturing those more casual employment relationships that are on the increase today – an individual who is not an employee, but neither are they genuinely self-employed'.

Table 9.1 Gig economy case law

Issue	Commentary	Impact and approach to reform
Uber London Limited ("ULL") v Transport for London ("TfL") (2018). The regulatory body The Public Carriage Office (PCO) (part of TfL) refused Uber London Ltd (ULL) its private hire vehicle operator's licence on the basis that it was not fit and proper to hold a licence due to its approach to: • reporting serious criminal offences; • how medical certificates are obtained; • how Enhanced Disclosure and Barring Service (DBS) checks are obtained; • explaining the use of Greyball in London – software that could be used to block regulatory bodies from gaining full access to the app and prevent officials from undertaking regulatory or law enforcement duties.	There was considerable social outcry at the thought of Uber exiting the private hire market in London and the thought of losing the convenience of travelling using the Uber app. Uber seized on its popularity and presence, as well as the reliance placed on it by society, to start a petition using Change.org to ask the public to put pressure on the PCO/TfL and the Mayor of London to reverse its decision. The judge remarked at paragraph 20: '[Uber] launched a public attack on the decision to refuse to renew the licence by launching a petition aimed at the Mayor of London. It was of concern that instead of accepting the blame it tried to whip up a public outcry whilst in fact ULL had brought the refusal of the renewal on itself.' Change.org said that this was one of the fastest growing petitions that they had seen in the UK for the year. When the petition closed, it had 858,203 supporters. This demonstrates how powerful online campaigning can be and how ordinary citizens can add pressure to a situation very quickly. The danger of using the public voice in this way is that it can quickly mask safety concerns such as sexual assaults taking place in taxis. In fact the highest number of sexual offences reported in 2016, which are the latest statistics available, show that Uber had the largest number of drivers against which a claim was made.	The interesting aspect of this case is Uber's disdain for TfL's regulation of the industry; almost treating itself as beyond the scope of regulation due to its huge popularity, Uber saw an opportunity to lobby the public and pressurise TfL through online petitions, which seem to be an increasingly popular approach to bringing about change. It would seem that Uber were focusing less on the legality of the decision and more on the unpopularity of the decision. Incidentally, Uber have been granted a 15-month as opposed to the usual five-year private hire vehicle operator's licence, having given assurances to TfL and demonstrated a change in their practices.

Issue	Commentary	Impact and approach to reform
Aslam v Uber BV and others (2016). This case centred around whether Uber drivers are self-employed or employed. Aslam and others argued that as Uber drivers, they should be classified as 'workers' rather than 'self-employed'. This classification is very significant as workers have more rights from the company that they work for by comparison to self-employed people. According to the Employment Rights Act 1996, s. 230 a worker is as follows: (3) In this Act "worker" (except in the phrases "shop worker" and "betting worker") means an individual who has entered into or works under (or, where the employment has ceased, worked under)— (a) a contract of employment, or (b) any other contract, whether express or implied and (if it is express) whether oral or in writing, whereby the individual undertakes to do or perform personally any work or services for another party to the contract whose status is not by virtue of the contract that of a client or customer of any profession or business undertaking carried on by the individual; and any reference to a worker's contract shall be construed accordingly. A worker is entitled to basic employment rights such as entitlement to minimum wage and paid annual leave.	Those who are self-employed do not benefit from employment law in general in the same way as employees do, as self-employed persons are their own boss. Employers often tend to describe the people that work for them as independent contractors as a way of formalising the relationship when in actual fact the relationship is one of employer and worker. Uber were well aware of this and the position is neatly summed up at paragraph 96 of the Employment Tribunal's judgment: '. . . the terms that Uber rely do not correspond with the reality of the relationship between the organisation and the drivers. . . as is often the case, the problem stems at least in part from the unequal bargaining positions of the contracting parties . . . Many Uber drivers (a substantial proportion of whom . . . do not speak English as their first language) will not be accustomed to reading and interpreting dense legal documents in impenetrable prose.' Uber have since appealed the decision to the Employment Appeal Tribunal but this was further dismissed and Uber then attempted to apply for a leapfrog appeal to the Supreme Court rather than appeal the decision to the Court of Appeal. The Supreme Court rejected this application for a leapfrog appeal and sent it back to the Court of Appeal where it should be considered. At the time of writing this appeal is pending. It is interesting though to remind ourselves of when the leapfrog procedure should be used (see Glossary). Supreme Court Practice Direction 3 on Applications for Permission to Appeal states that:	Predictably this case involving Uber has attracted a lot of publicity. However the publicity doesn't just surround the high profile of Uber but also the implications that this decision will have on the gig economy in general and how this decision will reverberate throughout businesses that rely on a similar business model as Uber. Moreover, this is a stark reminder that no matter how the employer might frame the relationship, the reality of the relationship will be examined to determine whether there is an employment relationship or whether the party working is indeed self-employed. The type of factors that are looked for in making this determination include: control, how integral the party is to the business, the ability to set charges for the service or product offered, the ability to negotiate and the level of freedom in determining the scope and pattern of work. Although this case is of immense significance given the way people choose to work using a digital platform, it is ironic that the judiciary has classified the drivers as workers whereas the Taylor Review is premised on the basis that those who work within the gig economy are essentially self-employed and use that freedom to design their working lives around the modern way of work. Having said that, the decisions thus far only help to support those who choose to work in the gig economy as they have better rights than they first thought. However, it is not clear how Uber or indeed any party operating a business within the gig economy, could continue to function on the basis that the parties they use to provide the service are workers. The sheer scale of the number of drivers that Uber has, which is about 40,000 in the UK, makes it unfathomable.

(continued)

9

LAW REFORM

Table 9.1 Gig economy case law (Continued)

Issue	Commentary	Impact and approach to reform
	Leapfrog appeals 3.6.1 In certain cases an appeal lies direct to the Supreme Court see paragraph 1.2.17 of Practice Direction 1. A certificate must first be obtained and the permission of the Supreme Court then given before the appeal may proceed. Such appeals are known as "leapfrog" appeals. Importantly, Part 3.6.12 of the Practice Direction goes on to say: In applications where the certificate has been granted by the judge under section 12(3)(a) of the 1969 Act, the Appeal Panel only grants permission to appeal where: there is an urgent need to obtain an authoritative interpretation by the Supreme Court; the case is one in which permission to appeal to the Supreme Court would have been granted if it had not been brought direct to the Supreme Court and the judgment had been that of the Court of Appeal; and it does not appear likely that any additional assistance could be derived from a judgment of the Court of Appeal. This case was not deemed to be of an urgent nature or one that the Court of Appeal would not have been able to provide assistance in understanding the nuances between worker and a self-employed worker. The decision in *Pimlico Plumber Ltd v Smith* (2018) which raises similar issues that has been heard in the Supreme Court really sets out clearly the position of workers in the gig economy. This is discussed next.	There is also the stigma that comes with being a big powerful business, and its perceived control or influence over the mere worker. Often the picture is painted that the business will not hesitate in taking advantage of the workers but in this case, the business model itself might be what makes it essential for a driver to be deemed self-employed. Furthermore, there is the societal pressure at work, which might also bring about a change in our perception of big businesses like Uber. Uber have appealed the decision to the Court of Appeal and it is currently set to be heard on 30 October 2018.

Issue	Commentary	Impact and approach to reform
Pimlico Plumbers v Smith (2018). This case raised similar issues to that of the case against Uber in relation to the status of the people that worked for Pimlico Plumbers. Were they self-employed, employed or workers? Pimlico Plumbers argued that such workers were self-employed.	The Supreme Court again looked at the characteristics of the work being performed. It was clear that the work was being performed personally, and personal performance of work is indicative of worker status. Assistance could of course be sought but essentially all jobs assigned were to be performed by the assignee. In this case there were a number of classic features which are looked for in determining the status and this is iterated at paragraph 48 of the judgment: > On the other hand, there were features of the contract which strongly militated against recognition of Pimlico as a client or customer of Mr Smith. Its tight control over him was reflected in its requirements that he should wear the branded Pimlico uniform; drive its branded van, to which Pimlico applied a tracker; carry its identity card; and closely follow the administrative instructions of its control room. The severe terms as to when and how much it was obliged to pay him, on which it relied, betrayed a grip on his economy inconsistent with his being a truly independent contractor. The contract made references to "wages", "gross misconduct" and "dismissal". Were these terms ill-considered lapses which shed light on its true nature? And then there was a suite of covenants restrictive of his working activities following termination.	Initially there was speculation that Uber's appeal would be joined to Pimlico Plumber's appeal as they raised the same issue in relation to the status of the parties that work for them. As it happens, Uber's appeal is yet to be heard. On the one hand this case affirms and injects further certainty into the law confirming what we know about how to distinguish a self-employed party. But it does not allow any room for accommodating modern business practices such as ones that use a digital platform. The Taylor Review in fact commended the strength of the economy and the levels of employment in the years that followed the financial downturn about 10 years ago. This was in part attributable to this flexible type of work that could be picked up. If this type of work is made more difficult and/or expensive to provide, it leads one to wonder whether such businesses can sustain themselves in the long-term.

9

LAW REFORM

(continued)

Table 9.1 Gig economy case law (Continued)

Issue	Commentary	Impact and approach to reform
Independent Workers' Union of Great Britain (IWGB) v RooFoods Limited T/A Deliveroo (2016). This case raises similar issues to the cases above. Deliveroo argued that its couriers are independent contractors, as opposed to workers, and therefore cannot avail themselves of benefits that are available to those who are deemed to be workers, particularly the benefit of having representation through a union, and that is why the case was brought by the Independent Workers' Union of Great Britain (IWGB) on behalf of Deliveroo couriers.	This case was initially heard in the Central Arbitration Committee (CAC). The reason why this case was heard in the CAC and not the Employment Appeal Tribunal is because the CAC is a specialist in trade union matters. The point that Deliveroo pressed upon was that its contracts set out extensively that its couriers can appoint a substitute to perform its work. This is what the matter turned on for the CAC. That was in November 2017. Since then, IWGB has turned to CrowdJustice to raise £50,000 to fund its legal challenge to the CAC's decision. At the time of writing, with three weeks to go, the fund had reached £31,410. The High Court has since granted permission for the IWGB to apply for judicial review of workers' rights as per Article 11 of the ECHR which protects the right to join a trade union.	Much attention was given to this case as it is one of the few decisions which favour the companies that rely on such a business model. This decision was seen as an important victory for these companies especially in light of the previous decisions which were decided in favour of the workers. The IWGB may have been able to apply for judicial review on the grounds of human rights but it does not change the fundamental point that the couriers were, and still are, classified as self-employed. This is a case which is also significant because it is bringing about important discussions in the Government and other leading forums about the status of such companies *vis-à-vis* their staff.

The Taylor Review further states that: 'In developing the test for the new "dependent contractor" status, control should be of greater importance, with less emphasis placed on the requirement to perform work personally.' This is in light of its earlier point in its report that as a first principle, the Government must make legislation clearer. The employment statuses should also be distinct and not open to as much interpretation as currently, nor be so ambiguous that only a court can fully understand the basic principles. In addition to this there are a number of reforms recommended by the Taylor Review and it would seem that reform in this area has to be undertaken sooner rather than later given the flurry of cases going through the courts. Moreover, with concerns over the economy in light of Brexit and a slight downturn in the economy, it is ever more important to ensure that greater mutuality can be established within the gig economy so that businesses can continue to operate on their business models but not to the disadvantage of their workers / dependent contractors.

9.4.3 Political parties

Some of the most high-profile legislation is that passed in order to implement the Government party's election manifesto, or its general ideology – examples include the privatisations of gas and water and the creation of the Poll Tax by the Conservative Government, which began in 1989.

9.4.4 The civil service

Although technically neutral, the civil service nevertheless has a great effect on legislation in general. It may not have party political goals, but various departments will have their own views as to what type of legislation enables them to achieve departmental goals most efficiently – which strategies might help the Home Office control the prison population, for example, or the Department of Health make the NHS more efficient. Ministers rely heavily on senior civil servants for advice and information on the issues of the day, and few would consistently turn down their suggestions.

9.4.5 Treaty obligations

The UK's obligations under the treaties establishing the EU and the European Convention on Human Rights both influence changes in British law.

9.4.6 Public opinion and media pressure

As well as taking part in campaigns organised by pressure groups, members of the public make their feelings known by writing to their MPs, to Ministers and to newspapers. This is most likely to lead to reform where the ruling party has a small majority. The media can also be a very powerful force for law reform, by highlighting issues of concern. In 1997, media pressure helped secure a judicial inquiry into the racially motivated killing of South London teenager Stephen Lawrence. The inquiry was authorised to look not only at the Lawrence case itself, but also at the general issue of how racially motivated killings are investigated.

Public opinion and media pressure interact; the media often claims to reflect public opinion, but can also whip it up. What appears to be a major epidemic of a particular crime may in fact be no more than a reflection of the fact that once one interesting example of it hits the news, newspapers and broadcasting organisations are more likely to report others. An example of this is the rash of stories during 1993 about parents going on holiday and leaving their children alone, which caught the headlines largely because of a popular film about just such a situation, *Home Alone*. Leaving children alone like this may have been common practice for years, or it may be something done by a tiny minority of parents, but the media's selection of stories gave the impression of a sudden epidemic of parental negligence. In 2000, there was a high-profile campaign by the *News of the World* to 'name and shame' paedophiles. The Government subsequently introduced a limited reform of the law.

The Bigger Picture: Reforming the law on abortion

A recent example of pressure for law reform is the current wave for change on abortion law in the UK. It is currently a criminal offence punishable by life imprisonment for a woman to terminate her pregnancy. The Offences Against the Person Act 1861, ss. 58 and 59 make it illegal to carry out an abortion. It is only legal to carry out an abortion pursuant to the Abortion Act 1967 with the involvement of doctors up until 24 weeks into the pregnancy. This is to say that should a woman attempt to undertake an abortion using pills in the privacy of her own home, at whatever stage of her pregnancy, she could be punished by life imprisonment. In 2017 the MP Diana Johnson successfully introduced a Bill called the Abortion (Foetus Protection) Bill. The first reading took

9

LAW REFORM

place on 5 July 2017, which marked the start of its journey through the House of Lords. If the Bill becomes an Act, it will see the decriminalisation of (non-doctor assisted) termination of unwanted pregnancies up until 12 weeks. This Bill has thus far courted a lot of public interest especially because many feel that women should have autonomy in making decisions about their lives and that the old law reflects a time when abortions were being carried out using unsafe practices by sometimes unqualified individuals. These were commonly referred to as backstreet abortions. This no longer reflects the state of affairs today. Even the British Medical Association has sought to influence the laws on abortion, arguing that its doctors should not face criminal sanctions for assisting in a termination of an unwanted pregnancy. Heightened public and media interest, as well as interest from the parties involved such as the British Medical Association, will no doubt maintain the momentum for reform in this area.

9.5 Agencies of law reform

Much law reform happens as a direct response to pressure from one or more of the above sources, but there are also a number of agencies set up to consider the need for reform in areas referred to them by the Government. Often problems are referred to them as a result of the kind of pressures listed above – the Royal Commission on Criminal Justice 1993 was set up as a result of public concern and media pressure about high-profile miscarriages of justice, such as the Birmingham Six and the Guildford Four.

9.5.1 The Law Commission

Established in 1965 (along with another for Scotland), the Law Commission is a permanent body, comprising five people drawn from the judiciary, the legal profession and legal academics. In practice, the chairman tends to be a High Court judge, and the other four members to include a QC experienced in criminal law, a solicitor with experience of land law and equity, and two legal academics. They are assisted by legally qualified civil servants.

Under the Law Commissions Act 1965, the Law Commission's task is to:

- codify the law;
- remove anomalies in the law;
- repeal obsolete and unnecessary legislation;
- consolidate the law; and
- simplify and modernise the law.

The Commission works on reform projects referred to it by the Lord Chancellor or a Government department, or on projects which the Commission itself has decided would be suitable for its consideration. At any one time the Commission will be engaged on between 20 and 30 projects of law reform.

A typical project will begin with a study of the area of law in question, and an attempt to identify its defects. Foreign legal systems will be examined to see how they deal with similar problems. The Commission normally publishes a consultation paper inviting comments on the subject. The consultation paper describes the present law and its shortcomings and sets out

Figure 9.2 Pressures for reform

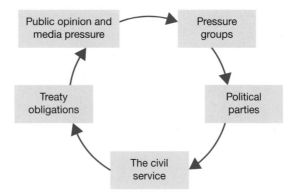

possible options for reform. The Commission's final recommendations are set out in a report which contains a draft Bill where legislation is proposed. It is then essentially for the Government to decide whether it accepts the recommendations and to introduce any necessary Bill in Parliament.

9.6 Royal Commissions

These are set up to study particular areas of law reform, usually as a result of criticism and concern about the relevant area. They are made up of a wide cross-section of people: most have some expertise in the area concerned, but usually only a minority are legally qualified. The Commissions are supposed to be independent and non-political.

A Royal Commission can commission research, and also take submissions from interested parties. It produces a final report detailing its recommendations, which the Government can then choose to act upon or not. Usually a majority of proposals are acted upon, sometimes in amended form.

Important Royal Commissions include the 1981 Royal Commission on Criminal Procedure, the Royal Commission on Criminal Justice, which reported in 1993, and the Royal Commission on Reform of the House of Lords, which reported in 2000.

9.6.1 Public inquiries

Where a particular problem or incident is causing social concern, the Government may set up a one-off, temporary committee to examine possible options for dealing with it. Major disasters, such as the Hillsborough football stadium disaster, the sinking of the ferry *Herald of Free Enterprise* and railway accidents; events such as the Brixton riots during the 1980s; and advances in technology, especially medical technology (such as the ability to fertilise human eggs outside the body and produce 'test tube babies') may all be investigated by bodies set up especially for the job. In recent years inquiries have been set up following the BSE crisis, the murder of Victoria Climbié (a young girl living away from her parents),

Photo 9.3 Brixton riots

Source: © Trinity Mirror/Mirrorpix/Alamy Stock Photo

and the conviction of the serial killer Harold Shipman. These inquiries usually comprise individuals who are independent of Government, often with expertise in the particular area. Academics are frequent choices, as are judges – Lord Scarman headed the inquiry into the Brixton riots and Lord Hutton (2004) headed the inquiry into the suicide of Dr David Kelly following the war in Iraq. The Leveson Inquiry was set up following the News International phone hacking scandal, where private phone calls of celebrities had been listened to by journalists employed by the *News of the World*.

Public inquiries consult interested groups, and attempt to discover the truth, conducting their investigation as far as possible in a non-political way. Unlike a court, an inquiry is not required to reach a decision in favour of one party or the other. Instead, a report is produced which states the facts as the inquiry finds them to be and puts forward recommendations as to how problems could be avoided in the future.

The Bigger Picture: The independent inquiry into child sexual abuse

In 2014, the Home Secretary announced that an independent inquiry into child sexual abuse would be established because of the growing evidence of organised child sexual abuse, conducted over many years, and institutional failures to protect children from this abuse. The inquiry is intended to be an overarching investigation into how state and non-state institutions handled their duty of care to protect children from sexual abuse; it will consider the extent to which any failings have since been addressed; and identify further action needed to address these failings. The institutions to be scrutinised include the police, the courts, the education system, the BBC and the NHS.

Initially the inquiry was going to be relatively informal with only limited powers, but following complaints by sex abuse victims and campaigners this is now a statutory inquiry established under the Inquiries Act 2005 with the power to compel witnesses to attend to give evidence in person and to order individuals and institutions to produce evidence. The inquiry will therefore have the powers it needs to penetrate deeply into the institutions that have failed children in the past, and to identify those institutions that are reportedly continuing to fail children today.

The first person to be appointed as the chair of the inquiry was Baroness Butler-Sloss who was a retired judge. Her selection was criticised as she was a member of the House of Lords and her brother, Lord Havers, was the Attorney General of England and Wales during the 1980s, so his conduct in the handling of sex abuse files could have fallen within the inquiry. She was therefore viewed by some victims of sex abuse as being part of the 'establishment' that the inquiry was being set up to look at. In 2011, she had carried out a review of sex abuse in the Church of England and had been criticised as being biased in favour of the Church. She therefore stood down. The corporate lawyer and Lord Mayor of London, Fiona Woolf, was appointed. But she lived in the same street and was an acquaintance of Lord Brittan, a former Home Secretary whose handling of sex abuse accusations would fall within the inquiry. As a result, she was not seen as sufficiently independent and she stood down. A High Court judge from New Zealand, Justice Dame Lowell Goddard was then appointed as the chair, but she resigned after a year in office. She had been criticised in the media for the number of days she had spent abroad, and she blamed a 'legacy of failure'. The current chair is Professor Alexis Jay, who has 30 years' experience in child protection and led the inquiry into child sexual exploitation and abuse in the town of Rotherham. The inquiry is expected to take three years to complete.

9.6.2 Other temporary inquiries

From time to time, various Government departments set up temporary projects to investigate specific areas of law. One of the most important examples is the inquiry by Lord Woolf into the Civil Justice System (p. 628).

Figure 9.3 Agencies of law reform

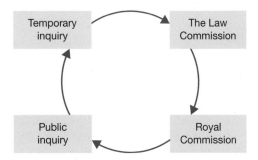

9.7 Performance of the law reform bodies

9.7.1 The Law Commission

One of the principal tasks of the Commission at its inception was codification, and this programme has not on the whole been a success. The Commission's programme was ambitious: in 1965 it announced that it would begin codifying family law, contract, landlord and tenant, and evidence. Attempts in the first three were abandoned – family in 1970, contract in 1973 and landlord and tenant in 1978. Evidence was never begun.

Zander (1988) suggests the reasons for the failure are 'a mixture of conservatism and a realisation on the part of draftsmen, legislators and even judges that [codification] simply did not fit the English style of lawmaking'. The draftsmen were not keen on the idea that codes would have to be drawn up in a broader manner than was normal for traditional statutes. Legislators were doubtful of the concept of a huge Bill which would attempt to state the law in a vast area such as landlord and tenant. The judges objected to the vision promoted by Lord Scarman, the Commission's first chairman, of the code coming down like an iron curtain making all pre-code law irrelevant. As Zander explains, this appeared to the judges like 'throwing the baby out with the bathwater – losing the priceless heritage of the past and wasting the fruits of legislation and litigation on numerous points which would still be relevant to interpret the new code'.

The Law Commission is particularly concerned with the Government's failure to codify the criminal law. Between 1968 and 1974 the Commission produced a series of working papers, but in 1980 announced that its shortage of resources would not allow it to continue, and appealed for help with the task. The Society of Public Teachers of Law responded, and set up a four-person committee, which by 1985 had produced a draft code. But this has never been legislated as law. In most countries criminal law is contained in a single code so that it is accessible to the people against whom it will be applied. The Commission has now embarked upon a programme to produce a series of draft Bills, based on the code but incorporating appropriate law reform proposals, which will in themselves make substantial improvements in the law. If enacted, these Bills will form a criminal code. But at the moment there is no tangible sign of progress in implementation of any of their major reports dating back to 1993. Decisions of the courts continue to draw attention to defects in the substantive law in areas on which they have already reported. One ray of hope has been the passing of legislation consolidating the sentencing regime, and further impetus for codification has been given by the review of criminal procedure under Lord Justice Auld (2001). In the Home Office White Paper, *Criminal Justice: the Way Ahead* (2001) it stated that it did intend to codify the criminal law as part of its modernisation process.

However, opinions are mixed on whether codification would prove to be of very great value even if it ever becomes possible. Supporters say it would provide accessibility, comprehensibility, consistency and certainty. A code allows people to see their rights and liabilities more clearly than a mixture of case law and separate statutes could, and should encourage judges and others who use it to look for and expect to find answers within it. Lord Hailsham has said that a good codification would save a great deal of judicial time and so reduce costs, and the academic Glanville Williams (1983) makes the point that criminal law is not like the law of procedure, meant for lawyers only, but is addressed to all classes of society, and so the greater accessibility and clarity of a code should be particularly welcomed in this area.

Critics say a very detailed codification could make the law too rigid, losing the flexibility of the common law. And if it were insufficiently detailed, as Zander (2004) points out, it would need to be interpreted by the courts, so creating a new body of case law around it, which would defeat the object of codification and make the law neither more accessible nor more certain. It may be that the Law Commission's failure to codify the law signifies a problem with codification, not with the Law Commission.

Instead of proceeding with large-scale codification, the Law Commission has chosen to clarify areas of law piece by piece, with the aim of eventual codification if possible. Family law in particular has been significantly reformed in this way, even if the results are, as Zander points out, a 'jumble of disconnected statutes rather than a spanking new code'.

As far as general law reform is concerned, as well as the major family law reforms, the Commission has radically changed contract law by recommending control of exclusion clauses which led to the passing of the Unfair Contract Terms Act 1977. Its report, *Criminal Law: Conspiracy and Criminal Law Reform* (1976), helped shape the Criminal Law Act 1977 and its working paper, *Offences Against Public Order* (1982), was instrumental in creating the Public Order Act 1986. Following its recommendations, the Computer Misuse Act 1990 introduced new criminal offences relating to the misuse of computers; and the Family Law Act 1996 changed the law on domestic violence and divorce.

In recent years, however, there has been a major problem with lack of implementation of Law Commission proposals. By 1999, 102 law reform reports had been implemented, which represented two-thirds of their final reports. There is a better chance of proposals from the Law Commission becoming legislation if the subject concerned comes within the remit of the Ministry of Justice; there is less chance if they concern other departments, particularly the Home Office. In any case, it has been pointed out that implementation of proposals is not the only benefit of a permanent law reform body. Stephen Cretney (1998), a legal academic who has been a Law Commissioner, suggests that one of its most important contributions has simply been getting law reform under discussion and examination, and drawing attention to the needs of various areas of law.

In its White Paper, *Governance of Britain: Constitutional Renewal* (2008), the Labour Government laid out plans to strengthen the Law Commission's role. The Law Commission Act 2009 has now been passed which places a statutory duty on the Lord Chancellor to report annually to Parliament on the Government's intentions regarding outstanding Law Commission recommendations. The 2009 Act has been supplemented by a protocol agreed between the Government and the Commission designed to ensure closer collaboration between the two. In 2008, the House of Lords introduced an accelerated procedure for legislating uncontroversial Law Commission recommendations. Parliament's annual report, published in 2013, on the progress of Law Commission reform proposals, noted that the new House of Lords procedure for Law Commission Bills is proving to be effective in implementing uncontroversial changes to the law.

9.7.2 Royal Commissions

These have had mixed success. The 1978 Royal Commission on Civil Liability and Compensation for Personal Injury produced a report that won neither public nor Government support, and few of its proposals were implemented.

The Royal Commission on Criminal Procedure had most of its recommendations implemented by the Police and Criminal Evidence Act 1984 (PACE), but subsequent criticisms of

PACE mean this is less of a success than it appears. The Royal Commission stated that the aim behind its proposals was to secure a balance between the rights of individuals suspected of crime, and the need to bring guilty people to justice. PACE has, however, been criticised by the police as leaning too far towards suspects' rights, and by civil liberties campaigners as not leaning far enough.

Perhaps the most successful Royal Commission in recent years has been the Royal Commission on Assizes and Quarter Sessions, which reported in 1969. Its proposals for the reorganisation of criminal courts were speedily implemented.

As regards the 1993 Royal Commission on Criminal Justice, this has met with mixed results. Some of its recommendations were introduced in the Criminal Justice and Public Order Act 1994 and the Criminal Appeal Act 1995, which created the Criminal Cases Review Commission (see p. 613) in response to the Commission's criticism of the criminal appeals system. On the other hand, the Government has ignored some of its proposals and has proceeded to introduce changes that the Royal Commission was specifically opposed to, for example the abolition of the right to silence.

9.7.3 Public inquiries and other temporary committees

These rely to a great extent on political will, and the best committees in the world may be ineffective if they propose changes that a Government dislikes. Lord Scarman's investigation into the Brixton riots is seen as a particularly effective public inquiry, getting to the root of the problem by going out to ask the people involved what caused it (his Lordship, then retired, shocked his previous colleagues by taking to the streets of Brixton and being shown on television chatting to residents and cuddling their babies). His

Photo 9.4 Stephen Lawrence

Source: © Handout/Getty Images

proposals produced some of the steps towards police accountability in PACE. But the subsequent inquiry into the case of Stephen Lawrence shows that the progress made was not sufficient. The Civil Justice Review was also instrumental in bringing about reform, though views on the success of the changes are mixed and the area has subsequently been tackled again by Lord Woolf.

Public inquiries are often set up after a major disaster or matter of controversy, where there is suspicion on the part of the community involved. For example, an inquiry was set up into the fire at Grenfell Tower.

Another inquiry was that concerning Harold Shipman, who was convicted of murdering a large number of his elderly patients. People demanding an inquiry are usually looking for an independent and open examination of the facts to determine what exactly happened and to prevent this happening again. In practice, public inquiries can put forward a large number of recommendations that the Government may appear to accept but then nothing is done to implement these recommendations, so that the risks of reoccurrence remain. For example, Dame Janet Smith's inquiry into the Shipman case made many recommendations that have not been acted upon.

Governments can refuse to hold a public inquiry which they feel may prove politically embarrassing. The parents of four soldiers killed in Iraq wanted there to be a public inquiry into whether the war in Iraq was illegal. The Labour Government refused to establish such an inquiry and the families sought a judicial review of this decision, arguing that they had a right to a public inquiry under Art. 2 of the European Convention on Human Rights which guarantees the right to life: *R (on the application of Gentle)* v *Prime Minister* (2008). Their application was rejected by the House of Lords, which held that Art. 2 could not restrict a nation's decision to go to war. Ultimately, the decision as to whether or not to hold a public inquiry is normally a political one, not a legal one. An exception to this is where there is a potential breach of the right to life and the right not to be subjected to torture, inhuman or degrading treatment where the European Convention imposes an obligation on the state to investigate. Following accusations of abuse by British soldiers of Iraqi prisoners, the Defence Minister had set up an internal inquiry. However, this inquiry was being carried out by a unit of the army which was itself implicated in the abuse. As a result, in *R (on the application of Mousa)* v *Secretary of State for Defence* (2011) the Court of Appeal held that this inquiry was inadequate to satisfy the Convention obligation and the Government Minister was instructed to look at the matter again.

The Bigger Picture: Streamlining public inquiries

The Labour Government was concerned by the inefficiency and cost of recent public inquiries. For example, the inquiry into Bloody Sunday in Ireland took twelve years and is reported to have cost £195 million. By contrast, Lord Hutton's inquiry into the death of Dr David Kelly cost £2.5 million and lasted six weeks. The Government decided to introduce legislation to improve the inquiry process, partly in an attempt to keep costs down. In 2004, a consultation paper was issued on the subject called *Effective Inquiries*. Following this consultation process, the Inquiries Act 2005 was passed. The stated aim of the legislation was to modernise procedures, control costs and give more effective powers to those chairing the inquiries. Despite this, the legislation has been criticised; Amnesty International has claimed that any inquiries established under this legislation would be a 'sham' and urged judges to refuse appointments to them. It is worried that the legislation fails to allow adequate public scrutiny and 'undermines the rule of law, the separation of powers and human rights protection'. The Act arguably gives too much power to the executive, as the executive will be able to decide whether or not to publish the final report of any inquiry, whether to exclude evidence if this is deemed 'in the public interest', and whether the inquiry, or part of it, will be held in public or private.

The first inquiry to be set up under this legislation looked at allegations of state collusion in the murder of Patrick Finucane, who was an outspoken human rights lawyer in Northern Ireland. Amnesty International was concerned that this inquiry was ineffective because of the limitations of the Inquiries Act 2005.

9.8 Problems with law reform agencies

9.8.1 Lack of power

There is no obligation for Government to consult the permanent law reform bodies, or to set up Royal Commissions or other committees when considering major law reforms. Mrs Thatcher set up no Royal Commissions during her terms of office, despite the fact that important and controversial legislation – such as that abolishing the Greater London Council – was being passed.

9.8.2 Political difficulties

Governments also have no obligation to follow recommendations, and perfectly well-thought-out proposals may be rejected on the grounds that they do not fit in with a Government's political position. An example was the recommendation of the Law Commission in 1978 that changes be made to the rule that interest is not payable on a contract debt unless the parties agreed otherwise. The idea was supported by the House of Lords in *President of India* v *La Pintada* (1984), but the Government was persuaded not to implement the proposals after lobbying from the Confederation of British Industry and consumer organisations.

Even where general suggestions for areas of new legislation are implemented, the detailed proposals may be radically altered. The recommendations of law reform agencies may act as justification for introducing new legislation yet, as Zander (2004) points out, often when the Bill is published it becomes clear that the carefully constructed proposal put together by the law reform agency 'has been unstitched and a new and different package has been constructed'.

9.8.3 Lack of influence on results

Where proposals are implemented, ideas that are effective in themselves may be weakened if they are insufficiently funded when put into practice – a matter on which law reform bodies can have little or no influence. The 1981 Royal Commission on Criminal Procedure's recommendations were largely implemented in the Police and Criminal Evidence Act 1984, and one of them was that suspects questioned in a police station should have the right to free legal advice, leading to the setting up of the duty solicitor scheme. While the idea of the scheme was seen as a good one, underfunding has brought it close to collapse, and meant that in practice relatively small numbers of suspects actually get advice from qualified, experienced solicitors within a reasonable waiting time. This has clearly frustrated the aims of the Royal Commission's recommendation.

9.8.4 Too much compromise

Royal Commissions and temporary committees have the advantage of drawing members from wide backgrounds, with a good spread of experience and expertise. However, in some cases this can result in proposals that try too hard to represent a compromise. The result can be a lack of political support and little chance of implementation. It is generally agreed that this was the problem with the Pearson Report, the report of the Royal Commission on Civil Liability and Compensation for Personal Injury.

9.8.5 Influence of the legal profession

Where temporary law reform committees have a high proportion of non-lawyers, the result can be more innovative, imaginative ideas than might come from legally trained people who, however open-minded, are within 'the system' and accustomed to seeing the problems in a particular framework. However, this benefit is heavily diluted by the fact that the strong influence of the legal profession on any type of reform can defeat such proposals even before they reach an official report.

An example was the suggestion of the Civil Justice Review in its consultation paper that the County Courts and High Court might merge, with some High Court judges being stationed in the provinces to deal with the more complex cases there. Despite a warm welcome from consumer groups and the National Association of Citizens Advice Bureaux, the proposals were effectively shot down by the outcry from senior judges who were concerned that their status and way of life might be adversely affected, and the Bar, which was worried that it might lose too much work to solicitors. In the event the proposal was not included in the final report.

9.8.6 Waste of expertise

Royal Commissions and temporary committees are disbanded after producing their report, and take no part in the rest of the law-making process. This is in many ways a waste of the expertise they have built up.

9.8.7 Lack of ministerial involvement

There is no single ministry responsible for law reform so that often no Minister makes it his or her priority.

Answering questions

1   To what extent is the English Law Commission effective?

2   Critically evaluate the agencies of law reform in England and Wales.

3   Despite the influence of, for example, pressure groups, public opinion and the media, numerous problems with law reform agencies have resulted in a lack of implementation of reform proposals, especially those advanced by the Law Commission. What factors have contributed towards this lack of implementation?

For answers to these questions, visit the companion website at www.pearsoned.co.uk/ elliottquinn

SUMMARY OF CHAPTER 9: LAW REFORM

The law needs to change to reflect the changes in society. Changes in the law can be made through the process of case law or by Parliament. The four ways in which Parliament can change the law are:

- repeal;
- creation;
- consolidation; and
- codification.

Pressures for reform

The inspiration for reform may come from a variety of sources, including:

- pressure groups;
- political parties;
- the civil service;
- treaty obligations; and
- public opinion and media pressure, particularly social media pressure.

Agencies of law reform

There are a number of agencies set up to consider the need for reform in areas referred to them by the Government. These agencies are:

- the Law Commission;
- Royal Commissions;
- public inquiries; and
- other temporary inquiries.

The level of success of these agencies has varied considerably. Governments have no obligation to follow their recommendations. Some of the recommendations involve too many compromises and, where lawyers dominate, the resulting reforms may be under-ambitious.

Reading list

Auld, Sir R. (2001) *Review of the Criminal Courts.* London: HMSO.

Cretney, S. (1998) *Law, Law Reform and the Family.* Oxford: Clarendon Press.

Halliday, J. (2001) *Making Punishment Work: Report of the Review of the Sentencing Framework for England and Wales.* London: Home Office.

Home Office (2001) *Criminal Justice: The Way Ahead.* Cm 5074. London: Stationery Office.

Hutton, Lord (2004) *Report of the Inquiry into the Circumstances Surrounding the Death of Dr David Kelly CMG.* London: Stationery Office.

Law Commission (1976) *Criminal Law: Report on Conspiracy and Criminal Law Reform.* London: HMSO.

(1982) *Offences against Public Order.* London: HMSO.

Marsh, N. (1971) Law reform in the United Kingdom: a new institutional approach. *William and Mary Law Review,* 13: 263.

Williams, G. (1983) *Textbook of Criminal Law.* London: Stevens and Sons.

Zander, M. (1988) *A Matter of Justice.* Oxford: Oxford University Press.

The Law-Making Process. London: Butterworths.

(2004) *The Law-Making Process.* London: Butterworths.

On the internet

The White Paper on constitutional reform. The governance of Britain: constitutional renewal (2008) is available on the website of gov.uk at:

https://www.gov.uk/government/publications/the-governance-of-britainconstitutional-renewal--9

The Law Commission's website is:

https://www.lawcom.gov.uk/

Rights Info website, article on Gina Martin case:

https://rightsinfo.org/gina-martin-upskirting/

Website of the Undercover Policing Inquiry:

https://www.ucpi.org.uk/

Guardian newspaper editorial on police spies:

https://www.theguardian.com/commentisfree/2018/sep/23/the-guardian-view-on-police-spies-victims-need-answers

Change.org Uber petition:

https://www.change.org/p/save-your-uber-in-london-saveyouruber

Link to report and judgment on *Uber London Limited* v *Transport for London*, 26 June 2018, Westminster Magistrates Court:

http://content.tfl.gov.uk/uber-licensing-appeal-final-judgment.pdf

Case Tracker for Civil Appeals – Case Reference: A2/2017/3467, Title: *Uber B.V. and ors* v *Aslam and ors*:

https://casetracker.justice.gov.uk/getDetail.do?case_id=20173467

Recorded crime figures for Taxi and Private Hire journey-related sexual offences are available on TfL's website at:

https://tfl.gov.uk/corporate/safety-and-security/security-on-the-network/tph-related-sexual-offences

Supreme Court Practice Direction 3: Applications for Permission to Appeal:

https://www.supremecourt.uk/procedures/practice-direction-03.html

UK Supreme Court Blog: New Judgment: *Pimlico Plumbers Ltd & Anor* v *Smith* [2018] UKSC 29:

http://ukscblog.com/new-judgment-pimlico-plumbers-ltd-anor-v-smith-2018-uksc-29/

Central Arbitration Committee (CAC) website:

https://www.gov.uk/government/organisations/central-arbitration-committee

CAC Report on *IWGB* v *Deliveroo*:

https://assets.publishing.service.gov.uk/government/uploads/system/uploads/attachment_data/file/663126/Acceptance_Decision.pdf

Part 2
People working in the legal system

This Part of the book looks at the different people involved in the English legal system. Some of these are in paid employment, such as the professional judges, barristers, solicitors and legal executives. Others are essentially unpaid and include jurors and magistrates.

Chapter 10
The judges

This chapter discusses:

- the role of the judges;
- the different types of judges, known as the 'judicial hierarchy';
- how judges are appointed and trained;
- the five ways in which a judge may cease to be a judge;
- the independence of the judiciary; and
- criticisms of the judiciary and options for reform.

10.1 The role of the judges

The judges play a central role under the British constitution. A basic principle of our constitution is known as the rule of law (discussed at p. 7). Under the rule of law judges are expected to deliver judgments in a completely impartial manner, applying the law strictly, without allowing any personal preferences to affect their decision-making.

The judges play a vital but sensitive role in controlling the exercise of power by the state. They do this in particular through the procedure of judicial review. The passing of the Human Rights Act 1998 significantly increased the powers of the judges to control the work of Parliament and the executive. A controversial judicial decision which highlights the tension between the roles of the judges, Parliament and the executive is *A and X and others* v *Secretary of State for the Home Department* (2004). Following fear over the increased risks of terrorism, Parliament had passed the Anti-Terrorism, Crime and Security Act 2001. This allowed the Government to detain in prison suspected terrorists without trial. The subsequent detention of nine foreign nationals was challenged through the courts and the House of Lords ruled that their detention was unlawful because it violated the Human Rights Act. As a result, the relevant provisions within the legislation were repealed.

10.2 Judicial hierarchy

The judges are at the centre of any legal system, as they sit in court and decide the cases. At the head of the judiciary is the President of the Courts of England and Wales. This position was created by the Constitutional Reform Act 2005. Before that Act was passed, the Lord Chancellor (a Government Minister) had been the head of the judiciary. The new President of the Courts of England and Wales (in practice the Lord Chief Justice, discussed below) is now the head of the judiciary, being officially the president of the Court of Appeal, the High Court, the Crown Court, the County Courts and the magistrates' courts. He or she is technically allowed to hear cases in any of these courts, though in practice he or she is only likely to choose to sit in the Court of Appeal. Under s. 7 of the Act, the President's role is to represent the views of the judiciary to Parliament and to Government Ministers. He or she is also responsible for the maintenance of appropriate arrangements for the welfare, training and guidance of the judiciary and for arranging where judges work and their workload.

The most senior judges are the 12 Justices of the Supreme Court. They sit in the Supreme Court and the Privy Council.

At the next level down, sitting in the Court of Appeal, are 39 judges (or full-time equivalent if some are part-time) known as Lords Justices of Appeal and Lady Justices of Appeal. The Criminal Division of the Court of Appeal is presided over by the Lord Chief Justice who, following the Constitutional Reform Act 2005, is also known as the President of the Courts of England and Wales (discussed above). He or she can at the same time act as the Head of Criminal Justice or appoint another Court of Appeal judge to take this role.

The Civil Division of the Court of Appeal is presided over by the Master of the Rolls. There is also a Head of Civil Justice and a Head of Family Justice.

In the High Court, there are 110 judges (or full-time equivalent if some are part-time). These judges are sometimes called puisne (pronounced 'puny') judges. As well as sitting in the High Court itself, they hear the most serious criminal cases in the Crown Court. Although – like judges in the Court of Appeal and the Supreme Court – High Court judges receive a knighthood, they are referred to as Mr or Mrs Justice Smith (or whatever their surname is), which is written as Smith J.

Table 10.1 The hierarchy of the judiciary

Judge	*Usual court*
Justice of the Supreme Court	Supreme Court and Privy Council
Lord Chief Justice	Criminal Division of the Court of Appeal
Master of the Rolls	Civil Division of the Court of Appeal
Lord Justice of Appeal	Court of Appeal
High Court judge	High Court and Crown Court
Circuit judge	County Court and Crown Court
District judge	County Court and High Court
District judge (magistrates' court)	Magistrates' court
Recorder	County Court and Crown Court

10

THE JUDGES

The next rank down concerns the circuit judges, who travel around the country, sitting in the County Court and also hearing the middle-ranking Crown Court cases. The Criminal Justice and Public Order Act 1994 added a further role, allowing them occasionally to sit in the Criminal Division of the Court of Appeal.

Figure 10.1 Court of Appeal: proportion of types of judges sitting on Court of Appeal cases, 2017

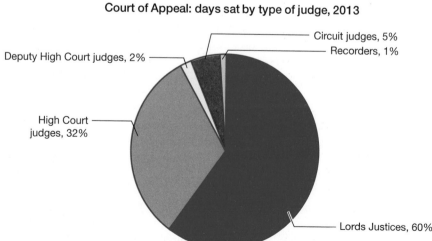

Court of Appeal: days sat by type of judge, 2013

Circuit judges, 5%
Recorders, 1%
Deputy High Court judges, 2%
High Court judges, 32%
Lords Justices, 60%

Source: Ministry of Justice, Civil Justice Statistics (quarterly) January – March 2018. Graph created from data contained in the Court Statistics, Table 5.2 'Royal Courts of Justice tables' (https://www.gov.uk/government/statistics/civil-justice-statistics-quarterly-january-to-march-2018)

The slightly less serious Crown Court criminal cases are heard by recorders, who are part-time judges. Recorders are usually still working as barristers or solicitors, and the role is often used as a kind of apprenticeship before becoming a circuit judge. Because of the number of minor cases coming before the Crown Court, there are now assistant recorders as well, and at times retired circuit judges have been called upon to help out. Finally, in larger cities there are district judges (magistrates' courts), who were previously known as stipendiary magistrates, and are full-time, legally qualified judges working in magistrates' courts.

In practice, there is some flexibility between the courts, so that judges sometimes sit in more senior courts than their status would suggest. This practice is illustrated in Figure 10.1.

10.3 Appointments to the judiciary

The way in which judges are appointed has been radically reformed by provisions in the Constitutional Reform Act 2005. In order to evaluate the new appointment procedures, it is useful to understand how judges were appointed before these reforms were introduced. We will therefore look first at the old procedures before looking at the new ones.

10.3.1 The old appointment procedures

Prior to the 2005 Act, the Lord Chancellor played a central role in the appointment of judges. The Lords of Appeal in Ordinary (the judges in the House of Lords) and the Lords Justices of Appeal were appointed by the Queen on the advice of the Prime Minister, who in turn was advised by the Lord Chancellor. High Court judges, circuit judges and recorders were appointed by the Queen on the advice of the Lord Chancellor.

Over the years there had been considerable criticism of the way in which judges were appointed and, as a result, changes had been made even before the more radical reforms of the 2005 Act. In the past only barristers could become senior judges. The Courts and Legal Services Act 1990 widened entry to the judiciary, reflecting the changes in rights of audience (see p. 218), and (at least in theory) opening up the higher reaches of the profession to solicitors as well as barristers. In 2009, Lord Justice Collins was the first solicitor to be appointed as a judge in the House of Lords (now the Supreme Court). The selection process for judges in the High Court involved the old Lord Chancellor's Department gathering information about potential candidates over a period of time by making informal inquiries (known as 'secret soundings') from leading barristers and judges.

The normal procedure for recruiting for a job is to place an advertisement in a newspaper and to allow people to apply. By contrast, until recently, there were no advertisements for judicial office: you simply waited to be invited to the post.

The three main criticisms of the old system of selecting judges were that it was dominated by politicians, secretive and discriminatory. On the first issue, the Lord Chancellor and the Prime Minister played central roles in this process but they were politicians and could be swayed by political factors in the selection of judges. The Lord Chancellor presented the Prime Minister with a shortlist of two or three names, listing them in the order of his or her own preference. Mrs Thatcher is known to have selected Lord Hailsham's second choice on one occasion.

On the second issue, the constitutional reform organisation Charter 88, among others, criticised the old selection process for being secretive and lacking clearly defined selection criteria. The process was handled by a small group of civil servants who, although they consulted widely with judges and senior barristers, nevertheless wielded a great deal of power. This process was considered to be unfair because it favoured people who had a good network of contacts, perhaps because of their school and family, rather than focusing on the individual's strength as a future judge. There was also a danger that too much reliance was placed on a collection of anecdotal reports from fellow lawyers, with candidates being given no opportunity to challenge damning things said about them.

Since 1999, the Law Society had refused to participate in the secret soundings process. The president of the Law Society described the system as having 'all the elements of an old boys' network', and being inconsistent with an open and objective recruitment process. 'We suspect we were being used to legitimise a system where other people's views were more important than ours. It didn't really matter what we thought, it was the views of the senior judiciary and the Bar which counted.' The Judicial Diversity Statistics 2018 note that just 3 per cent of Lord Justices of Appeal come from a non-barrister background.

As regards the third criticism, that the old appointments process was discriminatory, a 1997 study commissioned by the Association of Women Barristers is of interest. It found that there was a strong tendency for judges to recommend candidates from their own former chambers. The study looked at appointments to the High Court over a 10-year period (1986–96) and found that of the 104 judges appointed, 70 (67.3 per cent) came from a set of chambers which had at least one ex-member among the judges likely to be consulted. In addition, a strikingly high percentage of appointments came from the same handful of chambers: 28.8 per cent of new judges from chambers which represented 1.8 per cent of the total number of chambers in England and Wales. The fact that those who advised on appointments were already well established within the system could make it unlikely that they would encourage appointment from a wider base: Lord Bridge, the retired Law Lord, commented in a 1992 television programme that they tend to look for 'chaps like ourselves'. As Helena Kennedy QC (1992) has put it, 'the potential for cloning is overwhelming', and the outlook for potential female judges and those from the ethnic minorities not promising.

The process of 'secret soundings' gave real scope for discrimination, with lawyers instinctively falling back on gender and racial stereotypes in concluding whether someone was appropriate for judicial office. For example, individuals were asked whether they thought candidates showed 'decisiveness' and 'authority'. But these are very subjective concepts and as the judiciary is seen as a male profession, perceptions of judicial characteristics, such as 'authority', are also seen as male characteristics. 'Authority' is dependent more on what others think than on the person's own qualities. Indeed, research published by the Bar Council in 1992 concluded:

> It is unlikely that the judicial appointment system offers equal access to women or fair access to promotion to women judges . . . The system depends on patronage, being noticed and being known. (Holland and Spencer, 1992, para. 48(1))

However, in his book *The Judge,* Lord Devlin (1979) says that, while it would be good to open up the legal profession, so that it could get the very best candidates from all walks of life, the nature of the job means that judges will still be the same type of people whether they come from public schools and Oxbridge or not, namely those 'who do not seriously question the status quo'.

A report published in 2003 by the Commission for Judicial Appointments concluded that there was systemic bias in the way that the judiciary and the legal profession operated. This bias prevented women, ethnic minorities and solicitors from applying successfully for judicial office. The Commission was fundamentally unhappy with the appointment process for High Court judges and recommended that it should be stopped immediately because it was 'opaque, out-dated and not demonstrably based on merit'.

10.3.2 The current appointment procedures

The Labour Government published a consultation paper, *Constitutional Reform: a new way of appointing judges* (2003). While some improvements had been made in recent years to the appointment procedures, the Government concluded that:

> The most fundamental features of the system . . . remain rooted in the past. Incremental changes to the system can only achieve limited results, because the fundamental problem with the current system is that a Government minister, the Lord Chancellor, has sole responsibility for the appointments process and for making or recommending those appointments. However well this has worked in practice, this system no longer commands public confidence, and is increasingly hard to reconcile with the demands of the Human Rights Act.

The consultation paper considered the creation of three possible types of commission:

- an Appointing Commission;
- a Recommending Commission; and
- a Hybrid Commission.

An Appointing Commission would itself make the decision whom to appoint with no involvement of a Minister at any stage. This is similar to the arrangements that exist in some Continental European countries.

A Recommending Commission would make suggestions to a Minister as to whom he or she should appoint (or recommend that the Queen appoints). The final decision on whom to appoint would rest with the Minister.

A Hybrid Commission would act as an Appointing Commission in relation to the more junior appointments and as a Recommending Commission for the more senior appointments.

Ultimately, the Labour Government favoured the creation of a Recommending Commission, but an Appointing Commission would have more effectively removed Government interference in the judicial appointment process.

The Constitutional Reform Act 2005 was passed containing provisions for the establishment of a Judicial Appointments Commission (JAC) responsible for a new judicial appointments process. Its creation aimed to put an end to the breaches of the principle of the separation of powers and reinforce judicial independence. The pressure group Civil Liberties had concerns that the Judicial Appointments Commission was only an advisory panel, as the ultimate decision to appoint is still made by the Government Minister (or effectively the Prime Minister for Court of Appeal and Supreme Court judges).

Candidates must be selected on the basis of merit and be of good character. Part 2 of the Tribunals, Courts and Enforcement Act 2007 contains provisions to try to widen the pool of lawyers eligible to become judges. In the past, to be eligible for appointment as a judge a person needed to have experience as a judge in a more junior court or rights of audience in a court (which effectively limited judicial appointments to barristers and solicitors). If these professions were dominated by white men from an upper-middle class background, then the judiciary would inevitably share this profile. Under the 2007 Act, eligibility is no longer based on the number of years candidates have had rights of audience before a court, but instead on their number of years' post-qualification experience. The latter is a much broader concept but equally reflects a person's experience of the law. The required number of years' experience has been reduced from seven to five years and ten to seven years, depending on the seniority of the judicial office. In order to be considered for judicial office, a person must have a relevant qualification. Following the 2007 Act, the Lord Chancellor issued regulations stating that the qualification of a legal executive is sufficient for judicial appointment in the county courts, magistrates' courts and tribunals. As a larger proportion of legal executives are women (73 per cent of CILEx members in 2015), this will help to increase the number of female judges.

Government lawyers are now allowed to become judges. These lawyers include people employed in the Crown Prosecution Service, Serious Fraud Office and the Government Legal Service. They are able to sit as civil recorders (part-time judges), deputy district judges in the magistrates' court and as tribunal judges, provided their own department is not involved in the case. This is a major development, since such lawyers have a wide range of backgrounds, with women and ethnic minorities well represented, and the majority state-educated. Their recruitment as junior judges will hopefully make the profession at this level more representative of society, but it is not clear that there is any real justification for not making the more senior judicial posts open to these lawyers.

In performing its functions, the Judicial Appointments Commission must have regard to the need to encourage diversity in the range of persons available for selection (s. 64). The Crime and Courts Act 2013 (Schedule 13, Part 2) introduced a range of reforms to the appointment process to increase diversity and further reduce the role of the Lord Chancellor. Where two candidates are of equal merit, the Commission can appoint the candidate from a minority background to increase judicial diversity (known as positive discrimination). It is allowed to encourage people it believes should apply for judicial posts to apply. The Lord Chancellor is able to issue guidance which the Commission must have considered. This guidance can include directions on increasing diversity in the judiciary. Between 1 April 2017 and 31 March 2018, the Judicial Appointments Commission made three recommendations following the application of the equal merit provision (all of whom were women). They noted that for all other incidences during that period, candidates were not of equal merit.

The 2013 Act enabled judges to be appointed part-time for senior courts as well as lower courts, aiming to facilitate women with childcare responsibilities being able to hold this office. With regard to the composition of the Judicial Appointments Commission, the Act states that the number of Commissioners who are judicial office holders must not be greater than the number of non-judicial office holders. The aim is to reduce the risk of the Commission simply appointing more 'chaps like us', though there must always be at least one judicial member involved in the selection process. The Lord Chancellor's powers with regard to judicial appointments to positions below the High Court are transferred to the Lord Chief Justice and for tribunal judges to the Senior President of the Tribunals. Tribunal judges have not in the past been allowed to sit in the courts and their career path has been separate from the courts. The Crime and Courts Act 2013 provides for judges to work flexibly in different courts and tribunals of equivalent or lower status to respond efficiently to the needs of the legal system.

In the past, the final selection process consisted of a traditional job interview. For the appointment of most judges, this was replaced in 2003 with attendance at an assessment centre for a whole day. The centres require judicial applicants to sit through a panel interview, tackle questions on scenarios you may face as a judge, participate in role play and undertake a presentation. This is designed to offer applicants a fairer opportunity to demonstrate their knowledge and skills and thereby reduce the danger of subjective judgments and consequent discrimination. You can access some examples of the selection day tasks on the Commission's website (see Selection Process).

The Commission evaluates candidates and recommends, on the basis of merit, only one individual for each vacancy. The Lord Chief Justice appoints the judges below the position of High Court judge, while the Lord Chancellor retains the power to appoint the High Court and more senior judges. The Lord Chief Justice and the Lord Chancellor are not able to appoint someone who has not been recommended to them by the Commission. They, however, are able to ask for a candidate who is not initially recommended by the Commission to be reconsidered, and can refuse the appointment of someone recommended and ask for a new name to be put forward.

There is special provision for the appointment of the Lord Chief Justice, the heads of Division and the Lords Justices of Appeal (for the Court of Appeal).

Appointments of Lords Justices and above are formally made by the Queen on the advice of the Prime Minister, after the Commission has made a recommendation to the Minister. Provisions were contained in the Constitutional Reform and Governance Bill to remove the role of the Prime Minister altogether, but this reform was not included in the Act when it was passed in 2010.

The Judicial Appointments Commission is not involved in the appointment of judges to the Supreme Court. Instead, when there is a vacancy, the Lord Chancellor can convene a temporary selection commission. This temporary commission will have a minimum of five members, and will be chaired by the President of the Supreme Court. Its members must include at least one senior judge nominated by the President (who will not be a justice from the Supreme Court), one person without legal qualifications (a lay person) and one member of each of the three judicial appointing bodies of England and Wales, Scotland and Northern Ireland. The temporary commission will put forward the name of the recommended candidate to the Lord Chancellor, according to prescribed criteria. The Lord Chancellor is under a statutory duty to consult with the senior judges, the First Minister in Scotland, the First Minister in Wales, and the Secretary of State for Northern Ireland. If the Lord Chancellor is content with the recommendation, they will afterwards notify the name of the selected candidate to the Prime Minister who must recommend this candidate to the Queen for appointment.

The Law Society thinks that a choice of up to five gives too much scope for political interference, and considers that only one name should be put forward for each job vacancy.

In practice, appointments to the Supreme Court tend to be made from people with experience of being a judge in the Court of Appeal, although this is not a legal requirement. When a senior barrister, Jonathan Sumption QC, applied in 2010 to be appointed as a Justice of the Supreme Court, the Court of Appeal judges were very unhappy about this development. He withdrew his application and a judge from the Court of Appeal was appointed instead. His appointment was successful, however, the following year.

A Judicial Appointments and Conduct Ombudsman now oversees the recruitment process and has the power to investigate individual complaints about judicial appointments.

10.3.3 Judicial selection in other countries

In civil law systems, such as France, there is normally a career judiciary. Individuals opt to become judges at an early stage, and are specifically trained for the job, rather than becoming lawyers first as they do here. The judiciary is organised on a hierarchical basis, and judges start in junior posts, dealing with the least serious cases, and work up through the system as they gain experience. One drawback is that they can be viewed as part of the civil service, rather than as independent of Government.

In the US there are two basic methods of selection; appointment and election, although a compromise between the two methods is often made. All federal judges are appointed by the President, subject to confirmation by the Senate, which may include examining a prospective judge's character and past life, as the confirmation of Clarence Thomas, the judge accused of sexual harassment, did in the 1990s. In July 2018 the US President nominated Brett Kavanaugh to serve on the Supreme Court, but he was accused publicly of historic sexual assault by Christine Blasey Ford, a university professor (and later two other women). This led to both Kavanaugh and his accuser giving testimony to the Senate Judiciary Committee (livestreamed to the nation), before a hastily organised FBI investigation and then a Senate vote which saw Kavanaugh sworn into office. There were widespread protests at the way in which the allegations were dealt with, as well as the unprecedented mockery of Ford's account by the US President, Donald Trump, at a campaign rally. (For further discussion of the #MeToo movement, see Chapter 9.) Most state and local judges are elected, although genuine competition for a post is rare. In a number of states elections are used to confirm in office judges who have been in their posts for a limited period.

The Bill of Rights leads Americans to favour single-issue pressure groups which mount legal campaigns – most famously in the case of the 1954 decision to end racial segregation in schools – to achieve political aims. These groups realise the vital importance of the person who decides such cases and therefore spend a lot of time and money researching potential candidates to see whether their views fit and, if not, whether there is any damaging information which could be used to prevent their appointment. There are also associations which are interested simply in enhancing the reputation of the court, so that the American Bar Association, in particular, launches extensive inquiries of every nominee, involving hundreds of interviews with judges and academics, and commissioning studies of a candidate's opinions.

Although most US judicial nominations are confirmed, 20 per cent of nominees are rejected and, more importantly, Presidents are discouraged from proposing people who might fall at this hurdle. The knowledge that one will have to submit oneself to such public examination might affect the way in which judges behave earlier in their careers.

The Bigger Picture: Judicial appointments and Parliament

In 2008, the Minister for Justice published a White Paper looking at ways to improve the current constitution: *The Governance of Britain: Judicial Appointments* (2007), which considered whether selection should be subject to the advice and consent of Parliament to increase accountability if the role of Government Ministers was reduced. It concluded:

> To adopt such an approach in this country could lead to the strong perception that judicial appointments were being politicised, and such a perception could have an impact on confidence in the independence of the judiciary . . . [T]here would . . . be the risk that the decision to confirm or reject could be based on factors other than the candidate's ability to do the job effectively.

The consultation paper also pointed out that such a process would lead to delays, discourage some candidates from applying, use up scarce resources of parliamentary time and damage the status of the judges appointed because they could have been publicly criticised by Parliament during the appointment process.

Photo 10.1 Robes for male judges

Source: www.judiciary.gov.uk

10.4 Wigs and gowns

Traditionally judges have been required to wear a wig made of horse hair and a gown when sitting in court. The Labour Government became concerned that this tradition could make the judges appear old-fashioned to court users. Following a consultation process, it has been decided that from 2008 onwards judges hearing civil court cases are no longer required to wear a wig. Judges hearing criminal cases will continue to wear a wig because the wig provides a degree of anonymity for judges, so that they are less likely to be recognised by defendants or their associates outside court, and also an important element of dignity to the court proceedings.

10.5 Training

Although new judges have the benefit of many years' experience as barristers or solicitors, they traditionally received a surprisingly small amount of training for their new role, limited to a brief training period, organised by the Judicial College (before 2011 it was called the 'Judicial Studies Board'). In more recent years, this has been supplemented in several ways: the advent of the Children Act 1989 has meant that social workers, psychiatrists and paediatricians have shared their expertise with new judges, while concern about the perception of judges as racist, or at best racially unaware, has led to the introduction of training on race issues. The reforms to the civil justice system and the passing of the Human Rights Act 1998 also led to the provision of special training to prepare for those legal reforms. The Strategy of the Judicial College 2018–20 lists judicial training as having three elements:

- substantive law, evidence and procedure and other expertise;
- acquisition and improvement of judicial skills including any leadership and management skills;
- social context of judging.

On the last element, they note the importance of judges being able to relate to and communicate effectively with people from varied backgrounds 'with different capacities, needs and expectations'.

10.6 Pay

Judges are paid large salaries – £181,566 at High Court level – which are not subject to an annual vote in Parliament. The official justification for this is the need to attract an adequate supply of candidates of sufficient calibre for appointment to judicial office, and in fact some top barristers can earn more by staying in practice. One of the attractions for a barrister of becoming a judge is the security of a pensionable position after years of self-employment. While judges earn more than most in salaried employment, their earnings and pensions

Table 10.2 Judicial salaries (as of 1 April 2017)

Judge	Pay
Justices of the Supreme Court	£217,409
Lord Chief Justice of England and Wales	£252,079
Master of the Rolls	£225,091
Lord Justice of Appeal	£206,742
High Court judge	£181,566
Circuit judge	£134,841
District judge	£108,171
District judge (magistrates' court)	£108,171

Source: Ministry of Justice Judicial salaries from 1 April 2017

10

THE JUDGES

have reduced in value in real terms over the last five years. As a result, in 2015 a survey of all judges found that a third of them were considering retiring early as they felt underpaid, overworked and undervalued.

In January 2017 more than 200 judges took the Ministry of Justice to a tribunal hearing, alleging they were discriminated against because of their age. Younger judges were required by the Ministry to move to a new pension scheme while older judges could remain on the previous (more generous) scheme.

A major review was undertaken regarding judicial salaries by the Senior Salaries Review Body. A recommendation emerging in October 2018 that judges in the high court should see an increase of more than 30 per cent in their pay was not welcomed by other public sector workers, but has been promoted as the only way to beat the recruitment crisis. Days later the Lord Chancellor announced a 2 per cent pay rise for judges. Critics note that pay is only one element of the current dissatisfaction in judicial ranks (see later section on Morale).

10.7 Promotion

The traditional view has been that there is no system of promotion of judges, on the ground that holders of judicial office might allow their promotion prospects to affect their decision-making. In practice, judges are promoted from lower courts to higher courts. Potential recorders generally have to have proved themselves as assistant recorders; circuit judges as recorders. Those appointed to the High Court have usually served as a recorder or deputy High Court judge. The process is the same as for an initial judicial appointment, with the involvement of the Judicial Appointments Commission.

10.8 Termination of appointment

There are five ways in which a judge may leave office.

10.8.1 Dismissal

Judges of the High Court and above are covered by the Act of Settlement 1700, which provides that they may only be removed from office by the Queen on the petition of both Houses of Parliament. The machinery for dismissal has been used successfully only once, when in 1830 Sir Jonah Barrington, a judge of the High Court of Admiralty in Ireland, was charged with appropriating £922 to his own use. Proceedings against the judge were conducted in each House and each passed a resolution against the judge calling for his dismissal, which was then confirmed by the king. No judge has been removed by petition of Parliament during the twentieth or twenty-first centuries.

Under the Courts Act 1971, circuit judges and district judges can be dismissed by the Lord Chancellor, if the Lord Chief Justice agrees, for 'inability' or 'misbehaviour'. In fact this has occurred rarely since the passing of the Act: Judge Bruce Campbell (a circuit judge) was sacked in 1983 after being convicted of smuggling spirits, cigarettes and tobacco into England in his yacht; Judge Margaret Short was sacked in 2009 following complaints that she had been petulant and rude towards solicitors; Judge Constance Briscoe (a recorder and tribunal judge) was sacked in 2014 after being jailed for perverting the course of justice.

Judge Briscoe had, during a criminal investigation of a politician, provided police with two inaccurate statements, altered a witness statement, and sent a false document to an expert witness. In July 2016, part-time recorder Francis Evans QC was removed from judicial office for consuming alcohol during the day on court premises and defaulting on orders to pay child maintenance. The Judicial Conduct Investigations Office noted that the drinking 'created significant problems for the court staff assisting him'. Misbehaviour can include a conviction for drink-driving or any offence involving violence, dishonesty or moral turpitude. It would also include any behaviour likely to cause offence, particularly on religious or racial grounds or behaviour that amounted to sexual harassment. In 2015, three judges were sacked for viewing pornography on their office computers.

In dismissing a judge, s. 108(1) of the Constitutional Reform Act 2005 provides that the Lord Chancellor will have to comply with any procedures that have been laid down to regulate this process. Judges who have been sacked for breaching the judicial code of conduct will, since 2009, have their names and the reasons for their removals made public.

In addition to dismissal there is, of course, also the power not to reappoint those who have been appointed for a limited period only.

10.8.2 Discipline

In practice the mechanisms for disciplining judges who misbehave are more significant than those for dismissal, which is generally a last resort. There was concern in the past that there were no formal disciplinary procedures for judges. Over the years there had been a few judges whose conduct had been frequently criticised, but who had nevertheless remained on the Bench, and the lack of a formal machinery for complaints was seen as protecting incompetent judges. The pressure group JUSTICE had recommended the establishment of a formal disciplinary procedure in its report on the judiciary in 1972. The Constitutional Reform Act 2005 contains provision for the establishment of such procedures. The Act gives the Lord Chancellor and the Lord Chief Justice joint responsibility for judicial discipline. Section 108(3) states:

> The Lord Chief Justice may give a judicial office holder formal advice, or a formal warning or reprimand, for disciplinary purposes (but this section does not restrict what he may do informally or for other purposes or where any advice or warning is not addressed to a particular office holder).

The Office for Judicial Complaints (OJC) was set up in 2006 to handle complaints about judges and provide advice and assistance to the Lord Chancellor and Lord Chief Justice in the performance of their joint role in this context under the Constitutional Reform Act. In 2013 the Judicial Conduct and Investigations Office (JCIO) took over the responsibilities of the OJC. A complaint will be dismissed by the JCIO if it fails to meet the criteria set out in the judicial discipline regulations. If the case is not dismissed by that Office, the Lord Chancellor and the Lord Chief Justice will consider the evidence and decide what action, if any, is appropriate. In certain complex cases the matter may be referred to a senior judge for a judicial investigation. If the complaint is upheld the Lord Chief Justice and the Lord Chancellor may decide that disciplinary action is required.

A person can be suspended from judicial office for any period when they are subject to criminal proceedings, have been convicted, are serving a criminal sentence, are subject to disciplinary procedures or where it has been determined under prescribed procedures that a person should not be removed from office, but it appears to the Lord Chief Justice, with the agreement of the Lord Chancellor, that the suspension is necessary for maintaining public confidence in the judiciary.

The Judicial Appointments and Conduct Ombudsman is able to review the handling of complaints about judicial conduct.

The JCIO received 2,126 complaints about judicial office holders in the 2016–17 period, representing a significant reduction from the previous year, when complaints totalled 2,609. Of those, almost half related to the judicial decision itself or case management and were therefore dismissed because they were outside the scope of the complaint system. A minority of complaints led to disciplinary action and exceptionally to the judge being removed from office. In 2016–17 only 42 investigations resulted in disciplinary action being taken by the Lord Chancellor and Lord Chief Justice. In 2009, a Crown Court judge was suspended by the Office for Judicial Complaints pending its investigations into accusations published in the *News of the World* newspaper that he allowed a male prostitute with whom he was having a relationship to sit beside him on the bench, pretending that he was a law student. The investigation concluded that the judge's actions had brought the judiciary into disrepute and he subsequently resigned before the disciplinary process to remove him from office was completed. Investigations from 2017 include a circuit judge (Simon Newell) who got involved in a dispute with a local bar owner over his dog, a recorder of the Crown Court (Donald Peter Herbert OBE) who made inappropriate comments in a public speech and a magistrate (Ms June Wilson) who failed to report her own arrest and the separate conviction of a close family member. Several judges have been subject to investigation in 2018 over their delays in producing a judgment (His Honour John Hand QC and The Honourable Mr Justice Timothy King) and Judge Karen Holt was reprimanded for accessing confidential files in a case where her daughter was a witness.

As well as the formal procedures discussed above, judges may be criticised in Parliament, or rebuked in the appellate courts, and are often censured in the press. There may be complaints from barristers, solicitors or litigants, made either in court or in private to the judge personally.

10.8.3 Resignation

Serious misbehaviour has on occasion been dealt with not by dismissal, but by the Lord Chancellor suggesting to the judge that he or she should resign.

10.8.4 Retirement

Judges usually retire at 70, although they are sometimes allowed to work part-time up to the age of 75. There have been calls to permit judges to sit beyond the age of 70 to help ease the problem with judicial recruitment. Both Lord Neuberger, the past President of the Supreme Court, and Lady Hale, the current President, have called for the retirement age to be extended, particularly considering the significant number of fellow Justices due to retire in the next couple of years. Lady Hale has spoken of this as a great shame when 'they are at the height of their powers'. The advert for the role of Lord Chief Justice was controversial in February 2017 as it stipulated that the candidate must be able to serve for at least four years. Heavyweight candidates such as Sir Brian Leveson (68) and Lady Justice Hallett (67) were ineligible.

Figure 10.2 Termination of appointment

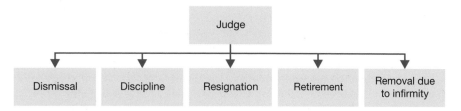

10.8.5 Removal due to infirmity

The Lord Chancellor has powers to remove a judge who is disabled by permanent infirmity from the performance of his or her duties and who is incapacitated from resigning his or her post.

10.9 Independence of the judiciary

In our legal system great importance is attached to the idea that judges should be independent and be seen to be independent. In addition to the common-sense view that they should be independent of pressure from the Government and political groups, and in order to decide cases impartially, judicial independence is required by the constitutional doctrine known as the separation of powers (discussed on p. 5).

In the past, the broad role of the Lord Chancellor was seen as both a threat to judicial independence and as the protector of judicial independence. He was a threat because he breached the doctrine of the separation of powers, but, at the same time, as the head of the judiciary he was responsible for defending judges from Government influence. When the Labour Government announced in 2003 that it planned to introduce major constitutional changes, including the abolition of the position of Lord Chancellor, this caused some concern among the judges. They were worried that, without the Lord Chancellor, there would be nobody with responsibility for protecting their independence, and that as a result their independence could be threatened. In response to these concerns, the Lord Chancellor signed an agreement with the senior judge, the Lord Chief Justice, known as the Concordat. This agreement provided that some of the key judicial functions of the Lord Chancellor would be handed to the Lord Chief Justice when the constitutional reforms were introduced and that key aspects of this agreement would be incorporated into the legislation, which was subsequently done. Following political negotiations, the post of Lord Chancellor was not actually abolished, though the role of the Lord Chancellor has significantly changed. With the changes in the role of the Lord Chancellor introduced by the Constitutional Reform Act 2005, the Government sought to reassure judges that their independence would still be guaranteed, by introducing a statutory guarantee of the independence of the judiciary. Section 3 states:

> The Lord Chancellor, other Ministers of the Crown and all with responsibility for matters relating to the judiciary or otherwise to the administration of justice must uphold the continued independence of the judiciary.

It also provides that:

> The Lord Chancellor and other Ministers for the Crown must not seek to influence a particular judicial decision through any special access to the judiciary.

10

THE JUDGES

The Bigger Picture

The role of the Lord Chancellor has become increasingly criticised since the role was given to non-lawyers – Grayling and Gove both coming in for critical shots, but it was Elizabeth Truss who really shocked.

Truss was seen by many to have failed in her statutory duty to protect the independence of the judiciary in the wake of the Article 50 case, *R (Miller and Dos Santos)* v *Secretary of State for Exiting the European Union* (2017) (see Chapter 5). Judges were subject to unprecedented personal attacks in the media, and also from politicians. Judges were branded 'Enemies of the people' on the front page of the *Daily Mail*.

A statement from Truss was not forthcoming until two days later. It said:

> The independence of the judiciary is the foundation upon which our rule of law is built and our judiciary is rightly respected the world over for its independence and impartiality.

Her tardiness to jump to the defence of the judiciary was widely condemned by the legal profession. Lord Judge (the former Lord Chief Justice) stated in an interview that Truss's response was 'a little too late – and quite a lot too little'. A letter from 17 QCs at One Crown Office Row had further reproof for Truss's 'inadequate defence':

> The judges have been publicly accused of bias and in effect of breaking their judicial oath. The accusations have come not only from the press but from MPs.

When Truss was unsurprisingly shunted from her role in a cabinet reshuffle (June 2017), David Lidington replaced her, carefully stating:

> I will be resolute and unflinching as Lord Chancellor in upholding the rule of law and defending the independence of the judiciary.

(For more on the media and freedom of expression see the 'Bigger Picture' section on p. 204.)

Other safeguards of judicial independence include the security of tenure given to judges, which ensures they cannot be removed at the whim of one of the other branches of power; the fact that their salaries are not subject to a parliamentary vote; and the rule that they cannot be sued for anything done while acting in their judicial capacity. Independence in decision-making is provided through the fact that judges are only accountable to higher judges in appellate courts.

Because the Lord Chancellor is, first and foremost, a politician, there is concern that if the Lord Chancellor is involved in selecting the judges then this could undermine his or her independence. The creation of the Judicial Appointments Commission in 2005 reduced the role of the Lord Chancellor in the selection process. The Crime and Courts Act 2013 has transferred to the Lord Chief Justice (a senior judge) some of these powers with regard to junior judicial appointments, but has strengthened the Lord Chancellor's role with regard to the appointment of more senior judges.

The importance of the independence of the judiciary can be seen, for example, in judicial review, where the courts can scrutinise the behaviour of the executive, and in some cases declare it illegal. However, there are problems with the idea of the judiciary being independent (see p. 193). Litigation that raises the question of judicial bias is discussed on p. 714.

10.10 Criticisms of the judiciary

10.10.1 Background, ethnic origin, sex and age

Judges are overwhelmingly white, male and middle to upper class, and frequently elderly, leading to accusations that they are unrepresentative of, and distanced from, the majority of society. According to research carried out by the Sutton Trust in 2016, 74 per cent of senior judges (High Court and Court of Appeal) attended Oxford or Cambridge University and 74 per cent attended private schools. This figure has barely changed – from 76 per cent in the late 1980s and 75 per cent in the 2000s. The appointments made by the Labour Government did not break the mould. The narrow background of the judges does mean that they can be frighteningly out of touch with the world in which they are working. Mr Justice Harman, who resigned in 1998, said in three different cases that he had not heard of the footballer Paul Gascoigne, the rock band Oasis and the singer Bruce Springsteen. In 2016 however Judge Patricia Lynch was hailed a legend and a hero after sentencing a defendant for racist abuse and finding herself on the receiving end of an expletive-ridden rant. She responded back: 'You are a bit of a c*** yourself. Being offensive to me does not help'.

In 2010 only 20 per cent of judges were women. There are eight women sitting as judges in the Court of Justice of the European Union. The first female judge was appointed to the House of Lords in 2004, Lady Justice Hale. She is now the President of the Supreme Court. Excitingly, she was joined by Lady Black and Lady Arden in 2018 and, on 3 October of that year, the UK's highest court heard their first case with a female majority. Only 24 per cent of Court of Appeal judges are women and 24 per cent of High Court judges are women. In 2006, the Equal Opportunities Commission warned that it would take 40 years for women to achieve equality in the senior judiciary. In October 2016 a report by the Council of Europe showed England and Wales as one of the systems with the lowest percentage of women among the judiciary (30 per cent) along with Azerbaijan (11 per cent), Armenia (23 per cent) Northern Ireland (23 per cent) Scotland (23 per cent) and Ireland (33 per cent). This compares to a Europe average of 51 per cent. According to the Judicial Diversity Statistics 2018, 7 per cent of the judiciary are from an ethnic minority, while for the High Court, just 3 per cent of judges are black, Asian and minority ethnic (BAME); there are however 14 per cent of deputy High Court judges who are BAME. By comparison, 14 per cent of the population of England and Wales comes from an ethnic minority. Lord Lane, the former Lord Chief Justice, said after his retirement that his regret at being forced off the bench was due, at least partly, to the fact that his colleagues were 'a jolly nice bunch of chaps'. This remark reinforces the view of many that the judiciary is actually a sort of rarefied gentlemen's club.

The age of the full-time judiciary has remained constant over many years with the average age of a judge being 58. With a retirement age of 70, judges are allowed to retire five years later than most other professions. Despite this, there was much sniping when it was confirmed that two of the front-runners for Supreme Court appointments opening up in 2017 (Leveson and Hallett LJ) would be ineligible, as their age would mean they would be unable to serve a full five-year term. This was a decision taken by the JAC selection panel following consultation with the Lord Chancellor. David Pannick (1987) has written in his book, *Judges*, that 'a judiciary composed predominantly of senior citizens cannot hope to apply contemporary standards or to understand contemporary concerns'.

Before the Courts and Legal Services Act 1990, judges were almost exclusively selected from practising barristers. Since it is difficult for anyone without a private income to survive the first years of practice, successful barristers have tended to come from reasonably well-to-do families, who are of course more likely to send their sons or daughters to public schools and then to Oxford or Cambridge. The background of the Bar is however gradually changing; the Judicial Appointments Commission reported that in the 2017–18 application period 66 per cent of applicants attended a state school, compared with 28 per cent from fee-paying schools and 6 per cent from overseas. The figures for those actually appointed differed only marginally: 62 per cent (state), 34 per cent (fee-paying) and 4 per cent (overseas). *The Times* reported in June 2018 that the seven new Court of Appeal judges included two judges who were first in their family to attend university or become lawyers, three of the new judges were women and one of these trained as a solicitor.

The Courts and Legal Services Act 1990 provided new opportunities for solicitors to join the judiciary, and the new right of Government lawyers to become junior judges will in time help to alter the traditional judicial background, since there are larger numbers of women, members of the ethnic minorities and those from less privileged backgrounds working as solicitors and Government lawyers than in the barrister's profession. Since April 2005 judges below High Court level are able to sit part-time, which should prove attractive to women combining work with childcare responsibilities.

Research has been carried out by Dame Hazel Genn into why senior lawyers are not seeking judicial office (*The attractiveness of senior judicial appointment to highly qualified practitioners* (2008)). Her research concluded that:

> Female solicitors who had reached partnership in magic circle firms, and who felt that their professional journey had been something of a struggle, were reluctant to begin again, and perhaps have to struggle to re-establish their credibility, in a world that they perceived to be even more antediluvian than City commercial law practice.

An important practical obstacle to attracting a wider range of people to become judges is the general requirement that individuals work at least three weeks a year as a part-time judge for a probationary period of at least two years before they are considered for a permanent position. This can be problematic for solicitors and single parents and reflects the flexibility of the barrister profession rather than other potential candidates. Hazel Genn's research identified this requirement to undertake part-time work as a particular obstacle for women solicitors. She noted:

> First, the time commitment might be more than their co-partners felt could be spared from the practice. Second, they would have to forego a significant amount of salary to compensate for the time out of practice. Third, they would have to work very hard to make up the time spent while sitting. Finally, they were concerned that taking a part-time judicial appointment might be interpreted by their partners as reflecting a lack of commitment to the practice.

This requirement to work part time before being considered for a permanent position could simply be abolished, as it does not exist for appointments to other senior professional positions.

With the arrival of the first solicitor Lord Chancellor, David Gauke, there is more focus than ever on promoting the judiciary as a future career path to this branch of the profession. The Chairman of the City of London Law Society, Edward Sparrow, has spoken about cherry-picking and fast-tracking senior City solicitors to the High Court bench: 'In a commercial setting where commitment to the firm and one's partners is important, to make this request requires courage . . . City law firms can't make partners and associates apply for judicial appointments'. Sparrow emphasises that there needs to be 'radical overhaul of the job to make it more attractive and a fairer process for solicitors'.

Section 64 of the Constitutional Reform Act 2005 provides that the Judicial Appointments Commission 'must have regard to the need to encourage diversity in the range of persons available for selection for appointments'. The Lord Chancellor can issue guidance for the Commission in order to encourage a range of persons to be available for selection (s. 65). The Labour Government issued a consultation paper, *Increasing Diversity in the Judiciary* (2004). At the launch of this paper, the Minister for Constitutional Affairs stated:

> It is a matter of great concern that the judiciary in England and Wales – while held in high regard for its ability, independence and probity – is not representative of the diverse society it serves. A more diverse judiciary is essential if the public's confidence in its judges is to be maintained and strengthened.
>
> We need to find out why people from diverse backgrounds and with disabilities are not applying for judicial appointment in the numbers we might expect and, once we have identified the barriers, we need to do something about removing them. Judicial appointments will continue to be made on merit. But I do not believe that there is any conflict between merit and diversity.

A diversity strategy was launched by the Lord Chancellor in 2006 which aimed to increase the number of women and black and ethnic minority judges. The strategy seeks to achieve this by promoting fair and open selection processes based solely on merit and by ensuring that the culture and working environment for judicial office holders encourages and supports a diverse judiciary. Flexible working hours have been introduced for some judicial appointments and a work-shadowing scheme established in order to try to attract a more diverse range of people to a judicial career.

10

THE JUDGES

Photo 10.2 Lady Hale

Source: Dan Kitwood/Getty Images

Part 2 of the Tribunals, Courts and Enforcement Act 2007 aimed to widen the pool of lawyers eligible for the judiciary (see p. 184).

Unfortunately, the appointments made by the Judicial Appointments Commission have failed to significantly increase diversity, particularly in the higher realms of the judiciary. Although the statistics show a rise in women and ethnic minority judicial appointments, these are mostly at low or part-time levels. The Commission has argued that the legal profession itself must become more diverse if further progress is to be made.

In 2011, the Ministry of Justice (2011b) published a consultation document entitled *Appointments and Diversity: A Judiciary for the 21st Century.* Following this consultation process, the Crime and Courts Act 2013 was passed. The Act amends the Constitutional Reform Act 2005 to allow the selecting panels to positively favour those from under-represented backgrounds, if two candidates are of equal merit. In other words, if a white and a black candidate are of roughly similar merit, the black candidate can be appointed to increase judicial diversity. Likewise, if there were a male and a female candidate of equal merit, the woman should get the job.

Lady Hale gave a speech in 2015 at Birmingham University at which she noted there would be six vacancies on the Supreme Court between September 2016 and December 2018 and that 'if we do not manage to achieve a (much) more diverse court in the process of filling them we ought to be ashamed of ourselves'.

10.10.2 Training

Considering the importance of their work, judges receive very little training, even with recent changes. They may be experienced as lawyers, but the skills needed by a good lawyer are not identical to those required by a good judge. Unlike the career judge system seen on the Continent, where judges cut their judicial teeth in the lower courts, and gain experience as they move up to more serious cases, our judges often begin their judicial careers with cases that may involve substantial loss of liberty for the individual. Nor are they required to have shown expertise in the areas of law they will be required to consider: it is perfectly possible for a High Court judge to try a serious criminal case, and possibly pass a sentence of a long term of imprisonment, without ever having done a criminal case as a lawyer in practice.

The most serious cases of all in the civil courts are not being heard by High Court judges but by deputy High Court judges. These deputies are circuit judges spending a few days in London or, more likely, barristers filling time between cases. The only thing to be said about this system is that it is cheaper for the Treasury.

Judges could benefit from receiving more training, not just at the beginning of their careers, but at frequent intervals throughout. Helena Kennedy (1992) suggests judges might also benefit from sabbaticals, in which they could study the practices of other jurisdictions, and the work of social agencies and reform groups.

Judge Pickles (1988) put forward the view that the judiciary needs more training in sociology, psychology, penology and criminology, and to learn more about how criminals are dealt with in other systems.

Technology

The upcoming move to digital justice and the online courts has meant that there is an urgent need for the judiciary to receive comprehensive training in this area. In August 2018 Lord Burnett of Maldon (Lord Chief Justice) and Lord Justice Ryder (President of the Tribunals) reported back on a private consultation carried out with over 10,000 members of the judiciary and magistrates. Observations were that judges welcomed the technology and new ways of working, but that 'thinking about and planning for tomorrow should not come at the expense of delivering justice in the proceedings that come before us today'. The court closure programme has alarmed many within the judiciary; and the focus on online dispute resolution raises concerns about access to justice and transparency. Sir Geoffrey Vos, head of the High Court's Chancery Division, cautioned that 'under no circumstances can justice be delivered behind closed doors'; care must be taken to ensure that technology does not exclude anyone.

The Commons Public Accounts Committee had raised concerns about the £1.2 billion court modernisation programme in their *Transforming courts and tribunals* report (July 2018), questioning how much meaningful stakeholder consultation had taken place and due consideration given to access to justice issues.

The drive for public legal education and transparency has led to increased calls for live-streaming and broadcasting of legal proceedings; virtually all Supreme Court hearings are now available to view and many from the Court of Appeal. The Lord Chief Justice, Lord Burnett has outlined the importance of this to ensure public support for judicial independence, calling for expansion of broadcasts and more engagement with the media: 'Judicial independence is strong when the public understands its importance and supports it.'

10.10.3 Morale

Even before the Brexit backlash there were signs that the judiciary were having a difficult time. The Lord Chief Justice, Lord Thomas of Cwmgiedd, spoke of the 'very substantial deterrents' to joining the bench in 2016, noting the pension changes, low pay (compared to private practice) and increasing volume of work. Judges have needed to take on case management responsibilities and significant administration, while the increased number of litigants in person has also contributed to the soaring workload of the judiciary (as discussed in Part 5: Civil justice system).

This ebbing morale has contributed to a recruitment crisis within the judiciary; the Lord Chief Justice reported at the annual judges' dinner in July 2018 that for a fourth year running, vacancies would not be filled, and the likelihood was that for the following year the High Court would be operating with 20 per cent fewer judges than it needed. Lord Burnett pointed out: 'That is unsustainable. There is an urgent need to act now if we are to avoid serious and lasting damage to the High Court and to the international position of the jurisdiction of England and Wales, with knock on consequences for the professional services industry and the City.' The President of the Family Division of the High Court has also spoken out about the rising workload; noting that hearings about children were now at record levels with child arrangement orders increasing by 10,000 in the past two years.

The Bigger Picture: Judges and emotions

Being a judge can actually be emotionally quite draining and judges might benefit from more psychological support during their careers. Research carried out by Sharyn Roach Anleu and Kathy Mack (2005) looks at the emotional distress felt by magistrates in Australia when carrying out their work. One magistrate characterised his work as 'seeing absolute misery passing in front of you day in, day out, month in, month out, year in, year out'.

10

THE JUDGES

> Another judge in child welfare cases spoke of relentless sadness and observed that there is 'no good news'. In the murder case of the teenager Becky Watts, the trial judge became visibly upset when concluding his sentencing remarks, his voice started to tremble, tears came into his eyes and he swiftly rose and left the court. The American academic, Terry Maroney (2011), has argued judges need more help in learning to cope with their emotions.
>
> The Judicial College now offers an online course in helping the judiciary deal with the stress, as well as offering professional support. There has been increased acknowledgement of the toll of the often-harrowing cases judges deal with; particularly with the increasing number of sexual offence cases (many involving children) now occupying the Crown Court.

10.10.4 Problems with judicial independence

While the Constitutional Reform Act 2005 has now given statutory recognition to the independence of the judiciary, there remain a number of threats to judicial independence.

Supremacy of Parliament

Apart from where European law is involved, it is never possible for the courts to question the validity of existing Acts of Parliament. In the UK all Acts of Parliament are treated as absolutely binding by the courts, until such time as any particular Act is repealed or altered by Parliament itself in another statute or by a Minister under the special fast-track procedure provided for under the Human Rights Act 1998. The judiciary are therefore ultimately subordinate to the will of Parliament – unlike, for example, judges in the US, who may declare legislation unconstitutional. Dworkin (1978) has argued that if judges had the power to set aside legislation as unconstitutional, judicial appointments would become undesirably political, and judges would be seen as politicians themselves. He points to the political character of high judicial appointments in the US.

Treasury counsel

Those barristers retained to represent the Government in court actions in which the Government are involved – called Treasury counsel – are very likely to be offered High Court judgeships in due course.

Non-judicial work

Judges also get involved in non-judicial areas with political implications, for example, chairing inquiries into events such as Bloody Sunday in Londonderry, the Brixton riots or the Zeebrugge ferry disaster. Thus, Lord Justice Scott chaired the high-profile inquiry into the arms-to-Iraq affair and the High Court Judge, Sir William Macpherson, headed the inquiry into the handling of the police investigation of the death of the black teenager Stephen Lawrence, who was murdered in South London. This function can often be seen to undermine the political neutrality of the judiciary – in the early 1970s, for example, Lord Diplock headed an inquiry into the administration of justice in Northern Ireland, the report of which led to the abolition of jury trials for terrorist offences in the region. To this day such hearings are known as Diplock courts, which does nothing to uphold the reputation for independence of the judiciary.

The Hutton inquiry, following the war against Iraq and Dr David Kelly's death, raised questions about the future role of judges in public inquiries. There was wide public dissatisfaction with the Hutton Report (2004), and a general unease as to how independent the judge and chair, Lord Hutton, had been. As a result, the former Lord Chief Justice, Lord Woolf, wrote a memo to the House of Commons Public Administration Select Committee expressing concern that Lord Hutton had been used as a political tool by the Government: 'I have no doubt that Lord Hutton was drawn into the most difficult area after he gave his report. He found himself being criticised.'

The problem arose again in 2010 when the Government announced that it would set up an inquiry looking at the involvement of the British security services in the use of torture on terrorist suspects abroad. Sir Peter Gibson, a retired senior judge, was appointed to chair the inquiry, but his appointment was the subject of some criticism. It seems that he had already undertaken a secret inquiry into allegations of misconduct by the secret services and had concluded that the security services were 'trustworthy, conscientious and dependable'. In these circumstances he might be better as a witness to the new inquiry rather than as an impartial chairperson.

It is interesting to note that the Hillsborough Independent Panel, which looked into the circumstances surrounding the tragic Hillsborough Football disaster, was not chaired by a judge, but by the Bishop of Liverpool. The Panel did not follow the usual procedures for a public inquiry, witnesses were not called to give evidence and much of the process took place behind closed doors, but its report, which was published in 2013, gained considerable public support as an honest and accurate statement of what actually occurred on that fateful day in 1989.

The public inquiry into the Grenfell Tower fire disaster (2017) prompted outcry when the judge was announced. Residents, survivors and local people want those responsible for this tragedy brought to justice and the appointment of Sir Martin Moore-Bick, a retired Court of Appeal judge, gave rise to a flood of demands for him to be replaced. The local Labour MP Emma Dent Coad said: 'How anybody like that could have empathy for what those people have been through, I don't understand . . . A technocrat is really not what we need right now.' David Lammy, Labour MP for Tottenham, described Sir Martin as 'a white, upper-middle-class man who I suspect has never, ever visited a tower block housing estate and certainly hasn't slept the night on the 20th floor of one'.

Cases with political implications

Although judges generally refrain from airing their political views, they are sometimes forced to make political decisions, affecting the balance between individuals and the state, the allocation of resources, and the relative powers of local and national government. Despite the official view of judges as apolitical, the fact that these decisions have political ramifications cannot be avoided; judges do not have the option of refusing to decide a case because it has political implications, and have to make a choice one way or the other.

However, concerns have been expressed that too often such decisions defend the interests of the Government of the day, sometimes at the expense of individual liberties. In the wartime case of *Liversidge* v *Anderson* (1942), Lord Atkin voiced concern about the decision by a majority of judges in the House of Lords that the Home Secretary was not required to give reasons to justify the detention of a citizen, commenting that the judges had shown themselves 'more executive minded than the executive'.

Certain cases have borne out this concern. In *McIlkenny* v *Chief Constable of the West Midlands* (1980), Lord Denning dismissed allegations of police brutality against the six men accused of the Birmingham pub bombings with the words:

> Just consider the course of events if this action were to go to trial . . . If the six men fail, it will mean that much time and money and worry will have been expended by many people for no good purpose. If the six men win, it will mean that the police were guilty of perjury, that they were guilty of violence and threats, that the confessions were involuntary and were improperly admitted in evidence: and that the convictions were erroneous. That would mean that the Home Secretary would have either to recommend they be pardoned or he would have to remit the case to the Court of Appeal under section 17 of the Criminal Appeal Act 1968. This is such an appalling vista that every sensible person in the land would say: it cannot be right that these actions should go any further. They should be struck out.

In other words, Lord Denning was saying, the allegations should not be addressed because, if proved true, the result would be to bring the legal system into disrepute.

In *R* v *Ponting* (1985), the civil servant Clive Ponting was accused of leaking documents revealing that the Government had covered up the circumstances in which the Argentine ship the *General Belgrano* was sunk during the Falklands war. Ponting argued that he had acted 'in the interests of the state' (a defence laid down in the Official Secrets Act at the time), but Mr Justice McGowan directed the jury that 'interests of the state' meant nothing more or less than the policies of the Government of the day. Nevertheless the jury acquitted Ponting (see p. 285).

The danger of political bias has been increased as a result of the Human Rights Act 1998 coming into force. While judges have already decided some politically sensitive cases, the number is likely to increase, with litigation directly accusing Government actions and legislation of breaching fundamental human rights. The journalist Hugo Young argues that we will see the emergence of the 'political judge'.

Over time the changing role of the judiciary is most likely to be visible in the Supreme Court. The House of Lords' judges decided about 100 cases a year, usually on technical commercial and tax matters, though with the implementation of the Human Rights Act 1998 it was increasingly hearing cases raising human rights issues. The Supreme Court is moving closer to the US Supreme Court, deciding fundamental issues on the rights of the individual against the state.

The greatest tensions between the judges and the Government often emerge with regard to the application of the terrorist legislation and the judges' approach to sentencing. In 2006, the Attorney General published a list of more than 200 judges who have given 'unduly lenient' sentences to criminals. The list was drawn up by looking at successful appeals against lenient sentences made by the Attorney General to the Court of Appeal. In response, a spokesperson from the Judicial Communications Office stated:

> Figures on successful appeals against a judge's sentencing can only begin to have relevance if they are set against the total number of sentencing decisions made by the judge in question, and those where there has been no appeal or an appeal has been rejected. It should also be borne in mind that some judges have caseloads involving more complex and serious cases, so they might be more likely to feature in appeal cases. In any event, there are many cases where the Court of Appeal reduces sentences without implying any criticism of the sentencing judges, sometimes indeed because of changes of circumstances – such as new evidence – after the original sentencing decision.

At the same time, the then Constitutional Affairs Minister, Vera Baird, criticised the judiciary during an appearance on BBC Radio 4's *Any Questions* programme. Baird attacked a trial judge for giving a convicted paedophile, Craig Sweeney, a sentence which potentially allowed him to be released after six years' imprisonment. The Lord Chancellor came to the defence of the trial judge and pointed out that he had simply applied the relevant sentencing guidelines to the case. Vera Baird subsequently apologised for her remarks in a letter to the Lord Chancellor.

The pressure group, JUSTICE, published a report in 2007 entitled *The Future of the Rule of Law*. This document sought to remind politicians that there is a constitutional convention that the Government should refrain from criticising the judiciary in any manner that would diminish public confidence. This convention was repeatedly breached by the former Home Secretaries John Reid and David Blunkett. Under their own rules of professional conduct, judges are not usually allowed to respond publicly to criticisms so such criticisms do not lead to a constructive debate. In addition, it is in everyone's interests that the judges who enforce the law are respected in society.

The backlash to the *Miller* judgment saw questionable media output as well as the arguably inadequate defence of judges by the Lord Chancellor (see the 'Bigger Picture' section on p. 194). Another important aspect of this situation was the way in which politicians reacted; speaking against the judges to curry favour with the public, seemingly with no understanding of basic constitutional law principles. Iain Duncan Smith, MP for Chingford and Woodford Green and former Leader of the Conservative Party (2001–03) alarmingly had this to say in January 2017:

> You've got to understand that, of course, there's the European issue but there's also the issue about who is Supreme – Parliament or a self-appointed court. This is the issue here right now, so I was intrigued that it was a split judgment, I'm disappointed they've tried to tell Parliament how to run its business . . . they've stepped into new territory where they've actually told Parliament not just that they should do something but actually what they should do and I think that leads further down the road to real constitutional issues about who is supreme in this role.

In October 2018 a case emerged where judicial impartiality was called into question; judge Robert Altham sentenced three protestors over their participation in a demonstration against fracking, where they climbed on top of lorries and refused to move for several days. It later emerged that the family business (JC Altham & Sons) run by his sister and parents, was a current supplier to the oil and gas industry. In an expedited hearing at the Court of Appeal, their sentences were later quashed for being 'manifestly excessive'. The appellants' barrister, Kirsty Brimelow QC drew attention to a letter addressed to Lancashire Council and signed by the judge's sister, which called on them to approve fracking: 'He should not have sentenced, because there is sufficient evidence here to raise apparent bias.'

10.10.5 Judges speaking out

In recent years there have been a number of incidences where judges have taken the opportunity to send a message to the executive about cases which have an impact on society. Sir James Munby's judgment in the 2016 case of *Re D (A Child)* told the world what an impossible situation the government's legal aid cuts were putting ordinary citizens in (see Chapter 15: Paying for legal services). In 2017 his judgment in *Re X (A Child)* was damning in its criticism of mental health provision in the UK, warning that the country will have 'blood on its

10

THE JUDGES

hands' if it fails to find a hospital bed for X, a teenager at risk of taking her own life, when she leaves a secure unit in youth custody:

> What this case demonstrates, as if further demonstration is still required of what is a well-known scandal, is the disgraceful and utterly shaming lack of proper provision in this country of the clinical, residential and other support services so desperately needed by the increasing numbers of children and young people afflicted with the same kind of difficulties as X is burdened with. We are, even in these times of austerity, one of the richest countries in the world. Our children and young people are our future. X is part of our future. It is a disgrace to any country with pretensions to civilisation, compassion and, dare one say it, basic human decency, that a judge in 2017 should be faced with the problems thrown up by this case and should have to express himself in such terms.
>
> . . .
>
> If, when in eleven days' time she is released from ZX, we, the system, society, the State, are unable to provide X with the supportive and *safe* placement she so desperately needs, and if, in consequence, she is enabled to make another attempt on her life, then I can only say, with bleak emphasis: we will have blood on our hands.

The uncertainty around Brexit has prompted a number of the Supreme Court justices to speak out in speeches and interviews.

As these instances become more frequent, we also see judges challenging the idea of them being 'out of touch' through communications. Mr Justice Peter Jackson broke from convention in the case of a 14-year-old boy who had applied to the court to leave the home of his mother and stepfather, in order to move to Scandinavia with his father. Jackson J gave his judgment in the form of a letter directly written to the boy, clearly explaining his decision and the reasons for it (***Re A (Letter to a Young Person)*** (Rev 1) (2017)). This example was followed by the deputy District Judge Lucy Reed in 2018 in an adoption case, who wrote her judgment in order that the baby's father, who had a learning disability, would understand her decision (***A Council v Jack's Mother, Jack's Dad and Jack*** (2018)).

In ***R (Unison) v Lord Chancellor*** (2017) we saw the Supreme Court make a finding that employment tribunal fees introduced by the government in 2013 were unlawful. Lord Reed's judgment on the importance of access to the courts, as a core element of the rule of law, was very powerful indeed (for more on this, see Chapter 15: Paying for legal services).

Judges also regularly speak out on developments within the court service; judicial commentary for 2018 included the slippage of advocacy skills for solicitor-advocates and in-house barristers (for a study commissioned by the SRA/BSB), the crisis in the family justice system (Sir Andrew McFarlane, President of the Family Division), the withdrawal of Government funding for the problem-solving Family Drug and Alcohol Court (Sir James Munby) and immigration lawyers who use litigation to delay removal proceedings (Mr Justice Green).

The Bigger Picture: The media and freedom of expression

The media (including newspapers, television and radio) hold considerable power and their role depends on them having the right to inform the public. Any restriction on their freedom of expression is an irritation to the media and it is the judges who are required to police the scope of this freedom. In recent years the right to privacy has been extended by the courts. This was highlighted in the judgment of Mr Justice Eady in the High Court when he ruled that the *News of the World* had been wrong to publish a story about Max Mosley (the president of the body that regulates Formula 1 racing) paying prostitutes to act out sadomasochistic activities. Mosley's parents were well-known Fascist sympathisers who had reportedly been friends and supporters of Adolf Hitler. The newspaper suggested that the sexual activities had a Nazi-style theme. This judgment of Mr Justice Eady was publicly criticised by the editor of the *Daily Mail* in 2009, who made a very personal attack on the judge himself, and the tone of this attack raises questions about how far the independence of the judiciary is sufficiently protected from the pressures of the media. In 1900 a newspaper editor was convicted for contempt of court for calling a judge an 'impudent little man in horsehair', but such a response would seem disproportionate today. The Judicial Communications Office acts as the press office for the judiciary and it issued the following statement in response to the editor's speech:

> Judges determine privacy cases in accordance with the law and the particular evidence presented by both parties. Any High Court judgment can be appealed to the Court of Appeal.

It is understandable that the judges would not want to enter into a public dispute with a newspaper editor, but it is also noteworthy that Government Ministers, and in particular the Lord Chancellor who under the Constitutional Reform Act 2005 is responsible for protecting the independence of the judiciary, did not speak up in support of the judges in relation to the ruling in the **Miller** case. As a politician, the Lord Chancellor will be anxious to keep the media on his or her side ready for the next general election.

In relation to the **Miller** press coverage (see p. 194), the way in which the press 'stirred up' the public both pre- and post-judgment was largely unprecedented. The online version of the *Daily Mail,* MailOnline, essentially 'trolled' the judges ruling at the High Court: Lord Chief Justice Lord Thomas, Lord Justice Sales and Master of the Rolls Sir Terence Etherton. Running a profile on the 'judges that blocked Brexit' the paper turned the focus on the judges themselves with large photographs and an accompanying line that read:

> One founded a EUROPEAN law group, another charged the taxpayer millions for advice and the third is an openly gay ex-Olympic fencer.

This onslaught wasn't the reserve of the tabloid press however – the *Telegraph* ran with a similar headline: 'The judges versus the people', again accompanied by photographs of the three High Court judges.

This seeming attempt to pit the 'common man' against the judiciary highlights a real issue in terms of public understanding of the law and constitutional principles – something the media were happy to exploit. Former Attorney General Dominic Grieve noted:

> There is something smacking of the fascist state about them [the headlines attacking judges] . . . It shows either a total misunderstanding of the UK constitution, which such critics periodically extol – or a deliberate desire to destroy it.

Some might suggest that a mere newspaper headline doesn't have the power to influence people or indeed impact society – though *The Sun*'s coverage of the 1989 Hillsborough disaster would suggest otherwise.

The tension between judges and the media has increased as judges have sought to strengthen the protection of celebrities' right to privacy, considering that there is no public interest in allowing, for example, the publication of a celebrity footballer's sex life. Judges have been prepared to issue what have become known as 'super injunctions', preventing any publication that would identify the relevant celebrity. These injunctions have been undermined by the use of social networking sites, such as Twitter, to publish the name regardless of the injunction. In addition, politicians have chosen to name the relevant celebrities in Parliament, relying on the legal protection offered to them under the doctrine of parliamentary privilege. The risk is that the authority of judges is being undermined and the public will be less willing to respect the decisions of judges more generally.

10

THE JUDGES

10.10.6 Right-wing bias

In addition to an alleged readiness to support the Government of the day, the judiciary has been accused of being particularly biased towards the interests traditionally represented by the right wing of the political spectrum. In his influential book *The Politics of the Judiciary*, Griffith (1997) states that:

> . . . in every major social issue which has come before the courts in the last thirty years – concerning industrial relations, political protest, race relations, government secrecy, police powers, moral behaviour – the judges have supported the conventional, settled and established interests.

Among the cases he cites in support of this theory is ***Bromley London Borough Council v Greater London Council*** (1982). In this case the Labour-run GLC had won an election with a promise to cut bus and tube fares by 25 per cent. The move necessitated an increase in the rates levied on the London boroughs, and one of those boroughs, Conservative-controlled Bromley, challenged the GLC's right to do this. The challenge failed in the High Court, but succeeded on appeal. The Court of Appeal judges condemned the fare reduction as 'a crude abuse of power', and quashed the supplementary rate that the GLC had levied on the London boroughs to pay for it. The House of Lords agreed, the Law Lords holding unanimously that the GLC was bound by a statute requiring it to 'promote the provision of integrated, efficient and economic transport facilities and services in Greater London', which they interpreted to mean that the bus and tube system must be run according to 'ordinary business principles' of cost-effectiveness. The decision represented a political defeat for the Labour leaders of the GLC and a victory for the Conservative councillors of Bromley.

Other cases cited by Griffith include: ***Council of Civil Service Unions v Minister for the Civil Service*** (1984) – the 'GCHQ' case in which the House of Lords supported the withdrawal of certain civil servants' rights to belong to a trade union; ***Attorney General v Guardian Newspapers Ltd*** (1987), which banned publication of *Spycatcher*, a book on the security services, even though it was generally available in America and Australia; and several cases arising out of the 1984 miners' strike, such as ***Thomas v NUM (South Wales Area)*** (1985), in which injunctions were sought to prevent protesters collecting at pit gates and shouting abuse at those going to work. The judge in that case, according to Griffith, had some difficulty in finding the conduct illegal, but eventually decided that it amounted to 'a species of private nuisance, namely unreasonable interference with the victim's right to use the highway'; Griffith describes the decision as 'judicial creativity at its most blatant'.

Commentators have also noted that the great advances in judicial review in the 1960s and 1970s came almost entirely at the expense of Labour policies, and that judicial reluctance to review Government decisions of the executive is most likely to be decisive in cases where the Government in question is a Conservative one. However, the past quarter of a century has seen a shift; the decisions of the mid-1990s Conservative Home Secretary, Michael Howard, were several times found illegal by the courts. Legal journalist and writer Joshua Rozenberg argued that the bias at least in favour of the establishment has broken down.

The early-2000s Labour Home Secretary, David Blunkett, expressed displeasure on a number of occasions with the decisions of the courts, particularly where these decisions ran counter to his policies on sentencing and immigration.

10.10.7 Bias against women

In her book *Eve was Framed*, Helena Kennedy (1992) argues that the attitude of many judges to women is outdated, and sometimes prejudiced. The problems are particularly apparent in cases involving sexual offences: Kennedy cites the comments of Cassell J in 1990, that a man who had unlawful intercourse with his 12-year-old stepdaughter was understandably driven to it by his pregnant wife's loss of interest in sex.

Kennedy alleges that women are judged according to how well they fit traditional female stereotypes. Because crime is seen as stepping outside the feminine role, women are more severely punished than men, and women who do not fit traditional stereotypes are treated most harshly.

The Judicial Studies Board, responsible for the training of judges, has issued judges with the *Equal Treatment Bench Book*. This advises judges on equal treatment of people in court and the appropriate use of language to avoid causing offence by, for example, being sexist.

10.10.8 Influence of Freemasonry

Freemasonry is a fraternal organisation which is viewed in popular culture as a secret society. It does not ordinarily allow women to join. Among its stated aims is the mutual self-improvement of members, and there has long been concern about the extent of membership

Figure 10.3 The offices of the Freemasons in central London

Source: © Alex Segre/Alamy

10

THE JUDGES

among the police as well as the judiciary, on the basis that loyalty to other Masons – who might be parties in a case, or colleagues seeking promotion – could have a corrupting influence. Josephine Hayes, former chairwoman of the Association of Women Barristers, told newspapers that anecdotal evidence suggested there was public concern about the influence that Masonic membership might have on judges: clients whose opponents were Freemasons had been known to express worries that the judge might also be one. She pointed out that, although fears of actual influence might be unfounded, the concern that it might exist weakened confidence in the legal system.

The Association of Women Barristers also suggests that Freemasonry may have a discriminatory effect on women lawyers' chances of appointment to the Bench. It points out that because the current system of appointment looks at recommendations by existing judges, men benefited by the opportunities which Freemasonry provides to meet senior judges. Such opportunities, it points out, have become even more valuable now that the practising Bar has grown to over 16,000, so that judges no longer necessarily know all candidates for the judiciary personally. The Association has argued that judges should be obliged to resign from the Freemasons on appointment to the bench. The former Lord Chancellor, Lord McKay, opposed such a rule, arguing that as a matter of principle individuals should be free to join any lawful organisation they wished. He pointed out that the judicial oath requires all judges to swear 'to do right to all manner of people . . . without fear or favour, affection or ill will'. He suggested that this meant there was no conflict of interest between membership of the Freemasons and judicial office.

In an attempt to introduce greater transparency, a questionnaire was sent in 1998 to all members of the judiciary asking them to declare their 'Masonic status'. Five per cent of those who responded stated that they were Freemasons. In 2009 the government decided to stop collecting this information.

10.10.9 Lack of specialisation

A very distinctive feature of the English system is that judges tend not to specialise: instead, they are organised in terms of the hierarchy of the courts in which they work. In France, for example, every region has its own court structure, and there will be hundreds of judges of equal status, instead of the elite group that forms the pinnacle of our judiciary. It has been argued that this arrangement prevents our judiciary from developing the kind of expertise that, in France, has contributed to the development of specialist courts such as the *Conseil d'État,* which deals with administrative law; the development of our administrative law is said to have suffered as a result. However, it can also be argued that the English model gives the highest judges an overview of the whole system, which helps ensure that different branches of law remain fundamentally consistent with each other.

In any case, there are some signs that the system is changing. First, the growth of tribunals has removed many specialist areas from the ordinary courts: most tribunals are presided over by people with specialist knowledge of the relevant areas. The growth of mediation systems as an alternative method of dispute resolution (see Chapter 25) has also contributed to this. Secondly, Lord Woolf's report on the civil justice system recommended that High Court and circuit judges should concentrate on fewer areas of work, though he did not suggest that they actually became specialists in particular subjects.

10.10.10 Shortage of time

There is a growing concern that judges currently have insufficient time allocated for them to read the papers for a case. Court of Appeal judges are allocated only four reading days a month when they can do legal research. The rest of the time they are expected to be hearing court cases. This is in striking contrast with some appellate judges in the US who only hear cases four days per month.

Answering questions

Questions about the judiciary generally focus on their independence, but as this is closely related to appointments, background and selection, you need to know more than just the information under the heading of 'Independence of the judiciary', as the following examples show.

1   What are the roles and responsibilities of the judiciary? Does the selection process in England and Wales ensure that appropriate people are selected to carry these out? *University of London, International Programmes LLB*

2   The position of Lord Chancellor in the past clearly breached the doctrine of separation of powers. How have the reforms contained in the Constitutional Reform Act 2005 addressed this breach of a fundamental constitutional principle? In your view, have these reforms been successful?

3   'For nearly 300 years, the English judge has been guaranteed his independence.' How far is this true? In your opinion, can the decisions of our judges be regarded as satisfactory to all members of society?

4   What measures have been taken to make the judiciary more representative of society?

For answers to these questions, visit the companion website at www.pearsoned.co.uk/ elliottquinn

SUMMARY OF CHAPTER 10: THE JUDGES

The role of the judges

The judges play a central role under the British constitution, playing a vital but sensitive role in controlling the exercise of power by the state.

Judicial hierarchy

At the head of the judiciary is the President of the Courts of England and Wales. The most senior judges are the Justices of the Supreme Court. At the next level down, sitting in the Court of Appeal, are 39 judges known as Lords Justices of Appeal and Lady Justices of Appeal.

Appointing the judges

The way in which judges are appointed has been radically reformed by provisions in the Constitutional Reform Act 2005. The Act contains provisions for the establishment of a new Judicial Appointments Commission. It is hoped that the creation of this body will help to put an end to the breaches of the principle of separation of powers and reinforce judicial independence. Depending on their rank, judges are appointed by the Queen on the advice of the Prime Minister or by the Lord Chancellor.

Training

Training is provided by the Judicial College.

Termination of appointment

There are five ways in which a judge may leave office:

- dismissal;
- discipline;
- resignation;
- retirement; and
- removal due to infirmity.

Independence of the judiciary

In our legal system great importance is attached to the idea that judges should be independent and be seen to be independent. Section 3 of the Constitutional Reform Act 2005 states:

> The Lord Chancellor, other Ministers of the Crown and all with responsibility for matters relating to the judiciary or otherwise to the administration of justice must uphold the continued independence of the judiciary.

Criticisms of the judiciary

Judges are overwhelmingly white, male and middle to upper class, and frequently elderly, leading to accusations that they are unrepresentative of the society they serve. The situation is changing, but slowly. The appointments process has been criticised for being dominated by politicians, secretive and discriminatory. Judges receive very little training. There are real concerns that the independence of the judiciary is not sufficiently protected. The academic, Griffith, has accused judges of being biased towards the interests traditionally represented by the right wing of the political spectrum. The lawyer, Baroness Helena Kennedy, has argued that the attitude of many judges to women is outdated and sometimes prejudiced. There is also concern that some judges are members of the Freemasons.

Reading list

Anleu, S. and Mack, K. (2005), Magistrates' everyday work and emotional labour. *Journal of Law and Society,* 32: 590–614.

Blom-Cooper, L. (2009) Bias: malfunction in judicial decision-making. *Public Law,* 199.

Darbyshire, P. (2011) *Sitting in Judgment.* Oxford: Hart Publishing.

Devlin, P. (1979) *The Judge.* Oxford: Oxford University Press.

Dworkin, R. (1978) Political judges and the rule of law. *Proceedings of the British Academy,* 259.

Gee, G. and Rackley, E. (2017) *Debating Judicial Appointments in an Age of Diversity.* Abingdon: Routledge

Genn, H. (2008) (see website, below).

Griffith, J.A.G. (1997) *The Politics of the Judiciary.* London: Fontana.

Hailsham, Lord (1989) The Office of Lord Chancellor and the separation of powers. *Civil Justice Quarterly,* 8: 308.

Hedley, Sir M. (2016) *The Modern Judge: Power Responsibility and Society's Expectations.* Bristol: LexisNexis.

Holland, L. and Spencer, L. (1992) *Without Prejudice?* Sex *Equality at the Bar and in the Judiciary.* London: Bar Council.

Hutton, Lord (2004) *Report of the Inquiry into the Circumstances Surrounding the Death of Dr David Kelly CMG.* London: Stationery Office.

JUSTICE (2007) *The Future of the Rule of Law.* London: JUSTICE.

Kennedy, H. (1992) *Eve was Framed: Women and British Justice.* London: Chatto.

Malleson, K. (1997) Judicial training and performance appraisal: the problem of judicial independence. *Modern Law Review,* 60: 655.

      (1999) *The New Judiciary – The Effect of Expansion and Activism.* Aldershot: Ashgate.

Malleson, K. and Banda, F. (2000) *Factors Affecting the Decision to Apply for Silk.* London: Lord Chancellor's Department.

Maroney, T. (2011) Emotional regulation and judicial behaviour. *Californian Law Review,* 99: 1485.

Pannick, D. (1987) *Judges.* Oxford: Oxford University Press.

Partington, M. (1994) Training the judiciary in England and Wales: the work of the Judicial Studies Board. *Civil Justice Quarterly* 319.

Paterson, A. (2013) *Final Judgment: The Last Law Lords and the Supreme Court.* Oxford: Hart Publishing.

Peach, Sir L. (1999) *Appointment Processes of Judges and Queen's Counsel in England and Wales.* London: HMSO.

Pickles, J. (1988) *Straight from the Bench.* London: Coronet.

Windlesham, Lord (2005) The Constitutional Reform Act 2005: ministers, judges and constitutional change, Part 1. *Public Law,* 806.

Woodhouse, D. (2007) The Constitutional Reform Act 2005 – defending judicial independence the English way. *International Journal of Constitutional Law,* 5(1): 153.

Woolf, Lord (1996) *Access to Justice.* London: Lord Chancellor's Department.

10

THE JUDGES

On the internet

The White Paper on constitutional reform. *The governance of Britain: constitutional renewal* (2008) is available on the website of gov.uk at:

https://www.gov.uk/government/publications/the-governance-of-britain-constitutional-renewal--9

The report by Hazel Genn, *The attractiveness of senior judicial appointment to highly qualified practitioners* (2008) has been published on the UCL website at:

https://studylib.net/doc/11990641/the-attractiveness-of-senior-judicial-appointment-to-high...

The report of the House of Lords Parliamentary Committee, *Relations between the executive, the judiciary and Parliament* (2007), is available on Parliament's website at:

https://publications.parliament.uk/pa/ld200607/ldselect/ldconst/151/151.pdf

The consultation paper *Appointments and Diversity: A Judiciary for the 21st Century* (2011) can be accessed on the website of the Ministry of Justice at:

https://webarchive.nationalarchives.gov.uk/20130206211835/http:/www.justice.gov.uk/downloads/consultations/judicial-appointments-consultation-1911.pdf

The 2010 report of the Advisory Panel on Judicial Diversity is available at:

https://www.judiciary.gov.uk/publications/advisory-panel-recommendations/

The consultation paper *The Governance of Britain: Judicial Appointments* (2007) is available at:

http://webarchive.nationalarchives.gov.uk/+/http://www.justice.gov.uk/publications/cp2507.htm

The website of the Judicial Appointments Commission is available at:

https://www.judicialappointments.gov.uk/

The consultation paper *Constitutional reform: a new way of appointing judges* (2003) is available at:

https://webarchive.nationalarchives.gov.uk/+/http://www.dca.gov.uk/consult/jacommission/index.htm

General information on the Courts and Tribunals Judiciary is available on:

https://www.judiciary.gov.uk

The booklet *Judicial Appointments in England and Wales: Policies and Procedures* is available at:

https://webarchive.nationalarchives.gov.uk/+/http://www.dca.gov.uk/judicial/appointments/jappinfr.htm

The website of the Judicial College can be found at:

https://www.judiciary.gov.uk/about-the-judiciary/training-support/judicial-college/

Statistics on the judges are published via the Publications tab (filter by type: Statistics) at:

https://www.judiciary.gov.uk/publications/

Videos of judges talking about their work are available at:

https://www.judiciary.uk/about-the-judiciary/judges-career-paths/videos-high-court-judges-talk-about-their-work/

The Official Statistics (1 April 2017 to 31 March 2018) for the Judicial Appointments Commission on Judicial Selection and Recmmendations for Appointment can be found at:

https://www.judicialappointments.gov.uk/sites/default/files/sync/about_the_jac/official_statistics/statistics-bulletin-jac-2017-18.pdf

The Judicial Diversity Statistics 2018 can be found at:

https://www.judiciary.uk/about-the-judiciary/who-are-the-judiciary/diversity/judicial-diversity-statistics-2018/

The disciplinary statements for the Judicial Conduct Investigations Office are published at:
https://judicialconduct.judiciary.gov.uk/disciplinary-statements/2018/

The Judicial Conduct Investigations Office Annual Report 2016–17 is available at:
https://judicialconduct.judiciary.gov.uk/reports-publications/

The report by Dr Philip Kirby for the Sutton Trust, *Leading People 2016: The educational backgrounds of the UK professional elite* (February 2016) is available at:
https://www.suttontrust.com/wp-content/uploads/2016/02/Leading-People_ Feb16.pdf

The European Commission for the Efficiency of Justice report *European Judicial systems – Efficiency and quality of justice*, CEPEJ Studies No. 23 (2016) is available at:
https://rm.coe.int/european-judicial-systems-efficiency-and-quality-of-justice- cepej-stud/1680786b58

The speech by Lord Hodge *Upholding the rule of law: how we preserve judicial independence in the United Kingdom* (7 November 2016) is published here:
https://www.supremecourt.uk/docs/speech-161107.pdf

The speech by Lord Neuberger *Reflections on significant moments in the role of the Judiciary* (16 March 2017) is published here:
https://www.supremecourt.uk/docs/speech-170316.pdf

The report commissioned by the SRA and BSB by Gillian Hunter, Jessica Jacobson & Amy Kirby, *Judicial Perceptions of the Quality of Criminal Advocacy* (June 2018) is available here:
https://www.sra.org.uk/sra/how-we-work/reports/criminal-advocacy.page

The speech by Sir Geoffrey Vos to the Foundation for Science and Technology: *Debate on how the adoption of new technology can be accelerated to improve the efficiency of the justice system* (20 June 2018) is published here:
https://www.judiciary.uk/wp-content/uploads/2018/06/speech-chc-the-foundation- for-science-and-technology.pdf

The speech from Lord Burnett of Maldon *Becoming Stronger Together* to the Commonwealth Judges and Magistrates' Association Annual Conference in Brisbane (10 September 2018) can be accessed here:
https://www.judiciary.uk/wp-content/uploads/2018/09/lcj-speech-brisbane- lecture-20180910.pdf

The full report of the Commons Public Accounts Committee, *Transforming courts and tribunals* (20 July 2018) is available here:
https://www.parliament.uk/business/committees/committees-a-z/commons- select/public-accounts-committee/news-parliament-2017/transforming- courts-tribunals-report-published-17-19/

The speech Lord Burnett of Maldon gave at the annual judges' dinner (Mansion House, 4 July 2018) can be found here:
https://www.judiciary.uk/wp-content/uploads/2018/07/20180704-lcj-speech- mansion-house-speech.pdf

Grenfell Tower Inquiry website:
https://www.grenfelltowerinquiry.org.uk/

10

THE JUDGES

Chapter 11
The legal professions

This chapter discusses:

- solicitors – their work, qualifications and training;

- the handling of complaints against solicitors;

- barristers – their work, qualifications and training;

- senior barristers, known as Queen's Counsel;

- the handling of complaints against barristers;

- the background of barristers and solicitors;

- attempts to increase diversity in the legal professions through educational reforms;

- the regulation of the professions;

- changes to the business structures in which the professions are organised;

- moves towards fusing the solicitor and barrister professions into a single profession; and

- legal executives – their work, qualifications and training.

11.1 Introduction

The British legal profession, unlike that of most other countries, includes two separate branches: barristers and solicitors (the term 'lawyer' is a general one which covers both branches). They each do the same type of work – advocacy, which means representing clients in court, and paperwork, including drafting legal documents and giving written advice – but the proportions differ, with barristers generally spending a higher proportion of their time in court.

In addition, some types of work have traditionally been available to only one branch (conveyancing to solicitors, and advocacy in the higher courts to barristers, for example), and barristers are not usually hired directly by clients – a client's first point of contact will usually be a solicitor, who then engages a barrister on their behalf if it proves necessary. As we shall see, though, these divisions are beginning to break down.

In the past, the two branches of the profession have been fairly free to arrange their own affairs but, over the past 20 years, this situation has changed significantly with the Government directly and indirectly exercising increased controls over the profession, most recently with the passing of the Legal Services Act 2007.

11.2 Solicitors

There are around 130,000 practising solicitors. The solicitor profession has been growing rapidly, so that since 1970 it has more than trebled in size. Their governing body is the Law Society. Until recently, the Law Society acted both as the representative of solicitors and as the solicitor's regulator. A Government-commissioned report by Sir David Clementi (2004) raised concerns that this dual function could cause a conflict of interests with the Law Society putting the solicitor first, rather than the consumer, when making decisions regarding the regulation of the profession. In response to these concerns, in 2005 membership of the Law Society became voluntary and the Law Society decided to separate its representative function from its regulatory function. The profession is now regulated by the Solicitors Regulation Authority. This Authority has seven lay members and nine solicitor members. It deals with all regulatory and disciplinary matters, setting monitoring and enforcing standards for solicitors. Its stated purpose is to set, promote and secure in the public interest standards of behaviour and professional performance necessary to ensure that clients receive a good service and that the rule of law is upheld. As a result of these changes, the Law Society has shifted from being a mandatory governing body for solicitors to a voluntary trade association. It aims to protect and promote solicitors by, for example, lobbying Government.

11.2.1 Work

For most solicitors, paperwork takes up much of their time. It includes conveyancing (legal aspects of the buying and selling of houses and other property) and drawing up wills and contracts, as well as giving written and oral legal advice. Until 1985, solicitors were the only people allowed to do conveyancing work, but this is no longer the case – people from different occupations can qualify as licensed conveyancers, and the service is often offered by banks and building societies. Probate work (which concerns wills) can now also be done by banks, building societies, insurance companies and legal executives, and consequently the proportions of work done by solicitors are changing.

Photo 11.1 The Law Society

Source: © Spiroview Inc/Shutterstock

Figure 11.1 Trends in the number of solicitors with and without practising certificates

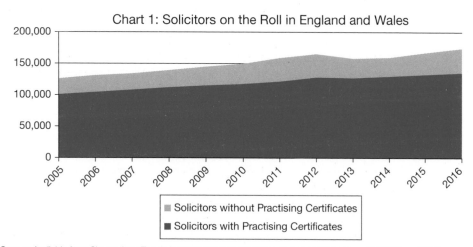

Source: Available from Chart 1 from Trends in the solicitors' profession, Annual Statistics Report 2016 (June 2017). The report can be accessed at https://www.lawsociety.org.uk/support-services/research-trends/documents/annual-statistics-report-2016-executive-summary/

Solicitors have traditionally been able to do advocacy work in the magistrates' court and the County Court, but not generally in the higher courts. This situation was changed by the Courts and Legal Services Act 1990 and the Access to Justice Act 1999. These Acts put in place the mechanics for equalising rights of audience between barristers and solicitors. Now all barristers and solicitors acquire full rights of audience when they are admitted to the Roll (an official register of qualified lawyers entitled to practise), though they will only be able to exercise these rights on completion of the necessary training. When undertaking advocacy work, solicitors can, since 2008, wear wigs in court, just like barristers, which reinforces the fact that they are of equal status. There are currently 5,500 solicitor-advocates. Many firms are sending their solicitors on courses, making advocacy training compulsory and designating individuals as in-house advocates. Thus, solicitors are increasingly doing the advocacy work themselves rather than sending it to a barrister. Where Government funding has established fixed fees for work, solicitors are faced with a simple choice: keep the money or give it away. Even those solicitors who do not have full rights of audience can appear in the High Court in bankruptcy proceedings, or to read out a formal, unchallenged statement; and in the Crown Court if the case is an appeal from the magistrates' court, or has been committed to the Crown Court for sentence, and they appeared in the same case in the magistrates' court. They can also appear before a single judge of the Court of Appeal, and in High Court proceedings held in chambers.

Traditionally, an individual solicitor did much less advocacy work than a barrister but, as more solicitors gain the necessary training to become solicitor-advocates, this is changing. In any case, solicitors as a group do more advocacy than barristers, simply because 98 per cent of criminal cases are tried in the magistrates' court, where the advocate is usually a solicitor. The amount of advocacy done by solicitors is also growing as a result of the removal of many contract and tort cases from the High Court to the County Court, following the Courts and Legal Services Act 1990.

Solicitors can, and usually do, form partnerships with other solicitors. Alternatively, since 2001, they can form a Limited Liability Partnership. Under an ordinary partnership a solicitor can be personally liable (even after retirement) for a claim in negligence against the solicitor firm, even if he or she was not involved in the transaction giving rise to the claim. Under the Limited Liability Partnership (LLP) a partner's liability is limited to negligence for which he or she was personally responsible. Law firms are increasingly converting into LLPs, though some are reluctant to do so as it would require them to be more open about how much senior staff earn.

Solicitors work in ordinary offices, with, in general, the same support staff as any office-based business, and have offices all over England and Wales and in all towns. Practices range from huge London-based firms dealing only with large corporations, to small partnerships or individual solicitors, dealing with the conveyancing, wills, divorces and minor crime of a country town. The top City law firms are known as the 'Magic Circle' and a recent Sweet and Maxwell survey found nearly a quarter of all law students wanted to join one when they qualified, though in practice a much smaller percentage will succeed in doing so. Most law firms are small, with 85 per cent of them having four or fewer partners, and nearly half having only one partner. Some solicitors work in law centres and other advice agencies, Government departments, private industry and education rather than in private practice. Those solicitors who are employed in a salaried position to provide legal advice to their employer (such as a private company) are known as in-house lawyers. The number of in-house lawyers has been growing rapidly, so that in 2011 a quarter of all practising solicitors were in-house lawyers.

Over 1,300 people working for City law firms take home more than £1 million a year, though the chances of a trainee solicitor becoming an equity partner in one of these firms is sometimes only 3 per cent. In 2008, partners in a City law firm charged their clients between £600 and £750 an hour. But these figures have to be seen in the context of a profession that has over 120,000 members. The average annual salary for a solicitor is £45,000.

11.2.2 Qualifications and training

There are two routes to qualifying as a solicitor: with a university degree and without a university degree. Almost all solicitors begin with a degree, though not necessarily in law. A number of law schools introduced an admissions test in 2004, the National Admissions Test for Law (LNAT), to help select students onto their law degrees. The test consists of a series of multiple choice comprehension questions and an essay question. The use of aptitude tests for selection purposes is controversial. The arguments in favour of their use are that they are quick and cheap to run and provide additional information about students' potential, to distinguish between students who have achieved A grades in all their 'A' levels. Critics point out that they provide only a limited portrait of a candidate's skills and miss out important skills needed in law students such as their level of conscientiousness. Practice and coaching on aptitude tests can increase people's scores significantly which can introduce bias in favour of those from privileged family backgrounds. Although no minimum degree classification is laid down, increased competition for entry to the profession means that most successful applicants now have an upper second class degree, and very few get in with less than a lower second.

Students whose degree is not in law have to take a one-year conversion course leading to the Common Professional Examination (CPE). It is possible for non-graduate mature students, who have demonstrated some professional or business achievements, to enter the profession without a degree. They take a broad, two-year CPE course. Only a very small number of people take this two-year route and it is not a route the Law Society encourages – they suggest that, for most people, it is worth putting in the extra year to do a law degree and enter in the conventional manner, especially bearing in mind that many universities and colleges now offer mature students law degrees which can be studied part time, so that students do not have to give up paid employment. It is also possible for legal executives (discussed at p. 256) to become solicitors without first taking a degree course.

The next step, for law graduates and those who have passed the CPE, is a one-year Legal Practice Course (LPC), designed to provide practical skills, including advocacy, as well as legal and procedural knowledge. Since 2009 the LPC has been divided into two stages. Stage one covers the core areas: business law and practice; property law and practice; litigation; professional conduct and regulation; taxation; wills and administration of estates; and skills elements (writing, drafting, interviewing, advising, advocacy and practical legal research). Stage two consists of three vocational electives which can be studied at different institutions if wished. The two stages will normally be completed within a year, but students can take breaks in their studies as long as they complete the course within five years. Fees for the LPC now exceed £16,000 in London but can start upwards of £12,000 outside of London. The CPE and the LPC are not covered by the Government's student loan scheme. The Law Society provides a very small number of bursaries, and has also negotiated a loans scheme with certain high street banks, which offers up to £5,000, that students do not begin paying back until they have finished studying; a few large London firms also offer assistance to those students they wish to attract into employment. The vast majority of students, however, are obliged to fund themselves or rely on expensive loans.

After passing the Legal Practice exams, the prospective solicitor must undertake a period of recognised training. The work of a trainee solicitor can be very demanding, and a survey carried out for the Law Society found that a third work more than 50 hours a week. In 2014, the minimum wage for trainee solicitors was abolished (£17,000 in London). Trainees can now be paid the national minimum wage of £7.38 an hour (approximately £13,500 a year) if a law firm so chooses. In practice, the average salary of a trainee solicitor is around £27,000.

In 2014, the training regulations were changed: most trainee solicitors will continue to undertake a training contract, but this is no longer compulsory; what matters is that a person has undertaken a period of recognised training. This change has been introduced because many people who had completed the Legal Practice Course were failing to find training contracts, especially in times of economic difficulty when firms are reluctant to invest in training. In 2017 there were 5,719 training contracts, but the number of students taking the LPC far exceed that number. Candidates must demonstrate that they have achieved the outcomes required to be a professional solicitor. They must demonstrate to the Solicitors Regulation Authority that their learned experiences in their work experience are equivalent to what is required from a training contract. Candidates will do this by, for example, showing how they have worked alongside solicitors, the legal nature of the work they have undertaken, the level of supervision they have received, feedback, appraisals and interaction with clients. Paralegals (see p. 255) are expected to be the main beneficiaries of this route to qualification. The difficulty for a paralegal seeking to qualify as a solicitor by this route is that much paralegal work is specialist while the period of recognised training requires a breadth of experience.

The majority of solicitors qualifying each year are still law graduates – in 2009 a quarter of newly qualified solicitors had degrees that were not in law. However, the Law Society says that the non-law degree and CPE route is becoming more popular, with a third of places on Legal Practice Courses currently being taken by people aiming to qualify this way. Legal academics have expressed some concern about this, but the Law Society points out that, in some years, pass rates for non-law graduates in solicitors' finals have been higher than those for law graduates.

Figure 11.2 Qualifying as a solicitor with a university degree

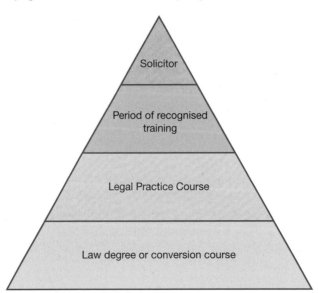

Solicitor

Period of recognised training

Legal Practice Course

Law degree or conversion course

Lord Woolf has observed that the solicitor profession is becoming 'increasingly polarised' depending on the nature of the work carried out, with lawyers working in City firms earning significantly more than those in High Street practices. Specialist LPC courses are now being offered for City law firms. Lord Woolf has criticised this development, as he fears it could undermine the concept of a single solicitor profession with a single professional qualification. Such courses may, over time, create a barrier which prevents students from other colleges from entering a big commercial practice. Lord Woolf has observed that given the quality of the trainees attracted by the City firms, it should be possible for them to provide any enhanced training they require after the end of the Legal Practice Course.

11.2.3 Qualifying without a university degree

You can qualify to become a solicitor without having a university degree. You can do this by completing the academic study of law through the professional examinations set by the Chartered Institute of Legal Executives (see p. 255). After completing these examinations you then have to complete the Legal Practice Course as normal. Chartered Legal Executive lawyers may be exempt from undertaking the two-year training contract depending on the work experience they have already acquired as legal executives.

Alternatively, the Government, with the Solicitors Regulation Authority, has created new apprenticeships which can ultimately lead to qualification as a solicitor. Under the Trailblazer route, qualification as a solicitor will take a number of years and will involve a combination of study and work experience. To qualify as a solicitor through the Trailblazer scheme a person will have to demonstrate to the Solicitors Regulation Authority that they meet the same standards as anyone who has come through more traditional paths to qualification.

Another form of apprenticeship is the High Apprenticeship in Legal Practice. After completing this with the Chartered Institute of Legal Executives, students could take additional examinations with the Chartered Institute as a stepping stone to becoming a solicitor, though it will still be necessary to complete the Legal Practice Course on this route.

The Government and the Solicitors Regulation Authority are keen to develop routes into the profession without a degree. The main aim is to encourage diversity in the profession, because the traditional route of qualifying with a university degree and the Legal Practice Course is extremely expensive and risks pricing people from poorer backgrounds out of the profession. It is interesting to note that apprenticeships have long been used in the accountancy industry. Thus, possible advantages of the apprenticeship route are that people can earn as they learn, avoid paying heavy tuition fees for a degree and LPC and become more commercially aware with their hands-on learning. Potential disadvantages are that this could amount to a very heavy workload for frequently quite young individuals, who miss out on the opportunities provided by a university education. There is a risk that people taking this route may suffer a stigma compared to those who have taken the more traditional route to qualification, and as a result their career progression could be limited. Internationally, the norm is to have a graduate legal profession.

11.2.4 Qualified Lawyers Transfer Scheme

Certain lawyers qualified abroad, particularly in Europe, and English barristers, can convert to become English solicitors by passing the Qualified Lawyers Transfer Scheme (QLTS). In 2018, 11 per cent of admissions as a solicitor (724 lawyers) were through this route. Many of the lawyers entering by this route are employed in international City law firms keen to employ talent from abroad. Applicants under this route must be fully qualified to practise as a lawyer in a country where the role of lawyers is similar to that of England and Wales. They will have to pass a range of tests to show they have the same knowledge and skills as lawyers qualified in the English system.

11.2.5 Continuing competence

The arrangements for continuing professional education have changed. Before November 2016 all solicitors were required to participate in 16 hours a year of Continuing Professional Development (CPD) throughout their careers, with the subjects covered depending on each individual's areas of interest or need. Twenty-five per cent of the time had to be spent attending relevant courses with records kept of courses attended. The remainder of the time could be used to undertake a range of other activities, such as carrying out research and watching DVDs or webcasts.

There had been concern that some solicitors could be tempted to take quite a minimalist approach to Continuing Professional Development to save time and money. The Legal Education and Training Review (discussed on p. 237) considered that the professions placed too great a reliance on initial training and not enough on post-qualification training to guarantee ongoing competence and quality. It recommended that CPD requirements should no longer be measured by imposing a minimum number of hours to be completed each year.

In the light of these recommendations, the old CPD system has been replaced. From November 2016, all solicitors must comply with the new system of continuing competence. Under the new system, instead of an hours-based scheme, the requirements are measured in terms of personal outcomes. Solicitors are required to plan, implement, evaluate and reflect annually on their training needs. This personal development plan is supervised by their employers. Solicitors have to make an annual declaration when renewing their practising certificate that they have considered their educational needs and taken appropriate measures to ensure continuing competence. These new arrangements are likely to be more flexible than the old arrangements. It is hoped the new system will encourage solicitors to take responsibility for planning their training and that the training will be more focused and relevant for their work.

11.2.6 Promotion to the judiciary

In the past, solicitors were only eligible to become circuit judges, but the Courts and Legal Services Act 1990 has opened the way for them to become judges in the higher courts (see Chapter 10: The judges).

The Bigger Picture: Claims management companies

Claims management companies are companies that find people who have a legal problem (for example, by placing adverts on the television and radio asking whether you have suffered an accident in the last three years). They then refer these people to solicitors, who pay the company on average £800 for the referral. Insurance companies have become involved in this business because after a road accident they will have all the victims' details and are making billions of pounds in selling this information to lawyers. The Law Society relaxed its restrictions on advertising in 1986, but law firms have been slow to take up this opportunity, relying heavily on the advertising of claims management companies instead. In the past, the payment of referral fees had been banned, but there was a strong suspicion that this ban was being breached in practice. In 2004, the Law Society decided to lift this ban, providing the Law Society an opportunity to control how referral fees were used.

Many people who suffer a personal injury respond to an advertisement placed by a claims management company. Personal injury litigation is no longer spread evenly across law firms, but instead a smaller number of law firms are paying the claims management companies to do large quantities of personal injury cases. This has led to investment in computer technology to manage the cases which are more likely to be dealt with by lawyers who are specialists in the field; but there is less face-to-face contact with the client. Conveyancing work is also increasingly reaching lawyers through a referral arrangement.

Looking on the positive side, claims management companies can be seen as having successfully broadened access to justice. The large-scale advertising has led to a significant growth in legal claims for personal injury. However, there has been concern that some of these companies have behaved inappropriately, for instance, by encouraging members of the public to start litigation when they do not have a genuine claim, or by pushing people to take out expensive loans to pay for legal insurance premiums they cannot really afford. Most recently, there have been a large number of complaints about the tactics of companies pursuing claims regarding the mis-selling of Payment Protection Insurance.

To try to put an end to unscrupulous practices by claims management companies, they are now required to have a licence and are regulated by the Claims Management Regulation Unit in the Ministry of Justice in accordance with provisions in Part 2 of the Compensation Act 2006. They have to comply with new rules of conduct covering advertising, marketing, soliciting of business and complaints procedures. Any unauthorised provision of claims services is punishable by up to two years' imprisonment. There are a number of exceptions from the requirement for authorisation under the 2006 Act to cover professions whose conduct is already regulated: for example, insurance companies and trade unions.

Lord Jackson's report into court costs which was published in 2010 recommended that referral fees be banned because he thought they added to the client's legal costs unnecessarily. Lord Young was asked by the Prime Minister to investigate 'the rise of the compensation culture over the last decade'. His report *Common Sense, Common Safety* (2010) recommended restricting the operation of referral agencies, including controlling the volume and type of advertising. The Law Society wanted referral fees to be banned, arguing that the choice of lawyer should be made according to quality and not according to who has paid the most to a claims management company, while the Solicitors Regulation Authority opposed a ban.

The Legal Services Board published a report on the subject entitled *Referral Fees, Referral Arrangements and Fee Sharing* (2010) in which it ruled out a complete ban; instead it decided that front-line regulators could impose their own bans if they could provide sufficient evidence to explain their actions. The Board was concerned that a complete ban would push unethical practices underground, with payments being made 'under the counter'. Instead, it pushed for more openness about the payment of referral fees so that the public understood what was going on – the agreements between lawyers and claims management companies should be in writing and a client should be told how much the law firm paid to have their case and that they could choose a different lawyer to avoid paying that fee. In practice one regulator alone will not choose to ban referral fees as this would place its members at a disadvantage to other professionals with a different regulator.

The Government, however, decided that referral fees should be banned with the hope that this could reduce the cost of motor insurance, which all car drivers have to pay for. A provision to this effect was added to the Legal Aid, Sentencing and Punishment of Offenders Act 2012. This ban only applies to the personal injury sector. Some have suggested that it should be extended to, for example, conveyancing, or be a blanket ban on all referral fees.

With the move to alternative business structures for lawyers (discussed on p. 246) in 2011, it is likely that claims management companies will increasingly employ lawyers in-house so there will be no need for referral fees to be paid. Also, established brands (such as insurance companies) entering into the legal service market as an alternative business structure may not need to use claims management companies because they will have their own developed marketing strategy.

11.3 Barristers

There are around 13,076 barristers in independent practice, known collectively as the Bar. Its governing body is the Bar Council, which acts as a kind of trade union, safeguarding the interests of barristers. The Bar Council, like the Law Society, has tried to separate its representative functions from its regulatory functions, and has therefore established a Bar Standards Board responsible for regulating the Bar. The Board makes the rules and takes the decisions affecting entry to, training for, and practice at the Bar, including disciplinary issues.

11.3.1 Work

Advocacy is the main function of barristers, and much of their time will be spent in court or preparing for it. Until the changes made under the Courts and Legal Services Act in 1990, barristers were, with a few exceptions, the only people allowed to advocate in the superior courts – the Supreme Court, the Court of Appeal, the High Court, the Crown Court and the Employment Appeal Tribunal. We have seen that this has now changed, and they are increasingly having to compete with solicitors for this work. Barristers also do some paperwork, drafting legal documents and giving written opinions on legal problems.

Barristers must be self-employed and, under Bar rules, cannot form partnerships, but they usually share offices, called chambers, with other barristers. All the barristers in a particular chambers share a clerk, who is a type of business manager, arranging meetings with the client and the solicitor and also negotiating the barristers' fees. Around 70 per cent of practising barristers are based in London chambers, though they may travel to courts in the provinces; the rest are based in the other big cities. A new commercial vehicle in which barristers can work is a ProcureCo (discussed on p. 363).

Not all qualified barristers work as advocates at the Bar. Like solicitors, some are employed by law centres and other advice agencies, Government departments or private industry, and some teach. Some go into these jobs after practising at the Bar for a time, others never practise at the Bar.

Traditionally, a client could not approach a barrister directly, but had to see a solicitor first, who would then refer the case to a barrister. In 2004, the ban on direct access to barristers was abolished. Members of the public can now contact a barrister without using a solicitor as an intermediary. Barristers are today able to provide specialist advice, drafting and advocacy without a solicitor acting as a 'middleman', although the management of litigation will still generally be handled by solicitors. Direct access to the client is permitted where the barrister has been in practice for three years, and has undertaken a short course preparing them for this new mode of operation.

Barristers work under what is called the 'cab rank' rule. Technically, this means that if they are not already committed for the time in question, they must accept any case which falls within their claimed area of specialisation and for which a reasonable fee is offered. The aim is to ensure that a client can be represented by the barrister of their choice. Professors Flood and Hviid (2013) have argued the rule has too many exceptions, so that barristers can in practice avoid taking on clients they do not want to represent and that there was no justification for the cab rank rule in a modern legal system.

Barristers' pay varies considerably. Average earnings of barristers are apparently very high at the top end at around £300,000 a year but they are reported to earning anything between £25,000–£300,000. In some cases it is suggested that after 10 years' call, earnings can reach £1,000,000. But those working in the criminal and family sector earn much less than those relying on private clients. For those relying on private clients there have been some questions raised as to the value of the claims and costs involved in any legal action. In a case involving the well-known QC David Pannick, there was a lot of criticism around the fees that he charged. In *Fawaz Al Attiya* v *Hamad Bin Jassim Bin Jabber Al Thani* (2016) he reportedly charged over £400,000 for a two day trial which he did not attend. The judge reportedly reminded those involved, that the court was a 'court of justice not a casino'. Likewise, Jonathan Sumption reportedly was paid over £5,000,000 for his representation of Roman Abramovich in a 2012 case which lasted 10 months. This information is however reported and not verified. Shortly after this case Jonathan Sumption became a Supreme Court Judge and is only one of five people to ever be appointed as a judge to the highest court directly from the Bar. Perhaps then it is not so unreasonable for someone so prominent in the profession with such influence and credibility to charge fees such as those mentioned given the value that we attach to their work in shaping the law? Similarly, David Pannick QC is really considered the best in his field and was the barrister that successfully represented Gina Miller in the now infamous *Miller* v *Secretary of State for Exiting the EU* case. Perhaps more than anything, this further crystallises the divide between barristers that work with private clients as opposed to those that work for clients that are either funded through legal aid or have limited financial resources, say in criminal and family law practices. Having said all of this, it is worthy of note that some judges have complained about the quality of advocacy exhibited by some advocates and that perhaps some are taking on work that they cannot manage. This is largely in reference to the work of criminal barristers. This adds insult to injury as criminal barristers are paid far less than their counterparts who can take on private clients and are not subject to the same pressures that criminal barristers are. The quality and performance of their work is inevitably likely to be threatened as a result.

11.3.2 Qualifications and training

The starting point is (at least) an upper second class degree. If this degree is not in law, applicants must do the one-year course leading to the Common Professional Examination (the same course taken by would-be solicitors with degrees in subjects other than law). Mature students may be accepted without a degree, but applications are subject to very stringent consideration, and this is not a likely route to the Bar.

All students then have to join one of the four Inns of Court: Inner Temple; Middle Temple; Gray's Inn; or Lincoln's Inn, all of which are in London. The Inns of Court first emerged in the thirteenth century and their role has evolved over time. Their main functions now cover the provision of professional accommodation for barristers' chambers and residential accommodation for judges, discipline, the provision of law libraries and the promotion of collegiate activities.

Students take the year-long Bar Professional Training Course (BPTC, previously known as the Bar Vocational Course). Until 1996 this course was only available at the Inns of Court School of Law in London, but can now be taken at eight different institutions around the country. The vocational course was reviewed by the Bar Standards Board which published a report, *Entry to the Bar*, in 2007 and some changes to the course were made. The course includes oral exercises and tuition in interviewing and negotiating skills and, as with solicitors' training, more emphasis has been laid on these practical aspects in recent years. The 2007 report suggested that consideration should be given as to whether students should be required to have an upper second class degree in order to undertake the course. It also suggested that students should be required to sit an entrance examination checking their aptitude for the barrister profession, by looking in particular at their communication and written skills. This raises the same debates as for the LNAT aptitude test (discussed on p. 219). The report recommended that there should be a single, unified final examination, set and marked externally and overseen by a board of examiners, to deal with the perceived differences in standards between different providers.

Following this report, the Bar Standards Board introduced an aptitude test and an English language test which have to be passed in order to be allowed to take the BPTC.

The national student loan scheme is not available for the one-year conversion courses or the BPTC. The Inns of Court between them provide around £4 million in sponsorship. Approximately 25 per cent of students will receive assistance from their Inn, with about half of these obtaining a sum of between £3,000 and £6,000. Around 2,917 apply and just over 1,400 applicants take the BPTC each year with around 800 of those being successful and only half of these obtaining a pupillage. Each student has to pay approximately between £15,000 to £19,000 for the course alone, and then find living expenses on top.

Students have to dine at their Inn 12 times. This rather old-fashioned and much criticised custom stems from the idea that students will benefit from the wisdom and experience of their elders if they sit among them at mealtimes. The dinners are linked to seminars, lectures and training weekends, in order to provide genuine educational benefit.

After this, the applicant is called to the Bar, and must then find a place in a chambers to serve his or her pupillage. This is a one-year apprenticeship in which pupils assist a qualified barrister, who is known as their pupil master. In the past funding for pupillage has been a problem. But pupils should now normally be paid a minimum of £12,000 a year in accordance with the Living Wage Foundation's benchmark. Again, there is a large disparity between the wage a pupil can expect depending on whether they work in in private law such as for a commercial set or a criminal set. Some commercial sets offer around £70,000 to their pupils. Competition for pupillage places can be fierce, with only around 450 pupillage vacancies available each year for the 1,400 students completing the BPTC course. Pupillage is usually done in two six-month blocks, with different pupil masters and usually in different chambers. Pupils are required to take courses on advocacy, advice to counsel and forensic accountancy, as part of the increased emphasis on practical skills.

Pupillage completed, the newly qualified barrister must find a permanent place in a chambers, known as a tenancy. This can be the most difficult part, and some are forced to 'squat' – remaining in their pupillage chambers for as long as they are allowed, without becoming a full member – until they find a permanent place. There are less than 300 tenancies available each year – one to every two pupils.

In 1993, the Royal Commission on Criminal Justice recommended that barristers should have to undertake further training during the course of their careers, after noting that both preparation of cases and advocacy were failing to reach acceptable standards. In response, the Bar Council introduced a continuing education programme. Barristers must now complete a minimum of 45 hours of continuing education in the prescribed subjects by the end of their first three years of practice. They have to study four subjects:

- Case Preparation and Procedure;
- Substantive Law or Training relating to Practice;
- Ethics;
- Advocacy Training.

The Bar Council has also introduced an established practitioners' programme under which all barristers who have been qualified for over three years must undertake each year a minimum of 24 hours' study.

11.3.3 Promotion to the judiciary

Suitably experienced barristers are eligible for appointment to all judicial posts, and the majority of current judges have practised at the Bar (for details of appointments, see Chapter 10: The judges).

11.3.4 Queen's Counsel

After 15 years in practice, barristers and solicitors may apply to become a Queen's Counsel, or QC (sometimes called a silk, as they wear gowns made of silk). This usually means they will be offered higher-paid cases, and need do less preliminary paperwork. The average annual earnings of a QC are £270,000, with a small group earning over £1 million a year. At the moment most QCs are barristers, though not all barristers attempt or manage to become QCs – those that do not are called juniors, even up to retirement age. Juniors may assist QCs in big cases, as well as working alone. Since 1995, solicitors can also be appointed as QCs, but they form the minority. In 2017, 119 QCs were appointed of which six were solicitor advocates.

The future of the QC system was put in doubt when the Office of Fair Trading in 2001 suggested the system was merely a means of artificially raising the price of a barrister's services. The Bar Council counter-argued that, actually, the system was an important quality mark which directs the client to experienced, specialist lawyers where required.

In the past the appointment process for QCs was similar to that for senior judges, including the system of secret soundings, and with civil servants, a Cabinet Minister and the Queen all involved. In 2003 the appointment process was suspended, following criticism of the QC system. Appointments were recommended in 2004 but relying on a new appointment process. The Government is no longer involved. Instead, responsibility for appointments has been placed in the hands of the two professional bodies: the Bar Council and the Law Society. They select candidates on the basis of merit, following an open competition. The secret soundings system has been abolished and replaced by structured references from judges, lawyers and clients who have seen the candidate in action. The title of QC has been retained for the time being, though the Law Society would like to see it replaced with another name,

Figure 11.3 Qualifying as a barrister

to mark a clean break from the past, when the system clearly favoured barristers. Commenting on the new appointment procedures, the Law Society president stated:

> Consumers can be assured that holders of the QC designation under the new scheme have been awarded it because of what they know not who they know, and that their superior expertise and experience has been evaluated by an independent panel on an objective basis.

The current view of the Ministry of Justice is that the badge of QC is a well-recognised and respected 'kite-mark' of quality both at home and abroad. The existence of QCs helps to enhance London's status as the centre of international litigation and arbitration.

Sadly, research carried out by Dr Michael Blackwell (2012) has found that Oxbridge-educated, London-based male barristers are still far more likely to make silk. He concluded:

> Because of the failure of the QC system to appoint the best advocates it does not operate as a perfect kite-mark of quality for consumers. Nor does it equally distribute the awards of QC status on any equitable basis. Finally, it might be thought to inhibit judicial diversity by restricting the pool from which the senior judiciary is traditionally recruited.

He also noted:

> The award of QC status is effectively for life, which might be thought to make the claim that it is a kite-mark of quality dubious.

The Bigger Picture: Quality Assurance Scheme for Advocates (QASA)

There has been some concern about the quality of advocacy in the courts. The quality of some solicitor-advocates has been questioned, particularly by barristers. Lord Carter produced a report in 2006 in which he stated that market forces alone can no longer be relied upon to eliminate under-performing advocates. The Law Society asked a consultant, Nick Smedley, to undertake a review of this issue (2009). He concluded that the qualification process needed to be tightened up, so that solicitor-advocates received more intense training before they could undertake higher rights of audience.

The regulators of the barristers, solicitors and legal executives are together establishing a Quality Assurance Scheme for Advocates (QASA) to respond to these concerns. The details of the scheme were finalised in August 2013 and the scheme was expected to be up and running in 2015. Implementation has been repeatedly delayed due to strong opposition from criminal lawyers. Its implementation has been postponed following a court challenge to the scheme carried out by the Criminal Bar Association (CBA), which claims that the scheme risks exposing advocates to inappropriate pressure, resulting in a 'chilling effect' on advocacy. Initially it will only apply to criminal law advocates. Under the scheme, everybody wishing to undertake criminal law advocacy work (both prosecution and defence) will have to register with QASA. The aim is to systematically assess the quality of advocacy measured by agreed standards regardless of the advocate's previous education and training. Advocates will be accredited at one of four levels. A Level 1 advocate will be able to undertake work in the magistrates' court and a Level 4 advocate will be able to undertake the most serious cases in the Crown Court. Advocates may progress through the four levels (subject to rights of audience of their professional status) by demonstrating through formal assessments that they meet the required standard for the next level. Advocates who choose to remain at their current level will be required to re-accredit at that level every five years. Assessment will be by continuing professional development tests, independent assessors and judges to determine whether they are competent to act at a certain level. Trained judges in the Crown Courts may assess advocates of their own initiative if they have concerns about performance, and submit such evaluations directly to the regulators for consideration.

If there is sufficient evidence to conclude that an advocate is acting above their competence, they can undertake training to address concerns. If a regulator decides that an advocate is not competent, the advocate's accreditation at that level can be removed and, in appropriate circumstances, they can be given accreditation at a lower level. There would be a right to appeal in these circumstances.

One area of controversy has been the involvement of judges in this process. Those in favour of judicial involvement point to the benefits of assessing advocates at work in a live situation rather than artificially in an assessment centre. Also, as the judges are already being paid to watch the advocates their involvement would be relatively cheap. Solicitors fear that, as many judges originally trained as barristers, they will favour the Bar. Others have argued that judges in criminal cases should be focusing on determining the innocence or guilt of the defendant before them in court, rather than being distracted by grading the quality of the advocates. Barristers in the north of England have voted unanimously to boycott the scheme. Barristers may not be opposed to a system of quality control for advocacy in itself, but they may fear the scheme will be used as part of the price-competitive tendering process for legal aid (see p. 361). QASA would stop cheap lawyers being used who were not of the requisite standard. An appeal on the legality of the QASA scheme was rejected by the Supreme Court. In November 2017 it was decided that QASA would no longer be implemented.

In 2015, the Government issued a consultation paper, *Enhancing the quality of criminal advocacy*. This considered banning the payment of referral fees for criminal defence advocacy work; introducing a panel of lawyers who would be the only lawyers entitled to undertake publicly funded criminal defence work in the Crown Court and appellate courts; and restricting the use of in-house lawyers for criminal defence advocacy. The Law Society expressed its concerns that these reform proposals seem to favour the interests of the barrister profession over other legal professionals.

11.3.5 Reserved activities

Under the Legal Services Act 2007 some services are called 'reserved legal activities'. These activities can only be undertaken by professionally qualified lawyers or members of other professions who are authorised to provide such services. These include the conduct of litigation and probate activities (following a person's death). This amounts to a significant restriction on freedom of competition, but aims to ensure the professional standard of work in sensitive areas where a lay person might not be in a position to judge the quality of the work.

The Law Society campaigned for wills and estate administration to become reserved legal activities. They argued that, at the moment, anybody could, for example, charge for will-writing services and the standard of some of these wills was unsatisfactory. Consumers can be subjected to high-pressure sales tactics and poorly drafted wills, and problems usually only come to light after someone has died. By then, it is very difficult to put matters right. Will-writers need not be members of any professional body and are therefore not necessarily subject to any professional regulations. One consequence is that consumers are not able to complain about these services to the Legal Ombudsman if the services are not provided by professional lawyers. There is a risk of fraud with unregulated estate administration. The Institute of Professional Willwriters (IPW) has campaigned for more than 20 years for will-writing to be regulated. It launched a voluntary code of practice for will-writers in 2010, but only a minority of practitioners joined the scheme. The Solicitors Regulation Authority is in favour of more services becoming reserved activities and the Legal Services Board favoured making will-writing a reserved activity. However, the Lord Chancellor has decided that will-writing should not become a reserved activity because there was no evidence that regulation would improve the quality of will-writing, but it would certainly push up the cost. Most wills are actually quite straightforward to prepare and do not need advanced legal skills. The arrival on the scene of alternative business structures (see p. 246) is likely to add to the importance of this debate.

11.4 Complaints

Until recently the individual professions were responsible for dealing with complaints, but these procedures were heavily criticised. Problems with the handling of complaints were highlighted by the fallout from the Coal Health Compensation Scheme. This scheme was set up by the Labour Government in 1999 to compensate miners for respiratory disease and vibration white finger suffered as a result of working for the national coal industry. The scheme was expected to cost the Government £1 billion. Solicitors were criticised for deducting large sums of money as legal fees from money that was intended to be paid to their clients as compensation. In 65 per cent of the cases that had been settled by March 2008, the solicitors' legal fees had been greater than the compensation received by the client. Many complaints were made to the Legal Complaints Service but there was criticism of the inconsistent way these complaints were handled.

Sir David Clementi (2004) looked at the complaints system and concluded that it favoured the lawyer over the complainant. He recommended establishing a completely independent body that would consider complaints against all lawyers.

The position of Legal Ombudsman was therefore created in 2010 to investigate and resolve complaints about the service provided by lawyers, including barristers and solicitors.

The Legal Ombudsman provides a free service and is required to look at complaints in a fair and independent way. Complaints should be made to the lawyer first and it is only if the internal complaints handling procedure is unable to resolve the dispute that the complaint should be made to the Legal Ombudsman. Many complaints about lawyers arise from a collision between what lawyers are used to providing and what the modern users of professional services are increasingly accustomed to expect. When investigating a complaint, the key questions the Ombudsman asks are: Was the information the lawyer provided clear? Did the lawyer treat their client fairly? Did the lawyer keep their client advised so that they could make informed decisions? The Ombudsman can recommend any remedy from a simple apology, a refund, or up to £50,000 compensation. It resolves the majority of complaints informally, but where this is not possible the Ombudsman imposes a decision on the parties.

The Legal Ombudsman publishes the names of lawyers against whom there has been a pattern of complaints or where this is in the public interest, under a process of 'naming and shaming'. By doing this the Ombudsman is both providing a remedy for the individual who submitted the complaint, but also providing a service to the wider public by providing them with information when choosing which solicitor to instruct. This in turn should act as an incentive for lawyers to maintain high standards. The Legal Ombudsman is, thereby, providing a level of transparency which might be a viable alternative to market-driven developments such as the controversial 'Solicitors from Hell' website where unhappy clients chose to publish their complaints, damaging some law firms' reputations.

At the moment only the lawyer's clients can make a complaint to the Legal Ombudsman. The Legal Services Board Consumer Panel has recommended that third parties should also be able to make a complaint: for example, a home owner whose house sale fell through because of delays by the purchaser's lawyer, or where the claimant's lawyer used bullying tactics against the defendant during litigation proceedings. The aim would be to encourage ethical conduct and raise professional standards. Without this it is difficult for third parties to get a remedy against lawyers. The Legal Ombudsman would also like to expand its remit to include complaints about any legal service provider.

While the establishment of the Legal Ombudsman has improved the handling of complaints and saved money, the Office of Fair Trading still considered in 2013 that the complaints system was too complicated, with a third of dissatisfied clients stating they had not complained because they did not understand how to make a complaint.

Where there is an allegation against a solicitor of professional misconduct or breach of the Rules, Regulations or Code relating to professional practice, proceedings can be brought before the Solicitors Disciplinary Tribunal. Such proceedings are usually commenced by the Solicitors Regulation Authority, though private parties can also make an application. In appropriate cases the tribunal can ban the individual from practising as a solicitor.

Lawyers can also be sued for negligent work like most other professionals. Following the House of Lords' judgment in *Arthur JS Hall & Co v Simons* (2000) lawyers no longer enjoy any immunity from liability for work connected to the conduct of a case in court. Until that case, barristers enjoyed immunity from liability for negligent work in court. This immunity had been recognised by the courts in the case of *Rondel v Worsley* (1969). The main justification for the immunity was that a negligence action would effectively result in a retrial of the case that gave rise to the allegation of negligence, which would damage the certainty and finality of the original verdict. In other words, clients would seek to use litigation against their barrister to reopen indirectly litigation that had already been lost.

Figure 11.4 Complaint categories investigated by the Ombudsman, 2017–2018

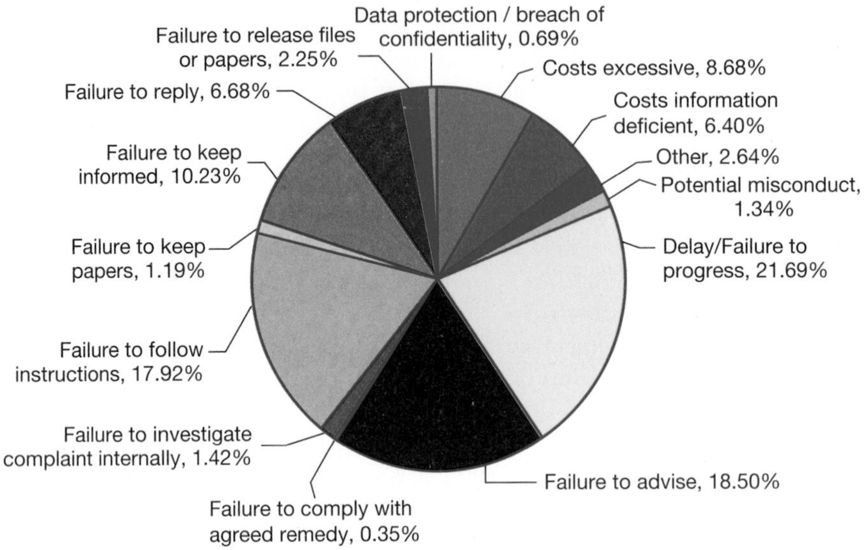

Data protection / breach of confidentiality, 0.69%
Failure to release files or papers, 2.25%
Failure to reply, 6.68%
Failure to keep informed, 10.23%
Failure to keep papers, 1.19%
Failure to follow instructions, 17.92%
Failure to investigate complaint internally, 1.42%
Failure to comply with agreed remedy, 0.35%
Costs excessive, 8.68%
Costs information deficient, 6.40%
Other, 2.64%
Potential misconduct, 1.34%
Delay/Failure to progress, 21.69%
Failure to advise, 18.50%

Source: Graph created from data held in the table labelled 'What the complaints were about' which is hosted on the following page: http://www.legalombudsman.org.uk/raising-standards/data-and-decisions/\#complaints-data.

Key case

The immunity of barristers from liability for negligence was dramatically abolished by the House of Lords in *Arthur JS Hall & Co v Simons* (2000). There was no longer any good reason to treat barristers differently from other professionals – their negligence could give rise to liability in tort.

Legal principle
Barristers can be liable for negligent work.

11.5 Background of barristers and solicitors

Lawyers have, in the past, come from a very narrow social background, in terms of sex, race and class; there have also been significant barriers to entrants with disabilities. In recent years the professions have succeeded in opening their doors to a wider range of people, so that they are more representative of the society in which they work.

White, middle-class men dominate in most professions, excluding many people who would be highly suited to such careers. A narrow social profile created particular problems for the legal professions in the past. First, it meant that the legal professions have been seen as unapproachable and elitist, which put off some people from using lawyers and thereby benefiting from their legal rights (this issue is examined in Chapter 15). Secondly, the English judiciary is drawn from the legal professions and, if their background is narrow, that of the judiciary will be too (this issue is examined in Chapter 10). Increasingly, the professions are becoming representative of the society in which they function.

Research carried out by InterLaw Diversity Forum (2011) has found a general improvement in attitudes to gay lawyers within the profession.

11.5.1 Women

Women were only allowed to become lawyers with the passing of the Sex Disqualification (Removal) Act 1919, which allowed women to enter all professions. Up until then, the Law Society had been anxious to keep women out to protect the financial interests of the existing male solicitors. Thirty-five years later there were still only 350 practising women solicitors. At that time, many male solicitors with their own practices saw training for the legal profession as an easy way to educate and provide for their daughters and their own retirement. Thus these female solicitors tended to work in family firms.

The number of women in the professions has increased dramatically since the 1970s. In 1987 women accounted for less than 20 per cent of all solicitors; now 48 per cent of solicitors are women. Today there are more women qualifying for the solicitor profession than men, and nearly 70 per cent of all law students are female, and women hold over 60 per cent of registered training contracts.

For the barrister profession in 2017, just over 60 per cent of those called to the Bar were women and just over 50 per cent of those who commenced a pupillage were women. Overall around just over 35 per cent of barristers are women.

The problem now, for women, is less about entry into the professions and more about pay, promotion and working conditions. Female solicitors earn less than male solicitors. Right from the beginning of their career, men are earning more than women, with male trainees having a starting salary which is 5.7 per cent more than female trainees. Statistics published by the Law Society show that male solicitors are earning 50 per cent more than female solicitors: on average a male solicitor is earning £60,000 compared with £41,000 for a female solicitor.

The statistics of 2017 show that fewer women are being promoted to become partners in their law firm. Women make up 48 per cent of all lawyers but only 33 per cent of partners are women, with women making up 59 per cent of non-partner solicitors. There is quite a stark difference between 59 per cent and 33 per cent and this percentage of women partners goes down further still in the largest firms to 29 per cent. There is a similar problem in the barrister profession. In 2017 only just over 15 per cent of Queen's Counsel were women: there were 1,409 silks and only 254 were women.

A growing problem exists of women choosing to leave the profession early. This is either because they find it impossible to combine the demands of motherhood with a legal career or because they are frustrated at the 'glass ceiling' which seems to prevent women lawyers from achieving the same success as their male counterparts. Solicitor firms do not tend to have provisions in place for flexible or part-time working for solicitors. Those that do tend to discourage solicitors from taking advantage of them (*Research Study No. 26 of the Law Society Research and Policy Planning Unit* (1997)). Research by Insight Oxford (2010) found that the profession's long hours culture disadvantaged those with family responsibilities. The female lawyers questioned stated that the biggest barrier to advancing their career was the 'mindset and values of the senior partners' and there was 'no real impetus for change from male colleagues'. By the ninth year after qualification, 40 per cent of women have left the profession. There is a risk that young women are in effect being employed as cheap, temporary labour. The Law Society has recognised that in order to retain women and to ensure that the investment in their training is not lost, the profession must consider more flexible work arrangements (including career breaks) to allow women (and men) to continue to work alongside caring responsibilities.

The solicitor, Elizabeth Cruickshank (2007), has commented:

> We have been encouraged to think that there would be a 'trickle up' effect because of the sheer numbers of women entering the profession, so that we would no longer be held back by the 'sticky floor', bump our heads against the 'glass ceiling' or fall off the 'glass cliff'. Reflection shows that apparently the floor, the ceiling and the cliff are still in place and that the trickle upwards is almost inexorably slowed by social gravity.

11.5.2 Ethnic minorities

Again, the picture is improving. Since 2013, the Legal Services Board requires legal regulators to collect diversity data for their profession. The number of solicitors from a black, Asian and minority ethnic (BAME) background has increased recently. In 2017, 21 per cent of practising solicitors came from an ethnic minority. This compares with 4 per cent in 1995. In 2017, approximately 14 per cent of trainee solicitors were from an Asian background. There are still, however, very few male Afro-Caribbean solicitors, with black solicitors only representing 3 per cent of the solicitor population.

As regards the Bar, in 1989, 5 per cent of practising barristers came from a BAME background; by 2017 this has increased with incredible slow progress to 12.5 per cent.

Regrettably, there have in the past been reports in the media of black candidates doing less well in legal examinations than white candidates, particularly at the Bar. It has been suggested that oral examinations may be particularly vulnerable to subjective marking.

The Law Society has recognised that obstacles still exist for ethnic minorities in the solicitor profession. This is because most solicitor firms do not follow proper recruitment procedures, do not have an equal opportunities policy and practice, and the levels of discrimination within society at large are reflected in the perception of solicitors and their clients. Only 20 per cent of black and minority ethnic solicitors are partners in their firms. Just 8 per cent of partners in the top 150 law firms are from an ethnic minority and only 7 per cent of Queen's Counsel. Research carried out for the Legal Services Commission in 2008 suggests that ethnic minority barristers were earning on average £50,000 less than their white counterparts. Statistics published by the Law Society show that white solicitors are earning 25 per cent more than black solicitors: on average a white solicitor is earning £60,000 compared with £41,000 for a black solicitor. Black solicitors often practise in areas of work such as legal aid and in small law firms which are coming under increased economic pressure, with the risk that they will be forced out of the profession.

11.5.3 Class

The biggest obstacle to a career in law now seems to be a person's social background. Law degree students are predominantly middle class, with less than one in five coming from a working class background. In 2009, an official report, *Unleashing Aspiration: The Final Report of the Panel on Fair Access to the Professions*, identified that lawyers were increasingly coming from wealthy families. Lawyers born in 1958 tended to come from families whose income was 40 per cent higher than average. Lawyers born in the 1970s grew up in households whose income was 64 per cent higher than average, so the problem is getting worse

Table 11.1 Ethnicity of practising certificate (PC) holders (2015)

Ethnicity	Men	Women	Total	% of all PC holders
White European	52,428	48,546	100,974	75.7%
African-Caribbean	249	658	907	0.7%
Asian	4,943	5,752	10,695	8.0%
Chinese	641	1,062	1,703	1.3%
African	835	1,096	1,931	1.4%
Other ethnic origin	1,369	1,942	3,311	2.5%
All solicitors for whom ethnic origin is known	60,465	59,056	119,521	
% of all solicitors with PCs for whom ethnic origin is known	88.6%	90.7%		89.6%
Ethnicity unknown	7,755	6,091	13,846	10.4%
All PC holders	68,220	65,147	133,367	100%
All PC holders from minority ethnic groups known to the Law Society	8,037	10,510	18,547	
% of all solicitors with PCs	11.8%	16.1%		13.9%

Annual Statistical Report 2015

Source: Page 9 of the Law Society report 'Diversity Profile of the Profession 2014, A Short Synopsis' published in June 2015. The report can be accessed at: http://www.lawsociety.org.uk/support-services/research-trends/diversity-in-the-profession/

rather than better, with even average middle-class students finding it difficult to build a career in law. A 1989 Law Society Survey found that over a third of solicitors had come from private schools, despite the fact that only 7 per cent of the population attend such schools. In recent years, more lawyers have been educated in the state sector, but this progress could soon be reversed. This is because the lack of funding for legal training has made it very difficult for students without well-off parents to qualify, especially as barristers. Seventy-eight per cent of Queen's Counsel attended Oxford or Cambridge University.

Research carried out by Louise Ashley (2010) of City University London has concluded that part of the problem for working-class candidates is that law firms tend to recruit applicants on the basis of how they look and sound. Law firms believe that clients have difficulty in assessing the quality of the legal advice they have received. They therefore consider that portraying a 'high class' image is important to convincing the client that they have received a good quality service. The research suggests that this attitude might be misguided because it is restricting the firm to a limited range of candidates with copy-cat skills that only attract one segment of the market. If the firms diversified their recruitment this could be a means of diversifying their market.

11.5.4 Disability

Much attention has been paid to the under-representation of working-class people, ethnic minorities and women in the legal profession, but disabled people are less often discussed. Skill as a lawyer requires brains, not physical strength or dexterity, yet it seems there are still significant barriers to entry for disabled students, particularly to the Bar. Part of the problem is simply practical: a quarter of court buildings are over 100 years old and were never designed to offer disabled access. Most now have rooms adapted for disabled people, but need notice if they are to be used, which is hardly feasible for junior barristers, who often get cases at very short notice. The other main barrier is effectively the same as that for ethnic minorities, working-class people and women: with fierce competition for places, 'traditional' applicants have the advantage.

Steps are being taken to address the problems of disabled applicants to the Bar. In 1992, the Bar's Disability Panel was established. This offers help to disabled people who are already within the profession or are hoping to enter it, by matching them to people who have overcome or managed to accommodate similar problems. The Inner Temple also gives grants for reading devices, special furniture and other aids, with the aim of creating a 'level playing field' for disabled and able-bodied people.

11.5.5 Social mobility

In addition to matters concerning diversity in terms of ethnicity and gender, there is further the issue of social mobility. Social mobility considers the ease at which one can move within and through the social spectrum. Data collected by the SRA indicates that 22 per cent of all lawyers attended a fee-paying school, which compares with 7 per cent of the general population. Further, 24 per cent of partners attended a fee-paying school and 20 per cent of solicitors attended a fee-paying school. In City firms, 36 per cent of partners attended a fee-paying school. Further still, there is a divide between the type of work undertaken, with corporate firms having the lowest proportion of state-educated lawyers at 56 per cent whereas in firms undertaking criminal and litigation work, around 77 per cent of the solicitors are from state-educated schools. Attendance at fee-paying schools indicates such people already come from a level of financial stability and have a certain preferred characteristic for the profession. This can serve as a further barrier to enter the profession.

In addition to attendance at fee-paying schools, the proportion of partners who were the first generation to attend university is highest within the smallest firms according to the information available from the SRA.

In the summer of 2018, the Bar Council launched a campaign called 'I am the Bar'. This examines the profile of those who have succeeded at the Bar but who are from what is described as a 'non-traditional' background, that is, those who are not white and the first generation to attend university amongst some other factors. The campaign states that it designed to:

1   Raise the profile of social mobility and support fair access to the Bar, to encourage aspiring barristers from non-traditional backgrounds.
2   Highlight efforts made to improve access to, and diversity within, the profession.
3   Support efforts to improve insight into the profession by drawing together profession-wide social mobility efforts across chambers, Inns, other organisations and individual barristers.

The Bigger Picture: Educational reform

In 2011 a Legal Education and Training Review (LETR) was established by the Solicitors Regulation Authority (SRA), the Bar Standards Board (BSB) and ILEX Professional Standards (IPS). The Review looked at the education and training requirements of the legal professions for the provision of legal services in England and Wales. The legal services sector is experiencing an unprecedented degree of change. The LETR was intended to ensure that the future system of legal education and training will be effective and efficient in preparing legal service providers to meet the needs of consumers. England and Wales need a legal education and training system which both protects and promotes the interests of consumers and ensures an independent, strong, diverse and effective legal profession. It looked at all stages of legal education and training, including the academic stage of qualification at university, professional training and continuing professional development post-qualification.

During the preliminary consultation process the LETR considered a range of quite radical reforms, including abolishing the need to have a qualifying law degree or equivalent qualification. The proposals in its final report, published in 2013, are actually less radical and it does not recommend any major change to the existing system. The Review seems to have concluded that major changes are not actually required, because there are no fundamental problems with the current arrangements for legal education. Instead, it recommends a range of small changes to enhance quality, accessibility and flexibility to make sure the system remains fit for the future. Furthermore, it has recommended that learning outcomes for the different qualification routes should be established, based on occupational analysis of the range of knowledge, skills and attributes required for the different professional roles. Upon completion of their qualification, trainees should demonstrate competence based on these professional criterion before they can qualify. This is called 'day one learning outcomes'. The report concluded that the current system for legal education and training 'provides, for the most part, a good standard of education and training enabling the development of the core knowledge and skills needed for practice across the range of regulated professions'.

The Review noted that professional ethics are central to professional practice but the current quality of training in this field was of a variable standard. There should be a strengthening in requirements for education and training in legal ethics, values and professionalism. The current education provision left some skills gaps: students needed to develop greater legal research skills, critical thinking and communication skills. The initial stages of training needed more writing, drafting and advocacy practice. Students should therefore complete a project or dissertation in the second or final year of their degree. They needed to develop management skills and greater commercial awareness. Students also needed to receive equality and diversity awareness training.

It was also noted that there should be more opportunity to mix formal education and supervised legal practice. This could respond to the concern that the Legal Practice Course struggles to mirror real practice at work. Flexibility of access, particularly through non-graduate entry (apprenticeships) and progression from paralegal roles, should be improved and the consistency and transparency of transfer rules between authorised occupations enhanced. There should be increased standardisation of assessments. Guidance on offering work experience should be introduced to improve equality of access.

A one-stop information hub should be created to facilitate access to information on the education and training available.

LETR was the latest stage in a long discussion on the future of legal education and training. It is now up to each of the front-line regulators to decide what action to take in response to the review's recommendations. The LETR proposals will not tackle the problem of the cost of getting the academic and vocational qualifications, which will continue to act as a barrier to

11

THE LEGAL PROFESSIONS

students from lower income families. The current arrangements favour applicants from wealthy backgrounds who can afford to undertake the lengthy and expensive training process. It is undoubtedly important that the legal profession should be a career option for all able students from a wide range of backgrounds, and that people should not be prevented from entering the profession because their family is not rich.

The Charter 88 constitutional reform pressure group has argued that students should be funded throughout their legal training. The Law Society and the Bar Council have made representations to the Government, pointing out that training for other professions, such as medicine and teaching, is paid or involves reduced fees. In her book *Eve was Framed* (1992), Helena Kennedy QC argues that selection for the Bar in particular has always been based too much on 'connections' and financial resources than on ability. She recommends public funding for legal education and that there should be incentives for barristers' chambers to take on less conventional candidates.

In 2005 the Law Society published a consultation paper, *Qualifying as a Solicitor – a Framework for the Future.* The consultation paper suggested that it should no longer be necessary for a future solicitor to complete a Legal Practice Course or, in fact, to have any academic legal qualifications (such as a law degree). Instead, candidates would simply need to demonstrate they had acquired the necessary skills and knowledge by passing assessments set by the Law Society. These proposals were the subject of considerable criticism, in particular that, without the course structure of the Legal Practice Course, consistent standards would not be maintained.

The former Advisory Committee on Legal Education and Conduct (ACLEC) examined the issue of legal training in a report it published in 1996. It suggested that the two branches should no longer have completely separate training programmes at the postgraduate stage. Instead, after either a law degree or a degree in another subject plus the CPE, all students would take a Professional Legal Studies course, lasting around 18 weeks. Only then would they decide which branch of the profession to choose, going on to a Legal Practice Course (for solicitors) or Bar Vocational Course (for barristers) which would be only 15–18 weeks long. This, the ACLEC suggested, would prevent the problem of students having to specialise too early. It also recommended that funding should be made available for the CPE course and the vocational stage of training.

The Legal Services Consumer Panel criticised the 'general practitioner' style of training for lawyers in its submission to LETR:

> The GP-style qualification model fails to respond to a market which is hugely varied in terms of its provider base and range of activities. It is impossible for a single qualification to prepare an individual for the sheer diversity of roles they might, perhaps much later, come to occupy. It is in danger of providing adequate preparation for nothing instead of providing a readiness to tackle anything – the principle to which it aspires.

The Panel has argued that a 'modular approach' to qualification should be taken, where those approved to practise would gain a limited permission to provide certain legal services, but authorisation to provide others would be granted separately on the completion of further training. The consumer panel would like to see a single regulatory badge under which the professional titles of solicitor and barrister would 'lose meaning'. While the professional titles have powerful brand appeal for consumers and strongly influence their choice of legal adviser, they create misleading distinctions between regulated providers. For example, a solicitor is likely to be seen by the average consumer wishing to buy a home as being more qualified than a licensed conveyancer for this task, but both have demonstrated they are sufficiently competent to perform the role.

In 2015 the Solicitors Regulation Authority suggested a new examination for solicitors could be introduced, called the Solicitors Qualifying Examination (SQE). This would be a national examination which would have to be passed by anyone who wished to become a solicitor. It would not be necessary to have a degree or to study the Legal Practice Course (LPC) in order to sit this examination. The aim would be to provide a consistent standard that had to be achieved in order to become a solicitor. At the same time it would potentially remove some of the financial obstacles of becoming a solicitor because a candidate would not need to pay the fees for a university degree or LPC qualification, though in practice they might find it difficult to pass this examination without any formal education in law. While other professions, such as nursing and teaching, have moved to become graduate professions, it is surprising that solicitors would move backwards to being a non-graduate profession. The barrister profession has not suggested it would remove the requirement of a degree from its qualification process.

It is anticipated that the SQE will consist of two parts: SQE stage 1 and SQE stage 2. Stage 1 requires the completion of 6 functioning legal knowledge assessments and 1 practical legal skills assessment. Stage 2 requires 5 practical legal skills assessments taken in practical skills contexts which will constitute another 5 assessments so there will be a total of 10 assessments in stage 2. The SRA plans for there to be two points in the year when these exams can be taken and anticipates the new SQE to come into effect in 2020.

11.6 Performance of the legal professions

Over the past 30 years, the performance of lawyers has come in for a great deal of criticism. The last good report was given by the 1979 Royal Commission on Legal Services, which found that 84 per cent of clients were satisfied with the work done by their lawyers, and only 13 per cent were actually dissatisfied. The Commission interpreted this as a vote of confidence for the profession, but as Zander (1988) pointed out, the research was not entirely reliable, since ordinary individuals are unlikely to have sufficient knowledge or experience to make informed judgements about the service they received – they might recognise very bad legal work, but were unlikely to know whether they had received the best advice or help for their situation. Significantly, a similar survey among corporate clients, who use lawyers more frequently, reported a higher level of dissatisfaction.

Since the 1979 Royal Commission, many different criticisms of the profession have been made, from many different quarters. In 1995, the Consumers' Association magazine *Which?* caused a stir with a survey of the standards of advice provided by solicitors. Its researchers phoned a number of solicitors, posing as members of the public seeking advice about simple consumer problems, and the advice given was assessed by the Association's own legal team. The verdict was not good, with much of the advice given being assessed as inadequate or simply wrong. Two years later, the magazine repeated the test and, once again, the results were bad: of the 79 solicitors approached by researchers, the majority gave advice which was incomplete, or in some cases incorrect. In several cases, researchers were incorrectly told that their situation gave them no claim in law; the magazine points out that real-life clients told this would probably not pursue the matter further and would therefore not take advantage of their full legal rights. *Which?* accepted that lawyers cannot be expected to be experts in every area of law, but argued that, if asked something outside their area of expertise, they should admit that and either find out the answer or refer the client to someone else. The Law Society criticised both surveys, arguing that the methods employed were not realistic; and after complaints about the first survey, *Which?* admitted that its allegations against one firm had proved to be wrong.

The number of complaints made about lawyers continues to rise, according to the 2003 annual report from the Legal Services Ombudsman. Complaints are not spread evenly across the whole profession. Instead, 80 per cent of complaints concern the same 950 firms, out of the 8,500 in practice.

A survey undertaken for the Law Society in 2001 found that the public perceive lawyers as formal, expensive and predatory. It may be that they are now being accused of being predatory because of the intensive television advertising by companies who pass work on to solicitors.

One of the most common areas for complaint to the Legal Ombudsman is costs. The nineteenth-century novelist, Charles Dickens, was particularly critical of the legal professions in his novel *Bleak House*. He wrote:

> The one great principle of the English law is, to make business for itself. There is no other principle distinctly, certainly, and consistently maintained through all its narrow turnings. Viewed by this light it becomes a coherent scheme, and not the monstrous maze the laity are apt to think it. Let them but once clearly perceive that its grand principle is to make business for itself at their expense, and surely they will cease to grumble.

One way that services can be improved is through 'consumer power': people making intelligent choices about which lawyer to use, so that bad lawyers go out of business. In practice, the public find it difficult to distinguish good lawyers from bad lawyers (Legal Services Consumer Panel (2013)). It is difficult to develop price comparison websites for lawyers because there are so many practising lawyers to compare and often they do not have fixed prices for their services. People turn to lawyers when they are in distress, when they do not have the confidence or time to choose between lawyers.

The Law Society's Written Practice Standard requires solicitors to give clients written information about all aspects of financing their case, including how the fee is calculated, arrangements for payment and liability for the other side's costs. However, a 1995 report by the National Association of Citizens Advice Bureaux (NACAB), *Barriers to Justice*, concluded that few clients actually received clear information about costs, and that this was part of the reason why fees were so often the cause of complaints. NACAB recommended that solicitors should have to agree with clients a timetable for regular updates on costs, confirm the arrangement in writing and provide leaflets giving information about costs. Research carried out in 2005 for the consumer group *Which?* showed that three out of ten people did not feel they got value for money from solicitors and a third did not feel they received a good service. People going to see a solicitor may be told that it is not possible to put a price on what the whole service may cost but the lawyer will charge, say, £200 per hour plus VAT, with fees and disbursements being extra. An hourly pricing rate with no limit tells the client nothing about how much they can expect to pay.

The Legal Ombudsman has suggested that traditional views of lawyers as experts, separated from other businesses by the notion of professionalism, dominate the legal sector and the public's approach. The term 'client' embodies the traditional view of the relationship between lawyers and those they represent. By contrast, most businesses view the public as potential consumers or customers who have the power to choose which services to buy from which provider. The traditions of the law are different, and many lawyers have historically been able to treat the notion of customer service as somehow lesser than their professional obligations. Market changes are forcing lawyers to reassess their approach to the general public. While lawyers are increasingly bowing to consumer expectations by offering estimates of how much the service might cost, they do not regard these as in any way binding: an initial estimate of £5,000 can end up being a final bill for £50,000. Lawyers would argue in their defence that it is difficult to predict how a case will progress. But actually many transactions, such as writing a will or selling a home, are completely predictable and costs could be safely calculated in advance. The Legal Ombudsman has commented:

> And as the legal services market continues to change, with the arrival of commercial giants and big high street brands, and the increasing cross-selling of financial, legal and other services by banks and insurers, it is the lawyers who show that they can adapt their traditional view of clients and put customers at the heart of their business who stand the best chance of prospering. There are risks in that new market: no one wants 'pile 'em high and flog 'em cheap' law, particularly not when our children, our homes or even our freedom are at stake. But if it means cheaper, more predictable pricing, one of the key barriers between citizens and legal services will be removed.

With the introduction of alternative business structures, lawyers are increasingly agreeing to do work for a fixed fee, particularly conveyancing and wills: 42 per cent of legal work is now carried out under a fixed fee.

Barristers' prices have also been the subject of considerable criticism and, in particular, the fees charged by what the press have called 'super silks' – QCs whose annual earnings can top £1 million, as mentioned earlier in this chapter. As a result of this criticism, the House of Lords looked into the issue, and reported in October 1998 that the fees being charged in some cases were excessive. The report accused barristers' clerks of 'deliberately pitching fees at a very high level' (a conclusion which was not all that surprising, since securing the best possible fee for his or her barrister is part of a clerk's job). The report was welcomed by the Legal Action Group, which said that the excessively high fees charged by some QCs were undermining public confidence in the legal system.

The legal profession suffers from a negative public image. A survey of over 1,000 consumers and 100 lawyers carried out in 2005 found that while most lawyers consider themselves forward-thinking and up to date, the public think quite the opposite. The consumers said the main attributes they associated with lawyers were that they were good with people but also ruthless and ambitious. The Law Society launched a national advertising campaign in 2005 to try to change the public's view of the profession. The adverts portrayed solicitors as heroes to encourage the public to consult solicitors about their legal problems.

On a more positive note, in 2010 the Ministry of Justice published a research paper entitled *Baseline Survey to Assess the Impact of Legal Services Reform*. It found that 95 per cent of respondents agreed that the lawyer acted in a professional manner, 96 per cent agreed that the lawyer explained things in a way the client could understand, 94 per cent agreed that the lawyer was approachable and 91 per cent felt they had received a good service.

11.7 The future of the professions

A number of Government reports have been published in recent years pushing for changes in the professions. In 2001, the Office of Fair Trading (OFT) issued a report entitled *Competition in Professions* (2001). This looked primarily at the restrictive practices of barristers and solicitors. These professions were criticised for imposing unjustified restrictions on competition and were urged to take prompt action to put an end to these practices.

Professor Zander (2001b) criticised the report, stating:

> What is deplorable about these developments is the simplistic belief that equating the work done by professional people to business will necessarily improve the position of the consumer, when the reality is that sometimes it may rather worsen it. Certainly one wants competition to ensure that professional fees are no higher than they need to be and that the professional rules did not unnecessarily inhibit efficiency. But what one looks for from the professional even more is standards, integrity and concern for the client of a higher order than that offered in the business world. To damage those even more important values in the name of value for the consumer in purely economic terms may be to throw out the baby with the bath water.

The former Labour Government accepted that the legal professions should be subject to competition law. It subsequently issued a consultation paper, *In the Public Interest?* (2002), which questioned the competitiveness of legal services given primarily by solicitors working in solicitor firms.

The Bar Council has made some changes in the light of the OFT report, but has rejected many of its key recommendations. Direct access to the Bar has been increased (see p. 224).

In July 2003, the Labour Government established an independent review into the regulation of legal services. The review was chaired by Sir David Clementi and considered which regulatory framework 'would best promote competition, innovation and the public and consumer interest in an efficient, effective and independent legal sector'. Sir David Clementi published his final report in 2004, *Report of the Review of the Regulatory Framework for Legal Services in England and Wales.* The Labour Government subsequently published a White Paper in 2005 entitled *The Future of Legal Services – Putting Consumers First,* in which it accepted most of Sir David Clementi's recommendations. The Legal Services Act 2007 contains the key reforms, which will be considered in turn below.

11.7.1 Regulation of the legal professions

Regulation is the process by which the standards of the profession are set and maintained, protecting both the interests of the members of the profession and the clients of the professionals. When clients are using a regulated professional they should be able to trust the work of that professional.

Sir David Clementi looked at how improvements in the provision of legal services could be made through changes to the regulation of the professions. Historically the professions regulated themselves. Sir David Clementi considered that the established regulatory arrangements did not prioritise the public's interest. He therefore looked at whether the professions should be stripped of their right to regulate themselves and whether instead an independent regulator should be created. The professional bodies would merely represent their professions and not regulate them. Clementi commented:

> Among the suggested advantages of this approach are the clear independence of the regulator, clarity of purposes for both regulator and representative bodies and consistency of rules and standards across the profession and services. An independent regulator would be well placed to make tough, fair enforcement decisions and to facilitate lay/consumer input into the decision making processes.
>
> Disadvantages might include creating an overly bureaucratic and inefficient organisation, with consequent issues of costs and unwieldy procedure. A further argument is that it fails to recognise the significance of strong roots within the profession and their importance on the

international stage. Divorcing the regulatory functions from the profession might lessen the feeling of responsibility professionals have for the high standard of their profession and their willingness to give time freely to support the system.

Ultimately, Clementi concluded that an independent Legal Services Board should be set up and provisions for the establishment of this Board are contained in the Legal Services Act 2007. The Legal Services Board was established in 2009.

The new Board oversees the way the existing professional bodies regulate the professions. It has a duty to promote the public and consumer interests as well as protecting the independence of the legal profession and supporting access to justice. It has statutory responsibility to ensure standards of regulation, training and education of the legal professions. It is led by a part-time chair and a full-time chief executive, who are both non-lawyers, as are the majority of the Board's members. All the members of the Board are selected on merit by the Lord Chancellor after consultation with the Lord Chief Justice. It is hoped that the involvement of the Lord Chief Justice in the appointment process will support the Board's independence from the Government. Politicians must not have too much control over the lawyers whose challenges to possible abuses of power are essential in a free and democratic society. For example, lawyers represent members of the public in criminal cases, when children are being taken into care and when local authorities seek to evict anti-social tenants. The Law Society had unsuccessfully argued that members of the Legal Services Board should be appointed by an independent appointment panel.

The professional bodies are now required by the 2007 Act to separate their regulatory and representative functions. As an immediate response to Sir David Clementi's report on the regulation of the professions, the professional bodies went ahead and separated their regulatory functions from their representative functions. Thus the Law Society set up the Solicitors Regulation Authority and the Bar Council set up the Bar Standards Board.

While the Legal Services Board does not replace the Bar Standards Board and the Solicitors Regulation Authority, it holds them to account for the work they do. The new Board takes only a light-touch, supervisory approach to regulation (as recommended by Sir David Clementi), intervening merely when it is in the public interest. This light-touch approach avoids costly duplication of effort, stifling innovation and burdening the front-line regulators. The Legal Services Act 2007 gives the Legal Services Board the power to set targets for front-line regulators and it has the power to remove a body's authorisation to regulate if these targets are not met. Front-line regulators have to apply to the Legal Services Board for permission to carry out regulatory functions, such as the regulation of alternative business structures.

The aim of this reform is to achieve consistency and transparency, while keeping costs down and leaving day-to-day regulation close to those who provide the services. The reform has been generally well received, though the Bar is unhappy that it has lost the power to regulate itself.

The Bar Standards Board has pointed to the Quality Assurance Scheme for Advocates (see p. 229) and the Legal and Education and Training Review (see p. 237) as evidence that the Legal Services Board is exceeding its intended role, sometimes described as 'mission creep'. It considers that the Board is getting too involved in the detailed management of the professions, known as 'micromanaging', which risks duplicating the work of the front-line regulators. It has also accused the Board of putting too much emphasis on economic liberalisation. It has proposed replacing the Legal Services Board with a College of Regulators to avoid this micromanagement occurring in the future.

11

THE LEGAL PROFESSIONS

At the moment the Legal Services Board is overseeing nine different regulatory bodies responsible for a range of different legal professionals. These bodies are:

- The Solicitors Regulation Authority (solicitors)
- The Bar Standards Board (barristers)
- CILEx Regulation (legal executives)
- Council for Licensed Conveyancers (licensed conveyancers)
- Intellectual Property Regulation Board (patent and trademark attorneys)
- Costs Lawyer Standards Board (law costs draftsmen)
- Master of the Faculties (notaries)
- Institute of Chartered Accountants in England and Wales (accountants doing probate work)
- Institute of Chartered Accountants of Scotland.

In practice, 85 per cent of the legal professionals regulated are solicitors and the Solicitors Regulation Authority has suggested that the eight front-line regulators are duplicating each other, amounting to an inefficient use of resources, and it would make more sense to have a single front-line regulator. There is a risk that in competing to have clients to regulate, regulators might be tempted to take a very light approach to regulation. It is arguable that the new outcome-focused approach to regulation introduced by the Solicitors Regulation Authority is evidence of this. The Legal Services Board has been critical of some of the smaller legal regulators in its annual reports. The current arrangements have been criticised by MPs as unduly bureaucratic and complicated – red tape upon red tape. The chair of the Legal Services Board has suggested that the front-line regulators should be replaced by a single regulator for the whole legal services sector. The review considered whether regulations should be based on function rather than title. A new legal services authority could divide its work into divisions based on functions. So, rather than regulating barristers, solicitors, or legal executives, the regulator could regulate advocacy, or will writing, or the conduct of litigation, irrespective of the title of the provider. The Bar has suggested that the Legal Services Board should be abolished and replaced by a College of Regulators. The Ministry of Justice has stated it has no immediate plans to introduce either of these reforms and does not want to return to self-regulation based around the professional bodies. Instead, the current arrangements for professional regulation will be left unchanged because there is no consensus on the longer term vision for regulation amongst the professionals who responded to the review.

Since its creation, the Solicitors Regulation Authority has had quite difficult relations with the Law Society itself and the large corporate law firms based in the City of London (often known as the 'Magic Circle'). The Law Society still wants to retain some control over the broader issues concerning regulation, while the Solicitors Regulation Authority is anxious to enjoy complete independence from the Law Society. The Solicitors Regulation Authority considers that if the regulation of the solicitor profession is to be credible in the eyes of the public, it must be genuinely independent of pressures from solicitors via the Law Society. The chair of the Solicitors Regulation Authority has stated: 'We need to move away from the perception that lawyers are regulated by lawyers for their own benefit. Section 30 of the Legal Services Act 2007 requires the Legal Services Board to make rules which create adequate separation of the various professional bodies' representative and regulatory functions.

In 2009, the Law Society announced that it had established a review of the regulation of law firms. When asked why the Law Society rather than the Solicitors Regulation Authority were conducting this review, the chief executive of the Law Society stated:

> The Solicitors Regulation Authority is not a legal person, it is a body of the Law Society. The obligation of the Law Society is to make sure the Solicitors Regulation Authority is properly dealing with those tasks delegated to it.

This statement would seem to suggest that the Law Society does not wish to view the Solicitors Regulation Authority as completely independent. The Legal Services Board appears to be unhappy with the level of control being exercised over the Solicitors Regulation Authority by the Law Society.

The review set up by the Law Society into the regulation of solicitors has been carried out by Lord Hunt (a solicitor and former Government Minister). A particular issue that this review considered was how the Magic Circle law firms should be regulated. This was partly in response to signs that some of the biggest corporate law firms were considering alternatives to the existing system of regulation and representation. As these firms were increasingly opening offices overseas, their representation nationally by the Law Society was becoming less important. They are anxious to remain competitive at an international level and they do not want a heavy-handed regulatory system to obstruct their global expansion.

A key debate has been whether the large corporate law firms should be regulated separately by a new regulator, which would work alongside the Solicitors Regulation Authority. This partly depends on whether the regulatory issues and risks associated with City law firms are different from those of small firms and firms with significant private-client work rather than corporate-client work. It has been argued that corporate purchasers of legal services do not need the same regulatory protections as a private individual. At least on the surface, a large City law firm is a very different work environment from a small high street firm of solicitors. Lord Hunt recommended the introduction of Authorised Internal Regulation. Initially, this would apply to larger law firms, but with time it would apply to all law firms. Thus, law firms would progressively be allowed to self-regulate on the understanding that they developed strong internal regulatory systems with careful checks being imposed to make sure this was being carried out effectively. Thus, under these proposals, with time, law firms would continue to be regulated in the same way regardless of their size. The reason for this is that ultimately the same ethical standards apply.

Lord Hunt rejected the earlier proposals in a report published by the Law Society in 2009, and produced by a former civil servant, Nick Smedley. This report had concluded that the Solicitors Regulation Authority was not up to the job of regulating corporate law firms and needed to be fundamentally restructured to equip it for the task. Smedley had recommended the creation of a 'quasi-autonomous' body called the Corporate Regulation Group within the Solicitors Regulation Authority, based not in the Authority's premises in the Midlands but in a separate building in London, to regulate the big corporate law firms. Employees of this group would have to be better paid than other employees of the Authority so that it could recruit and retain staff with knowledge and experience of the corporate law sector. This would not amount to the more radical option of a completely separate regulator for corporate firms.

Smedley (2009) warned that if his recommendations were not accepted, the City law firms might themselves set up a separate regulator. This is a serious risk. It would amount to a split away from the Law Society and the established solicitor profession, effectively creating a new City legal profession. This would constitute a public divorce in what is already in practice quite a divided profession. The current financial crisis and in particular the problems in the banking sector have partly arisen due to weak regulation. It has highlighted that a careful balance needs to be reached between protecting consumers from risk and the freedom needed to grow businesses. The City law firms are anxious to remain competitive during the worst world recession since the 1930s, but it would seem to be in nobody's interests for the regulation of City law firms to be weakened, though it is understandable that their regulation needs to be appropriate to their international work and their risks. In the current economic climate any change to the regulation of City lawyers needs to be perceived as a strengthening in professional regulation and not a weakening. The current economic environment would not seem to be the right time for City lawyers to be seen to be breaking away from the historical controls of the Law Society and the new Solicitors Regulation Authority.

The Solicitors Regulation Authority has moved in the direction recommended by Lord Hunt. It has appointed more City lawyers to its board and set up a Corporate Regulation Group to regulate the major commercial firms. Thus, the Law Society and the Solicitors Regulation Authority have recognised that they need to pay more attention to the concerns of the City law firms. For the time being these firms seem to have decided to give the new arrangements a chance.

In addition, the approach taken by the Solicitors Regulation Authority has changed for all law firms, both large and small. In the past, the Code of Conduct laid down specific rules that had to be followed and firms would be inspected to check the rules had not been broken. In 2011, a new Code of Conduct was published which lays down in broad terms the desired outcomes of the regulatory process, but the individual law firms are allowed a lot of flexibility as to how they achieve these objectives. The focus is on the firms self-regulating through establishing internal governance and compliance systems.

In 2013 the Government announced that it would carry out a review of the regulation of legal services, due to the fact that they are currently extremely complicated and bureaucratic. The review examined the entire legislative framework, which covered at least 10 pieces of primary legislation and over 30 statutory instruments. Professionals in the sector were asked for their opinions on the subject and their ideas for change. Following the review, the Ministry of Justice announced it would make no immediate changes to the regulation of the legal professions.

11.7.2 Alternative business structures

Currently, most legal services are delivered to the public by solicitors working in a law firm or by barristers in independent practice at the Bar. Sir David Clementi considered two new business structures through which legal services could be delivered to the public: legal disciplinary practices (LDPs) and multi-disciplinary partnerships (MDPs). The Government decided to go further, with the introduction of 'alternative business structures' provided for in the Legal Services Act 2007.

Legal disciplinary practices were permitted since 2009. Under these, 25 per cent of the partners can be non-lawyers and thereby share ownership in the legal practice. Over 300 were created primarily to allow the promotion of a non-lawyer to the position of a partner. LDPs which have a solicitor partner were converted automatically to become alternative business structures in 2012.

Multi-disciplinary partnerships bring together lawyers with other professionals, such as accountants, surveyors and estate agents. These organisations can provide legal and non-legal services, so that they could be described as a 'one-stop shop', offering a range of services to their clients. Sir David Clementi did not recommend that these should be allowed. He was cautious about them and said the Government should only consider introducing MDPs once some experience had been gained from the introduction of LDPs.

In fact, the Labour Government went one step further, with provisions in the Legal Services Act 2007 for the creation of alternative business structures. The legislation allows legal services to be provided to the public through a wide range of alternative business structures, which can include multi-disciplinary partnerships. A key difference between legal disciplinary practices which were introduced in 2009 and alternative business structures is that the latter allow external ownership (for example, a law business can be owned by Tesco) while the former must be owned by the partners to the practice. As a result, potentially a large amount of external funding could be invested into an alternative business structure.

Alternative business structures do not really fit a single model; instead they can consist of any alternative to the traditional partnership model of delivering legal services. Thus it could take the form of Tesco providing direct legal services to the public but also, for example, claims management companies could start providing these services, or insurance companies could do so.

The relevant provisions of the Legal Services Act 2007 were brought into force in October 2011. The Solicitors Regulation Authority commenced approving alternative business structures in January 2012. The first alternative business structure to be established was Premier Property Lawyers in 2011, which was approved by the Council of Licensed Conveyancers. About 450 alternative business structures have been approved to date.

The aim is to increase competition to the benefit of consumers and to increase investment in legal service providers, so that they can improve such areas as their use of IT for the delivery of legal services and expand to provide a better quality of service to the consumer. The impact of these changes has been considered by research commissioned by the Government – James Dow and Carlos Lapuerta (2005) *The Benefits of Multiple Ownership Models in Law Services*. A central conclusion of this research was that external investment would lead to an increased use of IT for the delivery of legal services. Law firms have been using automated document creation for a number of years. It is likely that these automated systems will be accessed directly by the public using tailored websites, making the process quicker and cheaper. The public has become used to buying products and services online and will be increasingly keen to buy certain legal services, such as wills, in this way.

The Chair of the Solicitors Regulation Authority has suggested that the establishment of alternative business structures 'could well be the legal profession's equivalent of the financial world's Big Bang', with big business getting involved in the provision of legal services. Increasingly, alternative business structures are looking like a real threat to the traditional high street law firms. The Co-op, Halifax and the AA all initially expanded their activities to offer legal advice and assistance directly to the public. The large accountancy firm, KPMG, has become an alternative business structure. The Co-op has established 'Co-operative Legal Services', offering a range of legal services, including conveyancing and will-writing. It is based in Bristol and employs approximately 150 people, including a team of 30 lawyers. It has for a number of years offered a free legal services helpline to its customers which has been praised by consumer groups but criticised by the Law Society for not offering face-to-face advice to its clients.

The Co-op's research into the legal market found that there was a general distrust of traditional legal service providers. This is exacerbated by the media's portrayal of the legal system, but it also stems from clients' experiences. Unlike many other businesses, the solicitor profession has often not moved with the times to take into account the development of internet services and mobile phones. The Co-op considers it can succeed in this market because people like to deal with a business which they feel is a trusted brand, with which they have an existing relationship, and where they know what to expect. Customers want all this combined with the professionalism, skill and *gravitas* of a properly qualified lawyer. The Co-op aims to be the country's biggest provider of legal services by 2022.

Halifax has launched 'Halifax Legal Express', which provides online legal services at fixed prices. Halifax has recognised that the banks and building societies, with their network of branded, highly visible shop fronts on every high street, have a huge advantage over local solicitors operating in isolation.

The AA has opened an online legal shop where people can access legal services via the internet. About 150 different legal documents are available from the website. Customers are asked a series of questions and then the computer software produces a document. Some of these documents will be checked by a lawyer before being issued to the client. For example, a tenancy agreement costs £39.99, a letter to the council about noisy neighbours costs £2.99, a will costs £59.99 and a pre-nuptial agreement costs £99.99. What will be attractive to the public is that these documents are available at a pre-agreed price and lawyers will increasingly have to work for fixed fees to compete, rather than leaving the client uncertain how much the bill will be until after the work is completed. The public is increasingly comfortable with buying goods and services over the internet and may not want to spend time physically visiting a law firm to get legal advice. For such people, online legal services delivered by a recognised and trusted brand might look very attractive.

The Labour Government considered that bigger organisations might provide advice more efficiently than the traditional business structures for lawyers. The reform has become known as the 'Tesco Law' because big organisations will be able to buy law firms. The Bar Council is unhappy with this reform. It has pointed out that outside commercial involvement does not always mean better and cheaper services. External investment will also come at a price – the investors will expect a share of the profits which in the past belonged to the partners. Large, wealthy companies could choose to employ a few solicitors and lots of paralegals (individuals with more limited legal qualifications) to offer these services. This could be primarily a telephone service, offered from a centralised location and focused at only the better paid work. Legal work would increasingly be treated like a commodity from which to make a profit. This is already the case with conveyancing and personal injury cases, where an impersonal service may be offered at a fixed price. Just as out-of-town supermarkets have forced the closure of local greengrocers and chemists, alternative business structures for legal advisers could lead to the closure of many high street solicitor firms. The Lord Chancellor has admitted that the new business structures could affect the future of small high street solicitor firms, but the Labour Government did not seem keen on small firms, pointing out in its 2005 White Paper that research by Paul Grout (2005) found that complaints of dishonest practice are disproportionately generated by smaller law firms.

The employment prospects for lawyers employed in an alternative business structure will be different from those in a law firm. A traditional law firm is owned by solicitors. While new recruits have the status of employees, if they get promoted over time to become an equitable partner in the firm then they become joint owners of the firm, sharing the firm's profits each year. In the large city firms, this can be very large sums. In an alternative business structure the owner is often an external investor and any profit is paid to the shareholders in dividends. The senior solicitors might be given shares in the company but they are unlikely to achieve the same earnings as they would have done as partners. This could have implications for recruitment, with junior lawyers preferring to join traditional solicitor firms because of the better long-term financial prospects.

The Bar Council has stated that the historical ban on barristers forming partnerships actually promoted competition between the 10,000 barristers in private practice, and preserved their independence. It is unhappy that non-lawyers could become owners and investors in legal practices. The Bar has argued that non-lawyers would not be bound by the ethical codes of standard that apply to legal professionals and that the independence of the legal practice would be put at risk. It considers that the current proposed safeguards would be inadequate to prevent improper interference by external investors with the delivery of legal services.

A parliamentary joint committee looked at the proposed introduction of alternative business structures contained in the then Legal Services Bill. The committee was concerned that there was a risk of a conflict of interest between the different participants in alternative business structures and inappropriate pressure could be placed on lawyers within such structures to sell products, such as insurance policies, from other branches of the organisation. The evidence presented to the committee suggested that alternative business structures might not be allowed to practise in America and some European countries. Certainly, at this stage, America is not inclined to allow its own law firms to become alternative business structures, due to concerns over client confidentiality, client service and legal ethics.

While some professionals have been quick to attack the introduction of alternative business structures, it may be that the quality of their current services has made them vulnerable to this type of reform. Most people would be perfectly happy to go through life without ever having to instruct a solicitor. They only turn to a legal professional out of necessity and frequently at times of distress: for example, to get a divorce, or because they have been in an accident or have been arrested by the police. The Lord Chancellor's introduction to the White Paper, *The Future of Legal Services: Putting the Consumer First* (2005), observes:

> The professional competence of lawyers is not in doubt. The calibre of many of our legal professionals is among the best in the world. But despite this, too many consumers are finding that they are not receiving a good or a fair deal.

In practice, much of the work in solicitor firms is already being done by paralegals rather than solicitors themselves. The personal contact between the solicitor and client has been reduced through the use of claims management companies (see p. 222), who refer cases to solicitors at a fee and the solicitor will have never met the client personally but merely receive a paper file on the case. Thus solicitors themselves are not always providing a personal, face-to-face service.

Solicitors have to confront the fact that customers want easy access to legal advice at the right price and delivered in a way and at a time which suits them (not the lawyer). If they cannot get this from their local solicitor firm they will look elsewhere. Solicitors are trying to respond to the challenge of new competition from established companies (such as banks, accountancy firms, insurance companies, claims management companies and retailers) by trying to create their own recognised brands. The solicitor brand with perhaps the highest profile at the moment is QualitySolicitors, which was created in 2009. Existing law firms can pay to run their firm as a franchise of QualitySolicitors. They benefit from a centralised

Figure 11.5 Business structures

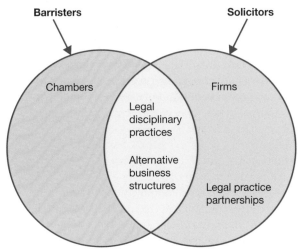

computer system, strategic planning and marketing support. Over 150 law firms have become a QualitySolicitors franchise. Other similar solicitor brands that have been created are ContactLaw, Quindell, GetSolicitors, highstreetlawyers.com and Face2Face Solicitors, though few have proved commercially successful.

To date, alternative business structures have not had the impact expected on the legal services market. Legal services continue to be provided by lawyers in predominantly traditional law firms and barristers' chambers. Despite this, research by Roper and others (2015) has concluded that alternative business structures have been a success in promoting innovation and diversity in the provision of legal services. Though the report did note that alternative business structures were not typically used to lower costs, which had been a key reason for their introduction.

11.7.3 Legal ombudsman

A Legal Ombudsman has been established under the Legal Services Act 2007 to hear complaints against all legal professions (this reform is discussed on p. 230).

11.8 Fusion of the professions

The divided legal profession dates from the nineteenth century, when the Bar agreed to give all conveyancing work and all direct access to clients to the solicitors, in return for sole rights of audience in the higher courts and the sole right to become senior judges for barristers. However, since the late 1960s, there has been a series of moves towards breaking down this division. Following the Access to Justice Act 1999, solicitors automatically have rights of audience, though they still have to undertake training in order to exercise these rights. It is likely that an increasing number of solicitors will undertake this training to become solicitor-advocates.

There has been much discussion over recent years as to whether the professions will eventually fuse. When the Courts and Legal Services Act 1990 was passed, it was thought that it might be the first step in Government plans to fuse the two professions by legislation. Until 1985, the two branches had been largely left alone to divide work between themselves, and had made their own arrangements for this; the abolition of the solicitors' monopoly on conveyancing was the first major Government interference in this situation, and the Courts and Legal Services Act was obviously a much bigger step towards regulation by Government rather than the professions themselves. Even if the Government did not force fusion, it has been suggested, it could happen anyway if large numbers of solicitors take up rights of audience.

Alternatively, it has been suggested that the Bar might survive, but in a much reduced form, and there is much debate about which areas would suffer most. Barristers generally fall into two groups: those who specialise in commercial fields, such as company law, tax and patents; and those who have what is called a common law practice, which means that they deal with a fairly wide range of common legal issues, such as crime, housing and family law. Some legal experts believed that commercial lawyers would be most likely to survive, since they have a specialist knowledge that solicitors cannot provide. However, for several years now, solicitors in City firms have been becoming more specialist themselves and, if able to combine specialist knowledge with rights of audience, they would clearly be a threat to the commercial Bar. In addition, such firms offer high incomes, without the insecurity of self-employment at the Bar, and therefore they are able to attract first-rate students who once would have automatically been attracted to the more prestigious Bar. As these entrants work their way up through law firms, the Bar's traditional claim to offer the best expertise in high-level legal analysis will be difficult to sustain.

Others have suggested that common law barristers have a better chance of surviving competition from solicitors. They cater for the needs of ordinary high street solicitors, who generally have a wide-ranging practice, and spend much of their time seeing clients and gathering case information. This leaves little opportunity to swot up on the finer details of every area of law with which clients need help so, where specialist legal analysis is needed, they refer the client to a barrister with experience in the relevant area.

The Inns of Court (discussed on p. 225) set up a Working Party on the future of the Inns of Court which reported in 2000. The aim of the Working Party was to review the impact of the Access to Justice Act 1999, which has made it easier for more solicitors and employed barristers to qualify to appear in the higher courts. It recommended that membership of the Inns should be offered to solicitors entitled to appear in the higher courts, on payment of an entrance fee of £1,000. The report warns that if the Inns cease to be of relevance to the profession they run the risk of decline. The Inns are financially dependent on rents from their properties, which are priced at the very top of the market. If the Bar does decline in numbers – as many predict – they could well find themselves left with property they cannot let at rents no one wants to pay. One of the greatest threats to the future of the Bar is the fact that employed lawyers' rights of audience have increased. Much of the work that the Bar currently gets from the Crown Prosecution Service in particular is likely to disappear as the advocacy will be done 'in-house'.

When Sir David Clementi was appointed in 2003 to review the legal professions, there were fears that this might be the moment when the Government forced the two professions to fuse and abolished the Bar Council and Law Society. In fact these fears proved ill-founded. Below we look at some of the arguments for and against fusion of the two professions.

11.8.1 Arguments for fusion of the professions

Expense

With the divided profession a client often has to pay both a solicitor and a barrister, sometimes a solicitor and two barristers. However, the Bar Council prepared a report called *The Economic Case for the Bar: A Comparison of the Costs of Barristers and Solicitors* (2000). This paper claimed that it was generally more economical to employ the services of a barrister, particularly a junior, for work within his or her area of expertise than to use a solicitor. In broad terms it stated that the differences in charge-out rates make it from 25 per cent to 50 per cent cheaper to employ the services of a junior barrister than an assistant solicitor in London. A major factor is that barristers' overheads are approximately half those of solicitors. However, the paper is misleading, as without direct access to clients for barristers it is not an either/or situation. The reality is that a client does not pay for either a solicitor or a barrister, but if they employ a barrister they must pay for both, along with the cost of the solicitor preparing the papers for the barrister.

Inefficiency

A two-tier system means work may be duplicated unnecessarily, and the solicitor prepares the case with little or no input from the barrister who will have to argue it in court. Barristers are often selected and instructed at the last moment – research by Bottoms and McLean (1976) in Sheffield revealed that in 96 per cent of cases where the plea was guilty, and 79 per cent where it was not guilty, clients saw their barrister for the first time on the morning of the trial. In this situation important points may be passed over or misunderstood.

Table 11.2 Moves towards fusion

Year	Moves towards fusion
1969	Following the Royal Commission on Assizes and Quarter Sessions, the Lord Chancellor was given the power to allow solicitors extended rights of audience where there were not enough barristers.
1972	A Practice Direction from the Lord Chancellor's Department stated that solicitors could appear in appeals or committals for sentencing from the magistrates' to the Crown Court, where they had appeared for that client in the magistrates' court.
1979	The Royal Commission on Legal Services unanimously rejected a proposal for the fusion of the professions.
1985	A Practice Direction permitted solicitors to appear in the Supreme Court in formal or unopposed proceedings, and when judgment is given in open court.
1986	The Law Society document, *Lawyers and the Courts: Time for Some Changes*, proposed that all lawyers should undergo the same training, work two or three years in 'general practice', and then choose to go on to train as barristers if they wished. The Bar Council rejected this idea.

Table 11.2 Moves towards fusion (Continued)

Year	Moves towards fusion
1988	The Marre Committee was set up by the Bar Council and the Law Society to look at, among other things, whether any changes were needed in the structure of the profession. It largely advocated maintaining the status quo.
1990	The Courts and Legal Services Act contained the following provisions. • Direct access to barristers by certain professional clients • Access to the higher levels of the judiciary for solicitors • Multi-disciplinary partnerships to be allowed, subject to the agreement of the professions' ruling bodies • Rights of audience in all courts should be extended to 'suitably qualified' persons, not necessarily barristers or solicitors. Applications for this right had to be made to the Lord Chancellor's Advisory Committee and then approved by the Lord Chancellor and four judges.
1992	Solicitor-advocates were introduced (discussed on p. 218).
1999	Following the Lord Chancellor's report, *Modernising Justice* (1998), the Access to Justice Act 1999 was passed. This replaces the Lord Chancellor's Advisory Committee with the new Legal Services Consultative Panel, which takes over the role of regulating rights of audience. The procedure for approving changes to the rules on rights of audience is simplified and the Lord Chancellor has a new power, subject to parliamentary approval, to change rules which are unduly restrictive. This last power is designed to ensure that the legal professions themselves cannot cling on to restrictive rules and prevent reform. All barristers and solicitors now automatically acquire full rights of audience, though they are only able to exercise them by successfully completing the necessary training.
2001	The Office of Fair Trading issued its report on anti-competitive practices in the professions (discussed on p. 241).
2004	The Clementi Committee issued its report into the regulation of the professions.
2007	The Legal Services Act 2007, containing provisions for alternative business structures, receives Royal Assent.

Waste of talent

Prospective lawyers must decide very early on which branch of the profession they wish to enter, and if, having chosen to be a solicitor, the lawyer later discovers a talent for advocacy, they may be denied the chance to use it to the full.

Other countries

All common law countries have bodies of specialist advocates, and possibly need them, but no other country divides its legal profession in two as England does.

11.8.2 Arguments against fusion

Specialisation

Two professions can each do their different jobs better than one profession doing both.

Independence

The Bar has traditionally argued that its cab rank principle guarantees this, ensuring that no defendant, however heinous the charges, goes undefended; and that no individual should lack representation because of the wealth or power of the opponent. The fact that barristers operate independently, rather than in partnerships, also contributes. However, the Courts and Legal Services Act 1990 does provide for solicitors with advocacy certificates to operate on a cab rank basis, which has somewhat weakened the Bar's argument. In addition, successful barristers do get round the cab rank rule in practice.

Importance of good advocacy

Our adversarial system means that the presentation of oral evidence is important; judges have no investigative powers and must rely on the lawyers to present the case properly.

The 1979 Royal Commission suggested that fusion would lead to a fall in the quality of the advocacy, arguing that although many solicitors were competent to advocate in the magistrates' and County Courts, arguing before a jury required different skills and greater expertise, and if rights were extended it was unlikely that many solicitors would get sufficient practice to develop these.

Access to the Bar

Critics of moves towards fusion argued that it may result in many leading barristers joining the large firms of commercial solicitors, so making their specialist skills less accessible to the average person. Smaller practices might generate insufficient business to justify partnership with a barrister and find it difficult to secure a barrister of equal standing to the opponent's; they would be reluctant to refer a client to a large firm, for fear of losing them permanently. A major drift towards large firms could worsen the already uneven distribution of solicitors throughout the country.

Table 11.3 Comparison of barristers and solicitors

	Barrister	**Solicitor**
Number	12,700	130,000
Professional organisation	Bar Council	Law Society
Professional course	Bar Professional Training Course (BPTC)	Legal Practice Course (LPC)
Apprenticeship	Pupillage	Training contract

The judiciary

A reduction in the number of specialist advocates might make it more difficult to make suitable appointments to the Bench; although the potential candidates would increase, they would not be as well known to those carrying out the selection process. On the other hand this might eventually mean appointments would have to be made on a more open, regulated system, and from a wider social base.

Use of court time

Court cases are not given a fixed time, only a date; depending on the progress of previous cases they may appear at any time during a morning or afternoon session, or be held over until another day – the idea behind this is that the clients and their lawyers should wait for courts, rather than the other way round. It has been suggested that barristers are best organised for this, though there seems no reason why, within a united profession, those lawyers who specialise in court work could not organise themselves accordingly.

11.9 Other legal personnel

11.9.1 Chartered legal executives

There are 22,000 trainee and qualified legal executives. Traditionally, legal executives were employed by solicitors but, following the Legal Services Act 2007, legal executives can work independently in an alternative business structure. They can undertake work in litigation, advocacy, conveyancing, probate and immigration. Most firms of solicitors employ legal executives (sometimes called paralegals) who do much of the same basic work as solicitors. Their professional body is the Chartered Institute of Legal Executives (CILEx). Although technically they are under the supervision of their employers, in practice many experienced executives specialise in particular areas – such as conveyancing – and take almost sole charge of that area. From the firm's point of view, they are a cheaper option than solicitors for getting this work done, and in many cases will be more experienced in their particular area than a solicitor. However, clients are usually unaware that, when they pay for a solicitor, they may be receiving the services of a legal executive.

As part of the Government's efforts to increase judicial diversity, legal executives have been given the right to become judges in the Tribunals, Courts and Enforcement Act 2007. Three-quarters of legal executives are women and a third are from a black or ethnic minority background.

Legal executives are generally less well paid than solicitors. The CILEx Omnibus Member Survey 2015 asserts that legal executives can expect to earn between £15,000 and £28,000 although post-qualification they can earn £38,000 upwards.

11.9.2 Qualifications and training

To qualify as a legal executive, a person works full time and studies part time. Studying will either be undertaken at a local college or through distance learning with the Chartered Institute of Legal Executives Law School. It takes on average six years to qualify fully as a legal executive, though students with a law degree benefit from exemptions from some of the examinations. Only about 600 people qualify each year as legal executives, with many people failing to complete their education. It is much cheaper to qualify as a legal executive than for the other legal professions and no university degree is required. Once qualified as a legal executive, a person can undertake further part-time study to become a solicitor, unless they had unsuccessfully attempted the Legal Practice Course before becoming a legal executive.

11.9.3 Legal apprentices

Legal apprenticeships are aimed in particular at school leavers who are employed in the legal sector and undertake training at the same time. The training may be at a local college or a specialist training organisation, or through distance learning providers. This off-the-job training is usually done on weekly day release or over a number of days in a block. Depending on the scheme that the apprentice follows and the number of years and studies completed, the apprentice can become a solicitor (see p. 221), a chartered legal executive (see p. 255) or a paralegal (see next 'Bigger Picture' box). There are two levels of apprenticeships in Legal Services that students can embark upon. The Level 3 Advanced Apprenticeship in Legal Services is equivalent to A-level standard and takes about 18 months to complete. The Level 4 Higher Apprenticeship in Legal Services is equivalent to the first year of a degree and takes about two and a half years to complete. There is also a one-year apprenticeship in legal administration. The emphasis of the Legal Services qualifications is on both workplace competence and legal knowledge and understanding specific to a particular role. The legal understanding required to achieve the Legal Services knowledge qualification is more specialised than that required to achieve the Chartered Legal Executive professional qualifications, though there are some common units for both qualifications.

11.9.4 Licensed conveyancers

The Courts and Legal Services Act 1990 abolished the solicitor's monopoly of conveyancing and paved the way for a new profession, licensed conveyancers. As their name suggests, these professionals are purely involved in conveyancing and are increasingly being used by people buying and selling a home. The Council for Licensed Conveyancers (CLC) supervises apprenticeships to become Conveyancing Technicians.

The Bigger Picture: Paralegals

Paralegals are not a recognised legal profession as such, but they are people who are carrying out legal work in the legal sector. They may have legal qualifications or they may have been purely trained 'on the job'. Some paralegals are people who have completed their academic and vocational training but have been unable to secure a pupillage or training contract to become barristers or solicitors. They may be using the position of paralegal to get a foot in the door in a law firm with the hope that they will be selected for a training contract with the firm at a future date. Indeed, some law firms are using the position of paralegal as part of their selection process for the allocation of training contracts. In this context, the training contract looks like an artificial barrier to career progression, as often the work that a paralegal will perform will be very similar to that of a trainee solicitor. The Legal Education and Training Review (LETR) has failed to respond to this concern. Paralegals have historically been employed by solicitors to perform narrow areas of legal work such as conveyancing or personal injury claims. The Legal Services

Board has calculated that 40 per cent of staff carrying out legal work in solicitor firms are not legally qualified (Legal Services Board (2012)). A lot of paralegals are employed by the Crown Prosecution Service. With the development of alternative business structures, the expectation is that their numbers will increase as organisations compete to provide cheaper services at fixed costs. Increasingly, paralegals will deliver the legal services to clients, with solicitors becoming supervisors and managers.

The LETR recognised that the apparent expansion in the number of paralegals poses a challenge. Research carried out for the Review highlighted concerns about the quality of supervision and training of paralegals, and the lack of progression from paralegal roles into a professional qualification. LETR suggested that thought needs to be given to voluntary certification of paralegals based on a common set of paralegal outcomes and standards. A voluntary process keeps the flexibility of paralegals but will be less effective at ensuring consistent standards. The development of apprenticeships to increase diversity is considered, though LETR recognised the risk that these might not apply a consistent standard and therefore need to be monitored.

11.10 Do we need legal professionals?

In many areas, non-legally qualified people do the work of lawyers as well as professionals could, and sometimes more effectively – an obvious example is the large number of volunteer and employed lay advisers in Citizens Advice who provide an accessible, economic and uncomplicated service to deal with legal and other queries. Legal executives often become so well experienced in particular areas that they need no supervision from their legally qualified colleagues, and take on much of the work that the general public assumes only solicitors can do. Some work may even be better done by clients themselves. So why should we need a profession (or two), and why should that profession be allowed sole access to certain types of work?

Where litigants choose to represent themselves in court, they may take along someone (who may not be a lawyer) to advise them (see p. 659). They are called a 'McKenzie friend' after the case in which the court made it clear that the attendance of a lay adviser was permissible: *McKenzie* v *McKenzie* (1970). Workers from Citizens Advice Bureaux, Law Centres and law student groups are among those who commonly act as McKenzie friends, though anyone (including friends and relatives) requested by the litigant could do so. Heather Mills used a McKenzie friend when she represented herself during her divorce from Paul McCartney. If a person acting for themselves in legal proceedings (known as a 'litigant in person') wishes to use a McKenzie friend they need to make this request to the judge. The judge will give permission for this provided the assistance is not contrary to the interests of justice and a fair trial. For example, Dr Pelling was a campaigner for fathers' rights, and on a number of occasions he has been refused permission to act as a McKenzie friend on the basis that his campaigning agenda had a tendency to take over and his experience led to him, rather than the litigant, running the case (*R* v *Bow County Court, ex parte Pelling (No. 1)* (1999)). McKenzie friends may assist a litigant by providing quiet advice and support in court and, in exceptional circumstances with the court's permission, they can act as the litigant's advocate by directly addressing the court. With increasing numbers of litigants in person because of the reduced availability of legal aid, the use of McKenzie friends is likely to increase.

Increasingly, information about the law is available online. The Legal Services Consumer Panel (2013) has suggested that online services might be cheap to deliver but may not always be the best means of helping people to fix their legal needs. While digital technologies have a role to play, the Panel suggests they should be seen as a supplement to the traditional personalised advice format, rather than a substitute.

Research by Pleasence and Balmer (2013) found that small businesses still preferred to get legal advice from solicitor firms rather than other alternatives, such as banks and accountancy firms, though only 13 per cent of respondents considered lawyers provided a cost-effective means of resolving legal disputes.

There are many reasons why a legal profession might be considered desirable, but two broad theories shed some interesting light on the reasons why we maintain it. The first, functionalism, emphasises the importance of keeping society together, and it sees one important way of doing this as maintaining the status quo, keeping the structure of society the same. Functionalists believe professions in general contribute to this process. They say those within a profession will share certain values, put public service before profit, and use expert knowledge for the good of society – the implication is that professionals have higher moral standards than ordinary people. They are supposed to believe in 'public service' and 'shared professional ethics', while plumbers, car manufacturers and shopkeepers, for example, are only interested in money. This is used to justify the fact that they are the only people to have access to certain types of work. It is difficult to reconcile this view with the fact that many lawyers compete to work for the big legal firms, working for the most powerful members of society – not because the work is interesting or socially useful, but because it pays so well.

A second theory, that of market control, has a very different view of the role played by professionals. It takes as its starting point the marketplace, where different suppliers compete with each other to get consumers to buy their goods and services. Economic theory reasons that at any given level of quality, consumers will choose the cheapest goods or services, so those offering good quality services cheaply will sell a lot, and the rest will go bust.

This may be good news for consumers, but tough for producers, who must be constantly striving to provide a better product for less money, while looking over their shoulder to make sure that someone else is not providing it cheaper or better than they can. Consequently, producers try to get round this competitive situation, and they can do so in a number of different ways – by forming monopolies and cartels, or by controlling the raw materials or the patents to a manufacturing process, for example.

Market control theory suggests that having professions is just one of those ways of escaping uncontrolled competition. Professions restrict access to their market by controlling who enters the profession, saying that only those with complicated qualifications can offer services in this area; they control the way in which professionals offer their services, for example by stopping members of the profession using aggressive advertising to compete with each other; and they keep their own special area of expertise as complex and as obscure as they can.

One of the leading proponents of this point of view is Richard Abel, Professor of Law at the University of California. His book on the legal profession in England and Wales (1988) describes in great detail how solicitors and barristers have controlled who become lawyers, how they operate and what they sell. He suggests that they have done this in their own interests, to keep the price of legal services high. An example of this process is that during the current difficult economic situation, when there is increased competition for jobs, the Bar Council has raised its entry requirement for the vocational course. Similarly, Abel (1988) has shown that the pass rate for the Law Society exams goes up when there is a shortage of jobs, and down when there is a shortage of recruits.

Answering questions

1 Do you consider that the current system of legal education and training can provide the lawyers that this country needs?

2 Critically evaluate the recent reforms to the governance of the legal professions.

3 It is arguable that the once separate professions of barrister and solicitor have been covertly and gradually fused over recent years. Use your knowledge of the different roles that barristers and solicitors serve in the legal system to either support or oppose the above statement.

For answers to these questions, visit the companion website at www.pearsoned.co.uk/ elliottquinn

SUMMARY OF CHAPTER 11: THE LEGAL PROFESSIONS

The three main professions in the legal field are:

- solicitors;
- barristers; and
- legal executives.

Solicitors

- *Work:* traditionally solicitors focused primarily on paperwork but they are now doing more advocacy.
- *Qualifications and training:* usually a university degree, followed by a conversion course if this was not in law. Then they take the one-year Legal Practice Course and period of recognised training.

Barristers

- *Work:* traditionally advocacy, but they also do some paperwork.
- *Qualifications and training:* usually a university degree, followed by a conversion course if this is not in law. Then they take the one-year Bar Professional Training Course and one-year pupillage.

Claims management companies

Claims management companies are companies that find people who have a legal problem and refer them to solicitors who pay the company on average £800 for the referral. The payment of referral fees for personal injury claims was banned by the Legal Aid, Sentencing and Punishment of Offenders Act 2012.

Quality Assurance Scheme for Advocates

The regulators of the legal professions are together establishing a Quality Assurance Scheme for Advocates (QASA) to respond to concerns over the quality of advocacy in the courts.

Complaints

The position of Legal Ombudsman was created in 2010 to investigate and resolve complaints about the service provided by lawyers.

Background of barristers and solicitors

Barristers and solicitors have traditionally come from a very narrow social background, in terms of class, race and sex, and disabled people are under-represented. They now come from a wider range of backgrounds, but there is a problem with promotion and retention of women and people from minority groups.

Educational reform

In 2013 the Legal Education and Training Review published its report on the education and training requirements of the legal professions. The aim is to ensure that the future system of education and training is effective and efficient in preparing legal service providers to meet the needs of consumers.

The future of the professions

A number of Government reports have been published in recent years pushing for changes in the professions. In July 2003, the Labour Government established an independent review into the regulation of legal services, chaired by Sir David Clementi. A range of reforms has subsequently been introduced in the Legal Services Act 2007.

Regulation of the legal professions

The Legal Services Act 2007 has led to the establishment of a Legal Services Board to oversee the way the existing professional bodies regulate the professions.

Alternative business structures

Under the Legal Services Act 2007 legal services can be provided to the public through a wide range of alternative business structures where the owners and investors do not need to be lawyers.

Moves towards fusion?

Since the late 1960s there has been a series of moves towards breaking down the division between barristers and solicitors.

Reading list

ACLEC (1996) *First Report on Legal Education and Training.* London: Lord Chancellor's Advisory Committee for Legal Education and Conduct.

Abel, R. (1988) *The Legal Profession in England and Wales.* Oxford: Blackwell.

Ashley, L. (2010) Making a difference? The use (and abuse) of diversity management at the UK's elite law firms. *Work, Employment and Society,* 24: 711.

Bar Council (2000) *The Economic Case for the Bar: A Comparison of the Costs of Barristers and Solicitors.* London: General Council of the Bar.

Bar Council Working Party (2007) *Entry to the Bar: Working Party Final Report.* London: Bar Council.

Blackwell, M. (2012) Old boys' networks, family connections and the English legal profession. *Public Law,* 3: 426.

          (2015) Taking silk: an empirical study of the award of Queen's Counsel status 1981–2015. *Modern Law Review,* 78(6): 971.

Boon, A. and Levin, J. (2008) *Ethics and Conduct of Lawyers in the UK.* Oxford: Hart.

Bottoms, A.E., and McLean, J.D. (1976) *Defendants in the Criminal Process.* London: Routledge & K. Paul.

Clementi, D. (2004) (see website, below).

Cruickshank, E. (2007) Sisters in the law, *Solicitors Journal,* 1510.

Dow, J. and Lapuerta, C. (2005) *The Benefits of Multiple Ownership Models in Law Services.* London: Brattle Group.

Grout, P.A. (2005) *The Clementi Report: Potential Risks of External Ownership and Regulatory Responses – A Report to the Department for Constitutional Affairs.* London: Department for Constitutional Affairs.

Insight Oxford Ltd (2010) (see website, below).

Jackson, Lord (2009) *The Review of Civil Litigation Costs: Final Report.* Norwich: Stationery Office.

Johnson, N. (2005) The training framework review – what's all the fuss about? *New Law Journal,* 155: 357.

Joseph, M. (1985) *Lawyers Can Seriously Damage Your Health.* London: Michael Joseph.

Kennedy, H. (1992) *Eve Was Framed: Women and British Justice.* London: Chatto.

Law Society (2005) *Qualifying as a Solicitor – A Framework for the Future.* London: Law Society.

Legal Education and Training Review (2013) *Setting Standards: The Future of Legal Services Education and Training Regulation in England and Wales.* London: Legal Education and Training Review.

Legal Services Board (2010) *Referral Fees, Referral Arrangements and Fee Sharing.* London: Legal Services Board.

          (2012) *Market Impacts of the Legal Services Act – Interim Baseline Report.* London: Legal Services Board.

Legal Services Consumer Panel (2013) *Empowering Consumers.* London: Legal Services Board.

Lord Chancellor's Department (2005) *The Future of Legal Services: Putting the Consumer First.* London: Lord Chancellor's Department.

11

THE LEGAL PROFESSIONS

Modernising Justice (1997) Cm 4155, London: Home Office.

National Association of Citizens Advice Bureaux (1995) *Barriers to Justice: CAB Clients' Experience of Legal Services.* London: NACAB.

Office of Fair Trading (2001) (see website, below).

Pleasence, P. and Balmer, N. (2013) *In Need of Advice? Findings of a Small Business Legal Needs Benchmarking Survey.* London: Legal Services Board.

Research Study No. 26 of the Law Society Research and Policy Planning Unit (1997).

Roper, S., Love, J., Rieger, P. and Bourke, J. (2015) *Innovation in legal services: A report for the Solicitors Regulation Authority and the Legal Services Board.* Warwick: Enterprise Research Centre.

Ryan, E. (2007) The unmet need: focus on the future. *New Law Journal,* 157: 134.

Smedley, N. (2009) *Review of the Regulation of Corporate Legal Work.* London: Law Society.

Susskind, R. (1996) *The Future of Law.* Oxford: Oxford University Press.

(2008) *The End of Lawyers? Rethinking the Nature of Legal Services.* Oxford: Oxford University Press.

Young, Lord (2010) *Common Sense, Common Safety.* Oxford: Oxford University Press.

Young, S. (2005) Clementi: in practice. *New Law Journal,* 155: 45.

Zander, M. (1988) *A Matter of Justice.* London: Cabinet Office.

(2001a) Should the legal profession be shaking in its boots? *New Law Journal,* 151: 369.

(2001b) A question of trust. *Solicitors Journal,* 1100.

On the internet

The report by Flood and Hviid (2013), *The Cab Rank Rule: Its Meaning and Purpose in the New Legal Services Market,* is available on the Legal Services Board website at:

> **https://research.legalservicesboard.org.uk/wp-content/media/Cab-Rank-Rule_final-copy.pdf**

The Law Society's Annual Statistics Report (2017) is available on its website at:

> **https://www.lawsociety.org.uk/support-services/research-trends/annual-statistics-report-2017/**

Sir David Clementi's report, *Report of the Review of the Regulatory Framework for Legal Services in England and Wales* (2004), is available at:

> **https://webarchive.nationalarchives.gov.uk/+/http://www.legal-services-review.org.uk/content/report/index.htm**

The report of the Office of Fair Trading, *Competition in Professions* (2001), is available at:

> **https://webarchive.nationalarchives.gov.uk/20140402172414/http://oft.gov.uk/shared_oft/reports/professional_bodies/oft328.pdf**

Insight Oxford Ltd's 2010 report *Obstacles and Barriers to the career development of woman solicitors* can be downloaded from the Law Society website at:

> **https://www.lawsociety.org.uk/support-services/research-trends/documents/obstacles-and-barriers-to-the-career-development-of-women-solicitors/**

Research by the InterLaw Diversity Forum can be found on its website at:

https://interlawdiversityforum.org/interlaw/2012-career-progression-legal-sector/

The Bar Council website can be found at:

https://www.barcouncil.org.uk/

The website of the Bar Standards Board is available at:

https://www.barstandardsboard.org.uk

Statistics for the practising barrister profession are published by the Bar Standards Board at:

https://www.barstandardsboard.org.uk/media-centre/research-and-statistics/ statistics/practising-barrister-statistics/

The link to the *Report of the Royal Commission on Criminal Justice* (1993) is:

https://www.gov.uk/government/publications/report-of-the-royal-commission-on-criminal-justice

The Chartered Institute of Legal Executives (CILEx) Omnibus Member Survey 2015 is available on its website at:

https://www.cilex.org.uk/pdf/2015_Omnibus_summary.pdf

The Law Society's website can be found at:

https://www.lawsociety.org.uk/home.law

SRA's route to admission statistics are available at:

https://www.sra.org.uk/sra/how-we-work/reports/data/routes_admission.page

Prospects profile of barristers job is available at:

https://www.prospects.ac.uk/job-profiles/barrister

Guardian article '"This is a court of justice not a casino," judge tells lawyers over £1.1m fees' is available at:

https://www.theguardian.com/law/2016/mar/03/court-of-justice-not-casino-judge-tells-lawyers-over-huge-fees

The Times article 'Advocacy skills are slipping in court, judges warn' is available at:

https://www.thetimes.co.uk/article/advocacy-skills-are-slipping-in-court-judges-warn-8hmdx33sh

Bar Council response to the Bar Standards Board Consultation on Future Bar Training: Shaping the education and training requirements for prospective barristers (January 2018) is available at:

https://www.barcouncil.org.uk/media/627546/bar_council_future_bar_training_response_0118.pdf

Diversity data is available on the SRA website at:

https://www.sra.org.uk/sra/equality-diversity/key-findings/law-firms-2017.page

Law undergraduate entry data is available from the Law Society website:

https://www.lawsociety.org.uk/law-careers/becoming-a-solicitor/entry-trends/

Data on diversity in the solicitor's profession can be found on the SRA website:

https://www.sra.org.uk/solicitors/diversity-toolkit/diverse-law-firms.page

The Bar Council publication *I am the Bar: A Bar of all, for all*, is available at:

https://www.barcouncil.org.uk/careers/i-am-the-bar-social-mobility/

11

THE LEGAL PROFESSIONS

Chapter 12
The jury

This chapter discusses:

- the role of the jury in civil and criminal cases;

- who can serve as a juror;

- the jury selection process;

- how the jury works in secret and reaches its verdict;

- the advantages and disadvantages of jury service; and

- some possible ways in which the jury system could be reformed.

12.1 History

The jury system was imported to Britain after the Norman Conquest in 1066. The right for a man to be punished only pursuant to 'the lawful judgment of his equals' is enshrined in the Magna Carta of 1215 which lays down our democratic rights. But the functions of the jury have changed significantly over the years. The first jurors acted as witnesses, providing information about local matters, and were largely used for administrative business – gathering information for the Domesday Book for example. Later, under Henry II (1133–89), the jury began to take on an important judicial function, moving from reporting on events they knew about, to deliberating on evidence produced by the parties involved in a dispute. Gradually it became accepted that a juror should know as little as possible about the facts of the case before the trial, and this is the case today.

The importance of the juror's right to give a verdict according to their conscience is that juries may acquit a defendant, even when the law demands a guilty verdict. This right was recently reinforced by the House of Lords' decision of ***R v Wang*** (2005). The House confirmed that a judge can never tell a jury to convict. Mr Wang's bag had been stolen from a train station. When it was retrieved, it was found to contain a large martial arts sword and knife. Mr Wang was prosecuted for having 'an article with a blade . . . in a public place'. At his trial, he argued in his defence that he was a Buddhist practising Shaolin – an ancient martial art which requires the mastery of nearly 20 weapons. He stated that he had taken the weapons with him because he did not like to leave them unsupervised in his flat. The trial judge rejected this defence and told the jury: 'As a matter of law, the offences themselves are proved and I direct that you return guilty verdicts'. The House of Lords allowed Mr Wang's appeal. The trial judge had been wrong to direct the jury members that they had to convict. The judge should have told the jury that the jurors alone were to decide what the evidence

Key case

A major milestone in the history of the jury was in ***Bushell's Case*** (1670). Before this, judges would try to bully juries into convicting the defendant, particularly where the crime had political overtones, but in ***Bushell's Case*** it was established that the jurors were the sole judges of fact, with the right to give a verdict according to their conscience, and could not be penalised for taking a view of the facts opposed to that of the judge.

The facts of the case were that two Quakers had stood and preached in a public street in central London. They were arrested and charged with causing an unlawful assembly. At the time religious assemblies (other than an assembly of members of the Church of England) of more than five people were banned by legislation. The judge told the jury to find the men guilty, but they refused. The judge warned the jurors that they would be locked up 'without meat, drink, fire and tobacco' until they reached a guilty verdict. The jury still refused to convict and the jury foreman, Bushell, petitioned another court for their release. This court accepted the application and ruled that judges could not punish jurors for reaching a verdict that the judge did not like.

Legal principle
Jurors can give a verdict according to their conscience.

was and how to apply the law. It is for the jury and not the judge to decide whether the defendant was guilty. In answer to the Court of Appeal's question: 'In what circumstances, if any, is a judge entitled to direct a jury to return a verdict of guilty?', the House of Lords replied, 'none'.

Today the jury is considered a fundamental part of the English legal system, though, as we shall see, only a minority of cases is tried by jury. It is considered to play a vital role in making sure that the criminal justice system works for the benefit of the public rather than for the benefit of unjust leaders. This has implications not just for a healthy criminal justice system but also for a healthy society because the criminal justice system can potentially be abused by political leaders to silence their opponents. The French philosopher Alexis de Tocqueville (1835) wrote in his book *Democracy in America*:

> . . . to regard the jury simply as a judicial institution would be taking a very narrow view of the matter, for great though its influence on the outcome of lawsuits, its influence on the fate of society is much greater still. The jury is above all a political institution, and it is from that point of view that it must always be judged.

It has attained symbolic importance, so that Lord Devlin wrote in 1956:

> Trial by jury is more than an instrument of justice and more than one wheel of the constitution; it is the lamp that shows that freedom lives.

This statement led to a classic rebuttal by the academic Penny Darbyshire (1991), who wrote an article entitled 'The lamp that shows that freedom lives – is it worth the candle?' She argued in that article that:

> juries are not random, not representative, but anti-democratic, irrational and haphazard legislators, whose erratic and secret decisions run counter to the rule of law.

The main Act that now governs jury trial is the Juries Act 1974.

12.2 The function of the jury

The jury has to weigh up the evidence and decide what are the true facts of the case – in other words, what actually happened. The judge directs the jury as to what is the relevant law, and the jury then has to apply the law to the facts that it has found and thereby reach a verdict. A judge in a jury trial can give directions about the law at any time which will help the jurors to evaluate the evidence they hear. When summing up the case for the jury the judge can give directions on the law, focusing on what is directly relevant and necessary to the case. If it is a criminal case and the jury has given a verdict of guilty, the judge will then decide on the appropriate sentence. In civil cases the jury can be asked to decide on how much money should be awarded in damages.

In reaching a verdict, the jury is only entitled to take into account evidence that arose in court. In *R v F* (2009), two members of a jury were seen talking to a law student who had been watching the trial. The conviction was quashed on appeal because of the appearance of a risk that the jury could have been influenced by evidence not heard in court.

The Bigger Picture: The jury and the internet

The rule that jurors are banned from taking into account evidence not raised in court exists to ensure defendants get a fair trial and are not convicted on the basis of, for example, whispered gossip to which they have not had an opportunity to respond. In practice, the greatest challenge to this rule is now the internet. In the past, finding information outside the courtroom about a case would have been a lengthy and inconvenient exercise with a higher risk of discovery. Now temptation is greater because materials, such as past newspaper reports, can be accessed quickly and easily. Jurors are warned before and during their trial not to research their case on the internet and that to do so will amount to the offence of contempt. In **R v Marshall and Crump** (2007), two defendants had been convicted of offences including robbery and manslaughter. After their conviction, material printed off the internet was found in the jury room. The defendants appealed on the basis that their convictions were unsafe as they had no opportunity to discuss this material in open court. While it was accepted that in principle a jury should not consider material which had not been considered in court, on the facts of the case the evidence had been printed off legitimate websites to which the public had general access and only concerned issues as to sentencing. Therefore, on the facts of the particular case, the convictions were found to have been safe.

Professor Thomas's research published in 2010 found that in 12 per cent of high-profile cases jurors looked for information on the internet. For ordinary cases, 5 per cent of jurors admitted doing so. Professor Thomas suggests that the results of her research are likely to show the 'minimum numbers of jurors' as others may not have admitted to such conduct if they had realised it was prohibited. Her research in 2013 found that three-quarters of jurors understood the rules limiting access to the internet during the trial, but the remaining quarter were confused. A fifth thought they were not allowed to look at the internet at all during the trial, including their own emails, while 5 per cent thought there were no restrictions on the use of the internet during the trial. Some jurors may not understand the logic behind the ban and therefore see no harm in ignoring it.

What must be unacceptable is any communication over the internet between jurors and defendants. In **Attorney General v Fraill and Sewart** (2011), a juror chatted with a defendant on Facebook after she had been acquitted but while the jury was still considering the verdict of a co-defendant. In these communications the juror discussed the jury's ongoing deliberations in the jury room. The juror was a vulnerable woman of low intelligence, but she knew what she was doing was wrong and was sentenced to eight months' custody for contempt of court.

In **Attorney General v Dallas** (2012) a juror was sentenced to six months' imprisonment after researching online a defendant's previous convictions and then sharing them in the jury deliberations. She suggested she may not have understood the judge's directions regarding use of the internet as her English was 'not that good' but held a job as a psychology lecturer at the University of Bedfordshire.

'An avalanche of prejudicial comments' posted on Facebook pages was declared the cause for the judge discharging the jury in the 2015 case of two girls on trial for the murder of a vulnerable woman (**R v F and D** (2016)). Sir Henry Globe QC was notified of more than 500 comments about the case and he, along with the prosecution and defence agreed there was a risk that the defendants would be unable to have a fair trial.

At the new trial, an order was placed banning any reporting of the trial until verdicts were returned, which was challenged by media organisations including *The Times* and Sky News (**Re BBC and Others** (2016)). This was on the basis of the principle of open justice, as well as the fact that this order would not prevent the general public from posting about the case online regardless of the lack of news stories. Their appeal was granted but restrictions were placed on reporting; including the disabling of the comments feature under any news story.

> **Criminal offences committed by jurors**
>
> In the past, juror misconduct was mainly dealt with as contempt of court. The Law Commission published a report in 2013 looking at the jury and modern media. It recommended there should be a specific offence when a juror intentionally seeks information relating to the case being tried, to tackle the problem of internet use by jurors. The Law Commission preferred creating a new criminal offence so that people are only punished after 'normal' criminal proceedings with their inbuilt safeguards had been followed, instead of relying on the general offence of contempt. Following this report, the Criminal Justice and Courts Act 2015 was passed. This created four criminal offences replacing the former contempt of court punishments. These new offences criminalise jurors researching details of a case a court is trying, sharing details of that research with others, disclosing details of deliberations and behaving in a way that shows they intend to try the issue otherwise than on the basis of the evidence presented in the proceedings. This expansion of the criminal law is another challenge to a juror's freedom of expression and might discourage other jurors from reporting misconduct of this nature. It is arguable that, instead of criminalising this behaviour, the courts should adapt to the reality that the internet is easily accessible in jurors' homes.
>
> The Attorney General called for evidence from individuals and organisations who work within the criminal justice system at the end of 2017 with the publication of 'The Impact of Social Media on the Administration of Justice', however at the time of writing no summary of findings or recommendations have been published.

12.3 When are juries used?

12.3.1 Criminal cases

Though juries are symbolically important in the criminal justice system, they actually operate only in a minority of cases and their role is constantly being reduced to save money. Criminal offences are classified into three groups: summary only offences, which are tried in the magistrates' courts; indictable offences, which are tried in the Crown Court; and either way offences, which, as the name suggests, may be tried in either the magistrates' courts or the Crown Court. The majority of criminal offences are summary only, and because these are, in general, the least serious offences, they are also the ones most commonly committed (most road traffic offences, for example, are summary only). As a result, 95 per cent of criminal cases are heard in the magistrates' courts, where juries have no role (this proportion also includes cases involving either way offences where the defendant chooses to be tried by magistrates). Juries only decide cases heard in the Crown Court. Even among the 5 per cent of cases heard there, in a high proportion of these the defendant will plead guilty, which means there is no need for a jury and, on top of that, there are cases where the judge directs the jury that the law demands that they acquit the defendant, so that the jury effectively makes no decision here either. The result is that juries actually decide only around 1 per cent of criminal cases.

On the other hand, it is important to realise that even this 1 per cent amounts to 30,000 trials, and that these are usually the most serious ones to come before the courts – though here too the picture can be misleading, since some serious offences, such as assaulting a police officer or drink-driving, are dealt with only by magistrates, while even the most trivial theft can be tried in the Crown Court if the defendant wishes.

Despite its historical role in the English legal system, and the almost sacred place it occupies in the public imagination, the jury has come under increasing attack in recent years. Successive governments have attempted to reduce the use of juries in criminal cases in order to save money. The Criminal Law Act 1977 removed the right to jury trial in a significant number of offences, by making most driving offences and relatively minor criminal damage cases summary only. Since 1977, more and more offences have been removed from the realm of jury trial by being made summary only. The sentencing powers of magistrates (currently a maximum of six months' imprisonment for a single offence) were meant to have been increased by the Criminal Justice Act 2003. However s. 154, which includes provision to increase this to twelve months' imprisonment, has never been brought into force. By increasing the magistrates' sentencing powers, the aim was for more cases to be tried in the magistrates' court rather than being referred up to the Crown Court to be tried by an expensive jury. This push to double magistrates' sentencing powers was backed by the Justice Select Committee in October 2016 and also by the then Lord Chief Justice, Lord Thomas of Cwmgiedd in September 2017. Lord Thomas dismissed concerns that any such change would result in an increased prison population: 'We do have a serious problem with those sentenced long-term . . . but there is not a problem with that part [short-term prisoners] of the prison population.'

Photo 12.1 The Old Bailey, the Central Criminal Court in London

Source: © BasPhoto/Shutterstock.com

Legislating to reduce the role of the jury

The Criminal Justice Act 2003 provides for trial by judge alone in the Crown Court in two situations:

- where a serious risk of jury tampering exists (s. 44); or
- where the case involves complex or lengthy financial and commercial arrangements (s. 43).

In this second scenario, trial by judge alone would be possible where the trial would be so burdensome upon a jury that it is necessary in the interests of justice for the case to be heard without a jury. Alternatively, it would be possible where the trial would be likely to place an excessive burden on the life of a typical juror. While s. 44 has been brought into force, the former Labour Government agreed with the then opposition not to implement s. 43 while alternative proposals for specialist juries and judges sitting in panels were investigated. The legislative provision can only be brought into force by a parliamentary order approving its implementation, which will require debates and a vote in both Houses of Parliament. This process was initiated at the end of 2005, but following strong opposition the provision was not brought into force. Instead, the Labour Government introduced in 2006 a single issue Bill, the Fraud (Trials without a Jury) Bill, aimed solely at abolishing the jury in a limited range of serious and complex fraud trials. This Bill did not complete its progress through Parliament before Parliament closed for the summer of 2007. The Protection of Freedoms Act 2012 repealed s. 43 of the Criminal Justice Act 2003 before it was ever brought into force.

The justification for trial without jury where there has been jury tampering, was explained by the Court of Appeal in *R* v *JSM* (2010), where it stated:

> The principle of trial by jury is precious, but in the end any defendant who is responsible for abusing the principle by attempting to subvert the process, has no justified complaint that he has been deprived of a right which, by his own actions, he himself has spurned.

The first Crown Court trial to be ordered without a jury in England and Wales under s. 44 occurred in the case of *R* v *Twomey* in 2009. The trial was concerned with an attempted robbery that occurred in Heathrow in 2004. The defendants had originally been put on trial in 2008, but the trial had been stopped after six months when two jurors had been approached. The cost of that first, unsuccessful trial had been £22 million. The cost of giving a new jury adequate protection would have been £1.5 million. The Court of Appeal concluded that in those circumstances s. 44 applied and the trial was ordered to proceed without a jury. The Court of Appeal stated that 'save in unusual circumstances, the judge faced with this problem [of jury tampering] should order not only the discharge of the jury but that he should continue the trial'. The case went to the European Court of Human Rights (*Twomey* v *UK* (2013)) which noted there is no right under Art. 6 (protecting the right to a fair trial) to have a jury trial. The Court stated that trial with a judge and jury and trial with a judge alone, were two forms of trial which are equally acceptable under Art. 6.

An exceptional case, where it was not appropriate for the judge to proceed to hear the case alone after jury tampering was *R* v *KS* (2009). In that case there had been a suggestion of jury tampering so the jury had been discharged but the judge had decided to proceed with the fraud trial, even though he had seen evidence which would not have been heard by a jury because of its sensitive nature for the security service. He had also sat on nine earlier trials concerned with different aspects of the fraud in which KS was portrayed as being central to the criminal enterprise. In sentencing those other individuals, the judge had made negative comments about KS. In those circumstances, the Court of Appeal considered that there was an appearance of bias and the conviction was quashed. The case should not have been allowed to continue with the judge sitting alone.

12.3.2 Civil cases

In the past most civil cases were tried by juries, but trial by jury in the civil system is now almost obsolete. The erosion of the use of juries in civil cases was very gradual and appears to have started in the middle of the nineteenth century, when judges were given the right, in certain situations, to refuse to let a case be heard before a jury and insist that it be heard in front of a sole judge instead. Now less than 1 per cent of civil cases are tried by a jury. Today the Senior Courts Act 1981 gives a qualified right to jury trial of civil cases in three types of case:

- malicious prosecution;
- false imprisonment;
- fraud.

In these cases jury trial is to be granted, unless the court is of the opinion that the trial requires any prolonged examination of documents or accounts, or any scientific or local investigation which cannot conveniently be made with a jury.

In all other cases (including defamation cases following the Defamation Act 2013), the right to jury trial is at the discretion of the court. In **Ward** v **James** (1966), the Court of Appeal stated that in personal injury cases (which constitute the majority of civil actions), trial should be by judge alone unless there were special considerations. In **Singh** v **London Underground** (1990), an application for trial by jury of a personal injury claim arising from the King's Cross underground fire of November 1987 was refused on the ground that a case involving such wide issues and technical topics was unsuitable for a jury.

There has been criticism of the distinction drawn between the types of case which carry a qualified right to trial by jury and other civil cases. In the past, there was also a qualified right

Figure 12.1 Role of the jury

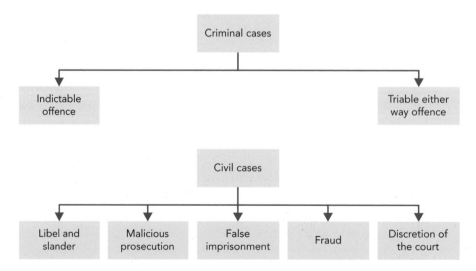

to jury trial in defamation cases. The Faulks Committee on Defamation in 1975 rejected arguments for the complete abolition of juries in defamation cases, but recommended that in such cases the court should have the same discretion to order jury trial as it does in other civil cases. The same recommendation was made by Lord Jackson in 2010 in his review of civil court costs. The Defamation Act 2013 introduced this reform.

12.4 Qualifications for jury service

Before 1972, only those who owned a home which was over a prescribed rateable value were eligible for jury service. The Morris Committee in 1965 estimated that 78 per cent of the names on the electoral register did not qualify for jury service under this criterion, and 95 per cent of women were ineligible. This was either because they lived in rented accommodation or because they were wives or other relatives of the person in whose name the property was held. The Committee recommended that the right to do jury service correspond with the right to vote. This reform was introduced in 1972. Despite this reform, there continued to be the problem that, in practice, juries were not truly representative of the society which they served. While it was understandable that some people with criminal convictions were disqualified from jury service, a wide range of other people were either excluded or excused from jury service. A wide range of people were automatically excluded from doing jury service, including the clergy and all those involved in the administration of justice, such as judges, barristers, solicitors, prison officers and the police.

12.4.1 The qualification rules today

The basis of the use of juries in serious criminal cases is that the 12 people are randomly selected, and should therefore comprise a representative sample of the population as a whole. This ideal came closer with the abolition of the property qualification and with the use of computers for the random selection process. Despite this, research carried out for the Home Office (*Jury Excusal and Deferral* (2000)) found that only two-thirds of the people summoned for jury service made themselves available to do it each year. About 15 per cent of summoned jurors failed to attend court on the day or had their summonses returned as 'undelivered'. Because enforcement has been poor, it became widely known that a jury summons could be ignored with impunity.

In his *Review of the Criminal Courts* (2001), Sir Robin Auld argued that the many exclusions and excusals from jury service deprived juries of the experience and skills of a wide range of professional and successful people. Their absence created the impression that jury service was only for those not important or clever enough to get out of it. He was keen to make juries more representative of the general population. He wanted jury service to become a compulsory public duty for all, to stop middle-class professionals opting out. He proposed that everyone should be eligible for jury service, save for the mentally ill.

The Government accepted these recommendations. The Criminal Justice Act 2003, s. 321 and Sched. 33 amended the Juries Act 1974. This Act now provides that potential jury members must be:

- aged 18 to 75;
- on the electoral register;

- resident in the UK, Channel Islands or Isle of Man for at least five years since the age of 13;
- not a mentally disordered person; and
- not disqualified from jury service.

Most of the grounds for ineligibility and excusal have been removed. Today the sole category of people who are ineligible for jury service are the mentally disordered. People can now be disqualified or excused from jury service due to age, residency, mental disability, criminal record, language or medical reasons. While these reforms have made juries more representative, the inclusive nature of the reforms has created new problems. Cases have been brought arguing that having police officers or prosecutors sitting as jurors creates the risk of bias. Before 2003, the police, prosecutors, barristers, solicitors and prison officers were ineligible to sit as jurors so this problem was avoided. Sir Robin Auld, who recommended this reform, considered that the danger of a police officer or prosecutor being biased was no greater than for any other member of the public, such as home owners who had been burgled in the past, or people with controversial views on drugs.

Key case

Membership of the jury of people who ordinarily work within the criminal justice system was considered by the House of Lords in *R v Abdroikof* (2007). The majority of the judges applied the basic principle that justice must not only be done, but manifestly be seen to be done. Legislation cannot override that principle. The House of Lords stated that the issue in each case was not actual bias but whether a fair-minded and informed observer would conclude that there was a real possibility that the jury was biased. The question was the appearance of bias. It would be for the trial judge to decide whether there was any special danger of apprehension of bias that distinguished the individual from other members of the jury. The House of Lords observed that most adults harboured prejudices, both conscious and unconscious. The assumption is that the 12 jurors will be able to neutralise any bias on the part of one or more members and so reach an impartial verdict.

The case involved three separate appeals which were heard together as they raised the same legal issues. The first appellant had been convicted of attempted murder. A minor issue in the six-day trial concerned one aspect of the evidence of a police witness. While the jury were considering their verdict, the foreman sent a note to the judge revealing that he was a serving police officer. He was supposed to report for duty at the Notting Hill Carnival on the following bank holiday Monday when the court would not be sitting. His concern was the possibility that he might meet officers who had given evidence in the case. The defence did not object to the case going forward. The first appellant's appeal was not allowed. The House noted:

> It is difficult to see what argument defence counsel could have urged other than the general undesirability of police officers serving on juries, a difficult argument to advance in face of the parliamentary enactment. It was not a case which turned on a contest between the evidence of the police and that of the appellant, and it would have been hard to suggest that the case was one in which unconscious prejudice, even if present, would have been likely to operate to the disadvantage of the appellant, and it makes no difference that the officer was the foreman of the jury.

The second appellant appealed against their conviction for assault occasioning actual bodily harm committed against a police officer. The officer had pricked himself against a syringe during a search of the person. There was a crucial dispute on the evidence between the appellant and the officer about the way in which he was searched and what had been said. After the trial, his solicitor discovered by chance that a policeman had sat on the jury. This policeman had not known the victim, but had previously served in the same police station at the same time. The House of Lords noted that, unlike the first appellant, there was a link between the case and the police officer serving on the jury and an important issue turned on a conflict between police and defence evidence:

> In this context the instinct (however unconscious) of a police officer on the jury to prefer the evidence of a brother officer to that of a drug-addicted defendant would be judged by the fair-minded and informed observer to be a real and possible source of unfairness, beyond the reach of standard judicial warnings and directions. The second appellant was not tried by a tribunal which was and appeared to be impartial.

The third appellant had been convicted of rape. The jury included a solicitor employed by the Crown Prosecution Service. Before the trial began he wrote informing the court of this fact. The defence counsel challenged the juror on the ground of potential bias, but the judge rejected this challenge and the third appellant was selected to be the foreman of the jury. The conviction was quashed and the House of Lords commented:

> It must, perhaps, be doubted whether Lord Justice Auld or Parliament contemplated that employed Crown prosecutors would sit as jurors in prosecutions brought by their own authority. It is in my opinion clear that justice is not seen to be done if one discharging the very important neutral role of juror is a full-time, salaried, long-serving employee of the prosecutor.

Legal principle

People will not be allowed to sit as a juror if their ordinary employment would lead a fair-minded and informed observer to conclude that there was a real possibility that they would be biased.

The case of **R v Abdroikof** did not lay down any hard and fast rules regarding whether CPS lawyers and police officers could sit on juries. Instead, the issue had to be decided on a case-by-case basis. Because in practice most prosecutions are brought by the CPS, most CPS lawyers will be unable to sit on a jury. The case of **Abdroikof** had suggested that where a personal connection between a juror and witness has been identified, the judge should be satisfied the evidence of the witness will play no contested part in the trial. Only if this cannot be established with certainty should the juror stand down. However, this issue has now been considered by the European Court of Human Rights, which took a more restrictive view. It ruled that people cannot act as jurors if they have a personal connection with someone involved in prosecuting the case. In **Hanif and Khan v UK** (2011) a juror in a trial was a police officer. He sent a note to the trial judge stating he had worked with a police officer who had given evidence for the prosecution. The judge allowed the juror to continue, with a warning about impartiality. The defendant appealed to the European Court, which ruled there had been a breach of Art. 6 of the Convention. A judicial warning was insufficient to guard against the risk that the juror may, albeit subconsciously, favour the police evidence. A tribunal must be objectively, as well as subjectively, impartial. The European Court noted that no other common law countries had chosen to follow the English example in allowing police officers to sit as jurors. However, more recently in **Armstrong v UK** (2015) the European Court of Human Rights ruled that the presence of retired and serving police officers on a jury did not, in itself, violate the right of a defendant to a fair trial as guaranteed by Art. 6 of the European Convention on Human Rights.

When interpreting legislation, the national courts have to take into account the decisions of the European Court of Human Rights. Thus it is likely a more restrictive approach will be taken to this matter than was initially done in the case of *R v Abdroikof.* A future court will probably take the view that police officers on the jury, having any acquaintance with individuals involved in the prosecution of the case, will not be allowed to remain in the jury to avoid a breach of Art. 6.

Trial judges should identify any risk of juror partiality before the start of a trial. People summoned for jury service must write to inform the court if they are employed in the criminal justice system so that the trial judge can consider whether there would be apparent bias before the trial begins.

Research carried out by Thomas and Balmer (2007) into jury service has found that juries are today representative of the communities they serve. The most significant factors predicting whether a summoned juror will serve or not are income and employment status. Among all people summoned, those with the lowest household income and those who were economically inactive were the least likely to serve. The highest income earners and those in higher status professions were fully represented among serving jurors. The employed in general are over-represented among serving jurors, while it is the retired and unemployed that are under-represented. The proportion of men and women serving as jurors was exactly the same (50 per cent), and gender had no significant impact on whether those summoned served or not.

12.5 Summoning the jury

Every year almost half a million people are summoned to do jury service. In 2001, a Central Juror Summoning Bureau was established to administer the juror summoning process for the whole of the country. Computers are used to produce a random list of potential jurors from the electoral register. Summons are sent out (with a form to return confirming that the person does not fall into any of the disqualified or ineligible groups), and from the resulting list the jury panel is produced. This is made public for both sides in forthcoming cases to inspect, although only names and addresses are shown (before 1977 the occupation of the juror was also stated). It is at this stage that jury vetting may take place (see below). Jurors also receive a set of notes which explain a little of the procedure of the jury service and the functions of the juror.

Jury service is compulsory and failure to attend on the specified date, or unfitness for service through drink or drugs, is contempt of court and can result in a fine. In terms of deferral of jury duty, common grounds include having a holiday booked, that you are in a temporary job which you would lose or if you are having a hospital operation.

The jury for a particular case is chosen by random ballot in open court – the clerk has each panel member's name on a card, the cards are shuffled and the first 12 names called out. Unless there are any challenges (see p. 278), these 12 people will be sworn in. In a criminal case there are usually 12 jurors and there must never be fewer than nine. In civil cases in the County Court there are eight jurors.

Sir Robin Auld also recommended that potential jurors no longer only be selected from the electoral register. Many people are not registered to vote in elections, even though they are entitled to do so. To reach as many people as possible he therefore proposed that a range of publicly maintained lists and directories be used. The Government has not adopted this recommendation.

12.6 Jury vetting

Jury vetting consists of checking that the potential juror does not hold 'extremist' views which some feel would make them unsuitable for hearing a case. It is done by checking police and security service records.

This controversial practice first came to light in the 1978 'ABC Trial' (*R v Aubrey, Berry and Campbell* (1978)), in which two journalists and a soldier were accused of collecting secret information, in breach of the Official Secrets Act. During the trial it became known that the jury had been vetted to check their 'loyalty', under guidelines laid down by the Attorney General, and a new trial was ordered.

The ensuing publicity eventually led to the publication of the Attorney General's guidelines, which it was admitted had been in use since 1974. These guidelines were revised in 1988. They confirm that, as a rule, juries should be chosen at random, with people being excluded only under the statutory exceptions, and that the proper way for the prosecution to exclude a juror was challenge for cause in open court (see below). But it was also stated that vetting might be necessary in certain special cases: those involving terrorism, where it was felt a juror's political beliefs might prevent him or her being impartial or lead to undue pressure on other jurors; and those concerning national security, where in addition to the problem of strong political beliefs there was the danger that some jurors might reveal evidence given *in camera* (that is heard in private and not in open court). Jurors could only be 'stood by' (see below) if the vetting revealed a very strong reason for doing so. In order to vet a jury in these cases authorisation from the Attorney General is required, who will be acting on the advice of the Director of Public Prosecutions. Checking whether a person has a criminal record is permissible in a much wider range of cases without special permission.

The legality of vetting was considered by the Court of Appeal in two cases during 1980. In *R v Sheffield Crown Court, ex parte Brownlow*, the defendants were police officers, and the defence wanted the jury vetted for previous convictions. The prosecution opposed it, but the Crown Court judge ordered that vetting should take place, and this decision was upheld by the Court of Appeal. Lords Denning and Shaw, *obiter dicta*, vigorously condemned vetting in security and terrorist cases as unconstitutional (because it was not provided for in the Juries Act 1974), and an invasion of privacy.

In *R v Mason* (1980), a convicted burglar appealed on the ground that the jury had been vetted for previous convictions, a common practice in the particular court at the time. The Court of Appeal decreed that vetting for previous convictions was necessary in order to ensure that disqualified persons could not serve. In such situations Lord Lawton described vetting as 'just common sense', although it should not be used to gain tactical advantage in minor cases.

The limits on vetting for previous convictions were, however, stressed again in *R v Obellim* (1996). The case concerned a criminal trial in which the judge had received a written question from the jury, which displayed a lot of knowledge about police powers and led him to suspect that one of the jurors might have such previous convictions as should have disqualified him or her. The judge ordered a security check on the jury, without telling the defence counsel, who only discovered the check had taken place when the jury complained about it after delivering their verdict.

The defendant, who was convicted, appealed on the grounds that the check on jury members might have prejudiced them. The Court of Appeal agreed, and quashed the conviction, stating that it was questionable whether the check should have been ordered at all on such grounds, and it certainly should not have been without informing defence counsel.

12

THE JURY

Vetting for any purpose remains controversial. Supporters claim that it can promote impartiality by excluding those whose views might bias the other members of the jury, and make them put pressure on others, as well as protecting national security and preventing disqualified persons from serving. Opponents say it infringes the individual's right to privacy, and gives the prosecution an unfair advantage, since it is too expensive for most defendants to undertake, and they do not have access to the same sources of information as the prosecution. Only on very rare occasions has the defence been granted legal aid to make its inquiries into the panel.

The whole process is still not sanctioned by legislation and, despite the publication of the Attorney General's guidelines, it is impossible to know whether they are being followed – 60 potential jurors were vetted by MI5 for the Clive Ponting case (see p. 284), despite the fact that there was no apparent threat to national security.

12.7 Challenges

As members of the jury panel are called, and before they are sworn in, they may be challenged in one of two ways.

12.7.1 Challenge for cause

Either side may challenge for cause, on the grounds of privilege of peerage, disqualification, ineligibility or assumed bias. Jurors cannot be questioned before being challenged to ascertain whether there are grounds for a challenge. A successful challenge for cause is therefore only likely to succeed if the juror is personally known, or if jury vetting has been undertaken. If a challenge for cause is made, it is tried by the trial judge.

12.7.2 Stand by

Only the prosecution may ask jurors to stand by for the Crown. Although there are specified grounds for this, in practice no reason need be given, and this is generally how the information supplied by jury vetting is used. The use of the power to stand by has been limited by guidelines issued by the Attorney General which specifically state that the abolition of the peremptory challenge (see below) means that the power to stand by should only be used in connection with jury vetting or where the juror is manifestly unsuitable and the defence agrees with the exercise of the power.

Until 1988, there was a third type of challenge, peremptory challenge, available only to the defence. This meant that the defence could challenge up to three jurors without showing cause, which was equivalent to the prosecution's power to 'stand by' a juror. This was abolished, amid much opposition, on the recommendation of the Roskill Committee (1986) on fraud trials, on the grounds that it interfered with the random selection process and allowed defence lawyers to 'pack' the jury with those they thought were likely to be sympathetic. This was felt to be a particular problem when there were several defendants as (theoretically) they could combine their rights to peremptory challenge.

This limited process of challenging the jury should be contrasted with the system in the US where it can take days to empanel a jury, particularly where the case has received a lot of pre-trial media coverage. Potential jury members can be asked a wide range of questions about their attitudes to the issues raised by a case, and a great deal of money may be spent employing special consultants who claim to be able to judge which way people are likely to vote, based on their age, sex, politics, religion and other personal information.

In a high-profile 1998 case, *R v Andrews*, the defence wanted to use the American approach to establish whether members of the jury panel were likely to be biased against the defendant. She was accused of murdering her boyfriend, and the case had received an enormous amount of publicity since Ms Andrews had initially told police that her boyfriend was killed by an unknown assailant in a 'road rage' incident, sparking off a media hunt for the killer. Her lawyers wanted to issue questionnaires to the jury panel to check whether any of them showed a prejudice against her. The trial judge refused the request and when Ms Andrews was convicted, she appealed, arguing that the failure to allow questioning of the jury meant her conviction was unsafe. The argument was rejected by the Court of Appeal, which stated that questioning of the jury panel, whether orally or by written questionnaire, should be avoided in all but the most exceptional cases, such as where potential jurors might have a direct or indirect connection to the facts of the trial (for example, if they were related to someone involved in the trial, or had lost money as a result of the defendant's actions).

12.8 Discharging the jury

The judge may discharge any juror, or even the whole jury, to prevent scandal or the perversion of justice. The courts have had to consider whether a jury needs to be discharged where there is a risk of racism. In *Gregory v United Kingdom* (1997), Gregory was a black defendant accused of robbery. During his trial, the jury had handed the judge a note asking that one juror be excused because of racial bias. The judge did not excuse the juror, but instead issued a strong direction to the jury to decide the case on the evidence alone. Gregory was convicted on a majority verdict and brought a case before the European Court of Human Rights, claiming that the judge should have discharged the whole jury, and that failure to do so infringed his right to a fair trial under the European Convention on Human Rights. The European Court of Human Rights, however, held that, in the circumstances, issuing a clear and carefully worded warning to the jury was sufficient to ensure a fair trial.

This case was distinguished in *Sander v United Kingdom* (2001). The applicant was an Asian man, who had been tried in the Crown Court with another Asian man on a charge of conspiracy to defraud. During the trial, a juror passed a note to the judge alleging that certain of his fellow jurors had made racist remarks and jokes. The juror who made the complaint was initially segregated from the rest of the jury while the court considered representations made by the lawyers. The judge then asked the complainant to re-join the other jurors and instructed them to consider whether they were able to put aside any prejudices which they had and to try the case solely on the evidence. All of the jurors signed a letter to the judge stating:

> We utterly refute the allegation of possible racial bias. We are deeply offended by the allegation. We assure the Court that we intend to reach a verdict solely according to the evidence and without racial bias.

One juror, who believed that the allegations were directed at him, wrote a separate letter to confirm that he was not racially biased. The judge concluded that there was no real risk of bias and allowed the trial to continue with the same jury, and rejected the defence request to discharge the jury. At first instance, the applicant was convicted and his co-accused was acquitted.

The applicant appealed against his conviction up to the European Court of Human Rights. He complained that he had been denied the right to a fair trial before an impartial court, guaranteed by Art. 6(1) of the European Convention on Human Rights. The European Court held that it was not possible to state whether some of the jurors were actually biased as the matter had not been investigated. The fact that at least one juror had made comments that could be construed as jokes about Asians was not evidence of actual bias. But it was also important for the jurors to be viewed as objectively impartial, in other words, that they were not just as a matter of fact impartial, but also that they would appear to an observer to be impartial. There was doubt as to the credibility of the letter which denied the allegations because the juror who had made the allegations also signed the letter. The identity of the juror who had made the allegations was revealed by his separation from the other jurors and this must have compromised his position with his fellow jurors, and inhibited him in the further discussion of the case. An admonition by a judge 'however clear, detailed and forceful would not change racist views overnight'. Even though it was not established that the jurors had such views, the judge's direction could not dispel the reasonable impression and fear of a lack of impartiality based on the original note. The fact that the jury had acquitted one Asian defendant was irrelevant since the case against him was much weaker. The judge should have discharged the jury. Thus, the court concluded that the appellant had not received a fair trial and Art. 6(1) had been breached.

The court distinguished its earlier decision of *Gregory* v *United Kingdom* (1997), mainly on the ground that in that case there was no admission by a juror that he had made racist comments, nor an indication as to which juror had made the complaint and the complaint was vague and imprecise.

Professor Zander (2000) has criticised the decision in *Sander* v *United Kingdom*. He controversially argues that the Strasbourg court does not understand the English jury system and the measures in place to ensure that the jury deliberate fairly free from prejudices.

12.9 The secrecy of the jury

Once they retire to consider their verdict, jurors are not allowed to communicate with anyone other than the judge and an assigned court official, until after the verdict is delivered. Afterwards they are forbidden by the Criminal Justice and Courts Act 2015 from revealing anything that was said or done during their deliberations. Breach of this ban amounts to a criminal offence.

The arguments in favour of secrecy are that:

- it ensures freedom of discussion in the jury room;
- it protects jurors from outside influences, and from harassment;
- if the public knew how juries reached their verdict they might respect the decision less;
- without secrecy citizens would be reluctant to serve as jurors;
- it ensures the finality of the verdict;
- it enables jurors to bring in unpopular verdicts; and
- it prevents unreliable disclosures by jurors and misunderstanding of verdicts.

The arguments against secrecy and in favour of disclosure are that this reform would:

- make juries more accountable;
- make it easier to inquire into the reliability of convictions and rectify injustices;
- show where reform is required;
- educate the public; and
- ensure each juror's freedom of expression.

In ***Attorney General* v *Seckerson and Times Newspapers Ltd*** (2009) a jury foreman revealed to *The Times* newspaper that he had concerns with how the guilty verdict was reached in a high-profile criminal case. The case involved a childminder who was convicted of the manslaughter of a baby, following expert evidence on the injuries suffered when a child is shaken. Both the juror and the newspaper were fined for committing a criminal offence. In its defence, the newspaper sought unsuccessfully to rely on the right to freedom of expression guaranteed by Art. 10 of the European Convention on Human Rights.

The House of Lords case of ***R* v *Mirza*** (2004) drew attention to the problem of jury secrecy where, after the trial, a juror writes to the court expressing their concern with how the verdict was reached. Now that a majority verdict is possible, a letter after verdict is often the only option open to a juror where a verdict has been reached which they did not agree with. There was a suggestion in one of the cases being considered in ***R* v *Mirza*** that some of the jurors were racist. The House of Lords took the view that, due to the secrecy of the jury, it could not investigate what had happened in the jury room. However, the trial court could make such an inquiry before a verdict was reached and, if an appeal was launched, the Court of Appeal could ask a judge to provide a report about the trial. A Practice Direction has now been issued stating that trial judges should ensure that the jury is alerted to the need to bring any concerns about fellow jurors to the attention of the judge immediately, and not to wait until the case is concluded. The point should be made that, unless that is done while the case is continuing, it may be impossible to put matters right.

In ***Attorney General* v *Scotcher*** (2005), Scotcher had been a juror on a trial of two brothers. After the brothers were convicted, he wrote to the mother suggesting that he was unhappy with the way the jury had reached its verdict and that there might have been a miscarriage of justice. He was subsequently successfully prosecuted for the old offence under s. 8 of the Contempt of Court Act 1981. His defence that this offence breached his right to freedom of expression under Art. 10 of the European Convention on Human Rights was rejected by the House of Lords.

Research into the work of juries has always been made difficult by the requirement for secrecy. The Runciman Commission recommended that the 1981 Act be amended so that valid research can be carried out into the way juries reach their verdicts. The Government issued a consultation paper, *Jury Research and Impropriety* (2005), considering when it was appropriate to allow the secrecy of the jury room to be breached, particularly for the purposes of research into juries. About 75 per cent of respondents opposed allowing researchers any form of access to the jury room itself. The majority of respondents were happy, however, to allow more research into jurors to take place provided it did not involve access to the jury room. In Cheryl Thomas's research (2010), 82 per cent of jurors believed that what happens in the deliberating room should remain secret.

The Government's conclusions are that initially more research should be carried out into the jury within the confines of the present law, for example, by using shadow juries and mock trials. This initial research could generate questions which subsequently need to be answered by allowing researchers access to the jury room. The academic, Michael Zander (2000), had expressed concern that if jury rooms could be 'bugged' for research purposes, it risked undermining the public's confidence in the jury system and therefore could ultimately lead to its abolition.

The American case of *Peña-Rodriguez* v *Colorado* (2017) saw for the first time an exception to the understanding that jurors cannot be challenged on their secret deliberations, opening up the possibility of greater post-trial analysis of jury verdicts. After the conviction of Peña-Rodriguez for harassment and unlawful sexual contact, two jurors came forward to state that one of their fellow jurors had made a succession of comments about 'Mexicans' and 'illegals', stating that in his job as a former law enforcement officer 'nine times out of ten Mexican men were guilty of being aggressive to women and young girls'. In a five to three decision by the United States Supreme Court, Justice Anthony M. Kennedy wrote:

> A constitutional rule that racial bias in the justice system must be addressed – including, in some instances, after the verdict has been entered – is necessary to prevent a systemic loss of confidence in jury verdicts.

The possibility of jurors being influenced by racial bias was also a factor in the recent review of the case of Keith Leroy Tharpe, who had been on death row since being convicted of the death of his sister-in-law in 1990. A juror in his case was said to have commented: 'I have wondered whether black people even have souls.'

12.10 The verdict

Ideally, juries should produce a unanimous verdict, but in 1967 majority verdicts were introduced of ten to two (or nine to one if the jury has been reduced during the trial). This is now provided for in the Juries Act 1974. When the jury withdraws to consider its verdict, the jurors must be told by the judge to reach a unanimous verdict. If, however, the jury has failed to reach a unanimous verdict after what the judge considers a reasonable period of deliberation, given the complexity of the case (not less than two hours), the judge can direct that the jury may reach a majority verdict. The foreman of the jury must state in open court the numbers of the jurors agreeing and disagreeing with the verdict. Professor Cheryl Thomas's research (2010) found that only 0.6 per cent of jury cases result in a hung jury where the jurors are unable to reach a majority verdict. Jurors convicted in 64 per cent of all cases. Majority verdicts were intended to help prevent jury 'nobbling' (where someone involved in the trial puts pressure on jurors to vote in a particular way, by bribes or threats). It also avoids the problem of one juror with extreme or intractable views holding out against the rest, and should lessen the need for expensive and time-consuming retrials. However, Brown and Neal's 1988 research found that the introduction of majority verdicts has not substantially affected the number of hung juries and consequent retrials. Freeman (1981) has suggested that majority verdicts dilute the concept of proof beyond reasonable doubt – on the grounds that if one juror is not satisfied, a doubt must exist – and give less protection against the risk of convicting the innocent. This in turn weakens public confidence in the system.

In Scotland, the jury consists of 15 people and a conviction can be based on a simple majority verdict.

12.11 Strengths of the jury system

12.11.1 Public participation

Juries allow the ordinary citizen to take part in the administration of justice, so that verdicts are seen to be those of society rather than of the judicial system, and satisfy the constitutional tradition of judgment by one's peers. Lord Denning described jury service as giving 'ordinary folk their finest lesson in citizenship'. This has particular importance when one considers the background of magistrates, which continues to be largely white and middle class. A defendant who does not come from this sector of society may well prefer to be judged by a jury, which is more likely to include members of his or her own race and/or class: a 1990 study by the Runnymede Trust found that black defendants charged with either way offences were more likely to opt for jury trial than white defendants in the same position. This is not to say that magistrates are biased against those from outside their race and/or class, and so unable to give them a fair trial, merely that, if defendants believe this to be the case, trust in the legal system is reduced, and reduced even more if the option to choose a mode of trial which looks fairer is taken away.

The Home Office has carried out research into the experience of being a juror: Matthews, Hancock and Briggs, *Jurors' Perceptions, Understanding, Confidence and Satisfaction in the Jury System: A Study in Six Courts* (2004). The research questioned 361 jurors about their jury service. More than half (55 per cent) said they would be happy to do it again, 19 per cent said they would not mind doing jury service again, but 25 per cent said they would never want to be a juror again. About two-thirds felt that their experience had boosted their opinion of the jury system and they were impressed by the professionalism and helpfulness of the court staff and the performance of the judge. A minority was unhappy with the delays in the system, the trivial nature of some cases and the standard of facilities. Thirty-six per cent of jurors felt intimidated or very uncomfortable in the courtroom, primarily because they were worried about meeting defendants or their family members coming out of court or in the street.

When questioned by Professor Lloyd-Bostock (2007) about their experience, the jurors in the collapsed Jubilee Line case (see p. 294) were found to be enthusiastic about their role, committed to it, and furious when the trial was aborted. They were a remarkably cooperative and mutually supportive group. Two compared being on the jury with being on *Big Brother*. However, as the trial progressed the jurors felt increasingly like 'jury fodder', on tap but not informed. They would be telephoned at short notice and told not to turn up for several days but no explanation would be given. Even more frustrating was when they turned up for jury service and then, after a lengthy delay, were sent home again. The main difficulties suffered by the jurors were in relation to their employment. All seven jurors who were employed said their employers were very unhappy about the long trial. Most felt that the court should have more responsibility for communicating directly with their employers rather than placing the onus on the jurors. Uncooperative employers could cause problems over claims for allowances. One juror had been made redundant, one was in an employment dispute, one had missed a definite and much desired promotion and was required to undertake extensive retraining, and one had been signed off by his doctor as suffering from stress as a result of his work situation. Most of the jurors had suffered financially as a result of the trial. One suggestion is that a juror liaison person could be appointed for long jury trials whose remit is to look after jurors' needs and alleviate the burden of jury service as much as possible.

It is important to realise that despite the symbolic importance of juries, the system remains dominated by judges and magistrates. Only a small proportion of cases is tried by juries and, even in such cases, judges can exert considerable influence.

12.11.2 Certainty

The jury adds certainty to the law, since it gives a general verdict which cannot give rise to misinterpretation. In a criminal case the jury simply states that the accused is guilty or not guilty, and gives no reasons. Consequently, the decision is not open to dispute.

12.11.3 Ability to judge according to conscience

Because juries have the ultimate right to find defendants innocent or guilty, they have been seen as a vital protection against oppressive or politically motivated prosecutions, and as a kind of safety valve for those cases where the law demands a guilty verdict, but it can be argued that genuine justice does not. For example, in the early nineteenth century, all felonies (a classification of crimes used at the time, marking out those considered most serious) were in theory punishable by death. Theft of goods or money above the value of a shilling was a felony, but juries were frequently reluctant to allow the death penalty to be imposed in what seemed to them trivial cases, so they would often find that the defendant was guilty, but the property stolen was worth less than a shilling.

There are several well-known cases of juries using their right to find according to their consciences, often concerning issues of political and moral controversy, such as *R v Kronlid* (1996). The defendants here were three women who broke into a British Aerospace factory and caused damage costing over £1.5 million to a Hawk fighter plane. The women admitted doing this – they had left a video explaining their actions in the plane's cockpit – but claimed that they had a defence under s. 3 of the Criminal Law Act 1967, which provides that it is lawful to commit a crime in order to prevent another (usually more serious) crime being committed, and that this may involve using 'such force as is reasonable in all the circumstances'.

The defendants pointed out that the plane was part of a consignment due to be sold to the Government of Indonesia, which was involved in oppressive measures against the population of East Timor, a region forcibly annexed by Indonesia in 1975. They further explained that Amnesty International had estimated that the Indonesians have killed at least a third of the population of East Timor, and that the jet was likely to be used in a genocidal attack against the survivors. Genocide is a crime and therefore, they argued, their criminal damage was done in order to prevent a crime. However, the prosecution gave evidence that the Indonesian Government had given assurances that the planes would not be used against the East Timorese, and the British Government had accepted this and granted an export licence. Acquitting the women was therefore a criticism of the British Government's position on the issue, as well as the actions of the Indonesian Government and, in the face of the clear evidence that they had caused the damage, they were widely expected to be convicted. The jury found them all not guilty.

Other cases have involved what were seen to be oppressive prosecutions in matters involving the Government, such as *R v Ponting* (1985), where the defendant, a civil servant, was prosecuted for breaking the Official Secrets Act after passing confidential information to a journalist – even though doing so exposed a matter of public interest, namely the fact that the then Government had lied to Parliament about the circumstances in which an Argentinian warship, the *General Belgrano*, was sunk by a British submarine during the Falklands war. At his trial, Ponting admitted that he had leaked the confidential information, but said in his defence that he was acting in the public interest. The trial judge directed the jury to convict, dismissing Ponting's public interest defence with the words: 'the public interest is what the government of the day says it is.' Ponting had apparently brought his toothbrush with him to court on the day the verdict was due, expecting to be convicted, but the jury acquitted. As juries do not give reasons for their decisions, we do not know why the jury acquitted in the case, but it may have been because it considered Ponting had done the right thing and thereby it protected a private citizen against the oppressive use of power by the state.

Not all cases in which juries exercise this right are overtly political. In *R v Owen* (1991), the defendant was a man whose son had been knocked down and killed by a lorry driver who had never taken a driving test, and had a long criminal record for drink-driving and violence. The driver, who apparently showed no remorse for killing the boy, was convicted of a driving offence, sentenced to 18 months in prison and released after a year. He then resumed driving his lorry unlawfully. After contacting a number of different authorities to try to secure what he considered to be some sort of justice for his son's death, Mr Owen eventually took a shotgun and injured the lorry driver. He was charged with a number of offences, including attempted murder but, despite a great deal of evidence against him, the jury acquitted.

The importance of this aspect of the jury's involvement in criminal justice is very difficult to assess. In high-profile cases such as ***Ponting*** and ***Kronlid***, it can be a valuable statement of public feeling to those in authority, but, even in this kind of case, it cannot be relied on. The defendant in the earlier case of *R v Tisdall* (1984) was a junior civil servant who leaked information which exposed Government wrongdoing. It was admitted that the leak was no threat to national security, yet she was convicted and sentenced to imprisonment for six months, which was seen as overly severe in the circumstances.

Juries are never actually told that they can acquit if their consciences suggest they should: their instructions are quite the opposite and, before the case begins, they must swear to try the case according to the evidence. Nor do they give reasons for their decisions, so there is no way of knowing how often juries acquit defendants out of a sense of justice, even though they know that the law demands a guilty verdict. Where the verdict does clearly seem perverse in the face of the evidence, there may be other reasons for an acquittal, such as not understanding the evidence or the law.

However, there is one modern example of law reform being brought about at least partly in response to the actions of juries. This is the creation of the offence of causing death by dangerous driving, which was introduced after juries proved reluctant to convict of manslaughter those who had killed people by dangerous driving. It can be argued, however, that this example shows that allowing the jury such freedom is not always a good thing, since the reason for the reluctance was thought to be that many jurors who were motorists could see how easily they could have found themselves in the dock: Sir Robin Auld (2001) appears to consider perverse verdicts by juries an affront to the criminal justice system, and has recommended reforms which would seek to prevent juries handing down such verdicts.

12.12 Criticisms of the jury system

12.12.1 Lack of competence

Lord Denning argued in *What Next in the Law?* (1982) that the selection of jurors is too wide, resulting in jurors that are not competent to perform their task. Praising the 'Golden Age' of jury service when only 'responsible heads of household from a select band of the middle classes' were eligible to serve, he claimed that the 1972 changes have led to jurors being summoned who are not sufficiently intelligent or educated to perform their task properly. In one unfortunate case a jury hearing a murder trial had apparently set up a Ouija board in an attempt to make contact with the spirit of the deceased: *R v Young* (1995). Stephen Young was a financial adviser who was alleged to have shot dead Mr and Mrs Fuller for their money. He was prosecuted and the jury had to stay overnight in a hotel while they considered their verdict. In the hotel they used a Ouija board (a board with numbers and letters on) to try and contact the victims' spirits. At the séance it was suggested that the late Mr Fuller (who, in life, had been dyslexic) spelt out the name of his killer and urged the jury to 'vote guilty tomorrow'. The subsequent guilty verdict was overturned but a new jury found Mr Young guilty at his retrial (without the help of a Ouija board). Lord Denning suggested that jurors should be selected in much the same way as magistrates are, with interviews and references required. This throws up several obvious problems: a more complicated selection process would be more time-consuming and costly; finding sufficient people willing to take part might prove difficult; and a jury that is intelligent and educated can still be biased, and may be more likely to be so if drawn from a narrow social group.

Professor Cheryl Thomas published a major piece of research into jury trials entitled *Are Juries Fair?*, which was funded by the Ministry of Justice and published in 2010. This concluded that juries found it easier to understand a case when they had been issued with written guidance. Only 31 per cent understood the legal questions in a case when no written summary was provided. But even when jurors were given a one-page summary of the judge's directions, only 48 per cent were able to identify correctly both questions the judge said needed to be answered. The former Judicial Studies Board recommended that written directions be given to juries in all but the simplest cases, and this has become standard practice.

New guidance for judges on summing up was issued to crown court judges and recorders in the 'Crown Court Compendium' in February 2017, in order to aid the jurors' comprehension of trials.

Particular concern has been expressed about the average jury's understanding of complex fraud cases. The Roskill Committee concluded that trial by random jury was not a satisfactory way of achieving justice in such cases, with many jurors 'out of their depth'. However, the Roskill Committee was unable to find accurate evidence of a higher proportion of acquittals in complex fraud cases than in any other kind of case – many of their conclusions were based on research by Baldwin and McConville (1979), yet none of the questionable acquittals reported there was in a complex fraud case. Evidence of the police to the Runciman Commission stated that the conviction rates for serious fraud, when compared with the overall conviction rate for cases that are considered by a jury, show that in serious fraud trials the jury are actually convicting a slightly higher percentage. The academic, Terry Honess, conducted an extended simulation study of jurors' comprehension of some of the evidence in the Maxwell fraud trial (Honess, Charman and Levi, 2003). He estimated that four out of five of the participants could be regarded as competent to serve on a major fraud trial, and concluded that abolition of the jury system for complex fraud trials was not justified on the grounds of 'cognitive unfitness'.

Following the collapse of the trial of six men prosecuted for alleged fraud in the awarding of contracts for the construction of the extension to the Jubilee underground line, *R v Rayment and others* (2005), the jurors were questioned about their experience of the trial as part of a Government review of the case. This review found that 'when the case collapsed this jury, taken as a group, had a good understanding of the case, the issues and the evidence so far, as presented to them'. The jurors said they had no problem with technical language or documents. They displayed quite impressive familiarity with the charges, issues and evidence, and were able to engage in detailed discussion of the prosecution case nearly a year after it had closed. The chief difficulty expressed by the jurors was not in finding evidence too technical or complex, but in finding the pace of the trial extremely slow and parts of the defence evidence tedious. It is questionable whether the trial needed to be unmanageably long. In the preface to his report on the case, Stephen Wooler (2006) describes it as 'probably one of the best examples' of cases 'which are neither sufficiently complex to be beyond the comprehension of juries, nor necessarily lengthy'. Discussion was evidently facilitated by the provision of a jury deliberating room for much of the trial, where the jury went while at court but not in court. The jurors said they found discussion much more difficult, if not impossible, when they did not have use of this room. The jurors were not allowed to take their notes from the courtroom and several said it would have been helpful to do so. The academic, Professor Findlay (2001) has noted that juror comprehension and memory for complex evidence can be assisted through, for example, the use of visual aids. Discussion among jurors, taking notes and asking questions can enhance juror comprehension (Horowitz and Fosterlee, 2001). Professor Lloyd-Bostock (2007) has concluded:

> . . . where the jury is concerned, the 'problem' with the Jubilee Line case was not the jury's ability to cope, but the unnecessarily excessive length of the case with its consequences for the jurors' lives, together with some aspects of their treatment at court . . . Taken in context, the jurors' perspective on the ill-fated Jubilee Line trial does not indicate that the solution is to abandon jury trial for such cases. Rather, it confirms that jury trial is valued, and that improvements through trial preparation, and trial and jury management, should be fully explored before the jury itself is threatened.

An American lawyer, Robert Julian (2007), interviewed all the judges who had tried a fraud case prosecuted by the Serious Fraud Office over a one-year period. They were unanimously in favour of jury trials of serious fraud cases and did not want them to be replaced by judge-alone trials. They were not convinced that judge-alone trials would automatically be shorter, as the prosecution would not have the same pressure to prune the case to make it manageable for a jury. As one judge observed:

> I have no reason to doubt that juries understand the issues in serious fraud cases . . . Fundamentally we are talking about honesty and dishonesty. That's very well suited to the jury trial process.

Many of the judges gave objective bases for their favourable opinions about the juries' understanding of the issues, pointing to the pertinent questions asked by jurors and the fact that they discriminated between different defendants, convicting some, while acquitting others.

The Bigger Picture: The Vicky Pryce fiasco

The competency of jurors was called into question following the high-profile trial of Vicky Pryce. Vicky Pryce had been married to the senior politician Chris Huhne. During a bitter divorce process, she revealed she had agreed to pretend she was driving a car which had been caught speeding instead of her husband, so the speeding points would go on her licence and he would not lose his licence. When she was prosecuted for perverting the course of justice, she argued an antiquated defence that she had acted under marital coercion. The jury were directed by the trial judge on the law but returned, after a number of hours of deliberation, to ask the judge a number of questions. The judge concluded that the questions demonstrated the jury's failure to understand the most basic aspects of the case and decided to halt the trial. The judge made some very critical comments about the jury and their 'absolutely fundamental deficits in understanding'. A retrial was subsequently ordered with a different jury and Vicky Pryce was convicted. Some commentators have suggested this case illustrates the incompetence of jurors. But another view is that the judge showed a lack of respect for the jury. For example, the judge was concerned that the jury asked for a definition of 'reasonable doubt' but was this question simply reflecting how seriously the jury were taking their civic duty? The test for the burden of proof might be understood by lawyers but a non-lawyer could, upon reflection, quite reasonably wonder what exactly it meant. Jurors should feel that they can ask questions, without fear of being publicly ridiculed.

12.12.2 The 'perverse verdicts' problem

It is a matter of fact that juries acquit proportionately more defendants than magistrates do; research from the Home Office Planning Unit suggests that an acquittal is approximately twice as likely in a jury trial. Many critics of the jury system argue that this is a major failing on the part of juries, arising either from their inability to perform their role properly, as discussed above, or from their sympathy with defendants, or both. Others would argue that apparently 'perverse' judgments are frequently just the juries deciding the case according to their conscience (see p. 284).

This is a difficult area to research, as the Contempt of Court Act 1981 prohibits asking jurors about the basis on which they reached their decision. What research there is generally involves comparing actual jury decisions with those reached by legal professionals, or by shadow juries, who sit in on the case and reach their own decision just as the official jurors are asked to do.

A piece of research commissioned by the Roskill Committee on fraud trials concluded that jurors who found difficulty in comprehending the complex issues involved in fraud prosecution were more likely to acquit. They suggested that the jurors characterised their own confusions as a form of 'reasonable doubt' leading them to a decision to acquit.

A study by McCabe and Purves, *The Jury at Work* (1972), looked at 173 acquittals, and concluded that 15 (9 per cent) defied the evidence, the rest being attributable to weakness of the prosecution case or failure of their witnesses, or the credibility of the accused's explanation. McCabe and Purves viewed the proportion of apparently perverse verdicts as quite small and, from their observations of shadow juries, concluded that jurors did work methodically and rationally through the evidence, and try to put aside their own prejudices.

However, Baldwin and McConville's 1979 study (*Jury Trials*) examined 500 cases, both convictions and acquittals, and found up to 25 per cent of acquittals were questionable (as well as 5 per cent of convictions), and concluded that, given the serious nature of the cases concerned, this was a problem. They describe trial by jury as 'an arbitrary and unpredictable business'.

Zander (1988) points out that the high rate of acquittals must be seen in the light of the high number of guilty pleas in the Crown Court. It must also be noted that many acquittals are directed or ordered by the judge: according to evidence from the Lord Chancellor's Department to the Runciman Commission, 40 per cent of all acquittals in 1990–91 were ordered by the judge because the prosecution offered no evidence at the start of the trial.

A further 16 per cent of the acquittals were directed by the judge after the prosecution had made their case as there was insufficient evidence to leave to the jury. Thus the jury were only responsible for 41 per cent of the acquittals, which was merely 7 per cent of all cases in the Crown Court. Bearing in mind the pressures on defendants to plead guilty, it is not surprising that those who resist tend to be those with the strongest cases – and of course the standard of proof required is very high. Nor is it beyond the bounds of possibility that part of the difference in conviction rates between magistrates and juries is due to magistrates convicting the innocent rather than juries acquitting the guilty.

In a high-profile case the Court of Appeal overturned a jury decision in civil proceedings on the basis that the jury decision had been perverse. In **Grobbelaar v News Group Newspapers Ltd** (2001) a jury had awarded the former goalkeeper for Liverpool FC, Bruce Grobbelaar, £85,000 on the basis that he had been defamed in *The Sun* newspaper. *The Sun* had published a story claiming that Bruce Grobbelaar had received cash to fix football matches. They had obtained secretly taped videos of Grobbelaar where he apparently admitted receiving money in the past to lose matches, and appeared to accept cash following a proposal to fix matches in the future. A criminal prosecution of Grobbelaar had failed and he had sued in the civil courts for defamation. Grobbelaar accepted that he had made the confessions and accepted cash, but claimed that he had done so as a trick in order to bring the other person to justice. The jury accepted his claim and awarded damages. *The Sun*'s appeal was allowed on the basis that the jury's decision had been perverse. The Court of Appeal found Grobbelaar's story 'incredible'. The House of Lords allowed a further appeal. It considered it wrong to overturn the jury's verdict as perverse, as the verdict could have been given an alternative explanation.

12.12.3 Bias

Ingman (2008) suggests that jurors may be biased for or against certain groups – for example, they may favour attractive members of the opposite sex, or be prejudiced against the police in cases of malicious prosecution or false imprisonment (and, of course, some jurors may also be biased towards the police, and other figures of authority such as customs officers).

Bias appears to be a particular problem in libel cases, where juries prejudiced against newspapers award huge damages, apparently using them punitively rather than as compensation for the victim. Examples include the £500,000 awarded to Jeffrey Archer in 1987, and the £300,000 to Koo Stark a year later, as well as **Sutcliffe v Pressdram Ltd** (1990), in which *Private Eye* was ordered to pay £600,000 to the wife of the Yorkshire Ripper. In the latter case, Lord Donaldson described the award as irrational, and suggested that judges should give more guidance on the amounts to be awarded – not by referring to previous cases or specific amounts, but by asking juries to think about the real value of money (such as what income the capital would produce, or what could be bought with it). The Courts and Legal Services Act 1990 now allows the Court of Appeal to reduce damages considered excessive.

(For a discussion of cases concerned with potentially racist jurors see p. 279.)

The spotlight has been very firmly focused on sexual assault and rape cases in the past couple of years; whether in relation to the #MeToo movement or linked to discussions around disclosure (more on this in Chapter 19: The criminal trial process). The Crime Survey for England and Wales reported almost 51,833 offences of rape and 93,564 other sexual offences in 2017 but ever-lowering conviction rates. There have been calls to abandon jury trials in cases of rape in order to combat juror bias, which some suggest occurs in cases where the sexual assault is carried out by someone known to the victim, resulting in high numbers of acquittals.

12.12.4 Representation of ethnic minorities

Black defendants have no right to have black people sitting on the jury. In *R v Bansal* (1985) the case involved an Anti-National Front demonstration and the trial judge ordered that the jury should be drawn from an area with a large Asian population. However, this approach was rejected as wrong in *R v Ford* (1989). The Court of Appeal held that race could not be taken into account when selecting jurors, and that a judge could not discharge jurors in order to achieve a racially representative jury as this would undermine the principle that juries should be randomly selected.

Research carried out by Professor Cheryl Thomas (2007) found that there is today no significant under-representation of black and minority ethnic groups (BME) among those summoned for jury service. The process of computerised random summoning from the electoral lists provided by local authorities is successfully reaching an ethnically representative group of potential jurors in almost every court. In most courts there is no significant difference between the proportion of BME jurors serving and the BME population levels in the juror catchment area for each court. Ethnicity was only relevant as to whether a summoned juror serves or not where English was not a first language because those without a sufficient command of English are excused from jury service. However, the research found that the ethnicity of summoned jurors may be more problematic for some Crown Courts where ethnic minorities make up less than 10 per cent of the entire juror catchment area. Unfortunately, only 21 per cent of Crown Courts in England and Wales (mainly in London) have juror catchment areas where ethnic minorities comprise more than 10 per cent of the population. This is a particular problem where the catchment has large pockets of ethnic minorities within a catchment area but which represents less than 10 per cent of the total population in that area. The people living in that 'pocket' might have an expectation that they will be tried by some of their ethnic peers but find that they are faced by an all-white jury.

In this context it is significant that Professor Thomas's 2007 research found that the defendant's race had a significant impact on the individual votes of some jurors. In certain

Figure 12.2 Jury conviction rate by defendant ethnicity and offence type: 2006–14

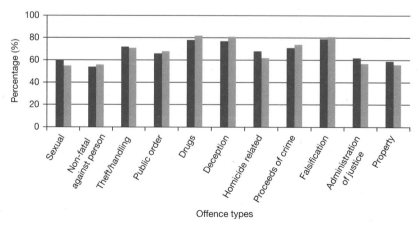

Source: The Lammy Review: An independent review into the treatment of, and outcomes for, Black, Asian and Minority Ethnic individuals in the Criminal Justice System (8 September 2017) https://www.gov.uk/government/publications/lammy-review-final-report

cases black and minority ethnic (BME) jurors were significantly less likely to vote to convict a BME defendant than a white one, though this did not affect the outcome of the trial because the BME jurors were in the minority and the defendant was convicted regardless.

Research carried out by Professor Thomas in 2010 for the Ministry of Justice organised 68 pretend trials (called jury simulations) where only the race of the defendant was altered. This showed that all-white juries did not discriminate against BME defendants – they were not convicted any more often than white defendants. She also looked at all the cases in the Crown Court between 2006 and 2008 and found that white and Asian defendants were equally likely to be convicted (63 per cent), although a slightly higher proportion of black defendants was convicted (67 per cent). She concluded that this was not a significant difference in conviction rates.

More recently, David Lammy MP carried out an independent review into the treatment of, and outcomes for, black, Asian and minority ethnic (BAME) individuals in the criminal justice system. There is more that can be said of the Lammy Review (2017) in a broader criminal justice system context (discussed in Chapter 19), but important here are his investigations regarding the impact of race on jury decision-making. Researchers looked at a wide range of offences over an eight year period, to see the percentage of those convicted among white or BAME defendants. Happily, the conclusion was (by analysing over 400,000 cases) that juries are consistent in their decisions, regardless of the defendant's ethnicity. This was not the case however in relation to judicial sentencing.

12.12.5 Manipulation by defendants

The Government's consultation paper, *Determining Mode of Trial in Either Way Cases* (Lord Chancellor's Department, 1998a), suggests that manipulation of the right to jury trial by defendants is a major problem. It claims that many guilty defendants choose jury trial in a bid to make use of the delay such a choice provides. The report puts forward three reasons why guilty defendants want to do this. First, delay may put pressure on the Crown Prosecution Service to reduce the charge in exchange for the defendant pleading guilty and so speeding up the process. Secondly, it may make it more likely that prosecution witnesses will fail to attend the eventual trial, or at least weaken their recollections if they do attend, so making an acquittal more likely. Thirdly, if a defendant is being held on remand, they are kept at a local prison, and allowed additional visits and other privileges not given to convicted prisoners; time spent on remand is deducted from any eventual prison sentence, so for a defendant on remand who calculates that he or she is likely to be found guilty and sentenced to imprisonment, putting off the trial for as long as possible will maximise the amount of the sentence that can be spent under the more favourable conditions. Such manipulation is obviously undesirable from the point of view of justice, and it also wastes a great deal of time and money, since many defendants who manipulate the system in this way end up pleading guilty at the last minute (resulting in what is known as a 'cracked trial'), so that the time and money spent preparing the prosecution's case is wasted; in most cases, state funding will also have been spent on the defence case.

However, those who support jury trials argue that this is a declining problem, as a result of the decision in *R* v *Hollington and Emmens* (1986). Where a defendant has pleaded guilty to an offence, the courts generally impose a lesser sentence than they otherwise would, but in this case, the Court of Appeal stated that a defendant charged with an either way offence who opts for Crown Court trial in an attempt to benefit by the subsequent delay cannot expect to receive the same reduction in sentence as someone who pleads guilty in the magistrates' court (this decision has now been incorporated into s. 48 of the Criminal Justice and Public Order Act 1994, which allows courts to take account of the stage at which a guilty plea was made when deciding how far to reduce the sentence). Lawyers were obviously bound to warn their clients that if they chose Crown Court trial and then pleaded guilty, they would receive heavier sentences than if they simply pleaded guilty in the magistrates' court. The Government's own consultation paper points out that, since 1986, there has been a steady decline in the number of defendants in either way cases choosing jury trial. In 1987, defendants choosing jury trial accounted for 53 per cent of either way cases sent to the Crown Court, but by 1997 the proportion had fallen to 28 per cent.

12.12.6 Jury nobbling

This problem led to the suspension of jury trials for terrorist offences in Northern Ireland, and has caused problems in some English trials. In 1982, several Old Bailey trials had to be stopped because of attempted 'nobbling', one after seven months, and the problem became so serious that juries had to sit out of sight of the public gallery, brown paper was stuck over the windows in court doors, and jurors were warned to avoid local pubs and cafés and eat only in their own canteen. In 1984, jurors in the Brinks-Mat trial had to have police protection to and from the court, and their telephone calls intercepted, while in August 1994 a four-month fraud trial at Southwark Crown Court had to be abandoned after the jury had already delivered their verdict on one of the charges.

A new criminal offence was created under the Criminal Justice and Public Order Act 1994 to try to give additional protection to the jury. This provides under s. 51 that it is an offence to intimidate or threaten to harm, either physically or financially, certain people involved in a trial including jurors.

A more radical reform was introduced in the Criminal Procedure and Investigations Act 1996. Section 54 of the Act provides that where a person has been acquitted of an offence and someone is subsequently convicted of interfering with or intimidating jurors or witnesses in the case, then the High Court can quash the acquittal and the person can be retried. This is a wholly exceptional development in the law since traditionally acquittals were considered final, and subsequent retrial a breach of fundamental human rights. Following the Criminal Justice Act 2003, where there is a real risk of jury nobbling a case can be heard by a single judge.

2017 saw only the second instance of using s. 46 of the Criminal Justice Act 2003 to proceed without a jury in the Crown Court. Mr Justice Goss in *R v Hussain and Others* stated there had been a 'concerted attempt to tamper with the jury' in a 'cash for crash' case, after he heard of various approaches being made to jury members.

In April 2018 a Scottish juror was jailed for corrupt behaviour after accepting bribes in a money-laundering and drug-trafficking trial. Catherine Leahy was the spokeswoman on the jury which acquitted the defendant, and was found to have received almost £3,000 for her manipulation of the outcome after a tip-off led to covert surveillance recordings at her home.

12.12.7 Absence of reasons

When judges sit alone, their judgment consists of a detailed and explicit finding of fact and a summary of the relevant law applied. When there is a jury in a criminal trial, the jury simply states whether it finds the defendant 'guilty' or 'not guilty' and provides no reasons for its decision. The former is more easily reviewed by appellate courts because the reasons for the trial judge's decision are clearly stated in public and published. But when the appellate court is faced with a jury's verdict, it cannot dispute the jury's reasonable interpretation of the evidence. Instead, the appeals have to focus on the judge's directions to the jury on the law and argue that the judge made an error on the relevant law.

Article 6 of the European Convention on Human Rights guarantees a defendant a fair trial which includes a requirement for courts to give reasons for their judgments. In *Taxquet v Belgium* (2010) the European Court of Human Rights held that there is no Convention requirement that lay jurors should give reasons for their decisions, but the accused and the public must be able to understand the jury's verdict if the trial is to be regarded as fair. Thus there must be sufficient safeguards in place, such as directions from the judge to the jury on the law and evidence and the right to appeal, in order for there to be a fair trial when a jury does not give reasons for its decision. The case itself concerned the assassination of a politician in Belgium.

12.12.8 Problems with compulsory jury service

Jury service is often unpopular but a refusal to act as a juror amounts to a contempt of court. Resentful jurors might make unsatisfactory decisions: in particular, jurors keen to get away as soon as possible are likely simply to go along with what the majority say, whether they agree or not.

12.12.9 Excessive damages

In the past juries in civil cases have awarded very high damages. The Court of Appeal now has the power either to order a new trial on the ground that damages awarded by a jury are excessive or, without the agreement of the parties, to substitute for the sum awarded by the jury such sum as appears to the court to be proper.

12.12.10 Cost and time

A Crown Court trial currently costs the taxpayer around £7,400 per day, as opposed to £1,000 per day for trial by magistrates. The jury process is time-consuming for all involved, with juries spending much of their time waiting around to be summoned into court.

12.12.11 Distress to jury members

Juries trying cases involving serious crimes of violence, particularly rape, murder or child abuse may have to listen to deeply distressing evidence and, in some cases, to inspect photographs of injuries. One juror in a particularly gruesome murder case told a newspaper how horrific it was to listen to a tape of the last words of the victim as, fatally injured, she struggled to make herself understood on the phone to the emergency services.

At the end of the case, most members of the jury were in tears and, after delivering their verdict, it was over an hour before they could compose themselves sufficiently to leave the jury room. The problem is made worse by the fact that jurors are told not to discuss the case with anyone else.

The potential for distress to jurors was recognised in the trials of Rosemary West and the killers of James Bulger, where the jurors were offered counselling afterwards, and since these cases the Ministry of Justice has provided that court-appointed welfare officers should be made available. However, these are provided only in cases judges deem to be exceptional, and only if jurors request their help.

12.12.12 Other criticisms

See also the notes on jury vetting, the non-representative nature of juries, and the termination of peremptory challenges. The material on the allocation procedure (discussed in Chapter 19) and jurors using the internet (p. 269) is also relevant.

12.13 Reform of the jury

A wide range of proposals has been put forward for the reform of the jury system.

12.13.1 Serious fraud trials

The Government would have liked to remove jury trials from most serious fraud cases (see p. 271), a reform that has been heavily criticised. There has been an ongoing debate as to whether juries are suitable for such cases and the issue was considered in the Roskill Fraud Trials Committee Report of 1986. Public attention was drawn to this issue by the collapse of the trial of six men accused of fraud relating to the awarding of contracts for the construction of the Jubilee Line extension on the London Underground system (***R v Rayment and others*** (2005)). The trial lasted two years – the longest ever jury trial – before it collapsed, having cost the taxpayer £60 million. It had suffered from a range of delays due to illness, scheduled holidays and paternity leave among the jury and lawyers, since it began in February 2000. Legal arguments also involved substantial periods where the jury was not required to hear evidence. In the last seven months before the case was dropped, the jury heard evidence on only 13 days of the 140 available. The prosecution eventually dropped the case after deciding there had been so many interruptions that a fair trial had become impossible.

To try to prevent such a waste of time and money occurring again, the Lord Chief Justice issued a Protocol requiring judges to exercise strong case management over cases likely to last more than eight weeks, including strict deadlines. The aim is to reduce the length of such trials to a maximum of three months. Trials will only be allowed to go on longer than six months in 'exceptional circumstances'. In addition, since April 2005 large criminal cases are monitored by a case management panel chaired by the Director of Public Prosecutions. Research carried out by Robert Julian (2008) has found that the judges involved in hearing fraud trials consider that the Protocol and judicial case management have been successful in reducing the length of complex fraud trials and have brought about a cultural change in the approach to this type of case.

The Government had not wanted to wait to see whether this new Protocol would lead to shorter fraud trials and instead tried to remove juries from such cases by introducing the Fraud (Trials Without a Jury) Bill into Parliament in 2007. However, it faced strong opposition to this Bill and the Bill did not become law, and has not been debated in Parliament since.

A Scottish fraud trial (***HMA v Edwin McLaren and Lorraine McLaren*** (2017)) commencing in September 2015 re-opened discussion on this matter when it took 20 months to conclude, losing three jurors along the way (15 are needed for a Scottish criminal trial).

A former chief executive of the Law Society in Scotland, Douglas Mill, told the BBC that fraud was so specialised that everyone involved in the case was an expert (the police, the lawyers and the CPS), everyone that is, except the jury:

> It is left to 15 very lay people who are being asked to assimilate vast numbers of documents over an endless number of days . . . Is that in the interests of justice? Big question.

The use of a single judge has the advantages of making trials quicker, reducing the likelihood of 'perverse' verdicts, and defeating the problem of 'jury nobbling' (in Northern Ireland single judges have long been used in some cases because of the problem of jury nobbling). However, the benefits of public participation in the legal system would be lost, and all the problems associated with judicial bias and the restricted social background of judges (described in Chapter 10) would be let loose on cases which involve vital questions for both the individuals concerned and society as a whole. The Bar Council believes that juries should be retained in all cases where the defendant faces serious loss of liberty or reputation. It considers that fraud cases can appear complex but, if they are properly managed, juries are capable of deciding the case, which usually comes down to determining whether the defendant has been dishonest.

Using a bench of perhaps three or five judges would give a little more protection against individual bias, but would still not give the benefit of community participation that the jury offers (and would also require massive investment to train the increased number of judges that would be required).

12.13.2 Abolishing juries

It can be argued that since juries have already been abolished in all but a handful of civil cases with no apparent ill effects, and that they decide only 1 per cent of criminal cases anyway, the system really no longer needs them at all and they should be abolished. The pros and cons of this argument naturally depend on what would be put in their place.

Lay participation and increased speed (and lower costs) could be achieved by allowing magistrates to decide all criminal cases, but it is highly unlikely that society would ever wish to trust decisions on the most serious crimes to non-legally qualified judges. Of course, it could be argued that that is exactly what the jury system does, but in that case the number of jurors, and the advantages of random selection in terms of representing society as a whole, is thought by supporters to outweigh the amateur status of jurors – and in jury trials, the judge is always there to offer guidance on matters of law, and to decide the sentence in criminal cases.

The Government's 1998 consultation paper on the criminal justice system considered four possible options for serious fraud trials:

- abolishing the use of juries in fraud trials completely and replacing them with a specially trained single judge and two lay people with expertise in commercial affairs;
- replacing juries with a specially trained single judge or panel of judges, possibly with access to advisers on commercial matters;
- retaining jury trial but restricting the jury's role to deciding questions of dishonesty, with the judge deciding other matters; or
- replacing the traditional, randomly selected jury with a special jury, selected on the basis of qualifications or tests, or drawn from those who can demonstrate specialist knowledge of business and finance.

In his review of the criminal justice system in 2001, Sir Robin Auld favoured the first option of a specially trained single judge and two lay people with expertise on the subject. Under his recommendations, a panel of experts would be set up and the trial judge would select the lay members after giving the parties the opportunity to make written representations as to their suitability. The judge would be the sole judge of law, procedure, admissibility of evidence and sentence. All three would be judges of fact and they would therefore decide the verdict together. A majority of any two would suffice for a conviction. The defendant would always have the option of choosing, with the consent of the court, a trial by judge alone.

There are weaknesses in this proposal. The selection process and limited powers of the lay members would risk undermining their stature in the eyes of the public. The power to convict on a majority of two to one could be seen as undermining the usual requirement in criminal law that, in order to convict, a defendant should be found guilty beyond reasonable doubt.

Sir Brian Leveson's *Review of Efficiency in Criminal Proceedings* (2015) proposed further reductions in jury involvement by limiting the circumstances in which a defendant could ask for a jury trial. Leveson notes that:

> . . . jurors required to give up their time to undertake that important civic duty not infrequently at considerable personal cost (on the basis that the allowances do not reach the level of their earnings) are equally not infrequently concerned that their time is 'wasted' by what are perceived to be trivial cases, whether the value of the sum stolen or the loss caused is far exceeded by the cost to the public purse of the trial.

The Bigger Picture

In 2014, the world was gripped by the trial in South Africa of the disabled athlete, Oscar Pistorius, for the murder of his girlfriend Reeva Steenkamp. Ultimately on appeal he was found guilty of murder. In England the case would have been heard before a jury. In South Africa juries were abolished in 1969 because they could not work effectively under the apartheid system. Instead, serious cases, such as murder, are heard by a judge. The judge can either hear the case alone or can choose to appoint two assessors to sit alongside him or her. The assessors can be lawyers but they do not have to be so. People who wish to be considered as assessors have to put their name forward with their CV. The judge then selects two people, from a pool of potential assessors, who the judge considers will be of use. The assessor might be a non-lawyer with a relevant field of expertise: for example, an accountant could be an assessor to assist with a fraud trial. In the Oscar Pistorius case both the assessors were lawyers, one a legal academic, the other an experienced advocate. The role of the assessors is to assist the judge in deciding the case. If both the assessors disagree with the judge on the facts, then they can overrule the judge on the facts, but the judge has the sole responsibility of deciding the law. The assessors have no involvement in deciding the sentence.

12.13.3 Improving the performance of the jury

As well as favouring a reduction in the role of the jury (discussed above), Sir Robin Auld made a range of specific recommendations to improve the performance of the jury.

Help the jury to work effectively

The Auld Review (2001) recommended that, in order to assist a jury in their work, the judge should sum up the case at the end of the trial by forming questions which need to be considered by the jurors. Juries would reach verdicts by answering these questions during their deliberations. Where the judge thought it appropriate, he or she would be able to require the jury publicly to answer each of the questions and to declare a verdict in accordance with those answers. Sir Robin Auld argued that this would strengthen the jury as a tribunal of fact, provide a reasoned basis for jury verdicts and reduce the risk of perverse verdicts. While there can only be benefits from presenting the case more clearly to the jury, the use of questions which the jury may be forced to answer publicly seems to be an unnecessary restriction on the jury's freedom to reach a decision in accordance with their conscience as well as in accordance with the law.

Research was carried out for the Law Commission in New Zealand. This research included watching juries deliberate their verdict, a process that would be illegal in the UK. In the light of this research the New Zealand Law Commission has recommended in its Report on *Juries in Criminal Trials* (2001) that reforms should be introduced to assist the work of a criminal jury. These reforms include changing the ways in which evidence is put before the jury. Evidence should be put before a jury in the same way that other information is given to them in their everyday lives. For example, clear explanations of legal terms ought to be given in writing. The court should make notes of the evidence and give these to the jury. If appropriate, visual aids should be supplied. Where possible, the court should set out briefly in writing what decisions the jury need to make, and in what order – a 'decision tree' where the verdict flows logically from the answers to the questions. The court should tell the jury what the key issues are between the parties. Sir Robin Auld seems to have been attracted to this approach.

Professor Zander (2001b) has criticised Sir Robin Auld's recommendations on the subject. He argues persuasively that Sir Robin Auld demonstrates:

> an authoritarian attitude that disregards history and reveals a grievously misjudged sense of the proper balance of the criminal justice system. For centuries the role of the jury has included the power to stand between the citizen and unjust law . . . [G]etting it right does not necessarily mean giving the verdict a judge would have given . . . To want to inquire whether they reached their decision in the 'right' way, is foolish because it ignores the nature of the institution.

While the courts have not gone as far as providing a 'decision tree' where the verdict flows logically from the answer to the questions posed, they are making increasing use of 'route to verdict directions'. These also pose a logical series of questions to the jury but they leave to the jury the final determination of innocence or guilt. Their use still reflects a lack of trust in the jury and concern with 'perverse verdicts' (Crosby (2012)). In *R v Thompson* (2010) the Court of Appeal stated that it is at the discretion of the trial judge whether any written materials are provided to the jury to clarify judicial directions given in the courtroom. Any such materials have to be discussed with the parties' lawyers before they are given to the jury.

Prevent perverse verdicts

The Auld Review was concerned by the risk of juries reaching perverse verdicts. Rather than seeing these as a potential safeguard of civil liberties, the Review seems to consider these as an insult to the law. It has therefore recommended that legislation should declare that juries have no right to acquit defendants in defiance of the law or in disregard of the evidence. The prosecution would be given a right to appeal against what it considered to be a perverse acquittal by a jury.

Sir Robin Auld recommended that, where appropriate, the trial judge and the Court of Appeal should be allowed to investigate any alleged impropriety or failure in the way the jury reached their verdict, even where this is supposed to have happened during the traditionally secret deliberations of the jury. Such an investigation might look at accusations that some jurors ignored or slept through the deliberation or that the jury reached their verdict because of an irrational prejudice or whim, deliberately ignoring the evidence.

These recommendations show insufficient respect for the jurors and have been rejected by the Government.

Reserve jurors

One recommendation of the *Review of the Criminal Courts* was that, where appropriate, for long cases judges should be able to swear in extra jurors. These reserve jurors would be able to replace jurors who are unable to continue to hear a case, for example, because of illness.

12.13.4 Black jurors

It has been argued by the Commission for Racial Equality that consideration needs to be given to the racial balance in particular cases. They suggest that where a case has a racial dimension and the defendant reasonably believes that he or she cannot receive a fair trial from an all-white jury, then the judge should have the power to order that three of the jurors come from the same ethnic minority as the defendant or the victim. Both the Runciman Commission (1993) and the *Review of the Criminal Courts* (2001) have given their endorsement to this proposal but it has never been implemented.

The Society of Black Lawyers had, in addition, submitted to the Runciman Commission that there should always be a right to a multi-racial trial, that peremptory challenges should be reinstated and that certain cases with a black defendant should be tried by courts in areas with high black populations, and panels of black jurors who would be available at short notice should be set up. These proposals have not been implemented either.

The problems caused by lack of racial representation on juries can be seen in the high-profile Rodney King case in Los Angeles, where a policeman was found not guilty of assaulting a black motorist despite a videotape of the incident showing brutal conduct. The case was tried in an area with a very high white population, while the incident itself had occurred in an area with a high black population. However, the decision in *R v Ford* (1989), that there is no principle that a jury should be racially balanced, still holds.

Peremptory challenge was abolished because it was said to have interfered with the principle of random selection, especially in multi-defendant trials. However, Vennard and Riley's study (1988a) found that the peremptory challenge was only used in 22 per cent of cases, with no evidence of widespread pooling of challenges, and research for the Crown Prosecution Service in 1987 showed that the use of peremptory challenge had no significant effect on the rate of acquittals.

Peremptory challenge could in fact be used to make juries more balanced in terms of race and sex, and it seems rather unjust that, while the defence have had their right to a peremptory challenge removed, the prosecution is still allowed to stand by for the Crown.

Answering questions

1   'Those who argued for restricting the right to jury trial misunderstood the symbolic role of the jury – this symbolic role is as important as the need for just decision-making.' Discuss. *University of London, International Programmes LLB*

2   'The jury is often described as "the jewel in the Crown" or "the corner-stone" of the British criminal justice system. It is a hallowed institution which, because of its ancient origin and involvement of 12 randomly selected lay people in the criminal process, commands much public confidence.' (Lord Justice Auld (2001) *Review of the Criminal Courts of England and Wales,* Chapter 5, para. 1)

   Is this confidence in the jury misplaced? *University of London, International Programmes LLB*

3   'We believe that twelve persons selected at random are likely to be a cross-selection of the people as a whole and thus represent the views of the common man.' (Lord Denning MR in ***R v Sheffield Crown Court, ex parte Brownlow*** (1980))

   Do you consider that this statement justifies the use of juries in criminal cases? Is there any other satisfactory justification?

4   Critically discuss the impact of the jury composition provisions, contained in the Criminal Justice Act 2003, on the efficacy of criminal jury trials.

5   What is the role of the jury in a criminal trial and to what extent may it ignore the law?

For the answers to these questions, visit the companion website at www.pearsoned.co.uk/ elliottquinn

SUMMARY OF CHAPTER 12: THE JURY

When are juries used?

Juries decide only about 1 per cent of criminal cases and a very small number of civil cases.

Qualifications for jury service

Potential jury members must be:

- aged 18–75;
- on the electoral register; and
- resident in the UK, Channel Islands or Isle of Man for at least five years since the age of 13.

Jury vetting

Jury vetting consists of checking that the potential juror does not hold 'extremist' views which some feel would make them unsuitable for hearing a case. It is done by checking police and security service records.

The secrecy of the jury

Once they retire to consider their verdict, jurors are not allowed to communicate with anyone other than the judge and an assigned court official, until after the verdict is delivered.

Arguments in favour of the jury system

Juries allow ordinary citizens to participate in the administration of justice and decide cases according to their conscience.

Criticisms of the jury system

In practice, juries are not representative of the general population. Some of their judgments are perverse; they can be biased and susceptible to manipulation.

Reform of the jury

Proposals have been put forward for restricting the role of juries or abolishing juries altogether. Significant reform proposals were drawn up by Sir Robin Auld, but many of these were rejected by the former Labour Government. It introduced the Fraud (Trials Without a Jury) Bill, which aimed to abolish the use of juries for many fraud trials. After facing strong opposition, the Bill was not passed. This was also touched on in Leveson's 2015 *Review of Efficiency in Criminal Proceedings*.

Reading list

Auld, Sir R. (2001) *Review of the Criminal Courts*. London: HMSO.

Baldwin, J. and McConville, M. (1979) *Jury Trials*. Oxford: Clarendon.

Bornstein, B., Miller, M., Nemeth, R., Page, G. and Musil, S. (2005) Juror reactions to jury duty: perceptions of the system and potential stressors, *Behavioral Sciences and the Law*, 23: 321.

Brown, D. and Neal, D. (1988) Show trials: the media and the Gang of Twelve. In: Findlay, M. and Duff, P. (eds) *The Jury under Attack*. London: Butterworths.

Crosby, K. (2012) Controlling Devlin's jury: what the jury thinks, and what the jury sees online. *Criminal Law Review*, 15.

Darbyshire, P. (1991) The lamp that shows that freedom lives – is it worth the candle? *Criminal Law Review*, 740.

de Tocqueville, A. (2000) *Democracy in America* (Lawrence, G. (trans.); Mayer, J.P. (ed.)). New York: Perennial Classics (first published 1835).

Denning, A. (1982) *What Next in the Law?* London: Butterworths.

Devlin, P. (1956) *Trial by Jury*. London: Stevens.

Findlay, M. (2001) Juror comprehension and complexity: strategies to enhance understanding. *British Journal of Criminology*, 41: 56.

Freeman, M.D.A. (1981) The jury on trial. *Current Legal Problems*, 34: 65.

Home Office Research Development and Statistics Directorate (2000) *Jury Excusal and Deferral* (Research Findings No. 102). London: Home Office.

Honess, T., Charman, E. and Levi, M. (2003) Factual and affective/evaluative recall of pretrial publicity. *Journal of Applied Social Psychology,* 33(7): 1404.

Horowitz, I. and Fosterlee, L. (2001) The effects of note-taking and trial transcript access on mock jury decisions in a complex civil trial. *Law and Human Behaviour,* 25:373.

Hungerford-Welch, P. (2012) Police officers as jurors. *Criminal Law Review,* 320.

Ingman, T. (2008) *The English Legal Process.* Oxford: Oxford University Press.

Julian, R. (2007) Judicial perspectives on the conduct of serious fraud trials. *Criminal Law Review,* 751.

Julian, R. (2008) Judicial perspectives in serious fraud cases – the present status of and problems posed by case management practices, jury selection rules, juror expertise, plea bargaining and choice of mode of trial. *Criminal Law Review,* 764.

Levi, M. (1988) The role of the jury in complex cases. In: Findlay, M. and Duff, P. (eds) *The Jury under Attack.* London: Butterworths.

Levi, M. (1992) *The Investigation, Prosecution and Trial of Serious Fraud.* London: HMSO.

Lloyd-Bostock, S. (2007) The Jubilee Line jurors: does their experience strengthen the argument for judge-only trial in long and complex fraud cases? *Criminal Law Review,* 255.

Lord Chancellor's Department (1998a) *Determining Mode of Trial in Either Way Cases.* London: Lord Chancellor's Department.

Matthews, R., Hancock, L. and Briggs, D. (2004) *Jurors' Perceptions, Understanding, Confidence and Satisfaction in the Jury Systems: A Study in Six Courts.* London: Home Office.

McCabe, S. and Purves, R. (1972) *The Jury at Work: A Study of a Series of Jury Trials in which the Defendant was Acquitted.* Oxford: Blackwell.

New Zealand Law Commission (2001) *Juries in Criminal Trials.* Wellington, NZ: New Zealand Law Commission.

Roberts, P. (2011) Does Article 6 of the European Convention on Human Rights require reasoned verdicts in criminal trials? *Human Rights Law Review,* 11: 213.

Roskill Committee (1986) *Report of the Committee on Fraud Trials.* London: HMSO.

Spencer, J. (2012) Police officers on juries. *Cambridge Law Journal,* 71: 251.

Thomas, C. (2007) *Diversity and fairness in the jury system.* Ministry of Justice Research Series 2/07. London: Ministry of Justice.

(2008) Exposing the myths of jury service. *Criminal Law Review,* 415.

(2010) *Are Juries Fair?* London: Ministry of Justice.

(2013) Avoiding the perfect storm of juror contempt. *Criminal Law Review,* 483.

Thomas, C. and Balmer, N. J. (2007) (see website, below).

Vennard, J. and Riley, D. (1988a) The use of peremptory challenge and stand by of jurors and their relationships with trial outcome. *Criminal Law Review,* 723.

Wooler, S. (2006) *Review of the Investigation and Criminal Proceedings Relating to the Jubilee Line Cases.* London: HM CPS Inspectorate.

(1988) *A Matter of Justice.* Oxford: Oxford University Press.

(2000) The complaining juror. *New Law Journal,* 150: 723.

(2001b) A question of trust. *Solicitors Journal,* 1100.

Zander, M. (1988) The Government's plans on civil justice. *Modern Law Review,* 61: 382.

(2000) The complaining juror. *New Law Journal,* 150: 723.

12

THE JURY

On the internet

The report of Professor Cheryl Thomas and Nigel Balmer, *Diversity and Fairness in the Jury System,* Ministry of Justice Research Series 02/07 (2007) is available at:

https://webarchive.nationalarchives.gov.uk/+/http://www.justice.gov.uk/publications/research130607.htm

The consultation document *Jury Research and Impropriety* (2005), considering when the law should allow the secrecy of jury deliberations to be broken, is available at:

http://webarchive.nationalarchives.gov.uk/+/http://www.dca.gov.uk/consult/juryresearch/juryresearch_cp0405.htm

Leaflets on jury service are published on the Court Service website at:

https://www.gov.uk/jury-service

The Blackstone Lecture *Trial by Jury – Past and Present* (Lady Justice Hallett) 20 May 2017 can be found at:

https://www.judiciary.uk/wp-content/uploads/2017/05/hallett-lj-blackstone-lecture-20170522-1.pdf

The House of Commons Justice Committee report *The role of the magistracy* (October 2016) is available at:

https://publications.parliament.uk/pa/cm201617/cmselect/cmjust/165/165.pdf

The Lammy Review: An independent review into the treatment of, and outcomes for, Black, Asian and Minority Ethnic individuals in the Criminal Justice System (8 September 2017) is available at:

https://www.gov.uk/government/publications/lammy-review-final-report

More information about the Society of Black Lawyers is available on its website at:

https://societyofblacklawyers.co.uk/

Sir Brian Leveson's *Review of Efficiency in Criminal Proceedings* (2015) can be found at:

https://www.judiciary.gov.uk/wp-content/uploads/2015/01/review-of-efficiency-in-criminal-proceedings-20151.pdf

Maddison, Ormerod, Tonking & Wait, *The Crown Court Compendium, Part I: Jury and Trial Management and Summing Up* can be found at:

https://www.judiciary.gov.uk/wp-content/uploads/2016/05/crown-court-compendium-part-i-jury-and-trial-management-and-summing-up.pdf

The Attorney General's Office Call for Evidence, *The Impact of Social Media on the Administration of Justice* (September 2017) is found at:

https://assets.publishing.service.gov.uk/government/uploads/system/uploads/attachment_data/file/645032/Call_for_Evidence__Final_.pdf

Dominic Willmott, University of Huddersfield, *An Investigation of the role of juror bias in rape trial verdict outcomes* (2017) is available at:

https://whatworks.college.police.uk/Research/Research-Map/Pages/ResearchProject.aspx?projectid=645

Penny Darbyshire, Andy Maughan and Angus Stewart, *What can the English Legal System learn from Jury Research published up to 2001?* is available here:

https://eprints.kingston.ac.uk/23/1/Darbyshire-P-23.pdf

Chapter 13
Magistrates

This chapter discusses:

- the organisation of the magistrates' courts;

- the selection and appointment of lay magistrates;

- their social background;

- the training provided;

- their role in criminal and civil cases;

- the work of justices' clerks and legal advisers;

- whether lay magistrates or professional judges should work in the magistrates' court; and

- possible reforms to the magistrates' system.

13.1 The magistrates' courts

The magistrates' courts are managed by the Ministry of Justice. The legislative provisions concerning the organisation of these courts are contained in the Courts Act 2003, which introduced significant reforms. These reforms are broadly in line with recommendations on the subject made by Sir Robin Auld in his *Review of the Criminal Courts* in 2001.

The Act introduces a central administration for all the courts (except the Supreme Court), so that they are managed at a national rather than a local level. The Lord Chancellor has a general duty to maintain an efficient and effective court system. The country is divided into local justice areas (previously known as commission and petty sessional areas – the name 'local justice area' is considered to be a more modern and more appropriate title for these administrative areas). Each local justice area has its own courthouse and justices' clerk.

In the past, the courthouses were essentially run by local committees consisting of up to 35 magistrates. But this approach was criticised by a Scrutiny Report carried out for the Home Office in 1989. The study concluded that at the time there was no coherent management structure; the system was inefficient and not giving value for money. These local committees were therefore replaced in 1994 by Magistrates' Courts Committees, which had a smaller membership and a wider range of members. A justices' chief executive carried out the day-to-day administration of the local justice area.

The Magistrates' Court Committees and the position of justices' chief executives were abolished by the Courts Act 2003. They were replaced by Her Majesty's Court Service (now called Her Majesty's Courts and Tribunals Service (HMCTS)), which is a single national executive agency which administers all the courts (excluding the Supreme Court). A limited local input is provided by local 'courts' boards'. These are made up of local community representatives and the judiciary, but their power is limited to offering recommendations to the Lord Chief Justice as to the local needs of the courts. The Lord Chief Justice was given the power to appoint magistrates by the Crime and Courts Act 2013. Prior to October 2013, it was the Lord Chancellor who had the power to appoint magistrates. The magistrates themselves no longer play a significant role in the administration of the courts.

The reforms have incited considerable debate. The Government hoped that the changes would create a cohesive, national court system within which personnel, buildings and facilities can be interchanged to make the most of resources. Professor Zander (2004) has commented:

> If sensitively implemented over the coming years this piece of legislation could provide a good basis for a courts system that combines the advantages of a centrally managed national system with the right amount of recognition of local concerns and interests.

Critics have argued that courts should be managed locally so that they reflect the local needs of the community, and that the courts' boards will have insufficient powers compared to the central court agency to achieve this. The Magistrates' Association has described the courts' boards as 'impotent and insufficiently representative of the lay magistracy'.

As regards the financial arrangements for the magistrates' courts, 60 per cent of their funding is now allocated on the basis of their workload, 25 per cent according to their efficiency in fine enforcement, 10 per cent depends on the time taken to deal with cases and the remaining 5 per cent for 'quality of service'. Performance targets have also been introduced. These arrangements have led to fears that the independence of the courts is threatened. Magistrates' courts' accounts can be reviewed by the Audit Commission.

> ## The Bigger Picture: Closing local courts
>
> Concern has been expressed at the closure of small local courts which have been rehoused in large new complexes. The justification for these closures is that the smaller courthouses were expensive to run, had poor facilities and the new multi-jurisdictional centres were modern with separate waiting areas for victims, witnesses and defendants and better access for the disabled. They also offer a pleasant environment for court staff to work in. The downside is that the smaller courts were local courts offering local justice to the local community, while the larger multi-jurisdictional centres can be inconvenient for users to travel to and be perceived as remote. The Law Society opposed the plans, concerned by the impact this would have on public transport users, citing the example of a return journey from one closed court to the alternative in Milton Keynes. They reported a ticket price of £71 and a five-hour round trip.
>
> Justice Minister Shailesh Vara justified the extensive closures (which amounted to almost a fifth of courts and tribunals in England and Wales) in a written statement in February 2016:
>
> > Court closures are difficult decisions; local communities have strong allegiances to their local courts and I understand their concerns. But changes to the estate are vital if we are to modernise a system which everyone accepts is unwieldy, inefficient, slow, expensive to maintain and unduly bureaucratic.
>
> These court closures have also had an impact on the morale of magistrates themselves (see p. 319).

13.2 Magistrates

13.2.1 History

Like juries, lay magistrates have a long history in the English legal system, dating back to the Justices of the Peace Act 1361, which, probably in response to a crime wave, gave judicial powers to appointed lay people. Their main role then, as now, was dealing with criminals, but they also exercised certain administrative functions, and until the nineteenth century the business of local government was largely entrusted to them. A few of these administrative powers remain today.

There are over 16,000 lay magistrates (also called justices of the peace, or JPs), hearing over 1 million criminal cases a year – 95 per cent of all criminal trials, with the remaining being heard in the Crown Court. They are therefore often described as the backbone of the English criminal justice system. Lay magistrates do not receive a salary, but they receive travel, subsistence and financial loss allowances.

There are also 140 professional judges who sit in the magistrates' courts. These are called 'district judges (magistrates' courts)' following a reform introduced by the Access to Justice Act 1999. They had previously been known as stipendiary magistrates. They receive a salary of over £108,000. On top of the permanent district judges (magistrates' courts) there are also deputy district judges who work part-time, usually with a view to establishing their competence in order to get a full-time position in the future. These professional judges are appointed by the Queen on the recommendation of the Lord Chancellor. Following the passing of the Constitutional Reform Act 2005, the Judicial Appointments Commission is involved in the appointment process of these professional judges. Applicants must have had a five-year right of audience. Often, they will also have previously held the role of deputy district judge (magistrates' courts) for at least two years, or 30 days' sittings. Under the Access to Justice Act 1999, they are appointed to a single bench with national jurisdiction. They act as sole judge in their particular court, mostly in the large cities and London in particular, where 46 are based. They are part of the professional judiciary, and most of the comments about magistrates in this chapter do not apply to them.

Upon appointment magistrates are required to take an oath that they will apply the law of the land. They, therefore, are not allowed to refuse to hear cases because of their personal beliefs. Thus, in 2008, a Christian magistrate could not require cases to be filtered so that he did not have to hear cases involving adoptions by same-sex couples.

13.2.2 Selection and appointment

Lay magistrates are appointed by the Lord Chief Justice in the name of the Crown, on the advice of local Advisory Committees (of which there are 47). Candidates are interviewed by the Committee, which then makes a recommendation to the Minister, who usually follows the recommendation.

Members of the local Advisory Committees are appointed by the Minister for Justice. Two-thirds of them are magistrates, and should have good local knowledge, and represent a balance of political opinion. Their identity was at one time kept secret, but names are now available to the public.

Candidates are usually put forward to the Committee by local political parties, voluntary groups, trade unions and other organisations, though individuals may apply in person. The only qualifications laid down for appointment to the magistracy are that the applicants must be under 65 and live or work within a reasonable distance of the court in which they will work. These qualifications may be dispensed with if it is considered to be in the public interest to do so. In practice they must also be able to devote at least 26 half-day sittings a year, although many can undertake more. They usually only receive expenses and a small loss of earnings allowance for this work. Legal knowledge or experience is not required; nor is any level of academic qualification.

Certain people are excluded from appointment, including: police officers, traffic wardens and members of the armed forces; anyone whose work is considered incompatible with the duties of a magistrate; anyone who due to a disability could not carry out all the duties of a magistrate; undischarged bankrupts; and those who have a close relative who is already a magistrate on the same bench. Updated guidance to would-be magistrates in September 2018, states that a civil order or past conviction would not necessarily curtail your ambition; we are told that the Advisory Committee and Senior Presiding Judge will consider various elements (nature and seriousness of the matter, when it occurred, and the penalty or order imposed). Appendix D of the guidelines provides further detail.

In 1998 the procedures for appointing lay magistrates were revised. The reforms aimed to make the appointment criteria open and clear. Thus a job description for magistrates was introduced which declares that the six key qualities defining the personal suitability of candidates are: having good character; understanding and communication; social awareness; maturity and sound temperament; sound judgement; and commitment and reliability. Positions are now advertised widely, including in publications such as *Inside Soaps* magazine, to attract a wider range of people.

Following the Courts Act 2003, magistrates are appointed nationally rather than locally. The Judicial Appointments Commission established by the Constitutional Reform Act 2005 is not currently involved in the appointment of lay magistrates, though it is responsible for the appointment of district judges (magistrates' court).

13.2.3 Removal and retirement

Magistrates usually have to retire at 70. Under powers in the Courts Act 2003 and the Constitutional Reform Act 2005, the Lord Chancellor with the concurrence of the Lord Chief Justice has the statutory power to remove a magistrate for the following reasons:

- on the ground of incapacity or misbehaviour;
- on the ground of a persistent failure to meet the prescribed standards of competence;
- if the Minister is satisfied that the lay justice is declining or neglecting to take a proper part in the exercise of his or her functions as a magistrate.

In addition, magistrates are prevented from exercising their functions if they suffer from an incapacity.

Social media seems to be the undoing of a number of magistrates; in 2009 a magistrate resigned after his inappropriate use of Twitter. One message he posted stated: 'Called into court today to deal with those arrested last night and held in custody. I guess they will be mostly drunks but you never know.' No prizes for guessing how he announced his resignation . . . on Twitter. More recently the Judicial Conduct Investigations Office reprimanded two magistrates; one for his involvement in an 'inappropriate conversation' and the other for posting a photo complete with caption, which 'could have created the impression that he did not take his role as a magistrate seriously'. The first, Mr Roger Warrington JP, was told he had 'not upheld the high standards of behaviour expected of a judicial office holder'.

13.2.4 Background

Class

The 1948 Report of the Royal Commission on Justices of the Peace showed that approximately three-quarters of all magistrates came from professional or middle-class occupations. Little seems to have changed since: research carried out by Rod Morgan and Neil Russell (2000) found that more than two-thirds of lay magistrates were, or had been until retirement, employed in a professional or managerial position. Their social backgrounds were not representative of the community in which they served. For example, in a deprived metropolitan area, 79 per cent of the bench members were professionals or managers compared with only 20 per cent of the local population.

One of the reasons for this may be financial; while employers are required to give an employee who is appointed as a magistrate reasonable time off work, not all employers are able or willing to pay wages during their absence. To meet this difficulty, lay magistrates receive a loss of earnings allowance, but this is not overly generous and will usually be less than the employee would have earned. This can be for financial loss, travel or subsistence.

A further problem is that employees who take up the appointment against the wishes of their employer may find their promotion prospects jeopardised. This means that only those who are self-employed, or sufficiently far up the career ladder to have some power of their own, can serve as magistrates without risking damage to their own employment prospects. The outcome is that those outside the professional and managerial classes are proportionately under-represented on the bench, which is still predominantly drawn from the more middle-class occupations. The maximum age for appointment has been raised to 65 in the hope that working-class people, who were prevented from serving during their working lives, will do so in retirement, though so far the change has had little impact.

13

MAGISTRATES

In the past the Government sought to achieve a social balance on the bench by taking into account a person's political affiliation when making appointments. This stemmed from the time when people tended to vote along class lines, with people from the working class voting predominantly for the Labour Party. Political opinion is no longer a reliable gauge of a person's social background and the Government has replaced, therefore, the question about 'political associations' on the application form for magistrates. It has been replaced by a question about the applicant's employment. The Ministry of Justice believes that this will provide a better means of achieving a socially balanced bench.

A 2005 White Paper, *Supporting Magistrates' Courts to Provide Justice* included proposals to encourage the recruitment of more young magistrates to make them representative of the communities they serve. Section 50(1) of the Employment Rights Act 1996 requires an employer to allow an employee to take reasonable time off during working hours to perform his or her duties as a magistrate. The employer doesn't however have to pay for this time.

Proposals on how to encourage employers to support those employees who also serve on the bench, were discussed in *The Role of the Magistracy* report published by the House of Commons Select Committee (2016). Suggestions included creating a 'kitemark' scheme to recognise those employers who support the magistracy, and reviewing the rates of financial loss allowance available.

Age

There are few young magistrates – most are middle-aged or older. 55 per cent of magistrates are aged 60 or over and will retire within a decade (only 4 per cent of magistrates are under the age of 40). The problems concerning employment are likely to have an effect on the age as well as the social class of magistrates; people at the beginning of their careers are most dependent on the goodwill of employers for promotion, and least likely to be able to take regular time off without damaging their career prospects. They are also more likely to be busy bringing up families.

While a certain maturity is obviously a necessity for magistrates, younger justices would bring some understanding of the lifestyles of a younger generation. The youngest person to be appointed as a magistrate was Alex Hyne, who was 18 years old when appointed in 2015. Prior to his appointment the record was held by Lucy Tate, who was 19 years old when she was appointed in 2006.

Figure 13.1 The percentage of magistrates by age band, 1 April 2017

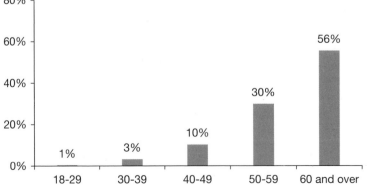

Source: https://www.judiciary.uk/wp-content/uploads/2017/07/judicial-diversity-statistics-2017-1.pdf

Politics

Government figures released in 1995 showed that a high proportion of magistrates were Conservative supporters, and few voted Labour. A sample survey of 218 new appointments as magistrates in England and Wales showed that 91 were Conservative voters, 56 Labour, 41 Liberal Democrat, 24 had no political affiliation and four voted for the Welsh party, Plaid Cymru. A report analysing the figures for 1992 compared the proportion of Conservative voters among magistrates to the proportion in their local area: in two Oldham constituencies, 52 per cent of the local people voted Labour, but only 27 per cent of magistrates, and slightly more magistrates than constituents in general voted Conservative. In Bristol, Labour had won 40 per cent of the votes, slightly more than the Tories; of the magistrates, 142 said they were Tory, and only 85 described themselves as Labour supporters.

Race

The Government reported in 1987 that the proportion of black magistrates was only 2 per cent. The figures for 2018 show that lay magistrates increasingly reflect the ethnic diversity of contemporary Britain: 12 per cent of magistrates come from ethnic minority communities, who make up 14 per cent of the general population. But there is a considerable variation locally and the fit between the local benches and the local communities they serve is, in several instances, very wide (see Figure 13.2).

In terms of the professional magistracy, figures from the Judicial Appointments Commission indicated that Black, Asian and Minority Ethnic (BAME) candidates actually constituted 23 per cent of deputy district judge applicants but only 6 per cent of these were appointed.

In previous years the Magistrates' Association has seen age as the biggest problem in terms of under-representation, but their attentions have turned to a lack of ethnic representation. John Bache, chairman of the Association has highlighted a need for better promotion of opportunities:

> Actually we do have a good social mix on benches — plenty of magistrates are not from typically middle-class professional backgrounds. But encouraging more from minority groups is a challenge.

Figure 13.2 BAME representation of magistrates, by region as at 1 April 2017

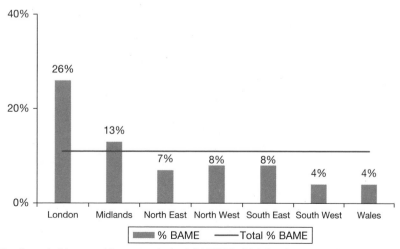

Source: https://www.judiciary.gov.uk/wp-content/uploads/2017/07/judicial-diversity-statistics-2017-1.pdf

> Generally it's getting the message to those groups and convincing them that they can be magistrates: what we hear is that 'magistrates are not from our background'. We want to rectify that. It is really important, because we want to reflect society. It is as simple as that. (*The Times,* 12 July 2018)

One of the findings of David Lammy's report was that a lack of diversity within the judiciary was one of the factors for BAME distrust of the criminal justice system. The government rejected Lammy's recommendations to set targets for BAME judges in December 2017.

Sex

The sexes are fairly evenly balanced among lay magistrates, with 45 per cent men and 55 per cent women. Thirty-five per cent of district judges (magistrates' courts) are women.

13.2.5 Training

The Magistrates' Commission Committees are responsible for providing training under the supervision of the Judicial College. Magistrates are not expected to be experts on the law, and the aim of their training is mainly to familiarise them with court procedure, the techniques of chairing, and the theory and practice of sentencing. They undergo a short induction course on appointment, and have to undergo basic continuous training comprising six hours every three years. Magistrates who sit in juvenile courts or on domestic court panels receive additional training.

Appraisals happen every three years and are carried out by another member of the same bench, who takes on an observational role. This was seen by many of those who contributed to *The Role of the Magistracy* report as being inadequate and a 'tick-box exercise'.

In order to chair a court hearing a magistrate must, since 1996, take a Chairmanship Course the syllabus of which is set by the Judicial College. Since 1998 the training has included more 'hands on' practical experience, sessions in equality awareness, and experienced magistrates act as monitors of more junior members of the bench.

The Role of the Magistracy report notes that funding available for the training of magistrates has been drastically reduced, from £72 per sitting magistrate in 2009/10 to just £30 in 2013/14. More recent figures were not available but it is likely that this downward trend has continued. There were also concerns regarding the quality of training offered. The report pushed for a future continuing professional development (CPD) programme and a review of training needs.

13.2.6 Criminal jurisdiction

Magistrates have three main functions in criminal cases:

- Dealing with the first appearance of any defendant, dealing with procedural issues and hearing initial applications for bail.
- Trial. Magistrates mainly try the least serious criminal cases. They are advised on matters of law by a justices' clerk, but they alone decide the facts, the law and the sentence.
- Appeals. In ordinary appeals from the magistrates' court to the Crown Court, magistrates sit with a judge. But, following a reform by the Access to Justice Act 1999, they no longer have this role in relation to appeals against sentence.

Magistrates also exercise some control over the investigation of crime, since they deal with applications for bail and requests by the police for arrest and search warrants.

Lay magistrates generally sit in groups of three. However, s. 49 of the Crime and Disorder Act 1998 provides that certain pre-trial judicial powers may be exercised by a single justice of the peace sitting alone. These include decisions to extend or vary the conditions of bail, to remit an offender to another court for sentence and to give directions as to the timetable for proceedings, the attendance of the parties, the service of documents and the manner in which evidence is to be given. These powers of single justices were tested in six pilot studies and, having proved to be successful, were applied nationally in November 1999.

It is not uncommon for defendants in some relatively minor cases to choose not to attend court – they are specifically given an option not to. In the past, this still necessitated a hearings which would take place in a courtroom, with only magistrates, prosecutors and court staff present. The defendant's written account might be read out. To prevent such waste, the Magistrates' Courts Act 1980 s. 16A (inserted by the Criminal Justice and Courts Act 2015), provides that cases involving adults charged with summary-only, non-imprisonable offences can be considered by a Lay Magistrate upon the papers, without the need for a rehearsal in open court. Neither the prosecutor nor defendant will be present. The aim is to deal quickly and cheaply with straightforward, uncontested cases, involving offences such as failure to register a new vehicle keeper, driving without insurance, exceeding a 30mph speed limit, and TV licence evasion. The new procedure is outlined under Explanatory notes 58–60 of the 2015 Act:

> 58. Cases which prosecutors identify as being suitable for this process will be commenced by a written charge and a new type of document called a 'single justice procedure notice'. This notice will give a defendant a date to respond in writing to the allegation rather than a date to attend court; it will also be accompanied by the evidence . . . which the prosecutor would be relying on to prove the case.
>
> 59. If a defendant pleads guilty and indicates they would like to have the matter dealt with in their absence, or does not respond to the notice, then a single magistrate will consider the case on the basis of the evidence submitted in writing by the prosecutor, and any written mitigation from the defendant. . . .
>
> 60. If a defendant wishes to plead not guilty, or otherwise wants to have a hearing in a traditional courtroom, they can indicate their wishes and the current arrangements [a traditional court hearing] will apply.

The role of magistrates in the criminal justice system has been effectively increased in recent years. Some offences which were previously triable either way have been made summary only, notably in the Criminal Law Act 1977, where most motoring offences, and criminal damage worth less than £2,000, were made summary only. The Government proposed at the time that thefts involving small amounts of money should also be made summary offences, but there was great opposition to the idea of removing the right to jury trial for offences which reflected on the accused's honesty. The proposal was dropped, but is still suggested from time to time.

The vast majority of new offences are summary only – there was controversy over the fact that the first offence created to deal with so-called 'joyriding' was summary, given that the problem appeared to be a serious one, and critics assume that it was made a summary offence in the interests of keeping costs down. Since then, the more serious joyriding offence, known as aggravated vehicle-taking, which occurs when joyriding causes serious personal injury or death, has been reduced to a summary offence by the Criminal Justice and Public Order Act 1994. Other serious offences which are summary only include assaulting a police officer, and many of the offences under the Public Order Act 1986.

The Courts Act 2003 has given district judges (magistrates' court) for the first time limited powers to sit in the Crown Court. This is in order to deal with some preliminary administrative matters.

13.2.7 Civil jurisdiction

Magistrates' courts are responsible for granting licences to betting shops and casinos, and hearing appeals from local authority decisions regarding the issuing of pub and restaurant licences.

Magistrates' courts used to deal with domestic matters, including adoption, but in 2014 this was changed, and all domestic matters now commence in a specialised Family Court.

The fact that for domestic matters different procedures and law are applied in the different courts, and cases are generally assigned to the magistrates' court because they fall within certain financial limits, has led to the criticism that there is a second class system of domestic courts for the poor, with the better off using the High Court and County Courts where cases are heard by professional and highly qualified judges. Because of this, magistrates sitting in domestic cases must receive special training and the bench must contain both male and female magistrates.

Figure 13.3 Defendants prosecuted at magistrates' courts, 12 months ending March 2008 to 12 months ending March 2018 by type of offence

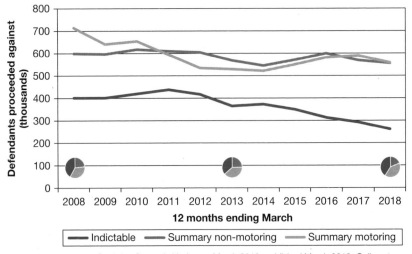

Source: Page 4, Criminal Justice Statistics Quarterly Update to March 2018, published March 2018. Online at: https://assets.publishing.service.gov.uk/government/uploads/system/uploads/attachment_data/file/734069/ criminal-justice-statistics-quarterly-march-2018.pdf

13.2.8 The justices' clerk and legal advisers

There are about 250 justices' clerks in the country. Most must have a five-year magistrates' court qualification, that is to say they must be qualified as barristers or solicitors with a right of audience in relation to all proceedings in the magistrates' courts for at least five years, though some hold office by reason of their length of service. In the past, there have been problems with recruiting suitably qualified people, partly because the local organisation of the courts meant there was no clear career structure. This led many clerks to leave for the Crown Prosecution Service where pay and promotion prospects were better.

The justices' clerks delegate many of their powers in practice to assistant justices' clerks, who are also known as legal advisers. This wide delegation has caused concerns about the qualifications of the people to whom these powers are being delegated. In an effort to raise standards, since 1 January 1999 all newly appointed legal advisers must be qualified solicitors or barristers. Those in post prior to this date who have a specialist diploma in magisterial law have 10 years in which to requalify. There is an exemption for legal advisers aged 40 or over on 1 January 1999. Not surprisingly, this reform was angrily received by legal advisers who did not have the requisite qualification.

The primary function of the justices' clerk and legal adviser is to advise the lay magistrates on law and procedure. They are not supposed to take any part in the actual decision of the bench; legal and procedural advice should be given in open court, and the justices' clerk and legal adviser should not accompany the magistrates if they retire to consider their decision. Section 49(2) of the Crime and Disorder Act 1998 provides that many of the pre-trial judicial powers that are exercisable by a single justice of the peace can be delegated to a justices' clerk. Their independence is guaranteed by s. 29 of the Courts Act 2003. In the past the justices' clerk also had considerable administrative functions, but these are increasingly being passed to other staff.

A Practice Direction was issued by the High Court in 2000 clarifying the powers of the justices' clerk – **Practice Direction (Justices: Clerk to Court) (2000)**. This was issued to make it clear that their powers conform with the European Convention on Human Rights following the passing of the Human Rights Act 1998.

The Magistrates' Association (which represents lay magistrates) has suggested that in a democratic country judicial and executive functions should be separate and that the role of justices' clerks and legal advisers needs to be rethought.

The Courts and Tribunals (Judiciary and Functions of Staff) Bill (HL Bill 108) seeks to make the role of Justices' Clerk a non-statutory one, which would mean them being able to give advice outside of the magistrates' court.

13.2.9 Lay magistrates versus professional judges

In recent years, there has been some discussion as to whether lay magistrates should be replaced by professional judges. There have been suspicions that this may be on the political agenda. These suspicions have been fuelled by the increasing role of justices' clerks. The academics, Rod Morgan and Neil Russell, carried out research on the subject and produced a report, *The Judiciary in the Magistrates' Courts* (2000). That research concluded:

> At no stage during the study was it suggested that . . . the magistrates' courts do not work well or fail to command general confidence. It is our view, therefore, that eliminating or greatly diminishing the role of lay magistrates would not be widely understood or supported.

The Ministry of Justice commissioned further research in 2011, which was undertaken by the market research company Ipsos MORI and published in the report *The Strengths and Skills of the Judiciary in the Magistrates' Courts.* The conclusions of this report also seemed to favour the retention of lay magistrates.

In Australia lay magistrates were often only used because of a shortage of professional judges and have been phased out in some states. In New Zealand the role of magistrates is now limited in practice to witnessing documents. There was no formal decision to downgrade their role but over time their judicial functions have increasingly been carried out by professional judges.

13.2.10 Advantages of lay magistrates

Cost

It has traditionally been assumed that because lay magistrates are unpaid volunteers, they are necessarily cheaper than their stipendiary colleagues. However, it is not clear that this is the case. The research by Rod Morgan and Neil Russell (2000) found that a simple analysis of the direct costs for the Magistrates' Courts Service of using the two types of magistrates shows that lay magistrates are extraordinarily cheap compared with professional judges. The direct average cost of a lay justice is £495 per annum, that of a district judge £90,000. However, lay magistrates incur more indirect costs than professional judges. They are much slower than professional judges in hearing cases, as one professional judge handles as much work as 30 lay magistrates. Lay magistrates therefore make greater proportionate use of the court buildings. They need the support of legally qualified legal advisers. Administrative support is required for their recruitment, training and rota arrangements. When all the overheads are brought into the equation the cost per appearance for lay and professional magistrates becomes £52.10 and £61.78 respectively. These figures have to be seen in the context that professional judges are currently more likely to send someone to prison which is more expensive than the alternative sentences frequently imposed by lay magistrates. They are almost twice as likely to remand defendants in custody and they are also twice as likely to sentence defendants to immediate custody, a finding that may be partly attributable to their hearing the most serious cases.

Table 13.1 The cost of appearing before lay and professional magistrates (per appearance)

	Lay magistrates	Professional magistrates
	£	£
Direct costs (salary, expenses, training)	3.59	20.96
Indirect costs (premises, administration staff etc.)	48.51	40.82
Direct & indirect costs	52.10	61.78

Source: Morgan and Russell (2000) *The Judiciary in the Magistrates' Courts,* Home Office RDS Occasional Paper No. 66

Switching to Crown Court trials would be extremely expensive. The Home Office Research and Planning Unit has estimated that the average cost of a contested trial in the Crown Court is around £13,500, with guilty pleas costing about £2,500. By contrast, the costs of trial by lay magistrates are £1,500 and £500 respectively. This is partly a reflection of the more serious nature of cases tried in the Crown Court, but clearly Crown Court trials are a great deal more expensive overall.

Lay involvement

This is the same point as that cited in favour of the jury (see p. 283). Lay magistrates are an ancient and important tradition of voluntary public service. They can also be seen as an example of participatory democracy. Lay involvement in judicial decision-making ensures that the courts are aware of community concerns. However, given the restricted social background of magistrates, and their alleged bias towards the police, the true value of this may be doubtful. Magistrates do not have the option, as juries do, of delivering a verdict according to their conscience.

The Ipsos MORI research (2011) concluded that lay magistrates were widely perceived as having a greater connection with the local community compared to district judges, being fair, less 'case hardened' or fatigued and more open-minded than professional judges. Some people associated a bench of three people with 'a greater degree of democracy'.

Weight of numbers

The simple fact that magistrates must usually sit in threes may make a balanced view more likely.

Local knowledge

Magistrates must live within a reasonable distance of the court in which they sit, and therefore may have a more informed picture of local life than professional judges.

13.2.11 Disadvantages of lay magistrates

Inconsistent

Historically there has been concern that magistrates' courts around the country were not treating like cases alike. To achieve the fundamental goal of a fair trial, similar crimes committed in similar circumstance by offenders with similar backgrounds should receive a similar punishment. In 1985, the Home Office noted in *Managing Criminal Justice* (edited by David Moxon) that although benches tried to ensure that their own decisions were consistent, they did not strive to achieve consistency with other benches. The researchers Flood-Page and Mackie found in 1998 that district judges (magistrates' courts) sentenced a higher proportion of offenders to custody than lay magistrates after allowing for other factors. There are also marked variations in the granting of bail applications: in 1985, magistrates' courts in Hampshire granted 89 per cent of bail applications, while in Dorset only 63 per cent were allowed.

The Government has tried to put an end to the differences in sentencing patterns in different areas, a situation which was described as 'postcode sentencing'. In order to do this, the Sentencing Guidelines Council was established and more recently the Sentencing Council (see p. 531), to ensure greater consistency in sentencing across England and Wales. These bodies were not intended to be a threat to the independence of the magistracy who need to be able to take into account individual circumstances. But where circumstances are similar, the aim is to reduce the regional disparity in sentencing. Legally binding sentencing guidelines have now been issued for magistrates. Magistrates have to take into account any relevant guideline, and if a decision is reached that the particular facts of a case justify a sentence outside the range indicated, they must state their reasons for doing so.

Inefficient

The Ipsos MORI research (2011) found that professional judges were both speedier and perceived to be speedier in handling cases; they were considered by lawyers using the courts as being better at case management.

Most of the public sampled in the research by Rod Morgan and Neil Russell (2000) was largely unaware that there were two types of magistrate. When enlightened and questioned, a majority considered that magistrates' court work should be divided equally between the two types of magistrate or that the type of magistrate did not matter. However, professional court users have significantly greater levels of confidence in the district judges (magistrates' courts). They regard these judges as quicker than lay justices, more efficient and consistent in their decision-making, better able to control unruly defendants and better at questioning CPS and defence lawyers appropriately. In practice, straightforward guilty pleas to minor matters are normally dealt with by panels of lay magistrates whereas serious contested matters are increasingly dealt with by a single, professional judge who decides questions of both guilt and sentence. Rod Morgan and Neil Russell question whether the work should be distributed in the opposite way. The Ipsos MORI research (2011) suggested that:

> deployment of magistrates and District Judges could be made more effective and efficient by adopting a more systematic, evidence-based approach . . . Specifically, District Judges could be deployed more exclusively on more difficult or complicated cases (though determining this can be difficult), where their training and experience were widely seen as offering notable advantages.

Bias towards the police

Police officers are frequent witnesses, and become well known to members of the bench, and it is alleged that this results in an almost automatic tendency to believe police evidence. One magistrate was incautious enough to admit this: in *R* v *Bingham Justices, ex parte Jowitt* (1974), a speeding case where the only evidence was that of the motorist and a police constable, the chairman of the bench said: 'Quite the most unpleasant cases that we have to decide are those where the evidence is a direct conflict between a police officer and a member of the public. My principle in such cases has always been to believe the evidence of the police officer, and therefore we find the case proved.' The conviction was quashed on appeal because of this remark.

Magistrates were particularly criticised in this respect during the 1984 miners' strike for imposing wide bail conditions which prevented attendance on picket lines, and dispensing what appeared to be conveyor-belt justice. Following the riots in 2011, some magistrates' courts stayed open all night to deal with rioters and they were under pressure to impose custodial sentences.

Background

Despite the recommendations of two Royal Commissions (1910 and 1948) and the *Review of the Criminal Courts* (Auld, 2001), that magistrates should come from varied social backgrounds, magistrates still appear to be predominantly middle class and middle-aged, with a strong Conservative bias.

The selection process has been blamed for the general narrowness of magistrates' backgrounds: Elizabeth Burney's 1979 study into selection methods concluded that the process was almost entirely dominated by existing magistrates who over and over again simply appointed people with similar backgrounds to their own.

The effect of their narrow background on the quality and fairness of magistrates' decisions is unclear. A survey of 160 magistrates by Bond and Lemon (1979) found no real evidence of significant differences in approach between those of different classes, but they did conclude that political affiliation had a noticeable effect on magistrates' attitudes to sentencing, with Conservatives tending to take a harder line. The research did not reveal whether these differences actually influenced the way magistrates carried out their duties in practice, but there is obviously a risk that they would do so.

In 1997, there was a slight controversy when, on winning the general election, the Labour Lord Chancellor called for more Labour-voting candidates to be recommended for appointment as magistrates by Advisory Committees. His reasoning was that the political make-up of the magistrates needed to reflect that of the general population which had shifted towards Labour. The Labour Government later reversed its position, having concluded that it is no longer necessary to seek a political balance among magistrates because people no longer vote along class lines.

Some feel that the background of the bench is not a particular problem: in *The Machinery of Justice in England* (1989) Jackson points out that: 'Benches do tend to be largely middle to upper class, but that is a characteristic of those set in authority over us, whether in the town hall, Whitehall, hospitals and all manner of institutions.'

However, a predominantly old and middle-class bench is unrepresentative of the general public and may weaken confidence in its decisions, on the part of society in general as well as the defendants before them. Jackson's argument that those 'set in authority over us' always tend to be middle to upper class is not a good reason for not trying to change things.

13

MAGISTRATES

The Bigger Picture

There is a crisis of morale within the ranks of the magistrates, with numbers falling from around 30,000 in 2009 to 16,000 in 2018. Varied reasons have been noted as contributing to this; *The Role of the Magistracy* reports 'top-down administration' undermining the ability of magistrates to deliver a high-quality service, as there was a feeling that they were not consulted about potential reforms of the justice system or management of the courts. Magistrates report feeling unappreciated and ignored, with their resources being constantly cut back; the court closure programme and budget cuts all adding to this perception. Over 50 magistrates resigned in 2015 after the criminal court charges were introduced by the then Justice Secretary, Chris Grayling. These controversial charges were later scrapped by Michael Gove, Grayling's replacement. A lack of investment in training was another factor in magistrates' dispiritedness.

The Chairman of the Magistrates' Association has estimated a further 9,000 magistrates are needed in the next decade just to 'stand still'.

13.3 Suggested reforms

13.3.1 Professional judges

Professional judges could either replace lay magistrates, or sit together with them. In no other jurisdiction do lay judges alone or in panels deal with offences of the seriousness dealt with in the English and Welsh magistrates' courts by lay magistrates. But putting a professional judge in all magistrates' courts would be very expensive, and is unlikely to happen, though the Royal Commission on Criminal Justice did recommend in 1993 that more use should be made of professional judges. Rod Morgan and Neil Russell (2000) calculated that if the work of lay magistrates was transferred to professional judges, one professional judge would be needed for every 30 magistrates replaced.

13.3.2 The role of the justices' clerk

Justices' clerks have slowly been allowed to have more powers to manage cases, while limiting their administrative functions. These reforms could be taken further by appointing them to the bench, making them legally qualified chairpersons, or giving them formal powers to rule on all points of law, while leaving the determination of the facts to the lay justices. The academic Penny Darbyshire has, however, sounded a note of caution to such developments. In an article in 1999 she argues that case management is not an administrative activity but a judicial one. She considers that such powers should not be delegated to justices' clerks unless they are selected and screened in the same way as judges and given the same protection as judges to ensure their independence.

In its submission to the Auld Review of the Criminal Courts in 2001, the Association of Magisterial Officers, which represents staff in magistrates' courts, called for a major transfer of powers from lay magistrates to justices' clerks. The union argued that the role of lay magistrates should be restricted to arbiters of fact. Justices' clerks would take on full responsibility for all pre-trial issues apart from the grant or removal of bail. Where lay magistrates were involved, they would act as 'wingers' in three-person tribunals chaired by justices' clerks. The clerks' decision on points of law would be final, but any decision on the facts would be by simple majority. Sir Robin Auld rejected this submission and essentially recommended that the role of justices' clerks should remain unchanged.

13.3.3 The selection process

The *Review of the Criminal Courts* (Auld, 2001) recommended that steps should be taken to make magistrates reflect more broadly than at present the communities they serve. Increased loss of earnings allowances and crèche facilities at courts (to help young parents) are all ways of attracting a more varied range of candidates. Legislation preventing employers from discriminating against magistrates would be difficult to enforce, but might at least make employers more wary about being seen to discriminate, and thus encourage more working class and younger applicants.

Membership of local Advisory Committees could be broadened to include members of the ethnic minorities and the working class, perhaps drawn from community organisations and trade unions.

The Auld Review (2001) recommended that local Advisory Committees should be equipped with the information they need to enable them to submit for consideration for appointment candidates that will produce and maintain benches broadly reflective of the communities they serve. This would include the establishment and maintenance of national and local databases of information on the make-up of the local community and on the composition of the local magistracy.

13.3.4 A District Division

A major review of the criminal courts was undertaken by Sir Robin Auld. The Review was primarily focused on the practices and procedures of the criminal courts and a wide range of recommendations was made. The central recommendation of the report was essentially that a new criminal court should be created (though it would for administrative purposes be a division of a court), which would be called the District Division.

Instead of having a separate Crown Court and magistrates' court, there would be a single unified criminal court containing three divisions. The three divisions would be the Crown Division (currently the Crown Court), the Magistrates' Division (currently the magistrates' court) and a new intermediate District Division.

Cases before the District Division would be heard by a judge and two lay magistrates. The District Division would deal with a middle range of either way cases which were unlikely to attract a sentence of more than two years' imprisonment. This would include most burglaries and thefts as well as some assault cases.

Only the judge would be able to determine questions of law, but the judge and lay magistrates would together be judges of fact. The order of proceedings would be broadly the same as in the Crown Division. The judge would rule on matters of law, procedure and inadmissibility of evidence, in the absence of the magistrates where it would be potentially unfair to the defendant to do so in their presence. The judge would not sum up the case to the magistrates, but would retire with them to consider the court's decision. They would reach their verdicts together, each having an equal vote. The judge would give a reasoned judgment and he or she would have sole responsibility for determining the sentence.

Defendants would lose their right to insist on a jury trial. Instead, cases would be allocated by magistrates to the relevant Division according to their seriousness.

These recommendations of Sir Robin Auld would have significantly increased the role of magistrates in the criminal justice system, but also represented a major attack on jury trials, since they would have significantly reduced the number of cases being heard by a jury. The proposals were heavily criticised by supporters of the jury system. It is questionable whether they would have produced any financial savings. The Law Society expressed its concern that an intermediate court 'would add an unnecessary level of bureaucracy'. After reflection, the Government rejected these recommendations.

The Ipsos MORI research (2011) found that most interviewees were not in favour of mixed benches of a professional judge with two lay justices but were more favourable to the idea of a District Division.

In 2012 the Government issued a consultation paper entitled *Swift and Sure Justice*. In this paper it considers allowing single magistrates to rule on uncontested, low-level criminal cases. Some pilot community justice centres have been set up which are modelled on similar centres that have been established in the US. These centres seek to bring together the courts and a range of relevant agencies, such as the social services and drug charities, to tackle the underlying problems in a community that lead to crime and anti-social behaviour. As well as bringing offenders to justice, the centres aim to develop crime prevention, solve community problems and offer mediation for minor disputes. The consultation paper is looking at extending the use of community justice centres nationally. It is considering allowing magistrates, sitting on their own, to operate from community centres and police stations as well as hearing cases via video link to cells, to deal (potentially within hours of arrest) with low-level cases where the defendant has pleaded guilty. At the moment the average time between an offence and sentencing is 140 days. Magistrates would sit in the evenings and earlier in the mornings as well as at weekends to speed up the justice system, depending on local demands. Lawyers would not necessarily be involved in the case. These reform proposals are partly inspired by how efficiently the magistrates' courts reacted to the riots in the summer of 2011, sitting through the night to process rioters rapidly through the system. The plans also aim to increase the role of magistrates in out-of-court disposals, currently handled by the police.

13.3.5 Sentencing

Another recommendation within *The Role of the Magistracy* report was that the sentencing powers of magistrates should be increased. This was supported in a September 2017 speech from the Lord Chief Justice, Lord Thomas of Cwmgiedd, just before he retired. Provision was made within the Criminal Justice Act 2003 for these sentencing powers to be increased for up to one year for a single offence, but s. 154 has not been brought into force. Lord Thomas indicated extending these powers would save time and money, but not everyone agrees. There are fears about a rise in the prison population if this was to be changed. Frances Crook, chief executive of the Howard League for Penal Reform has previously suggested that the magistrates' role should be one of problem-solving rather than punishments, and commented on increased powers a year earlier:

> Justice is not served by conferring the awesome power to incarcerate a citizen on magistrates. As well as the moral argument, the practical implications of short prison sentences are devastating on the individual, counterproductive and costly to the public.

Answering questions

As well as the following examples, the role of magistrates may also be considered as part of a question on lay involvement in the criminal justice system generally, and in questions on the criminal justice system itself.

1 While magistrates may be cheap, is it right that matters of vital concern to the citizen are being decided by amateurs?

2 Discussions about increasing the powers of magistrates in the criminal justice system have once again come to the fore. If these were implemented would their powers be too great – or too small?

3 To what extent do lay magistrates provide justice 'on the cheap'?

4 Discuss the extent to which lay magistrates are representative of society.

For answers to these questions, visit the companion website at www.pearsoned.co.uk/ elliottquinn

SUMMARY OF CHAPTER 13: MAGISTRATES

Introduction

There are over 16,000 lay magistrates and 140 professional judges who sit in the magistrates' courts.

Selection and appointment

Lay magistrates are appointed by the Lord Chief Justice in the name of the Crown, on the advice of local Advisory Committees.

Background

More than two-thirds of lay magistrates are employed in a professional or managerial position, or were until they retired. Almost a third of magistrates are in their sixties. A high proportion are Conservative voters. Lay magistrates do, however, increasingly reflect the ethnic diversity of contemporary Britain and the sexes are fairly evenly balanced.

Training

The Magistrates' Commission Committees are responsible for providing training under the supervision of the Judicial College.

Jurisdiction

Magistrates are primarily concerned with criminal matters but they exercise a limited jurisdiction over some civil matters.

The justices' clerk and legal adviser

The primary function of the justices' clerk and legal adviser is to advise the lay magistrates on law and procedure. They are not supposed to take any part in the actual decision of the bench.

Lay magistrates versus professional judges

In recent years there has been some discussion as to whether lay magistrates should be replaced by professional judges.

Reading list

Auld, Sir R. (2001) *Review of the Criminal Courts.* London: HMSO.

Bond, R.A. and Lemon, N.F. (1979) Changes in magistrates' attitudes during the first year on the bench. In: Farrington, D.P. *et al.* (eds) *Psychology, Law and Legal Processes.* London: Macmillan.

Burney, E. (1979) *Magistrates, Court and Community.* London: Hutchinson.

Darbyshire, P. (1999) A comment on the powers of magistrates' clerks. *Criminal Law Review*, 377.

Flood-Page, C. and Mackie, A. (1998) *Sentencing During the Nineties.* London: Home Office Research and Statistics Directorate.

Hedderman, C. and Moxon, D. (1992) *Magistrates' Court or Crown Court? Mode of Trial Decisions and Sentencing.* London: HMSO.

Herbert, A. (2003) Mode of trial and magistrates' sentencing powers: will increased powers inevitably lead to a reduction in the committal rate? *Criminal Law Review*, 314.

Jackson, R.M. (1989) *The Machinery of Justice in England.* Cambridge: Cambridge University Press.

King, M. and May, C. (1985) *Black Magistrates: A Study of Selection and Appointment.* London: Cobden Trust.

Lidstone, K. (1984) *Magisterial Review of the Pre-Trial Criminal Process: A Research Report.* Sheffield: University of Sheffield Centre for Criminological and Socio-Legal Studies.

Morgan, R. and Russell, N. (2000) *The Judiciary in the Magistrates' Courts.* Home Office RDS Occasional Paper No. 66. London: Home Office.

Moxon, D. (ed.) (1985) *Managing Criminal Justice: A Collection of Papers.* London: HMSO.

Sanders, A. (2001) Modernizing the magistracy. *JPN*, 165: 57.

Seago, P., Walker, C. and Wall, D. (2000) The development of the professional magistracy in England and Wales. *Criminal Law Review*, 631.

Ward, J. (2017) *Transforming Summary Justice: Modernisation in the Lower Criminal Courts.* Oxon: Routledge.

Zander, M. (2004) *The Law-Making Process.* London: Butterworths.

On the internet

The research undertaken by Ipsos MORI commissioned by the Ministry of Justice *The Strengths and Skills of the Judiciary in the Magistrates' Courts* (2011) is available at:

> http://webarchive.nationalarchives.gov.uk/20120215123124/http://www.justice.gov.uk/publications/research-and-analysis/moj/strengths-skills-judiciary.htm

The research of Rod Morgan and Neil Russell, *The Judiciary in the Magistrates' Courts* (2000), is available on the internet at:

> http://webarchive.nationalarchives.gov.uk/20011220104429/http://www.homeoffice.gov.uk:80/rds/adhocpubs1.html

The website of the Magistrates' Association, which represents the interests of magistrates, is available at:

> https://www.magistrates-association.org.uk/

General information about magistrates is available on the following website:

https://www.gov.uk/become-magistrate

The report *Delivering Simple, Speedy, Summary Justice – An Evaluation of the Magistrates' Courts Tests* (2006) is available on the internet at:

http://webarchive.nationalarchives.gov.uk/+/http:/www.dca.gov.uk/publications/ reports_reviews/delivery-simple-speedy.pdf

The report *Supporting Magistrates' Courts to Provide Justice* (2005) is available on the internet at:

https://assets.publishing.service.gov.uk/government/uploads/system/uploads/ attachment_data/file/272197/6681.pdf

The report *The Role of the Magistracy* (2016) is available at:

https://publications.parliament.uk/pa/cm201617/cmselect/cmjust/165/165.pdf

Penelope Gibbs, Transform Justice and Amy Kirby, Birkbeck, University of London, *Judged by peers? The diversity of lay magistrates in England and Wales* (Howard League Working Paper 6/2014) is available at:

https://howardleague.org/wp-content/uploads/2016/04/HLWP_6_2014.pdf

Chapter 14
Administration of justice

This chapter discusses:

- national changes to the arrangements for the administration of justice;
- the separate roles of the Home Office and the Ministry of Justice;
- the Lord Chancellor; and
- the Attorney General.

14.1 The Ministry of Justice and the Home Office

In recent years, the Government has made radical reforms to the administration of the English legal system. Historically, this system was administered by both the Lord Chancellor's Department and the Home Office.

In 2003, the Lord Chancellor's Department was abolished and replaced by a Department for Constitutional Affairs. The Department for Constitutional Affairs had similar responsibilities to its predecessor. It was responsible for the appointment of judges, judicial salaries and the disciplining of the lower judiciary. It administered the courts, oversaw the state funding of legal services and contributed to the work on law reform.

The Home Office was responsible for the police, national security, reform of the criminal law, prisons, immigration, elections and civil rights.

The division of most of the important legal work between the Home Office and the Department for Constitutional Affairs was subsequently criticised as illogical. Why should two different departments each play a leading role in the same area? Under these complex arrangements legal matters could be easily ignored when the Government was unenthusiastic about them, since there was no single Minister who could be pressurised in Parliament. An example is the issue of funding for law centres: while the Department of the Environment had given grants to set up law centres, their continued funding appeared not to be the responsibility of any department, and so they were forced to rely on local authorities – themselves under severe financial restraints – and any other sources of funding they could drum up themselves.

In 2006, following a number of scandals relating to the prison service and immigration, the Home Secretary announced that the Home Office was 'not fit for purpose'. In 2007, the Department for Constitutional Affairs was abolished and replaced by a larger Ministry of Justice. There had long been a debate as to whether the UK should have a Ministry of Justice and the Government appears to have accepted the arguments in favour of this. The new Ministry is responsible for all the matters that fell within the remit of the Department for Constitutional Affairs, but in addition it has taken over responsibility for prisons and the probation service from the Home Office. Following the Courts Act 2003, the courts (apart from the Supreme Court) are administered by Her Majesty's Courts and Tribunals Service (HMCTS). This executive body falls within the responsibilities of the Ministry of Justice.

In summary, the Ministry of Justice has responsibility for three core policy areas:

- the court service (including the judges);
- the penal system (both prisons and community punishments); and
- legal aid.

The Home Office is now responsible for:

- counter-terrorism;
- security;
- policing;
- immigration; and
- asylum.

The hope is that the new Ministry of Justice will focus on reducing crime and run an effective penal system. A key focus of the Home Office will be on the detection of crime, while the Ministry of Justice will concentrate on the task of delivering a fair trial and sentence.

Figure 14.1 Home Office and Ministry of Justice responsibilities

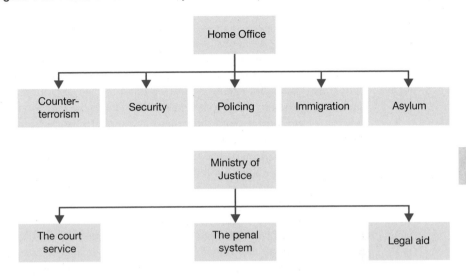

Members of the senior judiciary expressed concern that these new administrative arrangements could pose a threat to the independence of the judiciary. They were particularly anxious to avoid any pressure to impose sentences that the judges considered inappropriate now that the courts were being administered by the same department as the prisons. They demanded that the structures be put in place to prevent any threat to their independence from arising. They failed to get any guarantees for the funding of the court service, but a new board has been established to provide leadership for Her Majesty's Courts and Tribunal Service whose members include three judges and a representative of the Ministry of Justice. The aims of the Courts Service are agreed by the Lord Chancellor and the Lord Chief Justice.

Some of the work involved in administering the English legal system is not directly carried out by a government ministry, but is instead carried out by a 'quango', a public body to which specific responsibilities have been delegated. The Public Bodies Act 2011 contains a list of all non-departmental public bodies, executive agencies and non-ministerial departments (often termed 'quangos') which the Government is entitled to abolish by delegated legislation. This list includes the Judicial Appointments Commission, the Law Commission, the Legal Services Board, the Civil Justice Council and the Official Solicitor. A cloud is now hanging over all of these organisations which will have an impact on their independence.

14.2 The Lord Chancellor

The position of Lord Chancellor has existed for over 1,400 years. He or she (there has only ever been one female Lord Chancellor, Elizabeth Truss, who served from July 2016 to June 2017) has played a central role in the English legal system, but the position has been significantly reformed following persistent criticism. This criticism was based on the constitutional doctrine of the separation of powers. Under this doctrine, the power of the state has to be divided between three separate and independent arms: the judiciary (comprising the judges), the legislature (Parliament in the UK); and the executive (the Government of the day). The idea is that the separate arms of the state should operate independently, so that each one is checked and balanced by the other two, and none becomes all-powerful. The doctrine of the separation of powers was first put forward in the eighteenth century by the French political theorist, Montesquieu. Montesquieu argued that if all the powers were concentrated in the hands of one group, the result would be tyranny. Therefore, the doctrine requires that individuals should not occupy a position in more than one of the three arms of the state – judiciary, legislature and executive; each should exercise its functions independently of any control or interference from the others; and one arm of the state should not exercise the functions of either of the others.

The Lord Chancellor had such wide powers, which extended to all three arms of the state, that his existence was a clear breach of the doctrine of the separation of powers. We will look first at his judicial powers. Until recently, he was at the head of the whole judiciary, and effectively appointed all the other judges. He was President of the High Court, the Crown Court and the Court of Appeal. He was also officially President of the Chancery Division of the High Court, although in practice the Vice-Chancellor usually performed this role. The Lord Chancellor was also himself a judge. When he chose to sit as a judge, it was in the House of Lords or the Privy Council, but recent Lord Chancellors chose only to do this occasionally or not at all, and the House of Lords in its judicial capacity has now been abolished.

As regards his political role, the Lord Chancellor was a Cabinet Minister and Speaker of the House of Lords. Although technically appointed by the Queen, the Lord Chancellor is actually chosen by the Prime Minister and goes out of office when that party loses an election, as well as being eligible for removal by the Prime Minister, just like any other Minister.

In relation to his executive functions, he was at the head of the Lord Chancellor's Department, now the Ministry of Justice. Most controversially, he had control over judicial appointments. Politically, the most important judicial appointment is that of the Master of the Rolls; as president of the Court of Appeal his or her view on the proper relationship between the executive Government and the individual is crucial. The appointment of Lord Donaldson in 1982 was seen as a strongly political appointment and one which the then Prime Minister favoured: he had been a Conservative councillor, and was not promoted during the years of the previous Labour Government, 1974–79. There was some publicity concerning Lord Donaldson's political views at the time of the high-profile GCHQ union membership case, *Council of Civil Service Unions* v *Minister for the Civil Service* (1985) and, as a result, his Lordship declined to preside over the Court of Appeal when it considered the Government's appeal in that case.

So the position of the Lord Chancellor as a member of the judiciary, the executive and the legislature clearly went against the idea that no individual should be part of all three arms of the state. The conflicting roles of the Lord Chancellor were highlighted in 2001 when the media drew attention to the fact that the Lord Chancellor had been involved in political fundraising. Guests to a dinner he had organised were invited to make donations to the Labour Party and there were concerns that lawyers might seek promotion by giving substantial donations. Legal Action Group, a pressure group, argued that the various roles of the Lord Chancellor put him in breach of the European Convention on Human Rights.

In 2003, the Government announced that it intended to abolish the office of Lord Chancellor, and replace the position with a Minister for Constitutional Affairs. Following debate over this reform, the Government agreed to retain the position of Lord Chancellor, but the role has been significantly reduced so that the incumbent has become a more conventional Cabinet Minister and head of department. This reform was contained in the Constitutional

Table 14.1 Past role of the Lord Chancellor

Branch of Government	Role of the Lord Chancellor
Legislature	Speaker of the House of Lords
Executive	Government Minister
Judiciary	Judge in the House of Lords and Privy Council. He was also President of the group of courts formerly known as the Supreme Court and President of the Chancery Division of the High Court.

14

Reform Act 2005. Since 2007, the Lord Chancellor also has the title of Minister for Justice and is at the head of the Ministry of Justice. The new Minister is intended to be a more traditional member of the executive to satisfy the principle of the separation of powers. Four major changes to the role of the Lord Chancellor have been made, so that he or she no longer:

- sits as a judge;
- heads the judiciary;
- takes a central role in the judicial appointments process; or
- automatically becomes the Speaker of the House of Lords.

As regards the Lord Chancellor's historical function as Speaker of the House of Lords, it is now up to the House of Lords in its parliamentary capacity to determine who will be the Speaker of the House. The Lord Chancellor is no longer required to be a member of the House of Lords, but could be a member of the House of Commons instead. This could lead to the position becoming more political.

In the past, the Lord Chancellor had to be a lawyer, but under s. 2 of the Constitutional Reform Act 2005, the Lord Chancellor must simply appear to the Prime Minister to be qualified 'by experience'. Subsection (2) states that this experience could have been gained as a Government Minister, a member of either House of Parliament, a qualified lawyer, a teacher of law in a university or 'other experience that the Prime Minister considers relevant'. Thus, the Lord Chancellor no longer needs to be a lawyer and in 2012 a non-lawyer was appointed for the first time since 1558.

14.3 The Law Officers' Department

There is a small Law Officers' Department. The Law Officers are the Attorney General and the Solicitor General, who are both Ministers, though not members of the Cabinet. The Attorney General is the Government's main legal adviser and advised the Government on the legality of going to war against Iraq, which the Government initially refused to publish. He or she is responsible for major domestic and international litigation involving the Government. Other functions of the post include appealing against lenient sentences and bringing contempt proceedings when media coverage risks jeopardising a fair trial. As regards the prosecution process, the consent of the Attorney General is required for certain categories of prosecution (see p. 485); he or she grants immunities from prosecution and terminates prosecutions where appropriate, through a process known as *nolle prosequi*. The Director of

Public Prosecutions answers to the Attorney General in relation to the running of the Crown Prosecution Service.

The Solicitor General used to carry out such functions as the Attorney General delegated to that office. Following the Law Officers Act 1997, the Law Officers can agree a general division of labour between them, as the Act specifically empowers the Solicitor General to perform all the functions of the Attorney General. Thus, formal authorisation for any delegation is no longer required.

The Bigger Picture: The Attorney General

At the moment the Attorney General is chief Government legal adviser, a Government Minister and superintendent of the prosecuting authorities. Due to the breadth of the Attorney General's role and the fundamental violations of the principle of the separation of powers (discussed on p. 5), there has been suspicion of political interference in his or her decisions, even where there has not actually been any. The Attorney General's powers in relation to prosecutions have proved particularly controversial. At the time of the police investigation as to whether politicians had put forward individuals for peerages in return for financial payments (known as the 'cash-for-peerages' investigation), the Attorney General was, under statute, the person who would make the final decision as to whether to prosecute the politicians. This looked very uncomfortable when he was himself closely linked to those politicians. Although the Attorney General of the day, Lord Goldsmith, stated that as he could not delegate his statutory responsibility to make this decision to someone else, he would take and publish independent legal advice on the subject, there remained the risk that the decision looked political rather than legal. In 2007, the Attorney General made a controversial decision that no prosecution should be brought against BAE Systems following a police investigation over the possible payment of huge bribes to a member of the Saudi royal family, in order to be awarded a valuable contract for the supply of weapons.

The Government issued a Green Paper, *The Governance of Britain: A Consultation on the Role of the Attorney General* (2007). This was followed in 2008 by a White Paper looking at ways to improve the current constitution: *The Governance of Britain: Constitutional Renewal* (2008); along with a Draft Constitutional Renewal Bill. The White Paper considered possible reforms to the role of the Attorney General in order to enhance public trust and confidence. It suggested that the person holding this office could remain the Government's chief legal adviser, but changes could be made to their role with regard to prosecutions. The Attorney General would lose the power to give directions on the prosecution of individual criminal cases, including the power to prevent cases going ahead (the *nolle prosequi* power). These powers would be handed over to the directors of the different prosecuting authorities – the Crown Prosecution Service, Serious Fraud Office and Revenue and Customs Prosecution Office. The Attorney General would only retain a power to give directions in individual cases where they involved national security. The consent of the Attorney General to begin prosecutions would only be required where there was a particularly powerful public interest argument involved, such as in official secrets or war crimes cases.

The consultation paper suggested that 'both in perception and reality, it would improve the independence and public confidence in the impartial nature and authority of the provision of legal advice if it were not the responsibility of someone in political life'. However, the White Paper concluded that the Attorney General should continue to operate as the Government's legal adviser and remain as a Government Minister within Parliament.

Ultimately, the Government has decided to pursue more limited reforms, with the Attorney General simply required to issue a protocol making it clear that he or she will not be consulted in criminal cases concerning an MP or peer or where there is a personal or professional conflict of interest.

Answering questions

1   To what extent has the creation of a Ministry of Justice improved the administration of justice?

2   Has the creation of the Ministry of Justice facilitated or – as alleged by some members of the judiciary – threatened the independence of the judiciary?

For answers to these questions, visit the companion website at www.pearsoned.co.uk/ elliottquinn

SUMMARY OF CHAPTER 14: ADMINISTRATION OF JUSTICE

In 2003, the Government commenced a radical reform of the administration of the English legal system. The Lord Chancellor's Department was abolished and replaced by a Ministry for Constitutional Affairs. The office of Lord Chancellor was reformed so that it respects the principle of the separation of powers. In 2006, the Home Secretary stated that the Home Office was 'not fit for purpose' and in 2007 the Ministry of Justice was established, with legal work redistributed between that department and the Home Office. There is also a small Law Officers' Department. The Law Officers are the Attorney General and the Solicitor General, who are both Ministers, though not members of the Cabinet.

Reading list

Brazier, R. (1998) *Constitutional Reform*. Oxford: Oxford University Press.

Drewry, G. (1987) The debate about a Ministry of Justice – A Joad's eye view. *Public Law*, 502.

Jackson, R.M. (1989) *The Machinery of Justice in England*. Cambridge: Cambridge University Press.

Montesquieu, C. (1989) *The Spirit of the Laws*. Cambridge: Cambridge University Press.

On the internet

The consultation paper *The Governance of Britain: A Consultation on the Role of the Attorney General* (2007) is available at:

> **http://www.official-documents.gov.uk/document/cm71/7192/7192.pdf**

The consultation paper *The Governance of Britain: Constitutional Renewal* (2008) is available at

> **https://assets.publishing.service.gov.uk/government/uploads/system/uploads/ attachment_data/file/250803/7342_i.pdf**

The website for the Ministry of Justice is at:

> **https://www.gov.uk/government/organisations/ministry-of-justice**

The Home Office website is at:

> **https://www.gov.uk/government/organisations/home-office**

Chapter 15
Paying for legal services

This chapter discusses:

- the unmet need for legal services;

- legal aid under the Access to Justice Act 1999;

- cuts to the legal aid system;

- civil legal aid;

- criminal legal aid;

- the Public Defender Service;

- conditional and contingency fee agreements as alternative methods of funding legal proceedings;

- alternative sources of legal advice; and

- criticisms and reform of the current funding arrangements.

15.1 Introduction

Since society requires all its members keep the law, it follows that all members of society should be not only equally bound by, but also equally served by, the legal system. Legal rights are worthless unless they can be enforced. Justice may be open to all, but only in the same way as the Ritz Hotel. In other words, anyone can go there, but only if they can afford it – and, just like the Ritz Hotel, legal advice and help can be very expensive. As a result, many people simply cannot afford to enforce their legal rights and are therefore denied access to justice.

What is more, cost is not the only thing which stops many people from using the legal system. Other issues such as awareness of legal rights, the elitist image of the legal profession and even its geographical situation all contribute to the problem which legal writers call 'unmet legal need'. In the following section, we look at what unmet legal need really means, and the causes of it. Later in the chapter we consider the various attempts which have been made to resolve the problem, including the provision of state funding. Legislation was passed in 2012 to drastically cut the provision of legal aid, which has meant that very few people are now eligible for legal assistance, leaving us with what Amnesty International in their report *Cuts that Hurt* (2016) call 'a two-tier justice system: open to those who can afford it, but, increasingly closed to the poorest, most vulnerable and most in need of its protection'.

15.2 Unmet need for legal services

Unmet legal need describes the situation where people have problems that could potentially be solved through the law, but they fail to get whatever help they need to use the legal system. Research carried out by Pascoe Pleasence *et al.* for the Legal Services Commission in 2004 found that over a three-and-a-half-year period, more than one in three adults experienced a civil law problem; one in five took no action to solve their problem; and around 1 million problems went unsolved because people did not understand their basic rights or know how to seek help. About 15 per cent of people who sought advice did not succeed in obtaining any. The research revealed that civil law problems are not evenly distributed. Groups vulnerable to social exclusion suffer more problems more often. The survey showed civil justice problems were experienced by:

- four in five people living in temporary accommodation;
- two in three lone parents; and
- more than half of unemployed people.

Many civil justice problems trigger other problems and increase the risk of social exclusion. For example, an accident could lead to personal injury, which could lead to loss of income and then the loss of a person's home. This is reinforced by Organ and Sigafoos (2018) whose research on the impact of the legislation passed in 2012 indicated that the financial impact of unresolved legal problems escalated steeply; something which could have been avoided if specialist advice had been accessed earlier.

Research by Richard White in 1973 suggested four situations where someone would fail to get the legal help they needed:

1 The person fails to recognise a problem as having legal implications and so does not seek out legal advice.

2 The problem is recognised as being a legal one, but the person involved does not know of the existence of a legal service that could help, or their own eligibility to use it.

3   The person knows the problem is a legal one, and knows of the service that could help with it, but chooses not to make use of it because of some barrier, such as cost, ignorance of state funding or the unapproachable image of solicitors.

4   The person knows there is a legal problem and wants legal help, but fails to get it because they cannot find a service to deal with it.

Of these reasons, the barrier of cost has traditionally received most attention, and it is an important one. With court costs going up and eligibility for legal aid decreasing, access to justice risks becoming more of an aspiration than a reality. Simply obtaining legal advice from a private solicitor is expensive, and taking a case to court much more so. This gives the rich three major advantages: they can hire good lawyers and pay for the time needed to do the job properly; they can afford to take the risk of losing litigation; and they can use their wealth to bully a less well-off opponent, by dragging out the case or making it more complex (and therefore more expensive). Bear in mind that 'the rich' does not just mean the millionaire in the Rolls-Royce, but also the employer you might want to sue for unfair dismissal, the company whose products could make you ill or the builder who left you with a leaky roof, and you can see the problem. Pereira *et al.* (2015) found that with limited availability of legal aid, access to money is a significant factor in determining whether a person has access to justice. Some legal problems are so complex, such as employment and family finance, that the use of a lawyer is perceived as unavoidable. This presents challenges for people without adequate financial resources.

However, as White's research shows, cost is not the only reason why people fail to secure help with their legal problems. This is backed up by the research of Abel-Smith *et al.* (1973), which compared people's own perception of their need for legal help and the action they took to get it. Almost all the respondents consulted a solicitor when they felt they needed advice on buying a house (though, of course, this only includes those with sufficient means to buy their own home). For employment problems, though, only 4 per cent consulted a solicitor; 34 per cent took advice from some other source and 62 per cent took no advice at all. For welfare benefit problems, solicitors were consulted by even fewer people: just 3 per cent saw a solicitor, while 16 per cent took other advice and 81 per cent took none at all. Yet, in all these cases, the people surveyed realised they did need some legal advice.

Similarly, Zander (1988) has pointed out that even the poorest members of society consult solicitors about divorce, while the middle classes seem no more likely than working class people to consult solicitors about employment or consumer problems.

Research by Pleasence and Balmer (2013) found that 91 per cent of small businesses said they took action when identifying a legal issue. While 52 per cent decided to handle the matter alone, 12 per cent sought advice from a solicitor, 8 per cent from accountants and 4 per cent from trade or professional bodies.

American sociologists, Mayhew and Reiss (1969), put forward a 'social organisation' theory to explain why solicitors are consulted in some cases and not others. This theory suggests that certain types of work are related to social contact – most people know people who have used solicitors for conveyancing and divorce, and it becomes an obvious step to take. As Zander points out, lawyers adjust the services they offer to demand and so it becomes a self-fulfilling prophecy.

Supportive family and friends help access to justice. Pereira *et al.* (2015) have noted:

Social networks supported participants across all problem types. Participants reported turning to friends and family for a range of reasons along their pathway. They provided guidance on where to look for help, signposted to professional advice services and were a source of advice themselves. Friends and family enhanced the resources available to participants to resolve their problems – through providing money to pay for legal representation, offering support in informal mediation and intervening in domestic abuse problems. This has implications for access to justice for those without established social networks, who may find it difficult to take the first steps to resolve their justice problems or find themselves with fewer options to access the resources required.

Critical obstacles preventing people from solving their legal problems were difficulties accessing information about their options and the relevant processes to follow:

Across the study, participants in diverse situations reported that they needed information on the options available to them (including related costs), required guidance on the meaning of legal terminology and wanted information on the legal process, including for courts and tribunals. They required this information in order to understand what their next steps could be to resolve their justice issue and what to expect at each stage . . . Participants felt that authoritative online resources were hard to identify; such resources were typically not clear or comprehensive and could be contradictory.

The research by Pereira *et al.* (2015) also found that:

Low levels of individual capability with skills such as comprehension and communication were a key barrier to resolving justice problems. There was considerable evidence that participants with limited ability to understand complex written information and those who were vulnerable or distressed were not able to understand their options fully and make informed choices. Confidence was also important. Participants who felt they lacked capability could be easily discouraged if unable to access the information they needed, and tended to let the matter drop even if they would have preferred to pursue it.

The research identified how important it was for these people to receive support through advocacy and representation, particularly where there was an emotional trigger, such as personal injury or family child arrangements. Independent advocacy offered vital support to people in these processes, enabling them to pursue a case if they felt unable to do so alone.

Research carried out by Professor Hazel Genn in 1982 categorised the different types of people who are confronted by a legal problem. Five per cent were labelled as 'lumpers'. This group had low incomes, low education levels and were frequently unemployed. They were unable to see any way out of their money and employment problems and therefore did absolutely nothing. This could lead to a 'cluster' of problems where the person becomes increasingly incapable of helping him- or herself. The next group were described as 'self-helpers' and only had a 50 per cent chance of resolving their legal problems. They often believed, until the last minute, that nothing could be done to help them and, when they tried to take action, found they had gone, or been sent, to the wrong place; or were confronted by queues, unanswered telephones and restricted opening times. Professor Genn noted that social distress could be caused where legal problems were left unresolved. By contrast, if people got good-quality early advice they could help themselves.

Another problem is the uneven geographical distribution of solicitors throughout the country: a third of all solicitors practise in London. The Royal Commission on Legal Services (1979) highlighted research showing that while there was one solicitor's office for every 4,700 people in England and Wales, their distribution varied enormously, from one office for every 2,000 people in prosperous owner-occupier areas such as Bournemouth and Guildford, to one for every 66,000 in working class areas such as Huyton in Liverpool. The Commission concluded that the low rates for state-funded work had much to do with this; most private firms need to subsidise such work with privately funded work, and the poorer areas may not provide enough of this to keep more than a few solicitors in each area in business. Other advice agencies, such as law centres and Citizens Advice Bureaux, may also be thin on the ground in some, particularly rural, areas. The image of lawyers as predominantly white, male and from privileged backgrounds may contribute to the problem, making them unapproachable to many people.

In its 1999 report, *A Balancing Act: Surviving the Risk Society*, the National Association of Citizens Advice Bureaux (NACAB) suggested the problem of unmet legal need may still be growing. It pointed out that changes in society are forcing people to take on responsibility for their own welfare in areas where the state would once have made provision, while insecurity in work, housing and family relationships is increasing. This means more and more people are placed in situations where they need to assert their legal rights – divorce, homelessness, debt or employment problems, for example – but are unable to do so because there is too little access to free, independent, legal advice.

15.3 The historical development of legal aid

After the Second World War a system of legal aid was introduced to try and respond to the problem of unmet legal need. During this period, the Labour Government introduced a range of measures designed to address the huge inequalities between rich and poor. These included the National Health Service, the beginnings of today's social security system and, in 1949, the first state-funded legal aid scheme. The legal aid scheme was designed to allow poorer people access to legal advice and representation in court: this would be provided by solicitors in private practice, but the state, rather than the client, would pay all or part of the fees. By the 1980s, the system had developed into six different schemes, covering most kinds of legal case, and administered by the Legal Aid Board. But the growing cost of these schemes was causing concern. In the 1990s the Government sought to keep the escalating costs down by reducing financial eligibility for the schemes, which in turn led to criticisms they were also reducing access to justice. The Access to Justice Act 1999 introduced major changes to the legal aid system. Through these reforms the Government hoped to improve the quality and accessibility of the legal services on offer, while keeping a tighter control on their budget.

Before 1999, legal aid in civil cases was available on a demand-led basis (meaning that all cases which met the merits and means tests would be funded). After 1999, there was a fixed legal aid fund, containing a fixed amount of money, set each year as part of the normal round of Government spending plans. A means test applied so that people earning more than £2,300 a month or with more than £8,000 savings were not entitled to legal aid. In practice, the proportion of the population entitled to legal aid was reducing, from 80 per cent of the population in 1949, to 52 per cent in 1998 and then to 29 per cent in 2007. Of those entitled to legal aid, most were on income support and where they were in low paid employment, they were often required to pay part of their legal costs.

A Funding Code set out the priorities on how the money should be spent. Once all the money had been spent for the year, no more funding would be available, however strong the merits of a case might be. Only solicitors or advice agencies holding a contract with the former Legal Services Commission were able to provide state-funded advice or representation.

Certain types of case were removed from the state-funded system, including personal injury cases (unless they involved clinical negligence), defamation and disputes arising in the course of a business. These cases were not considered sufficiently important to justify public funding, but people could seek to fund litigation with a private conditional fee agreement with a solicitor (discussed on p. 355). Personal injury cases accounted for around 60 per cent of cases previously funded by legal aid, so this was a particularly important restriction in the availability of legal aid.

Even after the 1999 reforms, the cost of legal aid continued to grow and the Legal Aid, Sentencing and Punishment of Offenders Act 2012 (LASPO 2012) was subsequently passed introducing further cuts to the civil legal aid system. The 2012 Act was passed as part of the coalition Government's austerity programme, which sought to reduce the UK's budget deficit, caused in part by the 2008 global financial crisis.

15.4 Legal aid today

Spending on legal aid increased from £536 million in 1982 to around £2 billion in 2012 – an average annual growth of over 5 per cent in real terms. England and Wales were spending at least four times more on legal aid than any other European country, according to a survey carried out by the European Commission for the Efficiency of Justice (2008). It spent more per person on legal aid than many countries outside Europe, including Australia, Canada and New Zealand (Bowles and Perry, 2009). The Legal Aid, Sentencing and Punishment of Offenders Act 2012 has drastically reduced the availability of civil legal aid, and criminal legal aid is gradually being reduced. The aim of the provisions in this Act was to save £570 million a year on the cost of legal aid but the cuts amount to the most radical attack on the legal aid system since its foundation in 1949.

Legal aid is administered by the Legal Aid Agency (LAA). This is an executive agency under the direct control of the Ministry of Justice, which has given rise to some concern that there is a risk of political interference, with legal aid being withdrawn from politically sensitive cases. These fears were realised in a story broken by the well-respected journalist on social justice issues, Emily Dugan (BuzzFeed, 5 October 2018). Access to internal emails from LAA staff marked as 'Official sensitive' helped her expose the fact that a number of those bringing legal challenges against the government had their legal aid applications rejected once the Ministry of Justice was made aware of their applications by the 'independent' LAA.

15.4.1 Civil legal aid

Legal aid is now available only where the subject area is listed in Schedule 1 to the Legal Aid, Sentencing and Punishment of Offenders Act 2012. These are areas where the Government believes it necessary to meet its minimum legal obligations – primarily cases directly concerned with an individual's human rights. This amounts to little more than an emergency service. Most areas of social welfare law have been removed from the system altogether. This is particularly unfortunate when this reduction in legal aid is happening at a time when people's welfare benefits are being cut or removed and they might desperately need legal advice to understand these changes in the law.

Civil legal aid is no longer available for cases involving medical negligence, welfare benefits, employment, consumer disputes, education (except special needs cases), immigration (unless clients are in detention) and housing cases (unless they involve homelessness or serious disrepair). Private family law cases (such as divorce and child contact) do not qualify for legal aid funding unless the case involves domestic violence, child abduction or a forced marriage. Instead, funding is provided for mediation as an alternative to family disputes going to court. This would remove entitlement to legal advice from 650,000 people.

Legal aid has been retained for environmental law, asylum, mental health and child welfare cases, including where children may be taken into care, and judicial review. It is only available for clinical negligence cases where the negligence occurred during the first weeks of life. In summary, civil legal aid is only available where a person's life or liberty is at stake, or where they are at risk of serious harm or immediate loss of their home. A fund has been set up for cases where legal aid would not normally be available, but where it is necessary to provide funding to meet domestic or international legal obligations.

The means test for civil legal aid has been tightened, including taking into account the value of a person's family home. A minimum £100 contribution to their legal costs has been introduced for all successful applicants with £1,000 or more disposable income. The number of people entitled to legal aid has, as a result of these changes, been reduced by more than half. Payments to lawyers for civil legal aid work have been cut by 10 per cent. Most people will remember the harrowing case of Charlie Gard as it played out in court during 2017. This case concerned whether treatment on the baby with a rare genetic condition, should continue. Charlie's parents wanted to remove their son from the care of Great Ormond Street hospital in order to travel to the United States for experimental treatment. Despite not working (as they were caring for their son), Charlie's parents did not qualify for legal aid, and would not have had legal representation were it not for lawyers stepping in to work on a pro bono basis. Non-means-tested legal aid is only available in certain circumstances in family law cases.

There was massive opposition to the reforms embedded within the Legal Aid, Sentencing and Punishment of Offenders Act 2012, even before it came into force, with many organisations warning against its far-reaching effects on society. The Legal Action Group observed that the changes to civil legal aid meant that those who will need it at some point in their lives are unlikely to be able to access it. They suggest that it is now largely reserved for those cases that directly engage fundamental human rights.

The Law Society has also commented:

> The attack on civil legal aid is horrific. Huge swathes of a system which helped vulnerable people will be completely eliminated.

In the years following the passing of the Act those fears have been realised. In 2016, the amount spent on legal aid was £950 million less than in 2010. The voices criticising the Act come from the judiciary, MPs, charities and legal representative groups, as well as campaigning organisations like Amnesty International. The Ministry of Justice is due to review LASPO 2012 sometime in 2018.

Ironically, at a time when the UK Government is cutting the legal aid system, the European Union has pledged to set mandatory levels of civil and criminal legal aid for member states. Under Art. 47 of the European Charter of Fundamental Rights (see p. 394), all member states will be required to make legal aid funding available to parties in civil and criminal cases who otherwise could not afford representation.

Civil legal advice

Civil Legal Advice (CLA) is a national telephone and website service providing free legal advice on civil law matters. Members of the public can telephone the helpline on 0345 345 4345 (or enter their details online for a CLA call-back) for advice on matters such as housing, special educational needs, discrimination, debt and certain family matters. Civil Legal Advice is intended to provide an alternative to face-to-face advice, which will be particularly attractive to those with mobility problems, caring responsibilities or accommodation in a remote area. In addition, some people may feel more comfortable talking about their problems with the relative anonymity of a telephone line, rather than in a face-to-face meeting.

People with problems involving debt, discrimination and special educational needs will no longer be able to go directly to a solicitor. Instead, they have to call the CLA national helpline. An operator will only refer the person for face-to-face advice if this is appropriate. Such a referral will be considered appropriate where the case is too complex to be dealt with by telephone or where a client's needs cannot be met through a telephone service, for example, because of a mental impairment. The service deals with around 1,500 new cases each month.

15.4.2 Criminal legal aid

Unlike legal aid in civil cases, state-funded criminal defence work is still given on a demand-led basis; there is no set budget and all cases which fit the merits criteria and the means test are funded. After passing the Legal Aid, Sentencing and Punishment of Offenders Act 2012, the Ministry of Justice announced changes to the operation of criminal legal aid in 2013. The Ministry of Justice originally proposed reforms to the eligibility criteria for criminal legal aid, a reduction in the fees for criminal legal aid and the introduction of competition into the criminal legal aid market. The LAA directly funds the provision of criminal legal services, employs public defenders and pays for duty solicitor schemes. Thus, legal services are provided by both lawyers in private practice and employed lawyers. The Government believes that a mixed system of public and private lawyers will provide the best value for money for the taxpayer. The salaried service is intended to provide a benchmark to assess whether prices charged by private practice lawyers are reasonable, as well as filling in gaps in the system. In order to save a further £220 million in the legal aid budget, in addition to the £350 million of savings made in the civil legal aid budget, the Ministry of Justice argued that the best way to ensure long-term sustainability and value for money in the legal aid market was to move away from set fees and towards competition.

Contracts for criminal legal aid

Previously, only solicitor firms having a contract with the LAA were able to offer state-funded criminal defence work. Unlike the contracts for civil matters, the contracts for criminal defence matters did not limit the number of cases that could be taken on, or the total value of the payments that might be made. Contracted solicitors were paid for all work actually undertaken in accordance with the contract. The Ministry of Justice originally proposed the introduction of price-competitive tendering for contracts for criminal legal aid. This involved law firms bidding for contracts to provide legal aid work in specific areas. Many law firms opposed this proposal, arguing that competition based upon price would undermine the quality of legal representation given to clients. As a result of this opposition, the Ministry of Justice changed its plans. There are now two different contract types for criminal legal aid.

First, a set number of Duty Provider contracts are awarded in each geographic area through a competitive tendering process. This means clients do not have a choice regarding which law firm represents them under the duty solicitor scheme (see p. 344). Secondly, an unlimited number of Own Client Work contracts are available to any provider who satisfies certain quality requirements. These contracts allow law firms to undertake work anywhere in the country, and allow clients to choose a solicitor. All contracts are for four years.

Means test

Before the Access to Justice Act 1999, criminal legal aid was means tested. The means test was criticised because most defendants were too poor to pay for their defence lawyers – only 1 per cent of applicants were refused criminal legal aid. As a result, the cost of administering the means test was more than the sum that was collected by defendants and the process also caused delays in the criminal system. The 1999 Act therefore abolished the means test for criminal cases. Instead, for cases heard in the Crown Court, orders could be issued at the end of a trial to recover the defence costs against wealthy people who had been convicted of an offence. Abolition of the means test led to concern in the media that some wealthy defendants were receiving legal aid when they could have comfortably afforded to pay themselves. Following such criticisms, the Criminal Defence Service Act 2006 reintroduced a means test for criminal cases in the magistrates' courts (apart from the first hearing, to avoid court delays). A means test was reintroduced for Crown Court cases in 2010. The Legal Aid, Sentencing and Punishment of Offenders Act 2012 introduced a further financial eligibility threshold in the Crown Court, which will further restrict the availability of legal aid in Crown Court trials. If the defendant is acquitted their contributions will be refunded. There remains a risk that means testing will cause delays in the criminal system, both because evidence of means will need to be obtained and because the number of unrepresented defendants is likely to increase.

A client in receipt of one of the following benefits will automatically receive legal aid. The same applies for those under 18 years old.

- Income Support;
- Income-based Jobseekers Allowance;
- Universal Credit;
- State Pension Guarantee Credit;
- Income-based Employment and Support Allowance.

For others, the means test will look at the client's income, their family circumstances and essential living costs, in order to establish whether they can receive legal aid to cover some or all of their defence costs.

Public defenders

Since May 2001, the Legal Services Commission (now the LAA) directly employs a number of criminal defence lawyers, known as public defenders. Eight regional offices were piloted. The public defenders can provide the same services as lawyers in private practice and have to compete for work.

There was strong opposition to the introduction of public defenders. The explanatory notes to the Access to Justice Act 1999 state that the idea is to provide flexibility, so that employed lawyers can be used if, for example, there is a shortage of suitable private lawyers in remoter areas. The notes point out that using salaried lawyers will also produce better information about the real costs of providing the services. Public defenders provide an element of competition with solicitors in private practice. They are required to follow a code of conduct guaranteeing certain standards of professional behaviour, including duties to avoid discrimination, to protect the interests of those whom they are defending, to avoid conflicts of interest and to maintain confidentiality.

The Labour Government had planned to eventually set up a national network of public defender offices. People suspected of crime would then have had a choice only between these public defenders and lawyers who had a contract to undertake legal aid work, though within that limited range it was intended there would be some choice in all but the most exceptional circumstances. However, following research carried out by Lee Bridges *et al.* entitled *Evaluation of the Public Defender Service in England and Wales* (2007), the Government concluded that four of the public defender offices were not delivering value for money and decided to close these down. There are therefore four offices remaining (Cheltenham, Darlington, Pontypridd and Swansea); however, a job advert released in August 2018 hinted at future expansion of the service to other parts of the UK.

Duty solicitor schemes

Duty solicitors are available at police stations and magistrates' courts and offer free legal advice (see p. 444).

Criminal Defence Direct

A telephone service, known as Criminal Defence Direct (CDD), was established in 2005 to provide free telephone advice primarily to people detained by police for non-imprisonable offences. If people request to see their own solicitor, they will have to pay for this themselves. The Government considers that telephone advice is a modern and appropriate way to assist people detained at police stations who are accused of less serious offences. It is also much cheaper than face-to-face advice. CDD attempts to contact the client within 15 minutes of being informed of the case. Unfortunately, in over half of cases the police fail to pick up the telephone, which causes delay.

The academics Lee Bridges and Ed Cape have published research into this telephone service: *CDS Direct: Flying in the Face of the Evidence* (2008). They have argued that the telephone service is of 'questionable legality', as it could breach the European Convention on Human Rights and does not satisfy the requirements of the Police and Criminal Evidence Act 1984 (PACE). While s. 58 of PACE states that suspects in a police station are entitled to consult a solicitor, the telephone service is not manned by solicitors, but instead by paralegals. Bridges and Cape argue that the right to consult a solicitor has been 'undermined' by the introduction of the telephone service. They conclude that, while the Government has paid lip service to quality, its main aims are to reduce costs, secure convictions and limit access to legal services.

Even before the telephone service was introduced, it was increasingly only a paralegal from the solicitor's office who was attending the police station, not solicitors themselves. The telephone service is saving taxpayers £8 million a year. As increasing numbers of cases are being handled by the police instead of going to court because of the use of cautions, fixed-penalty notices and police bail, the legal controls over what happens in the police station are increasingly important.

15.5 Problems with the legal aid system

15.5.1 Litigants in person

The cuts in legal aid are leading to a large number of court cases with unrepresented litigants (sometimes called litigants in person). This leads to delays and increased court costs, wiping out any savings made by cutting legal aid. In divorce cases, the husband is often wealthier than his ex-wife, so the husband can afford a lawyer while the wife can no longer get a lawyer through legal aid. This risks causing an imbalance in the litigation and the wife may not get a fair hearing.

Figures from the Ministry of Justice family court statistics show that incidences of so-called 'DIY-justice' are rising steeply. It was reported that 37 per cent of divorcing couples who end up in court in disputes over children or finances, do so without a lawyer to represent them (this represents a rise of 21 per cent since the cuts were introduced). It is worth remembering too that there will be many others who just throw in the towel, feeling that without legal aid and legal representation they don't stand a chance. Sir Andrew McFarlane, President of the Family Division of the High Court has commented on the impact within the family courts, stating his concern for parents 'who walk away because they simply cannot face the court process'.

15

PAYING FOR LEGAL SERVICES

Figure 15.1 Proportion of private law disposals by type of legal representation of the parties, January–March 2012 to January–March 2018.

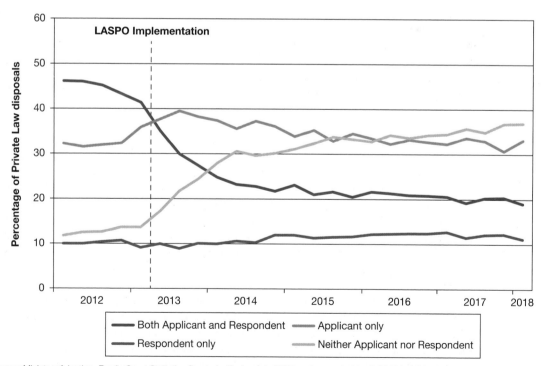

Source: Ministry of Justice, *Family Court Statistics Quarterly, England and Wales, January to March 2018* (published 28 June 2018) available at: https://assets.publishing.service.gov.uk/government/uploads/system/uploads/attachment_data/file/720100/FCSQ_January_to_March_2018.pdf

The Judges Council, which represents judges in England and Wales, has stated that a large increase in litigants in person has serious implications for the administration of justice, at a time when the courts are already having to cope with closures, budget cuts and reductions in staff. The judiciary have become more outspoken on legal aid as the years post-LASPO go by. In 2017 Lady Justice Hale stated cuts had probably been a 'false economy' and Lady Justice Hallett has spoken of the 'huge burden' for her colleagues, lawyers and the litigants themselves. Mr Justice Bodey used the occasion of his retirement to say the following: 'I find it shaming that in this country, with its fine record of justice and fairness, that I should be presiding over such cases.' Back in 2014 of course, Sir James Munby, the president of the family division, used his judgment in *Re D (A Child)* to draw attention to the impact cuts had on vulnerable people.

> What I have to grapple with is the profoundly disturbing fact that the parents do not qualify for legal aid but lack the financial resources to pay for legal representation in circumstances where, to speak plainly, it is unthinkable that they should have to face the local authority's application without proper representation.
>
> . . .
>
> To require them to do so would be unconscionable; it would be unjust; it would involve a breach of their rights under Articles 6 and 8 of the [ECHR]; it would be a denial of justice.
>
> . . .
>
> He [the child] is entitled to a fair trial.

Munby went on to make it plain where the blame lay for the terrible situation:

> Thus far the State has simply washed its hands of the problem, leaving the solution to the problem which the State itself has created – for the State has brought the proceedings but declined all responsibility for ensuring that the parents are able to participate effectively in the proceedings it has brought – to the goodwill, the charity, of the legal profession.

Having confused individuals in court who are unrepresented and mystified by proceedings is difficult for everyone concerned; the litigant-in-person themselves, the judge, as well as the lawyer representing the other party. The Government hoped that parents would seek to use alternative methods for resolving their disputes but this has not been the case. (For a further discussion of litigants in person see p. 658.)

15.5.2 Access to justice

Since 2013, many people may have a legal problem but not be entitled to state-funded legal services. In 2012, some form of legal aid was received by 573,000 people. In 2013, that number went down to 172,000. In terms of civil legal aid, there were in excess of 130,000 legal aid cases every quarter, yet by the summer this had plummeted to 40,000. Even where a person is still entitled to legal aid, they may find it difficult to get access to a lawyer with the right specialism. Because many state-funded legal services can only be obtained from lawyers who have a contract with the LAA, members of the public are finding it increasingly difficult to find a state-funded lawyer with the relevant expertise close to their home.

Part of the problem is that many law firms have in the past done a small amount of legal aid work alongside their privately funded work. Such firms have not wanted to bid for block contracts because they have not wanted to increase the amount of comparatively poorly paid state-funded work they take on. There are now only 5,000 solicitor firms offering state-funded legal services, compared with 11,000 in 1998. One result, many fear, will be the creation of a two-tier legal profession, with one set of firms doing poorly paid state-funded work and another doing exclusively private work.

A study undertaken by the Citizens Advice Bureau (2004a) has reinforced this picture of growing gaps in the supply of state-funded legal services, what it calls 'advice deserts'. Their survey found that people were often having to travel up to 50 miles to find a lawyer. The Minister for Justice commented in 2009:

> I think access is at risk of being confused with physical proximity. People have grown used to a far wider range of telephone and internet-based services – and demand more rapid and convenient access to services, but not necessarily an office on the street corner.

The situation has worsened significantly since then: The Joint Parliamentary Committee on Human Rights (composed of MPs and peers) published their 'Enforcing Human Rights' report in July 2018 and stated that these vast legal aid deserts in the UK meant human rights were often 'unenforceable'. The Committee noted they had 'grave concerns for access to justice, the rule of law and enforcement of human rights in the UK'. They called for urgent review of both the financial eligibility for legal aid and the exceptional case funding scheme.

The Law Society carried out their own review (*Access Denied? LASPO four years on* (June 2017)) around the impact of legal aid changes under LASPO, concluding the following:

- Legal aid is no longer available for many of those who need it.
- Those eligible for legal aid find it hard to access it.
- Wide gaps in provision are not being addressed.
- LASPO has had a wider and detrimental impact on the state and society.

State funding is not available for legal representation at most tribunals. In *R (on the application of Unison)* v *Lord Chancellor* (2017) it was held by the Supreme Court that fees were charged to bring a case to the Employment Tribunal/Employment Appeal Tribunal which had the effect of preventing access to justice. The judgment of Lord Reed outlined that it was not enough to provide independent courts for the rule of law to be upheld; the people had to have meaningful access to them.

> Courts exist in order to ensure that the laws made by parliament, and the common law created by the courts themselves, are applied and enforced. That role includes ensuring that the executive branch of government carries out its functions in accordance with the law. In order for the courts to perform that role, people must in principle have unimpeded access to them. Without such access, laws are liable to become a dead letter, the work done by parliament may be rendered nugatory, and the democratic election of members of parliament may become a meaningless charade. That is why the courts do not merely provide a public service like any other.

15.5.3 Public defenders

The legal profession has fiercely opposed the idea of the state employing its own lawyers to do criminal defence work. Both the Bar Council and the Criminal Law Solicitors Association have expressed concern that lawyers who are wholly dependent on the state for their income cannot be sufficiently independent to defend properly people suspected of crime – people who, by definition, are on the opposite side to the state. Interviewed by *The Lawyer* newspaper in December 1998, the Bar Council chairperson pointed to the example of the US, where public defenders have been used for some years, arguing that, as a result, the justice system there has become geared towards administrative convenience and cost-cutting, leading to an emphasis on plea bargaining and uncontested cases.

The experience of foreign jurisdictions such as the US and Canada shows that any system of public defenders must be properly funded and staffed if it is to retain the confidence of providers, users and the courts. Unfortunately, they are frequently underfunded in practice, relying as a result on inexperienced lawyers with excessive caseloads and who are not respected by their clients, opponents or the court.

Research carried out by Cyrus Tata *et al.* (2004) has evaluated the success of the Public Defence Solicitors Office in Scotland in its first three years. The research compared the performance of the public defenders with that of solicitors in private practice receiving state funding. The conclusions of this research were mixed. It found that public defender clients pleaded guilty earlier than clients of solicitors in private practice. But it found no evidence to suggest that public defenders put explicit pressure on clients to plead guilty. Instead, the clients criticised the public defenders for being too neutral and too willing to go along with whatever the client decided. The change in economic incentives involved in receiving a salary rather than a legal aid payment appeared to produce a change in behaviour, because solicitors in private practice earn very little if a client immediately pleads guilty, so ending the case, compared to where there is a late guilty plea. Public defender clients were more likely to be convicted. Representation by a public defender increased the chances of a client being convicted from around 83 per cent to 88 per cent. This was primarily because clients of private solicitors were more likely to plead late, allowing for a greater chance in the meantime for the case against them to be dropped by the prosecution, for example, because a witness fails to attend the trial. There was no difference between the sentences handed down.

The levels of trust and satisfaction expressed by public defender clients who had not volunteered to use the service, but been obliged to do so, were consistently lower than those expressed by clients using private practitioners. They were less likely to say that their solicitor had done 'a very good job' in listening to what they had to say; telling them what was happening; being there when they wanted them; or having enough time for them. They were also less likely to agree strongly that the solicitor had told the court their side of the story or treated them as though they mattered. Part of the problem appears to have been that clients resented not being able to choose their solicitor, and this choice has now been reinstated. Those who had chosen to use the public defender service were more positive about the service. However, they were still significantly less likely than private clients to agree strongly that their lawyer had told the court their side of the story or had treated them as if they mattered, rather than as 'a job to be done'. Public defenders tended to be seen as more 'business-like' and less personally committed than private solicitors. Public defender clients were less likely to say they would use the service again compared to clients of private solicitors. The research concluded:

> From a managerial perspective, the fact that public defenders resolved cases at an earlier stage has advantages. It has the potential to save legal aid costs and also reduce court and prosecution costs, inconveniencing fewer witnesses. Clients were spared the wait and worry of repeated court [hearings] and were less likely to be held in detention pending the resolution of their case.

At the moment, surprisingly, the public defender service is proving more expensive than private solicitors. The average cost of a case handled by the public defender service is over £800, compared with £506 for private practice. The Legal Aid Practitioners Group has suggested this is because the taxpayer has to pay the salary of public defenders even if they have failed to attract clients, while private solicitors are only paid for the work they do. A job advert from the Ministry of Justice in 2014 prompted criticism after offering salaries between £46,036 and £125,000 with extra benefits for lawyers for the public defender service. In the context of severe fee cuts for the criminal bar and decimation of legal aid support, this was seen as an attempt by the Government to fix their problem without engaging effectively with the criminal bar. Criminal barrister and peer, Lord Carlile, said at the time: 'I'm shocked by the way the government is behaving. It is proposing to pay salaries that far exceed the amount paid in the legal aid sector, bearing in mind the additional benefits, such as paid holidays, secretaries, pensions and paid sick leave.' The advert followed the appointment of two QCs to the public defender service (PDS). Desmond Hudson (then Law Society chief executive) added his voice to the disquiet: 'Evidence shows that solicitors in private practice offer substantially better value for money than solicitor services delivered through the PDS. We continue to make the case to the MoJ that the most effective way to safeguard the future of high quality criminal defence is by facilitating a diverse supplier base and a market underpinned by client choice.'

15.5.4 Small businesses

Research has been carried out at the Institute of Advanced Legal Studies into the impact of the removal of legal aid for business disputes by the Access to Justice Act 1999: *Breaking the Code: The Impact of Legal Aid Reforms on General Civil Litigation* (Goriely and Gysta, 2001). The removal of state funding in this area has attracted little attention, which has led the researchers to comment:

> The problem with any discussion of 'businessmen' is that the phrase is laden with overtones. It conjures up an image of a man in a 'business suit', possibly flying 'business class' to a 'business meeting'.

While this is an accurate picture of some business people, it is far from accurate for many others. The Labour Government justified excluding business disputes from state funding on the basis that such cases did not lead to social exclusion and, according to the Government, 'it is not thought justified to spend public money helping businessmen, who fail to insure against the risk of facing legal costs'.

In fact, the research has found that the withdrawal of state funding for business disputes is leaving low-paid workers, such as self-employed cleaners and taxi drivers, with no means of redress if their businesses run into legal difficulties. The researchers found that '[b]usiness failure is a fast track to social exclusion'. When small businesses fail, the impact on a person's life can be enormous. People often end up losing 'their homes, their savings, their marriages, their health and their self-esteem'. Legal expenses insurance is often too expensive and specifically excludes the kinds of difficulties that failing small businesses face. Many policies have clearly been developed for businesses with million-pound turnovers, not for self-employed builders and taxi drivers.

15.5.5 Lack of independence from Government

State-funded work is likely to become the most important source of income for those firms which hold contracts – in some cases, even the only source of income. There are therefore concerns that the threat of losing their contract if they make themselves unpopular with the

Government might lead firms to shy away from taking on cases that challenge Government action, or might in any other way embarrass or annoy the Government.

15.5.6 Poorer standards of work

In 2001 the Consumers' Association undertook research into the experiences of people seeking state-funded civil legal aid. The research consisted of in-depth interviews of people who had sought help from the service, particularly those from vulnerable groups in society. It found that community centres and law centres provided the best help and advice, but many people felt the legal system gave them a second-rate service. The research criticised the apparent lack of commitment and poor communication of some solicitors. There were still not enough solicitors and advisers specialising in areas like social security, housing, disability discrimination, employment and immigration law. People with disabilities complained of poor physical access to buildings.

Some research has been carried out into the impact of different funding arrangements on the quality of the provision of legal services (*Quality and Cost: Final Report on the Contracting of Civil, Non-family Advice and Assistance Pilot* (2001)). A study was undertaken over two years of 80,000 cases handled by 43 not-for-profit agencies and 100 solicitors' firms. The solicitors' firms were randomly allocated to one of three payment groups: those who continued to be paid as under the old legal aid system; those paid a fixed sum and left to determine how many cases it was reasonable for them to do for the money; and those paid a fixed sum and given a specific number of cases which had to be undertaken. The research concluded that where the payment system gave firms an incentive to do work cheaply, the quality of work suffered. Thus firms in the third group performed worst on most indicators, with 20 per cent of the contracted advisers doing poor quality work. Group 2, in general, performed better than Group 1.

In his *Review of the Criminal Courts* (2001), Sir Robin Auld recommended that changes should be made to the arrangements for the payment of defence lawyers so that they are rewarded for carrying out adequate case preparation.

15.5.7 The cost of criminal cases

Criminal legal aid was becoming increasingly expensive, which is what prompted the coalition Government to pass the Legal Aid, Sentencing and Punishment of Offenders Act 2012 and seek to cut £220 million from the criminal legal aid budget. Research on the subject has been carried out by Professors Richard Moorhead and Ed Cape, *Demand Induced Supply? Identifying Cost Drivers in Criminal Defence Work* (2005). The study concluded that much of the increase in the cost of criminal legal aid was the result of endless changes to the system made by Government. This conclusion is ironic, considering that the 2012 Act has introduced further substantive changes to the system of legal aid in order to reduce costs.

In 2002, 1 per cent of criminal cases consumed 49 per cent of the budget for criminal legal aid. Following the publication of a consultation paper, *Delivering Value for Money in the Criminal Defence Service* (Lord Chancellor's Department, 2003), the Government tried to reduce the cost of these cases. Lawyers working on cases lasting more than five weeks, or costing more than £150,000, had to negotiate contracts for payment at each stage of the case.

In 2005, criminal barristers, considering themselves underpaid for their work, effectively took strike action (they could not officially strike because they were self-employed and not members of a trade union). Fixed fees for Crown Court trials lasting up to 10 days were introduced in 1997, but the remuneration for these cases has not been increased since they came into force. In a controversial move, the 2012 Act reduced fees by 17.5 per cent. It has been estimated that junior criminal barristers relying on legal aid work, with up to five years' experience, are earning only between £15,000 and £30,000 a year. As a result of these cuts, in 2013, more than 1,000 barristers and solicitors took unofficial strike action twice, disrupting court proceedings across England and Wales. In March 2014, further unofficial strike action was avoided when criminal barristers reached a deal with the Ministry of Justice to suspend further criminal legal aid budget cuts until after the general election in May 2015. A cut of 8.75 per cent to fees was implemented in March 2014.

15

PAYING FOR LEGAL SERVICES

The Bigger Picture: The demise of the criminal bar?

The Law Society and the Criminal Bar Association have been pitted against the Ministry of Justice for much of 2017 and 2018. A month-long strike of criminal barristers resulted in the government offering to invest an additional £15 million on fees. However, consultation due to take place on how this should be allocated was fraught with ill-feeling, with the solicitor advocates feeling excluded and the Criminal Bar Association citing continued postponement by the Ministry of Justice.

Solicitors have also been heavily impacted by reforms to the payment scheme for criminal defence solicitors, reducing legal aid payments significantly for complex cases. The Law Society president reports:

> Criminal duty solicitors offer a vital public service, but cuts and the fact they have had no pay rises for more than 20 years are driving more and more of them away from criminal defence work.

In a judicial review action brought by the organisation, the High Court ruled this attempt to cut fees was unlawful. It was noted that a consultation carried out on the proposals revealed they were opposed by a massive 97 per cent of participants, and yet the Government went ahead regardless. Fees were cut in relation to evidence work; with solicitors only being paid for reading the first 6,000 pages of evidence, rather than 10,000 as it had been previously.

A Commons Justice Committee report into criminal legal aid highlighted the starkness of the situation, with chairman Bob Neill stating:

> In criminal cases, there is a common law right to legal advice, and a right to legal representation under the ECHR.
>
> There is compelling evidence of the fragility of the Criminal Bar and criminal defence solicitors' firms, which places these rights at risk – a risk that can no longer be ignored. We heard first-hand the deep unhappiness among barristers about their situation and the future of the criminal justice system as a whole.
>
> The Government cannot kick these problems down the road any longer and they must carry out comprehensive reviews to develop policies that are sustainable in the long term.
>
> An effective criminal justice system is one of the pillars on which the rule of law is built.
>
> Underfunding of the criminal justice system in England and Wales threatens its effectiveness, tarnishing the reputation of our justice system as a whole, and undermining the rule of law.

The Justice Committee have called on the Government to commission an independent review to find ways to avert the current crisis.

15.5.8 Reliance on private practice

When the legal aid system was first set up, the Government had a choice between using the existing private practice structures or setting up a totally separate system of lawyers, who would be paid salaries from public funds (as doctors are in the NHS), rather than being paid on a case-by-case basis. They chose to give legal aid work to lawyers in private practice. This continues to be the case for state funding, with the sole exception of the criminal defenders. Kate Markus, writing in *The Critical Lawyer's Handbook* (1992), argues that this causes five main problems. First, rather than responding to need, state-funded practitioners in private practice are ruled by the requirements of running a business in a highly competitive marketplace. Private practitioners have to make a profit, even where they are paid by the state, and therefore often feel that they must limit the time they spend on state-funded cases. This problem severely limits the services they can offer to their clients. It is also the reason why so many lawyers have refused to do state-funded work which, given the funding problems, has never been able to compete with privately paid work in terms of the salaries paid.

Secondly, private solicitors' practices are very much geared towards legal problems concerning money and property, which means that, as far as general high street solicitors are concerned, their expertise is often not developed in those areas affecting the poorer client.

The third problem, which we have mentioned before, is that solicitors in private practice may be seen as intimidating by the majority of poorer clients. They are then put off bringing their problems to them, especially in areas where they are not sure whether it is appropriate to involve a lawyer.

The fourth issue Markus highlights is that private practice is geared largely to litigation (bringing cases to court), which is not always the best solution to the kind of problems facing the poorer members of society. Let us say, for example, that a local council is failing to fulfil its obligations to tenants, with the result that many of them are living in unacceptable housing. Each affected family could take the council to court, but that would be expensive and time-consuming, and only solve the problem for those families who actually did so. But with access to good legal advice on their rights, the tenants could get together and put pressure on the council themselves, potentially solving a problem affecting lots of people in one action, and much more cheaply. Law centres (see p. 353) often work this way, but the working practices of private practitioners, and the case-by-case way in which legal aid was funded, made it impossible for them to do much, if any, of this kind of work.

Finally, Markus makes the point that any system which seeks to make justice truly accessible has to address the problem of widespread ignorance of legal rights and how to assert them; after all, if a person with a legal problem is unaware there might be a legal right which could solve it, he or she will not even think of getting legal help in the first place. That means educating people about their rights, and private practice, where every task a lawyer does has to be paid for, is simply not set up to do that kind of work.

15.5.9 Unfair trials

Where legal aid is refused, a subsequent trial may prove to be unfair if one party is unrepresented by a lawyer as a result, and the other party benefited from legal representation. This can amount to a breach of Art. 6 of the European Convention, which guarantees the right to a fair trial.

Key case

The problem of unrepresented defendants was highlighted by the case which has come to be known as the McLibel Two (***Steel v United Kingdom*** (2005)). The defendants were two environmental campaigners who had distributed leaflets outside McDonald's restaurants. These leaflets criticised the nutritional content of the food sold in the restaurants. McDonald's sued the two defendants for defamation. The defendants were refused legal aid because it is not generally available for defamation cases. They therefore represented themselves throughout the proceedings, with only limited help from some sympathetic lawyers who provided a small amount of assistance for free. McDonald's were represented by a team of specialist lawyers. The libel trial lasted for 313 days and was the longest civil action in English legal history. The defendants lost the case and were ordered to pay £60,000 in damages (later reduced to £40,000 on appeal). They challenged the fairness of the UK proceedings in the European Court of Human Rights. That challenge was successful. The European Court held that the McLibel Two had not had a fair trial, in breach of Art. 6 of the European Convention on Human Rights, and there had been a breach of their right to freedom of expression under Art. 10 of the Convention.

Legal principle

Where state-funded legal representation is unavailable to a private individual in legal proceedings, there may sometimes be a breach of the European Convention guaranteeing the right to a fair trial and freedom of expression.

15.6 Not-for-profit agencies

There are a number of non-profit-making agencies which give legal advice and sometimes representation, and initiatives by the legal profession and other commercial organisations also address the issue of access to justice.

15.6.1 Law centres

Law centres traditionally offer a free, non-means-tested service to people who live or work in their area. Following the legal aid cuts, some law centres are charging small fees for some of their services. They aim to be accessible to anyone who needs legal help, and in order to achieve this they usually operate from ground floor, high street premises, stay open beyond office hours, employ a high proportion of lay people as well as lawyers and generally encourage a more relaxed atmosphere than that found in most private solicitors' offices. Most law centres are run by a management committee drawn from the local area, so that they have direct links with the community.

The first law centres were established in 1969 and today there are 43 of them in England, Wales and Northern Ireland. The Law Society allowed them to advertise (before the restriction on advertising was lifted for solicitors in general) in exchange for the centres not undertaking certain areas of work which were the mainstay of the average high street solicitor – small personal injury cases, wills and conveyancing. Their main areas of work are housing, welfare, immigration and employment.

Law centres are funded by a mixture of grants from central and local government, legal aid and donations from large local private firms. This method of funding means they do not have to work on a case-by-case basis but can allocate funding according to community priorities.

Because they do not depend purely on case-by-case funding, law centres have developed innovative ways of solving legal problems. As well as dealing with individual cases, they run campaigns designed to make local people aware of their legal rights, act as a pressure group on local issues such as bad housing, and take action where appropriate on behalf of groups as well as individuals. The reasoning behind this approach is that resources and time are better used tackling problems as a whole, rather than aspects of those problems as they appear case by case. For example, if a council has failed to replace lead piping or asbestos in its council houses, it would seem more efficient to approach the council about all the properties rather than take out individual cases for each tenant as they become aware that they have a problem.

Law centres also provide valuable services in areas not covered by the statutory schemes, such as inquests, and several have set up duty solicitor schemes to deal with housing cases in the County Court and help prevent evictions. They may offer a 24-hour, general emergency service.

Most law centres face long-term problems with funding; some have been forced to close due to a lack of money and others go through periodic struggles for survival. The cuts to legal aid have reduced by 60 per cent the income that law centres receive from legal aid funding. This, in turn, has led to some closures. For example, the Legal Aid, Sentencing and Punishment of Offenders Act 2012 removed most of social welfare law from the legal aid scheme.

15.6.2 Citizens Advice

Citizens Advice (CA) offer their services across the country, offering free advice and help with a whole range of problems, though the most common areas currently are social security and debt. They are largely staffed by trained volunteers, who can become expert in the areas they most frequently deal with. Where professional legal help is required, some CA centres employ solicitors, some have regular help from solicitor volunteers and others refer individuals to local solicitors who undertake state-funded work. The CA is a network of 316 independent charities and the UK's largest advice provider.

One of their major advantages is a very high level of public awareness – because they are frequently mentioned in the press and have easily recognisable high street offices, most people know where they are and what they do.

Like law centres, they have come under considerable financial pressure in recent years, with the result that many can only open for a very limited number of hours a week.

The Bigger Picture: Demand, supply and value for money

Increase in demand is seen across the not-for-profit legal advice sector. The Personal Support Unit are a charity based within court buildings who provide free support in the civil and family courts. They report a 520% increase in those seeking their help since 2011.

More startling statistics, in relation to the quantity of not-for-profit legal advice centres, emerged in the Bach Commission Report (mentioned later in this chapter); they highlight Ministry of Justice research which showed that there was a drop in the total number of centres from 3,226 in 2005 to just 1,462 in 2015. As legal aid was withdrawn and demand went up, centres were struggling to meet demand. More than half of those who responded to the MoJ survey stated they had client groups they were unable to help, either through 'lack of resources, expertise or because they fell outside the centre's remit'.

The Bach Commission report also made strong arguments for the benefit of early legal help in order to stem problems further down the line. A Citizens Advice report *Modelling our value to society in 2015/16* included some very persuasive figures: for every £1 invested in Citizens Advice, there are £1.52 savings to the government, £8.08 in wider economic and social benefits and almost £11 value to the clients. Essentially spending that £1, pays dividends in the long run.

15.6.3 Alternative sources of legal help

Some lawyers will offer their services for free to vulnerable members of society. This is traditionally known as 'pro bono' work. Some university law faculties run 'law clinics', where students, supervised by their tutors, give free help and advice to members of the public.

Some local authorities run money, welfare, consumer and housing advice centres to provide both advice and a mechanism for dealing with complaints, while charities such as Shelter, the Child Poverty Action Group and MIND often offer legal help in their specialist areas. Other organisations, such as trade unions, motoring organisations (including the AA and RAC) and the Consumers' Association give free or inexpensive legal help to their members.

There are a growing number of internet sites giving basic legal advice for free, but the websites need to be improved so that they do not just provide information, but help take legal service users through the legal process: this is the approach taken in Holland which is the world leader in publicly funded advice on the web. Some magazines publish legal advice telephone lines, which charge a premium rate for readers to phone and get one-to-one legal advice from qualified solicitors. It is also possible to insure against legal expenses, either as a stand-alone policy, or more usually, as part of household, credit card or motor insurance.

As we saw earlier, cost is not the only cause of unmet legal needs; a reluctance among many ordinary people to bring problems to lawyers is also recognised. In recent years the profession has taken steps to address the issue, including the use of advertising and public relations campaigns. Many high street firms now advertise their services locally, while some of the firms involved in suing cigarette manufacturers for illnesses caused by smoking attracted potential clients by advertising specifically for people with smoking-related diseases.

15.7 Conditional fee agreements

In 1990 the Courts and Legal Services Act (CLSA) made provision for the introduction of conditional fee agreements, sometimes known as 'no win, no fee' agreements. Under this arrangement, solicitors can contract to take no fee or a reduced fee from their client if they lose, and raise their fee by an agreed percentage if they win, up to a maximum of double the usual fee. The solicitor calculates the extra fee (usually called the 'uplift' or 'success fee') on the basis of the size of the risk involved – if the client seems very likely to win, the uplift should be lower than in a case where the outcome is more difficult to predict. A 1997 report by the Policy Studies Institute found that the average uplift was 43 per cent. The author of the study, Stella Yarrow, commented that the number of cases assessed as having a low chance of success was surprisingly large, suggesting that solicitors might be underestimating the chances of winning, in order to increase the uplift. A party using a conditional fee agreement will sometimes take out insurance to cover the risk of losing the case and having to pay the other side's costs. This is known as after the event insurance (ATE insurance) because it is taken out after the legal dispute arises. The Access to Justice Act 1999 made conditional fee agreements available for all cases apart from medical negligence.

There is no means test to determine whether a person is entitled to bring litigation on the basis of a conditional fee agreement, though their use by a wealthy individual has been criticised by the European Court of Human Rights. The 'supermodel' Naomi Campbell brought legal proceedings against the publishers of the *Daily Mirror*, claiming that the newspaper had breached her right to privacy because it had published pictures of her leaving a support group for recovering drug users. Her claim was rejected by the Court of Appeal and she proceeded to appeal to the House of Lords. To pay for this appeal she reached a conditional fee agreement with her solicitors and her barrister. Her appeal to the House of Lords was successful and the publishing company was ordered to pay her £3,500 in damages and her costs. Her costs were £1,086,295.47 in total! The size of the bill for the appeal to the House of Lords was particularly high because the conditional fee agreement allowed for a success fee of 95 per cent for her solicitor and 100 per cent for her barrister. The publishers contested these costs, arguing that the success fee was so disproportionate that it infringed their rights to free speech under Art. 10 of the European Convention on Human Rights. It argued that, as Naomi Campbell was a rich celebrity, she could have afforded to fund her litigation without a conditional fee agreement, while the conditional fee agreement scheme was intended to help people who could not otherwise afford to sue. The House of Lords rejected this argument: conditional fee agreements were not means tested, and the publishers had to pay all the costs. The publisher took the case to the European Court of Human Rights. It ruled in *MGN Ltd* v *UK* (2011) that the legal costs order under the conditional fee agreement was disproportionate and amounted to a breach of the publisher's right to freedom of expression. Naomi Campbell was wealthy and did not need to use such an agreement to bring the litigation. The court did not overturn the House of Lords' ruling that, on the facts, there had been a breach of confidentiality.

There have been problems with conditional fee agreements. There has been concern that conditional fees have inflated costs to such a degree that, in many cases, it is simply cheaper to buy off a claim through settling it, than fighting the claim, even where the claim is weak. The cost of after the event insurance has increased considerably, and some clients are finding it difficult to get such insurance. There has been a lot of litigation over paying these extra costs by the losing party (known as satellite litigation because it is a spin-off from the main litigation). There may also be pressure to settle from insurance companies, some of whom have been known to threaten to withdraw their cover if a client refuses to accept an offer of settlement that the insurance company considers reasonable. Clearly the insurance company's primary interest will be to avoid having to pay out, so it is not difficult to see that their idea of a reasonable settlement might be very different from the client's – or from what the client could expect to get if the case continued.

Some lawyers are not working on a genuine 'no win, no fee' basis, but rather they are agreeing to take a low fee if the case is lost but will charge a success fee if it is won. This is difficult to justify: the risk being run by the lawyer is minimal since a fee will still be payable if the case is lost. Professor Richard Moorhead (2011) has produced some fairly damning research showing the public are being misled when they are encouraged to sign up to a 'no win, no fee' agreement because actually they will find they have to pay their lawyer even if they lose their case. This was because the lawyers would charge the clients for what were described as 'disbursements' no matter the outcome of the case, as this was billed for separately from the percentage success fee. When the client was told they would have to pay 'disbursements', they did not understand this bit of legal jargon. It basically means they will have to pay the lawyer's expenses, which could include such things as court fees, photocopying and a barrister's fee. Even VAT was frequently added onto the percentage success fee, and as VAT is 20 per cent this is a significant increase in the lawyer's bill. Professor Moorhead recommends regulations should require the agreed percentage fee to include VAT and all other costs.

The Citizens Advice Bureau issued a report entitled *No Win, No Fee, No Chance* (2004b). This also expressed concern that consumers were being misled by the term 'no win, no fee'. Often consumers find the system costs them more than they gain. Consumers are subjected to aggressive and high-pressured sales tactics from unqualified employees of claims management companies. These companies receive a fee from solicitors for passing them a case. Consumers can be subjected to inappropriate marketing tactics; for example, accident victims have been approached in hospital. They are not informed clearly of the financial risks the legal proceedings will involve, and are misled into believing the system will genuinely be 'no win, no fee' when they might find they have to pay the lawyer's expenses, for example.

In *Coventry v Lawrence (No. 2)* (2014) the Supreme Court suggested costs arrangements for conditional fee agreements might breach a defendant's right to a fair trial under Art. 6 of the European Convention on Human Rights. This is because defendants who lose their case have to pay the lawyer's success fee and after the event insurance premiums of the winning party which can be excessively costly. In *Coventry v Lawrence (No. 2)* homeowners had won a claim for nuisance against a small business operating a noisy speedway racing track near their home. The claim was worth £74,000, but the costs order against the business was £640,000.

Following the recommendations by Lord Justice Jackson and the subsequent Legal Aid, Sentencing and Punishment of Offenders Act 2012, conditional fee agreements will be used less often. The success fee for conditional fee agreements is no longer recoverable from the losing party. If a party chooses to enter into a conditional fee agreement with their solicitor, they will have to pay the fee uplift themselves, even if they win their case. Tighter limits on the success fees that can be charged by lawyers have been imposed because there were suggestions that lawyers were abusing the system to increase their earnings. For personal injury cases (excluding asbestos cases), the success fee is capped at 25 per cent. For all other cases, the success fee can be 100 per cent of the lawyer's usual fee. To partially offset the fees claimants now face, there was an uplift in the amount of compensation received of 10 per cent. There was a warning however issued to lawyers who habitually charge 100 per cent success fees without a risk assessment in *A and M v Royal Mail Group* (2015), particularly when the likelihood of success is 'virtually certain'.

15

PAYING FOR LEGAL SERVICES

The Bigger Picture: The biggest costs case in legal history

A large amount of satellite litigation has arisen involving disputes over the legal costs of the case. In other words, once the main case has finished, the parties sometimes start arguing over how much legal costs the losing party should have to pay and this argument ends up back in court. In *Motto v Trafigura* (2011) a firm of solicitors brought a claim on behalf of 30,000 Africans who claimed they had suffered health problems when a contractor of the oil giant Trafigura had illegally dumped a shipload of toxic waste into the sea near the capital city of Ivory Coast, Abidjan. The claim was successful and damages of £30 million were awarded, which meant that each claimant received about £1,000 in compensation. Their lawyers had worked under a conditional fee agreement and were charging a 100 per cent success fee which took their bill to over £100 million. The defendants challenged this bill and the court decided that the success fee should have been 58 per cent because, as the claim progressed, it became clear there was a good chance of success. The bill was therefore reduced by 40 per cent. This is the biggest costs case in legal history.

The 2012 Act is now allowing contingency agreements to be used (discussed next), which are intended to replace conditional fee agreements.

15.8 Contingency fees

While a conditional fee agreement allows the lawyer to be paid an increased fee if the action is successful, under a contingency fee agreement, lawyers receive a share of the successful claimant's award of damages. The name 'contingency fee' comes from the fact that payment of the lawyer is contingent on the claim succeeding and an award of damages being paid. Before 2012, contingency fees were generally unlawful. They were banned from being used for litigation in the High Court and County Court, though they could be used in Employment Tribunals and were commonly used in America.

Following concern over increasing legal costs and disputes over costs, the president of the civil courts, known as the Master of the Rolls, asked another judge, Lord Justice Jackson, to carry out an independent review of civil litigation costs. His report was published in 2010. He recommended the introduction of contingency fees for litigation and the coalition Government accepted this recommendation. The Legal Aid, Sentencing and Punishment of Offenders Act 2012 now allows lawyers to enter into contingency fee agreements, known as damages-based agreements (DBAs), with their clients. Under the 2012 Act, lawyers are allowed to receive up to 25 per cent of the award of damages as legal fees for personal injury cases, 35 per cent for employment cases and 50 per cent for all other cases (including commercial cases).

Under the traditional cost-shifting rule, the loser pays the winner's costs. This has now been replaced by the qualified one-way cost-shifting rule (QOCS). Under this, if defendants lose, they pay the claimants' costs, but if the claimants lose, each side bears their own costs. Thus, defendants no longer have the right to recover their costs from unsuccessful claimants. While this might appear unfair to defendants, it means that after the event insurance is often no longer required. Claimants are now responsible for paying the success fee as this is no longer recoverable from the unsuccessful defendant, but will be paid out of the winner's award of damages. Damages have been increased by 10 per cent to take into account this change.

15.8.1 Advantages of contingency fees

Reduce satellite litigation

The hope is that the introduction of contingency fees will eliminate much of the satellite litigation over costs associated with conditional fee cases. Contingency fees are intended to provide a cleaner and less complicated model of litigation than their predecessors. When claimants enter into a conditional fee agreement they are not concerned about the amount of the success fee because they will not themselves ever have to pay it; only the defendant who loses will have to pay this. Such a situation can be compared to going shopping with someone else's credit card. As a result lawyers have been able to make disproportionate profits under conditional fee agreements, which the public end up paying for indirectly through higher insurance premiums. For contingency fees, the successful party will often have to pay their lawyers' fees and will therefore be keen to keep their lawyers' costs down.

No cost to the state

Contingency fees (and conditional fee agreements) cost the state nothing – the costs are entirely borne by the solicitor or the losing party, depending on the outcome.

Wider access to justice

Contingency fee agreements are available where legal aid is not. These agreements allow many people to bring or defend cases who would not have been eligible for state funding and who could not previously have afforded to bring cases at their own expense. As long as they can persuade a solicitor that the case is worth the risk, anyone can bring or defend a case for damages.

Contingency fees have always been allowed in Employment Tribunals and they do not appear to have given rise to major problems. Research by Professor Moorhead (Moorhead and Cumming, 2008) on contingency fees in tribunals found they provide a very slight improvement in access to justice. There was no evidence they led to an increase in weak tribunal claims, or that the percentage fees charged were excessive. Moorhead suggested there needed to be greater openness in the way lawyers' fees were calculated and there was some evidence that the contingency fee arrangements increased the pressure to settle, leading to cases being compromised inappropriately.

On the other hand, research carried out for the Civil Justice Council by Professor Moorhead and Senior Costs Judge Peter Hurst (2008) did find there was a risk that contingency fees could narrow access to justice, particularly for low-value cases, risky cases and cases that are not seeking a financial remedy, as these are less likely to be brought under a contingency fee arrangement. The research found there was no evidence that in the US contingency fees discouraged the parties from reaching an out-of-court settlement or that they led to high rates of litigation, frivolous claims or a litigation culture. There was no evidence the use of contingency fees had led to excessive awards of damages to take into account the lawyers' fees that needed to be deducted.

Performance incentives

Supporters claim that contingency fees encourage solicitors to perform better, since they have a financial interest in winning cases funded this way.

15.8.2 Disadvantages of contingency fee agreements

Low take-up rate

Contingency fees have not proved popular with lawyers. The cap on the percentage of damages that can be taken as the lawyer's fees is considered too small. Fewer low-value cases are being brought, such as low-value public liability cases (often involving trips and slips) because the damages are too small to justify bringing on the basis of a contingency fee. Thus, in 2014, the number of cases started in the road traffic portal dropped by 10 per cent on the previous year. Some lawyers have suggested that hybrid contingency fees should be introduced where clients could be charged some upfront fees for their work as well as having to pay the lawyers a percentage of their damages if their litigation was successful. This had been possible for conditional fee agreements. However, the Ministry of Justice has rejected this suggestion as it is concerned such arrangements could encourage a litigation culture.

Lawyers are unwilling to take cases which are genuinely 'no win, no fee' because of the risk of an all or nothing approach. This raises real problems for access to justice: because legal aid has been cut, conditional fee agreements are no longer attractive to clients and contingency fees are not attractive to lawyers.

Lawyer's financial interests

A criticism of contingency fees is that they give the lawyer a direct personal interest in the level of damages and it has been suggested this is partly responsible for the soaring levels of damages seen in American courts. Critics of contingency fees have argued they could have unintended consequences, they could significantly reduce access to justice and increase costs for those who do go to court. A one-way costs-shifting rule may encourage the pursuit of claims with no merit and claimants may not be motivated to settle their claims. For example, the one-way costs-shifting rule could open the floodgates to speculative litigation against the NHS, with the NHS forced to settle cases to reduce their legal costs and thereby indirectly give rise to no-fault compensation.

In reality, most funding methods create a tension between the interests of the lawyer and the interests of the client. Even where a private client is directly paying the lawyer under the traditional payment arrangements, there is a conflict between the claimant who wishes to recover the largest amount of damages as quickly and cheaply as possible, and the lawyer who has no direct interest in the damages recovered but a clear interest in maximising the level of costs incurred.

Uncertain cases

Solicitors will only want to take on cases under contingency fee agreements where there is a very high chance of winning. They will not want to take on cases which have enormous public importance, but which need large amounts of work, are difficult to win, and may attract relatively low levels of damages even if successful. These include some types of action against the police and Government, such as complaints by prisoners about their treatment.

15.9 Third party funding

Third party funding is an umbrella label used to describe investment in litigation by third parties unconnected with the case. This means lawyers may not be paid by their client's money, but with someone else's money. These third parties are funding the litigation as an investment on the basis they will receive a share of the damages awarded by the court if the claim is successful, which will be greater than the original sum invested in the case. In the past, the courts treated contracts for third party funding as illegal. They considered them to be against the interests of justice because, for example, they might encourage frivolous litigation or the funders might push the parties to settle early to secure their profit. However, in recent times the courts are allowing third party investment: a third party can fund another party's litigation as long as they simply provide the funding and do not interfere with the litigation itself. Thus, in **Arkin v Borchard Lines** (2005) the Court of Appeal gave tacit approval for litigation funding, though pointing out that such a funder should also be liable to the risk of paying the other side's costs (proportionate to the amount of funding) if the case was unsuccessful. In practice, to date, third party investors have been companies which have only been interested in funding commercial litigation worth over £100,000.

A voluntary code of conduct has been developed for third party litigation to try to make sure those involved behave ethically.

Litigation funding was given a boost in the Court of Appeal in *Excalibur Ventures* v *Psari Holdings* (2016) when Tomlinson J described it as 'an accepted and judicially sanctioned activity perceived to be in the public interest'. Here, third party funders were held to be jointly and severally liable for the defendants' costs on an indemnity basis, after unsuccessful litigation. Distinction was drawn between professional funders and those who were inexperienced and ill-equipped for assessing the merits of the case.

There are far more incidences of third party funding in the commercial sector than for public interest litigation.

15.9.1 Crowdfunding

The erosion of legal aid and increased recognition of the innovations possible when using technology have led to a new way of funding legal action: crowdfunding. Various platforms have sprung up to facilitate this, including CrowdJustice, which retains 5 per cent of donations to cover expenses. Its front page notes the successes: 100,000+ pledges, over £8 million raised and several Supreme Court cases, including The People's Challenge to the Government regarding Brexit (raised over £170,000). Other examples where CrowdJustice has provided a platform to raise money for legal representation include: the challenge to the UK Government for excluding child refugees from the Dubs Amendment, and helping those caught up in the US Travel Ban early in 2017. Rebecca Steinfeld and Charles Keidan – whose fight to be permitted a civil partnership resulted in success at the UK Supreme Court, when justices ruled the Civil Partnership Act 2004 to be incompatible with the European Convention on Human Rights (Articles 8 and 14) – used CrowdJustice to help fund their case.

CrowdJustice insists on a lawyer or regulated NGO being in place before any appeal goes live, but this isn't always the case with other platforms. This arrangement is low risk for both backers and instructed lawyers; as Julia Salasky, a former Linklaters associate explains: 'For backers this means there is a high level of trust – they can be assured that the legal matter they are donating to has been taken on by a firm . . . for lawyers it also means they get paid up front, and that funds are collected compliantly.'

Unlike the third party funding detailed above, it is less obvious what benefits there are for those who contribute. If an action is successful and costs are recovered, there may be some reimbursement for those donating large sums (£1,000 or more), but for most the reward is simply contributing to a fight for justice. People are used to donating online to races and challenges to raise money for charities, and this is an obvious next step. Worth noting however, is that the courts have not ultimately ruled on whether any backer to a fund could find themselves liable to costs.

15.10 Reform

15.10.1 Price-competitive tendering

In 2005, the Lord Chancellor asked Lord Carter to carry out a review of the legal aid system. Major reforms were recommended in his report, *Legal Aid: A Market-Based Approach to Reform* (2006). Lord Carter criticised the current criminal legal aid system for spending money on 'unproductive time and anomalies in the system'. Payment is calculated on the basis of the number of hours spent on a case and, therefore, does not reward efficiency. He recommended that criminal legal aid lawyers no longer be paid by the hour but by the case. Fixed fees would be introduced across the board for criminal cases, calculated according to the type of case. Fees would be front-loaded to encourage early preparation and discourage trials. It was argued that a fixed-fee regime would allow efficient firms to be more profitable, since they expend less input to produce the same quality service and get the same fee as a less efficient firm:

> Fixed pricing rewards efficiency and suppliers who deliver increased volumes of work. How-
> ever, pricing should be graduated for more complex work so that cases genuinely requiring
> more expertise and effort are priced fairly.

Lord Carter recommended the introduction of a new procurement process for state-funded legal aid, known as 'best value tendering' or 'price-competitive tendering' (PCT). This would involve asking legal service providers to make bids for contracts to deliver categories of state-funded legal services in a particular geographical area, known as 'block contracts'. The tendering competition would be decided according to which firm bid to do the most work for the lowest price by an online auction process.

Contracts for criminal legal aid would only be issued for large volumes of work, so a smaller number of contracts would be awarded. The hope is that larger law firms will be more efficient, but the result is likely to be the closure of many small and medium-sized law firms which the Government considers inefficient. There are currently 1,700 criminal law firms but this could be reduced to just 400. Lord Carter argued that it is uneconomic for solicitors to deliver small amounts of legal aid work. He argued that a move towards larger law practices would be in the interests of legal aid lawyers, saying that sole practitioners (lawyers working in an office on their own) are likely to earn between £36,000 and £55,000 a year, while equity partners in a legal aid firm with 40 fee earners could expect to earn between £120,000 and £150,000.

The aim of these proposed reforms was to control the cost and quality of legal aid and to promote efficiency of service in the public interest. Lord Carter predicted that implementation of his proposals could lead to a saving of £100 million a year. He suggested that, without these new procurement reforms, the same sort of price inflation as had been seen in the previous decade would be repeated in the future.

The coalition Government announced it intended to introduce price-competitive tendering. This reform was included in its consultation paper, *Transforming Legal Aid* (2014). Following strong opposition from the legal profession, the Government decided to amend their proposals, and not introduce price-competitive tendering. Instead, a limited number of contracts for Duty Provider Work would be introduced, which would be awarded through a competitive tendering process based upon quality and capacity, rather than price.

Legal aid lawyers are strongly opposed to the introduction of competitive tendering and have pointed to hospital cleaning, school dinners and prison transport as examples of why tendering should not be used as a procurement mechanism. Lord Carter's strategy was dismissed by critics as 'pile them high, sell them cheap'. Black and minority ethnic solicitors frequently work as sole practitioners or in small legal aid firms, and this led to concern that such firms would suffer if these reforms were introduced. The reforms were likely to lead to a legal aid client having a narrower choice of lawyer. The contracts would only last for one or two years. Initially, there would be intense competition to obtain one of these contracts. Once the contracts had been allocated, a monopoly would have been created in each geographical area for the contract period – economically, an extremely unhealthy market structure and quite the opposite of the 'diverse and competitive market' intended. A criminal law firm that failed to get a contract would be unlikely to survive six months and it would be difficult for any new solicitors to enter the market given the emphasis on larger firms being preferred suppliers. The contracts introduced under the 2012 Act last for four years.

The US already has some experience of contracting out criminal defence services through competitive bidding. Research into their experience was carried out by Roger Smith (1998), who subsequently became the director of the pressure group JUSTICE. This concluded that the process led to reductions in quality, the compromising of professional ethics and the creation of cartels leading to an increase in costs. The US Department of Justice produced a special report on the subject in 2000 and found that such schemes led to an increase of complaints by defendants, partly because the contracting process encouraged lawyers to take on too many cases. It also led to an increase in costs as some legal service providers submitted a low bid to win a contract and then raised the bid in the second and subsequent bidding rounds, once the local competition had been destroyed.

Under the competitive tendering process allocating a single fee for each case (one case, one fee), barristers were worried the work will be allocated to solicitors and not much of it will be referred on to them, as the solicitor would probably prefer to keep the whole fee. The Bar Council therefore created a business structure called a ProcureCo which could be used by a barrister's chambers to bid for legal aid contracts. The ProcureCo would then distribute the work under the contract to barristers and solicitors. Nothing was heard of ProcureCo two years after launch.

15.10.2 A national legal service?

Perhaps the most radical reform would be to take the statutory scheme entirely out of the hands of private practice and establish a nationwide network of salaried lawyers on the law centre model. All funding could be given on a block rather than case-by-case basis, for centres to use in whatever ways best met the needs of their own locality, in consultation with management committees representing the community. The nationalisation of criminal defence work was considered briefly in the Government's consultation paper *Best Value Tendering for Criminal Defence Services* (2007).

The nationalisation of state-funded legal services would deal with some of the criticisms of the current schemes made by Kate Markus and discussed earlier (p. 352). In particular, the advantages of this idea include:

- state-funded work would no longer have to compete with private work for lawyers' time;
- state funding would no longer have to include an element of profit for the lawyer;
- resources could be more flexibly employed, on a combination of individual casework and litigation, education and campaigning, or any other approach that suited particular problems;
- this more flexible approach to dealing with problems would get away from the over-emphasis on litigation of solicitors in private practice;
- the ability to run educative campaigns would help deal with public ignorance of legal rights;

- law centres appear not to suffer from the unapproachable image of the legal profession in general;
- law centres have been successful in attracting problems not previously brought to lawyers, especially welfare and employment cases; and
- a nationwide network of such centres would help overcome the uneven distribution of solicitors' firms.

The 1979 Royal Commission on Legal Services did suggest the establishment of a nation-wide network of centrally financed Citizens Law Centres, but felt that these should be restricted to individual casework only and not get involved in general work for the community. This idea would fail to take advantage of one of the real strengths of the law centre movement, and the fact that solicitors in private practice would still be allowed to undertake state-funded work would limit the improvements to be made in cost-efficiency. The Law Centres Federation rejected the idea.

In a 1995 article for the *Guardian* newspaper, barrister Daniel Stilitz argued for a similar scheme, though not necessarily based on law centres. Under his National Justice Service, anyone seeking to bring a legal action would need to show a reasonable cause. If the case had a reasonable prospect of success, the National Justice Service would decide what services were needed, fix a budget and allocate a lawyer on the basis of suitability and availability. Stilitz points out that for such a scheme to equalise access to justice, it would have to be compulsory – if one side was allowed to 'go private', the scales might be tipped unfairly in their favour. So, both sides would be obliged to use National Justice Service lawyers. The service would be means-tested, with contributions of up to 100 per cent, ensuring that those who could afford to pay the whole cost did so, but could not use that wealth to secure an advantage in the justice system. Those who could not afford to pay would receive free or subsidised help. The result, says Stilitz, would be a level playing field, with cases decided on merit and wasteful tactics designed to drive up costs eliminated.

Stilitz acknowledges the plan would remove client choice, but argues improving access to justice is more important. He also points out that while many might object to the loss of independence involved in tying lawyers so closely to the state, this cannot have a worse effect on individual rights than the current system, under which financial pressures mean many citizens' rights are useless because they cannot afford to enforce them.

15.10.3 No-fault compensation

Instead of looking to contingency fees to secure justice for those injured in accidents, such cases could be removed from the litigation arena by the establishment of a system of no-fault compensation for personal injury cases, as was done in New Zealand.

15.10.4 Alternative funding arrangements

The Access to Justice Act 1999 allows for a new way of funding legal help for individuals, which at present the Government has no plans to use. It provides for a scheme in which people could be given state funding, but required to agree that if they win their case they will pay back the state funding (which they would presumably claim from the losing party). They would also pay a contribution to a fund that would help pay the costs of those parties in receipt of state funding who lose their claims.

> ## The Bigger Picture: Class actions
>
> Sometimes one unlawful act harms not just a single individual but a large group of people. In these circumstances it can be much more efficient for a single group action to be brought to the courts, rather than lots of individual cases. However, at the moment there are many obstacles in the way of bringing successful group actions in England, unlike in America. In particular, the Legal Aid Agency imposes tight controls on the award of public funds for multi-party actions and only £3 million is allocated each year for such cases. Class actions can only be brought in the UK on behalf of a clearly identified claimant group. This is known as the opt-in system as you are only entitled to damages if you first commence your own litigation against the defence, and your case is then managed collectively under a Group Litigation Order or representative action provided for by the Civil Procedure Rules. The damages awarded are calculated on an individual basis looking at the entitlement of each of the individual claimants. Examples include a Group Litigation Order being issued for Tesco shareholders in connection with its overstated accounts, and in the Volkswagen emissions scandal. In America an opt-out system is used, where the court can make an award taking into account any potential claimant and then, once the award is made, relevant claimants can come forward to receive their share of the damages (otherwise they opt out if they do not want to be involved). In practice, this is much easier to administer than the UK opt-in system. Under the American system, aggregate damages can be awarded which are calculated to take into account the loss suffered by the whole class of claimant, rather than just that of the individual claimants before the court. Class members are then notified after the judgment of their entitlement to a share of the settlement.
>
> The Civil Justice Council has issued a report on this subject – *Improving Access to Justice through Collective Actions* (2008) – calling for legislation enabling class actions for groups of consumers or businesses to be possible on an opt-out basis. Cases would only be allowed to proceed with the permission of a court. Class actions would be subject to an enhanced form of case management by specialist judges and any settlement agreed should be approved by the court by means of a 'fairness hearing'. The Civil Justice Council has found there is overwhelming evidence that valid consumer claims are not being pursued at the moment and it has recommended that class actions should be possible for such cases.
>
> While group litigation has been successful in America against cigarette manufacturers, it has not been successful in the United Kingdom. In November 2007 the drugs manufacturer, Merck, announced plans to pay more than $4.85 billion to Americans who claim to have suffered heart attacks and strokes after taking a drug for arthritis. The pharmaceutical company has refused to make any payments to the UK claimants (and claimants elsewhere) who took their legal action in the United Kingdom where they had been refused legal aid. When the Italian company Parmalat collapsed in 2003, group litigation was brought in America because this was considered more effective than the litigation options in Europe. There is, therefore, a risk that the American system could be introduced through the back door.
>
> In order to implement European legislation, the Consumer Rights Act 2015 has introduced class actions in competition law. Opt-out collective actions can now be brought for infringements of competition rules. This is likely to lead to a significant increase in claims for damages in this field and such class actions may be extended in future to a wider range of cases.

15

PAYING FOR LEGAL SERVICES

The Bach Commission Report

Published in September 2017, this report analysed the impact of the legal aid reforms brought in by the Legal Aid, Sentencing and Punishment of Offenders Act 2012. More than 100 individuals and organisations within the justice system were interviewed. Describing the legal aid system as 'creaking at the seams' the report concludes that 'the problems are so deep-rooted, commonplace and various that piecemeal reforms alone would simply be papering over the cracks'. The Commission state the cost of implementing their recommendations as £400 million a year. Some of the headline recommendations are:

- a new statute: the Right to Justice Act. The Commission state this would 'codify our existing rights to justice and establish a new right for individuals to receive reasonable legal assistance' – this would incorporate the creation of a new independent body, the Justice Commission;

- reform of legal aid assessment – a simpler and more generous scheme which would mean those in receipt of a means tested benefit would automatically be eligible for legal aid;

- reform of legal aid means test;

- restoration of legal aid for early legal assistance in social welfare and family law cases;

- replacement of the Legal Aid Agency with an independent body (described in the report as 'at arm's length from government');

- better legal education in schools; and

- universally accessible advice.

Time will tell how many of these recommendations the Government decide to embrace.

15.10.5 Are lawyers always necessary?

As we have seen, many of the non-statutory advice schemes use advisers who are not legally qualified. Some of these lay advisers appear as advocates in tribunals and in some cases have been granted discretionary rights of audience in the County Courts, as well as giving legal advice. In particular, advisers for charities such as MIND have shown themselves to be more than a match for most solicitors in their knowledge of the law in their fields. Many solicitor firms also employ non-qualified workers to do legal work.

The skills of a good adviser are not always the same as those of a good lawyer; what the client needs is someone who can interview sympathetically, ascertain the pertinent facts from what may be a long, rambling and in some cases emotional story, analyse the problem and suggest a course of action. The preliminary skills are just as likely to be possessed by a lay person as by a lawyer, even if a lawyer may be needed to advise on the course of action.

Nor are lawyers considered to be the best advocates in every situation. The National Consumer Council advised against allowing them to represent clients in the Small Claims Court, on the grounds that they could make the procedure unnecessarily long-winded and legalistic.

However, critics identify two possible problems in the growing use of lay advisers. First, although most organisations are scrupulous in training their advisers, some may be more casual, and there is no obligatory check on advisers before they are allowed to deal with cases. The general public may not always be in a position to assess the quality of the advice they are given. Secondly, the large number of overlapping agencies means it can be difficult for consumers of legal advice to find the best provider for them and can be wasteful of scarce resources.

Answering questions

1 Recent reforms in legal aid are motivated by financial concerns rather than the desire to ensure access to justice for all. Discuss. *University of London, International Programmes LLB*

2 Should all state funding for legal services be replaced by contingency fee agreements?

For the answers to these questions, visit the companion website at www.pearsoned.co.uk/ elliottquinn

SUMMARY OF CHAPTER 15: PAYING FOR LEGAL SERVICES

Unmet need for legal services

Unmet legal need essentially describes the situation where a person has a problem that could potentially be solved through the law, but the person is unable to get whatever help he or she needs to use the legal system.

Legal aid today

With the passing of the Access to Justice Act 1999 the Labour Government introduced some major reforms to the provision of state-funded legal services. Further reforms were introduced by the Legal Aid, Sentencing and Punishment of Offenders Act 2012, which drastically cut the civil legal aid and criminal legal aid systems. The Legal Aid Agency administers two schemes: civil legal aid and criminal legal aid. In addition, the Legal Aid Agency employs public defenders.

Conditional fee agreements

In 1990 the Courts and Legal Services Act made provision for the introduction of conditional fee agreements which are sometimes referred to as 'no win, no fee' agreements.

Contingency fees

The Legal Aid, Sentencing and Punishment of Offenders Act 2012 effectively replaces conditional fees with contingency fees. While a conditional fee agreement allows the lawyer to be paid an increased fee if the action is successful, under a contingency fee agreement, lawyers receive a share of the successful claimant's award of damages.

Reform

In his report, *Legal Aid: A Market-Based Approach to Reform* (2006), Lord Carter recommended the introduction of some important, money-saving reforms to the system of state-funded legal services, in particular price-competitive tendering. We eagerly await the outcome of the government review into the impact of the LASPO reforms.

Reading list

Abel-Smith, B., Zander, M. and Brooke, R. (1973) *Legal Problems and the Citizen*. London: Heinemann-Educational.

Advice Services Alliance (2004) *The Independent Review of the Community Legal Service*. London: ASA.

Auld, Sir R. (2001) *Review of the Criminal Courts*. London: HMSO.

Bowles, R. and Perry, A. (2009) *International Comparison of Publicly Funded Legal Services and Justice Systems*. Ministry of Justice Research Series 14/09.

Bridges, L. and Cape, E. (2008) *CDS Direct: Flying in the Face of the Evidence*. London: Centre for Crime and Justice Studies at King's College London.

Bridges, L. *et al.* (2007) (see website, below).

Carter, Lord (2006) *Legal Aid: A Market-Based Approach to Reform*. London: Department for Constitutional Affairs.

Citizens Advice Bureau (2004a) *Geography of Advice*. London: Citizens Advice Bureau.

　　　　　(2004b) *No Win, No Fee, No Chance*. London: Citizens Advice Bureau.

Civil Justice Council (2008) *Improving Access to Justice through Collective Action*s. London: Ministry of Justice.

Department for Constitutional Affairs (2004) *Making Simple CFAs a Reality*. London: Department for Constitutional Affairs.

Epstein, H. (2003) The liberalisation of claim financing. *New Law Journal*, 153: 153.

Genn, H. (1982) *Meeting Legal Needs? An Evaluation of a Scheme for Personal Injury Victims*. Oxford: SSRC Centre for Socio-Legal Studies.

Goriely, T. and Gysta, P. (2001) *Breaking the Code: The Impact of Legal Aid Reforms on General Civil Litigation*. London: Institute of Advanced Legal Studies.

Hynes, S. and Robins, J. (2009) *The Justice Gap: Whatever Happened to Legal Aid?* London: Legal Action Group.

Jackson, Lord Justice (2010) *Civil Litigation Costs Review*. Norwich: Stationery Office.

Kemp, V. (2011) *Transforming Legal Aid – Access to Legal Defence Services*. London: Legal Services Commission.

Law Society (2008) *Conditional Fees: A Guide to CFAs and Other Funding Options*. London: Law Society.

Legal Services Commission (2001) *Quality and Cost: Final Report on the Contracting of Civil, Non-family Advice and Assistance Pilot*. London: Legal Services Commission.

　　　　　(2007) *Best Value Tendering for Criminal Defence Services*. London: Legal Services Commission

Lord Chancellor's Department (2003) *Delivering Value for Money in the Criminal Defence Service*. Consultation Paper. London: Lord Chancellor's Department.

Markus, K. (1992) The politics of legal aid. In: *The Critical Lawyer's Handbook*. London: Pluto.

Mayhew, L. and Reiss, A. (1969) The social organisation of legal contacts. *American Sociological Review*, 34: 309.

Moorhead, R. (2011) Filthy lucre: lawyers' fees and lawyers' ethics – what is wrong with informed consent? *Legal Studies,* 31: 345.

Moorhead, R. and Cape, E. (2005) *Demand Induced Supply? Identifying Cost Drivers in Criminal Defence Work.* London: Legal Services Commission.

Moorhead, R. and Cumming, R. (2008) *Damage-Based Contingency Fees in Employment Cases.* Cardiff Law School Research Paper No. 6. Cardiff: Cardiff University.

Moorhead, R. and Hurst, P. (2008) *Improving Access to Justice: Contingency Fees. A Study of their Operation in the United States of America.* London: Civil Justice Council.

National Association of Citizens Advice Bureaux (1999) *A Balancing Act: Surviving the Risk Society.* London: NACAB.

National Audit Office (2003) *Community Legal Service: The Introduction of Contracting.* HC 89, 2002–03. London: HMSO.

Pereira, I., Perry, C., Greevy, H. and Shrimpton, H. (2015), *The varying paths to justice. Mapping problem resolution routes for users and non-users of the civil, administrative and family justice systems.* London: Ministry of Justice Analytical Series.

Pleasence, P., Buck, A., Balmer. N., O'Grady, A., Genn, H. and Smith, M. (2004) *Causes of Action: Civil Law and Social Justice.* London: HMSO.

Pleasence, P. and Balmer, N. (2013) *In Need of Advice? Findings of a Small Business Legal Needs Benchmarking Survey.* Cambridge: PPSR.

Sanders, A. and Bridge, L. (1993) Access to legal advice. In: Walker, C. and Starmer, K. (eds) *Justice in Error.* London: Blackstone.

Smith, R. (1998) *Legal Aid Contracting: Lessons from North America.* London: Legal Action Group.

      (2007) Ever decreasing circles. *New Law Journal,* 157: 1437.

Tata, C. *et al.* (2004) Does mode of delivery make a difference to criminal case outcomes and clients' satisfaction? The public defence solicitor experiment. *Criminal Law Review,* 120.

White, R. (1973) Lawyers and the enforcement of rights. In: Morris, P., White, R. and Lewis, P. (eds) *Social Needs and Legal Action.* Oxford: Martin Robertson.

Yarrow, S. (1997) *The Price of Success: Lawyers, Clients and Conditional Fees.* London: Policy Studies Institute.

Zander, M. (1988) *A Matter of Justice.* Oxford: Oxford University Press.

      (2007a) Carter's wake (1). *New Law Journal,* 157: 872.

      (2007b) Carter's wake (2) *New Law Journal,* 157: 912.

      (2007c) Full speed ahead? *New Law Journal,* 157: 992.

Zuckerman, A. (2014) No justice without lawyers – the myth of an inquisitorial solution. *Civil Justice Quarterly,* 355.

15

PAYING FOR LEGAL SERVICES

On the internet

The report by Lee Bridges *et al.* (2007), *Evaluation of the Public Defender Service in England and Wales* is available at:

    https://orca.cf.ac.uk/44472/1/1622.pdf

The report *Proposals for reform of Legal Aid in England and Wales* (2010) is available on the Ministry of Justice website at:

> https://www.gov.uk/government/publications/proposals-for-reform-of-legal-aid-in-england-and-wales

The report of the Ministry of Justice *Proposals for Reform of Civil Litigation Funding and Costs in England and Wales: Implementation of Lord Justice Jackson's Recommendations* is published on the Ministry of Justice website at:

> https://www.gov.uk/government/uploads/system/uploads/attachment_data/file/238368/7947.pdf

Lord Jackson's report *Review of Civil Litigation Costs: Final Report* (2009) is available on the website for the judiciary of England and Wales at:

> http://www.judiciary.gov.uk/wp-content/uploads/JCO/Documents/Reports/jackson-final-report-140110.pdf

The Royal Commission on Legal Services (1979) can be found at:

> http://discovery.nationalarchives.gov.uk/details/r/C10257

The Judicial Working Group on Litigants in Person: Report (2013) is at:

> https://www.judiciary.gov.uk/wp-content/uploads/JCO/Documents/Reports/lip_2013.pdf

The judgment of the European Court of Human Rights in the 'McLibel Two' case can be found on HUDOC (the ECHR database of judgments) by clicking on Advanced Search and typing 'Steel and Morris v the United Kingdom' into the Case Title box:

> https://hudoc.echr.coe.int/

The website of the Legal Aid Agency is available at:

> https://www.gov.uk/government/organisations/legal-aid-agency

The report by Roger Smith and Alan Paterson *Face to Face Legal Services and their Alternatives: Global Lessons from the Digital Revolution* (2014) is available on the University of Strathclyde's website at:

> https://strathprints.strath.ac.uk/56496/

Citizens Advice, *Modelling our value to society in 2015/16* is available at:

> https://www.citizensadvice.org.uk/Global/Public/Impact/ModellingthevalueoftheCitizensAdviceservicein201516.pdf

Amnesty International, *Cuts that hurt: The impact of legal aid cuts in England on access to justice* (2016) can be downloaded at:

> https://www.amnesty.org/en/documents/eur45/4936/2016/en/

The Bach Commission Final Report, *The Right to Justice* (2017) can be obtained at:

> http://www.fabians.org.uk/wp-content/uploads/2017/09/Bach-Commission_Right-to-Justice-Report-WEB.pdf

The excellent BuzzFeed article on the impact of legal aid by Emily Dugan, *A Record Number of People are Representing Themselves in Court – This is What It's Like,* can be found at:

> https://www.buzzfeed.com/emilydugan/a-record-number-of-people-are-representing-themselves-in?utm_term=.nlkXd7Jn8Z\#.kr46ZEnWQJ

Henry Brooke, retired Lord Justice of Appeal, was the Vice-Chair on the Bach Commission. His blog, *Musings, Memories and Miscellanea* features a whole series of posts to accompany the report. It is available (via the Bach Commission tab) at:

> https://sirhenrybrooke.me/

More information about CrowdJustice can be found on its website at:
>https://www.crowdjustice.com/

Read the Emily Dugan story *People Suing the Government were Denied Legal Aid after the Government was Briefed on their Cases* (Buzzfeed, 5 October 2018) here:
>https://www.buzzfeed.com/emilydugan/people-suing-government-denied-legal-aid-political

The Joint Committee on Human Rights report *Enforcing Human Rights* (10th report HC 669 HL 171, 19 July 2018) is available at:
>https://publications.parliament.uk/pa/jt201719/jtselect/jtrights/669/669.pdf

For more on crowdfunding, read the useful Law Society piece *Strength in numbers* by Melanie Newman (23 July 2018), available at:
>https://www.lawgazette.co.uk/features/strength-in-numbers/5066950.article

The Law Society *review Access Denied? LASPO four years on* is accessed here:
>https://www.lawsociety.org.uk/support-services/research-trends/laspo-4-years-on/

The research report carried out by Dr James Organ and Dr Jennifer Sigafoos for the Equality and Human Rights Commission, *The Impact of LASPO on Routes to Justice* (Research Report 118, 2018) is accessible here:
>https://www.equalityhumanrights.com/sites/default/files/the-impact-of-laspo-on-routes-to-justice-september-2018.pdf

The House of Commons Justice Committee Report on *Criminal Legal Aid* (HC 1069, 26 July 2018) is available here:
>https://publications.parliament.uk/pa/cm201719/cmselect/cmjust/1069/1069.pdf

The Association of Litigation Funders can be found at:
>http://associationoflitigationfunders.com

15

PAYING FOR LEGAL SERVICES

Part 3
Human rights

In democratic societies, it is usually felt that there are certain basic rights – often called civil liberties, civil rights or human rights – which should be available to everyone. Exactly what these rights are varies in different legal systems, but they generally include such freedoms as the right to say, think and believe what you like (freedom of expression, thought and conscience); to form groups with others, such as trade unions and pressure groups (freedom of assembly); to protest peacefully; and to be imprisoned or otherwise punished only for breaking the law and after a fair trial. Part of the reason why these freedoms are considered important is the nature of democracy: citizens can only make the kind of free choice of government required by a democratic system if there is open discussion and debate.

In this Part we consider the place of human rights in England and Wales.

Chapter 16
Introduction to human rights

This chapter discusses:

- the European Convention on Human Rights;
- the Human Rights Act 1998;
- recent developments in human rights law; and
- whether the UK needs a Bill of Rights.

16.1 Introduction

Most democratic countries have a written Bill of Rights, which lays down the rights which, by law, can be enjoyed by citizens of that country. These rights have to be respected by the courts, Parliament, the police and private citizens, unless the Bill of Rights allows otherwise (for example, some rights may be suspended in times of war or when it is necessary in the interests of national security). Such a Bill may form part of a written constitution or sit alongside such a constitution: either way, it will usually have a status which is superior to that of ordinary law, in that it can only be changed by a special procedure. This will vary from country to country, but might involve holding a referendum, or securing a larger than usual majority in Parliament. Legislation which is protected in this way is said to be entrenched.

Britain is unusual among democratic countries in having, to date, neither a Bill of Rights nor a written constitution. In this country, our rights and freedoms are traditionally considered to be protected by a presumption that we are free to do whatever is not specifically forbidden by either legislation or the common law. Anyone prevented by the state from doing something which they are legally entitled to do should have a remedy against the state – an example is that a person wrongly detained in a police station can sue for false imprisonment. Citizens' rights in the UK were described as residual, in that they consisted of what was left after taking into account the lawful limitations.

The system of residual freedoms had shown itself to be seriously flawed over the past couple of decades. The idea that a person is free to do anything not specifically prohibited by law also applies to the state, so that the Government may violate individual freedom even though it is not formally empowered to do so, on the ground that it is doing nothing which is prohibited. An example of this is *Malone* v *Metropolitan Police Commissioner* (1979). Mr Malone's telephone had been tapped, and he was able to prove that this was done without any lawful authority – that is, there was no law which allowed the Government or its agencies to tap his phone. But equally, there was no law which forbade them to do so as English law gives no general right to privacy. Therefore, Mr Malone's action failed.

A significant change in the British position was made by the Human Rights Act 1998. This came into force in October 2000. The Act makes the European Convention on Human Rights (ECHR) part of the law of the UK. While the Convention had been part of the international law that is recognised by the UK, it had never been integrated as part of our domestic law. While the Human Rights Act represents a major shift in approach to civil liberties it still fails to give the UK a Bill of Rights. A Bill of Rights is the supreme authority on human rights in a country and is entrenched, which means that it cannot be changed by legislation and amounts to a significant limitation on the powers of the elected legislature. The Human Rights Act and the European Convention are not entrenched in the UK, though there is some debate as to how exactly the Human Rights Act could be repealed. Lord Justice Laws stated in *Thoburn* v *Sunderland City Council* (2002) that the Human Rights Act was a constitutional Act which could only be repealed by express provisions of an Act of Parliament (and not by implication). This could be described as a 'soft' form of entrenchment.

Even before the passing of the Human Rights Act 1998, English law was being influenced by the European Convention. With the passing of the 1998 Act this process has gathered momentum. The Act has raised the importance of human rights law in the UK, provides a clear legal basis for human rights challenges and has led to greater scrutiny of such matters during the progress of Bills through Parliament.

16.2 The European Convention on Human Rights

The ECHR was drawn up by the Council of Europe, which was established after the Second World War when countries tried to unite to prevent such horrors from ever happening again. The Council now has 47 members, including the 28 members of the EU. Signed in Rome in 1950, the Convention was ratified by the UK in 1951 and became binding on those states which had ratified it in 1953.

A special court, known as the European Court of Human Rights, was set up to deal with claims concerning breaches of the ECHR. The Court sits in Strasbourg, and handles claims made by one state against another and by individuals against a state. It only hears individual claims where the relevant state has accepted the right of individuals to bring such cases; not all states accept this right of individual petition, though the UK Government agreed to this in 1966.

The fact that a state has ratified the Convention does not mean it has to incorporate Convention provisions into its domestic law: each state can choose whether or not to do this, and about half have done so. In these cases, citizens can claim their rights under the Convention through domestic courts and the national parliaments cannot usually legislate in conflict with the Convention.

The UK refused for many years to incorporate the Convention and so it was not recognised by the national courts as part of English law. UK citizens who believed that their rights under the Convention had been breached could not bring their claim through the normal domestic courts, but had to take their case to the European Court of Human Rights; if they succeeded there, the UK Government was expected to amend whatever aspect of domestic law caused the problem. But such litigation is slow and expensive and the eventual remedies often inadequate. As with any other international treaty, British courts could take the Convention into account when interpreting UK legislation, and presume that Parliament did not intend to legislate inconsistently with it. Where a statute was ambiguous, they could use the Convention as a guide to its correct interpretation; an example of this is provided by **_Waddington_ v _Miah_** (1974), where the House of Lords referred to Art. 7 of the Convention to support its view that s. 34 of the Immigration Act 1971 could not be interpreted as having retrospective effect. Where the words of a statute were clear, domestic courts had to apply them, even if they obviously conflicted with the Convention. This position has changed radically with the passing of the Human Rights Act 1998 incorporating the Convention into domestic law.

16.3 The scope of the Convention

The rights protected by the ECHR include: the right to life (Art. 2); freedom from torture, inhuman or degrading treatment (Art. 3); freedom from slavery or forced labour (Art. 4); the right to liberty and security of the person (Art. 5); the right to a fair trial (Art. 6); the prohibition of retrospective criminal laws (Art. 7); the right to respect for a person's private and family life, home and correspondence (Art. 8); freedom of thought, conscience and religion (Art. 9); freedom of expression (Art. 10); freedom of peaceful assembly and association, including the right to join a trade union (Art. 11); and the right to marry and have a family (Art. 12).

The Convention provides that people should be able to enjoy these rights without discrimination (Art. 14). Some additions, known as Protocols, have been made to the ECHR since it was first drawn up. The First Protocol was written in 1952 and provides three new rights: the right to peaceful enjoyment of one's possessions (Art. 1); the right to education (Art. 2); and the right to take part in free elections by secret ballot (Art. 3). The other important Protocol is the fourth, concluded in 1963, which guarantees freedom of movement within a state and freedom to leave any country; it precludes a country from expelling or refusing to admit its own nationals. This Protocol has not been ratified by the UK and, in the past, some citizens from Northern Ireland have been excluded from mainland Britain.

Many of the rights provided under the Convention contain specific restrictions and exemptions. For example, Art. 10 allows restrictions on freedom of expression where they are:

> necessary in a democratic society, in the interests of national security, territorial integrity or public safety, for the prevention of disorder or crime, for the protection of health or morals, for the protection of the reputation or rights of others, for preventing the disclosure of information received in confidence, or for maintaining the authority and impartiality of the judiciary.

Member states may decline to carry out most of their obligations under the Convention in time of war or some other national emergency if this is strictly required by the situation. The UK has done so in respect of Northern Ireland. In such cases a state must inform the Secretary-General of the Council of Europe with its reasons (Art. 15). There are some rights, most importantly freedom from torture, inhuman or degrading treatment, from which states are never permitted to derogate. The Convention does not cover the whole field of human rights. It omits general economic and social rights, such as a right to housing, a minimum income and free health care, which some would argue should be guaranteed in a civilised society. This is because there is less agreement between different countries on such issues than there is on the traditional freedoms currently protected by the ECHR.

16.4 The administration

The European Court of Human Rights (ECtHR) has the same number of judges as contracting states, which is currently 47. The court is divided into four Sections, there are Committees of three judges and Chambers of seven judges. There is also a Grand Chamber of 17 judges. Any contracting state or individual claiming to be a victim of a violation of the Convention by a contracting state may lodge an application directly with the court in Strasbourg. Each individual application is assigned to a Section and a judge, called a rapporteur, makes a preliminary examination of the case and decides whether it should be dealt with by a three-member Committee or by a Chamber. A Committee may decide, by unanimous vote, to declare an application inadmissible or strike it out. Cases are admissible only after the applicant has exhausted all available domestic remedies and makes the application no more than six months after the final national decision (Art. 26). The Committee will also reject as inadmissible any petition which is outside the scope of the Convention or manifestly ill-founded (Art. 27). Apart from those cases that are struck out by a Committee, all the other cases are heard by a Chamber. Chambers may at any time relinquish jurisdiction in favour of a Grand Chamber where a case raises a serious question of interpretation of the Convention or where there is a risk of departing from existing case law, unless one of the parties objects to this transfer.

Within three months of delivery of the judgment of a Chamber, any party may request that a case be referred to the Grand Chamber if it raises a serious question of interpretation

Photo 16.1 European Court of Human Rights in Strasbourg

Source: © Arseniy Chervonenkis/123RF

or application or a serious issue of general importance. Such requests are examined by a panel of judges of the Grand Chamber. If the panel accepts the request the case will be heard by the Grand Chamber of 17 judges. The decision of the Grand Chamber is final. As well as deciding whether a state is in breach of the Convention, the court can award compensation or other 'just satisfaction' of the complaint (Art. 50). Responsibility for supervising the execution of judgments lies with the Committee of Ministers of the Council of Europe.

Unfortunately, the ECtHR has become a victim of its own success – in 2011 it had a backlog of 120,000 cases. In order to reduce this backlog, the 47 member nations of the Council of Europe agreed a package of reforms at a conference in Brighton in 2012. These reforms were published in the Brighton Declaration. Following this agreement the introduction to the European Convention on Human Rights (known as the preamble) has been amended to include the principle of subsidiarity, a principle developed in the ECtHR's case law and which under these reforms is expressly mentioned in the Convention. There is some disagreement about what exactly is meant by the 'principle of subsidiarity', but the Brighton Declaration refers to a shared responsibility between State Parties and the European Court of Human Rights for realising the effective implementation of the Convention and the fact that State Parties may choose how to fulfil their obligations under the Convention. This reflects the fact that the Convention system is subsidiary to the safeguarding of human rights at national level and that national authorities are in principle better placed than an international court to evaluate local needs and conditions.

The Preamble has also been amended to expressly lay down that State Parties enjoy a margin of appreciation in how they apply and implement the Convention, depending on the circumstances of the case and the rights and freedoms engaged.

The Brighton Declaration has led to reforms to the court process to try and reduce the backlog of cases. Applicants may be charged a fee to bring a case to the court, and a tighter admissibility test will be applied to filter out weak cases. An application will be rejected as manifestly ill-founded 'unless the Court finds that it raises a serious question affecting the interpretation or application of the Convention'. The time limit for bringing claims has been reduced from six to four months. As a result of these reforms, the backlog of the Court has fallen considerably, and at the end of 2013 fell below 100,000. Further reforms have been initiated with the purpose of reducing the backlog of cases, which has seen some success although the crises occurring in Europe have impacted on the number of cases, although the number of cases has now come back down again to just over 56,000 cases pending at the close of 2018. The Court has taken the approach of joining certain claims which raise similar legal questions by considering them together to increase its efficiency.

16.5 The Human Rights Act 1998

The Human Rights Act 1998 incorporated the ECHR (and its first Protocol) into domestic law. The effect of this is to strengthen the protection of individual rights by UK courts and provide improved remedies where these are violated. The Convention is now applicable directly in the UK courts (s. 7), so that it is no longer necessary to go all the way to Strasbourg, though it is still possible. Under s. 2 of the Human Rights Act, the domestic judiciary 'must take into account' any relevant Strasbourg jurisprudence, although they are not bound by it (see p. 26).

The UK courts are required to interpret all legislation in a way which is compatible with Convention rights 'so far as it is possible to do so' (s. 3). This goes much further than the previous position of allowing ambiguities to be interpreted in favour of the Convention.

It is unlawful for public authorities to act in a way which is incompatible with Convention rights (s. 6). A public authority includes central and local government, the police and the NHS. In addition, a private body can be regarded as a public authority for the purposes of the Human Rights Act if, under s. 6(3)(b), it performs 'functions of a public nature'. Such a body is described as a hybrid public authority. The obligation on such hybrid bodies to observe Convention rights attaches only to functions which are of a public nature; other work that it carries out will not be affected.

There has been some debate as to whether the Act allows individual citizens to enforce Convention rights in proceedings against other individuals (known as 'horizontal effect'). Section 6 states that public authorities cannot breach Convention rights. It is therefore clear from s. 6 that citizens can rely on their Convention rights against the state (known as 'vertical effect'). The reference primarily to 'public authorities' would suggest that individual citizens can breach the Convention with impunity. But the courts are public authorities. It is therefore arguable that if a civil court failed to apply a Convention right in legal proceedings between private parties it would be in breach of the Human Rights Act. Academic opinion on this issue has been sharply divided.

The courts appear to have accepted that the Convention has a limited form of horizontal effect. Thus, in ***Douglas v Hello!*** (2001) photographs of the marriage of the Hollywood celebrities Michael Douglas and Catherine Zeta-Jones had been published without their

Table 16.1 The European Convention on Human Rights

Article	Rights and freedoms
2	The right to life
3	Freedom from torture or inhuman or degrading treatment
4	Freedom from slavery and forced labour
5	The right to liberty and security of the person
6	The right to a fair trial
7	Protection from the criminal law having retrospective effect
8	The right to respect of one's private and family life
9	Freedom of thought, conscience and religion
10	Freedom of expression
11	Freedom of assembly and association
12	The right to marry
14	The right to enjoy Convention rights without discrimination on the grounds of sex, race, colour, language, religion, political or other opinion, national or social origin, association with a national minority, property, birth or other status.
The First Protocol	
1	The right to peaceful enjoyment of one's possessions
2	The right to education
3	The right to free elections.

authority by the popular magazine *Hello!* The legal proceedings were between private parties, but all the judges treated the Convention as relevant to the case because of the Human Rights Act 1998.

In *R (on the application of Al-Skeini) v Secretary of State for Defence* (2007) the House of Lords considered whether Iraqi civilians arrested and detained by British soldiers had the protection of the 1998 Act. It concluded that the Act has a potentially wide geographical application, beyond the physical boundaries of the United Kingdom itself, to places where the UK has effective control. The Supreme Court extended this extraterritorial application of the 1998 Act in *Smith v Ministry of Defence* (2013), when it held that the Act also applies to British soldiers serving abroad. Given that the House of Lords in *Al-Skeini* held that civilians detained by soldiers abroad were covered by the 1998 Act, it only makes sense that the Act also applies to soldiers.

Key case

The application of s. 6(3)(b) of the Human Rights Act was considered by the House of Lords in **YL v Birmingham City Council** (2007). It did not lay down a single test to be applied to determine this issue, but said that the question had to be decided on a case- by-case basis, though it identified the sort of factors that would be taken into account. The case involved an appeal of an 84-year-old lady suffering from dementia. Under the National Assistance Act 1948, Birmingham City Council had a statutory obligation to make residential arrangements for elderly people in need of care. She had been placed by the council in a private care home operated by a company called Southern Cross Healthcare Ltd. Unfortunately, the relationship between some of the elderly lady's family and the care home's management deteriorated, and Southern Cross gave notice that she would have to leave the home. The House of Lords had to decide whether Southern Cross was required to respect Convention rights when exercising its powers in relation to the elderly lady. The majority of the Law Lords concluded that it was not. It noted that in determining the scope of s. 6 it should reflect the extent of the UK Government's liabilities before the European Court of Human Rights, as the section aimed to allow UK citizens remedies in the UK to avoid the need for them to go to Strasbourg to get a remedy. Section 6, therefore, is designed to mirror the scope of state responsibility at Strasbourg. The fact that public funding was used to pay Southern Cross was not decisive, as on the facts this was equivalent to a payment for services. The greater the powers given to the private body, the more likely that it is exercising a public function. For example, a private prison has the power to detain individuals and, therefore, is exercising a public function, whereas Southern Cross had no such power. The House concluded that Southern Cross was not carrying out a public function and its state-funded residents, therefore, could not benefit from Convention rights. The House of Lords observed that a finding to the contrary would have created rights which sat uneasily with the ordinary private law freedom of contract enjoyed in the private sector.

Legal principle

A private body can be regarded as a public authority for the purposes of the Human Rights Act 1998 under s. 6(3)(b), if it performs functions of a public nature, and this will be determined on a case-by-case basis.

Under s. 19 Government Ministers have to publish a written statement as to whether or not a Bill is compatible with the Convention. The House of Lords Parliamentary Committee has issued a report *Relations between the executive, the judiciary and Parliament* (2007) in which it suggested that there have been cases where Ministers had adopted a 'far too optimistic view' about the compatibility of provisions in Bills with the European Convention. It recommended that in cases of doubt about compatibility, Ministers should seek the involvement of the Law Officers (discussed on p. 331) to ensure that the Bill is compatible.

While the Human Rights Act represents an important advance for civil liberties in the UK, there are still significant limitations on the impact that the Act will have. In particular, legislation which is incompatible with the Convention is still valid; judges do not have the power to strike down offending statutes as unconstitutional. Thus, the principle of parliamentary sovereignty remains intact. If a higher court does find that legislation is incompatible with the Convention, then it can choose to make a declaration to this effect (s. 4) and a Minister can subsequently amend the offending legislation by a fast-track procedure which avoids the full parliamentary process (s. 10). An early example of a declaration of incompatibility is provided by the case of **Wilson v First County Trust Ltd** (2003) where the House of Lords declared that a provision of the Consumer Credit Act 1974 violated the Convention. The Ministry of Justice report *Responding to Human Rights judgments* notes that as of July 2017 39 declarations of incompatibility have been made, of which ten were overturned on appeal and two are subject to appeal. Of the remaining 27:

- 11 have been remedied by a subsequent Act of Parliament or secondary legislation;
- five related to provisions that had already been remedied by primary legislation at the time of the declaration;
- three have been remedied by a remedial order provided for by s. 10 of the Act;
- one has been addressed by administrative measures;
- the Government has notified the Joint Committee on Human Rights that it intends to address four declarations of incompatibility through a remedial order; and
- three are under consideration as to how to remedy the incompatibility.

The judiciary has a lot of power in determining the impact and success of the Human Rights Act 1998. The Convention rights are very loosely drafted and through their interpretation the judges could easily dilute them and render them ineffective. The Government is clearly aware of the central role of the judges in the success or failure of the Act. It spent £4.5 million training the judges, magistrates and tribunal chairpersons ready for the implementation of the Act. The Lord Chancellor wrote directly to all the judges pointing out their vital role. The letter stated:

> With proper training and planning, I am confident that all courts and tribunals will be able to give full effect to the rights recognised by the Convention and to make their distinctive contribution to fostering a culture of awareness of, and respect for, human rights throughout the whole of society. I hope you look forward to playing your part in making those rights real, as do I.

The Human Rights Act 1998 appears to have been successfully implemented and has engendered a stronger human rights culture in the courts. Research has been carried out by Raine and Walker (2002) into the impact of the Act in its first 18 months. Their research points to 'the comparative success with which the courts managed the implementation process and the ways in which they have adapted their practices'. Prior to the Act's implementation, there had been fears that the courts would be overrun with speculative human rights claims. This has not in fact happened. The report states that:

> . . . the general picture from the research was one of relatively limited impact of the Human Rights Act in terms of challenges and additional workload for the courts, although it had invoked a number of significant and specific policy and practice changes.

A statistical analysis has been published of the first effects of the Human Rights Act 1998 on the work of the civil courts. In the last three months of the year 2000, 76 claims for damages were issued in the civil courts relying wholly on the Human Rights Act 1998, out of a total of 467,000 claims.

One of the first cases to seek to rely on the Human Rights Act 1998 was **Procurator Fiscal v Brown** (2000), which started in the Scottish courts. Under the road traffic legislation, Ms Brown had been required to inform the police of the identity of the person driving her car on the evening she was questioned. It would have been a criminal offence for her not to have answered the question. She admitted that she had been driving her car and was prosecuted for drink-driving. She claimed at her trial that her confession should not be admissible as evidence as she had been forced to incriminate herself in breach of her right to a fair trial in Art. 6 of the European Convention. The High Court in Scotland accepted this argument. This decision was highly controversial as it threatened the credibility of the Human Rights Act. It appeared to justify fears that the Act would create a large amount of litigation and give people rights that went against the general interests of society. However, on appeal the Privy Council ruled that the road traffic legislation did not breach the European Convention and the evidence was admissible at her trial. Reviewing the case law of the European Court of Human Rights, Lord Bingham concluded:

> The jurisprudence of the European Court very clearly established that while the overall fairness of a criminal trial cannot be compromised, the constituent rights comprised, whether expressly or implicitly, within Art. 6 [such as freedom from self-incrimination] are not themselves absolute.

The privilege against self-incrimination was not absolute, but had to be balanced against the wider interests of the community, in particular public safety. The Privy Council found that the obligation to state who was driving the vehicle represented a proportionate response to the serious social problem of death and injury on the roads. The case was distinguished from *Saunders* v *UK* (1997) (discussed at p. 386) where the UK legislation had allowed prolonged questioning, as opposed to the answering of a single question in this case. The decision shows that the courts will not tolerate attempts to misuse provisions of the Convention in ways which are contrary to the public interest.

Key case

In **Wilson v Secretary of State for Trade and Industry** (2003) the House of Lords took a slightly more flexible view as to whether the Human Rights Act could have retrospective effect. It cited with approval a statement of Staughton LJ in **Secretary of State for Social Security v Tunnicliffe** (1991) on the presumption that Acts of Parliament will not have retrospective effect:

> [T]he true principle is that Parliament is presumed not to have intended to alter the law applicable to past events and transactions in a manner which is unfair to those concerned in them, unless a contrary intention appears. It is not simply a question of classifying an enactment as retrospective or not retrospective. Rather it may well be a matter of degree – the greater the unfairness, the more it is to be expected that Parliament will make it clear if that is intended.

Thus, some of the provisions of the Human Rights Act 1998 could have retrospective effect if that would not be unfair to the parties in a particular case.

Legal principle

Provisions of the Human Rights Act 1998 can have retrospective effect if it would not be unfair to the parties in a particular case.

16.5.1 Retrospective effect?

The Human Rights Act 1998 was brought into force in October 2000. In *R v Lambert* (2001) the House of Lords ruled that the Act did not have retrospective effect.

16.5.2 Commission for Equality and Human Rights

When preparing the Human Rights Act, the Labour Government considered establishing a Human Rights Commission, but then rejected this idea. However, in 2004, the Labour Government announced that it intended to establish a Commission for Equality and Human Rights. A consultation paper, *Fairness for All: A New Commission for Equality and Human Rights,* was published in 2004 by the Department for Trade and Industry. Following this consultation process, the Equality Act 2006 was passed by Parliament which contained provisions for the creation of the new Commission. It has replaced the Commission for Racial Equality, the Disability Rights Commission and the Equal Opportunities Commission, which had fought against racism, disability discrimination and sexism. The Commission is responsible for promoting both human rights and equality of opportunity. It seeks to prevent a wider range of discriminatory behaviour, including discrimination on the grounds of religion, age and sexual orientation. The new body was launched in October 2007. Its functions include:

- providing advice and guidance to people wishing to assert their rights;
- conducting inquiries;
- bringing legal proceedings;
- monitoring the operation of the ECHR in domestic law;
- scrutinising new legislation; and
- publishing regular reports on the state of the nation.

16.6 Advantages of the Human Rights Act 1998

16.6.1 Improved access

Bringing a case to Strasbourg can take up to six years and can be very expensive. Through incorporation, UK citizens are now able to enforce their rights under the Convention directly before the domestic courts (though applications to Strasbourg are still possible as a last resort).

16.6.2 Remedies

The remedies available from the European Court of Human Rights are inadequate. Also, the long delays mean that the remedies awarded can be too late to be effective. The national courts are able to provide quicker and more effective remedies.

16.6.3 Tried and tested

The ECHR has already been tried and tested over the last 60 years. The UK courts have developed some knowledge of its provisions as their decisions have been challenged in Strasbourg. The Privy Council has also developed case law in relation to similar provisions to be found in the written constitutions of Commonwealth countries, which were often drafted with the Convention in mind. It is therefore likely to prove easier to incorporate the Convention into domestic law than a completely new Bill of Rights.

16.6.4 Avoid conflict between domestic and international law

Problems were highlighted in the case of **R v Saunders** (1996). In this case, evidence obtained by Government inspectors under s. 177 of the Financial Services Act 1986 was used against Saunders in criminal proceedings for insider dealing. The English courts ruled that in English law this evidence was admissible at a criminal trial. The court in Strasbourg ruled that this evidence had been obtained by an unfair procedure and should have been excluded from the trial – **Saunders v UK** (1997). Evidence obtained in the same way was accepted by the trial court in **R v Morrissey** and **R v Staines** (1997). The Court of Appeal stated that it was 'an unsatisfactory position' that it was obliged to follow the domestic decision, which had held Saunders's evidence was admissible, despite the fact that the European Court had subsequently ruled that this breached the Convention. Now, under ss. 2 and 3 of the Human Rights Act 1998 a court would be able to take into account the Strasbourg jurisprudence and interpret relevant legislation in a way which is compatible with Convention rights 'so far as it is possible to do so'.

16.6.5 Encouraging conformity

While there are many instances of UK Governments changing the law as a result of losing cases in the European Court of Human Rights, they are not always keen to do so. In **Brogan v United Kingdom** (1988) the provisions of the Prevention of Terrorism (Temporary Provisions) Act 1984, allowing detention of suspects for up to seven days without judicial authority, were found to violate Art. 5, protecting freedom of the person. The Government responded by declaring that the power was necessary on security grounds and by depositing at Strasbourg a limited derogation under Art. 15 from the Convention to the extent that the legislation violated Art. 5.

In **Abdulaziz v United Kingdom** (1985) the Government technically complied with the European Court of Human Rights' decision, but in such a way as to decrease rather than increase rights. The case alleged that British immigration rules discriminated against women, because men permanently settled in the UK were allowed to bring their wives and fiancées to live with them here, but women in the same position could not bring their husbands and fiancés into the country. The European Court agreed, but the Government was determined not to increase immigration rights. Instead of allowing husbands and fiancés to settle here, they removed the right of wives and fiancées to do so, thereby ending the sexual discrimination but making the immigration laws even more restrictive.

Incorporation has reduced the problem of bringing domestic law into line with the ECHR. The courts are contributing to this process in every case where a conflict arises between the Convention and domestic law. But tensions can still arise between the European Court of Human Rights and the British Government, and on occasion the British Government is still prepared to ignore a decision of the European Court. In 2008, two men, Faisal Al-Saadoon and Khalaf Mufdhi were being held prisoner by UK soldiers in Iraq, accused of being responsible for the deaths of two British soldiers. The UK Government wished to transfer these men to the Iraqi Government as part of the process of handing back power in Iraq in accordance with a United Nations mandate. The two prisoners objected to the handover, claiming that the Iraqi Government tortured prisoners and if they were convicted they faced the death penalty. They took their case to the European Court of Human Rights and before the Court had time to give a final judgment it issued an injunction ordering the UK Government not to hand over the men until the Court had heard the case. The UK Government was concerned that if it continued to detain the men after 1 January 2009 it would be in breach of the UN mandate. It therefore went ahead and handed over the men to the Iraqi Government in breach of the European Court's injunction.

16.6.6 International image

It is not good for the UK's image abroad frequently to be found in error by a 'foreign' court, as it has been many times.

16.6.7 Clarity and accessibility

The law on civil rights has been complex and disorderly. For example, there has been no clear definition of the right to freedom of expression, only a collection of statutes and cases which state when and how such a freedom can be restricted. The ECHR provides a comprehensive and easily accessible statement of rights and freedoms enforceable in the UK.

16.6.8 Education

The ECHR sets out for citizens, Government and the judiciary the basic rights and freedoms we are all entitled to expect. This should lead to better awareness by citizens of their legal rights, and to legislation and judicial decisions which take those rights as their starting point, rather than just one of many things to be considered.

16.7 Disadvantages of the Human Rights Act 1998

16.7.1 Judicial power

Politicians have been unhappy with some of the decisions handed down by the judges relying on the Human Rights Act, which undermine national policies. While Members of Parliament have been elected to make and change law, judges are not elected and are supposed to apply the law, not make it. For example, the High Court ruled that the Government of the day had breached the human rights of some Afghan nationals who had hijacked an aircraft in order to escape to the UK. The High Court held that the Home Secretary had behaved unlawfully when he had denied the applicants leave to enter the UK after they had already successfully claimed before the courts that it would be in breach of their human rights to return them to Afghanistan. Instead, the Home Secretary had sought to delay granting the men leave to enter so that the rules could be changed and the men refused leave to enter. The High Court considered this to amount to an abuse of power. Following this case, the then Prime Minister described the judgment as an 'abuse of common sense' and announced that he would consider restricting the rights granted in the Human Rights Act.

Problems arise when politicians refuse or delay changing domestic law to bring it into line with Convention rights where problems have been identified by judges. For example, in *Greens and MT* v *UK* (2010) the European Court of Human Rights ruled that a blanket ban on prisoners voting in elections breached the European Convention. In *R (on the application of Chester)* v *Secretary of State for Justice; McGeoch* v *The Lord President of the Council* (2013) the Supreme Court acknowledged that s. 2 of the 1998 Act meant that they had to 'take into account' decisions of the European Court of Human Rights, but that did not mean they necessarily had to follow them. Here, two prisoners were unsuccessful in overturning the ban on prisoner voting as a draft Bill had been prepared by the Government which would allow certain prisoners the right to vote. However, to date this Bill has not been introduced for debate in Parliament.

16.7.2 Legal status

Incorporation of the ECHR would have had more impact if it had been entrenched. Any legislation which did not comply with it would have been struck down by the courts, and the ECHR itself could only have been changed in domestic law by special procedures, such as a referendum or an increased parliamentary majority. The American constitution is entrenched and as a result the American Supreme Court can strike down legislation which conflicts with the constitution. The Human Rights Act 1998 does not give UK citizens a Bill of Rights.

Many experts believe it would be constitutionally impossible to make the ECHR an entrenched Bill of Rights. This is because the doctrine of parliamentary sovereignty provides that no sitting Parliament can bind a future one: in other words, every Parliament is free to unmake laws made by their predecessors. This means that a future Parliament could simply abolish a Bill of Rights and any arrangements for entrenchment could be legislated away.

Not everybody agrees that such entrenchment would be impossible. Many Commonwealth countries which have inherited ideas of parliamentary sovereignty from the UK have enacted entrenched Bills of Rights without any constitutional problems arising. Alternatively, the ECHR could have been partially entrenched so that it was treated in the same way as EU law is today.

As the Labour Government decided not to entrench or partly entrench the ECHR into domestic law, so the legal protections provided by it are limited. Real weight would be given to the Convention both if it was entrenched and if a constitutional court were created.

Because the Convention is not entrenched into domestic law, the UK Government can derogate from it (which means they can obtain permission to breach a provision of the Convention with impunity). It has chosen to do this in order to be able to detain terrorist suspects without trial for indefinite periods under the Anti-Terrorism, Crime and Security Act 2001. To enable the above legislation to be passed, the Government obtained a derogation from Art. 5 of the European Convention which guarantees the right to liberty of the person. This piece of legislation followed the attacks on the US on 11 September 2001 and constitutes a significant violation of an individual's human rights. By January 2002, 11 individuals had been detained under these powers. Investigators from the European Committee for the Prevention of Torture and Degrading Treatment or Punishment visited the UK amid concerns over the treatment of these suspects. The Committee raised a number of concerns, including the fact that the detainees were being denied access to their family and lawyers for long periods of time.

16.7.3 Limited scope

The ECHR is over 60 years old and, since its creation, new rights have become important – for example, the Convention makes limited provision for preventing racial discrimination and none at all for preventing discrimination on the basis of disability or sexual orientation. Some people feel that a UK Bill of Rights should be broader, including environmental, economic and social rights.

The Convention is proving to be totally ineffective in the face of international violations of human rights. UK citizens and residents were held by the US at Camp X-Ray on Guantanamo Bay in Cuba for years, with no effective human rights.

16.8 A Bill of Rights for the UK?

It has been observed that the ECHR does not constitute a Bill of Rights for the UK because it has not been entrenched. Many people feel that while the Human Rights Act 1998 is a first step in the right direction, ultimately the UK needs a properly entrenched Bill of Rights to protect its citizens. Among developed Western countries, Israel and the UK are the only ones without such a Bill.

16.8.1 Arguments in favour of a Bill of Rights

Curbs on the executive

A Bill of Rights provides an important check on the enormous powers of the executive (the Government of the day and its agencies, such as the police, the army and Government departments). Constitutional writers of the nineteenth century, such as Dicey, made much of the role of Parliament as a watchdog over the executive, ensuring that oppressive legislation could not be passed. Since Dicey's time, the growth of a strong party system has fundamentally altered the nature of Parliament; in the vast majority of cases, a Government can expect its own members to obey party discipline, so that Government proposals will almost invariably be passed – during the 1980s, for example, only one Government Bill was defeated. Not only do those in opposition lack the numbers to prevent this, but the pressures of parliamentary time may even curtail a detailed scrutiny of proposed legislation. This can result in Governments being able to legislate against individual rights and freedoms almost at will.

The movement in favour of a Bill of Rights gained considerable support during the later years of the Thatcher regime, when the Government showed itself willing to compromise many important civil liberties. Many commentators were alarmed as they watched the banning of trade unions at Government Communications Headquarters (GCHQ), the attempts to ban the publication of *Spycatcher* (the memoirs of a retired security service agent) and the use of the Official Secrets Act 1911 to prosecute civil servants Sarah Tisdall and Clive Ponting who leaked official information the Government had wished to keep secret.

The fact that, given a decent majority in Parliament, Governments can make whatever law they like, means that they can simply legislate freedoms away, secure in the knowledge that the courts cannot refuse to apply their legislation, as they can in countries which have a Bill of Rights or written constitution. The Public Order Act 1986 and the Criminal Justice and Public Order Act 1994, for example, severely restrict rights of peaceful protest, of assembly and of movement, but English courts must apply this legislation nevertheless.

Supporters of a Bill of Rights claim it would curb executive powers, since the courts could simply refuse to apply laws which conflicted with it. This in turn would be a powerful incentive for a Government to avoid introducing such legislative provisions in the first place.

While the provision in s. 19 of the Human Rights Act 1998, requiring Ministers to state whether a Bill conforms with the 1998 Act, will discourage the executive in some circumstances from introducing legislation that breaches the ECHR, they are still able to do so.

Attitude of the judiciary

Even where the constitution does allow for judicial protection of civil rights, British judges have frequently proved themselves unequal to the task. As Griffith (1997) has famously pointed out, they show a tendency to view the public interest as the maintenance of established authority and traditional values. Though exceptions can always be found, the overall result has been that the maintenance of 'order' and the suppression of challenges to established authority – whether of trade unions or terrorists – have taken precedence over the kind of liberties a Bill of Rights might seek to protect. For example, in *R v Secretary of State for the Home Department, ex parte Brind* (1989), the judiciary upheld a broadcasting ban on members of a legitimate political party in Northern Ireland; in *Council of Civil Service Unions v Minister for the Civil Service* (1984), the ban on trade unions at GCHQ was accepted; and in *Kent v Metropolitan Police Commissioner* (1981) a blanket ban on protest marches through an area of London was allowed.

The numerous miscarriages of justice suggest there is little protection of the right to a fair trial, nor, given the treatment of some of those involved while in police custody, to freedom from torture and inhuman treatment. The wide powers of surveillance permitted under statute to the police and security services prove the right to privacy a fallacy.

The Human Rights Act 1998 only requires the UK courts to interpret legislation in a way which is compatible with Convention rights 'so far as it is possible to do so' (s. 3). If a judge decides that the Act breaches a Convention right, the Act prevails.

16.8.2 Arguments against a Bill of Rights

Unnecessary

The previous Conservative Government was among those who asserted that civil liberties were already adequately protected in this country. However, the present Conservative Government has gone from debating leaving the ECHR altogether to adopting a Bill of Rights in its place which will remain faithful to protecting fundamental rights. This debate now stands in abeyance until the details for Brexit are negotiated and focus can return to the need for a Bill of Rights.

Increased power for the judiciary

Among those who oppose a Bill of Rights, mistrust of the judiciary and constitutional objections to taking power from Parliament and giving it to judges, are perhaps the most frequent reasons given. There is no doubt that such a Bill would considerably increase judicial power. Unlike British statutes, the language of a Bill of Rights is typically open and imprecise, setting out broad principles rather than detailed provisions. This gives judges a wide discretion in interpretation – so wide that in the US, for example, the provisions against racial discrimination in the American Bill of Rights were once held to allow a form of apartheid, yet since 1954 such a system has been held to violate the Bill. Even within recent decades, the US Bill of Rights has been interpreted to allow discrimination against minorities. Thus, in the Supreme Court's decision in *Bowers v Hardwick* (1986), the constitutional right of privacy was effectively denied to homosexuals. However, it should be noted that *Bowers* was overruled by the Supreme Court in 1996, and in recent years the court has given much wider protections to homosexuals. More recently, in *United States v Windsor* (2013), the court held that it was unconstitutional to define 'marriage' as being between one man and one woman, meaning that the United States Government must recognise same-sex marriages which have taken place in specific states (such as California) as valid.

A Bill of Rights also calls upon judges to decide the relative importance of protected rights where two of them clash. Should, for example, the right to free expression of members of the British National Party override or give way to that of ethnic minorities to be free of racial harassment? Does a foetus have a right to life which overrides its mother's right to liberty and security of the person? There are no obvious right or wrong answers to questions like these and nor are there always obvious legal answers, even where there is a Bill of Rights. In many such cases the real problem is not what the law is, but what the law should be. Many people believe that is not a question which should be answered by judges, who are not elected but appointed from a narrow social elite by a secretive procedure. As Griffith (1997) has pointed out, these questions are political and political questions should, as far as possible, be answered by politicians elected to do so.

Supporters of such a Bill argue that the problems associated with greater judicial power could be dealt with by reforming judicial selection and drawing judges from a wider spread of the population. While this is clearly desirable in itself, it would not remove the fundamental objection that judges are not elected and nor, whatever the reforms, is it likely to avoid the fact that, by virtue of their education and their lifestyle, judges would be unrepresentative of the mass of the population. Commentators like Griffith, who oppose a Bill of Rights, argue that what is needed is not so much reform of the judiciary, but political reforms that would allow a democratically elected legislature genuinely to supervise the acts of the executive and to fetter the exercise of executive discretion. The protection of fundamental freedoms and rights should not be for the individual to establish in court, but for the legislature to safeguard as part of its job.

Inflexibility

Supporters of our current constitutional arrangements argue that, without a written constitution, our system can adapt over time, meeting new needs as they arise. They contend that a Bill of Rights would lack this flexibility. Two responses to this are that, first, the open and imprecise language of a Bill of Rights allows flexibility; and, secondly, the Bills can be changed when necessary: the arrangements for entrenchment will usually set down a special procedure that can be used to make amendments. The fact that these procedures may be long and difficult simply protects those rights originally laid down from rash or unpopular change; it does not set them in stone.

Too much flexibility

Ironically, it is also argued that the imprecise language typical of a Bill of Rights would lead to uncertainty about the law, leading to increased litigation with no clear objectives as to how general principles might emerge and policies be interpreted. This is clearly linked to the problem of mistrust of the judiciary.

Rights are not powers

A more fundamental problem is the idea that merely granting rights is not enough to secure individual freedom and empowerment. It is all very well to grant rights but, unless they are underpinned by economic and social provision, they may prove to be useless. Freedom of labour is effectively useless in times of high unemployment, when it becomes nothing more

16

INTRODUCTION TO HUMAN RIGHTS

than the freedom to live in poverty. Freedom of movement fails to help disabled people who cannot use public transport or afford their own. Freedom of association offers little advantage if employers refuse to recognise trade unions, and liberty of the person means nothing for the battered wife or abused child who has neither the personal nor the practical resources to escape.

Where there are huge imbalances in power in society, giving equal rights to all may be of limited use because those who have the most power can use it to find a way round the rights of those who are less powerful. For example, recent compensation payments made to women sacked for being pregnant have led to speculation that as a result employers may simply become even less keen than before to employ women; cases on racial discrimination may have had similar effects on the employment prospects of members of ethnic minorities. While it should not be denied that this kind of provision helps people, it can be argued that in focusing on individual rights, rather than social duties, a Bill of Rights might detract attention from any real commitment to a just society. The point is not that a Bill of Rights is undesirable but that, on its own, it cannot make the kind of changes sought by its supporters.

There is also the question of whether the same Bill of Rights would be appropriate for all parts of the UK. Northern Ireland may require special treatment given the intensity of religious and political animosity.

Drafting style

The ECHR follows the more general, looser European style of legislative drafting, in contrast to the more tightly worded legislation our courts are used to applying – though, British courts are gaining more experience of this approach.

The Bigger Picture: A British Bill of Rights

The Conservative Party has pledged to repeal the Human Rights Act 1998 and replace it with a British Bill of Rights. It is also considering withdrawing from the European Convention on Human Rights. The Government is concerned that the Human Rights Act is hindering the fight against crime and terrorism and undermines national sovereignty. It was particularly angered by the European Court of Human Rights temporarily blocking the deportation of Abu Qatada, a Muslim cleric who was suspected of having terrorist links. The European court was concerned that, if deported, evidence obtained by torture was likely to be relied on in a subsequent trial in Jordan. This would amount to a breach of his Art. 6 right to a fair trial: ***Othman (Abu Qatada) v UK*** (2012). As regards national sovereignty, the Conservatives oppose the influence of European human rights law over UK law, through the incorporation of the European Convention on Human Rights. The European Court has been accused of 'mission creep', by expanding its jurisdiction beyond that contemplated by the member states. Its supporters have counter-argued that the Convention is a living instrument which must be constantly re-interpreted to take into account social change; and that sovereignty is not surrendered merely by entering into international commitments. Lord Lester has observed that:

> The political commitment to an enduring system is fragile and uncertain because of constant challenges to the legitimacy of the Human Rights Act. From its birth, powerful sections of the British media have attacked the Human Rights Act on a daily basis, because they oppose its protection of personal privacy against media intrusion on private lives and because they wish the UK to withdraw from the European Convention and the European Union.

The Government established a Commission to look at whether the Human Rights Act should be repealed and a British Bill of Rights created in its place. The Commission published its final report in 2012, entitled *A UK Bill of Rights? The Choice Before Us.* The majority of its members recommended establishing a UK Bill of Rights, because of the 'lack of ownership by the public' of the Human Rights Act 1998 and the European Convention. This problem would be overcome if a home-grown Bill of Rights was produced which would not be entrenched to respect the principle of the sovereignty of Parliament. A minority opposed this recommendation, fearing it could lead to the diminution of rights and be the first step towards withdrawing from the European system altogether.

In its manifesto for the 2015 elections, the Conservative Party pledged to repeal the Human Rights Act and establish a UK Bill of Rights. This Bill of Rights would re-enact the Convention rights but with clarification and more precise definition, in order, for example, to prevent foreign nationals from using human rights to resist deportation. It would remove the UK courts' obligation to 'take account' of decisions of the Strasbourg Court and remove the requirement to interpret domestic legislation compatibly with Convention rights. The new Bill would also require UK courts to strike out 'trivial' rights cases. Judgments of the European Court of Human Rights would be 'advisory', becoming binding only if Parliament agreed to them. The Conservative Party is also considering withdrawing from the European Convention on Human Rights. The only country to withdraw from the Convention to date was Greece in 1970 when it was governed by military colonels who had been found to have tortured political opponents in breach of the European Convention. It rejoined the Convention when democracy was restored to the country. The momentum for withdrawing from the ECHR has slowed down considerably after the decision was made to withdraw from the EU. The Conservative Party has said that it does not want there to be any distractions while negations for Brexit are underway and that withdrawal from the ECHR will firmly be on their 2020 election campaign agenda.

Those in favour of retaining the Human Rights Act argue it has been the victim of a sustained campaign of misinformation. If the Act was repealed the UK would return to its previous position of being a signatory to the Convention, giving individuals merely a right to take cases to the European Court of Human Rights. Individuals in UK courts would have to rely on the new Bill of Rights, rather than being able to rely on the European Convention. The international reputation of the UK as a liberal democracy could be damaged. A complication in trying to 'nationalise' human rights, is that the European Union has now established its Charter of Rights which is based on the Convention. The Charter will not have any effect in the UK when it officially withdraws from the EU. A former Conservative Attorney General considered that it was an incoherent policy to remain a signatory to the European Convention but refuse to recognise the rulings of the court which enforces it. The former Lord Chancellor, Kenneth Clarke, has commented: 'Modern government is big, powerful and bureaucratic. It interferes with every aspect of our lives. We need the ECHR more now than we did when it was created.'

Due to opposition by some Conservative Members of Parliament, these reforms were not included in the first Parliamentary session under the new Conservative Government because of concerns it would be difficult to get these changes passed in Parliament. Instead the Government has simply stated it will 'bring forward proposals for a British Bill of Rights'.

16.9 The European Court of Human Rights and the CJEU

The European Court of Human Rights in Strasbourg is often confused with the Court of Justice of the European Union (CJEU) in Luxembourg, but these are quite separate institutions, as are the Commission of Human Rights and the Commission of the European

Union. The phrase 'taking your case to Europe' tends to be used broadly, but the process and grounds for bringing an action to the CJEU are quite distinct from those for the European Court of Human Rights.

There are, however, growing links between the ECHR and European Union law. Article 164 of the Treaty of Rome provides that one of the functions of the CJEU is to ensure observance of the general principles of law contained in that treaty. In recent cases the CJEU has suggested that respect for human rights is one of these principles, and that for guidance in understanding the scope of this principle they can look to the Convention. For example, in *P v S and Cornwall County Council* (1996) P was dismissed from her employment because she was a transsexual. Her application to the UK courts for sex discrimination was rejected. When the case was heard by the CJEU the Court referred to the European Court of Human Rights' judgment in *Re Rees* (1986). It concluded that the European Equal Treatment Directive had been breached, as this directive encapsulated the fundamental principle of equality.

16.10 The European Charter of Fundamental Rights

The European Union looks set to become more involved in the protection of human rights within Europe. Article 6 of the Lisbon Treaty came into force in 2009 and recognises the rights and freedoms set out in the European Charter of Fundamental Rights. Thus the treaty provides for the incorporation of the Charter into EU law. It also states that the fundamental rights guaranteed by the European Convention on Human Rights 'constitute general principles of the Union's law'.

Where the Charter lays down rights contained in the European Convention, these rights will be interpreted in accordance with the Convention right, even if the Charter is worded slightly differently. Thus, Art. 53(2) of the Charter states:

> so far as this Charter contains rights which correspond to rights guaranteed by the [Convention], the meaning and scope of those rights shall be the same as those laid down by the said Convention.

The Charter lays down more extensive rights than those contained in the European Convention because, as well as containing civil and political rights, it lays down social and economic rights, such as freedom of information, freedom of the arts and sciences and rights for children and the elderly. The Charter also extends some of the existing Convention rights to a more modern context. Thus it includes the established right to life and prohibition of torture, but also prohibits more modern problems of human trafficking, forced labour, human cloning and the sale of body parts. The rights in the Charter are divided into six sections:

- dignity;
- freedoms;
- equality;
- solidarity;
- citizens' rights;
- justice.

In the section on 'justice' it explicitly requires criminal sentences to be proportionate to the offence and lays down a right not to be tried twice for the same offence (known as the double jeopardy rule). The section entitled 'solidarity' deals with workers' rights, including a right to consultation, protection from unjustified dismissals, fair and just working conditions, parental leave and, most importantly, the right to strike (a right which has never been recognised in this country).

The Charter applies to the acts of EU institutions and member states when implementing EU law (Art. 51 of the Charter). It is not clear whether the Charter can be relied on between private citizens (horizontal effect) or whether it can only be relied on against member states and EU institutions.

McB v *E* (2011) is the first case in which the European Court looks at the impact of the Charter. It noted that 'it is called upon to interpret, in the light of the Charter, the law of the European Union within the limits of the powers conferred on it'. So the Charter would only be looked at for the purposes of interpreting the European Regulation that was relevant to the case, and would not be used to assess the national law as such. On the facts of the case, the Charter did not actually affect the Court's interpretation of the Regulation. In the subsequent case of *Volker und Markus Schecke* v *Land Hessen* (2012) the European Court used the Charter to strike down a piece of EU legislation.

The UK has obtained a legally binding protocol, which states that no court can rule that UK laws or practices are inconsistent with the principles laid down in the Charter and the Charter will not therefore create new legal rights in the UK.

The European Union has established a Fundamental Rights Agency. There has been some criticism of this organisation on the basis that the new agency might simply duplicate much of the work being done by existing bodies, particularly the European Court of Human Rights. However, with the current backlash to terrorist activity, greater involvement of the EU in the protection of human rights might be desirable.

16.11 Today's debates

16.11.1 Responding to the threat of terrorism

If one person extends their rights, it tends to be at the expense of another person's rights. For example, when a newspaper exercises its right to freedom of expression, this will frequently be to the detriment of another person's right to privacy. Thus careful controls need to be in place to make sure that one person or organisation does not extend their rights too far at the expense of another. This is particularly the case where a Government is seeking to extend its rights over its citizens. In recent years there has been particular concern that in its fight against terrorism the Government has not been respecting human rights. After the bombing of the public transport system in London in July 2005, Tony Blair stated that the 'rules of the game have changed' and outlined some of his ideas for amending the law in the UK to tackle this threat to our society. At the same time, civil liberties organisations are concerned that the Government might respond to these attacks in a way that amounted to a significant attack on an individual's human rights, while at the same time proving to be counter-productive in the fight against terrorism. In 2008, the Labour Government was forced to drop its provision in the Counter-Terrorism Bill to allow the detention of suspected terrorists for 42 days without charge, but the judges will still be placed in a very sensitive position when interpreting this piece of legislation.

16

INTRODUCTION TO HUMAN RIGHTS

Following the 11 September 2001 attacks on the United States, there was international concern about terrorism. This led the UK Government to pass the Anti-Terrorism, Crime and Security Act 2001, which allowed it to detain in prison suspected terrorists without trial. This was in breach of their right to freedom of movement which is guaranteed under Art. 5 of the European Convention. The UK Government therefore gained permission from the European Council to not comply with this article on the basis that there was a national emergency under Art. 15.

Under this legislation, nine foreign nationals were certified as suspected terrorists and detained without trial. The legality of the detention was challenged through the courts in ***A and X and others* v *Secretary of State for the Home Department*** (2004). Some of the applicants had been detained in a high security prison for three years, with no prospect of release or a trial. Because the case was so important, nine judges in the House of Lords heard the case instead of the usual five. The House held that the detentions were unlawful. It accepted that there was a national emergency justifying derogation under Art. 15, but the measures taken were not strictly required. Indefinite detention without trial was not strictly required because it was being imposed only on foreign nationals unable to leave Britain and not on foreign nationals who could leave for another country or on British nationals. The legislation also therefore discriminated against foreign nationals and so breached Art. 14 of the Convention.

As a result, the legislation was repealed and replaced by the Prevention of Terrorism Act 2005. This established control orders (sometimes called 'gag and tag orders'), which can potentially amount to house arrest – the first time we have seen this measure in the UK. The people who had been detained without trial were released and were allowed to return home, but they were placed under control orders (not amounting to house arrest). Up to

Photo 16.2 The aftermath of the London bus bombing on 7 July 2005

Source: © DBURKE/Alamy Stock Photo

16 different restrictions can be placed on an individual who is subjected to a control order, such as the use of electronic tagging, surveillance, permission to search their premises and a curfew. The order is usually made by the High Court following an application by the Home Secretary. It will be imposed where the individuals are suspected of having been involved in terrorism-related activity but it is thought that, due to the sensitivity surrounding Security Service involvement, evidence demonstrating suspicions against the person, and the high standard of proof required in criminal trials, a criminal conviction cannot be obtained. Breach of a control order without reasonable excuse is a criminal offence punishable by up to five years' imprisonment.

In *Secretary of State for the Home Department* v *JJ* (2007) control orders had been imposed on six suspects, under which they were electronically tagged, required to remain at home for 18 hours a day and have all visitors vetted by the Home Office. The House of Lords concluded that these orders amounted to a deprivation of liberty in breach of Art. 5 of the Convention. As a result of this decision, the Home Office has amended the restrictions imposed on the complainants under the control orders and they are currently subjected to a 16-hour curfew.

In *Secretary of State for the Home Department* v *MB* (2007), the High Court described control orders as an 'affront to justice'. MB is a British Muslim who was arrested when trying to leave the country in March 2005. The judge concluded that he could not quash the order due to the 'one-sided information' available to the court. However, he criticised the control orders for allowing a suspect's rights to be determined by 'executive decision-making, untrammelled by any prospect of effective judicial supervision'.

> To say that the [Prevention of Terrorism] Act does not give the respondent in the case . . . a 'fair hearing' . . . would be an understatement. The court would be failing in its duty under the Human Rights Act, a duty imposed upon the court by Parliament, if it did not say, loud and clear that the procedure under the Act whereby the court merely reviews the lawfulness of the Secretary of State's decision to make the order upon the basis of the material available to him at the early stage is conspicuously unfair.

An appeal against the High Court decision was subsequently successful before the Court of Appeal, which held that the control order procedures did not breach a right to a fair trial under Art. 6 of the Convention. MB appealed to the House of Lords, which held that a control order review hearing would only be fair if the Home Office disclosed the allegation against the individual along with enough information for the person to have sufficient knowledge of the case against them to be able to contest the allegation. The House sent the case back to the High Court to consider whether the control order was fair in the light of this ruling. Forty-eight control orders had been issued by 2011, with eight people remaining under a control order in that year and seven people who were placed under a control order having disappeared altogether.

In 2006, Lord Carlile, the Government's independent terrorism watchdog, issued his first annual review of the Prevention of Terrorism Act 2005. With access to secret security service papers, he made clear that '[t]he nature of the activities is sufficiently alarming for me to re-emphasise . . . the real and present danger of shocking terrorism acts involving suicide bombers'. He considered that further suicide bombings in the UK must be expected and that in his view such an ongoing threat meant that 'as a last resort (only), in my view the control order system as operated currently in its non-derogating form is a justifiable and proportionate safety valve for the proper protection of civil society'.

The coalition Government set up a review to look at the impact of anti-terrorist legislation on civil liberties. The review published its final report in 2011: *Review of Counter-Terrorism and Security Powers*. In light of the review's recommendations, the coalition Government abolished control orders and replaced them with terrorism prevention and investigation measures (TPIMs). These new measures are contained in the Terrorism Prevention and Investigation Measures Act 2011. They look very similar to control orders, but suspects under these measures are allowed to leave home for longer periods; they can only be required to stay at home at night for 8 hours (instead of 16 hours); they can no longer be asked to move to another part of the country away from their family and friends; and internet and phone use can be restricted but not banned altogether. The similarities with control orders has led to the suggestion that this reform amounts to little more than rebranding.

The former Labour Government planned to introduce compulsory identity cards into the UK and the Identity Cards Act 2006 was passed by Parliament. The justification for ID cards is that they would help to fight terrorism, organised crime, illegal immigration, identity fraud and benefit fraud. On the other hand, ID cards can be a dangerous tool for controlling a population and their absence in this country has to date been seen as a sign of our freedom. The coalition Government scrapped the identity cards scheme by passing the Identity Documents Act 2010, after deciding that the arguments against identity cards outweighed their perceived benefits.

16.11.2 The right to privacy

Another very different area that has given rise to considerable debate is whether the European Convention protects the right to privacy of celebrities. While the courts are recognising that the Convention does provide a right to privacy they are anxious to balance this against the right to freedom of expression. In April 2005, the celebrities Victoria and David Beckham tried to prevent the publication by the *News of the World* of revelations by their former nanny about their private lives. The court allowed the newspaper to publish, pointing to the public interest in the publication of the stories, despite the fact that the story was merely trivial information primarily about the state of their marriage and Victoria's cosmetic surgery.

The courts are prepared to recognise that the European Convention protects the right to privacy and has sought to seek a balance between this right and the right to freedom of expression. This has caused particular tensions where newspapers have wanted to publish details of celebrities' sex lives and the celebrities have sought to prevent publication. The approach that the court seems to be taking is that there needs to be a public interest in details being published. The very well-publicised controversy of topless photos of the Duchess of Cambridge, Kate Middleton, being published by the magazine *Closer* in France ended in the magazine having to pay out significant sums to the Duke and Duchess of Cambridge. The pair were holidaying in a private chateau owned by the Queen's nephew, Viscount Linley, and the waiting paparazzi used long lens cameras to be able to take intrusive photos of the couple. Prince William has remarked that this intrusion of privacy is particularly shocking because it reminded him of the harassment that led to the death of his mother, Diana, Princess of Wales. The case was heard in France and the court held that the taking of such photos was an unjustified intrusion of the couple's privacy. Some critics have argued, however, that knowing all about the royals and the strength of their marriage, is in fact in the public interest.

The approach of the courts has been that there is no public interest in the public knowing details of, for example, a footballer's extra-marital affairs. ***CTB*** v ***News Group Newspapers Ltd*** (2011) concerned a case brought against a newspaper company which was seeking to publish a story about an affair between the *Big Brother* TV programme contestant, Imogen Thomas, and a footballer (who was named by an MP in Parliament). The High Court stated that in determining whether to allow publication the court had to consider whether publication would contribute to a debate of general interest – for instance, whether it would help achieve a social purpose, such as the prevention or detection of crime or whether it would in some way prevent the public from being seriously misled. On the facts of the case, the High Court concluded that no public interest would be served by allowing publication.

16

INTRODUCTION TO HUMAN RIGHTS

The Bigger Picture: Your rights in school and university

Young people are actually quite vulnerable members of our society and it is important that they realise they benefit from human rights as well as adults. The Equality Act 2006 gives children the right not to be discriminated against, Art. 9 of the European Convention protects the rights to freedom of religion and Art. 2 of Protocol 1 to the Convention protects the right to education.

English schools often require pupils to wear a school uniform. They also frequently lay down rules about how the children should wear their hair, known as a 'hair policy'. The schools have to be careful that in setting the rules about uniform and hair that they respect the rights of all the children in the school. Discrimination can take different forms: it can be direct (for example, banning black children from a school) or indirect (where there may be no racist intent, but a rule has a greater impact on black children). In **SG v St Gregory's Catholic Science College** (2011) a school's hair policy banned boys from having cornrows (traditional plaits). The High Court ruled that this ban was illegal because it indirectly discriminated against black boys. While the policy theoretically applied to all children in the school, in practice black boys were being treated differently from white boys because the policy had a greater impact on them, as their cultural traditions included wearing plaits. The legal principle in this case will equally apply to an

Photo 16.3 Various hairstyles

Source: (from L-R) Blend Images/Shutterstock; Duplass/Shutterstock; Sophie Bluy/Pearson Education Ltd

afro and neatly shaved black hair. A boys' school cannot, therefore, have a policy stating all hair must be between 1 and 3 cm long, because this amounts to indirect discrimination. Instead, schools have moved to having hair policies that simply require a boy's hair to be cut above the collar. Some people might argue that a hairstyle is a very trivial issue and the courts should not waste their time on this. But actually this is a very important issue because racism stems from a person looking physically different from the majority: black children do not just have a different skin colour but they also often have different hair. A British multicultural society celebrates these differences, it does not try to repress them.

In *R (on the application of Shabina Begum) v Headteacher and Governors of Denbigh High School* (2006) a Muslim schoolgirl, Shabina Begum, wanted to wear a jilbab (a full-length gown) to school instead of the agreed school uniform, because of her religious beliefs. In 2002, she had arrived at school wearing a jilbab, but she was told to go home and change. Because of her continued refusal to wear a school uniform, she was excluded from school for two years. Pupils at the school were allowed to wear a shalwar kameez (trousers and tunic) but not a jilbab. The House of Lords concluded that the school's conduct did not amount to a breach of her right to freedom of religion or right to education. She had not attended school for two years, but her school was entitled to exclude her while she refused to comply with the uniform and she could have attended another local school where the jilbab was allowed. But this case is not necessarily the final word on this issue. In *Eweida v UK* (2013) the ECtHR accepted that simply because a person could go elsewhere did not in itself prevent there being a breach of a human right. Instead, the possibility of going elsewhere would be one factor that could be taken into account when deciding whether the restriction was proportionate.

In *Ali v Head Teacher and Governors of Lord Grey School* (2006) the House of Lords held a pupil's exclusion from school for eight months did not amount to a breach of his right to education. Following the exclusion, the 13-year-old pupil had access to educational facilities outside the school (including homework and tuition in a pupil referral unit) and failed to attend a meeting to re-integrate him back into the school. Schools can insist on compliance with rules: as long as alternative educational facilities are made available to excluded pupils, their Convention rights have not been breached. The House of Lords said that the right to education would only be breached in extreme cases, where virtually no education had been provided.

The process of excluding a pupil from school does not amount to criminal proceedings, so Art. 6 does not apply guaranteeing the right to a fair hearing. In *R (on the application of LG) v Independent Appeal Panel for Tom Hood School* (2010), a boy had been excluded from school because he had threatened a teacher with a knife. Article 6 did not apply because this was a disciplinary case, not a criminal case.

Answering questions

1   Critically evaluate the impact of the Human Rights Act 1998 upon the English legal system.

2   What has been the effect of s. 2 of the Human Rights Act 1998 on the exercise of precedent by UK judges?

3   To what extent would a Bill of Rights provide additional protection of human rights in the United Kingdom?

For answers to these questions, visit the companion website at www.pearsoned.co.uk/ elliottquinn

SUMMARY OF CHAPTER 16: INTRODUCTION TO HUMAN RIGHTS

Introduction

Most democratic countries have a written Bill of Rights. Britain is unusual among democratic countries in having, to date, neither a Bill of Rights nor a written constitution. In this country, our rights and freedoms are traditionally considered to be protected by a presumption that we are free to do whatever is not specifically forbidden either by legislation or by the common law. A significant change in the British position was made by the Human Rights Act 1998, which makes the European Convention on Human Rights (ECHR) part of the law of the UK.

The European Convention on Human Rights

The ECHR was drawn up by the Council of Europe, which was established after the Second World War. A special court, known as the European Court of Human Rights, was set up to deal with claims concerning breaches of the ECHR.

The Human Rights Act 1998

The Convention is now applicable directly in the UK courts under s. 7 of the Human Rights Act. Under s. 2 of the Act, the domestic judiciary 'must take into account' any relevant Strasbourg jurisprudence, although they are not bound by it. The UK courts are required to interpret all legislation in a way which is compatible with Convention rights 'so far as it is possible to do so' (s. 3). It is unlawful for public authorities to act in a way which is incompatible with Convention rights (s. 6).

Retrospective effect?

Following the case of *Wilson v Secretary of State for Trade and Industry* (2003) some provisions of the Human Rights Act 1998 could have retrospective effect if that would not be unfair to the parties in a particular case.

The scope of the convention

The rights protected by the ECHR include the right to life (Art. 2); freedom from torture, inhuman or degrading treatment (Art. 3); freedom from slavery or forced labour (Art. 4); the right to liberty and security of the person (Art. 5); the right to a fair trial (Art. 6); the prohibition of retrospective criminal laws (Art. 7); the right to respect for a person's private and family life, home and correspondence (Art. 8); freedom of thought, conscience and religion (Art. 9); freedom of expression (Art. 10); freedom of peaceful assembly and association, including the right to join a trade union (Art. 11); and the right to marry and have a family (Art. 12).

A Bill of Rights for the UK?

It has been observed that the ECHR does not constitute a Bill of Rights for the UK because it has not been entrenched. Many people feel that while the Human Rights Act 1998 is a first step in the right direction, ultimately the UK needs a properly entrenched Bill of Rights to protect its citizens. Among developed Western countries, Israel and the UK are the only ones without such a Bill.

Reform

The European Union is becoming more involved in the protection of human rights within Europe.

Reading list

Clayton, R. (2015) The empire strikes back: common law rights and the Human Rights Act [2015]. *Public Law*, 3.

Department for Trade and Industry (2004) *Fairness for All: A New Commission for Equality and Human Rights*, Cm 6185. London: Stationery Office.

Griffith, J.A.G. (1997) *The Politics of the Judiciary*. London: Fontana.

Hoffmann, Lord (2009) The universality of human rights. *Law Quarterly Review*, 125: 416.

House of Lords Parliamentary Committee (2007) *Relations Between the Executive, the Judiciary and Parliament*, London: Stationery Office.

Laws, J. (1998) The limitations of human rights. *Public Law*, 254.

Raine, J. and Walker, C. (2002) *The Impact on the Courts and the Administration of Justice of the Human Rights Act 1998*. London: Lord Chancellor's Department, Research Secretariat.

Tickell, A. (2015) More 'efficient' justice at the European Court of Human Rights: but at whose expense? *Public Law*, 206.

Wright, J. (2009) Interpreting section 2 of the Human Rights Act 1998: towards an indigenous jurisprudence of human rights. *Public Law*, 595.

On the internet

The Human Rights Act 1998 is available on the legislation.gov.uk website at:
www.legislation.gov.uk/ukpga/1998/42/contents

The website of the European Court of Human Rights is:
http://www.echr.coe.int

The Ministry of Justice report *Responding to Human Rights judgments* (2016) is available at:
https://assets.publishing.service.gov.uk/government/uploads/system/uploads/attachment_data/file/570754/responding-to-human-rights-judgments-2014-to-2016-print.pdf

The *Review of Counter-Terrorism and Security Powers* (2011) has been published on the Home Office website at:

> https://assets.publishing.service.gov.uk/government/uploads/system/uploads/attachment_data/file/97971/report-by-lord-mcdonald.pdf

The report of the Commission on a Bill of Rights entitled *A UK Bill of Rights? The Choice Before Us* (2012) is available at:

> http://webarchive.nationalarchives.gov.uk/20130206065653/https://www.justice.gov.uk/downloads/about/cbr/uk-bill-rights-vol-1.pdf

A useful source of information on human rights in England is:

> https://www.equalityhumanrights.com/en/human-rights/human-rights-act

The European Court of Human Rights' Annual Report 2016 can be found at:

> http://www.echr.coe.int/Documents/Annual_report_2016_ENG.pdf

Chapter 17
Remedies for infringement of human rights

This chapter discusses:

- the different remedies available when a person's human rights have been breached, including:

  - judicial review;

  - *habeas corpus;*

  - civil proceedings;

  - compensation paid by the state;

  - criminal proceedings;

  - the Criminal Injuries Compensation Scheme;

  - the European Court of Human Rights;

  - disciplinary proceedings against the police;

  - the exclusion of evidence from the criminal courts;

  - the right to use force in self-defence; and

  - parliamentary controls.

17.1 Introduction

Rights are only worthwhile if there are adequate remedies for their enforcement. The fact that we do not yet have a Bill of Rights, but only a collection of laws detailing what we may not do, has inevitably meant that remedies are similarly scattered. Some of the main remedies available in English law for unlawful infringement of basic rights are the subject of this section.

17.2 Judicial review

Where a public body – such as a local authority, the police, or a Government department – acts illegally, the result will often be an infringement of an individual's rights, and in some cases the remedy for this is a procedure known as judicial review. (This is discussed in Chapter 26.)

17.3 *Habeas corpus*

Personal liberty is regarded as the most fundamental of all freedoms, and where individuals are wrongfully deprived of their liberty, the fact that, on release, they can sue their captor for damages under the ordinary civil law is not regarded as sufficient. *Habeas corpus* is an ancient remedy which allows a person detained to challenge the legality of detention and, if successful, get themselves quickly released. It does not punish the person responsible for the detention, but once the detainee is set free, they can still pursue any other available remedies for compensation or punishment.

Habeas corpus may be sought by, among others, convicted prisoners; those detained in custody pending trial or held by the police during criminal investigations; those awaiting extradition; psychiatric patients; and those with excessive bail conditions imposed on them. Application is made to the Divisional Court, and takes priority over all other court business.

17.4 Civil action for negligence

Where a public body breaches a person's rights in such a way as to amount to a tort, that body may be sued in the same way as a private citizen would be; since the Crown Proceedings Act 1947, this includes the Crown.

As far as civil rights are concerned, this remedy is of particular importance in relation to illegal behaviour by the police: possible actions include assault, malicious prosecution, false imprisonment, wrongful arrest and trespass to property or goods. Exemplary damages may be awarded against the police even where there has been no oppressive behaviour or other aggravating circumstances. These cases are usually heard by a jury.

In the past the police have benefited from an effective immunity from liability for negligence in their investigations. This immunity stems from the case of **Hill v Chief Constable of West Yorkshire** (1989). The case looked at whether the police owed a duty of care to a victim of Peter Sutcliffe, known as the Yorkshire Ripper. The House of Lords ruled that public policy prevented any action for negligence lying in respect of police strategies for the investigation and prevention of crime.

In *Osman* v *UK* (1998) the European Court of Human Rights threw into doubt the future of this immunity. In that case, a teacher had developed a fixation with a 14-year-old boy at his school. He gave him money, took photographs of him and sometimes followed him home. Graffiti of a sexual nature appeared in the neighbourhood and the parents' house and car suffered criminal damage but the teacher denied any involvement. The teacher changed his name by deed poll to include the boy's name. He was suspended from his position as a teacher and he indicated that he was thinking of 'doing a Hungerford' by which it was assumed he meant he might use firearms to kill the deputy headmaster and other victims at random. In December 1987, the police sought to interview the man in connection with allegations of criminal damage but he had disappeared. Two months later he went to the boy's home, shot and wounded him and killed his father. He also went to the home of the deputy headmaster and shot and wounded him and killed his son. He was convicted of manslaughter and placed in a psychiatric hospital.

The pupil with whom he had had an obsession and the mother brought a civil action against the Metropolitan Police for negligence. They claimed that the police had been negligent in not apprehending the man before the incident that led to the killing. Relying on *Hill* v *Chief Constable of West Yorkshire* the Court of Appeal upheld a ruling to strike out the case as disclosing no cause of action. The Court of Appeal treated that case as laying down a watertight defence. It was contended before the European Court of Human Rights that the rule of public policy preventing the action for negligence breached the European Convention on Human Rights. The European Court ruled that Art. 6 of the Convention, which guarantees the right to a fair trial, had been violated. It considered that the exclusionary rule formulated in the *Hill* case should not be used as a blanket immunity, but that the existence of competing public policy issues had to be considered. The approach of the Court of Appeal had amounted to an unjustifiable restriction on the right of access to a court to have a claim determined on its merits.

In *Brooks* v *Metropolitan Police Commissioner* (2005) the House of Lords clarified that *Hill* was laying down a rule of substantive law (that the police did not owe a duty of care on the facts), rather than a rule of procedure (which is associated with an 'immunity' from proceedings). The right to a fair trial in Art. 6 is restricted to rules of procedure and should not interfere with the substantive law in a country. In *Z* v *UK* (2001) the European Court acknowledged it had not fully understood the English law as laid down in *Hill* because it had thought it was laying down a procedural immunity that was covered by Art. 6.

The policy aims which underlie the decision in *Hill* are that the police should make their operational decisions on the basis of what is best to provide protection to the community at large. But the absolute rule that the House of Lords seemed to have laid down in *Hill* has been subject to some modest backtracking by the courts in subsequent years. In *Brooks* the House of Lords did accept that the court in *Hill* may have overstated the position to some degree. There was one circumstance in which the police may have a duty to individuals in relation to their role in the investigation and suppression of crime and that was where there was an assumption of responsibility by the police to that individual. In addition, even where no negligence liability may be imposed, the courts may be prepared to impose liability on the basis that there has been a separate breach of the European Convention following the Human Rights Act 1998.

17

REMEDIES FOR INFRINGEMENT OF HUMAN RIGHTS

17.4.1 The Human Rights Act 1998

Claimants may be entitled to compensation for breach of the European Convention under the Human Rights Act 1998. For example, a woman may be the victim of domestic abuse over a number of years to the knowledge of the police. If she rings the police telling them she is about to be stabbed by her partner and the police do not respond appropriately and she is killed, then her family may be entitled to compensation for breach of her right to life under Art. 2 of the European Convention. On the basis of the leading case of *Osman* v *UK*, Art. 2 applies where the authorities knew or ought to have known of the existence of a 'real and immediate risk to the life of an identified individual . . . from the criminal acts of a third party'.

The number of actions against the London Metropolitan Police has risen considerably over the years, reaching 5,836 in 2017. In 1995/96, £2,014,000 was paid out in damages and settlements; 1996 saw a number of very high awards of damages in civil actions by the courts of first instance. For example, in *Goswell* v *Commissioner of Police for the Metropolis* (1998) Mr Goswell was waiting in his car for his girlfriend when PC Trigg approached. Mr Goswell complained about the police failure to investigate an arson attack on his home. He was handcuffed to another officer, struck by PC Trigg (causing injuries which required stitches and left a permanent scar) and then arrested for assault and threatening behaviour. His prosecution for these charges failed and when he brought a civil action he was awarded £120,000 damages for assault, £12,000 for false imprisonment and £170,000 exemplary damages for arbitrary and oppressive behaviour.

Appeals were lodged against the more substantial payments in damages and they were reduced by the Court of Appeal to £47,600. Strict guidelines were laid down for future allocations of damages by a jury, including figures as a starting point in their deliberations for different types of cases. For example, basic damages for false imprisonment should be between £500 for one hour and £3,000 for 24 hours with an upper limit of £50,000 on exemplary damages. Their Lordships claimed to be at pains to establish a proper balance between the need to add teeth to the damages paid by the defendant and the fact that this money has to be drawn from public funds. Lawyers have taken issue with the likely impact of a £50,000 award on an institution with an annual budget in excess of £3 billion.

In 2018, the High Court handed down a particularly extensive judgment involving the well-known entertainer Sir Cliff Richard. It was widely publicised that Cliff's house in Berkshire was the subject of a raid as part of Operation Yewtree which concerns historical child sex allegations. In summary, the BBC and South Yorkshire Police were in communication with each other so that the police could benefit from the publicity to further Operation Yewtree, and the BBC could benefit from media publicity. The BBC were informed about an intended search of Cliff's home which took place on 14 August 2014. The BBC immediately gave prominent and extensive television coverage to it. Cliff complained that this was an invasion of his privacy under Art. 8 of the ECHR which protects the right to private and family life. The BBC argued that they have their freedom of expression protected under the ECHR as well under Art. 10 which secures the right to express yourself freely. It was held that there was no genuine public interest to suppress Cliff's right to privacy over the BBC's freedom of expression. Just because he is a public figure that does not mean that he loses his right to privacy especially in an investigation that can damage his reputation. Damages were awarded in favour of Cliff for infringement of his Art. 8 rights which were to be apportioned between the BBC and South Yorkshire Police. Notably South Yorkshire Police, who accepted liability for its part, apologised and made a statement in open court accepting liability. It paid Cliff damages of £400,000 and agreed to pay his costs.

The Bigger Picture: *Lee v Ashers Baking Company* (2018) – is it discriminatory to refuse to supply a cake with a message that is contrary to your religious beliefs?

Mr and Mrs McArthur are Christians and are firm believers that marriage should be between a man and a woman. They own a company called Ashers Baking Company Ltd. They offer a service called 'Build-a-cake', by which customers can request images or inscriptions to be iced onto a cake. Mr Lee, who is a gay man, ordered a cake for an event as part of a campaign supporting gay marriage. On this cake Mr Lee requested a picture of Sesame Street characters Bert and Ernie with the words 'Support Gay Marriage'. Mrs McArthur initially took the order but then refused to fulfil the order.

It was noted at paragraph 9 of the judgment that: 'The McArthurs are Christians, who hold the religious beliefs that: (a) the only form of full sexual expression which is consistent with Biblical

Photo 17.1

Source: © Ivonne Wierink/Shutterstock

teaching (and therefore acceptable to God) is that between a man and a woman within marriage; and (b) the only form of marriage consistent with Biblical teaching (and therefore acceptable to God) is that between a man and a woman.'

Mrs McArthur took the order but raised no objection at the time as she wanted to think about it. The McArthurs decided that they could not in conscience produce a cake with that slogan as it was contrary to their religious beliefs. They objected to the message and not to the messenger. Mr Lee then complained to the Equality Commission in Northern Ireland that he had been subject to discrimination on grounds of sexual orientation, religious belief or political opinion contrary to the Equality Act (Sexual Orientation) Regulations (Northern Ireland) 2006 ('the SORs') and/or on grounds of religious belief or political opinion, contrary to the Fair Employment and Treatment (Northern Ireland) Order 1998 ('FETO'). Initially it was found that there was direct discrimination on all three grounds. The McArthur's appeal rested on such a finding being contrary to their rights under Arts. 9 and 10 of the ECHR which protect freedom of religion and freedom of expression respectively. The Court of Appeal held that it was not necessary to take into account these rights of the owners in determining whether there had been discrimination. The Supreme Court held that Arts. 9 and 10 include the right not to be obliged to manifest beliefs one does not hold. The point is neatly summarised at paragraph 55 of the judgment that the bakery could not refuse to provide a cake – or any other of their products – to Mr Lee because he was a gay man or because he supported gay marriage. But that important fact does not amount to a justification for something completely different – obliging them to supply a cake iced with a message with which they profoundly disagreed. This was the crux of the case. It was held that this distinction is key. As the McArthurs were not refusing to supply the cake on the grounds of sexual orientation but rather what the message on the cake conveyed, the Supreme Court upheld their appeal in that the McArthurs' refusal to supply a cake with such a message was not discriminatory.

17.5 Compensation

Compensation should be paid to a person whose conviction has been reversed or whom has been pardoned on the grounds that 'a new or newly discovered fact shows beyond reasonable doubt that there has been a miscarriage of justice' (s. 133 of the Criminal Justice Act 1988). There has been a miscarriage of justice 'if and only if the new or newly discovered fact shows beyond reasonable doubt that the person did not commit the offence'.

The sums awarded were reduced in 2006 and the maximum payable is now £1 million. Controversially, when calculating the award, the House of Lords confirmed in *R (on the application of O'Brien)* v *Independent Assessor* (2007) that deductions can be made to take into account the fact that the claimant did not have to pay for food and lodging while in prison, and previous criminal convictions and conduct leading to their wrongful imprisonment. Under the Criminal Justice and Immigration Act 2008, deductions can be made from an award of compensation to take into account the claimant's conduct that contributed to their wrongful conviction and any previous convictions.

In the past, discretionary payments could also be awarded by the Home Secretary where there had been gross misconduct that fell outside the statutory scheme. This discretionary scheme was abolished in 2006, on the pretext that the money should be spent on the victims of crime, ignoring the fact that people who have been wrongly held in prison are themselves victims.

17.6 Criminal proceedings

Criminal proceedings may be brought for false imprisonment or assault, if necessary by means of a private prosecution. In 2003, 195 police officers were convicted of a criminal offence; of these, 61 were for non-traffic offences. Sadly, not one police officer accused of malpractice arising from the many high-profile miscarriages of justice put right by the Court of Appeal since 1989 has been convicted of a criminal offence.

> **The Bigger Picture:** The shooting of Jean Charles de Menezes
>
> Following the fatal shooting by a police officer of Jean Charles de Menezes, who was mistaken for a suicide bomber, the Metropolitan Police was found guilty of breaching Health and Safety Rules and fined £175,000. Section 3 of the Health and Safety at Work etc. Act 1974 provides that it is:
>
> > the duty of every employer to conduct his undertaking in such a way as to ensure, so far as reasonably practicable, that persons not in his employment who may be affected are not thereby exposed to risks to their health and safety.
>
> Members of the de Menezes family would have preferred to have seen a prosecution for a homicide offence, but this would have been unlikely to succeed. No individuals were prosecuted for the death and no disciplinary proceedings were brought against those involved in the surveillance and shooting. At the inquest into Jean Charles's death, the coroner controversially instructed the jury that they could not find that the death was an unlawful killing.

17.7 Criminal Injuries Compensation Scheme

The Criminal Injuries Compensation Scheme (CICS) aims to compensate innocent victims of violent crime. Compensation is awarded by the Criminal Injuries Compensation Authority according to a tariff system. The CICS currently pays £170 million each year in compensation to about 40,000 victims, which is more than all the other equivalent schemes in Europe put together. Two-thirds of the awards are for less than £3,000. The maximum that can be awarded is £500,000. The award seeks to provide financial assistance while at the same time showing solidarity for the victim from the community.

These arrangements for compensation were subject to some criticism following the 7 July 2005 bombing in Central London. Many of the victims of the bombing had to wait a considerable amount of time before receiving any compensation and when they did receive compensation this was considered inadequate for those who had been more seriously injured. Where a person was killed, their families were only eligible for £11,000 compared to the £1.13 million paid to the victims of the 9/11 bombing in America.

Proposals for reforming the scheme have been published in a consultation paper, *Rebuilding Lives, Supporting Victims of Crime* (2005). One of the proposals in the consultation paper is that if an employee is assaulted while at work, and sustains injury, it should be the employer rather than the state that compensates the victim. The paper considers removing the maximum limit for compensation awards to allow very serious cases to receive adequate financial support, while giving no financial compensation for minor injuries, about two-thirds of cases. Instead, such victims would receive more practical and emotional help (such as professional counselling and help with insurance claims). But for victims the crime is always serious and a denial of compensation on the basis that the injury was not serious will be adding insult to injury. One benefit of the proposed arrangements is that those people with more serious injuries should receive compensation more swiftly.

17.8 The Independent Office for Police Conduct

In the past, complaints against the police could be made to the Police Complaints Authority. Following persistent criticism of this organisation both by the public and the police, the Police Reform Act 2002 abolished this body and replaced it with the Independent Police Complaints Commission (IPCC) subsequently renamed as the Independent Office for Police Conduct (IOPC). It was hoped this body would be more accessible, open and independent than its predecessor.

The primary responsibility for recording complaints against the police and civilian staff remains with the police. Certain complaints can be handled informally (called 'local resolution'). There are three situations in which a complaint must be referred to the IOPC. These are where:

- the conduct complained of is alleged to have resulted in death or serious injury;
- the complainant falls into a specified category of people; or
- the IOPC requires the complaint to be referred to it.

There is a discretion to refer a complaint to the IOPC due to the gravity of the subject matter, or exceptional circumstances. These provisions have been criticised as too narrow, as, for example, complaints of assault, corruption and racism will not automatically be referred to the IOPC.

The IOPC has the power to determine, according to the seriousness of the case and the public interest, the form the investigation should take. There are four options:

- a police investigation on behalf of the appropriate authority;
- a police investigation supervised by the IOPC;
- a police investigation managed by the IOPC; or
- an investigation by the IOPC, independent of the police.

Investigations by the IOPC are carried out for the most serious complaints. The investigators have the same powers as the police. The most high-profile case to be the subject of such an investigation is the fatal shooting in 2005 by a police officer of Jean Charles de Menezes, who was mistaken for a suicide bomber at Stockwell tube station. Initially, the Metropolitan Police were reluctant to allow an independent investigation to take place and there were clear tensions between the police and the IPCC (as it then was) during the course of the investigation.

Misconduct by the police can be punished by internal disciplinary procedures. The Home Office report, *Police Complaints and Discipline* (Cotton and Povey, 2004) found that, in 2003, disciplinary misconduct charges were brought against 1,529 police officers and these led to 115 police officers being dismissed or required to resign.

Complainants have a right to appeal against a decision taken concerning the handling of a complaint.

The IPCC has been the subject of some criticism, as being ineffective and too close to the police. The Legal Action Group produced a damaging report on the subject in 2007. In

2008 a hundred lawyers refused to continue to work with the organisation because they were concerned the IPCC was not handling complaints effectively. It was criticised by a report of the Home Affairs Select Committee in 2013 for being 'woefully under-equipped' and lacking the investigative resources necessary to get to the truth, which was harming public confidence in the police.

Further reforms to the complaints system have been introduced by the Police Reform and Social Responsibility Act 2011. The police are no longer required to record every complaint they receive. Instead, they have an unfettered discretion to determine which complaints they wish to record. While the aim is to reduce bureaucracy, there is a risk that the complaints system will be undermined.

17.9 The admissibility of evidence

Where police officers commit serious infringements of a suspect's rights during the investigation of an offence, the courts may hold that evidence obtained as a result of such misbehaviour is inadmissible in court, the idea being to remove any incentive for the police to break the rules.

Under s. 76(2) of the Police and Criminal Evidence Act 1984 (PACE), confession evidence is inadmissible where it was obtained by oppression or in circumstances likely to render it unreliable and, if the defence alleges that this is the case, the onus is on the prosecution to establish otherwise (s. 76(1)). Oppression is defined as including 'torture, inhuman or degrading treatment, and the use or threat of violence (whether or not amounting to torture)' (s. 76(8)). The definition of 'oppression' was considered in *R* v *Fulling* (1987). In that case, the police had persuaded a woman to make a confession by telling her that her lover was being unfaithful. The court held that this did not amount to oppression, and stated that the term should carry its ordinary meaning, that of unjust treatment or cruelty, or the wrongful use of power. Excluding evidence is potentially a powerful safeguard against oppressive treatment by the police, since there is little point in pressurising a suspect to confess if that confession cannot be used to obtain a conviction. However, the extent of this protection is diluted by s. 76(4), which states that, even if a confession is excluded, any facts discovered as a result of it may still be admissible. Parts of an excluded confession may also be allowed if relevant to show that the defendant speaks or writes in a particular way. This means that the police can use oppressive treatment to secure a confession which will help them find other evidence.

Section 78 provides that in any proceedings the court may refuse to admit evidence 'if it appears to the court that, having regard to all the circumstances, including the circumstances in which the evidence was obtained, the admission of the evidence would have such an adverse effect on the fairness of the proceedings that the court ought not to admit it'. This provision covers all types of evidence, not just confessions. It is generally invoked only if the police have committed serious breaches of PACE, such as refusing a suspect access to legal advice over a long period.

17.10 The right to exercise self-defence

Any citizen may use reasonable force to prevent unlawful interference with their person or property, or to protect others from such interference. This can affect both civil and criminal liability.

17.11 Parliamentary controls

One of the basic functions of Parliament is to act as a watchdog over the rights of citizens, protecting them from undue interference by Government. A number of methods are available, from questions directed to Ministers in Parliament, to committees designed to scrutinise legislation. However, this function has suffered as a result of the strength of party discipline, which means that many MPs appear to put loyalty to their party above loyalty to the citizens they represent. The result is that even measures which clearly restrict fundamental rights can be voted through if the Government has a clear majority.

17.12 The Ombudsman

The Parliamentary Commissioner for Administration, known as the Ombudsman, has a role in protecting individual rights.

Answering questions

1   Critically discuss the effectiveness of remedies available to individuals for infringement of human rights by the police.

2   Mary had been convicted in the past of theft and burglary, but had no convictions for violence. One Friday afternoon the police received an urgent telephone call telling them that someone had been stabbed in a car park. Two young women had been seen running away from the car park and the description of one of the women bore similarities to Mary's appearance. Police officer Percy saw Mary walking down the street with her friend Kelly two miles away from the car park. He grabbed hold of Mary's arm and said that she had to empty her pockets so that he could check whether she was carrying a knife. Mary refused to do so and Kelly kicked Percy to help her friend run away, but was unsuccessful and ran off herself. Percy then pushed Mary against a wall and carried out a thorough search of her person. He found that she was carrying nothing suspicious, but told Mary that she had to give her friend's name and address or she would have to go down to the police station. Mary gave him the details and together they went round to Kelly's house. Percy told Mary to pretend she was alone so that Kelly would open the door. When Kelly opened the door, Percy rushed inside and searched the house. He found a number of televisions with their serial numbers rubbed out and seized them all, despite Kelly's claims that she was just a lodger and the televisions were in the homeowner's bedroom and she had no knowledge of them. Mary and Kelly were then taken down to the police station where they were detained for 28 hours. They were only allowed to see a duty solicitor briefly on one occasion and were subjected to lengthy questioning about the stabbing and the televisions. They were finally released without charge when two other women were arrested for the stabbing and Kelly's landlady provided a satisfactory explanation for the presence of the televisions in her bedroom.

    Consider whether the police were legally entitled to act as they did and whether Mary and Kelly have any remedies for their ordeal.

3   Explain how people can obtain a remedy when they consider that the state has breached one of their human rights.

For answers to these questions, see the companion website at www.pearsoned.co.uk/ elliottquinn

SUMMARY OF CHAPTER 17: REMEDIES FOR INFRINGEMENT OF HUMAN RIGHTS

Introduction

Rights are only worthwhile if there are adequate remedies for their enforcement. Some of the main remedies available in English law for unlawful infringement of basic rights are the subject of this chapter.

Judicial review

Where a public body acts illegally a remedy may be available through the procedure of judicial review.

Habeas corpus

Habeas corpus is an ancient remedy which allows people detained to challenge the legality of their detention and, if successful, get themselves quickly released.

Civil action for negligence

Where a public body breaches a person's rights it may be sued in the civil courts.

Compensation

If there has been a miscarriage of justice an award of compensation can be made by the state under s. 133 of the Criminal Justice Act 1988.

The Human Rights Act 1998

Claimants may be entitled to compensation for breach of the European Convention.

Criminal proceedings

Criminal proceedings may be brought for false imprisonment or assault, if necessary by means of a private prosecution.

The Independent Office for Police Conduct

Misconduct by the police can be punished by internal disciplinary procedures. Complaints against the police can be made to the Independent Office for Police Conduct (IOPC).

The admissibility of evidence

Where police officers commit serious infringements of a suspect's rights during the investigation of an offence, the courts may hold that evidence obtained as a result of such misbehaviour is inadmissible in court.

The right to exercise self-defence

Any citizen may use reasonable force to prevent unlawful interference with their person or property, or to protect others from such interference. This can affect both civil and criminal liability.

Parliamentary controls

One of the basic functions of Parliament is to act as a watchdog over the rights of citizens, protecting them from undue interference by Government.

The Ombudsman

The Parliamentary Commissioner for Administration, known as the Ombudsman, has a role in protecting individual rights.

Reading list

Cotton, J. and Povey, D. (2004) *Police Complaints and Discipline.* London: Home Office.

Ormerod, D. (2003) ECHR and the exclusion of evidence: trial remedies for article 8 breaches? *Criminal Law Review,* 61.

Spencer, J. (2010) Compensation for wrongful imprisonment. *Criminal Law Review,* 803.

On the internet

The consultation paper, *Rebuilding Lives – supporting victims of crime* (2005), looking at the future of the Criminal Injuries Compensation Scheme, is available at:
   http://www.official-documents.gov.uk/document/cm67/6705/6705.pdf

The website address of the Independent Office for Police Conduct is:
   https://policeconduct.gov.uk/

Part 4
Criminal justice system

This Part looks at how the criminal justice system works in practice. It starts by looking at the role of the police, what powers they enjoy above those of an ordinary citizen and the problems that can arise in the way these powers are exercised. The criminal trial process is then examined, including the role of the Crown Prosecution Service, the rules of criminal procedure, the possibility of plea bargaining and the trial hearing. The different types of sentencing available to the courts are discussed, in particular the frequent use of fines and prisons. Finally, some of the special rules applying to young offenders are considered.

Chapter 18
The police

This chapter discusses:

- miscarriages of justice, where an appropriate balance has not been achieved between an individual's rights and police powers, so that innocent people have been convicted of a criminal offence they did not commit;

- the police powers of stop and search, arrest and detention;

- the treatment of suspects at the police station;

- the safeguards of the suspect; and

- problems with the police.

18.1 Introduction

The criminal justice system is one of the most important tools available to society for the control of anti-social behaviour. It is also the area of the English legal system which has most potential for controversy given that, through the criminal justice system, the state has the means to interfere with individual freedom in the strongest way: by removing people's liberty, that is, sending them to prison.

An effective criminal justice system needs to strike a balance between punishing the guilty and protecting the innocent; our systems of investigating crime need safeguards which prevent the innocent being found guilty, but those safeguards must not make it impossible to convict those who are guilty. This balance has been the subject of much debate in recent years: a large number of miscarriages of justice, where innocent people were sent to prison, suggested the system was weighted too heavily towards proving guilt, yet, shortly after these cases had been uncovered, there were claims, particularly from the police, that the balance had tipped too far in the other direction. It may be that the formal incorporation into English law, under the Human Rights Act, of the European Convention on Human Rights has arguably led to a further shift in the balance, as the courts interpret such rights as the right to a 'fair trial' contained in Art. 6 of the Convention.

18.2 Miscarriages of justice

In the 1980s and 1990s, confidence in the criminal justice system was seriously dented by the revelation that innocent people had been wrongly convicted and sentenced to long periods in prison. The academics Walker and Starmer (1999) have suggested that miscarriages of justice can result from: an eyewitness, and even multiple eyewitnesses, identifying the wrong person; misconduct or errors by the prosecution; faulty forensic evidence; false confessions; unreliable evidence of people with a criminal background; and inadequate legal representation. High-profile cases have included the 'Guildford Four', the 'Birmingham Six' and the 'Tottenham Three'. We will look closely at just two of these cases, to see where the system went wrong, before examining in detail the rules that govern the criminal justice system.

18.2.1 The Guildford Four

In October 1974, the IRA bombed a pub in Guildford. A year later, Patrick Armstrong, Paul Hill, Carole Richardson, Gerard Conlon and two others were convicted of the five murders arising from the bombing. Mr Armstrong and Mr Hill were also convicted of two murders arising from an explosion in November 1974 at a pub in Woolwich. All were sentenced to life imprisonment.

The prosecution case was based almost entirely on confessions which were alleged to have been made while the four were in police custody. There was no other evidence that any of the four were members of the IRA, and they were certainly not the type of people that an effective terrorist organisation would choose to carry out such an important part of its campaign – Patrick Armstrong and Carole Richardson, for example, took drugs, lived in a squat and were involved in petty crime. They all vehemently denied the charges and maintained their innocence in prison, even though to have admitted their guilt would have permitted their earlier release on parole.

Like the other victims of miscarriages of justice, they tried to get their convictions referred to the Court of Appeal under s. 17 of the Criminal Appeal Act 1968 (since repealed), but were initially unsuccessful. In 1987, a Home Office memorandum recognised that the Four were unlikely terrorists, but the Home Office concluded that this could not be considered to be new evidence justifying referral to the Court of Appeal.

Then, in 1989, a police detective looking into the case found a set of typed notes of interviews with Patrick Armstrong, which contained deletions and additions, both typed and handwritten, as well as some rearrangements of material. At the original trial the police evidence had consisted of a set of handwritten notes which they said were made at the time of the interview, and a typed version of these notes; both incorporated the corrections made on the newly discovered typewritten set, suggesting that the handwritten version was actually made after the interviews had been conducted. The implication was that the notes had been constructed so as to fit in with the case the police wished to present.

Patrick Armstrong's confession was central to the prosecution case. Anything which cast doubt on it would undermine all four convictions. The Director of Public Prosecutions, Alan Green, decided that he should not oppose a further appeal, and this took place in 1989. Giving judgment, the Lord Chief Justice said there were two possible explanations. The first was that the typescripts were a complete fabrication, amended to make them more effective and then written out by hand to appear as if they were contemporaneous. Alternatively, the police had started with a contemporaneous note, typed it up to improve legibility, amended it to make it read better and then converted it back to a manuscript note. Either way, the police officers had not told the truth. The Lord Chief Justice concluded: 'If they were prepared to tell this sort of lie, then the whole of their evidence becomes suspect.' As a result, the Guildford Four were released, after having spent 15 years in prison for crimes which they did not commit.

18.2.2 The Birmingham Six

In November 1974, 21 people died and 162 were injured when IRA bombs exploded in two crowded pubs in the centre of Birmingham. The bombs caused outrage in Britain, and led to a wave of anti-Irish feeling.

The six Irishmen who became known as the Birmingham Six were arrested after police kept a watch on ports immediately after the bombings. The police asked them to undergo forensic tests in order to eliminate them from their inquiries. The men had told the police that they were travelling to Northern Ireland to see relatives; this was partly true, but their main reason for travelling was to attend the funeral of James McDade, an IRA man. Although some of the Six may well have had Republican sympathies, none was actually a member of the IRA. They were unaware, until McDade was killed, that he was involved in terrorism. Nevertheless, they all knew his family, and intended to go to the funeral as a mark of respect, a normal practice in Northern Ireland which would not necessarily suggest support for the dead person's political views.

Perhaps not surprisingly given the situation at the time, the men did not mention the funeral when the police asked why they were travelling and, equally unsurprisingly, when the police searched their luggage and found evidence of the real reason for their journey, they became extremely suspicious. When the forensic tests, conducted by a Dr Skuse, indicated that the men had been handling explosives, the police were convinced their suspicions were right.

Photo 18.1 Scenes from the Hillsborough disaster

Source: © David Cannon Collection/Getty Images

At their trial, the case rested on two main pieces of evidence: the forensic tests and confessions which the men had made to the police. The Six claimed that, while at the police station, they had been beaten, kicked and threatened with death; they were also told that their families were in danger and would only be protected if the men confessed. There was clear evidence that the Six were beaten up; photos taken three days after their admission on remand to Winston Green prison show serious scars. However, the men were also beaten up by prison officers once they were remanded in custody, and the prosecution used this beating to explain the photographic evidence, stating that there had been no physical abuse by the police and that, therefore, the confessions were valid. Yet a close examination of the confessions would have made it obvious that they were made by people who knew nothing about the bombings: they contradicted each other, none of them revealed anything about the way the terrorist attacks were carried out that the police did not know already, and some of the 'revelations' proved to be untrue – for example, three of the men said the bombs were left in carrier bags, when forensic evidence later showed them to have been in holdalls. The men were never put on identity parades, even though at least one person who had been present in one of the bombed pubs felt he could have identified the bombers. Nevertheless, the Six were convicted and sentenced to life imprisonment, the judge commenting: 'You have been convicted on the clearest and most overwhelming evidence I have ever heard in a case of murder.' On appeal, the judges reprimanded the trial judge for aspects of his summing up and a character attack on a defence witness; they acknowledged the weaknesses in the forensic evidence, yet concluded that this evidence would have played a small part in the jury's decision; and as far as the confession evidence was concerned, a judge mentioned the black eye on one of the defendants, 'the origin of which I have forgotten', but said 'I do not think it matters much anyway'. The appeal was dismissed.

Fourteen prison officers were subsequently tried for assaulting the Six; their victims were not allowed to appear as witnesses, and they were all acquitted. Evidence given suggested that the men had already been injured when they arrived at the prison. The Six then brought a civil action for assault against the police force. This claim was struck out. Lord Denning's judgment summed up the legal system's attitude to the case, pointing out that if the Six won, and proved they had been assaulted in order to secure their confessions, this would mean the police had lied, used violence and threats, and that the convictions were false; the Home Secretary would have to recommend a pardon or send the case back to the Court of Appeal. The general feeling seemed to be that such serious miscarriages were simply unthinkable, and so the system for a long time turned its back on the growing claims that the unthinkable had actually happened.

In January 1987, the Home Secretary referred the case back to the Court of Appeal. The appeal took a year; the convictions were upheld. The Lord Chief Justice Lord Lane ended the court's judgment with remarks which were to become notorious: 'The longer this hearing has gone on, the more convinced this court has become that the verdict of the jury was correct. We have no doubt that these convictions were both safe and satisfactory.'

In the end, it took 16 years for the Six to get their convictions quashed. In 1990, another Home Secretary referred the case back to the Court of Appeal. A new technique had been developed, known as electrostatic document analysis (ESDA), which could examine the indentations made on paper by writing on the sheets above. The test suggested that notes of a police interview with one of the Six had not been recorded contemporaneously, as West Midlands detectives had claimed in court. The prosecution decided not to seek to sustain the convictions and the Six were finally freed in 1991.

The Bigger Picture: The Hillsborough disaster

Ninety-six Liverpool football fans were crushed to death in 1989 in the Hillsborough disaster. The tragedy unfolded at the FA Cup semi-final between Liverpool and Nottingham Forest, which was held at Hillsborough football stadium in Sheffield. In 2016 an inquest concluded they were unlawfully killed. The jury ruled the chief superintendent in charge of policing the match had been grossly negligent. It criticised the 'slow and uncoordinated' police response to the over-crowding and found that officers should have closed a tunnel leading to the overcrowded area before ordering an exit gate to be opened. Families had battled for decades to have the truth exposed and certain individuals held accountable, and in June 2017 the Crown Prosecution Service announced that six would finally face criminal charges in relation to the disaster and its repercussions. The six included a former Match Commander, Chief Superintendent, Detective Chief Inspector and police officer from South Yorkshire Police, the solicitor acting for South Yorkshire Police during the earlier inquests/Taylor Inquiry and the individual who was Company Secretary/Safety Officer for Sheffield Wednesday Football Club at the time of the disaster.

18.3 The response to the miscarriages of justice

The miscarriages of justice just described, and others, showed that there was something seriously wrong with the criminal justice system. On 14 March 1991, when the Court of Appeal quashed the convictions of the Birmingham Six, the Home Secretary announced that a Royal Commission on Criminal Justice (RCCJ) would be set up to examine the penal process from start to finish – from the time the police first investigate to the final appeal.

The RCCJ (sometimes called the Runciman Commission, after its chairperson) considered these issues for two years, during which they received evidence from over 600 organisations and asked academics to carry out 22 research studies on how the system works in practice. In July 1993 they published their final report. It received a mixed reception, as Steven Greer sums up for us in his article, *Miscarriages of Criminal Justice Reconsidered*: '. . . it was warmly welcomed by the police, the agency most criticised for its role in the miscarriage cases, and heavily criticised by lawyers, civil libertarians, academics and others for having increased rather than decreased the risk of convicting the innocent.'

In more recent miscarriage of justice cases, attention has been drawn on the issue of what happens next for those exonerated. Organisations such as JUSTICE have investigated what levels of support those who have been wrongly imprisoned receive on the outside. Their report *Supporting Exonerees: ensuring accessible, continuing and consistent support* (2018) looks into the failings of the criminal justice system and makes recommendations.

The Criminal Cases Review Commission have stated that non-disclosure of evidence is now the single biggest cause of miscarriages of justice. A review carried out by the Crown Prosecution Service of 3,637 rape and serious sexual assault cases found 47 cases where evidence was not properly shared with the defence.

18.4 Human Rights Act 1998

The passing of the Human Rights Act 1998, incorporating the European Convention on Human Rights into domestic law, has had a significant impact on all stages of the criminal justice system. The provisions of the European Convention provide an important safeguard against abuses and excesses within the system. Of particular relevance in this field are Art. 3 prohibiting torture and inhuman or degrading treatment; Art. 5 protecting the right to liberty including the right not to be arrested or detained by the police without lawful authority; Art. 6 guaranteeing a fair trial; and Art. 8 which recognises the right to respect of an individual's right to private and family life. The powers of arrest, stop and search and the refusal of bail have been the subject of legal challenges on the basis that their exercise has breached the Convention. For example, in *Caballero* v *UK* (2000) the UK Government accepted that the law on bail breached Art. 5 of the Convention and the domestic law was reformed as a result.

18.5 The organisation of the police

In England and Wales the tradition is to have local police forces, rather than one single national police force. This decentralisation was considered to help build the links between the police and the local community that is being policed, and to reduce the risk of the police behaving oppressively. However, a step towards centralisation was taken when the Police and Magistrates' Courts Act 1994 provided that the Home Secretary was allowed to 'determine objectives for the policing of the areas of all police authorities'. The Police Reform Act 2002 has continued to increase the power of central Government over the police. The Home Secretary is now required to produce an annual National Policing Plan. This will set out strategic policing priorities generally for police forces in England and Wales. He or she is given additional supervisory powers over the police, with increased powers to issue codes of practice and regulations relating to the discharge of police functions. In an inquiry into police failures leading up to the murder of Soham schoolgirls Holly Wells and Jessica Chapman, the police force of Humberside was heavily criticised. The chief constable of Humberside refused to resign, and the Home Secretary ordered his suspension. He challenged in the courts the Home Secretary's power to do this, and the courts accepted that the Home Secretary held this power under legislation. The Police and Justice Act 2006 further increased the Home Secretary's powers over the police. Furthermore the two truly national, and arguably most powerful law enforcement agencies – the Metropolitan Police and the National Crime Agency – also report directly to the Home Secretary.

Following the publication of a consultation paper, *One Step Ahead: A 21st Century Strategy to Defeat Organised Criminals* (2004), Parliament passed the Serious Organised Crime and Police Act 2005. This Act contained provisions for the establishment in April 2006 of the Serious Organised Crime Agency (SOCA). It was chaired by a former head of MI5, Stephen Lander, and consisted of a national team of about 4,000 specialist investigators who were not formally police officers and who had more powers than ordinary police constables. They could issue disclosure notices to compel witnesses to answer questions, or be the subject of a criminal conviction themselves, and could strike deals with informants to give evidence against other offenders (known as 'Queen's evidence'). Their role was to tackle the people at the head of criminal gangs, whose illegal enterprises range from drug-trafficking, paedophile rings and people smuggling, to fraud and money laundering. A specialist team of prosecutors helped the organisation secure convictions. SOCA was compared with the FBI in America. The Police Federation was unhappy with the creation of SOCA, commenting:

> There is a huge difference between an officer of the Crown who bears personal responsibility to the law, and a civilian employee. The blurring of these boundaries sets a dangerous precedent for the future and will further erode the status of police.

The academics Ben Bowling and James Ross (2006) suggested that SOCA had too much power, commenting that it had 'unprecedented powers for surveillance, intrusion and coercion'. Particularly controversial sections of the Act were those which extended to SOCA the use of 'compulsory powers', which are investigatory powers to require an individual to answer questions, provide information or produce documents. A refusal to comply with one of these compulsory powers amounts to a criminal offence. They also pointed out that SOCA may have taken advantage of the absence of a definition of what constitutes 'serious organised crime' in the Act, by deciding its own mandate and functions and not restricting itself to combating classic mafia-style activities such as drugs and violence.

SOCA has been replaced with a more powerful National Crime Agency to strengthen the fight against organised crime. Provisions for this reform were contained in the Legal Aid, Sentencing and Punishment of Offenders Act 2012.

At the same time, the Government has sought to encourage a stronger local input into policing by creating directly elected commissioners known as police and crime commissioners (PCC). Statutory provisions for their establishment are contained in the Police Reform and Social Responsibility Act 2011 which have been brought into force and the first elections have taken place. In London the equivalent role is fulfilled by the London Mayor. Under s. 1(2) the core functions of the PCC are to secure the maintenance of an efficient and effective police force and to hold the Chief Constable to account. Local police authorities which have up to now fulfilled this role, are being abolished. The PCC is able to set police force budgets, determine policing priorities and appoint (and, if necessary, fire) the Chief Constable. They have been described in the popular press as 'local sheriffs'! Their creation has prompted several concerns. One of the most immediate problems is the apparent lack of public awareness and understanding of the new PCCs, with low turn-outs for their elections.

The Bigger Picture: Civilian support staff

The Police Reform Act 2002 allows a range of civilians to exercise police powers. The most significant in practice are likely to be the community support officers (CSOs). These are civilians who are employed by a police authority. The only qualifications required for the post are that the chief officer is satisfied the person is suitable, capable and has been adequately trained. They are paid two-thirds of a regular police officer's salary. Their powers, extended by the Police and Justice Act 2006 and the Policing and Crime Act 2017, include the right to issue fixed penalty notices for such anti-social behaviour as dropping litter, cycling on footpaths, dog fouling and drinking in public. They are able to carry out searches and road checks and to stop and detain school truants. Where a suspect fails to provide his name and address, or if the community support officer reasonably suspects the details to be inaccurate, the community support officer may deprive the individual of their liberty (using reasonable force if necessary) for up to 30 minutes until a police officer arrives.

The Police Federation was unhappy that community support officers were given this power to detain suspects, commenting:

> Community Support Officers are supposed to just be the eyes and ears of the police service and therefore should not be placed in potentially confrontational situations, which detaining someone clearly is. They do not have the appropriate experience, the right training or adequate safety equipment to deal with this, which places the wellbeing of the public, police officers and themselves in jeopardy. By giving them more powers, we are effectively taking them away from the communities they serve and creating even greater confusion as to the differences between CSOs and police officers.

Chief officers can also establish accreditation schemes to support community safety and to combat nuisance. Under these schemes private employees are given some police powers. The employer must have adequate training facilities and mechanisms for handling complaints. Shops and shopping centres are likely to seek accreditation for their security guards. They will then have broader powers to deal with low-level criminal behaviour. Accredited individuals can issue fixed penalty notices for trivial offences, prevent alcohol consumption in designated places and confiscate alcohol and tobacco from children. They are allowed to require provision of the name and address of those reasonably suspected of committing one of a limited range of offences or of behaving in an anti-social manner. Failure to comply with this request is an offence.

These reforms have been highly controversial. The Labour Government's view was that the use of civilians for matters that were essentially administrative and routine would allow more police time for investigative work. In addition, the police role in the establishment of community safety accreditation schemes may lead to a greater degree of police influence over the activities of private security guards and store detectives. But some have criticised this development as a step towards privatising policing. The Home Affairs Committee (2002) saw a danger of:

> civilians with insufficient training, working in poor conditions, for less money while doing jobs that until recently were undertaken by police officers.

The shops and shopping centres which are likely to seek accreditation are, ironically, areas in which there is arguably adequate policing and private security. This reform may result in over-policing of safe areas without increasing the protection in areas in real need of extra reassurance policing.

The Government wants to encourage volunteers, known as reservists, to accompany police officers on patrol. As the Government plans to reduce spending on the police, it is possible that these reservists would in time replace some community support officers.

18.6 Police powers

Most people's first contact with the criminal justice system involves the police and, because they have responsibility for investigating crimes, gathering evidence and deciding whether to charge a suspect, they play an important part in its overall operation. They also have wide powers over suspects, which may be used to help convict the guilty or, as the miscarriages of justice have shown, abused to convict the innocent.

The main piece of legislation regulating police powers is the Police and Criminal Evidence Act 1984 (PACE). The Act was the product of a Royal Commission set up following an earlier miscarriage of justice, concerning the murder in 1977 of a man called Maxwell Confait. Confait was found strangled with electric flex in a burning house, and three boys, aged 14, 15 and 18, one of whom had learning difficulties, were arrested, interrogated and, as a result of their confessions, charged with murder. Three years later, they were all released after an official report into the case (the Fisher Report) concluded that they had nothing to do with the killing.

In the light of concern over the police conduct of this case, and in particular the interrogation process, the then Labour Government set up the Royal Commission on Criminal Procedure (RCCP), sometimes known as the Philips Commission, to examine police procedures. It concluded in its report of 1981 that a balance needed to be reached between 'the interests of the community in bringing offenders to justice and the rights and liberties of persons suspected or accused of crime'. A criminal justice system that achieved this balance would reach the required standards of fairness, openness and accountability. However, the Commission,and the subsequent Act (PACE), were criticised by some as unjustifiably extending police powers, especially in the areas of stop and search, arrest and detention at the police station.

PACE was intended to replace a confusing mixture of common law, legislation and local bye-laws on pre-trial procedure with a single coherent statute. The Act provides a

Photo 18.2 A Police Officer (left) and Community Support Officer (right) in their respective uniforms

Source: © pcruciatti/Shutterstock.com (left), miamia/Shutterstock.com (right)

comprehensive code of police powers to stop, search, arrest, detain and interrogate members of the public. It also lays down the suspects' rights. The Criminal Justice and Public Order Act 1994 (CJPOA) extended police powers significantly. It introduced some of the recommendations of the Royal Commission on Criminal Justice, and other changes that the RCCJ was opposed to: for example, the abolition of the right to silence. Police powers have been further increased by the Serious Organised Crime and Police Act 2005.

As well as the statutory rules on police powers, contained in PACE and the CJPOA, there are Codes of Practice, drawn up by the Home Office under s. 66 of PACE, which do not form part of the law, but which provide extra detail on the provisions of the legislation. Breach of these Codes cannot be the ground for a legal action, but can give rise to disciplinary procedures and, if they are breached in very serious ways, evidence obtained as a result of such a breach may be (but is not automatically) excluded in a criminal trial. It has been argued that some of the Code provisions should be legally enforceable and form part of PACE itself.

18.6.1 Pre-arrest powers

Police officers are always free to ask members of the public questions in order to prevent and detect crime, but members of the public are not obliged to answer such questions, nor to go to a police station unless they are lawfully arrested. This type of contact with the police is sometimes called a 'stop and account'. The police Code of Practice A states:

> There is no national requirement for an officer who requests a person in a public place to account for themselves . . . to make any record of the encounter, or to give the person a receipt.

Key case

In *Rice v Connolly* (1966), the appellant was spotted by police officers in the early hours of the morning, behaving suspiciously in an area where burglaries had taken place that night. The officers asked where he was going and where he had come from; he refused to answer, or to give his full name and address, though he did give a name and the name of a road, which were not untrue. The officers asked him to go with them to a police box for identification purposes, but he refused, saying, 'If you want me, you will have to arrest me.' He was arrested and eventually convicted of obstructing a police officer in the execution of his duty. His conviction was quashed on appeal on the basis that nobody is obliged in common law to answer police questions.

Legal principle
Nobody is obliged in common law to answer police questions.

The line between maintaining the freedom not to answer questions and actually obstructing the police would appear to be a thin one. In *Ricketts v Cox* (1982), two police officers, who were looking for youths responsible for a serious assault, approached the defendant and another man in the early hours of the morning. The defendant was said to have been abusive, uncooperative and hostile to the officers, using obscene language which was designed to provoke and antagonise the officers and eventually trying to walk away from them.

The magistrates found that the police acted in a proper manner and were entitled to put questions to the two men; the defendant's behaviour and attitude amounted to an obstruction of the police officers in the execution of their duty. An appeal was dismissed, and the implication appears to be that, while merely refusing to answer questions is lawful, rudely refusing to do so may amount to the offence of obstruction.

An even more problematic area is the question of how far the police are allowed to detain a person without arresting them. The courts appear to have concluded that under common law the police cannot actually prevent a person from moving away, though they can touch them to attract their attention (they also have some statutory powers in this area, discussed below). Two schoolboys, in *Kenlin* v *Gardiner* (1967), were going from house to house to remind members of their rugby team about a game. Two plain-clothes police officers became suspicious and, producing a warrant card, asked what they were doing. The boys did not believe the men were police officers, and one of them appeared to try to run away. A police officer caught hold of his arm, and the boy responded by struggling violently, punching and kicking the officer, at which point the second boy got involved and struck the other officer. Both boys were convicted in the magistrates' court of assaulting a police constable in the execution of his duty, but an appeal was allowed, on the ground that the police did not have the power to detain the boys prior to arrest, and so the boys were merely acting in self-defence.

In *Donnelly* v *Jackman* (1970), the appellant was walking along a road one Saturday evening at about 11.15 pm, when a uniformed police officer came up to him, intending to make inquiries about an offence which the officer had reason to believe the appellant might have committed. The officer asked the appellant whether he could have a word with him, but the appellant ignored him and walked on. The officer followed close behind him, repeated the request and, on being ignored, tapped him on the shoulder. The appellant turned round and tapped the officer on the chest saying 'Now we are even, copper.' When the officer tapped him on the shoulder a second time, the appellant turned round again, and this time hit him with force. He was convicted of assaulting an officer in the execution of his duty, and argued in his defence that in tapping him on the shoulder the officer had acted outside his duty. The Court of Appeal held that what the officer had done was not unlawful detention but merely 'a trivial interference with liberty', and the conviction was upheld. The primary distinction between the powers of the police and ordinary citizens, such as security guards, is that the police can exercise their powers on the basis of their reasonable belief, even if that belief is ultimately shown to be incorrect. However, if a security guard touches you, and you have not in fact done anything wrong, they commit an assault; if a police officer does so, reasonably believing you may have done something wrong, they are acting lawfully.

Under s. 50 of the Police Reform Act 2002, a uniformed police officer can require a person who has behaved in an anti-social manner to give their name and address. Failure to comply is an offence and may form the basis for an arrest under s. 25 of PACE. This is a significant extension of police powers, which could be abused to harass young people.

Stop and search under PACE

PACE repealed a variety of often obscure and unsatisfactory statutory provisions on stop and search; the main powers in this area are now contained in s. 1 of PACE. Under s. 1 a constable may search a person or vehicle in public for stolen or prohibited articles (defined as offensive weapons, articles used for the purpose of burglary or related crimes and professional display fireworks). This power can only be used where the police have 'reasonable grounds for suspecting that they will find stolen or prohibited articles' (s. 1(3)). The Criminal Justice

Act 2003 extended the power to stop and search to cover searches for articles intended to cause criminal damage. This reform is aimed at people suspected of causing graffiti and who might be carrying cans of spray paint in their pockets.

The exercise of the power to stop and search is also governed by Code of Practice A. This Code states:

> 1.1 Powers to stop and search must be used fairly, responsibly, with respect for people being searched and without unlawful discrimination. Under the Equality Act 2010, section 149, when police officers are carrying out their functions, they also have a duty to have due regard to the need to eliminate unlawful discrimination, harassment and victimisation, to advance equality of opportunity between people who share a 'relevant protected characteristic' and people who do not share it, and to take steps to foster good relations between those persons. . . . The Children Act 2004, section 11, also requires chief police officers and other specified persons and bodies to ensure that in the discharge of their functions they have regard to the need to safeguard and promote the welfare of all persons under the age of 18.

The threshold for establishing reasonable suspicion is a low one because the police are at an early stage in the investigative process so they do not need strong evidence to support their suspicions. The requirement of reasonable suspicion is intended to protect individuals from being subject to stop and search on a random basis, or on grounds that the law rightly finds unacceptable, such as age or racial background. Code of Practice A provides guidance on the meaning of 'reasonable grounds for suspecting':

> 2.2B Reasonable suspicion can never be supported on the basis of personal factors. This means that unless the police have information or intelligence which provides a description of a person suspected of carrying an article for which there is a power to stop and search, the following cannot be used, alone or in combination with each other, or in combination with any other factor, as the reason for stopping and searching any individual, including any vehicle which they are driving or are being carried in:
>
> (a) A person's physical appearance with regard, for example, to any of the 'relevant protected characteristics' set out in the Equality Act 2010, section 149, which are age, disability, gender reassignment, pregnancy and maternity, race, religion or belief, sex and sexual orientation . . . , or the fact that the person is known to have a previous conviction; and
>
> (b) Generalisations or stereotypical images that certain groups or categories of people are more likely to be involved in criminal activity.

Before searching under these powers, police officers must, among other things, identify themselves and the station where they are based, and tell the person to be searched the grounds for the search (s. 2). If not in uniform, police officers must provide documentary identification (s. 2(3)). In *R v Bristol* (2007) the Court of Appeal confirmed that a failure to provide the necessary information would render a stop and search unlawful. The appellant was in a street where there was a problem with drug dealing. A police officer saw him and thought that he was carrying drugs in his mouth, ready to supply to a customer. The policeman asked the appellant what he had in his mouth and he replied it was chewing gum. Not satisfied with this response, the officer immediately applied pressure to his throat to stop him swallowing and said 'Drugs search, spit it out.' A struggle ensued and the appellant was arrested. He was subsequently convicted of intentionally obstructing a police officer in carrying out a search for drugs and sentenced to 12 months' imprisonment. The appellant appealed. The appeal was allowed because the search was unlawful as the police officer had failed to give his name and station. The Court of Appeal pointed out that the police officer

Figure 18.1 Image of local police

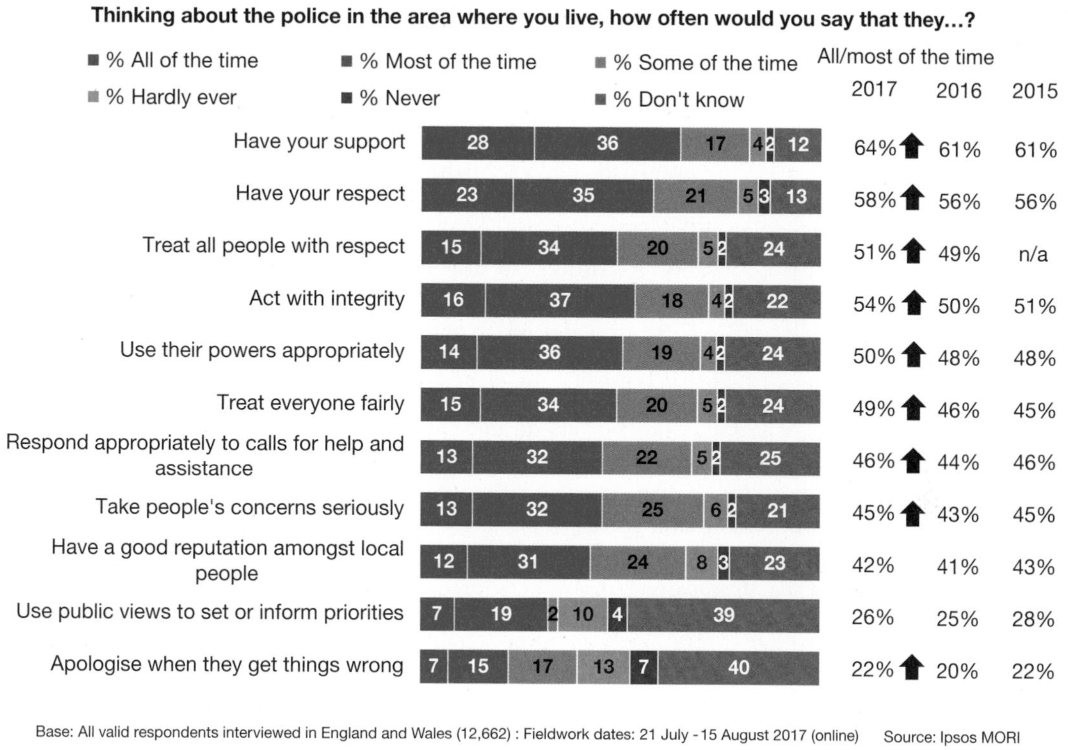

Thinking about the police in the area where you live, how often would you say that they...?

	All/most of the time		
	2017	2016	2015
Have your support	64% ↑	61%	61%
Have your respect	58% ↑	56%	56%
Treat all people with respect	51% ↑	49%	n/a
Act with integrity	54% ↑	50%	51%
Use their powers appropriately	50% ↑	48%	48%
Treat everyone fairly	49% ↑	46%	45%
Respond appropriately to calls for help and assistance	46% ↑	44%	46%
Take people's concerns seriously	45% ↑	43%	45%
Have a good reputation amongst local people	42%	41%	43%
Use public views to set or inform priorities	26%	25%	28%
Apologise when they get things wrong	22% ↑	20%	22%

Legend: ■ % All of the time ■ % Most of the time ■ % Some of the time ■ % Hardly ever ■ % Never ■ % Don't know

Bar values:
- Have your support: 28, 36, 17, 4, 2, 12
- Have your respect: 23, 35, 21, 5, 3, 13
- Treat all people with respect: 15, 34, 20, 5, 2, 24
- Act with integrity: 16, 37, 18, 4, 2, 22
- Use their powers appropriately: 14, 36, 19, 4, 2, 24
- Treat everyone fairly: 15, 34, 20, 5, 2, 24
- Respond appropriately to calls for help and assistance: 13, 32, 22, 5, 2, 25
- Take people's concerns seriously: 13, 32, 25, 6, 2, 21
- Have a good reputation amongst local people: 12, 31, 24, 8, 3, 23
- Use public views to set or inform priorities: 7, 19, 2, 10, 4, 39
- Apologise when they get things wrong: 7, 15, 17, 13, 7, 40

Base: All valid respondents interviewed in England and Wales (12,662) : Fieldwork dates: 21 July - 15 August 2017 (online)   Source: Ipsos MORI

Source: Ipsos MORI Report for Her Majesty's Inspectorate of Constabulary and Fire & Rescue Services, Public Perceptions of Policing in England and Wales 2017 Page 18. https://www.ipsos.com/sites/default/files/ct/publication/documents/2017-12/public-perceptions-of-policing-in-england-and-wales-2017.pdf

could have satisfied the statutory requirements by simply adding three words – 'Mason, Charing Cross' – before commencing the search.

Reasonable force may be used during a stop and search (s. 117), but the suspect cannot be required to remove any clothing in public, except for an outer coat, jacket or gloves (s. 2(9)). Police officers must ask anyone stopped to give their name, address and define their ethnicity.

Any stolen or prohibited articles discovered by the police during the search may be seized (s. 1(6)). In the past, when a stop and search had been carried out the police had to make quite a detailed written record of this immediately and give the person searched a copy of this. Following the Crime and Security Act 2010, s. 1, a record is simply made of the ethnic origin of the person searched and this record can be made at the police station if the person is arrested. The record no longer states the name and address of the person searched or any damage or injury caused during the stop and search. If someone is stopped but not searched then the police do not need to make a record of the encounter.

Under s. 117 of the Serious Organised Crime and Police Act 2005, the police are allowed to fingerprint people on the street using a handheld device to check the identity of a person. Once checked, the fingerprint has to be destroyed.

In the past the police could, and frequently did, carry out a search where there was no statutory power to search but with the member of the public's consent. These searches could then take place without any of the legislative safeguards. In practice, some people would 'consent' to a search in that they would offer no resistance to it, because they did not know their legal rights. Since 2003, voluntary searches are no longer allowed.

Other powers to stop and search

Various statutes give specific stop and search powers regarding particular offences. For example, the Misuse of Drugs Act 1971, s. 23, allows the police to stop and search anyone who is suspected on reasonable grounds to be in unlawful possession of a controlled drug. It is this form of stop and search which is most frequently used by the police. The Sporting Events (Control of Alcohol etc.) Act 1985 contains a power to stop and search people before entry into certain sporting events such as a football match. Section 60 of the Criminal Justice and Public Order Act 1994 provides that where a senior police officer reasonably believes that serious violence may take place in an area, they may, in order to prevent its occurrence, give written authorisation for officers to stop and search persons and vehicles in that area for up to 24 hours. This can be extended by a further 24 hours. When such authorisation is in place, police officers can stop and search any pedestrian or vehicle for offensive weapons or dangerous instruments. Offensive weapon bears the same meaning as in s. 1 of PACE; a dangerous instrument refers to an object which has a blade or is sharply pointed (s. 60(11)). Unlike s. 1 of PACE, these powers do not require reasonable grounds for suspicion. The police can also be authorised to stop and search randomly any pedestrian or vehicle in an area where it is suspected that knives or offensive weapons are being carried without good reason.

The power to stop and search under s. 60 was found not to be in breach of the European Convention on Human Rights in ***R (on the application of Roberts) v Commissioner of Police of the Metropolis*** (2015). The Supreme Court stated that even though reasonable suspicion was not required, there were other safeguards to prevent the power from being used in a discriminatory manner, such as the guidelines contained in Code of Practice A (see p. 432).

Under s. 65 of the Criminal Justice and Public Order Act 1994, an officer can stop anyone on their way to a 'rave' and direct them not to proceed. Similar powers exist under s. 71, in relation to trespassory assemblies. These rather draconian powers can be exercised within five miles of the rave or assembly.

There are clearly potential dangers in granting wide stop and search powers to the police if there is a possibility that the powers will be abused, with harassment of ethnic minority groups being a particular concern. In August 2014, the coalition Government introduced a new police code of conduct on the use of their powers to stop and search members of the public. The then Home Secretary Theresa May had said the technique was being misused so often that it was damaging relations between the public and police (discussed in detail at p. 461). Police now record every outcome resulting from stop and search. The continuing public concern at the disproportionate use of stop and search against members of ethnic minority groups has arguably driven the adoption of body-worn cameras, which are now routinely used by the Metropolitan Police. Complaints regarding such encounters are now markedly reduced.

The Bigger Picture: Terrorism and stop and search

Under s. 44 of the Terrorism Act 2000, the Home Secretary could secretly authorise the police to carry out random stops and searches for 28 days in designated areas as part of the fight against terrorism. There was no requirement that the police have reasonable suspicion against the person being searched. These powers were in practice being used extensively and controversially by the police. The Home Secretary continuously approved the use of this power in the whole of the London area since the legislation came into force in 2001. Thousands of people were being stopped each year under this provision, but only a very small number of these stops and searches resulted in an arrest and none that were connected to terrorism. For example, in 2008 over 41,000 people were subjected to a stop and search under s. 44, but only 28 people were arrested as a result.

The legality of the exercise of this power to stop and search was challenged before the House of Lords in *R (on the application of Gillan) v Commissioner of Police for the Metropolis* (2006). Kevin Gillan and Pennie Quinton were students who attended a peaceful demonstration against an arms fair in East London. The police stopped and searched them using their power under s. 44. With the support of the civil rights group Liberty, the students challenged the legality of the stop and search. They argued that Parliament only intended these powers to be used exceptionally and for short periods, but they were in fact being used as an everyday tool of public order. The House of Lords rejected this application and concluded that the stop and search powers were lawful. The case was taken to the European Court of Human Rights which held that the power under s. 44 was in fact unlawful. The exercise of the power amounted to a breach of the right to privacy guaranteed by Art. 8 of the European Convention on Human Rights. This breach could only be permitted under the Convention if it was in accordance with the law, which meant that the relevant law had to be foreseeable, accessible and compatible with the rule of law. As the stop and search under s. 44 could be undertaken without reasonable suspicion, it could be carried out in an arbitrary and discriminatory way. In conclusion, the s. 44 power was not subject to adequate legal safeguards to prevent abuse.

In addition, Lord Carlile, the Government's terrorist watchdog, stated in his annual report for 2005 that the s. 44 powers to stop and search were unnecessary. There was no evidence that the use of s. 44 had a greater potential to prevent an act of terrorism than the existing powers to stop and search founded on a police officer having reasonable suspicion. In 2007, he suggested that the Home Office be more cautious in authorising this type of stop and search.

As a result s. 44 has now been repealed and replaced by a new power to stop and search without reasonable suspicion, contained in the Protection of Freedoms Act 2012. The new stop and search powers are inserted as s. 47A of the Terrorism Act 2000. The new provisions are disappointingly similar to the old ones, but it is hoped that they are compatible with the European Convention. The senior police officer's authorisation for use of the new powers may only be given where he or she reasonably suspects that an act of terrorism 'will take place' and only where the powers are considered to be 'necessary to prevent such an act'. The maximum period for any authorisation is reduced from 28 to 14 days. The purposes for which the search may be conducted are narrowed to looking for evidence that the person is a terrorist or that the vehicle is being used for terrorist purposes.

18.6.2 Powers of arrest

Powers of arrest allow people to be detained against their will. Such detention is only lawful if the arrest is carried out in accordance with the law. An arrest can take place either with or without a warrant. As well as the relevant legislative provisions, guidance for the police on the use of their power of arrest is provided in Code of Practice G.

Arrest with a warrant

Under s. 1 of the Magistrates' Courts Act 1980, criminal proceedings may be initiated either by the issue of a summons requiring the accused to attend court on a particular day or, in more serious cases, by a warrant of arrest issued by the magistrates' court. The police obtain a warrant by applying in writing to a magistrate, and backing up the application with an oral statement made on oath. The warrant issued must specify the name of the person to be arrested and general particulars of the offence. When an arrest warrant has been granted, a constable may enter and search premises to make the arrest, using such reasonable force as is necessary (PACE, s. 117).

Controversially, a private individual can apply to the magistrates for an arrest warrant to be issued. Such a warrant was issued by a magistrates' court in London against the former Israeli foreign minister, Tzipi Livni, in 2009 for an alleged international war crime committed by bombing carried out in Gaza. This caused diplomatic tensions between the UK and Israel. The Police Reform and Social Responsibility Act 2011 has added a requirement for the Director of Public Prosecutions to consent to the issue of an arrest warrant for an international crime to prevent the courts being used as a political tool.

Arrest without a warrant

The powers of the police to arrest without a warrant were increased by the Serious Organised Crime and Police Act 2005. The extension of police arrest powers were considered in the consultation paper, *Modernising Police Powers to Meet Community Needs* (Home Office, 2004b). The reforms have simplified the police powers of arrest, but at the same time they have given the police more powers than they need, and are open to abuse.

In the past s. 24 of PACE allowed a person to be arrested only for quite serious offences, known as arrestable offences, unless certain additional requirements were satisfied when an arrest would also be possible for a minor offence. The 2005 Act amended PACE so that now a police officer can arrest a person for committing any offence if this is necessary. Police officers must reasonably suspect that a person has committed, is committing, or is about to commit an offence and have reasonable grounds for believing that it is necessary to arrest that person. It will be necessary to carry out an arrest:

- if the person will not give their name and address, or the police officer reasonably suspects that the name or address given is false;
- if the arrest will prevent the person from causing physical injury to him- or herself or another person; suffering physical injury; causing loss or damage to property; committing an offence against public decency; or obstructing the highway;
- to protect a child or other vulnerable person;
- to allow the prompt and effective investigation of the offence or of the conduct of the person in question; or
- to prevent the person disappearing.

These last two reasons – and in particular the penultimate one – are most likely to justify an arrest in the majority of cases. Further guidance on the issue is contained in paragraph 2.9 of Code of Practice G. In *G v DPP* (1989) it was held that a belief of the police officer concerned that suspects generally give false names was not sufficient to satisfy the general arrest conditions.

In *Richardson* v *Chief Constable of West Midlands Police* (2011) a teacher had been accused of assaulting a pupil. He agreed to attend with his solicitor at an appointment at a police station to answer questions. On arriving at the police station he was arrested. The arresting officer said he thought arrest was necessary because the teacher might have tried to leave the interview room. The High Court held that on the facts there was no evidence an arrest was necessary because the teacher was willing to attend the police station voluntarily. As a result the arrest amounted to false imprisonment and the police force had to pay compensation. The lawfulness of an arrest will be assessed against three questions:

1   Did the officer believe that an arrest was necessary?

2   Did the officer have reasonable grounds for that belief?

3   Was the decision to arrest exercised in a reasonable way? Another way of putting this last question is to ask whether the officer had exercised his or her executive discretion in a reasonable way (known as the 'Wednesbury reasonableness test', discussed on p. 716).

On the facts, the decision to arrest was not exercised in a reasonable way because a blanket decision had been made that if a person was to be questioned they must always be arrested.

In *Lord Hanningfield* v *Chief Constable of Essex Police* (2013), Lord Hanningfield had recently come out of prison following his conviction for false accounting with regard to his House of Lords' expenses. At 6.45 am, five police officers arrived in unmarked cars outside his bungalow, woke him up, arrested him and searched his home. He took the police to court, arguing that his arrest had been unlawful because it was not necessary. The police argued that it had been necessary 'to allow the prompt and effective investigation of the offence' under s. 24 of PACE. The police were investigating a claim he had committed fraud with regard to his expenses when he was the leader of Essex County Council. His claim for unlawful arrest was successful and he was awarded £3,500 in damages. The High Court ruled it had not been necessary to arrest him because he would have voluntarily attended the police station and there was no risk at this stage that evidence would be tampered with or potential witnesses contacted. The police officer in charge might have believed the arrest was necessary, but on an objective assessment it was not: while the arrest was convenient for the police, it was not necessary. If the police wanted to search his home they should have got a warrant to do this from the magistrates' court.

The same rules apply to the concept of reasonable suspicion for arrest as were discussed for stop and search powers. Its meaning in the context of an arrest was considered by the House of Lords in *O'Hara* v *Chief Constable of the Royal Ulster Constabulary* (1996). A two-stage test was identified. First, there must be actual suspicion on the part of the arresting officer (the subjective test) and, secondly, there must be reasonable grounds for that suspicion (the objective test). This approach was upheld by the European Court of Human Rights in *O'Hara* v *UK* (2002).

Citizen's arrest

A member of the public is entitled to arrest a person in certain circumstances. This power to carry out a citizen's arrest is contained in s. 24A of PACE. The exercise of the citizen's power of arrest is limited to indictable offences. The person must have reasonable grounds for believing that an arrest is necessary and that it is not reasonably practicable for a police officer to carry out the arrest instead. If the citizen has made a mistake, and an offence has not actually been committed by anyone, the citizen may be liable for damages (*Walters* v *WH Smith & Son Ltd* (1914)). For example, if a man hears somebody shout 'Stop thief!' and seeing a woman running away with a handbag wrongly assumes she is the thief, he can be sued for damages by that woman if he tries to grab her.

18

THE POLICE

Manner of arrest

Arrest requires that it is made clear to the subject that they are no longer at liberty – this is usually achieved by some form of tacit or more comprehensive restraint, such as taking someone by the arm, or placing them in handcuffs. PACE requires that at the time of, or as soon as practicable after, the arrest the person arrested must be informed that they are under arrest, and given the grounds for that arrest, even if it is perfectly obvious that they are being arrested and why (s. 28). This is in line with the pre-existing case law, where in *Christie* v *Leachinsky* (1947) Viscount Simon said: 'No one, I think, would approve a situation in which when the person arrested asked for the reason, the policeman replied "that has nothing to do with you: come along with me" . . .'

There is no set form of words that must be used, and colloquial language such as 'You're nicked for mugging' may be acceptable.

In carrying out the arrest, the police are entitled to use reasonable force under s. 117 of PACE and s. 3 of the Criminal Law Act 1967. In assessing the reasonableness of the force used, the courts will consider two issues:

- Was it necessary to use force?
- Was the force used reasonable or excessive in the circumstances?

Section 76 of the Criminal Justice and Immigration Act 2008 seeks to clarify when force has been used reasonably. It provides that the courts can take into account any genuine mistakes as to the circumstances made by the defendant unless the mistake was made under the influence of drink or drugs. The force will not be viewed as reasonable if it is 'disproportionate'. In determining whether reasonable force has been used, the courts will remember:

(a) that a person acting for a legitimate purpose may not be able to weigh to a nicety the exact measure of any necessary action; and

(b) that evidence of a person's having only done what the person honestly and instinctively thought was necessary for a legitimate purpose constitutes strong evidence that only reasonable action was taken by that person for that purpose.

The Bigger Picture: Taser guns

On occasion, the police will use a taser gun to assist the arrest process. Taser guns are weapons which aim to incapacitate a person temporarily by giving them a short electric shock. The Association of Chief Police Officers has published guidance on when taser guns should be used. This states that they should only be used:

> when officers would be facing violence or threats of violence of such severity that they would need to use force to protect the public, themselves or the subject(s).

In *R (on the application of Morrison)* v *Independent Police Complaints Commission* (2009), a taser gun was used to carry out an arrest of Daniel Morrison. The High Court judge accepted that because of the intense pain involved in tasering, its use could potentially amount to a breach of Art. 3 of the European Convention, which lays down the right not to be subjected to torture or inhuman or degrading treatment. Under s. 134 of the Criminal Justice Act 1988, the criminal offence of torture is committed where a person acting in an official capacity 'intentionally inflicts severe pain or suffering on another in the performance or purported performance of his official duties'.

Photo 18.3 A taser gun

Source: © Kbiros/Shutterstock.com

The use of taser guns was the subject of much debate when the fugitive Raoul Moat shot himself after a six-hour stand-off with police. It subsequently emerged that the police had shot Raoul Moat twice with a taser gun around the time that he had shot himself.

Encounters with armed terrorists in the Westminster and London Bridge attacks of 2017 have opened the debate on whether more police on the frontline should be given tasers.

18.6.3 Police detention

Apart from powers given by anti-terrorist legislation, before 1984 the police in England and Wales had no express power to detain suspects for further investigations to be carried out, nor did they have a general power to detain individuals for questioning, whether as suspects or potential witnesses. In practice, the police often acted as if they had these powers.

The 1981 Royal Commission on Criminal Procedure (Philips, 1981) recommended that the police should be given express powers to detain suspects for questioning, with safeguards to ensure that those powers were not abused. These express powers were granted by PACE. Before PACE, it was generally thought that the police were obliged to bring a suspect before a court within 24 hours, or release them; the Act allows suspects to be detained without charge for up to four days, although there are some safeguards designed to prevent abuse of this power. PACE provides that an arrested person must be brought to a police station as soon as practicable after the arrest, though this may be delayed if their presence elsewhere is necessary for an immediate investigation (s. 30). Alternatively, the police can put the person on bail to attend a police station at a future date. Conditions can be attached to the granting of bail (PACE, ss. 30A–30D). On arrival at the police station, they should usually be taken to the custody officer, who has to decide whether sufficient evidence exists to charge the person. If, on arrest, there is already sufficient evidence to charge the suspect, they must be charged and then released on bail unless there are reasons why this is not appropriate. Such reasons include the fact that the defendant's name and address are not known, there are reasonable grounds for believing that the address given is false, or that the suspect may commit an offence while on bail (s. 38(1)). A person who has been charged and is being held in custody must be brought before magistrates as soon as practicable, and in any event not later than the first sitting after being charged with the offence (s. 46).

If there is not sufficient evidence to charge the suspect, then the person can be detained for the purpose of securing or obtaining such evidence – often through questioning (s. 37). Where a person is being detained and has not been charged, a review officer should assess whether there are grounds for continued detention after the first six hours and then at intervals of not more than nine hours (s. 40). These reviews can sometimes be carried out by telephone. As a basic rule, the police can detain a person for up to 36 hours from the time of arrival at the police station (this was increased from 24 hours by the Criminal Justice Act 2003). After this time the suspect should generally be either released or charged (s. 41). However, there are major exceptions to this. Continued detention for a further 12 hours can be authorised by the police themselves, if the detention is necessary to secure or preserve evidence and the offence is an indictable offence (meaning an offence which can be tried in the Crown Court rather than the magistrates' court).

Further periods of continued detention, up to 96 hours, are possible with approval from the magistrates' court. After 96 hours the suspect must be charged or released. In fact prolonged detention is rare, with only 5 per cent of suspects detained for more than 18 hours, and 1 per cent for more than 24 hours.

In terrorist cases, under the Terrorism Act 2006, a person can be detained for up to 14 days, reduced from 28 days by the coalition Government.

The custody officer is an officer entirely independent from the investigation, whose responsibility it is for keeping the custody record (which records the various stages of detention) and checks that the provisions of PACE in relation to the detention are complied with. These theoretical safeguards for the suspect have proved weak in practice. PACE seems to contemplate that custody officers will be quasi-judicial figures, who can distance themselves from the needs of the investigation and put the rights of the suspect first. In practice this has never been realistic; custody officers are ordinary members of the station staff. They are in practice unlikely to refuse to allow the detention of a suspect.

Once a person has been charged, they cannot normally be subject to further questioning by the police. Post-charge questioning is currently allowed only if an interview is necessary to prevent or minimise harm or loss, to clear up an ambiguity in a previous statement, or where it is in the interests of justice for a person to be given the opportunity to comment on information that has come to light following charge. If suspects are interviewed in these circumstances, inferences cannot be drawn under ss. 34, 36 or 37 of CJPOA 1994 so they have a genuine right to silence.

The current ban on post-charge questioning aims to reduce the risk of false confessions, which become increasingly likely the longer a person is detained or questioned. In a consultation paper, *Modernising Police Powers: Review of the Police and Criminal Evidence Act 1984* (2007a), the Home Office considered whether the ban on further questioning should be lifted in the future, combined with the possibility of inferring guilt when a person refuses to answer questions (see p. 448). Several pilot studies were set up where post-charge questioning was permitted. The aim of this reform is to increase police powers to question suspects about new evidence as it emerges. Concerns about such a development included the fact that after charge the suspect should be under the authority of the courts not the police, as well as the risk that the questioning could be oppressive as the suspect might have been held on remand in custody for a long time between the time of charge and the trial hearing. Despite this, the restriction on post-charge questioning was lifted in 2012 via s. 22 of the Counter-Terrorism Act 2008. Guidance is also included in the PACE Code of Practice H.

Police interrogation

The usual reason for detaining a suspect is so that the police can question them, in the hope of securing a confession (or at least an account which the investigation can then disprove, for example an alibi). This has come to be a very important investigative tool, since it is cheap (compared, for example, with scientific evidence) and the end result, a confession, is seen as reliable and convincing evidence by judges and juries alike. Research by Mitchell (1983) suggests that a high proportion of suspects do make either partial or complete confessions. For example they may accept large parts of the allegation – their presence, confirming their identity, their possession of an item, etc. – while denying a particular element. This enables the police to focus on the disputed area.

Unfortunately, as the miscarriages of justice show, relying too much on confession evidence can have severe drawbacks. Instances of police completely falsifying confessions, or threatening or beating suspects so that they confess even when they are innocent, may be rare but the miscarriages show that police have been willing to use these techniques where they think they can get away with it. In addition, there are less dramatic, but probably more widespread problems. The 1993 Royal Commission raised questions about the poor standard of police interviewing; research by John Baldwin (*Video Taping Police Interviews with Suspects: An Evaluation* (1992b)) suggested that police officers went into the interview situation not with the aim of finding out whether the person was guilty, but on the assumption that they were and with the intention of securing a confession to that effect. Interviews were often rambling and repetitious; police officers dismissed the suspect's explanations and asked the same questions over and over again until they were given the answer they wanted. In some cases the researchers felt this treatment amounted to bullying or harassment and in several cases the 'admissions' were one-word answers given in response to leading questions. Suspects were also offered inducements to confess, such as lighter sentences – which the police are not in a position to guarantee. The police may misrepresent the importance of an interview – 'this is your chance to tell your side of the story'; or seek to disregard explicitly stated legal advice given by a solicitor – 'it's only advice, you don't have to follow it, it's your decision'. The reality is that interview transcripts are very often edited to remedy such unfairness – the admissible evidence consists of the *answers* given by the suspect, *not* the questions asked.

Obviously, the implication here is that, under this kind of pressure, suspects might confess to crimes they did not commit – as many of the miscarriage of justice victims did. But such false confessions do not only occur where the suspects are physically threatened. A study by psychologist G.H. Gudjonsson (*The Psychology of Interrogations, Confessions and Testimony,* 1992) found that there were four situations in which people were likely to confess to crimes they did not commit. First, a minority may make confessions quite voluntarily, out of a disturbed desire for publicity, to relieve general feelings of guilt or because they cannot distinguish between reality and fantasy. Secondly, they may want to protect someone else, perhaps a friend or relative, from interrogation and prosecution. Thirdly, they may be unable to see further than a desire to put the questioning to an end and get away from the police station, which can, after all, be a frightening place for those who are not accustomed to it. A psychologist giving evidence to the 1993 Royal Commission commented that: 'Some children are brought up in such a way that confession always seems to produce forgiveness, in which case a false confession may be one way of bringing an unpleasant situation [the interrogation] to an end.' Among this group there may also be a feeling that, once they get out of the police station, they will be able to make everyone see sense, and realise their innocence: unfortunately this does not always happen.

Finally, the pressure of questioning, and the fact that the police seem convinced of their case, may temporarily persuade the suspect that they must have done the act in question. Obviously the young and the mentally ill are likely to be particularly vulnerable to this last situation, but Gudjonsson's research found that its effects were not confined to those who might be considered abnormally suggestible. His subjects included people of reasonable intelligence who scored highly in tests on suggestibility, showing that they were particularly prepared to go along with what someone in authority was saying. Under hostile interrogation in the psychologically intimidating environment of a police station, even non-vulnerable people are likely to make admissions which are not true, failing to realise that once a statement has been made it will be extremely difficult to retract.

18.6.4 Safeguards for the suspect

Certain safeguards are contained in PACE to try to protect the suspect in the police station. Some of these – the custody officer, the custody record, and the time limits for detention – have already been mentioned, and we will now look at the rest. It has been claimed that these safeguards would prevent miscarriages of justice in the future, yet the police station where Winston Silcott was questioned as part of investigations into the Broadwater Farm riots (see Chapter 22) was meant to be following the PACE guidelines on a pilot basis.

Broadwater Farm is a housing estate in Tottenham, north London and riots there in October 1985 led to the horrific death of PC Keith Blakelock, who was sent there with colleagues to protect firefighters tackling the various fires raging across the estate. PC Blakelock was stabbed over 40 times. PACE officially came into force in January 1986 and yet when Mark Braithwaite, another suspect, was arrested in February of that year, he was denied access to the legal advice guaranteed by the Act. The three convicted of PC Blakelock's murder in 1987 (Silcott, Braithwaite and Raghip – the 'Tottenham Three') had their convictions quashed in 1991 due to concerns about police interviews and fabricated evidence.

The caution

Under Code of Practice C, a person must normally be cautioned on arrest, and a person whom there are grounds to suspect of an offence must be cautioned before being asked any questions regarding involvement, or suspected involvement, in that offence. The caution used to be: 'You do not have to say anything unless you wish to do so but what you say may be given in evidence.' Since the abolition of the right to silence (see p. 447), the correct wording is: 'You do not have to say anything, but it may harm your defence if you do not mention when questioned anything which you later rely on in court. Anything that you do say may be given in evidence.'

Audio-recording

Section 60 of PACE states that interviews must be audio-recorded. Guidance is provided in PACE Code of Practice E. This measure was designed to ensure that oppressive treatment and threats could not be used, nor confessions made up by the police. Sadly, it has proved a weaker safeguard than it might seem. In the first place, research presented to the RCCJ showed that police routinely got round the provision by beginning their questioning outside the interview room – in the car on the way to the police station, for example. In addition, they appeared quite willing to use oppressive questioning methods even once the tape-recorder was running – the RCCJ listened to tapes of interviews with the Cardiff Three, victims of another miscarriage of justice whose convictions were quashed in December 1992, and expressed concern at the continuous repetitive questioning that the tapes revealed.

The Home Office is carrying out pilot schemes for the use of video recordings in interviews. However, video recording is unlikely to be introduced at a national level in the near future as the cost of establishing such a scheme would be about £100 million.

The right to inform someone of the detention

Section 56 of PACE provides that, on arrival at a police station, a suspect is entitled to have someone, such as a relative, informed of their arrest. The person who the suspect chooses must be told of the arrest, and where the suspect is being held, without delay.

This right may be suspended for up to 36 hours if the detention is in connection with an indictable offence, and the authorising officer reasonably believes that informing the person chosen by the suspect would lead to: interference with, or harm to, evidence connected with a serious arrestable offence; the alerting of other suspects; interference with or injury to others; hindrance in recovering any property gained as a result of a serious arrestable offence; or, in drug-trafficking offences, hindrance in recovering the profits of that offence.

The right to consult a legal adviser

Under s. 58 of PACE, a person held in custody is entitled to consult a legal adviser, privately and free of charge. About 1.5 million people are arrested every year, of which about a half choose to receive free legal advice. Since 2004, for non-imprisonable offences, this advice is usually given over the telephone by Criminal Defence Direct (see p. 344). Those accused of an imprisonable offence are entitled to see a lawyer in person. In addition, those accused of a non-imprisonable offence continue to have the right to see a legal adviser in person where:

- a police interview or ID procedure is to take place;
- they are entitled to the assistance of an appropriate adult (see p. 445);
- they need an interpreter or cannot communicate on the telephone;
- they complain that they have been maltreated by the police; or
- their preferred solicitor is already at the police station.

The House of Lords ruled in **R v *Chief Constable of the RUC, ex parte Begley*** (1997) that there was no equivalent right to consult a lawyer under common law. The legal adviser will be either a solicitor or, since 1995, an 'accredited representative'. To become an accredited representative a person must register with the Legal Services Commission with a signed undertaking from a solicitor that they are 'suitable' for this work. Once registered they can attend police stations on behalf of their solicitor and deal with summary or either way offences, but not indictable only offences. Within six months the representative must complete and submit a portfolio of work undertaken. This will include two police station visits where they observed their instructing solicitor, two visits where the solicitor observed them and five visits which they completed on their own. If they pass the portfolio stage they then have to take a written and an oral examination, at which point they are fully qualified to represent clients in the police station for any criminal matters.

Where the legal advice is to be given over the telephone by a Criminal Defence Direct adviser, the adviser will start the telephone conversation with the following statement:

> My name is [first name and surname]. I am an accredited representative [or solicitor] working for CD Direct. My job is to give you free and independent legal advice on the telephone. I have nothing to do with the police. You may have asked to speak to a particular solicitor. Your call

has been put through to CD Direct because the type of offence you have been arrested for is one where the necessary advice is provided by telephone. If the police decide to interview you then we will arrange for the solicitor of your choice to attend free of charge at the police station to advise you in person. If you wish to speak to your own solicitor at this stage then it is possible you may have to pay as the call will not be covered by legal aid. Do you wish to continue with free advice from me?

If the suspect answers yes to the question, then the accredited representative will proceed to advise the individual. If, during the conversation, it becomes apparent that the person is entitled to see a legal adviser in person at the police station (for example, because they are about to be interviewed by the police) then the case will either be referred to the particular solicitor requested by the suspect, or to a duty solicitor (including where the requested solicitor could not be contacted within two hours).

The right to speak to a legal adviser may be suspended for up to 36 hours on the same grounds as the right to have another person informed.

Key case

In *R* v *Samuel* (1988) the appellant was detained for six hours on suspicion of armed robbery and then refused access to a lawyer because the police claimed there was a danger that other suspects might be warned. He was interviewed on two further occasions, and denied the suspected offence but admitted carrying out two burglaries. After 48 hours, a lawyer sent by Samuel's mother arrived at the police station, but was refused access to Samuel for a further three hours, during which time he confessed to the armed robbery. The Court of Appeal said that the denial of access to legal advice was unjustified and the confession obtained as a result was inadmissible. They stated that a police officer who sought to justify refusal of legal advice had to do so by reference to the specific circumstances of the case. It was not enough to believe that giving access to a solicitor might generally lead to the alerting of accomplices; there had to be a belief that in the specific case it probably would, and such cases would be very rare – especially where the lawyer called was the duty solicitor.

Legal principle

Under the Police and Criminal Evidence Act 1984, access to a legal adviser can only be refused where this is justified by the specific facts of the case.

On the other hand, in *R* v *Alladice* (1988), a suspect was refused access to a lawyer. Despite this clear breach of PACE, the court held that the interview was in fact conducted with propriety, and that legal advice would have added nothing to the defendant's knowledge of his rights, so the suspect's confession was allowed in evidence.

Before the Police and Criminal Evidence Act 1984 was passed, no more than 20 per cent of suspects asked for legal advice. Since PACE, the uptake has gradually been increasing. By 1990 the figure was over 30 per cent. In 1991, the PACE Code of Practice C was changed requiring the suspect to be told that legal advice was free regardless of means; it stated that police officers were not allowed to try to dissuade the suspect from asking for legal advice and a poster about free legal advice had to be displayed – the poster currently says 'You need a solicitor'. These changes appear to have had some effect. A Home Office study by Bucke and Brown in 1997 showed that the proportion of suspects asking for legal advice rose to

40 per cent. Research carried out by Dr Vicky Kemp (2011) suggests that this has now increased to over 50 per cent. Of those who did not ask to contact a legal adviser, the majority said they did not need one either because they were innocent or because they were guilty. One in five said they did not have a solicitor because they were concerned about delays; police may lead a suspect to believe that 'getting a lawyer will only delay matters – you could be out of here before they arrive . . . '. Indeed, suspects currently perceive solicitors as the main cause of delay (Kemp, 2013). As a result, uptake of legal advice increases where solicitors are visible in the waiting areas in police stations.

In the past there had been concern as to the quality of the legal advice given in the police station. Research by Baldwin (1992a) found that in 66 per cent of interviews the legal representative said nothing at all, and in only 9 per cent of cases did they actively intervene on behalf of the suspect or object to police questions. Baldwin comments:

> The interview takes place on police territory and it is police officers who are in charge of it . . . Passivity and compliance on the part of lawyers are therefore the normal, the expected, almost the required responses at the police station. Solicitors are conditioned by their history, their experience, even their professional training and guidance, to be passive in the police interview room, and the existing rules reinforce this by giving police officers the upper hand. The junior staff who mainly turn up to police stations are more inclined to facilitate police questioning than they are to challenge it.

Research by McConville and Hodgson (1993) noted that legal advisers sometimes appeared to identify more with the police than with the suspect. They were usually told very little about the case by the police, and had only minimal discussions with their client beforehand (around half spent less than ten minutes alone with the client). They were therefore rarely in a position to give useful advice.

In the light of concerns about the quality of advice given by solicitors' representatives, the accreditation scheme was introduced in 1995 to raise the standard of legal advice offered at this vital stage in the criminal system. This scheme seems to have led to significant improvements in the advice given. Research carried out by Lee Bridges and Satnam Choongh (*Improving Police Station Legal Advice* (1998)) found that accredited representatives performed as well as duty solicitors and other solicitors, though there were still high rates of non-compliance with the Law Society's standards of performance. In particular, they observed failures to ask suspects about their treatment by the police, to inform them of their right to break interviews for further advice, and to intervene where police questioning was inappropriate. There remains a danger that the police may have questioned the suspect before the official interview, and may continue to do so after a lawyer has visited.

An 'appropriate adult'

PACE and Code of Practice C provide that young people and adults with a mental disorder or mental disability must have an 'appropriate adult' with them during a police interview, as well as having the usual right to legal advice. This may be a parent, but is often a social worker. Surprisingly, Evans's 1993 research for the RCCJ found that parents were not necessarily a protection for the suspect, since they often took the side of the police and helped them to produce a confession.

It is reported that mental health conditions make up around 23 per cent of the total burden of disease in the UK but the percentage allocated to care for those with such conditions within the NHS is just 11 per cent (BMA Report: *Breaking down barriers – the challenge of improving mental health outcomes,* 2017). The gap in support is wide and many mentally vulnerable adults are finding themselves in police stations. Unlike children, they may be difficult to identify, making it likely that the required safeguards will not be in place when they are interviewed. Research by the psychologist Gudjonsson (1992) calculated that between 15 and 20 per cent of suspects may need an appropriate adult present – considerably more than the 4 per cent whom the police currently identify.

The RCCJ recommended that the police ought to be given clearer guidelines and special training in identifying vulnerable individuals, and that there should be a full review of who should be considered an 'appropriate adult', and what their role in the police station should be. They also raised the possibility of establishing duty psychiatrist schemes at busy police stations in city centres, and felt that, in any event, all police stations should have arrangements for calling in psychiatric help where necessary.

The National Appropriate Adult Network carried out analysis on police data (*There to help: Ensuring provision of appropriate adults for mentally vulnerable adults detained or interviewed by the police,* 2015), finding that appropriate adults were used in 45,000 detentions and voluntary interviews during the course of a year, despite the fact that 280,000 involved the mentally vulnerable.

Treatment of suspects

PACE Codes stipulate that interview rooms must be adequately lit, heated and ventilated, that suspects must be allowed to sit during questioning, and that adequate breaks for meals, refreshments and sleep must be given.

Record of the interview

After the interview is over, the police must make a record of it, which is kept on file. Baldwin's (1992b) research checked a sample of such records against the taped recordings, and concluded that even those police forces considered to be more progressive were often failing to produce good quality records of interviews. Half the records were faulty or misleading, and the longer the interview, the more likely the record was to be inaccurate. These findings were backed up by a separate study carried out by Roger Evans (1993). He found that, in some summaries, the police stated that suspects had confessed during the interview, but, on listening to the tape recordings the researchers could find no evidence of this, and felt that the suspects were in fact denying the offence.

Baldwin points out that the job of police officers is to catch criminals, and their temperament, aptitude and training are focused on this; the skills required for making careful summaries of complex material are not among those generally thought to be required in the job. Since police officers would inevitably summarise interviews from the point of view of a prosecution, defence lawyers should be prepared to take this into account and, rather than taking the summaries on trust, need to listen to the interview tapes themselves. In practice, solicitors request interview tapes in only 10 per cent of cases. Increasingly, and sometimes with judicial encouragement, the use of such police-authored 'summaries' – which may reduce an hour of questioning to a few paragraphs – as evidence placed before the court is replacing the admission of a full transcript of what the suspect *actually* said. Given the importance of any account advanced by a suspect in an interview, whether this practice advances a suspect's interests is perhaps doubtful. But a defendant is entitled to require the court to play the actual tape recording – for that is the evidence – although this is something which is now rarely done.

Exclusion of evidence

One of the most important safeguards in PACE is the possibility for the courts to refuse to admit evidence which has been improperly obtained. Given that the reason why police officers bend or break the rules is to secure a conviction, preventing them from using the evidence obtained in this way is likely to constitute an effective deterrent.

PACE contains two provisions on the admissibility of evidence. Section 76(2) requires the prosecution to prove beyond reasonable doubt that a confession was not obtained by oppression (which is defined in s. 76(8) as torture, inhuman or degrading treatment or the use or threat of violence), or otherwise in circumstances likely to render the confession unreliable. The broader, and much more regularly deployed exclusionary provisions set out at s. 78 allows the court to refuse evidence (of any kind) if it appears to the court that the admission of such evidence would have such an adverse effect on the fairness of the proceedings that the court ought not to admit it.

These provisions have been used to render evidence inadmissible when the police have breached PACE or its Codes, although breaches of the Codes alone must be 'serious and substantial' in order to make evidence inadmissible. Such breaches were found in *R v Canale* (1990), where the court refused to accept evidence of interviews which were not contemporaneously written up, describing this breach of a Code as 'flagrant, deliberate and cynical'. In *R v Latif and Shahzad* (1996) the House of Lords took a very narrow approach to s. 78. The appellants had been convicted of being knowingly concerned in the importation of heroin into the UK from Pakistan. An undercover police officer had assisted in the importation in order to trick Shahzad into entering the UK so that he could be prosecuted here, there being no extradition treaty with Pakistan. Despite the fact that the court found that the police officer's conduct had been criminal and had involved trickery and deception, the House of Lords refused to exclude his evidence under s. 78. Unlike, for example, the admissibility criteria in the United States, in the United Kingdom evidence obtained in breach of PACE Codes of Practice can, and very often is, ruled nonetheless admissible. The counter-argument is that tribunals can judge for themselves whether breaches of procedure affect the weight of such evidence.

The House of Lords in *A v Secretary of State for the Home Department* (2005) held that, if it was established that evidence had been obtained by torture abroad, such as from detainees of Guantanamo Bay, this evidence would not be admissible in proceedings in English courts.

Article 8 of the European Convention on Human Rights protects the right to privacy. Article 8(2) adds that interference with that right is permitted if it is in accordance with the law and necessary in a democratic society for the prevention of crime. A careful balance has to be drawn by the law where surveillance techniques are used: for example, by bugging a private home. Breach of Art. 8 can give rise to a right to damages, but there is no guarantee that the evidence will be excluded at trial as the ordinary rules in s. 76 and s. 78 of PACE apply.

The right to silence

Until 1994, the law provided a further safeguard for those suspected of criminal conduct, in the form of the traditional 'right to silence'. This essentially meant that suspects were free to say nothing at all in response to police questioning, and the prosecution could not suggest in court that this silence implied guilt (with some very limited exceptions).

Once PACE was introduced, the police argued that its safeguards, especially the right of access to legal advice, had tipped the balance too far in favour of suspects, so that the right to silence was no longer needed. Despite the fact that the Royal Commission on Criminal Justice (1993) opposed this view, the Government agreed with the police, and the right to silence was abolished by the Criminal Justice and Public Order Act 1994. This does not mean that suspects can be forced to speak, but it provides four situations in which, if the suspect chooses not to speak, the court will be entitled to draw such inferences from that silence as appear proper. The four situations are where suspects:

- when questioned under caution or charge, fail to mention facts which they later rely on as part of their defence and which it is reasonable to expect them to have mentioned (s. 34);

- are silent during the trial, including choosing not to give evidence or to answer any question without good cause (s. 35);

- following arrest, fail to account for objects, substances or marks on clothing when requested to do so (s. 36);

- following arrest, fail to account for their presence at a particular place when requested to do so (s. 37).

No inferences from silence can be drawn where a suspect was at a police station and has been denied access to legal advice (s. 34(2A)).

The legislative provisions which allow inferences to be drawn from silence have created an expectation of defendant participation in the criminal justice process, and the onus has been placed squarely on the defence to justify any lack of participation. Where inferences can be drawn from silence, the jury is effectively invited to penalise defendants for their failure to participate. The obvious assumption underlying the legislation is that the innocent, with nothing to hide, will want to assert their innocence.

Key case

The European Court of Human Rights stated in **Murray v United Kingdom** (1996) that, in the context of the anti-terrorist legislation, the abolition of the right to silence was not in breach of the European Convention, because of the existence of a range of other safeguards ensuring that the defendant had a fair trial.

Legal principle

The abolition of the right to silence by the Criminal Justice and Public Order Act 1994 did not amount to a breach of the European Convention on Human Rights.

Adverse inferences cannot always be drawn from silence. Where the statute does not apply, the judge should explicitly direct the jury that they should not draw adverse inferences from the defendant's silence, as the old common law applies. In **R v McGarry** (1998) the defendant, on leaving a club, had punched a man in the face. When questioned by the police about the incident after being cautioned, he had provided a short written statement that he had acted in self-defence and then had answered 'no comment' to all subsequent questions. At his trial he relied on the defence of self-defence and the jury heard the tape of his interview when he had refused to answer questions. The Court of Appeal ruled that he fell outside

s. 34 as he had not failed to mention facts that he later relied on at his trial in his defence. The judge should therefore have directed the jury not to draw adverse inferences from his refusal to answer questions.

In *R* v *N* (1998) the defendant was prosecuted for indecent assault. At his trial the judge informed the jury that they could draw an adverse inference from the appellant's failure in the police interview to provide the explanation for the presence of semen on the victim's nightdress that he had given at his trial. The appellant was convicted and appealed. The Court of Appeal ruled that the trial judge had made a mistake since, at the time of the interview, it was not known that there were semen stains on the nightdress, and so the appellant was not asked to explain them. Section 34 of the CJPOA had to be limited to its express terms: an adverse inference could only be drawn from a failure to mention a fact when being questioned in relation to it. Merely failing to mention a fact during the police interview was not sufficient.

If suspects remain silent on the advice of their solicitor then no adverse inferences can be drawn from this fact. Normally, discussions between solicitors and their clients are private (known as 'privileged'). The courts can only find out what was said between a lawyer and a client if this privilege is waived by the client. Following the case of *R* v *Condron* (1997) there was some confusion as to whether, when suspects stated they had remained silent because of their lawyer's advice, this amounted to a waiver of their lawyer/client privilege so that their conversation could be the subject of detailed cross-examination by the court. However, in *R* v *Seaton* (2010) the Court of Appeal clarified that suspects could state they had relied on their lawyer's advice and remain silent without having to reveal any details about the conversation between themselves and their lawyer which led to this advice being given. While this can in certain circumstances prevent the unjust application of s. 34, it does not prohibit it.

Figure 18.2 Safeguards for the suspect

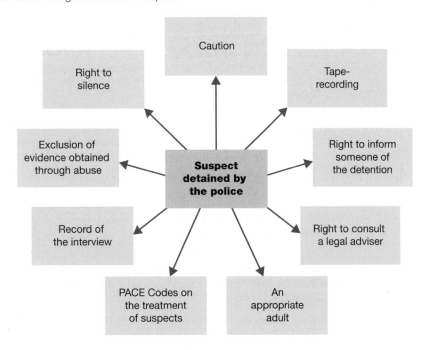

The tribunal (for example jury) are invited to consider whether the decision to accept the advice was reasonable. Furthermore, unless there is a prepared statement, or the legal adviser specifically states that such advice was given on the interview record, a defendant may be left in a position where they have to give evidence at trial as to the fact of such advice being given. Section 34 remains a very powerful and often-used legislative tool in the armoury of the prosecution in seeking to prove a defendant's guilt at trial.

Interviews outside the police station

PACE states that, where practicable, interviews with arrested suspects should always take place at a police station. However, evidence obtained by questioning or voluntary statements outside the police station may still be admissible. Since such interviews are not subject to most of the safeguards explained above, the obvious danger is that police may evade PACE requirements by conducting 'unofficial' interviews – such as the practice known as taking the 'scenic route' to the station, in which suspects are questioned in the police car. The RCCJ found that about 30 per cent of suspects report being questioned prior to arrest.

Even at the police station, research by McConville (Videotaping interrogations: police behaviour on and off camera (1992)) shows that illegal, informal and unrecorded visits were made to suspects in cells to prepare the ground for an interview and to persuade them not to raise a defence. Sometimes suspects themselves ask to see police officers informally, in the hope of doing some kind of deal. In some cases the formal interview that followed was little more than a set piece, scripted by the police. Yet, defence lawyers often accepted the police version of these events as the truth. Despite the obvious dangers of these practices, the RCCJ did not recommend excluding evidence obtained in this way, but merely discussed the possibility of requiring tape-recording of all contact between a suspect and the police. The PACE Codes of Practice do, however, provide for a procedure whereby such 'significant statements' – made after caution, but prior to interview – need to be recorded, offered to the suspect to sign (to indicate accuracy), and must be re-canvassed in any interview. Failure to follow such procedures may well lead to the exclusion of evidence; whether suspects appreciate the significance of signing an officer's notebook, without the benefit of legal advice, is more doubtful.

18.6.5 Non-intimate samples

Urine and other non-intimate samples can be taken after arrest for a trigger offence, such as theft and burglary, to test for the presence of Class A drugs.

18.6.6 Search of the person after arrest

Section 32 of PACE provides that the police may search an arrested person at a place other than a police station if there are reasonable grounds for believing they are in possession of evidence, or anything that might assist escape or present a danger.

The police have the power to search arrested persons on arrival at the police station, and to seize anything which they reasonably believe the suspect might use to injure anyone, or use to make an escape, or that is evidence of an offence or has been obtained as the result of an offence (s. 54).

18.6.7 Searches in school

Under the Violent Crime Reduction Act 2006, school staff, with the permission of the head teacher, are able to carry out a search of school pupils for knives and other offensive weapons. If an offensive weapon is found, or any other evidence of an offence, the police must be immediately informed. Thus, the school does not have the option of merely dealing with this as an internal disciplinary matter.

18.6.8 Intimate searches

Section 55 of PACE gives police the power to conduct intimate searches of a suspect, which means searches of the body's orifices. Such a search must be authorised by a superintendent, who must have reasonable grounds for believing that a weapon or drug is concealed, and must be carried out by a registered health care professional.

The safeguards on the use of this power caused problems for the police when confronted with drug dealers. The dealers frequently stored drugs in their mouths, knowing that search of the mouth was regarded as an intimate search needing to be carried out by a member of the medical profession with special authorisation. To address this problem, s. 65 of PACE, as amended by the CJPOA 1994, now provides that a search of the mouth is not an intimate search.

The Criminal Justice and Court Services Act 2000 allows the compulsory drug testing of alleged offenders.

The Bigger Picture: DNA samples and fingerprints

Sections 61–64 of PACE allow the police to take DNA samples and fingerprints. DNA information is stored on a national database and constitutes an invaluable investigative tool, allowing the police to check for a match on the database with DNA taken from the scene of a crime. Even where there is no match, the DNA profile enables the police to determine the gender, ethnicity and certain medical conditions of a suspect.

The National DNA Database (NDNAD) is proportionately the largest in the world, holding over 4 million samples (about 6 per cent of the population). There is concern that the database could add to the problem of race discrimination in the criminal justice system, with a high proportion of the black population retained on the database. This imbalance may be the result of discriminatory police practices. Figures updated to September 2018 are included in Table 18.1

In *S. and Michael Marper v UK* (2008) the European Court of Human Rights held that the retention of DNA samples where there is no conviction breached the European Convention. As a result, provisions were included in the Protection of Freedoms Act 2012 amending PACE. Under these provisions DNA samples and fingerprints must be destroyed if it appears to the police that the material was taken unlawfully. DNA samples and fingerprints of those arrested but not convicted must normally be removed from the police DNA database. If a person was arrested but not convicted of certain sexual or violent offences, their DNA and fingerprint details may be retained for up to five years.

▶

Table 18.1 Number of DNA profiles retained by ethnicity

ETHNIC APPEARANCE

The ethnic appearance data is based on the judgement of the police officers taking the samples as to which of seven broad ethnic appearance categories they consider the individuals belong.

It is recorded solely for police intelligence purposes, to assist in subsequent identification of a suspect identified through a match on the NDNAD. Ethnic appearance has only been recorded for volunteer samples since 2005.

'Unknown' means that no ethnic appearance was recorded by the officer taking the sample.

All Forces

Ethnic Appearance	Subject Profiles	%
Unknown	502,059	7.97%
Asian	331,529	5.26%
Black	476,513	7.56%
Chinese, Japanese or SE Asian	39,233	0.62%
Middle Eastern	51,297	0.81%
White North European	4,760,586	75.55%
White South European	139,616	2.22%
Total	6,300,833	

England and Wales plus BTP

Ethnic Appearance	Subject Profiles	%
Unknown	162,128	2.82%
Asian	329,089	5.73%
Black	471,017	8.20%
Chinese, Japanese or SE Asian	38,092	0.66%
Middle Eastern	50,816	0.88%
White North European	4,554,986	79.30%
White South European	137,714	2.40%
Total	5,743,842	

Source: NDNAD Statistics 30 September 2018

Figure 18.3 Number of DNA profiles retained from all UK enforcement agencies, by ethnicity, as of 30 September 2018

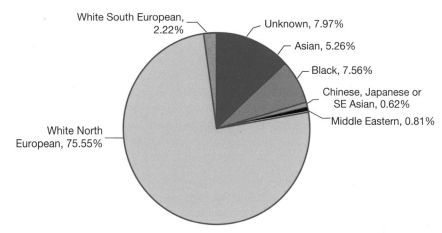

Source: Graph created from the gov.uk National DNA Database Statistics site, made available by clicking on National DNA Database Statistics, Q2, 2018–2019 https://www.gov.uk/government/statistics/national-dna-database-statistics

Photo 18.4 Taking a DNA sample

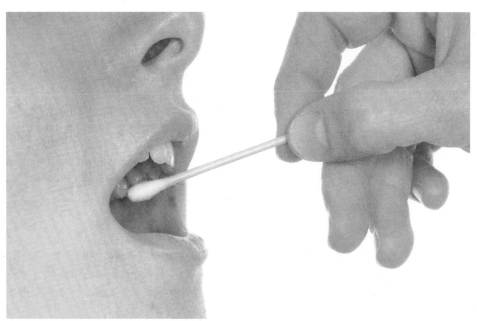

Source: © PeJo/Shutterstock.com

18.6.9 Powers to search premises

The police can always search premises if the occupier consents to this. In addition, Part II of PACE (ss. 8–18) provides the police with statutory powers to enter and search premises for evidence. These powers can be executed either with or without a warrant.

Search with a warrant

A number of statutes allow the granting of search warrants, but the main provisions are to be found in s. 8 of PACE. The police apply for the warrant to a magistrate, who must be satisfied that the police reasonably believe an indictable offence has been committed, and that the premises concerned contain relevant evidence or material likely to be of substantial use to the investigation. In addition, it must be impractical to make the search without a warrant (which means with the consent of the person entitled to grant entry or access to evidence), because:

- it is not practicable to communicate with that person;
- entry would not be granted without a warrant; or
- the purpose of the search would be frustrated or seriously prejudiced if immediate entry could not be obtained on arrival.

The search warrant may allow entry to:

- specific premises;
- any premises occupied or controlled by the person specified on the application;
- premises on more than one occasion. The number of entries may be specified or unlimited.

The latter two search powers were created by the Serious Organised Crime and Police Act 2005 and are known colloquially as 'super-warrants'.

In practice, research by Lidstone (1984) indicates that magistrates rarely refuse to grant a warrant; if certain magistrates were known to refuse applications, the police would simply stop applying to them and go to another magistrate instead. About 12 per cent of searches are made with a warrant.

There are certain classes of material for which these basic powers cannot be used:

- privileged material (communications between lawyers and their clients);
- excluded material (medical records and journalistic material held in confidence); and
- special procedure material (other journalistic material and material acquired through business and held in confidence).

Once the warrant is issued, entry and search must take place within three months, and must be undertaken at a reasonable hour, unless that would frustrate the search. Reasonable force may be used (PACE, s. 117). The officers concerned should provide documentary evidence of their status, plus a copy of the warrant, unless it is impracticable to do so. The Codes also require that police hand out a notice giving information about the grounds for and powers of search, and the rights of the occupier, including rights to compensation for any damage done.

Search without a warrant

PACE provides a range of powers of search which can be exercised without a warrant. Section 17 allows the police to enter and search to execute a warrant of arrest; to make an arrest without warrant; to capture a person unlawfully at large; or to protect people from serious injury or prevent serious damage to property.

Under s. 18, after an arrest for an indictable offence, the police can search premises occupied or controlled by the suspect if they reasonably suspect that there is evidence of the immediate offence or other offences on the premises.

Section 32 provides that, after an arrest for an indictable offence, an officer can lawfully enter and search premises where the person was when arrested or immediately before they were arrested, if the constable reasonably suspects that there is evidence relating to the offence in question on the premises.

There is also a common law power to enter and remain on premises 'to deal with or prevent a breach of the peace'. This is based on *Thomas* v *Sawkins* (1935), where it was held to be lawful for police to enter and insist on remaining in a hall where a political meeting was taking place, because their past experience of such meetings gave them reasonable grounds to apprehend a breach of the peace.

In *McLeod* v *UK* (1998), Mrs McLeod was ordered by the County Court to deliver certain property to her ex-husband. Mr McLeod mistakenly believed he had the right to collect the property from her home. His solicitors asked two police officers to escort him to prevent a breach of the peace. Mrs McLeod was not actually at home when he arrived and he entered her house escorted by two police officers. The Court of Appeal found that the police entry was lawful. Lord Neill commented:

> I am satisfied that Parliament in s. 17(6) has now recognised that there is a power to enter premises to prevent a breach of the peace as a form of preventive justice. I can see no satisfactory basis for restricting that power to particular classes of premises such as those where public meetings are held. If the police reasonably believe that a breach of the peace is likely to take place on private premises, they have power to enter those premises to prevent it. The apprehension must, of course, be genuine and it must relate to the near future.

Mrs McLeod took her case to the European Court of Human Rights. That court ruled that Art. 8 of the European Convention on Human Rights, which protects the right to privacy, had been violated. While the breach of the peace doctrine could in certain circumstances justify an interference with a person's privacy, on the facts of the case there were almost no grounds to apprehend that a breach of the peace would occur, and so it provided no justification for the interference with Mrs McLeod's privacy. As soon as it became apparent that she was away from home, the officers should not have entered her house since it should have been clear that there was no risk of a breach of the peace.

Searches of premises are governed by Code of Practice B, which states that searches should be made at a reasonable time, that only reasonable force should be used and that the police should show due consideration and courtesy towards the property and privacy of the occupier. How far this is observed in practice might be doubted by anyone who watched television news coverage of the anti-burglary campaign Operation Bumblebee, in which police broke down suspects' doors with sledgehammers at 6 am. The fact that in high-profile cases such searches are often accompanied by TV cameras suggests that the media may be tipped off by the police, which, whether such tip-offs are official or not, suggests little regard for the suspects' privacy.

Once the police are lawfully on premises, then under s. 19 of PACE they may seize and retain any item that is evidence of a crime.

18.6.10 Surveillance operations

In recent years a combination of developing technology, concern about confession evidence, the changing nature of financial and drug-related crime and the growing threat of terrorism, has led the police to adopt increasingly sophisticated and intrusive methods of investigation. Surveillance operations can include the placing of bugging devices on private property, the interception of communications (including mobile phones and e-mails), and the use of under-cover police officers. Such surveillance activities were in the past unregulated, which may have been in breach of Art. 8 of the European Convention on Human Rights, protecting the right to privacy. Legislation was therefore required. The relevant legislative provisions are now contained in the Police Act 1997 and the Regulation of Investigatory Powers Act 2000. Except in the case of an emergency, the police have to obtain the authorisation of an independent Commissioner before they can use intrusive surveillance techniques. Even if such techniques are authorised, only very limited types of evidence are admissible, though they may be used for intelligence purposes. In the United Kingdom, for example, transcripts of intercepted telephone calls (unless obtained using physical bugging devices) are not admissible as evidence.

The pressure group, JUSTICE, has produced a report *Freedom from Suspicion: Surveillance Reform for a Digital Age* (2011) drawing attention to the problems with the law in this field. The phone hacking scandal – involving journalists hacking into private telephone calls – and the widespread use of CCTV cameras around the country, have raised concerns about the effective control of surveillance activities.

In 2012 the Government published a draft Communications Bill with a view to updating the powers of the police and security agencies to monitor e-mails, phone calls and the internet. This reform was nicknamed a 'snooper's charter' and has not been introduced due to strong political and public opposition.

In 2013 the whistleblower, Edward Snowden, leaked details of the US and UK mass surveillance programmes, under which they are indiscriminately intercepting huge amounts of internet and phone messages. The UK Government claims all these interceptions have been carried out lawfully, in particular a Government Minister has authorised these interceptions under s. 8(4) of the Regulation of Investigatory Powers Act 2000. Critics have argued that such broad surveillance is excessive and completely undermines our right to privacy.

In 2014 the Court of Justice of the European Union ruled that regulations allowing blanket data retention of electronic communications (telephone, e-mail, texts and web-based communications) went beyond what was strictly necessary for the purposes of national security and therefore breached our basic human right to privacy. However, the Government considers that such retention is necessary for the purposes of national security and the fight against serious crime. It therefore hastily passed the Data Retention and Investigatory Powers Act 2014 which the Government considers contains sufficient safeguards to respond to the concerns of the Court of Justice. The legislation requires internet and phone companies to store the communications data of the entire population of the United Kingdom for 12 months and make it accessible to the police and security services.

> ## The Bigger Picture: Undercover police operations
>
> Undercover police officers are used to detect and prevent crime. Their roles can vary considerably. They can be used to gather intelligence in gangs or to collect evidence about people suspected of serious crimes; they may be 'test purchase officers' who buy drugs from drug dealers prior to arrest, or undercover online officers who establish online relationships to gather information to fight crime. The activities of undercover officers are governed by the Regulation of Investigatory Powers Act 2000 (see above). The legislation refers to an undercover officer as a 'covert human intelligence source' (CHIS). There has been concern over how plain-clothed police officers have behaved during undercover police operations. It has come to light that undercover officers have adopted the identities of dead children to create their covert identity and some have had sexual relations with members of the group they are infiltrating. It has been alleged that undercover officers provided information on trade union activists who were then blacklisted by employers and that they sought to gain information that might be used to 'smear' the Stephen Lawrence family (see p. 153) and their friends.
>
> In the light of such concerns, the Home Secretary established a public inquiry in 2015 to look into the activities of undercover officers. Originally chaired by Lord Justice Pitchford, the inquiry was taken over by Sir John Mitting in 2017 after Lord Pitchford became ill. Sir John will continue the existing work, which will include looking at whether undercover police operations have targeted political and social justice campaigners.
>
> There is frustration from the activists at the length of time the inquiry is taking, and accusations that the Metropolitan Police are attempting to suppress materials. Lord Pitchford however, attributed this to the force's incompetence rather than deliberate sabotage. It was announced in 2018 that the final report will not be delivered until 2023.

18.6.11 Cautions

In appropriate cases an offender can be issued with a caution rather than being subjected to a full criminal prosecution. This is a formal warning to offenders about what they have done, and their conduct in the future. To avoid overuse of cautions, the Criminal Justice and Courts Act 2015 bans police cautions being given to adults for indictable and either-way offences except in exceptional circumstances. Home Office guidelines lay down the criteria on which the decision to caution should be made. A caution can only be given where the offender admits guilt, and there would be a realistic prospect of a successful prosecution. In the case of a juvenile, the parents or guardian must consent to a caution being given. If these criteria are met, other factors to be taken into account are the seriousness of the offence and the extent of the damage done; the interests and desires of the victim; the previous conduct of the offender; the family background of the offender; and the offender's conduct after the offence, such as a willingness to make reparation to the victim.

Formal cautions are recorded and, if the person is convicted of another offence afterwards, can be cited as part of their criminal record. The 1980s saw a substantial increase in the use of cautioning, with the number of cautions given doubling between 1983 and 1993, peaking at 311,300 cautions for that year, primarily to juveniles. There has subsequently been a slight decline in their use, with the figures for 1995 showing a 6 per cent reduction in the use of cautions.

The Criminal Justice Act 2003 introduced conditional cautions. Conditions can seek either to facilitate rehabilitation or ensure that reparation is made. Failure to comply with the conditions can trigger a criminal trial for the offence. This is a dangerous reform, as cautions

Figure 18.4 Offenders cautioned for indictable offences by offence group, March 2007–March 2017

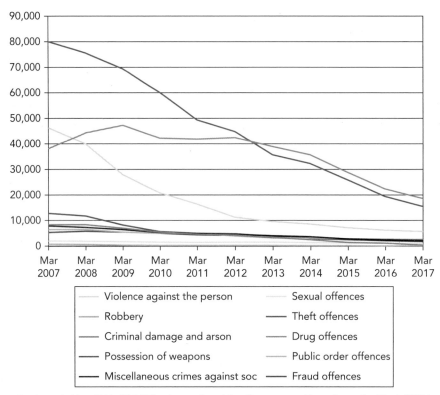

Source: Graph created from Table Q2.2 'Offenders cautioned, by offence group, 12 months ending March 2008 to 12 months ending March 2018' which is available by clicking on 'Overview tables' on the following Ministry of Justice website: https://www.gov.uk/government/statistics/criminal-justice-system-statistics-quarterly-march-2018

will take on the form of a punishment administered outside the court system. As such, they might well breach the European Convention on Human Rights.

Cautioning appears to be effective in terms of preventing reoffending: 87 per cent of those cautioned in 1985 were not convicted of a standard list offence within two years of the caution. However, this may reflect the kind of individuals and offences that are seen as suitable for a caution: for example, 80 per cent of those cautioned had no previous cautions or convictions, but for those who had been previously convicted there was a much greater likelihood that they would reoffend. Prosecution is the most expensive method of dealing with offenders. The Royal Commission on Criminal Justice (RCCJ, 1993) recognised the value of diversionary schemes, stating that there could safely be more cautioning of petty offenders. They were concerned, though, that rates of cautioning varied widely across the country, and recommended the introduction of statutory guidelines. The initial decision on whether to caution should remain with the police, but the Crown Prosecution Service (CPS) should be able to require the police to caution instead of bringing a prosecution.

Despite the RCCJ's recommendations for more cautioning, the national guidelines that were subsequently introduced are more restrictive than previous practice, removing any presumption that juveniles should be cautioned, and discouraging repeat cautions and cautions for serious offences. Problems with variations in the use of cautioning continue – the Criminal Statistics 1995 showed that there were big differences in police caution rates between different police forces, with Gloucestershire, Suffolk and Warwickshire having a rate of over 54 per cent, while Merseyside, Durham, Dorset, South Wales and Cumbria had a rate of 30 per cent or less.

18.6.12 Bail

A person accused, convicted or under arrest for an offence may be granted bail, which means they are released under a duty to attend court or the police station at a given time. There is no time limit on how long a person can be kept on bail before being charged with an offence. Fourteen per cent of those bailed to appear at court fail to do so (*Criminal Justice Statistics 2003*) and nearly 25 per cent of defendants commit at least one offence while on bail (Brown (1998)). The criteria for granting or refusing bail are contained in the Bail Act 1976. There is a general presumption in favour of bail for unconvicted defendants, and they should be released on bail if there is no real prospect of a custodial sentence if subsequently convicted. There are some important exceptions to the presumption in favour of bail. Bail need not be granted where there are substantial grounds for believing that, unless kept in custody, the accused would fail to surrender to bail, or would commit an offence, interfere with witnesses or otherwise obstruct the course of justice. In assessing these risks, the court may take account of the nature and seriousness of the offence and the probable sentence, along with the character, antecedents, associations and community ties of the defendant. A court considering the question of bail must take into account any drug misuse by the defendant. The Criminal Justice Act 2003 has created a presumption against bail for a person charged with an imprisonable offence, who tests positive for a specified Class A drug and refuses treatment, unless there are exceptional circumstances. This provision may breach Art. 5 of the European Convention on Human Rights, which guarantees the right to freedom of the person.

The courts need not grant bail when the accused should be kept in custody for their own protection, where the accused is already serving a prison sentence or where there has been insufficient time to obtain information as to the criteria for bail. If the court does choose to grant bail in such cases, its reasons for doing so must be included in the bail record. The presumption in favour of bail is reversed where someone is charged with a further indictable offence which appears to have been committed while on bail.

The Criminal Justice and Public Order Act 1994, following concern at offences being committed by accused while on bail, provided that a person charged or convicted of murder, manslaughter, rape, attempted murder or attempted rape could never be granted bail if they had a previous conviction for such an offence. This complete ban breached the European Convention on Human Rights. The law has now been reformed by the Crime and Disorder Act 1998, under which such a person may only be granted bail where there are exceptional circumstances which justify doing so. Thus Sion Jenkins, who was put on trial for the murder of his foster-daughter Billy-Jo, was on bail throughout most of the proceedings.

When bail is refused for any of the stated reasons, other than insufficient information, the accused will usually be allowed only one further bail application; the court does not have to hear further applications unless there has been a change in circumstances. Where the remand in custody is on the basis of insufficient information, this is not technically a refusal of bail, so the accused may still make two applications.

Bail can be granted subject to conditions, such as that the accused obtain legal advice before their next court appearance or that the accused or a third party gives a security (which is a payment into court that will be forfeited if the accused fails to attend a court hearing). The Police and Justice Act 2006 significantly increased the range of conditions that can be imposed when granting bail. When a defendant fails to attend court any money held by the court is immediately forfeited and it is up to the person who paid that money to show why it should not be forfeited. A defendant refused bail, or who objects to the conditions under which it is offered, must be told the reasons for the decision, and informed of their right to appeal. The prosecution also has increasing rights to appeal against a decision to grant bail.

The Criminal Justice Act 2003 has given the police the power to grant bail at the place of arrest. This is called 'street bail'. It means that the police do not have to take suspects to the police station and undertake lengthy paperwork. A form is completed on the street and later entered in police records. The power has not been used much by the police and is unlikely to be used much while we do not have compulsory ID cards.

To try to reduce the prison population, Lord Carter (2007) recommended that pre-trial custody be used primarily for individuals being prosecuted for dangerous and serious offences and only as a last resort for women. Under the Criminal Justice and Immigration Act 2008, half the time spent on bail with an electronically tagged curfew of at least eight hours a day can be deducted from any subsequent custodial sentence.

18.7 Criticism and reform

Criticisms and suggestions for reform have been made throughout this chapter, but the following have been the subject of particular debate.

18.7.1 A graduate profession

The work of a police officer requires a wide range of skills, both intellectual and personal. At the moment, a candidate does not need any formal qualifications to join the police force. Now that increasing numbers of young people are going to university, it is time to transform the police force into a graduate profession? Only then would the United Kingdom have an efficient police force with the skills to combat crime effectively. The police force currently struggles with the paperwork that their job requires because they have an inadequate education. Without better preparation for their career, the police will continue to be perceived by many in the public as slow, lazy and inefficient. With the creation of community support officers, the higher pay and status of the police can only be justified if they actually have better qualifications and skills. Police Now is a two-year national leadership programme for graduates. The mission?: '. . . to transform communities, reduce crime and increase the public's confidence in policing, by recruiting and developing an outstanding and diverse group of individuals to be leaders in society and on the policing frontline.'

The Bigger Picture: Racism and the police

Britain is a multicultural and ethnically diverse community. Three per cent of the population aged ten and over is of black ethnic origin, 5 per cent of Asian origin. Successful policing requires that all members of British society must have confidence in the police force. Following the fatal stabbing of Stephen Lawrence, a black teenager who was an A-level student from south London, by a group of racist youths in 1993, defects in several aspects of the English legal system initially failed to bring his killers to justice. A fresh prosecution was brought against two suspects, 18 years after the murder, which led to their conviction (see p. 608). Following concern at the handling of the police investigation into the killing, a judicial inquiry headed by a former High Court judge, Sir William Macpherson, was set up by the Labour Government in 1997 and its report was published in February 1999. It found that the Metropolitan Police suffered from 'institutional racism'.

This is defined as existing where there is a 'collective failure of an organisation to provide an appropriate and professional service to people because of their colour, culture and ethnic origin. It can be seen or detected in processes, attitudes and behaviour which amount to discrimination through unwitting prejudice, ignorance, thoughtlessness and racist stereotypical behaviour.'

The presence of institutional racism was reflected in the fact that the first senior officer at the scene of the crime assumed that what had occurred had been a fight; it was also expressed in the absence of adequate family liaison and the 'patronising and thoughtless approach' of some officers to Mr and Mrs Lawrence; and it could be seen in the side-lining of Stephen Lawrence's friend, the surviving victim of the attack. There was, furthermore, a refusal to accept, by at least five officers involved in the case, that this was a racist murder. Finally, there was the use of inappropriate and offensive language by police officers, including, on occasion, during their appearance before the inquiry itself. It found that racism awareness training was 'almost non-existent at every level', and concluded that institutional racism could only be tackled effectively if there was an 'unequivocal acceptance that the problem actually exists'.

The inquiry, however, concluded that institutional racism was not 'universally the cause of the failure of this investigation'. The investigation by the Metropolitan Police was 'marred by a combination of professional incompetence, institutional racism and a failure of leadership by senior officers'.

The report contained 20 recommendations for reform. In March 1999, the Labour Government issued its Action Plan in response to the Macpherson Report. A steering group, chaired by the Home Secretary, was established to oversee the programme of reform. In the past the Race Relations Act 1976 did not apply to the police, so that there was no legal remedy if a black person thought they had been stopped by the police because of racial prejudice. Now the Equality Act 2010 makes it unlawful for a public authority, including the police, to discriminate in carrying out any of their functions. Police forces have reviewed their provision of racism awareness training. Targets have been set for the recruitment and retention of ethnic minority police officers. Currently 6.6 per cent of police officers are from an ethnic minority.

While the Macpherson Report is one step towards tackling institutional racism in the police, it is worrying that Lord Scarman's report into the Brixton riots of 1981 had already identified this problem, and though some progress was subsequently made, this had clearly not been sufficient. In 1999/2000 the British Crime Survey suggested that there were 143,000 racially motivated crimes committed and yet only 1,832 defendants were prosecuted for such offences.

A particularly sensitive area of policing is the power to stop and search. A police operation against street robberies in Lambeth (south London) in 1981, codenamed SWAMP 81, involved 943 stops, mostly of young black men, over a period of two weeks. Of these, only 118 led to arrests and 75 to charges, one of which was for robbery. The operation, which had no noticeable effect on the crime figures, shattered relations between the police and the ethnic community, and was one of the triggers of the Brixton riots that occurred soon afterwards. Nevertheless, in his report on the Brixton disorders, Lord Scarman thought such powers necessary to combat street crime, provided that the safeguard of 'reasonable suspicion' was properly and objectively applied. But in 1999 the Macpherson Report concluded that the 'perception and experience of the minority communities that discrimination is a major element in the stop and search problem is correct'.

In accordance with recommendations made by Macpherson, the police are now required to monitor the use of stop and search powers, and 'consider in particular whether there is any evidence that they are being exercised on the basis of stereotyped images or inappropriate generalisations'. Regrettably, these statistics show that an increasing proportion of those stopped and searched by the police are black. These Home Office statistics show that if you are from a black or a minority ethnic background you are seven times more likely to be stopped and searched by the police than if you are white. A report by Her Majesty's Inspectorate of Constabulary, *Stop and search powers: are the police using them effectively and fairly?* (2013), found disturbingly low levels of supervision by senior officers of the conduct of stop and search encounters. Twenty-seven per cent of stop and search records did not contain reasonable grounds to search the person.

In response to these criticisms of the stop and search power, the coalition Government introduced a new police code of conduct in August 2014. This code of conduct applies to all police forces in the UK. The then Home Secretary Theresa May declared that the stop and search powers were being misused and that was damaging the public's trust in the police. All police forces in England and Wales signed up to the Best Use of Stop and Search scheme, making them more accountable to their communities. Stop and search outcomes had to be published via the website data.police. uk and if there were a large number of complaints, forces would be required to explain to their local community scrutiny group how they were using their powers. Members of the community were also able to accompany police on patrol to see first-hand how they use stop and search. It was hoped that greater levels of transparency may ease the tensions between police and the communities they serve.

In October 2016 the College of Policing announced new training to address officers' 'unconscious bias' based on age, race and nationality.

Fast forward to 2018 and as violent crime increases, communities worry about gangs and knife crime, and there are more voices calling for stop and search to increase again. However, research carried out by Stopwatch, Release and the LSE *The Colour of Injustice: 'Race', drugs and law enforcement in England and Wales* (2018), shows that the calls for change in 2014 were ignored and the situation has in fact worsened.

Although stop and search declined, disproportionality flourished, with statistics showing that black people were stopped and searched at more than eight times the rate of whites in 2016/17. Asian people and those described as 'mixed' groups were twice as likely to be stopped than white people. Stop and search for drugs made for even wider disparity; with searches on black people at nine times the rate of whites.

18.7.2 Police corruption

The police exercise an extremely delicate role in society and, as criminals are able to generate large sums of money from their criminal conduct, the danger of corruption is real. High risk areas include the handling of informers and positions within drug, vice and crime squads where constant vigilance is required. Where corruption is rife, one can no longer fall back on the idea of a few rotten apples and must accept that the system itself must be corrupting its members.

Sir Paul Condon made anti-corruption a touchstone of his tenure as Commissioner of the Metropolitan Police. He estimated that there may have been as many as 250 corrupt officers in his force, some of whom were directly involved in very serious criminal activity, and dedicated resources to their detection. A more proactive approach can be expected at a national level, as New Scotland Yard has established a special squad concentrating on corruption in the police, and the Association of Chief Police Officers established in 1998 a Taskforce on Corruption. During the course of that year, 28 police officers were convicted of corruption-related offences and, at the end of the year, 153 police officers were suspended for alleged corruption and similar matters. These issues have not gone away, and somewhat ironically, in 2018 the media reported the anti-corruption unit at Scotland Yard was being investigated over claims of serious corruption and malpractice.

18.7.3 Armed officers

There is an ongoing debate as to whether our police officers should carry guns. The majority of police in other countries do carry guns. In the UK the tradition is that police do not carry guns, and only 5 per cent have carried out special training to be authorised to carry them. They work, for example, in armed response vehicles, so that they can provide swift support to their colleagues where necessary. Following the fatal shooting in Bradford of police officer Sharon Beshenivsky, who was investigating a robbery at a travel agent, the Police Federation and the Association of Chief Police Officers called for more police to be armed in the UK. Arming the police with guns can be viewed as a militarisation of the police. It raises concerns about whether we are moving away from a system of 'policing by consent' to one of 'policing by compliance'. The fatal shooting of Jean Charles de Menezes at Stockwell tube station in the summer of 2005 highlighted the risks of police officers being armed, as the police are only human and can make mistakes.

18.7.4 'Bobbies on the beat'

Four billion pounds is spent each year on police patrols, but the reality is that at any one time only 5 per cent of police officers are out on patrol. The Audit Commission report, *Streetwise: Effective Police Patrol* (1996), notes that the public are keen to see more 'bobbies on the beat' and that this provides the public with a feeling of security. A review of research in 1998 found that random patrols are ineffective in reducing crime but that targeted patrols on crime hot spots can be effective (Nuttall, Goldblatt and Lewis, *Reducing Offending: An Assessment of Research Evidence on Ways of Dealing with Offending Behaviour* (1998)). It is unsurprising to note that not seeing uniformed officers walking the streets in local communities is one of the biggest causes for dissatisfaction with the police.

Figure 18.5 Perceived performance of local police services across a range of areas

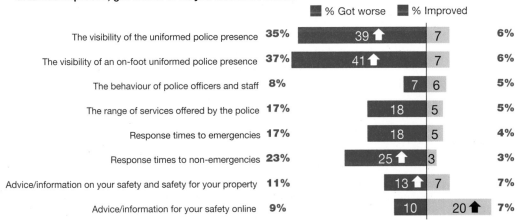

Over the past 12 months do you think each of the following aspects of policing in in your local area has improved, got worse or stayed about the same?

■ % Got worse　■ % Improved

	% Got worse		% Improved
The visibility of the uniformed police presence	35%	39 ⬆ 7	6%
The visibility of an on-foot uniformed police presence	37%	41 ⬆ 7	6%
The behaviour of police officers and staff	8%	7 6	5%
The range of services offered by the police	17%	18 5	5%
Response times to emergencies	17%	18 5	4%
Response times to non-emergencies	23%	25 ⬆ 3	3%
Advice/information on your safety and safety for your property	11%	13 ⬆ 7	7%
Advice/information for your safety online	9%	10 20 ⬆	7%

Base: All valid respondents interviewed in England and Wales (12,662) : Fieldwork dates: 21 July-15 August 2017 (online) Source: Ipsos MORI

18

THE POLICE

18.7.5 Police conduct

During 1997, well over 6,000 complaints of alleged rudeness and incivility by police officers were recorded. Her Majesty's Inspectorate of Constabulary undertook a wide-ranging exploration of the level of integrity in the police because it was recognised that 'public confidence was becoming seriously affected by the bad behaviour of a small minority of police'. In *Police Integrity: Securing and Maintaining Public Confidence* (1999) Her Majesty's Inspectorate reported that: 'Numerous examples were found in all forces visited of poor behaviour towards members of the public and colleagues alike, including rudeness, arrogance and discriminatory comment.' In the Inspectorate's view, one consequence of tolerating bullying, rudeness and racist or sexist behaviour is that 'corruption and other wrongdoing will flourish'. In 2018, the Independent Office for Police Conduct (IOPC) replaced the Independent Police Complaints Commission.

18.7.6 Police as witnesses

In ***R v Momodou and Limani*** (2005) the principle was confirmed that discussions between witnesses should not take place before a trial and statements of one witness should not be disclosed to any other witness, to prevent them tailoring their evidence in the light of what others are saying. But when the police are to act as witnesses in court they are allowed to confer together. This occurred following the shooting of Jean Charles de Menezes and led the jury at his inquest to be unhappy with the police evidence. It also occurred following

---

The Bigger Picture: Policing demonstrations

The death of Ian Tomlinson at the G20 summit demonstrations in 2009 highlighted concerns about the current policing arrangements for demonstrations. The right to demonstrate forms an important part of a democratic system. When Ian Tomlinson died, the public was originally told that he had suffered a heart attack. It was only after video footage was published in the media showing that Ian Tomlinson had been pushed violently from behind by a police officer that a second autopsy was ordered, and it was revealed he had died as a result of internal injuries. Ian Tomlinson himself was not part of the G20 demonstration but just looking for a route to get back from work to the hostel where he was living. Following an inquest finding that Tomlinson had been unlawfully killed, a police officer was charged with manslaughter and subsequently cleared.

The controversy surrounding his death has also drawn attention to the police tactic of containment, referred to often as 'kettling', whereby demonstrators are cordoned off and not allowed to leave for a number of hours until they are released in small groups. This method of policing has proved effective at reducing the risk of demonstrations becoming violent riots, but also constitutes a significant restriction on a person's freedom of movement and right to demonstrate. It was held to be lawful by the House of Lords in ***Austin v Metropolitan Police Commissioner*** (2009). Austin had attended a demonstration in Oxford Street when the police had cordoned off the demonstrators and refused to allow them to leave for seven hours, with no access to toilet facilities. The House of Lords held that there was no breach of the right to liberty in Art. 5 of the European Convention on Human Rights. The police are entitled to restrict the movement of demonstrators provided their actions are proportionate and reasonable and any confinement is restricted to the minimum necessary to prevent serious public disorder and violence. If a cordon was maintained beyond the time necessary for crowd control, in order to punish the demonstrators, then there would be a breach of Art. 5.

the shooting dead of a barrister at his home in Chelsea by the police, after the barrister had started shooting at random from the window of his home. The barrister was naked at the time and appears to have had a mental breakdown. His family brought legal proceedings questioning the legality of the police conferring together when they were preparing their notes of the incident – no other category of eyewitness would be permitted, let alone encouraged, to confer (some would argue, collude) in this manner prior to making witness statements – indeed, such conduct may well render their evidence inadmissible. The High Court held that the police had acted legally: *R (on the application of Saunders)* v *IPCC* (2008).

18.7.7 The right to silence

The abolition of the right to silence has been one of the most severely criticised changes to the criminal justice system in recent years. As the academic John Fitzpatrick has written, the basis of the right to silence is the presumption of innocence, which places the burden of proof on the prosecution: 'this burden begins to shift, and the presumption of innocence to dwindle, as soon as we are obliged to explain or justify our actions in any way' (*Legal Action,* May 1994).

Those who objected to the right to silence claimed that only the guilty would have anything to hide and that the innocent should therefore have no objection to answering questions. It was suggested that the calculated use of this right by professional criminals was leading to serious cases being dropped for lack of evidence, and that 'ambush' defences (in which defendants remain silent till the last moment and then produce an unexpected defence) were leading to acquittals because the prosecution had no time to prepare for the defence.

These arguments were put to the RCCJ, by a Home Office Working Group among others, but after commissioning its own research into the subject the RCCJ rejected the idea of abolishing the right to silence. This research, by Leng (1993), and McConville and Hodgson (1993), showed that in fact only 5 per cent of suspects exercised their right to silence, and there was no evidence of an unacceptable acquittal rate for these defendants. Nor was there any serious problem with ambush defences.

As we have seen, the Conservative Government of the 1990s decided to ignore the RCCJ's recommendations and abolish the right to silence – a somewhat strange decision considering that it was the same Government which set up the Commission in the first place. The law reform body, JUSTICE, has claimed that this decision will lead to increased pressure on suspects and, in turn, to more miscarriages of justice. It studied the effects of removing the right to silence in Northern Ireland (which took place five years before removal of the right in England and Wales). Apparently, suspects frequently failed to understand the new caution and were put under unfair pressure to speak, while lawyers found it difficult to advise suspects when they did not know the full case against them. Most importantly, JUSTICE claims that while at first trial judges were cautious about drawing inferences of guilt from a suspect's silence, five years on, they were giving such silence considerable weight, and in some cases treating it almost as a presumption of guilt.

18.7.8 Deaths following contact with the police

Controversial deaths following contact with the police can arise in a number of situations. They include a death in a road traffic accident after a high-speed police pursuit; deaths following a police response to public disorder; deaths caused by a police officer using a gun and deaths in police custody.

The group Inquest states that 1,092 people have died in police custody since 1990. An additional 599 have died in that period after contact with the police in relation to shooting, pursuit or road traffic incidents. Some deaths are natural and unavoidable but there can sometimes be concern over the amount of physical restraint used against the victim or inadequate monitoring of an intoxicated or mentally disturbed person. The majority of those who die in police custody have been arrested for drink or drug-related offences or minor thefts (Leigh and others, 1998). Very few police officers have been prosecuted following a death in custody, and none has been convicted. A report on the subject by Vogt and Wadham, *Deaths in Custody: Redress and Remedies* (2003) for the pressure group Liberty, concluded that these deaths were not being adequately investigated. The police, the Independent Police Complaints Commission, and the coroner could all be involved. These investigations were ineffective, secretive, slow and insufficiently independent. Deaths in custody can now be the subject of a criminal prosecution under the Corporate Manslaughter and Corporate Homicide Act 2007 which may help to combat this problem. In 2009 the Government created a Ministerial Council on Deaths in Custody. The aim of the Council is to bring about a continuing and sustained reduction in the number and rate of deaths in all forms of state custody in England and Wales.

A report into deaths in police custody was ordered by Theresa May as Home Secretary in 2015 and published in October 2017. The *Report of the Independent Review of Deaths and Serious Incidents in Police Custody* by Dame Elish Angiolini QC contains 110 recommendations for the police, justice system and health service. It includes a startling observation:

> Of eight prosecutions of police officers in connection with a death in custody in the last 15 years, all have ended with acquittals. These include prosecutions for murder and manslaughter. In fact, there has never been a successful prosecution for manslaughter in this context, despite unlawful killing verdicts in Coroner's Inquests. This does not prove that the criminal justice system has failed to deliver justice, but it goes to the heart of why families so often feel let down by the system.

Dame Elish's recommendations have been widely welcomed and focus strongly on mental health. Selected recommendations include the following.

- Those held under mental health powers should not be held in police cells or transported in police vehicles.
- The same standard of mental health training should be provided to all police forces, with the addition of regular top-up training.
- Video cameras should be worn by every frontline officer and be integrated into every police vehicle.
- Ex-police officers should be phased out as lead investigators of the Independent Police Complaints Commission (IPCC).
- Mandatory and consistent training of restraint techniques across all forces, with additional focus on supervision of vital signs during restraint.
- Police officers involved in a death in custody or other serious incident should not confer prior to making their statements.
- Reconsideration by Government of the viability of drying-out centres – where those who are under the influence of alcohol or drugs can be properly supervised.

The report also notes the disproportionality of BAME people in restraint-related deaths.

Figure 18.6 Deaths in police custody in England and Wales, 2007–2017

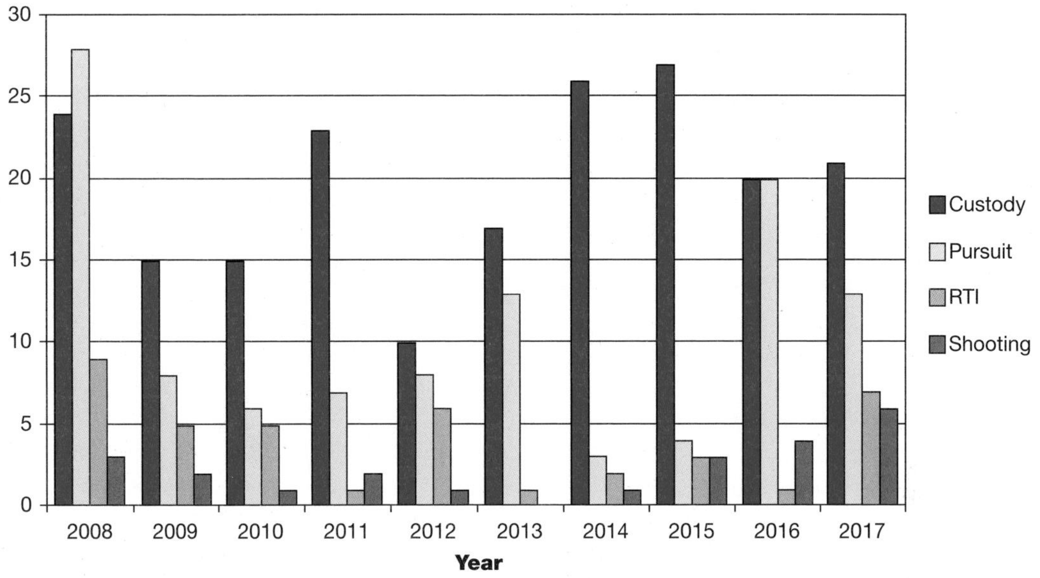

Source: From Inquest, statistics and monitoring, at: https://www.inquest.org.uk/deaths-in-police-custody

The Independent Office for Police Conduct (IOPC) reported that deaths in custody were the highest in a decade in 2017, with 23 people dying, 11 of whom had been exposed to the use of force or restraint by officers.

Answering questions

1   Simon is 15 years old. He is walking home at 3 am after playing computer games at a friend's house when a police officer stops him in the street and asks to see what he is carrying in his pockets. Simon is fed up with the police in his neighbourhood and ignores the police officer and keeps walking. The police officer takes Simon by the arm, pushes him into the police car and drives him to the police station.

    (a) Explain when the police have the power to stop and search, and when they have the right to arrest someone.

    (b) Advise Simon on whether the police officer acted lawfully.

2   Sir William Macpherson's inquiry into the investigation of Stephen Lawrence's murder concluded that the Metropolitan Police was institutionally racist. On a national level, is the police force racist? *University of London, International Programmes LLB*

3   How successful, in reality, are the PACE safeguards in protecting suspects held at police stations?

4   Critically contrast the powers of arrest exercisable by a police officer and a citizen.

For answers to these questions, visit the companion website at www.pearsoned.co.uk/ elliottquinn

SUMMARY OF CHAPTER 18: THE POLICE

Introduction

The criminal justice system needs to strike a balance between punishing the guilty and protecting the innocent. Recent miscarriages of justice have raised concerns as to whether this balance is being achieved.

The organisation of the police

The organisation of the police is becoming increasingly centralised.

Civilian support staff

The Police Reform Act 2002 allows a range of civilians to exercise police powers.

Pre-arrest powers of the police

Even without carrying out an arrest, the police enjoy a range of powers to stop and search a member of the public, in particular under s. 1 of PACE.

Powers of arrest

An arrest can take place either with or without a warrant. The powers of the police to arrest without a warrant were increased by the Serious Organised Crime and Police Act 2005.

Citizen's arrest

A member of the public is entitled to arrest a person in certain circumstances. This power to carry out a citizen's arrest is contained in s. 24A of PACE.

Police detention

Under PACE the police can detain a suspect for up to four days without charge.

Police interrogation

The usual reason for detaining suspects is so that the police can question them, in the hope of securing a confession. Certain safeguards exist to protect people while they are being detained and questioned. These include the tape-recording of police interviews in the police station and the right to inform someone of the detention. Since 1994 the right to silence has been effectively abolished.

Bail

A person accused, convicted or under arrest for an offence may be granted bail, which means the person is released under a duty to attend court or the police station at a given time.

Criticism and reform

A range of criticisms and reform proposals have been put forward relating to the police.

A graduate profession

Now that increasing numbers of young people are going to university, it is time to transform the police force into a graduate profession. Only then would the United Kingdom have an efficient police force with the skills to combat crime effectively.

Racism and the police

Following the unsuccessful police investigation into the murder of the black teenager Stephen Lawrence, Sir William Macpherson found that the Metropolitan Police suffered from 'institutional racism'. A particularly sensitive area of policing is the power to stop and search and the targeting of black people can have a detrimental effect on the relationship of the police with black people generally.

Police corruption

The police exercise an extremely delicate role in society and, as criminals are able to generate large sums of money from their criminal conduct, the danger of corruption is real.

The right to silence

The abolition of the right to silence has been one of the most severely criticised changes to the criminal justice system in recent years.

Deaths following contact with the police

More than 1,000 people have died in police custody or in contact with the police since 1990. Very few police officers have been prosecuted following a death in custody, and none have been convicted.

18

THE POLICE

Reading list

Audit Commission (1996) *Streetwise: Effective Police Patrol*. London: HMSO.

(2003) *Victims and Witnesses*. London: Audit Commission.

Austin, R. (2007) The new powers of arrest: *plus ça change:* more of the same or major change? *Criminal Law Review*, 459.

Baldwin, J. (1992a) *The Role of Legal Representatives at the Police Station*. Royal Commission on Criminal Justice Research Study No. 2. London: HMSO.

(1992b) *Video Taping Police Interviews with Suspects: An Evaluation*. London: Home Office.

Baldwin, J. and Moloney, T. (1992) *Supervision of Police Investigations in Serious Criminal Cases.* Royal Commission on Criminal Justice Research Study No. 4. London: HMSO.

Bowling, B. and Ross, J. (2006) The serious organised crime agency – should we be afraid? *Criminal Law Review,* 1019.

Bridges, L. and Cape, E. (2008) *CDS Direct: Flying in the Face of the Evidence.* London: Centre for Crime and Justice Studies at King's College London.

Bridges, L. and Choongh, S. (1998) *Improving Police Station Legal Advice: The Impact of the Accreditation Scheme for Police Station Legal Advisers.* London: Law Society's Research and Planning Unit: Legal Aid Board.

Brown, D. (1998) *Offending While on Bail.* Home Office, Report No. 72. London: Home Office.

Brownlee, I. (2004) The statutory charging scheme in England and Wales: towards a unified prosecution system. *Criminal Law Review,* 896.

Bucke, T. and Brown, D. (1997) *In Police Custody: Police Powers and Suspects' Rights Under the Revised PACE Codes of Practice.* Home Office Research Study 174. London: Home Office.

Campbell, L. (2010) A rights-based analysis of DNA retention: 'non-conviction' databases and the liberal state. *Criminal Law Review,* 889.

Cape, E. (2007) Modernising police powers – again? *Criminal Law Review,* 934.

(2013) The Protection of Freedoms Act 2012: the retention and use of biometric data provisions. *Criminal Law Review,* 23.

Cape, E. and Young, R. (2008) *Regulation Policing: The Police and Criminal Evidence Act 1984 Past, Present and Future.* Oxford: Hart.

Carter, Lord (2007) *Securing the Future – Proposals for the Efficient and Sustainable Use of Custody in England and Wales.* London: Ministry of Justice.

Cotton, J. and Povey, D. (2004) *Police Complaints and Discipline, April 2002–March 2003.* London: Home Office.

Doak, J. (2008) *Victims' Rights, Human Rights and Criminal Justice: Reconceiving the Role of Third Parties.* Oxford: Hart.

Evans, R. (1993) *The Conduct of Police Interviews with Juveniles.* London: HMSO.

Greer, S. (1994) Miscarriages of justice reconsidered. 57:1 *Modern Law Review* 58

Gudjonsson, G.H. (1992) *The Psychology of Interrogations, Confessions and Testimony.* Chichester: Wiley.

(2010) Psychological vulnerabilities during police interviews. Why are they important? *Legal and Criminological Psychology,* 15: 161.

Hamer, D. (2009) The expectation of incorrect acquittals and the 'new and compelling evidence' exception to double jeopardy. *Criminal Law Review,* 63.

HM Inspectorate (1999) *Police Integrity: Securing and Maintaining Public Confidence.* London: Home Office Communication Directorate.

Home Office (2004b) *Modernising Police Powers to Meet Community Needs.* London: Home Office.

(2004c) *One Step Ahead: A 21st Century Strategy to Defeat Organised Crime.* Cm 6167. Norwich: Stationery Office.

(2006b) *Rebalancing the Criminal Justice System in Favour of the Law-Abiding Majority.* London: Home Office.

(2007a) *Modernising Police Powers: Review of the Police and Criminal Evidence Act 1984.* London: Home Office.

(2009) *Keeping the Right People on the DNA Database: Science and Public Protection*. London: Home Office.

Hucklesby, A. (2004) Not necessarily a trip to the police station: the introduction of street bail. *Criminal Law Review,* 803.

Idriss, M. (2004) Police perceptions of race relations in the West Midlands. *Criminal Law Review,* 814.

Jackson, J. (2003) Justice for all: putting victims at the heart of criminal justice? *Journal of Law and Society,* 30: 309.

Kemp, V. (2011) *Transforming Legal Aid – Access to Legal Defence Services*. London: Legal Services Research Commission.

(2013) "No time for a solicitor": implications for delays on the take-up of legal advice. *Criminal Law Review,* 184.

Kemp, V., Balmer, N. and Pleasence, P. (2012) Whose time is it anyway? Factors associated with duration in police custody. *Criminal Law Review,* 736.

Law Commission (1999) *Bail and the Human Rights Act 1998*. Report No. 157. London: HMSO.

(2010b) *The Admissibility of Expert Evidence in Criminal Proceedings in England and Wales*. Law Commission Consultation Paper No. 190. London: Law Commission.

Leigh, A. *et al.* (1998) *Deaths in Police Custody: Learning the Lessons*. London: Home Office.

Leigh, L. and Zedner, L. (1992) *A Report on the Administration of Criminal Justice in the Pretrial Phase in London, France and Germany*. London: HMSO.

Leng, R. (1993) *The Right to Silence in Police Interrogation*. Royal Commission on Criminal Justice Research Study No. 10. London: HMSO.

Lidstone, K. (1984) *Magisterial Review of the Pre-Trial Criminal Process*. Sheffield: University of Sheffield Centre for Criminological and Socio-Legal Studies.

McConville, M. (1992) Videotaping interrogations: police behaviour on and off camera. *Criminal Law Review,* 532.

McConville, M. and Hodgson, J. (1993) *Custodial Legal Advice and the Right to Silence*. Royal Commission on Criminal Justice Research Study No. 16. London: HMSO.

McConville, M., Sanders, A. and Leng, P. (1993) *The Case for the Prosecution: Police Suspects and the Construction of Criminality*. London: Routledge.

McEwan, J. (2013) Vulnerable defendants and the fairness of trials. *Criminal Law Review,* 100.

Miller, J. (2000) *Upping the PACE? An Evaluation of the Recommendations of the Stephen Lawrence Inquiry on Stop and Search*. Police Research Series Paper 128. London: Home Office.

Miller, J., Bland, N. and Quinton, P. (2000) *The Impact of Stop and Search on Crime and the Community*. Police Research Series Paper 127. London: Home Office.

Mitchell, B. (1983) Confessions and police interrogation of suspects. *Criminal Law Review,* 596.

Mullins, C. (1990) *Error of Judgement: The Truth About the Birmingham Bombings*. Dublin: Poolbeg Press.

Nuttal, C., Goldblatt, P. and Lewis, C. (1998) *Reducing Offending: An Assessment of Research Evidence on Ways of Dealing with Offending Behaviour*. Home Office Research Study No. 187. London: Home Office.

Ormerod, D. and Roberts, A. (2003) The Police Reform Act 2002 – increasing centralisation, maintaining confidence and contracting out crime control. *Criminal Law Review,* 141.

Pattenden, R. and Skinns, L. (2010) Choice, privacy and publicly-funded legal advice at the police station. *Modern Law Review,* 73: 349.

18

THE POLICE

Philips, C. (1981) *The Royal Commission on Criminal Procedure*. Cmnd 8092. London: HMSO.

Pleasence, P., Kemp V. and Balmer, N. (2011) The justice lottery? Police station advice 25 years on from PACE. *Criminal Law Review*, 1.

Quinton, P., Bland, N. and Miller, J. (2000) *Police Stops, Decision-Making and Practice*. Police Research Series Paper 130. London: Home Office.

Roberts, P. and Saunders, C. (2008) Introducing pre-trial witness interviews: a flexible new fixture in the Crown Prosecutor's toolkit. *Criminal Law Review*, 831.

Rock, P. (2004) *Constructing Victims' Rights*. Oxford: Oxford University Press.

Royal Commission on Criminal Justice (1993) Report. Cm 2263. London: HMSO.

Sanders, A. (1993) Controlling the discretion of the individual officer. In: Reiner, R. and Spencer, S. (eds) *Accountable Policing*. London: Institute for Public Policy Research.

Skinns, L. (2009) I'm a detainee; get me out of here. *British Journal of Criminology*, 399.

        (2010) *Police Custody: Governance, Legitimacy and Reform in the Criminal Justice Process*. London: Routledge.

        (2011) The right to legal advice in the police station: past, present and future. *Criminal Law Review*, 19.

Vogt, G. and Wadham, J. (2003) *Deaths in Custody: Redress and Remedies*. London: Liberty.

Walker, C. (2008) Post-charge questioning of suspects. *Criminal Law Review*, 509.

Walker, C. and Starmer, K. (1999) *Miscarriages of Justice: A Review of Justice in Error*. London: Blackstone.

Zander, M. (2007d) Change of PACE. *New Law Journal*, 157: 504.

On the internet

The Police Codes of Practice are available on the Government website at:

https://www.gov.uk/guidance/police-and-criminal-evidence-act-1984-pace-codes-of-practice

Useful information about the police is available on the Government website at:

https://www.gov.uk/crime-justice-and-law/policing

The report by Ramona Franklyn, *Satisfaction and willingness to engage with the criminal justice system: Findings from the witness and victim experience survey, 2009–10* (2012) is available on the website of the Ministry of Justice at:

https://assets.publishing.service.gov.uk/government/uploads/system/uploads/attachment_data/file/197099/satisfaction-willingness-to-engage-with-cjs.pdf

A useful source of information on the criminal justice system is:

https://www.gov.uk/browse/justice

The report by Her Majesty's Inspectorate of Constabulary *Stop and Search Powers: Are the police using them effectively and fairly?* (2013) can be found at:

https://www.justiceinspectorates.gov.uk/hmic/publications/stop-and-search-powers-20130709/

The *Report of the Independent Review of Deaths and Serious Incidents in Police Custody* (2017) by Dame Elish Angiolini QC is available on the Home Office website at:

https://www.gov.uk/government/publications/deaths-and-serious-incidents-in-police-custody

JUSTICE, *Supporting Exonerees: ensuring accessible, continuing and consistent support* (April 2018)

https://justice.org.uk/our-work/areas-of-work/criminal-justice-system/supporting-exonerees-ensuring-accessible-continuing-and-consistent-support/

Ipsos MORI Report for Her Majesty's Inspectorate of Constabulary and Fire & Rescue Services, *Public Perceptions of Policing in England and Wales 2017*: can be found at:

https://www.ipsos.com/sites/default/files/ct/publication/documents/2017-12/public-perceptions-of-policing-in-england-and-wales-2017.pdf

National Appropriate Adult Network, *There to help: Ensuring provision of appropriate adults for mentally vulnerable adults detained or interviewed by police* (2015) is available at:

http://www.appropriateadult.org.uk/index.php/news/9-public-articles/154-theretohelp

Stopwatch, Release and the LSE, *The Colour of Injustice: 'Race', drugs and law enforcement in England and Wales* (2018) can be found at:

http://www.stop-watch.org/news-comment/story/the-colour-of-injustice

18

THE POLICE

Chapter 19
The criminal trial process

This chapter discusses:

- the adversarial process followed in the criminal justice system;

- the Crown Prosecution Service;

- the classification of offences as summary, indictable or either way offences;

- the pre-trial hearings – mode of trial hearings, case management hearings and sending for trial and plea;

- disclosure of evidence between the prosecution and the defence;

- plea bargaining;

- the criminal trial; and

- criticisms and possible reforms of the criminal trial process.

19.1 The adversarial process

The English system of justice can be described as adversarial. In the criminal justice system there is the presumption of innocence. In criminal cases where the state (the prosecution) enjoys vast resources and advantages they hold the 'burden of proof'. This means that the prosecution bring the case and they alone must prove it until the jury are sure. The defendant needs to prove nothing but to rigorously test the prosecution case. This means that the prosecution is responsible for establishing the case against the accused. They investigate and provide the evidence that the accused committed the offence. The defendant does not have to call witnesses or give evidence or establish innocence, although in most instances they will. In court both the prosecution and defence will present their own evidence, usually in form of a live witness and they will attempt to undermine their opponent's evidence by cross-examining their adversary's witnesses. Both parties call only those witnesses likely to advance their cause and both parties are permitted to attack the credibility and reliability of the witnesses testifying for the other side. The judge is impartial and has the role of ensuring fair play, and to make sure that the rules on procedure and evidence are followed. The judge may ask questions to clarify evidence if it is unclear, but is not there to investigate. The adversarial system is typical of common law countries. The alternative is an inquisitorial system, which exists in most of the rest of Europe while an adversarial system is designed to establish proof. An inquisitorial system is seen as a search for the truth. Under that system, a judge (known in France as the *juge d'instruction*) plays the dominant role in collecting evidence before the trial. During the course of a lengthy investigation, the judge will interview witnesses and inspect documents, and the final trial is often just to 'rubber stamp' the investigating judge's findings.

In the light of the recent miscarriages of justice, some people suggested that we should introduce an inquisitorial system into England, or at least elements of an inquisitorial system. Arguments were put forward that the inquisitorial system provides a properly organised and regulated pre-trial phase, with an independent figure supervising the whole investigation. The Royal Commission on Criminal Justice (RCCJ) ordered research into the French and German criminal justice systems (Leigh and Zedner, 1992). The researchers rejected the idea of introducing the inquisitorial system into England. They did not think that the *juge d'instruction* was a real protection against overbearing police practices, except in rare cases where physical brutality was involved. Furthermore, despite the fact that only 10 per cent of cases go before the *juge d'instruction* in France, the system is overburdened and works slowly. In Germany and Italy, the powers of the investigating judge have been transferred to the public prosecutor, to avoid potential conflict between the functions of investigator and judge.

In recent years the English system has shifted slightly towards an inquisitorial system. This shift towards an inquisitorial system has been the result of the influence of European human rights law, the development of new managerial models for the administration of justice, such as judicial case management and judicial input on how child and vulnerable witnesses should be questioned in ground rules hearings. These changes are primarily aimed at achieving greater efficiency and producing the best evidence. Interestingly, this move is not one-sided. A focus on 'efficiency' has also simultaneously pushed the traditionally inquisitorial French criminal justice system to incorporate adversarial elements.

19.2 Criminal Procedure Rules

In 2005, the main rules on criminal procedure that apply to the trial and pre-trial process were brought together in new Criminal Procedure Rules. These rules did not introduce any radical changes to the law and practice, but they aim to make the relevant rules more accessible as they are all now brought together in one place.

Rule 1 lays down that:

1   The overriding objective of this procedural code is that criminal cases be dealt with justly.

2   Dealing with a criminal case justly includes:

    (a) acquitting the innocent and convicting the guilty;

    (b) dealing with the prosecution and the defence fairly;

    (c) recognising the rights of a defendant, particularly those under Article 6 of the European Convention on Human Rights;

    (d) respecting the interests of witnesses, victims and jurors and keeping them informed of the progress of the case;

    (e) dealing with the case efficiently and expeditiously;

    (f) ensuring that appropriate information is available to the court when bail and sentence are considered; and

    (g) dealing with the case in ways that take into account:

        (i)   the gravity of the offence alleged,

        (ii) the complexity of what is in issue,

        (iii) the severity of the consequences for the defendant and others affected, and

        (iv) the needs of other cases.

The procedural rules emphasise that judges need to take an active role in case management. Rule 3 states that active case management includes:

(a) the early identification of the real issues;

(b) the early identification of the needs of witnesses;

(c) achieving certainty as to what must be done, by whom, and when, in particular by the early setting of a timetable for the progress of the case;

(d) monitoring the progress of the case and compliance with directions;

(e) ensuring that evidence, whether disputed or not, is presented in the shortest and clearest way;

(f) discouraging delay, dealing with as many aspects of the case as possible on the same occasion, and avoiding unnecessary hearings;

(g) encouraging the participants to cooperate in the progression of the case; and

(h) making use of technology.

The emphasis on case management in criminal proceedings is clearly influenced by its relative success in the civil system. It is hoped that through the use of active case management, cases will progress more rapidly through the criminal system and fewer cases will collapse.

19

THE CRIMINAL TRIAL PROCESS

The Courts Act 2003 established a Rules Committee which updates the Criminal Procedure Rules twice a year. The Committee hopes eventually to develop a criminal procedure code.

The rules of criminal procedure must be respected, but the courts are trying to achieve a balance between the importance of following these rules and the requirements of justice. Cases can be thrown out for breach of a technicality where that breach undermines justice or where there is at least a real possibility of the defendant suffering prejudice as a consequence of a procedural failure. But if no damage is done, the procedural irregularity can be corrected after the event and the case can proceed.

Key case

In the case of **R v Clarke and McDaid** (2008) an appeal against conviction was allowed when an indictment had not been signed because this procedural requirement was not viewed by the court as a meaningless formality, but as a requirement that made sure the prosecution had given careful consideration to the case. The House of Lords noted:

> technicality is always distasteful when it appears to contradict the merits of a case. But the duty of the court is to apply the law, which is sometimes technical, and it may be thought that if the state exercises its coercive power to put a citizen on trial for serious crime a certain degree of formality is not out of place.

At the same time, the House of Lords acknowledged that their decision:

> will produce from time to time unsatisfactory results. Guilty men may go free or, if not free, have to be retried . . . A retrial will involve delay, expense and inconvenience and may cause particular witnesses . . . considerable distress.

Legal principle

An appeal against conviction will be allowed where there has been a breach of a technical procedural rule which does not amount to a meaningless formality.

Research by Darbyshire (2014) into the use of judicial case management in ten Crown Courts has shown that the Criminal Procedure Rules are applied in different ways and with differing levels of strictness in different courts around the country. Darbyshire's study emphasises the difference between the law in the books and the law in the real world and shows the need for Crown Court judges to develop expertise in such case management for criminal cases.

19.3 The Crown Prosecution Service

Until 1986, criminal prosecutions were officially brought by private citizens rather than by the state; in practice most prosecutions were brought by the police (though technically they were prosecuting as private citizens, albeit as employees of the state – hence in the magistrates' court, a case would bear a title such as 'Chief Constable of Police v A'; while cases in the Crown Court are brought in the name of the Queen, for example 'Regina (or R.) v A'). Although the police obviously employed solicitors to help them in this task, their relationship with those solicitors was a normal client relationship, and so the police were not obliged to act on the solicitors' advice. Prior to 1986, in magistrates' courts the prosecutor would ordinarily be the police officer who investigated the case.

In 1970, a report by the law reform pressure group, JUSTICE, criticised the role of the police in the prosecution process (*The Prosecution in England and Wales*, 1970). It argued that it was not in the interests of justice for the same body to be responsible for the two very different functions of investigation and prosecution. This dual role prevented the prosecution from being independent and impartial: the police had become concerned with winning or losing, when the aim of the prosecution should be the discovery of the truth. As a result, there was a danger of the police withholding from the defence information that might make a conviction less likely.

The prosecution process was reviewed by the Royal Commission on Criminal Procedure (RCCP) in 1981. Their report highlighted a range of problems. There was a lack of uniformity, with differing procedures and standards applied across the country on such matters as whether to prosecute or caution, and the system prevented a consistent national prosecution policy. The process was inefficient, with inadequate preparation of cases. The RCCP agreed with JUSTICE that, in principle, investigation and prosecution should be separate processes, conducted by different people. As a result of these findings, the RCCP recommended the establishment of a Crown Prosecution Service, divided into separate local services for each police force area.

The Government followed the main recommendations, though it opposed the establishment of separate local services. The Crown Prosecution Service (CPS) was set up under the Prosecution of Offences Act 1985, as a national prosecution service for England and Wales. The service as a whole is headed by the Director of Public Prosecutions (DPP). The DPP reports on the running of the service to the Attorney General. The only formal mechanism for accountability of the CPS is the requirement that an annual report must be presented to the Attorney General, who is obliged to lay it before Parliament. The Attorney General is responsible in Parliament for general policy, but not for individual cases.

The establishment of the CPS means that the prosecution of offences is now separated from their detection and investigation, which is undertaken by the police.

19.3.1 Administration of the CPS

When the CPS first started to operate in 1986, it was organised into 31 areas, each with a Chief Crown Prosecutor. These were subsequently increased to 38, but in 1993, in an effort to improve efficiency, the areas were enlarged into just 13 across the country. The administration was centralised around headquarters in London, with the DPP playing an increased role in the direct administration of the CPS. In the light of continuing concern over the functioning of the CPS, a review was carried out by a body chaired by Sir Iain Glidewell which reported in 1998. The *Review of the Crown Prosecution Service* (also known as the Glidewell Report) heavily criticised the CPS. It concluded that the 1993 reform had been a mistake, as it made the organisation too centralised and excessively bureaucratic. It found that there was a problem with judge-ordered acquittals (where the case is too weak to be left to the jury), which constituted over 20 per cent of acquittals in 1996. Not all of these were due to poor case preparation by the CPS, as some involved errors in witness warnings by the police. But many were due to inadequate compilation of case papers between committal and trial by non-qualified staff who lacked supervision; the drafting of inadequate or erroneous indictments; and counsel being briefed too late to put things right.

Glidewell concluded that the CPS 'has the potential to become a lively, successful and esteemed part of the criminal justice system, but . . . sadly none of these adjectives applies to the service as a whole at present'.

The key recommendation of the Report was that there should be a devolution of powers from the centre to the regions, with the London headquarters playing a more limited role. This would involve replacing the 13 CPS areas with 42 areas corresponding to police force areas.

The Glidewell Report proposed that teams of CPS lawyers, police and administrative caseworkers (together known as a Criminal Justice Unit), should be established to prepare and deal with many straightforward cases in their entirety (in other words, both the case preparation and the court advocacy); the section which dealt with the most serious cases, called Central Casework, needed more staff, with more training and closer monitoring; there should be at least one full-time CPS lawyer in each Crown Court; CPS lawyers should be allowed to concentrate more on court work rather than paperwork; and that the DPP ought to play less of a role in the administration of the CPS and concentrate largely on the prosecution and legal process.

The Government accepted the main recommendations of the Glidewell Report and the new 42 areas of the CPS came into effect on 22 April 1999.

In 2010 the CPS came under pressure with significant cuts to its budget. In December 2015, the then Director of Public Prosecutions, Alison Saunders told the justice committee that the CPS budget had been reduced by 23 per cent since 2010. Former Shadow Attorney General Karl Turner, said that CPS staff are 'highly committed, talented individuals who are being asked to do more for less and working hard to keep a sinking ship afloat'.

19.3.2 Powers of CPS employees

In the past, barristers from the independent Bar had to be paid by the CPS to carry out the advocacy required for prosecutions in the Crown Court, because lawyers employed in the CPS, including qualified barristers, did not have rights of audience in the Crown Court. The Access to Justice Act 1999 allows CPS lawyers to carry out this work themselves, with the aim of achieving greater efficiency while saving money. This was heavily criticised, particularly by the Bar Council and Professor Michael Zander, on the basis that, as full-time salaried employees with performance targets, CPS lawyers would sometimes be tempted to get convictions using dubious tactics because their jobs and prospects of promotion would depend on conviction success rates. To reduce this risk, s. 37 of the Act states that every advocate 'has a duty to the court to act in the interests of justice', which overrides any inconsistent duty, for example, to an employer. Professor Zander dismissed these as 'mere words', writing in a letter to *The Times* (29 December 1998), that:

> The CPS as an organisation is constantly under pressure in regard to proportion of discontinuances, acquittal and conviction rates. These are factors in the day to day work of any CPS lawyer. It is disingenuous to imagine they will not have a powerful effect on decision making.

Despite these criticisms, CPS employees are increasingly carrying out the advocacy themselves in the Crown Court and less work is being passed on to the Bar. In the magistrates' court, s. 55 of the Criminal Justice and Immigration Act 2008 allows associate prosecutors (employees of the CPS who are not qualified lawyers) to undertake advocacy work in the magistrates' court, including contested trials of summary, non-imprisonable offences. Trials of triable either way offences will continue to be prosecuted by qualified lawyers. These associate prosecutors currently handle 20 per cent of the prosecution advocacy work in the magistrates' courts. A key reason why the CPS chooses to use associate prosecutors is that they are considerably cheaper than qualified lawyers. The Law Society has pointed out that as a result of these reforms a large proportion of criminal cases could be prosecuted and decided by unqualified individuals – lay magistrates hearing a case prosecuted by an associate prosecutor against an unrepresented defendant.

19.3.3 Charging and prosecuting defendants

The normal practice had been for the police to decide whether to charge a defendant and then after charge send the file to the CPS to proceed with the prosecution. The Criminal Justice Act 2003 amended s. 37 of the Police and Criminal Evidence Act 1984, moving the decision to charge from the police to the CPS. The police only retained the right to charge for certain minor offences. Lord Auld recommended this reform in his *Review of the Criminal Courts*. The hope was to improve the relationship between the CPS and the police so that they worked efficiently together in the preparation of cases for trial. The police had in the past felt very unhappy about the number of prosecutions that were discontinued after they had decided to charge a suspect. Six pilot schemes were established around the country where the decision to charge was moved from the police to the CPS, and these proved to be very successful. Convictions rose by 15 per cent. The instances of charges being reduced or dropped fell from 51 per cent to 18 per cent. The Attorney General concluded that: 'Getting cases right from the start means less abandoned prosecution, less of the frustrating delays and more criminals brought to justice.' Now, if the police wish to charge a detainee, they must ordinarily obtain authorisation from a CPS subsidiary called CPS Direct – a 24-hour telephone-based service which is manned by prosecution lawyers.

When the CPS receives the file, it reviews whether a prosecution should be brought on the basis of criteria set out in the Code for Crown Prosecutors. This Code is issued by the CPS under s. 10 of the Prosecution of Offences Act 1985. The latest edition of the Code explains that this decision is taken in two stages. First, prosecutors must ask whether there is enough evidence to provide a 'realistic prospect of conviction', that is to say that a court is more likely than not to convict. If the case does not pass this evidential test, the prosecution must not go ahead, no matter how important or serious the case may be. If the case does pass the evidential test, the CPS must then consider whether the public interest requires a prosecution. For example, a prosecution is more likely to be in the public interest if a conviction is likely to result in a significant sentence, if the offence was committed against a person serving the public (such as a police officer) or if the offence is widespread in the area where it was committed. On the other hand, a prosecution is less likely to be in the public interest where the defendant is elderly, or suffering from significant mental or physical ill-health.

At the end of this two-stage test, the CPS may decide to go ahead with the prosecution, send the case back to the police for a caution instead of a prosecution, or take no further action. The decision is theirs, and the police need not be consulted.

In 2008, a review was carried out by Her Majesty's Crown Prosecution Service Inspectorate and Her Majesty's Inspectorate of Constabulary. Their report concluded that the vast majority of those working on the ground felt the new charging system had brought about better working practices between the police and prosecutors, better quality charging decisions, and led to fewer weak cases going to court. Despite this, the power to charge suspects for summary and either way offences has been returned to the police.

The clear distinction that was initially drawn between the police and the CPS has been weakened by subsequent reforms. Following the Glidewell Report and the Narey Report (*Review of Delay in the Criminal Justice System* (1997)), some CPS staff now work alongside police officers in Criminal Justice Units to prepare cases for court.

Key case

A decision not to prosecute can be as sensitive as a decision to prosecute. The case of ***R (on the application of Corner House Research and others)* v *Director of the Serious Fraud Office*** (2008) concerned a decision not to prosecute following allegations of corruption. The Serious Fraud Office had carried out an investigation into an allegation that a bribe was paid by the company BAE in order to secure a contract worth £43 billion to sell military aircraft to Saudi Arabia. In July 2006, a Saudi representative made a specific threat to the Prime Minister's chief of staff – that if the police investigation was not stopped the UK would lose a valuable contract for military aircraft and the previous close intelligence and diplomatic relationship would cease, putting the UK at an increased risk of suffering terrorist attacks. As a result, the director of the Serious Fraud Office decided to stop the investigation on the grounds of national security. The claimants applied to challenge that decision by way of judicial review.

The High Court had held that any decision as to whether the investigation and prosecution should continue in these circumstances should have been taken by the court and not by the executive, as the threat amounted to a threat to the court system, as well as a threat to the UK's commercial, diplomatic and security interests:

> No one, whether within the country or outside, is entitled to interfere with the course of our justice.

Under the rule of law, the decision to discontinue the case should have been reached as an exercise of independent judgment of the court. The director of the Serious Fraud Office had submitted too readily to the threat because he had not focused on the need to fight corruption. The House of Lords allowed an appeal against the High Court's decision, finding that in the circumstances the director of the Serious Fraud Office was entitled to take the decision to discontinue the investigation.

Legal principle

A prosecutor is entitled to decide to discontinue a prosecution, to avoid a threat to national security.

19.3.4 Deferred prosecution agreements

The Crime and Courts Act 2013 introduced deferred prosecution agreements (DPAs). These are available as a response to corporate crime (crimes committed by companies). They involve an agreement being reached between the prosecution and company under which a prosecution for an economic crime (such as fraud, bribery or money laundering) will be dropped if a company pays a fine and implements specified corporate reforms. The DPA Code of Practice states that before entering into a DPA, a prosecutor must be satisfied that there is at least a reasonable suspicion based upon some admissible evidence that an offence has been committed. The DPA must be approved by a judge in a public hearing where a company admits wrongdoing, though the procedure will not amount to an admission of guilt or a criminal conviction. The court must declare that the DPA is in the interests of justice and that the terms are fair, reasonable and proportionate.

The aim of this procedure is to improve the state's response to corporate crime, a problem that was highlighted with the failed prosecution of BAE for overseas corruption (see p. 482). It seeks to tackle the limitation of plea bargaining seen in cases such as *R v Innospec* (2010) (see p. 494).

An equivalent procedure is available in America, and where America claims global jurisdiction and reaches an agreement with a company under a DPA equivalent, then a prosecution cannot be brought in England under the principle of double jeopardy (see p. 607). This creates a risk that a multinational company might forum shop for the lightest penalty, which might be in America. As England now has its own DPA system, the legal procedures have become similar and one court system might not be preferred over the other. The risk is that DPAs could lead to under-investigation, undue leniency, lack of transparency and a shift of power from the judge to the prosecutor: the public might view DPAs as allowing companies to buy themselves out of trouble.

In 2016, Standard Bank negotiated with the Serious Fraud Office the first DPA. Employees of the bank had paid a bribe in Tanzania in breach of the Bribery Act 2010. The benefit for Standard Bank was limited publicity and a relatively speedy settlement, but they were shown no leniency on the size of the financial penalties imposed. The US Department of Justice issued a statement that if a DPA was agreed in England then it would not itself investigate the matter.

On 17 January 2017, the Serious Fraud Office applied for a DPA with Rolls-Royce plc and this was authorised by Sir Brian Leveson, the President of the Queen's Bench Division. He described the case as 'egregious criminality over decades, involving countries around the world, making truly vast corrupt payments and, consequentially, even greater profits'. Rolls-Royce as a company apologised 'unreservedly' in open court for the bribery and corruption that occurred in the company for over two decades. How was it then, that it was in the interest of justice for Rolls-Royce to avoid prosecution? What Rolls did, it appears, to enable them to achieve a DPA, was that they were frank about what had happened and cooperated fully with the Serious Fraud Office's investigation. Further guidance was given by the court on the 'interests of justice' criteria for a DPA. The court stated that there will be cases where the use of a DPA would be 'inappropriate and contrary to the public interests of justice'. In considering the interests of justice, the court considered:

(a) the seriousness of the predicate offence or offences;

(b) the importance of incentivising the exposure and self-reporting of corporate wrongdoing;

(c) the history (or otherwise) of similar conduct;

(d) the attention paid to corporate compliance prior to, at the time of, and subsequent to the offending;

(e) the extent to which the entity has changed both in its culture and in relation to relevant personnel;

(f) the impact of prosecution on employees and others innocent of any misconduct.

These decisions to date undoubtedly exhibit a progressively increasing willingness on the part of the court to approve DPAs for very serious corporate crimes.

It seems that cooperation and transparency with the Serious Fraud Office may enable a DPA to be seen as an appropriate sanction.

19

THE CRIMINAL TRIAL PROCESS

19.3.5 Private prosecutions

Most prosecutions are commenced either by the police and the Crown Prosecution Service (CPS) or by governmental organisations. However, a prosecution may also be commenced by individuals or commercial or charitable organisations.

Private prosecutions should not, it has been argued, take the place of a properly funded police service and an independent CPS. The Metropolitan Police Crime Assessment Policy of 2017 set out how the police may no longer investigate low-level crimes including some public order offences, some offences of shoplifting, and low-level criminal damage. It also imposed a 20-minute limit on examining CCTV for 'petty' crimes. It has been reported that wealthy neighbourhoods are recruiting private police officers and launching private prosecutions. Private prosecutions can of course play an important role, particularly in highlighting or encouraging public concern over relevant issues.

In 1974, a Police Constable Joy stopped a motorist and reported him for a motoring offence. The motorist was a Member of Parliament and PC Joy's superiors refused to pursue the case; PC Joy thought this unjust and successfully brought a private prosecution. Mary Whitehouse (a campaigner against a permissive, sexual culture) also brought important private prosecutions in the past. More recently, the family of Stephen Lawrence, the teenager murdered in south London, took out a private prosecution against three men suspected of the killing, after the CPS dropped the case because it said there was insufficient evidence. Unfortunately, the private prosecution was unsuccessful for lack of evidence. The case primarily relied on the identification evidence of Duwayne Brooks. This was weak because the attack had lasted for only a matter of seconds. He was unable to be specific about the number of attackers, saying that it was a 'group of four to six'. In his initial statement to the police, he said that, 'Of the group of six youths, I can only really describe one of them.' At one identification parade, he identified a member of the public. At another he identified no one although there was a suspect present. He had originally said Stephen had been hit on the head with an iron bar although he was later found to have sustained no head injuries. The judge summed up by saying: 'Where recognition or identification is concerned, [Brooks] simply does not know whether he is on his head or his heels . . . Adding one injustice to another does not cure the first injustice done to the Lawrence family.' The judge withdrew the case from the jury and ordered an acquittal. A retrial of one of the defendants in 2011 later led to his conviction.

When a private prosecution is brought, the Director of Public Prosecutions (DPP) may choose to take over the case and can then discontinue it (Prosecution of Offences Act 1985, s. 23(3)). Thus, the right to bring a private prosecution might best be viewed as a right to simply commence a prosecution, but there is actually no right to continue the prosecution. In deciding whether to discontinue a private prosecution, the DPP applies guidance that a case should be discontinued unless it was more likely than not that the prosecution would result in a conviction (there needs to be a reasonable prospect of success) and the prosecution is in the public interest. In *R (on the application of Gujra)* v *Crown Prosecution Service* (2012) the claimant had commenced a private prosecution against two men for common assault and against a third man for the use of threatening, abusive or insulting words or behaviour. The DPP concluded there was insufficient evidence to provide a realistic prospect of conviction against any of the three men and, therefore, he took over and discontinued the private prosecutions. This decision was challenged through the courts, but the challenge was rejected by a majority of the Supreme Court.

There is growing concern that private prosecutions could be abused and could indirectly be leading to the privatisation of the criminal justice system. There is concern particularly regarding the use of private prosecutions as 'tactical' proceedings, which are run alongside otherwise non-criminal disputes (such as seeking to prosecute an allegation of fraud, alongside and in the context of an existing civil or commercial dispute). In *R (on the application of Virgin Media Ltd) v Zinga* (2014), Virgin Media brought a private prosecution against Mr Zinga for conspiracy to defraud. The Court of Appeal expressed its concern that private prosecutions should not be used as an alternative to civil proceedings against commercial competitors. It tried to remove any financial incentive for favouring a private prosecution by stating that while a confiscation order in a private prosecution could strip the accused of any benefit, they had obtained from their criminality; any resultant monies were payable only to the state.

19.3.6 Historical powers of the attorney general and director of public prosecutions

We have noted that, with the creation of the CPS, the Director of Public Prosecutions (DPP) was placed at its head. However, before the creation of this body, the DPP and the Attorney General had certain powers to control the bringing of prosecutions and both have kept these powers despite the existence of the CPS.

For certain offences prosecutions can be brought only if the Attorney General or the DPP has given their consent. The sensitivity of the decision whether or not to consent to a prosecution has been highlighted in the context of prosecutions against family members who have assisted a seriously ill relative to die. Under the Suicide Act 1961 prosecutions can only be brought for the offence of assisting a person to commit suicide with the consent of the DPP. *R (on the application of Purdy) v DPP* (2009) concerned Debbie Purdy, a sufferer of multiple sclerosis. When her condition became unbearable for her, she wanted her husband to go with her to Switzerland where there are facilities for a person to be assisted to commit suicide. She was concerned that her husband might be prosecuted under the Suicide Act on his return to the UK. She brought legal proceedings arguing that the DPP should be required to issue guidelines which explained when he would give consent to such a prosecution so that she and her husband would know the legal consequences of their conduct. The House of Lords declared that the DPP was required to issue guidelines on this subject, which the DPP has since done.

The Attorney General has the power to stop proceedings that would be brought before the Crown Court. This is known as granting a *nolle prosequi* and is not actually an acquittal, so a prosecution can be brought in the future on the same charge. It is most often used in cases where the defendant is physically or mentally unfit to be produced at court and the defendant's incapacity is likely to be permanent. Traditionally, it has also been used to protect a person to whom an undertaking or immunity has been given. Controversy was caused in 1998 when the Attorney General entered a *nolle prosequi* in the trial of Justice Richard Gee who had been accused of a £1 million fraud.

The position of the Attorney General attracted attention during the 'cash for honours' scandal. The police carried out an investigation into whether cash had been paid by wealthy individuals in return for the promise that they would receive the prestigious title of 'Sir' or 'Lord'. The Prime Minister of the day, Tony Blair, himself was questioned as part of this investigation. If the police had decided that there was sufficient evidence to show that a crime had been committed then they would have passed the papers for the case to the Crown Prosecution Service. But the final decision as to whether a prosecution should be brought in such a case would normally be taken by the Attorney General. Unfortunately, as the Attorney General is effectively a political appointment, it would be difficult for the public to have confidence that this was an impartial decision, particularly if he had decided that it was not appropriate to proceed. In fact, the police themselves decided that there was insufficient evidence to take the case further. The role of the Attorney General was only subject to limited reforms that are discussed above.

19.3.7 Public defenders

The Access to Justice Act 1999 provides for the appointment of public defenders. For a discussion of public defenders see p. 343.

19.4 Appearance in court

To start criminal proceedings, a person can either be arrested and charged at the police station, or be sent a written charge along with a requisition requiring them to attend the magistrates' court to answer the charge. If a person on bail fails to attend court as required under s. 1 of the Magistrates' Courts Act 1980, a magistrate can issue an arrest warrant.

The defendant is entitled to plead guilty by post for any summary offence for which the maximum penalty does not exceed three months' imprisonment (s. 12 of the Magistrates' Courts Act 1980). In this situation the defendant does not need to attend court, and the procedure is frequently used for traffic offences. In the past, delays were caused when people failed to respond to the summons in which they were given the opportunity to plead guilty by post: neither pleading guilty by post nor turning up for the court hearing. This led to the case being adjourned while witness statements were prepared or arrangements made for witnesses to attend. To avoid such adjournments in future, the Magistrates' Courts (Procedure) Act 1998 was passed which allows witness statements to be served with the original correspondence, so that if the defendant fails to respond the case can be tried at the first hearing.

Under s. 57 of the Crime and Disorder Act 1998, if an accused is being held in custody, all pre-trial hearings can take place using a live TV link between the court and the prison or the police station. Increasingly, preliminary hearings are being conducted by video-link. While the judge is in a court room, the defendant is in a room in a prison or in a police station and communicates with the court on camera. The defendants' lawyers have a private video discussion with their client beforehand. This process saves money as it avoids the transport and security costs of physically bringing a defendant to court. However, the conference which a lawyer would ordinarily have with their client in person is arguably restricted by this procedure in the following ways.

- The conferences are strictly time-limited.
- The parties are unable to exchange documents.
- The technology has on occasion proved less than dependable.

There has been little research on the effect of virtual courts on a fair hearing but the pilot of virtual courts conducted by the Ministry of Justice in 2010 found that 'virtual court cases were more likely to receive a custodial sentence and less likely to receive a community sentence. Analysis at the level of individual offence types suggests that the difference between community and custody penalties occurs across the board: it was not offence-specific.' In a study by Penelope Gibbs she concludes that defendants cannot communicate their best evidence on a video screen, that there are numerous technical problems and that there are no reasonable adjustments made for vulnerable people, in particular for those with mental health disabilities. There may be a suggestion that it could breach Article 6 (and the right of a defendant to participate in their trial) of ECHR. It is also seen as being a challenge to unrepresented defendants. Gibbs further states that judges are concerned that sentencing over video limits both its importance and their own ability to engage with the defendant. Further research is required, she states, to determine if this is an 'optimal method of justice either fiscally or in terms of serving the interests of justice'.

As a rule, the accused has a right to be present at trial. Prior to 2008, there was always a broad discretion for a magistrates' court to proceed with a trial in the absence of a defendant. The Criminal Justice and Immigration Act 2008 amended s. 11 of the Magistrates' Court Act 1980, which means that there is now a requirement to proceed in the defendant's absence with a trial, unless it appears to the court to be against the interests of justice to do so. Magistrates' courts rarely find it unjust to do so, while Crown Courts appear to be more resistant, save for the clearest circumstances, which is perhaps a reflection of the gravity of offences each jurisdiction deals with. According to the Criminal Practice Direction 14E.2:

> The court has a discretion as to whether a trial should take place or continue in the defendant's absence and must exercise its discretion with due regard for the interests of justice. The overriding concern must be to ensure that such a trial is as fair as circumstances permit and leads to a just outcome. If the defendant's absence is due to involuntary illness or incapacity it would very rarely, if ever, be right to exercise the discretion in favour of commencing or continuing the trial.

The court must therefore ensure that it is fair to proceed in the absence of the defendant.

19.5 Classification of offences

There are three different categories of criminal offence.

19.5.1 Summary offences

These are the most minor crimes, and are only triable summarily in the magistrates' court. 'Summary' refers to the process of ordering the defendant to attend the court by summons, a written order usually delivered by post which is the most frequent procedure adopted in the magistrates' courts. There has been some criticism of the fact that more and more offences have been made summary only, reducing the right to trial by jury.

19

THE CRIMINAL TRIAL PROCESS

19.5.2 Offences triable either way

These offences may be tried in either the magistrates' court or the Crown Court. Common examples are theft and burglary.

Figure 19.1 The criminal court system

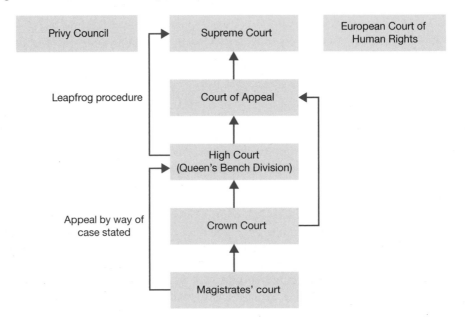

Figure 19.2 Crown Court receipts by case type, 2011–2017

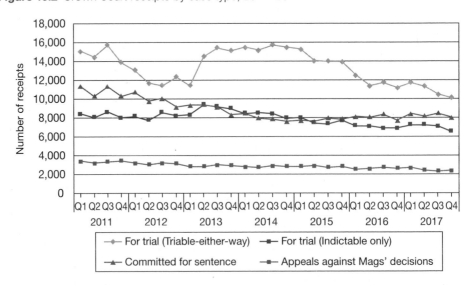

Source: Graph created from data in Table C1 'Receipts, disposals and outstanding criminal cases in the Crown Court' Criminal Court Statistics Quarterly, England and Wales, April to June 2018, published by Ministry of Justice on 27 September 2018, available at https://www.gov.uk/government/statistics/criminal-court-statistics-quarterly-april-to-june-2018 (Main Tables > C1)

Figure 19.3 Trial courts

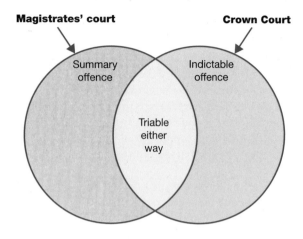

19.5.3 Indictable offences

Indictable offences are very serious offences, such as rape, robbery and murder. These are offences that can only be heard by the Crown Court for adult defendants. The indictment is the document containing the charges against the defendant for trial in the Crown Court. Each charge is listed on the indictment and each separate offence is called a count. A count is a statement of the offence that describes the offence in ordinary language and identifies any legislation that creates it.

19.6 Allocation procedure

Where a person is charged with a triable either way offence, he or she can insist on a trial by jury. He or she cannot choose to be tried by the magistrates. If the case is too serious or too complicated to be tried by the magistrates, it must be sent to the Crown Court. In reaching this decision, the magistrates will take into account the seriousness of the offence and whether they are likely to have sufficient sentencing powers to deal with it.

When deciding whether the case should stay in the magistrates' court, the magistrates will be informed of the defendant's prior convictions, if any. If they decide summary trial is appropriate, the defendant has the right to ask for an indication of sentence on plea of guilty before deciding which court to choose.

There are three main reasons why defendants may choose to be dealt with by the Crown Court. First, it can put off the day of trial. This has particular benefits to those who are remanded in custody and believe they will be found guilty and sent back to prison, because remand prisoners are entitled to privileges which are not available to sentenced prisoners (and time spent on remand is included in the time the prisoner eventually serves).

Secondly, many defendants believe they stand a better chance of acquittal in the Crown Court with a trial by jury, with the jury consisting of their own peers. A study by Vennard in 1985 ('The outcome of contested trials') suggests that they may be right: acquittal rates were significantly higher in the Crown Court (57 per cent) than in magistrates' courts (30 per cent). More recent statistics show at the Crown Court the conviction rate was 80 per cent and at the magistrates' court the conviction rate was 84.8 per cent. However, many of those who choose to be tried in the Crown Court then proceeded to plead guilty.

Thirdly, around a half of defendants are under the mistaken impression that they will get lighter sentences in the Crown Court. The Royal Commission on Criminal Justice noted that, in fact, judges were three times more likely to impose prison sentences, and their sentences were, on average, two-and-a-half times longer than those imposed by magistrates. Perhaps not surprisingly, a third of the defendants who chose Crown Court trial thought that they had made a mistake and would have been better off being dealt with by magistrates.

The Lammy Review argued that BAME defendants were consistently more likely than white defendants to plead not guilty in court. It also reported that BAME defendants sought trial by jury and lacked trust in the magistrates' court in some cases. This means that defendants were pleading not guilty in the magistrates' court and then electing for a jury trial at the Crown Court, rather than be tried in a magistrates' court, despite the higher sentencing powers available at the Crown Court.

19.7 Sending for trial

For every adult charged with an indictable offence their first appearance is in the magistrates' court. This is to determine issues concerning legal aid, bail and the use of statements and exhibits. The magistrates' court then provides defendants with a statement of the evidence against them so far, as well as a notice setting out the offence(s) for which they are to be sent for trial and the court where they are to be tried. They are then sent immediately for trial in the Crown Court. The Crown Court has taken over from the magistrates' court all remaining case management duties.

19.8 Plea and trial preparation hearing

The plea and trial preparation hearing takes place in the Crown Court within 28 days of the sending of a case from the magistrates' court. These hearings aim to encourage early preparation of cases before trial, with a view to reducing the number of 'cracked' trials (see p. 505). They are held in open court with the defendants present, and whom are ordinarily expected to enter a plea of guilty or not guilty to the counts on the indictment. This process is known as the 'arraignment'. If the defendants plead guilty, the judge will proceed to sentence. Where they plead not guilty the prosecution and defence will have to identify the key issues, and provide any additional information required to organise the actual trial, such as which witnesses will have to attend, facts that are admitted by both sides and issues of law that are likely to arise. The trial date will be set and there will not usually be any further case management hearings before the trial itself. The Court then sets a series of 'stage dates', which reflect a standardised chronology of how a Crown Court case should proceed.

19.9 Disclosure

The issue of disclosure is concerned with the responsibility of primarily the prosecution, but also in certain circumstances the defence, to reveal information related to the case prior to the trial.

Disclosure by the prosecution is governed by the Criminal Procedure and Investigations Act 1996 (the CPIA) and the CPIA Code of Practice. Mark George QC states that:

> The current scheme for disclosure was introduced as a direct response to failures of disclosure in cases as those of the Birmingham 6 and the Guildford 4.

Disclosure refers to the serving on the defence copies of any prosecution material (evidence) which 'might reasonably be considered capable of undermining the case for the prosecution against the accused', or 'of assisting the case for the accused, and which has not previously been disclosed'.

Section 3(1) of the CPIA provides that the prosecutor must:

(a) disclose to the accused any prosecution material which has not previously been disclosed to the accused and which might reasonably be considered capable of undermining the case for the prosecution or of assisting the case for the accused, or

(b) give to the accused a written statement that there is no material of a description mentioned in paragraph (a).

The prosecution is under a continuing duty to disclose material that might reasonably be considered capable of undermining its case or assisting the defence case. This does not end until the verdict has been reached, or the case is otherwise discontinued.

Under the Criminal Justice Act 2003 the defence has an obligation to broadly disclose the nature of the defence to be advanced to the prosecution. They must identify any defences they intend to rely on and any points of law they intend to raise. They must give the prosecution the names and addresses of all the witnesses they intend to call and the name of any expert witness they have consulted. If they do not, the judge may direct the jury to hold that against the defendant when deciding if the prosecution have proved their case. The prosecution (or the defence) may request to interview any witness in the trial. In *Rochford* (2011), the Court of Appeal ruled that the combination of the provisions concerning notification of details of defence witnesses and the Criminal Procedure Rules are designed to abolish 'trial by ambush'. If the police wish to interview an alibi witness, the CPS advise the police that they should give the solicitor for the defence a reasonable opportunity for their solicitor to attend. If the defendant does not have a solicitor, the police should try and arrange for an independent person attend.

Research carried out by Dr Hannah Quirk (2006) has shown that there have been difficulties with the implementation of the disclosure legislation. The police do not have enough training to perform this duty satisfactorily and the CPS lawyers often do not have sufficient time to check this process. A Protocol for the Control and Management of Unused Material in the Crown Court has been produced, but Professor Zander (2006) has argued that this is unlikely to be successful in improving the disclosure system. Disclosure, particularly inadequate disclosure by the prosecution, is an aspect of the trial process which can often lead to adjournments, even abuse of process applications. It is an area to which defence lawyers need to be particularly alive.

19

THE CRIMINAL TRIAL PROCESS

The Bigger Picture: Disclosure, miscarriages of justice and the criminal justice system at breaking point . . . cuts coming home to roost?

Failure to disclose vital information to the defence has come into sharp focus this year after the collapse of a series of rape cases. The most notorious of these cases was Liam Allan who was charged with 12 counts of rape and sexual assault. Failing to disclose evidence and failing to comply with the directions of the court can mean that trials collapse and that not only are potentially innocent people accused without a proper review of all the evidence, but also means that guilty people can be found not guilty.

The disclosure scandal did not operate in a vacuum and the criminal justice system has been described as being at 'breaking point'. *Stories of the Law and How It's Broken* (2018), point us to the fact that between 2009 and 2017 CPS net expenditure fell by 27 per cent, from £672m to £491m. Between 2014 and 2017 the number of full-time equivalent staff employed by the CPS fell 11 per cent, from around 6,200 to around 5,500. In real terms between 2010 and 2016, central Government funding to Police and Crime Commissioners fell by 25 per cent. Between March 2010 and March 2017 the police workforce reduced by more than 45,000 (19 per cent). Just before the collapse of Liam Allan's trial early in December 2017, the Government had announced that the Attorney General would conduct a review of the disclosure regime.

Liam Allan was a 22-year-old criminology student who was charged with 12 counts of rape and sexual assault. He was on bail for two years awaiting his trial. Over the course of those two years, a time that he described as 'mental torture', Allan claimed that there was telephone evidence on the complainant's mobile phone, exonerating him. The defence sought this evidence from the complainant's phone, specifically asking the CPS for all text messages between Liam Allan and the complainant. They were told that there was nothing of relevance and a few Snapchat messages were eventually disclosed.

The phone messages did not come to light, but the defence state that they did not stop asking for them, and once the trial began, they made a request to the judge. The analysis of the complainant's mobile phone was finally disclosed to his defence barrister, Julia Smart, after the trial had begun. The disclosed evidence was 2,500 pages long and it contained 40,000 text messages downloaded by police from the complainant's mobile phone. This was irrefutably disclosable evidence under the CPIA and should have been disclosed to the defence. Ms Smart had one night to read through all 2,500 pages of evidence. Her diligence and perseverance found, amongst the 40,000 or so messages, communications to Mr Allan from the complainant pestering him for sex, and one to a friend stating: 'It wasn't against my will or anything.' The prosecutor was informed in the morning and the Crown 'offered no evidence' against Mr Allan and he was found not guilty.

The *Guardian* newspaper reported that a CPS review of the case found that the officer in the Liam Allan case had conducted a search of the phone download to identify relevant material. He did not record the method he used to conduct this search and the only reference to the phone and phone download was on the Crime Reporting Information System (CRIS) report which is not routinely disclosed to the defence. After Liam Allan had been charged, the officer did not list the complainant's mobile phone or phone download on the disclosure schedule. The review found that he should have done this, as the phone download unsurprisingly met the definition of relevant material. In an internal review of the CPS it was subsequently revealed that an internal review discovered that 47 rape or sexual assault cases had been stopped because evidence had not been properly disclosed to the defence.

In January 2018 the Justice Committee launched an inquiry following these reports of cases which had collapsed, or guilty verdicts which had been overturned on appeal, due to errors in the disclosure process. The committee called for evidence regarding the disclosure regime. The Criminal Bar Association (an organisation that represents the views and interests of the practising members of the Criminal Bar in England and Wales) stated that the disclosure regime was sufficiently 'clear, well balanced and satisfactory'. However, it noted that the CPIA was introduced when the internet was in its infancy. The select committee referred to the amount of data generated by the average person as 'the digital crater'. Policing Minister Nick Hurd stated: 'The average mobile phone today is capable of holding the data equivalent of about 5 million A4 pages.'

The Centre for Criminal Appeals, a law charity, on giving evidence to the select committee, felt that the CPIA was asking too much of the police, as it required the police and prosecution 'to act in an impartial manner', when in practice they act as 'adversaries to the defence'. They pointed out that police officers are not legally trained in any way, yet are expected to make crucial legal decisions. The suggestion seems to be that the police will be subconsciously susceptible to what is called 'confirmation bias' and 'selectivity' in considering the evidence before them.

When she gave evidence to the committee, Angela Rafferty QC, then Chair of the Criminal Bar Association, commented on a Public Accounts Committee report from 2016 that stated that 'the criminal justice system is close to breaking point'. She highlighted that 'what is happening right now [with disclosure] is that the effects of those cuts are coming home to roost'.

On 20 July 2018 the select committee published its report on disclosure. The select committee stated in its conclusions that it felt that the issues raised in the inquiry 'were symptomatic of a criminal justice system under significant strain'. It appeared that the police and the CPS were not reviewing the relevant material, and when the defence finally received it, they were not paid to review it. They also stated that problems with disclosure might be driven in part by 'wider changes to the justice system, and notably a reduction in resources available across the system, including funding for the CPS and police and public funding for criminal defence'. It also concluded that 'long-term failures in the disclosure of evidence have gone unresolved, in part, because of insufficient focus and leadership, and that the Government must consider whether funding across the system is enough to ensure a good disclosure regime'.

The Liam Allan case generated a huge amount of review and discussion. Sir Brian Leveson (currently the President of the Queen's Bench Division and Head of Criminal Justice) suggested in a speech at UCL in April 2018 that:

> If you are part of a team, directly or indirectly, the extent to which you can carry out a genuinely objective and independent assessment could be questioned. The unconscious bias of expert witnesses is a well-known phenomenon. To what extent might, unconsciously, a similar phenomenon influence the role played by the disclosure officer?

He suggested that an independent assessment for unused material in serious offences is required and that there should perhaps be sanctions for failure to disclose. Professor Dennis at UCL also suggests that the police force may not be the best party to oversee disclosure in an adversarial system. This reminds us that additional research has shown that the police see themselves as 'owning an investigation'. They identify a suspect and build a case against them. He argues that this is not stated as a criticism, just a statement of fact and one that is difficult to challenge. Professor Dennis also states that it makes sense to have this culture as it 'incentivises the police to bring criminals to justice'. He suggests that there should be independent oversight of the disclosure decisions by an independent judge or lawyer who could act as an 'impartial reviewer'.

A report from the current Attorney General was published in November 2018. There was no mention at that point of any further investment in the CPS or the police service. As a lack of funding has been a thread throughout the criticisms, it is suspected that the recommendations alone may not solve the problem. The chairperson of the Bar Council, Andrew Walker QC, said:

> Those at the highest levels in Government need to accept their responsibility for what a decade of disinvestment in justice has caused. Victims of crime, the tax payer, those wrongly accused, and the whole of society, are all being short-changed . . . But this will also require the CPS to be funded properly, so that it can employ the necessary staff.

In the absence of any such recommendations by the Attorney General and without funding and real change, it may be that future miscarriages of justice will not be avoided. Police failure to disclose relevant evidence across all types of case is now very well documented. There is a long-held maxim in English Law, 'it is better that ten guilty persons escape than that one innocent suffer'. There may be a real risk that innocent parties are suffering. The objective of the criminal justice system, as stated in the Criminal Procedure Rules, is to deal with cases justly. This includes acquitting the innocent and convicting the guilty. This objective may not be served, if the innocent are not acquitted, nor the guilty convicted. Andrew Walker leaves us with this thought: 'Our politicians and the public have a choice to make. They must make it wisely. If they take all this for granted, then I fear that we will all pay the price.'

19.10 Plea bargaining

Plea bargaining is the name given to negotiations between the prosecution and defence lawyers over the outcome of a case; for example, where a defendant is choosing to plead not guilty, the prosecution may offer to reduce the charge to a similar offence with a smaller maximum sentence, in return for the defendant pleading guilty. Although plea bargaining is well known in the US criminal justice system, for many years the official view was that it did not happen here, although those involved in the system knew that in fact it happened all the time. Its existence in the English penal system was confirmed in a 1977 study by McConville and Baldwin, and it is now recognised to be a widespread phenomenon.

Effective plea bargaining requires the active cooperation of the judge but following the Court of Appeal case of *R v Turner* (1970) judges were not allowed to get involved in plea bargaining in the UK. That case effectively banned judges from indicating what sentence they would give if a defendant pleaded guilty. The case was not always followed in practice. In the 1993 Crown Court Study carried out by Zander and Henderson, 86 per cent of prosecution barristers, 88 per cent of defence barristers and 67 per cent of judges thought that *Turner* should be reformed to permit realistic discussion of plea, and especially sentence, between the defence and prosecution lawyers and the judge.

Key case

The ban against plea bargaining was dramatically removed by the Court of Appeal case of *R v Goodyear* (2005). Defendants can now request in writing an indication from the judge of their likely sentence if they plead guilty. Following such a request, trial judges are allowed to indicate in public the maximum sentence they would give on the agreed facts of the case. This indication binds the judge, so that a higher sentence cannot subsequently be given. Judges cannot state what sentence they would give if the case went to trial, as this risks placing undue pressure on defendants to plead guilty.

Legal principle
Defendants can request in writing an indication from the judge of their likely sentence if they plead guilty.

During the investigation, before going to court, the prosecution cannot make promises to a suspect about what type of sentence they will get, because the judge is not involved at this stage: *R v Innospec Ltd* (2010). This type of negotiation is sometimes allowed in

America. The introduction of deferred prosecution agreements (DPAs) following the Crime and Courts Act 2013 seeks to tackle the limitations of plea bargaining. They came into force in early 2014 (and are discussed in detail at p. 482).

19.10.1 Should plea bargaining be allowed?

It can be argued that plea bargaining offers benefits on all sides: for the defendant, there is obviously a shorter sentence; for the courts, the police and ultimately the taxpayers, there are the financial savings made by drastically shortening trials. In fact, without a high proportion of guilty pleas, the courts would be seriously overloaded, causing severe delays which in turn would raise costs still further, especially given the number of prisoners remanded in custody awaiting trial.

Despite this, plea bargaining has been widely criticised as being against the interests of justice. Several studies have shown that the practice may place undue pressure on the accused and persuade innocent people to plead guilty: Zander and Henderson (1993) concluded that each year there were some 1,400 possibly innocent persons whose counsel felt they had pleaded guilty in order to achieve a reduction in the charges faced or in the sentence. Critics also point out that the judge should be, and be seen to be, an impartial referee, acting in accordance with the law rather than the dictates of cost-efficiency. In addition, plea bargaining goes against the principle that offenders should be punished for what they have actually done. As well as leading to cases where people are punished more leniently than their conduct would seem to demand, it may lead to quite inappropriate punishments. For example, the high rate of acquittals in rape trials frequently leads to the prosecution reducing the charge to an ordinary offence against the person, in exchange for a guilty plea; this means that offenders who might usefully be given psychiatric help never receive it.

These criticisms are backed up by the fact that, in practice, plea bargaining does not necessarily save time or money because, in many cases, it occurs at the last moment, so there is no time to arrange for another case to slot into the court timetable. Such cases are often known as 'cracked trials', and Zander and Henderson's study found that 43 per cent of those cases listed as not guilty pleas 'cracked', which represented 26 per cent of listed cases overall.

19.11 The trial

Apart from the role played by the jury in the Crown Court, the law and procedure in the Crown Court and magistrates' court are essentially the same. The burden of proof is on the prosecution, which means that they must prove, beyond reasonable doubt, that the accused is guilty; the defendant is not required to prove his or her innocence.

Defendants should normally be present at the trial, though the trial can proceed without them if they have chosen to abscond. A lawyer should usually represent them in their absence (*R* v *Jones* (2002)).

The trial begins with the prosecution outlining the case against the accused (this is given in their opening speech) and then producing evidence to prove its case. The prosecution calls its witnesses, who will give their evidence in response to questions from the prosecution (called examination-in-chief). These witnesses can then be questioned by the defence (called cross-examination), and then, if required, re-examined by the prosecution to address any points brought up in cross-examination. Currently, witnesses are required to swear an oath before testimony, either on a Holy Book such as the Bible or Qur'an, or affirm a secular oath. In 2013, the Magistrates' Association introduced a proposal to abolish the option to swear a religious oath in court, replacing it entirely with a secular oath, but this was discarded following opposition. This means that defendants have the option today to either swear or affirm an oath in court.

When the prosecution has presented all its evidence it is the end of their case so they 'close their case'. The defence may submit that there is no case to answer, which means that they will argue that, on the prosecution evidence, no reasonable jury (or bench of magistrates) could convict. If the submission is successful, a verdict of not guilty will be given straight away. If no such submission is made, or if the submission is unsuccessful, the defence case starts. It puts forward its case, using the same procedure for examining witnesses as the prosecution did. The accused (and their spouse or civil partner) are the only witnesses who cannot be forced to give evidence.

Once the defence has presented all its evidence, each side usually makes a closing speech, outlining their case and seeking to persuade the magistrates or jury of it. In the Crown Court, this is followed by the judge's summing up to the jury. It is not always the case that the judge will only sum up at the end of the trial. The judge can identify for the jury, the issues in the case, even before the evidence is called. The judge can give directions of law at points in the trial when they are of most use to the jury.

When the judge sums up, they should review the evidence, draw the jury's attention to the important points of the case, and direct them on the law. At the end of the trial the judge must remind the jury that the prosecution must prove its case beyond reasonable doubt and must explain to them in simple terms what this means. The judge may give the jury a 'route to verdict'. This is described by the Crown Court Compendium as: 'a series of written factual questions, the answers to which logically lead to an appropriate verdict in the case. Each question should be tailored to the law as the judge understands it to be and to the issues and evidence in the case'. The court may also give written directions. These could be bullet point summaries of the law, longer summaries of the law, a written transcript of judge's legal directions, or a diagram illustrating the routes to verdicts. All written and oral directions given to the jury must be discussed, and preferably agreed, with the advocates well before they are provided to the jury.

The jury then retires and decides if the prosecution has proved its case. When a decision has been made the verdict is given by the foreman of the jury. The verdict is 'guilty' or 'not guilty'; there is no 'finding' of innocence.

The Youth Justice and Criminal Evidence Act 1999 contains a range of measures to make it easier for disabled and vulnerable witnesses to give evidence, including children under 17 and victims of sexual offences. The special arrangements that can be made for such witnesses include the use of screens, the giving of evidence by live television link, the abandoning of formal court dress and the use of pre-recorded video evidence. Special measures may also be introduced for those witnesses who, for religious reasons, wear a face veil, or niqab. This follows two Crown Court trials where a female Muslim defendant and a witness were each asked to remove their niqabs during sentencing and when giving evidence respectively. The trial judges noted that there was no clear guidance on this issue. Following this, the Lord Chief Justice declared that a Practice Direction would be drawn up and put out for consultation on when niqabs should be worn in court by defendants and witnesses. Central to the effective management of a case involving child and vulnerable witnesses will be the potential of a 'ground rules hearing' which should, amongst other things, establish the style, limits and duration of questioning child and vulnerable witnesses. It should also seek to guard against repetitive or aggressive cross-examination. The questions will often be written out and agreed by the judge and the advocates.

19.11.1 Evidence of bad character and previous convictions

In the past, previous convictions have only been exceptionally available to the court when determining guilt. Following the passing of ss. 101–103 of the Criminal Justice Act 2003, this evidence will be more widely available. The Court of Appeal stated in *R v Hanson* (2005) that the legislation required the consideration of three questions, namely:

1   Did the defendant's history of offending show a propensity to commit offences?

2   Did that propensity make it more likely the defendant committed the current offence? and

3   Is it just to rely on convictions of the same description or category having in mind the overriding principle that proceedings must be fair?

About 70 per cent of defendants have past convictions, so this reform will be important in practice. Critics argue that admitting this evidence undermines the presumption of innocence. It increases the risk of miscarriages of justice, with the courts being distracted by

The Bigger Picture: Giving 'Queen's evidence'

The US law enforcement agencies have traditionally favoured the practice of using those who admit offences to provide evidence against others, in exchange for a substantially reduced sentence or immunity from prosecution. This has enabled them to prosecute corporate crime successfully, particularly in relation to cartel offences (where businesses in the same sector reach secret agreements to artificially inflate prices). Historically, the UK law enforcement agencies were reluctant to do the same because of the risk that people might tell lies about a purported accomplice to avoid liability themselves. However, influenced by successes in America, the Serious Organised Crime and Police Act 2005, ss. 71–75 provide that an offender can benefit from a reduced sentence or even immunity from sentence, if they give evidence against other criminals (sometimes called 'Queen's evidence').

A person assisting the prosecution in this way is colloquially described as a 'supergrass'. This term tends to be used where the informant is a serious criminal or terrorist who informs on a large number of his or her partners in crime and is the prosecutor's principal witness in any subsequent trial. The evidence of these individuals can disrupt and dismantle the most powerful organised criminal gangs and terrorist organisations. The process has given rise to some concern due to the risk of police corruption when they are working with criminals, failures in witness protection arrangements for the supergrass and the reliability of any evidence of a supergrass who, by definition, is a serious criminal whose motivation for giving evidence is to reduce their own punishment, not to achieve justice. The 2005 Act seeks to reduce some of these risks by formalising the arrangements to create greater transparency and accountability. The supergrass is now convicted and sentenced before testifying, with the details of the agreement and the extent of the sentence reduction being officially recorded and made available to the court. There remain concerns where individuals are convicted purely on the basis of supergrass evidence, without any corroborating evidence.

the defendant's past convictions, rather than focusing on the actual evidence about whether the defendant committed the particular offence before the court.

19.11.2 Expert witnesses and miscarriages of justice

In court only, experts can give their 'opinion'. Lay witnesses can only give evidence about what they saw and what they heard.

The case of Sally Clark and others highlighted potential problems with the use of expert witnesses. Sally Clark was a solicitor who was convicted of killing her two young sons. The evidence of three medical experts helped to convict her.

Clark's first son died suddenly in December 1996 shortly after his birth, and in January 1998 her second child died, also seemingly of a cot death. However, a month later she was arrested for their murder. The prosecution case relied on statistical evidence presented by charismatic expert paediatrician, Professor Sir Roy Meadow. Sir Roy Meadow coined the term Munchausen syndrome by proxy (MSBP), a very rare form of child abuse in which mothers or other care-givers fabricate or cause symptoms of illness in their children to gain sympathy. Notably he was not an expert statistician nor an expert epidemiologist. However he gave, and was allowed to give, his expert opinion evidence that the chance of two children from a middle-class family suffering sudden infant death syndrome was 1 in 73 million. However, the actual probability of two babies dying of cot death in a family like Mrs Clark's is actually said to be 1 in 77.

In 2003 the Court of Appeal found her conviction to be unsafe (***R v Clark*** (2003)). It stated that it had already decided to set aside her conviction because a Home Office pathologist, Dr Alan Williams, had not disclosed crucial medical evidence to the defence. Namely, he had withheld exculpatory evidence of tests that showed that her second child had died from the bacterial infection staphylococcus aureus, an illness that could have accounted for his death.

They stated however that the evidence of the prosecution expert, Professor Sir Roy Meadow, 'grossly overstates the chance of two sudden deaths within the same family from unexplained but natural causes'. He was said to have given very misleading evidence about the chances of a woman having two of her children die naturally from unexplained causes. He stated the chances of a second child dying from natural causes in the same family were one in 73 million. Why would an expert put forward such misleading evidence? One of the reasons put forward for experts putting forward misleading evidence is that: 'Some experts are crusaders: they are so convinced of a general truth that they have difficulty in descending to the particular case before them.'

Astonishingly, after Sally Clark was freed on appeal but despite the criticism of the evidence of Sir Roy Meadow, the Crown Prosecution Service still chose to use him as an expert in another case of 'cot death' in the case of Trupti Patel. She was acquitted in 90 minutes by the jury.

On the back of Sally Clark's conviction, a number of women appealed their convictions for murdering their babies. One of those wrongly convicted was Angela Cannings. Jean Golding, the professor of epidemiology at Bristol University, was originally, reported *The Scotsman*, asked to be a prosecution witness in Angela Cannings' trial where Sir Roy Meadow was again a prosecution witness. Once she read the pre-trial evidence, Golding became a witness for the defence. In court she critiqued Sir Roy's original research methodology, saying that 81 cases on which he based his outlook did not stand up to scrutiny, because he had no control group. In December 2003 Angela Cannings' conviction for the murder of her infant sons was quashed after Professor Michael Patton, a geneticist, told the Court of Appeal that an 'undiscovered genetic disorder' could have been the cause of their deaths. Lord Justice Judge gave the full reasons for allowing Cannings' appeal:

> Therefore, the flawed evidence he gave at Sally Clark's trial serves to undermine his high reputation and authority as a witness in the forensic process. It also, and not unimportantly for present purposes, demonstrates not only that in this particular field which we summarise as 'cot deaths', even the most distinguished expert can be wrong, but also provides a salutary warning against the possible dangers of an over-dogmatic expert approach.

On the back of this appeal the law was changed so that in the future, no prosecutions should be brought where medical experts are in dispute and there is no other cogent evidence. The court held that:

> All this suggests that, for the time being, where a full investigation into two or more sudden unexplained infant deaths in the same family is followed by a serious disagreement between reputable experts about the cause of death, and a body of such expert opinion concludes that natural causes, whether explained or unexplained, cannot be excluded as a reasonable (and not a fanciful) possibility, the prosecution of a parent or parents for murder should not be started, or continued, unless there is additional cogent evidence, extraneous to the expert evidence, (such as we have exemplified in paragraph 10) which tends to support the conclusion that the infant, or where there is more than one death, one of the infants, was deliberately harmed. In cases like the present, if the outcome of the trial depends exclusively or almost exclusively on a serious disagreement between distinguished and reputable experts, it will often be unwise, and therefore unsafe, to proceed . . . Unless we are sure of guilt the dreadful possibility always remains that a mother, already brutally scarred by the unexplained death or deaths of her babies, may find herself in prison for life for killing them when she should not be there at all. In our community, and in any civilised community, that is abhorrent.

When Sally Clark was released she had already spent three years in custody and never recovered from her ordeal. She died four years later age 48.

As previously mentioned, following the appeal of Sally Clark, Alan Williams the Home Office pathologist was found guilty of serious professional misconduct by the General Medical Council (GMC) and banned from undertaking any Home Office pathology work or coroners' cases for three years. This was upheld by the High Court. The GMC also struck Professor Meadow off the medical register after finding him guilty of serious professional misconduct. The council decided that he gave 'erroneous' and 'misleading' evidence at Mrs Clark's trial. However, he appealed to the Court of Appeal, who granted his appeal, stating the GMC should not have brought misconduct proceedings against him because expert witnesses should be 'immune' from prosecution or disciplinary action. Laying down new law, Mr Justice Collins explained that this was based on the principle that a witness could not be sued over remarks made in court. Otherwise, the judge said, experts would be deterred from giving evidence.

In its annual report for 2004, the Criminal Cases Review Commission criticised expert witnesses. It considered high fees were tempting experts to give strong evidence to please their client, to ensure they would be asked to give expert evidence in the future. Some experts earn more than £1,500 a day and are keen to keep this source of income. They are frequently doctors who are employed by the NHS and earn some extra money by working privately as expert witnesses at the same time. The Criminal Cases Review Commission was concerned that unless expert witnesses were more tightly regulated, there would be a risk of more miscarriages of justice.

The Law Commission issued a report entitled *Expert Evidence in Criminal Proceedings in England and Wales* (2011a). It looked at how to resolve some of the problems associated with the use of expert evidence. It suggested judges should look more closely at the expert's ability to provide useful and reliable evidence to the court; such evidence would only be admissible if it satisfied a reliability test. It also recommended that experts for the defence and prosecution should give evidence at the same time so they have an opportunity to discuss with each other the differences in their evidence. This approach is sometimes called 'concurrent evidence' or 'hot-tubbing' and has been used in Australia. The hope is that this will give the court a clearer understanding of the expert evidence, but the risk is that the

Photo 19.1 Sally Clark

Source: © Trinity Mirror/Mirrorpix

evidence becomes less clear during the discussion between the experts and the impact of that evidence might depend more on the strength of their individual personalities rather than the quality of the evidence. The Law Commission recommendations on expert reliability and concurrent evidence are effectively implemented by changes to the Criminal Procedure Rules and a Practice Direction issued by the Court of Appeal. Under the Practice Direction there must be 'a sufficiently reliable scientific basis for the evidence to be admitted' and the courts are entitled to consider the reliability of expert evidence.

In the early 2000s, ear print evidence, which had previously been used to convict in a number of trials, was discredited, and a man who had been imprisoned for life on the basis of such evidence, was released (**R v Dallagher** (2002)). The CPS offer guidance on how much weight a jury should give to expert evidence regarding an ear print, due to the flexibility and its susceptibility to change dependent on how much pressure is placed (for example as someone squeezes through a window). The defence barrister in the Dallagher case, James Sturman QC, said: 'This is yet another example of the dangers of police perhaps following science too closely when scientists are building a science . . . '.

19.12 Models of criminal justice systems

In order to judge the effectiveness of a criminal justice system (or anything else for that matter), you need first to know what that system sets out to do. The academic Herbert Packer (1968) identified two quite different potential aims for criminal justice systems: the 'due process' model; and the 'crime control' model. The former gives priority to fairness of procedure and to protecting the innocent from wrongful conviction, accepting that a high level of protection for suspects makes it more difficult to convict the guilty, and that some guilty people will therefore go free. The latter places most importance on convicting the guilty, taking the risk that occasionally some innocent people will be convicted. Obviously, criminal justice systems tend not to fall completely within one model or the other: most seek to strike a balance between the two. This is not always easy: imagine for a moment that you are put in charge of our criminal justice system, and you have to decide the balance at which it should aim. How many innocent people do you believe it is acceptable to convict? Bear in mind that if you answer 'none', the chances are that protections against this may have to be so strong that very few guilty people will be convicted either. Would it be acceptable for 10 per cent of innocent people to be convicted if that means 50 per cent of the guilty were also convicted? If that 10 per cent seems totally unacceptable, does it become more reasonable if it means that 90 per cent of the guilty are convicted? It is not an easy choice to make.

Looking at the balance which a criminal justice system seeks to strike, and how well that balance is in fact struck, is a useful way to assess the system's effectiveness. As mentioned at the beginning of Chapter 18, in recent years this balance has been the subject of much debate and disagreement as regards our criminal justice system, with the police, magistrates and the Government claiming that the balance has been tipped too far in favour of suspects' rights, at the expense of convicting the guilty. On the other hand, civil liberties organisations, many academics and the lawyers involved in the well-known miscarriages of justice feel that the system has not learned from those miscarriages, and that the protections for suspects are still inadequate.

The latter group have particularly criticised the findings of the RCCJ. Sean Enright (1993) has written: 'One would not guess from a reading of the Commission's proposals that this Royal Commission was set up in response to some astonishing miscarriages of justice. Rather, the abiding impression is that this Commission was primarily concerned with a ruthlessly efficient and cost-effective disposal of criminal business.' The barrister Michael Mansfield, who represented some of the Birmingham Six, among others, agrees, pointing out that the RCCJ proposals and the subsequent changes made to the criminal justice system are 'a complete denial of the basic principle of the presumption of innocence . . . the position has deteriorated to such an extent that further wrongful convictions are guaranteed' (*Presumed Guilty* (1993)).

19.13 Criticism and reform

The following criticisms and suggestions for reform have been the subject of particular debate.

19.13.1 Racism and the CPS

A report prepared by the Crown Prosecution Inspectorate in 2003 has criticised the CPS for failing to weed out weaker cases against ethnic minorities. The report says acquittal rates for black and Asian defendants stand at 42 per cent, compared to 30 per cent for white defendants. The CPS is therefore failing in its duty to eliminate differential treatment. The Inspectorate is of the view that, as members of minority groups are more likely to be stopped by the police, the CPS should consider whether the behaviour of the arresting officer 'might have been inappropriate or provocative'. It concludes:

> The CPS would appear to be discriminating against ethnic minority defendants by failing to correct the bias [of police] and allowing a disproportionate number of weak cases against ethnic minority defendants to go to trial.

19.13.2 Racism and the courts

Research was undertaken in 2003 by Roger Hood *et al.*, which was published in a paper called *Ethnic Minorities in the Criminal Courts: Perceptions of Fairness and Equality of Treatment*. The research found that, over recent years, members of the ethnic minorities were increasingly satisfied that the criminal courts were racially impartial. Several judges said that attitudes had changed a lot and many lawyers also reported that racial bias or inappropriate language was becoming a thing of the past. This improvement was partly due to the fact that judges and magistrates are increasingly receiving training in racial awareness, and partly due to improvements in society as a whole.

While there has been this improvement in the courts, there still remains a significant minority of defendants who consider that they have been treated unfairly because of their race. One in five black defendants in the Crown Court, one in ten in the magistrates' courts and one in eight Asian defendants in both types of court, considered they had been treated unfairly because of their race. Most complaints were about sentencing, which was perceived to be higher than for white defendants. Very few perceived racial bias in the conduct or attitude of judges or magistrates – only 3 per cent in the Crown Court and 1 per cent in the magistrates' courts. There were no complaints about racist remarks from the bench. Of some concern is the fact that black lawyers had a more negative view of proceedings. A third of black lawyers said they had personally witnessed incidents in court that they regarded as 'racist'.

Black defendants and lawyers felt that the authority and legitimacy of the courts would be strengthened if more ethnic minorities were employed in the criminal justice system. Many judges agreed that more could be done to avoid the impression that the courts were 'white dominated institutions'.

19.13.3 The Lammy Review

David Lammy, in his 2017 review into the treatment of black, Asian and minority ethnic (BAME) individuals within the criminal justice system, covered a wide spectrum of organisations: the role of CPS, the court system, prisons and young offender institutions, the Parole Board, the Probation Service and Youth Offending Teams. The statistics presented were sobering:

> Despite making up just 14% of the population, BAME men and women make up 25% of prisoners, while over 40% of young people in custody are from BAME backgrounds. If our prison population reflected the make-up of England and Wales we would have over 9,000 fewer people in prison – the equivalent of 12 average-sized prisons. There is greater disproportionality in the number of Black people in prisons here than in the United States.

A 'chronic trust deficit' was seen as a significant part of the problem by Lammy, who states:

> they see the system in terms of 'them and us'. Many do not trust the promises made to them by their own solicitors, let alone the officers in a police station warning them to admit guilt. What begins as a 'no comment' interview can quickly become a Crown Court trial.

Findings showed that BAME individuals are more likely to plead not guilty in order for their case to go before a jury, as they fear injustice from a magistrate. This leaves missing out on the possibility of a reduced sentence.

Key recommendations included:

- introduction of a deferment system where first-time low-level offenders have the option of completing a rehabilitation programme – when the programme is completed the charges are dropped;
- publishing of all Crown Court sentencing remarks to increase transparency;
- making the charging decision 'race-blind' through redaction of identifying information from case files that are passed from the police to the CPS;
- stating national targets for an ethnically representative judiciary and magistracy, as well as other organisations within the criminal justice system (currently 6 per cent within the police and prison service, 7 per cent in judiciary, 11 per cent among magistrates and 19 per cent in the CPS);
- consideration of a US-style system for 'sealing' criminal records where individuals have rehabilitated since an initial conviction as a young person. This would take the form of a hearing where the reasons for wanting the record sealed would be weighed up against the reasons why the public should have a right to be aware of it.

(Lammy's findings are further discussed in Chapter 20: Sentencing and Chapter 21: Young offenders.)

19.13.4 The crown prosecution service

It is perhaps the case that the CPS ran into problems from the very beginning. It has been suggested that this is because the Home Office had apparently underestimated the cost of the new service. In 1996 a MORI poll found that 70 per cent of CPS lawyers responding to a questionnaire considered that the CPS was either below average or one of the worst places to work. In 1990 the House of Commons Public Accounts Committee noted that the CPS appeared to be costing almost twice as much as the previous prosecution arrangements, and the number of staff required was practically double that originally envisaged.

Relations between the police and the CPS have not always been good: the police resented the new service and its demands for a higher standard of case preparation from police. While the CPS saw a high rate of discontinued cases as a success story, the police saw this as letting offenders off the hook. Reforms introduced following the Glidewell Report aim to improve police/CPS relations, with police and CPS staff working in integrated teams and the creation of 42 prosecuting authorities which correlate with the 42 police forces. Following the 1997 Narey Report into delay in the criminal justice system, CPS staff now work alongside police officers in police stations to prepare cases for court. However, it may be that these reforms could go to the opposite extreme. The CPS was created to put an end to the close and often cosy relations between police officers and the lawyers who used to prosecute their cases, as this could lead to malpractice.

Some of the teething problems have now been ironed out, but problems still remain. There is doubt as to how far the CPS provides an independent perspective on deciding whether or not to prosecute. The CPS has no control over the police decision to caution rather than to prosecute.

In 1990 the Home Affairs Committee expressed concern at the large proportion of discontinued cases which were not dropped until the court hearing, and was surprised that the CPS undertook no systematic analysis of the reasons for discontinuance. In 1993 the RCCJ found that the CPS did exercise the power to discontinue appropriately, citing one study (Moxon and Crisp, 1994) which suggested that nearly a third of discontinuances were dropped on public interest grounds. Of these, nearly half were discontinued because the offence was trivial and/or the likely penalty was nominal. Only 5 per cent of the cases were discontinued before any court appearance and, where cases were terminated at the court, the decision to discontinue was often taken before the hearing but not communicated to the defendant in time to save a court appearance – either because the decision had been taken too late in the day or because the CPS did not know where the defendant was.

In assessing the incidence of weak cases in the Crown Court (which may be cases that should have been discontinued), the numbers of ordered and directed acquittals are relevant. According to the 1996 Judicial Statistics, in one in every five cases a judge ordered an acquittal.

19.13.5 Disclosure

The intention of the Criminal Procedure and Investigations Act 1996 (CPIA 1996) was to redress the balance between the prosecution and defence, but there is a danger that it has gone too far in favour of the prosecution. The new rules allow considerable discretion to the prosecution to decide what should be disclosed to the defence solicitor. There is a risk that they will not disclose information highlighting weaknesses in the prosecution case. Such a failure was one of the main causes of the high-profile miscarriages of justice. For example, Judith Ward's conviction was quashed after 18 years of incarceration for a terrorist attack she did not commit when medical evidence came to light which ought to have been disclosed by the prosecution at the time of her original trial. The Law Society fears that the changes in prosecution disclosure may leave future miscarriages of justice undetected.

Prosecution disclosure does not have to take place until after the defendant has pleaded not guilty and identified what the defence consider the relevant issues in the case are (in what is called a 'Defence Statement' – see s.6 of CPIA 1996 as amended by the Criminal Justice Act 2003). Many have argued that the defendant, or rather his or her lawyers, need to see this information before they can sensibly decide their plea, or indeed make informed requests for disclosure. There may, for example, be significant problems for the prosecution in one area of the case (such as the identity of an informant, or the conduct of officers or other prosecution witnesses). But if the defence, without any inkling of such problems, fail to identify that area as one of concern, the material will ordinarily not be disclosed. The fairness and transparency of such an approach has often been questioned.

The new rules providing for defence disclosure have given rise to considerable controversy, as many feel that they further undermine the right to silence, and the fundamental principle that the prosecution can be invited to prove their case. According to the consultation paper that preceded CPIA 1996, the reforms are intended to prevent defendants 'ambushing' the trial by producing an unexpected defence at the last moment which the prosecution is unprepared for, and therefore enabling the defendant to be wrongly acquitted. In fact, research prepared for the RCCJ suggested that there was little evidence of this happening in practice. Sir Robin Auld has recommended some limited changes to the existing system of disclosure. These include that prosecutors should be made responsible for identifying all potentially disclosable material and automatic prosecution disclosure of certain documents. As noted above, alleged failures in prosecution disclosure continue to lead to a considerable amount of argument during the trial process. It is perhaps the most common reason Crown Court trials are halted by the judge by reason of the prosecution's conduct amounting to an abuse of the Court's process.

19.13.6 Cracked and ineffective trials

The Labour Government was concerned by the problem of 'cracked and ineffective trials'. Cracked trials occur when a case is concluded without a trial, usually because the defendant has pleaded guilty at a very late stage. An ineffective trial happens when a hearing is cancelled on the day it was due to go ahead.

The Crown Prosecution Service is responsible for 20 per cent of all ineffective trials in the magistrates' courts (National Audit Office, 2006). This was due to insufficient oversight of cases, urgent cases not being prioritised, incomplete evidence and mislaid files. Over a quarter of Crown Court hearings are cancelled on the day of the trial. In 1999, it was noted that in a quarter of these cases, this was due to a witness not attending (*Criminal Justice: Working Together*, National Audit Office, 1999). This is sometimes because they are too frightened to give evidence. However, vulnerable and intimidated witnesses are now routinely entitled to the benefit of what are termed 'special measures', which can range from their giving evidence from behind a screen, hidden from the defendant, to providing the majority of their evidence in a pre-recorded interview or by live link. The Government is piloting the pre-recording of cross-examination in certain types of case.

With rising numbers of witnesses not turning up to court, The HM Crown Prosecution Service Inspectorate (*Witness for the Prosecution*, 2016) audited 120 cases to see if the CPS were using witness summonses correctly. They found that despite a 12.4 per cent increase in the numbers of summons being issued between 2013/14 and 2014/15, there was no evidence of a corresponding increase in the number of witnesses attending court. The report found evidence of good practice from the CPS but also many areas for improvement, including increasing the background reports carried out on the witness and consideration of other options for the witness to present their evidence (for example, video link). Figures from this report note that the number of Crown Court trials which crack due to the witness being absent or withdrawing on the day of trial has increased, from 1.8 per cent of all trials in 2013/14 to 2.1 per cent of all trials in 2014/15. The numbers are higher in the magistrates' court (6.3 per cent in 2013/14 and 6.8 per cent in 2014/15).

When cracked or ineffective trials occur, it is frequently too late to arrange for another case to slot into the court timetable. Cracked and ineffective trials are a considerable waste of public money and resources and can cause unnecessary stress for victims and witnesses keen for justice to be done without delay.

Figures contained in the report *Facing justice: tackling defendants' non-attendance at court* (2005) prepared by the Committee of Public Accounts, show that a defendant failing to attend court was the second highest cause of ineffective trials. Unfortunately, of the 15 per cent of defendants that failed to attend court hearings, only 45 per cent had bail warrants executed against them within three months.

Following the introduction of the plea before venue procedure, and the reduction in sentence for early pleas, the number of cracked trials was halved but remains a problem.

To try to deal with the problem of cracked trials, the Courts Act 2003 has given the criminal courts a power to award costs against third parties who cause a case to collapse or be delayed.

Recent criminal court statistics (see Figure 19.4) show a slight improvement in trial effectiveness, with the number of cracked trials falling from 43 per cent in 2010 to 34 per cent in 2017, but ineffective trials increased marginally from 14 per cent in 2010 to 15 per cent in 2017.

19.13.7 A corroboration rule?

Figure 19.4 Effectiveness of Crown Court trials in England & Wales, 2010–17

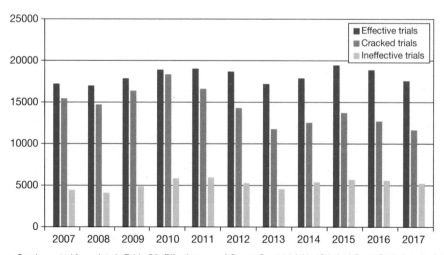

Source: Graph created from data in Table C2 'Effectiveness of Crown Court trials' in 'Criminal Court Statistics: April to June 2018 which can be found online at: https://www.gov.uk/government/statistics/criminal-court-statistics-quarterly-april-to-june-2018 (Main Tables > C2)

The major role played by confession evidence in the miscarriages of justice has led to suggestions that confession evidence alone should be regarded as insufficient to secure a conviction; in other words, the prosecution would be required to produce other evidence (such as witnesses, or forensic evidence) to support the confession.

Research by McConville for the RCCJ (1992) suggests that in 95 per cent of cases where confession evidence played a part, supporting evidence was available, indicating that a requirement for such extra evidence would lead to automatic acquittals in only a handful of cases. He calculated that, even without changes in police investigative practices, only 8 per cent of prosecutions would be affected, and these would mostly be less serious cases: a reasonable price to pay for avoiding more miscarriages of justice.

Three members of the RCCJ agreed that there should be a requirement for corroborating evidence of confessions. However, the majority merely recommended that judges should warn juries that care was needed in convicting on the basis of the confession alone, and explain the reasons why people might confess to crimes that they did not commit.

Confession evidence usually consists of confessions given to the police, but the case of Michael Stone also highlighted the danger of courts relying on uncorroborated evidence of confessions given to other prisoners. Michael Stone was convicted in 1998 of the murder of Lin Russell and her daughter Megan. They had been walking home from school through a cornfield with the other daughter Josie, when they were brutally attacked. Josie had been left for dead but had survived. While Josie had regained some memory of the incident, she was not able to pick out Stone from the identity parade. Apart from circumstantial evidence, the main evidence against Michael Stone were statements that Stone had allegedly made to three other prisoners while in prison on remand. One of these prisoners subsequently told the *Daily Mirror* newspaper that he had lied to the court. Confessions made to fellow prisoners have none of the protections surrounding confessions made to the police that are laid down in PACE. As the defence lawyer pointed out to the jury in Michael Stone's trial: 'In an unconscious way you may think that everyone desperately wants Michael Stone to be guilty. If he's guilty the police guessed right and if he's guilty then the killer's caught and if he's guilty then all of us can sleep a little sounder in our beds tonight.' Confession evidence may be attractive but it does not necessarily do justice.

19.13.8 Conviction rates

Recent years have seen a large rise in reported crime but falling conviction rates. For example, for sexual offences there were 21,107 cases reported in 1980 and 31,284 by 1993. By contrast, the convictions in those years were 8,000 in 1980 and only 4,300 in 1993. In 2002 the Audit Commission reported that criminals only have a 1 in 16 chance of being caught and convicted.

19.13.9 Victims and witnesses

Victims and other witnesses play a vital role in getting convictions and thereby achieving justice. In 2003, more than 5 per cent of Crown Court cases did not go ahead on the first day because a witness failed to turn up. Twenty-two per cent of Crown Court cases and more than a quarter of magistrates' court cases that collapsed did so because prosecution witnesses failed to come to court.

There is now a growing awareness that the criminal justice system has paid insufficient attention to the needs of victims and witnesses of crime, with lawyers taking the centre stage in legal proceedings instead. For many years, victims of crime had virtually no rights. In English legal theory and practice, victims are not parties to the prosecution, but are only witnesses. Traditionally, victims have had no legal right to participation, consultation or even information about their cases. By comparison, suspects and defendants do have rights, even if not all of them are enforceable in practice.

Victims have repeatedly complained about the lack of information they received from the criminal justice system about the progress of their case. The Witness Satisfaction Survey in 2000 showed that more than half of prosecution witnesses were not kept informed about the progress of the case and over 40 per cent were not told the verdict but had to find out for themselves.

Organisations such as Victim Support campaigned for many years to persuade the Government to recognise that victims should have distinct rights and as a result victims' rights have gradually been increased. These rights have been put together in a Code of Practice for Victims of Crime. The Code sets out the services victims should expect to receive from the criminal justice system, including the right to be notified of any arrests and court hearings related to their case, if charges are being dropped, and whether or not they are eligible for compensation.

The Criminal Injuries Compensation Scheme provides limited financial compensation to the victims of some forms of crime (see p. 411). It is perhaps of note that the state will compensate a 'complainant' (the preferred term used in court) even where the defendant is not found guilty. Dedicated Witness Care Units have been set up to improve the experience of victims and witnesses of crime. Their needs should be assessed at the start of the criminal process, to identify their specific requirements, such as childcare needs and the risk of intimidation. Witness care officers should then help to guide individuals through the criminal justice system.

The Audit Commission (2003) found that the majority of victims and witnesses felt they had been treated with respect by the police, but were less complimentary about their treatment by the courts. Many witnesses were unaware they could reclaim travel and other expenses incurred, and said their expenses were increased by delays in the court system. Once at court, witnesses reported intimidation, such as name-calling by the defendant's family and friends who were around in the corridors. Non-smoking policies meant people (including defendants and victims) gathered around the entrance to the court, causing stress not only to those wanting to smoke, but also to witnesses arriving at the building. The report concludes:

> There is a tension between supporting victims and witnesses through a court case and the adversarial nature of a trial. Many witnesses have no idea what to expect in court, and perceptions are often based on media and dramatic portrayals. Many also perceive that the current culture of the court is not one that responds to witness needs and demands as readily as it does to those of court professionals and the defence.

In response to these concerns, Her Majesty's Courts Service is striving to provide separate facilities for victims and prosecution witnesses at court. A victim can now make a Victim Personal Statement, which is a written statement presented to the trial court. This should be considered by the court prior to passing sentence. The court can take into account the effect of the offence on the victim when passing sentence, but not the victim's opinions on what the sentence should be. Research carried out by the National Centre for Social Research in 2004 on the Victim Personal Statement Scheme revealed that take-up and understanding of the scheme was patchy, and that worryingly, the purpose of the scheme was unclear. The research suggests if the purpose was clarified, then the scheme might prove more successful. Many people involved in the criminal justice system simply view the scheme as a political gimmick, but the reality is that these have become routine in the Crown Court and the areas they cover are increasingly an addendum at the end of the ordinary statement.

In 2008, public protection advocates were introduced. These communicate victims' views at oral hearings of the Parole Board in cases where a prisoner serving an open-ended sentence (called an indeterminate sentence) is applying for release or transfer to open conditions. Victims will be able to attend and speak in person at an oral hearing, but they will also be subject to cross-examination by the prisoner's advocate and to questioning by the panel.

In 2010 a Victims' Commissioner was appointed who works across the criminal justice system to improve the support for victims. A National Victims' Service was created in 2013, replaced by the Victim and Witness Information website in 2018. The website was created to provide victims of crime with a comprehensive and dedicated support service. There is information on what happens after a crime, how victims can seek support and what the steps are towards claiming compensation. They can also find out about restorative justice. The associated telephone helpline is run by the charity Victim Support.

In 2013 a Victims' Right to Review Scheme was introduced. Under this scheme, whenever a prosecutor decides not to bring charges against a suspect, or to stop a case that has already started, the victim of the offence must be informed of their right to request a review of that decision.

The European Commission passed a directive in 2012 to establish minimum standards on the rights, support and protection of victims of crime. The United Kingdom has to make sure its domestic law complies with this directive.

As victims have been allowed a greater say in criminal proceedings, the question has been raised as to whether the right balance has been achieved between the defendant's and victim's interests. In his response to the Home Office consultation paper, *Modernising Police Powers: Review of the Police and Criminal Evidence Act 1984* (2007a), Professor Zander (2007d) has commented:

> I do not accept that the interests of victims should be a central concern of the criminal justice system. Where relevant they should of course be taken into account. But in regard to the investigation and evidence gathering processes of the criminal justice system the interests of victims as victims (as opposed to potential witnesses), have little, if any, relevance. The victim is of course likely to have an entirely legitimate concern that the person responsible for the crime be apprehended and convicted. But it is as wrong to make that personal interest the basis for altering the balance of the criminal justice system as it would be to do so because of the personal interest of the victim's mother.

19.13.10 The role of the media and public opinion

It is noticeable that all the serious miscarriages of justice occurred in cases where a particular crime had outraged public opinion and led to enormous pressure on the police to find the culprits. In the case of the Birmingham Six, feelings ran so high that the trial judge consented to the case being heard away from Birmingham, on the ground that a Birmingham jury might be 'unable to bring to the trial that degree of detachment that is necessary to reach a dispassionate and objective verdict'. Given the graphic media descriptions of the carnage the real bombers had left behind them, it was in fact debatable whether any jury, anywhere, would have found it easy to summon up such detachment. The chances of a fair trial must have decreased even further when, halfway through the trial, the *Daily Mirror* devoted an entire front page to photographs of the Six, boasting that they were the 'first pictures' (implying that they were the first pictures of the bombers).

The miscarriages of justice were characterised by a reluctance to refer cases back to appeal. While campaigning by some newspapers and television programmes was eventually to help bring about the successful appeals, other sections of the media, and in particular the tabloid newspapers, were keen to dismiss the idea that miscarriages of justice might have occurred. Nor was there a great amount of public interest in the alleged plight of the Birmingham Six or the other victims – in stark contrast to the petitioning on behalf of Private Lee Clegg during 1995. There was a common feeling of satisfaction that someone had been punished for such terrible crimes, and the public did not want to hear that the system had punished the wrong people.

The Bigger Picture: Anonymous witnesses

The Youth Justice and Criminal Evidence Act 1999 allows courts to issue special measures directions. These directions seek to reduce the stress and problems experienced by vulnerable and intimidated witnesses giving evidence to courts. The directions can allow the courts to put up a screen between the witness and the defendant, their evidence can be video-recorded in advance and submitted as a video to the court, or it can be given by a live TV link, the public can be asked to leave the court and the lawyers can remove their wigs and gowns.

One special arrangement to prevent the intimidation of witnesses which has caused problems in the criminal courts is where witnesses have been granted complete anonymity when giving evidence. Anonymity can be secured by, for example, putting up a screen and electronically disguising the voice of the witness. The House of Lords concluded in ***R v Davis*** (2008) that this arrangement was unlawful because the defendant had not been given a fair trial. The Law Lords were concerned that without knowing the identity of the person giving evidence against them, defendants were unable to effectively reply to the accusations. If they knew who their accuser was, they might, for example, be able to show that the individual had a personal vendetta against them which provided the motive to tell lies to the court. The facts of the actual case were that two men had been shot and killed at a party. Davis had been prosecuted, but argued that his ex-girlfriend had told lies about him to the police and had arranged for others also to tell lies about him. Three witnesses gave evidence against Davis anonymously and, as a result, he was not allowed to ask them questions which might reveal their identity. He, therefore, was unable to find out whether they were acquaintances of his ex-girlfriend, which had hindered the presentation of his defence.

The Labour Government considered that this ruling went too far in protecting the rights of defendants at the expense of the rights of witnesses. Following the House of Lords' judgment, it quickly pushed through Parliament emergency legislation, the Criminal Evidence (Witness Anonymity) Act 2008, which allowed witnesses in sensitive criminal trials to give evidence anonymously. This Act has now been replaced by more detailed provisions for the protection of anonymous witnesses in the Coroners and Justice Act 2009.

The Home Office has undertaken research into the use of special measures by the courts: *Are Special Measures Working? Evidence from Surveys of Vulnerable and Intimidated Witnesses* (2004a). This found that a large number of witnesses are getting the benefit of these special measures. The vast majority of people who used these arrangements to give evidence

> found them helpful, particularly live link TV and video-recorded evidence. One-third of witnesses using special measures said that they would not have been willing and able to give evidence without them.
>
> The downside of these methods of giving evidence is that it can look less convincing in court compared to the witness giving evidence and answering questions directly in the courtroom. Hearing evidence from a video can create a distance between the victim and the jury, and the real experience of the victim can seem more like a story on television.

Even when the miscarriages of justice were finally uncovered, a lingering 'whispering campaign' suggested that the victims of those miscarriages had been let off on some kind of technicality – that there had been police misbehaviour, but that those accused of the bombings and so on were really guilty. Again, tabloid newspapers were only too pleased to contribute to this view. On the day that the report of the Royal Commission on Criminal Justice was published, the *Daily Mail* printed an article entitled 'The true victims of injustice'. In it, victims of the bombings expressed anger that the Guildford Four and the Birmingham Six had been released – as though justice for those wrongly convicted of a crime somehow meant less justice for the victims of that crime – and raised doubts as to their innocence. The newspaper commented that 'the decent majority' were more concerned to see measures designed to convict criminals than to prevent further miscarriages of justice.

On the other hand, in the case of Stephen Lawrence, the young black student murdered at a bus stop in south London in an apparently racially motivated attack, one branch of the media saw itself as a vital tool in fighting for justice. The refusal of five youths, whom many suspected to be the murderers, to give evidence at the coroner's court led to the *Daily Mail* labelling them as the killers on its front pages, despite the fact that they had already been acquitted by a criminal court.

The implications of all this for the criminal justice system are important. Clearly such a system does not operate in a vacuum and, in jury trials in particular, public opinion can never really be kept out of the courtroom. That does not mean that juries should not be used in emotive cases, nor that the media should be gagged. What it does mean is that, in those cases which arouse strong public opinion, the police, the prosecution, judges and defence lawyers must all be extra vigilant to ensure that the natural desire to find a culprit does not take the place of the need to find the truth – and to make clear to juries that they must do the same. To that end, the Judicial Studies Board, a panel set up to review and encourage best practice in such areas, has provided guidance in such areas – juries are given very detailed legal directions in such cases. Recently, perhaps belatedly, the Courts have begun issuing to juries written instructions on how to approach such different topics. In addition, measures must be taken to prevent 'trial by newspaper' – the Contempt of Court Act 1981 already provides powers in this respect but, in using these powers, the courts must be able to take into account the profits to be made from crime 'scoops' by newspapers, and punish breaches of the law accordingly. Rather than impose fines, which can be paid from the increased profits, preventing newspapers from publishing for a day or more might be a greater deterrent.

Fears that the media are prejudicing the course of justice led the Labour Government to issue a consultation document on proposals to ban payments by the media to potential witnesses in criminal trials. The issue was highlighted by breaches of the Press Complaints Commission's Code of Practice during the trial of Rosemary West. The Code of Practice has

Figure 19.5 Trends in confidence in the Criminal Justice System, Crime Survey of England and Wales 2007/08 to 2013/14

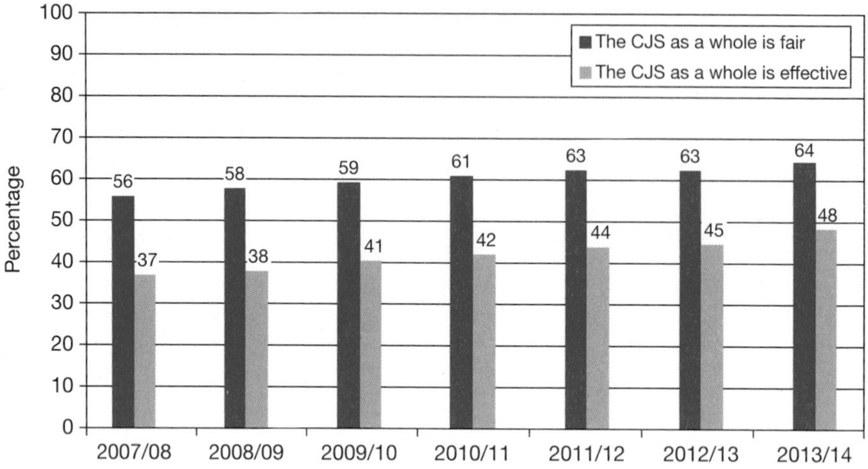

Source: Page 3, Ministry of Justice, Analytical Summary 2015, available at https://www.gov.uk/government/uploads/system/uploads/attachment_data/file/449444/public-confidence.pdf

since been tightened up to ban any payments to potential witnesses. Under the Courts Act 2003, newspapers which publish material that causes trials to collapse can now be punished with a heavy fine. Also, under the Coroners and Justice Act 2009, a civil exploitation proceeds order can be made against convicted criminals who seek to derive a financial benefit from exploiting material connected to their crime. For example, if a murderer published an autobiography, the profits from this book can be confiscated.

The Bigger Picture: Television in court

Televisions have been allowed in many American courts since 1953. While many people in England watched on television parts of the trial of Michael Jackson's doctor for manslaughter, television cameras have historically not been allowed in English courts. The Government published a consultation paper, *Broadcasting Courts* (2004). This paper considered whether television cameras should be allowed into courts so that the public can gain an insight into the workings of the law, in order to educate the public and to boost their confidence in the court system. The Lord Chancellor commented:

> Most people's knowledge and perception of what goes on in court comes from court reporting and from fictionalized accounts of trials. But the medium that gives most access to most people, television, is not allowed in court. Is there a public interest in allowing people, through television, to see what actually happens in our courts in their name?

For the first time ever, cameras were permitted into an English courtroom when a pilot study was carried out in the Court of Appeal. Criminal and civil cases were filmed and edited for mock news pieces and documentaries. These pictures were not broadcast to the public, but circulated to Ministers, senior judges and representatives from legal professional bodies so that they could consider their impact. Post-pilot, broadcasting continues, with cases filmed regularly and sometimes used by news bulletins.

The response to the consultation paper was mixed, with the views of respondents very much split over the issue. The conclusions of research into TV cameras in court are generally quite mixed. Research by William Petkanas (1990) found that public confidence did not increase as a result of having cameras in court. Roberta Entner's research (1993) suggested that the emphasis of courtroom broadcasting was on entertainment at the expense of impartiality, with the defendant being presented unfairly. The Lord Chancellor has commented:

> We don't want our courts turned into US-style media circuses. We will not have OJ Simpson-style trials in Britain. Justice should be seen to be done. But our priority must be that justice is done.

Television cameras are now allowed into the Supreme Court but in practice the public have not been very interested in watching this. A judge in Scotland was filmed for the first time handing down his sentence in a murder case. It was not broadcast live but shortly afterwards on the same day so that it could be edited. All the background noise was deleted, including the shouts from the public gallery when the murderer was led away to prison. There were no pictures of the murderer himself or of the public gallery where the victim's family were sitting; instead the focus was purely on the judge, who spoke with a quiet, calm voice. This is not really what the public want to see; the public want to watch the full drama of the courtroom, with all its potential emotion, tension and anger.

Provisions are contained in the Crime and Courts Act 2013 allowing the Lord Chancellor to make regulations permitting television cameras into courtrooms. Regulations have been made which permit broadcasting of the opening and closing legal arguments and judgments in the Court of Appeal. This may later be extended to judges' sentencing remarks at the Crown Court, and a three-month trial was launched across eight courts in England and Wales in June 2016 to pilot this. Detailed evaluation will follow. Victims, witnesses, offenders and jurors were not to be filmed, and safeguards put in place to ensure victims were supported and the administration of justice unaffected. The trial itself would not be broadcast, partly because if only select extracts were screened (such as the prosecution case) from a lengthy trial, there is a risk that the viewer could get a very one-sided view of the case. The Government is anxious that the reporting must not give offenders opportunities for theatrical public display.

The trial of Anders Breivik for the mass murder of 77 people in Norway showed some of the pitfalls of televising criminal court cases. When the defendant's handcuffs were removed he did a clenched fist salute (an implicitly political statement that he was involved in a popular struggle). Television broadcasting was temporarily stopped as a result, which was unfortunate when one of his arguments was that there was no freedom of expression in Norway.

19.13.11 Recommendations of Sir Robin Auld

In his *Review of the Criminal Courts* (2001) Sir Robin Auld made a wide range of recommendations, some of which have already been considered at relevant points in this text. Other interesting recommendations have included codification, increased use of information technology and the introduction of standard timetables.

Codification

Sir Robin Auld recommended that the law covering offences, court procedures, evidence and sentencing should be codified. This would make the law simpler and more accessible for the legal professions and members of the public to whom these rules can be applied.

The Lord Chief Justice's Report for 2016 announced that the Criminal Procedure Rule Committee was close to finishing the collating of all materials relating to the conduct of criminal proceedings. This will now be available in one document: *The Rules and Practice Directions.* The Law Commission continue to work on codifying the law of sentencing. The final report and draft Bill was published in November 2018; it is now a matter for the Government to decide whether to enact the Sentencing Code.

Information technology

Sir Robin Auld emphasised the need for much greater use to be made of information technology in the criminal justice system. He was particularly keen to see the introduction of single electronic case files, managed by a new criminal case management agency.

Lord Justice Leveson produced a report, *Review of Efficiency in Criminal Proceedings* (2015), in which he placed a strong emphasis on the use of IT to simplify court procedure. For example, he recommended that adequate IT should be provided for preparatory Crown Court hearings to take place out of court. The Crown Court Digital Case System enables the easy online exchange of information and evidence between parties and the court. In 2016 the Government announced a plan to digitise criminal case handling via the *Transforming Our Justice System* report. This stated that the digitisation of the entire criminal justice system was underway, in partnership with the Crown Prosecution Service and the police, and was due to be completed in 2019. Investment in this venture has been set at £270 million. Among its aims, the report notes that:

> All participants in a case, from the judge to the jurors, the Crown Prosecution Service and the defence, legal advisers and court staff, will soon become 'digital by default'.

More generally the plan is for current paper and court-based practices to be moved online wherever possible, in order to save time and increase efficiency. The *Transforming Our Justice System* vision for Her Majesty's Courts and Tribunals Service (HMCTS) looks to increase the use of video link and telephone/video conferencing technology. In order to make the courts more convenient and efficient (as well as cheaper), there is a real possibility that, in cases where offenders are to plead guilty, they could go on to be convicted and sentenced without going to court. The process would take place entirely by video link between the court and the police station where they are held. More controversial is the proposal that for low-level, summary, non-imprisonable offences with no identifiable victim, defendants should be able to log on to view the evidence against them and enter a plea for the offence. Concerns during the initial consultation included: there being no facility for mitigating circumstances to be considered; and safeguarding those citizens who may be unable to understand the system (the elderly, people with learning difficulties, those with low literacy or English language skills and those who cannot access a computer). A pilot of this scheme pushed ahead in 2017 for railway fare evasion; HMCTS collaborating with London Transport in a paperless operation.

Standard timetables

The Auld Review proposed that there should be a move away from all forms of pre-trial hearings. Instead, standard timetables would be issued and the parties would be required to cooperate with each other in order to comply with these timetables. There would then be a written or electronic 'pre-trial assessment' by the court (discretionary for the magistrates' court) of the parties' readiness for trial. Only if the court or the parties are unable to resolve all matters in this way would there be a pre-trial hearing.

Video-recorded evidence

The traditional approach to evidence from a witness is for them to give live evidence in court under questioning from lawyers. Today, in some cases, the courts will allow a video-recording to be used of the witness being questioned by the police. Westera *et al.* (2013) carried out research on the use of video-recorded evidence in rape trials in New Zealand. They concluded that the evidence from the video-recording was significantly more detailed than that provided by live witnesses. Over two-thirds of the details in the video-recording that were central to establishing innocence or guilt were later omitted from live evidence. The police approach of using open questions generated longer narrative answers which were more complete than the lawyers managed in court. The police were also questioning soon after the offence had been committed, so the facts were fresh in the witness's mind and the interview room was less formal than the court. The researchers concluded that the video interview provides the most complete evidence from a witness, and hence may improve just outcomes if used as evidence in court.

Pilots into pre-recording of cross-examinations of children and other vulnerable witnesses have been rolled out in Crown Courts across the country. This initiative forms part of the joint vision paper *Transforming Our Justice System* (2016), launched by the Lord Chancellor, the Senior President of Tribunals and the Lord Chief Justice. Benefits include reducing distress for vulnerable witnesses (and victims) but also greater efficiencies – early observations of the pilots showed evidence was given in half the time it would take at trial.

Unrepresented defendants, legal aid and LASPO

Access to justice – Will we all pay the price?

In 2018 a report commissioned by the (naturally conservative) Bar Council stated that an observer might well conclude that the UK Government has taken 'a conscious decision to substantially withdraw public funding for the support of the justice system and promoting access to justice'. The report, written by Professor Chalkley, is suggesting that the reduction in funds to the justice system is a political strategy and not a necessity at all.

As a result of the report a bombshell speech was made by Andrew Walker QC, Chair of the Bar, on 24 November 2018. He spoke about access to justice and asked the audience:

> . . . can we tolerate this state of affairs? We have had a huge withdrawal of public support from a fundamental part of the state's functions and obligations. Our politicians and the public have a choice to make. They must make it wisely. If they take all this for granted, then I fear that we will all pay the price.

How did we get here? Before the introduction of LASPO, legal aid in Crown Court proceedings was available for all defendants.

In 2012 the Ministry of Justice introduced reforms to legal aid under the Legal Aid, Sentencing and Punishment of Offenders (LASPO) Act. The Act was designed to reduce spending on legal aid, and to promote alternatives to litigation. Regarding criminal legal aid it included one significant change in respect of the Crown Court. Defendants whose disposable household income was £37,500 or more, were not eligible at all for criminal legal aid. This meant that if a person is accused of a crime, and their familial disposable income is more than £37,500, that person would not get legal aid. This means that they would have to pay a barrister or solicitor's firm private rates. These rates are significantly more expensive than legal aid rates. If there was a trial and the defendant was found not guilty then the defendant would only recover legal aid rates from the state. The defendant could be left many thousands of pounds in debt. Nigel Evans, Conservative MP for the Ribble Valley in Lancashire was left £130,000 out of pocket when he was found not guilty of sexual offences. The Secret Barrister calls this 'the innocence tax'. Inevitably, this has caused an increase in unrepresented defendants in the Crown Court. Not only has legal aid been removed from defendants but investment into court buildings has ground to a halt with reports of trials being stopped due to collapsing ceilings, leaks and rodents being a daily feature of working in the criminal justice system. Transform Justice, a charity, reported that Lady Justice Macur, the Senior Presiding Judge for England and Wales, agreed that conditions are 'scandalous – court estate cells sometimes have no heating' and that she has had, on occasion, to order them to be closed. The Lord Chief Justice in his 2017 annual report wrote that 'the public should not be expected to visit dilapidated buildings and neither is it reasonable to expect staff or judges to work in conditions which would not be tolerated elsewhere', and partly blamed the dilapidation for the low morale of the judiciary. There is investment in technology but there is reported concern that this may in fact compromise justice. The chair of the Bar reiterated that technology must be used as 'a tool, not as an end in itself, or as a misplaced attempt to supplant human advice and judgment and it need not and must not mean compromising on justice itself'.

In 2017 the Bar Council of England and Wales commissioned the aforementioned research study by Professor Chalkley. He found that 'whilst the last decade has been characterised as one of austerity, it is nevertheless a period during which the economy has grown both in cash and in real terms', and stated that it would not be unreasonable for the justice system to grow along with the economy. He concluded that the Ministry of Justice accounted for only 1 per cent of government spending. He found that the overall reduction in cash and real terms for the Ministry of Justice in the 10 years from 2008–2018 was approaching 30 per cent. The biggest losers within the Ministry of Justice were legal aid with a 32 per cent real decline and the Youth Justice Board with a staggering 79 per cent real decline. What do we make from this? It is certainly a fact that a 32 per cent decline in real terms is a choice and that the suggestion that it is a political strategy may not be as far-fetched as it may initially appear.

In 2015 the Ministry of Justice commissioned a report on unrepresented defendants in the Crown Courts. This was not published. The full report was eventually released, two years after it was created and after repeated requests to the Information Commissioner. The report was utterly damning, reported Buzzfeed News UK senior reporter Emily Dugan, in both demonstrating that removing legal aid did nothing to save money because the cases took longer but also that the right to a fair trial was being compromised for defendants. It also revealed that unrepresented defendants were risking the 'dignity of complainants and the safety of members of the prosecution team'.

In the report, Crown Court judges and CPS representatives were interviewed and their concerns regarding the risks to a fair trial were recorded. Describing the risk to unrepresented defendants, one judge described a lay person performing their own advocacy as: 'It's like saying if you felt unwell would you want to go and ask someone with no medical qualification how to cure yourself.' A judicial interviewee clearly stated that a lay person could not follow the intricacies of a Crown Court trial: 'Some of them just sit there looking like a rabbit in the headlights and they have not got a clue what is going on and you really have to check that they are following and are in a position to make any relevant comments they need to. Others will be jumping up every five seconds even when it's not their turn to talk.' It is a reported concern of the judiciary that unrepresented defendants were getting more punitive sentences as a result of not understanding how to mitigate or that they are entering a plea to the wrong offence. Some CPS interviewees said that they were concerned that an unrepresented defendant may not get a fair trial, as they are not properly qualified to put their case forward. This raises the question: are unrepresented defendants having a fair trial and is Article 6 of ECHR being breached? The hypothesis being, no they are not and yes, it is.

Giving evidence in court can be traumatic. There is evidence that unrepresented defendants are making this experience traumatic for complainants. A judge interviewed by Ministry of Justice researchers described that the impact of witnesses being questioned by a defendant is 'almost like committing the offence all over again'. The MoJ report described judges giving examples of defendants being 'aggressive, rude, and asking unnecessary questions'. The common perception of these interviewees was 'that this led to an unpleasant cross examination experience for witnesses'.

Although the element of danger was not covered in the report, it must be considered. Some unrepresented defendants are people in the Crown Courts charged with serious criminal offences. Some of them may be dangerous. If there is no defence representative, then the prosecutor will have to liaise directly with the defendant, something that would never happen when the defendant is represented. The behaviour of some defendants towards prosecutors was been described as 'openly hostile'.

Alarmingly it seemed that no money was being saved by removing access to legal aid. All the CPS and nearly all judicial interviewees thought unrepresented hearings take longer than those with legal representation. Some interviewees said they usually last double the time, one said half as much again. Interviewees also stated that they believed that unrepresented defendant numbers have increased, and this is disproportionally reducing the efficiency of courts.

Perhaps we can reflect on the words of the chair of the Bar: 'in truth, in the last two decades, we have been following a course that has set its face against justice, by political design, political folly and political expediency. This now presents a huge threat to access to justice in our country.' If we take it for granted, will we all pay the price?

19

THE CRIMINAL TRIAL PROCESS

Answering questions

1   Why was the Crown Prosecution Service created and how successful has the CPS proved to be?

2   Who, in the UK, has the authority to decide whether a defendant should be prosecuted?

3   Peter has been charged with murder.

   (a) Explain the role of his solicitor and barrister as his case progresses through the courts;

   (b) Describe the work of the Crown Prosecution Service in relation to his case; and

   (c) What criticisms have been made of the Crown Prosecution Service?

4   Can plea bargaining ever be justified?

For answers to these questions, visit the companion website at www.pearsoned.co.uk/ elliottquinn

SUMMARY OF CHAPTER 19: THE CRIMINAL TRIAL PROCESS

The adversarial process

The English system of criminal justice can be described as adversarial. This means each side is responsible for putting their own case. The judge is impartial. The adversarial system is typical of common law countries. The alternative is an inquisitorial system, which exists in most of the rest of Europe.

Criminal Procedure Rules

In 2005, the main rules on criminal procedure that apply to the trial and pre-trial process were brought together in new Criminal Procedure Rules.

The Crown Prosecution Service

Most prosecutions are now brought by the Crown Prosecution Service. Significant reforms of this body were introduced following the Glidewell Report, which was published in 1998.

Appearance in court

Persons charged with an offence can be called to court by means of a summons, or by a charge following arrest without a warrant.

Classification of offences

There are three different categories of offence: summary offences, indictable offences and offences triable either way.

Mode of trial

Where a person is charged with a triable either way offence, they can insist on a trial by jury, otherwise the decision is for the magistrates.

Disclosure

The issue of disclosure is concerned with the responsibility of the prosecution and defence to reveal information related to the case prior to the trial.

Plea bargaining

Plea bargaining is the name given to negotiations between the prosecution and defence lawyers over the outcome of a case.

The trial

Apart from the role played by the jury in the Crown Court, the law and procedure in the Crown Court and magistrates' court are essentially the same. The burden of proof is on the prosecution.

Models of criminal justice systems

The academic, Herbert Packer (1968) has identified two quite different potential aims for criminal justice systems: the 'due process' model; and the 'crime control' model.

Criticism and reform

The following issues have been the subject of particular debate:

Racism and the CPS

The CPS is failing to weed out weak cases against ethnic minorities.

Racism and the courts

Over recent years members of the ethnic minorities are increasingly satisfied that the criminal courts are racially impartial.

The Lammy Review

David Lammy's 2017 review of the treatment of BAME individuals in the criminal justice system found there to be a disproportionate number of BAME prisoners and a 'chronic trust deficit' among BAME individuals towards the police, their own solicitors and magistrates.

The Crown Prosecution Service

The CPS ran into problems from the very beginning and has continued to be the subject of much controversy.

Cracked and ineffective trials

The Government has been concerned by the problem of 'cracked and ineffective trials'.

Conviction rates

Recent years have seen a large rise in reported crime but falling conviction rates.

Victims and witnesses

There is now a growing awareness that the criminal justice system has paid insufficient attention to the needs of victims and witnesses of crime.

Reading list

Audit Commission (2003) *Victims and Witnesses.* London: Audit Commission.

Auld, Sir R. (2001) *Review of the Criminal Courts.* London: HMSO.

Committee of Public Accounts (2005) *Facing justice: tackling defendants' non-attendance at court.* 22nd Report, HC 103. London: Stationery Office.

Criminal Justice System Race Unit (2005) *Race and the Criminal Justice System: An Overview to the Complete Statistics 2003–2004.* London: Criminal Justice System Race Unit.

Darbyshire, P. (2014) Judicial case management in ten Crown Courts. *Criminal Law Review,* 30.

Dennis, I. (2018) Prosecution disclosure: are the problems insoluble? *Criminal Law Review* 829

Department for Constitutional Affairs (2004a) *Broadcasting Courts.* CP28/04. London: DCA.

Duff, A., Farmer, L., Marshall, S. and Tadros, V. (2007) *The Trial on Trial (Volume 3): Towards a Normative Theory of the Criminal Trial.* Oxford: Hart.

Enright, S. (1993) Cost effective criminal justice. *New Law Journal,* 143: 1023.

Entner, R. (1993) Encoding the Image of the American Judiciary Institution: A Semiotic Analysis of the Broadcast Trials to Ascertain Its Definition of the Court System. PhD thesis. New York: New York University.

Glidewell, Sir I. (1998) *Review of the Crown Prosecution Service.* Cm 3960. London: Stationery Office.

Hall, M. (2010) The relationship between victims and prosecutors: defending victims' rights? *Criminal Law Review,* 31.

Hedderman, C. and Hough, M. (1994) *Does the Criminal Justice System Treat Men and Women Differently?* London: Home Office Research and Planning Unit.

Hedderman, C. and Moxon, D. (1992) *Magistrates' Court or Crown Court? Mode of Trial Decisions and Sentencing.* London: HMSO.

Herbert, A. (2003) Mode of trial and magistrates' sentencing powers: will increased powers inevitably lead to a reduction in the committal rate? *Criminal Law Review,* 314.

Home Office (2001) *Criminal Justice: The Way Ahead.* Cm 5074. London: Stationery Office.

(2003b) *Statistics on Women and the Criminal Justice System.* London: Home Office.

(2004a) *Are Special Measures Working? Evidence from Surveys of Vulnerable and Intimidated Witnesses.* Home Office Research Study 283. London: Home Office.

(2004c) *One Step Ahead: A 21st Century Strategy to Defeat Organised Crime.* London: Stationery Office.

(2007a) *Modernising Police Powers: Review of the Police and Criminal Evidence Act 1984.* London: Home Office.

Hood, R., Shute, S. and Seemungal, F. (2003) *Ethnic Minorities in the Criminal Courts: Perceptions of Fairness and Equality of Treatment.* London: Lord Chancellor's Department.

Hungerford-Welch, P. (2019) Criminal Procedure and Sentencing (9th edition). London: Routledge.

Jeremy, D. (2008) The prosecutor's rock and hard place. *Criminal Law Review,* 925.

Jones, D. and Brown, J. (2010) The relationship between victims and prosecutors: defending victims' rights? A CPS response. *Criminal Law Review,* 212.

JUSTICE (1970) *The Prosecution in England and Wales.* London: JUSTICE.

Law Commission (2011a) *Expert Evidence in Criminal Proceedings in England and Wales.* London: Law Commission.

Leigh, L. and Zedner, L. (1992) *A Report on the Administration of Criminal Justice in the Pretrial Phase in London, France and Germany*. London: HMSO.

Lippke, R. (2011) *The Ethics of Plea Bargaining*. Oxford: Oxford University Press.

Mansfield, M. (1993) *Presumed Guilty: The British Legal System Exposed*. London: Heinemann.

McConville, M. (1992) Videotaping interrogations: police behaviour on and off camera. *Criminal Law Review*, 532.

McConville, M. and Baldwin, J. (1977) *Negotiated Justice: Pressures to Plead Guilty*. Oxford: Martin Robertson.

(1981) *Courts, Prosecution and Conviction*. Oxford: Oxford University Press.

McConville, M., Sanders, A. and Leng, R. (1991) *The Case for the Prosecution*. London: Routledge, especially Ch.35.

Moxon, D. and Crisp, D. (1994) *Case Screening by the Crown Prosecution Service: How and Why Cases are Terminated*. London: HMSO.

Narey, M. (1997) *Review of Delay in the Criminal Justice System*. London: Home Office.

National Audit Office (1999) *Criminal Justice: Working Together*. London: Stationery Office.

(2006) *CPS: Effective Use of Magistrates' Court Hearings*. London: Stationery Office.

Office for Criminal Justice Reform (2004) *Cutting Crime, Delivering Justice: A Strategic Plan for Criminal Justice 2004–08*. Cm 6288. London: Home Office.

Packer, H. (1968) *The Limits of the Criminal Sanction*. Stanford, CA: Stanford University Press.

Petkanas, W. (1990) Cameras on Trial: An Assessment of the Educational Affect of News Cameras in Trial Courts. PhD thesis. New York: New York University.

Philips, C. (1981) *The Royal Commission on Criminal Procedure*, Cmnd 8092, London: HMSO.

Quirk, H. (2006) The significance of culture in criminal procedure reform: why the revised disclosure scheme cannot work. *International Journal of Evidence and Proof*, 10: 42.

Ridout, F. (2010) Virtual courts – virtual justice? *JPN*, 174: 602.

The Secret Barrister (2018) *Stories of the Law and How It's Broken*. Pan Macmillan.

Vennard, J. (1985) The outcome of contested trials. In: Moxon, D. (ed.) *Managing Criminal Justice*. London: HMSO.

Westera, N., Kebbell, M. and Milne, B. (2013) Losing two thirds of the story: a comparison of the video-recorded police interview and live evidence of rape complainants. *Criminal Law Review*, 290.

Zander, M. (2006) Mission impossible. *New Law Journal*, 156: 618.

(2007d) Change of PACE. *New Law Journal*, 157: 504.

Zander, M. and Henderson, P. (1993) *Crown Court Study*. London: HMSO.

19

THE CRIMINAL TRIAL PROCESS

On the internet

The executive summary of the *Joint Thematic Review of the New Charging Arrangements* carried out by Her Majesty's Inspectorate of Constabulary 1 (HMIC) and Her Majesty's Crown Prosecution Service Inspectorate is available on the internet at:

https://www.justiceinspectorates.gov.uk/cjji/inspections/joint-thematic-review-of-the-new-charging-arrangements/

The Code of Practice for Victims of Crime (2015) is published at:

> https://www.gov.uk/government/uploads/system/uploads/attachment_data/file/476900/code-of-practice-for-victims-of-crime.PDF

The Home Office statistical bulletin *Crime in England and Wales* is published on the website of the Office for National Statistics at:

> https://www.ons.gov.uk/peoplepopulationandcommunity/crimeandjustice/bulletins/crimeinenglandandwales/previousReleases

The Code for Crown Prosecutors is available on the Crown Prosecution Service's website at:

> http://www.cps.gov.uk

The Witness summons report, *Witness for the Prosecution* (2016) is available on the website of HM Crown Prosecution Service Inspectorate at:

> https://www.justiceinspectorates.gov.uk/hmcpsi/inspections/witness-summons/

The Victim and Witness Information website is:

> https://www.victimandwitnessinformation.org.uk/

The Lammy Review: An independent review into the treatment of, and outcomes for, Black, Asian and Minority Ethnic individuals in the Criminal Justice System (2017) is available at:

> https://assets.publishing.service.gov.uk/government/uploads/system/uploads/attachment_data/file/643001/lammy-review-final-report.pdf

The Ministry of Justice vision paper *Transforming Our Justice System* (2016) is available at:

> https://assets.publishing.service.gov.uk/government/uploads/system/uploads/attachment_data/file/553261/joint-vision-statement.pdf

The report by Rt Hon Sir Brian Leveson, *Review of Efficiency in Criminal Proceedings* (2015) can be found at:

> https://www.judiciary.gov.uk/wp-content/uploads/2015/01/review-of-efficiency-in-criminal-proceedings-20151.pdf

The Criminal Cases Review Commission's annual lecture for 2018 was given by Sir Brian Leveson on *The Pursuit of Criminal Justice* (2018). It is accessible online:

> https://www.judiciary.uk/wp-content/uploads/2018/04/speech-leveson-ccrc-lecture-april-2018.pdf

The CPS and the Met Police collaborated on *A Joint Review of the Disclosure Process in the case of R v Allan* (January 2018), which is available at:

> https://www.cps.gov.uk/sites/default/files/documents/publications/joint-review-disclosure-Allan.pdf

Ministry of Justice *Virtual Court pilot Outcome evaluation* (December 2010) (authors Terry, Johnson and Thompson), Ministry of Justice Research Series 21/10 is available online:

> https://assets.publishing.service.gov.uk/government/uploads/system/uploads/attachment_data/file/193633/virtual-courts-pilot-outcome-evaluation.pdf

The Transform Justice report by Penelope Gibbs (2017) *Defendants on video – conveyor belt justice or a revolution in access?* can be found via:

> http://www.transformjustice.org.uk/wp-content/uploads/2017/10/Disconnected-Thumbnail-2.pdf

The Commons Select Committee report on *Disclosure of Evidence in Criminal Cases* (July 2018) is available at:

> https://publications.parliament.uk/pa/cm201719/cmselect/cmjust/859/85905.htm

The report commissioned by the Bar Council, *Funding for Justice 2008 to 2018: Justice in the age of austerity* by Martin Chalkley (Nov 2018) is accessible via:

> https://www.barcouncil.org.uk/media/688940/funding_for_justice-_the_last_10_years_version_-_professor_martin_chalkley.pdf

Another Transform Justice report of interest is *Justice denied? The experience of unrepresented defendants in the criminal courts* (April 2016). Access it via:

> http://www.transformjustice.org.uk/wp-content/uploads/2016/04/TJ-APRIL_Singles.pdf

The Ministry of Justice report on *Unrepresented Defendants: Perceived effects on the Crown Court in England and Wales and indicative volumes in magistrates' courts* (Feb 2016) can be found at:

> https://www.documentcloud.org/documents/4489882-DRAFT-29-02-16-Unrepresented-Defendants.html

The speech to the Annual Bar and Young Bar Conference by Chair of the Bar, Andrew Walker QC (November 2018) can be found at:

> https://www.barcouncil.org.uk/media/693814/awqc_chair_s_speech_to_annual_bar_conference_2018.pdf

The speech to the Annual Bar and Young Bar Conference by Chair of the Bar, Andrew Walker QC (November 2018) can be found at:

> https://www.barcouncil.org.uk/media/693814/awqc_chair_s_speech_to_annual_bar_conference_2018.pdf

The Crown Court Compendium (updated December 2018) is available at:

> https://www.judiciary.uk/publications/crown-court-compendium-published-december-2018/

Buzzfeed's Emily Dugan piece on the Government's attempt to hide judges' warnings about defendants without a lawyer is available at:

> https://www.buzzfeed.com/emilydugan/the-government-tried-to-conceal-this-testimony-from-judges

The Justice Committee report, *Disclosure of evidence in criminal cases inquiry* (2018) is accessible via:

> https://www.parliament.uk/business/committees/committees-a-z/commons-select/justice-committee/inquiries/parliament-2017/disclosure-criminal-cases-17-19/

Find out more about the work of the Centre for Criminal Appeals at:

> http://www.criminalappeals.org.uk/

Chapter 20
Sentencing

'Restorative justice' can be a replacement for criminal proceedings altogether or it can be part of a custodial or community sentence. It can also be part of a deferred sentence. The Ministry of Justice describes restorative justice as 'the process that brings those harmed by crime, and those responsible for the harm, into communication, enabling everyone affected by a particular incident to play a part in repairing the harm and finding a positive way forward'.

The Government has based their 'vision' for restorative justice on John Braithwaite's work on 'the good society', stating that the fundamental 'element is the dialogue between the victim and the offender. With crime, restorative justice is about the idea that because crime hurts, justice should heal. It follows that conversations with those who have been hurt and with those who have afflicted the harm must be central to the process'.

Intensive research was carried out into the effectiveness of restorative justice, which was published in a report called *Restorative Justice: The Evidence* (Sherman and Strang, 2007). This concluded that many violent criminals are less likely to commit further offences after participating in a restorative justice programme. The victim's symptoms of post-traumatic stress were reduced, it was argued partly because meeting their offender demystified the offence. Restorative justice was also found to be cheaper than traditional criminal sentences. Research carried out by Professor Joanna Shapland (2008) found that offenders who participated in restorative justice were reconvicted for significantly fewer offences in the subsequent two years than those who had not. The research concluded that restorative justice provides an opportunity for offenders who want to put a stop to their criminal lifestyle to use the process to gain support for that decision, particularly where the outcome of the process is an agreement targeting problems relating to their reoffending. As regards the question of value for money, the conclusions of the research are mixed, with one scheme saving a significant amount of money but two others not leading to any savings, though there were high levels of victim and offender satisfaction. For a discussion of some of the potential limitations of restorative justice, see Gerry Johnstone's article, *Restorative Justice For Victims: Inherent Limits?* Here, a tension is discussed between the two objectives of restorative justice that are seen as 'helping offenders to become really aware of the harm their actions have caused and helping victims to recover from the trauma they have suffered as a result of a crime' and a suggestion that the goal of reforming offenders may inadvertently be prioritised over helping victims of crime. The CRCs (Community Rehabilitation Companies) who are tasked with delivering restorative justice have no formal responsibility for victims and supporting them is not part of their remit. Furthermore, as CRCs are paid by results and many are reported to be struggling, it is not surprising that restorative justice may not focus on the victims sufficiently.

20.2 Sentencing practice

The jury is not involved in the sentencing procedure. It is the trial judge or magistrates who determine the appropriate sentence.

On conviction in the magistrates' court, the magistrates can determine the sentence themselves or, with certain more serious offences, the defendant can be committed to the Crown Court for sentence. If sentenced by the magistrates' court, the maximum sentence that can be imposed for a summary offence is 6 months.

Once the defendant has been convicted, it must be decided first what category of sentence is appropriate and then the amount, duration and form of that sentence.

20.2.1 Guidance for sentencers

In recent years there has been a considerable amount of legislation that guides the sentencing practices of judges, the aim of this being said to develop transparency and consistency in sentencing.

20.2.2 Legislation

Parliamentary legislation has, for a minority of offences, fixed the sentence that must be imposed. Since 1997 it has applied minimum sentences to some offenders.

20.2.3 Mandatory sentences

Certain offences have mandatory sentences that are required by law to be given when committed. The most notable example of this is murder, which has a mandatory sentence of life imprisonment. A court passing a mandatory life sentence must make an order specifying the time that the prisoner must serve before being considered for parole. Where the offender was aged 21 or over at the time of the offence, and the court thinks the offence is so serious that the offender ought to spend the rest of their life in prison, they can make what is known as a 'whole life order'.

A court must impose an automatic life sentence where an offender has been convicted of two very serious, violent or sexual offences. This could be described as a 'two strikes and you're out' policy. A life sentence need not be imposed if it is unjust in all the circumstances. It will be rare that the conditions for the automatic life sentence will be satisfied.

20.2.4 Minimum sentences

For some offences, minimum sentences are prescribed by law. Minimum sentences have been seen as politically populist as they 'show' the public that the Government of the day is tough on crime.

Minimum sentences were introduced in 2003 to tackle the growing problem of criminals using guns, but arguably have caught within their definition defendants to whom they are inappropriate to apply. The Firearms Act minimum provisions are the most misapplied – with a large percentage of cases found to be 'exceptional', this allows the judge to avoid imposing a five-year sentence. The minimum sentence is in place for the purposes of deterrence but a report from the Centre for Crime and Justice Studies, *'Gun crime' A review of evidence and policy* (2008), found 'no compelling evidence' that the imposition of mandatory minimum sentences addressed the wider causes of such violence. The five-year sentence was imposed on the defendant (a grandmother) in the Scottish case of **Cochrane v HM Advocate** (2010). In this case, the defendant was in possession of a Second World War handgun brought back by her father after his active service. She owned no ammunition for the gun and had rarely removed it from its box, despite her father dying 28 years earlier. She was also unaware of the requirement for a firearms licence. Exceptional circumstances were considered, and her sentence was reduced on appeal.

20.3 Guidance for the court when sentencing

In most sentencing exercises Courts use two sources of guidance: judgments of the Court of Appeal (consolidated judicial guidance), and the guidelines put down by the Sentencing Council.

20.3.1 Sentencing guidelines

Sentencing guidelines are designed to enable the courts to approach sentencing from a common starting point and enable practitioners and the public to know the starting point for each offence. They originated from the time when judges in the Court of Appeal laid down sentencing guidelines to assist the lower courts to determine the appropriate sentence for certain types of offence and offender.

In 1998, a Sentencing Advisory Panel was established to assist the Court of Appeal with the development of these guidelines. Some judges were initially unhappy about the imposition of guidelines and others felt that the 'government is too often concerned with votes and the civil service with the Treasury – when it comes to sentencing considerations' (Hough, *Time to rethink the role of the Sentencing Council?*).

The Criminal Justice Act 2003 created a Sentencing Guidelines Council which itself established sentencing guidelines rather than having to pass these on for the Court of Appeal to establish. Judges were instructed that they had to 'have regard' to these guidelines and had to give reasons if they chose to depart from these guidelines.

The Coroners and Justice Act 2009 abolished both the Sentencing Advisory Panel and the Sentencing Guidelines Council and replaced them with the Sentencing Council, which is what we have today. The Sentencing Council describes itself as responsible for developing sentencing guidelines and monitoring their use.

The Council has 14 members: eight are members of the judiciary and six non-judicial with extensive experience in the criminal justice system. Some of the non-judicial members hold or have held part-time judicial posts. There has been some academic criticism of the constitution of the Council and suggestions have been made that it should include more people with experience in helping people with addiction issues and mental health problems, and more people who are involved in the prison system.

This body sets sentencing guidelines and the courts must 'follow' these guidelines unless the judge is satisfied that it would be contrary to the interests of justice to do so. In *R v Blackshaw* (2011), the Court of Appeal stated that the word *follow* does not require *slavish adherence* to the guidelines; the main function of the guidelines was to provide 'starting points' for the court and thereby to foster consistency of approach 'without sacrificing the obligation to do justice in the individual and specific case'. The overriding obligation of the judge is to 'achieve a just result'. Previous guidelines are deemed to be guidelines of the Council, until they are reconsidered.

The guidelines must also include aggravating and mitigating factors to be taken into consideration and these should include criteria, and provide guidance, for determining the weight to be given to previous convictions and such other aggravating or mitigating factors as the Council considers to be of particular significance in relation to the offence or the offender. What also assists is that each offence has its own guideline. The clear step-by-step methodology in determining sentence is explained in the next section. One point that has been noted by many academics and journalists regarding the guidelines is that they provide a more restrictive range than that prescribed by statute. For example, the statutory maximum for actual bodily harm is five years imprisonment, whereas the maximum sentence if a judge follows the guideline is only three years. As the removal of legal aid for many offences has created a considerable number of self-represented defendants concerns have also been raised that these offenders are getting more severe sentences because, without a lawyer, they don't understand the guidelines. Penelope Gibbs of Transform Justice, a national charity working for a 'fair, humane, open and effective justice system', states that 'unrepresented defendants make decisions which can easily lead to a tougher sentence. If they go to trial when there is no chance they will be acquitted, they lose potential credit for a guilty plea. If they accept the "wrong" charge, or if they don't provide the right mitigation, they will get a higher sentence'. Ms Gibbs interviewed judges and prosecutors. One prosecutor stated: 'So poor are unrepresented defendants at mitigation that they sometimes make the situation worse.' Most people, states Ms Gibbs, 'think it is mitigation to say they were drunk at the time. The sentencing guidelines say that is an aggravating feature. 'This suggests that the guidelines are not entirely comprehensible to the lay person and this may work against them in mitigation.

20.3.2 Determining the seriousness of the offence

The Criminal Justice Act 2003 provides that when passing sentence, the court must ensure that it is commensurate with the seriousness of the offence, with seriousness being determined by:

- the culpability of the offender, and
- the harm caused, risked or intended by the offending.

In considering the seriousness of any offence, the court must consider the offender's culpability in committing the offence and any harm which the offence caused, was intended to cause, or might foreseeably have caused.

20.3.3 Steps taken when sentencing using the guidelines

The Sentencing Council state that the key decisions involved in sentencing are:

1 Determining the offence category. The guidelines state that the first step is to determine the offence category by means of an assessment of the offender's culpability and the harm caused, or intended, by reference only to the factors set out at step one in each guideline.

2 Starting point and category range: The guidelines state that they provide a starting point which applies to all offenders irrespective of plea or previous convictions. The guidelines also specify a category range for each offence category. The guidelines provide non-exhaustive lists of aggravating and mitigating factors relating to the context of the offence and to the offender. Sentencers should identify whether any combination of these, or other relevant factors, should result in an upward or downward adjustment from the starting point. In some cases, it may be appropriate to move outside the identified category range when reaching a provisional sentence. Once the sentencer has reached a provisional sentence they may then consider the next steps.

3 The guidelines state that there can be a reduction in sentence for any assistance to the prosecution.

4 The guidelines state that the sentencer should give a reduction for a guilty plea. The court should take account of any potential reduction for a guilty plea in accordance with s. 144 of the Criminal Justice Act 2003 and have regard to the guideline for Reduction in Sentence for a Guilty Plea. The court will reduce the sentence by up to a third if the offender pleads guilty at the first opportunity. It is reduced thereafter on a sliding scale.

5 The guidelines state that where an offender is being sentenced for multiple offences, the court's assessment of the totality of the offending may result in a sentence above the range indicated for the individual offences, including a sentence of a different type. This is called the principal of totality and must have regard to whether the sentence is just and proportionate.

6 The court must then consider compensation and ancillary orders appropriate to the case.

7 The court states its reasons for, and explains the effect of, the sentence. It then gives credit for any time spent on remand.

20.4 Types of sentence

Sentences are divided into five categories: custodial sentences, community sentences, fines, discharges and certain miscellaneous sentences. A custodial or community sentence can only be ordered where the offence is sufficiently serious to justify such a sentence.

20.4.1 Custodial sentences

For a person aged 21 or over, a custodial sentence is a sentence of imprisonment or a suspended sentence. When an offender is 18–20 inclusive, the custodial sentence that is available is detention in a young offenders' institution. For a person under 18, a custodial sentence includes detention in a young offenders' institution or a sentence of custody for life.

A court should not pass a custodial sentence unless it considers that the crime was so serious that only a custodial sentence is justified. Section 153 of the Criminal Justice Act 2003 directs the court to impose the shortest custodial term that is commensurate with the seriousness of the offence(s), subject to certain exceptions. Section 143 of the 2003 Act states that:

> In considering the seriousness of any offence, the court must consider the offender's culpability in committing the offence and any harm which the offence caused, was intended to cause, or might foreseeably have caused.

The court must also consider previous convictions, failure to respond to previous sentences and the commission of an offence while on bail (CJA 2003, s. 143).

If the court decides to suspend the period of imprisonment and impose a suspended sentence, the offender must be told that the court would have had to impose an immediate custodial sentence if the power to suspend were not available. In 2017 the Sentencing Council reported that 53,148 offenders had a suspended sentence order imposed, representing only four per cent of all individuals sentenced.

Where a judge intends to impose a custodial sentence (unless the sentence is fixed by law), a pre-sentence report must normally be prepared by the probation service, containing background information about the offender and the risks they pose. This will assist the judge in selecting the appropriate sentence.

Imprisonment

Most sentences of imprisonment are determinate (for a fixed length of time) but some can be indeterminate (there is no fixed length of time, for example a life sentence). If the offence is very serious and the offender so dangerous that the court feels that they ought never to be released, the offender may be sentenced to a 'whole life order'.

A sentencer passing a mandatory life sentence must normally make an order specifying the minimum number of years to be served before the offender can be considered for release on licence.

It is the case that most offenders who are given immediate custodial sentences do not serve the full sentence in custody. They are released part way through their sentence on licence. When an offender is released on licence this means that the offender will serve the remainder of their sentence in the community supervised by a probation officer. They must also comply with the conditions of the licence. The licence must expire when the sentence expires. Offenders sentenced to life imprisonment when released, will remain on licence for the rest of their lives.

Sentences of imprisonment of less than two years

Where a sentence of less than two years is imposed, the offender must comply with 'supervision requirements' during the 'supervision period'. All short-term prisoners have 12 months' supervision in the community. The supervision period begins with the expiry of the custodial period (the time that the offender has been in prison), and lasts for 12 months. For example, if an offender was sentenced to a six month sentence of imprisonment, they would serve three months in custody. On their release they would have a nine months' licence plus three months' post-sentence supervision. The offender will serve three months of imprisonment and a total of 12 months' supervision.

Sentences of imprisonment of more than two years

A fixed-term prisoner must be released on licence after serving half of their sentence. The licence remains in force for the second-half remainder of the sentence (i.e. the second half). Fixed-term prisoners must comply with the conditions of their licence, for example to be of *good behaviour* and not behave in a way which *undermines the purpose of the licence period*. If the terms of that licence are breached, then the offender can be recalled to prison to serve the remainder or a period of the licence in custody.

Extended sentences

In certain circumstances, a court has the discretion to order an extended sentence. This applies where a person is convicted of a specified offence and when the court considers there to be a significant risk to members of the public of serious harm occasioned by the offender by committing further specified offences. What this means is that instead of the offender being released half way through their sentence on licence, if the court deems the offender to be dangerous, the offender remains in custody and can only be released automatically, or be entitled to apply for parole, at the two thirds point of their custodial sentence. If parole is refused, the offender will be released at the end of the prison term. When the offender is released from custody they are also subject to an extended licence period set by the judge when sentencing the offender at the sentencing hearing. This means that the offender will be on licence, and will be under the supervision of a probation officer until the expiry of the extended period.

The total length of the extended sentence (including the extension period) cannot exceed the maximum sentence for the offence committed.

In 2017, a total of 575 offenders were given an extended sentence.

Life sentences

Most prison sentences are for a fixed term, for example a sentence of five years imprisonment. However, in some scenarios the court can sentence an offender to an indeterminate sentence, a sentence with no fixed period of time. Some indeterminate sentences are mandatory (murder), this means that the judge has no choice but to impose a life sentence. Some are discretionary (for example, rape or robbery), which means that the maximum sentence for the offence is life but the judge may only impose this sentence when appropriate to do so. When imposing a discretionary life sentence, the judge will specify a minimum number of years which the offender must serve before the parole board considers release on licence.

The Bigger Picture: The Parole Board and John Worboys

The Parole Board describes itself as 'an independent body that carries out risk assessments on prisoners to determine whether they can be safely released into the community'. It was established in 1968 under the Criminal Justice Act 1967 and became an independent, executive, non-departmental public body on 1 July 1996 under the Criminal Justice and Public Order Act 1994. It describes its main responsibilities as protecting the public and that it manages:

- the early release of prisoners serving fixed-length sentences of four years or more;
- the release of prisoners who are serving life sentences or indeterminate sentences for public protection; and
- the re-release of prisoners who were given life or indeterminate sentences and were then re-imprisoned.

The role of the Parole Board exploded when it was reported that John Worboys was to be released. Between 2003 and 2008, Warboys, the driver of a black cab in London, committed 'a legion' of sexual offences on women. Worboys picked up women as passengers after dark in central London. He plied them with alcohol that had been laced with sedative and then sexually assaulted or raped them. There were first reports to police regarding disturbing incidents in black cabs dating back to 2002. Over a period of six years, 14 women reported assaults and other frightening experiences to the police, all of which had similar factors, including that they took place in a black cab in London. The police did not link the assaults and in one case laughed at a victim when she reported her assault. In 2007 a series of reports finally convinced police that they were dealing with a serial sex offender and they made a public appeal. Worboys was subsequently arrested. A rape kit was found in his car, along with sleeping tablets and other paraphernalia. He pleaded not guilty at his trial and therefore forced the victims to give evidence in court. He was convicted on 13 March 2009 of 19 sexual offences involving 12 victims. He received an indeterminate sentence of imprisonment and was to serve a minimum term of eight years. On sentencing, the trial judge said that Worboys would not be released until the Parole Board decided that he did not pose a threat to women. The police investigation was brought before the IPCC (see Chapter 17) who stated that some of the attacks could have been prevented if the reports had been properly investigated by the police. After conviction, the police appealed for other victims who may have been assaulted by John Worboys to contact them. By 2010 over 100 women had come forward.

John Worboys maintained his innocence for six years, including appealing to the Court of Appeal against his conviction. He then admitted the offences, except for the assault by penetration, when he was nearing the end of his minimum term at the point that he could apply to the Parole Board for release. In August 2017 he was rejected in his application for a transfer to an open prison by the Justice Secretary because of the level of risk he posed. Six months later, still a Category A prisoner, he applied for a Parole Board hearing. At the hearing, the Parole Board had police material referring to 80-plus victims; however, ***DSD v Commissioner of Police of the Metropolis*** (2014), which found that he had committed over 100 assaults, was not in the material provided to the Parole Board. Also not provided were the judge's sentencing remarks or the prosecution's opening speech in the Crown Court Tribunal. It was alleged that in the Parole Hearing, Worboys was not asked a single question to test his position. On 26 December 2017 the Parole Board directed his that he be released. A lawyer who represented two of Worboys' victims at the time of the subsequent hearing, said neither woman had received a letter or any form of notification to inform them that he would be released. Parties, including two of the victims, applied for a judicial review of the decision. The victims could not find out the reasons for the decision because the decision and the reasons of the Parole Board (under the then rule 25 of the Parole Board Rules) were prohibited from being published.

Judicial review proceedings were brought to challenge the decision to release him, stating that the Parole Board should have undertaken further enquiry into the level of his offending and remorse. Proceedings were also brought to challenge the legality of rule 25.

The High Court determined that is was very rare for a Category A prisoner to be released with no intervening periods at lower categorisation, and there were striking features, including Worboys' admissions after six years of maintaining his innocence. They stated that:

> The psychologists did not seem to have probed the possibility that he was not being honest. The board did not ask him questions directed to his credibility . . . he was not probed to any extent if at all . . . And in the instant case it ought to have carried out further inquiry. And that a key issue was whether he was being open and honest.

The release decision was quashed. Regarding rule 25, the Parole Board argued that they were not a court, they were a government body and that the proceedings were protected because they had always been held in private. Proceedings often involved wards of court, the mentally ill and matters of national security, and therefore the principle of open justice did not apply. The High Court ruled that the principle of open justice did apply because the Parole Board 'exercises the judicial power of the state'. It ruled that the victims did have the right (in some circumstances) to receive information about the decision. It found that:

> r. 25(1) was so broad that it embraced non-confidential information and information which could be presented in a way that respected individual rights. It was not objectively necessary and was *ultra vires*.

The Parole Board's decision to release Worboys was quashed and a 'fresh determination' in his case was ordered.

After the judgment was released, the Chair of the Parole Board, Nick Hardwick, who had previously called for greater transparency in Parole Board decisions, resigned. In his resignation letter, Hardwick made it clear he was forced to resign by the then Justice Secretary, David Gauke; he wrote:

> You told me that you thought my position was untenable, I had no role in the decision of the panel in the case and believe I am capable of leading the Parole Board through the changes, many of which I have advocated, that will now be necessary.

The victims of John Worboys changed the law. The blanket ban in rule 25 on disclosure of information was removed as a direct result of their action (see more on this in Chapter 9). The Parole Board are now able to make available summaries of their reasons for decisions to release or to continue to detain an offender, to victims. A full review of the Parole Board Rules has been promised.

On 21 February 2018 the judgment was released in **Commissioner of Police of the Metropolis v DSD and another**. The Metropolitan Police had appealed to the Supreme Court against a ruling of the Court of Appeal regarding the awarding of damages to Worboys' victims relating to their negligence. The Supreme Court case confirmed the award of damages against the police for the failure to conduct an effective investigation. Lord Hughes stated in his judgment: 'Although only a small proportion (ten) of his many attacks were reported to the police at the time, it is now known that he raped more than 100 women, employing a similar method.'

Children and young people

There are three types of custodial sentence which apply children and young people (see Chapter 21):

- a detention and training order (children and young people under 18);

- long-term detention (children and young people under 18 convicted of 'grave' crimes);

- detention in a young offender institution, under s. 96 of the Powers of Criminal Courts (Sentencing) Act 2000 (18–20-year-olds).

The Bigger Picture: Sentencing rioters

The summer of 2011 saw serious rioting across the United Kingdom, which took many people by surprise. Rioters communicated and planned their activities using modern technology, such as Facebook, Twitter or Blackberry messaging (BBM). Magistrates' courts stayed open through the night to deal with the rioters and heavy sentences were handed down. At the time of the rioting a Crown Court judge, Judge Gilbart, appeared to issue sentencing guidelines for the courts, stating that heavier sentences than normal should be imposed where offences had been committed in the context of riots. The Court of Appeal subsequently stated in *R v Blackshaw* (2011) that it was inappropriate for the Crown Court judge to appear to issue sentencing guidelines. The Prison Governors Association, with the prisons struggling to cope with a bulge in the prison population, accused lay magistrates of 'naked popularism', caught up in a 'feeding frenzy' of disproportionate sentencing in the wake of the riots.

The country seemed quite divided by these riots. While the media took a firm law and order stance, demonising the rioters, it also recognised that there was public discomfort at the heavy sentences imposed on young people for quite trivial behaviour. The sentences of two young men, Jordan Blackshaw and Perry Sutcliffe-Keenan, caused particular consternation. They had created Facebook pages, such as 'Smash down in Northwick Town', in which they encouraged rioting in their local area and became known as the 'Facebook rioters'. The riot never took place but they were put on trial for encouraging the commission of crimes and were sentenced to four years' imprisonment. The aim of the sentence was undoubtedly deterrence, because social networking sites had played an important role in generating the riots. Ten people, including the Facebook rioters, appealed against their sentences in *R v Blackshaw*. The Court of Appeal stated that the context of the riots 'hugely aggravates the seriousness of each individual offence'. It upheld most of these sentences, stating that sentences beyond the range indicated in the sentencing guidelines were inevitable where there was the aggravating factor of widespread public disorder. Such sentences 'should be designed to deter others from similar criminal activity'. The defence lawyers had argued that the sentencing court should 'distinguish between tangible acts of criminality and incitement which, in fact, leads to nothing', but this argument was rejected.

Three appellants had been convicted of handling stolen goods. The Court of Appeal halved their sentences, but still gave them custodial sentences, stating that the guideline judgment on sentencing handling offences which suggested a non-custodial sentence on these facts was not relevant as the offences were linked to rioting.

Councils announced that they would seek to evict rioters from their homes on the basis that, by rioting, they had wilfully damaged their local neighbourhood. In fact, many of the rioters were still living with their parents and the tenancy agreement was with the parents, not the rioters.

▶

Landlords are not supposed to be law enforcement agencies. A consultation paper was published in 2011, looking at facilitating evictions for anti-social behaviour, even where the relevant behaviour was committed far from the person's home. It is arguable that evicting rioters and their families, making them homeless, would be a disproportionate response and only further marginalise individuals and move the problem elsewhere. A former Director of Public Prosecutions commented:

> To have young former rioters bereft of income and homeless roaming the streets, with their families also rendered homeless. . . I'm not quite sure how that would help us to improve social harmony.

The Blackshaw principles have been confirmed in *R v Suleimanov (Ucha)* (2013) and *R v Ellis (Alexander Tyrone)* (2013), where the arguments that the custodial sentence lengths for riot convictions were 'manifestly excessive' were rejected on appeal.

Critics of the heavy sentences have argued that if the courts wanted to sentence people for rioting, they should have been prosecuted for rioting, rather than offences such as handling, burglary and theft. However, a concern about handing out deterrent sentences is that the courts are not focusing on the individual before them; instead, the defendant is treated as a faceless representative of social breakdown.

Suspended sentence

Under ss. 189–194 of the Criminal Justice Act 2003, a custodial sentence can be suspended. A court can suspend a short custodial sentence for between six months and two years. The offender can be required to undertake certain activities in the community. If the offender breaches the terms of the suspension, the suspended sentence will be activated. Committal of a further offence during the entire length of suspension will also count as breach, and the offender's existing suspended sentence will be dealt with at the time the court sentences him or her for the new offence. Courts have a discretion to review an offender's progress under a suspended sentence.

Suspended sentences were created in 1967 and were intended to be used as an alternative to a custodial sentence. In practice, they have sometimes been used where a community sentence would have been adequate. If the offender then commits another offence the suspended sentence is activated, so that the offender ends up in prison. The Criminal Justice and Immigration Act 2008 abolished suspended sentences for summary only offences to reduce this problem.

Home detention curfew

Home detention curfews were introduced by the Crime and Disorder Act 1998 and the relevant statutory provisions are now contained in the Criminal Justice Act 2003. Prisoners sentenced to between three months and four years imprisonment can be released early (usually 90 days early) on a licence that includes a curfew condition. This requires the released prisoners to remain at a certain address at set times, during which period they will be subjected to electronic monitoring. Most curfews are set for 12 hours, between 7 pm and 7 am.

The person can be recalled to prison if there is a failure to comply with the conditions of the curfew condition or in order to protect the public from serious harm. Private contractors fit the tag to a person's ankle, install monitoring equipment which plugs into the telephone system in their home and connects with a central computer system, and notify the Prison Service of any breaches of curfew.

Research has been carried out by Dodgson *et al.* (2001) into the first 16 months' experience of home detention curfew. It found that only 5 per cent were recalled to prison. The main reasons for recall were breach of the curfew conditions (68 per cent) or a change of circumstances (25 per cent). The use of home detention curfew appeared to have eased the transition from prison to the community. Offenders were very positive about the scheme, with only 2 per cent saying that they would have preferred to have spent their time in prison. Prior to release, over a third of prisoners said that the prospect of being granted home detention curfew influenced their behaviour in prison. Other household members were also very positive about the scheme.

Advantages of custodial sentences

The previous Conservative Government claimed that prison 'works', in the sense that offenders cannot commit crime while they are in prison, and so the public is protected. The Labour Government claimed that prison could be made to work both by protecting the public and by making use of the opportunity for rehabilitation. The current Government is suggesting that prison should be used less for short sentences.

Disadvantages of custodial sentences

Fifty-nine per cent of prisoners are reconvicted within two years of being released. In her book, *Bricks of Shame* (1987), Vivien Stern highlights several reasons why imprisonment lacks any great reformative power, and may even make people more, rather than less, likely to reoffend. Prisoners spend time with other criminals, from whom they frequently acquire new ideas for criminal enterprises; budget cuts have meant there is now little effective training and education in prisons, while the stigma of having been in prison means their opportunities for employment are fewer when they are released, and families often break down, so that the ex-prisoner may become homeless. The result, says Stern, is that 'going straight can present the quite unattractive option of a boring, lonely existence in a hostel or rented room, eking out the Income Support'. All this can also mean that prison punishes the innocent as well as the guilty, with the prisoner's family suffering stigma, financial difficulties, the misery of being parted from the prisoner, and often family breakdown in the end. The research, *Poverty and Disadvantage Among Prisoners' Families* (Smith *et al.*, 2007) noted that about 4 per cent of children experience the imprisonment of their father during their school years. It found that this frequently caused them to suffer emotional and economic hardship, with a negative effect on their personal development.

Stern rejects the idea that prison works because it protects the public. She points out that, although it may prevent the individual offending for a while, the percentage of crime that is actually detected and prosecuted is so small that imprisonment has little effect on the crime rate.

Photo 20.1 Wormwood Scrubs, an example of a Victorian prison

Source: © David Hawgood

The Bigger Picture: Sentences for murder

All people convicted of murder are automatically sentenced to life imprisonment. But this does not actually mean that they spend life in prison: they can be released and spend the rest of their life in the community on licence. A breach of their licence will lead them to be recalled to prison. In the past the Home Secretary decided when a person sentenced to life should actually be released from prison. This was found to be in breach of the European Convention in the case of *R (on the application of Anderson)* v *Secretary of State for the Home Department* (2002). The danger was that Home Secretaries might be influenced by the issues of political popularity rather than the justice in the particular case. The matter was highlighted in the case of Myra Hindley, who was convicted for life in 1966 for the murder of two children and for her involvement in the killing of a third.

Home Secretaries, however, seem anxious to retain some control in this area. Provisions were added to the Criminal Justice Act 2003 in Sched. 21 which aim to promote consistency in the sentencing of murderers. Under these provisions, judges are required to slot offenders into one of three categories according to the severity of their crime. For the first category, actual life will be served by those convicted of the most serious and heinous crimes: multiple murderers, child killers and terrorist murderers. For the second category, there is a starting point of 30 years. This category includes murders of police and prison officers and murders with sexual, racial or religious motives. For the third category, the starting point is 15 years. In addition, there are 14 mitigating and aggravating factors which will affect the sentence imposed. Schedule 21 was criticised by the Government in its consultation paper *Breaking the Cycle: Effective Punishment, Rehabilitation and Sentencing of Offenders* (2010). The Schedule was described as unnecessarily complex and incoherent because it went into too much detail. Judges are able to ignore these guidelines, provided they explain why. Once the minimum term has expired, the Parole Board will consider the person's suitability for release. If the Parole Board considers that the person no longer poses a significant risk of reoffending, it can order their release. They are released on licence for the rest of their lives, and are supervised by the probation service until they are assessed as being fully reintegrated into the community. If they reoffend while under supervision, or if they fail to cooperate, or to keep in contact with the probation service, the licence is revoked by the Lifer Review and Recall Section at the Home Office; a warrant of arrest is issued by Scotland Yard, and they are classed as unlawfully at large until arrested and returned to prison.

The European Court of Human Rights (ECHR) ruled in *Vinter* v *UK* (2013) by 16 votes to 1 that prisoners cannot be given whole-life tariffs with no prospect of release. Such a sentence amounted to inhuman or degrading treatment in breach of Art. 3 of the Convention because it left the prisoner without hope. All prisoners must have the possibility of a review of their sentence and the possibility of a future release. To be compatible with the Convention, there should be a review within 25 years of the sentence being imposed. There are 56 prisoners in England and Wales who are serving whole-life tariffs. Unlike other life-term prisoners, they are not eligible for release on licence. At present they can only be released at the discretion of the Home Secretary in exceptional circumstances which justify a prisoner's release on compassionate grounds under s. 30 of the Crime (Sentences) Act 1997 – for example if they are terminally ill. Following the decision of the European Court, the Attorney General asked the Court of Appeal to decide on the legality of current whole-life sentences in the UK. In *R* v *McLoughlin*; *R* v *Newell* (2014), the Court of Appeal disagreed with the European Court of Human Rights, and held that whole-life terms do not amount to inhuman or degrading treatment under Art. 3 of the ECHR. This is because English law does not, as the European Court of Human Rights claimed, provide the possibility that a whole-life term could never be reduced. The Justice Secretary can release an individual imprisoned for a whole-life term in exceptional circumstances for compassionate reasons. The Court of Appeal held that the Justice Secretary must interpret 'compassionate grounds' in accordance with human rights law. This meant that whole-life terms did not breach Art. 3 of the ECHR.

The European Court of Human Rights overruled its decision in *Vinter* v *UK* in *Hutchinson* v *UK* (2015). The Court stated that whole-life sentences are only incompatible with the Convention if there is no possibility of a review. As the Home Secretary has the power to release those serving whole-life terms in exceptional circumstances, there remained a possibility of a review and there was no breach of the Convention.

There are currently over 12,000 people serving life sentences in England and Wales, which is more than in all 46 other Council of Europe member states combined. Twenty-two people are serving whole-life tariffs in England and Wales (in other words, they are expected to spend the rest of their lives in prison), none in Europe and 25,000 in America (along with 3,500 individuals under sentence of death).

20

SENTENCING

Prisons are also extremely expensive – at £37,500 a year per prisoner, three weeks in prison costs as much as a lengthy community sentence. The Lord Chief Justice pointed out in a public lecture in 2008 that by locking up a person in prison for 30 years, the state is investing a million pounds in punishing that individual. Prisons cost the taxpayer £1.9 billion every year. To this must be added the costs associated with the family breakdown and unemployment that imprisonment frequently causes. As well as those who find themselves in prison through non-payment of fines, many of those actually sentenced to prison have committed relatively minor offences and could be dealt with just as effectively, and far more cheaply, in the community.

The conditions within prisons continue to cause concern. While all prisoners are now supposed to have 24-hour access to toilet facilities, with the practice of 'slopping out' being ended in 1996, other problems remain. Major concerns were exposed in a findings paper from the HM Inspectorate of Prisons for 2017, including significant overcrowding (where two prisoners are held in a cell designed for one), and often squalid and unhygienic conditions within the cells. Prisoners experience very limited time outside of their cells – large numbers were found to be locked in their cells for more than 22 hours a day 'with limited access to association or purposeful activity'.

Where prison conditions are poor, there is an increased risk of suicide. In the 12 months preceding September 2017, a total of 77 people committed suicide in prison. There were over 41,103 incidents of self-harm recorded in the 12 months up to June of the same year, which represents an increase of 12 per cent from the previous year. This can be compared to the 16,000 incidents recorded in 2003. Women are far more at risk of self-harming, with Ministry of Justice figures showing the instance of self-harming at a rate of 1,914 incidents per 1,000 prisoners in female establishments, compared with a rate of 413 per 1,000 prisoners in male establishments. In December 2017 a leaked inspection report of horrendous

Figure 20.2 Persons sentenced to immediate custody, 12 months ending March 2010 to 12 months ending March 2017

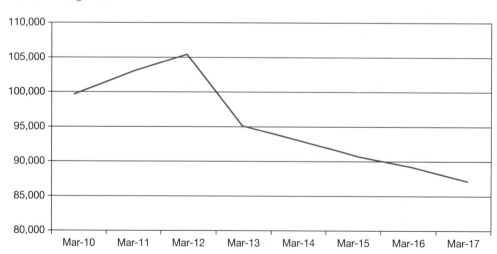

Source: Graph based on data contained in Table Q5.2 which can be accessed by clicking on 'Overview tables' at the following: https://www.gov.uk/government/statistics/criminal-justice-system-statistics-quarterly-march-2017

conditions in a Liverpool prison also highlighted the additional threat to those prisoners with existing mental health problems.

The number of people in prison has been growing at an alarming rate over recent years. In 1992 there were 44,000 people in prison, in 2013 that number had almost doubled to 85,000. Lord Carter (2007) has identified five reasons why the prison population has increased so dramatically:

- changes to legislation and sentencing;
- more offenders brought to justice (though the conviction rate has only increased by 5 per cent since 1995);
- increased sentence rates and longer terms;
- greater focus on enforcement of sentences (which means more licence recalls); and
- greater awareness of risk and increased political prominence of public protection.

A Council of Europe study revealed that defendants in English courts get longer sentences for assault, robbery or theft than they do elsewhere in Europe. Average prison populations in Europe are approximately a third lower as a proportion of the population to that of the UK. In 2015 America had a prison population of 458 per 100,000 of the population, England and Wales 148, Germany 77, Sweden 58 and France 98. Others higher than England and Wales include Turkey 220, Estonia 210 and Russia 439.

Figure 20.3 Trends in sentencing outcomes for indictable offences at all courts, 12 months ending March 2007 to 12 months ending March 2017

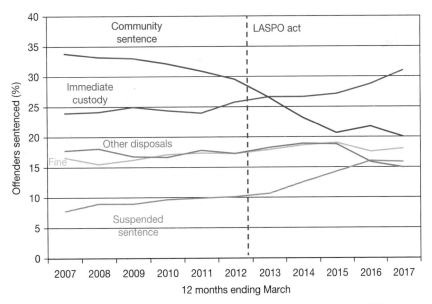

Source: Page 6, Criminal Justice Statistics Quarterly Update to March 2017, published 17 August 2017. Can be found online: https://www.gov.uk/government/uploads/system/uploads/attachment_data/file/638225/cjs-statistics-march-2017.pdf

The inevitable result of a growing prison population is prison overcrowding. In 2007 there was such a shortage of prison places that the Government decided to put some prisoners in police cells. This was an unsatisfactory solution to prison overcrowding because it is more expensive than prisons while providing no facilities for education and rehabilitation.

The benefits of locking more people up in prison are not clear. A report carried out by the businessman Patrick Carter in 2003 estimated that the increased use of custody had only reduced crime by 5 per cent at the most. The Chief Inspector of Prisons claimed in an interview for *The Guardian* in 2001 that the prison population could be cut to 40,000 if 'the kids, the elderly, the mentally ill, the asylum seekers, those inside for trivial shoplifting or drug offences' were taken away.

In recent years there has been concern that dangerous offenders have been released on licence and have subsequently reoffended (see our discussion of the issue of John Worboys). There have been suggestions that the Parole Board has been wrong to agree the release of certain individuals and, when they have been released, they have not been adequately supervised by the probation service. Such concerns were expressed in the media following the murder of the wealthy banker, John Monckton, at his home in Chelsea by Damien Hanson when he was on probation. The Parole Board may be giving undue weight to the human rights of the offender rather than the rights of potential victims, but they may also not have enough information to make a fully informed decision. Some of the criticism of the probation service may reflect an unrealistic expectation of the level of supervision that can be provided with the level of funding available. There have been significant cuts to the funding of the probation service and part of it has be privatised (see p. 558 for our discussions and further comment).

The Bigger picture: Prisoners' voting rights

Under English law, prisoners do not have the right to vote while they are being held in prison. In 2005, the European Court of Human Rights ruled, in **Hirst v UK (No. 2)**, that this blanket ban breached the European Convention on Human Rights. The Convention includes a Protocol guaranteeing the right to participate in free elections. In **Greens and MT v UK** (2010) the European Court ordered the UK to start working on legislative reforms to end the blanket ban.

In 2012, the Government published a draft Bill on prisoners' voting eligibility, entitled Draft Voting Eligibility (Prisoners) Bill. The draft Bill included three proposals:

1 a ban from voting for those sentenced to four years' imprisonment or more;

2 a ban from voting for those sentenced to more than six months; or

3 a ban from voting for all prisoners (the current position).

This draft Bill was submitted for pre-legislative scrutiny to a joint committee (its members are drawn from both Houses of Parliament) in 2012. The joint committee published its report in 2013, and recommended that the Government should introduce legislation to allow all prisoners serving sentences of 12 months or less to vote in all UK Parliamentary, local and European elections. To date, the Government has not acted upon the committee's recommendation.

20.4.3 Community sentences

In 2017 95,112 offenders were sentenced to a community sentence, representing only eight per cent of offenders sentenced.

Section 148 of the Criminal Justice Act 2003 states that a community sentence can only be imposed if the offence was 'serious enough to warrant such a sentence'. Where a court passes a community sentence, the requirements of the sentence must be the most suitable for the offender. The restrictions on liberty imposed by the order must be 'commensurate with the seriousness of the offence, or the combination of the offence and one or more offences associated with it'. The Crime and Courts Act 2013 amended the 2003 Act and made clear that in any community order the court must include at least one requirement which has been imposed for the purpose of punishment, or a fine, or both. This requirement would not apply where there are exceptional circumstances relating to the offence or offender which would make it unjust in the circumstances to impose such a punishment.

Recent Governments have been anxious to emphasise that community sentences impose substantial restrictions on the offender's freedom and should not be seen as 'soft options'. Following the Crime and Courts Act 2013, every community sentence must contain a punitive element, such as unpaid work or a curfew order. Home Office statistics show that 56 per cent of offenders given community sentences reoffend within two years. Reoffending means committing any offence, even one that resulted in a police caution. This is still a lower recidivist rate than those who were sentenced to custody.

The Criminal Justice Act 2003 has established a single community order which can be applied to an offender aged 16 or over who has committed an imprisonable offence. This order can contain a range of possible requirements. These are:

- an unpaid work requirement;
- a rehabilitation activity requirement;
- a programme requirement;
- a prohibited activity requirement;
- a curfew requirement;
- an exclusion requirement;
- a residence requirement;
- a mental health treatment requirement;
- a drug rehabilitation requirement;
- an alcohol treatment requirement;
- a foreign travel prohibition requirement.

Each of these requirements will now be considered in turn.

Unpaid work requirement

The offender can be required to perform, over a period of 12 months, a specified number of hours of unpaid work for the benefit of the community. The number of hours must be between 40 and 300. The kind of work done includes removing graffiti, clearing land of waste, and decorating public buildings. This requirement should allow for useful community work to be done and may give offenders a sense of achievement which it is suggested might help them stay out of trouble afterwards. However, with the contracting out to tender of much of the work of the probation services for low and medium risk offenders to CRCs (privately-run community rehabilitation companies), there has been serious criticism of the tasks set. In February 2019 the *Financial Times* reported that one of Britain's biggest private providers of probation services, Working Links, collapsed into administration and that inspectors had criticised the group for mishandling its operations to boost profits. There were reports that some offenders were being stood up by CRCs after attending at agreed times to carry out work, turning up to placements and finding no one there to supervise and nothing to do. Meanwhile, there are other reports of offenders being made to carry out meaningless unpaid work like moving mud from one pile to another in graveyards. There is direct evidence that sentencers have reduced the use of community sentences, preferring short custodial sentences because of the unproductive nature of the CRCs and the fear of poor supervision.

Rehabilitation activity requirement

When making a community or suspended sentence order, a court may include a rehabilitation activity requirement. This is a requirement that the offender participates in activity to reduce the prospect of reoffending. As discussed earlier in the chapter, rehabilitation activity requirements are known as RARs. The Sentencing Council Guidelines for RARs state that the court does not have to prescribe the activities undertaken when sentencing; they must simply state the maximum number of activity days the offender must complete. The probation officer will decide the rehabilitation activities to be undertaken (if any). The Guideline states that: 'where appropriate this requirement should be made in addition to, and not in place of, other requirements.' A recent report from the Inspectorate of Probation Services stated: 'We did not find that sufficient impact had been made on reducing the prospect of reoffending in the majority of cases inspected.'

Programme requirement

A programme requirement obliges the offender to participate in an accredited programme on a certain number of days. Programmes are courses which address offending behaviour, such as anger management, sex offending and drug abuse.

Prohibited activity requirement

The court can instruct an offender to refrain from participating in certain activities. For example, it might forbid an offender from contacting a certain person, or from participating in specified activities during a period of time. The court can make a prohibited activity requirement which prohibits a defendant from possessing, using, or carrying a firearm.

Curfew requirement

An offender can be ordered to remain in a specified place or places for periods of not less than two hours or more than 16 hours in any one day for up to 12 months. The court should avoid imposing conditions which would interfere with the offender's work or education, or cause conflict with their religious beliefs. A curfew requirement must be between two and 16 hours per day that the curfew applies. A specified person must be made responsible for monitoring the offender's whereabouts. Courts can require offenders to wear electronic tags, to monitor that they are conforming to their curfew order.

Advantages of curfew orders

Tagging costs about £4,000 a year compared with £37,500 for a prison place. Curfew orders have the potential to keep offenders out of trouble and protect the public, without the disruptive effects of imprisonment. In the US city of Atlanta, a night curfew has been imposed on anyone under 16. This was introduced to protect children but has also had the effect of considerably reducing juvenile crime. While such use of curfew orders on those who have not been convicted of crimes intrudes on the right to freedom of movement, the results show that, as a sentence, it could prove very useful.

Presently, the electronic tags set off an alarm if a curfew is breached but they cannot be used to identify where the offender has then gone. Since 2012 successive Governments have been considering a more technologically advanced system which can track the precise movements of the offender and GPS tags are being designed in a satellite tracking scheme. A 2018 Government report on the scheme found that it is already five years behind schedule. It is reported that the scheme will be rolled out in 2019 but with only 1,000 of the tags being in use at one time; this is estimated to cover up to 4,000 individuals over a calendar year. There are 60,000 offenders tagged under the old system so this will therefore enhance, but not replace the old system.

Disadvantages of curfew orders

Electronic tagging is a profitable business for private-sector companies. A report by the Inspector for the Probation Service (2013) has revealed that more than half of offenders ordered to wear electronic tags break the rules of their court-imposed orders. The Penal Affairs Consortium have argued that the money spent on electronic tagging would be better spent on constructive options, such as supervision requirements, which work to change offenders' long-term attitudes towards offending. Opponents to electronic tagging claim they are degrading to the person concerned, but their supporters – including one or two well-known former prisoners – point out that it is far less degrading than imprisonment. This argument applies only where tagging is used as an alternative to imprisonment: its opponents claim that it is likely to be used in practice to replace other non-custodial measures. The Government has increased the potential length of curfew orders from 12 hours to 16 hours. This raises questions about whether a person under such a long curfew would be able to go out to work or study and back without breaching their order.

Exclusion requirement

An offender can be required to stay away from a certain place or places at set times. Electronic tags can be used to monitor compliance with this requirement. It is aimed at people, such as stalkers, who present a danger or nuisance to a victim. An exclusion requirement is similar in many respects to a curfew requirement. However, whereas under a curfew requirement an offender has to remain at a specified place, an exclusion requirement prohibits an offender from entering a specific place. The maximum period of the requirement is two years.

Residence requirement

A residence requirement obliges the offender to reside (live and sleep) at a place specified in the order for a specified period.

Photo 20.2 An electronic tag

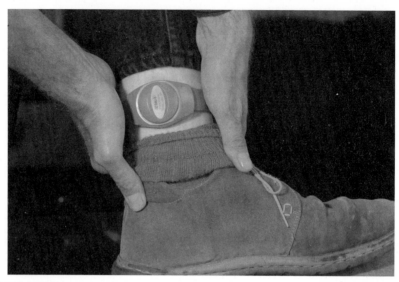

Source: © 67Photo/Alamy

Mental health treatment requirement

A court can direct an offender to undergo mental health treatment for certain periods as part of a community sentence or suspended sentence order, under the treatment of a registered medical practitioner or psychologist. Before including a mental health treatment requirement, the court must be satisfied that the mental condition of the offender requires treatment and may be helped by treatment but is not such that it warrants making a hospital or guardianship order (within the meaning of the Mental Health Act 1983). The offender's consent must be obtained before imposing the requirement.

Drug rehabilitation requirement

As part of a community sentence or suspended sentence the court may impose a drug reha-bilitation requirement, which includes drug treatment and testing. To impose such a require-ment, the court must be satisfied that the offender is dependent on, or has a propensity to misuse, any controlled drug and as such would benefit from treatment. In addition, the court must be satisfied that the necessary arrangements are or can be made for the treatment and that the offender has expressed a willingness to comply with the drug rehabilitation require-ment. The treatment provided must be for a minimum of six months.

A court may provide for the review of this requirement, and such reviews must take place if the order is for more than 12 months. Review hearings involve the individual appearing before the judge that sentenced them, to discuss their progress. The results of mandatory drug tests – often conducted weekly – are available to the court at these hearings.

Alcohol treatment requirement

A court can require an offender to undergo alcohol treatment to reduce or eliminate the offender's dependency on alcohol. The offender's consent is required. This requirement must last for at least six months.

Figure 20.4 Community sentence

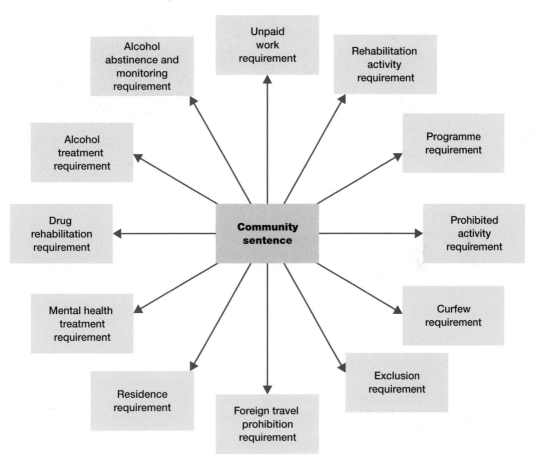

Foreign travel prohibition requirement

A foreign travel prohibition requirement bans the offender, expressly or on specified dates, from travelling overseas or to countries specified in the order, for up to 12 months.

20.4.4 Absolute and conditional discharges

If the court finds an offender guilty of any offence (except one for which the penalty is fixed by law) but believes that in the circumstances it is unnecessary to punish the person and a community rehabilitation order is inappropriate, it may discharge the defendant either absolutely or conditionally.

Absolute discharge

An absolute discharge effectively means that no action is taken at all and is generally made where the defendant's conduct is wrong in law, but no reasonable person would blame them for doing what they did.

Conditional discharge

A conditional discharge means that no further action will be taken unless the offender commits another offence within a specified period of up to three years. This order is commonly made where the court accepts that the offender's conduct was wrong as well as illegal, but the mitigating circumstances are very strong. If an offender who has received a conditional discharge is convicted of another offence during the specified period, they may, in addition to any other punishment imposed, be sentenced for the original offence.

20.4.5 Miscellaneous sentences

A range of other sentences are also available to the court. These include the following.

Compensation orders

Where an offence causes personal injury, loss or damage (unless it arises from a road accident), the courts have a duty to consider ordering the offender to pay compensation. Orders can also be made for the return of stolen property to its owner, or, where stolen property has been disposed of, for compensation to be paid to the victim from any money taken from the offender when arrested. If prisoners are employed while in prison, some of their earnings will be used to compensate their victims. In practice, compensation orders are frequently not made, simply because the offender has no money and no income.

Where the offender is appearing in a magistrates' court and is over 18, or is appearing in the Crown Court, there is no limit on the amount of the compensation order that can be made. The court must take account of the offender's means in deciding whether to make a compensation order and adjust the amount accordingly.

Confiscation orders

Confiscation orders under the Proceeds of Crime Act 2002 may only be made when an offender is sentenced by the Crown Court. Section 6 provides that, where an offender is being sentenced by the Crown Court, the court may decide whether the defendant has a 'criminal lifestyle' and, if so, whether the offender has benefited from 'general criminal conduct'.

Under s. 38 of the Act, the court will impose a term of imprisonment in default of payment. However, the punishment is for defaulting on the payment; the debt will continue to be owed.

The Bigger Picture: Serious crime prevention orders

Part 1 of the Serious Crime Act 2007 creates serious crime prevention orders (SCPOs). These are a new type of civil order aiming to prevent the commission of serious crime. The orders mandate or restrict the activities of individuals or organisations for up to five years. Section 5 lists the type of conduct that might be the subject of an order, including the compulsory provision of financial information and the imposition of travel restrictions, but the list is not definitive so the courts can add to this. The order can be made where the court is satisfied that a person over 18 years of age has been involved in serious crime (which includes facilitating another person to commit a serious crime, regardless of whether it was actually committed) and it has reasonable grounds to believe that the order would protect the public by preventing, restricting or disrupting involvement in such criminal activities. Whether a crime is 'serious' is left for the court to decide.

An order can be issued by the Crown Court following a criminal conviction. Where there is no criminal conviction, the prosecution may apply to the High Court for an order in cases where there is insufficient evidence to meet the required standard of proof for a criminal prosecution or, in respect of individuals suspected of being on the fringes of criminal activity, where the prospect of a criminal trial is unattractive for reasons of cost or public interest.

A failure to comply with the terms of an SCPO without reasonable excuse is a criminal offence punishable by up to five years' imprisonment. Critics have suggested that these orders amount to an unjustified invasion of a person's liberty, with insufficient safeguards to prevent injustice.

Binding over to be of good behaviour

This order dates to the fourteenth century and the relevant legislative provisions can be found in the Justices of the Peace Act 1361 and the Magistrates' Courts Act 1980. It can be made against any person who is before a court and has 'breached the peace'. People who are bound over have to put up a sum of money or find someone else to do so, which will be forfeited if the undertaking is broken. A person who refuses to be bound over can be imprisoned, even though they may not have been convicted of any offence. The order usually lasts for a year.

Key case

The power of the courts to bind people over to be of good behaviour was considered by the European Court of Human Rights in **Steel v UK** (1998). The first applicant, Ms Steel, was arrested in 1992 when she walked in front of an armed member of a grouse shoot, preventing him from shooting. She was charged with causing a breach of the peace and was detained for 44 hours. At her trial the complaint of breach of the peace was proved true and she was bound over to keep the peace for 12 months. Her appeal to the Crown Court was dismissed and when she refused to be bound over she was imprisoned for 28 days.

The second applicant was arrested while demonstrating against the building of a motorway. She had stood in front of a digging machine to stop it being used, and was charged with conduct likely to cause a breach of the peace. She was found to have committed a breach of the peace and was bound over for 12 months. She refused, and was sent to prison for seven days.

The other three applicants were all arrested for handing out leaflets and displaying banners against the sale of weapons at the 'Fighter Helicopter II Conference' in London in 1994.

The applicants claimed that their arrests and detention had not been 'prescribed by law' as required by Art. 5 of the European Convention on Human Rights and had amounted to a disproportionate interference with their freedom of expression in breach of Art. 10. The European Court of Human Rights found that the powers to bind over were compatible with the Convention. It was satisfied that the concept of breach of the peace was clear and that it had been established in English law that it was committed only when a person caused harm to persons or property, or acted in a manner the natural consequence of which was to provoke others to violence.

The court accepted that in the case of the first and second applicants the police had been justified in fearing that their behaviour might provoke others to violence. Bearing in mind the aim of deterrence, and also the importance in a democratic society of maintaining the rule of law and the authority of the judiciary, the court did not find it disproportionate that they were sent to prison.

However, concerning the three protesters at the arms fair, the court found that their behaviour had been entirely peaceful and could not have justified the police in fearing that a breach of the peace was likely to occur. For that reason, it found that their arrest and detention had been unlawful, under both the English law on breach of the peace and under Arts. 5 and 10 of the Convention. The arrest and detention of these protesters had been disproportionate to the aim of preventing disorder or of protecting the rights of others.

Legal principle

The English courts' power to bind people over to be of good behaviour does not breach the European Convention on Human Rights.

Deferred sentences

Section 1 of the PCC(S)A 2000 allows the courts to defer passing sentence for a period of up to six months after conviction. Sentence can only be deferred with the consent of the offender, and where deferring sentence is in the interests of justice. The power to defer passing sentence is exercisable only if offenders undertake to comply with any requirements as to their conduct that the court considers appropriate. Failure to comply with a requirement will result in the offender being brought back to court early for sentence. If the offender commits another offence during the deferment period, the court will deal with both sentences at once.

Deferred sentences are intended for situations where the sentencer has reason to believe that, within the deferral period, the offender's circumstances will materially change, with the result that no punishment will be necessary, or that the punishment imposed should be less than it would have been if imposed at the time of conviction. For example, offenders may make reparation to the victim, settle down to employment or otherwise demonstrate that they have changed for the better.

Disqualification

This is most common as a punishment for motoring offences when offenders can be disqualified from driving. Under ss. 146–147 of the PCC(S)A 2000, a court may disqualify a person from driving as a punishment for a non-motoring offence. A conviction for offences concerning cruelty to animals may also lead to disqualification from keeping pets or livestock.

Injunctions to prevent gang-related violence

Under the Policing and Crime Act 2009 police and local authorities have the power to apply to their local County Court for an injunction against local gang members. This is an order designed to prevent and protect the public from gang-related violence. The injunction can include any 'reasonable prohibition or requirement' to prevent an individual being involved in gang-related violence. A person could, for example, be prohibited from associating with certain people, going to certain places, wearing certain items of clothing or keeping a dangerous or threatening dog. Positive requirements could include attendance at anger management courses, counselling, job-preparedness coaching and mediation with rival gang members. Breaches of the injunction will be dealt with as a civil contempt of court, which is punishable by a prison sentence of up to two years, or an unlimited fine.

Criminal behaviour orders

Anti-social behaviour orders (ASBOs) were civil orders created in 1998 to deal with anti-social behaviour in local communities. These proved controversial, with concern they were being used disproportionately against the mentally ill and children, and that high rates of breach were leading to over-criminalisation.

The Anti-Social Behaviour, Crime and Policing Act 2014 abolished anti-social behaviour orders and replaced them with criminal behaviour orders (CBOs). A CBO is an order designed to tackle 'the most serious and persistent anti-social individuals where their behaviour has brought them before a criminal court'. The anti-social behaviour does not need to be linked to the offence which led to the criminal conviction. The court may only make a CBO if it is satisfied that two conditions are met:

1 The court must be satisfied, beyond reasonable doubt, that the offender has engaged in behaviour that caused, or was likely to cause, harassment, alarm or distress to one or more persons; and

2 That the court considers that making the order will help in preventing the offender from engaging in such behaviour.

The order can contain both requirements and prohibitions. It can prohibit the offender from doing anything described in the order or it can require the offender to do anything described in the order. Breach of the order is a criminal offence with a maximum of five years' imprisonment. There is a defence of reasonable excuse.

20.4.6 Fines

A fine may be imposed for almost any offence other than murder.

Crown court fines

When sentencing an offender, the Crown Court can impose a fine instead of, or as well as imposing any other type of sentence. This also applies when the offender pleaded guilty to an either-way matter in the magistrates' court but is committed for sentence, to the Crown Court. The powers of the Crown Court following such a committal are the same as if the offender has been convicted by the Crown Court.

There is no statutory limit on the amount of a fine imposed by the Crown Court.

Magistrates' court fines

Fines for offences tried in the magistrates' court carry a set maximum, depending on the offence. When assessing the fine, the court may take into consideration factors such as household income and financial circumstances. The standard scale for summary offences has five levels:

Level of current maximum fine (per offence):

1 £200

2 £500

3 £1,000

4 £2,500

5 Unlimited (for offences committed after 13 March 2015).

Where a magistrates' court convicts a person of an either-way offence, the magistrates' court may impose an unlimited fine of any amount, unless there is a provision for a maximum fine for the specific offence.

Fixed penalty fines

In order to clamp down on loutish behaviour, the Criminal Justice and Police Act 2001 has given the police the power to impose fixed penalty fines. These fines can be imposed for offences such as being drunk in a public place and being drunk and disorderly. A police officer may give a person a penalty notice if there is reason to believe that the person has committed a penalty offence (s. 2). The fine is usually £90 but can be as much as £500 for commercial establishments.

20.4.7 Problems with sentencing

The role of the judge

We have seen that the sentence in England is traditionally a decision for the judge, which can lead to inconsistent punishments, especially among magistrates' courts. We can see that the courts seem sometimes reluctant to impose community orders because of a perceived lack of confidence in what has been described as the failed privatisation of parts of the probation service.

The Government has tried to ensure consistency through legislative guidelines and has also set up a Sentencing Council and a Judicial College. Overseen by the Ministry of Justice, the functions of the Judicial College include running seminars on sentencing, which seek to reduce inconsistencies; courses for newly appointed judges; and refresher courses for more experienced members of the judiciary. The board also publishes a regular bulletin summarising recent legislation, sentencing decisions, research findings and developments in other countries, while the Magistrates' Association issues *Sentencing Guidelines* to its members.

Other jurisdictions generally allow judges less discretion in sentencing. In the US, for example, many states use 'indeterminate' sentencing by which a conviction automatically means a punishment of, say, one to five years' imprisonment, and the exact length of the sentence is decided by the prison authorities. However, in this country, control of sentencing is seen as an important aspect of judicial independence, and the introduction of more legislative controls has been criticised as interfering with the judiciary's constitutional position.

Racism

Critics of sentencing practice in England have frequently alleged that members of ethnic minorities are treated more harshly than white defendants. For example, in 2001, 21 per cent of the prison population was from an ethnic minority, which is significantly higher than their representation in the general population. This difference becomes much less if only UK nationals are considered, because one in four black people in prison is a foreign national, often imprisoned for illegally importing drugs. Whether these figures point to racial discrimination in sentencing is the subject of much debate.

What is clear from recent research is that some members of the ethnic minorities perceive the sentencing process as racist. Research undertaken in 2003 by Roger Hood *et al.* investigated how far black and Asian defendants considered that they had been treated unfairly by the courts because of their race. Most complaints about racial bias concerned sentences perceived to be more severe than those imposed on a white defendant for the same offence.

In addition to any racism in the system, the legal and procedural factors which affect sentencing may account for some of the differences in the punishment of black and white offenders. More black offenders elect for Crown Court trial and plead not guilty, which means that if convicted they would probably receive harsher sentences, because the sentences in the Crown Court are higher than those in the magistrates' court and they would not benefit from a discount for a guilty plea. Research by Flood-Page and Mackie in 1998 found that there was no evidence that black or Asian offenders were more likely than white offenders to receive a custodial sentence when all relevant factors were taken into account.

The experience of black people when in the prison system has also given rise to concern. An internal report commissioned by the Prison Service in 2000 found a blatantly racist regime at Brixton prison, where black staff as well as inmates suffered from bullying and harassment. The head of the Prison Service acknowledged that the service is 'institutionally racist' and that 'pockets of malicious racism exist'. He promised to sack all prison officers found to be members of extreme right-wing groups such as the British National Party. Prison officers' training now includes classes on race relations. Sentencing is a second area of concern.

A complex and advanced piece of research was conducted by the Ministry of Justice in 2015. It focused on ethnicity and sentencing in the Crown Court with defendants self-reporting their ethnic identity. The study focused on three groups of offences – offences involving acquisitive violence, sexual offences and drugs offences. This research demonstrated that for offenders during the time of the study, there was 'an association between ethnicity and being sentenced to prison' particularly with drugs offences, and that: 'Under similar criminal circumstances the odds of imprisonment for offenders from self-reported Black, Asian, and Chinese or other backgrounds were higher than for offenders from self-reported White backgrounds.' It concluded that Asian or Black defendants had a 50–55 per cent increase in the odds of imprisonment compared to White defendants and that Chinese defendants faced an 81 per cent increase in the odds of imprisonment.

The Lammy Review in 2017 found that BAME defendants, when charged with an offence, are more likely to request legal advice in a police station than their white counterparts. The report stated that many BAME defendants neither trust the advice that they are given, nor believe they will receive a fair hearing by magistrates. This means that when they had the choice of having their case heard by magistrates or the Crown Court (an either way offence) BAME defendants pleaded not guilty and elected trial by jury in the Crown Court. The report indicated that because the judge in the Crown Court had more extensive sentencing powers than the magistrates, the result was that BAME defendants were being sentenced more harshly than they need to be. This was due to mistrust of the advice (one assumes advice to plead guilty) to remain in the magistrates' court and have their trial there. It is a fact that pleading guilty at the very first opportunity in court, in almost all cases, guarantees a one-third discount from the final sentence.

One of the recommendations that the report made was that, 'as part of the court modernisation programme, all sentencing remarks in the Crown Court should be published in audio and/or written form'. This would, the report argued, build trust by making justice more transparent and comprehensible for victims, witnesses and offenders. What was also recommended is that there is a subtler scrutiny of sentencing decisions, to ensure that 'many finely balanced judgments do not add up to disproportionate sentencing of BAME defendants over time'. The pattern of sentencing decisions in each city and courtroom is now captured in Government statistics and can be further studied. In the future, the report argues, 'it should be possible to see whether this differs for defendants of different ethnicities'. The Government has responded to the report and has promised better capture of data in Government statistics.

Treatment of women

Women make up just under 5 per cent of the prison population in England and Wales, yet they are more likely than men to reoffend. Women tend to be given short prison sentences and because they are more often than not primary carers, they are also more likely to be disproportionately affected by a prison sentence, as well as being more likely to reoffend. The Ministry of Justice 2017 *Reoffending Report* found 'short-term sentences served by both men and women were consistently associated with higher rates of proven reoffending'.

There is enormous controversy over the treatment of women by sentencers. On the one hand, many claim that women are treated more leniently than men. A Home Office study carried out by Hedderman and Hough in 1994 reported that, regardless of their previous records, women were far less likely than men to receive a custodial sentence for virtually all indictable offences except those concerning drugs, and that when they do receive prison sentences these tend to be shorter than those imposed on men.

Several critics have suggested that women who step outside traditional female roles are treated more harshly than both men and other women. Sociologist Pat Carlen (1983) studied the sentencing of a large group of women and found that judges were more likely to imprison those who were seen as failing in their female role as wife and mother – those who were single, or divorced, or had children in care. This was reflected in the comments made by sentencers, including: 'It may not be necessary to send her to prison if she has a husband. He may tell her to stop it' and 'If she's a good mother we don't want to take her away. If she's not, it doesn't really matter.'

Flood-Page and Mackie also found in 1998 that women were less likely to receive a prison sentence or to be fined when all relevant factors were taken into account. This has been variously attributed to the fact that women are less likely to be tried in the Crown Court; assumptions that women are not really bad, but offend only as a result of mental illness or medical problems; and reluctance to harm children by sending their mothers, who more often than not are their primary carers, to prison.

London and the South in 2018 have been subject to a spate of murders, stabbings and serious offending around knife crime. Recent research shows that the children and young people who were the offenders in this recent spate of stabbings were children without any significant adult in their lives. The *Guardian* newspaper reported that (according to the minutes of the London Assembly's Police and Crime Committee), the interim findings of the research carried out by Croydon Council showed 'maternal absence was a very important feature in the cases of dozens of young people subject to serious case reviews after they were embroiled in serious youth violence'. There is persuasive evidence that removing children from their mothers has a very serious impact. Sending women to prison makes them more likely to reoffend and makes them also more likely to lose their children to the state or due to addictions and vulnerabilities.

A report undertaken by Reunite looked at children affected by maternal imprisonment. It found that each year about 17,000 children are separated from their mothers when they are put into prison. Only 25 per cent of children of women prisoners live with their fathers. Only 5 per cent of children of imprisoned mothers can stay in their own homes during their mother's absence. These children 'are exposed to family breakup, financial hardship, stigma and secrecy – leading to adverse outcomes'.

Hamida Ali, Croydon Council's cabinet member for community safety, told the London Assembly: 'Not one of those young people (involved in serous knife crime) had a relationship with a trusted adult. Forget a parent; not a grandparent, not an uncle or an aunt, not a neighbour, not a mentor, not a family friend. I think that is very powerful in terms of . . . love and attention for our young people.' It should be considered that removing children from their mothers can have a huge impact not just on the children but on society.

About one-fifth of the total female prison population have been sentenced as drugs couriers and, of these, some seven out of every ten are foreign nationals (Penny Green, *Drug Couriers: A New Perspective* (1996)). A former HM Chief Inspector of Prisons, Sir David Ramsbotham, has commented: 'There is considerable doubt whether all the women in custody [at Holloway] really needed to be there for the public to be protected' (*Report on Holloway Prison* (unpublished, 1997)). The vast majority of women in prison do not commit violent offences and much of their offending relates to addiction and poverty. Prison is not an appropriate, necessary or cost-effective way of dealing with these problems.

Following the deaths of six women in three years in one prison in Cheshire, Baroness Corston was asked by the Government to look at the issue of women in prison. She recommended that existing women's prisons should be closed and replaced with small multi-functional custodial centres, geographically dispersed, with no more than 20 to 30 women residents. These would be local units giving a chance for women and their families to stay connected during the sentence and offering rehabilitation services.

The Female Offender Strategy was first announced in the 2016 White Paper, *Prison Safety and Reform*. This included the building of five new community prisons for women. This plan caused outrage as Baroness Corston's report had focused on non-custodial options for female offenders. Many campaigners refused to give up on their demand for no new women's prisons and campaigned to overturn this decision.

In June 2018 the Ministry of Justice published its most recent Female Offender Strategy. It had reversed the decision to build the community prisons for women. It instead placed emphasis on community sentences for women. This was tentatively welcomed by campaigning organisations. There was no suggestion of sentencing reform, so it has been criticised for being light on measures that will bring the female prison population down. As has been discussed in this and other chapters, there have been significant court closures and privatisation of some of the services offered by probation, specifically for medium and lower risk offenders. This is reported to be causing a reluctance in the judiciary to sentence offenders to community sentences and this may have a more significant impact on women offenders than male offenders, due to the nature of their offending.

20

SENTENCING

There will need to be, it is suggested by campaigners, money and resources injected into community services like women's centres to ensure that the strategy is successful. Under austerity, these services are facing a serious and deepening funding crisis and without further investment this strategy will face challenges in implementation. However, it is a positive step forward and welcomed by many campaigning groups.

Women in the criminal justice system 'are more likely to be victims of abuse, and more likely to have been sentenced for offending related to their exploitation by a partner,' states Francis Crook, chief executive of the Howard League. It may be, in years to come, that many of the women who are sentenced to imprisonment now are seen in the future as victims of crime by the police and justice system, rather than offenders.

Privatisation

Criminal justice has, historically, been regarded as a matter for the state. Since the early 1990s, various parts of the system have been privatised, including 13 prisons, parts of the probation services, transport and security. Huge companies dominate the sector: G4S, Atos, Serco and Capita. They cover everything from security and transport, to welfare, prisons, technology and probation services. In some instances, private enterprises such as 'My Local Bobby' offer a private police force who will 'patrol the area and make citizens arrests' for communities that are prepared and able to pay for a 'Bobby on the beat'.

Prisons

In August 2018 the Ministry of Justice took over the running of Birmingham HMP from G4S after a damning inspection of the 'appalling state' of the prison, with 'high violence, widespread bullying, squalid living conditions and poor control' by scared staff. Staff vehicles were set alight during the inspection, rats and cockroaches were everywhere and the buildings were in a parlous state. Privatised prison escort services have also come in for severe criticism, with prisoners managing to escape or not being brought to the court on time or at all.

The prison population has doubled to more than 80,000 since 1993, when the Government began introducing more aggressive policies. The United Kingdom is now said to imprison twice as many people per capita as mainland Europe. The capacity of the prison services to cope with this has not risen in parallel. Quite the opposite: fiscal austerity has led to a marked reduction in the number of officers, and this is said to be one major cause of the widespread safety problems.

The probation service

In 2013 the then coalition Government claimed a 'rehabilitation revolution' in the form of their Transforming Rehabilitation Programme. The Government part-privatised its probation service in 2014, awarding contracts valued at £3.7 billion to private Community Rehabilitation Companies (CRCs) to oversee 200,000 medium and low risk offenders.

This was widely opposed by many because it split services between new CRCs and the publicly owned National Probation Service. For example, the probation staff union said the management of offenders should be 'left in the hands of skilled, experienced professionals, and not given to unqualified private sector providers'. These changes were criticised as creating a two-tier service. The Justice Committee summarised these aims as:

- extend statutory rehabilitation to offenders serving custodial sentences of less than 12 months;

- introduce nationwide 'Through the Gate' resettlement services for those leaving prison;

- open up the market to new rehabilitation providers to get the best out of the public, voluntary and private sectors;

- introduce new payment incentives for market providers to focus relentlessly on reforming offenders;

- split the delivery of probation services between the National Probation Service (offenders at high risk of harm) and CRCs (low and medium risk offenders); and

- reduce reoffending.

One of the key reforms was to support offenders who were serving short sentences of 12 months or less in their attempts to settle outside of prison and supervise them for a period of time. Another was the tendering out to private providers of the rehabilitation contracts by 'opening up' the market.

It has been widely accepted that this initiative has been 'chaotic and disastrous'. Reoffending is on the up, supervision has been neglected and the Government has bailed out some of the CRCs. The Public Accounts Committee found that CRCs were performing 'woefully' against their contracts, achieving only eight out of 24 targets on average.

The 2018 Government Select Committee report *Transforming Rehabilitation* stated that this initiative, like many before it, has 'failed to meet its aims to reduce reoffending and improve the management of offenders'. It found that short custodial sentences were being chosen over community rehabilitation options because of the lack of confidence by the sentencer in giving a community alternative from those that were being provided by the new rehabilitation providers. The report stated that:

> We find it extremely worrying that sentencer confidence in community alternatives to short custodial sentences is so low, particularly as the latter have worse outcomes in terms of reoffending. We recommend that the Government should introduce a presumption against short custodial sentences.

The resettlement initiative that was to support those leaving prison to find employment and accommodation was found to be being delivered in the form of a leaflet handed to the prisoner when they left prison, of which the report observed:

> One of the key components of the reforms was that all offenders would receive an element of continuous support from custody into the community. The current provision merely signposts offenders to other organisations and is wholly inadequate. We call on the Government to consider getting rid of this requirement. Offenders were receiving £46 and a leaflet rather than the services that it was suggested would be provided.

Since the reforms in 2014, a number of offenders who were supervised by CRCs were found to have committed a serious further offence. Reoffending at the time of the report's publication was found to have risen by 21 per cent, from 429 to 512 since 2013/14, as stated in the 2017 Annual Report of HM Inspectorate of Probation for England and Wales. A significant proportion of these were convicted of murder, manslaughter or sexual offences whilst under supervision by a CRC, the report found.

Some offenders were only undergoing one face-to-face meeting with CRCs before being assigned a risk category and pushed into 'remote offender monitoring' by telephone. The HM Chief Inspector of Probation, Dame Glenys Stacey, agreed in evidence to a question from the Committee that 'the system was fundamentally flawed'. In March 2018, companies told the Government they were 'forecasting losses of £443m for the remainder of their contracts, forcing the Ministry of Justice to adjust the agreements and commit additional funding of up to £343m. The current agreements are now due to end in 2020 but in August 2018 a further sum of £170m was given to cover huge losses in waived penalties and investments.

20.4.8 Out-of-court disposals

The number of crimes that are dealt with outside the formal criminal justice system has more than doubled in the last five years. Approximately a third of crimes which are dealt with in the criminal justice system are dealt with outside the formal court process. The most commonly used out-of-court disposals are warnings, cautions and penalty notices for disorder. Restorative justice solutions are also being adopted. While such processes can have the benefit of speed and efficiency in the fight against crime, they lack the safety procedures of an open court hearing.

20.5 Reform

20.5.1 A new code for sentencing

Sentencing law has been described as 'very complicated'. The Law Commission, the body that advises the Government on law in England and Wales, said: 'The current state of the law means that it is simply impossible to describe the governing sentencing procedure as clear, transparent, accessible or coherent.' Sentencing is currently reliant on a 'proliferation' of laws over 1,300 pages long and dating back to the 1300s. The Law Commission states that 'for a lay person to discover the law would be practically impossible'. The Law Commission say that this can lead to delays, costly appeals and unlawful sentences and that 'there is near unanimity from legal practitioners, judges and academic lawyers that the law in this area is in urgent need of reform'.

A Sentencing Code has been recommended by the Law Commission and this will, they submit, help stop unlawful sentences by providing a single reference point for the law of sentencing, simplifying many complex provisions and removing the need to refer to historic legislation.

The Rt Hon the Lord Thomas of Cwmgiedd, Lord Chief Justice of England and Wales stated:

> the Law Commission's project to codify sentencing law is a valuable and long-overdue stepping stone in the process of the rationalisation and clarification of the criminal law. The law on sentencing is highly complex and contained in a dizzying array of separate but overlapping sources. For that reason, sentencing procedure represents an obvious candidate for consolidation and simplification.

The Commission states that the code would:

- help stop unlawful sentences by providing a single reference point for the law of sentencing, simplify many complex provisions and remove the need to refer to historic legislation;
- save up to £255m over the next decade by avoiding unnecessary appeals and reducing delays in sentencing clogging up the court system;

- rewrite the law in modern language, improving public confidence and allowing non-lawyers to understand sentencing more easily;
- remove the unnecessary layers of historic legislation; and
- allow judges to use the modern sentencing powers for both current and historic cases, making cases simpler to deal with and ensuring justice is better served.

The aim is to ensure every part of the sentencing process is set out in a single, clear, logical structure in plain accessible language. The Commission envisages the new Sentencing Code laying down an exhaustive list of the available types of sentencing disposal and providing a framework for their imposition. It foresees that sentencing guidelines will still sit alongside the Code. The draft Sentencing Code has been published by the Law Commission and it is now, the Commission states, a matter for the Government as to whether they choose to enact the draft Code.

Answering questions

1 (a) What are the purposes of sentencing?

   (b) How much sentencing discretion does a judge have?

2 To what extent is there consistency in sentencing?

3 John, aged 40, is charged with manslaughter and has appeared before Claydon magistrates.

   (a) What are the powers of the magistrates' court to deal with John?

   (b) How may John obtain funding from the Legal Aid Agency?

   (c) If John is convicted, what sentences might be passed upon him?

4 After conviction, how do judges choose the defendant's sentence?

For answers to these questions, visit the companion website at www.pearsoned.co.uk/ elliottquinn

SUMMARY OF CHAPTER 20: SENTENCING

Purposes of sentencing

Section 142 of the Criminal Justice Act 2003 states that:

> any court dealing with an [adult] offender in respect of his offence must have regard to the following purposes of sentencing –
>
> (a) the punishment of offenders,
>
> (b) the reduction of crime (including its reduction by deterrence),
>
> (c) the reform and rehabilitation of offenders,
>
> (d) the protection of the public, and
>
> (e) the making of reparation by offenders to persons affected by their offences.

Sentencing practice

In recent years there has been a considerable amount of legislation trying to regulate the sentencing practices of the judges and to make it fairer to offenders.

Legislation

The legislation applies rules relating to:

- mandatory sentences;
- minimum sentences;
- general restrictions on sentencing; and
- dangerous offenders.

Types of sentence

The judge has the power to impose a wide range of sentences.

Custodial sentences

Adult offenders can be sent to prison. Some offenders will be released early on home detention curfew.

Community sentences

The Criminal Justice Act 2003 has established a single community order that can be applied to an offender. This order can contain a range of possible requirements. These are:

- Unpaid work for up to 300 hours
- Rehabilitation activity requirement (RAR) undertaking activities as instructed
- Undertaking a particular programme to help change offending behaviour
- Prohibition from doing particular activities
- Adherence to a curfew, so the offender is required to be in a particular place at certain times
- An exclusion requirement, so that the offender is not allowed to go to particular places
- A residence requirement so that the offender is obliged to live at a specified address
- A foreign travel prohibition requirement
- Mental health treatment with the offender's consent
- A drug rehabilitation requirement with the offender's consent
- An alcohol treatment requirement with the offender's consent
- An alcohol abstinence and monitoring requirement with the offender's consent
- Where offenders are under 25, they may be required to go to a centre at specific times over the course of their sentence.

In 2017 95,112 offenders were sentenced to a community sentence, representing only eight per cent of offenders sentenced.

Discharges

If the court finds an offender guilty of any offence (except one for which the penalty is fixed by law) but believes that in the circumstances it is unnecessary to punish the person and a community rehabilitation order is inappropriate, it may discharge the defendant either absolutely or conditionally. The Sentencing Council report that in 2017, 53,104 defendants were given a discharge, representing four per cent of all offences.

Miscellaneous sentences

A range of other sentences is also available to the court. These include:

- compensation orders;
- confiscation orders;
- financial reporting order;
- binding over to be of good behaviour;
- absolute and conditional discharges;
- deferred sentences;
- disqualification;
- injunctions to prevent gang-related violence; and
- criminal behaviour orders.

Fines

The fine is the most common sentence issued by the court, but there is a major problem with fines not being paid.

Problems with sentencing

The role of the judge

There has been concern that there is inconsistency in sentencing.

Racism

Critics of sentencing practice in England have frequently alleged that members of ethnic minorities are treated more harshly than white defendants.

Treatment of women

There is enormous controversy over the treatment of women by sentencers and an argument that many are victims rather than criminals.

Privatisation

Criminal justice has, historically, been regarded as a matter for the state. Recently, however, various parts of the system have been privatised, including 13 prisons and a disastrous privatisation of parts of the probation service.

Reading list

Ashworth, A. (2015) *Sentencing and Criminal Justice* Cambridge: Cambridge University Press

(2010) Coroners and Justice Act 2009: sentencing guidelines and the Sentencing Council. *Criminal Law Review*, 389.

(2002) Responsibilities, rights and restorative justice. *British Journal of Criminology*, 578.

Baker, M. (2014) Choices and consequences – an account of an experimental sentencing programme. *Criminal Law Review*, 51.

Bottoms, A.E. and Preston, R.H. (eds) (1980) *The Coming Penal Crisis*. Edinburgh: Scottish Academic Press.

Braithwaite, J. (2004) Restorative justice and de-professionalization. *The Good Society*, 13(4): 28–31

Campbell, S. (2002) *A Review of Anti-Social Behaviour Orders*. Home Office Research Study No. 236. London: Home Office.

Carlen, P. (1983) *Women's Imprisonment: A Study in Social Control*. London: Routledge.

(2003) *Managing Offenders, Reducing Crime*. London: Strategy Unit, Home Office.

Carter, Lord (2007) (see website, below).

Chalmers, J., Duff, P. and Leverick, F. (2007) Victim impact statements: can work, do work (for those who bother to make them). *Criminal Law Review*, 360.

Corston, J. (2007) *Women with Particular Vulnerabilities in the Criminal Justice System*. London: Home Office.

Dodgson, K. *et al.* (2001) *Electronic Monitoring of Released Prisoners: An Evaluation of the Home Detention Curfew Scheme*. London: Home Office.

Doob, A.N. and Webster, C.M. (2003) Sentence Severity and Crime: Accepting the Null Hypothesis. 30 *Crime and Justice: A Review of Research*, 143-195

Edwards, I. (2002) The place of victims' preferences in the sentencing of "their" offenders. *Criminal Law Review*, 689.

Ellis, T. and Hedderman, C. (1996) *Enforcing Community Sentences: Supervisors' Perspectives on Ensuring Compliance and Dealing with Breach*. London: Home Office.

Flood-Page, C. and Mackie, A. (1998) *Sentencing During the Nineties*. London: Home Office Research and Statistics Directorate.

Green, P. (1996) *Drug Couriers: A New Perspective*. London: Quartet.

Halliday, J. (2001) *Making Punishment Work: Report of a Review of the Sentencing Framework for England and Wales*. London: Home Office.

Hedderman, C. and Hough, M. (1994) *Does the Criminal Justice System Treat Men and Women Differently?* London: Home Office Research and Planning Unit.

Home Office (1990) *Crime, Justice and Protecting the Public*. Cm 965. London: HMSO.

(2007b) *Asset Recovery Action Plan*. London: Home Office.

(2011) *More Effective Responses to Anti-Social Behaviour*. London: Home Office.

Hood, R., Shute, S. and Seemungal, F. (2003) *Ethnic Minorities in the Criminal Courts*. London: Lord Chancellor's Department.

Hough, M. (2017) Time to Rethink the Role of the Sentencing Council? *Sentencing News* April: 6–8

Hungerford-Welch, P. (2019) *Criminal Procedure and Sentencing* (9th edition). London: Routledge.

Jacobson, J. and Hough, M. (2007) *Mitigation: The Role of Personal Factors in Sentencing.* London: Prison Reform Trust.

Johnstone, J. (2017) Restorative justice for victims: inherent limits? *Restorative Justice,* 5(3): 382–395

Lovegrove, A. (2010) The Sentencing Council, the public's sense of justice and personal mitigation. *Criminal Law Review,* 906.

Loveless, J. (2012) Women, sentencing and the drug offences definitive guidelines. *Criminal Law Review,* 592.

Mair, G. and May, C. (1997) *Offenders on Probation.* Home Office Research Study No. 167. London: HMSO.

Martin, R. (2013) The recent supergrass controversy: have we learnt from the troubled past? *Criminal Law Review,* 273.

Martinson, R. (1974) What works? – questions and answers about prison reform. *The Public Interest,* 35: 22–54.

McNeill, F., Raynor, P. and Trotter, C. (2010) *Offender Supervision: New Directions in Research, Theory and Practice.* Cullompton: Willan Publishing.

Ministry of Justice (2010a) *Breaking the Cycle: Effective Punishment, Rehabilitation and Sentencing of Offenders.* Cm 7972. Norwich: Stationery Office.

(2013) *Transforming Rehabilitation: A revolution in the way we manage offenders.* Consultation Paper CP1/2013, Cm 8517. Norwich: The Stationery Office.

Moore, R. (2003) The use of financial penalties and the amounts imposed: the need for a new approach. *Criminal Law Review,* 13.

(2004) The methods for enforcing financial penalties: the need for a multidimensional approach. *Criminal Law Review,* 728.

National Association of Probation Officers (NAPO) (2004) *Anti-Social Behaviour Orders: Analysis of the First Six Years.* London: NAPO (see website, below).

New Zealand Law Commission (2006) *Sentencing Guidelines and Parole Reform.* New Zealand: New Zealand Law Commission.

Nuttall, C., Goldblatt, P. and Lewis, C. (1998) *Reducing Offending: An Assessment of Research Evidence on Ways of Dealing with Offending Behaviour.* Home Office Research Study No. 187. London: Home Office.

Office for Criminal Justice Reform (2004) (see website, below).

Padfield, N. (2011) Time to bury the custody "threshold"? *Criminal Law Review,* 593.

Parliamentary Penal Affairs Group (1999) *Changing Offending Behaviour: Some Things Work.* London: Parliament.

Ramsbotham, Sir D. (1997) *Women in Prison: A Thematic Review.* London: Home Office.

Roberts, J. (2008) Aggravating and mitigating factors at sentencing: towards greater consistency of application. *Criminal Law Review,* 264.

(2012) Sentencing guidelines and judicial discretion: evolution of the duty of courts to comply in England and Wales. *British Journal of Criminology,* 50.

Roberts, J., Hough, M., Jacobson, J. and Moon, N. (2009) Public attitudes to sentencing purposes and sentencing factors: an empirical analysis. *Criminal Law Review,* 771.

20

SENTENCING

Sanders, A., Hoyle, C., Morgan, R. and Cape, E. (2001) Victim impact statements: don't work, can't work. *Criminal Law Review*, 447.

Shapland, J. (2008) *Does Restorative Justice Affect Reconviction?* Ministry of Justice Research Series 10/08. London: Ministry of Justice.

Sherman, L. and Strang, H. (2007) (see website, below).

Smith, J.C. and Hogan, B. (2002) *Criminal Law*. London: Butterworths.

Smith, R. *et al.* (2007) (see website, below).

Stern, V. (1987) *Bricks of Shame: Britain's Prisons*. London: Penguin.

The Secret Barrister (2018) *Stories of the Law and How It's Broken*. Pan Macmillan.

Thomas, D. (1970) *The Principles of Sentencing*. London: Heinemann.

(2004) The Criminal Justice Act 2003: custodial sentences. *Criminal Law Review*, 702.

Vogt, G. and Wadham, J. (2003) *Deaths in Custody: Redress and Remedies*. London: Liberty.

Von Hirsch, A., Ashworth, A. and Roberts, J. (2009), *Principled Sentencing. Readings on Theory and Policy*. Oxford: Hart.

Wasik, M. (2004) Going around in circles? Reflections on fifty years of change in sentencing. *Criminal Law Review*, 253.

(2008) Sentencing guidelines in England and Wales – state of the art? *Criminal Law Review*, 253.

(2017) Time to repeal the firearms minimum sentence provision. *Criminal Law Review*, 203.

White, P. and Power, I. (1998) *Revised Projections of Long Term Trends in the Prison Population to 2005*. London: Home Office.

White, P. and Woodbridge, J. (1998) *The Prison Population in 1997*. London: Home Office.

Whittaker, C. and Mackie, A. (1997) *Enforcing Financial Penalties*. London: Home Office.

Young, W. and Browning, C. (2008) New Zealand's Sentencing Council. *Criminal Law Review*, 287.

Zander, M. (2008) What's the rush? *New Law Journal*, 7317.

On the internet

You be the Judge, a great interactive website that gives you the opportunity to decide how you would sentence different offenders, can be found at:

http://ybtj.justice.gov.uk/

The consultation paper *Punishment and Reform: Effective Community Sentences* (2012) is available at:

https://assets.publishing.service.gov.uk/government/uploads/system/uploads/ attachment_data/file/228573/8334.pdf

The report *Breaking the Cycle: Effective Punishment, Rehabilitation and Sentencing of Offenders* (2010) is published on the website of the Ministry of Justice:

http://webarchive.nationalarchives.gov.uk/20111206103817/http://www.justice.gov. uk/consultations/docs/breaking-the-cycle.pdf

The guide entitled *Restorative justice: Helping to meet local needs* (2004), published by the Office for Criminal Justice Reform, is available on the Restorative Justice Council website at:

https://restorativejustice.org.uk/resources/restorative-justice-helping-meet-local-needs

The report *'Gun crime' A review of evidence and policy* (2008) is available on the Centre for Crime and Justice Studies website at:

> **https://www.crimeandjustice.org.uk/publications/gun-crime-review-evidence-and-policy**

A memorandum summarising the report of the National Association of Probation Officers entitled *Anti-Social Behaviour Orders – Analysis of the First Six Years* (2004), is available on the following website:

> **https://publications.parliament.uk/pa/cm200405/cmselect/cmhaff/80/80we20.htm**

The report by L. Sherman and H. Strang, *Restorative justice: the evidence* (2007), is available on the website of The Smith Institute at:

> **http://www.smith-institute.org.uk/book/restorative-justice-the-evidence/**

The report by R. Smith *et al., Poverty and disadvantage among prisoners' families* (2007) is available on the website of the Joseph Rowntree Foundation at:

> **https://www.jrf.org.uk/sites/default/files/jrf/migrated/files/2003-poverty-prisoners-families.pdf**

Life in prison: Living conditions – A findings paper by HM Inspectorate of Prisons (2017) can be found at:

> **https://www.justiceinspectorates.gov.uk/hmiprisons/wp-content/uploads/sites/4/2017/10/Findings-paper-Living-conditions-FINAL-.pdf**

Safety and Custody Statistics, England and Wales: Deaths in Prison Custody to September 2017; Assaults and Self-Harm to June 2017, published by the Ministry of Justice, are available at:

> **https://assets.publishing.service.gov.uk/government/uploads/system/uploads/attachment_data/file/654498/safety-in-custody-stats-q2-2017.pdf**

The *Council of Europe Annual Penal Statistics: SPACE I – Prison Populations Survey 2015* (updated 25 April 2017) is available at:

> **http://wp.unil.ch/space/files/2017/04/SPACE_I_2015_FinalReport_161215_REV170425.pdf**

Lord Carter's report, *Securing the future: Proposals for the efficient and sustainable use of custody in England and Wales* (2007), is available at:

> **http://webarchive.nationalarchives.gov.uk/+/http://www.justice.gov.uk/publications/securing-the-future.htm**

The consultation paper of the Sentencing Commission Working Group, *A structured sentencing framework and sentencing commission* (2008), is available at:

> **http://webarchive.nationalarchives.gov.uk/20080516191202/http://www.judiciary.gov.uk/docs/consultation_ssfsc_310308.pdf**

The Magistrates' Association's *Sentencing Guidelines* are available at:

> **https://www.magistrates-association.org.uk/sentencing-guidelines**

A report of HM Inspectorate of Constabulary and HM Crown Prosecution Service Inspectorate, called *Exercising Discretion: The Gateway to Justice* (2013), looking at out-of-court disposals, is available at:

> **https://www.justiceinspectorates.gov.uk/hmic/media/exercising-discretion-the-gateway-to-justice-20110609.pdf**

A thematic inspection report by the Criminal Justice Joint Inspection called *It's Complicated: The Management of Electronically Monitored Curfews* (2012) can be found at:

> **https://www.justiceinspectorates.gov.uk/probation/wp-content/uploads/sites/5/2014/03/electronic-monitoring-report-2012.pdf**

The Commons Select Committee: Public Accounts report on *Offender Monitoring Tags* from January 2018 is found here:

https://publications.parliament.uk/pa/cm201719/cmselect/cmpubacc/458/45802.htm

The Ministry of Justice report (authored by Kathryn Hopkins, Noah Uhrig and Matthew Colahan) on the *Associations between ethnic background and being sentenced to prison in the Crown Court in England and Wales in 2015* was published in November 2016 and is available at:

https://www.gov.uk/government/statistics/associations-between-ethnic-background-and-being-sentenced-to-prison-in-the-crown-court-in-england-and-wales-in-2015

Gibbs, P. *Justice Denied? Unrepresented defendants in the criminal courts* (5 May 2016) Guest blog for the Bar Council website is available at:

https://barcouncil.org.uk/media-centre/bar-blog/contributing-writers/2016/may/guest-blog-penelope-gibbs,-director-of-transform-justice

You can get insights into the different steps involved in the sentencing process via the Sentencing Council website:

https://www.sentencingcouncil.org.uk/explanatory-material/magistrates-court/item/using-the-mcsg/using-sentencing-council-guidelines/#

The excellent blog from the Secret Barrister is a useful source for accessible commentary. Read his take on the review of the John Worboys Parole Board decision:

https://thesecretbarrister.com/2018/03/29/your-questions-answered-on-the-john-worboys-judgment/

The Commons Select Committee inquiry into the Transforming Rehabilitation reforms is available at:

https://www.parliament.uk/business/committees/committees-a-z/commons-select/justice-committee/inquiries/parliament-2017/transforming-rehabilitation-17-19/

The Law Commission report (2018) on the Sentencing Code (LC382) is available at:

https://www.lawcom.gov.uk/project/sentencing-code/

The 2017 Annual Report from HM Inspectorate of Probation for England and Wales can be located at:

https://www.justiceinspectorates.gov.uk/hmiprobation/wp-content/uploads/sites/5/2017/12/HMI-Probation-Annual-Report-2017lowres.pdf

The article in the *Financial Times* by Wright and Warrell, 'Outsourcer's collapse stirs biggest crisis for probation service' (15 February 2019) is available at:

https://www.ft.com/content/092b0150-3136-11e9-ba00-0251022932c8

The report on the inspection of Dorset, Devon and Cornwall Community Rehabilitation Company (CRC) by HM Inspectorate of Probation can be located at:

https://www.justiceinspectorates.gov.uk/hmiprobation/inspections/ddccrc/

Find out more about the work of the Parole Board at:

https://www.gov.uk/government/organisations/parole-board/about

Chapter 21
Young offenders

This chapter discusses:

- when criminal liability can be imposed on young people;

- young offenders and the police;

- the imposition of bail on young people;

- reprimands and warnings;

- the criminal trial; and

- sentencing young offenders.

21.1 Introduction

Offenders who are under 18 years old are dealt with differently from adults by the criminal justice system. There have in the past been a number of reasons for this, including a belief that children are less responsible for their actions than adults, a wish to steer children away from any further involvement in crime, and the feeling that sentencing can be used to reform as well as, or instead of, punishing them. However, the mood towards young offenders has become more severe due to a widespread public perception of mounting youth crime and horrific cases which stick in the public consciousness, such as the killing of the toddler James Bulger by two 10-year-old boys in 1993.

The former Labour Government stated in its 1998 White Paper, *No More Excuses – A New Approach to Tackling Youth Crime in England and Wales* that it wanted to reverse the 'excuse culture' that had developed within the youth justice system. A change in approach was signalled by the passing of the Crime and Disorder Act 1998. This piece of legislation was central to the Labour Government's approach to youth crime. The Act sought to reduce offending by young people in two ways: first, by promoting strategies for the prevention of youth crime; and, secondly, by creating a range of extended powers available to the police and the courts to deal with young offenders and their parents. Many of its key provisions are now contained in the Powers of Criminal Courts (Sentencing) Act 2000.

Section 37 of the 1998 Act specifies that the aim of the youth justice system is to prevent offending by young people. A Youth Justice Board for England and Wales was established under s. 41 of the 1998 Act. Its principal functions are to monitor, set standards and promote good practice for the youth justice system. Its main focus to date has been to try to speed up the youth justice system, encourage the creation of programmes aimed at preventing youth crime and assist in the implementation of the provisions in the 1988 Act

Figure 21.1 Trends in arrests of children and young people for notifiable offences, England and Wales, years ending March 2007 to March 2017.

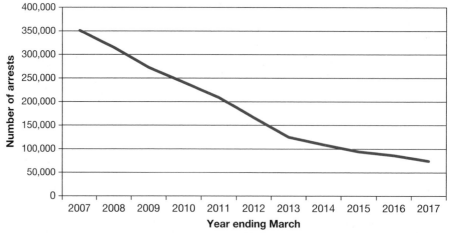

Source: Page 6 of Youth Justice Statistics 2016/17, which can be found online at: https://assets.publishing.service.gov.uk/government/uploads/system/uploads/attachment_data/file/676072/youth_justice_statistics_2016-17.pdf

concerning young offenders. Local authorities must formulate and implement a youth justice plan setting out how youth justice services are to be provided and funded (s. 40). They must, acting in cooperation with police authorities, probation committees and health authorities, establish one or more Youth Offending Teams whose duty it is to coordinate the provision of youth justice services and to carry out their functions under the youth justice plan (s. 39).

The number of children and young people being given a caution or sentence has dramatically reduced (by 85 per cent over the last decade) thanks to shifts in youth justice policy, and yet the numbers of young people committing offences with weapons has increased (up 11 per cent), and the numbers reoffending on release are very high (42.3 per cent reoffended within 12 months in the year ending March 2016). Various reports, including the Taylor Review (more on these at the end of the chapter) have highlighted that these low figures obscure the fact that those children in custody come from often tumultuous and dysfunctional backgrounds, and have multiple problems to overcome. We know from the Lammy Review that far-reaching reforms need to take place in order to reduce the numbers of BAME youth offenders.

In recent years we have also seen a renewed focus on young people in the older age bracket (18–25), recognising that their brains are still developing and that they have distinct needs which separate them from children and adults. It is certainly the case that the youth justice system has many challenges to grapple with.

21.2 Criminal liability

Under criminal law, children under 10 cannot be liable for a criminal offence at all. In the past, there was also a well-established presumption that children between the ages of 10 and 14 were not criminally liable. This presumption could be rebutted by the prosecution successfully adducing evidence that the child knew right from wrong and knew that what they were doing was more than just naughty. In 1998, this rebuttable presumption was repealed by the Crime and Disorder Act 1998. In this respect children aged 10 and above are now treated like adults. British children are almost alone in Europe in being regarded as criminals at the age of 10.

The United Nations Committee on the Rights of the Child has condemned the United Kingdom for imposing criminal liability on young children. In a report in 2002, it criticised the 'high and increasing numbers of children being held in custody at earlier ages for lesser offences and for longer custodial sentences'. It has called on the United Kingdom to raise the age of criminal responsibility to 14 or above, which would bring it into line with most other European countries.

21.3 Young people and the police

Most of the police powers concerning adults also apply to young suspects but, because they are thought to be more vulnerable, some extra rules apply. For example, Code of Practice C of the Police and Criminal Evidence Act 1984 (PACE) states that young suspects should not be arrested or interviewed at school and, when brought to a police station, they should not be held in a cell. The police must find out who is responsible for the young person's welfare

21

YOUNG OFFENDERS

as quickly as possible and then inform that person of the arrest, stating where and why the suspect is being held. If the person responsible for their welfare chooses not to come to the police station, the police must find another 'appropriate adult', who should be present during the various stages of cautioning, identification, intimate searches and questioning. Where the suspect's parent is not present, the appropriate adult will often be a social worker, although it may be anyone defined as a responsible adult, except someone involved in the offence, a person of low intelligence, someone hostile to the young person or a solicitor acting in a professional capacity. In *R (on the application of HC)* v *Secretary of State for the Home Department* (2013), a 17-year-old claimant challenged Code C of PACE. Under Code C, 17-year-olds were allowed to be treated as adults, rather than as juveniles, in a police station. The High Court held that Code C was inconsistent with Art. 8 of the European Convention on Human Rights (ECHR), which protects the right to a private and family life. In law, children are those under the age of 18, and, as such, the High Court ordered Code C be amended to reflect this.

The role of the adult is to ensure that the young person is aware of their rights, particularly to legal advice. The adult should be told that their function is not just that of observer, but also of adviser to the young person, ensuring that the interview is conducted properly and facilitating communication between suspect and interviewer. Unfortunately, research by Brown *et al.* (1992) suggests that some adults are so overawed by the whole process that they are of little use as advisers; they may even side with the interviewer.

21.4 Remand and bail

A young person charged with an offence has the right to be considered for bail under the Bail Act 1976 (see Chapter 18). Where the police refuse bail, young people under 18 should not be held in police custody. The Legal Aid, Sentencing and Punishment of Offenders Act 2012 made significant changes to the remand framework for 10–17-year-olds in criminal proceedings. Children between 12 and 18 are usually remanded to local authority accommodation, which can range from remand fostering schemes to accommodation with high levels of supervision. Youth detention accommodation, however, can be used in appropriate cases.

21.5 Youth cautions

People involved in administering the criminal justice system have been concerned to try to stop a young offender from a cycle of court appearances, punishments and further offending, often aggravated by contact with other offenders during the process. The police therefore try to divert the young offenders from the criminal justice system by issuing them with a caution rather than bringing a prosecution. A caution is an official warning about what the person has done, designed to make them see that they have done wrong and deter them from further offending (it is quite separate from the caution administered before questioning, concerning the right to silence).

There was concern that the caution procedure was being overused in practice, so that young repeat offenders were acting with a sense of impunity. Section 65 of the Crime and Disorder Act 1998, therefore, abolished the system of cautions for young offenders aged between 10 and 17, and replaced it with a system of reprimands and warnings. This system was subsequently found to be too rigid, so the Legal Aid, Sentencing and Punishment of Offenders Act 2012 has abolished it and reintroduced the old system of cautions (now s. 66ZA).

21.5.1 Youth conditional caution

Youth conditional cautions were introduced into the Crime and Disorder Act 1998 by the Criminal Justice and Immigration Act 2008, with further amendments courtesy of the Legal Aid, Sentencing and Punishment of Offenders Act 2012. They aim to reduce the number of young people being taken to court for a low-level offence. These cautions are available for children aged between 10 and 17. This type of caution can be issued where the offender admits guilt and consents to the caution. They may include a fine or an attendance requirement. If the offender does not satisfy the conditions, the prosecution has the right to bring a prosecution for the original offence.

21.6 Trial

Young offenders are usually tried in youth courts (formerly called juvenile courts), which are a branch of the magistrates' court. Other than those involved in the proceedings, the parents and the press, nobody may be present unless authorised by the court. Parents or guardians of children under 16 must attend court at all stages of the proceedings, and the court has the power to order parents of older children to attend.

Young persons can, in limited circumstances, be tried in a Crown Court: for example, if the offence charged is murder, manslaughter or causing death by dangerous driving. They may sometimes be tried in an adult magistrates' court or the Crown Court if there is a co-defendant in the case who is an adult. Following a Practice Direction, discussed below, a separate trial should be ordered unless it is in the interests of justice to do otherwise. If a joint trial is ordered, the ordinary procedures apply 'subject to such modifications (if any) as the court might see fit to order'.

Key case

The trial procedures for young offenders have been reformed in the light of a ruling of the European Court of Human Rights in *T v UK* and *V v UK* (2000). This found that Jon Venables and Robert Thompson, who were convicted by a Crown Court of murdering the two-year-old James Bulger in 1993, did not have a fair trial in accordance with Art. 6 of the European Convention on Human Rights. It concluded that the criminal procedures adopted in the trial prevented their participation:

> The public trial process in an adult court with attendant publicity was a severely intimidating procedure for 11-year-old children . . . The way in which the trial placed the accused in a raised dock as the focus of intense public attention over a period of three weeks, had impinged on their ability to participate in the proceedings in any meaningful manner.

Legal principle
Young defendants will not receive a fair trial in accordance with the European Convention unless the criminal court procedures are adapted to allow them to participate in a meaningful manner.

Following the decision in the Thompson and Venables case, a Practice Direction was issued by the Lord Chief Justice laying down guidance on how young offenders should be tried when their case is to be heard in the Crown Court. The language used by the Practice Direction follows closely that used in the European decision. It does not lay down fixed rules but states that the individual trial judge must decide what special measures are required by the particular case, taking into account 'the age, maturity and development (intellectual and emotional) of the young defendant on trial'. The trial process should not expose that defendant to avoidable intimidation, humiliation or distress. All possible steps should be taken to assist the defendant to understand and participate in the proceedings. It recommends that young defendants be brought into the court out of hours in order to become accustomed to its layout. Jon Venables and Robert Thompson had both benefited from these familiarisation visits. The police should make every effort to avoid exposure of the defendant to intimidation, vilification or abuse.

As regards the trial, it is recommended that wigs and gowns should not be worn and public access should be limited. The courtroom should be adapted so that, ordinarily, everyone sits on the same level. In the Bulger trial, the two defendants sat in a specially raised dock. The decision to raise the dock had been taken so that the defendants could view the proceedings, but the European Court of Human Rights noted that, while it did accomplish this, it also made the defendants aware that everyone was looking at them. Placing everyone on the same level should alleviate this problem. In addition, the Practice Direction states that young defendants should sit next to their families or an appropriate adult and near their lawyers.

The Practice Direction suggests that only those with a direct interest in the outcome of the trial should be permitted inside the courtroom. Where the press is restricted, provision should be made for the trial to be viewed through a CCTV link to another court area. Section 3G of the Criminal Practice Direction deals with the treatment of vulnerable defendants in court.

In 2010, when two boys aged 10 and 11 were put on trial and convicted in the Crown Court for the attempted rape of an 8-year-old girl in London, the Minister for Justice announced that a review would be carried out into how children are treated in a criminal court. He ruled out, however, raising the age of criminal liability. In most other European countries, children aged under 14 who commit offences do not appear before criminal courts, but are dealt with by civil family courts as children in need of compulsory measures of care.

21.7 Sentencing

Sentencing for young offenders has always posed a dilemma: should such offenders be seen as a product of their upbringing and have their problems treated, or are they to be regarded as bad, and have their actions punished? Over the past few decades, sentencing policy has swung between these two views. In 1969, the Labour Government took the approach that delinquency was a result of deprivation, which could be 'treated', and one of the aims of the Children and Young Persons Act of that year was to decriminalise the offending of young people. Instead of going through criminal proceedings, they would be handed over to the social services who would have the power to take the young person into some form of custody. The magistracy constantly fought against this approach and, when a Conservative

Government was elected in 1970, they declined to bring much of the Act into force and the care order provisions have now been repealed.

The opposite approach introduced by the Conservatives led to the UK having a higher number of young people locked up than any other west European country, but reconviction rates of 75–80 per cent suggested that this was benefiting neither the young offenders themselves, nor the country as a whole.

Since 1982, the philosophy behind the legislation has been that the sentencing of young people should be based on the offence committed and not on the offender's personal or social circumstances, or the consequent chances of reform. However following the passing of the Criminal Justice and Immigration Act 2008, when sentencing a young offender the courts must have regard to:

- the principal aim of the youth justice system to prevent offending;
- the welfare of the offender; and
- the purposes of sentencing.

The definitive sentencing guideline on children and young people was published in 2017 and we see a different approach emerging. Judges and magistrates are advised to 'avoid criminalising children unnecessarily' and the factors to consider are noted as follows:

- their age and maturity;
- the seriousness of the offence;
- their family circumstances;
- any previous offending history; and
- whether they admitted the offence.

The Law Commission have been working to produce a Sentencing Code for a number of years but were unable to incorporate fully the aspects relevant to children until the Taylor Review was completed. They note in the commentary that engaging children in the sentencing process is known to be a key factor in the prevention of reoffending, so we expect to see provision for this in the final report.

21.7.1 Custodial sentences

The courts cannot send a child under the age of 18 to prison. Instead, young offenders can be detained in a Young Offender Institution, a secure training centre or a secure children's home. In order to pass a custodial sentence of this kind, the court must satisfy the same conditions as for adults (discussed in Chapter 20) and in some cases, additional criteria as well.

The Bigger Picture: Young people in custody

In the year ending March 2017 there were 870 young offenders in custody, a large reduction from 2003 when this figure stood at over 3,000. The average cost of a place in a secure children's home is £211,000 a year, in a secure training centre it is £203,000 and in a Young Offender Institution it is £55,000. Placing young people in custody is hugely controversial as any criminal conduct is likely to be a reflection of an unsatisfactory childhood for which they themselves are not to blame.

In addition, young people are, by definition, vulnerable and when they are placed in custody the conditions of their detention are very important, or they risk being inhumane. The quality of the custodial accommodation has on occasion given rise to concern. For example, large sums of money have been spent developing the Feltham Young Offender Institution near Heathrow Airport. It is now the largest such institution in the UK, with places for 900 young offenders. In 1999, Sir David Ramsbotham was Her Majesty's Chief Inspector of Prisons. He reported that the conditions in Feltham were 'unacceptable in a civilised society'. As the inspector makes clear in a blistering report, the problem was not one of lack of resources, but of staff attitudes and management. This is exemplified by the Inspectorate finding two cases of appalling bedding conditions while there were new and unused mattresses being held in storage. Cell and common areas were dilapidated, dirty and cold. Despite ample stocks of available clothing in the central stores, the personal clothing provision was pitifully inadequate. All meals had to be taken not in dining rooms but in dirty cells with filthy toilets. Most of the youngsters were locked up for 22 hours a day. A 16-year-old boy who had been on the unit for three months told the inspector: 'I have nothing to do. I get hungry and there's nothing to distract me. If I get depressed, I talk to the chaplain and ask him to pray for me. Most of the time I sleep. My mum's not home during the day and I'm not allowed to phone her in the evening.' The report concluded that 'there were too many examples of distant and disinterested staff throughout the institution who were palpably failing to meet the health and welfare needs of the young people in their charge'. Sir David Ramsbotham has gone as far as describing the conditions in some institutions as 'institutionalised child abuse'.

An unannounced inspection at Feltham by HM Inspectorate of Prisons in June 2017 resulted in a finding that worrying levels of very serious violence had arisen. In July of the same year, a case of judicial review was brought (***R (on the application of B)* v *Secretary of State for Justice*** (2017)) after a 16-year-old young offender was kept in solitary confinement for 23-and-a-half hours. The UN Special Rapporteur of the Human Rights Council on Torture has previously condemned the imposition of solitary confinement, of any duration, on juveniles. Further media coverage of the use of solitary confinement in the youth justice system in 2018 led to this statement from the British Medical Association, the Royal College of Psychiatrists and the Royal College of Paediatrics and Child Health:

> Various studies indicate an increased risk of suicide or self-harm amongst those placed in solitary confinement. As children are still in the crucial stages of developing socially, psychologically and neurologically, there are serious risks of solitary confinement causing long-term psychiatric and developmental harm.

Figure 21.2 Average secure estate for children and young people population, 2000/01–2017/18[1]

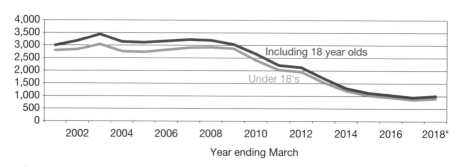

Source: Ministry of Justice Youth Custody report: August 2017

[1]2016/17 and 2017/18 data is provisional.

Twenty-nine children died in custody between 1990 and 2005. Of the children who died, 27 took their own lives, one boy died while being restrained by staff, and one young Asian boy, Zahid Mubarek, was killed by his cell mate. An inquiry was established to look at the death of Zahid Mubarek and a report was published in 2006. This concluded that his death could have been prevented and that improper attitudes to ethnic minority prisoners, particularly Muslims, contributed to the death. It recommended that a new concept of 'institutional religious intolerance' should be recognised by the Home Office, adapting the concept of institutional racism that had been developed by the Stephen Lawrence Inquiry, as institutional prejudice can be on the basis of religion as well as race. This recommendation has been adopted in the Equality Act 2006. The Act prohibits discrimination by public authorities on the grounds of religion or belief.

The organisation Inquest publishes statistics on the number of deaths of young people and children (aged 21 and under) in prisons and Young Offender Institutions. For recent years these stand at: 2016 – 8; 2015 – 7; 2014 – 9. Most of these deaths are classed as self-inflicted.

The Audit Commission (2004) concluded that placing young offenders in custody is the most expensive and least effective way of tackling crime. They noted at the time that 73 per cent of young offenders were reconvicted within one year after their release from custody, compared to 47 per cent of adult offenders. More recent figures from the Ministry of Justice (*Proven Reoffending Statistics Quarterly Bulletin, October 2014 to September 2015*) show no real improvement: just under 69 per cent of young offenders reoffend within a year of release from custody, compared with 58 per cent of adults released from a short sentence (less than 12 months) or 31 per cent for those on longer sentences.

21

YOUNG OFFENDERS

Detention 'during Her Majesty's pleasure'

Under the Powers of Criminal Courts (Sentencing) Act 2000, s. 90 an offender convicted of murder who was under 18 when the offence was committed must be sentenced to be detained indefinitely, known as 'during Her Majesty's pleasure'.

This form of sentence was considered by the House of Lords in *R v Secretary of State for the Home Department, ex parte* **Venables and Thompson** (1997), which we saw discussed earlier in the chapter. The two applicants had been convicted of the murder of James Bulger. They had been 10 years old at the time of the offence and were given a sentence of detention during Her Majesty's pleasure. The Home Secretary received several petitions signed by thousands of people demanding that the boys serve at least 25 years in custody. In 1994, the Home Secretary, applying the same procedures to children detained at Her Majesty's pleasure as to adults given a mandatory life sentence, decided that the minimum sentence that they should serve was 15 years. The case was taken to the European Court of Human Rights. In *T v UK* and *V v UK* (2000) the court held that it was not compatible with the Convention for the Home Secretary to set tariffs in the case of detention during Her Majesty's pleasure. In response to this finding the Criminal Justice and Court Services Act 2000 makes provision for the sentencing court to set the tariff in these cases.

Detention under PCC(S)A 2000, s. 91

The Powers of Criminal Courts (Sentencing) Act 2000, s. 91 provides that where a person aged 10 or over has been convicted in the Crown Court of an offence with a maximum sentence of 14 years' imprisonment or more, the court may pass a sentence not exceeding that maximum.

Detention and training orders

The only custodial sentence available in the youth court is a detention and training order of up to two years. The use of custody against young children is particularly controversial as, by definition, this involves their removal from their family. Under s. 100 of the PCC(S)A 2000, the courts can make a detention and training order. Such an order must be for a term of between 4 and 24 months. Half this period will be spent in detention and the other half under supervision. The detention period can be served in any secure accommodation deemed suitable by the Home Secretary: for example, a Young Offender Institution, Secure Training Centre, Youth Treatment Centre or local authority secure unit. The order will be available initially for offenders aged at least 12 years, but may be extended to 10- and 11-year-olds where the court 'is of the opinion that only a custodial sentence would be adequate to protect the public from further offending by him'. The sentence of detention in a Young Offender Institution will remain available for offenders aged 18 to 20 years.

The privately run Medway Secure Training Centre in Kent was completed in 1998 in order to detain 12–17-year-olds. This has places for 70 trainees. As the children detained are very young, it is important that they be able to maintain links with their families during their detention. Many will be detained far away from home and there is an assisted visits scheme financed by the Home Office for visits on a weekly basis and arrangements for contact through letters and telephone calls. The training and education programmes include education for 25 hours a week based on the national curriculum, one hour daily for tackling offending behaviour and crime avoidance and regular practical tuition in social skills and domestic training. This centre is set to close in early 2020, and the first of the Government's new £5 million Secure Schools will open here later that year. This will be run by not-for-profit academy trusts and is

Figure 21.3 Persons sentenced for indictable offences by age, years ending March 2006 to March 2016

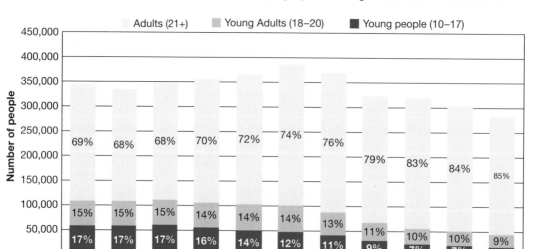

Source: Page 76, of the Youth Justice Statistics 2015/16 available online at: https://www.gov.uk/government/uploads/system/uploads/attachment_data/file/585897/youth-justice-statistics-2015-2016.pdf

the starting point for the Ministry of Justice to put education at the heart of youth custody. On announcing the development, Minister Dr Philip Lee said: 'Secure Schools will focus on the root cause of offending, by intervening early to help break the cycle of reoffending – making our streets safer and diverting young people away from a life of crime.'

It is debatable whether it is necessary to impose custodial sentences on children by means of a detention and training order. The vast majority of crimes committed by this age group are minor property offences, and for more serious cases s. 91 of the PCC(S)A 2000 applies. Given the problems associated with custodial sentences, putting young persons at risk of custody for more minor offences may not be effective in crime reduction in the long term.

The tariff

Because the maximum custodial sentences for young offenders are usually quite short, the tariff approach described in the chapter on sentencing (Chapter 20) is of limited application to the sentencing of young offenders, except in the sense that young offenders can usually rely on their youth as strong mitigation.

21.7.2 Referral orders

Most young offenders appearing before a youth court for the first time are given a mandatory referral to a youth offender panel if they plead guilty. Following a change made by the Criminal Justice and Immigration Act 2008, a referral order can also be made on a second conviction if the offender did not receive a referral order for the first conviction but was bound over to keep the peace or received a conditional discharge. Exceptionally, the courts can make a second referral order. This order was created by the Youth Justice and Criminal Evidence Act 1999, and the relevant legislative provisions are now contained in PCC(S)A 2000, s. 16. Referral orders are automatically made for first-time convictions where the offence is imprisonable, the sentence is not fixed by law and where a custodial sentence is not appropriate. The court has a discretion to make a referral order if the defendant has pleaded guilty to a single non-imprisonable offence and this is their first conviction. The youth offender panel agrees a 'programme of behaviour' with the young offender, the primary aims of which are the prevention of reoffending and restorative justice (in other words, that the offender pays back the victim or society in some way). Once agreed, the terms of the programme of behaviour are written in a youth offender contract. This may require the offender, among other things, to compensate financially or otherwise victims or other people whom the panel considers to have been affected by the offence; to attend mediation sessions with victims; to carry out unpaid work in the community; or to observe prescribed curfews. The order is administered by the local Youth Offending Team. Subsequent meetings will be arranged with the panel to review compliance with the contract and a final meeting will determine whether the contract has been satisfactorily completed. The courts have a discretion to discharge referral orders early for good behaviour or extend the term of the order for up to three months at the recommendation of the youth offender panel, for example, when dealing with cases of breach.

It was hoped that this procedure will prove more effective than the traditional court sentencing process, which the Home Secretary has criticised in Parliament, saying:

[T]he young offender is, at best, a spectator in a theatre where other people are the actors. At worst, the young offender is wholly detached and contemptuous of what is going on . . . never asked to engage his brain as to what he has done, or why he hurt the victim.

In many ways, the sentence provides the young offender with a second chance. They can admit their guilt knowing what sentence they will receive. Their future employment prospects are not unduly damaged as the offence is deemed spent on the completion of the sentence so that they do not have a criminal record.

21.7.3 Reparation orders

Under s. 73 of the PCC(S)A 2000, a court can hand down a reparation order requiring an offender under the age of 18 to make reparation commensurate with the seriousness of the offence, to the victim or to the community at large. Before making such an order, the court must obtain a report as to what type of work is suitable for the offender and the attitude of the victim or victims to the proposed requirements (PCC(S)A 2000, s. 74). Guidance from the Home Office indicates that the order may require the writing of a letter of apology to the victim, help to be given in repairing damage caused by the offending conduct, the cleaning of graffiti, weeding a garden, collecting litter or doing other work to help the community. The work required must not exceed 24 hours over a period of three months. Most importantly, the order may require a meeting with the victim in an attempt to make the offender understand the emotional and physical damage his or her actions have caused. For example, a burglar frequently thinks that a burglary will merely require the victim to make an insurance claim, not realising the fear and pain it actually causes, partly because traditionally the criminal justice system has been very impersonal. Reparation orders try to personalise the system, by putting offenders face to face with victims, forcing them to see the pain they have caused. The order may be combined with a compensation order if the court considers that financial compensation would also be appropriate. These orders are part of a system of restorative justice, and are becoming increasingly important in the youth justice system.

In the 1998 British Crime Survey, 60 per cent of respondents approved of the concept of reparation orders, though only 40 per cent would be prepared to meet the offender. The orders not only help to rehabilitate criminals but also help victims and their families come to terms with their feelings of fear and anger caused by the crime and give them positive input into the process of getting the offender to make amends. A small pilot study carried out in the Thames Valley area found that the young offenders who met the victims in controlled mediation sessions were half as likely to reoffend as those who were given police cautions. In Australia, where restorative justice is practised more widely, there has been a 38 per cent reduction in reoffending after violent criminals met their victims.

21.7.4 Youth rehabilitation orders

In 2003, the Labour Government published a consultation paper, *Youth Justice – the Next Steps*. This paper set out possible reforms to the youth justice system. Some of these reform proposals can now be found in the Criminal Justice and Immigration Act 2008. The Act created youth rehabilitation orders under which a young person undertakes a sentence in the community. The aim of this reform was both to simplify the law and to make the sentencing interventions more flexible. When imposing a youth rehabilitation order a court chooses from the following 'menu' of requirements that the offender must comply with:

- an activity requirement;
- a supervision requirement (the offender will be supervised by a probation officer or the social services department to assist the personal development of the young offender);

- an unpaid work requirement (if the offender is aged 16 or 17);

- a programme requirement (a new requirement for juveniles, designed to allow them to engage in programmes that address their offending behaviour or teach life skills);

- an attendance centre requirement (attendance centres are normally run by the police, and tend to involve attendance on Saturday afternoons for physical education classes or practical courses);

- a prohibited activity requirement (including a prohibition on carrying a gun);

- an exclusion requirement;

- a residence requirement (16–17-year-olds);

- a local authority residence requirement;

- a mental health treatment requirement;

- a drug treatment requirement;

- a drug testing requirement;

- an intoxicating substance requirement;

- an education requirement;

- an electronic monitoring requirement;

- intensive supervision and surveillance (for a minimum of six months);

- fostering;

- a curfew requirement.

A court can impose a curfew for up to 12 months on an offender under the age of 16 years. Compliance with the curfew can be monitored through the use of an electronic tag. The use of electronic tagging on young offenders was piloted in two schemes, the results of which were not particularly promising. In Manchester, 39 per cent of young offenders breached their curfew. The majority of the offenders spent their time at home watching television or sleeping. There is also a danger that some children will wear their tags with pride, seeing them as trophies to be shown off to their peers.

Initially introduced under the Anti-Social Behaviour Act 2003 (now repealed), curfews can be imposed on whole neighbourhoods. The curfew can ban, for a specified period, children under 16 from being in a public place between 9 pm and 6 am unless they are accompanied by an adult. A police officer who has reasonable cause to believe a child to be in contravention of the ban may inform the local authority of the contravention. To date, the police have imposed 150 local curfews, which cover large parts of the country including much of central London. These are the first curfews we have seen in Britain since the Second World War. No other European country imposes curfews on young people. The legality of a curfew order imposed in Richmond, Surrey, was challenged by a teenage boy in *R (on the application of W)* v *Metropolitan Police Commissioner* (2005). The Court of Appeal held that the Act allowed police to use reasonable force to remove children from a public place.

A youth rehabilitation order with intensive supervision and surveillance or intensive fostering can only be made if the offence committed was imprisonable and so serious that if that sentence was not available a sentence of custody would be appropriate; and, in addition, in the case of under-15-year-olds, the young person must be a persistent offender.

A youth rehabilitation order is the standard community sentence for the majority of young offenders. It is imposed if the court considers that:

- the offending was serious enough to warrant it;
- the requirements forming part of the order are the most suitable for the offender; and
- the restrictions on liberty imposed by the order are commensurate with the seriousness of the offence.

If the youth rehabilitation order is breached, the young person is issued with a warning. After the third warning (or earlier if appropriate), a young person can be returned to court. At court the offender can be given a custodial sentence if the original offence was imprisonable. If there is 'wilful and persistent' non-compliance with an order and the original offence was non-imprisonable, the young offender should be given intensive supervision and surveillance or placed in intensive fostering. If there is still wilful and persistent non-compliance, the young person can be placed in custody.

Parents of young offenders

Where a young offender is under 16, a parent or guardian must be required to attend the court hearing, unless the court considers that this would be unreasonable. If the offender is convicted, the court is required to bind over the parents to take proper care and exercise proper control over their child; the courts also have discretion to do this in the case of 16- or 17-year-olds. Although the consent of the parents is required, an unreasonable refusal can attract a fine of up to £1,000. Parents or guardians can also be bound over to ensure that the young offender complies with a community order (PCC(S)A 2000, s. 150).

Where an offender under 16 is sentenced to a fine, the parents are required to pay it. The court may also order parents to pay in the case of 16- and 17-year-old children. The fine will be assessed taking into account the financial situation of the parent, rather than the young offender. Where a local authority has parental responsibility for a young person who is in their care, or has provided accommodation for them, it is to be treated as the young person's parent for these purposes. Where a fine has not been paid, the courts can impose a youth default order, which requires a 16- or 17-year-old child to carry out unpaid work, or a curfew or attendance centre requirement.

In 1997 the Home Office published a study, *Women in Prison: A Thematic Review*, by Sir David Ramsbotham. It noted that when fines for juvenile offences are imposed on the parent or guardian, this is usually in practice the mother, often alone, and coping in difficult circumstances. If she does not (or cannot) pay the fine, she runs the risk of imprisonment. The report gives the example of Margaret, aged 46 and on income support. She had to pay fines imposed as a result of her son's criminal offences (he was then 16). Magistrates sentenced her to 27 days' imprisonment for a remaining debt of £170.50, despite the fact that she had not personally committed any crime.

Child safety orders

A local authority can commence civil proceedings for a child safety order to be made by a magistrates' court under ss. 11–13 of the Crime and Disorder Act 1998. It can require a child under the age of 10 to be at home at specified times or to avoid certain people or places to limit the risk of their involvement in crime. The order can be made if the child has committed or risks committing an act which would have constituted an offence if the child had been older, he or she has breached a curfew notice or behaved in an anti-social manner. The aim of this order is to divert children below the age of 10 from behaviour that would bring them into conflict with the criminal law. The child will be placed under the supervision of a social worker or member of a Youth Offending Team for up to three months (and, exceptionally, 12 months), and the child will be required to comply with the requirements in the order. These requirements are not specified in the Act and are whatever the court considers desirable in the interests of securing that the child receives appropriate care, protection and support and is subject to proper control, and to prevent the repetition of the offending behaviour. It is targeting those children who are 'running wild' but are too young to be the subject of criminal proceedings. Where longer-term intervention is required, care proceedings will be brought by the local authority instead, with a care order continuing until the child becomes an adult. If the child safety order is breached, care proceedings may also be brought.

Parenting orders

Under s. 8 of the Crime and Disorder Act 1998, a court may make a parenting order. The order is designed to help and support parents (or guardians) in addressing their child's anti-social behaviour. It is available in certain situations:

1   a court makes a child safety order;

2   a court makes a parental compensation order in relation to a child's behaviour;

3   an injunction is granted under s. 1 of the Anti-social Behaviour, Crime and Policing Act 2014, an order is made under s. 22 of that Act, or a sexual harm prevention order is made in respect of a child or young person;

4   a young person has been convicted of an offence;

5   a parent has been convicted for failing to secure his or her child's attendance at school.

The order can be for a maximum of 12 months and consists of two elements. First, the parent will have to attend counselling or guidance sessions for up to three months. Secondly, the parent must comply with certain specific requirements aimed at ensuring that they exercise control over their child. This may take the form of a residential course if this is likely to be more effective than a non-residential course and the interference with family life is proportionate. Parents convicted of failing to comply with a parenting order are liable to a fine.

Nearly 3,000 parents participated in 34 parenting programmes across England and Wales between 1999 and 2001. The Youth Justice Board found that parenting programmes, aimed at giving parents support and advice in child rearing, reduced reoffending by the children by one-third. They have concluded that while the introduction of these programmes was controversial, they actually provide a powerful way to reach parents who need help and who might otherwise never attend a parenting support service.

In its 'Respect Action Plan', published in 2006, the Government proposed the creation of a National Parenting Academy, to train social workers and other professionals to help families with anti-social children. The National Academy for Parenting Practitioners ran from 2007 to 2010 and was given £30 million funding by the Department of Education. Kings College London took over the research elements of this organisation and the National Academy for Parenting Research remains active today.

21

YOUNG OFFENDERS

21.7.5 Time limits

In 1998 the criminal justice system took, on average, four-and-a-half months to process a young offender from the time of arrest to sentence. The Audit Commission found that in 1997 cases were generally adjourned on four occasions before completion. The Crime and Disorder Act 1998 aimed to reduce this period as there is concern that delays in the system are undermining the impact of the sentence on the offender. In cases involving persons under the age of 18, s. 44 (now repealed) provided that time limits may be applied from arrest to the commencement of proceedings and from conviction to sentence. The then Home Secretary commented:

> Young people must be made to recognise and accept responsibility for their crimes – at the time, not many months later. Only when this happens will there be serious pressure on young offenders to change their behaviour rather than settle into a life of crime.

In order to assist practitioners in delivering those targets, the Government provided guidelines on the length of time each stage of the youth justice process should take in a straightforward case involving a persistent young offender. These were as follows:

Arrest to charge:	2 days
Charge to first appearance at court:	7 days
First appearance to start of trial:	28 days
Verdict to sentence:	14 days

The Government succeeded in cutting the average time taken to deal with most persistent young offenders in the magistrates' courts from 142 days in 1996 to 57 days in 2008.

Figure 21.4 Under 18 custody figures for England and Wales by ethnicity

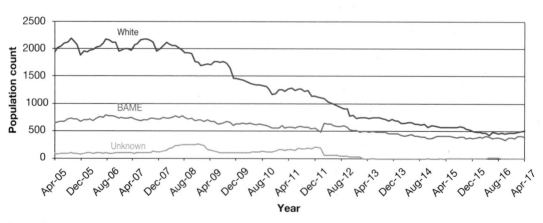

Source: Page 5, Under 18 secure population by ethnicity 2005/05–2017/18
https://www.gov.uk/government/uploads/system/uploads/attachment_data/file/643001/lammy-review-final-report.pdf

The Bigger Picture: Zero tolerance

The Labour Government described its approach to young offenders as being one of 'zero tolerance'. This is a concept that was developed by academics during the 1980s and was adopted by President Ronald Reagan as part of his war against drugs. The principle behind zero tolerance is the 'broken windows theory'. Under this theory, when a neighbourhood shows signs of decay such as graffiti, litter and broken windows, decent people leave, disorder takes over and the area slides into crime. The theory demands that even the most minor offences be pursued with the same vigilance as serious ones, to create a deterrent effect.

Zero tolerance policing was used in New York under the leadership of Mayor Giuliani. The results in New York were impressive, with falls of 50 per cent in overall crime and nearly two-thirds in the murder rate. But some of the police methods were criticised as aggressive by the pressure group Human Rights Watch. Critics also suggested that problematic people were simply shifted from rich to poor neighbourhoods – by putting thousands of homeless people onto buses and sending them to remote hostels. There may be other reasons for the drop in crime, such as a reduction in the number of young people in the general population, as this group is statistically more likely to offend. Thus, for example, San Diego saw a significant reduction in crime over a similar period without using zero tolerance policing, but by building partnerships between the police and the public. A recent use of 'zero tolerance' policy has been by the police in Los Angeles in an attempt to curtail the activities of gang members. Concern had developed that gangs in Los Angeles were disrupting neighbourhoods by dealing in drugs, painting graffiti on walls, urinating on private property, having all-night parties and committing violence and murder. The Los Angeles police, in conjunction with local prosecutors, strictly applied existing law by issuing civil court injunctions against gang members which prevented them from, for example, 'standing, sitting, walking, driving, gathering or appearing anywhere in public view' in a four-block area where their activities were disruptive. Since the imposition of the zero tolerance policy, some local residents say that the injunctions have returned their neighbourhoods to normal, allowing their children once again to play outside. Opponents of the policy claim that it breaches individuals' rights to freedom of association and speech.

One of the main forms of implementation of the zero tolerance policy by the Labour Government was through the introduction of anti-social behaviour orders, since replaced by criminal behaviour orders (discussed at p. 553). Zero tolerance policing was spearheaded in the UK in Cleveland. Home Office statistics suggest that the policing method was successful in reducing offences targeted by the policy. Between January and December 1997 reported burglary in Cleveland dropped by 26 per cent, robbery by 25 per cent and overall reported crime by 18 per cent. This was the highest reported reduction in England and Wales. At the same time, the area saw a threefold increase in the incidence of stop and searches. Its clear-up rate had also declined from 27 per cent in 1993 to 25 per cent in 1997, a figure that was 3 per cent below the British average.

In 2003 the Government issued a consultation paper entitled *Transforming Youth Custody: Putting Education at the Heart of Detention*. This paper notes that 88 per cent of boys aged 15–17 placed in custody have been excluded from school at some time, and some 18 per cent have special educational needs (compared with 3 per cent of the general population). Half the young people in custody aged 15–17 have a literacy level of a 7–11-year-old. Young people in a Young Offender Institution are supposed to receive 15 hours' education each week, but this rarely happens in practice. While educational opportunities are already available to young offenders, the Government wants to put a greater emphasis on education so that it is at the centre of the philosophy and practice of the youth system.

21.8 Key reports

There have been a number of significant reports in the 2016–17 period which focus on youth justice reform.

21.8.1 *Review of the Youth Justice System in England and Wales* (The Taylor Review)

Charlie Taylor's review focuses on two major recommendations: a far greater emphasis on education in the youth justice system and the adoption of a devolved structure. It highlights the vast drop in children being cautioned or convicted – a 79 per cent reduction in 2015 from only eight years previously – but makes clear that those remaining in the system are troubled, and emphasises the importance of rehabilitation and restoration for these young people:

> Among the children now in the youth justice system are high numbers of black, Muslim and white working class boys; many are in care, and mental and other health problems, and learning difficulties, are common . . . Many of the children in the system come from some of the most dysfunctional and chaotic families where drug and alcohol misuse, physical and emotional abuse and offending is common. Often they are victims of crime themselves. Though children's backgrounds should not be used as an excuse for their behaviour, it is clear that the failure of education, health, social care and other agencies to tackle these problems have contributed to their presence in the youth justice system.

In terms of education, the majority of those young people in custody are disengaged, with many either excluded from school or absent through long periods of truancy. The Government response to this report committed to agreeing to the majority of Taylor's recommendations, piloting secure schools and also to developing a Youth Custody Apprenticeship Pathway to ensure that all young people will be on a track into education, training or employment once released. A new role, the Youth Justice Officer, will be introduced, ensuring that there are more people trained specifically to work with young people.

There has been dissatisfaction at the slow response to implementing the reforms within the Taylor Review; the Standing Committee for Youth Justice said the Government has 'not gone far enough' in recommendation adoption, and the National Association for Youth Justice described the response as a 'missed opportunity'.

21.8.2 *The treatment of young adults in the criminal justice system* (House of Commons Justice Committee)

The Justice Committee put forward their 'blueprint for change', acknowledging that there is a strong case for dealing with young adults within the justice system differently and recognising that they are still developing neurologically up to the age of 25. The report notes that offenders in the 18–25 age bracket are overwhelmingly more likely to have 'cognitive difficulties with thinking, acting, and solving problems, emotional literacy and regulation, learning difficulties . . . and language disorders and head injuries'.

Recommendations include:

● extending statutory support currently provided to under-18-year-olds by a range of agencies up to the age of 25;

Table 21.1 Prevalence of neuro-developmental disorders amongst young people in the general population and those in custody

	Prevalence among young people in general population	Prevalence among young people in custody
Learning disability	2–4%	23–32%
Communication impairment	5–7%	60–90%
ADHD	1.7–9%	12%
Autism Spectrum Disorder	0.6–1.2%	15%
Any head injury	24–42%	49–72%
Head injury resulting in loss of consciousness	5–24%	32–50%

Source: Page 10, *The treatment of young adults in the criminal justice system,* House of Commons Justice Committee, available at: https://www.parliament.uk/business/committees/committees-a-z/commons-select/justice-committee/news-parliament-20151/young-adults-criminal-justice-system-report-launch-16-17/

- provision of more specialist staff within prison and probation services with experience of working with young people;
- further research regarding the treatment of adult offenders; and
- evaluating the impact of maturity as a possible mitigating factor in sentencing, and the testing of young adult courts.

June 2018 saw the publication of a follow-up report by the House of Commons Justice Committee: *Young adults in the criminal justice system.* This addresses the lack of commitment it perceived in the Government's response to the original report, which took a much narrower approach than proposed. They make further recommendations as well as reviewing the progress made by the Ministry of Justice in implementing their preferred approach.

The Howard League for Penal Reform/Barrow Cadbury Trust reports, *Judging Maturity* (2017) and *Sentencing Young Adults* (2018) also explore these areas and the organisations are pushing for young adults in the 18–25 age bracket to be seen as a distinct group and for maturity to be taken into account and seen as a mitigating factor when sentencing.

21.8.3 *The Lammy Review: An independent review into the treatment of, and outcomes for, Black, Asian and Minority Ethnic individuals in the Criminal Justice System*

David Lammy's independent report analyses data from the period 2006–16 and flags up the failings of the criminal justice system. Alarming figures are presented in relation to black, Asian and minority ethnic (BAME) individuals and youth justice, and these include the following.

- The BAME proportion of young people offending for the first time rose from 11 per cent (March 2006) to 19 per cent (March 2016).

- The BAME proportion of young people reoffending rose from 11 per cent (March 2006) to 19 per cent (March 2016).
- Despite making up just 14 per cent of the population, over 40 per cent of young people in custody are from BAME backgrounds.
- The BAME proportion of youth prisoners has risen from 25 per cent to 41 per cent in the decade 2006–16.

Lammy makes far-reaching and transformative proposals for reform, including the following.

- All sentencing remarks in the Crown Court should be published, making justice more transparent and building trust between BAME individuals and the justice system (Recommendation 13).
- Renaming youth offender panels as Local Justice Panels. These would take place within the community and have a strong emphasis on parenting (Recommendation 18).
- Allocating magistrates a certain number of cases in the youth justice system from start to finish, in order for them to gain a deeper understanding of how the rehabilitation process works (Recommendation 19).
- Rolling out a 'deferred prosecution' model. This would permit low-level offenders to receive targeted rehabilitation before entering a plea. Those who successfully followed the programme through would see the charges dropped (Recommendation 10).

The Government published its response to the Lammy Review in December 2017 and is pushing forward with some of Lammy's recommendations. Some though have already been dismissed, for example the prospect of targets for BAME judges.

Answering questions

1 How effectively does the criminal justice system deal with offenders under the age of 18 before trial?

2 Critically discuss the legislative provisions which have been put in place to protect child/youth offenders.

3 To what extent is a parent liable for the actions of an offender aged under 16?

4 Deborah, aged 15, has been seen by a police officer attacking an old man. He arrests her and takes her to the police station.

   (a) Explain the rules concerning the police powers to question Deborah about the offence.

   (b) If Deborah is charged and prosecuted, which courts are likely to deal with her case (excluding possible appeals)?

   (c) What sentencing powers do the courts have in respect of her offence?

5 Louise, aged 16, has been seen by a police officer stabbing an old lady and snatching her handbag. He arrests her and takes her to the police station.

   (a) Explain the rules concerning the police powers to question Louise about the offence.

   (b) If Louise is charged and prosecuted, which court(s) are likely to deal with her case at first instance?

For answers to these questions, visit the companion website at www.pearsoned.co.uk/elliottquinn

SUMMARY OF CHAPTER 21: YOUNG OFFENDERS

Introduction

Offenders under 18 are in some respects dealt with differently by the criminal justice system from adult offenders. In 1998, a Youth Justice Board was established to monitor, set standards and promote good practice.

Criminal liability

Children under the age of 10 cannot be liable for a criminal offence.

Young people and the police

An adult responsible for a young person's welfare or an appropriate adult should normally be present at the police station with the young person.

Remand and bail

Young offenders should usually be granted bail, and when bail is refused they should not be held in adult prisons or remand centres.

Youth cautions

Youth cautions are sometimes issued instead of a case being prosecuted to try to divert young offenders from the criminal justice system.

Youth conditional cautions

These cautions are combined with conditions, such as the payment of a fine, and were introduced in 2008.

Trial

Young offenders are usually tried in youth courts, and only occasionally can they be tried in the Crown Court. The European Court of Human Rights found that Jon Venables and Robert Thompson, who were convicted by a Crown Court of murdering the two-year-old, James Bulger, in 1993, did not receive a fair trial in accordance with Art. 6 of the European Convention on Human Rights. As a result, a Practice Direction was issued by the Lord Chief Justice which lays down guidance on how young offenders should be tried when their case is heard in the Crown Court.

Custodial sentences

The courts may not pass a sentence of imprisonment on an offender under the age of 18. Such offenders may be detained in other places, such as a Young Offender Institution or local authority accommodation.

Detention 'during Her Majesty's pleasure'

Under the Powers of Criminal Courts (Sentencing) Act 2000, an offender convicted of murder who was under 18 when the offence was committed must be sentenced to be detained indefinitely, known as 'during Her Majesty's pleasure'.

Detention under the Powers of Criminal Courts (Sentencing) Act 2000, s. 91

Where a person aged 10 or over has been convicted in the Crown Court of an offence with a maximum sentence of 14 years' imprisonment or more, the court may pass a sentence not exceeding that maximum.

Detention and training orders

Under the Powers of Criminal Courts (Sentencing) Act 2000 the courts can make a detention and training order against offenders aged between 12 and 17. Half the sentence will be spent in detention and the other half under supervision.

Referral orders

Most young offenders appearing before a youth court for the first time are given a mandatory referral to a youth offender panel if they plead guilty.

Reparation order

A reparation order requires an offender under the age of 18 to make reparation commensurate with the seriousness of the offence to the victim or to the community at large.

Youth rehabilitation orders

Youth rehabilitation orders were created by the Criminal Justice and Immigration Act 2008 and are a community sentence under which a range of requirements can be imposed on a young offender.

Parents of young offenders

Certain powers exist to coerce parents to take responsibility for the offending conduct of their children.

Time limits

The Government has set targets for the handling of cases involving young offenders to try to speed up the youth justice system.

Zero tolerance

The Labour Government described its approach to young offenders as being one of 'zero tolerance', which means that the law will be strictly enforced in order to reduce crime.

Key reports

A number of significant reports in the 2016–17 period have focused on youth justice reform:

- The Taylor Review recommends a far greater emphasis on education in the youth justice system and the adoption of a devolved structure.
- The Justice Committee notes there is a case for dealing with young adults within the justice system differently and recognising that they are still developing neurologically up to the age of 25.
- The Lammy Review identified alarming figures in relation to BAME individuals and youth justice, and proposed far-reaching and transformative proposals for reform.

Reading list

Audit Commission (1997) *Misspent Youth: Young People and Crime*. London: Audit Commission.

(2004) *Youth Justice*. London: Audit Commission.

Brown, D. *et al.* (1992) *Changing the Code: Police Detention under the Revised PACE Codes of Practice*. Home Office Research Study No. 129. London: HMSO.

Brown, K. (2012) "It is not as easy as ABC": examining practitioners' views on using behavioural contracts to encourage young people to accept responsibility for their anti-social behaviour. *Journal of Criminal Law*, 53.

Evans, R. (1993) *The Conduct of Police Interviews with Juveniles*. London: HMSO.

Field, S. (2008) Early intervention and the "new" youth justice: a study of initial decision-making. *Criminal Law Review*, 177.

Fionda, J. (2006) *Devils and Angels*. Oxford: Hart.

Home Office (1998a) *No More Excuses – A New Approach to Tackling Youth Crime in England and Wales*. London: Home Office.

Kemp, V., Pleasence, P. and Balmer, N. (2011) Children, young people and requests for police station legal advice: 25 years on from PACE. *Youth Justice*, 11(1): 28.

Ramsbotham, Sir D. (1997) *Women in Prison: A Thematic Review*. London: Home Office.

Thompson, R. (2012) Grave crimes – now it's personal. *Criminal Law Review*, 30.

On the internet

Research carried out for the Home Office on referral orders (*The Introduction of Referral Orders into the Youth Justice System* (2001), RDS Occasional Paper No. 70) is available at:
http://webarchive.nationalarchives.gov.uk/20011220104429/http://www.homeoffice.gov.uk:80/rds/adhocpubs1.html

The Youth Justice Board has a website that can be found at:

> https://www.gov.uk/government/organisations/youth-justice-board-for-england-and-wales

A report into young black people in the criminal justice system is available at:

> http://webarchive.nationalarchives.gov.uk/+/http:/www.justice.gov.uk/publications/docs/young-black-people-cjs-dec-08ii.pdf

The consultation paper *Transforming Youth Custody: Putting education at the heart of detention* (2013) is available at:

> https://consult.justice.gov.uk/digital-communications/transforming-youth-custody

The Ministry of Justice *Proven Reoffending Statistics Quarterly Bulletin, October 2014 to September 2015* (published 27 July 2017) is available at:

> https://assets.publishing.service.gov.uk/government/uploads/system/uploads/attachment_data/file/633194/proven-reoffending-2015-q3.pdf

The Howard League for Penal Reform report *Future insecure: Secure children's homes in England and Wales* (2016) can be found at:

> http://howardleague.org/wp-content/uploads/2016/05/Future-Insecure.pdf

Statistics from Inquest: *Deaths of children and young people in prison* can be found at:

> https://www.inquest.org.uk/deaths-of-children-and-young-people-in-prison

The Lammy Review: An independent review into the treatment of, and outcomes for, Black, Asian and Minority Ethnic individuals in the Criminal Justice System (2017) is available at:

> https://assets.publishing.service.gov.uk/government/uploads/system/uploads/attachment_data/file/643001/lammy-review-final-report.pdf

The Charlie Taylor report, *Review of the Youth Justice System in England and Wales* (December 2016) is available at:

> https://www.gov.uk/government/publications/review-of-the-youth-justice-system

The House of Commons Justice Committee report, *The treatment of young adults in the criminal justice system* (October 2016) is at:

> https://www.parliament.uk/business/committees/committees-a-z/commons-select/justice-committee/news-parliament-20151/young-adults-criminal-justice-system-report-launch-16-17/

Law Commission, *The Sentencing Code: Disposals relating to children and young persons* (Consultation Paper 234), is available at:

> https://www.lawcom.gov.uk/project/sentencing-code/

House of Commons Justice Committee, *Young adults in the criminal justice system*, (12 June 2018, HC 419), is available at:

> https://publications.parliament.uk/pa/cm201719/cmselect/cmjust/419/419.pdf

Chapter 22
Criminal appeals

This chapter discusses:

- appeals from the magistrates' court;
- appeals from the Crown Court;
- the powers of the prosecution to appeal;
- the role of the Privy Council;
- the Criminal Cases Review Commission; and
- criticism and reform of the appeal system.

22.1 Appeals

The appeals system provides a route for challenging the decisions of the lower courts and has two basic functions:

1   Reviewing potentially unjust or incorrect decisions which may make a conviction 'unsafe'. This would usually arise through the erroneous application of the law or procedure but may also be caused by errors of fact. An example of an error of law might be that the judge has wrongly defined an offence when directing the jury as to what needs to be proved, or more commonly, an incorrect determination by the trial judge as to the admissibility or exclusion of evidence. An error of fact might be that the prosecution advanced a case which was not justified or supported by the evidence. The test that the Court of Appeal applies is whether the conviction is 'unsafe'.

2   Promoting a consistent development of the law. Lower courts are bound by decisions of the Court of Appeal and higher courts, and appellate courts will often select certain cases (known as 'leading cases') to reiterate or clarify the correct approach to a certain area of law.

Significant reforms were introduced to the criminal appeal system in the light of heavy criticism following some high-profile miscarriages of justice. A wrongful conviction could arise for many reasons, for example because of police or prosecution malpractice, a misdirection by a judge, judicial bias, or because expert evidence, such as forensic evidence, was misleading.

22.1.1 From the magistrates' court

There are four routes of appeal.

1   The defendant may appeal to the Crown Court. If the defendant has entered a plea of guilty, they may only appeal against sentence. There is no route of appeal to the Crown Court for the prosecution.

    An appeal has to be made within 21 days of sentence. Permission is not required. These appeals are normally heard by a circuit judge or recorder sitting with two magistrates (not those who heard the original trial). Those individuals comprise the tribunal of fact (equivalent to a jury) and each person's vote has the same weight except where the court is equally divided, when the circuit judge has the casting vote. Importantly, the circuit judge determines the application of the law in such cases.

    An appeal to the Crown Court from the magistrates' court is an entire re-hearing of the case. The Crown Court approaches the matter afresh, and new evidence can be called. The trial is re-heard and the Court either confirms the verdict and/or sentence of the magistrates' court, or substitutes its own decision for that of the lower court. It can impose any sentence that the magistrates might have imposed – which can occasionally result in the accused's sentence being increased.

Under s. 48 of the SCA 1981, the Crown Court may:

(a) confirm, reverse, or vary *any* part of the decision appealed against.

(b) remit the matter with its opinion thereon to the authority whose decision is appealed against.

(c) make such other order in the matter as the court thinks just, and by such order exercise any power which the said authority might have exercised.

(d) if the appeal is against a conviction or a sentence, the (preceding provisions of this section) shall be construed as including power to award any punishment, whether more or less severe than that awarded by the magistrates' court whose decision is appealed against, if that is a punishment which that magistrates' court might have awarded.

What this means is that the Crown Court will review all decisions of the magistrates' court in the matter, not just the points on which the appeal rests. This means it has the power to increase the sentence of the offender, even if the sentence is not appealed, only the conviction.

2 Alternatively, the defendant or the prosecution may appeal to the High Court by way of case stated. This route is used when the magistrates are said to be wrong in law or acting in excess of their jurisdiction. Once an application to state a case to the High Court is made, the defendant's right to appeal to the Crown Court is lost. This route is seldom attempted. In *R* v *Mildenhall Magistrates' Court, ex parte Forest Heath DC* (1997), the Court of Appeal held that magistrates could refuse to state a case if they feel that the application is frivolous, which they defined as 'futile, misconceived, hopeless or academic'. They must inform the defendant why they have reached this conclusion.

Appeals by way of case stated are heard by up to three judges of the Queen's Bench Division and the sitting is known as a Divisional Court. The hearing consists of legal argument. The High Court may reverse, affirm or amend the determination in respect of which the case has been stated and it may remit the matter to the magistrates' court, with the opinion of the High Court, and may make any such order in relation to the matter (including as to costs) as it thinks fit.

3 A related form of appeal involves applying to the High Court for a judicial review of the proceedings. Judicial review is treated as a civil matter. The applicant for judicial review becomes a 'claimant'. This route is available to either party, where it is believed that the lower court has acted (a) 'unreasonably' (this term is defined in *Associated Provincial Picture Houses Ltd* v *Wednesbury Corporation* (1948) (see p. 716 for more on this)); (b) *ultra vires* – that is, entirely outside of its legal powers; or (c) irrationally, in that it has applied the law in an impermissible manner (for example it has failed to correctly approach the factual issue to be determined). Either party can apply on those grounds, but only on those grounds, for a judicial review of the proceedings. The High Court has similar powers to those it has upon appeal by way of case stated. However, this route of appeal is less frequently used for criminal cases than those outlined above and mainly used when it is alleged that there has been unfairness in the way that the trial in the magistrates' court had been conducted.

4 The Criminal Cases Review Commission can refer appeals from the magistrates' court to the Crown Court. This body is discussed in more detail below (see p. 613 onwards). In fact, only 5 per cent of new cases received by the Commission since 1997 have been against convictions by the magistrates.

If an appeal has been made to the Crown Court, either side may then appeal against the Crown Court's decision by way of case stated. If a party has already appealed to the High Court by way of case stated, they may not afterwards appeal to the Crown Court. The High Court has often been critical of appeals brought by way of case stated (or judicial review), which ought firstly to have been appealed to the Crown Court.

From the Divisional Court there is a further route of appeal, by either party, to the Supreme Court, but only if the Divisional Court certifies that the question of law is one of public importance and the Supreme Court or the Divisional Court gives permission – known as leave to appeal – for the appeal to be heard. The issue of leave to appeal is generally determined by the Supreme Court, and such cases are relatively rare.

In practice, appeals from the decisions of magistrates are taken in only 1 per cent of cases. This may be because the majority of defendants in the magistrates' court plead guilty and, since the offences are relatively minor and the punishment usually a fine, many of those who pleaded not guilty may prefer just to pay up and put the case behind them, avoiding the expense, publicity and embarrassment involved in an appeal. The magistrates' court also hears almost all offences of 'strict liability' – for example speeding offences, and so on – where the defences available are extremely limited.

A Home Office report (Taylor, *Cautions, Court Proceedings and Sentencing in England and Wales 1996* (1997)) found that the introduction of the right of magistrates to reopen cases to rectify their own mistakes by the Criminal Appeal Act 1995 had led to a significant reduction in both the number of appeals and the proportion of successful appeals. The number of appeals against conviction had fallen by 28 per cent from 14,100 in 1995 to 10,100 in 1996. The proportion of successful appeals – in other words, where the conviction was quashed or a retrial ordered – had fallen during the same period from a success rate of 41 per cent to 33 per cent.

22.1.2 From the Crown Court

There are three types of appeal for cases tried in the Crown Court.

1   An appeal against conviction, or sentence can be made to the Court of Appeal. The accused must apply for leave to appeal – this can technically be granted by the trial judge but in practice is almost exclusively determined by the Court of Appeal. If the appeal is dismissed, the original sentence will remain the same. If the appellant is successful, their conviction may be overturned or their sentence may be reduced.

As the aim of appeal is generally to avoid miscarriages of justice, which tend to affect the defendant, the routes of appeal available to the prosecution are far more limited. The prosecution can appeal against some rulings of law made by the Crown Court, if they agree that the ruling would otherwise require them to halt the prosecution ('offer no (or no further) evidence'). Appeals of this kind of 'terminating ruling' must be made within 48 hours of the decision, and in practice are rare.

More commonly used is the prosecution's ability to ask the Court of Appeal to review a sentence which they consider to be 'unduly lenient'. This procedure is restricted to more serious offences and requires the formal consent of the Government's Chief Legal Officer, the Attorney-General (though the procedural formalities are generally delegated to the very senior lawyers at the Crown Prosecution Service, for example the Director of Public Prosecutions). The case is then brought in the name of the Government and is termed an 'Attorney-General's Reference'. The Court of Appeal then reviews the sentence imposed and has the power to re-sentence the defendant – in reality, to increase the sentence (often significantly) – if it believes that the sentence imposed was 'unduly lenient'.

If either party is dissatisfied with the decision of the Court of Appeal, there again lies a further route of appeal on a point of law to the Supreme Court, provided that either the Court of Appeal or the Supreme Court grant permission for the appeal and that the Court of Appeal certifies that the case involves a matter of law of general public importance. The Royal Commission on Criminal Justice 1993 (RCCJ), set up after the release of the Birmingham Six, recommended that this latter requirement should be abolished.

2   The Criminal Appeal Act 1995 established the Criminal Cases Review Commission (CCRC), following a proposal made by the RCCJ. This body is not a court deciding appeals, rather it is responsible for bringing cases, where there may have been a miscarriage of justice, to the attention of the Court of Appeal if the case was originally heard by

the Crown Court (or the Crown Court if the case was originally heard by a magistrates' court). Either a person can apply to the Commission to consider their case or the Commission can consider it on their own initiative if an ordinary appeal is time-barred. The Commission can carry out an investigation into the case, which may involve asking the police to reinvestigate a crime. Before making a reference, the Commission is able to seek the Court of Appeal's opinion on any matter.

The decision whether to refer a case will be taken by a committee consisting of at least three members of the Commission. It can make such a reference in relation to a conviction where it appears to them that any argument or evidence, which was not raised in any relevant court proceedings, gives rise to a real possibility that the conviction would not be upheld were the reference to be made. A reference in relation to a sentence will be possible if 'any argument on a point of law, or any information' was not so raised and, again, there is a real possibility that the conviction might not be upheld. Where the Commission refers a conviction or sentence to the Court of Appeal, it is treated as a fresh appeal and the Commission has no further involvement in the case. Following the Criminal Justice and Immigration Act 2008, when a case is referred to the Court of Appeal by the Commission, the appeal can be dismissed if the only ground for allowing the appeal would have been because there has been a development in the law since the date of the conviction and in ordinary circumstances an application to appeal out of time would be rejected.

The Commission is based in Birmingham and consists of no fewer than 11 members, at least a third of whom are lawyers and one will have knowledge of the criminal justice system in Northern Ireland. They are appointed by the Queen on the advice of the Prime Minister.

3   A third possibility is appeal by way of case stated. There are only about 20 such cases each year heard by the High Court. The Law Commission has issued a report – *The High Court's Jurisdiction in Relation to Criminal Proceedings* (2010a) – in which it

Figure 22.1 Appellate Courts: overall caseload, 2003–2013

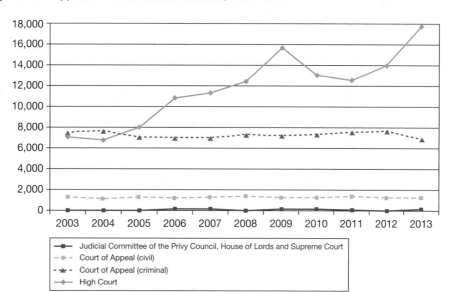

Source: Page 36 of Court Statistics Quarterly January to March 2014, Ministry of Justice Statistics bulletin, published 19 June 2014, available online at: https://www.gov.uk/government/uploads/system/uploads/attachment_data/file/321352/court-statistics-jan-mar-2014.pdf

22

CRIMINAL APPEALS

recommends that the appeal process should be simplified. It suggests that appeals (and judicial review hearings) from the Crown Court should no longer be heard by the High Court, but instead all appeals should be heard by the Court of Appeal.

22.1.3 Second appeal to the Court of Appeal

In exceptional circumstances, the Court of Appeal will be prepared to hear an appeal twice, in other words an appeal from its own earlier decision in the same case. This was decided in the landmark case of *Taylor* v *Lawrence* (2002). The Court of Appeal had dismissed the first appeal, which had been based on the fact that the judge at first instance had been a client of the claimants. After that first appeal, the appellant then discovered that the judge had not been asked to pay for work carried out the night before the case went to court. When this came to light, the Court of Appeal ruled that it would hear a second appeal. The Court of Appeal laid down guidelines for future cases on when it would be prepared to hear a second appeal in the same case. It must be clearly established that a significant injustice has probably been done, the circumstances are exceptional and there is no alternative effective remedy. There is no effective remedy if leave would not be available for an appeal to the Supreme Court. Leave to appeal would not have been given in *Taylor* v *Lawrence* because the case was not of sufficient general importance and merit.

The approach taken by the court in *Taylor* v *Lawrence* is now contained in Civil Procedure Rule 52.17.

22.1.4 Appeal against conviction

Grounds of appeal against conviction

Section 2(1) of the Criminal Appeal Act 1968 provides that the Court of Appeal:

(a) shall allow an appeal against conviction if they think that the conviction is unsafe; and

(b) shall dismiss such an appeal in any other case.

A person convicted in the Crown Court may appeal on the single ground that the conviction is 'unsafe'. If an appeal is to be made, it must be done within 28 days of conviction and the notice of application for leave (permission) to appeal should be lodged at the Crown Court at which the conviction took place. Permission to appeal against conviction is always required unless the Crown Court judge has certified that the case is fit for appeal or where the appeal has been referred by the Criminal Cases Review Commission.

It may be possible to argue that a conviction is unsafe for many reasons including:

(a) an error in the summing up;

(b) a procedural irregularity;

(c) incompetence or error on the part of the trial lawyer; or

(d) fresh evidence is discovered following the trial.

Errors in the summing up

After the closing speeches in a trial the judge sums up the evidence to the jury and directs them on the law. Errors in the summing up may give grounds for appeal. In *R* v *Williams*

(2001), Dyson LJ (at [28]) said that: 'A legal misdirection or non-direction is not significant unless it is possible that, but for the error of law, the jury would have acquitted.' Guidance for the judge relating to the content of the summing up can be found in *The Crown Court Compendium 2018*. If an error in the summing up is pleaded, the Court of Appeal will assess the alleged misdirections by setting them in the context of the whole summing up. They will not be looked at in isolation. In *R v Clarke* (2006), the appellant's convictions for murder and manslaughter were quashed. The court found that the judge had confused the meaning of murder and voluntary manslaughter in an opening passage. This not only served to confuse the jury but was also wrong in law. The judge also failed to guide the jury in relation to the appellant's bad character. The Court of Appeal concluded that the directions as to character were flawed. In short, the judge 'failed to do that which every summing-up must do, namely guide the jury as to how properly to deploy the evidence, whilst avoiding unnecessary prejudice'. In *R v Lambert* (2006), the Court of Appeal stated that the 'proper' question that must be asked, was whether, when viewed in the context of the trial as a whole, the safety of any verdict which had been given or was to be given, has been put in jeopardy, or the fairness of the trial has otherwise been prejudiced to an extent that calls for the discharge of the jury or the quashing of a verdict.

Following a procedural irregularity

If a mistake is made during the Crown Court trial this may give grounds for appeal. For example, a decision by the trial judge that certain evidence against the defendant was admissible when it was not, may make the conviction unsafe. If the Court of Appeal decides that this evidence should have been excluded, the court will consider what impact this mistake had on the trial overall. The Court of Appeal will determine whether the admission of this evidence made the appellant's conviction unsafe. Another example would be a wrongful rejection of a submission of no case to answer. If there is a submission of no case to answer (a legal submission made by the defence when the prosecution have presented the case against the defendant, before the defendant gives evidence) and the trial judge wrongly rejects it, the appeal is likely to succeed. The Court of Appeal will decide had the trial judge not made the error, would the defendant have been acquitted? In *R v Smith* (1999), the Court of Appeal quashed the conviction of the appellant, even though, in this case, the appellant had admitted guilt, as they considered the conviction was unsafe.

Errors by defence representative

An appellant can argue that the actions of his lawyers caused his conviction to be unsafe. The Court of Appeal will only allow an appeal for 'flagrantly' incompetent advocacy'. Essentially, that the effect on the trial is so unfair that the court should quash the conviction. What the court will do, is to look not just at the error but on the effect on the trial. Have they had a fair trial? *R v Boal* (1992) was an appeal on the grounds of flawed legal advice. This advice was that the appellant did not have a certain defence in law, and the appellant acted on this advice and did not assert the defence. The Court of Appeal stated that appeals 'will succeed only where the court believes the defence would quite probably have succeeded and concludes, therefore, that a clear injustice has been done'. In the case of *Ekaireb* (2015), there were serious criticisms of trial counsel's closing speech to the jury. The Court dismissed the appeal, holding that the appellant had to show that counsel's conduct had led to 'identifiable errors that resulted in an unsafe conviction and that incompetence was not enough'.

Admission of fresh evidence

An appeal against conviction is not a retrial, it is a review of the lower court's decision. One reason that a conviction may be unsafe is that new evidence has come to light which casts doubt on the safety of the conviction or it could be that the trial judge wrongly declared certain evidence to be inadmissible. This could, for example, be because of a disclosure failure pre-trial, or a lay witness may have been discovered. Not all 'fresh evidence' is oral evidence; however, if it is, the Court of Appeal has a discretion to hear the evidence which was not adduced at the trial.

The Court of Appeal can admit fresh evidence 'if they think it necessary or expedient in the interests of justice'. In deciding whether to admit fresh evidence, they must consider whether:

- the evidence is capable of belief;
- the evidence could afford a ground for allowing the appeal;
- the evidence would have been admissible at the trial; and
- there is a reasonable explanation why it was not so adduced.

Fresh evidence and post-conviction disclosure

It is argued by appeal lawyers that the post-conviction disclosure regime is not satisfactory and makes it extremely difficult for appeal lawyers to access prosecution documents post-conviction to find 'fresh evidence'. There is no right, in the law of England and Wales, to examine the prosecution materials post-conviction. If an appellant is seeking disclosure of this material, they must show that there 'exists a real prospect that further enquiry may reveal something affecting the safety of the conviction' and only then, 'that enquiry ought to be made': *R (Nunn)* v *Chief Constable of Suffolk Constabulary* [2014] UKSC 37. This can be seen as a no-win situation or a circular argument, as it is up to the CPS to decide whether or not to grant access to the materials and the appellant needs to access to these prosecution files to find the evidence that might exonerate them. This means it is very difficult, without significant funds and serious investigatory efforts, to be able to uncover the 'fresh evidence' that may exonerate an appellant.

In *R* v *Jones (Steven Martin)* (1996), the appellant had been convicted of his wife's murder and, on appeal, he had applied for the court to receive fresh expert evidence from three forensic pathologists. While on the facts of the case the evidence was allowed, the court stated that, in general, only new factual evidence (as opposed to expert evidence) would normally be admitted, noting that the test for admissibility was more appropriate to such evidence, as one could rarely consider expert evidence as 'incapable of belief'.

The Court of Appeal can direct the Criminal Cases Review Commission to investigate and report on any matter relevant to the determination of a case being considered by the court. Thus, the Court of Appeal has a radical power to seek out new evidence themselves, something that no other criminal court in England currently has been able to do, due to our traditional adversarial procedures.

In *Stafford* v *DPP* (1973), Viscount Dilhorne said that if the court was satisfied there was no reasonable doubt about the guilt of the accused, the conviction should not be quashed even though the jury might have come to a different view; the court was not bound to ask whether the evidence might have led to the jury returning a verdict of not guilty. The judges were, therefore, potentially replacing the jury's opinion with their own, which is viewed by some as weakening the right to trial by jury. This approach of second-guessing the outcome of jury deliberations has been criticised by the European Court of Human Rights in *Condron* v *United Kingdom* (2000). The case of *Stafford* v *DPP* was reconsidered in

R v *Pendleton* (2001). *Stafford* v *DPP* was not overruled but its interpretation needs to be reconsidered in the light of the later case which represents the law today. In 1986 Donald Pendleton was convicted of murdering a newspaper seller 15 years earlier. In 1999 the Criminal Cases Review Commission referred Mr Pendleton's conviction back to the Court of Appeal. The principal basis for the reference was that fresh evidence was available from an expert forensic psychologist to the effect that the appellant had psychological vulnerabilities which raised serious doubts about the reliability of his statements to the police. The Court of Appeal both received this evidence and accepted the opinion of the expert. However, the appeal was dismissed on the ground that the conviction was safe because the fresh evidence did not put a 'flavour of falsity' on the content of the interviews. His further appeal to the House of Lords was allowed.

While *Stafford* was not overruled, the House stated that the Court of Appeal had to remember it was a court of review and that the jury were the judges of fact. The Court of Appeal therefore had to bear in mind that:

> the question for its consideration is whether the conviction is safe and not whether the accused is guilty. . . It will usually be wise for the Court of Appeal, in a case of any difficulty, to test their own provisional view by asking whether the evidence, if given at the trial, might reasonably have affected the decision of the trial jury to convict. If it might, the conviction must be thought to be unsafe.

The appeal was allowed because the Court of Appeal had strayed beyond its role of simply reviewing the trial court's decision and had come perilously close to considering whether the appellant, in its judgment, was guilty. In other words, the Court of Appeal had to decide whether the jury's decision was safe, not whether the defendant was guilty. The *Pendleton* test effectively asks: does the Court of Appeal think the jury would have had a reasonable doubt about guilt? The Court of Appeal should not ask whether it itself has a reasonable doubt about guilt: to do so would be to take over the job of the jury without having had the benefit of hearing the live evidence in trial. *Pendleton* can best be understood as a middle course between, at one extreme, the quashing of all convictions where fresh evidence is received unless there is 100 per cent certainty that it would have made no difference to the verdict and, at the other extreme, a fresh determination of guilt by the appeal courts (arguably what had been suggested in *Stafford* v *DPP*). This middle course involves a 'risk assessment', gauging the potential impact of the fresh evidence on the jury: was there a real possibility that fresh evidence might reasonably have affected the jury's verdict?

The case of *R* v *Hanratty* (2002) was referred to the Court of Appeal by the Criminal Cases Review Commission. Hanratty had been convicted of murder and was later executed. A campaign was subsequently launched to establish his innocence. The Court of Appeal ordered that the body of the defendant be exhumed and samples of his DNA obtained. The prosecution made an application under the Criminal Appeal Act 1968, s. 23 to be allowed to submit fresh evidence consisting of the DNA analysis of evidence collected at the time of the murder. The defence argued against this application, primarily on the basis there was a risk the evidence had been contaminated after the defendant's arrest. The prosecution's application was successful: the defendant's DNA was found on some of the evidence collected at the time of the murder and Hanratty's appeal was rejected.

Procedure before the Court of Appeal

If the Court of Appeal is hearing an appeal against conviction, the court must comprise at least three judges and one or more of the judges must be a Lord Justice of Appeal. If the court is dealing with a case of exceptional difficulty, the court will consist of up to seven

22

CRIMINAL APPEALS

judges and It is rare for the court to deliver more than one judgment. This is to ensure for certainty of the law but is sometimes described as *prohibiting dissent*. Lady Justice Hale, President of the Supreme Court, states this about Court of Appeal judges: 'On occasions, it must place the dissenting judge in an intolerable position if he or she is to remain true to the judicial oath.'

At the appeal, the appellant's case is presented first, and the respondent then responds. The appeal takes the form of a submission based on the grounds of appeal, the relevant trial transcripts, usually the summing up and any other evidence that is relied upon. No witnesses can be heard by the court unless an application has successfully been made for fresh evidence.

Outcome of the appeal

The appellate court can allow the appeal or dismiss it (uphold the conviction or sentence). If the appeal is allowed, the court may order a new trial, or simply quash the conviction or sentence and terminate the proceedings. Under s. 2 of the Criminal Appeal Act 1968 (as amended by the 1995 Act), an appeal should be allowed if the court thinks that the conviction 'is unsafe'. There is conflicting case law as to whether, if a person is found to have had an unfair trial under Art. 6 of the European Convention on Human Rights, this will automatically mean that the conviction is unsafe and should be quashed. Some English judges prefer the view that if the defendant is clearly guilty, their conviction should be upheld as safe even if the trial was unfair. This seems to conflict with the view of the European Court of Human Rights, which suggested in *Condron* v *UK* (2000) that the conviction should always be quashed if there has been an unfair trial. The Court of Appeal may order a retrial where it feels this is required in the interests of justice. It will only do so if it accepts that the additional evidence is true but is not convinced that it is conclusive – in other words, that it would have led to a different verdict.

22.2 The power of the prosecution to appeal

22.2.1 Attorney General's reference

Appeal against excessively lenient sentences

The Criminal Justice Act 1988 enables the Attorney General to appeal against excessively lenient sentences imposed by the Crown Court. The Attorney General may, with the leave of the Court of Appeal, refer the case to them for them to review the sentencing of that person; and on such a reference the Court of Appeal may:

(i) quash any sentence passed on that person in the proceeding; and

(ii) in place of it pass such sentence as they think appropriate for the case and as the court below had power to pass when dealing with that person.

Three restrictions apply:

1   That the case is one to which this Part of this Act applies, that is, offences which are triable only on indictment, or have also been prescribed by statutory instrument.

2   It shall be made only with the permission of the Court of Appeal.

3   That the sentencing of a person in a proceeding in the Crown Court has been unduly lenient.

The prosecutors at the Crown Court, if they are of the view that a sentence was unduly lenient, must advise the Attorney General that they believe an unduly lenient sentence has been passed.

If the prosecution are successful and the Court of Appeal passes a new sentence, the court may consider the double jeopardy principle. This means that the court may choose to recognise that the defendant has already been sentenced once, and to reflect this in the new sentence. In *R v Deacon and Others AG Ref* (2014), in a case of conspiracy to possess firearm with intent to endanger life, Davis LJ stated:

> We should add that some mention was made before us of what counsel described as 'double jeopardy'. Indeed, one counsel before us rather hopefully sought to invoke what was, he said, considered to be a notional deduction for double jeopardy of the order of 20% to 30% which had some currency some time ago. We do not think that such considerations of double jeopardy in cases of this particular kind, where significant custodial sentences, on any view, were imposed and had to be imposed should feature to any great extent in the appropriate sentence now to be imposed by this court.

22.2.2 Attorney General's reference following acquittal

Where a defendant has been acquitted following trial in the Crown Court, the Attorney General refers the case to the Court of Appeal. The Court of Appeal cannot reverse the acquittal. The reference enables the Court of Appeal to clarify the law for future cases.

22.2.3 Appeal against a terminating ruling

The prosecution may appeal against the trial judge's 'terminating rulings'. As already discussed, these are rulings that stop the case. The Court of Appeal may confirm, reverse, or vary any ruling to which the appeal relates.

22

CRIMINAL APPEALS

The Bigger Picture: The double jeopardy rule

In the past there was a general rule that once a person had been tried and acquitted they could not be retried for the same offence, under the principle of double jeopardy. The rule aimed to prevent the oppressive use of the criminal justice system by public authorities. Following the unsuccessful private prosecution of three men suspected of killing Stephen Lawrence, the judicial inquiry into the affair recommended that the principle of double jeopardy should be abolished. It proposed that the Court of Appeal should have the power to permit prosecution after acquittal 'where fresh and viable evidence is presented'.

The Home Secretary referred the matter to the Law Commission. This body recommended that the double jeopardy rule should be limited. Under their recommendation, it would have been possible to retry someone acquitted of murder if new evidence was later discovered which made the prosecution case substantially stronger and the new evidence could not have been obtained before the first trial.

Sir Robin Auld's *Review of the Criminal Courts* (2001) also recommended that the double jeopardy rule should be abolished but for a wider range of offences.

The Criminal Justice Act 2003, s. 75 abolished the double jeopardy rule. The Act introduces an interlocutory prosecution right of appeal against a ruling by a Crown Court judge that there is no case to answer or any other ruling made before or during the trial that has the effect of

▶

terminating the trial. A retrial is permitted in cases of serious offences where there has been an acquittal in court, but compelling new evidence subsequently comes to light against the acquitted person. Twenty-nine serious offences are listed in a Schedule to the Act, and most of the offences carry a maximum sentence of life imprisonment. This is wider than the recommendations of the Law Commission and Sir Robin Auld. The consent of the Director of Public Prosecutions is required to reopen investigations and to apply to the Court of Appeal. There have only been two successful applications for an acquittal to be reversed, with the courts giving a strict interpretation to these statutory requirements. The first person in 800 years to be tried and convicted for a crime he was previously cleared of was a man called William Dunlop. He had been tried twice for the murder of Julie Hogg in 1989, but at these two earlier trials the jury were unable to reach a verdict and he had been formally acquitted at the end of the second trial. When new evidence arose, he was prosecuted again following the abolition of the double jeopardy rule and he pleaded guilty.

The second successful application concerned the murder of the teenager, Stephen Lawrence (see p. 460). Gary Dobson had been acquitted of his murder following a private prosecution in 1996. A fresh trial was ordered because new evidence had become available and it was in the interests of justice to allow a retrial.

Certain other exceptions to the double jeopardy rule also existed prior to the 2003 Act:

- The prosecution can state a case for consideration of the High Court following the acquittal of a defendant by the magistrates' court. This is restricted to a point of law or a dispute on jurisdiction.

- The prosecution can also, with leave, appeal to the Supreme Court against a decision of the Court of Appeal.

- The Criminal Justice Act 1972 gives the Attorney General powers to refer any point of law which has arisen in a case for the opinion of the Court of Appeal, even where the defendant was acquitted. Defendants are not identified (though they may be represented) and their acquittal remains unaffected even if the point of law goes against them – so this procedure is not, strictly speaking, an appeal. The purpose of this power is to enable the Court of Appeal to review a potentially incorrect legal ruling before it gains too wide a circulation in the trial courts.

- The Criminal Procedure and Investigations Act 1996 created a power to order a retrial where a person has been convicted of an offence involving interference with, or intimidation of, a juror, witness or potential witness, in any proceedings which led to an acquittal.

It is unlikely that the abolition of the double jeopardy rule breaches the European Convention as Art. 4(2) of Protocol 7 of the Convention expressly allows an appellate court to reopen a case in accordance with domestic law 'if there is evidence of new or newly discovered facts'.

22.3 The Supreme Court

The Supreme Court is the highest national appeal court for both civil and criminal matters. It was established in 2009 following the abolition of the House of Lords by the Constitutional Reform Act 2005 (see p. 14).

The prosecution or the defence can appeal to the Supreme Court against a decision of the Court of Appeal. This is subject to requirements: firstly, permission to appeal must be awarded by the Court of Appeal or by the Supreme Court itself; secondly, the Court of Appeal must certify that the case raises an arguable point of law of general public importance which ought to be considered by the Supreme Court at that time.

22.4 Privy Council

The Judicial Committee of the Privy Council hears:

- appeals from Commonwealth countries such as the Bahamas and Jamaica;
- appeals from Overseas Territories, such as the Falkland Islands and Gibraltar; and
- appeals from disciplinary proceedings by professional bodies and the courts of the Church of England.

The jurisdiction of the Privy Council has been significantly reduced over the years. Certain independent Commonwealth countries, including Australia, India, Malaysia, Nigeria, Pakistan and Singapore, have chosen to stop sending their final appeals to London. Most recently, a Caribbean Court of Justice has been established in Trinidad to hear final appeals from certain Caribbean islands. Many of these countries have retained the mandatory death penalty by hanging for the crime of murder. The Privy Council had been seen locally as an obstacle in the desire to execute those on death row. A landmark ruling by the Privy Council in London in 1993 stated that keeping someone on death row for more than five years was cruel and inhumane. Since then, defence lawyers have often managed to get death sentences reduced to life in prison by pursuing an appeals process that went beyond the five-year limit. The Privy Council was also viewed as a relic of England's colonial past; an alternative view is that it provides a significant and important safeguard to injustices which occur in less robust and rigorous jurisdictions.

22.5 Criticism and reform of the appeal system

22.5.1 A Supreme Court

Under provisions contained in the Constitutional Reform Act 2005, the judiciary function of the House of Lords has been abolished and replaced by a Supreme Court. This reform is discussed in detail in Chapter 1 (at p. 14).

22.5.2 Do we need a second appeal court?

Do we need two courts with purely appellate jurisdiction? Could the Supreme Court be abolished altogether, leaving the Court of Appeal as the final appellate court? Efforts to abolish the third tier of appeal date back over 100 years – in fact the Judicature Act of 1873 contained a section which did just that, but was never brought into force. The following are some of the arguments on both sides.

For abolition

- The Court of Appeal should be sufficient; a third tier is unnecessary and illogical. A.P. Herbert (1966) points out that giving appellants the chance to get their case decided by two appellate courts is like having one's appendix taken out by a distinguished surgeon and then being referred to another who might confirm the first surgeon's decision, but might just as easily recommend the appendix be replaced! Reversing legal decisions might not pose the same practical problems as medical ones but, nevertheless, it may seem odd that

Figure 22.2 An outline of the court structure in England and Wales

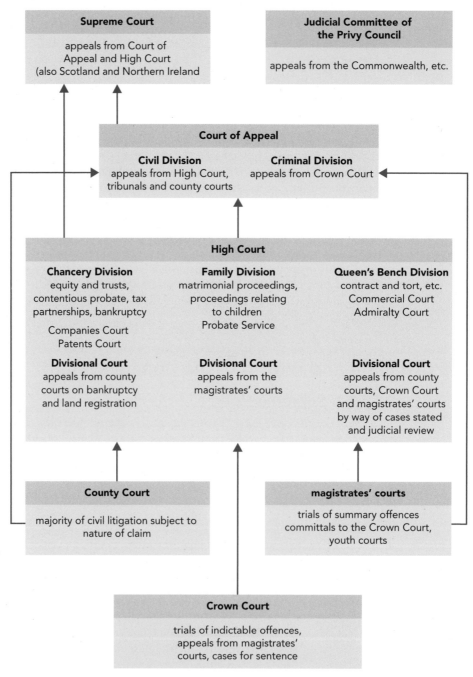

This diagram is, of necessity, much simplified and should not be taken as a comprehensive statement on the jurisdiction of any specific court.

Source: Judicial Statistics Annual Report 2004, p. 3

the decisions of the eminent judges in the Court of Appeal can be completely overturned by the Supreme Court.

- It adds cost and delay to achieving a decision. Usually, QCs are instructed in appeals to the Supreme Court, substantially increasing costs, and extra time is taken up.

- The former House of Lords has failed to make any adequate contribution to the development of the criminal law. This point is made by the eminent criminal law specialists J.C. Smith (Smith and Hogan, 2002) and Glanville Williams, and those criticisms are likely to be equally valid for the Supreme Court. Unlike the Court of Appeal, the House of Lords had no specialist divisions, and criticisms of the quality of their decisions in criminal appeals may stem from this. Williams (1983) points out that: 'It is particularly inapt that a Chancery judge should have the casting vote in the House of Lords in a criminal case, as Lord Cross did in Hyam.' He also suggests that the age of judges in the House of Lords is a problem, since old men are 'often fixed in their opinions' and 'tend to ignore the opinions of others'; this may be true, but the judges of the Court of Appeal are hardly in the first flush of youth either.

- Part of the problem relates to the strict conditions for appealing to the old House of Lords (and the new Supreme Court), which meant that few criminal cases got there, and the Law Lords actually had very little chance to make notable contributions to this area of the law. In 2009, Lord Judge suggested that the new Supreme Court should not hear criminal appeals, but this suggestion has not gained general support.

- The House of Lords tended to side with the establishment, and usually the Government. This is the argument advanced by Griffith (1997; see p. 30), but there is little evidence to suggest that the Court of Appeal would be very different in this respect if it became the highest court.

- The Supreme Court offers nothing beyond finality, and that could be more efficiently achieved without it. Jackson (1989), an academic in the field, examined the 15 appeals made to the House of Lords in 1972, and found that eight involved Government departments or national authorities and five were disputes between commercial concerns. He deduced that, in the case of both Government departments and commercial concerns, the reason for taking the case to the House of Lords was nothing more than the fact that it is the final court.

Against abolition

- Its small membership allows the Supreme Court to give a consistent leadership that the Court of Appeal, with its much greater number of judges, could not, and therefore to guide the harmonious development of the law. Louis Blom-Cooper QC (1972) has argued that, especially since the Practice Direction of 1966 allowing the third-tier appeal court to overrule its own decisions, the senior judges are in a unique position to be able to reform the law from the top. The much larger size of the Court of Appeal, and its division into different divisions, means that there would always be a danger of different divisions within it applying different views of the law.

- The combination of the two appellate courts allows the majority of appeals to be dealt with more quickly than the Supreme Court could hope to deal with them, while still retaining the smaller court for those matters which require further consideration, and for promoting consistent development of the law.

- The Supreme Court plays a valuable role in correcting decisions by the Court of Appeal. In 2007, the then House of Lords heard 58 decisions, of which 40 per cent were successful.

- The former House of Lords made some important contributions to the development of our law, including making marital rape a crime – in ***R v R*** (1991) – and confirming the restricted scope of parental rights in a modern society in ***Gillick v West Norfolk and Wisbech Area Health Authority*** (1985).

The Bigger Picture: Procedural irregularities

In his *Review of the Criminal Courts* (2001), Sir Robin Auld highlighted the difference between a conviction which was unsafe, in the sense that it was incorrect (or lacked supporting evidence), and one which was unsatisfactory because something had gone wrong in the trial process. He queried whether in the latter situation the conviction should be quashed. In September 2006, the Government issued a consultation paper, *Quashing convictions – report of a Review by the Home Secretary, Lord Chancellor and Attorney General.* This paper reviewed the legal test used by the Court of Appeal to quash criminal convictions. When the Government published the Criminal Justice and Immigration Bill, this initially contained provisions adopting Sir Robin Auld's recommendations on this subject. The Bill provided that 'a conviction is not unsafe if the Court of Appeal is satisfied that the appellant is guilty of the offence'. The Court of Appeal judges would have allowed an appeal against conviction 'where they think that it would be incompatible with the appellant's Convention Rights to dismiss the appeal'. Thus, as initially drafted, the Bill would have altered the test applied by the Court of Appeal when considering appeals against conviction. A conviction would not have been found unsafe if the Court of Appeal was satisfied that the appellant was guilty of the offence. If it appeared to the Court of Appeal, in determining an appeal, that there had been serious misconduct by any person involved in the investigation or prosecution of the offence, the court could refer the matter to the Attorney General.

These provisions in the Bill were highly controversial and the subject of considerable criticism. In the light of such strong opposition, the Labour Government removed these provisions from the Bill before the Criminal Justice and Immigration Act 2008 was passed. In support of the failed reform, the Labour Government had argued that to acquit defendants where the Court of Appeal considered they were guilty was itself an injustice to the victim and the public, because the guilty were being allowed to walk free without punishment; their convictions were being quashed 'on a technicality'. In its consultation paper, the Labour Government observed, 'if the system or those who operate it are at fault, it is they, and not the public, who should be punished or required to learn lessons, if appropriate'.

On the other hand, critics of the proposed reform, such as the academic Ian Dennis (2006), had argued that it would remove an important safeguard in the criminal justice system, which effectively discourages abuse of procedural rules by representatives of the state, such as the police or prosecution. They argued that a conviction is fundamentally unsatisfactory if it is gained in breach of the rule of law and to uphold such a conviction itself undermines the rule of law. They questioned whether the public would be happy to see the criminal courts appear to sanction a flagrant illegality by an agent of the state. The Court of Appeal does not rehear the evidence of a case and is not therefore in a strong position to reach a view on whether a person is innocent or guilty. Alternative sanctions of, for example, the police for procedural irregularities have not always proved effective. Alarmingly, in ***R (on the application of Mullen) v Secretary of State for the Home Department*** (2004), the Labour Government seemed to view unlawful rendition – when a person is removed from a country without following the lawful procedures – as a mere technicality, yet this constituted a major violation of an individual's human rights.

22.5.3 The single test for quashing convictions

Before the Criminal Appeal Act 1995, there used to be three grounds on which the Criminal Division of the Court of Appeal could allow an appeal. These were where the court thought that:

- the jury's verdict was unsafe and unsatisfactory; or
- there was an error of law; or
- there was a material irregularity in the course of the trial.

The old law was criticised by the Runciman Commission on the basis that it was unnecessarily complex and that the different grounds for quashing a conviction overlapped. For example, it felt that there was no real difference between the words 'unsafe' and 'unsatisfactory'. In the light of this criticism, the law has been reduced by the Criminal Appeal Act 1995 to a single test that the court thinks the conviction is unsafe. This is narrower than that recommended by the Runciman Commission as it had favoured a retrial where the conviction 'may' be unsafe. The Law Society, the Bar, Liberty and JUSTICE all unsuccessfully called on the Government to follow the RCCJ's proposal. The Government's expressed view was that any such doubt implied by the concept of 'may be unsafe' was already implicit in the idea of a conviction being 'unsafe'.

Government Ministers insisted that the effect of the new law was simply to restate or consolidate the existing practice of the Court of Appeal. However, the pressure group, JUSTICE, has criticised the new single test on the basis that if there is a danger, it will be interpreted more narrowly than the previous tests.

Michael Zander (one of the Commissioners and a leading academic on the English legal system), along with one other Commissioner, disagreed with the final proposal (Zander and Henderson, 1993). They took the view that where there had been serious police malpractice, then the conviction should always be quashed to discourage such conduct, and to prevent the police from believing that they could benefit in terms of getting convictions by such behaviour. This is a situation where, under the old law, the Court of Appeal might have stated that the conviction was safe but it would be quashed because it was unsatisfactory. This route is no longer open to the court.

22.5.4 The Criminal Cases Review Commission

The Criminal Appeal Act 1995 created the Criminal Cases Review Commission (CCRC). Its function is to investigate possible miscarriages of justice.

The Act states that where a person has been convicted by the Crown Court, the Commission may refer the conviction to the Court of Appeal. Where a person has been convicted by a magistrates' court, the Commission may, at any time, refer the conviction to the Crown Court. The power to refer a conviction to the Crown Court applies whether the defendant pleaded guilty or not guilty.

The CCRC was established to replace the old s. 17 procedure contained in the Criminal Appeal Act 1968 and repealed in 1995. Under the old procedure, the Home Office could receive applications about cases that had been previously heard in the Crown Court where the ordinary time limit for appeals had expired or an unsuccessful appeal had already been heard. The Home Secretary could refer cases to the Court of Appeal and had considerable discretion whether or not to make this referral: the statute simply required a reference to be made 'if he thinks fit'.

There were serious difficulties with the s. 17 procedure. The Home Secretary only usually referred cases where new evidence had come to light, and which were continuing to attract media comment and public concern long after the trial had taken place. Each year there were about 730 applications to the Home Office and its equivalent in Northern Ireland, but only 10–12 of those cases were actually referred to the Court of Appeal.

Problems with the process were highlighted by cases such as the Birmingham Six and the Tottenham Three, where references were only ordered after years of persuasion and publicity. The original appeal of the Birmingham Six was rejected in 1976. It was not until 1987 that the Home Secretary referred their case back to the Court of Appeal, though that appeal was rejected. Three years later, he again referred the case to the Court of Appeal and this time the Director of Public Prosecutions did not resist the application so that the court had little choice but to allow the appeal and quash the convictions.

The Court of Appeal showed a general reluctance to allow s. 17 appeals in cases where it had already dismissed an appeal, and in fact appeared to dislike s. 17 referrals generally. In the first (unsuccessful) s. 17 appeal from the Birmingham Six, the court stated that: 'As has happened before in references by the Home Secretary to this court, the longer the hearing has gone on the more convinced this court has become that the verdict of the jury was correct.' As MP Chris Mullins's book (1990) on the Birmingham Six points out, this seemed to be a thinly veiled message to the Home Secretary that referring such cases was a waste of time.

A further problem was that, once the reference was made, the appeal was governed by the Criminal Appeal Act 1968, and the expense and responsibility of preparing the appeal lay with the defendant, who would probably be in prison and have been there for quite some time. Legal aid might be available but investigation in these circumstances would be difficult.

The CCRC is a considerable improvement on the old s. 17 procedure. It is more open, giving detailed written reasons for its decisions and publishing an annual report about its activities. It refers cases back to the Court of Appeal where there is a real possibility the Court of Appeal will allow the appeal. Critics have argued that this threshold for referrals is set too high and that more cases should be referred. Another criticism of the Commission is that it cannot decide appeals, it can merely refer cases to the Court of Appeal. This was a weakness of the s. 17 procedure: even when the case was referred to the Court of Appeal the convictions were often upheld, even though later it was acknowledged there had been a miscarriage of justice. Thus, cases such as the Birmingham Six had to be repeatedly referred back to the Court of Appeal before they would eventually overturn the original conviction. In that case the appeal was allowed on the basis that there was 'fresh' evidence as to the police interrogation techniques and the forensic evidence. In reality this evidence had, in essence, been before the Court of Appeal in 1987; the difference was that the court was forced to accept that the evidence raised a lurking doubt in 1991. Only if the other provisions are adequate to improve the Court of Appeal process will the same problems be avoided. An alternative solution would have been to give the Commission the power to decide appeals themselves.

The CCRC has been criticised for placing too much reliance on desk-bound reviews and spending too little time interviewing witnesses and reconstructing crime scenes. The Centre for Criminal Appeals (CCA) a legal action charity, use the example of the case of Victor Nealon to illustrate this point. Mr Nealon, they report, was incarcerated for an additional 16 years due to failures or refusals to undertake DNA testing of the victims clothing which he stated would exonerate him. He appealed on two occasions to the CCRC and on both occasions they refused to undertake the required DNA tests on the evidence in his case, namely the clothing of the victim. His appeal team commissioned an independent analysis of the clothing. This exonerated Mr Nealon but 16 years too late. This criticism of desk-bound reviews is also linked to concerns that it is underfunded for the number of applications it receives each year. The CCA report that CCRC referred only 0.77 of its cases to the Court of Appeal in 2016/17.

The pressure group, JUSTICE, has criticised the fact that the CCRC has no power to assign in-house staff as investigating officers. It has argued that without this power the

Commission could not guarantee the independence of an inquiry. The CCRC has no independent powers to carry out searches of premises, to check criminal records, to use police computers, or to make an arrest. To do this, they would have to appoint someone who had these powers, usually a police officer. The fact that investigations carried out on behalf of the CCRC will be by the police has caused concern. Many allegations of a miscarriage of justice involve accusations of malpractice by the police. Experience of police investigations into the high-profile miscarriages of justice suggests that these are not always effective, with a tendency for the police to close ranks and try to protect each other. JUSTICE has also questioned the independence of the organisation as its members are Government appointees.

Over a third of applications made to the Criminal Cases Review Commission are concerned with murder convictions and a quarter relate to sex offences. The Commission receives

---

The Bigger Picture: Derek Bentley's appeal

One of the first referrals made by the Criminal Cases Review Commission concerned Derek Bentley. He had been involved with a friend in an unsuccessful burglary. This had resulted in a police chase when his friend had pointed a gun at a police officer and Derek Bentley had said 'let him have it', at which point the friend shot and killed the officer. Derek Bentley was convicted as an accomplice to the murder. He appealed but his appeal was rejected and he was hanged in January 1953.

The circumstances of his conviction gave rise to a long campaign by his family and numerous representations were made to the Home Office. He was given a royal pardon in 1993, but this was in respect of the sentence only. The family continued their campaign for the conviction itself to be quashed and in 1998 the CCRC referred the case to the Court of Appeal, which quashed the conviction. They found that the conviction was unsafe because of a defective summing-up by the trial judge to the jury, which had included such prejudicial comments about the defence case that Bentley had been denied a fair trial. This was a notable high-profile success for the CCRC.

---

over a thousand applications each year. In 2016–17, there were 1,397 applications made to the Commission, of which 12 were referred to an appeal court (the average is 33). Of these referrals, 46 per cent of the appeals were successful (down from 53 per cent in the previous year and as high as 70 per cent in earlier years) and led either to a conviction being quashed or a sentence being reduced.

Since beginning its operation in April 1997, the Commission has received 24,249 applications and referred less than 3 per cent of these to an appeal court. Of the 645 appeals heard by the Court of Appeal following a referral, 436 have been allowed.

Research shows that cuts to the budget of the CCRC have caused delays to the system. Between 2009 and 2015 the CCRC's funding fell from £6.5 million to £5.25 million. In real terms this amounted to a 30 per cent cut. At the same time, there was a 74 per cent increase in the number of applications. In 2005 there were 42 Case Review Managers and in 2014 the number had reduced to 34.

The CCRC has found the main reasons for it to refer cases back to the courts are:

- prosecution failings (such as breach of identification and interview procedures or the use of questionable witnesses);
- scientific evidence (such as DNA and fingerprint evidence);
- non-disclosure of evidence; and
- new evidence (such as alibis, eye-witnesses or confessions).

There is a problem of funding submissions to the Commission. Now, the Legal Aid Agency only pays for two hours of a solicitor's time, which is insufficient for the preparation of such an application. As a result, more than 90 per cent of applicants are not represented by a solicitor.

The Commission's workload could be reduced in the future by excluding applications about convictions of people who have died or received non-custodial sentences. The Justice Select Committee (2015) has concluded that the CCRC is struggling to cope with a sharp rise in its workload and is under-resourced.

The Bigger Picture: Jill Dando's murder

Jill Dando was a successful television presenter who worked for the BBC. She was shot dead outside her home in London in 1999. Barry George was convicted of her murder. Part of the evidence against Barry George was that a single microscopic particle of gunshot residue was found in his coat pocket. After his conviction witnesses came forward stating that armed police officers had been present when he was arrested. The police denied this, but if it was true then the gunshot residue could have come from the police rather than from the murder. His conviction was referred to the Court of Appeal by the Criminal Cases Review Commission and his conviction was quashed in 2007 and a retrial ordered. He was acquitted by the jury at his retrial.

22.5.5 Reluctance to overturn jury verdicts

The Court of Appeal seems to feel that overturning jury verdicts weakens public confidence in the jury system, and it is therefore very reluctant to do it. This view was spelt out during the final, successful appeal of the Birmingham Six in 1991, in which the Court of Appeal stated:

> Nothing in s. 2 of the Act, or anywhere else obliges or entitles us to say whether we think that the appellant is innocent. This is a point of great constitutional importance. The task of deciding whether a man is innocent or guilty falls on the jury. We are concerned solely with the question whether the verdict of the jury can stand.
>
> Rightly or wrongly (we think rightly) trial by jury is the foundation of our criminal justice system . . . The primacy of the jury in the criminal justice system is well illustrated by the difference between the Criminal and Civil Divisions of the Court of Appeal . . . A civil appeal is by way of rehearing of the whole of the case. So the court is concerned with fact as well as law . . . It follows that in a civil case the Court of Appeal may take a different view of the facts from the court below. In a criminal case this is not possible . . . the Criminal Division is perhaps more accurately described as a court of review.

The case of Winston Silcott illustrates the dangers. He had been convicted in 1985 of murdering PC Blakelock during the Tottenham riots. The offence had been committed by a group of 30 people. Six had gone on trial and only three were convicted, including Silcott. The only evidence against Silcott was a statement he was alleged to have made: 'You won't pin this on me . . . nobody will talk', which he had not signed. Despite these obvious weaknesses in the case, his conviction was initially upheld by the Court of Appeal and was only overturned in 1991.

The major problem with the appeal court's approach is that in many cases the fault lies not with the decision-making powers of the jury, but in the evidence presented to them. Where a jury has not seen all the evidence, or where the evidence it has heard has been falsified by the police (as was alleged in some of the well-known miscarriages of justice), or where the jury has in any other way failed to have the case properly presented to it, overturning the verdict should not automatically be viewed as a criticism of its ability to make correct decisions. A better way to demonstrate confidence in the jury system might be to order a retrial with a new jury.

The Runciman Commission concluded that the Court of Appeal should show greater willingness to substitute its judgment for that of the jury. They pointed out that in gauging the evidence juries could make errors, particularly in a high-profile case in which emotions run high. The trial of Winston Silcott is a classic case in point. The Criminal Appeal Act 1995 aims to instigate a change of philosophy in this regard, particularly through the changes to the rules on the admissibility of fresh evidence.

Up to 1995, the Court of Appeal was able to conclude that even if there was found to have been a material irregularity in the trial, they could still uphold the conviction if they felt that no miscarriage of justice had occurred. This was known as 'applying the proviso', but the relevant statutory provision has now been repealed, which may lead to a greater willingness to overturn a jury verdict.

22.5.6 Unwillingness to order retrials

Many have argued that the Court of Appeal should use its power to order retrials more often. The number of such retrials grew from 3 in 1990 to 23 in 1992, though they remain rare.

Lord Devlin has argued, as stated above, that a retrial should be ordered wherever fresh evidence could have made a difference to the verdict – the original verdict being clearly unsatisfactory since it was given without the jury hearing all the evidence.

Opponents argue that it may be unfair to the accused to reopen a decided case, and that a second trial cannot be a fair one, especially if some time has passed and/or the case has received a lot of publicity. But, as Lord Devlin argues, this does not stop retrials from being ordered where the jury has failed to agree a verdict, nor are prosecutions necessarily stifled because witnesses have to speak of events many years before. In fact, at the same time as the Birmingham Six were told that a retrial 13 years after the original one was inappropriate, the Government was debating the prosecution of war criminals, some 44 years after the end of the Second World War. Shortly after the Six's unsuccessful appeal, an IRA man was brought to trial on charges dating back 13 years.

As far as publicity is concerned, the second jury may well know of the defendant's record and have noted other adverse publicity, as well as knowing that the defendant has already been convicted on a previous occasion for the crime. On the other hand, in all the high-profile miscarriages of justice, no further publicity could have affected the attitudes of potential jurors more than that surrounding the original offences and trials.

Many wrongful convictions result from mistaken identity, and it is difficult for the Court of Appeal, which does not usually re-examine witnesses, to assess the strength of such evidence. Retrials might be the best way of dealing with this problem. A general power to order a retrial could also be a way of convicting offenders who escape on a technicality first time round, and might be a more obviously just solution than applying the old proviso, or letting such defendants go free, which has a negative effect on the public, the jury and the victim. However, it could also subject genuinely innocent defendants to a second ordeal.

It has been suggested that wider use of retrials would 'open the floodgates' to a deluge of appeals, yet this does not appear to be a problem in other countries with wider powers of retrial, including Scotland. In any case, as Lord Atkin pointed out in 1933, though it could equally apply to the law of today, 'Finality is a good thing but justice is better.'

The Runciman Commission considered the issue and concluded that the Court of Appeal should use the power to order a retrial more extensively.

22.5.7 Reluctance to address faults in the system

The problems outlined above can be seen as symptomatic of a more general reluctance to uncover the extent of miscarriages of justice in our system. This attitude was typified by Lord Denning's speech in *McIlkenny* v *Chief Constable of the West Midlands* (1980), the case in which the police successfully appealed against a civil action, brought against them by the Birmingham Six, in respect of injuries sustained after their arrest. Lord Denning said:

> If the six men win, it will mean that the police were guilty of perjury, that they were guilty of violence and threats . . . and that the convictions were erroneous . . . the Home Secretary would have either to recommend that they be pardoned or he would have to remit the case to the Court of Appeal . . . This is such an appalling vista that every sensible person in the land would say 'It cannot be right that these actions should go any further'.

The implication was that, even if the men were innocent, the damage such a revelation could do to confidence in the justice system meant it was better not known.

22.5.8 The Supreme Court in Scotland

By convention the Supreme Court has two Scottish judges. It hears appeals that raise devolution issues under the Scotland Act 1998 and criminal appeals from Scottish courts which raise human rights issues under the European Convention of Human Rights. Some Scots consider that this jurisdiction violates the 1707 Act of Union, which states that the English courts 'shall have no power to cognosce review or alter the acts or sentences of the judicatures within Scotland or stop the execution of the same'. There was anger in Scotland when a number of Supreme Court decisions held that the Scottish rules on criminal procedure breached suspects' human rights by, for example, questioning suspects in the police station without giving them access to a lawyer (*Cadder* v *HM Advocate* (2010)). In September 2014, the Scottish Independence Referendum was held and the Scottish electorate voted to remain in the UK. However, since the Referendum, Scotland has been promised greater autonomy by the UK Government. This move for more devolution may well lead to further calls for further independence for the Scottish legal system.

Answering questions

1 Assess the impact of the Criminal Cases Review Commission on the appeal process.

2 Martin is due to be tried at Margate Crown Court for robbing £10,000 from a newsagent.

   (a) Following his conviction, advise Martin about how he can appeal against his conviction.

   (b) Could the prosecution bring an appeal?

   (c) Critically analyse the current appeal system.

3 In criminal appeals to the Court of Appeal, does the fact that the court will only hear fresh evidence in limited circumstances disadvantage the appellant?

For answers to these questions, visit the companion website at www.pearsoned.co.uk/ elliottquinn

SUMMARY OF CHAPTER 22: CRIMINAL APPEALS

Appeals in criminal cases

From the magistrates' court (criminal jurisdiction)

There are four routes of appeal:

1   A defendant who has pleaded not guilty may appeal as of right to the Crown Court on the grounds of being wrongly convicted or too harshly sentenced.
2   Either the prosecution or the accused may appeal to the High Court by way of case stated.
3   Either the prosecution or the accused may apply to the High Court for a judicial review of the proceedings.
4   The Criminal Cases Review Commission can refer appeals from the magistrates' court to the Crown Court.

From the Crown Court

There are three types of appeal from the Crown Court:

1   An appeal to the Court of Appeal
2   An application to the Criminal Cases Review Commission
3   An appeal by way of case stated from the Crown Court to the High Court.

Powers of the prosecution following acquittal

The general rule is that once a person has been tried and acquitted, he or she cannot be retried for the same offence, under the principle of double jeopardy. Major exceptions have now been developed and can be found in Part 10 of the Criminal Justice Act 2003. The power to order a retrial applies in certain limited circumstances where a person has been acquitted of a 'qualifying offence' (for example, very serious offences such as murder and rape). The full range of qualifying offences are specified in the Act.

Criticism and reform of the appeal system

The appeal system has been the subject of considerable criticism. There has been concern over the working of the Criminal Cases Review Commission. The Court of Appeal has been criticised for being reluctant to overturn jury verdicts, admit fresh evidence and order retrials. The Government has abolished the judiciary function of the House of Lords and replaced it with a new, independent Supreme Court. The provisions for this reform were contained in the Constitutional Reform Act 2005.

Rejected reforms in the Criminal Justice and Immigration Bill would have altered the test applied by the Court of Appeal when considering appeals against conviction. Clause 26 of the Bill originally provided that 'a conviction is not unsafe if the Court of Appeal is satisfied that the appellant is guilty of the offence'.

Reading list

Auld, Sir R. (2001) *Review of the Criminal Courts.* London: HMSO.

Blom-Cooper, L. (1972) *Final Appeal: A Study of the House of Lords in its Judicial Capacity.* Oxford: Clarendon.

City Law School (2018) Criminal Litigation and Sentencing (Bar Manuals). Oxford: Oxford University Press.

Cooper, S. (2009) Appeals, referrals and substantial injustice. *Criminal Law Review,* 152.

Dennis, I. (2006) Convicting the guilty: outcomes, process and the Court of Appeal. *Criminal Law Review,* 955.

Devlin, P. (1979) *The Judge.* Oxford: Oxford University Press.

Elks, L. (2008) *Righting Miscarriages of Justice? Ten Years of the Criminal Cases Review Commission.* London: JUSTICE.

Griffith, J.A.G. (1997) *The Politics of the Judiciary.* London: Fontana.

Herbert, A.P. (1966) *Wigs at Work.* London: Penguin.

Hungerford-Welch, P. (2019) *Criminal Procedure and Sentencing* (9th edn). Oxon: Routledge.

Jackson, R.M. (1989) *The Machinery of Justice in England.* Cambridge: CUP.

Law Commission (2010a) *The High Court's Jurisdiction in Relation to Criminal Proceedings.* Law Com. No. 324. London: The Stationery Office.

Leigh, L.H. (2008) Injustice perpetuated? The contribution of the Court of Appeal. *Journal of Criminal Law,* 72: 40.

Malleson, K. (1993) *A Review of the Appeal Process.* Royal Commission on Criminal Justice Research Series No. 17. London: HMSO.

Malleson, K. and Roberts, S. (2002) Streamlining and clarifying the appellate process. *Criminal Law Review,* 272.

McPeake, R. (2017) *Criminal Litigation and Sentencing* (29th edn). Oxford: OUP.

Mullins, C. (1990) *Error of Judgement: The Truth about the Birmingham Bombings.* Dublin: Poolbeg.

Naughton, M. (2009) *Criminal Cases Review Commission. Hope for the Innocent?* London: Palgrave Macmillan.

Nobles, R. and Schiff, D. (2005) The Criminal Cases Review Commission: establishing a workable relationship with the Court of Appeal. *Criminal Law Review,* 173.

Owers, A. (1995) Not completely appealing. *New Law Journal,* 145: 353.

Pattenden, R. (2009) The standards of review for mistake of fact in the Court of Appeal, Criminal Division. *Criminal Law Review,* 15.

Plotnikoff, J. and Wilson, R. (1993) *Information and Advice for Prisoners about Grounds for Appeal and the Appeal Process.* Royal Commission on Criminal Justice Research Study No. 18. London: HMSO.

Roberts, A.J. (2006) Appeal: whether safety of verdict necessarily vitiated where jury direction omitted or where prejudicial or improper material placed before jury through oversight. *Criminal Law Review,* 995.

Robertson, G. (1993) *Freedom, the Individual and the Law.* London: Penguin.

Smith, J.C. and Hogan, B. (2002) *Criminal Law.* London: Butterworths.

Spencer, J.R. (2006) Does our present criminal appeal system make sense? *Criminal Law Review,* 677.

Taylor, R. (1997) *Cautions, Court Proceedings and Sentencing in England and Wales 1996.* London: Home Office.

The Secret Barrister (2018) *Stories of the Law and How It's Broken.* Pan Macmillan.

Williams, G. (1983) *Textbook of Criminal Law.* London: Stevens and Sons.

Zander, M. and Henderson, P. (1993) *Crown Court Study.* London: HMSO.

Zander, M. (2015) The Justice Select Committee's report on the CCRC – where do we go from here? *Criminal Law Review,* 473.

22

On the internet

The annual report of the Criminal Cases Review Commission is published on the Commission's website (via Corporate publications) at:
https://ccrc.gov.uk/publications/

The Crown Court Compendium (updated December 2018) is available at:
https://www.judiciary.uk/publications/crown-court-compendium-published december-2018/

CRIMINAL APPEALS

Part 5
Civil justice system

This Part looks at the repeated government efforts to modernise the civil justice system and the option of resolving civil disputes outside the civil court system through alternative methods of dispute resolution. It provides an overview of the opportunities to appeal against decisions of the lower courts and also explores the right to challenge decisions of the Government and the administration through judicial review.

Chapter 23
The civil trial process

This chapter discusses:

- the evolution of the civil justice system;

- the Civil Procedure Rules, including pre-action protocols, case management and sanctions for breach;

- Money Claim Online – a debt recovery service provided over the internet; and

- problems with the civil court system, along with possible reforms.

23.1 Introduction

The civil justice system is designed to sort out disputes between individuals or organisations. One party (the claimant) sues the other (the defendant) usually for money they claim is owed or for compensation for a harm to their interests. Typical examples might be the victim of a car accident suing the driver of the car for compensation, or one business suing another for payment due on goods supplied. The burden of proof is usually on the claimant, who must prove their case on a balance of probabilities – that it is more likely than not. This is a lower standard of proof than the 'beyond reasonable doubt' test used by the criminal courts and, for this reason, it is possible to be acquitted of a criminal charge yet still be found to have breached the civil law. This happened to O.J. Simpson in the US who, having been acquitted of murdering his ex-wife and her friend by the criminal courts, was successfully sued in the civil courts for damages by the victim's family.

Major changes have been made to the civil justice system in recent years. After the Civil Justice Review of 1988, reforms were made by the Courts and Legal Services Act 1990. Following continued criticism of the civil justice system, Lord Woolf was appointed to carry out a far-reaching review of the civil justice system. Lord Woolf's inquiry is the 63rd such review in 100 years. Lord Woolf made far-reaching recommendations in his report, *Access to Justice,* which was published in 1996. As with the Civil Justice Review, his aim was to reduce the cost, delay and complexity of the system and increase access to justice. Most of his recommendations were implemented in April 1999.

23.2 History

The legal process for civil cases developed in a rather piecemeal fashion, responding to different needs at different times with the result that, at the end of the eighteenth century, civil matters were being dealt with by several different series of courts. Three common law courts, supplemented by the Court of Chancery, did most of the work, but there was also a Court of Admiralty and the ecclesiastical (church) courts. They had separate, but often overlapping, jurisdictions and between them administered three different 'systems' of law: civilian law (based on Roman law), common law and equity. The courts were also largely centralised in London, making access difficult for those in the provinces.

With no coordination of the increasingly complex court system, inefficiency, incompetence and delays were common and the courts acquired a reputation for binding themselves up in cumbersome procedural rules. Until well into the nineteenth century, litigation in the higher courts was an extravagance which could be afforded only by the very rich and, in many respects, the system benefited the judges and the legal professions far more than litigants. Reform began in 1846, with the creation of a nationwide system of County Courts, designed to provide cheaper, quicker justice at a local level for businessmen. This was followed, in the early 1870s, by the creation of one Supreme Court consisting of the High Court, the Court of Appeal and the Crown Court, although the High Court was still divided into five divisions. In 1881, these were reduced to three: Queen's Bench, Chancery, and what is now known as the Family Division.

Figure 23.1 The civil court system

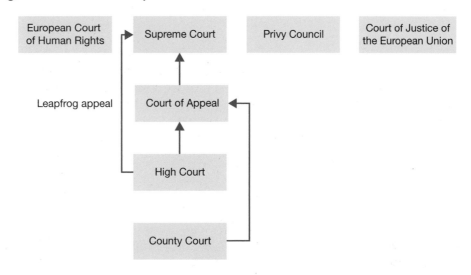

23.3 The civil courts

There are currently 173 hearing centres of the County Court concerned exclusively with civil work. All claims worth less than £100,000 and personal injury claims less than £50,000, must be issued in the County Court. High value cases are heard in the High Court.

In the High Court, the three divisions mentioned above remain today – they act as separate courts, with judges usually working within one division only. Lord Woolf recommended that these divisions should remain. The Chancery Division deals with matters of finance and property, such as tax and bankruptcy. The Queen's Bench Division is the biggest of the three, with the most varied jurisdiction. The major part of its work is handling those contract and tort cases which are unsuitable for the County Courts (see below). Sitting as the Divisional Court of the Queen's Bench, its judges also hear certain criminal appeals (originating primarily from the magistrates' courts) and applications for judicial review (for details see Chapter 1). High Court judges usually sit alone, but the Divisional Court is so important that two or three judges sit together.

Trials in the High Court are heard either in London or in one of the 26 provincial trial centres. In theory, they are all presided over by High Court judges, but in fact there are not enough High Court judges to cope with the case load. Some cases, therefore, have to be dealt with by circuit judges and others by barristers sitting as part-time, temporary, deputy judges.

Following the Woolf reforms, trial centres have been identified, headed by a Designated Civil Justice. They report to the Head of Civil Justice, a position currently held by Sir Terence Etherton.

Although most civil cases are dealt with by either the County Court or the High Court, magistrates' courts have a limited civil jurisdiction, and some types of cases are tried by tribunals.

In April 2014, a single Family Court was introduced through powers granted in the Crime and Courts Act 2013.

Photo 23.1 Lord Woolf

Source: © Alex Segre/Alamy

23.4 The civil justice system before April 1999

Before the implementation of the Woolf reforms, there were two separate sets of civil procedure rules: the Rules of the Supreme Court in the 'White Book' for the High Court and the Court of Appeal, and the County Court Rules in the 'Green Book' for the County Court. High Court actions were started with a writ, County Court ones by a summons, but there were also specialised procedures which required specific documents and formalities to be used. These documents were served on the defendant to a case, and informed the person that an action was being brought against them. The rules on serving documents were fairly restrictive and ignored modern modes of communication. Defendants had to acknowledge service. The claimant served a statement of claim if bringing an action in the High Court, or the particulars of a claim in the County Court. Both were formal pleadings which outlined the facts and legal basis of the action and the remedy sought. The defendant responded with a defence.

The Civil Justice Review was set up in 1985 by the Lord Chancellor in response to public criticism of the delay, cost and complexity of the civil court system. Unusually, it was chaired by a non-lawyer, Maurice Hodgson, the Chairman of BHS, and only a minority of its members were lawyers. They therefore tended to be less pro-lawyer than previous committees that had been dominated by judges and barristers, which may explain why many of the Review's more innovative suggestions were ignored or only partially implemented. Some important changes were made to the division of work between the County Courts and High Court by the Courts and Legal Services Act 1990 in response to some of the proposals of the 1985 Review.

One of the Review's main findings was that too many cases were being heard in the High Court rather than the cheaper and quicker County Courts, often for relatively small amounts of money. Consequently, the Review aimed to increase the number of cases heard in the County Court by increasing the value of cases it could hear.

23.4.1 Problems with the civil justice system before April 1999

Lord Woolf was appointed by the previous Conservative Government to carry out a far-reaching review of the civil justice system. In *Access to Justice: Final Report,* published in 1996, he stated that a civil justice system should:

- be just in the results it delivers;
- be fair in the way it treats litigants;
- offer appropriate procedures at a reasonable cost;
- deal with cases with reasonable speed;
- be understandable to those who use it;
- be responsive to the needs of those who use it;
- provide as much certainty as the nature of particular cases allows; and
- be effective, adequately resourced and organised.

Lord Woolf concluded that the system at the time failed to achieve all those goals. It is possible that this failure is inevitable, as some of the aims conflict with others. A system based on cost-efficiency alone would make it difficult to justify claims for comparatively small sums, yet these cases are very important to the parties involved, and wide access to justice is vital. Promoting efficiency in terms of speed can also conflict with the need for fairness. Making the courts more accessible could lead to a flood of cases which would make it impossible to provide a speedy resolution and keep costs down. One practical example of the conflict between different aims is that the availability of legal aid to one party, one of the aims of widening access to justice, can put pressure on the other side if they are funding themselves, and so clash with the need for fairness.

In addition, changes made to the civil justice system may have effects outside it – making it easier to bring personal injury actions, for example, could push up the costs of insurance, and it has been suggested that in the US this has led to unwillingness on the part of doctors to perform any risky medical treatment.

It is impossible to resolve all of these conflicts and a successful legal system must simply aim for the best possible balance.

In the final analysis, it is for the Government to decide the balance they wish to strike, and how much they are prepared to spend on it. While conflicting interests may mean it is impossible to achieve a civil justice system that satisfies everyone, there were serious concerns that the civil justice system before April 1999 was giving satisfaction to only a small minority of users for a range of reasons which will be considered in turn.

Too expensive

Research carried out for Lord Woolf's review found that one side's costs exceeded the amount in dispute in over 40 per cent of cases where the claim was for under £12,500. The simplest cases often incurred the highest costs in proportion to the value of the claim.

Because of the complexity of the process, lawyers were usually needed, making the process expensive. The sheer length of civil proceedings also affected the size of the bill at the end.

Lord Woolf has said that, 15 years before, his report would not have been necessary, because most lawyers made their money from other work, such as conveyancing, seeing litigation as a loss-maker that they would only undertake reluctantly. But, with the huge increase in the number of lawyers combined with the recession in the property market at the end of the 1980s, lawyers suddenly found that litigation could generate a steady income. He found that costs were now so high that even big companies were wary, with some preferring to fight cases in New York.

Delays

The Civil Justice Review observed that the time between the incident giving rise to the claim and the trial could be up to three years for the County Courts and five for the High Court. Time limits were laid down for every stage of an action but both lawyers and the courts disregarded them. Often time limits were waived by the lawyers to create an opportunity to negotiate, which was reasonable, but the problem was that there was no effective control of when and why it was done.

According to the Civil Justice Review, long delays placed intolerable psychological and financial burdens on accident victims and undermined the justice of the trial, by making it more difficult to gather evidence which was then unreliable because witnesses had to remember the events of several years before.

Injustice

Usually an out-of-court settlement is negotiated before the litigants ever reach the trial stage. Excluding personal injury cases, for every 100,000 writs issued before 1999, fewer than 300 actually came for trial. An out-of-court settlement can have the advantage of providing a quick end to the dispute, and a reduction in costs. But out-of-court settlements can be unfair – see the discussion on this subject below (p. 651).

The adversarial process

Many problems resulted from the adversarial process which encouraged tactical manoeuvring rather than cooperation. It would be far simpler and cheaper for each side to state precisely what it alleged in the pleadings, disclose all the documents they held, and give the other side copies of their witness statements. Attitudes did appear to be slowly changing, with a growing appreciation that the public interest demanded justice be provided as quickly and economically as possible. Some of the procedural rules, for example on expert witnesses, were changed and there was less scope for tactical manoeuvring.

Emphasis on oral evidence

Too much emphasis was placed on oral evidence at trial. This may have been appropriate when juries were commonly used in civil proceedings, but in the twentieth century much of the information the judge needed could be provided on paper and read before the trial. Oral evidence slowed down proceedings, adding to cost and delays.

23.5 The civil justice system after April 1999

On 26 April 1999 new Civil Procedure Rules and accompanying Practice Directions came into force. The new rules apply to any proceedings commenced after that date. They constitute a fundamental reform of the civil justice system, introducing the main recommendations of Lord Woolf in his final report, *Access to Justice*. He described his proposals as providing 'a new landscape for civil justice for the twenty-first century'.

The Woolf Report was the product of two years' intensive consultation, and was written with the help of expert working parties of experienced practitioners and academics. The recommendations of the Report received universal support from the senior judiciary, the Bar, the Law Society, consumer organisations and the media. In 1996, Sir Richard Scott was appointed as Head of Civil Justice with responsibility for implementing the reforms. The Civil Procedure Act 1997 was passed to implement the first stages of the Woolf Report. Following their election into office, the Labour Government set up their own review of the civil justice system and of Lord Woolf's proposed reforms. They quite reasonably wanted a second opinion before adopting the policies of their predecessors on those issues. The review was chaired by Sir Peter Middleton and took four months to complete. The final report was essentially in favour of implementation of Lord Woolf's proposals. His report placed an emphasis on the financial implications of the proposals and in particular the opportunities for cost-cutting. In November 1998, an intensive period of training for judges and court staff began, to prepare them for the changes, while the Treasury made available an additional £2 million to implement the reforms.

The reforms aim to eliminate unnecessary cost, delay and complexity in the civil justice system. The general approach of Lord Woolf is reflected in his statement: 'If "time and money are no object" was the right approach in the past, then it certainly is not today. Both lawyers and judges, in making decisions as to the conduct of litigation, must take into account more than they do at present, questions of cost and time and the means of the parties.' Lord Woolf suggested that the reforms should lead to a reduction in legal bills by as much as 75 per cent, though it might also mean some lawyers would lose their livelihoods.

The ultimate goal is to change fundamentally the litigation culture. Thus, the first rule of the new Civil Procedure Rules lays down an overriding objective which is to underpin the whole system. This overriding objective is that the rules should enable the courts to deal with cases 'justly and at proportionate cost'. This objective prevails over all other rules in case of a conflict. The parties and their legal representatives are expected to assist the judges in achieving this objective. The Woolf Report had heavily criticised practitioners, who were accused of manipulating the old system for their own convenience and causing delay and expense to both their clients and the users of the system as a whole. Lord Woolf felt that a change in attitude among the lawyers was vital for the new rules to succeed. Part 1 of the Civil Procedure Rules lays down the overriding objective of dealing with a case justly and at proportionate cost. According to r. 1.1(2):

Dealing with a case justly and at proportionate cost includes, so far as is practicable –

(a) ensuring that the parties are on an equal footing;

(b) saving expense;

23

THE CIVIL TRIAL PROCESS

(c) dealing with the case in ways which are proportionate –
  (i)   to the amount of money involved;
  (ii) to the importance of the case;
  (iii) to the complexity of the issues; and
  (iv) to the financial position of each party;

(d) ensuring that it is dealt with expeditiously and fairly;

(e) allotting to it an appropriate share of the court's resources, while taking into account the need to allot resources to other cases; and

(f) enforcing compliance with rules, practice directions and orders.

The emphasis of the new rules is on avoiding litigation through pre-trial settlements. Litigation is to be viewed as a last resort, with the court having a continuing obligation to encourage and facilitate settlement. Lord Woolf had observed that it was strange that, although the majority of disputes ended in settlement, the old rules had been mainly directed towards preparation for trial. Thus the new rules put a greater emphasis on preparing cases for settlement rather than a trial.

The new approach to civil procedure will now be examined in more detail.

23.5.1 Civil Procedure Rules

The Lord Chancellor appointed the Civil Procedure Rules Committee to produce and maintain one unified procedural code for both the County Court and the High Court. This produced the new Civil Procedure Rules which came into force in April 1999 and replaced the Rules of the Supreme Court and the County Court Rules. The new rules are simpler than their predecessors, providing a broad framework of general application rather than detailed rules covering every contingency. These framework rules are then fleshed out by a number of Practice Directions. There has been an attempt to write the rules in plain English, replacing old-fashioned terminology with more accessible terms. Lord Woolf hoped that the change in language would help to support a change in attitude, away from a legalistic, technical interpretation of words designed to give one party an advantage over their opponent, towards an attitude which was open and fair according to the overriding objective of the new rules.

While the new rules introduce some radical changes to the civil justice system, they also inherit much from the old system. In outline the procedure is as follows. Before proceedings are commenced, claimants should send a letter to defendants warning them that they are considering bringing legal proceedings. Proceedings should be brought within a fixed period (usually six years) from when the claimant suffered the harm. This period is known as the limitation period, and is laid down in the Limitation Act 1980. This area of the law has proved particularly problematic for people who have suffered sexual abuse while they were children. It was pointed out in *Ablett* v *Devon County Council* (2000) that:

> It is the nature of abuse of children by adults that it creates shame, fear and confusion, and these in turn produce silence. Silence is known to be one of the most pernicious fruits of abuse. It means that allegations commonly surface, if they do, only many years after the abuse has ceased.

In *A* v *Hoare* (2008) the House of Lords tried to avoid injustice by allowing a woman who had been raped in the 1970s by a serial rapist who had subsequently won the lottery in 2004, to bring a successful case for damages against her attacker.

Almost all proceedings start with the same document, called a claim form. This replaces the writ for the High Court and the summons for the County Court, and other specialist documents. The procedure for starting an action is thus undoubtedly simpler than under the old system. The claim form informs the defendant that an action is being brought against them. When claimants are making a claim for money, they must provide a statement as to the value of the claim in the claim form.

The Practice Direction supplementing Part 7 of the new Civil Procedure Rules (*How to start proceedings – the Claim Form*) specifies in which court proceedings should be started. For non-personal injury actions, a claim may be started in the High Court where the claimant expects to recover more than £25,000. For personal injury actions, a claim can only be started in the High Court where the claimant expects to recover at least £50,000 for pain, suffering and loss of amenity.

The claim form is served on the defendant to a case. The methods of service have been liberalised to reflect modern modes of communication, including the use of fax, emails and even Facebook. Service will normally be carried out by the court through postage by first-class post, unless a party notifies the court that they will serve the documents. Defendants must acknowledge service. The claimant must then serve on the defendant the particulars of claim.

The defendant should respond within 14 days by either filing an acknowledgement of service or a defence with the court. If the defendant fails to do either of these within that period of time, the claimant can enter judgment in default against the defendant (r. 12.3). The mechanics of pleading a defence are now regulated more strictly. Defendants may no longer simply deny an allegation, but must state their reasons for the denial and, if they intend to put forward a different version of events from that given by the claimant, then they must state their own version.

If the defendant files a defence, the court will serve an allocation questionnaire on each party (r. 24.4(1)). This is designed to enable the court to allocate each claim to one of the three tracks discussed below (at p. 637).

The disclosure procedures are then followed (as discussed on p. 640). Either party may seek more details from the other, through a 'request for information'. This procedure merges the old system of interrogatories and requests for further and better particulars.

Normally a cost budget should be filed and served seven days before the first case management conference. If a party fails to do this they can only claim back their court fees.

At any stage of the proceedings the parties can enter into 'without prejudice' negotiations to try to settle the dispute out of court. The without prejudice rule makes all negotiations genuinely aimed at settlement, whether oral or in writing, inadmissible in evidence at any subsequent trial. The rule lets litigants make whatever concessions or admissions are necessary to achieve a compromise, without fear of these being held against them if negotiations break down and the case goes to court. It is hoped that this will help and encourage the parties to settle their disputes early.

If defendants wish to settle a claim, they can simply make a written offer to settle at any time including before legal proceedings have commenced. This is known as a Part 36 offer. Parties frequently make Part 36 applications in both small and large value cases. An accepted offer must then be paid by the defendant within 14 days. A Part 36 offer can be withdrawn after 21 days. If the case is not settled out of court, the case proceeds to trial. If the claimant fails to receive an award for more than an earlier Part 36 offer, then he or she will not receive any of their legal costs from the date that the offer was made, even though they have technically won the case. The matter of what costs are recoverable when the claimant does beat a Part 36 offer was the central issue in the decision of

Figure 23.2 A claim form

Table 23.1 Changes in terminology

Old term	New term
Writ	Claim form
Discovery	Disclosure
Plaintiff	Claimant
Statement of claim	Particulars of claim
Payment into court procedures	Part 36 procedures

Broadhurst v *Tan* (2016). Here the claimant beat the Part 36 offer and sought to recover costs in the usual way, that is, outside of the fixed costs regime as this would be more favourable. (The fixed costs regime is considered later in this chapter at p. 638.) The claimant was allowed to recover his costs outside of the fixed costs regime as the rules around costs surrounding Part 36 are unchanged by the introduction of fixed costs and such claimants should not be penalised by fixed costs, especially when they were seeking to settle rather than to litigate. Lord Dyson held that:

> fixed costs and assessed costs are conceptually different. Fixed costs are awarded whether or not they were incurred, and whether or not they represent reasonable or proportionate compensation . . . assessed costs reflect the work actually done.

This may then have the impact of making parties strongly consider making reasonable Part 36 offers early in their claims so as to avoid paying higher than the fixed costs. This may then lead to more settlements and less litigation.

The different formal documents are described as the statement of case, while in the past they were called the pleadings. All statements of case must be verified by a statement of truth. This is a statement signed by the claimant (or their legal representative), in the following words: 'I believe that the facts stated in these particulars of claim are true.' The purpose of such a statement is to prevent a party from putting in facts for purely tactical purposes which they have no intention of relying upon. If a party makes a false statement in a statement of case verified by a statement of truth, the party will be guilty of contempt of court (r. 28.14).

Either party can apply for a summary judgment on the ground that the claim or defence has no real prospect of success. The court can also reach this conclusion on its own initiative.

The emphasis of the new procedural rules is to encourage an early settlement of proceedings. A MORI poll of 100 solicitors carried out in 2000 found that 76 per cent of solicitors believed that the reforms had increased the chances of an early settlement. The majority felt that the reforms had cut the amount of litigation. Between May 1999 and January 2000 there was a 25 per cent reduction in the number of cases issued in the County Courts compared with the same period the previous year.

23

THE CIVIL TRIAL PROCESS

23.5.2 Pre-action protocols

The pre-trial procedure is, perhaps, the most important area of the civil process, since few civil cases actually come to trial. To push the parties into behaving reasonably during the pre-trial stage, Lord Woolf recommended the development of pre-action protocols to lay down a code of conduct for this stage of the proceedings. Fourteen pre-action protocols have been produced so far which cover such areas of practice as personal injury, medical negligence and housing. They were developed in consultation with most of the key players in the relevant fields, including legal, health and insurance professionals. The Civil Justice Council is currently producing a general protocol to cover all those cases that are not caught by the existing protocols.

Pre-action protocols are a major innovation and aim to encourage:

- more pre-action contact between the parties;
- an earlier and fuller exchange of information;
- improved pre-action investigation; and
- a settlement before proceedings have commenced.

They strive to achieve this through establishing a timetable for the exchange of information, by setting standards for the content of correspondence, providing schedules of documents that should be disclosed along with a mechanism for agreeing on a single joint expert. The pre-action protocols seek to encourage a culture of openness between the parties. This should lead to the parties being better informed as to the merits of their case so that they will be in a position to settle cases fairly, so reducing the need for litigation. If settlement is not reached, the parties should be able to proceed to litigation on a more informed basis. Pre-action protocols should also enable proceedings to run to timetable, and efficiently, if litigation proves to be necessary.

Compliance with a pre-action protocol is not compulsory but, if a party unreasonably refuses to comply, then this can be taken into account when the court makes orders for costs. It may be that these protocols will need 'sharper teeth' in order to be effective.

A Practice Direction on pre-action conduct has also been issued by the Civil Justice Council giving general guidance on how the parties should behave at the early stages of litigation. The Practice Direction seeks to encourage the parties to settle their claim out of court. A letter before claim must be sent and responded to within a reasonable time. This must be acknowledged within 14 to 90 days depending on the complexity of the dispute. The parties must attempt to resolve the dispute through alternative dispute resolution.

23.5.3 Alternative dispute resolution

At various stages in a dispute's history, the court will actively promote settlement by alternative dispute resolution (ADR). (For a detailed discussion of ADR in the English legal system see Chapter 25.) There is a general statement in the new rules that the court's duty to further the overriding objective by active case management includes both encouraging the parties to use an alternative dispute resolution procedure (if the court considers that appropriate) and facilitating the use of that procedure (r. 1.4(2)(e)). Also, when filling in the allocation questionnaire, the parties can request a one-month stay of proceedings while they try to settle the case by ADR or other means (r. 26.4). The parties will have to show that they genuinely attempted to resolve their dispute through ADR and have not just paid lip service to the ideal, as has been the tendency in the past.

23.5.4 Case management

This is the most significant innovation of the 1999 reforms. Case management means that the court will be the active manager of the litigation. The main aim of this approach is to bring cases to trial quickly and efficiently. Traditionally, it has been left to the parties and their lawyers to manage the cases. In 1995, the courts had made a move towards case management following a Practice Direction encouraging such methods, but it was only with the new Civil Procedure Rules that case management came fully into force. The new Rules firmly place the management of a case in the hands of the judges, with r. 1.4 emphasising that the court's duty is to take a proactive role in the management of each case. The judges are given considerable discretion in the exercise of their case management role. Lord Woolf does not feel that this will undermine the adversarial tradition, but he sees the legal professions fulfilling their adversarial functions in a more controlled environment.

Once proceedings have commenced, the court's powers of case management will be triggered by the filing of a defence. When the defence has been filed and case management has started, the parties are on a moving train, trial dates will be fixed and will be difficult to postpone, and litigants will not normally be able to slow down or stop unless they settle. The court first needs to allocate the case to one of the three tracks: the small claims track, the fast track or the multi-track (r. 24.6(1)), which will determine the future conduct of the proceedings. To determine which is the appropriate track, the court will serve a directions questionnaire on each party. The answers to this questionnaire will form the basis for deciding the appropriate track. When considering the answers to the questionnaire, the judge will determine whether a case should be subject to summary judgment, or whether a stay of proceedings should be given for alternative dispute resolution; and, if neither of these matters applies, whether there should be an allocation hearing called or whether the matter can be the subject of a paper determination of the allocation to a particular track.

The three tracks

The court allocates the case to the most appropriate track depending primarily on the financial value of the claim, but other factors that can be taken into account include the case's importance and complexity (r. 26.6). Normally:

- Small claims track cases deal with actions with a value of less than £10,000 (or £1,000 for repairs to a rented residential property). If it is a personal injury case, the claim must be for less than £10,000, of which no more than £1,000 must be for the personal injuries themselves.
- Fast-track cases deal with actions of a value between £10,000 and £25,000 (and equity proceedings up to £350,000).
- Multi-track cases deal with actions with a value higher than £25,000.

The three tracks will now be considered in turn. (In addition see p. 647 for details on the proposed fourth track: the intermediate track.)

The small claims track

The handling of small claims is largely unchanged by the Woolf reforms. In the small claims track, directions are issued for each case providing a date for the hearing and an estimate of the hearing time, unless the case requires a preliminary hearing appointment to assist the parties in the conduct of the case. This track was previously known as the small claims court, though it was never actually a separate court, but a procedure used by County Courts to deal with relatively small claims. It was introduced in response to a report from the Consumers' Association in 1967 claiming that the County Court was being used primarily as a debt collection agency for businesses: 89.2 per cent of the summonses were taken out by firms and only 9 per cent by individuals, who were put off by costs and complexity.

Established in 1973, this special procedure aims to provide a cheap, simple mechanism for resolving small-scale consumer disputes. Disclosure is dispensed with and, if the litigation continues to trial, it is usually held in private rather than in open court. The hearing is simple and informal, with few rules about the admissibility or presentation of evidence. No experts may be used without leave. It is usually a very quick process, with 60 per cent of hearings taking less than 30 minutes. Costs are limited except where, by consent, a case with a financial value such that it would normally be allocated to the fast track was allocated to the small claims track. The procedure is designed to make it easy for parties to represent themselves without the aid of a lawyer, and legal aid for representation is not available. A party can choose to be represented by a lay person, though the party must also attend.

The fast track

Fast-track cases will normally be dealt with by the County Court. Upon allocation to the fast track the court gives directions for the management of the case, and sets a timetable for the disclosure of documents, the exchange of witness statements, the exchange (and number) of expert reports, and the trial date or a period within which the trial will take place, which will be no more than 30 weeks later (compared to an average of 80 weeks before 1999).

A Practice Direction gives an example of a typical timetable that a court may give:

- Disclosure: 4 weeks
- Exchange of witness statements: 10 weeks
- Exchange of experts' reports: 14 weeks
- Hearing: 30 weeks.

Although the parties can vary certain matters by agreement, such as disclosure or the exchange of witness statements, the rules are quite clear that an application must be made to court if a party wishes to vary the date for the trial.

Under this track the maximum length of the trial is normally one day. The relevant Practice Direction states that the judge will normally have read the papers in the trial bundle and may dispense with an opening address. Witness statements will usually stand as evidence-in-chief. Oral expert evidence will be limited to one expert per party in relation to any expert field and expert evidence will be limited to two expert fields.

In an attempt to keep lawyers' bills down, fixed costs for 'fast-track' trials have been introduced, but the introduction of pre-trial fixed costs has been delayed until additional information is available to inform the development of the revised costs regime. Lord Woolf had recommended that there should be a £2,500 limit on costs for fast-track cases (though clients could enter into a written agreement to pay more to their solicitors). Apart from the trial itself, litigants are still committing themselves to open-ended payment by the hour, which Lord Woolf described as being equivalent to handing out a blank cheque. He observed: 'If you and I are having our house repaired, we don't do it on a time and materials basis, because we know it will be a disaster. There is no incentive for the builder to do it in the least time and do it with the most economical materials.'

The multi-track

Upon allocation to the multi-track, the court can give directions for the management of the case and set a timetable for those steps to be taken. Alternatively, for heavier cases, the court may fix a case management conference or a pre-trial review or both. Unlike the fast-track, the court does not at this stage automatically set a trial date or a period within which the trial will take place. Instead it will fix this as soon as it is practicable to do so. Thus, this track offers individual case management with tailor-made directions according to the needs of the case. The High Court only hears multi-track cases.

Since April 2013, more extensive cost management procedures have been introduced to the multi-track (excluding commercial cases). Parties are now required to exchange detailed budgets following the service of a defence. These budgets will, if not agreed, be approved or revised by the court. When assessing costs at the end of the case, the court will have regard to a party's last approved or agreed budget and will not depart from it unless satisfied there is good reason to do so.

Table 23.2 Average number of weeks from claim being issued to initial hearing date, Q2 (January to March) 2009 to Q3 (July to September) 2018

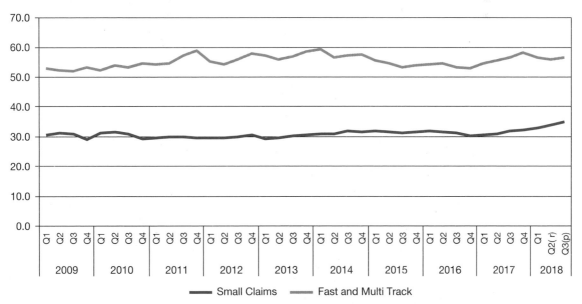

Small Claims   Fast and Multi Track

Source: Page 7 of Civil Justice Statistics Quarterly July to September 2018, Ministry of Justice Statistics bulletin, published 6 December 2018, available online at: https://assets.publishing.service.gov.uk/government/uploads/system/uploads/attachment_data/file/761869/civil-justice-statistics-quarterly-Jul-Sep-2018.pdf

Figure 23.3 Small claims – average time from issue to hearing, 2009–2013

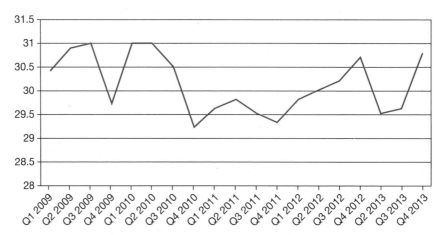

Source: Graph created from data contained in file 'csv_timeliness_national_final.csv', which can be found by clicking on 'Civil' at the following link: https://www.gov.uk/government/statistics/court-statistics-quarterly-january-to-march-2014

A proactive approach

Gone are the days when the court waited for the lawyers to bring the case back before it or allowed the lawyers to dictate without question the number of witnesses or the amount of costs incurred. In managing litigation the court must have regard to the overriding objective, set out in Part 1, which is to deal with cases justly. To fulfil this key objective of the reformed civil justice system, the court is required to:

- identify the issues at an early stage;
- decide promptly which issues require full investigation and dispose summarily of the others;
- encourage the parties to seek alternative dispute resolution where appropriate;
- encourage the parties to cooperate with each other in the conduct of the procedures;
- help the parties to settle the whole or part of the case;
- decide the order in which issues are to be resolved;
- fix timetables or otherwise control the progress of the case;
- consider whether the likely benefits of taking a particular step will justify the cost of taking it;
- deal with a case without the parties' attendance at court if this is possible;
- make appropriate use of technology; and
- give directions to ensure that the trial of a case proceeds quickly and efficiently.

Many of the preliminary hearings, such as allocation hearings and case management conferences, are now dealt with by the judge over the telephone, rather than people having to attend court. This saves time and money by taking advantage of modern technology.

23.5.5 Disclosure

Before the 1999 reforms, disclosure was known as 'discovery'. The procedure used to involve each party providing the other with a list of all the documents which they had in relation to the action. The parties could then ask to see some or all of this material. The process could be time-consuming and costly. Pre-action disclosure was also available in claims for personal injury and death. Lord Woolf recommended that disclosure should generally be limited to documents which were readily available and which to a 'material extent' adversely affected or supported a party's case, though this could be extended for multi-track cases. This change would have altered significantly the disclosure process and risked going against the philosophy of openness between the parties generally advocated by Lord Woolf. He also favoured extending pre-action disclosure to be available for all proceedings and against people who would not have been parties to the future proceedings. However, the new Civil Procedure Rules are actually very similar to the old rules. These require the disclosure of documents on which they rely or which adversely affected or supported a party's case. It is not necessary for this impact to be to a 'material extent'. As under the old rules, additional disclosure will be ordered where it is 'necessary in order to dispose fairly of the claim or to save costs.' The availability of pre-action disclosure was not extended despite the fact that the Civil Procedure Act 1997 provided for its extension. The pre-action protocols are designed to ensure voluntary disclosure is made between likely parties. It seems that the Government wishes to see how the pre-action protocols operate in practice before implementing such changes.

23.5.6 Sanctions

Tough rules on sanctions give the courts stringent powers to enforce the new rules on civil procedure to ensure that litigation is pursued diligently. The two main sanctions are an adverse award of costs and an order for a case or part of a case to be struck out. These sanctions were available under the old rules, but the novelty of the new regime lies in the commitment to enforce strict compliance. There is an increasing willingness of the courts to manage cases with a stick rather than a carrot. The courts can treat the standards set in the pre-action protocols as the normal approach to pre-action conduct and have the power to penalise parties for non-compliance.

A further significant change to the civil system made by the Woolf reforms concerned the approach to legal costs. Under the old system there was a basic principle that the loser paid the winner's costs. This principle was only departed from in exceptional circumstances. Although this principle still exists under the new system, it is now treated only as a starting point which the court can readily depart from. Where a party has not complied with court directions, particularly as to time, they can be penalised by being ordered to pay heavier costs, or by losing the right to have some or all of their costs paid.

A party who fails to comply with the case timetable or court orders may have their claim struck out. The court has power to strike out a party's statement of case, or part of it, where there has been a failure to comply with a rule, Practice Direction or court order (r. 3.4). This power can be exercised on an application from a party, or on the court's own initiative. Mere delay will be enough in itself to deprive a party of the power to bring or defend an action.

It is up to the defaulting party to apply for relief from sanctions using the procedure contained in r. 3.9. This is dramatically different from the previous state of affairs where a party in default of a court order was not the subject of any sanction unless the innocent party brought the matter to the court's attention.

Where, during the trial, any representative of a party incurs costs as a result of their own improper, unreasonable or negligent conduct, they will not receive payment for those wasted costs. A wasted costs order is essentially a power to 'fine' practitioners who incur the disapproval of the court.

Under the Criminal Justice and Courts Act 2015, where claimants have been 'fundamentally dishonest' in relation to their claim, the claim must be dismissed unless the court is satisfied the claimants would suffer substantial injustice. They are also likely to lose the costs protection offered by the qualified one-way costs shifting rule. This provision is aimed, for example, at claimants who exaggerate their injuries after a car crash. Even though some of the claim may be legitimate, the whole claim will be thrown out.

23.5.7 Court fees

Court fees have been increased significantly over the last three decades. The aim is that civil courts should be self-financing and managed according to business principles. The Labour Government introduced a 'pay-as-you-go' system, which requires parties to pay for each stage of a civil action, with the costs obviously mounting if a party chooses to proceed all the way to a trial. The aim is both that the courts should be self-financing and that people should be encouraged to settle.

The increased court fees have been criticised on the ground that they will deter many lower-income households from pursuing reasonable claims for justice. Some observers point out that payments are not made by members of the public at the point of use in the education and health systems and that justice can be seen as being just as important as those services.

The civil justice watchdog, the Civil Justice Council, has called upon the Government to abandon its policy of making litigants pay almost the full cost of the civil courts through fees. It has stated: 'access to the civil courts must be seen as providing a social and collective benefit, as well as a service to the individual citizen.' The senior judiciary have criticised High Court fees as undermining access to justice.

23.5.8 Money Claim Online

In 2002, Money Claim Online (MCOL) was established. It provides a debt recovery service over the internet for sums up to £100,000. The debts might be for unpaid goods or services, or rent arrears, for example. Claimants can issue money claims via the internet at www.moneyclaim.gov.uk. Fees are paid electronically by debit or credit card. The defence can use the online service to acknowledge service and file a defence. Most debt claims are undefended, and if no defence is filed, the claimant can apply online for a judgment and enforcement. If the case is defended, the litigation reverts to the old-fashioned paper system. The parties can use the website to check the progress of their case, such as whether a defence has been filed. The service is available 24 hours a day, seven days a week. The new service has proved very popular with creditors, who have issued thousands of claims to date using the new service.

The Bigger Picture: An automated claims portal

A streamlined claims system was introduced in 2010 for personal injury cases following road traffic accidents for between £1,000 and £25,000 where the defendant does not dispute liability and the only dispute is with regard to how much damages should be paid. This is an online system which is sometimes described as an automated claims portal. A consultation paper on the subject was published in 2007 entitled *Case Track Limits and the Claims Process for Personal Injury Claims.* If the defendant denies responsibility or fails to respond to the notification of the claim within 15 days, the case will be removed from this automated system and be dealt with under the ordinary fast-track system. The aim is to provide a swift and cheap resolution procedure. The process is divided into three stages. The first stage involves the issuing of the claim and the defence response. If the defendant (usually an insurer) does not respond within the required 15 days, denies liability, alleges contributory negligence (other than a failure to wear a seat belt) or asserts that the information on the claim form is inadequate, the claim falls out of the process. If liability is admitted, the claim moves on to stage two. Stage two is an attempt to settle the case. The claimant submits a settlement pack comprising the medical report, financial receipts for expenses incurred and the claimant's valuation of the claim. If the case is not settled at this stage, the case moves on to stage three. Stage three is the court hearing. There is normally only a paper hearing of the case, though the parties have the right to request an oral hearing. The whole process should normally be completed within three months. The parties use standard template documents which are submitted electronically. They are entitled to use lawyers, but only fixed costs are payable of a maximum of £500.

The scheme handles 70 per cent of all road accident claims. Over a quarter of a million claims were registered on the system in the first six months of it being established. In practice, a third of claims are exiting the system at the first stage. In 60 per cent of cases this is because the insurer has not responded, rather than there actually being a dispute over liability. Almost half the cases (47 per cent) exit the system before they settle. Ninety-seven per cent of the claims that settle in the portal system do so for under £3,500.

Since 2016, all parties have to use the MedCo portal to select experts and medical agencies for soft tissue injury claims entering the Road Traffic Accidents Portal. The MedCo portal produces a randomised list of seven independent medical experts within a 30-mile radius of the injured party. MedCo was introduced to try to stop fraudulent whiplash claims by making sure all medical reports are above suspicion. The Government is now planning to stop compensation for minor whiplash and soft tissue injuries altogether in its new Civil Liability Bill (see p. 654).

In 2013 the scope of the portal was extended to include employer and public liability cases up to a value of £25,000. These cases are carried out on a fixed costs basis. Although the sums involved can be quite small, employer and public liability cases cover a wide variety of circumstances, are often complex and may be less suitable for a blanket approach. The impact of this reform might be limited because while these cases may start in the automated portal system they are likely to drop out of the system as the case progresses due to their complexity.

The Bigger Picture: The family justice system

The family court system has undergone major reforms in recent years, with moves to make them more open, unify the family court system and limit the availability of legal aid. We will look at these three issues in turn.

Openness

The family courts have been the subject of considerable criticism, particularly from fathers of children who felt they had been treated unfairly by the courts. They argued the legal system was biased in favour of mothers when determining such issues as access to their children and financial contributions. Some fathers managed to get support for their cause in the media, but there were suggestions that actually the public were not able to get a full picture of the case, because many of the court proceedings took place in private; so journalists might not be aware of good reasons why access to the father's children was being restricted, such as that he had been violent in the past. These issues raised the question of whether the public would have a better understanding of the court proceedings if they were open to the public. A balance needs to be achieved between the public's interest and the interests of the children in a case. This balance has been highlighted where children have been taken into care by social services following a suspicion of abuse and the family have claimed their innocence. While the family are free to speak to the media and put their side of the case, the social services have an obligation to respect the privacy of the children and fear the public are getting a very one-sided perspective of the case.

In 2009 the media were given greater access to family proceedings except adoption cases. At any stage of the proceedings the court may direct that a journalist cannot attend if this is necessary to respect the interests of a child, protect the parties or witnesses, enable the orderly conduct of proceedings or prevent the obstruction of justice. While journalists with a press card are being allowed to attend family court hearings, the tight restrictions on reporting remain. They are permitted to publish details of the family court process, but are prohibited from publishing details of individual cases. In particular, no information must be published which would identify any children involved in court proceedings. As a result of these restrictions, the public is not very interested in what the journalists are allowed to publish and very few cases are being reported from the family courts.

The media has inevitably been pushing for increased access to the family courts but, in practice, it will only be interested in reporting a narrow range of family cases, particularly celebrity divorces. Most family cases are of interest to nobody apart from the parties themselves (and perhaps a few nosy neighbours). Restrictions to media access to divorce courts were introduced in 1926 because of the lurid details of divorce cases then appearing in the press. It has to be remembered that the priority of the media is usually to make money. It may be that the risk of media exposure will prompt a greater number of out-of-court settlements, as a person's desire to keep their personal life private outweighs their desire to achieve the best possible outcome for themselves in a case.

In *Appleton and Gallagher v News Group Newspapers* (2015) two famous popstars were getting divorced, Nicole Appleton from the 'girl band' All Saints, and Liam Gallagher from the Britpop group, Oasis. The litigation was sorting out the financial settlement between the parties. The trial court imposed reporting restrictions and the newspaper company sought unsuccessfully to have this ban removed.

Unification

Until recently family cases could be heard in the magistrates' court, the County Court or the High Court. A former senior civil servant, David Norgrove, produced a report in 2011 and stated that the family justice system was 'a system that isn't a system', made up of a series of 'quite disparate organisations'. He recommended that a unified family justice service should be established with a single family court. This reform was introduced by the Crime and Courts Act 2013. The aim is to promote efficiency and avoid forum shopping. The risk is increased bureaucracy with too much centralisation.

Legal aid cuts

Following reforms to the legal aid system under the Legal Aid, Sentencing and Rehabilitation of Offenders Act 2013, legal aid is not available for many family cases, including divorce cases. As a result family courts are rapidly becoming lawyer-free zones. In 2014, 60 per cent of parents went to court without a lawyer to contest arrangements for their children, such as child contact, residency and maintenance payments. The number of cases going to court over child arrangements dropped by 40 per cent in 2014 compared to 2013 and there was also a drop of 50 per cent in the number of cases referred to mediation. Thus, whole sections of society are being denied access to justice and are being left to try and resolve matters themselves without the assistance of professionals. The risk is that by failing to resolve these disputes through the formal legal routes, society is building up problems for the future.

Photo 23.2 A stunt at Buckingham Palace by the campaign group Fathers 4 Justice

Source: © Scott Barbour/Getty Images

23.5.9 Costs: Lord Jackson's reforms

There has been some concern that Lord Woolf's reforms increased rather than reduced costs. *The Woolf Network Questionnaire* (Law Society, 2002) suggested that the cost of engaging in civil litigation had not been reduced by the civil justice reforms. The pre-action protocols combined with case management may have front-loaded costs onto cases which would have settled anyway before reaching court. In the past, lawyers could keep their early costs down while waiting to see whether the case would settle, but this is not possible when pre-action protocols and case management directions need to be complied with. There has been an increasing problem that after a legal dispute has been resolved, the parties then enter into separate litigation as to the amount of legal costs that should be paid by the losing party – known as satellite litigation.

As a result, the senior judge who is the president of the civil courts (the Master of the Rolls) asked another judge, Lord Justice Jackson, to carry out an independent review of civil litigation costs. His report, entitled *Review of Civil Litigation Costs: Final Report*, was published in 2010. He took the view that the right to access to justice required costs incurred during the civil litigation process to be proportionate to the value of the case; it is discouraging if the costs of bringing a claim should outweigh the actual value of the claim. Lord Jackson indicated that reforms to costs will have to take place in stages, with his report focusing on broad proposals on amendments to costs and that the matter would have to be revisited once his first set of proposals are embedded within the system to understand how the system takes to such change. He noted that 'there are serious problems of non-compliance with pre-action protocols' and that the courts had become 'too tolerant of delays and non-compliance with orders'. The Government accepted his key recommendations and relevant provisions were contained in the Legal Aid, Sentencing and Punishment of Offenders Act 2012 (LASPO). In January 2017, it was announced by the then Justice Minister that the Ministry of Justice will be undertaking a post-implementation review of the effects of the LASPO. This review is currently underway and will be telling of the impact that the withdrawal of legal aid has had on access to justice and whether the changes introduced thus far meet the objectives of Part 2 of LASPO in respect of the changes that impact on funding for civil litigation.

In 2016, Lord Jackson was asked to continue with his review of costs but with the narrow focus of fixed recoverable costs in low value claims. This culminated in his 2017 report entitled *Review of Civil Litigation Costs: Supplemental Report – Fixed Recoverable Costs*. It is important, he says, that there is control and a level of restriction over recoverable costs, namely the costs that the winning party will seek to recover from the losing party; and that there is an overall reduction in the actual litigation costs, that is, the costs which each party pays to its own lawyers. He believes that the will for such change is there both from the judiciary and the profession. He is mindful that lawyers should be adequately remunerated for their work while at the same time ensuring that costs are not so high that they impede access to justice for those involved in the claim. He considers that the profession is now steadily coming on board with his proposals to cost reforms, primarily because this saves both time and money for all involved.

Lord Jackson was anxious to reduce satellite litigation over costs. His reforms aimed to reduce the use of conditional fee agreements because the parties would themselves have to pay any uplift in their lawyers' fees under such an agreement. Instead, he paved the way for the use of contingency fee agreements where the lawyer will be paid a percentage of any award of damages to their client (see p. 358).

The traditional approach to costs has been for the winner to ask the loser to pay their costs (known as the indemnity principle). If the loser thought the costs were unreasonable and no agreement could be reached, then the matter would go to a judge to determine retrospectively whether the costs were reasonable. Lord Jackson identified a peculiarity of litigation: at the time when costs were being run up, no one knew who would be paying the bill or how much that bill would be. In his view it was no longer acceptable for questions of costs to be left to the end of litigation – some judicial control of costs during the course of the litigation had to be introduced as part of the case management process. Litigation should be run on a budget just like any other commercial venture.

Following Lord Jackson's recommendations, a qualified one-way cost-shifting rule (QOCS) for personal injury cases has been introduced, whereby an unsuccessful claimant will not be required to pay the defendant's costs, but the defendant will have to pay the costs of a successful claimant. The reforms will lead to a significant reduction in fees earned by lawyers acting for the victims of personal injury. While fees have been reduced by over half, the amount of compensation claimants can obtain has not been affected. To make up for the shortfall, claimants are now routinely billed for up to 25 per cent of all damages, to cover the costs of the law firm representing them. This cut in legal fees could see law firms close or merge, or even move away from billing clients by the hour to introducing fixed-fee services. The ability to bring a personal injury claim without an obvious costs downside is likely to encourage people to bring claims. This may be a sign of greater access to justice and/or it may open the door to unmeritorious claims, creating a risk of people pursuing weak claims as their costs exposure would be fixed and modest. Defendants who win will still effectively lose as they will be liable to bear their own costs. They will be under pressure to settle even weak cases to avoid incurring legal costs.

In his 2010 report Lord Justice Jackson pressed for the introduction of fixed fees in any case up to £250,000 as this would remove any arguments about proportionality and produce greater consistency. Efficiency would be rewarded by ditching the hourly rate. Critics have argued that this change would be an oversimplification, treating a complex medical negligence case in the same way as a debt claim. Lord Justice Briggs in his *Civil Courts Structure Review: Final Report* (2016) states that:

> a fixed or budgeted recoverable costs regime, backed by Qualified One-way Costs Shifting ('QOCS') plus uplifted damages has, in the sphere of personal injury (including clinical negligence) ligation been a powerful promoter of access to justice, in an area where the playing field is at first sight sharply tilted against the individual claimant, facing a sophisticated insurance company as the real (even if not nominal) defendant.

While such measures have been welcome, since the Jackson reforms, lawyers have expressed concerns about rising costs and access to justice. In 2013, the London Solicitors Litigation Association (LSLA) polled 1,500 lawyers in London, asking them for their opinion of the Jackson reforms: 93 per cent of those polled said that the reforms had not increased access to justice, and, worryingly, 73 per cent said that civil litigation costs have increased, not decreased, since the reforms. The need for absolute compliance with rules, orders and time-tables has led law firms to put more resources towards ensuring they meet this compliance, which increases costs. Lawyers have set more cautious deadlines for case management, making cases last longer, because of a fear of being hit with punitive sanctions if they miss the date. Despite this, the Government is seeking further reform to costs. In 2014, QOCS was extended to apply to defamation and invasion of privacy cases, as well as personal injury cases. In other cases, the old rule that the loser pays the winner's costs will still apply.

Costs must be proportionate and a new test of proportionality has been introduced. This means that only costs that are reasonable and proportionate can be recovered from the losing party. This is designed to prevent parties, or their advisers, from engaging in work that is disproportionate to the 'value, complexity and importance' of the claim. The question of what amounts to 'disproportionate' costs is, as of yet, unclear. In *Willis v MRJ Rundell* (2013), the High Court declined to accept 'unreasonable' costs budgets on both sides of a £1.6 million professional negligence claim, because the costs claimed were higher than the amount which was claimed and recovered.

For fast-track cases, Lord Jackson recommended a full fixed recoverable costs (FRC) regime for all fast track cases, that is, cases that are expected not to last any longer than one day and where the value of the claim does not exceed £25,000. This regime will involve a grid where parties can read off from it what the recoverable costs will be in their case. This is very similar to the German system. This will help to promote certainty for those who would like to know in advance what the likely amount of recoverable costs might be. If it is going to be a low amount, the parties may want to think carefully about embarking on litigation. They may prefer instead to look at alternative ways of resolving their claim, such as ADR. The figures in the grid are to be reviewed every three years to ensure that they are set at the right levels which continue to ensure the right balance.

Lord Jackson also recommends the introduction of a new track altogether which is to be known as the 'intermediate' track. This will be for claims up to £100,000, that are of modest complexity and which can be tried in three days or less. This track will also have a FRC grid for parties to consider the likely amount of costs that they may be able to recover. It is important to understand that the spirit of the system is to avoid allowing wealthy defendants to manipulate the system and thereby impede access to justice for those who need it the most. This track is largely designed to avoid litigation of lower value cases in the multi-track where the cost in relation to the claim is disproportionate

For multi-track cases the Jackson report recommends the introduction of costs management. The parties will now have to produce a costs budget for their case, which is approved by the judge. The judges have to actively control the parties' costs from the start of litigation to its conclusion. The parties normally have to stick to their budgets and any costs incurred which go beyond the budget are not normally recoverable from the losing party. The costs management process involves each party, early in the proceedings, producing an estimate of their costs. They set out how many hours are likely to be spent – and by which seniority of lawyer – on each stage of the action from pre-issue of claim until trial or settlement. The budgets are approved by a judge if they are proportionate to the remedy being sought or amended as appropriate. Budgets can be updated if necessary during the course of the litigation. If parties do not adhere to the costs budgeting procedure, or make a mistake in their budgeting, then the court may refuse to allow them to recover any extra costs they have accumulated. In *Elvanite Full Circle Ltd* v *AMEC Earth and Environmental (UK) Ltd* (2013), the High Court refused the request of a defendant to recover extra costs. The Court had approved a costs budget of £268,488, only for the defendant to realise a few weeks later that they had made a terrible mistake, and that the costs of the trial would actually amount to £531,946.18. The High Court refused the defendant's request for extra costs, in part because the defendant made the request after the trial, and the whole point of costs budgeting was that costs would be finalised before the end of the trial.

A high-profile case which caused considerable disquiet among the legal profession was the case of *Mitchell* v *News Group Newspapers* (2013). In this case, Andrew Mitchell MP, formerly a minister in the coalition Government, had brought a claim against *The Sun* newspaper, which reported that Mr Mitchell had insulted police officers in Downing Street in an incident which became known as 'Plebgate' because Mr Mitchell was accused of calling a police officer a 'pleb'. In March 2013, Mr Mitchell brought defamation proceedings against *The Sun* newspaper. The proceedings had to comply with the Civil Procedure Rules which stipulated that the parties had to file their costs budget seven days before the date of the hearing. Mr Mitchell's solicitors were late in submitting the costs budget. As a sanction, the High Court ruled Mr Mitchell could recover only his court fees as costs, and not the fees of his lawyers. This meant that Mr Mitchell had to pay for the vast majority of his legal fees, which amounted to £590,000 in total. The Court of Appeal upheld the High Court judgment. The Master of the Rolls, Lord Dyson, said he wanted to 'send out a clear message' about the importance of complying with the costs budget rules.

This decision caused practical problems. Judges took the view that if a breach was not trivial or there was no good reason for it, then they were bound by *Mitchell* to impose a sanction. Breaches of court orders were rarely found to be trivial or for good reason so draconian sanctions were imposed for these technical breaches. Lawyers started trying to get cases thrown out of court on the basis of a technical breach of a court deadline. Litigants were made to suffer severe sanctions for relatively minor procedural failures. Parties to litigation ceased to cooperate with each other and adopted a policy of 'spot the breach' in the hope they might win the case because of a technical breach by the other party. This then led to satellite litigation by parties against their lawyers for negligence, such as missing a time limit, leading to them losing their case.

The Court of Appeal therefore revisited the *Mitchell* decision in *Denton* v *TH White Ltd* (2014). This case laid down a three-stage approach to be taken to a breach of court directions. Where there has been a failure to comply with any rule, practice direction or court order, the first stage is to identify and assess the seriousness and significance of this failure to comply. If the breach is not serious or significant, then relief from sanctions will usually be granted. If the breach in respect of which relief from sanctions is sought is serious or significant, the second stage is to consider why the failure or the default occurred. The third stage is to consider all the circumstances of the case so as to enable the court to deal justly with the application for relief. In particular, the court will take into account the promptness of any application for relief and other past or current breaches of rules, practice directions and court orders. The Court emphasised that opportunistic behaviour by litigants seeking to take advantage of minor failures to comply by others was wrong. All parties to litigation have an obligation to cooperate to ensure it is conducted efficiently and at proportionate cost. This case has helped to restore sensible collaboration between litigators which had been in danger of being irreparably undermined by the *Mitchell* decision. The courts are now permitted to take a more flexible approach to the grant of relief from sanctions, one that permits an outcome which better reflects the gravity of the breach and the justice of the individual case.

The pilot schemes which tested out the new budgeting arrangements identified a problem with the expense and time involved in creating and approving the budgets, and that some judges were hostile to the idea of managing costs. However, weighed against this was the clear benefit to clients of being forewarned of the extent of their potential liability for not only their own, but also their opponent's costs.

In response to the potentially conflicting decisions of the lower courts as they implement the Jackson reforms, five Court of Appeal judges, including the Master of the Rolls and Lord Justice Jackson himself, have been appointed to hear all appeals arising from the reforms. This should ensure that the Court of Appeal takes a consistent line on how to interpret and apply the new Civil Procedure Rules, reducing uncertainty for lawyers and litigants. This is particularly welcome, as lawyers around the country have reported discrepancies among County Courts in applying the costs budgeting and other new rules, which may lead to a larger number of appeals to the Court of Appeal in the future.

Upon Lord Jackson's recommendation, the courts have increased general damages by 10 per cent to make sure claimants are properly compensated, as some of their damages will now be paid to their lawyer. The Court of Appeal announced in *Simmons* v *Castle* (2012) that the increase in damages would take effect from 1 April 2013. It applies to all torts which cause suffering, inconvenience or distress to individuals.

Claimants who fail to beat a Part 36 offer to settle by defendants (see p. 635) lose the protection of the qualified one-way cost-shifting rule (see *Broadhurst* v *Tan* on p. 635). Under s. 55 of the Legal Aid, Sentencing and Punishment of Offenders Act 2012 a damages mark-up of 10 per cent can be awarded to the claimant on top of the *Simmons* v *Castle* mark-up of 10 per cent. This mark-up applies for the first £500,000 awarded and is reduced to 5 per cent between £500,000 and £1 million. The additional 10 per cent has to be paid by the defendant when the claimant is awarded more than his own Part 36 offer to settle. For example, a claimant in a claim for damages offers to accept £85,000. The defendant will not pay. At trial, the claimant is awarded £100,000. Since the claimant has secured a better outcome than their Part 36 proposal, they will in fact recover £110,000. The aim is to put pressure on the parties to accept a pre-trial offer to settle.

Normally, the same judge should deal with the case from any pre-trial hearings and case management directions to the trial itself.

Following Lord Jackson's recommendation, referral fees have been abolished for personal injury cases because these 'add to the cost of litigation without adding any real benefit to it' (see p. 223).

Lord Jackson wanted to see the abolition of the general pre-action protocol on the basis that one size does not fit all, but this recommendation has not been acted upon. Like Lord Woolf, he wanted to see fixed costs applied to all personal injury cases on the fast track (which, in practice, is most personal injury cases): lawyers would not be able to decide for themselves how much to charge for a case. Again, this reform has not been introduced, but more cases are dealt with on the automated portals where fixed costs apply. Germany has a system of fixed costs which works well in practice.

Upon Lord Jackson's recommendation, to improve the quality of evidence from expert witnesses, experts can give evidence at the same time – this is known as 'hot-tubbing'. This process allows experts to discuss in open court between each other the differences in their evidence.

23.6 Interim assessment of LASPO

This momentum of reform has not slowed down and has been compounded by the post-implementation review (PIR) of Part 2 of LASPO and the initial assessment by the MoJ. The PIR aims to consider whether the legislation has met its objectives, and whether there are unintended consequences that need addressing.

The initial review states that:

The overall aims of the costs and litigation funding reforms in LASPO Part 2 were: to reduce the costs of civil litigation and to rebalance the costs liabilities between claimants and defendants while ensuring that parties with a valid case can still bring or defend a claim. There was also an ambition to encourage early settlement; and to discourage unmeritorious claims. The Part 2 reforms were based on recommendations made by Sir Rupert Jackson in his Review of Civil Litigation Costs . . . [which included] a package of reforms (commonly known as the Jackson reforms) 'to control costs and promote access to justice', which were the thrust of LASPO Part 2 . . . The intention, then, was for meritorious claims to be allowed to proceed at more proportionate cost, whilst discouraging unmeritorious claims. As Sir Rupert Jackson put it rather more pithily: 'access to justice at proportionate cost'.

Data and information are still being collected in order to present the impact of the changes brought in by LASPO.

23.7 Criticism of the civil justice system

Some aspects of the civil justice system are working very well. It is pleasing to see that foreign nationals who have a choice of jurisdiction are choosing to use the English courts and arbitrators to resolve their disputes. An example of this is the high-profile litigation between Boris Berezovsky and Roman Abramovich (the Russian billionaire owner of Chelsea Football Club). In approximately half the cases heard by the Commercial Court in London, all the parties are from outside the UK. Reasons for this include the fact that the legal services sector in London has developed to meet the demands of the sophisticated markets and industries located there and, accordingly, international litigants find London lawyers have a wide range of relevant expertise. Our judges have a global reputation for impartiality and honesty: they are not suspected of being influenced by the Government of the day or by private interests.

23.7.1 Standards

A pilot simulation carried out by civil litigators on behalf of the old Lord Chancellor's Department to try to predict the impact of the Woolf reforms on the civil justice system was not encouraging (*Report of the Fast Track Simulation Pilot* (1998b)). Those involved expressed the fear that pressures on practitioners in terms of both time and costs might lead to corner-cutting, devolution of cases to less experienced fee earners, insufficient time for proper investigation of the claim, and the incurring of irrecoverable costs. They worried too that the openness that Lord Woolf was so keen to encourage as a fundamental principle underlying his reforms might be prejudiced by the 'fear factor'. In other words, solicitors might be secretive during the early stages of the litigation so as to avoid client criticism and potential negligence claims; and be reluctant to tell a client about the weakness of a case.

23.7.2 Enforcement

The enforcement of judgments continues to be a problem. Research carried out by Professor John Baldwin (2003) of Birmingham University highlighted this weakness in the civil justice system. He concluded that the difficulties with enforcing civil judgments were leaving many claimants disillusioned with the legal system. The danger is that if the system of enforcement is inadequate creditors will look to other methods of securing payment.

23.7.3 Out-of-court settlements

The *Judicial Statistics* show that there has been a significant drop in the number of cases reaching the courts since the Woolf reforms were introduced. In 1995 over 150,000 claims were commenced in the High Court. By 2007, the number had fallen to 64,000. The number of claims issued in the County Courts has also dropped significantly. In 1998 the number of claims issued nationally was over 2,200,000 but by 2005 the number of annual claims had fallen to less than 1,900,000. This drop was partly due to the favourable economic climate at the time, and 2006 saw a slight increase in the number of claims being brought as the economic climate turned sour with the global credit crunch starting to bite.

The use of pre-action protocols and claimant offers to encourage pre-trial settlements has diverted cases from being litigated in the courts. As a result only 8 per cent of cases listed for trial settle at the trial, while 70 per cent settle much earlier. The reforms put considerable emphasis on the use of out-of-court settlements, which can have the advantage of providing a quick end to the dispute, and a reduction in costs. For the claimant, a settlement means they are sure of getting something, and do not have to risk losing the case altogether and probably having to pay the other side's costs as well as their own. But they must weigh this up against the chances of being awarded a better settlement if the case goes to trial and they win. The defendant risks the possibility that they might have won and therefore had to pay nothing, or that they may be paying more than the judge would have awarded if the claimant had won the case, against the chance that the claimant wins and is awarded more than the settlement would have cost.

The high number of out-of-court settlements creates injustice, because the parties usually hold very unequal bargaining positions. In the first place, one party might be in a better financial position than the other, and therefore under less pressure to keep costs down by settling quickly.

Figure 23.4 Civil claims, defences, allocations and hearings and trials, January 2009 to June 2016 (quarterly)

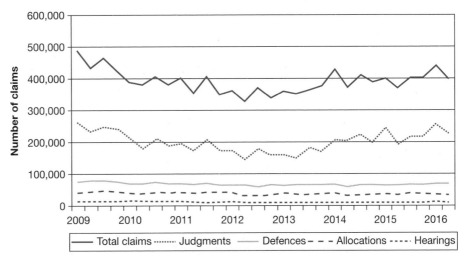

Source: Page 10, of the *Civil Justice Statistics Quarterly*, England and Wales, April to June 2016 published 1 September 2016 and available online at: https://www.gov.uk/government/statistics/civil-justice-statistics-quarterly-april-to-june-2016

23

THE CIVIL TRIAL PROCESS

Secondly, as Galanter's 1984 study revealed, litigants can often be divided into 'one-shotters' and 'repeat players'. One-shotters are individuals involved in litigation for probably the only time in their life, for whom the procedure is unfamiliar and traumatic; the case is very important to them and tends to occupy most of their thoughts while it continues. Repeat players, on the other hand, include companies and businesses (particularly insurance companies), for whom litigation is routine. They are used to working with the law and lawyers and, while they obviously want to win the case for financial reasons, they do not have the same emotional investment in it as the individual one-shotter. Where a repeat player and a one-shotter are on opposing sides – as is often the case in personal injury litigation, where an individual is fighting an insurance company – the repeat player is likely to have the upper hand in out-of-court bargaining.

A third factor was highlighted by Hazel Genn's 1987 study of negotiated settlements of accident claims. She found that having a non-specialist lawyer could seriously prejudice a client's interests when an out-of-court settlement is made. Non-specialists may be unfamiliar with court procedure and reluctant to fight the case in court. They may, therefore, not encourage their client to hold out against an unsatisfactory settlement. Specialist lawyers on the other side may take advantage of this inexperience, putting on pressure for the acceptance of a low settlement. Repeat players are more likely to have access to their own specialist lawyers, whereas, for the one-shotter, finding a suitable lawyer can be something of a lottery, since they have little information on which to base their choice.

In many cases, especially those involving personal injury, the defendant's costs, and sometimes those of the claimant, will be paid by an insurance company – for example, the parties in a car accident are likely to have been insured and professionals such as doctors are insured against negligence claims. As Hazel Genn's 1987 study showed, where only one party is insured, this can place great pressure on the other, unless they have been granted state funding. Given the recent cuts to legal aid, this is less likely to be granted. The insured side may try to drag out the proceedings for as long as possible, in the hope of exhausting the other party's financial reserves and forcing a low settlement.

Clearly, these factors affect the fairness of out-of-court settlements. In court, the judge can treat the parties as equals, but for out-of-court negotiations one party often has a very obvious advantage.

The Labour Government's first evaluation of the new Civil Procedure Rules, *Emerging Findings: an early evaluation of the Civil Justice Reforms* (2001) found that overall the reforms have been beneficial. It seems that cases are settling earlier, rather than at the door of the court. Lawyers and clients are now regarding litigation as a last resort, and making more use of alternative methods of dispute resolution. The pre-action protocols have been a success. Their effect has been to concentrate the minds of defendants and make them deal properly with a claim at the early stages rather than months after the issue of proceedings (conditional fee agreements could also be an explanation for this). While generally cases are being heard more quickly after the issue of the claim, small claims are taking longer. But the picture is not quite as straightforward as it looks. Lawyers know that as soon as they issue the claim form they will lose control of the pace of the negotiations and are going to be locked into timetables and procedures which they may find burdensome as well as costly. There is evidence that lawyers are therefore delaying issuing the claim. It is not yet clear whether litigation has become cheaper. The report quotes practitioners who believe the front-end loading of costs caused by the pre-action protocols means that overall costs have actually gone up.

In their research paper, *More Civil Justice: The Impact of the Woolf Reforms on Pre-Action Behaviour* (2002), the Law Society and the Civil Justice Council assessed the success of the new pre-action procedures. Most of the respondents were positive about their introduction.

In particular, personal injury practitioners and insurers have welcomed the additional information the protocol requires to be disclosed during the early stages of proceedings, as it facilitates early settlement.

Important research into the civil justice system, *The Management of Civil Cases: The Courts and the Post-Woolf Landscape* (Peysner and Seneviratne, 2005), concludes that the reforms have led to a better litigation culture. They have significantly reduced the amount of litigation going to court from 2.2 million cases in 1997 to 1.5 million cases in 2003. However, costs have increased, they have become front loaded (in other words, more costs are incurred at the earlier stages of the litigation process) and the cost of each case is higher overall.

23.7.4 Small claims track

The small claims procedure is an important part of the civil procedure system, involving around 80,000 actions each year. The procedure is quicker, simpler and cheaper than the full County Court process, which is helpful to both litigants and the overworked court system. It gives individuals and small businesses a useful lever against creditors or for consumer complaints. Without it, threats to sue over small amounts would be ignored on the basis that going to court would cost more than the value of the debt or compensation claimed. Public confidence is also increased, by proving that the legal system is not only accessible to the rich and powerful. The academic, Professor John Baldwin, has carried out research into the small claims track, *Lay and Judicial Perspectives on the Expansion of the Small Claims Regime* (2002). He noted that the official statistics show that the recent rises in the small claims limit have not led, as many feared, to the County Courts being inundated with new cases. There has only been a slight increase in the number of small claims cases. Most small claims litigants involved in relatively high value claims are satisfied with the experience. However, there are long-standing concerns about the small claims procedure, which have not been tackled by the 1999 reforms. Small claims are not necessarily simple claims; they may involve complex and unusual points of law. Is the small claimant entitled to be judged by the law of the land or by speedier, more rough-and-ready concepts of fairness?

The small claims procedure is not simple enough. The Civil Justice Review recommended that court forms and leaflets should be simplified. The system is still largely used by small businesses chasing debtors, rather than by the individual consumer for whom it was set up. A consultation paper was issued in 1995 suggesting that, in limited cases, the judge might be given the power to award an additional sum of up to £135 to cover the cost of legal advice and assistance in the preparation of the case. If this reform were to be introduced, it might assist individual consumers to bring their cases.

There are also problems with enforcement. A report by the Consumers' Association (November 1997) suggests that many people using the small claims procedure are being denied justice because of slow and inefficient enforcement procedures. The court is not responsible for enforcement, which is left to the winning party to secure. The report found that only a minority of defendants paid up on time and that after six months a substantial minority of people still had not paid their debts. Baldwin concluded that the enforcement problem was so serious that it threatened to undermine the small claims procedure itself by deterring people from using it.

The Civil Justice Council spent three years looking at the funding of civil claims and how to keep costs in proportion. In 2005 it published its report, *Improved Access to Justice – Funding Options and Proportionate Costs* (2005). It recommended that the small claims track limit for personal injury cases should be retained at £1,000. In 2013, the overall cap for the small claims track was increased from £5,000 to £10,000, and while the claim for personal injuries themselves must be below £1,000, the total sum claimed (for example, for loss of earnings) can be up to £10,000. Before this reform, most personal injury cases were heard under the fast-track procedure, which meant that costs could be recovered and lawyers could represent clients on a 'no win, no fee' basis. With the change to the financial limits, about 70 per cent of personal injury cases will now be heard under the small claims procedure where lawyers' fees cannot be recovered.

Baldwin's research concluded that the informal small claims procedures inevitably involve a sacrifice in the standards of judicial decision-making. He questioned whether this could be justified in claims involving more than £5,000.

Whiplash injuries are generally neck injuries caused by a sudden movement of the head in a road accident. Apparently, 1,500 whiplash claims are made each day, adding £90 to the average annual motor insurance premium. There has been concern that some claims for compensation for whiplash injuries are fraudulent. The Ministry of Justice issued a consultation paper entitled *Reducing the Number and Cost of Whiplash Claims* (2013). This looked at whether the small claims limit for all personal injury cases should be increased to £5,000, or whether it should be increased for whiplash claims only. The first option was preferred. Despite this, following pressure from Parliament's Transport Select Committee, Justice Secretary Chris Grayling decided in 2014 not to increase the small claims limit for whiplash cases from £1,000. This was partly due to the Government's own statistics, which showed that there were 488,281 whiplash claims in 2012/13, compared with 547,405 in 2011/12. This contradicted Government concerns about a whiplash epidemic pushing up premiums. The Government is moving to stop compensation for minor whiplash injuries altogether in its proposed Civil Liability Bill.

23.7.5 Civil Liability Bill

The Queen announced in her 2017 speech the introduction of the Civil Liability Bill:

> This Bill will crack down on fraudulent whiplash claims and is expected to reduce motor insurance premiums by about £35 per year. The Bill will ban offers to settle claims without the support of medical evidence and introduce a new fixed tariff of compensation for whiplash injuries with a duration of up to 2 years.

What this Bill is intended to do is to drive a move away from the notion that where there is blame there is a claim. We do not want our society to become embedded in the compensation culture that is prevalent in other countries, most notably in the US. The Bill will aim to prevent fraudulent and undeserving claims from getting through the system. It is therefore anticipated that if only the most deserving claims succeed, motor insurance premiums will go down.

The Justice Committee considered the impact of raising the small claims limit for personal injury claims from £1,000 to £2,000 and to £5,000 for road traffic accidents which result in personal injury. It determined earlier in July 2018 that any such personal injury reforms will be delayed until 2020 in order to be done correctly rather than quickly. This additional time will allow for large scale user testing of an online platform for small claims. Moreover, this extra time will dovetail with the consideration of the post-implementation review of Part 2 of LASPO (see p. 649). Some particular reasons as to why the reforms have been delayed also include the fact that there is a need to gain further reliable data to establish that there is indeed a growing compensation culture that needs to be addressed.

The Bigger Picture: Compensation culture

There has been some concern that the UK might be developing a compensation culture, which has historically been associated with the US. A compensation culture implies that people with frivolous and unwarranted claims bring cases to court with a view to making easy money. The phenomenon of a more litigious society can be interpreted in two very different ways. It can be seen as a good thing because more people are asserting their rights and obtaining stronger legal protection. At the same time it can be seen as a bad thing because the law is pushing people into relationships which lack trust and creating confrontational communities.

It is questionable whether the UK has an unhealthy compensation culture (accident claims actually fell by 10 per cent in 2004), but the increased number of threats to sue and the resulting fear of being sued is having a negative effect on people's work and behaviour, and this trend needs to be reversed. In 2004 the Lord Chancellor of the day commented:

> If you have a genuine claim – where someone else is to blame – you should be able to get compensation from those at fault. This is only fair. The victim or taxpayer shouldn't have to pay out where someone else is to blame. But there is not always someone else to blame. Genuine accidents do happen. People should not be encouraged to always 'have a go' however meritless the claim. The perception that there is easy money just waiting to be had – the so called 'compensation culture' – creates very real problems. People become scared of being sued; organizations avoid taking risks and stop perfectly sensible activities. It creates burdens for those handling claims and critically it also undermines genuine claims.

The Compensation Act 2006 contains provisions to encourage the courts to consider whether a successful negligence claim in a particular case might prevent a desirable activity, such as a school trip, from taking place in future.

The Ministry of Justice is concerned that the problems relating to a compensation culture are being aggravated by the unscrupulous sales tactics of some claims management companies, which encourage people who have suffered minor personal injuries to bring litigation. Advertisements are frequently broadcast on television, asking the viewers whether they have suffered an accident in the last three years. A report on the issue, *Better Routes to Redress*, was published in 2004. This recommended that stronger guidelines regarding appropriate advertisements needed to be issued, and the claims management companies needed to be more carefully regulated. However, it did feel that these companies and advertisements should be allowed to continue, as they helped improve access to legal services by spreading information about the services available and the ways that these could be paid for. The Labour Government decided that claims management companies need to be regulated and relevant provisions are contained in the Compensation Act 2006.

The insurer, Norwich Union (now known as Aviva), has suggested a radical solution to the compensation culture, of abolishing all claims for under £1,000 (*A Modern Compensation System: Moving from Concept to Reality* (2004)). The Law Society has rejected this suggestion, pointing out that denying people their right to seek compensation for claims under £1,000 would prevent the courts from getting to the root cause of injuries and falsely assumes that a loss of £1,000 is a trivial matter.

The Bar Council is concerned that allowing private companies to own law firms will fuel the move towards a compensation culture, as such companies will seek to grow demand for legal services to increase profits. The legal sector may as a result become more commercialised, with franchising, national brand-building and more television advertising.

At the request of the coalition Government, Lord Young produced a report entitled *Common Sense, Common Safety* (2010). This report agreed with many of the recommendations made

> by Lord Jackson with regards to making changes to the civil justice system as one aspect of tackling the compensation culture. He also recommended that there should be restrictions on advertising by claims management companies.

23.7.6 Professor Zander's concerns

Professor Zander (1998), a leading academic, felt that the reforms were fundamentally flawed, rather than prone to temporary hiccups, and was very vociferous in expressing his opposition to the reforms prior to their implementation. He is reported to have said that they amounted to taking a sledgehammer to crack a nut. Below is an analysis of the main concerns he has expressed.

The causes of delay

Lord Woolf's view was that the chief cause of delay was the way the adversarial system was played by the lawyers. Zander has criticised this analysis, pointing out that it is only supported by 'unsubstantiated opinion' rather than real evidence, despite the fact that it forms the basis for most of the subsequent proposals. By contrast, Zander has drawn attention to research carried out for the Lord Chancellor's Department in 1994 into the causes of delay. It identified seven causes: the type of case; the parties; the judiciary; court procedures; court administration; the lawyers (mainly due to pressure of work, inexperience or inefficiency); and external factors such as the difficulty of getting experts' reports, including medical reports. Of these seven factors, the last two factors were felt to be the most significant. Not all the reasons for the delay were the fault of the system: for example, in some cases it may be necessary to wait for an accident victim's medical condition to stabilise in order to assess the long-term prognosis. Accident victims in particular often do not seek legal advice until some time after the accident has occurred.

Clearly, if Lord Woolf has wrongly diagnosed the causes of delay, it is unlikely that his reforms will resolve these problems. The *Judicial Statistics* published in 2002 show that, in the High Court, the time taken between issue and trial went up to 173 weeks, but delays had reduced in the County Court, where the average time from issue to trial had fallen from 640 days in 1997 to 500 in 2000/01.

Case management

Zander feels that court management is appropriate for only a minority of cases and that the key is to identify these. He has remarked that judges do not have the time, skills or inclination to undertake the task of case management. The court does not know enough about the workings of a solicitor's office to be able to set appropriate timetables. In addition, litigants on the fast track may feel that the brisk way in which a three-hour hearing deals with the dispute is inadequate. Most will not feel that justice has been done by a short, sharp trial with restricted oral evidence and an interventionist judge chivvying the parties to a resolution of their dispute.

A move towards judicial management has already been seen in the US, Australia and Canada. A major official study was published by the Institute of Civil Justice at the Rand Corporation in California (Kakalik *et al.*, 1996). This research was not available to Lord

Woolf while he was compiling his report. The study was based on a five-year survey of 10,000 cases looking at the effect of the American Civil Justice Reform Act 1990. This Act required certain federal courts to practise case management. Judicial case management has been part of the US system for many years so that, compared with this country, the procedural innovations being studied operated from a different starting point.

The study found that judicial case management did lead to a reduced time to disposition. Its early use yielded a reduction of one-and-a-half or two months to resolution for cases that lasted at least nine months. Also, having a discovery timetable and reducing the time within which discovery took place both significantly reduced time to disposition and significantly reduced the amount of hours spent on the case by a lawyer. These benefits were achieved without any significant change in the lawyers' or litigants' satisfaction or views of fairness.

On the other hand, case management led to an approximate 20-hour increase in lawyer work hours overall. Their work increased with the need to respond to the court's management directions. In addition, once judicial case management had begun, a discovery cut-off date had usually been established and lawyers felt an obligation to begin discovery on a case which might be settled. Thus, the Rand Report found that case management, by generating more work for lawyers, tended to increase rather than reduce costs.

The Rand Report noted that the effectiveness of implementation depended on judicial attitudes. Some judges viewed these procedural innovations as an attack on judicial independence and felt that it emphasised speed and efficiency at the possible expense of justice. The Report concluded, among other things, that judicial management should wait a month after the defence has been entered in case the action settles.

In research carried out for the Law Society, *The Woolf Network Questionnaire* (2002), 84 per cent of solicitors questioned said they thought the new procedures were quicker and 70 per cent said they were more efficient than the old ones. Greater use of telephone case management conferences was cited as leading to greater efficiency.

Sanctions

Procedural timetables for the fast track are, according to Professor Zander, doomed to failure because a huge proportion of firms, for a range of reasons, will fail to keep to the prescribed timetables. This will necessitate enforcement procedures and sanctions on a vast scale which, in turn, will lead to innumerable appeals. Sanctions will be imposed that are disproportionate and therefore unjust, and will cause injustice to clients for the failings of the lawyers. Furthermore, if the judges did impose severe sanctions when lawyers failed to comply with timetable deadlines, it would usually be the litigants rather than the lawyers who would be penalised.

Professor Zander has pointed to the courts' experience of Ord. 17 under the old County Court Rules as evidence that lawyers are not good at time limits and sanctions were unlikely to change that. Under that order an action would be automatically struck out if the claimant failed to take certain steps within the time limits set by the rule. From its introduction in 1990 until 1998, roughly 20,000 cases had been struck out on this basis, leaving 20,000 people either to sue their lawyers for negligence or to start all over again. In relation to Ord. 17, the Court of Appeal stated in ***Bannister* v *SGB plc*** (1997):

> This rule has given rise to great difficulties and has generated an immense amount of litigation devoted to the question whether a particular action has been struck out and if so, whether it should be reinstated. In short, the rule has in a large number of cases achieved the opposite of its object, which was to speed up the litigation process in the County Courts.

There is the danger that, if the court does not exercise its power temperately and judiciously then, in its eagerness to dispose of litigation, it will actually generate more litigation. This danger is particularly acute where the court exercises powers on its own initiative. If, for example, the court moves to strike out a statement of case on its own initiative, the likely result is that the party affected will apply to have its case reinstated; and if, in fact, it was not a suitable case for striking out, unnecessary cost and delay will be the result.

There is a risk that unrealistic trial dates and timetables will be set, particularly in heavy litigation, at an early stage, and of the judges insisting on their being adhered to thereafter, regardless of the consequences.

In the research for the Law Society, *The Woolf Network Questionnaire* (2002), some solicitors said they were reluctant to apply for sanctions against those who did not stick to the pre-action protocols. This was because they felt that the courts were unwilling to impose sanctions for non-compliance in all but the most serious cases, judges were inconsistent in their approach to sanctions and an application for sanctions was likely to cause more delays and additional costs.

The Bigger Picture: Litigants in person

Litigants in person (nicknamed LIPs) are sometimes more formally referred to as 'self-represented litigants', though an alternative label would be 'DIY litigants'. They are people who represent themselves in court instead of employing a lawyer to do so. The number of litigants in person has been increasing and the expectation is that their numbers will increase further with the implementation of the cuts in the legal aid system contained in the Legal Aid, Sentencing and Punishment of Offenders Act 2012. Lord Woolf commented back in 1995 that lawyers had a tendency to dismiss unrepresented litigants as 'a problem for judges and for the court system rather than the person to whom the system of civil justice exists'. In his eyes, the true problem was that the court system was often inaccessible. The difficulty is that the court system has been developed with the expectation that people will be represented by a lawyer. Litigants in person can find it very difficult to understand the procedural rules on their own and their breach can have serious repercussions for the progression of their case: potentially, a case can be thrown out for breach of procedure without the court even considering the merits of the case. Litigants in person can feel very passionately about their case. Without a lawyer to separate the facts from the emotions, a person's emotional involvement in a case can sometimes stop them from making rational decisions about whether and how they should settle their case. The Ministry of Justice commissioned some research on the subject and a report was produced entitled *Litigants in person in private family cases* (2013). This research looked at 151 cases involving litigants in person. It concluded that only a small minority were able to represent themselves competently. Even those with high levels of education or professional experience struggled with aspects of the legal process. Most were challenged by the court procedures and some had 'no real capacity to advocate for their own or their children's interests'. While litigants in person were heavily reliant on internet searches for advice and research, there was a lack of useful online information available. Litigants in person may not have the skills to deal with the paperwork generated by the case to present their case orally to the court. One consequence of this is that cases are often slower when one party is not represented by a lawyer, more is required by the judge to make sure that justice is done and that both sides have a fair opportunity to present their case. Achieving a balance between the parties can be very difficult when one party has employed a lawyer and another has not. For example, in **Feltham v Commissioners for HM**

Revenue and Customs (2011) the tax tribunal identified a legal argument that supported the case of the litigant in person but had not been presented to the court. The tribunal considered this issue on its own initiative, observing:

> Very often, particularly with litigants in person, the law is not understood and the arguments which need to be pursued are either not made at all or are confused. Flexibility and justice required the tribunal to deal with arguments omitted from the grounds of appeal and those patent or latent in the appeal.

Where litigants in person have made a procedural error, they are less likely to be sanctioned than if they had been represented by a lawyer. Thus in **Kinsley v Commissioner of Police for the Metropolis** (2010) a case had been struck out because of a procedural error but the Court of Appeal overturned this decision as the error had been made by a litigant in person.

Research by Pereira *et al.* (2015) found those litigants in person who were most comfortable with the experience had been assisted by staff at their local court. Some people could adapt to having to bring cases without a lawyer, but they still needed support.

In **Veluppillai v Veluppillai** (2015) the High Court judge criticised a litigant in person in a divorce case who had threatened the judge (calling for him to be 'executed in a gas chamber'), sent abusive emails, threatened to kill his ex-wife and her lawyer and had to be removed from the courtroom by security staff.

The Civil Justice Council (2011) has produced a report looking at how the civil justice system can adapt to cope with litigants in person, though it has concluded that, even if its recommendations are all adopted, in some situations there will still be a denial of justice. Its recommendations include that there should be a systematic review of all court forms and leaflets to ensure they are suitable for litigants in person; the publishing of a nutshell guide for self-represented litigants; and promoting the use of free volunteer support services. In America the majority of litigants represent themselves because of the cost of using lawyers, and websites and helpdesks are available to help them cope.

In 2013, the jurisdiction of the small claims track was increased from £5,000 to £10,000. It is hoped that this more informal procedure will be better suited to litigants in person and this track does not impose heavy cost orders against the losing parties. In 2013, senior judges also called for special procedural rules to be introduced to make the civil court process more inquisitorial. This change would avoid the delays and disruptions caused by lay persons running their own cases, and potentially not understanding legal terminology or the requirements of the Civil Procedure Rules. A report of the National Audit Office *Implementing reforms to civil legal aid* (2015) found that cases take 50 per cent longer when they involve unrepresented parties. The family court has already adopted a more inquisitorial process to assist litigants in person involved in disputes.

McKenzie friend

Litigants in person may seek the help of a lay adviser – frequently known as a McKenzie friend (see p. 257). The involvement of non-lawyers has been described by one MP as the 'cult of the amateur', and they have been criticised as untrained, uninsured and unregulated. In a focus group of judges for the research *Litigants in person in private family cases* (2013) some judges commented that McKenzie friends were 'obviously better than nobody' and 'actually did help'. But another judge described some of them as 'mad as a bag of frogs'. The Chair of the Legal Services Board has stated they are a 'legitimate feature' of an evolving legal services market. In the past, the 'McKenzie friend' was frequently just a family friend offering a bit of moral support, but today the system is becoming a more organised 'cottage industry'. Most are sole traders without legal qualifications or insurance, but some are larger businesses. This has led the Legal Services Board (now replaced by the Legal Aid Agency) to suggest that those involved should be required to invest in safeguards such as an accreditation scheme with a trade association and insurance. A typical hourly rate for a fee-charging McKenzie friend is between £35 and £60, and day rates tend to be between £150 and £200.

The Legal Services Consumer Panel (2014) noted that there are four types of McKenzie friends:

1   The family member or friend providing one-off assistance
2   The volunteer attached to an institution or charity
3   The fee-charging McKenzie friend offering support and advice, but not advocacy
4   The fee-charging McKenzie friend offering a wide range of services including advocacy in court.

The Judicial Executive Board in 2016 published a consultation paper in which it considered whether the McKenzie friend should be renamed to something more easily understood by the public, such as lay supporter or court supporter. The Judicial Executive Board would like to ban the recovery of fees by McKenzie friends, considering that such payment undermines the Legal Services Act 2007 which regulates rights of audience. By contrast, the Legal Services Consumer Panel considers they should continue to be allowed to be paid for their services. Inevitably, the legal professions are unhappy to see their members being undercut by those who have no legal education, professional training, insurance or professional code of conduct.

23.7.7 Vexatious litigants

Vexatious litigants are people who repeatedly make unfounded claims in the court system. They are frequently litigants in person. The leading authority on the subject is ***Bhamjee* v *Forsdick (No. 2)*** (2003), where the Court of Appeal created a range of civil restraint orders to try to prevent vexatious litigants from abusing the court system. The restraint orders restrict the person from bringing claims to a court for up to two years. The Court of Appeal justified these restrictions on the basis that the overriding objective of the Civil Procedure Rules is to deal with cases justly. This meant dealing with them quickly and allotting them an appropriate share of resources. That would not be possible if vexatious litigants were bombarding the courts with hopeless applications.

A restraint order was issued in ***Perotti* v *Collyer-Bristow*** (2004), where the Court of Appeal noted that Perotti had made 80 applications to the Court of Appeal in the previous seven years, of which only two applications had been successful. It therefore ordered that, for the next two years, any further application from Perotti would only be dealt with on paper, with no right of appeal.

The Bigger Picture: Keeping secrets

The English legal system has traditionally respected the principle of open justice. Article 6 of the European Convention on Human Rights guarantees the right to a fair trial. This is interpreted as guaranteeing the right to a fair and public hearing before an independent court. Thus the courts should be open to the public and all evidence presented in open court. A public hearing is a form of democratic control which should be constantly putting pressure on those involved in the administration of justice to perform their duties to a professional standard. The legal philosopher, Jeremy Bentham wrote that 'publicity is the very soul of justice'. In **Attorney General v Leveller Magazine** (1979) Lord Diplock concluded that, 'if the way that courts behave cannot be hidden from the public ear and eye, this provides a safeguard against judicial arbitrariness or idiosyncrasy and maintains the public confidence in the administration of justice'.

Tensions can arise between the desire to achieve justice and open court proceedings. This tension has been noted in the context of the family justice system, particularly where children are involved. Civil Procedure Rule 39.2 lays down a general presumption that court hearings will be in public, but then lists a range of exceptions when the hearing can be in private:

39.2 1 The general rule is that a hearing is to be in public.

   2 The requirement for a hearing to be in public does not require the court to make special arrangements for accommodating members of the public.

   3 A hearing, or any part of it, may be in private if –

   (a) publicity would defeat the object of the hearing;

   (b) it involves matters relating to national security;

   (c) it involves confidential information (including information relating to personal financial matters) and publicity would damage that confidentiality;

   (d) a private hearing is necessary to protect the interests of any child or protected party;

   (e) it is a hearing of an application made without notice and it would be unjust to any respondent for there to be a public hearing;

   (f) it involves uncontentious matters arising in the administration of trusts or in the administration of a deceased person's estate; or

   (g) the court considers this to be necessary, in the interests of justice.

   4 The court may order that the identity of any party or witness must not be disclosed if it considers non-disclosure necessary in order to protect the interests of that party or witness.

The heightened threat of terrorist activity and the resulting increased work for the security services has led to tensions with the courts. In **Al Rawi v Security Service** (2011) former Guantanamo Bay detention camp detainees were seeking compensation. The Government wanted to rely on national security material to defend the claim. The Security Service argued that the court should have the power to use a closed material procedure in exceptional circumstances and where it was in the interests of justice. This submission was rejected by the Supreme Court, which suggested that such a change to the rules on civil procedure would have to be made by Parliament, not the courts. Having been refused permission to keep evidence secret by the lower courts, the Government settled the case outside court. But the Supreme Court went ahead with the case as there was an important issue that needed to be resolved for the future.

In **R (on the application of Mohamed) v Secretary of State for Foreign and Commonwealth Affairs** (2008) a former Guantanamo Bay detainee, Binyam Mohamed, sought a court order for disclosure of materials held by the UK Government regarding his allegations of torture during his detention. The UK Government argued that disclosure would damage intelligence sharing with the US. Despite this, the court ordered the Government to release a seven-paragraph CIA summary showing what the UK knew of the torture allegations.

Following these cases, the Justice and Security Act 2013 was passed. This introduces a new and controversial exception to the principle of open justice in the civil courts: the closed material procedure (CMP). This procedure is only available where it is absolutely necessary in civil proceedings involving, in the Secretary of State's opinion, sensitive material which might, if

23

THE CIVIL TRIAL PROCESS

made public, cause damage to the public interest. Under a CMP, the sensitive material is never disclosed to the defence. A Special Advocate is appointed on behalf of the defendant and, once they have seen the material, the Special Advocate is only allowed to speak to the defendant with express court permission.

The normal procedure for dealing with sensitive information is an application for Public Interest Immunity (PII) which is a system developed in the case of **Conway v Rimmer** (1968). PII involves the prosecution giving the judge sensitive information (that might, for example, reveal the identity of an informant or military secrets) so that he can assess whether this is so relevant to the proper conduct of the defence case that it has to be disclosed. The defence barrister is excluded from court when that material is discussed. If the trial judge orders that the material should be disclosed to achieve a fair trial then in a criminal case the prosecution can choose to either follow this order or drop the case. In a civil case, if the state is the defendant then the state cannot stop the claim proceeding. PII operates to exclude sensitive evidence from proceedings altogether, so that none of the parties can rely on it. By contrast, a closed material procedure excludes the party that would normally receive such disclosure from the proceedings, so the sensitive evidence can be heard by the judge and taken into account.

CMPs have been used for some time in a range of procedures, and in particular by the Special Immigration Appeals Commission since 1997 when handling appeals against deportation by people considered to be a threat to national security. The Special Advocates from that system have responded to the consultation paper by saying that CMPs undermine justice and the system should not be extended.

23.8 Reform

Clearly the civil justice system underwent significant reforms in 1999, but further reforms are on the horizon.

23.8.1 The Briggs Review

Lord Justice Briggs produced a report entitled, *Civil Courts Structure Review: Final Report* (2016). Whereas the Jackson report focuses on the procedural mechanisms that need to be changed within civil litigation in order to save costs, the Briggs report focuses on the structural changes required within the civil courts to save costs. In the report, he makes some 62 recommendations. According to the Briggs report there are five main weaknesses in the provision of an effective civil justice system.

> The first is the lack of adequate access to justice [in lower value cases] due to the combination of the excessive costs expenditure and costs risk of civil litigation . . . and the lawyerish culture and procedure of the civil courts, which makes litigation without lawyers impracticable.

Briggs recommends that this can be in part addressed by setting up an online vourt for claims up to £25,000, which litigants could access without lawyers. The objective of this recommendation is to provide 'an effective overall remedy for the adverse effects upon access to justice constituted by the continuing disproportionality between costs and value at risk in large parts of the workload of the civil courts'. At the moment it is hard for a case worth less than £25,000 to be conducted by lawyers at a proportionate cost. An online court in which lawyers play no part is a radical, if drastic, solution. It would process cases in three stages:

- first, a largely automated, interactive process to identify the issues and provide documentary evidence;
- second, conciliation and case management by case officers; and
- third, resolution by judges.

On-screen, telephone, face-to-face and video meetings would be held to discuss each case. The case officers would take over some of the judge's more routine tasks, but parties would have a right to have these decisions reconsidered by a judge. The Law Society has expressed concern that civil servants will be carrying out judicial roles while not being part of an independent judiciary. The training of case officers will be critical in ensuring procedural decisions are consistent and of a high standard. This might be a branch of the County Court, or an entirely separate court. We already have an automated portal but this merely deals with processing and settling cases over the internet. The proposed court would aim to achieve online adjudication of the case from beginning to end. The online court would not deal with personal injury cases, its use would not be compulsory and there would only be limited recoverable costs. The Bar Council has suggested this proposal risks entrenching a two-tier system of justice. Not being able to recover costs for advice or representation will mean leaving those who need it most, to litigate without any legal assistance, which would put them at a significant disadvantage. Not everyone has access to technology to participate in an online court. The concept of an online court could potentially become a barrier to accessing the justice system, rather than a way to make it easier.

The second weakness identified in the Briggs report 'consists of the inefficiencies arising from the continuing tyranny of paper, coupled with the use of obsolete and inadequate IT facilities in most of the civil courts'. Lord Justice Briggs has recommended that IT provision should be improved for all the civil courts with the digitisation of the processes going through these courts.

The third weakness relates to 'the unacceptable delays in the Court of Appeal, caused by its excessive workload'. The appeal courts, particularly the Court of Appeal, are clogged up and the wait for a hearing can be years. Briggs suggests that the Court of Appeal should be given more resources, but the government has already taken action by ending the right to automatic oral renewal for permission to appeal applications from 3 October 2016. He further recommends that there should be an increase in the threshold for issuing a claim in the High Court from £100,000 (£50,000 for personal injury claims) to £250,000 with a view to increasing this to £500,000.

The fourth weakness concerns 'the under-investment in provision for civil justice outside London'. Briggs is of the view that no case is too big to be resolved in the regions. He would like all civil work with a regional connection to be tried in the regions, regardless of value.

The fifth weakness relates to 'the widespread weaknesses in the processes for the enforcement of judgments and orders'. Lord Briggs recommends unifying enforcement processes within the County Courts.

In response to the Briggs report, the Ministry of Justice have committed to an investment of £700 million in the courts and tribunals. In relation to the civil justice system, this investment will see the introduction of a cross-jurisdictional Online Solutions Court and the promotion of alternative dispute resolution.

23.8.2 Integration

A proposal to integrate the High Court and the County Court to produce a simpler system was considered by the Gorell Committee on County Court procedure back in 1912, but rejected, mainly on the grounds that hearing big cases in the County Courts would prejudice the handling of smaller ones.

The proposal was also considered by the Civil Justice Review, which pointed out that the two-court system was inflexible, making it difficult to make rational allocations of judges' and administrators' time between the different courts. Consequently, some courts have much longer delays than others. In a unified court, all cases would start in the same way and be allocated to different sorts of judges on the basis of their complexity. Judges could be sent where they were needed most, and some higher level judges could be based outside London.

The recommendation was supported by solicitors, advice centres and consumer organisations but strongly opposed by barristers and judges, for rather unattractive reasons. Barristers feared that solicitors would have greater rights of audience in the unified court and that the London Bar would lose business to provincial solicitors; High Court judges thought that the proposals would reduce their standing and destroy their special way of life, especially if they were expected to be based for long periods of time in the provinces.

In the end the Review rejected the idea of a unified court, on the grounds that there was no general support for it, the financial implications were uncertain, a unified court would require major legislation and a lengthy implementation period and it might have adverse effects on the standing of the High Court judiciary. But the former Head of Civil Justice, Sir Richard Scott VC, has predicted that ultimately the High Court and County Courts will merge.

The Labour Government looked again at this issue in a consultation paper, *A Single Civil Court?* (2005). That report considered abolishing the County Courts, while giving the High Court a wider jurisdiction to hear all civil cases at first instance. The Labour Government was concerned that it is inefficient and costly for the Courts Service to administer two separate civil court systems. The President of the Courts of England and Wales asked a senior judge, Sir Henry Brooke, to look at whether the civil courts should be unified, but he concluded in 2009 that they should not.

23.8.3 Abolish pre-action protocols

The Bar Council has suggested, in a discussion document, *Reforming Civil Litigation* (2013), that pre-action protocols should be abolished:

> It is our view that formalising the pre-action process adds to the length, and thus the expense, of proceedings, and is thus against the interests of legal consumers.

23.8.4 An inquisitorial system

In theory, the civil justice system could move to an inquisitorial system, in which the judge would take a more investigative role and the two parties would be required to cooperate by revealing all their evidence to each other. Tactics would become less important and, since delay is often a part of these tactics, the whole process could be speeded up. Some would suggest that this system might also be fairer, since being able to afford the best lawyer would be less important.

In fact, a full change away from the adversarial system seems extremely unlikely, but there have been proposals for such movement in certain areas: the Civil Justice Review suggested that a paper adjudication scheme might be considered for handling certain claims, which would move to an oral hearing only if the adjudicator felt there were difficulties which made one necessary. The procedure would be compulsory for road accidents and claims under £5,000 and could also be used in other cases where the parties agreed. This idea has been opposed by both the National Consumer Council and the National Association of Citizens Advice Bureaux, on the ground that those who could afford a skilled lawyer to draft their papers would have too much of an advantage. Some of the Woolf proposals also favour a move towards an inquisitorial approach and a less aggressive form of litigation.

Progress towards full pre-trial disclosure of evidence, and the fact that small claims court arbitrators now take a more interventionist approach, can be seen as moves towards a more inquisitorial system.

23.8.5 Reform of compensation for personal injury

Tort law dictates that the victims of an accident (other than industrial accidents, which are covered by a compensation scheme) can get compensation only if they can prove that the harm caused to them was somebody else's fault. The result of this is that individuals with identical injuries may receive hundreds of thousands of pounds in compensation, or nothing more than state benefits, depending not on their needs but on whether they can prove fault – often very difficult to do conclusively. In many cases, the state has to spend money, in the form of legal aid, but if the case is lost, the only person to benefit from that expenditure is the lawyer. Given the recent cuts to civil legal aid, many individuals who have suffered accidents may not now be able to claim state funding and will have to pay for their cases themselves or represent themselves. Because of this, it is often suggested that the tort action for personal injury should be abolished and the financial savings should be used to provide improved welfare benefits for all those injured by accidents. New Zealand has adopted such an approach and established a no-fault system of compensation.

The National Health Service Redress Act 2006 contains provisions for the establishment of a National Health Service Redress Scheme. The scheme has not yet been established and it may be that it never will be set up. The idea was that the new scheme would provide a quick and simple process for compensating people with small claims (up to £20,000) against the NHS without the need to go to court. The scheme would have been overseen by the NHS Litigation Authority. Compensation would only have been awarded where a tort had been committed, so it would not have amounted to a no-fault system of compensation. Patients would have been able to withdraw from the scheme if they decided they would rather take their claim to court, but if they did withdraw they might find legal aid was not available for legal proceedings. If patients accepted an offer of redress, they waived their right to bring subsequent legal proceedings. At the moment, over three-quarters of claims valued between £10,000 and £15,000 cost more to settle than the amount awarded. Lord Jackson, in his report entitled *Review of Civil Litigation Costs: Final Report* (2010), recommended that the regulations be passed so that this scheme could start working. While the scheme itself has not been introduced, the NHS is trying to foster a more open approach where errors in patient care have occurred. NHS staff are encouraged to report mistakes, taking the onus off patients to initiate claims. Where financial compensation is not appropriate, patients can still be provided with an explanation, apology and remedial care.

Answering questions

1   To what extent has the adoption of the Woolf reforms changed the nature of the civil justice process? *University of London, International Programmes LLB*

2   **(a)** Discuss the advantages and disadvantages of the civil court system.

   (b) What new reforms might further improve the civil justice system?

3   Reforms to the civil justice system introduced after Lord Woolf's review and report, *Access to Justice* (1996), were aimed at eliminating unnecessary cost, delay and complexity from the system. Briefly explain what the main reforms were. In your view, have these reforms achieved their intended aims?

4   Why has the small claims court proved so popular?

For answers to these questions, see the companion website at www.pearsoned.co.uk/ elliottquinn

SUMMARY OF CHAPTER 23: THE CIVIL TRIAL PROCESS

Civil courts

There are two main civil courts which hear civil cases at first instance. These are the County Courts and the High Court.

The civil justice system before April 1999

Before the implementation of the Woolf reforms, there were two separate sets of civil procedure rules for the County Courts and the High Court and Court of Appeal. The system was heavily criticised for being too expensive and slow.

The civil justice system after April 1999

In April 1999 new Civil Procedure Rules and accompanying Practice Directions came into force. The new rules introduce the main recommendations of Lord Woolf in his final report, *Access to Justice*. The reforms aim to eliminate unnecessary cost, delay and complexity in the civil justice system. The ultimate goal is to change fundamentally the litigation culture. Thus, the first rule of the new Civil Procedure Rules lays down an overriding objective which is to underpin the whole system. This overriding objective is that the rules should enable the courts to deal with cases justly. The emphasis of the new rules is on avoiding litigation through pre-trial settlements.

Civil Procedure Rules

For non-personal injury actions, a claim may be started in the High Court, where the claimant expects to recover more than £25,000. For personal injury actions a claim can only be started in the High Court where the claimant expects to recover at least £50,000.

Pre-action protocols

To push the parties into behaving reasonably during the pre-trial stage, pre-action protocols have been developed. These lay down a code of conduct for this stage of proceedings.

Alternative dispute resolution

At various stages in a dispute's history, the court will actively promote settlement by alternative dispute resolution (ADR).

Case management

Case management has been introduced, whereby the court plays an active role in managing the litigation. To determine the level and form of case management, cases have been divided into three types:

- small claims track;
- fast track; and
- multi-track.

Costs: Lord Jackson's reforms

Reforms have been introduced, following Lord Jackson's recommendations, to try and reduce the cost of civil litigation.

Criticism of the civil justice system

The 1999 reforms were generally well received, though Professor Zander has been a vociferous critic of the changes, suggesting that they would not succeed in reducing delays and expense.

Sanctions

The courts now have tough powers to enforce the civil procedure rules to ensure that litigation is pursued diligently.

Litigants in person

The number of people who represent themselves in court is increasing.

Vexatious litigants

Vexatious litigants are people who repeatedly make unfounded claims in the court system.

Keeping secrets

There are currently tensions between the state's desire to keep certain matters secret in the public's interest and the principle of open justice.

Reform

The civil justice system underwent significant reforms in 1999, but further reforms could be made.

Reading list

Baldwin, J. (1997) *Small Claims in County Courts in England and Wales: The Bargain Basement of Civil Justice?* Oxford: Clarendon.

(1998) Small claims hearings: the interventionist role played by district judges. *Civil Justice Quarterly,* 17: 20.

(2002) *Lay and Judicial Perspectives on the Expansion of the Small Claims Regime.* London: Lord Chancellor's Department.

(2003) *Evaluating the Effectiveness of Enforcement Procedures in Undefended Claims in the Civil Courts.* London: Lord Chancellor's Department.

Bar Council (2013) *Reforming Civil Litigation: Discussion Document.* London: Bar Council.

Barton, A. (2001) Medical litigation: who benefits? *British Medical Journal,* 322: 1189.

Better Regulation Taskforce (2004) *Better Routes to Redress.* London: Better Regulation Taskforce.

Civil Justice Council (2011) *Access to Justice for Litigants in Person (or self-represented litigants).* London: Civil Justice Council.

(2005) *Improved Access to Justice – Funding Options and Proportionate Costs,* London: Ministry of Justice.

Denvir, C., Balmer, N.J. and Buck, A. (2012) Informed citizens? Knowledge of rights and the resolution of civil justice problems. *Journal of Social Policy,* 41(3): 591.

Department for Constitutional Affairs (2005a) *A Single Civil Court?* London: Department for Constitutional Affairs.

Galanter, M. (1984) *The Emergence of the Judge as a Mediator in Civil Cases.* Madison: University of Wisconsin.

Genn, H. (1987) *Hard Bargaining: Out of Court Settlement in Personal Injury Actions.* Oxford: Clarendon.

(1987) Understanding civil justice. *Current Legal Problems,* 50: 155.

(2013) Getting to the truth: Experts and judges in the "hot tub". *Civil Justice Quarterly,* 32: 275.

Jolowicz, J. (1996) The Woolf Report and the adversary system. *Civil Justice Quarterly,* 15: 198.

Kakalik, J. *et al.* (1996) *An Evaluation of Judicial Case Management under the Civil Justice Reform Act.* California: Rand Corporation.

Law Society (2002) *The Woolf Network Questionnaire.* London: Law Society.

Law Society and Civil Justice Council (2002) *More Civil Justice: The Impact of the Woolf Reforms on Pre-Action Behaviour.* Research Study 43. London: Law Society.

Lord Chancellor's Department (1998b) *Report of the Fast Truck Simulation Pilot.* London: Lord Chancellor's Department.

              (2002) *Further Findings: A Continuing Evaluation of the Civil Justice Report.* London: Lord Chancellor's Department.

Ministry of Justice (2008b) *Family Justice in View.* London: Ministry of Justice.

Morris, A. (2007) Spiralling or stabilising? The compensation culture and our propensity to claim damages for personal injury. *Modern Law Review,* 70: 349.

Norwich Union (2004) *A Modern Compensation System: Moving from Concept to Reality.* Norwich: Norwich Union.

Pereira, I., Harvey, P., Dawes, W. and Greevy, H. (2014) *The role of court fees in affecting users' decisions to bring cases to the civil and family courts: A qualitative study of claimants and applicants.* London: Ministry of Justice.

Peysner, J. and Seneviratne, M. (2005) *The Management of Civil Cases: The Courts and the Post-Woolf Landscape.* London: Department for Constitutional Affairs.

Pleasence, P. (2004) *Causes of Action: Civil Law and Social Justice.* London: HMSO.

Pleasence, P. and Balmer, N.J. (2014) *How people resolve 'legal' problems.* London: Legal Services Board.

Pleasence, P., Balmer, N.J. and Sandefur, R.L. (2013) *Paths to justice: A past, present and future roadmap.* London: Nuffield Foundation.

Sorabji, J. (2014) *English Civil Justice After the Woolf and Jackson reforms: A critical analysis.* Cambridge: Cambridge University Press.

Trinder, L., Hunter, R., Hitchings, E., Miles, J., Moorhead, R., Smith, L., Sefton, M., Hinchly, V., Bader, K. and Pearce, J. (2013) *Litigants in person in private family law cases.* London: Ministry of Justice.

Woolf, Lord Justice H. (1996) *Access to Justice.* London: Lord Chancellor's Department.

              (2008) *The Pursuit of Justice.* Oxford: Oxford University Press.

Zander, M. (1997) The Woolf Report: forwards or backwards for the new Lord Chancellor? *Civil Justice Quarterly,* 17: 208.

              (1998) The government's plans on civil justice. *Modern Law Review,* 61: 382.

              (2004) *The Law-Making Process.* London: Butterworths.

Zuckerman, A. (1995) A reform of civil procedure – rationing procedure rather than access to justice. *Journal of Legal Studies,* 22: 156.

              (1996) Lord Woolf's Access to Justice: plus ça change . . . *Modern Law Review,* 59: 773.

23

THE CIVIL TRIAL PROCESS

On the internet

A number of videos on using the family courts have been prepared by the Ministry of Justice and are available at:

> https://www.youtube.com/watch?v=wUi7CsoeOE8&index=2&list=PL5g5
> tPp-sxrjOlwV_7gA0yELB1gw2TpW1

> https://www.youtube.com/watch?v=woVeTe2_Ga8&index=3&list=PL5g5tPp-
> sxrjOlwV_7gA0yELB1gw2TpW1

> https://www.youtube.com/watch?v=aM2LAgz2a4I&list=PL5g5tPp-sxrjOlwV_7gA0y
> ELB1gw2TpW1&index=4

Lord Jackson's report *Review of Civil Litigation Costs: Final Report* (2010) is available on the website of the judiciary of England and Wales at:

> http://www.judiciary.uk/wp-content/uploads/JCO/Documents/Reports/jackson-
> final-report-140110.pdf

Lord Jackson's report *Review of Civil Litigation Costs: Supplemental Report – Fixed Recoverable Costs* (2017) is available at:

> https://www.judiciary.uk/wp-content/uploads/2017/07/fixed-recoverable-costs-
> supplemental-report-online-3.pdf

Lord Briggs's *Civil Courts Structure Review: Final Report* (2016) is available at:

> https://www.judiciary.uk/wp-content/uploads/2016/07/civil-courts-structure-review-
> final-report-jul-16-final-1.pdf

Lord Young's report *Common Sense, Common Safety* (2010) is available on the Government website at:

> https://webarchive.nationalarchives.gov.uk/20130104180141/
> http://www.number10.gov.uk/wp-content/uploads/402906_CommonSense_acc.pdf

The report by David Norgrove, *Family Justice Review: Final Report* (2011) is available on the Ministry of Justice website at:

> https://assets.publishing.service.gov.uk/government/uploads/system/uploads/
> attachment_data/file/217343/family-justice-review-final-report.pdf

The consultation paper *Solving disputes in the county courts: creating a simpler, quicker and more proportionate system* (2011) is available on the Ministry of Justice website at:

> https://assets.publishing.service.gov.uk/government/uploads/system/uploads/
> attachment_data/file/238301/8045.pdf

The report of the Constitutional Affairs Committee, *Family Justice: the operation of the family courts revisited* (2006), is available at:

> https://publications.parliament.uk/pa/cm200506/cmselect/cmconst/1086/1086.pdf

The policy paper, *Queen's Speech 2017: what it means for you* (published 21 June 2017) can be found on the Government website at:

> https://www.gov.uk/government/publications/queens-speech-2017-what-it-means-for-
> you/queens-speech-2017-what-it-means-for-you

A copy of the post-implementation review (PIR) of Part 2 of LASPO: Initial assessment by the MoJ is available at:

> https://assets.publishing.service.gov.uk/government/uploads/system/uploads/
> attachment_data/file/719140/pir-part-2-laspo-initial-assessment.pdf

Chapter 24
Tribunals

This chapter discusses:

- the history of tribunals;
- tribunals today following the Tribunals, Courts and Enforcement Act 2007;
- tribunal procedure, composition and status;
- the Employment Tribunals;
- the availability of appeals and judicial review; and
- the advantages and disadvantages of the tribunal system.

24.1 Introduction

Many claims and disputes are settled not by the courts, but by tribunals, each specialising in a particular area of law. The tribunal system handles over a million cases each year. Three times as many cases are decided by tribunals as go before the criminal courts. Although tribunals have often been seen as an unimportant part of the legal system, this caseload clearly shows they are now playing a major role. They deal with fundamental issues in people's lives including housing, employment and education. Employment Tribunals are probably the best-known example, but there are many others, dealing with subjects ranging from social security and tax to forestry and patents. Not all are actually called tribunals – the category includes the Criminal Injuries Compensation Authority, which assesses applications for compensation for victims of violent crime. The majority deal with disputes between the citizen and the state, though the Employment Tribunal is an obvious exception.

Tribunals are generally distinguished from the other courts by less formal procedures, and by the fact that they specialise. However, they are all expected to conduct themselves according to the same principles of natural justice used by the courts: a fair hearing for both sides and open and impartial decision-making.

24.2 History

Tribunals were in existence as long ago as 1799, but the present system has really grown up since the Second World War. The main reason for this was the growth of legislation in areas which were previously considered private, and therefore rarely addressed by the state, such as Social Security benefits, housing, town and country planning, education and employment.

This legislation gave people rights – to a school place, to unemployment benefit or not to be unfairly sacked, for example – but its rules also placed limits on these rights. Naturally, this leads to disputes: employer and employee disagree on whether the latter's dismissal was unfair under the terms of the legislation; a Social Security claimant believes he or she has been wrongly denied benefit; a landowner disputes the right of the local authority to purchase her field compulsorily.

Given the potentially vast number of disputes likely to arise, and the detailed nature of the legislation concerning them, it was felt that the ordinary court system would neither have been able to cope with the workload nor be the best forum for sorting out such problems, hence the growth of tribunals.

As well as the administrative tribunals dealing with this kind of dispute, there are domestic tribunals, which deal with disputes and matters of discipline within particular professions – trade unions and the medical and legal professions all have tribunals like this. The decisions of these tribunals are based on the particular rules of the organisation concerned, but they are still required to subscribe to the same standards of justice as the ordinary courts and, in the case of those set up by statute, their decisions can be appealed to the ordinary courts – as can those of most administrative tribunals.

24.2.1 The Franks Report

In 1957, the Franks Committee investigated the workings of tribunals. It reported that the tribunal system was likely to become an increasingly important part of the legal system, and recommended that tribunal procedures should be marked by 'openness, fairness and impartiality'. Openness required, where possible, hearings in public and explanations of the reasoning behind decisions. Fairness entailed the adoption of clear procedures, which allowed parties to know their rights, present their case fully, and be aware of the case against them. Impartiality meant that tribunals should be free of undue influence from any Government departments concerned with their subject area. The Committee was particularly concerned that tribunals were often on Ministry premises, with Ministry staff.

The Committee also recommended the establishment of two permanent Councils on Tribunals, one for England and Wales and one for Scotland, to supervise procedures. A Council was subsequently set up (with a Scottish committee), consisting of 10–15 members. It reviewed and reported on the constitution and workings of certain specified tribunals, and was consulted before any changes to their procedural rules were made. It also considered and reported on matters referred to it concerning any tribunal. However, it had no firm say in any of these matters, and could not overrule any decisions. Its functions were only advisory – it had little real power, and could not reverse or even direct further consideration of individual tribunal decisions. The Council was, therefore, a watchdog with no teeth. In 1980, it put forward a report asking for further powers, but these were not granted.

24.3 Reforming the tribunals

Tribunals were the subject of a major reform with the passing of the Tribunals, Courts and Enforcement Act 2007. This piece of legislation followed a lengthy review of the tribunal service undertaken by the Labour Government. First, in 2000, the Labour Government asked Sir Andrew Leggatt, a retired Lord Justice of Appeal, to look at the tribunal service. This was the first systematic examination of tribunals since the Franks Report in 1957. He was asked to look at the funding and management of tribunals, their structure and standards, and whether they complied with the Human Rights Act 1998.

Leggatt issued a consultation document in which he agreed with the Franks Committee that the main characteristics required of tribunals are fairness, openness and impartiality, though he saw openness and impartiality as components of the overarching requirement of fairness. The Review proposed certain benchmarks against which the achievement of fairness could be tested. These benchmarks included:

- independence from sponsoring departments;
- an accessible and supportive system;
- tribunals exercising a jurisdiction suitable for the area that each is intended to cover;
- simple procedures;
- effective decision-making;
- ensuring that the decision-making process is suitable for the type of dispute;
- providing proportionate remedies;
- speed in reaching finality;
- authority and expertise appropriate for their task; and
- cost-effectiveness.

The final report of the Review, *Tribunals for Users: One System, One Service*, was published in 2001. Of the 70 different administrative tribunals in England and Wales, it found that their quality varied 'from excellent to inadequate'. It identified some significant weaknesses in the tribunal system. In particular, it was concerned that the tribunals were not always accessible or user-friendly, they were not independent from the Ministries whose decisions were the subject of the tribunal work and the tribunal system lacked coherence. These criticisms will be considered in turn.

24.3.1 The Leggatt Review criticisms

Lack of accessibility

The Franks Committee recommendation that tribunals should be 'open' requires more than just a rule that hearings should usually be held in public; it also demands that citizens should be aware of tribunals and their right to use them. In cases where the dispute is between a citizen and the Government, the citizen will usually be notified of procedures to deal with disputes, but in other cases more thought needed to be given to publicising citizens' rights.

Not user-friendly

The tribunals were originally intended to be user-friendly, providing easy access to justice. Over time many had become increasingly like courts and it is difficult as a result for claimants, without professional legal help, to take their case to a tribunal.

Dependent

The relevant Ministry responsible frequently provided the administrative support for the tribunal having jurisdiction over its decisions, selected the tribunal members, paid their fees and expenses and laid down the tribunal procedures. This meant that tribunals neither appeared to be nor were in fact, independent. Responsibility for tribunals and their administration should not lie with those whose policies or decisions it is the tribunals' duty to consider. Otherwise, for users every case is an 'away game'. Such arrangements could be the subject of a successful challenge under Art. 6 of the European Convention on Human Rights, which guarantees the right to a fair trial.

Lack of coherence

Each tribunal had evolved as a solution to a particular problem, adapted to one particular area of law. Most tribunals were, therefore, entirely self-contained and operated separately from each other, using different practices and procedures. The result was a system that lacked coherence and which was not providing a uniformly high standard of service.

24.3.2 The Review proposals

The Review concluded that the tribunals had to be rationalised and modernised, and that a radical approach was both necessary and justified. The main proposal of the Review was that a single Tribunal Service should be established which would be responsible for the administration of all the tribunals. According to the Review, this would achieve efficiency, coherence and independence. Any citizen who wished to apply to a tribunal would simply have to submit their case to the Tribunal Service and the case would be allocated to the appropriate tribunal. This would be a considerable advance in clarity and simplicity for users and their advisers. The single system would enable a coherent, user-focused approach to the provision of information which would enable tribunals to meet the claim that they operate in ways which enable citizens to participate directly in preparing and presenting their own cases.

The Review hoped that a Tribunal Service would raise the status of tribunals, while preserving their distinctness from the courts. It could also yield considerable economies of scale, particularly in relation to the provision of premises for all tribunals, common basic training and the use of information technology. It would provide a single point of contact for users, improved geographical distribution of tribunal centres, common standards, an enhanced corporate image and a greater prospect of job satisfaction for employees on account of the size and coherence of the Tribunal Service.

The Review recommended that the Tribunal Service should be an executive agency of the Lord Chancellor's Department (now the Ministry of Justice). It considered that the independence of tribunals would best be safeguarded by having their administrative support provided by this Department with its extensive experience of managing courts.

24.4 Tribunals today

Following the Leggatt Review, the former Labour Government issued a White Paper, *Transforming Public Services: Complaints, Redress and Tribunals* (2004b), containing significant plans to reform the tribunal system. Many of these reforms are now contained in the Tribunals, Courts and Enforcement Act 2007. Before that Act was passed, tribunals had been created by individual pieces of primary legislation, without any overarching framework. The reforms amount to the establishment of an administrative legal system which can be compared to that found in many European countries.

Part 1 of the Act creates a new, simplified statutory framework for tribunals. The Leggatt Review had recommended that there should be a single Tribunal Service and the Act moves in this direction by creating two new, generic tribunals: the First-tier Tribunal and the Upper Tribunal. The Upper Tribunal is primarily, but not exclusively, an appellate tribunal from the First-tier Tribunal. The Act gives the Lord Chancellor power to transfer the jurisdiction of existing tribunals to the two new tribunals. Schedule 6 to the 2007 Act lists the tribunals which it is intended will be abolished and their jurisdiction transferred to one of the two new tribunals. These tribunals consist of most of the tribunals that have been administered by central Government. The Act provides for the establishment of 'chambers' within the two tribunals so that the many jurisdictions that will be transferred into the tribunals can be grouped together appropriately. To date, seven chambers have been set up in the First-tier Tribunal:

- the Social Entitlement Chamber;
- the Health, Education and Social Care Chamber;
- the War Pensions and Armed Forces Compensation Chamber;
- the Tax Chamber;
- the Property Chamber;
- the Immigration and Asylum Chamber; and
- the General Regulatory Chamber.

There are around 60 hearing centres around the country so that many of the cases will be heard locally rather than in London.

The Upper Tribunal currently has four chambers:

- the Administrative Appeals Chamber;
- the Tax and Chancery Chamber;
- the Lands Chamber; and
- the Immigration and Asylum Chamber.

Each chamber is headed by a Chamber President and the tribunals' judiciary is headed by a Senior President of Tribunals. The Senior President is a new office and he or she is the judicial leader of the tribunal system.

Some tribunals have been excluded from the new structures because of their specialist nature, and tribunals run by local government have not been included for the time being while further consideration is given to their financial situation. The Employment Tribunals (discussed below) and the Employment Appeal Tribunal will keep their separate identity, though they will share the administrative arrangements of the new tribunals. These two tribunals have been retained because of the nature of the cases that come before them, which involve one private party against another, unlike most other tribunals which hear applications from citizens against decisions of the state.

Figure 24.1 Tribunals structure chart 2017

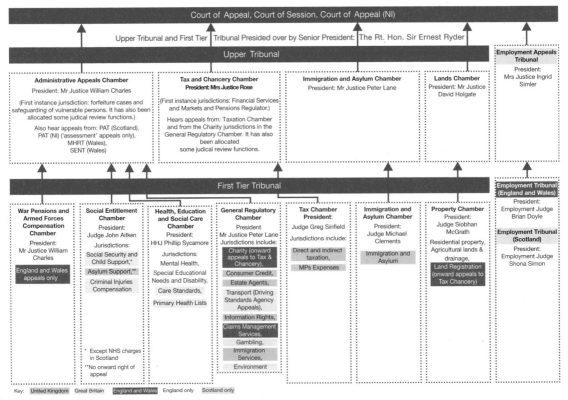

Source: https://www.judiciary.gov.uk/wp-content/uploads/2010/02/tribunals-chart-171005.pdf

All the tribunals that fall within the responsibility of central government will increasingly be administered by Her Majesty's Courts and Tribunal Service.

In 2007, the Council on Tribunals was abolished and replaced by the Administrative Justice and Tribunals Council. This was given a broader remit than its predecessor. The new Council had a similar role of supervising the tribunals to the old Council, but in addition it had responsibility for keeping the administrative justice system as a whole under review. It was required to consider and advise the Government on how to make the system more accessible, fair and efficient. However, the Administrative Justice and Tribunals Council was itself abolished in 2011 as part of the coalition Government's drive to cut the national debt.

Until recently most tribunals were free, but fees have been introduced through powers granted in the Legal Aid, Sentencing and Punishment of Offenders Act 2012. The Government has also introduced fee remissions, which are available for individuals who rely on state benefits, or whose household income falls below a financial threshold. Most controversially, the coalition Government introduced fees in the Employment Tribunal and Employment Appeals Tribunal from 2013. The Administrative Justice and Tribunals Council (2011) argued such fees are inappropriate where the tribunal is handling cases against the state, on the basis that the public should not have to pay for the state to look at its own mistakes. Fees have appeared to create a problem of access to justice for low income families, for example those applying to the employment tribunal for unfair dismissal, where they have, by definition, lost their job. After the introduction of fees for the Employment Tribunal, the number of claims received by the tribunals fell by 79 per cent. Fees are payable when an individual lodges a claim, launches an appeal and has a hearing. Coupled with the cuts made to legal aid, it is now cheaper to commence claims in the County Court, rather than at the employment tribunal. But the Government considers that such fees simply bring the tribunal service into line with the civil court system, where fees are always charged.

24.4.1 Tribunal procedure

Before 2007 the tribunals all had their own rules of procedure. Under the 2007 Act a new Tribunal Procedure Committee has been established with responsibility for tribunal rules of procedure. It has produced a unified set of procedural rules for the tribunals, which are heavily influenced by the civil procedural rules introduced by Lord Woolf (see p. 632). For example, the new rules contain a similar overriding objective.

24.4.2 Composition

Most tribunals consist of a judge and two lay people who have some particular expertise in the relevant subject area – doctors sit on some cases in the Health, Education and Social Care Chamber, for example, and representatives of both employees' and employers' organisations in the Employment Tribunal. The lay members take an active part in decision-making. Tribunals composed entirely of lay people are considered to have been less effective than those with a judge.

While the norm is for cases to be heard by a panel of three, consisting of a professional judge and two lay persons, some cases can now be heard by a judge sitting on his or her own. Since 2012, unfair dismissal cases in the Employment Tribunal are heard by a judge sitting on his or her own. In addition, the Enterprise and Regulatory Reform Act 2013 contains provisions for legal officers to make pre-trial case management decisions. It is not clear whether these legal officers have to be legally qualified or whether they can simply be experienced administrators. While these developments may be good for efficiency, they do raise concerns about the quality of the decision-making in the tribunals. Further, 40 per cent of tribunal judges and members are women, and 10 per cent are from an ethnic minority.

The Bigger Picture: Employment Tribunals

Employment Tribunals (ETs) provide one example of a powerful tribunal playing a central role in today's society. The role of Employment Tribunals has altered radically since they were first established in 1964. The procedure is quicker than the civil courts, with 75 per cent of cases being heard within 26 weeks of receipt, and only 4 per cent of cases are appealed. A MORI users' survey in 2002 found that both applicants and respondents were satisfied that cases were dealt with impartially and professionally. However, research into the Employment Tribunals has been carried out for the employers' organisation, the Confederation of British Industry (CBI). This research, *A Matter of Confidence: Restoring Faith in Employment Tribunals* (2005), concluded that employers lacked confidence in the Employment Tribunal system and often chose to settle weak and vexatious claims to avoid using it. Among the 450 employers polled, the research found that all firms with fewer than 50 staff settled every claim, despite advice that they would win almost half the cases. Most employers felt that the tribunal system had become too adversarial and legalistic, no longer satisfying the original idea that tribunals should hold quick, informal hearings. The coalition Government's introduction of fees for Employment Tribunals in 2013 has led to a sharp decline in the number of claims made by more than half. Until the coming into force of the Employment Tribunals and the Employment Appeal Tribunal (EAT) Fees Order 2013, SI 2013/1893 ('the Fees Order'), a claimant could bring and pursue proceedings in an ET and appeal to the EAT without paying any fee. The Fees Order prescribes various fees. The long-term impact of the fees is yet to be seen, but it could be that many people are now financially unable to bring cases of unfair dismissal and workplace discrimination and achieve redress.

There were many concerns that the introduction of fees created a major barrier to access to justice. This issue has since reached its climax in the case of *R (UNISON) v Lord Chancellor* (2017) in which UNISON, supported by the Equality and Human Rights Commission and the Independent Workers Union of Great Britain, challenged the lawfulness of the Fees Order. It was argued that the making of the Fees Order was not a lawful exercise of the Lord Chancellor's statutory powers, because the prescribed fees interfere unjustifiably with the right of access to justice under both the common law and EU law, frustrate the operation of parliamentary legislation granting employment rights, and discriminate unlawfully against women and other protected groups. Part of the thinking behind the introduction of such fees was to transfer some of the cost of the EAT from the taxpayer to those whom use it as well as to deter unmeritorious or vexatious claims and encourage settlements. The Supreme Court agreed with UNISON and declared that the charging of such fees was indeed prohibitive and hindered access to justice which is a fundamental constitutional right. It also held that such fees meant that it was unaffordable for some to pursue their claim which they otherwise would have been able to if the fees were not imposed.

As a result of this decision, the Government stopped charging fees and agreed to reimburse any fees that had been charged from when the Fees Order came into force, which amounts to something between £30–35 million. This of course also serves as an example of the interplay between the judiciary and the executive but some might say predictably, the number of claims saw a year on year increase. In the second quarter of 2018, there was a 165 per cent increase in claims and an increase of 130 per cent in cases outstanding. Not all of these increases can be attributable to the removal of fees as there are other social movements at work, such as the #MeToo movement concerning sexual harassment in the workspace, but the removal of fees has had a significant impact.

A headline figure to note, taken from the MoJs statistics: From the launch of the ET fee refund scheme in October 2017 to 30 June 2018, there were 14,500 applications for refunds received and 12,400 refund payments made, with a total monetary value of £10,615,000. Between 1 April 2018 and 30 June 2018, 5,100 refund applications were received and 4,700 refund payments were made with a total value of £4,018,300.

24.4.3 Appeals and judicial review

Historically, there was no uniform appeals procedure from tribunals and there was no absolute right of appeal from a tribunal, though most did allow some right of appeal. An example of where there was no right of appeal was the Vaccine Damage Tribunal, set up under the Vaccine Damage Payments Act 1971 to assess claimants' rights to damages for disabilities caused by a vaccination. The Tribunals and Inquiries Act 1992 provided for appeals to the High Court on points of law from some of the most important tribunals. These appeals are heard by the Queen's Bench Division. However, appeals to the High Court are expensive, complex and time-consuming, and are therefore inconsistent with the basic aims of tribunals. Some tribunal appeals could only be made to the relevant Minister, who could hardly be seen as a disinterested party.

In a report *Right First Time* (2011), the Administrative Justice and Tribunals Council commented that too many appeals are successful. It points out that in some tribunals up to 40 per cent of appeals are successful and suggests that this is evidence public bodies are not learning from their mistakes. Public bodies could thereby save money by getting their decisions right first time. In addition to appeal rights, decisions of tribunals are sometimes subject to judicial review on the grounds that they have not been made in accordance with the rules of natural justice or are not within the powers of the tribunal to make (see p. 719). The controlling effect of the potential for judicial review is limited by the fact that it cannot consider the merits of decisions and that, where wide discretionary powers are given to a Minister, Government department or local authority, the court will find it difficult to prove that many decisions are outside those powers. The continued availability of judicial review following the implementation of the 2007 Act was confirmed by the Supreme Court in *R (on the application of Cart)* v *Upper Tribunal* (2011). While the new tribunal system is intended to be respected and independent, parties still have a last resort option of challenging a tribunal's decision through the courts under the system of judicial review. However, judicial review will only be allowed where the application raises an important point of principle or practice or some other legally compelling reason.

The Tribunals, Courts and Enforcement Act 2007 now provides a unified appeal structure for the tribunal system. Under the Act, in most cases, a decision of the First-tier Tribunal may be appealed to the Upper Tribunal and a decision of the Upper Tribunal may be appealed to the Court of Appeal. The grounds of appeal must relate to a point of law. The rights to appeal may only be exercised with permission from the tribunal being appealed from, or the tribunal or court being appealed to. Exceptionally, a leapfrog appeal is possible from the Upper Tribunal to the Supreme Court. It is hoped that this simplified appeal structure will enable the law to develop more consistently.

It is also now possible for the Upper Tribunal to deal with some judicial review cases which would in the past have been dealt with by the High Court. The Upper Tribunal has this jurisdiction only where a case falls within a class specified in a direction given by the Lord

Chief Justice or transferred by the High Court. It is possible that in the future all judicial review cases could be heard by the Upper Tribunal, which would be a logical way to develop the new administrative legal system.

24.5 Advantages of tribunals

24.5.1 Speed

Tribunal cases come to court fairly quickly, and many are dealt with within a day. Many tribunals are able to specify the exact date and time at which a case will be heard, so minimising time-wasting for the parties.

24.5.2 Cost

Tribunals usually do not charge fees, and each party usually pays their own costs, rather than the loser having to pay all. The simpler procedures of tribunals should mean that legal representation is unnecessary, so reducing cost, but that is not always the case (see below).

24.5.3 Informality

This varies between different tribunals, but as a general rule, wigs are not worn, the strict rules of evidence do not apply, and attempts are made to create an unintimidating atmosphere. This is obviously a help where individuals are representing themselves. A risk of the reforms introduced by the 2007 Act is that the tribunal system may become increasingly formal, particularly now cases are heard by judges.

24.5.4 Flexibility

Although they obviously aim to apply fairly consistent principles, tribunals do not operate strict rules of precedent, so are able to respond more flexibly than courts.

24.5.5 Specialisation

Tribunal members already have expertise in the relevant subject area, and, through sitting on tribunals, are able to build up a depth of knowledge of that area that judges in ordinary courts could not hope to match.

24.5.6 Relief of congestion in the ordinary courts

If the volume of cases heard by tribunals was transferred to the ordinary courts, the system would be completely overloaded.

24.5.7 Awareness of policy

The expertise of tribunal members means they are likely to understand the policy behind legislation in their area, and they often have wide discretionary powers which allow them to put this into practice.

24.5.8 Privacy

Tribunals may, in some circumstances, meet in private, so that the individual is not obliged to have their circumstances broadcast to the general public (but see the first disadvantage below).

24.6 Disadvantages of tribunals

Despite the improvements made to the tribunal system by the Tribunals, Courts and Enforcement Act 2007, problems still remain with the tribunal system:

24.6.1 Lack of openness

The fact that some tribunals are held in private can lead to suspicion about the fairness of their decisions.

24.6.2 Unavailability of state funding

While state funding is now available for representation at the majority of hearings in the Upper Tribunal dealing with issues of law, it is only available for the minority of hearings in the First-Tier Tribunal. Tribunals are of course designed to do away with the need for representation, but in many of them the ordinary individual will be facing an opponent with access to the very best representation – an employer, for example, or a Government department – and this clearly places them at a serious disadvantage. Even though the procedures are generally informal compared with those in ordinary courts, the average person is likely to be very much out of their depth, and research by Genn and Genn in 1989 found that much of the law with which tribunals were concerned was complex, and their adjudicative process sometimes highly technical; individuals who were represented had a much better chance of winning their case. The cuts to legal aid funding will doubtless impact this position further. The cuts to civil legal aid remove state funding from over 600,000 of the 1 million people who were previously eligible to receive it.

There is, however, some dispute as to the desirability of such representation necessarily involving lawyers; although in some cases this will be the more appropriate form of representation, there are fears that introducing lawyers could detract from the aims of speed and informality. If money for tribunal representation were to become available, it may be better spent on developing lay representation, such as that offered by specialist agencies like the UK Immigration Advisory Service, or the Child Poverty Action Group, who can develop real expertise in specific areas, as well as general agencies such as the Citizens Advice Bureaux.

Answering questions

1   Sir Andrew Leggatt carried out a review of tribunals for the Lord Chancellor's Department. In his report, *Tribunals for Users: One System, One Service* (2001), he painted a picture of an incoherent and inefficient set of institutions which provided a service to the public which was well short of what people are entitled to expect. Do you agree with Sir Andrew Leggatt and, if so, were the reforms contained in the Tribunals, Courts and Enforcement Act 2007 sufficient?

2 Evaluate the role of tribunals in the English legal system.

3 Tribunals play a significant role in deflecting disputes away from the traditional court system. This may be particularly true following the Leggatt recommendations and the Government's response thereto. Discuss with particular reference to:

(a) the advantages and disadvantages of the tribunal system; and

(b) the provisions for appeal and review of tribunal decisions.

For answers to these questions, see the companion website at www.pearsoned.co.uk/ elliottquinn

SUMMARY OF CHAPTER 24: TRIBUNALS

Introduction

Tribunals are generally different from ordinary courts because of their less formal procedures and the fact that they are very specialist.

History

Tribunals were in existence as long ago as 1799, but the present system has really grown up since the Second World War.

The Franks Report

In 1957 the Franks Committee investigated the workings of tribunals. It recommended that tribunal procedures should be marked by 'openness, fairness and impartiality'. Following the Committee's report, the Council on Tribunals was established.

Reforming the tribunals

Tribunals have recently been the subject of a major reform with the passing of the Tribunals, Courts and Enforcement Act 2007. This piece of legislation followed a lengthy review of the tribunal service undertaken by the Government. First, in 2000, the Government asked Sir Andrew Leggatt, a retired Lord Justice of Appeal, to look at the tribunal service. The report of the Review, *Tribunals for Users: One System, One Service*, was published in 2001. It identified some significant weaknesses in the current system. In particular, it was concerned that the tribunals were not always accessible or user-friendly, they were not independent from the Ministries whose decisions were the subject of the tribunal work and the tribunal system lacked coherence. The Review concluded that the tribunals had to be rationalised and modernised.

Tribunals today

Following the Leggatt Review, the former Labour Government issued a White Paper, *Transforming Public Services: Complaints, Redress and Tribunals* (2004), containing significant plans to reform the tribunal system. Many of these reforms are contained in the Tribunals, Courts and Enforcement Act 2007. Part 1 of the Act creates a new, simplified statutory framework for tribunals. The Act establishes two new, generic tribunals: the First-tier Tribunal and the Upper Tribunal. The Upper Tribunal is primarily, but not exclusively, an appellate tribunal from the First-tier Tribunal. The Act provides for the establishment of 'chambers' within the two tribunals so that the many jurisdictions that are being transferred into the new tribunals can be grouped together appropriately. The tribunals' judiciary is headed by a Senior President of Tribunals.

The Council on Tribunals was replaced by the Administrative Justice and Tribunals Council, but this was also abolished in 2011.

Tribunal procedure

Under the 2007 Act, a Tribunal Procedure Committee has been established with responsibility for tribunal rules of procedure.

Composition

Most tribunals consist of a legally trained chairperson, and two lay people who have some particular expertise in the relevant subject area.

Status

Tribunals are generally regarded as inferior to the ordinary courts.

Employment Tribunals

Employment Tribunals provide one example of a powerful tribunal playing a central role in today's society. The Government introduced fees for the Employment Tribunals in 2013, but has swiftly stopped charging fees as they were prohibitive to accessing justice.

Appeals from tribunals

Historically there was no uniform appeals procedure from tribunals, though most did allow some right of appeal. Improvements to the appeal system have been made by the Tribunals, Courts and Enforcement Act 2007.

Advantages of tribunals

The advantages of tribunals include:

- speed;
- cost;
- informality;
- flexibility;
- specialisation;
- relief of congestion in the ordinary courts;
- awareness of policy; and
- privacy.

Disadvantages of tribunals

The disadvantages of tribunals include:

- lack of openness; and
- unavailability of funding from the Legal Aid Agency.

Reading list

Administrative Justice and Tribunals Council (2011) *Right first time.* London: Administrative Justice and Tribunals Council.

Confederation of British Industry (2005) *A Matter of Confidence: Restoring Faith in Employment Tribunals.* London: CBI.

Department for Constitutional Affairs (2004b) *Transforming Public Services: Complaints, Redress and Tribunals.* London: Stationery Office.

Dickens, L. (1985) *Dismissed: A Study of Unfair Dismissal and the Industrial System.* Oxford: Blackwell.

Genn, H. and Genn, Y. (1989) *The Effect of Representation at Tribunals.* London: Lord Chancellor's Department.

Leggatt, Sir A. (2001) (see website, below).

On the internet

The Report of the Review of Tribunals *Tribunals for Users: One System, One Service,* by Sir Andrew Leggatt is available at:

http://webarchive.nationalarchives.gov.uk/+/http://www.tribunals-review.org.uk

A video, *Employer guidance for the Employment Tribunal,* has been prepared by the Ministry of Justice and is available at:

http://www.youtube.com/watch?v=oyQkvdju0c8&list=PLF7E46C0A7B86C7E9

The Tribunals, Courts and Enforcement Act 2007 is published on the legislation.gov.uk website at:

http://www.legislation.gov.uk/ukpga/2007/15/contents

The explanatory notes to the Tribunals, Courts and Enforcement Act 2007 are published on the legislation.gov.uk website at:

http://www.legislation.gov.uk/ukpga/2007/15/notes/contents

The consultation paper *Resolving Workplace Disputes: Government response to the consultation* (2011) is available at:

https://assets.publishing.service.gov.uk/government/uploads/system/uploads/attachment_data/file/229952/11-1365-resolving-workplace-disputes-government-response.pdf

Ministry of Justice *Guide to Tribunals and Gender Recognition Certificate Statistics Quarterly* (September 2018), is available at:

https://assets.publishing.service.gov.uk/government/uploads/system/uploads/ attachment_data/file/740316/Tribunal_and_GRC_statistics_supporting_document_ Q1_201819.pdf

Chapter 25
Alternative methods of dispute resolution

This chapter considers:

- the problems with court hearings;

- the three main alternative dispute resolution (ADR) mechanisms;

- examples of ADR; and

- advantages and disadvantages of using ADR.

25.1 Introduction

Court hearings are not always the best way to resolve a dispute, and their disadvantages mean that, for some types of problem, alternative mechanisms may be more suitable. The main uses of these at present are in family, consumer, commercial, construction and employment cases but, following Lord Woolf's reforms of the civil justice system, these alternative mechanisms should play a more important role in solving all types of civil disputes. Civil Procedure Rule 1.4 requires the court to undertake case management which is stated to include:

> (2) (e) encouraging the parties to use an ADR procedure if the Court considers that appropriate and facilitating the use of such procedure;
>   (f) helping the parties to settle the whole or part of the case.

In addition, Civil Procedure Rule 26.4 allows the court to grant a stay for settlement by ADR or other means either when one or all of the parties request this, or when the court considers this would be appropriate. If a party fails to use ADR where the court thinks this would have been appropriate, then it can be penalised through a costs order (Civil Procedure Rule 44.5).

Key case

In **Halsey v Milton Keynes General NHS Trust** (2004) the Court of Appeal held that the courts do not have the power to force parties to try ADR, as this might amount to a breach of a person's right to a fair trial under Art. 6 of the European Convention on Human Rights.

> It is one thing to encourage the parties to agree to mediation, even to encourage them in the strongest terms. It is another to order them to do so. It seems to us that to oblige truly unwilling parties to refer their disputes to mediation would be to impose an unacceptable obstruction on their right of access to the Court.

By contrast, in many other countries, such as the US and Australia, the courts are prepared to force the parties to try ADR. Despite the decision in **Halsey**, the Court of Appeal has made clear that a failure to respond at all to an invitation to engage in ADR is itself unreasonable. Given the power of the civil courts to issue sanctions against parties who behave unreasonably in litigation, this situation does almost make trying ADR compulsory.

Legal principle
The courts do not have the power to force parties to try ADR.

The case of **Halsey** was applied and extended in **PGF II SA v OMFS Co 1 Ltd** (2013). In that case the Court of Appeal stated that failure to respond to an invitation for mediation would generally be viewed as unreasonable and could therefore lead to cost sanctions. This case was considered in **R (on the application of Crawford) v University of Newcastle Upon Tyne** (2014). A medical student was in dispute with his university. During the dispute he suggested the parties should consider mediation. The university did not respond to this suggestion. However, the High Court stated that on the facts this was one of the rare cases when silence in the face of this refusal was reasonable because the parties were already engaged at the time of the invitation to mediate, in another form of alternative dispute resolution. In the decision of **Laporte v Commissioner of Police of the Metropolis** (2015), the police were invited to engage in ADR with the claimants. The claimants claimed that they had suffered assault, battery, false imprisonment and a contravention of their Article 10 and 11 rights under the European Convention on Human Rights. This claim failed entirely. The claimants nevertheless argued that they should not have to pay the costs of the winning side because the defendants had failed to engage in ADR with them. The High Court endorsed the decision in *Halsey* and decided that there was indeed a reasonable chance that ADR would have been successful in these circumstances and that this possibility should therefore be reflected in the costs ordered against the claimants, that is, a reduction. Similarly in the case of *Kupeli* **v** *Sirketi* (2016), Mrs Justice Whipple remarked that:

> This case was crying out for some sensible attempt at negotiation before costs racked up and the parties' attitudes hardened . . . Even if the case could not be settled, an early meeting would surely have focussed the minds of those involved, and is likely to have led at least to some narrowing of issues, which would in the end have saved costs . . . there is a world of difference between a case which comes to trial after reasonable efforts at settlement have been made but settlement has proved impossible, and a case where one party has simply refused to engage, preferring to take the view that it will see its opponents in Court.

Contrast this decision with that in *Briggs* **v** *First Choice Holidays & Flights Limited* (2017). This was a group action in which holidaymakers claimed to have suffered a sub-standard holiday for which the defendants were responsible. The defendants argued that the claimants should have mediated through the Association of British Travel Agents (ABTA), which would have meant that the matter could have been resolved at a reasonable cost relative to the claim. The High Court held that the mere availability of ADR is not sufficient to deny a successful party costs owed. The claimants had won and just because they chose to litigate instead of engage in mediation that did not automatically mean that they were acting unreasonably.

25.2 Problems with court hearings

Alternative methods of dispute resolution have become increasingly popular because of the difficulties of trying to resolve disputes through court hearings. Below are some of the specific problems posed by court hearings.

25.2.1 The adversarial process

A trial necessarily involves a winner and a loser, and the adversarial procedure combined with the often aggressive atmosphere of court proceedings divides the parties, making them end up enemies even where they did not start out that way. This can be a disadvantage where there is some reason for the parties to sustain a relationship after the problem under discussion is sorted out – child custody cases are the obvious example but, in business too, there may be advantages in resolving a dispute in a way which does not make enemies of the parties. The court system is often said to be best suited to areas where the parties are strangers and happy to remain so – it is interesting to note that in small-scale societies with close kinship links, court-type procedures are rarely used, and disputes are usually settled by negotiation processes that aim to satisfy both parties, and thus maintain the harmony of the group.

25.2.2 Technical cases

Some types of dispute rest on detailed technical points, such as the way in which a machine should be made, or the details of a medical problem, rather than on points of law. The significance of such technical details may not be readily understandable by an ordinary judge. Expert witnesses or advisers may be brought in to advise on these points, but this takes time, and so raises costs. Where detailed technical evidence is at issue, alternative methods of dispute resolution can employ experts in a particular field to take the place of a judge.

25.2.3 Inflexible

In a court hearing, the rules of procedure lay down a fixed framework for the way in which problems are addressed. This may be inappropriate in areas which are of largely private concern to the parties involved. Alternative methods can allow the parties themselves to take more control of the process.

25.2.4 Imposed solutions

Court hearings impose a solution on the parties which, since it does not involve their consent, may need to be enforced. If the parties are able to negotiate a settlement between them, to which they both agree, this should be less of a problem.

25.2.5 Publicity

The majority of court hearings are public. This may be undesirable in some business disputes, where one or both of the parties may prefer not to make public the details of their financial situation or business practices because of competition.

25.3 Alternative dispute resolution mechanisms

Where, for one or more of the reasons explained above, court action is not the best way of solving a dispute, a wide range of alternative methods of dispute resolution (often known as ADR) may be used. Three main forms of ADR can be identified: arbitration, mediation and conciliation:

- **Arbitration** is a procedure whereby both sides to a dispute agree to let a third party, the arbitrator, decide. The arbitrator may be a lawyer, or may be an expert in the field of the dispute. He or she will make a decision according to the law and the decision is legally binding.

- **Mediation** involves the appointment of a mediator to help the parties to a dispute reach an agreement which each considers acceptable. Mediation can be 'evaluative', where the mediator gives an assessment of the legal strength of a case, or 'facilitative', where the mediator helps the parties to find a settlement that is in all the parties' best interests. When a mediation is successful and an agreement is reached, it is written down and forms a legally binding contract unless the parties state otherwise.

- **Conciliation** is similar to mediation but the conciliator takes a more interventionist role than the mediator in bringing the two parties together and in suggesting possible solutions to help achieve an agreed settlement. The term conciliation is gradually falling into disuse and the process is regarded as a form of mediation.

One of the simplest forms of ADR is, of course, informal negotiation between the parties themselves, with or without the help of lawyers – the high number of civil cases settled out of court are examples of this. Formal schemes include the Advisory, Conciliation and Arbitration Service (ACAS) which mediates in many industrial disputes and unfair dismissal cases; the role of Ombudsmen in dealing with disputes in the fields of insurance and banking, and in complaints against central and local government and public services; the work done by trade organisations such as the Association of British Travel Agents (ABTA) in settling consumer complaints; inquiries into such areas as objections concerning compulsory purchase or town and country planning; the conciliation schemes offered by courts and voluntary organisations to divorcing couples; and the arbitration schemes run by the Chartered Institute of Arbitrators for business disputes. We will look at some of these in more detail below. Though procedural details vary widely, what they all have in common is that they are attempting to provide a method of settling disagreements that avoids some or all of the disadvantages of the court system listed above.

The Ministry of Justice is keen to promote ADR. It has set up a working party to draw up plans to increase awareness of the availability of ADR and intends to launch a wide-ranging awareness campaign. As part of the Government's commitment to promote alternative dispute resolution, Government legal disputes should be settled by mediation or arbitration whenever possible. Government departments should only go to court as a last resort.

25.3.1 Pressure to use ADR

Following the Woolf reforms of the civil justice system (see p. 631), the Civil Procedure Rules positively encourage the use of ADR. The pre-action protocols direct the parties to consider ADR. When filling out the allocation questionnaire, the parties are invited to apply for a one-month stay of proceedings in order to explore settlement through ADR. Active case management under Civil Procedure Rule 1.4 involves '. . . encouraging the parties to use an alternative dispute resolution procedure if the court considers that to be appropriate and facilitating the use of such procedure . . . ' The courts will order a stay of the proceedings for ADR if the parties request it.

Figure 25.1 The ABTA logo

Source: ABTA – The Travel Association

The Court of Appeal is now prepared to punish parties who refuse to use ADR by depriving them of costs, even if they are successful in the action: ***Dunnett*** v ***Railtrack plc*** (2002). A party may turn down an opponent's offer to mediate with impunity if it can satisfy the court that it has compelling reasons for doing so. Thus, in ***Hurst*** v ***Leeming*** (2002) the court held that when mediation can have no real prospect of success a party may, with impunity, refuse to proceed to mediation.

In ***Rolf*** v ***De Guerin*** (2011) the claimant contracted with a builder (the defendant) for an extension to be built on her house. The claimant's husband was expected to oversee the work. The builder stopped work, citing the husband's aggressive behaviour. The claimant therefore stopped paying the builder and sued him for breach of contract. The builder refused to mediate and won at trial. The claimant appealed on a number of grounds including the costs order which the trial judge had made in favour of the defendant. When asked by the Court of Appeal why he had been unwilling to mediate, the builder stated that he would not have been able to demonstrate to a mediator what the claimant's husband was like, which could only be done at trial. In addition, he wanted his 'day in court'. The Court of Appeal allowed the appeal against costs, stating the refusal to mediate amounted to unreasonable behaviour, even where the mediation was unlikely to succeed in producing an agreed settlement. A party's unreasonable refusal to engage in mediation would be a relevant factor when assessing costs. The Court of Appeal commented:

> As for wanting his day in court, that of course is a reason why the courts have been unwilling to compel parties to mediate rather than litigate: but it does not seem to me to be an adequate response to a proper judicial concern that parties should respond reasonably to offers to mediate or settle and that their conduct in this respect can be taken into account in awarding costs.

Cases such as small building disputes should only go through the courts as a last resort because a trial can lead to disproportionate costs and anxiety.

25.4 Examples of ADR

Following are some examples of ADR being used in practice.

25.4.1 Conciliation in unfair dismissal cases

A statutory conciliation scheme administered by ACAS operates before cases of unfair dismissal can be taken to an Employment Tribunal. ACAS conciliation officers talk to both sides with the aim of settling the dispute without a tribunal hearing; they are supposed to procure reinstatement of the employee where possible, but in practice most settlements are only for damages.

A conciliation officer contacts each party or their representatives to discuss the case and advise each side on the strength or weakness of their position. They may tell each side what the other has said, but, if the case does eventually go to a tribunal, none of this information is admissible without the consent of the party who gave it.

In 2014 a new ACAS early conciliation service was introduced. This service requires claimants to obtain a certificate from ACAS before they can bring a claim at an Employment Tribunal. This service is attractive to employers as it is cheaper than heading to a tribunal, and it is also useful for litigants in person.

Evaluation

The success of the scheme is sometimes measured by the fact that two-thirds of cases are either withdrawn or settled by the conciliation process. However, this ignores the imbalance in power between the employer and the employee, especially where the employee has no legal representation – the fact that there has been a settlement does not necessarily mean it is a fair one, when one party is under far more pressure to agree than the other. Dickens's 1985 study of unfair dismissal cases found that awards after a hearing were generally higher than those achieved by conciliation, implying that employees may feel under pressure to agree to any settlement. The study suggested that the scheme would be more effective in promoting fair settlements – rather than settlement at any price – if conciliation officers had a less neutral stance and instead tried to help enforce the worker's rights.

The Bigger Picture: Mediation in divorce cases

In many ways, the court system is an undesirable forum for divorce and its attendant disputes over property and children, since the adversarial nature of the system can aggravate the differences between the parties. This makes the whole process more traumatic for those involved, and clearly is especially harmful where there are children. Consequently, conciliation has for some time been made available to divorcing couples, not necessarily to get them back together (though this can happen), but to try to ensure that any arrangements between them can be made as amicably as possible, reducing the strain on the parties themselves as well as their children.

The Family Law Act 1996 made changes to the divorce laws and placed a greater emphasis on mediation. The Act requires those seeking legal aid for representation in family proceedings to attend a meeting with a mediator to consider whether mediation might be suitable in their case. This requirement was extended to all divorcing couples in 2011. Thus under a pre-action protocol, parties in a family law dispute involving children or finances are required to attend a mediation information and assessment meeting (MIAM). The parties are therefore forced to consider mediation, but they are not actually forced into mediation. The parties will not be required to attend this meeting if the case is a simple divorce with no dispute over access to children or financial arrangements, where there is a history of intimidation or domestic violence or where relevant children are in contact with social services for their protection.

The information and assessment meeting is held with a mediator, who looks at the background circumstances of the case, and the process of mediation is explained. The parties then consider whether mediation would be appropriate as a means of resolving the case.

If no solution to the case is reached through mediation, the parties can apply for their case to be heard by a court. Under the pre-action protocol, the parties must provide the court with evidence they have attended a MIAM, though in practice this pre-action protocol is not always being followed.

In divorce cases generally, the success of mediation depends on the parties themselves and their willingness to cooperate. The parties may find that meeting in a neutral environment, with the assistance of an experienced, impartial professional, helps them communicate calmly. It can make the process of divorce less painful for the couple and their children, by avoiding the need for a court battle in which each feels obliged to accuse the other of being unfit to look after their children – a battle which can be as expensive as it is unpleasant, at a time when one or both parties may be under considerable financial strain.

In 2014, eight out of ten of those who began mediation reached agreement. According to the Ministry of Justice, the average cost of a legally aided mediation is £535, compared to just over £2,800 for cases going to court. However, the Solicitors Family Law Association points out that because men are usually the main earners in a family, and women's earning abilities may be limited by the demands of childcare, women may need lawyers to get a fair deal financially; in fact the Association says the emphasis on mediation may well turn out to be a 'rogue's charter for unscrupulous husbands'.

The Legal Aid, Sentencing and Punishment of Offenders Act 2012 has abolished legal aid for most family law cases but will still fund mediation. The Ministry of Justice expected that slashing family legal aid would keep people out of court and drive up mediation referrals by 9,000 a year. However, mediation referrals dropped by 56 per cent in 2013. The lack of legal aid means fewer people are talking to solicitors about their separation, and solicitors would previously have signposted them towards mediation.

Research carried out by Pereira *et al.* (2015) looked at examples of mediation in the family and employment context. It concluded:

> Participants were receptive to resolution of their problems through mediation, although experiences and the sustainability of agreements varied. In employment cases, all relevant settlements agreed through mediation had held at the point of interview, whereas for family cases none had done so. To at least some extent this was related to the nature of the sampling for this study. However, participants' reports of the mediation process demonstrated that there was a qualitative difference between the two types of agreement. In mediated employment settlements, participants were offered and agreed to take a certain number of months' pay, which ended the matter – the terms of the offer were simple. In family mediations, the process was often not successful because it started too late, when relations between ex-partners had become antagonistic, and because the dynamics of the settlement were complex, involving contact with children and the separation of assets. The limited sustainability of mediated family arrangements was a barrier to participants adopting their preferred pathway in family justice cases, which was to avoid court.

25.4.2 Online dispute resolution

The European Union has established an online dispute resolution (ODR) IT platform. This allows consumers to complain about cross-border online sales and service contracts. An online business must provide a link to the ODR platform and state the online trader's email address.

25.4.3 Trade association arbitration schemes

The Fair Trading Act 1973 provides that the Director-General of Fair Trading has a duty to promote codes of practice for trade associations, which include arrangements for handling complaints. So far, more than 20 codes have received approval from the Office of Fair Trading (OFT), and there are many other voluntary schemes not yet approved. Many include provisions for an initial conciliation procedure between consumers and retailers or suppliers in case of complaints, often followed by independent arbitration if conciliation fails.

One of the best-known examples is that set up by ABTA which, in the case of disputes between tour operators and consumers, offers impartial conciliation. If this fails, disputes may be referred to a special arbitration scheme – about half of all claims referred to it succeed, though not always winning the amount originally claimed. See the decision in *Briggs* as discussed above.

Evaluation

The best of the schemes offer quick, simple dispute resolution procedures, but standards do vary – the National Consumer Council has reported that some are very slow, and there is some concern about the impartiality of arbitrators. These problems could be addressed relatively easily, but the main drawback is the diversity of the codes, and widespread ignorance of their existence, not only among consumers but even among some of the retailers covered by them! Tighter controls by the OFT and better publicity could make them much more useful mechanisms.

25.4.4 Commercial arbitration

Many commercial contracts contain an arbitration agreement, requiring any dispute to be referred to arbitration before court proceedings are undertaken – the aim being to do away with the need for going to court. Arbitrators may have expertise in the relevant field, and lists of suitable individuals are kept by the Chartered Institute of Arbitrators. The parties themselves choose their arbitrator, ensuring that the person has the necessary expertise in their area and is not connected to either of them. Once appointed, the arbitrator is required to act in an impartial, judicial manner just as a judge would, but the difference is that they will not usually need to have technical points explained to them, so there is less need for expert witnesses.

Disputes may involve disagreement over the quality of goods supplied, interpretation of a trade clause or point of law, or a mixture of the two. Where points of law are involved the arbitrator may be a lawyer. The Arbitration Act 1996 aims to promote commercial arbitration by providing a clear framework for its use. It sets out the powers of the parties to shape the process according to their needs, and provides that they must each do everything necessary to allow the arbitration to proceed properly and without delay. It also spells out the powers of arbitrators, which include limiting the costs to be recoverable by either party and making orders which are equivalent to High Court injunctions if the parties agree. Arbitrators are also authorised to play an inquisitorial role, investigating the facts of the case – many of them are, after all, experts in the relevant fields.

Arbitration hearings must be conducted in a judicial manner, in accordance with the rules of natural justice, but proceedings are held in private, with the time and place decided by the parties. The arbitrator's decision, known as the award, is often delivered immediately, and is as binding on the parties as a High Court judgment would be, and if necessary can be enforced as one.

25

ALTERNATIVE METHODS OF DISPUTE RESOLUTION

Table 25.1 Commercial Court mediation statistics

	Apr 98–Mar 99	Apr 99–Mar 00	Apr 00–Mar 01	Apr 01–Mar 02
Number of commercial mediations	190	462	467	338
% referred by courts	not known	19	27	31

Based on Civil Justice Reform Evaluation Further Findings (2002) [Figure 8]

The award is usually to be considered as final, but appeal may be made to the High Court on a question of law, with the consent of all the parties, or with the permission of the court. Permission will only be given if the case could substantially affect the rights of one of the parties, and provided (with some exceptions) that they had not initially agreed to restrict rights of appeal. The High Court may confirm, vary or reverse the award, or send it back to the arbitrator for reconsideration.

Evaluation

Arbitration fees can be high, but for companies this may be outweighed by the money they save through being able to get the problem solved as soon as it arises, rather than having to wait months for a court hearing. The arbitration hearing itself tends to be quicker than a court case, because of the expertise of the arbitrator – in a court hearing, time and therefore money can be wasted in explanation of technical points to the judge. Despite this, arbitration costs in certain cases may still be as high as or higher than litigation. It may be that the confidential nature of arbitration is considered by companies to be as attractive as or more attractive than the potential monetary savings.

Privacy ensures that business secrets are not made known to competitors. Around 10,000 commercial cases a year go to arbitration, which tends to suggest that business people are fairly happy with the system and the more detailed framework set out by the 1996 Act has supported the use of arbitration. Arbitration has proved popular in international disputes because it does not have the national ties of one of the parties' national courts. London is a major arbitration centre. Many international companies with few links to the UK include arbitration clauses in their commercial contracts stating that, in the event of a dispute, arbitration is to take place in London under English law.

25.4.5 Commercial Court ADR scheme

The Commercial Court has taken a robust approach to the use of ADR. Since 1993, it issues ADR orders for commercial disputes regarded as suitable for ADR. It requires each party to inform the court by letter what steps were taken to resolve the case by ADR and why those efforts failed. This has been the subject of research by the academic, Hazel Genn, which was published in 2002 – *Court-based ADR Initiatives for Non-Family Civil Disputes: the Commercial Court and the Court of Appeal*. ADR was undertaken in a little over half of the cases in which an ADR order had been issued, though the research found that the take-up was increasing in recent years.

Of the cases in which ADR was attempted, 52 per cent settled through ADR, 5 per cent proceeded to trial following unsuccessful ADR, 20 per cent settled some time after the conclusion of the ADR procedure, and the case was still live or the outcome unknown in 23 per cent of cases. Among cases in which ADR was not attempted following an ADR order, about 63 per cent eventually settled. About one-fifth of these said that the settlement had been as a result of the ADR order being made. However, the rate of trials among the group of cases not attempting ADR following an ADR order was 15 per cent, compared with only 5 per cent of cases proceeding to trial following unsuccessful ADR.

ADR orders were generally thought to have had a positive or neutral impact on settlement. Orders can have a positive effect in opening up communication between the parties, and may avoid the fear of one side showing weakness by being the first to suggest settlement.

25.4.6 The Court of Appeal mediation scheme

In 1996 the Court of Appeal established a voluntary mediation scheme. Cases are not individually selected, but, with the exception of certain categories of case, a standard letter of invitation is sent to parties involved in appeals. Since 1999, parties refusing to mediate have been asked to give their reasons for refusal. If both parties agree to mediate, the Court of Appeal arranges mediations and mediators provide their services without charge. This scheme was also the subject of Hazel Genn's research that was published in 2002.

Between November 1997 and April 2000, 38 appeal cases were mediated following agreement by both sides. When the scheme had the benefit of a full-time manager, there was a significant increase in the proportion of cases in which both sides agreed to mediate.

About half of the mediated appeal cases settled either at the mediation appointment or shortly afterwards. Among those cases in which the mediation did not achieve a settlement, a high proportion (62 per cent) went on to trial. This suggests that there are special characteristics of appeal cases that need to be considered in selecting cases for mediation. Blanket invitations to mediate, particularly with an implicit threat of penalties for refusal, may not be the most effective approach for encouraging ADR at appellate level. There was some concern that clients felt they were being pushed into mediation and sometimes being pressured to settle. Although solicitors generally approved of the Court of Appeal taking the initiative in encouraging the use of ADR in appropriate cases, it was felt that there was a need for the adoption of a more selective approach, such as that being used in the Commercial Court.

In 2012 a pilot scheme was established to push parties involved in an appeal in a personal injury or contract claim worth up to £100,000 to use mediation. Unless a judge directs otherwise, such cases are automatically referred to the Centre for Dispute Resolution to attempt mediation. If this is unsuccessful, the case will be referred back to the Court of Appeal. In 2014 the pilot scheme was made permanent. Road traffic, personal injury and housing repair claims are excluded, but for all other small claims mediation is strongly encouraged before the case is listed for trial.

25.4.7 Small claims mediation service

In 2005 the Ministry of Justice introduced a small claims mediation service. The mediators are not lawyers, but administrative staff employed by the Ministry who have received some basic mediator training. The mediation hearing is increasingly carried out over the telephone. The scheme was evaluated by the academic Susan Prince in 2007. She found that the telephone mediation sessions lost the benefits of face-to-face mediation as the parties were not able to actively participate in the negotiations. Teleconferencing equipment was not used so there was no shared telephone line; instead the parties relied on the mediator to relay to them what the other party had said. The mediators were found to place too much emphasis on Government targets emphasising efficiency and the research questioned whether parties who did not have a lawyer were receiving a fair and just alternative to court procedures.

The Ministry of Justice issued a consultation paper, *Solving Disputes in the County Courts: Creating a Simpler, Quicker and More Proportionate System* (2011), in which it considered making mediation compulsory. The Government has now made engagement with mediation compulsory for most small claims cases. This does not make mediation itself compulsory, but it makes it compulsory to communicate with a mediator. Once it is clear there is little prospect of a settlement, the case can be referred back to the court system.

25.4.8 Ombudsmen

Ombudsmen provide a non-litigious avenue for individuals to call on for the scrutiny of the decisions of public bodies. A range of different ombudsman schemes exist. For example, there is the Parliamentary Commissioner, the Local Government Ombudsman, the Health Service Ombudsman and the Housing Ombudsman. These are all looking at complaints about public sector administration. There are also ombudsmen in the private sector, such as the banking ombudsman and the insurance ombudsman. These are independent individuals who can investigate complaints into maladministration.

The Parliamentary Commissioner was established by the Parliamentary Commissioner Act 1967. He or she can investigate actions of Government departments and certain other authorities, such as the Electoral Commission. In order to reach the Commissioner, members of the public must make a complaint to their Member of Parliament who refers it to the Commissioner. The Commissioner will investigate whether the complainant has sustained injustice in consequence of maladministration. The Commissioner cannot purely look at the merits of the decision taken: the emphasis is on maladministration. Lord Denning in *R v Local Commissioner for Administration for the North and East Area of England, ex parte Bradford City Council* (1979) held that maladministration will cover 'bias, neglect, inattention, delay, incompetence, ineptitude, perversity, turpitude, arbitrariness and so on'. After investigating a complaint, the Commissioner sends a report to the Member of Parliament who referred it and to the department or authority that is the subject of the complaint. The Commissioner also lays an annual report before each House of Parliament on the performance of his or her functions. A special report can also be laid before each House of Parliament if it appears that injustice caused by maladministration has not been or will not be remedied. The ombudsman is therefore an additional means for MPs to call the executive to account. In its consultation paper *Public Services Ombudsmen* (2011) the Law Commission noted that the main tool available to public service ombudsmen for the implementation of their recommendations is publicity in the media.

In 2014, the Legal Ombudsman called for the UK's system of ADR to be made more coherent, and less complex for firms and consumers. If this was not done, the Legal Ombudsman proposed that the jurisdiction of the Ombudsman be extended to cover areas where ADR does not exist.

The Bigger Picture: Religious and cultural arbitration

Religious and cultural organisations can set up their own systems of alternative dispute resolution under which disputes are resolved by applying laws and rules associated with their religion or culture. For example, Jewish people have their own rabbinical laws, known as Beth Din and Muslims have Sharia law. They can choose to enter into private agreements whereby their disputes are resolved by private arbitration. It can be agreed that the arbitrator will not apply English law to the dispute but will apply, for example, Sharia law. In the same way, a commercial dispute involving businessmen from France could choose to arbitrate their dispute in England but apply French law to the arbitration procedure. The decisions of the arbitrators will only be enforced in England if there is no fundamental conflict with English law. For example, if an arbitrator decided that under Sharia law a wife could not inherit any of her husband's property, then this decision might be found to be unenforceable if it was held to discriminate against women. In *AI v MT* (2013) the High Court approved a divorce settlement for a Jewish couple which had been decided by an arbitrator applying rabbinical law. The decision of the arbitrator was not in itself binding, but was subsequently approved by the High Court. The judge commented that this process was an example of religion and the law working in harmony at a time when 'there is much comment about the antagonism between the religious and secular elements of society'.

25.5 Advantages of ADR

25.5.1 Cost

Many procedures try to work without any need for legal representation, and even those that do involve lawyers may be quicker and therefore cheaper than going to court.

In 1998, Professor Hazel Genn carried out research into a mediation scheme at Central London County Court. The scheme's objective was to offer virtually cost-free, court-annexed mediation to disputing parties at an early stage in litigation. This involved a three-hour session with a trained mediator assisting parties to reach a settlement, with or without legal representation. The scheme's purpose was to promote swift dispute settlement and a reduction in legal costs through an informal process that parties might prefer to court proceedings. Professor Genn's research did not find clear evidence that mediation saved costs. The overall cost of cases which were settled through mediation was significantly less than those which were litigated; but where mediation was used and the parties failed to reach an agreement, and then went on to litigate, it was possible for costs to be increased.

25.5.2 Accessibility

Alternative methods tend to be more informal than court procedures, without complicated rules of evidence. The process can therefore be less intimidating and less stressful than court proceedings.

25.5.3 Speed

The delays in the civil court system are well known, and waiting for a case to come to court may, especially in commercial cases, add considerably to the overall cost, and adversely affect business.

The research carried out by Professor Genn (1998) found that mediation was able to promote and speed up settlement. The majority (62 per cent) of mediated cases settled at the mediation appointment. This is why the judge took a dim view of the actions of the defendant in the case of *Thakkar* v *Patel* (2017) where although both sides had expressed a willingness to mediate, the claimants had taken active steps but the defendants had 'dragged their feet to the point where mediation was abandoned'. A key objective of mediation is to speed up the resolution of disputes and not to waste time.

25.5.4 Expertise

Those who run alternative dispute resolution schemes often have specialist knowledge of the relevant areas, which can promote a fairer as well as a quicker settlement.

25

ALTERNATIVE METHODS OF DISPUTE RESOLUTION

25.5.5 Conciliation of the parties

Most alternative methods of dispute resolution aim to avoid irrevocably dividing the parties, so enabling business or family relationships to be maintained.

25.5.6 Customer satisfaction

The research by Hazel Genn (2002) found that ADR generally results in a high level of customer satisfaction.

25.6 Problems with ADR

25.6.1 Imbalances of power

As the unfair dismissal conciliation scheme shows, the benefits of voluntarily negotiating agreement may be undermined where there is a serious imbalance of power between the parties – in effect, one party is acting less voluntarily than the other. Hazel Genn (2009) has also pointed out that the diversion of a case into alternative dispute resolution often amounts to removing the case from the state sector into the private sector. The priority of the private sector is normally profit not justice:

> The push for less law is supported by the growing ADR profession which professes a mission to rid society of conflict but which is more interested in the profits to be made from large commercial dispute settlement than the small change of the County Courts.

25.6.2 Lack of legal expertise

Where a dispute hinges on difficult points of law, an arbitrator may not have the required legal expertise to judge, although a legal expert can be appointed to advise an arbitrator if necessary.

25.6.3 No system of precedent

There is no doctrine of precedent, and each case is judged on its merits, providing no real guidelines for future cases. While arbitrators have a duty to apply the law contained in court judgments, the decisions of the arbitrators themselves do not act as precedents.

25.6.4 Enforcement

Decisions not made by courts may be difficult to enforce. While an arbitration award can be enforced just like a judgment, to enforce a mediation settlement a party may need to go to court to obtain a judgment which can then be enforced.

25.6.5 Low take-up rate

There is a relatively low take-up rate for ADR, and the numbers have not increased as much as expected following the introduction of the Woolf reforms. Research carried out for the Government, *Further Findings: A Continuing Evaluation of the Civil Justice Reforms* (2002), has found that after a substantial rise in the first year following the introduction of the Civil Procedure Rules 1998, there has been a levelling off in the number of cases in which alternative dispute resolution is used. In particular, there is low take-up for mediation between divorcing couples. Of the 300,000 couples that separate every year, very few opt for mediation. For most people, solicitors remain the first port of call. Many couples, believing incorrectly that mediation is not covered by legal aid at all, self-filter out of legal advice altogether.

Hazel Genn's research (2002) found that outside commercial practice, 'the profession remains very cautious about the use of ADR. Positive experience of ADR does not appear to be producing armies of converts'. She looked at the reasons why parties choose not to use ADR. For the Commercial Court ADR scheme, the most common reasons given for refusal to mediate were:

- a judgment was required for policy reasons;
- the appeal turned on a point of law; or
- the past history or behaviour of the opponent.

The most common reasons given for not trying ADR following an ADR order in the Court of Appeal were:

- the case was not appropriate for ADR;
- the parties did not want to try ADR;
- the timing of the order was wrong (too early or too late); or
- there was no faith in ADR as a process in general.

In addition, Professor Genn has suggested that following the Woolf reforms the increased number of pre-trial settlements might mean that fewer people feel the need for ADR in 'run of the mill' cases. The research concluded that an individualised approach to the direction of cases towards ADR is likely to be more effective than general invitations at an early stage in the litigation process. This would require the development of clearly articulated selection principles. The timing of invitations or directions to mediate is crucial. The early stages of proceedings may not be the best time, and should not be the only opportunity to consider using ADR.

25.7 The future for ADR

Although ADR appears to meet many of the principles for effective civil justice, the proportion of people with legal problems who choose to use ADR has remained very low, even when there are convenient and free schemes available. It is not altogether clear why this is so. Professor Genn's research (1998) found that in only 5 per cent of cases did the parties agree to try mediation, despite vigorous attempts to stimulate demand. It was least likely to be used where both parties had legal representation.

At present, many of those contemplating litigation will go first to a solicitor, and Professor Genn's research shows widespread misunderstanding about mediation processes amongst solicitors. Many did not know what was involved and were therefore not able to advise clients on whether their case was suitable for any form of ADR, or the benefits that might flow from seeking to use it. Solicitors were apprehensive about showing weakness through accepting mediation in the context of traditional adversarial litigation. Litigants were also hostile to the idea of compromise, particularly in the early stages of litigation.

It is likely that in the future ADR will play an increasingly important role in the resolution of disputes. It is already widely used in the US where the law frequently requires parties to try mediation before their case can be set down for trial. It is generally accepted that the UK will see a similar expansion in the use of ADR, as both the courts and the legal profession begin to take ADR more seriously than they once did. Following Lord Woolf's reforms of the civil justice system, the new rules of procedure in the civil courts impose on the judges a duty to encourage parties in appropriate cases to use ADR and to facilitate its use. Parties can request that court proceedings be postponed while they try ADR, and the court can also order a postponement for this reason. Lord Justice Briggs's 2016 report (see Chapter 23) identifies that there certainly needs to be a change in culture to promote and encourage the use of ADR. He believes that parties should be further encouraged to embark on ADR through the case management process.

25.7.1 European consumer ADR and Brexit

Increasingly we are buying goods online from around the world. The European Union is keen to encourage this type of cross-border trade. The EU passed a directive and a regulation on ADR in 2013. ADR organisations must now be available in member states to resolve consumer complaints. Traders are legally obligated to inform consumers about the ADR organisations that are competent to deal with potential disputes. All ADR entities have to comply with the following procedural principles.

- **Impartiality:** consumers and traders must be equally represented in the organisation.
- **Transparency:** they must publish an annual report and have a website that displays information to the parties before they agree to participate in the process.
- **Effectiveness:** all ADR entities must offer easy access regardless of their location; they cannot require legal representation; the ADR process must be free of charge or moderately priced for consumers; and disputes should normally be resolved within 90 days.
- **Fairness:** member states must ensure parties are aware of their rights and decisions must be reasoned and given in writing. Consumers must be given time for reflection before they agree to an amicable solution.

The European Commission established a European Online Dispute Resolution (ODR) website to facilitate the resolution of consumer disputes related to the online sale of goods and provision of services arising from e-commerce. The website acts as a hub to deal with complaints where parties will be invited to agree on using an ADR process to settle their disputes. Traders have to inform consumers about the existence of the website. Consumers are able to submit complaints free of cost and in their own language, but the subsequent ADR process may charge a reasonable fee and offer their services in a different language to that of the consumer. While the UK is still a member state, it will have to maintain its commitment to both the Regulation on ODR for consumers and the Directive on ADR for consumers. Post-Brexit however, the UK will not be compelled to abide by these laws. So what will be the anticipated impact of Brexit and ADR? The culture of using ADR and mediation is increasing within the UK and parties in dispute who unreasonably fail to engage in ADR can be penalised by not being awarded their full costs. That said, the culture to engage in ADR is not where we would like it to be and should be used with greater rigor to save cost and time. It is envisaged that it is unlikely that Brexit will have any major impact on the culture of ADR in the UK, although the UK will be excluded from further implementing ODR.

The UK has implemented the 2008 EU Mediation Directive for national proceedings. The application of this directive is only compulsory for cross-border disputes. The directive's implementation involves making mediation settlement agreements binding without needing to go to court for a separate order to this effect. Mediators would be protected from having to give evidence in civil proceedings about the mediation process. This immunity would prevent the reopening of settlement agreements after a mediation. Extending the application of the directive to national disputes would also require extending the limitation period during the mediation window.

As the use of mediation is increased, the Ministry of Justice suggests that mediators should be properly regulated with a code of conduct, possibly through the Civil Mediation Council.

Answering questions

1   Do you think that the courts offer the best means of solving disputes?

2   Should people be obliged to use ADR before being allowed to pursue their case in court? *University of London, International Programmes LLB*

3   Compare and contrast arbitration, mediation and conciliation as effective methods of ADR.

4   'Alternative Dispute Resolution (ADR) is an alternative means of resolving disputes without reference to the traditional court system.' Critically analyse this statement with particular reference to (i) the context in which ADR operates; and (ii) its non-enforceability.

For answers to these questions, visit the companion website at www.pearsoned.co.uk/ elliottquinn

SUMMARY OF CHAPTER 25: ALTERNATIVE METHODS OF DISPUTE RESOLUTION

Introduction

Following Lord Woolf's reforms of the civil justice system, ADR should play a more important role in solving all types of civil disputes. ADR has become increasingly popular because of problems resolving disputes through court hearings.

Alternative dispute resolution mechanisms

Three main forms of ADR can be identified:

- arbitration;
- mediation; and
- conciliation.

Conciliation in unfair dismissal cases

A statutory conciliation scheme administered by the Advisory, Conciliation and Arbitration Service (ACAS) operates before cases of unfair dismissal can be taken to an employment tribunal.

Mediation in divorce cases

The Family Law Act 1996 has made changes to the divorce laws and places a greater emphasis on mediation.

Trade association arbitration schemes

The Fair Trading Act 1973 provides that the Director-General of Fair Trading has a duty to promote codes of practice for trade associations. Many include provisions for an initial conciliation procedure, often followed by independent arbitration if conciliation fails.

Commercial contracts

Many commercial contracts contain an arbitration agreement, requiring any dispute to be referred to arbitration before court proceedings are undertaken.

Commercial Court ADR scheme

Since 1993 the Commercial Court has issued ADR orders for disputes regarded as suitable for ADR.

The Court of Appeal mediation scheme

The Court of Appeal has a voluntary mediation scheme, under which a standard letter is sent to the parties inviting them to enter mediation.

Ombudsmen

Ombudsmen provide a non-litigious avenue for individuals to call for the scrutiny of the decisions of public bodies.

Advantages of ADR

The advantages of ADR include:

- cost;
- accessibility;
- speed;
- expertise;
- conciliation of the parties; and
- customer satisfaction.

Problems with ADR

The problems with ADR are that:

- there may be a serious imbalance of power between the parties;
- an arbitrator may lack legal expertise;
- there is no system of precedent;
- enforcement may be difficult; and
- there is a low take-up rate.

The future of ADR

It is likely that in the future ADR will play an increasingly important role in the resolution of disputes.

25

ALTERNATIVE METHODS OF DISPUTE RESOLUTION

Reading list

Boyron, S. (2006) The rise of mediation in administrative law disputes: experiences from England, France and Germany. *Public Law,* 230.

Dickens, L. (1985) *Dismissed: A Study of Unfair Dismissal and the Industrial System.* Oxford: Blackwell.

Evans, Sir A. (2003) Forget ADR – think A or D. *Civil Justice Quarterly,* 230.

Fricker, N. and Walker, J. (1993) Alternative dispute resolution – state responsibility or second best? *Civil Justice Quarterly,* 29.

Genn, H. (1998) *The Central London County Court Pilot Mediation Scheme: Evaluation Report.* London: Lord Chancellor's Department.

(2002) *Court-based ADR Initiatives for Non-Family Civil Disputes: The Commercial Court and the Court of Appeal.* London: Lord Chancellor's Department.

(2009) *Judging Civil Justice.* Hamlyn Lectures 2008. Cambridge: Cambridge University Press.

Law Commission (2011b) *Public Services Ombudsmen.* HC 1136. London: Stationery Office.

Lightman, J. (2003) The civil justice system and legal profession – the challenges ahead. *Civil Justice Quarterly,* 235.

Lord Chancellor's Department (1999) *Alternative Dispute Resolution – A Discussion Paper.* London: Lord Chancellor's Department.

(2002) *Further Findings: A Continuing Evaluation of the Civil Justice Reforms.* London: Lord Chancellor's Department.

Ministry of Justice (2011) *Solving Disputes in the County Courts.* London: Ministry of Justice.

Partington, M. (2004) Alternative dispute resolution: recent developments, future challenges. *Civil Justice Quarterly,* 99.

Pereira, I., Perry C., Greevy, H. and Shrimpton, H. (2015), *The Varying Paths to Justice Mapping problem resolution routes for users and non-users of the civil, administrative and family justice systems.* Ministry of Justice Analytical Series.

Prince, S. (2007) Mediating small claims: are we on the right track? *Civil Justice Quarterly,* 26: 328.

Supperstone, M., Stilitz, D. and Sheldon, C. (2006) ADR and public law. *Public Law,* 299.

On the internet

For information about ombudsman systems, see the website of the Ombudsman Association:
http://www.ombudsmanassociation.org/

The Family Mediation Council has a website at:
www.familymediationcouncil.org.uk

Chapter 26
Civil appeals and judicial review

This chapter discusses:

- appeals in civil law cases from the County Court, the High Court and the civil jurisdiction of the magistrates' court;

- the power of the courts to quash a decision of a public body where it had no power to make that decision, under the procedure known as judicial review; and

- the remedies available following a successful application for judicial review.

26.1 Appeals in civil law cases

Civil appeals may be made by either party to a dispute. There has been concern at the increasing number of appeals being brought in civil proceedings. In 1990 there were 954 appeals heard and 573 applications outstanding. By 1996, 1,825 appeals were heard and 1,288 applications were outstanding. There has also been a slight increase in the number of appeals following the passing of the Human Rights Act 1998. A review of the Civil Division of the Court of Appeal was undertaken by a Committee chaired by Sir Jeffrey Bowman. It produced a report in the spring of 1997. A number of problems were identified as besetting the Court of Appeal. In particular, the court was being asked to consider numerous appeals which were not of sufficient weight or complexity for two or three of the country's most senior judges, and which had sometimes already been through one or more levels of appeal. Additionally, existing provisions concerning the constitution of the court were too inflexible to deal appropriately with its workload. Recommendations were made, designed to reduce the delays in the hearing of civil appeals, and the former Labour Government accepted many of its proposals. The Access to Justice Act 1999 introduced some significant reforms to the civil appeal process. By 2003 the number of civil appeals had been reduced to 1,075.

In the past, permission was required for most cases going to the Civil Division of the Court of Appeal, but not elsewhere. Following the Access to Justice Act 1999, court rule 52 requires permission to appeal to be obtained for almost all appeals. This permission can be obtained either from the court of first instance or from the appellate court itself. Permission will be given where the appeal has a realistic prospect of success or where there is some other compelling reason why the appeal should be heard. More stringent conditions are applied for the granting of permission to appeal case management decisions. The main situation where permission to appeal is not required is where the liberty of the subject is at stake: for example, following the rejection of a *habeas corpus* application. The general rule is that appeal lies to the next level of judge in the court hierarchy.

The Access to Justice Act 1999 provides that in normal circumstances there will be only one level of appeal to the courts. Where the County Court or High Court has already reached a decision in a case brought on appeal, there will be no further possibility for the case to be considered by the Court of Appeal, unless it considers that the appeal would raise an important point of principle or practice, or there is some other compelling reason for the Court of Appeal to hear it. Thus in future second appeals will become a rarity. Only the Court of Appeal can grant permission for this second appeal.

In the Court of Appeal, cases are normally heard by three judges, but following the Access to Justice Act 1999 some smaller cases can be heard by a single judge.

Civil appeals will normally simply be a review of the decision of the lower court, rather than a full rehearing, unless the appeal court considers that it is in the interests of justice to hold a rehearing. The appeal will only be allowed where the decision of the lower court was wrong, or where it was unjust because of a serious procedural or other irregularity in the proceedings of the lower court.

The role of the Supreme Court is discussed in detail in Chapter 22 and the Privy Council is discussed on p. 609.

26.1.1 From the County Court

Appeals based on alleged errors of law or fact are made to the Civil Division of the Court of Appeal. Appeals from a district judge's decision usually go first to a circuit judge and then to the High Court (though exceptionally they will go to the Court of Appeal instead of the High Court).

The Court of Appeal does not hear all the evidence again, calling witnesses and so forth, but considers the appeal on the basis of the notes made by the trial judge, and/or other documentary evidence of the proceedings. Written skeleton arguments should be provided to the court so that oral submissions can be kept brief to save time and costs.

The Court of Appeal may affirm, vary (for example, by altering the amount of damages) or reverse the judgment of the County Court. It is generally reluctant to overturn the trial judge's finding of fact because it does not hold a complete rehearing. As the trial judge will have had the advantage of observing the demeanour of witnesses giving their evidence, the Court of Appeal will hardly ever question his or her findings about their veracity and reliability as witnesses. From the Court of Appeal, there may be a further appeal to the Supreme Court, for which leave must be granted.

Judicial review (discussed on p. 714) by the High Court is also possible.

26.1.2 From the High Court

Cases started in the High Court may be appealed to the Civil Division of the Court of Appeal. The case is examined through transcripts rather than being reheard, as above. Following the case of *Taylor* v *Lawrence* (discussed on p. 602) a second appeal can exceptionally be made to the Court of Appeal. This rule is now contained in Civil Procedure Rule 52.17. From the Court of Appeal, a further appeal on questions of law or fact may be made, with leave, to the Supreme Court.

The exception to this process is the 'leapfrog' procedure, provided for in the Administration of Justice Act 1969. Under this procedure, an appeal can go directly from the High Court to the Supreme Court, missing out the Court of Appeal. The underlying rationale is that the Court of Appeal may be bound by a decision of the Supreme Court (or former House of Lords), so that money and time would be wasted by going to the Court of Appeal when the only court that could look at the issue afresh is the Supreme Court. In order to use this procedure, a High Court judge must give permission for the leapfrog. A leapfrog appeal may be granted if the appeal involves a point of law of general public importance and one or more of three conditions is satisfied:

1   The appeal raises issues of national importance.
2   The result is of particular significance.
3   The benefits of early consideration by the Supreme Court outweigh the benefits of consideration by the Court of Appeal.

26.1.3 From the civil jurisdiction of the magistrates' court

Appeals concerning family proceedings go to a County Court. From there, appeal with leave lies to the Court of Appeal and the Supreme Court. Appeals on licensing matters are heard by the Crown Court.

26

CIVIL APPEALS AND JUDICIAL REVIEW

It is also possible for the magistrates to state a case (see p. 599) and for judicial review to be applied.

26.2 Judicial review

The system of judicial review is one of the main ways by which public bodies are held to account. Through judicial review the High Court, and occasionally the Upper Tribunal, oversee the decisions of public bodies and officials, such as inferior courts and tribunals, local councils, and members of the executive including police officers and Government Ministers. Controversially, the Criminal Justice and Courts Act 2015 restricts the right to bring judicial review cases and thereby restricts the public's ability to hold public bodies to account. Cases in the High Court are heard by the Queen's Bench Division either in London or in administrative court centres in Birmingham, Manchester, Cardiff and Leeds.

Certain public bodies are exempt from judicial review. For example, in ***R v Parliamentary Commissioner for Standards, ex parte Al-Fayed*** (1998) the Court of Appeal ruled that the Parliamentary Commissioner for Standards could not be subjected to judicial review. One of the functions of the Commissioner is to receive and, where appropriate, investigate complaints from the public in relation to the conduct of Members of Parliament. Mohamed Al-Fayed, the then owner of Harrods, had made such a complaint that Michael Howard, while Home Secretary, had received a corrupt payment. The complaint had been investigated and then rejected and Al-Fayed had sought judicial review of this decision. The Court of Appeal ruled that the Parliamentary Commissioner for Standards operated as part of the proceedings of Parliament and its activities were non-justiciable. This is because of the principles of the separation of powers (discussed at p. 5).

Unlike the appeal process, judicial review does not examine the merits of the decision. It can only quash a decision if the public body had no power to make it, known as *ultra vires* (*ultra* is Latin for 'beyond' and *vires* is Latin for 'powers'). There are two forms of *ultra vires*: procedural *ultra vires* and substantive *ultra vires*.

26.2.1 Procedural *ultra vires*

Where there has been procedural *ultra vires* it is often said that there has been a breach of natural justice. This means either that the body reaching the particular decision complained of was biased, or that procedures had been unfair. These requirements have been bolstered by Art. 6 of the European Convention on Human Rights which lays down the right to a fair and impartial hearing.

Bias

In ***Dimes*** v ***Grand Junction Canal Proprietors*** (1852), a dispute about land, Lord Chancellor Cottenham found in favour of the canal company. It was then discovered that he owned several thousand pounds worth of shares in Grand Junction Canal Proprietors, and the decision was set aside. This was the principle that was applied in the litigation concerning the extradition of Pinochet, the former dictator of Chile. In those proceedings the House of Lords had handed down a judgment that Pinochet could be extradited to Spain. It was subsequently discovered that one of the judges, Lord Hoffmann, had links with Amnesty International, a human rights organisation that was involved in the proceedings.

Because the process could as a result be viewed as unfair, the House of Lords reopened the case and gave a fresh judgment several months later. Note, there is no need to prove the decision was in fact biased, only that there is a financial interest or some other reason why bias is likely – this is on the grounds that justice must be seen to be done as well as actually be done – *R v Bow Street Metropolitan Stipendiary Magistrate, ex parte Pinochet Ugarte (No. 2)* (1999).

Following the *Pinochet* decision a series of cases has arisen where a litigant has challenged the impartiality of the judge. In *Director General of Fair Trading v Proprietary Association of Great Britain* (2001) the Court of Appeal amended the test for bias. It stated that the court should:

- ascertain all the circumstances that had a bearing on the suggestion that the tribunal was biased; and
- ask whether those circumstances would lead a fair-minded and informed observer to conclude that there was a real possibility that the tribunal was biased.

Unfairness

In *R v National Lottery Commission, ex parte Camelot Group plc* (2000) the National Lottery Commission had established a competition for the award of a new licence to operate the National Lottery. The Commission received bids from Camelot and The People's Lottery (TPL). After a long evaluation process and with only one month of Camelot's existing seven-year licence left to run, the Commission announced that neither bid met the statutory criteria for granting a licence. It declared that the competition was at an end, and stated that it would establish a new procedure under which it would negotiate exclusively with TPL for one month.

Camelot commenced judicial review proceedings, claiming that the Commission's decision to operate this new procedure was unfair. The court accepted that the Commission had tried to be fair. It had decided to negotiate only with TPL because it believed that the deficiencies in TPL's bid (unlike Camelot's) were capable of being addressed within the time constraints. Despite this, the court found that the decision to negotiate exclusively with TPL had been 'conspicuously unfair to Camelot' and was therefore unlawful.

26.2.2 Substantive *ultra vires*

This occurs where the content of the decision was outside the power of the public body that made it. Sometimes legislation may make it clear what the limits on the public body's powers are. Thus, the limits on the magistrates' jurisdiction are clearly laid down in legislation. If a magistrates' court decides to hear a case which is indictable only, and should therefore have been heard in the Crown Court, the magistrates' decision can be ruled *ultra vires* and quashed.

Often, however, the legislation does not lay down clear limits on the public body's powers. For example, the legislation might simply say that the Minister can appoint 'who he thinks fit'. If the Minister then appoints someone who is totally unqualified for the job, it is very difficult for the court to prove that the Minister did not think he was fit for the job. To get round some of the problems caused by broadly drafted powers such as these, the courts are prepared to imply certain limitations on the official's power even where they are not laid down by the relevant legislation.

Wednesbury unreasonable

Key case

A decision will be held to be outside the public body's power if it was so unreasonable that no reasonable public body could have reached the decision. This is known as the Wednesbury principle and was laid down in **Associated Provincial Picture Houses Ltd v Wednesbury Corporation** (1948). The Wednesbury Corporation had been given the power under statute to decide whether cinemas could be allowed to open on Sundays. The Corporation had decided the claimant's cinemas could not admit children under the age of 15 into their cinemas on Sundays. The court upheld the decision of the Corporation because it was not so unreasonable that no reasonable authority could have made this decision.

Legal principle
A decision is *ultra vires* if it is so unreasonable that no reasonable public body could have reached the decision.

Lord Diplock described such an executive decision in **Council of Civil Service Unions v Minister for the Civil Service** (1984) as 'a decision which is so outrageous in its defiance of logic or of accepted moral standards that no sensible person . . . could have arrived at it'.

In **R v Chief Constable of Sussex, ex parte International Trader's Ferry Ltd** (1998) lorries carrying livestock for export required police protection from animal rights protesters in order to gain access to the ferries. The Chief Constable decided to reduce the protection to certain days of the week due to insufficient police resources. The ferry company sought judicial review of this decision but it was held by the Court of Appeal and the House of Lords that the decision was not unreasonable.

If a decision interferes with fundamental human rights then the court applies a more stringent test in determining whether the decision was reasonable. The relevant test is whether a reasonable body could, on the material before it, have reasonably concluded that such interference was justifiable. The more substantial the interference with human rights, the more the courts require by way of justification before they are satisfied that a decision is reasonable. **R v Lord Saville of Newdigate, ex parte B** (1999) arose from the events of 'Bloody Sunday' when 13 people were killed and many others injured when British soldiers opened fire on a demonstration in Northern Ireland. In 1972, the Widgery tribunal was set up to inquire into the incident. The majority of soldiers giving evidence in that inquiry were allowed to remain anonymous. The subsequent report was criticised and eventually in 1998 a further inquiry was set up presided over by Lord Saville. In May 1999 the Ministry of Defence asked the tribunal to permit military witnesses to give their evidence again without disclosing their names, primarily on the grounds that such disclosure would endanger their lives as they would be exposed to the threat of revenge attacks by terrorist organisations. While the tribunal accepted that anonymity would not prevent it from discovering the truth, it refused to grant this request. An application was then made to the High Court by soldiers who had fired live bullets on 'Bloody Sunday' for judicial review of the tribunal's decisions, contending that it was unreasonable. The High Court accepted that the tribunal's decision potentially interfered with fundamental human rights, those rights being the rights to life, safety and to live free of fear. The question for the court was, given the tribunal's clear finding that anonymity would not impede it in its fundamental task of discovering the truth, could a reasonable tribunal conclude that the additional degree of openness to be gained by disclosure of the names of the 17 soldiers who fired the shots amount to so compelling a public interest as to justify subjecting the soldiers and their families to a significant danger to their lives. The authorities established that where fundamental human rights might be affected by a decision of a public authority, the law gave those rights precedence. The law was that such rights were to prevail unless either the threat that they would be infringed was slight or there was a compelling reason why they should yield. The High Court found that the tribunal had not accorded the applicants' fundamental human rights the required weight. The tribunal's decision was quashed and a subsequent appeal to the Court of Appeal was dismissed.

Irrelevant considerations

If the court concludes that a public body took into account irrelevant considerations, then its decision may be quashed. For example, in *R v Somerset County Council, ex parte Fewings* (1995) Somerset County Council passed a resolution prohibiting stag hunting on its land. The ban was challenged on the ground that it was acting outside its statutory authority; the power under s. 120(1)(b) of the Local Government Act 1972, to manage its land for the benefit of the authority's area, did not extend to banning stag hunting on the ground that it was cruel or unethical. The Court of Appeal held that the ban was illegal. It found that, while the assertion that hunting was cruel was not a completely irrelevant consideration when exercising its discretion, the council may have given undue weight to the moral question concerning the desirability of hunting, at the expense of the statutory requirement to manage the land for the benefit of the authority's area.

Improper purpose

The idea of a body acting outside its powers has been extended to include abusing those powers by using them for an improper purpose. In *R v Derbyshire County Council, ex parte Times Supplements* (1990), *The Times* challenged Derbyshire County Council's decision to withdraw its advertising for educational appointments from *The Times* publications, after the *Sunday Times* had printed two articles accusing the council of improper and legally doubtful behaviour. The Divisional Court held that the council's decision had been motivated by bad faith and vindictiveness, and was therefore an abuse of power.

Fettered discretion

Where the public body does have a discretion, that is to say a choice, they must exercise that choice. In *British Oxygen Co v Minister of Technology* (1971) a scheme had been set up where grants towards capital expenditure (the purchase of large pieces of machinery, etc.) by industry could be awarded from the Ministry of Trade at the Ministry's discretion. The Ministry developed a rule that grants would not be given for machinery costing less than £25. The British Oxygen Company had spent over £4 million on gas cylinders which cost £20 each. They applied for a grant to assist with the expenditure and, applying this blanket rule, the Ministry rejected their application. On appeal, the House of Lords concluded that a public body with a general legislative discretion was only allowed to develop such internal policies if it was prepared to listen to arguments for the exercise of individual discretion in particular cases.

In *R v Southwark London Borough Council, ex parte Udu* (1995) the applicant had obtained a law degree from South Bank University. The applicant applied to his local authority for a discretionary maintenance award in order to study the Legal Practice Course at the College of Law to qualify as a solicitor. The authority rejected the application in accordance with its policy of not providing grants for study at private institutions. The application for judicial review was dismissed. The authority could have a policy on the award of postgraduate grants provided it was rational and flexible, and rejected the argument that the result of the policy was that only children of wealthy parents could enter the legal profession.

Error on the face of the record

Where the decision-making body's own record of the proceedings reveals it has made a mistake concerning the law, the decision may be quashed.

Proportionality

The case law of the European Court of Human Rights and the Court of Justice of the European Union will only allow a public body to use discretionary powers to do what is proportionate to the end to be achieved. In other words, they will not allow a public body to cause a greater degree of interference with the rights or interests of individuals than is required to deal with the state's objectives.

Traditionally, the English courts have been reluctant to adopt this test of proportionality, for fear that it can amount to the judges taking decisions instead of the executive, with judges starting to look at the factual merits of a particular decision. They have preferred to use the more restrictive test of reasonableness.

The courts are now prepared to apply the proportionality test to determine the legality of the actions of public authorities, particularly where these are regulated by European law or touch on rights protected by the European Convention on Human Rights.

Following the Supreme Court decision of *Pham v Secretary of State of the Home Department* (2015) the courts are now prepared to look at the issue of proportionality more generally under the common law. In *Kennedy v Charity Commission* (2014) the Supreme Court noted the advantages of the proportionality test in directing attention to factors such as appropriateness, necessity and the balance of the benefits and disadvantages.

26.2.3 Remedies

In addition to any of the ordinary civil law remedies of damages, an injunction, or a declaration, the High Court may order a public law remedy only available through the judicial review proceedings. These remedies are often called prerogative orders, and three such remedies exist:

Quashing order

This order used to be called *certiorari*. It quashes (nullifies) an *ultra vires* decision. For example, it might be used to quash the refusal to pay child benefit. It is not available against the Crown, but usually a declaration in that situation will be sufficient.

Mandatory order

This is an order to do something and might be used, for example, to force a local authority to produce its accounts for inspection by a local resident, or to compel a tribunal to hear a previously refused appeal. A mandatory order is not available against the Crown. Often an applicant will seek both a quashing order and a mandatory order. A quashing order could quash an *ultra vires* decision and a mandatory order could compel the public body to decide the case according to its legal powers.

Prohibiting order

This can order a body not to act unlawfully in the future. Thus, while a quashing order quashes decisions already made, a prohibiting order prevents a decision from being made which, if made, would be subject to a quashing order. For example, it can prohibit an inferior court or tribunal from starting or continuing proceedings which are, or threaten to be, outside their jurisdiction, or in breach of natural justice.

The former Labour leader Michael Foot made an unsuccessful application for a prohibiting order in *R v Boundary Commission for England, ex parte Foot* (1983). He had challenged the recommendations of the Boundary Commission on amendments to the boundaries of electoral constituencies, as he thought they were unjust. His application was rejected.

26.2.4 Discretion

All the prerogative remedies are discretionary, so even if an applicant proves that the public body behaved illegally, the court can still refuse a remedy. Thus, in deciding whether to grant a remedy, the court should take into account whether it would be detrimental to good administration. If an alternative remedy is available, such as through the appeals process or a specialised tribunal, the court is unlikely to grant a prerogative order. Examples of other factors that might influence their use are consistency with other cases, the nature of the remedy sought, delay, and the motive of the applicant.

26.2.5 Procedure

Part 54 of the Civil Procedure Rules lays down the procedures to be followed for judicial review. The rules contain safeguards to protect public authorities from unreasonable or frivolous complaints and to prevent abuse of the legal process.

Time limit

An application should normally be made within three months of the date when the grounds for the application arose. Even where the application is made within this time, if the court concludes that it was not made promptly it may still not be allowed. On the other hand, the court has a discretion to allow applications made outside the three-month time limit if there was good reason for the delay. In 2013, the coalition Government cut the time limit for the judicial review of planning decisions from three months to six weeks. The Government was concerned that judicial review was being used frivolously, and as a campaigning tool which hinders national policy. This change was designed to remove spurious challenges to planning decisions.

Leave

Before the case can be heard, leave must be obtained from a single judge in the High Court. To obtain leave, the applicants must prove that they have an arguable case. This is quite a low threshold, but the aim is to sift out very weak cases at an early stage to avoid too much unnecessary inconvenience to the administration.

Locus standi

The applicant must have 'a sufficient interest in the matter to which the application relates'. They must, therefore, have a close connection with the subject of the action. This is known as *locus standi*. Again, this rule aims to prevent time from being wasted by vexatious litigants or unworthy cases. The issue can be considered both when leave is sought and at the main hearing.

The coalition Government proposed amending the 'sufficient interest' test, narrowing its scope so fewer people would have standing to bring a claim of judicial review. Following widespread opposition from lawyers and interest groups, the Government did not move forward with this proposal.

Key case

An important case on the subject of *locus standi* is **R v Inland Revenue Commissioners, ex parte National Federation of Self-Employed and Small Businesses** (1982), often called the Fleet Street Casuals case. An application for judicial review had been made by a taxpayers' association. They wanted to challenge an agreement that had been made by the Inland Revenue to waive the income tax arrears for 6,000 freelance workers in the newspaper printing industry, based at the time in Fleet Street, if they declared their earnings fully in the future. The House of Lords held that the applicant lacked *locus standi*. In deciding whether there was *locus standi* the merits of the case could be taken into account and the case had no merit as the Inland Revenue had no duty to collect every penny of tax due. The taxpayers' association did not have a sufficient interest in other taxpayers' affairs.

Legal principle

In determining whether a party has *locus standi* to bring judicial review proceedings, the court can take into account the merits of a case.

Since the Fleet Street Casuals case, the concept of *locus standi* has been broadened to include some interest and pressure groups. The Attorney General always has *locus standi*. If a party has failed to prove *locus standi* the Attorney General can choose to permit the action through a proceeding known as a 'relator action'. Under this mechanism the action officially proceeds under the Attorney General's name.

There is limited discovery of documents and cross-examination is only allowed in certain circumstances.

Where an application for judicial review is refused by the Divisional Court, application may be made to the Court of Appeal, which, if it accepts that the case should be heard, may refer it back to the Divisional Court, or conduct the hearing itself. Decisions made in a judicial review case may be appealed to the Court of Appeal, and from there to the Supreme Court.

26.2.6 Criticisms of judicial review

Problems with control of wide discretionary powers

While the courts have been prepared to imply certain limits to apparently broad discretionary powers of public bodies, it is still very difficult for such powers to be controlled. The Housing Act 1980, for example, empowers the Secretary of State for the Environment to 'do all such things as appear to him necessary or expedient' to enable council tenants to buy their council houses. In 1982, the then Secretary of State decided that this allowed him to take the sale of council houses out of the hands of local authorities who were not proceeding with such sales as quickly as he wished, and in *R v Secretary of State for the Environment, ex parte Norwich City Council* (1982), the courts had to agree. The powers granted were so wide that very little could be considered *ultra vires*.

Strictness of 'Wednesbury principles'

As Geoffrey Robertson points out in his book *Freedom, the Individual and the Law* (1993), the very narrow test of unreasonableness severely limits the court's power to supervise the executive. For example, in *R v Ministry of Defence, ex parte Smith* (1995) the applicants had been dismissed from the armed forces because they were homosexuals and sought judicial review of the Ministry of Defence's policy of banning homosexuals. The ban was held to be legal as it was not *Wednesbury* unreasonable; the decision was not completely irrational even if the reasons for the ban did not appear convincing. This illustrates how weak the test renders judicial review for protecting fundamental human rights. The approach of the English courts was subsequently heavily criticised by the European Court of Human Rights on the basis that the test of unreasonableness was set too high (*Smith and Grady v United Kingdom* (1999)).

From time to time the courts have toyed with the idea of adopting the principle of proportionality as a ground for judicial review. This principle, which is recognised by the administrative law of many European countries, would allow a decision to be struck down on the grounds that, although not irrational on *Wednesbury* terms, it is out of proportion to the benefit it seeks to obtain, or the harm it wishes to avoid – in other words, where a sledgehammer is being used to crack a nut. Clearly, this would provide a wider test than the *Wednesbury* principle and could lead to more decisions being struck down.

The idea of proportionality as a criterion for judicial review has been mentioned in *Council of Civil Service Unions v Minister for the Civil Service* (1984). It was also raised in *R v Secretary of State for the Home Department, ex parte Brind* (1991), where journalists unsuccessfully sought to challenge the Home Secretary's ban on broadcasting direct interviews with members of the IRA and other groups from Northern Ireland. In both cases the courts felt it was not open to them to accept it as a criterion at the time, but indicated that case-by-case development might eventually bring it into consideration.

When the courts are considering European law in the domestic context, they are prepared to take into account the issue of proportionality. In *R v Chief Constable of Sussex, ex parte International Trader's Ferry Ltd* (1997) (discussed at p. 716) the House of Lords made direct reference to the concept of proportionality. One of the basic precepts of Europe is free movement of goods. But this free movement can be restricted on the grounds of public policy. To fall within this concept the authority's conduct must have been proportionate to the risk involved. This required a balance to be reached between the restriction on the fundamental freedom, the right of local residents to protection from crime and disorder and the right to hold lawful demonstrations. On the facts, the House of Lords held the particular decision to have been lawful.

26.2.7 Political nature of decisions

The nature of cases brought under judicial review means they inevitably become political at times. Critics, notably Griffith (1997), have noted that the judiciary seem more reluctant to interfere in decisions made by the executive where the executive concerned is a Conservative one. Cases such as *R v Boundary Commission for England, ex parte Foot* (1983) (see p. 719) would support this argument.

Restrictions on applications

The procedural limitations on applications for judicial review can be seen as necessary to safeguard good administration from unnecessary distractions, vexatious litigants and busy-bodies. One of the advantages of the judicial review procedure is that it is relatively quick and if the volume of cases were increased this would cease to be true. On the other hand, they can also be seen as ways to discourage ordinary people from seeking to challenge Government or other authorities. There is no leave requirement for ordinary civil proceedings. It could be argued that the current time limits are too short and the courts' discretion is too vague so that sometimes justice is not done.

The concept of national security

Some have criticised reliance on the requirements of national security to inhibit judicial review of Government decisions. In *Council of Civil Service Unions v Minister for the Civil Service* (1984), the Civil Service union challenged the Government's decision to ban employees of Government Communications Headquarters (GCHQ, the Government intelligence centre, which monitors communications from abroad and ensures security for UK military and official communications) from membership of trade unions. The Divisional Court upheld the complaint on the ground that the decision had been made unfairly, since the unions had not even been consulted. On appeal, the Government argued that its decision had been motivated by considerations of national security, because the centre had been disrupted by industrial action some years earlier. Despite the fact that this argument had not been advanced in the initial proceedings, and that a no-strike agreement was offered by the union, the House of Lords overturned the original decision and upheld the ban. The Government was not required to prove that the ban was necessary, or even justifiable in the interests of security; only that the decision had been motivated by national security concerns.

Similarly, in *R v Secretary of State for the Home Department, ex parte Hosenball* (1977), Mark Hosenball, an American journalist, was made the subject of a deportation order on the ground that his presence in the UK was not conducive to the public good. He challenged the order on the basis that he had been given no details of the case against him so that the rules of natural justice had not been followed. The Court of Appeal held that, although the proceedings had been unjust, the rules of natural justice were not to be applied to deportation decisions made on grounds of national security.

As Geoffrey Robertson (1993) points out, where national security is invoked, the courts are reluctant to assess the strength of evidence presented, even to assert whether decisions made on such grounds were made rationally. He alleges that, so long as there appears to be some evidence of national security concerns, however slight or dubious, the courts will take a 'hands-off' approach. Obviously this problem occurs in only a minority of cases but, as the above examples show, they may be those which affect fundamental civil liberties.

26.2.8 Reform

The number of judicial review cases has been increasing: in 1974 there were 160 cases, in 2000 there were 4,250 and in 2016 there were 17,672. The rise in the number of judicial reviews is the result of a range of factors including:

- an increase in the powers of the executive;
- new secondary legislation which can be the subject of a judicial review challenge;
- a growing awareness of human rights; and
- an increase in asylum and immigration cases, which account for at least half of all judicial review applications.

However, the nature of judicial review proceedings which challenge the decisions of the Government, mean the procedure can be unpopular with politicians. In 2011, the Ministry of Justice published a consultation paper looking at ways to cut the number of judicial review cases. As part of this process, under the Crime and Courts Act 2013, some cases which in the past would have been heard as judicial review applications by the High Court, are now heard by the Upper Tribunal, particularly with regard to immigration and asylum matters. The Criminal Justice and Courts Act 2015 has tightened the rules relating to leave and introduced fees for elements of the review process.

Answering questions

1 In 2017, a statute was passed authorising local authorities to make laws to 'ensure the safe use of pedestrianised areas'. The statute expressly stated that representatives of interested groups had to be consulted before any delegated legislation was passed. The local authority consulted market stallholders about passing legislation regulating street musicians. Following this consultation process, a bye-law was made requiring all street musicians to have a licence and to perform on designated platforms. Eight months after the legislation had been passed, only classical musicians had been granted a licence. When Mary, a punk rocker who had frequently played in a town centre subway, applied for a licence, her application was rejected on the ground that she was too noisy. Her appeal was rejected by a committee established by the local authority to hear complaints. Mary subsequently discovered that the president of the committee was related to a successful street musician who had been granted a licence. Advise Mary about how she can challenge the behaviour of the local authority.

2 To what extent is judicial review an alternative to an appeal from a lower civil court?

For answers to these questions, see the companion website at www.pearsoned.co.uk/ elliottquinn

SUMMARY OF CHAPTER 26: CIVIL APPEALS AND JUDICIAL REVIEW

Appeals in civil law cases

Following the report of Sir Jeffrey Bowman into the Civil Division of the Court of Appeal in 1998, the Access to Justice Act 1999 introduced some significant reforms to the civil appeal process. The Access to Justice Act provides that in normal circumstances there will be only one level of appeal.

From the County Court

Appeals based on alleged errors of law or fact are made to the Civil Division of the Court of Appeal. Appeals from a district judge's decision normally have to go first to a circuit judge and then to the High Court.

From the High Court

Cases started in the High Court may be appealed to the Civil Division of the Court of Appeal.

Judicial review

The system of judicial review by the High Court oversees the decisions of public bodies and officials. There are two forms of *ultra vires*:

* procedural *ultra vires*; and
* substantive *ultra vires*.

Remedies

In addition to the ordinary civil law remedies, three possible public law remedies can be ordered:

* quashing order;
* mandatory order;
* prohibiting order.

Reading list

Andrews, N. (2000) A New System of Civil Appeals and a New Set of Problems. *Cambridge Law Journal*, 464.

Bowman, Sir J. (1997) *Review of the Court of Appeal (Civil Division)*. London: Lord Chancellor's Department.

Griffith, J. A. G. (1997) *The Politics of the Judiciary*. London: Fontana.

Jolowicz, J. (2001) The New Appeal: Re-hearing or Revision or What? *Civil Justice Quarterly*, 20: 7.

Nobles, R. and Schiff, D. (2002) The Right to Appeal and Workable Systems of Justice. *Modern Law Review*, 65: 676.

Robertson, G. (1993) *Freedom, the Individual and the Law*. London: Penguin.

Woolf, Lord (1996) *Access to Justice*. London: Lord Chancellor's Department.

On the internet

Useful information on the High Court is available at:

https://www.judiciary.gov.uk/you-and-the-judiciary/going-to-court/high-court/

26

CIVIL APPEALS AND JUDICIAL REVIEW

Part 6
Concepts of law

Part 6 seeks to encourage a profound analysis of the very concept of law. Up to now we have explored some areas of law and practice without questioning what law actually is and why it exists in society. In this Part we will seek to provide answers to the questions 'What is law?' and 'Why do we have law?'

Chapter 27
Law and rules

This chapter looks at:

- the command theory developed by John Austin in the seventeenth century;

- Professor Hart's distinction between primary and secondary rules;

- Professor Dworkin's emphasis on legal principles;

- the natural law theory; and

- the importance that some writers have placed on the function of law.

27.1 Introduction

What is law? What do we mean when we say that something is the law? One answer is that a law is a type of rule, but clearly there are many rules which are not law: for example rules of etiquette, school or club rules and moral rules. One way to understand more about what law is, is to look at what distinguishes legal rules from other types of rules.

27.2 Austin: the command theory

The nineteenth-century writer John Austin, in his book *The Province of Jurisprudence Determined*, argued that law differed from other rules because it was the command of a sovereign body, which the state could enforce by means of punishment. The relevant sovereign body would vary in different countries; in Britain it was the Queen in Parliament, but in other countries it might be the monarch alone, or an emperor or president.

Austin's definition has fairly clear application to some areas of law, most obviously criminal law, where we are told we must do or not do certain things, with penalties for disobedience. But there are large areas which fall outside it. Contract law, for example, details the sanctions which can be imposed when contracts are broken, but it does not command us to make contracts in the first place. The law concerning marriage does not order anyone to marry; it simply sets out the conditions under which people may do so if they wish, the procedure they should follow to make the marriage legally valid, and the legal consequences of being married. The rules about marriage and contracts could be described as rules giving power, in contrast to the rules imposing duties which comprise criminal law; they have different functions, but both types are legal rules. As Professor Hart and other legal philosophers have pointed out, there are an enormous number of legal rules which neither make commands, nor impose sanctions. The complexity and variety of legal rules make it impossible to cover them all with the proposition that laws are commands.

27.3 Hart: primary and secondary rules

In his influential book *The Concept of Law* (1994, first published in 1961), Professor Hart attempted to link types of rules with types of legal systems. He divided legal rules into primary rules and secondary rules, and argued that the existence of secondary rules was a mark of a developed legal system.

Primary rules were described as those which any society needs in order to survive. These rules forbid the most socially destructive forms of behaviour – typically murder, theft and fraud – and also cover areas of civil law, such as tort. According to Hart, simple societies, which generally have a high degree of social cohesion, can survive with only these basic rules but, as a society becomes more complex, it will require what he described as secondary rules.

Secondary rules confer power rather than impose duties, and can be divided into three types: rules of adjudication, rules of change and rules of recognition.

27.3.1 Rules of adjudication

In simple societies, the primary rules can be applied and enforced by means of informal social pressures within the group; this works because the community is close-knit, and individuals rely on each other. As societies become larger and more complex, these bonds are broken, and social pressures will not be enough to shape behaviour. Therefore the community needs some means of giving authority to its rules, and the secondary rules of adjudication are designed to provide this. They enable officials (usually judges) to decide disputes, and to define the procedures to be followed and the sanctions which can be applied when rules are broken. Examples of secondary rules in our society are those which lay down what kind of issues can be decided by courts, who is qualified to be a judge and sentencing legislation for criminal cases; there are many more.

27.3.2 Rules of change

The second type of secondary rule is concerned with making new rules, both primary and secondary. A developed society will need these to respond to new situations – perhaps the clearest example in our society is the huge number of laws introduced over the last century as a result of the invention of motorised transport and the laws introduced to regulate the use of the internet. Rules of change lay down the procedure to be followed in making new rules or changing old ones. In our system, the main rules of change are those concerning how legislation is made and how judicial decisions become part of the common law.

There are also rules of change concerning the power of individuals to produce changes in the legal relationships they have with others.

27.3.3 Rules of recognition

The fact that in simple forms of society rules are enforced by social pressure means that they are only binding if the community as a whole accepts them. Within a small-scale, close-knit community it will generally be obvious to all what the accepted rules are. In a more complex society, this is not the case; there may be many rules, some of them complex, and individuals cannot be expected to know them all. To minimise uncertainty, the developed society, according to Hart, develops rules of recognition, which spell out which of the many rules that govern society actually have legal force. As Hart explains, in the simpler form of society we must wait and see whether a potential rule gets accepted as a rule or not; in a system with a basic rule of recognition we can say before a rule is actually made that it will be valid if it conforms to the requirements of the rule of recognition.

Hart described the UK as having a single rule of recognition: what the Queen in Parliament enacts is law. This leaves out the issue of judge-made law; the difficulties in pinpointing exactly how precedent works mean that a rule of recognition is more difficult to specify here, but it would certainly be inaccurate to say that only what the Queen in Parliament enacts is law.

27.4 Dworkin: legal principles

Professor Dworkin (1986) rejects Hart's analysis of law as consisting purely of rules. He argues that the rich fabric of law contains not just rules, but also a set of principles on which all legal rules are based. Dworkin defines rules as operating in an all or nothing manner, stating a particular answer to a particular question. Legal principles, on the other hand, are guidelines, giving a reason that argues in one direction, but does not dictate a decision. Take, for example, a hypothetical murder of a father by his son. One of the legal principles Dworkin advances is that no one should benefit from their own wrong, and this should clearly be taken into account in deciding this dispute. But it does not dictate a particular answer; there may be other aspects to the dispute which make other principles a stronger influence (perhaps the son killed in self-defence). By contrast, a rule that no one can inherit property from a person they have murdered is clear-cut and straightforward in application: the son cannot inherit from his father regardless of his motive.

Other differences between principles and rules, according to Dworkin, are that principles have a dimension of weight or importance – a suggestion of morality – that rules lack. Conflicts between principles can be weighed up by a judge, and the background guidance they give means that, even in hard cases, they should provide a fairly clear answer: if rules clash, a further rule will be needed to establish which should prevail (for example, the rule that if law and equity conflict, equity prevails). Finally, the strength of a principle can become eroded over time, whereas rules stand until they are removed.

27.5 The natural law theory

The theories of Austin (1954) and Hart (1963) attempt to define what law is, without examining what it says: they could be said to look at the outside appearance of law, rather than defining it by its content. This approach is called positivism. Another school of thought, the natural law theory, defines law by its content: only laws which conform to a particular moral code, seen as a higher form of law, can genuinely be called law. (This natural law theory is discussed in Chapter 28, p. 745.)

27.6 The function of law

Some writers have taken the view that law is best understood by looking at the role it plays in society: what is it for? The following are some of the key theories in this area.

27.6.1 Social cohesion

The nineteenth-century French sociologist Emile Durkheim (see Lukes and Scull, 1983) looked at the issue of social cohesion, searching for what keeps a society together, and concluded that law played an important role in this area. He looked at the role of law in two contrasting types of society: the first a relatively simple, technologically undeveloped society; the second highly developed in terms of technology and social structure.

Durkheim argued that in the first type of society, the whole group would have clearly identifiable common aims, and would all work to achieve them: the interests of any individual within the group would be exactly the same as those of the group as a whole. A moral and legal code based on these aims would be recognised and accepted by all, and would keep the group working together. Durkheim called this mechanical solidarity. An individual who deviated from this code would be punished, and their punishment would reinforce the code by reflecting the group's disapproval of the wrongdoing.

According to Durkheim's analysis, as social groups become larger and more complex, developing links with other social groups, the interests of individual members become less closely linked to those of the group as a whole. To take a simple example, members of a forest tribe might hunt together to provide food for everyone, whereas in a developed society individuals and families look after their own interests. Social solidarity does not disappear but becomes based on increasing interdependence, which itself stems from the division of labour. Whereas, for example, in the small-scale society, each family would make its own bread, in the developed society this task is shared between farmer, flour mill, bakery and retailer, all dependent on each other and the consumer. This interdependence means that the individual has social importance in their own right, rather than occupying a social position simply as one member of the group.

Durkheim argued that these changes would be accompanied by a corresponding change in the type of law present in the society. Penal law would become less important and would increasingly be replaced by compensatory law, where the object is not to punish but to resolve grievances by restoring the injured party to the position they were in before the dispute arose. There would be less need for resolution of disputes between the individual and society, and more for those between individuals.

Durkheim's analysis has been criticised for overestimating the extent to which criminal law would decline and give way to compensatory law in an industrialised society: if anything, industrialised societies have increased the application of criminal law and, indeed, industrialisation has created new crimes, such as corporate manslaughter and pollution. Anthropological studies have shown that he also underestimated the degree to which compensatory or civil law already exists in simple societies.

27.6.2 Survival

Professor Hart argues that the main function of law is simply to allow human beings to survive in a community. He suggests that there are certain truths about human existence which, without rules guiding our behaviour, would make life excessively dangerous. Each member of society has, more or less, the same physical strength and intelligence, and both our powers of self-restraint and willingness to help others are limited. We therefore all face the danger of attack from the others and competition for such resources as are available. Knowing this, any group of humans will soon recognise that it needs rules curbing individual desires and impulses. We realise that, if we attack people or take their goods when they are weak, the same could easily happen to us. To protect ourselves we must accept limitations on our behaviour. The alternative would be a degree of conflict that would make it impossible for the group to stay together, yet individual members might be even less safe if they had to face the world alone.

The realisation that we are not safe in the world alone and can only be safe in a community if there are rules of self-restraint, leads to the development of such rules, protecting the property and person of others. It also leads to acceptance of the idea that observance of the rules must be guaranteed by some kind of penalty directed against the rule-breaker. Hart maintains that such rules are the minimum necessary content of law in any society.

27.6.3 The maintenance of order

The German sociologist Max Weber (1979) argues that the primary role of law is to maintain order in society. Law makes individuals accept the legitimacy of their rules, and gives them the power to make law and coerce individuals into obeying it. Without this coercive power, argues Weber, order could not be maintained.

This idea has enjoyed much political support as political parties, from either side of the spectrum, are keen to present themselves as promoting law and order. But Weber's view can be criticised as overestimating the role of law in keeping order. If he is to be believed, a relaxation of law would result in the immediate degeneration of society into chaos and disorder; but this ignores the many other factors which make our society relatively orderly. In many cases we obey the law not because it is the law, but because of social or moral pressures – we do not steal, for example, because we have been brought up to think stealing is wrong, not because we might be caught and punished for it. Similarly, we may obey moral or social rules as strictly as we obey legal ones – we are unlikely to find ourselves in court for swearing at the vicar, but few of us would do it because of strong social and moral pressures.

Critics argue that Weber's theory fails to allow for the fact that societies are not just a loose group of independent individuals; they have clear patterns of behaviour, relationships and beliefs, which differ from society to society. These are what hold society together and, while law is one aspect of them, it is not the only force for social cohesion. Other social institutions which promote cohesion include the family and schools, which transmit social standards to new generations; political institutions (such as Parliament and political parties); economic and commercial institutions (such as trade unions, manufacturers' associations, patterns of production and trade); and religious and cultural institutions (such as literature and the arts, the press, television and radio). All of these play a part in establishing social rules.

The importance of these social rules can be seen if we compare a human society to a group of animals. Like animals, we have instincts to eat, sleep and mate. But whereas animals do all these things in response only to instinct and opportunity, our behaviour is controlled, directly and indirectly, through moral standards, religious doctrines, social traditions and legal rules. For example, like animals we are born with a mating instinct but, unlike animals, human societies attempt to channel this instinct into a form of relationship which has traditionally been seen as offering benefits for society: heterosexual marriage. As we have said, there are no legal rules commanding people to marry, but there are a great many social and moral pressures upholding heterosexual marriage as the desired form of relationship; the predominant religion in our history upholds it, and alternatives, such as homosexual relationships or heterosexual couples living together without marriage, have traditionally been seen as immoral and socially unacceptable. It can be argued that these pressures have, in the past, operated just as forcefully as laws do in other areas, though they now appear to be breaking down.

27.6.4 Balancing different interests

The US jurist Roscoe Pound (1968) saw law as a social institution, created and designed to satisfy human wants, both individual and social. Pound identified different interests in society, including individual, domestic, property, social and public interests. He argued that the law's main aim was to secure and balance these different and often competing interests.

Where interests on a different level conflicted – such as individual interests conflicting with social interests – they could not be weighed against each other, but where there is a conflict between interests on the same level, they must be weighed against one another with the aim of ensuring that as many as possible are satisfied.

27.6.5 'Law jobs'

Karl Llewellyn (1962) was a member of the US realist school of thought which, like the positivists, is concerned with what law is, rather than what it ought to be. Working with Hoebel, an anthropologist, Llewellyn studied Native American groups and, from this research, constructed a theory of 'law jobs' to explain the social functions of law.

Llewellyn's theory is that every social group has certain jobs which need to be done for it to survive, and law is one of the main ways in which these jobs are done. The jobs include preventing disruptive disputes within the group; providing a means of resolving disputes which do arise; allocating authority and providing mechanisms for constructing relationships between people, including ways of adjusting to change. Although these jobs are common to all societies, the ways in which the jobs are done will vary from society to society. For example, the allocation of authority in a simple society might be done by basic rules on electing or appointing a chief while, in a more complex society, this job can be done by a constitution.

Robert Summers (1992) also looked at law in terms of the various jobs it does for society, and identified five main uses of law: putting right grievances among members of a society; prohibiting and prosecuting forbidden behaviour; promoting certain defined activities; conferring social and governmental benefits, including education and welfare; and giving effect to private arrangements, such as contracts. Although their theses are different, both Llewellyn and Summers look at law in its social context, in contrast to writers such as Austin who believe rules, including legal rules, can be analysed without reference to their settings.

27.6.6 Exploitation

A radical alternative to the views of writers such as Durkheim and Weber is put forward by Karl Marx (1933). Durkheim and Weber disagreed about the precise functions of law, but they accepted the idea that law must in some way be of benefit to society as a whole. Marx, however, rejected the idea that there was a common interest in society which law could serve. He argued that society was composed of classes whose interests were fundamentally opposed to each other. Law, Marx maintained, was not made in the interests of society as a whole, but in the interests of the small group which dominates society; through law (and other social institutions, such as religion), this group is able to exploit the working class, which Marx called the proletariat.

Later Marxist writers, such as Althusser and Gramsci, have developed this thesis. They argue that the ruling class controls the ideology of society, including the beliefs and ideas which shape it. This ideology is expressed through social institutions such as the school, the family, religion and the law. By shaping the way in which people see the world around them, the ruling class is able to ensure that the working class see their exploitation as natural, as the only way things could be, rather than as the oppressive state of affairs that Marxists see. This minimises their resistance.

Law is seen as an important part of this process. Because, for example, the law protects private property, we come to view private property and all its implications as natural and inevitable. Take, for example, the acceptance of profit. If someone pays £100 for a set of raw materials, and pays an employee £100 to turn those materials into goods which they then sell for £600, it is quite acceptable in our society for the employer to keep the profit, because they purchased both the raw materials and the employee's labour. Clearly, an acceptance of people making a profit out of another's labour is fundamental to acceptance of the capitalist system as a whole, and the legal doctrine of private property is the basis of this acceptance. But Marxists point out that the situation can be looked at in another way, as the employer stealing from the worker the added value their labour gives to the raw materials. The fact that we would not usually think to see it this way is, Marxists say, because we see it through a capitalist ideology, and law plays a fundamental role in upholding this ideology.

Marx believed that law was only needed because of the fundamental clash of interests between those of the ruling class and those of the proletariat; once society was transformed by communism, these divisions would no longer exist, and law would wither away.

27.7 Why are laws obeyed?

Austin thought laws were obeyed because of the threat of sanction and out of a habit of obedience to the state. Hart rejects this explanation, arguing that acceptance of a rule is more important than possible sanctions. As well as the external aspect of obedience – recognition of the validity of the rule, and a potential sanction – Hart argues that there is an internal process, which inclines us to obey because we consider it right and proper to do so. Hart suggests that if a law is not internalised, an individual will feel no obligation to obey it. In our system there are many examples of laws which for some reason widely fail this internalisation test: parking offences, speeding, use of mobile phones whilst driving, tax evasion and drug legislation are obvious examples of laws which large numbers of people apparently feel no real compulsion to follow. He suggests that in order for law to promote social cohesion in a simple society with only primary rules, members must not only obey those rules, but also consciously see them as common standards of behaviour, breaches of which can legitimately be criticised: in other words, they internalise all the rules, following them not just because they are rules, but because they consider it right to do so. But, in a more developed legal system like ours, Hart believes individuals need not internalise every rule. It is clearly desirable for them to internalise as many as possible, but, failing this, the necessary functions can be served by officials internalising the rules and, thereby, becoming committed to their maintenance.

27.7.1 Fear and internalisation

If we obey laws because we internalise them, what makes us internalise some rules and not others? One theory, put forward by Professor Karl Olivecrona (1971), suggests that fear is a strong motivation. He points out that we are all aware from childhood of the consequences of breaking rules and, as a result, we experience a tension between temptation to break rules and fear of punishment. Olivecrona suggests that the human mind cannot accommodate such tension indefinitely, and so we gradually adjust psychologically to accept conformity to rules as a means of getting rid of the fear of punishment; eventually we do not believe we are acting out of fear at all, we have just become used to keeping the rules.

Perhaps because of the efficacy of this process, many writers have suggested that law can be used to shape moral and social ideas. Aristotle suggested that law could be used to educate citizens, commenting that: 'Legislators make citizens good by forming their habits.' On the other hand, social pressures can often bring about changes in conduct which legal rules have been unable to do. A recent example is that of drink-driving. At one time this offence was seen as being in a similar category to speeding or parking offences; it was against the law, but many still saw it as acceptable. Now, as a result of social pressures, partly driven by public information campaigns, it is viewed as highly anti-social behaviour, and the law is apparently more widely obeyed.

Answering questions

1   '. . . a law is a type of rule, but clearly there are many rules which are not law.' Discuss.

2   Is it possible to live in a society without law?

For answers to these questions, see the companion website at www.pearsoned.co.uk/ elliottquinn

SUMMARY OF CHAPTER 27: LAW AND RULES

One way to understand more about what law is, is to look at what distinguishes legal rules from other types of rules.

Austin: the command theory

The nineteenth-century writer John Austin argued that law differed from other rules because it was the command of a sovereign body, which the state could enforce by means of punishment.

Hart: primary and secondary rules

Professor Hart divided legal rules into primary rules and secondary rules, and argued that the existence of secondary rules was a mark of a developed legal system. Primary rules were described as those which any society needs in order to survive. Secondary rules confer power rather than impose duties, and can be divided into three types:

● rules of adjudication;

● rules of change; and

● rules of recognition.

Dworkin: legal principles

Professor Dworkin argues that the rich fabric of law contains a set of principles on which all legal rules are based. Legal principles are guidelines, giving a reason that argues in one direction, but does not dictate a decision.

The natural law theory

The natural law theory defines law by its content: only laws which conform to a particular moral code, seen as a higher form of law, can genuinely be called law.

The function of law

Some writers have taken the view that law is best understood by looking at the role it plays in society.

Social cohesion

The nineteenth-century French sociologist Emile Durkheim looked at the issue of social cohesion, searching for what keeps a society together, and concluded that law played an important role in this area.

Survival

Professor Hart argues that the main function of law is simply to allow human beings to survive in a community.

The maintenance of order

The German sociologist Max Weber argued that the primary role of law is to maintain order in society.

Balancing different interests

The US jurist Roscoe Pound saw law as a social institution, created and designed to satisfy human wants, both individual and social.

'Law jobs'

Karl Llewellyn's theory is that every social group has certain jobs which need to be done for it to survive, and law is one of the main ways in which these jobs are done.

Exploitation

Karl Marx argued that society was composed of classes whose interests were fundamentally opposed to each other. Law, Marx maintained, was not made in the interests of society as a whole, but in the interests of the small group which dominates society; through law (and other social institutions, such as religion), this group is able to exploit the working class.

Why are laws obeyed?

Austin thought laws were obeyed because of the threat of sanction and out of a habit of obedience to the state. Hart argues that there is an internal process, which inclines us to obey because we consider it right and proper to do so.

Fear and internalisation

If we obey laws because we internalise them, what makes us internalise some rules and not others? One theory, put forward by Professor Olivecrona, suggests that fear is a strong motivation.

Reading list

Austin, J. (1954) *The Province of Jurisprudence Determined*. London: Weidenfeld & Nicolson.

Dworkin, R. (1977) *Taking Rights Seriously,* London: Duckworth.

      (1986) *Law's Empire*. London: Fontana.

Hart, H.L.A. (1963) *Law, Liberty and Morality*. Oxford: Oxford University Press.

      (1994) *The Concept of Law*. Oxford: Clarendon.

Llewellyn, K. (1962) *Jurisprudence: Realism in Theory and Practice*. Chicago: University of Chicago Press.

Lukes, S. and Scull, A. (eds) (1983) *Durkheim and the Law*. Oxford: Robertson.

Marx, K. (1933) *Capital*. London: J.M. Dent.

Olivecrona, K. (1971) *Law as Fact*. London: Stevens.

Pound, R. (1968) *Social Control Through Law*. Hamden: Archon Books.

Summers, R. (1992) *Essays on the Nature of Law and Legal Reasoning*. Berlin: Duncker & Humblot.

Twining, W. and Miers, D. (1991) *How To Do Things With Rules*. London: Weidenfeld & Nicolson.

Weber, M. (1979) *Economy and Society*. Berkeley: University of California Press.

27

LAW AND RULES

Chapter 28
Law and morals

This chapter discusses:

- the relationship between law and morality;

- the evolution of law and morality;

- differences between law and morality;

- whether law and morality should be separate; and

- the impact of morality on law as seen through the work of the Human Fertilisation and Embryology Authority.

28.1 Introduction

Morals are beliefs and values which are shared by a society, or a section of a society; they tell those who share them what is right or wrong. In our society, moral values have been heavily influenced by the dominant religion, Christianity, though this is not our only source of moral values.

Debates about morals and morality often centre around sexual issues, such as sex outside marriage, homosexuality and pornography. The passing of the Marriage (Same Sex Couples) Act 2013, which legalised gay marriages, was the subject of considerable public discussion. But moral values also shape attitudes towards money and property, gender roles, friendship, behaviour at work – in fact it is difficult to think of any area of our lives where morality has no application. Mary Warnock (1986), an academic who has been involved in inquiries into issues of moral concern, says: 'I do not believe that there is a neat way of marking off moral issues from all others; some people, at some time, may regard things as matters of moral right or wrong, which at another time or in another place are thought to be matters of taste, or indeed to be matters of no importance at all.' However, she points out that in any society, at any time, questions relating to birth and death and to the establishing of families are regarded as morally significant. These can perhaps be regarded as core moral issues.

As Warnock has observed, moral attitudes tend to change over time. It is only within recent decades, for example, that the idea of couples living together without marriage has become widely accepted; even now acceptance is not total, but a generation or so ago it would have been unthinkable. Similar shifts have taken place with regard to homosexuality and women's liberation.

The French sociologist Durkheim (see Lukes and Scull, 1983) has highlighted the fact that in a modern, developed society it is difficult to pinpoint a set of moral values shared by all. In less developed societies, such as small tribal groups, Durkheim argued that all the members of the group are likely to share a moral code; but, in a technologically advanced society such as our own, where individuals differ widely in social status, income, occupation, ethnic background and so on, its members are unlikely to share identical moral values, even if they largely agree on some basic points. For example, most people in the UK agree that it is usually wrong to kill or steal, but there is much less consensus on whether it is wrong to take drugs, have abortions, experiment on animals or help a terminally ill person to die. Even on the basic crimes of theft and murder, some people will see these as always wrong, while others will believe there are situations in which they may be justified; among the latter, there will be disagreement as to what those situations are.

Criminologist Jock Young (1971) has pointed out that much depends on the standpoint of the observer, and how they see the norms of society. Looking at attitudes to illegal drug use, Young has observed that to those who see society's rules as based on a moral consensus, drug-taking was against that moral consensus, so those who indulged in it were therefore maladjusted and sick. But, if society's rules on deviant behaviour are seen simply as a yardstick of what that particular society considers normal, drug-taking is neither necessarily deviant nor necessarily a social problem: it is merely deviant to groups who condemn it and a problem to those who wish to eliminate it. What is being made is simply a value judgement, and values vary between people and over time.

28.2 Law and morality

Both law and morals are normative; they specify what ought to be done, and aim to mark the boundaries between acceptable and unacceptable conduct. While moral rules tend not to be backed by the obvious sanctions which make some legal rules enforceable, they are often reinforced by pressures which in some cases may be as strong, if not stronger: the disapproval of family and friends, loss of status and being shunned by the community are powerful disincentives against immoral conduct. Of course, many types of undesirable behaviour offend against both moral and legal rules – serious crimes are obvious examples.

Both law and morals are often presented as if they were the only possible responses to social or political problems and crises, yet both vary widely between societies. For example, in our society, private property is such a basic doctrine that we readily condemn any infringement of our rights – legal and moral – to acquire, possess and enjoy our personal property. Stealing is seen as immoral as well as illegal. But in a society where property is held communally, any attempt by one individual to treat property as their own private possession would be regarded as every bit as immoral as we would consider stealing. The idea of private property is not a basic part of human nature, as it is often presented, but a socially constructed value. Our society has for centuries been based on trade, and this requires a basis of private property.

Some areas of law are explicitly presented as raising moral issues and, when these areas arise in Parliament, MPs are allowed to vote according to their own beliefs, rather than according to party policy. This is called a vote of conscience and was used, for example, when the issue of capital punishment was debated. However, the kinds of issue on which a vote of conscience would be allowed are not the only ones to which moral values apply: when MPs vote on tax changes, the welfare state, employment or any number of issues before Parliament in every session, they are voting on moral issues, because they are voting on the way a Government treats its citizens, and the way in which citizens are allowed to treat each other.

Similarly, some areas of law, such as criminal law, have obvious moral implications, but these are also present in areas where morality is less obvious. Tort law, for example, and especially negligence, is built around the principle that those who harm others should compensate for the damage done; that, as Lord Atkin noted in the famous case of *Donoghue* v *Stevenson* (1932), the biblical principle of 'love thy neighbour' must include 'do not harm your neighbour'. Similarly, contract, as Atiyah (1979) has pointed out, is based around the principle that promises should be kept. Even land law which, on the surface, appears to consist of technicalities far removed from elevated questions of morality, has enormous moral importance because it is upholding the whole notion of property and ownership. Take the question of squatting: the property owner has all the rights to begin with but, if the squatting continues for long enough, the squatter can gain some rights. Is it moral that the property owner should lose rights to someone acting illegally? On the other hand, is it moral that some should be homeless while others have property they can afford to leave empty?

In *Re A (Children) (Conjoined Twins: Surgical Separation)* (2000), the Court of Appeal expressly stated that it was 'not a court of morals but a court of law and our decisions have to be taken from a solid base of legal principle'. But, in reality, law and morals were closely interlinked in that case. It concerned the legality of an operation to separate conjoined twins. The operation would inevitably lead to the death of the weaker twin, but was the sole chance of saving the life of the stronger twin. The judgment of the court is based on the principle of the sanctity of life, which itself is a moral commitment.

28.3 Changes in law and morality

As we have observed, the moral values of a society tend to change over time; the same applies to its laws. In the UK, legal changes have tended to lag behind moral ones, coming only when the process of moral acceptance is well advanced. Thus, the law was changed in 1991 to make rape within marriage a crime, the House of Lords stating that the change was necessary because marriages were now seen as equal partnerships, in which the husband could no longer enforce rights to sex. This shift in attitude had taken place long before 1991, but the time-lag between moral change and legal change was fairly typical. Often it is the possession of effective political power which finally determines which and whose definition of morality is reflected in the law.

On the other hand, law can sometimes bring about changes in social morality. Troy Duster, in *The Legislation of Morality* (1970), traced the history of drug use and its legal control in the US from the end of the nineteenth century. At that time, drug addiction was commonly restricted to the middle and upper classes, who had become dependent on morphine through the use of patented medicines; despite the fact that these contained morphine, it was perfectly legal to buy and sell them. Addiction carried no social stigma. However, when certain drugs were made illegal under the Harrison Act 1914, such drugs began to be supplied by the criminal underworld. Dependency on drugs became associated with this underworld and with the lower classes who had most contact with it. This in turn led to social stigma. Interestingly, this stigma, which was in a sense created by legal controls, was partly responsible for the calls for greater legal controls on drug-taking which have been heard over the last two decades, as more and more young people become involved in the drug culture.

Academics from the Scandinavian realist standpoint, such as Olivecrona (1971), argue that our morality is created by the law, rather than the law emerging from our morality. Olivecrona suggests that law has an influence on us from our earliest days, helping to mould our moral views. From the start, parents and teachers tell us what we must and must not do and we quickly learn the consequences of disobedience.

28.4 Differences between law and morality

Although law and morality are clearly closely linked, there are certain ways in which they differ. Many types of behaviour exist which may be widely considered to be immoral, yet we would be very surprised to find laws against them: telling lies, for example. Equally, some forms of behaviour are illegal, but would not usually be described as immoral, such as parking on a yellow line. Then there are areas where the law shares morality's disapproval, but not so far as to prohibit the relevant behaviour. Adultery, for example, is not illegal in this country, but it has long constituted grounds for a divorce, an important legal step for individuals.

Key case

The problem for the law in deciding whether to respond to appeals to morality is that there are very often conflicting moral views in a given situation. We can see this in the case of *Gillick v West Norfolk and Wisbech Area Health Authority* (1985). The claimant, Mrs Victoria Gillick, was a Roman Catholic. She objected to guidance given to doctors from the Department of Health and Social Security that, in exceptional cases, they could offer contraceptive advice and treatment to girls under 16, without parental consent. Mrs Gillick sought a declaration that these guidelines were illegal because they encouraged under-age sex.

Mrs Gillick lost at first instance, won in the Court of Appeal and lost by a majority in the House of Lords. The House held that the guidelines were lawful because they concerned what were essentially medical matters. In this field, girls under 16 had the legal capacity to consent to a medical examination and treatment, including contraceptive treatment, as long as they were sufficiently mature and intelligent to understand the nature and implications of the proposed treatment. The majority, in reaching this conclusion, stressed they were merely applying the law as it stood rather than taking a moral standpoint; the minority referred to the kind of moral arguments Mrs Gillick had advanced. This does not mean that, in rejecting Mrs Gillick's view, the majority ignored morality, even though they claimed to be making an objective decision. It could be argued that if teenage girls were likely to have sexual intercourse anyway, preventing doctors from giving contraceptive help would simply increase the chances of unwanted pregnancies and it would, therefore, be moral to protect girls from that. Neither approach is objectively wrong or right; in this, as in many areas, there are opposing moral views.

Legal principle

Children have the legal capacity to consent to medical treatment if they are sufficiently mature and intelligent to understand the nature and implications of the proposed treatment.

28

LAW AND MORALS

28.5 Should law and morality be separate?

The view taken by Mrs Gillick would seem to suggest that if something is immoral it should also be illegal and, to the person who holds strong moral opinions, this may seem a natural conclusion. But there are problems with it. First, moral opinions, however strongly held, are just that: moral opinions. Mrs Gillick believes under-age girls should not be given contraception and many people agree with her, but many others disagree. Which group's moral opinions should be adopted by the law?

Even if there were complete consensus, the logistics of enforcing as legal rules all the moral rules of our society would present enormous problems. How would we pay for the necessary manpower, both for policing and prosecutions? What sanctions would be severe enough to compel obedience, yet not too severe for the nature of the offences? Making every immoral act also illegal seems both impossible and undesirable, yet law with no connection to morality might find it difficult to command much respect. There is still much debate as to how far law should reflect morality; the following are some of the key suggestions.

28.5.1 Natural law

Natural law theorists argue that law should strongly reflect morality. Though their specific theories differ, their shared premise is that there is a kind of higher law, known as the natural law, to which we can turn for a basic moral code: some, such as St Thomas Aquinas, see this higher law as coming from God, others see it as simply the foundations of a human society. The principles in this higher law should be reflected in the laws societies make for themselves; laws which do not reflect these principles cannot really be called law at all, and in some cases need not be obeyed. The campaign, during the 1980s, against payment of the Poll Tax on the grounds that it was unfair might be seen as an example of this kind of disobedience.

Different natural law theorists disagree as to the actual content of natural law, but it is usually felt to embody basic human rights which governments should respect. Bills of Rights, like that in the US Constitution, could be seen as embodying natural law principles. Professor Fuller, in *The Morality of Law* (1969), talked about law's inner morality which he formulated in terms of eight procedural requirements of a legal system:

1   Generality: there should be rules, not *ad hoc* judgments.
2   Promulgation: the rules should be made known to all those affected by them.
3   Non-retroactivity: rules should not have retrospective effect.
4   Clarity: rules should be understandable.
5   Consistency: rules should not conflict.
6   Realism: people should not be required to do the impossible.
7   Constancy: rules should not be changed so frequently that people cannot use them to guide their behaviour.
8   Congruence: the actual administration of the rules should coincide with the information available to the public about them.

Fuller claims that a legal system which fails in any one of these areas is not just a bad system, it is not a legal system at all. As an example, he gives the legal system of Nazi Germany: although laws were made by recognised methods, in Fuller's view the system's failure to meet the above criteria meant that those laws were not really law at all.

28.5.2 Utilitarianism

During the nineteenth century, the rise of science and the beginning of the decline in the social importance of religion meant that natural law theories declined. In their place the theory of utilitarianism grew up, apparently offering a rational and scientific theory of law. One of the best-known exponents of this theory is John Stuart Mill (1859). He argued that rather than society imposing morality on individuals, individuals should be free to choose their own conduct, so long as in doing so they did not harm others or, if they did, that the harm done did not outweigh the harm which would be done by interfering with individual liberty.

The view that people should be left alone to do what they like so long as they do not harm others remains influential today, but it is open to criticism. First, the fact that someone's actions do not cause another direct and physical harm, in the way Mill envisaged, does not necessarily mean they do no harm at all. For example, opponents of pornography claim that while looking at pornography may not directly inspire individual users to rape, the fact that pornography is available and, to a degree, accepted, promotes the view that women are sexual objects which, in turn, promotes sexual violence against women.

Secondly, who counts as 'another'? This issue is clearly at the heart of debates over abortion and experimentation on embryos: does harming an unborn child count as harming another person, and from what point? The fact that abortion is legal up until a certain stage in pregnancy suggests that the law sees this as the moment at which the foetus becomes another: many people believe that point is reached earlier in pregnancy, and those opposed to abortion believe it is at the time of conception. On the other hand, many people who support the law on abortion nevertheless disapprove of experiments on embryos, even though their views of abortion might suggest that the embryo is not another at this point.

28.5.3 Crimes without victims

Modern theories which subscribe, at least partly, to Mill's view of individual liberty have tended to focus on what are often called victimless crimes. Using the examples of drug use, homosexuality and abortion, all of which were illegal at the time in which he was writing, in *Crimes without Victims* (1965) the academic Schur observes that the common characteristics of such crimes are that they involve no harm to anyone except the participants; they occur through the willing participation of those involved; and, as a result, there is no victim to make a complaint, rendering the law difficult to enforce. Schur argues that there is a social demand for these activities, which continues to be met despite illegality, through such means as back street abortions and black market drug supply. There is no proof that prohibition of such activities brought greater social benefits than decriminalisation, therefore there is no good reason to prohibit them.

As with John Stuart Mill, the main criticism of Schur's theory is his assertion that these activities harm no one who has not willingly taken part in them. Anti-abortionists would certainly dispute this as far as abortion is concerned. A further criticism is directed at the suggestion that participants join in these activities of their own free will; in the case of drug-taking, for example, that may be so at first, but can we really say that, once addicted, drug users take drugs of their own free will?

28.5.4 The Hart–Devlin debate

The issue of whether or not law should follow morality was hotly debated during the late 1950s, when there was public concern about what was perceived to be a decline in sexual morality. The Government of the day set up a commission to look at whether the laws on homosexuality and prostitution should be changed, and much debate was triggered by publication of the commission's findings, known as the Wolfenden Report (1957). Central to this debate were the writings of the leading judge, Lord Devlin, who opposed the report's findings, and Professor Hart who approved of them.

The Wolfenden Committee recommended that homosexuality and prostitution should be legalised, with some restrictions. Its reasoning was based on the notion that some areas of behaviour had to be left to individual morality, rather than being supervised by the law. The purpose of the criminal law, said the report, was:

> to preserve public order and decency, to protect the citizen from what is offensive and injurious and to provide sufficient safeguards against exploitation and corruption of others especially the vulnerable, that is the young, weak in body or mind, inexperienced or those in a state of physical, official or economic dependence. The law should not intervene in the private lives of citizens or seek to enforce any particular pattern of behaviour further than necessary to carry out the above purposes.

The reasoning is very like that of Mill: leave people to make their own choices, so long as they do not harm others. The Committee therefore recommended that prostitution itself should not be an offence, since the individual ought to be allowed to choose whether to take part in it, but activities associated with prostitution which could cause offence to others (such as soliciting in the street) were still to be regulated by the law.

Lord Devlin was opposed to this approach. He argued that some form of common morality, with basic agreement on good and evil, was necessary to keep society together. This being the case, the law had every right – and in fact a duty – to uphold that common morality.

He compared contravention of public morality to treason, in the sense that it was something society had to protect itself against. How are we to know what this public morality consists of? Devlin argued that we can judge immorality by the standard of the right-minded person, who could perhaps be thought of as the person in the jury box. Opinions should be reached after informed and educated discussion of all relevant points of view and, if there is still debate, the majority view should prevail, as it does in the ordinary legislative process.

In addition, said Devlin, there was a set of basic principles which should be followed by the legislature. First, individuals should be allowed the maximum of freedom consistent with the integrity of society, and privacy should be respected as much as possible. Secondly, punishment should be reserved for that which creates disgust among right-minded people, and society has the right to eradicate any practice which is so abominable that its very presence is an offence. Law-makers should be slow to change laws which protect morality. Thirdly, the law should set down a minimum standard of morality; society's standards should be higher.

Reaction to Devlin's thesis was mixed. Those who felt the Wolfenden Report had gone too far agreed with him, and there were many of them – the commission's recommendations seem rather tame now, but at the time they were ground-breaking. Others felt that his approach was out of step with the times. Hart, who was influenced by John Stuart Mill and, therefore, approved of the commission's approach, led this opposition. Hart argued that using law to enforce moral values was unnecessary, undesirable and morally unacceptable: unnecessary because society was capable of containing many moral standpoints without disintegrating; undesirable because it would freeze morality at a particular point; and morally unacceptable because it infringes the liberty of the individual. Devlin's response was that individual liberty could only flourish in a stable society: disintegration of our society through lack of a shared morality would, therefore, threaten individual freedom.

Hart pointed out that the standard of the right-minded person is a tenuous one. When people object to unusual behaviour, the response is not always prompted by rational moral objections, but often by prejudice, ignorance or misunderstanding. He gave four basic reasons why moral censure should not necessarily lead to legal sanctions. First, punishing the offender involves doing some harm to them, when they may have done no harm to others. Secondly, the exercise of free choice by individuals is a moral value in itself, with which it is wrong to interfere. Thirdly, this exercise of free choice can be valuable in that it allows individuals to experiment and learn. Finally, as far as sexual morality is concerned, the suppression of sexual impulses affects the development or balance of the individual's emotional life, happiness and personality and, thus, causes them harm. He objects strongly to the idea that the law should punish behaviour which does not harm others, but merely causes them distress or disgust by its very existence, even when conducted out of their sight: recognition of individual liberty as a value involves, as a minimum, acceptance of the principle that individuals may do what they want, even if others are distressed when they learn what it is that they do, unless, of course, there are other good grounds for forbidding it.

Judicial support for Devlin's view – and perhaps reaction against liberalising legislation – can be seen in some of the more high-profile cases which arose in its aftermath. In **Shaw v Director of Public Prosecutions** (1961), Shaw had published a booklet entitled *The Ladies' Directory*, which contained advertisements by prostitutes, featuring photographs and descriptions of the sexual practices they offered. He was convicted of the crime of conspiring to corrupt public morals, an offence which had not been prosecuted since the eighteenth century. The House of Lords upheld the conviction and, defending the court's power to uphold the recognition of such an antiquated offence, Viscount Simonds said: 'In the sphere of criminal law I entertain no doubt that there remains in the courts of law a residual power to enforce the supreme and fundamental purpose of the law, to conserve not only the safety and order but also the moral welfare of the State.' As an example of offences against this moral welfare, Viscount Simonds said:

> Let it be supposed that at some future, perhaps early, date homosexual practices between consenting adult males are no longer a crime. Would it not be an offence if, even without obscenity, such practices were publicly advocated and encouraged by pamphlet and advertisement?

This proved to be an uncannily accurate prediction: in 1967 the Sexual Offences Act was passed, which stated that homosexual acts between consenting adult males in private were no longer a criminal offence.

In *Knuller Ltd* v *Director of Public Prosecutions* (1972), the defendants were prosecuted for having published in their magazine, *International Times,* advertisements placed by readers inviting others to contact them for homosexual purposes. Once again, the charge was conspiracy to corrupt public morals and the court convicted. Lord Reid (who had dissented from the majority decision in *Shaw*'s case, but felt that *Shaw* should still apply to avoid inconsistency) recognised that the 1967 Act legalised homosexual acts, but said:

> I find nothing in that Act to indicate that Parliament thought or intended to lay down that indulgence in these practices is not corrupting. I read the Act as saying that, even though it may be corrupting, if people choose to corrupt themselves in this way that is their affair and the law will not interfere. But no licence is given to others to encourage the practice.

More recent decisions still show judicial support for the Devlin viewpoint that some acts are intrinsically immoral, regardless of whether they harm others. In *R* v *Gibson* (1990), an artist exhibited earrings made from freeze-dried foetuses of three to four months' gestation. A conviction for the common law offence of outraging public decency was upheld. The appellants in *R* v *Brown* (1992) were homosexual men who had willingly participated in the commission of acts of sado-masochistic violence against each other, involving the use of, among other things, heated wires, stinging nettles, nails, sandpaper and safety-pins. Evidence showed that all the men involved had consented; although the activities were videotaped by the participants, this was not for any profit or gain; none of the injuries was permanent and no medical attention had been sought; the activities were carried out in private; and none of the victims had complained to the police. They were convicted of committing a range of offences against the person and appealed to the House of Lords, arguing that, since all the participants had consented and the activities took place in private, the law had no reason to intervene. Their convictions were upheld; by a majority, the House held that public policy demanded such acts be treated as criminal offences. This decision was subsequently approved by the European Court of Human Rights.

28.5.5 The Warnock Committee

Despite the debate between Devlin and Hart, their two views are not always as opposed as they may seem, and in practice both are influential: a Government commission, the Warnock Committee, incorporates features of both approaches in its reasoning. The Committee was set up by the Government of the day to consider issues relating to scientific advances concerning conception and pregnancy. With the advent of *in vitro* fertilisation (the technique used to create test-tube babies) and other technological advances, new scientific possibilities have arisen. These include the possibility of creating embryos for use in medical experiments, sperm, egg and embryo donation by fertile men or women to those who are infertile, and the use of surrogate mothers – women who bear a child for another couple, using their own egg and the father's sperm. These practices raised a number of moral issues, including that of payment for surrogacy, and the parentage of children born from donated eggs and sperm.

The Committee's report, published in 1984, advised the setting up of an independent statutory body to monitor, regulate and license infertility services and embryo experiments. On the specific issues before them, they recommended that experiments on embryos up to 14 days old should be lawful; and that sperm, egg and embryo donation should be facilitated in that the babies born could be registered as the legitimate children of the non-contributing parent(s) on the birth certificate, and donors should be relieved of parental rights and duties in law. But surrogacy arrangements met with disapproval by the majority, who recommended that surrogacy agencies should be criminally prohibited, and private surrogacy arrangements between individuals should be illegal and unenforceable in the courts – although no criminal sanction would be imposed as it would be against the child's interests to be born into a family threatened by imprisonment. Many of the Committee's conclusions became law in the Human Fertilisation and Embryology Act 1990.

If we look at the reasoning behind the Committee's findings, we can see aspects of both Hart's utilitarian approach, and Devlin's upholding of common morality. In its conclusions on embryo research, it points out:

> We do not want to see a situation in which human embryos are frivolously or unnecessarily used in research but we are bound to take account of the fact that the advances in the treatment of infertility, which we have discussed in the earlier part of this report, could not have taken place without such research; and that continued research is essential, if advances in treatment and medical knowledge are to continue. A majority of us therefore agreed that research on human embryos should continue.

But this utilitarian approach is balanced against issues of morality.

> A strict utilitarian would suppose that, given procedures, it would be possible to calculate their benefits and their costs. Future advantages, therapeutic or scientific, should be weighed against present and future harm. However, even if such a calculation were possible, it could not provide a final or verifiable answer to the question whether it is right that such procedures should be carried out. There would still remain the possibility that they were unacceptable, whatever their long-term benefits were supposed to be. Moral questions, such as those with which we have been concerned are, by definition, questions that involve not only a calculation of consequences, but also strong sentiments with regard to the nature of the proposed activities themselves.

As the report shows, issues of law and morality cannot easily be separated into distinct theoretical approaches like those of Hart and Devlin; legislators in practice have to tread an uneasy path between the two.

The Bigger Picture: Infertility treatment

Modern science has made major developments in helping women who in the past would have been unable to have children, but these developments have themselves given rise to fundamental moral dilemmas. A case that caused some controversy is that of *R v Human Fertilisation and Embryology Authority, ex parte Blood* (1997). The husband of Diane Blood contracted meningitis and lapsed into a coma. Diane Blood asked for samples of his sperm to be collected for future use in artificial insemination. The samples were entrusted to a research trust for storage. The husband died and the Human Fertilisation and Embryology Authority prevented the research trust from releasing the samples from storage, on the ground that the written consent of the donor to the taking of his sperm had not been obtained as required by the relevant statute. The applicant sought judicial review of the Authority's decision. The Court of Appeal ruled that the applicant could have the sperm samples and undergo treatment for an artificially assisted pregnancy, provided she went abroad for the fertility treatment. The Authority's decision had been lawful under the terms of the statute but the circumstances were exceptional and had not been foreseen by Parliament when passing the regulatory legislation. Judicial discretion was sufficiently flexible to grant the remedy which the compassionate circumstances demanded, particularly as the legal situation had never before been explored.

In *Evans* v *Amicus Healthcare Ltd* (2004) Natalie Evans and her partner had no children and attended a fertility clinic for IVF treatment. During the course of treatment, it was discovered that Natalie had cancer in both her ovaries. Before her ovaries were removed, Natalie had some of her eggs fertilised with her partner's sperm and the resulting six embryos frozen. She and her partner had been engaged to be married, but they later split up and her partner wrote to the clinic stating that the embryos should now be destroyed. Natalie went to court to try to stop the embryos being destroyed as they were her only chance of having her own biological child. The Court of Appeal rejected her application. While it accepted that the destruction of the embryos was an interference with Natalie's private life under Art. 8 of the European Convention, it considered that this interference was necessary to respect the rights of her former partner. This seems quite a tough decision, as her former partner was able to have children with a future partner, but Natalie would not be able to, so perhaps the interference with her ex-partner's rights should have been justified to prevent the much greater interference with Natalie's rights.

Natalie took her case to the European Court of Human Rights, but again the European Court held there had not been any breach of the European Convention and rejected her application (*Evans* v *United Kingdom* (2007)).

28.5.6 The Human Fertilisation and Embryology Authority

The Human Fertilisation and Embryology Authority (HFEA) was set up in 1990. Areas of debate on morality and the need for law to prevent immorality have centred in recent years around scientific developments that the HFEA has to regulate. In the field of human genetics it is difficult for the law to keep up with the changes in scientific knowledge and the moral dilemmas to which these can give rise. The birth of Dolly, the cloned sheep, caused particular concern when it was announced in 1997. In January 1998 the Human Genetics Advisory Commission and the HFEA jointly published a consultation paper inviting views on various issues raised by cloning technology. The most troubling questions focused on the legality, ethics and practical consequences of human and reproductive cloning. The Authority's policy at the moment is not to license any research having reproductive cloning as its aim. The Human Reproductive Cloning Act 2001 was passed confirming this position.

The Human Genetics Advisory Commission has now recommended that controlled research using embryos (which are eggs that have been fertilised) should be allowed in order to increase understanding about human disease and disorders, and their treatment. It has recommended that reproductive cloning of human beings should remain a criminal offence. The Government has accepted these recommendations.

Another area of scientific activity that raises difficult moral questions concerns research which mixes human and animal tissue. This can take various forms:

- cybrids (where the nucleus of an animal egg is replaced with that from a human cell) – the resulting inter-species embryo is 99.9 per cent human;
- human transgenic embryos where a human embryo is altered by the introduction of animal genetic material;
- human–animal chimeras where a human embryo has been altered by the introduction of animal cells – chimeras can be made by fertilising an animal egg with human sperm.

There is public anxiety about such scientific developments, as these experiments evoke images of mad scientists creating half human/half animal monsters, such as the Minotaur – a half human/half bull monster from Greek mythology. There is also concern that these experiments fail to respect the moral status of human beings, including human embryos. HFEA has approved the creation of cybrids for research purposes by scientists at London University and the University of Newcastle. The creation of a cybrid involves the same cloning procedure that was used to create Dolly the sheep, but, instead of using cells from two animals of the same species, cells are used from two different species. The eggs are likely to come from farmyard animals, such as cows and sheep, since thousands of these animals are killed each day to be eaten. A key reason for using these eggs is simply that they are more easily available than human eggs. Two hundred and seventy sheep eggs were needed before the successful creation of Dolly the sheep.

Cybrid embryos will enable scientists to create cells useful for research into genetic diseases. It is hoped that this research could enable scientists in the future to grow tissues or organs that could replace damaged parts of the body of people suffering from such illnesses as spinal muscular atrophy, Alzheimer's disease or motor neurone disease. The recipient's immune system would not reject these transplants because they would be tissue compatible with the patient's body.

Another contentious issue is how far parents should be allowed to have 'designer babies' to provide living tissue to help cure a sibling. A high-profile case on this subject was that of *R (on the application of Quintavalle)* v *Human Fertilisation and Embryology Authority* (2005). The case concerned a young boy, Zain Hashmi, who had been born with a rare blood disorder. He would have died if he had not received stem cells from a compatible donor. These stem cells were taken from the umbilical cord of his healthy sibling, who had been conceived for this purpose. HFEA had licensed the procedure by which a genetically compatible embryo was selected for implantation in the body of the boy's mother. A pro-life campaigning organisation, Comment on Reproductive Ethics (CORE), had challenged the legality of HFEA's conduct, arguing that the procedure was opening the door to parents selecting 'designer babies' according to such criteria as sex, hair and eye colour. CORE's action succeeded in the High Court but the mother's appeal was successful before the Court of Appeal and the House of Lords. The House gave a purposive interpretation to the legislation containing HFEA's powers rather than a narrow literal reading, and thereby found that the Authority had the power to issue the licence. Zain Hashmi's life was saved both by the Law Lords and his 'saviour sibling', but CORE felt the medical procedure had been immoral.

In 2005, the House of Commons Science and Technology Select Committee published a review of the Human Fertilisation and Embryology Act 1990. The Department of Health issued a White Paper on the subject in 2006 and the Human Fertilisation and Embryology Act was passed in 2008. This Act replaces the provisions in the 1990 Act, updates and rationalises the law in this field to reflect developments in research and recent case law, and enshrines in the law some of the practices already adopted by HFEA and fertility clinics. It seeks to support medical research while respecting the dignity of human life and modern ethical values.

The Act extends the statutory storage period for embryos from five to ten years. If consent to storage and use of an embryo is withdrawn by one party, storage of the embryo will remain lawful for 12 months. This allows the parties time potentially to reach an agreement about the fate of the embryo after a relationship has broken down. Unfortunately, this will not resolve the type of problem that arose in the case of Natalie Evans where the parties were never able to reach an agreement. Sex-selection of an embryo for non-medical reasons is prohibited but is allowed in order to screen for gender specific diseases. The Act includes a 'saviour sibling' provision permitting the testing of embryos to establish whether the tissue from a child resulting from that embryo would be compatible for treating an existing sibling suffering from a serious medical condition.

The Act allows the creation of all three types of inter-species embryos: cybrids, human transgenic embryos and chimeras. They can be kept for a maximum of 14 days from the date of their creation. It is felt that this is both desirable and necessary for advanced medical research. A licence is necessary to carry out this type of research. Originally the Labour Government had planned to ban such activities but it was persuaded that the medical benefits outweighed any moral dilemma.

Other reforms in the Act aim to reflect changes in moral and social values. For instance, while the welfare of the child must be taken into account in cases of fertility treatment, the Act removes the reference to 'the need for a father' as a factor to be considered. Both partners in same-sex couples can be regarded as legal parents with parental responsibility, while in the past only the woman giving birth was regarded as the legal parent. The Act also introduces a new 'right to know' for children born as a result of fertility treatment who, on reaching majority, can apply for certain details of their biological origins.

Answering questions

1   Does morality play an important role in the development of the law?

2   Is civil disobedience ever justified?

3   How far should the law enforce morality?

For answers to these questions, see the companion website at www.pearsoned.co.uk/ elliottquinn

SUMMARY OF CHAPTER 28: LAW AND MORALS

Morals are beliefs and values which are shared by a society, or a section of a society; they tell those who share them what is right or wrong.

Law and morality

Both law and morals are normative; they specify what ought to be done, and aim to mark the boundaries between acceptable and unacceptable conduct. While moral rules tend not to be backed by the obvious sanctions which make some legal rules enforceable, they are often reinforced by pressures, such as the disapproval of family and friends.

Changes in law and morality

As we have observed, the moral values of a society tend to change over time; the same applies to its laws. In the UK, legal changes have tended to lag behind moral ones, coming only when the process of moral acceptance is well advanced. On the other hand, law can sometimes bring about changes in social morality.

Differences between law and morality

Although law and morality are clearly closely linked, there are certain ways in which they differ. Many types of behaviour exist which may be widely considered to be immoral, yet we would be very surprised to find laws against them: telling lies, for example. Equally, some forms of behaviour are illegal, but would not usually be described as immoral, such as parking on a yellow line. Then there are areas where the law shares morality's disapproval, but not so far as to prohibit the relevant behaviour.

Should law and morality be separate?

Making every immoral act also illegal seems both impossible and undesirable, yet law with no connection to morality might find it difficult to command much respect. There is still much debate as to how far law should reflect morality; the following are some of the key suggestions.

Natural law

Natural law theorists argue that law should strongly reflect morality. Though their specific theories differ, their shared premise is that there is a kind of higher law, known as the natural law, to which we can turn for a basic moral code.

Utilitarianism

One of the best-known exponents of this theory is John Stuart Mill (1859). He argued that, rather than society imposing morality on individuals, individuals should be free to choose their own conduct, so long as in doing so they did not harm others or, if they did, that the harm done did not outweigh the harm which would be done by interfering with individual liberty.

The Hart–Devlin debate

The issue of whether or not law should follow morality was hotly debated during the late 1950s, when there was public concern about what was perceived to be a decline in sexual morality. The Government of the day set up a commission to look at whether the laws on homosexuality and prostitution should be changed, and much debate was triggered by publication of the commission's findings, known as the Wolfenden Report (1957). Central to this debate were the writings of the leading judge, Lord Devlin, who opposed the report's findings, and Professor Hart who approved of them.

The Warnock Committee

The Warnock Committee was set up by the Government to consider issues relating to scientific advances concerning conception and pregnancy. Many of the Committee's conclusions became law in the Human Fertilisation and Embryology Act 1990. If we look at the reasoning behind the Committee's findings, we can see aspects of both Hart's utilitarian approach, and Devlin's upholding of common morality.

The Human Fertilisation and Embryology Authority

The Human Fertilisation and Embryology Act 1990 created the Human Fertilisation and Embryology Authority (HFEA). This body regulates scientific practice involving human genetics. The Human Fertilisation and Embryology Act 2008 has now replaced the provisions in the 1990 Act. It aims to update and rationalise the law in this field to reflect developments in research and recent case law.

28

LAW AND MORALS

Reading list

Aquinas, St T. (1942) *Summa Theologica*. London: Burns Oates & Washbourne.

Atiyah, P.S. (1979) *The Rise and Fall of Freedom of Contract*. Oxford: Clarendon.

Devlin, P. (1965) *The Enforcement of Morals*. Oxford: Oxford University Press.

Duster, T. (1970) *The Legislation of Morality*. New York: Free Press.

Fenton, A. and Dabell, F. (2007a) Time for change (1). *New Law Journal,* 157: 848.

          (2007b) Time for change (2). *New Law Journal,* 157: 964.

Fuller, L. (1969) *The Morality of Law*. London: Yale UP.

Hart, H.L.A. (1963) *Law, Liberty and Morality*. Oxford: Oxford University Press.

Lee, S. (1986) *Law and Morals*. Oxford: Oxford University Press.

Lukes, S. and Scull, A. (eds) (1983) *Durkheim and the Law*. Oxford: Robertson.

Mill, J.S. (1859) *On Liberty*. London: J.W. Parker.

Olivecrona, K. (1971) *Law as Fact*. London: Stevens.

Schur, E. (1965) *Crimes without Victims: Deviant Behaviour and Public Policy, Abortion, Homosexuality, Drug Addiction*. New York: Prentice-Hall.

Warnock, M. (1986) *Morality and the Law*. Cardiff: University College Cardiff.

Wolfenden, J. (1957) *Report of the Committee on Homosexual Offences and Prostitution*. Cm 2471. London: HMSO.

Young, J. (1971) *The Drugtakers: The Social Meaning of Drug Use*. London: Paladin.

On the internet

The website of the Human Fertilisation and Embryology Authority is:
http://www.hfea.gov.uk/

Chapter 29
Law and justice

This chapter explores:

- the ideas of the Greek philosopher Aristotle;
- the theory of natural law;
- utilitarianism;
- the economic analysis of law;
- Professor John Rawls's theory of justice; and
- the communist views of Karl Marx.

29.1 Introduction

Achieving justice is often seen as one of the most basic aims of a legal system. When areas of that system go wrong, the result is often described as injustice: for example, when people are convicted of crimes they have not committed, as in the cases of the Tottenham Three and the Birmingham Six, we say that a miscarriage of justice has occurred. But what is justice, and what is its relationship with law? These questions have been addressed by writers throughout the centuries, and we will look at some of the most important views in this chapter.

29.2 Aristotle

The Greek philosopher Aristotle is responsible for some of the earliest thinking on justice, and his work is still influential today. He considered that a just law was one which would allow individuals to fulfil themselves in society, and distinguished between distributive justice and corrective justice.

Distributive justice was concerned with the allocation of assets such as wealth and honour between members of the community. Here the aim of justice was to achieve proportion, but this did not mean equal shares; Aristotle thought that individuals should receive benefits in proportion to their claim on those benefits.

Corrective justice, on the other hand, applies when a situation that is distributively just, is disturbed – for example, by wrongdoing. A judge should discover what damage has been done, and then try to restore equality by imposing penalties to confiscate any gain made by the offence, and compensate for any damage caused.

29.3 Natural law theories

Natural law theories assume that there is a higher order of law, and if the laws of society follow this order they will be just. Aristotle supported this view, and believed that the higher law could be discovered from nature; others, such as the medieval scholar St Thomas Aquinas, thought that the higher law derived from God.

For Aquinas, there were two ways in which law could be unjust. First, a law which was contrary to human good, whether in its form or in its result, was, according to Aquinas, not true law at all. However, such laws might still be obeyed if to do so would avoid causing social disorder. Secondly, a law which was against God's will, and therefore a violation of the natural law, should be disregarded.

29.4 Utilitarianism

The utilitarian movement, which includes such writers as Mill and Bentham, is based on the idea that society should work towards the greatest happiness for the greatest number, even if this means that some individuals lose out. Utilitarians assess the justice of rules (and therefore law) by looking at their consequences; in their view, if a rule maximised happiness or well-being or had some other desirable effect, for the majority, it was just. A law could therefore be just even if it created social inequalities, or benefited some at the expense of others, so long as the benefits to the many exceeded the loss to the minority.

The utilitarian approach can be criticised as focusing only on justice for the community as a whole, and leaving out justice for individuals.

29.5 The economic analysis of law

This approach has developed mainly in the US, and attempts to offer a more sophisticated alternative to utilitarianism. While the goal of utilitarianism was to promote the greatest happiness of the greatest number, it offered no reliable way of calculating the effect of a law or policy on this goal, or measuring the relative benefits.

The economic analysis takes the view that a thing has value for a person when that person values it; its value can therefore be measured by how much the person is prepared to pay for it, or what would be required to make them give it up. As we have seen, a conflict exists between the concerns of utilitarianism and individual justice, and the same conflict exists here. Take the example of an NHS doctor with a limited budget, faced with one person who needs a life-saving operation costing £100,000, and ten others who each need more minor operations costing £10,000 each. On the face of it, doing the ten operations clearly seems to produce benefit for a greater number at the same cost, and in this sense may be the best way to spend public money. But can we say that this solution offers the first person justice?

A common criticism of the economic analysis of law is that it favours a particular ideology, that of market capitalism. It is based on the idea that the prices at which goods and services are bought and sold are the direct result of the value placed on them by buyer and seller, and therefore the result of free will; it presumes that sellers cannot exploit buyers, because nobody would pay more for something than it was worth to them. Critics of this approach point out that, in practice, power in the marketplace is frequently unequal; a seller may have the monopoly on particular goods, or sellers may collude to keep prices high. Equally, the idea that a thing has value because a person wants it ignores the question of where the desire for that thing originates; expensive advertising campaigns may produce the desire for what they sell, but can we objectively say that such publicity gives them value? In the same way, people may take low-paid jobs, not because they agree with that valuation of their labour, but because there are no other jobs and they have no power in the labour market.

29.6 Rawls: *A Theory of Justice*

Professor John Rawls first presented his ideas in *A Theory of Justice* which was published in 1971, and amended them slightly in his later book, *Political Liberalism* (1972). He approaches the question of justice through an imaginary situation in which the members of a society are to decide on a set of principles designed to make their society just, and advance the good of all its members. He describes this initial debate as the original position. The individuals involved will hold their discussions without knowing what their own position in the society is to be – whether they will be rich or poor, of high or low social status, old or young, and what will be the economic or political situation in the society. This veil of ignorance is designed to ensure that the ideas put forward really are the best for all members of society, since nobody will be willing to disadvantage a section of the community if they might find themselves a member of it.

Rawls believes that the principles which would result from such a discussion would include an equal distribution of what he calls social primary goods: these are the things which individuals are assumed to want in order to get the most out of their own lives, including rights, powers and freedoms, and, in Rawls's later work, self-respect. In addition to this, there would be two basic principles. The first involves liberty: a set of basic liberties – including freedom of thought, conscience, speech and assembly – would be available to all. Each person's freedom would be restricted only where the restriction on them was balanced out by greater liberty for the community as a whole. So, for example, the liberty of a person suspected of crime could be restricted by police powers of arrest, since these would increase the freedom from crime of society as a whole. The second basic principle is based on equality. This covers both equality of opportunity – offices and positions within society should be open to all equally – and equality of distribution. Rawls envisages an equal distribution of wealth, with inequalities allowed only where necessary to help the most disadvantaged.

If a social order is just, or nearly just, according to these principles, Rawls argues that those who accept its benefits are bound to accept its rules as well, even if they may disapprove of some of them, provided that those rules do not impose heavy burdens unequally, nor violate the basic principles. Professor Rawls would support limited disobedience, where the basic principles are violated, other means of obtaining redress fail, and no harm is done to others.

Rawls's theory has been extensively criticised. The clearest problem is simply its artificiality, particularly that of the veil of ignorance. As Dworkin has pointed out, even if we accept the scenario Rawls creates, the fact that individuals accept certain principles when they do not know what their position in society will be does not necessarily mean they will continue to live by them if they find themselves in a position to maximise their own advantage at the expense of others. Rawls's theory appears to view human beings as rather more perfect than they have in fact shown themselves to be.

29.7 Nozick and the minimal state

Robert Nozick's provocative essay, *Anarchy, State and Utopia* argues that, for a truly just society, the state should have the minimum possible right to interfere in the affairs of individuals; its functions should be limited to the basic needs, such as protecting the individual against force, theft and fraud, and enforcing contracts. Published in 1975, the essay revives a claim traditionally associated with the seventeenth-century writer John Locke, and has strong links with eighteenth-century individualism, and nineteenth-century capitalism.

Nozick's theory emphasises the importance of individual rights and, in particular, rights to property. He argues that the right to hold property is based on the way in which that property is obtained, either by just acquisition (such as inheritance) or just transfer (such as purchase from another), or by rectification of an unjust acquisition (for example, returning stolen property to its owner). Provided individuals have obtained their property in a just manner, the distribution of property throughout society is just; attempts to redistribute wealth are unjust because they interfere with the individual's right to hold justly obtained property. The state should, therefore, have no role in adjusting the distribution of wealth. In fact, Nozick rejects the idea that there are any goods belonging to society; goods belong only to individuals and the state has no right to interfere with them. Nozick's theories have been criticised, but they do reflect a growing disenchantment in Western society with the idea of redistributing wealth – in Britain we can see this in the emphasis placed by recent Governments on lowering taxes and expecting individuals to look after themselves, rather than taking taxes from the rich to help the poor.

29.8 Karl Marx

Marx held that it was impossible for a capitalist society to be just: such a society was organised with the aim of upholding the interests of the ruling class, rather than securing justice for all. For Marx, a just society would distribute wealth 'from each according to his capacity, to each according to his needs'; individuals should contribute what they can to society, and receive what they need in return. Marx's views are still influential, but the main criticism made of them is that so far no country has been able to put them into practice with sufficient success to bring about the fair society Marx envisaged.

29.9 Kelsen and positivism

For positivists, law can be separated from what is just or morally right. Parts of law may be based on, or incorporate ideas of, morality or justice, but this is not a necessary component of law; a law is still a law and should be obeyed even if it is completely immoral.

One of the best-known positivists is Kelsen, whose theories were first published in 1911, and further developed in his *General Theory of Law and State*, first published in 1945. Kelsen tried to develop a pure theory of law, to explain what law is rather than suggesting what it ought to be. He saw justice as simply the expression of individual preferences and values and, therefore, as an irrational ideal. Because of this, argued Kelsen, it is not possible scientifically to define justice.

29.10 Justice in practice

One of the most important aspects of the British legal system is parliamentary supremacy, which essentially means that Parliament is the ultimate law-maker, and can make or unmake any law it wishes. In most other developed countries, a written constitution sets down basic principles with which law should conform, and judges can strike down any legislation which conflicts with them. That is not the case in the UK; our constitution is unwritten and judges must apply the law that Parliament makes, even if they believe it is unjust. If Parliament wanted to make laws condemning all blonde women to death, banning old men from keeping pet dogs, or obliging parents to sell their eldest child into slavery, there would probably be political obstacles to doing so, but there would be no legal ones and judges would be obliged to apply the laws.

Clearly, this situation conflicts with the natural law approach we discussed earlier, where unjust laws were considered not to be true law and, in some circumstances, not to require application by the courts or obedience by the citizen. Arguments for a Bill of Rights, a statement of basic principles against which courts could measure legislation and strike down any in conflict with them, have something in common with the natural law approach, since they assume that some values are fundamental and those given the power to make law in a society should be bound to follow them, rather than being free to make any law they want.

As with most developed legal systems, ours is based on the idea that, to achieve justice, like cases must be treated alike – thus if two people commit a crime in identical circumstances, they should be punished in a similar way. This aim requires fixed rules, so that decision-makers base their verdicts on the application of those rules to the case before them, and not on arbitrary factors such as their own mood or what they personally think of the defendant. However, the downside of this approach is that fixed rules can make it difficult to do justice in individual cases. Take the crime of murder, for example: to commit a murder, a defendant must have intended to kill or to cause serious injury; if this intention is present, the motive for killing is largely irrelevant. While this promotes the idea of like cases being treated alike, allowing judges to opt out of assessing the pros and cons of different motives, which must of necessity involve personal views, it presents problems in individual cases – can we say it is just for someone who kills a terminally ill relative to spare them from pain to be treated in the same way as someone who kills another so they can rob them? They both have intention but are they equally blameworthy? Fixed rules can sometimes promote justice in the majority of cases at the expense of justice in the individual, out-of-the-ordinary one.

The problem of fixed rules preventing justice in individual cases was one which our legal system faced early on in its life, when the common law was first becoming established. Then the answer was to develop a special branch of law, equity, with the specific aim of providing justice in cases where the ordinary rules of law failed to do so. Equity is no longer a separate branch of law, but equitable principles are still important in some areas of the civil law, and allow the courts to use their discretion in order to do justice in individual cases. In the criminal law (though not for the offence of murder) discretion over sentencing can fulfil a similar role. The challenge is to maintain a balance between too much discretion, leading to the possibility of arbitrary decisions, and too little, leading to harsh results in individual cases.

Answering questions

1   Various writers, such as Aristotle, Mill, Bentham, Rawls, Nozick, Marx and Kelsen, have advocated individual theories of justice. Explain, evaluate and analyse three of these. Which theory do you prefer? Explain why.

For the answer to this question, see the companion website at www.pearsoned.co.uk/ elliottquinn

SUMMARY OF CHAPTER 29: LAW AND JUSTICE

Achieving justice is often seen as one of the most basic aims of a legal system. When areas of that system go wrong, the result is often described as injustice. But what is justice, and what is its relationship with law? These questions have been addressed by writers throughout the centuries.

Aristotle
....

Aristotle, the Greek philosopher, considered that a just law was one which would allow individuals to fulfil themselves in society, and distinguished between distributive justice and corrective justice.

Natural law theories

Natural law theories assume that there is a higher order of law, and if the laws of society follow this order they will be just.

Utilitarianism

The utilitarian movement is based on the idea that society should work towards the greatest happiness for the greatest number, even if this means that some individuals lose out. Utilitarians assess the justice of rules (and therefore law) by looking at their consequences; in their view, if a rule maximised happiness or well-being or had some other desirable effect, for the majority, it was just.

The economic analysis of law

The economic analysis takes the view that a thing has value for a person when that person values it; its value can therefore be measured by how much the person is prepared to pay for it, or what would be required to make them give it up.

Rawls: *A Theory of Justice*

Professor John Rawls approaches the question of justice through an imaginary situation in which the members of a society are to decide on a set of principles designed to make their society just, and advance the good of all its members. He describes this initial debate as the original position. Rawls believes that the principles which would result would include an equal distribution of what he calls social primary goods. In addition to this, there would be two basic principles: liberty and equality.

Nozick and the minimal state

Robert Nozick argues that, for a truly just society, the state should have the minimum possible right to interfere in the affairs of individuals; its functions should be limited to the basic needs, such as protecting the individual against force, theft and fraud, and enforcing contracts.

Karl Marx

Marx held that it was impossible for a capitalist society to be just: such a society was organised with the aim of upholding the interests of the ruling class, rather than securing justice for all. For Marx, a just society would distribute wealth 'from each according to his capacity, to each according to his needs'; individuals should contribute what they can to society, and receive what they need in return.

Kelsen and positivism

For positivists, law can be separated from what is just or morally right. Parts of law may be based on, or incorporate ideas of, morality or justice, but this is not a necessary component of law; a law is still a law and should be obeyed even if it is completely immoral.

Reading list

Hayek, F. (1982) *Law, Legislation and Liberty: A New Statement of the Liberal Principles of Justice and Political Economy*. London: Routledge.

Kelsen, H. (1945) *General Theory of Law and State*. Cambridge, MA: Harvard UP.

Locke, J. (1967) *Two Treatises of Government*. London: Cambridge University Press.

Nozick, R. (1975) *Anarchy, State, and Utopia*. Oxford: Blackwell.

Rawls, J. (1971) *A Theory of Justice*. Oxford: Oxford University Press.

(1972) *Political Liberalism, John Dewey Essays in Philosophy*. NY: Columbia University Press.

GLOSSARY

Administrative law   The body of law which deals with the rights and duties of the state and the limits of its powers over individuals.

Arraignment   The process whereby the accused is called to the Bar of the court to plead guilty or not guilty to the charges against him or her.

Bill of Rights   A statement of the basic rights which a citizen can expect to enjoy.

Case stated   Under the proceedings, a person who was a party to a proceeding before the magistrates (or the Crown Court when it is hearing an appeal from the magistrates) may question the proceeding of the court on the ground that there was an error of law or the court had acted outside its jurisdiction. The party asks the court to state a case for the opinion of the High Court on the question of law or jurisdiction.

Caution   1   A warning to an accused person administered on arrest or before police questioning. Since the abolition, by the Criminal Justice and Public Order Act 1994, of the right of silence, the correct wording is: 'You do not have to say anything. But it may harm your defence if you do not mention when questioned something which you later rely on in court. Anything you do say may be given in evidence.'

2   A formal warning given to an offender about what he or she has done, designed to make him see that he has done wrong and deter him from further offending. This process is used instead of proceeding with the prosecution.

Certiorari   An order quashing an *ultra vires* decision.

Chambers   The offices of a barrister.

Community sentence   This means a sentence that will be served in the community.

Constitution   A set of rules and customs which detail a country's system of government; in most cases it will be a written document but in some countries, including Britain, the constitution cannot be found written down in one document and is known as an unwritten constitution.

Contingency fee   A fee payable to a lawyer (who has taken on a case on a 'no win, no fee' basis) in the event of his or her winning the case.

Convention   1   A long-established tradition which tends to be followed although it does not have the force of law.
2   A treaty with a foreign power.

Corporation aggregate   This term covers groups of people with a single legal personality (for example, a company, university or local authority).

Corporation sole   This is a device which makes it possible to continue the official capacity of an individual beyond their lifetime or tenure of office: for example, the Crown is a corporation sole; its legal personality continues while individual monarchs come and go.

Counsel's opinion   A barrister's advice.

Custom   'Such usage as has obtained the force of law' (*Tanistry Case* (1608)).

Ejusdem generis rule   General words which follow specific ones are taken to include only things of the same kind.

Equity   In law it is a term which applies to a specific set of legal principles which were developed by the Chancery Court and add to those provided in the common law.

Habeas corpus   This is an ancient remedy which allows people detained to challenge the legality of their detention and, if successful, to get themselves quickly released.

He who comes to equity must come with clean hands   This means that a claimant who has been in the wrong in some way will not be granted an equitable remedy.

He who seeks equity must do equity   Anyone who seeks equitable relief must be prepared to act fairly towards their opponent.

Indictable offences   These are the more serious offences, such as rape and murder. They can only be heard by the Crown Court. The indictment is a formal document containing the alleged offences against the accused, supported by brief facts.

Law Officers   They are the Attorney General and the Solicitor General.

Lawyer   This is a general term which covers both branches of the legal profession, namely barristers and solicitors, as well as many people with a legal qualification.

Leapfrog procedure   This is the procedure provided for in the Administration of Justice Act 1969, whereby an appeal can go directly from the High Court to the Supreme Court, missing out the Court of Appeal.

Locus standi   The right to bring a case in court.

Natural law   A kind of higher law, to which we can turn for a basic moral code. Some, such as St Thomas Aquinas, see this higher law as coming from God; others see it simply as the basis of human society.

Noscitur a sociis   The meaning of a doubtful word may be ascertained by reference to the meaning of words associated with it.

Obiter dicta   Words in a judgment which are said 'by the way' and were not the basis on which the decision was made. They do not form part of the *ratio decidendi* and are not binding on future cases, but merely persuasive.

Parliament   Consists of the House of Commons, the House of Lords and the Monarch.

Per incuriam   Where a previous decision has been made in ignorance of a relevant law it is said to have been made *per incuriam*.

Plea bargaining   This is the name given to negotiations between the prosecution and defence lawyers over the outcome of a case: for example, where a defendant is choosing to plead not guilty, the prosecution may offer to reduce the charge to a similar offence with a smaller maximum sentence in return for the defendant pleading guilty to that offence.

Practice Direction   An official announcement by the court laying down rules as to how it should function.

Prohibition   An order prohibiting a body from acting unlawfully in the future: for example, it can prohibit an inferior court or tribunal from starting or continuing proceedings which are, or threaten to be, outside their jurisdiction, or in breach of natural justice.

Puisne judges   High Court judges are also known as puisne judges (pronounced puny) meaning junior judges.

Ratio decidendi   The legal principle on which a decision is based.

Relator action   A proceeding whereby a party, who has failed to prove *locus standi*, can choose to permit the action to be brought in the name of the Attorney General.

Small claims track   This is a procedure used by the County Courts to deal with claims under £10,000.

Sovereignty of Parliament   This has traditionally meant that the law which Parliament makes takes precedence over that from any other source, but this principle has been qualified by membership of the EU.

Stare decisis   Abiding by precedent: that is, in deciding a case a judge must follow any decision that has been made by a higher court in a case with similar facts. As well as being bound by decisions of courts above them, some courts must follow their own previous decisions.

Summary offences   These are most minor crimes and are only triable summarily in the magistrates' courts. 'Summary' refers to the process of ordering the defendant to attend court by summons, a written order usually delivered by post, which is the most frequent procedure adopted in the magistrates' court.

Ultra vires   Outside their powers.

Wednesbury principle   This principle, which was laid down in ***Associated Provincial Picture Houses Ltd* v *Wednesbury Corporation*** (1948), is that a decision will be held to be outside a public body's power if it is so unreasonable that no reasonable public body could have reached it.

Youth court   Young offenders are usually tried in youth courts (formerly called juvenile courts), which are a branch of the magistrates' court. Youth courts must sit in a separate courtroom, where no ordinary court proceedings have been held for at least one hour. Strict restrictions are imposed as to who may attend the sittings of the court.

SELECT BIBLIOGRAPHY

Abel, R. (1988) *The Legal Profession in England and Wales,* Oxford: Basil Blackwell.

Abel-Smith, B., Zander, M. and Brooke, R. (1973) *Legal Problems and the Citizen,* London: Heinemann-Educational.

Administrative Justice and Tribunals Council (2011) *Right First Time,* London: Administrative Justice and Tribunals Council.

Advice Services Alliance (2004) *The Independent Review of the Community Legal Service. The Advice Services Alliance's Response to the Department for Constitutional Affairs' Consultation on the Recommendations Made by Matrix Research and Consultancy,* London: ASA.

Aquinas, St T. (1942) *Summa Theologica,* London: Burns Oates & Washbourne.

Ashley, L. (2010) 'Making a difference? The use (and abuse) of diversity management at the UK's elite law firms', 24 *Work, Employment and Society* 711.

(2002) 'Responsibilities, rights and restorative justice', *British Journal of Criminology* 578.

Ashworth, A. (2010) 'Coroners and Justice Act 2009: sentencing guidelines and the sentencing council', *Criminal Law Review* 389.

Atiyah, P. S. (1979) *The Rise and Fall of Freedom of Contract,* Oxford: Clarendon.

Audit Commission (1996) *Streetwise: Effective Police Patrol,* London: HMSO.

(1997) *Misspent Youth: Young People and Crime,* London: Audit Commission.

(2003) *Victims and Witnesses,* London: Audit Commission.

(2004) *Youth Justice,* London: Audit Commission.

Auld, Sir R. (2001) *Review of the Criminal Courts,* London: HMSO.

Austin, J. (1954) *The Province of Jurisprudence Determined,* London: Weidenfeld & Nicolson.

Austin, R. (2007) 'The new powers of arrest: *plus ça change:* more of the same or major change?', *Criminal Law Review* 459.

Bailey, S. and Gunn, M. (2002) *Smith and Bailey on the Modern English Legal System* (2nd edn), London: Sweet & Maxwell.

Baker, M. (2014) 'Choices and consequences – an account of an experimental sentencing programme', *Criminal Law Review* 51.

Baldwin, J. (1992a) *The Role of Legal Representatives at the Police Station,* Royal Commission on Criminal Justice Research Study No. 2, London: HMSO.

(1992b) *Video Taping Police Interviews with Suspects: An Evaluation,* London: Home Office.

(1997) *Small Claims in County Courts in England and Wales: The Bargain Basement of Civil Justice?* Oxford: Clarendon.

(1998) 'Small claims hearings: the interventionist role played by district judges', 17 *Civil Justice Quarterly* 20.

(2002) *Lay and Judicial Perspectives on the Expansion of the Small Claims Regime,* London: Lord Chancellor's Department.

(2003) *Evaluating the Effectiveness of Enforcement Procedures in Undefended Claims in the Civil Courts,* London: Lord Chancellor's Department.

Baldwin, J. and McConville, M. (1979) *Jury Trials,* Oxford: Clarendon.

Baldwin, J. and Moloney, T. (1992) *Supervision of Police Investigations in Serious Criminal Cases,*

Royal Commission on Criminal Justice Research Study No. 4, London: HMSO.

Bar Council (2000) *The Economic Case for the Bar: A Comparison of the Costs of Barristers and Solicitors,* London: General Council of the Bar.

(2013) *Reforming Civil Litigation: Discussion Document,* London: Bar Council.

Bar Council Working Party (2007) *Entry to the Bar: Working Party Final Report,* London: Bar Council.

Barton, A. (2001) 'Medical litigation: who benefits?', 322 *British Medical Journal* 1189.

Bell, J. and Engle, G. (eds) (1995) *Cross: Statutory Interpretation* (3rd edn), London: LexisNexis/ Butterworths.

Bennion, F. A. R. (1999) 'A naked usurpation?', 149 *New Law Journal* 421.

(2005) *Statutory Interpretation,* London: Butterworths.

(2007) 'Executive estoppel: *Pepper v Hart* revisited', *Public Law,* Spring 1.

Better Regulation Taskforce (2004) *Better Routes to Redress,* London: Better Regulation Taskforce.

(2005) *Regulation – Less Is More,* London: Better Regulation Taskforce.

Blom-Cooper, L. (1972) *Final Appeal: A Study of the House of Lords in Its Judicial Capacity,* Oxford: Clarendon.

(2009) 'Bias, malfunction in judicial decision-making', *Public Law* 199.

Bond, R. A. and Lemon, N. F. (1979) 'Changes in magistrates' attitudes during the first year on the bench', in Farrington, D. P. *et al.* (eds) *Psychology, Law and Legal Processes,* London: Macmillan.

Boon, A. and Levin, J. (2008) *Ethics and Conduct of Lawyers in the UK,* Oxford: Hart.

Booth, A. (2002) 'Direct effect', *Solicitors Journal* 924.

Bornstein, B., Miller, M., Nemeth R., Page, G. and Musil, S. (2005) 'Juror reactions to jury duty: perceptions of the system and potential stressors', *Behavioral Sciences and the Law* 23, 321.

Bottoms, A. E. and Preston, R. H. (eds) (1980) *The Coming Penal Crisis: A Criminological and Theoretical Exploration,* Edinburgh: Scottish Academic Press.

Bowles, R. and Perry, A. (2009) *International Comparison of Publicly Funded Legal Services and Justice Systems,* Ministry of Justice Research Series 14/09, London: Ministry of Justice.

Bowling, B. and Ross, J. (2006) 'The serious organised crime agency – should we be afraid?', *Criminal Law Review* 1019.

Bowman, Sir J. (1997) *Review of the Court of Appeal (Civil Division),* London: Lord Chancellor's Department.

Boyron, S. (2006) 'The rise of mediation in administrative law disputes: experiences from England, France and Germany', *Public Law* 230.

Brazier, R. (1998) *Constitutional Reform,* Oxford: Oxford University Press.

Bridges, L. and Cape, E. (2008) *CDS Direct: Flying in the Face of the Evidence,* London: Centre for Crime and Justice Studies at King's College London.

Bridges, L. and Choongh, S. (1998) *Improving Police Station Legal Advice: The Impact of the Accreditation Scheme for Police Station Legal Advisers,* London: Law Society's Research and Planning Unit: Legal Aid Board.

Bridges, L. *et al.* (2007) *Evaluation of the Public Defender Service in England and Wales,* London: Stationery Office.

Brophy, J. (2007) *Openness and Transparency in Family Courts: Messages from Other Jurisdictions,* London: Ministry of Justice.

Brown, D. (1998) *Offending While on Bail,* Home Office, Report No. 72, London: Home Office.

Brown, D. and Neal, D. (1988) 'Show trials: the media and the gang of twelve', in Findlay, M. and Duff, P. (eds) *The Jury under Attack,* London: Butterworths.

Brown, D. *et al.* (1992) *Changing the Code: Police Detention under the Revised PACE Codes of Practice,* Home Office Research Study No. 129, London: HMSO.

Brown, K. (2012) ' "It is not as easy as ABC": examining practitioners' views on using behavioural contracts to encourage young people to accept responsibility for their anti-social behaviour', *Journal of Criminal Law* 53.

Brownlee, I. (2004) 'The statutory charging scheme in England and Wales: towards a unified prosecution system', *Criminal Law Review* 896.

Bucke, T. and Brown, D. (1997) *In Police Custody: Police Powers and Suspects' Rights Under the Revised PACE Codes of Practice.* Home Office Research Study 174. London: Home Office.

Burney, E. (1979) *Magistrates, Court and Community,* London: Hutchinson.

Burns, S. (2006) 'Tipping the balance', 156 *New Law Journal* 787.

(2008) 'An incoming tide', 158 *New Law Journal* 44.

Burrows, A. (2002) 'We do this at common law but that in equity', 22 *Oxford Journal of Legal Studies* 1.

Campbell, L. (2010) 'A rights-based analysis of DNA retention: "non-conviction" databases and the liberal state', *Criminal Law Review* 889.

Campbell, S. (2002) *A Review of Anti-Social Behaviour Orders,* Home Office Research Study No. 236, London: Home Office.

Cape, E. (2007) 'Modernising police powers – again?', *Criminal Law Review* 934.

Cape, E. and Young, R. (2008) *Regulation Policing: The Police and Criminal Evidence Act 1984 Past, Present and Future,* Oxford: Hart.

Carlen, P. (1983) *Women's Imprisonment: A Study in Social Control,* London: Routledge.

(2003) *Managing Offenders, Reducing Crime,* London: Strategy Unit, Home Office.

Carter, Lord (2006) *Legal Aid: A Market-Based Approach to Reform,* London: Department for Constitutional Affairs.

(2007) *Securing the Future – Proposals for the Efficient and Sustainable Use of Custody in England and Wales,* London: Ministry of Justice.

Chalmers, J., Duff, P. and Leverick, F. (2007) 'Victim impact statements: can work, do work (for those who bother to make them)', *Criminal Law Review* 360.

Citizens Advice Bureau (2004a) *Geography of Advice,* London: Citizens Advice Bureau.

(2004b) *No Win, No Fee, No Chance,* London: Citizens Advice Bureau.

Civil Justice Council (2005) *Improved Access to Justice – Funding Options and Proportionate Costs,* London: Ministry of Justice.

(2008) *Improving Access to Justice through Collective Actions,* London: Ministry of Justice.

(2011) *Access to Justice for Litigants in Person (or self-represented litigants),* London: Civil Justice Council.

Committee of Public Accounts (2005) *Facing Justice: Tackling Defendants' Non-Attendance at Court* (22nd Report, HC 103), London: Stationery Office.

Confederation of British Industry (2005) *A Matter of Confidence: Restoring Faith in Employment Tribunals,* London: CBI.

Constitutional Affairs Select Committee (2007) *Family Justice: The Operation of the Family Courts Revisited,* London: Stationery Office.

Consumer Council (1970) *Justice Out of Reach: A Case for Small Claims Courts: A Consumer Council Study,* London: HMSO.

Cooper, S. (2009) 'Appeals, referrals and substantial injustice', *Criminal Law Review* 152.

Corston, J. (2007) *Women with Particular Vulnerabilities in the Criminal Justice System,* London: Home Office.

Cotton, J. and Povey, D. (2004) *Police Complaints and Discipline, April 2002–March 2003,* London: Home Office.

Craig, P. and de Búrca, G. (2007) *EU Law: Text, Cases and Materials,* Oxford: Oxford University Press.

Cretney, S. (1998) *Law, Law Reform and the Family,* Oxford: Clarendon Press.

Crosby, K. (2012) 'Controlling Devlin's jury: what the jury thinks, and what the jury sees online', *Criminal Law Review* 15.

Cross, Sir R. (1995) *Statutory Interpretation,* Bell, J. and Engle, G. (eds), London: Butterworths.

Cruickshank, E. (2007) 'Sisters in the law', *Solicitors Journal* 1510.

Cutting Crime – Delivering Justice: Strategic Plan for Criminal Justice 2004–08 (2004) Cm 6288, London: Home Office.

Darbyshire, P. (1991) 'The lamp that shows that freedom lives – is it worth the candle?', *Criminal Law Review* 740.

——— (1999) 'A comment on the powers of magistrates' clerks', *Criminal Law Review* 377.

——— (2011) *Sitting in Judgment*, Oxford: Hart.

de Tocqueville, A. (2000) *Democracy in America* (George Lawrence, trans.; J. P. Mayer, ed.), New York: Perennial Classics (first published 1835).

Denning, A. (1952) 'The need for a new equity', 5 *Current Legal Problems* 1.

——— (1982) *What Next in the Law?* London: Butterworths.

Dennis, I. (2006) 'Convicting the guilty: outcomes, process and the Court of Appeal', *Criminal Law Review* 955.

Department for Business, Innovation and Skills (2011) *Resolving Workplace Disputes: A Consultation*, London: Department for Business, Innovation and Skills.

Department for Constitutional Affairs (2004) *Making Simple CFAs a Reality*, London: Department for Constitutional Affairs.

——— (2004a) *Broadcasting Courts*, CP 28/04, London: DCA.

——— (2004b) *Transforming Public Services: Complaints, Redress and Tribunals*, London: Stationery Office.

——— (2004c) *The Independent Review of the Community Legal Service*, London: DCA.

——— (2005a) *A Single Civil Court?*, London: Department for Constitutional Affairs.

——— (2005b) *Supporting Magistrates' Courts to Provide Justice*, Cm 6681, London: Stationery Office.

——— (2005c) *Focusing Judicial Resources Appropriately*, Consultation Paper CP25/05, London: DCA.

——— (2006a) *Delivering Simple, Speedy, Summary Justice*, 37/06, London: DCA.

——— (2006b) *Confidence and Confidentiality: Improving Transparency and Privacy in Family Courts*, London: Stationery Office.

——— (2007) *Case Track Limits and the Claims Process for Personal Injury Claims*, London: Stationery Office.

Department for Trade and Industry (2004) *Fairness for All: A New Commission for Equality and Human Rights*, Cm 6185, London: Stationery Office.

Devlin, P. (1956) *Trial by Jury*, London: Stevens.

——— (1965) *The Enforcement of Morals*, Oxford: Oxford University Press.

——— (1979) *The Judge*, Oxford: Oxford University Press.

Dicey, A. (1982) *Introduction to the Study of the Law of the Constitution*, Indianapolis: Liberty Classics.

Dickens, L. (1985) *Dismissed: A Study of Unfair Dismissal and the Industrial System*, Oxford: Blackwell.

Director General of Fair Trading (2001) *Competition in Professions*, OFT 328, London: OFT.

Doak, J. (2008) *Victims' Rights, Human Rights and Criminal Justice: Reconceiving the Role of Third Parties*, Oxford: Hart.

Dodgson, K. *et al.* (2001) *Electronic Monitoring of Released Prisoners: An Evaluation of the Home Detention Curfew Scheme*, London: Home Office.

Dow, J. and Lapuerta, C. (2005) *The Benefits of Multiple Ownership Models in Law Services*, London: Brattle Group.

Drewry, G. (1987) 'The debate about a Ministry of Justice – A Joad's Eye View', *Public Law* 502.

Duff, A., Farmer, L., Marshall, S. and Tadros, V. (2007) *The Trial on Trial (Volume 3): Towards a Normative Theory of the Criminal Trial*, Oxford: Hart.

Durkheim, E. (1983) *Durkheim and the Law*, Oxford: Robertson.

Duster, T. (1970) *The Legislation of Morality,* New York: Free Press.

Dworkin, R. (1977) *Taking Rights Seriously,* London: Duckworth.

(1978) 'Political judges and the rule of law', 64 *Proceedings of the British Academy* 259.

(1986) *Law's Empire,* London: Fontana.

Edwards, I. (2002) 'The place of victims' preferences in the sentencing of "their" offenders', *Criminal Law Review* 689.

Elks, L. (2008) *Righting Miscarriages of Justice? Ten Years of the Criminal Cases Review Commission,* London: JUSTICE.

Ellis, T. and Hedderman, C. (1996) *Enforcing Community Sentences: Supervisors' Perspectives on Ensuring Compliance and Dealing with Breach,* London: Home Office.

Enright, S. (1993) 'Cost effective criminal justice', 143 *New Law Journal* 1023.

Enter, R. (1993) *The image of the judiciary: a semiotic analysis of broadcast trials to ascertain its definition of the court system,* PhD, New York: New York University.

Epstein, H. (2003) 'The liberalisation of claim financing', 153 *New Law Journal* 153.

Evans, Sir A. (2003) 'Forget ADR – think A or D', *Civil Justice Quarterly* 230.

Evans, R. (1993) *The Conduct of Police Interviews with Juveniles,* London: HMSO.

Fenton, A. and Dabell, F. (2007a) 'Time for change (1)', 157 *New Law Journal* 848.

(2007b) 'Time for change (2)', 157 *New Law Journal* 964.

Field, S. (2008) 'Early intervention and the "new" youth justice: a study of initial decision-making', *Criminal Law Review* 177.

Findlay, M. (2001) 'Juror comprehension and complexity: strategies to enhance understanding', 41 *British Journal of Criminology* 56.

Fionda, J. (2006) *Devils and Angels,* Oxford: Hart.

Flood, J. and Hviid, M. (2013) *The Cab Rank Rule: Its Meaning and Purpose in the New Legal Services Market,* London: Legal Services Board.

Flood-Page, C. and Mackie, A. (1998) *Sentencing During the Nineties,* London: Home Office Research and Statistics Directorate.

Franklyn, R. (2012) *Satisfaction and Willingness to Engage with the Criminal Justice System: Findings from the Witness and Victim Experience Survey, 2009–10,* Ministry of Justice Research Series 1/12, London: Ministry of Justice.

Freeman, M. D. A. (1981) 'The jury on trial', 34 *Current Legal Problems* 65.

Fricker, N. and Walker, J. (1993) 'Alternative dispute resolution – state responsibility or second best?' *Civil Justice Quarterly* 29.

Fuller, L. (1969) *The Morality of Law,* London: Yale University Press.

Galanter, M. (1984) *The Emergence of the Judge as a Mediator in Civil Cases,* Madison: University of Wisconsin.

Genn, H. (1982) *Meeting Legal Needs? An Evaluation of a Scheme for Personal Injury Victims,* Oxford: SSRC Centre for Socio-Legal Studies.

(1987) *Hard Bargaining: Out of Court Settlement in Personal Injury Actions,* Oxford: Clarendon.

(1997) 'Understanding civil justice', 50 *Current Legal Problems* 155.

(1998) *The Central London County Court Pilot Mediation Scheme: Evaluation Report,* London: Lord Chancellor's Department.

(2002) *Court-based ADR Initiatives for Non-Family Civil Disputes: the Commercial Court and the Court of Appeal,* London: Lord Chancellor's Department.

(2008) *The Attractiveness of Senior Judicial Appointments to Highly Qualified Practitioners,* London: Directorate for Judicial Office.

(2009) *Judging Civil Justice* (Hamlyn Lectures 2008), Cambridge: Cambridge University Press.

Genn, H. and Genn, Y. (1989) *The Effect of Representation at Tribunals,* London: Lord Chancellor's Department.

Glidewell, Sir I. (1998) *Review of the Crown Prosecution Service,* Cm. 3960, London: Stationery Office.

Goriely, T. and Gysta, P. (2001) *Breaking the Code: The Impact of Legal Aid Reforms on General Civil Litigation,* London: Institute of Advanced Legal Studies.

Green, P. (ed.) (1996) *Drug Couriers: A New Perspective,* London: Quartet.

Griffith, J. A. G. (1997) *The Politics of the Judiciary,* London: Fontana.

Grout, Paul A. (2005) *The Clementi Report: Potential Risks of External Ownership and Regulatory Responses – A Report to the Department for Constitutional Affairs,* London: Department for Constitutional Affairs.

Gudjonsson, G. H. (1992) *The Psychology of Interrogations, Confessions and Testimony,* Chichester: Wiley.

(2010) 'Psychological vulnerabilities during police interviews. Why are they important?', 15 *Legal and Criminological Psychology* 161.

Hailsham, Lord (1989) 'The Office of Lord Chancellor and the separation of powers', 8 *Civil Justice Quarterly* 308.

Hale, Sir M. (1979) *The History of the Common Law of England,* Chicago: University of Chicago Press.

Hall, M. (2010) 'The relationship between victims and prosecutors: defending victims' rights?', *Criminal Law Review* 31.

Halliday, J. (2001) *Making Punishment Work, Report of the Review of the Sentencing Framework for England and Wales,* London: Home Office.

Hamer, D. (2009) 'The expectation of incorrect acquittals and the "new and compelling evidence" exception to double jeopardy', *Criminal Law Review* 63.

Hart, H. L. A. (1963) *Law, Liberty and Morality,* Oxford: Oxford University Press.

(1994) *The Concept of Law,* Oxford: Clarendon.

Hayek, F. (1982) *Law, Legislation and Liberty: A New Statement of the Liberal Principles of Justice and Political Economy,* London: Routledge.

Hedderman, C. and Hough, M. (1994) *Does the Criminal Justice System Treat Men and Women Differently?* London: Home Office Research and Planning Unit.

Hedderman, C. and Moxon, D. (1992) *Magistrates' Court or Crown Court? Mode of Trial Decisions and Sentencing,* London: HMSO.

Herbert, A. (2003) 'Mode of trial and magistrates' sentencing powers: will increased powers inevitably lead to a reduction in the committal rate?', *Criminal Law Review* 314.

Herbert, A. P. (1966) *Wigs at Work,* London: Penguin.

HM Crown Prosecution Service Inspectorate and HM Inspectorate of Constabulary (2008) *The Joint Thematic Review of the New Charging Arrangements,* Criminal Justice Joint Inspection, London: HM Crown Prosecution Inspectorate.

HM Inspectorate (1999) *Police Integrity: Securing and Maintaining Public Confidence,* London: Home Office Communication Directorate.

Hoffmann, Lord (2009) 'The universality of human rights', 125 *Law Quarterly Review* 416.

Hohfeld, W. N. and Cook, W. W. (1919) *Fundamental Legal Concepts as Applied in Judicial Reasoning,* London: Greenwood.

Holland, L. and Spencer, L. (1992) *Without Prejudice? Sex Equality at the Bar and in the Judiciary,* London: Bar Council.

Home Office (1990) *Crime, Justice and Protecting the Public,* Cm 965, London: HMSO.

(1998a) *No More Excuses – A New Approach to Tackling Youth Crime in England and Wales,* London: Home Office.

(1998b) *Violence: Reforming the Offences Against the Person Act 1861,* London: Home Office.

(2001) *Criminal Justice: The Way Ahead,* Cm 5074, London: Stationery Office.

(2003a) *Statistics on Race and the Criminal Justice System,* London: Home Office.

(2003b) *Statistics on Women and the Criminal Justice System,* London: Home Office.

(2004a) *Are Special Measures Working? Evidence from Surveys of Vulnerable and Intimidated Witnesses,* Home Office Research Study 283, London: Home Office.

(2004b) *Modernising Police Powers to Meet Community Needs,* London: Home Office.

(2004c) *One Step Ahead: A 21st Century Strategy to Defeat Organised Crime,* Cm 6167 Norwich: Stationery Office.

(2005) Exclusion or Deportation from the UK on *Non-conducive Grounds,* London: Home Office.

(2006a) *Making Sentencing Clearer,* London: Home Office.

(2006b) *Rebalancing the Criminal Justice System in Favour of the Law-Abiding Majority,* London: Home Office.

(2007a) *Modernising Police Powers: Review of the Police and Criminal Evidence Act 1984,* London: Home Office.

(2007b) *Asset Recovery Action Plan,* London: Home Office.

(2009) *Keeping the Right People on the DNA Database: Science and Public Protection,* London: Home Office.

(2011) *More Effective Responses to Anti-Social Behaviour,* London: Home Office.

Home Office Research Development and Statistics Directorate (2000) *Jury Excusal and Deferral* (Research Findings No. 102), London: Home Office.

Honess, T., Charman, E. and Levi, M. (2003) 'Factual and affective/evaluative recall of pretrial publicity: their relative influence on juror reasoning and verdict in a simulated fraud trial', 33 (7) *Journal of Applied Social Psychology* 1404.

Hood, R., Shute, S. and Seemungal, F. (2003) *Ethnic Minorities in the Criminal Courts: Perceptions of Fairness and Equality of Treatment,* London: Lord Chancellor's Department.

Horowitz, I. and Fosterlee, L. (2001) 'The effects of note-taking and trial transcript access on mock jury decisions in a complex civil trial', 25 *Law and Human Behaviour* 373.

Horowitz, M. J. (1977) 'The rule of law: an unqualified good?', 86 *Yale Law Journal* 561.

House of Lords Parliamentary Committee (2007) *Relations Between the Executive, the Judiciary and Parliament,* London: Stationery Office.

Hucklesby, A. (2004) 'Not necessarily a trip to the police station: the introduction of street bail', *Criminal Law Review* 803.

Hungerford-Welch, P. (2012) 'Police officers as jurors', *Criminal Law Review* 751.

Hutton, Lord (2004) *Report of the Inquiry into the Circumstances Surrounding the Death of Dr David Kelly CMG,* London: Stationery Office.

Hynes, S. and Robins, J. (2009) *The Justice Gap: Whatever Happened to Legal Aid?* London: Legal Action Group.

Idriss, M. (2004) 'Police perceptions of race relations in the West Midlands', *Criminal Law Review* 814.

Ingman, T. (2008) *The English Legal Process,* Oxford: Oxford University Press.

Jackson, J. (2003) 'Justice for all: putting victims at the heart of criminal justice?', 30 *Journal of Law and Society* 309.

Jackson, Lord (2009) *The Review of Civil Litigation Costs: Final Report,* Norwich: Stationery Office.

Jackson, Lord Justice (2010) *Review of Civil Justice Costs,* Norwich: Stationery Office.

Jackson, R. M. (1989) *The Machinery of Justice in England,* Cambridge: Cambridge University Press.

Jacobson, J. and Hough, M. (2007) *Mitigation: The Role of Personal Factors in Sentencing,* London: Prison Reform Trust.

Jeremy, D. (2008) 'The prosecutor's rock and hard place', *Criminal Law Review* 925.

Johnson, N. (2005) 'The training framework review – what's all the fuss about?', 155 *New Law Journal* 357.

Jolowicz, J. (1996) 'The Woolf Report and the adversary system', 15 *Civil Justice Quarterly* 198.

Jones, D. and Brown, J. (2010) 'The relationship between victims and prosecutors: defending victims' rights? A CPS response', *Criminal Law Review* 212.

Joseph, M. (1981) *The Conveyancing Fraud,* London: Woolwich.

(1985) *Lawyers Can Seriously Damage Your Health,* London: Michael Joseph.

Julian, R. (2007) 'Judicial perspectives on the conduct of serious fraud trials', *Criminal Law Review* 751.

(2008) 'Judicial perspectives in serious fraud cases: the present status of and problems posed by case management practices, jury selection rules, juror expertise, plea bargaining and choice of mode of trial', *Criminal Law Review* 764.

JUSTICE (1970) *The Prosecution in England and Wales,* London: JUSTICE.

(2007) *The Future of the Rule of Law,* London: JUSTICE.

Kairys, D. (1998) *The Politics of Law: A Progressive Critique,* New York: Basic Books.

Kakalik, J. *et al.* (1996) *An Evaluation of Judicial Case Management under the Civil Justice Reform Act,* California: Rand Corporation.

Kelsen, H. (1945) *General Theory of Law and State,* Cambridge, MA: Harvard University Press.

Kemp, V. (2011) *Transforming Legal Aid – Access to Legal Defence Services,* London: Legal Services Research Commission.

(2013) ' "No time for a solicitor": implications for delays on the take-up of legal advice', *Criminal Law Review* 184.

Kemp, V., Balmer, N. and Pleasence, P. (2012) 'Whose time is it anyway? Factors associated with duration in police custody', *Criminal Law Review* 736.

Kemp, V., Pleasence, P. and Balmer, N. (2011) 'Children, young people and requests for police station legal advice: 25 years on from PACE', 11(1) *Youth Justice* 28.

Kennedy, H. (1992) *Eve was Framed: Women and British Justice,* London: Chatto.

King, M. and May, C. (1985) *Black Magistrates: A Study of Selection and Appointment,* London: Cobden Trust.

Law Commission (1976) *Criminal Law: Report on Conspiracy and Criminal Law Reform,* London: HMSO.

(1982) *Offences Against Public Order,* London: HMSO.

(1999) *Bail and the Human Rights Act 1998* (Report No. 157), London: HMSO.

(2006) *Post-Legislative Scrutiny,* Cm 6945, London: HMSO.

(2007) *The High Court's Jurisdiction in Relation to Criminal Proceedings,* Law Com CP 184, London: Law Commission.

(2010a) *The High Court's Jurisdiction in Relation to Criminal Proceedings,* Law Com No. 324, London: The Stationery Office.

(2010b) *The Admissibility of Expert Evidence in Criminal Proceedings in England and Wales* (Consultation Paper No. 190), London: Law Commission.

(2011a) *Expert Evidence in Criminal Proceedings in England and Wales,* London: Law Commission.

(2011b) *Public Services Ombudsmen,* HC 1136: London: Stationery Office.

Law Society (2002) *The Woolf Network Questionnaire,* London: Law Society.

(2005) *Qualifying as a Solicitor – a Framework for the Future,* London: Law Society.

(2008) *Conditional Fees: A Guide to CFAs and Other Funding Options,* London: Law Society.

Law Society and Civil Justice Council (2002) *More Civil Justice: The Impact of the Woolf Reforms on Pre-Action Behaviour* (Research Study 43), London: Law Society.

Laws, J. (1998) 'The limitations of human rights', *Public Law* 254.

Lawson, C. M. (1982) 'The family affinities of common law and civil law legal systems', 6 *Hastings International Comparative Law Review* 85.

Lee, S. (1986) *Law and Morals,* Oxford: Oxford University Press.

Legal Services Board (2010) *Referral Fees, Referral Arrangements and Fee Sharing,* London: Legal Services Board.

(2012) *Market Impacts of the Legal Services Act – Interim Baseline Report,* London: Legal Services Board.

Legal Services Commission (2001) *Quality and Cost: Final Report on the Contracting of Civil, Non-Family Advice and Assistance Pilot,* London: Legal Services Commission.

(2007) *Best Value Tendering for Criminal Defence Services,* London: Legal Services Commission.

Legal Services Consumer Panel (2013) *Empowering Consumers,* London: Legal Services Board.

Leggatt, Sir Andrew (2001) *Tribunals for Users: One System, One Service,* London: Stationery Office.

Leigh, A. *et al.* (1998) *Deaths in Police Custody: Learning the Lessons,* London: Home Office.

Leigh, L. (2008) 'Injustice perpetuated? The contribution of the Court of Appeal', 72 *Journal of Criminal Law* 40.

Leigh, L. and Zedner, L. (1992) *A Report on the Administration of Criminal Justice in the Pretrial Phase in London, France and Germany,* London: HMSO.

Leng, R. (1993) *The Right to Silence in Police Interrogation,* Royal Commission on Criminal Justice Research Study No. 10, London: HMSO.

Lennan, J. (2010) 'A Supreme Court for the United Kingdom: a note on early days', *Civil Justice Quarterly* 139.

Lester, A. (1984) 'Fundamental rights: the United Kingdom isolated?', *Public Law* 46.

Levi, M. (1988) 'The role of the jury in complex cases', in Findlay, M. and Duff, P. (eds) *The Jury under Attack,* London: Butterworths.

(1992) *The Investigation, Prosecution and Trial of Serious Fraud,* London: HMSO.

Levitsky, J. (1994) 'The Europeanization of the British legal style', 42 *American Journal of Comparative Law* 347.

Lidstone, K. (1984) *Magisterial Review of the Pre-Trial Criminal Process: A Research Report,* Sheffield: University of Sheffield Centre for Criminological and Socio-Legal Studies.

Lightman, J. (2003) 'The civil justice system and legal profession – the challenges ahead', *Civil Justice Quarterly* 235.

Lippke, R. (2011) *The Ethics of Plea Bargaining,* Oxford: Oxford University Press.

Llewellyn, K. (1962) *Jurisprudence: Realism in Theory and Practice,* Chicago: University of Chicago Press.

Lloyd-Bostock, S. (2007) 'The Jubilee Line jurors: does their experience strengthen the argument for judge-only trial in long and complex fraud cases?', *Criminal Law Review* 255.

Locke, J. (1967) *Two Treatises of Government,* London: Cambridge University Press.

Lord Chancellor's Department (1998a) *Determining Mode of Trial in Either Way Cases,* London: Lord Chancellor's Department.

(1998b) *Report of the Fast Track Simulation Pilot,* London: Lord Chancellor's Department.

(1999) *Alternative Dispute Resolution – A Discussion Paper,* London: Lord Chancellor's Department.

(2000) *The House of Lords: Completing the Reform,* Cm 5291, London: Stationery Office.

(2002) *Further Findings: A Continuing Evaluation of the Civil Justice Reforms,* London: Lord Chancellor's Department.

(2003) *Delivering Value for Money in the Criminal Defence Service,* Consultation Paper, London: Lord Chancellor's Department.

(2005) *The Future of Legal Services: Putting the Consumer First,* London: Lord Chancellor's Department.

Lovegrove, A. (2010) 'The Sentencing Council, the public's sense of justice and personal mitigation', *Criminal Law Review* 906.

Loveless, J. (2012) 'Women, sentencing and the drug offences definitive guidelines', *Criminal Law Review* 592.

McCabe, S. and Purves, R. (1972) *The Jury at Work: A Study of a Series of Jury Trials in which the Defendant was Acquitted,* Oxford: Blackwell.

McConville, M. (1992) 'Videotaping interrogations: police behaviour on and off camera', *Criminal Law Review* 532.

McConville, M. and Baldwin, J. (1977) *Negotiated Justice: Pressures to Plead Guilty,* Oxford: Martin Robertson.

(1981) *Courts, Prosecution and Conviction,* Oxford: Oxford University Press.

McConville, M. and Hodgson, J. (1993) *Custodial Legal Advice and the Right to Silence,* Royal Commission on Criminal Justice Research Study No. 16, London: HMSO.

McConville, M., Sanders, A. and Leng, P. (1993) *The Case for the Prosecution: Police Suspects and the Construction of Criminality,* London: Routledge.

MacCormick, N. (1978) *Legal Rules and Legal Reasoning,* Oxford: Clarendon.

MacDonald, Lord (2011) *Review of Counter-Terrorism and Security Powers,* Cm 8003, London: Stationery Office.

McEwan, J. (2013) 'Vulnerable defendants and the fairness of trials', *Criminal Law Review* 100.

McHarg, A. (2006) 'What is delegated legislation?', *Public Law* 539.

McNeill, F., Raynor, P. and Trotter, C. (2010) *Offender Supervision: New Directions in Research, Theory and Practice,* Cullompton: Willan Publishing.

The Macpherson Report (1999) Cm 4262-I, London: HMSO.

Maine, Sir H. (2001) *Ancient Law,* London: Dent.

Mair, G. and May, C. (1997) *Offenders on Probation,* Home Office Research Study No. 167, London: HMSO.

Malleson, K. (1993) *A Review of the Appeal Process,* Royal Commission on Criminal Justice Research Series No. 17, London: HMSO.

(1997) 'Judicial training and performance appraisal: the problem of judicial independence', 60 *Modern Law Review* 655.

(1999) *The New Judiciary – The Effect of Expansion and Activism,* Aldershot: Ashgate.

Malleson, K. and Banda, F. (2000) *Factors Affecting the Decision to Apply for Silk,* London: Lord Chancellor's Department.

Malleson, K. and Roberts, S. (2002) 'Streamlining and clarifying the appellate process', *Criminal Law Review* 272.

Manchester, C., Salter, D. and Moodie, P. (2000) *Exploring the Law: The Dynamics of Precedent and Statutory Interpretation* (2nd edn), London: Sweet & Maxwell.

Mansfield, M. (1993) *Presumed Guilty: The British Legal System Exposed,* London: Heinemann.

Markus, K. (1992) 'The politics of legal aid', in *The Critical Lawyer's Handbook,* London: Pluto.

Marsh, N. (1971) 'Law reform in the United Kingdom: a new institutional approach', 13 *William and Mary Law Review* 263.

Martin, R. (2013) 'The recent supergrass controversy: have we learnt from the troubled past?', *Criminal Law Review* 273.

Martinson, R. (1974) 'What works? – questions and answers about prison reform', 35 *The Public Interest,* 22–54.

Marx, K. (1933) *Capital,* London: Dent.

Matthews, R., Hancock, L. and Briggs, D. (2004) *Jurors' Perceptions, Understanding, Confidence and Satisfaction in the Jury System: A Study in Six Courts,* London: Home Office.

Mayhew, L. and Reiss, A. (1969), 'The social organisation of legal contacts', 34 *American Sociological Review* 309.

Mendelle, P. (2005) 'No detention please, we're British?', 155 *New Law Journal* 77.

Mill, J. S. (1859) *On Liberty,* London: J.W. Parker.

Miller, J. (2000) *Upping the PACE? An Evaluation of the Recommendations of the Stephen Lawrence Inquiry on Stop and Search,* Police Research Series Paper 128, London: Home Office.

Miller, J., Bland, N. and Quinton, P. (2000) *The Impact of Stop and Search on Crime and the Community,* Police Research Series Paper 127, London: Home Office.

Millett, L. (2000) 'Modern equity: a means of escape', *Judicial Studies Board Journal* 21.

Ministry of Justice (2006) *Delivering Simple, Speedy, Summary Justice – An Evaluation of the Magistrates' Court Tests,* London: Ministry of Justice.

(2007a) *Confidence and Confidentiality: Openness in Family Courts – A New Approach,* London: Ministry of Justice.

(2007b) *The Governance of Britain: A Consultation on the Role of the Attorney General,* Cm 7197, London: Stationery Office.

(2007c) *The Governance of Britain: Judicial Appointments,* London: Ministry of Justice.

(2008a) *The Governance of Britain: Constitutional Renewal,* London: Ministry of Justice.

(2008b) *Family Justice in View,* London: Ministry of Justice.

(2010a) *Breaking the Cycle: Effective Punishment, Rehabilitation and Sentencing of Offenders,* Cm 7972, Norwich: Stationery Office.

(2010b) *Proposals for Reform of Civil Litigation Funding and Costs in England and Wales: Implementation of Lord Justice Jackson's Recommendations,* Cm 7947, Norwich: Stationery Office.

(2010c) *Proposals for the Reform of Legal Aid in England and Wales,* Consultation Paper, Cm 7967, Norwich: Stationery Office.

(2010d), *Report of the Advisory Panel on Judicial Diversity,* London: Ministry of Justice.

(2011a) *Solving Disputes in the County Court: Creating a Simpler, Quicker and More Proportionate System,* Consultation Paper, London: Ministry of Justice.

(2011b) *Appointments and diversity: A judiciary for the 21st Century,* Consultation Paper CP19/2011, London: Ministry of Justice.

(2012) *Punishment and Reform; Effective Community Sentences,* Consultation Paper CP8/2012, London: Ministry of Justice.

(2013) *Transforming Rehabilitation: A revolution in the way we manage offenders,* Consultation Paper CP1/2013, Cm 8517, Norwich: The Stationery Office.

Mitchell, B. (1983) 'Confessions and police interrogation of suspects', *Criminal Law Review* 596.

Modernising Justice (1997) Cm 4155, London: Home Office.

Montesquieu, C. (1989) *The Spirit of the Laws,* Cambridge: Cambridge University Press.

Moore, R. (2003) 'The use of financial penalties and the amounts imposed: the need for a new approach', *Criminal Law Review* 13.

(2004) 'The methods for enforcing financial penalties: the need for a multidimensional approach', *Criminal Law Review* 728.

Moorhead, R. (2011) 'Filthy lucre: lawyers' fees and lawyers' ethics – what is wrong with informed consent?' 31 *Legal Studies* 345.

Moorhead, R. and Cape, E. (2005) *Demand Induced Supply? Identifying Cost Drivers in Criminal Defence Work,* London: Legal Services Commission.

Moorhead, R. and Cumming, R. (2008) *Damage-Based Contingency Fees in Employment Cases: A Survey of Practitioners,* Cardiff Law School Research Paper No. 6, Cardiff: Cardiff University.

Moorhead, R. and Hurst, P. (2008) *Improving Access to Justice: Contingency Fees. A Study of their Operation in the United States of America,* London: Civil Justice Council.

Moorhead, R. *et al.* (2001) *Quality and Cost: Final Report on the Contracting of Civil, Non-Family Advice and Assistance,* London: Stationery Office.

Morgan, R. and Russell, N. (2000) *The Judiciary in the Magistrates' Courts* (Home Office RDS Occasional Paper No. 66), London: Home Office.

Morris, A. (2007) 'Spiralling or stabilising? The compensation culture and our propensity to claim damages for personal injury', 70 *Modern Law Review* 349.

Moxon, D. (ed.) (1985) *Managing Criminal Justice: A Collection of Papers,* London: HMSO.

Moxon, D. and Crisp, D. (1994) *Case Screening by the Crown Prosecution Service: How and Why Cases are Terminated,* London: HMSO.

Mullins, C. (1990) *Error of Judgement: The Truth about the Birmingham Bombings,* Dublin: Poolbeg Press.

Narey, M. (1997) *Review of Delay in the Criminal Justice System,* London: Home Office.

National Association of Citizens Advice Bureaux (1995), *Barriers to Justice: CAB Clients' Experience of Legal Services,* London: NACAB.

(1999) *A Balancing Act: Surviving the Risk Society,* London: NACAB.

National Association of Probation Officers (NAPO) (2004) *Anti-Social Behaviour Orders: Analysis of the First Six Years,* London: NAPO.

National Audit Office (1999) *Criminal Justice: Working Together,* London: Stationery Office.

(2003) *Community Legal Service: The Introduction of Contracting,* HC 89, 2002–03, London: HMSO.

(2005) *Facing Justice: Tackling Defendants: Non-Attendance at Court,* HC 1162, London: Stationery Office.

(2006) *CPS: Effective Use of Magistrates' Court Hearings:* London: Stationery Office.

Naughton, M. (2009) *Criminal Cases Review Commission. Hope for the Innocent?* London: Palgrave Macmillan.

New Zealand Law Commission (2001) *Juries in Criminal Trials,* Report 69, Wellington: New Zealand Law Commission.

(2006) *Sentencing Guidelines and Parole Reform,* New Zealand: New Zealand Law Commission.

Nobles, R. and Schiff, D. (2005) 'The Criminal Cases Review Commission: establishing a workable relationship with the Court of Appeal', *Criminal Law Review* 173.

Norgrove, D. (2011) *Family Justice Review: Final Report,* London: Ministry of Justice, Department of Education and the Welsh Government.

Norwich Union (2004) *A Modern Compensation System: Moving from Concept to Reality,* Norwich: Norwich Union.

Nozick, R. (1975) *Anarchy, State, and Utopia,* Oxford: Blackwell.

Nuttall, C., Goldblatt, P. and Lewis, C. (1998) *Reducing Offending: An Assessment of Research Evidence on Ways of Dealing with Offending Behaviour,* Home Office Research Study No. 187, London: Home Office.

Olivecrona, K. (1971) *Law as Fact,* London: Stevens.

Ormerod, D. (2003) 'ECHR and the exclusion of evidence: trial remedies for Article 8 breaches?', *Criminal Law Review* 61.

Ormerod, D. and Roberts, A. (2003) 'The Police Reform Act 2002 – increasing centralisation, maintaining confidence and contracting out crime control', *Criminal Law Review* 141.

Owers, A. (1995) 'Not completely appealing', 145 *New Law Journal* 353.

Packer, H. (1968) *The Limits of the Criminal Sanction,* Stanford, CA: Stanford University Press.

Padfield, N. (2011) 'Time to bury the custody "threshold"?', *Criminal Law Review* 593.

Pannick, D. (1987) *Judges,* Oxford: Oxford University Press.

Parliamentary Penal Affairs Group (1999) *Changing Offending Behaviour – Some Things Work,* London: Parliament.

Partington, M. (1994) 'Training the judiciary in England and Wales: the work of the Judicial Studies Board', *Civil Justice Quarterly* 319.

(2004) 'Alternative dispute resolution: recent developments, future challenges', *Civil Justice Quarterly* 99.

Paterson, A. (1982) *The Law Lords,* London: Macmillan.

Pattenden, R. (2009) 'The standards of review for mistake of fact in the Court of Appeal, Criminal Division', *Criminal Law Review* 15.

Pattenden, R. and Skinns, L. (2010) 'Choice, privacy and publicly-funded legal advice at the police station', 73 *Modern Law Review* 349.

Peach, Sir L. (1999) *Appointment Processes of Judges and Queen's Counsel in England and Wales,* London: HMSO.

Petkanas, W. (1990) *Cameras on Trial: An Assessment of the Educational Affect of News Cameras in Trial Courts,* PhD, New York: New York University.

Peysner, J. and Seneviratne, M. (2005) *The Management of Civil Cases: The Courts and the Post-Woolf Landscape.* London: Department for Constitutional Affairs.

Philips, C. (1981) *The Royal Commission on Criminal Procedure,* Cmnd 8092, London: HMSO.

Pickles, J. (1988) *Straight from the Bench,* London: Coronet.

Pleasence, P. (2004) *Causes of Action: Civil Law and Social Justice,* London: HMSO.

Pleasence, P. and Balmer, N. (2013) *In Need of Advice? Findings of a Small Business Legal Needs Benchmarking Survey,* Cambridge: PPSR.

Pleasence, P., Kemp V. and Balmer, N. (2011) 'The justice lottery? Police station advice 25 years on from PACE', *Criminal Law Review* 1.

Plotnikoff, J. and Wilson, R. (1993) *Information and Advice for Prisoners about Grounds for Appeal and the Appeal Process,* Royal Commission on Criminal Justice Research Study No. 18, London: HMSO.

Pound, R. (1968) *Social Control Through Law,* Hamden: Archon.

Prime, T. and Scanlan, G. (2004) 'Stare decisis and the Court of Appeal: judicial confusion and judicial reform', *Civil Justice Quarterly* 212.

Prince, S. (2007) 'Mediating small claims: are we on the right track?', 26 *Civil Justice Quarterly* 328.

Pywell, S. (2013) 'Untangling the law', 163 *New Law Journal* 321.

Quinton, P., Bland, N. and Miller, J. (2000) *Police Stops, Decision-making and Practice,* Police Research Series Paper 130, London: Home Office.

Quirk, H. (2006) 'The significance of culture in criminal procedure reform: why the revised disclosure scheme cannot work', 10 *International Journal of Evidence and Proof* 42.

Race and the Criminal Justice System: An Overview To The Complete Statistics 2003–2004 (2005) London: Criminal Justice System Race Unit.

Raine, J. and Walker, C. (2002) *The Impact on the Courts and the Administration of Justice of the Human Rights Act 1998,* London: Lord Chancellor's Department, Research Secretariat.

Ramsbotham, Sir D. (1997) *Women in Prison: A Thematic Review,* London: Home Office.

Rawls, J. (1971) *A Theory of Justice,* Oxford: Oxford University Press.

— (1972) *Political Liberalism, John Dewey Essays in Philosophy,* NY: Columbia University Press.

Raz, J. (1972) 'The rule of law and its virtue', 93 *Law Quarterly Review* 195.

Renton, D. (1975) *The Preparation of Legislation,* London: HMSO.

Restorative Justice: Helping to Meet Local Needs (2004), London: Office for Criminal Justice Reform.

Ridout, F. (2010) 'Virtual courts – virtual justice?', 174 *JPN* 602.

Rippon, Lord (1992) *Making the Law: Report of the Hansard Society Commission on the Legislative Process,* London: Hansard Society.

Roberts, J. (2008) 'Aggravating and mitigating factors at sentencing: towards greater consistency of application', *Criminal Law Review* 264.

— (2012) 'Sentencing guidelines and judicial discretion: evolution of the duty of courts to comply in England and Wales', 50 *British Journal of Criminology.*

Roberts, J., Hough, M., Jacobson, J. and Moon, N. (2009) 'Public attitudes to sentencing purposes and sentencing factors: an empirical analysis', *Criminal Law Review* 771.

Roberts, P. (2011) 'Does Article 6 of the European Convention on Human Rights require reasoned verdicts in criminal trials?', 11 *Human Rights Law Review* 213.

Roberts, P. and Saunders, C. (2008) 'Introducing pre-trial witness interviews: a flexible new fixture in the Crown Prosecutor's toolkit', *Criminal Law Review* 831.

Robertson, G. (1993) *Freedom, the Individual and the Law,* London: Penguin.

Rock, P. (2004) *Constructing Victims' Rights,* Oxford: Oxford University Press.

Roskill Committee (1986) *Report of the Committee on Fraud Trials,* London: HMSO.

Royal Commission for the Reform of the House of Lords, Report of the (2000) *A House for the Future,* Cm 4534, London: HMSO.

Royal Commission on Criminal Justice Report (1993), Cm 2263, London: HMSO.

Runciman, G. (1993) *Report of the Royal Commission on Criminal Justice,* London: HMSO.

Ryan, E. (2007) 'The unmet need: focus on the future', 157 *New Law Journal* 134.

Salter, M. and Doupe, M. (2006) 'Concealing the past? Questioning textbook interpretations of the history of equity and trusts', 22 *Liverpool Law Review* 253.

Sanders, A. (1993) 'Controlling the discretion of the individual officer', in Reiner, R. and Spencer, S. (eds) *Accountable Policing,* London: Institute for Public Policy Research.

(2001) 'Modernizing the magistracy', 165 JPN 57.

Sanders, A. and Bridge, L. (1993) 'Access to legal advice', in Walker, C. and Starmer, K. (eds) *Justice in Error,* London: Blackstone Press.

Sanders, A., Hoyle, C., Morgan, R. and Cape, E. (2001) 'Victim impact statements: don't work, can't work', *Criminal Law Review* 447.

Scarman, L. (1982) *The Scarman Report: The Brixton Disorders, 10–12 April, 1981,* London, Penguin Books.

Schur, E. (1965) *Crimes without Victims: Deviant Behaviour and Public Policy, Abortion, Homosexuality, Drug Addiction,* New York: Prentice-Hall.

Seago, P., Walker, C. and Wall, D. (2000) 'The development of the professional magistracy in England and Wales', *Criminal Law Review* 631.

Sentencing Commission Working Group (2008) *A Structured Sentencing Framework and Sentencing Commission,* London: Ministry of Justice.

Shapland, J. (2008) *Does Restorative Justice Affect Reconviction?,* Ministry of Justice Research Series 10/08, London: Ministry of Justice.

Sherman, L. and Strang, H. (2007) *Restorative Justice: The Evidence,* London: The Smith Institute.

Skinns, L. (2009) 'I'm a detainee; get me out of here', *British Journal of Criminology* 399.

(2010) *Police Custody: Governance, Legitimacy and Reform in the Criminal Justice Process,* London: Routledge.

(2011) 'The right to legal advice in the police station: past, present and future', *Criminal Law Review* 19.

Skyrme, Sir T. (1979) *The Changing Image of the Magistracy* (2nd edn, 1983), London: Macmillan.

Smedley, N. (2009) *Review of the Regulation of Corporate Legal Work,* London: Law Society.

Smith, D. and Gray, J. (1983) *Police and People in London* (The Policy Studies Institute), Aldershot: Gower.

Smith, J. C. and Hogan, B. (2002) *Criminal Law,* London: Butterworths.

Smith, R. (1998) *Legal Aid Contracting: Lessons from North America,* London: Legal Action Group.

(2007) 'Ever decreasing circles', 157 *New Law Journal* 1437.

Smith, R. *et al.* (2007) *Poverty and Disadvantage among Prisoners' Families,* London: Joseph Rowntree Foundation.

Spencer, J. (2006) 'Does our present criminal appeal system make sense?', *Criminal Law Review* 677.

(2010) 'Compensation for wrongful imprisonment', *Criminal Law Review* 803.

Stern, V. (1987) *Bricks of Shame: Britain's Prisons,* London: Penguin.

Steyn, J. (2001) '*Pepper* v *Hart:* a re-examination', *Oxford Journal of Legal Studies* 59.

Summers, R. (1992) *Essays on the Nature of Law and Legal Reasoning,* Berlin: Duncker & Humblot.

Supperstone, M., Stilitz, D. and Sheldon, C. (2006) 'ADR and public law', *Public Law* 299.

Susskind, R. (1996) *The Future of Law,* Oxford: Oxford University Press.

(2008) *The End of Lawyers? Rethinking the Nature of Legal Services,* Oxford: Oxford University Press.

Tain, P. (2003) 'Master of the game?', *Solicitors Journal* 192.

Tata, C. *et al.* (2004) 'Does mode of delivery make a difference to criminal case outcomes and clients' satisfaction? The public defence solicitor experiment', *Criminal Law Review* 120.

Taylor, R. (1997) *Cautions, Court Proceedings and Sentencing in England and Wales 1996,* London: Home Office.

Thomas, Cheryl (2007) *Diversity and Fairness in the Jury System,* Ministry of Justice Research Series 2/07, London: Ministry of Justice.

Thomas, C. (2008) 'Exposing the myths of jury service', *Criminal Law Review* 415.

(2010) *Are Juries Fair?* London: Ministry of Justice.

(2013) 'Avoiding the perfect storm of juror contempt', *Criminal Law Review* 483.

Thomas, C. and Balmer, N. J. (2007) *Diversity and Fairness in the Jury System,* London: Ministry of Justice.

Thomas, D. (1970) *Principles of Sentencing: The Sentencing Policy of the Court of Appeal Criminal Division,* London: Heinemann.

(2004) 'The Criminal Justice Act 2003: custodial sentences', *Criminal Law Review* 702.

Thompson, R. (2012) 'Grave crimes – now it's personal', *Criminal Law Review* 302.

Tonry, M. (1996) *Sentencing Matters,* Oxford: Oxford University Press.

Twining, W. and Miers, D. (1991) *How To Do Things With Rules,* London: Weidenfeld & Nicolson.

Vennard, J. (1985) 'The outcome of contested trials', in Moxon, D. (ed.) *Managing Criminal Justice,* London: HMSO.

Vennard, J. and Riley, D. (1988a) 'The use of peremptory challenge and stand by of jurors and their relationships with trial outcome', *Criminal Law Review* 723.

(1988b) *Triable Either Way Cases: Crown Court or Magistrates' Court?* London: HMSO.

Vogt, G. and Wadham, J. (2003) *Deaths in Custody: Redress and Remedies,* London: Liberty.

Von Hirsch, A., Ashworth, A. and Roberts, J. (2009) *Principled Sentencing: Readings on Theory and Policy,* Oxford: Hart.

Wade, Sir W. (2000) 'Horizons of horizontability', 116 *Law Quarterly Review* 217.

Wakeham, Lord (2000) *A House for the Future,* Cm 4534, London: HMSO.

Waldron, J. (1989) *The Law,* London: Routledge.

Walker, C. (2008) 'Post-charge questioning of suspects', *Criminal Law Review* 509.

Walker, C. and Starmer, K. (1999) *Miscarriages of Justice: A Review of Justice in Error,* London: Blackstone.

Warnock, M. (1986) *Morality and the Law,* Cardiff: University College Cardiff.

Wasik, M. (2004) 'Going around in circles? Reflections on fifty years of change in sentencing', *Criminal Law Review* 253.

(2008) 'Sentencing guidelines in England and Wales – state of the art?', *Criminal Law Review* 253.

Weber, M. (1979) *Economy and Society,* Berkeley: University of California Press.

Weinreb, L. (2004) *Legal Reason: The Use of Analogy in Legal Argument,* Cambridge: Cambridge University Press.

Westera, N., Kebbell, M. and Milne, B. (2013) 'Losing two thirds of the story: a comparison of the video-recorded police interview and live evidence of rape complainants', *Criminal Law Review* 290.

White, P. and Power, I. (1998) *Revised Projections of Long Term Trends in the Prison Population to 2005,* London: Home Office.

White, P. and Woodbridge, J. (1998) *The Prison Population in 1997,* London: Home Office.

White, R. (1973) 'Lawyers and the enforcement of rights', in Morris, P., White, R. and Lewis, P. (eds) *Social Needs and Legal Action,* Oxford: Martin Robertson.

Whittaker, C. and Mackie, A. (1997) *Enforcing Financial Penalties,* Home Office Research Study 165, London: Home Office.

Williams, G. (1983) *Textbook of Criminal Law,* London: Stevens and Sons.

Willis, J. (1938) 'Statute interpretation in a nutshell', 16 *Canadian Bar Review* 13.

Windlesham, Lord (2005) 'The Constitutional Reform Act 2005: ministers, judges and constitutional change, Part 1', *Public Law* 806.

Wolfenden, J. (1957) *Report of the Committee on Homosexual Offences and Prostitution,* Cmnd 2471, London: HMSO.

Woodhead, Sir P. (1998) *The Prison Ombudsman's Annual Report,* London: Home Office.

Woodhouse, D. (2007) 'The Constitutional Reform Act 2005 – defending judicial independence the English way', 5 (1) *International Journal of Constitutional Law* 153.

Wooler, S. (2006) *Review of the Investigation and Criminal Proceedings Relating to the Jubilee Line Cases,* London: HM Crown Prosecution Service Inspectorate.

Woolf, Lord Justice H. (1995) *Access to Justice: Interim Report to the Lord Chancellor on the Civil Justice System in England and Wales,* London: Lord Chancellor's Department.

(1996) *Access to Justice,* London: Lord Chancellor's Department.

(2008) *The Pursuit of Justice,* Oxford: Oxford University Press.

Wright, J. (2009) 'Interpreting section 2 of the Human Rights Act 1998: towards an indigenous jurisprudence of human rights', *Public Law* 595.

Yarrow, S. (1997) *The Price of Success: Lawyers, Clients and Conditional Fees,* London: Policy Studies Institute.

Young, J. (1971) *The Drugtakers: The Social Meaning of Drug Use,* London: Paladin.

Young, Lord (2010) *Common Sense, Common Safety,* London: Cabinet Office.

Young, S. (2005) 'Clementi: in practice', 155 *New Law Journal* 45.

Young, W. and Browning, C. (2008) 'New Zealand's Sentencing Council', *Criminal Law Review* 287.

Your Right to Know (1997) Cm 3818, London: HMSO.

Zander, M. (1988) *A Matter of Justice,* Oxford: Oxford University Press.

(1993) *Note of Dissent, Report of the Royal Commission on Criminal Justice* (Cmnd 2263), London: HMSO.

(1997) 'The Woolf Report: forwards or backwards for the new Lord Chancellor?', 17 *Civil Justice Quarterly* 208.

(1998) 'The Government's plans on civil justice', 61 *Modern Law Review* 382.

(2000) 'The complaining juror', 150 *New Law Journal* 723.

(2001a) 'Should the legal profession be shaking in its boots?', 151 *New Law Journal* 369.

(2001b) 'A question of trust', *Solicitors Journal* 1100.

(2004) *The Law-Making Process,* London: Butterworths.

(2005) 'The Prevention of Terrorism Act 2005', 155 *New Law Journal* 438.

(2006) 'Mission impossible', 156 *New Law Journal* 618.

(2007a) 'Carter's wake (1)', 157 *New Law Journal* 872.

(2007b) 'Carter's wake (2)', 157 *New Law Journal* 912.

(2007c) 'Full speed ahead?', 157 *New Law Journal* 992.

(2007d) 'Change of PACE', 157 *New Law Journal* 504.

(2008) 'What's the rush?', 158 *New Law Journal* 7317.

Zander, M. and Henderson, P. (1993) *Crown Court Study,* London: HMSO.

Zuckerman, A. (1995) 'A reform of civil procedure – rationing procedure rather than access to justice', 22 *Journal of Legal Studies* 156.

(1996) 'Lord Woolf's Access to Justice: plus ça change . . . ', 59 *Modern Law Review* 773.

INDEX

Abortion
    law reform, and 163–164
Absolute discharge 549
ABTA 693
Access to justice 346–347
Act of Parliament 49–56
    example: Criminal Defence Service (Advice
        and Assistance) Act 2001 50
    making 49–56
    policy development 49–51
Administration of justice 326–333
Adversarial process 476
Alternative business structures
    legal profession 246–250
Alternative dispute resolution 636–637,
        688–708
    accessibility 701
    Brexit, and 704–705
    conciliation of parties 702
    cost 701
    customer satisfaction 702
    enforcement 702
    expertise 701
    future for 703–704
    imbalances of power 702
    lack of legal expertise 702
    low take-up rate 702–703
    main uses 690
    mechanisms 692–694
    no system of precedent 702
    online dispute resolution 696
    pressure to use 693
    problems with court hearings 691–692
        adversarial process 691
        imposed solutions 692
        inflexibility 692
        publicity 692
        technical cases 692
    speed 701
    trade association arbitration schemes
        696–697
Alternative funding arrangements 364
Alternative sources of legal help 355
Appeals
    tribunals 681–682
Appearance in court 486–487
Appropriate adult
    requirement for 445–446
Arrest
    detention without 431
    search of the person after 450

Arrest powers 435–439
    citizen's arrest 437
    manner of arrest 438
    warrant, with 435–436
    warrant, without 436–437
Assisted voluntary euthanasia 36–37
Attorney General 332
    historical powers 485–486
Audio-recording
    police interviews, of 442–443
Auld Review 512–517
    codification 513–514
    information technology 514
    LASPO 515–517
    legal aid 515–517
    standard timetables 514
    unrepresented defendants 515–517
    video-recorded evidence 515

Bach Commission Report 365–366
Bail 459–460
    young offenders 574
Bar Standards Board 243
Barristers 224–229
    background 232–239
    cab rank rule 225
    class 234–235
    direct access 224
    disability 236
    ethnic minorities 234, 235
    fees 225
    promotion to judiciary 227
    qualifications 225–227
    reserved legal activities 230
    social mobility 236
    solicitors compared 254
    training 225–227
    women 233–234
    work 224–225
Bentley, Derek 615
Bias
    jury 289
Bill of Rights 389–393
    attitude of judiciary 390
    curbs on executive 389
    drafting style 392
    increased power for judiciary 390–391
    inflexibility 391
    rights are not powers 391–392
    too much flexibility 391
    unnecessary 390

Bills 51–53
    accelerated procedures 54
    Committee stage 52
    first reading 51
    House of Lords 52–53
    Private 51
    Private Members' 51
    Public 51
    report stage 52
    Royal Assent 53
    second reading 51
    third reading 52
Binding over 551–552
Birmingham Six 423–425
Black jurors 298
Blackstone, William
    case law, on 28–29
Bobbies on the beat 463
Brexit 102–103
    alternative dispute resolution, and
        704–705
Bye-laws 88

Case law 12–44
    advantages 37–38
    certainty 37
    chance, dependence on 39
    complexity 38
    critical theorists: precedent as
        legitimation 30
    detailed practical rules 38
    disadvantages 38–41
    Dworkin: seamless web of principles
        29–30
    flexibility 38
    free market in legal ideas 38
    Griffith: political choices 30–31
    historical background 14–18
    how do judges decide cases 28–31
    illogical distinctions 39
    judge-made law 31–39
    lack of research 39
    law reform 148–149
    retrospective effect 39–41
    rigidity 38
    statutory interpretation, and 63
    undemocratic 41
    unpredictability 39
    unsystematic progression 39
    volume 38
    Waldron: political choices 31

William Blackstone on 28–29
Case reference xxvi–xxvii
Case names xxiv–xxvii
    civil law xxiv–xxv
    criminal law xxiv
Cautions 442, 457–459
Central Criminal Court 270
Chartered legal executives 255–256
    qualifications 255–256
    training 255–256
Child safety orders 584–585
Children and young people
    custodial sentences 537
Citizen's arrest 437
Citizens Advice 354–355
Civil appeals 710–725
    county court, from 713
    High Court, from 713
    magistrates' court, from 713–714
Civil courts 627–628
Civil justice system
    after April 1999 631–649
    automated claims portal 642–643
    before April 1999 628–631
        adversarial process 630
        delays 630
        emphasis on oral evidence 630–631
        injustice 630
        problems with 628–631
        too expensive 630
    Briggs Review 662, 663
    case management 637–640
    changes in terminology 635
    Civil Liability Bill 654
    costs: Lord Jackson's reforms 645–649
    court fees 642
    criticism of 650–662
    disclosure 640–641
    enforcement 650
    fast track 638–639
    inquisitorial system 664–665
    integration 664
    multi-track 639
    out-of-court settlements 651
    pre-action protocols 636
    proactive approach 640
    Professor Zander's concerns 656
    proposed abolition of pre-action
        protocol 664
    sanctions 641–642
    small claims track 638, 640, 653–654
    standards 650
Civil legal aid 340–342
Civil Procedure Rules 632–635
Civil service
    law reform, and 163
Civil Service Tribunal 114
Civil trial process 624–670
    history 626
    nature of 626

Claim form 634
Claims management companies 222–224
Clark, Sally 498–501
Class
    barristers 234–235
    solicitors 234–235
Class actions 365
Commercial arbitration 697–698
Commercial Court ADR scheme 698
Commission for Equality and Human
        Rights 385
Common law
    equity, and 137–138
Community sentences 545–549
    alcohol treatment requirement 548
    curfew requirement 546–547
    drug rehabilitation requirement 548
    exclusion requirement 547
    foreign travel prohibition requirement
        549
    mental health treatment requirement
        548
    programme requirement 546
    prohibited activity requirement 546
    rehabilitation activity requirement 546
    residence requirement 547
    unpaid work requirement 545–546
Community Support Officer
    uniform 429
Compensation
    human rights, and 410
Compensation culture 655–656
Compensation orders 550
Competition in Professions 241
Conciliation
    unfair dismissal cases 694–695
Conditional discharge 550
Conditional fee agreements 355–358
    problems with 356
    success fee 357
Confiscation orders 550
Contingency fees 358–360
    advantages 358–359
    disadvantages 359–360
    lawyer's financial interests 360
    low take-up rate 359–360
    no cost to state 359
    performance incentives 359
    reduce satellite litigation 358
    uncertain cases 360
    wider access to justice 359
Costs
    Lord Jackson's reforms 645–649
    satellite litigation 357
Council of Ministers 109
Council on Tribunals 679
County Court 25
    appeals from 713
Court of Appeal 24–25
    appeal to 600–602

judges 181
    mediation scheme 699
    procedure before 605–606
    second appeal to 602
Court of Justice of the European Union
        19–20, 110–114, 393–394
    General Court 114
    judicial role 111
    supervisory role 111–114
Courts
    racism, and 502–503
Cracked trials 505–506
Criminal appeals 596–621
    Attorney-General's reference 606–607
        excessively lenient sentences
            606–607
        reference following acquittal 607
    conviction, against 602–608
        errors by defence representative 603
        errors in summing up 602–603
        fresh evidence 604–605
        grounds 602
        outcome of appeal 606
        procedural irregularity 603
    criticism of 609–612
    Crown Court, from 600–602
    magistrates' court, from 598–600
    procedural irregularities 612
    reform of 609
    reluctance to address faults in system 618
    reluctance to overturn jury verdicts
            616–617
    second appeal to Court of Appeal 602
    single test for quashing convictions 613
    terminating ruling, against 607
    unwillingness to order retrials 617
Criminal bar
    demise of 351
Criminal behaviour orders 553
Criminal cases
    cost of 350–351
    jury 269–272
Criminal Cases Review Commission
        613–616
Criminal Defence Direct 344
Criminal Defence Service (Advice and
        Assistance) Act 2001 50
Criminal court system 488
Criminal Injuries Compensation Scheme
        411–412
Criminal justice system
    features of 422
    Human Rights Act 1998, and 426
    models of 501–502
Criminal legal aid 342–344
    contracts for 342–343
    Criminal Defence Direct 344
    duty solicitor schemes 344
    means test 343
    public defenders 343–344

Criminal offences
    jurors, committed by 269
Criminal Procedure Rules 477–478
Criminal proceedings
    human rights, and 411
Criminal trial 495–501
    evidence of bad character and previous
        convictions 497
    expert witnesses and miscarriage of
        justice 498–501
    Queen's evidence 497
Criminal trial process 474–523
    allocation procedure 489–490
    conviction rates 507
    corroboration rule 506–507
    disclosure 491–494, 504–505
    media, and 509–513
    plea 490
    public opinion, and 509–513
    television 512–513
    trends in confidence 512
    trial preparation hearing 490
    victims 507–509
    witnesses 507–509
Crowdfunding 361
Crown Court 25
    appeals from 600–602
Crown Prosecution Service 478–486
    administration 479–480
    charging and prosecuting defendants
        481–482
    powers of employees 480–481
    problems 503–504
    racism, and 502
Custodial sentences 533–544
    advantages 539
    children and young people 537
    disadvantages 539
    extended sentences 534
    imprisonment 533–534
        less than two years 534
        more than two years 534
    life sentences 534
    statistics 542–544
    suspended 538
Custody officer 439–440
Custom 128–133
    certainty 131
    clarity 131
    conformity with statute 132
    consistency 131
    continuity 131
    exercised as of right 131
    international law, and 132
    locality 131
    obligatory 131
    reasonableness 130
    time immemorial 130

Damages
    excessive, jury and 293

Dando, Jill 616
Deaths
    contact with police, following 465–467
Deferred prosecution agreements
        482–483
Deferred sentences 552
Delegated legislation 86–99
    committee supervision 92
    confirmation by Government Minister
        94
    consultation 90–91
    control by courts 93–94
    control of 90–95
    criticism of 95–96
    flexibility 90
    future needs 90
    House of Lords, and 92–93
    insufficient parliamentary time 90
    judicial review 93–94
        procedural *ultra vires* 93
        substantive *ultra vires* 93–94
        unreasonableness 94
    lack of control 96
    lack of democratic involvement 95
    necessary, reasons for 90
    need for local knowledge 90
    negative resolution procedure 91–92
    overuse 96
    power to make 88–89
    publication 91
    questions from MPs 92
    revocation 91
    sources 89
    speed 90
    sub-delegation 96
    super-affirmative procedure 92
    supervision by Parliament 91–93
    technicality of subject matter 90
Demonstrations
    policing 464–465
Detention
    police 439–442
    right to inform someone 443
Detention and training orders
    young offenders 580–581
Detention during Her Majesty's pleasure
    young offenders 579
Devolution 55–56
Dictionaries
    statutory interpretation 74
Director of Public Prosecutions
    historical powers 485–486
Disability
    barristers 236
    solicitors 236
Disclosure
    criminal trial process 491–494,
        504–505
Disqualification 552
Distinct Division 321–322
DNA samples 451–453

Double jeopardy rule 607–608
Duty solicitors scheme 344
Dworkin, Ronald
    case law, on 29–30

Electronic tag 548
Employment tribunals 680–681
Equitable maxims 138–139
    delay defeats equity 138–139
    he who comes to equity must come
        with clean hands 138
    he who seeks equity must do equity
        138
Equitable remedies 139
Equity 134–141
    future of 140
    Judicature Acts 137
    common law, and 137
    origins 136
Ejusdem generis
    statutory interpretation 72
Ethnic minorities
    barristers 234, 235
    juries 290–291
    solicitors 234, 235
European Central Bank 114
European Charter of Fundamental Rights
        394–395
European Commission 108
European Convention on Human Rights
        377–380, 381
    administration 378–380
    origins 377
    scope 377–378
European Council 109
European Court of Human Rights 26–
        28, 378–380, 393–394
European flag 107
European law 100–127
    decisions 121
    directives 117–121
    effect on UK 121–125
        courts, role of 122
        future developments 124–
            125
        new sources of law 121–122
    impact 118–121
    making 114–115
    opinions 121
    recommendations 121
    regulations 117
    treaties 116–117
    types 115–121
European Parliament 109–110
European Union 100–127
    aims 105–107
    Commission 108
    Council of Ministers 109
    institutions 107–114
    membership 106, 113
    modernising 107

European Union (Notification of Withdrawal) Act 2017 104
Evidence, admissibility of human rights, and 413
Evidence, exclusion of improperly obtained 447
Expert witnesses miscarriages of justice, and 498–501
Expressio unius est exclusion alterius statutory interpretation 72

Family justice system 643–644
Fathers 4 Justice 645
Fines 553–554
Fingerprints 451
Franks Report 674–675
Freedom of expression judges, and 204–205
Freemasonry judges, and 207–208

Gang-related violence injunctions 552–553
Gig economy 156–162 case law 158–162
Glossary 766–768
Golden rule 65–66 advantages 66 disadvantages 66
Gowns judges 188
Guildford Four 422–423

Habeas corpus 408
Hansard statutory interpretation 75–78
Hierarchy of courts 19–28
county court 25
Court of Appeal 24–25
Court of Justice of the European Union 19–20
Crown Court 25
European Court of Human Rights 26–28
High Court 25
magistrates' courts 25
Privy Council 22–24
routes for civil and criminal cases 27
Supreme Court 20–21
High Court 25
appeals from 713
Hillsborough disaster 425
Home detention curfew 538–539
Home Office 328–329
House of Commons 48
House of Lords 48–49
Bills 52–53
delegated legislation, and 92–93
modernising 48–49
Human Fertilisation and Embryology Authority 751–753

Human rights
compensation 410
criminal proceedings 411
evidence, admissibility of 413
habeas corpus 408
judicial review 406
negligence, civil action for 406–407
Ombudsman 414
Parliamentary controls 414
residual freedoms 376
self-defence 413
terrorism, and 395–398
Human Rights Act 1998 376, 380–389
accessibility 387
advantages 385–387
avoid conflict between domestic and international law 386
clarity 387
criminal justice system, and 426
declarations of incompatibility 382–383
disadvantages 387–389
education 387
encouraging conformity 386–387
horizontal effect 380
improved access 385
international image 387
interpretation 70–71
judicial power 387–388
legal status 388
limited scope 388–389
public authority 381, 382
remedies 385, 408–410
retrospective effect 384
tried and tested 385

Independent Office for Police Conduct 412–413
Indictable offences 489
Ineffective trials 505–506
Injunction 139 gang-related violence 552–553
International law custom, and 132
Internet jury, and 268
Interrogation policy 440–442
Intimate searches 451

Jean Charles de Menezes shooting of 411
Judge-made law 31–39
adapting to social change 34–35
assisted voluntary euthanasia 36–37
consensus law-making 35–36
decisions 32
factors 33
protecting individual rights 37
respecting parliamentary opinion 36–37
types of law 35

Judges 178–213
age 195–198
appointment 182–188
civil law systems 186–187
current procedures 184–186
old procedures 182–184
Parliament, and 187
United States 187
background 195–198
barristers 227
cases with political implications 201–203
Court of Appeal 181
discipline 191–192
dismissal 190–191
emotions 199–200
ethnic origin 195–198
Freemasonry, and 207–208
hierarchy 180–182
independence 193–194
lack of specialisation 208
media and freedom of expression 204–205
morale 199
non-judicial work 200–201
pay 189–190
problems with independence 200–209
promotion 190
removal due to infirmity 193
resignation 192
retirement 192
right-wing bias 206
robes 188
role 180
sex 195–198
shortage of time 209
solicitors 222
speaking out 203–205
supremacy of Parliament, and 200
termination of appointment 190–193
training 188–189, 198–199
technology 198
Treasury counsel 200
wigs and gowns 188
women, bias against 207
Judicature Acts 137
Judicial precedent 18–19
overrule 19
reverse 19
Judicial review 406, 710–725
bias 714–715
delegated legislation, and *see* Delegated legislation
discretion 719
error on face of record 718
fettered discretion 717–718
improper purpose 717
irrelevant considerations 717
leave 720
locus standi 720
mandatory order 719

Judicial review (*continued*)
  national security, concept of 722–723
  political nature of decisions 722–723
  problems with control of wide
      discretionary powers 721
  procedural *ultra vires* 714–715
  procedure 719–720
  prohibiting order 719
  proportionality 718
  quashing order 718
  reform 723
  restrictions on applications 722
  strictness of Wednesbury principles 721
  substantive *ultra vires* 715–718
  time limit 719
  tribunals 681–682
  unfairness 715
  Wednesbury unreasonable 716–717
Jury 264–302
  abolishing 295–296
  absence of reasons 292–293
  bias 289
  black jurors 298
  challenge for cause 278
  challenges 278–279
  civil cases 272–273
  conviction rate 290
  cost 293
  criminal cases 269–272
  criticisms of system 285–294
  criminal offences committed by jurors
      269
  discharging 279–280
  distress to members 293–294
  excessive damages 293
  function 267
  helping to work effectively 297
  history 266
  importance of 267
  improving performance 296–298
  internet, and 268
  key case 266
  lack of competence 285–288
  legislating to reduce role of 271–272
  manipulation by defendants 291–292
  nobbling 292
  perverse verdicts problem 288–289
  preventing perverse verdicts 297–298
  problems with compulsory service 293
  qualifications for service 273–276
  reform 294–298
  representation of ethnic minorities
      290–291
  reserve jurors 298
  secrecy 280–282
  serious fraud trials 294–295
  strengths of system 283–285
  stand by 278–279
  summoning 276
  time 293

  verdict 282
  vetting 277–278
  Vicky Pryce fiasco 287–288
  when used 269–273
Justices' clerk 315
  proposed reform of role 320

Lady Hale 197
Lammy Review 503, 589–590
LASPO 649–650
Law and justice 758–764
  Aristotle 758
  economic analysis 759
  justice in practice 761–762
  Karl Marx 761
  Kelsen and positivism 761
  natural law theories 758
  Nozick and the minimal state 760
  Rawls: *A Theory of Justice* 759–760
  utilitarianism 758–759
Law and morals 740–755
Law and rules 728–739
  Austin: command theory 730
  balancing different interests 734–735
  changes in 744
  crimes without victims 747
  differences between 744–745
  Dworkin: legal principles 732
  exploitation 735–736
  fear and internalisation 736–737
  Hart: primary and secondary rules
      730–731
  Hart-Devlin debate 747–749
  infertility treatment 750–751
  law jobs 735
  maintenance of order 734
  moral implications 743
  natural law 745–746
  natural law theory 732
  rules of adjudication 731
  rules of change 731
  rules of recognition 731
  separation 745–753
  sexual issues 742
  social cohesion 732–733
  survival 733
  utilitarianism 746
  variation 743
  Warnock Committee 749–750
  why laws are obeyed 736–737
Law centres 353–354
Law Commission 164–165
Law Officers' Department 331–332
Law reform 146–175
  abortion 163–164
  agencies 164–165
  case law 148–149
  civil service 163
  gig economy 156–162
  judicial change 148–149

  legal profession, influence of 173
  MeToo protest 152
  media pressure 163–164
  Parliament, by 149–151
    codification 149
    consolidation 149
    creation of new law 149
    repeal 149
  political parties 162
  pressure groups 151–156
  pressures for 151–164, 165
  problems with agencies 172–173
    lack of influence 172
    lack of power 172
    lack of ministerial involvement 173
    political difficulties 172
    too much compromise 173
    waste of experience 173
  public inquiries 170–172
  public opinion 163–164
  Royal Commissions 165–167, 168–169
  sexual harassment 155
  temporary inquiries 170–172
  treaty obligations 163
  voyeurism 150–151
Law Reports xxv–xxvi
  neutral citation xxv–xxvi
Law Society 217
Lawrence inquiry 170
Lawyers necessary, whether 366
Legal adviser
  right to consult 443–445
Legal aid
  civil 340–342
  cost of criminal cases 350–351
  criminal 342–344
  historical development 339–340
  lack of independence from government
      349–350
  poorer standards of work 350
  problems with 345–353
  reform 361–366
  reliance on private practice 352
  small businesses 349
  today 340–344
  unfair trials 352–353
Legal apprentices 256
Legal executives 255–256
  qualifications 255–256
  training 255–256
Legal Ombudsman 230–232, 250
Legal professions 214–263
  alternative business structures 246–250
  Competition in Professions 241
  complaints 230–232
  educational reform 237–239
  fusion 250–255
    access to Bar 254
    arguments against 254–255
    arguments for 252–253

expense 252
importance of good advocacy 254
inefficiency 252
judiciary 255
moves towards 252–253
other countries 253
specialisation 254
use of court time 255
waste of talent 253
future of 241–250
law reform, and 173
necessary, whether 257–258
performance 239–241
regulation 242–245
separate branches 216
Tesco Law 248–249
unmet need 336–339
Legal Services Board 243
Legal system in context 4
Legislative procedures
reforms to 56
Legislative reform orders 89
Licensed conveyancers 256
Literal rule 63–65
advantages 64
disadvantages 64–65
Litigants in person 345–346, 658–660
Lord Chancellor 329–331
Lord Woolf 628

Magistrates 304–325
age 310
appointment 308
background 309
BAME representation 311
civil jurisdiction 314
class 309–310
criminal jurisdiction 312–314
defendants prosecuted March 2008 to
March 2018 314
history 307–308
justices' clerk 315
lay, advantages 316–317
cost 316–317
involvement 317
local knowledge 317
weight of numbers 317
lay, disadvantages 317–319
background 319
bias towards police 318
inconsistency 317–318
inefficiency 318
lay versus professional judges 315–316
legal advisers 315
percentage by age band 310
politics 311
race 311–312
removal 309
retirement 309
selection 308

sex 312
suggested reforms 320–322
Distinct Division 321–322
professional judges 320
role of justices' clerk 320
selection process 320–321
sentencing 322
training 312
Magistrates' courts 25, 306–307
appeals from 598–600
civil appeals from 713–714
closing local courts 307
McKenzie friends 257
Me Too protest
law reform 152
Media
judges, and 204–205
Media pressure
law reform, and 163–164
Media reports
statutory interpretation 77
Mediation
divorce cases 695–696
Ministry of Justice 328–329
Miscarriages of justice 422–426
expert witnesses, and 498–501
response to 425–426
Mischief rule 66–68
advantages 67
disadvantages 67–68
examples 67
Money Claim Online 642–645
Murder
sentencing 540–541

National legal service 363–364
Negligence, civil action for
human rights, and 406–407
No-fault compensation 364
Non-intimate samples 450
Noscitur a sociis
statutory interpretation 73

Offences triable ether way 488–489
Old Bailey 270
Ombudsman 700
human rights, and 414
Orders 88
Orders in Council 88

PACE
stop and search under 431–433
Paralegals 256–257
Parenting orders 585
Parliament
human rights, and 414
judicial appointments, and 187
law reform by 149–151
Parliament, supremacy of 5–7
judges, and 200

Parliamentary intention
meaning 62–63
statutory interpretation, and 78
Parole Board
John Worboys, and 535–536
Paying for legal services 334–371
Personal injury
reform of compensation for 665–666
Perverse verdicts 288–289
preventing 297–298
Plea bargaining 494–495
Police 420–473
armed officers 462–463
arrest powers *see* Arrest powers
bail 459–460
civilian support staff 428
custody officer 439–440
deaths following contact with 465–467
demonstration 464–465
detention 439–442
detention without arrest 431
graduate profession 460
interrogation 440–442
interview, record of 446
interviews outside police station 450
local forces 428
organisation 426–428
powers 429–460
pre-arrest powers 430–435
racism, and 460–462
right to silence, and 447–450
safeguards for suspect *see* Suspect,
safeguards for
stop and account 430
stop and search powers 434–435
stop and search under PACE 431–433
uniform 429
witnesses, as 464
young offenders, and 573–574
Police and crime commissioners 427
Police conduct 464
Police corruption 462
Political parties
law reform, and 162
Premises, search of 454–456
warrant, with 454
warrant, without 455–456
Pressure groups
law reform 151–156
Price-competitive tendering 361–363
Prisoners' voting rights 544
Privacy, right to 398–400
Private Bills 51
Private Members' Bills 51
Private practice
reliance on 352
Private prosecutions 484–485
Privatisation
sentencing, and 558–560
Privy Council 22–24, 609

Public Bills 51
Public defenders 343–344, 347–349, 486
Public inquiries
  law reform, and 170–172
  streaming 171–172
Public opinion
  law reform, and 163–164

Qualified Lawyers Transfer Scheme
    221–222
Quality Assurance Scheme for Advocates
    228–229
Queen's Counsel 227–228

Racism
  courts, and 502–503
  CPS, and 502
  police, and 460–462
  sentencing, and 555–556
Rectification 139
Referral orders
young offenders 581–582
Regulations 88
Religious and cultural arbitration
    700–701
Reparation orders
  young offenders 582
Rescission 139
Reserved legal activities 230
Right to silence 447–450, 465
Rioters 537–538
Royal Assent 53
Royal Commissions 165–167, 168–169
Rule of law 7–8
Rules 88

School
  searches in 451
Scotland
  Supreme Court 618
Search of the person
  arrest, after 450
  school, in 451
Self-defence
  human rights, and 413
Sending for trial 490
Sentencing 524–568
  custodial sentences 533–544
  guidance for court 530–532
  guidance for sentences 530
  guidelines 531–532
  judges, role of 554
  legislation 530
  mandatory sentences 530
  minimum sentences 530
  murder 540–541
  new code 560–561
  out-of-court disposals 560
  practice 529–530
  privatisation 558–560

protection of public 528
punishment of offenders 526–527
purposes 526–529
racism 555–556
reduction of crime 527
reform and rehabilitation 528
restorative justice 528–529
rioters 537–538
seriousness of offence 532
steps taken using guidelines 532
women 556–558
young offenders 576–587
Separation of powers 5
Serious Crime Prevention orders
    550–551
Serious fraud trials
  jury, and 294–295
Serious Organised Crime Agency
    (SOCA) 427
Sexual harassment
  law reform, and 155
Small business
  legal aid, and 349
Small claims mediation service 699
Social mobility
  barristers 236
  solicitors 236
Solicitors 216–224
  advocacy 218
  background 232–239
barristers compared 254
class 234–235
continuing competence 222
disability 236
ethnic minorities 234, 235
number of 217
promotion to judiciary 222
qualifications 2198–221
  without university degree 221
  reserved legal activities 230
  social mobility 236
  training 219–221
  women 233–234
  work 216–219
Solicitors Regulation Authority 244–246
Sources of law 10–11
Specific performance 139
Statute law 46–58
  devolution, and 55–56
  post-legislative scrutiny 54
Statutory instruments 88
  orders 88
  Orders in Council 88
  regulations 88
  Rules 88
Statutory interpretation 60–85
  aids 72–80
  approaches to 73
  case law, and 63
  Cross: a contextual approach 81

dictionaries 74
Dworkin: fitting in with principles 81
European legislation 72
external aids 74–80
factors causing uncertainty 62
golden rule 65–66
Griffith: political choices 81–82
guidance 63
Hansard 75–78
  lack of clarity 77
  parliamentary intention 78
  time and expense 78
  usefulness 77
historical setting 74
Human Rights Act 1998 70–71
internal aids 72–74
  ejusdem generis 72
  explanatory notes 72
  expressio unius est exclusion alterius
      72
  noscitur a sociis 73
  rules of language 72–73
  statute itself 72
literal rule 63–65
media reports 77
methods used by judges 80–82
mischief rule 66–68
other jurisdictions 77
parliamentary intention 62–63
presumptions 73–74
previous practice 74
purposive approach 68–69
rectification 69–71
reform 82–83
reports 74
rules 63–71
statutes are always speaking 79
textbooks 74
treaties 74
Willis: the just result 81
Stop and account 430
Stop and search 434–435
  PACE, under 431–433
  terrorism, and 434–435
Summary offences 487
Supreme Court 14–18, 20–21, 608
  jurisdiction 16
  membership 17
  Scotland 618
  separation from Parliament 15–16
  work of 17–18
Surveillance operations 456–457
Suspect, safeguards for 442–450
  appropriate adult 445–446
  audio-recording 442–443
  caution 442
  exclusion of evidence 447
  interviews outside police station 450
  record of interview 446
  right to consult legal adviser 443–445

right to inform someone of detention 443
right to silence 447–450
  treatment 446

Taser guns 438, 439
Taylor Review 588
Television
  in court 512–513
Temporary inquiries
  law reform, and 170–172
Terrorism
  human rights, and 395–398
  stop and search, and 434–435
Tesco Law 248–249
Textbooks
  statutory interpretation 100
Third party funding 360–361
Treasury counsel
  judiciary, and 200
Treaties 142–145
  implementation 144
  modern constitution, under 144
  statutory interpretation 74
Treaty obligations
  law reform, and 163
Trial
  young offenders 575–576
Tribunals 672–687
  appeals 681–682
  awareness of policy 682
  composition 679
  cost 682
  fees 679
  flexibility 682
  history 674–675
  informality 682
  judicial review 681–682
  lack of openness 683
  Leggatt Review criticisms 676–677
  privacy 683
  procedure 679
  reforming 675–677
  relief of congestion in ordinary courts 682
  role 674
  specialisation 682
  speed 682
  statutory framework 677
  structure 678
  unavailability of state funding 683

Undercover police operations 457
Unfair trials
  legal aid, and 352–353
United States
  judicial appointments 187
Unmet need for legal services 336–339
Unwritten constitution 4–8

Verdict 282
Vexatious litigants 660–662
Victims 507–509
Voyeurism
  law reform, and 150–151

Warrant
  arrest with 435–436
  arrest without 436–437
Wigs
  judges 188
Witnesses 507–509
  anonymous 510–511
  police as 464

Women
  barristers 233–234
  sentencing 556–558
  solicitors 233–234
Worboys, John
  Parole Board, and 535–536
Wormwood Scrubs 540
Written constitution 8

Young offenders 570–574
  bail 574
  criminal liability 573
  custodial sentences 577–591
  detention and training orders 580–581
  detention during Her Majesty's pleasure 579
  detention under PCC(S) A 2000, s.91 579–580
  House of Commons Justice Committee 588–589
  Lammy Review 589–590
  parents 584
  police, and 573–574
  referral orders 581–582
  remand 574
  reparation orders 582
  sentencing 576–587
    tariff 581
    time limits 586
    statistics 573
  Taylor Review 588
  trends 572
  trial 575–576
  zero tolerance 587
Youth cautions 574–575
Youth conditional caution 575
Youth rehabilitation orders 582–584